November 1–3, 2010
Melbourne, Australia

Association for Computing Machinery

Advancing Computing as a Science & Profession

IMC'10

Proceedings of the 2010 ACM Internet Measurement Conference

Sponsored by:

ACM SIGCOMM and ACM SIGMETRICS

In Cooperation with:

USENIX

Supported by:

NSF, Google, Akamai, NICTA, AT&T, HP, Technicolor, Intel, and Telefonica

Association for
Computing Machinery

Advancing Computing as a Science & Profession

The Association for Computing Machinery
2 Penn Plaza, Suite 701
New York, New York 10121-0701

ISBN: 978-1-4503-0057-5

Additional copies may be ordered prepaid from:

ACM Order Department
PO Box 11405
New York, NY 10286-1405

Phone: 1-800-342-6626 (USA and Canada)
+1-212-626-0500 (all other countries)
Fax: +1-212-944-1318
E-mail: acmhelp@acm.org

ACM Order Number 532102

Printed in the USA

Foreword

It is my great pleasure to welcome you to the 10th Internet Measurement Conference. This year's conference continues IMC's tradition of being the premier venue for dissemination empirical research results providing insight into how the Internet operates in practice, as well as disseminating new methodologies for increasing our understanding of networked systems. In putting together this year's program we explicitly tried to uphold IMC's best traditions, such as encouraging reappraisal of previous results, fostering papers that assess emerging uses (or mis-uses) of the Internet and including a broad variety of topics. Per usual, the program is a mix of long and short papers to encourage both deep treatment of topics and early exposure to fresh ideas.

This year's IMC program spans three full days and includes a record 47 papers (24 long papers and 23 short papers). The program was chosen by a highly skilled and dedicated program committee of 23 people. This year we received 211 submissions which represents a 16% increase over 2009. Interestingly, long submissions held fairly steady (110 this year vs. 115 last year) while the number of short submissions increased dramatically (101 this year vs. 68 last year). The review process proceeded in four steps. In the first round all papers were reviewed by two PC members which led to 125 papers being carried forward. The second round consisted of one additional review (and more in some specific cases). The PC then engaged in an online discussion which identified 11 papers that were "pre-accepted" and 61 papers to discuss at the PC meeting. The final decisions were made at the PC meeting which was held in Berkeley in July and attended by the vast majority of PC members. In certain cases we consulted with external reviewers for their expertise, however, this was a rare exception and nearly all reviews were conducted by the PC members themselves.

I would like to thank IMC's steering committee for their trust and support throughout this year's process. Both I and the community owe a debt to the program committee members who all sacrificed a great deal of time to review submissions, read background material, engage in discussions and travel to the PC meeting---only to be trapped in a windowless conference room at ICSI for 10 hours. The effort put forth to ensure this conference remains a premier venue is humbling. Thanks also go to the external reviewers who provided crucial expert input to our decision-making process. I also wish to thank Tom Callahan who setup and maintained the paper management system and acted as scribe during the PC meeting. Many thanks to Chris Switzer and his crew at ICSI for taking care of all the logistics for the PC meeting and keeping the committee happy enough to prevent a mutiny!

I hope you find this year's program exciting and thought provoking and that the conference provides you with a rewarding forum for fruitful discussions with colleagues from around the world.

Mark Allman

IMC 2010 Program Chair

ICSI

Table of Contents

Session 6: Topology

Session 7: Methodology II

Session 8: Edge Networks

Session 9: Wireless and Mobility

Session 10: Classification

Session 11: Methodology III

Session 12: Online Social Networks

Session 13: Path Properties and Dynamics

Session 14: Anomaly and Event Detection

IMC 2010 Conference Organization

Program Chair: Mark Allman (*International Computer Science Institute*)

Local Arrangements Chair: Darryl Veitch (*University of Melbourne*)

Steering Committee:
Paul Barford (*University of Wisconsin*)
Chen-Nee Chuah (*University of California, Davis*)
Bruce Maggs (*Duke University and Akamai Technologies*)
Renata Teixeira (*CNRS and UPMC Sorbonne*)

Program Committee:
Chadi Barakat (*INRIA*)
Paul Barford (*University of Wisconsin*)
Rob Beverly (*Naval Postgraduate School*)
Randy Bush (*Internet Initiative Japan*)
Mark Crovella (*Boston University*)
Anja Feldmann (*Deutsche Telekom Laboratory/TU Berlin*)
Saikat Guha (*Microsoft Research*)
Krishna Gummadi (*MPI-SWS*)
Minaxi Gupta (*Indiana University*)
Thomas Karagiannis (*Microsoft Research*)
Ramana Kompella (*Purdue University*)
Christian Kreibich (*International Computer Science Institute*)
Balachander Krishnamurthy (*AT&T Labs - Research*)
Simon Leinen (*SWITCH*)
Olaf Maennel (*Loughborough University*)
Ratul Mahajan (*Microsoft Research*)
Jelena Mirkovic (*USC/ISI*)
Craig Partridge (*Raytheon BBN Technologies*)
Michael Rabinovich (*Case Western Reserve University*)
Pablo Rodriguez (*Telefonica Research*)
Rob Sherwood (*Deutsche Telekom Inc. R&D Lab*)
Nina Taft (*Intel Labs*)
Walter Willinger (*AT&T Labs - Research*)

Technical Support: Tom Callahan (*Case Western Reserve University*)

Additional reviewers:
Aditya Akella
Kevin Bauer
Tom Callahan
Chris Dunn
Alex Gall
Kyle Jamieson
Andrew Kalafut
Stephen Kolek
Hangwei Qian
Pairoj Rattadilok
Matthew Roughan
Youngsang Shin
Zhihua Wen

IMC 2010 Sponsors & Supporters

Sponsors:

In Cooperation With:

Platinum Supporters:

Gold Supporters:

Silver Supporters:

CloudCmp: Comparing Public Cloud Providers

Ang Li Xiaowei Yang
Duke University
{angl, xwy}@cs.duke.edu

Srikanth Kandula Ming Zhang
Microsoft Research
{srikanth, mzh}@microsoft.com

ABSTRACT

While many public cloud providers offer pay-as-you-go computing, their varying approaches to infrastructure, virtualization, and software services lead to a problem of plenty. To help customers pick a cloud that fits their needs, we develop CloudCmp, a systematic comparator of the performance and cost of cloud providers. CloudCmp measures the elastic computing, persistent storage, and networking services offered by a cloud along metrics that directly reflect their impact on the performance of customer applications. CloudCmp strives to ensure fairness, representativeness, and compliance of these measurements while limiting measurement cost. Applying CloudCmp to four cloud providers that together account for most of the cloud customers today, we find that their offered services vary widely in performance and costs, underscoring the need for thoughtful provider selection. From case studies on three representative cloud applications, we show that CloudCmp can guide customers in selecting the best-performing provider for their applications.

Categories and Subject Descriptors

C.4 [**Performance of Systems**]: General—*measurement techniques, performance attributes*; C.2.3 [**Computer-Communication Networks**]: Network Operations—*network monitoring, public networks*; C.2.4 [**Computer-Communication Networks**]: Distributed Systems—*distributed applications, distributed databases*

General Terms

Measurement, Design, Performance, Economics.

Keywords

Cloud computing, comparison, performace, cost.

1. INTRODUCTION

Internet-based cloud computing has gained tremendous momentum in recent years. Cloud customers outsource their computation and storage to public providers and pay for the service usage on demand. Compared to the traditional computing model that uses dedicated, in-house infrastructure, cloud computing offers unprecedented advantages in terms of cost and reliability [22, 27]. A cloud customer need not pay a large upfront cost (*e.g.*, for hardware purchase) before launching services, or over-provision to accommodate future or peak demand. Instead, the cloud's pay-as-you-go charging model enables the customer to pay for what she actually uses and promises to scale with demand. Moreover, the customer can avoid the cost of maintaining an IT staff to manage her server and network infrastructure.

A growing number of companies are riding this wave to provide public cloud computing services, such as Amazon, Google, Microsoft, Rackspace, and GoGrid. These cloud providers offer a variety of options in pricing, performance, and feature set. For instance, some offer platform as a service (PaaS), where a cloud customer builds applications using the APIs provided by the cloud; others offer infrastructure as a service (IaaS), where a customer runs applications inside virtual machines (VMs), using the APIs provided by their chosen guest operating systems. Cloud providers also differ in pricing models. For example, Amazon's AWS charges by the number and duration of VM instances used by a customer, while Google's AppEngine charges by the number of CPU cycles consumed by a customer's application.

The diversity of cloud providers leads to a practical question: *how well does a cloud provider perform compared to the other providers?* Answering this question will benefit both cloud customers and providers. For a potential customer, the answer can help it choose a provider that best fits its performance and cost needs. For instance, it may choose one provider for storage intensive applications and another for computation intensive applications. For a cloud provider, such answers can point it in the right direction for improvements. For instance, a provider should pour more resources into optimizing table storage if the performance of its store lags behind competitors.

Despite the practical relevance of comparing cloud providers, there have been few studies on this topic. The challenge is that every provider has its own idiosyncratic ways of doing things, so finding a common ground needs some thought. A few efforts have characterized the performance of one IaaS provider (Amazon AWS) [24,34]. Some recent blog posts [6,15,36] compare Amazon AWS with one other provider each. These measurements are limited in scope; none of them cover enough of the dimensions (e.g., compute, storage, network, scaling) to yield meaningful conclusions. Further, some of the measurement methodologies do not extend to all providers, e.g., they would not work for PaaS providers.

In this paper, we consider the problem of systematically comparing the performance of cloud providers. We identify the key requirements for conducting a meaningful comparison (§2), develop

IMC'10, November 1–3, 2010, Melbourne, Australia.

a tool called CloudCmp, and use CloudCmp to evaluate a few cloud providers (§3– §4) that differ widely in implementation but together dominate the cloud market. Our results (§5) provide a customer with the performance-cost trade-offs across providers for a wide set of metrics. For providers, the results point out specific areas for improvement in their current infrastructures.

Several technical challenges arise in realizing a comparator for cloud providers. The first is the choice of what to measure. Rather than focusing on the nitty-gritty such as which virtualization technology a provider uses or how it implements its persistent storage, we take an end-to-end approach that focuses on the dimensions of performance that customers perceive. Doing so has the advantage that the measurement methodology remains stable even as the implementations change over time or differ widely across providers. To this end, we identify a common set of services offered by these providers, including elastic computing, persistent storage, and intra-cloud and wide-area networking (§3.2).

The second challenge is the choice of how to measure customer perceived performance of these services. For each service, we focus on a few important metrics, *e.g.*, speed of CPU, memory, and disk I/O, scaling latency, storage service response time, time to reach consistency, network latency, and available bandwidth (§3.3). We leverage pre-existing tools specific to each metric. However, when applying the tools, we had to be careful along several axes, such as using variable number of threads to test multi-core, piecing apart the interference from colocated tenants and the infrastructure itself, and covering the wide set of geographically distributed data centers offered by the providers. The individual tools *per se* are simple, but this specific collection of them that enables comparing cloud providers is novel.

Third, as with all significant measurement efforts, we trade off development cost to the completeness of the study. We skip functionality that is specific to small classes of applications but are comprehensive enough that our benchmark results allow predicting the performance of three representative applications: a storage intensive e-commerce web service, a computation intensive scientific computing application, and a latency sensitive website serving static objects. By deploying these applications on each cloud, we demonstrate that the predictions from CloudCmp align well with the actual application performance. CloudCmp enables predicting application performance without having to first port the application onto every cloud provider.

Finally, unlike other measurement efforts, we are constrained by the monetary cost of measuring the clouds and the acceptable use policies of the providers. We note that the results here were achieved under a modest budget by judicious choice of how many and how often to measure. CloudCmp complies with all acceptable use policies.

We used CloudCmp to perform a comprehensive measurement study over four major cloud providers, namely, Amazon AWS, Microsoft Azure, Google AppEngine, and Rackspace CloudServers. We emphasize that the infrastructure being measured is ephemeral. Providers periodically upgrade or regress in their software or hardware and customer demands vary over time. Hence, these results are relevant only for the time period in which they were generated. To keep the focus on the value of this comparison method and its implications rather than rank providers, our results use labels $C_1 - C_4$ instead of provider names.

From the comparison results, we find that the performance and price of the four providers vary significantly with no one provider standing out (§5). For instance, while the cloud provider C_1 has the highest intra-cloud bandwidth, its virtual instance is not the most cost-effective. The cloud provider C_2 has the most powerful virtual instances, but its network bandwidth is quite limited. C_3 offers the lowest wide-area network latency, but its storage service is slower than that of its competitors. We highlight a few interesting findings below:

- Cloud instances are not equally cost-effective. For example, while only 30% more expensive, C_4's virtual instance can be twice as fast as that of C_1.
- C_2 in our study allows a virtual instance to fully utilize the underlying physical machine when there is no local resource competition. Hence, an instance can attain high performance at low cost.
- The performance of the storage service can vary significantly across providers. For instance, C_1's table query operation is an order of magnitude faster than that of the others.
- The providers offer dramatically different intra-datacenter bandwidth, even though intra-datacenter traffic is free of charge. For instance, C_1's bandwidth is on average three times higher than C_2's.

The measurement data we collected is available at `http://www.cloudcmp.net`.

We believe that this is the first study to comprehensively characterize the performance and cost of the major cloud providers in today's market. Though we present results for four providers in this paper, we believe the techniques in CloudCmp can be extended to measure other providers. In future work, we plan to build performance prediction models based on CloudCmp's results to enable fast and accurate provider selection for arbitrary applications (§7).

2. GOALS AND APPROACH

In this section, we highlight the design goals of CloudCmp and briefly describe how we meet them.

1. **Guide a customer's choice of provider:** Our primary goal is to provide performance and cost information about various cloud providers to a customer. The customer can use this information to select the right provider for its applications. We choose the cost and performance metrics that are relevant to the typical cloud applications a customer deploys. These metrics cover the main cloud services, including elastic computing, persistent storage, and intra-cloud and wide-area networking.
2. **Relevant to cloud providers:** We aim to help a provider identify its under-performing services compared to its competitors. We not only present a comprehensive set of measurement results, but also attempt to explain what causes the performance differences between providers. This enables a provider to make targeted improvements to its services.
3. **Fair:** We strive to provide a fair comparison among various providers by characterizing all providers using the same set of workloads and metrics. This restricts our comparative study to the set of common services offered by all providers. The core functionality we study suffices to support a wide set of cloud applications. However, we skip specialized services specific to some applications that only a few providers offer. While support for functionality is a key decision factor that we will consider in future work, our focus here is on the performance-cost trade-off.
4. **Thoroughness vs. measurement cost:** For a thorough comparison of various cloud providers, we should measure all cloud providers continuously across all their data centers.

Provider	Elastic Cluster	Storage	Wide-area Network
Amazon AWS	Xen VM	SimpleDB (table), S3 (blob), SQS (queue)	3 DC locations (2 in US, 1 in EU)
Microsoft Azure	Azure VM	XStore (table, blob, queue)	6 DC locations (2 each in US, EU, and Asia)
Google AppEngine	Proprietary sandbox	DataStore (table)	Unpublished number of Google DCs
Rackspace CloudServers	Xen VM	CloudFiles (blob)	2 DC locations (all in US)

Table 1: The services offered by the cloud providers we study. The intra-cloud networks of all four providers is proprietary, and are omitted from the table.

This, however, incurs significant measurement overhead and monetary costs. In practice, we periodically (*e.g.*, once an hour) measure each provider at different times of day across all its locations. The measurements on different providers are loosely synchronized (*e.g.*, within the same hour), because the same measurement can take different amount of time to complete in different providers.

5. **Coverage vs. development cost:** Ideally, we would like to measure and compare all cloud providers on the market. Achieving this goal, however, can be cost and time prohibitive. We cover a representative set of cloud providers while restricting our development cost. We choose the cloud providers to compare based on two criteria: popularity and representativeness. That is, we pick the providers that have the largest number of customers and at the same time represent different models such as IaaS and PaaS. Our measurement methodology, however, is easily extensible to other providers.
6. **Compliant with acceptable use policies:** Finally, we aim to comply with cloud providers' use policies. We conduct experiments that resemble the workloads of legitimate customer applications. We do not overload the cloud infrastructures or disrupt other customer applications.

3. MEASUREMENT METHODOLOGY

In this section, we describe how we design CloudCmp to conduct a fair and application-relevant comparison among cloud providers. We first show how we select the providers to compare, and discuss how to choose the common services to ensure a fair comparison. Then for each type of service, we identify a set of performance metrics that are relevant to application performance and cost.

3.1 Selecting Providers

Our comparative study includes four popular and representative cloud providers: Amazon AWS [2], Microsoft Azure [12], Google AppEngine [7], and Rackspace CloudServers [14]. We choose Amazon AWS and Rackspace CloudServers because they are the top two providers that host the largest number of web services [19]. We choose Google AppEngine because it is a unique PaaS provider, and choose Microsoft Azure because it is a new entrant to the cloud computing market that offers the full spectrum of computation and storage services similar to AWS.

3.2 Identifying Common Services

Despite the complexity and idiosyncrasies of the various cloud providers, there is a common core set of functionality. In this section, we focus on identifying this common set, and describe the experience of a customer who uses each functionality. We defer commenting on the specifics of how the cloud achieves each functionality unless it is relevant. This allows us to compare the clouds from the end-to-end perspective of the customer and sheds light on the meaningful differences. The common set of functionality includes:

- **Elastic compute cluster.** The cluster includes a variable number of virtual instances that run application code.
- **Persistent storage.** The storage service keeps the state and data of an application and can be accessed by application instances through API calls.
- **Intra-cloud network.** The intra-cloud network connects application instances with each other and with shared services.
- **Wide-area network.** The content of an application is delivered to end users through the wide-area network from multiple data centers (DCs) at different geographical locations.

These services are offered by most cloud providers today because they are needed to support a broad spectrum of applications. For example, a web application can have its servers run in the elastic compute cluster, its data stored in the persistent storage, and its content delivered through the wide-area network. Other cloud applications such as document translation, file backup, and parallel computation impose different requirements on these same components. A few providers offer specialized services for specific applications (e.g., MapReduce). We skip evaluating these offerings to focus on the more general applications. Table 1 summarizes the services offered by the providers we study.

3.3 Choosing Performance Metrics

For each of these cloud services, we begin with some background and describe the performance and cost metrics we use to characterize that service.

3.3.1 Elastic Compute Cluster

A compute cluster provides virtual instances that host and run a customer's application code. Across providers, the virtual instances differ in their underlying server hardware, virtualization technology, and hosting environment. Even within a provider, multiple tiers of virtual instances are available, each with a different configuration. For example, the instances in the higher tier can have faster CPUs, more CPU cores, and faster disk I/O access. These differences do impact the performance of customer applications.

The compute cluster is charged per usage. There are two types of charging models among the providers we study. The IaaS providers (AWS, Azure, and CloudServers) charge based on how long an instance remains allocated, regardless of whether the instance is fully utilized or not. However, the PaaS provider (AppEngine) charges based on how many CPU cycles a customer's application consumes in excess of a few free CPU hours per application per day.

The compute cluster is also "elastic" in the sense that a customer can dynamically scale up and down the number of instances it uses to withstand its application's varying workload. Presently, there are two types of scaling mechanisms: opaque scaling and transparent scaling. The former requires a customer herself to manually change the number of instances or specify a scaling policy, such as creating a new instance when average CPU usage exceeds 60%. The latter automatically tunes the number of instances without customer intervention. AWS, Azure, and CloudServers support opaque scaling whereas AppEngine provides transparent scaling.

Service	Operation	Description
Table	get	fetch a single row using the primary key
	put	insert a single row
	query	lookup rows that satisfy a condition on a non-primary key field
Blob	download	download a single blob
	upload	upload a single blob
Queue	send	send a message to a queue
	receive	retrieve the next message from a queue

Table 2: The operations we use to measure the performance of each storage service.

We use three metrics to compare the performance of the compute clusters: benchmark finishing time, cost per benchmark, and scaling latency. These metrics reflect how fast an instance can run, how cost-effective it is, and how quickly it can scale.

Benchmark finishing time. Similar to conventional computational benchmark metrics for computer architectures [18], this metric measures how long the instance takes to complete the benchmark tasks. The benchmark has tasks that stress each of the main compute resources (CPU, memory, and disk I/O).

Cost. This is the monetary cost to complete each benchmark task. Because we use the same tasks across different instances provided by different clouds, customers can use this metric to compare the cost-effectiveness of the instances regardless of their prices and charging models. Together with the above metric, this provides customers with a view of the performance-cost trade-offs across providers. These metrics correspond to the criteria that customers use when choosing, such as best performance within a cost budget or lowest cost above a performance threshold.

Scaling latency. This is the time taken by a provider to allocate a new instance after a customer requests it. The scaling latency of a cluster can affect the performance and cost of running an application. An application can absorb workload spikes more quickly and can keep fewer number of instances running continuously if it can instantiate new instances quickly. With this metric, a customer can choose the compute cluster that scales the fastest or design better scaling strategies. She can also make more nuanced decisions based on what it would cost to provide good performance when the workload of her application varies.

There are a few other metrics, such as the customizability of a virtual instance and the degree of automation in management, that capture vital aspects of cloud providers. However, these are harder to quantify. Hence, we focus on the performance and costs of running an application and defer considering other metrics to future work.

3.3.2 Persistent Storage

Cloud providers offer persistent storage for application state and data. There are currently three common types of storage services: table, blob, and queue. The table storage is designed to store structural data in lieu of a conventional database, but with limited support for complex queries (*e.g.*, table join and group by). The blob storage is designed to store unstructured blobs, such as binary objects, user generated data, and application inputs and outputs. Finally, the queue storage implements a global message queue to pass messages between different instances. Most storage services are implemented over HTTP tunnels, and while not standardized, the usage interfaces are stable and similar across providers.

The cloud storage services have two advantages over their conventional counterparts: scalability and availability. The services are well-provisioned to handle load surges and the data is replicated [1] for high availability and robustness to failures. However, as a trade-off, cloud storage services do not offer strong consistency guarantees [25]. Therefore, an application can retrieve stale and inconsistent data when a `read` immediately follows a `write`.

There are presently two pricing models for storage operations. The table services of AWS and AppEngine charge based on the CPU cycles consumed to run an operation. Thus, a complex query costs more than a simple one. Azure and CloudServers have a fixed per-operation cost regardless of the operation's complexity.

We use three metrics to compare the performance and cost of storage services: operation response time, time to consistency, and cost per operation.

Operation response time. This metric measures how long it takes for a storage operation to finish. We measure operations that are commonly supported by providers and are popular with customers. Table 2 summarizes these operations. They include the basic `read` and `write` operations for each storage service. For table storage service, we also use an SQL-style `query` to test the performance of table lookup. In §6.1, we show that these operations account for over 90% of the storage operations used by a realistic e-commerce application.

Time to consistency. This metric measures the time between when a datum is written to the storage service and when all reads for the datum return consistent and valid results. Such information is useful to cloud customers, because their applications may require data to be immediately available with a strong consistency guarantee. Except for AppEngine, cloud providers do not support storage services that span multiple data centers. Therefore, we focus on consistency when the reads and writes are both done from instances inside the same data center.

Cost per operation. The final metric measures how much each storage operation costs. With this metric, a customer can compare the cost-effectiveness across providers.

3.3.3 Intra-cloud Network

The intra-cloud network connects a customer's instances among themselves and with the shared services offered by a cloud. The performance of the network is vital to the performance of distributed applications. Within a cloud, the intra-datacenter network often has quite different properties compared to the inter-datacenter network. Providers vary in the type of network equipment (NICs, switches) as well as in their choice of routing (layer 2 vs. layer 3) and configuration such as VLANs. All providers promise high intra-datacenter bandwidth (typically on the order of hundreds of Mbps to Gbps), approximating a private data center network.

To compare the performance of intra-cloud networks, we use path capacity and latency as metrics. We use TCP throughput as a measure of path capacity because TCP is the dominant traffic type of cloud applications. Path capacity impacts data transfer throughput and congestion events can lead to errors or delayed responses. Path latency impacts both TCP throughput [30] and end-to-end response time. Together, these metrics provide insight into how a provider's intra-cloud network is provisioned.

None of the providers charge for traffic within their data centers. Inter-datacenter traffic is charged based on the volume crossing the data center boundary. Since all providers charge similar amounts, comparing cost of network transfers becomes a moot point.

3.3.4 Wide-area Network

The wide-area network is defined as the collection of network paths between a cloud's data centers and external hosts on the Internet. All the providers we study offer multiple locations to host customer applications. Requests from an end user can be served by an instance close to that user to reduce latency. Uniquely, AppEngine offers a DNS-based service to automatically map requests to close-by locations. The others require manual configuration.

We use the *optimal wide-area network latency* to compare providers' wide-area networks. The optimal wide-area network latency is defined as the minimum latency between a vantage point and any data center owned by a provider. We use locations of PlanetLab nodes as vantage points. The more the data centers offered by a provider and the closer they are to population centers, the smaller the optimal network latency. The metric is useful for customers because it corresponds to the network latency an application may experience given an ideal mapping. For AppEngine, which provides automatic mapping of requests to locations, we also measure how close its automatic mapping is to the optimal mapping.

4. IMPLEMENTATION

In this section, we describe the implementation details of CloudCmp and highlight the practical challenges we address.

4.1 Computation Metrics

Benchmark tasks. As described above, we would like a suite of benchmark tasks that stresses various aspects of the compute infrastructure offered by cloud providers. In traditional computation performance measurement, any benchmark suite, such as the SPEC CPU2006 benchmarks [16], would fit this bill. However, the context of cloud computing poses new constraints. For example, AppEngine only provides sand-boxed environments for a few cross-platform programming languages, and applications have to be singled-threaded and finish within limited time.

To satisfy those constraints and be fair across different providers, we modified a set of Java-based benchmark tasks from SPECjvm2008 [17], a standard benchmark suite for Java virtual machines. We choose Java because it is supported by all cloud providers. The benchmark suite includes several CPU intensive tasks such as cryptographic operations and scientific computations. We augment it with memory and I/O intensive tasks. Each benchmark task runs in a single thread and finishes within 30 seconds so as to be compatible with all providers.

Benchmark finishing time. We run the benchmark tasks on each of the virtual instance types provided by the clouds, and measure their finishing time. Some instances offer multiple CPU cores for better parallel processing capability. For these instances, we also evaluate their multi-threading performance by running instances of the same benchmark task in multiple threads simultaneously, and measuring the amortized finishing time of the task. The number of threads is set to be equivalent to the number of available CPU cores.

Cost per benchmark. For cloud providers that charge based on time, we compute the cost of each benchmark task using the task's finishing time and the published per hour price. For AppEngine that charges by CPU cycles, we use its billing API to directly obtain the cost.

Scaling latency. We write our own scripts to repeatedly request new virtual instances and record the time from when the instance is requested to when it is available to use. We further divide the latency into two segments: a provisioning latency and a booting latency. The former measures the latency from when an instance is requested to when the instance is powered on. The latter measures the latency from the powered-on time to when the instance is ready to use. The separation of the two is useful for a cloud provider to pinpoint the performance bottleneck during instance allocation.

4.2 Storage Metrics

Benchmark tasks. Along with each storage service, comes an API to get, put or query data from the service. Most APIs are based on HTTP. To use the APIs, we wrote our own Java-based client based on the reference implementations from the providers [3,9,21]. The client has a few modifications over the reference implementations to improve latency. It uses persistent HTTP connections to avoid SSL and other connection set up overheads. It also skips a step in some implementations in which a client first sends a request header and waits an RTT until the server returns an HTTP 100 (Continue) message before proceeding with the request body. For comparison, we also tested other non-Java-based clients such as *wget* and C#-based clients. To avoid the potential impact of memory or disk bottlenecks at the client's instance, our clients mimic streaming workload that processes data as it arrives without retaining it in memory or writing it to disk.

Regarding the benchmark workload, we vary the size of the data fetched to understand the latency vs. throughput bottlenecks of the storage service. We vary the number of simultaneous requests to obtain maximum achievable throughput as well as measuring performance at scale. We vary the size of the working sets to observe both in- and out-of-cache performance. Because performance will be impacted by load on the client and in the network, we repeat each experiment at different times across different locations to get representative results. We also study the impact of the different client implementations described above.

Response time. The response time for an operation is the time from when the client instance begins the operation to when the last byte reaches the client.

Throughput. The throughput for an operation is the maximum rate that a client instance obtains from the storage service.

Time to Consistency. We implement a simple test to estimate the time to consistency. We first write an object to a storage service (the object can be a row in a table, a blob, or a message in a queue). We then repeatedly read the object and measure how long it takes before the read returns correct result.

Cost per operation. Similar to cost per benchmark task, we use the published prices and billing APIs to obtain the cost per storage operation.

4.3 Network Metrics

We use standard tools such as *iperf* [8] and *ping* to measure the network throughput and path latency of a provider. To measure intra-cloud throughput and latency, we allocate a pair of instances (in the same or different data centers), and run those tools between the two instances. Some providers further divide instances within the same data center into zones for a finer-grained control of instance location (e.g., not placing all instances in the same failure domain). In this case, we also deploy inter-zone and intra-zone instances respectively to measure their throughput and latency.

To prevent TCP throughput from being bottlenecked by flow control, we control the sizes of the TCP send and receive windows. Our measurements show that with a 16MB window, a single TCP flow is able to use up the available capacity along the paths measured in this paper. Larger window sizes do not result in higher throughput. For comparison, we also measure the throughput obtained by TCP clients that use the default window size configured by the instance's operating system.

To measure the optimal wide-area network latency, we instantiate an instance in each data center owned by the provider and ping these instances from over 200 vantage points on PlanetLab [13].

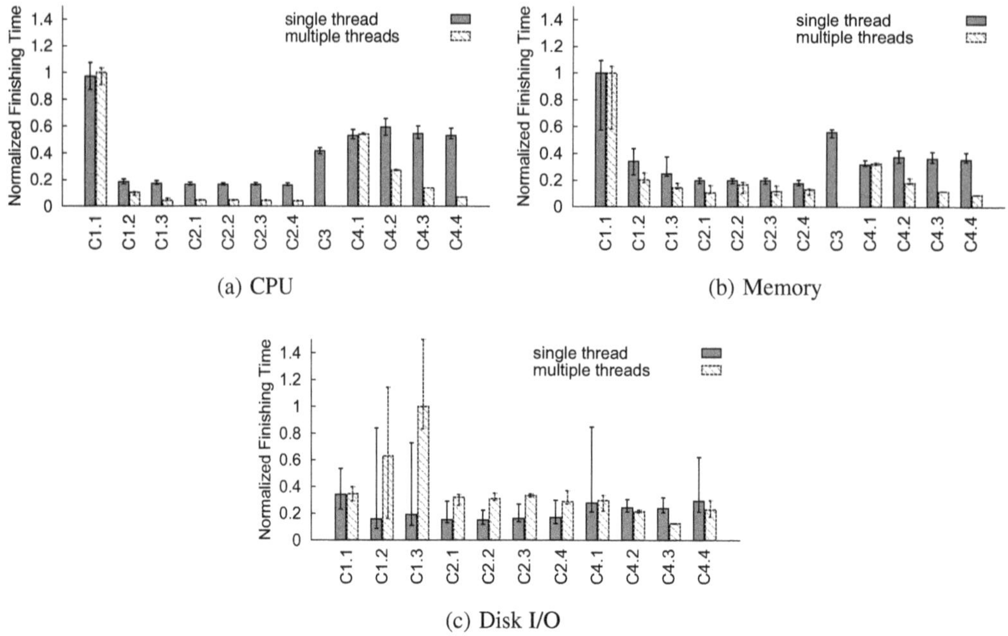

(a) CPU (b) Memory

(c) Disk I/O

Figure 1: The finishing time of benchmark tasks on various cloud instances. The time values are normalized using the longest finishing time to emphasize each provider's relative performance. We show both single-threaded and multi-threaded results. The multi-threaded and I/O results are missing for C_3 because it does not support multi-threading or accessing the local disk.

For each vantage point, the optimal latency to a provider is the smallest RTT to a data center of the provider. AppEngine automatically replicates our application to multiple instances at different data centers. By querying the DNS name corresponding to our application from each of the PlanetLab vantage points, we collect the IP addresses of the instance that AppEngine's automatic mapping service maps the request from each vantage point. Each of these IP addresses, we conjecture, corresponds to the virtual IP address of the front-end load balancer at a data center. We then ping all of these IP addresses from each of the PlanetLab vantage points to identify the best mapping that AppEngine might have achieved.

5. RESULTS

In this section, we present the comparison results between the four providers: AWS, Azure, AppEngine, and CloudServers. Due to legal concerns, we anonymize the identities of the providers in our results, and refer to them as C_1 to C_4. The data was collected over a two-month period from March to May 2010. We have made the data available for download from the project website [4].

5.1 Elastic Compute Cluster

We first measure the computation performance of different types of instances offered by cloud providers. Our naming convention refers to instance types as $provider.i$ where i denotes the tier of service with lower numerals corresponding to lower cost and computational speed. For instance, $C_1.1$ is the cheapest and slowest instance type offered by C_1.

Table 3 summarizes the instances we measure. We test all instance types offered by C_2 and C_4, and the general-purpose instances from C_1. C_1 also provides specialized instances with more memory or CPU or high bandwidth network, which we do not include in this study, as they have no counterparts from other providers. C_3 does not offer different instance types, so we use its default environment to run the benchmark tasks.

Cloud Provider	Instance Type	Number of Cores	Price
C_1	$C_1.1$	< 1	$0.085 / hr
	$C_1.2$	2	$0.34 / hr
	$C_1.3$	4	$0.68 / hr
C_2	$C_2.1$	4	$0.015 / hr
	$C_2.2$	4	$0.03 / hr
	$C_2.3$	4	$0.06 / hr
	$C_2.4$	4	$0.12 / hr
	$C_2.5$	4	$0.24 / hr
	$C_2.6$	4	$0.48 / hr
	$C_2.7$	4	$0.96 / hr
C_3	default	N/A	$0.10 / CPU hr
C_4	$C_4.1$	1	$0.12 / hr
	$C_4.2$	2	$0.24 / hr
	$C_4.3$	4	$0.48 / hr
	$C_4.4$	8	$0.96 / hr

Table 3: Information of the cloud instances we benchmark. With C_3, the first six CPU hours per day per application are free.

Some providers offer both Linux and Windows instances with the latter being slightly more expensive due to licensing fees. For experiments that depend on the type of OS, we compare instances from both OSes. For others, we choose Linux instances to reduce the cost of our experiment.

Figure 1 shows the finishing time of a CPU intensive task, a memory intensive task, and a disk I/O intensive task. Each bar shows the median and the 5th/95th percentiles of the measured samples. The same convention is used for all other figures without special notice. We omit the results of other benchmark tasks that show similar trends. For each instance type, we instantiate 10 instances and repeat each task 20 times per instance, i.e., a total of 200 samples per task per instance type. We only show the first four instance types of C_2 because the others have similar performance for the reason we soon describe. The I/O and multiple-threaded re-

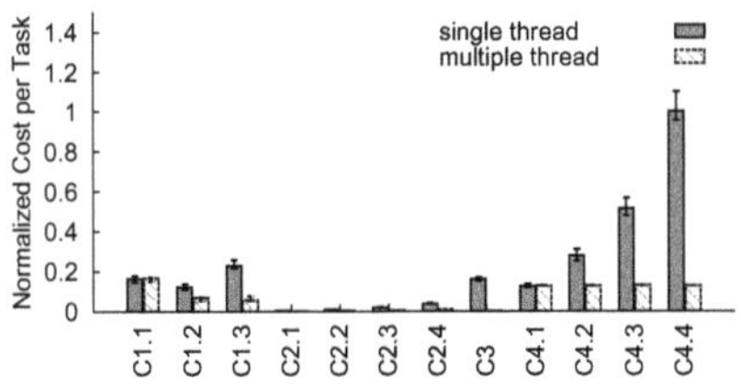

(a) CPU

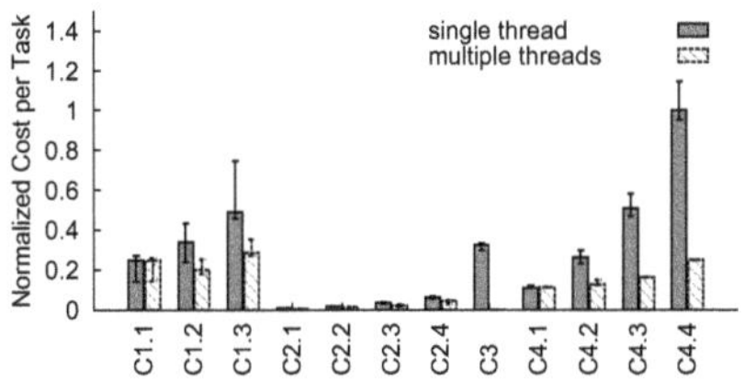

(b) Memory

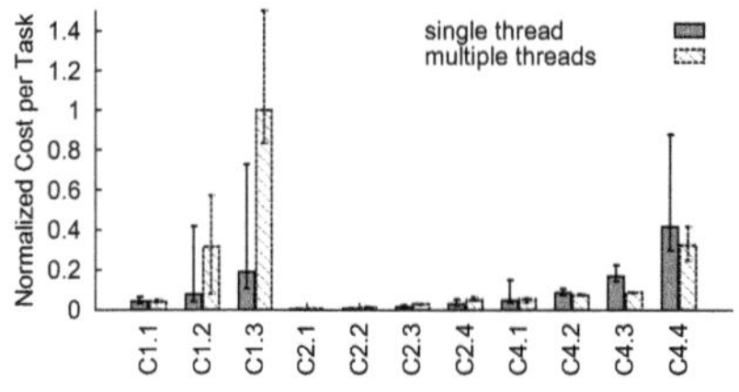

(c) Disk I/O

Figure 2: The per-task monetary cost on each type of cloud instance.

sults are not available for C_3 because it does not support local disk access or multi-threading.

From the results, we can see that price-comparable instances offered by different providers have widely different CPU and memory performance. For example, $C_4.1$ and $C_1.1$ are in the same pricing tier with the former being only 30% more expensive per hour per instance, but twice as fast as the latter. Alternatively, $C_1.2$ and $C_1.3$ offer better performance than their counterparts from C_4 and are on average 50% more expensive.

Note that across providers the instance types appear to be constructed in different ways. For C_1, the high-end instances ($C_1.2$ and $C_1.3$) have shorter finishing times in both single and multiple threaded CPU/memory tests. This is perhaps due to two reasons. First, besides having more CPU cores, the high-end instances may have faster CPUs. Second, the low-end instance may suffer from higher resource contention, due to high load and poor resource multiplexing techniques (e.g., CPU time sharing) that open a tenant to interference from other colocated tenants.

In contrast, for C_4, the finishing times do not improve significantly for the single threaded tests when we alter the instances from low-end to high-end, while the amortized running times of the multi-threaded tests are greatly reduced. This suggests that all the C_4 instances might share the same type of physical CPU and they either have similar levels of resource contention or are better at avoiding interference.

Interestingly, instances of C_2 have the same performance regardless of their prices. This might be explained by the work-conserving CPU sharing policy of C_2, where a virtual instance can fully use all physical CPUs on a machine if there is no contention, and when colocated instances compete for CPUs, the high-end instances are given larger weight in the competition. Under such policy, we expect to observe interference and poor performance at times of high load. However, we found this to never happen in our experiments, suggesting that C_2's data centers were lightly loaded throughout our experiment period.

Unlike CPU and memory intensive tasks, the disk I/O intensive task exhibits high variation on some C_1 and C_4 instances, probably due to interference from other colocated instances [22]. Further, the multi-threaded I/O performance is worse than the single-threaded performance, perhaps because interleaved requests from multiple threads are harder to optimize than requests from the same thread. On the contrary, instances from C_2 are much more stable perhaps due to better I/O scheduling techniques or lightly loaded physical machines.

5.1.1 Performance at Cost

Figure 2 shows the monetary cost to run each task. We see that for single-threaded tests, the smallest instances of most providers are the most cost-effective compared to other instances of the same providers. The only exception is $C_1.1$, which is not as cost-effective as $C_1.2$, because the latter has much higher performance due to faster CPU or lower contention.

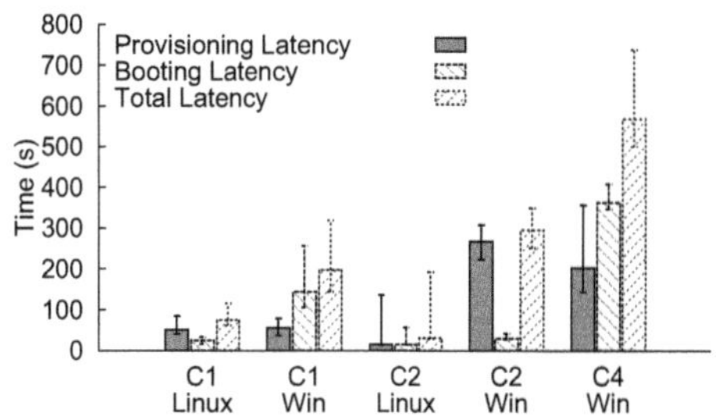

Figure 3: The scaling latencies of the lowest end instance of each cloud provider.

Surprisingly, for multi-threaded tests the high-end instances such as $C_1.3$ and $C_4.4$ with more CPU cores are not more cost-effective than the low-end ones. There are two possible reasons. First, the prices of high-end instances are proportional to the number of CPU cores, and thus do not provide any cost advantage per core. Second, although high-end instances are assigned more CPU cores, they still share other system resources such as memory bus and I/O bandwidth. Therefore, memory or I/O intensive applications do not gain much by using high-end instances as long as the applications do not run out of memory or disk space. This suggests that for parallel applications it might be more cost-effective to use more low-end instances rather than fewer high-end ones.

5.1.2 Scaling Latency

Finally, we compare the scaling latency of various providers' instances. To save cost, we only measure the scaling latency for the smallest instance of each provider. For providers that support both Linux and Windows instances, we test both choices to understand how different OSes affect the scaling latency, especially the booting latency. We run Ubuntu 9.04 for Linux instances and Windows Server 2008 for Windows ones. For each cloud and each OS type, we sequentially allocate 20 instances and measure the time between the request for a new instance and when that instance becomes reachable. We attribute the kernel uptime of the instance once it becomes available to be the time to boot and the remaining latency as the time to provision or otherwise set up the VM. We drop C_3 here because it does not allow manual requests for instances.

Figure 3 shows the scaling latencies for three clouds and different OS types. All cloud providers can allocate new instances quickly with the average scaling latency below 10 minutes. C_1 and C_2 can even achieve latency within 100 seconds for Linux instances. The latency of C_4 is larger. We see that across providers, Windows instances appear to take longer time to create than Linux

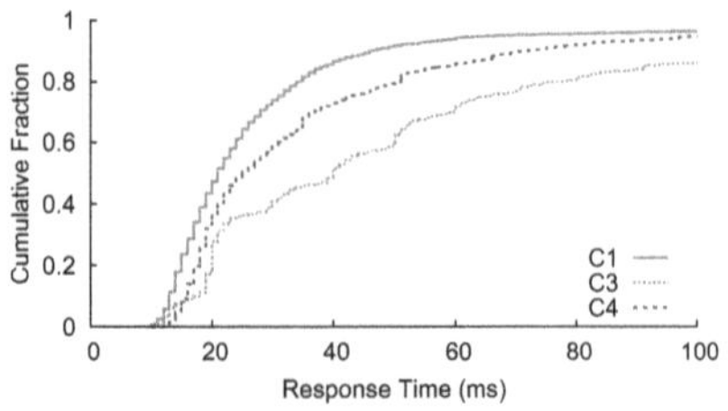

(a) Get

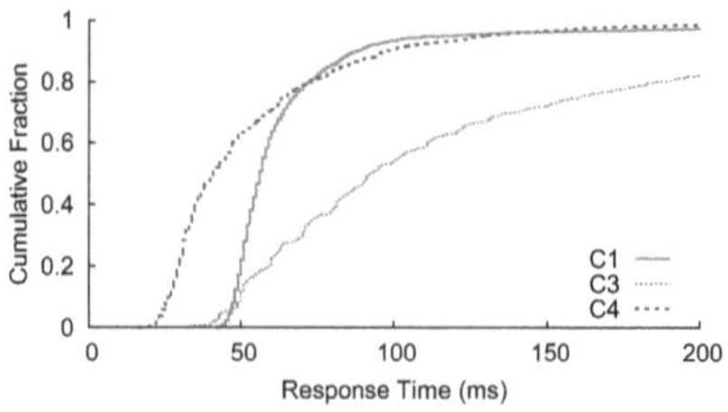

(b) Put

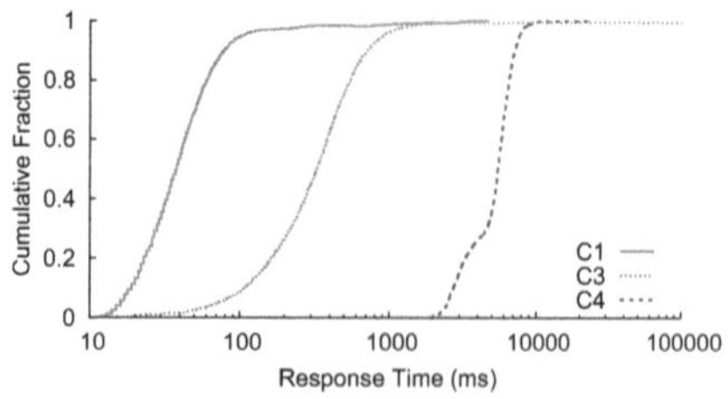

(c) Query

Figure 4: The cumulative distribution of the response time when using the large table with 100K entries. Note that for the query operation, the x-axis is in a logarithmic scale, due to the significant performance gaps between different services.

ones, but for different reasons. For C_1, the provisioning latency is similar for both instances, but the Windows ones have larger booting latency, possibly due to slower CPUs of the smallest instances. Windows Server 2008 R2 instances based on the Win7 code base can boot faster. For C_2, the booting latency is similar, while the provisioning latency of the Windows instances is much larger. It is unclear but likely that C_2 may have different infrastructures to provision Linux and Windows instances.

We note that a few other factors impacting scaling agility have not been considered here. Rather than focusing just on allocating instances quickly, some providers make it easy to update active instances or provide extensive monitoring and automatic recovery from faults during running. Another common goal is to create instances consistently within an SLA deadline even when they are brought up in large batches.

5.2 Persistent Storage

We measure and compare three types of storage services: table, blob, and queue, offered by various cloud providers.

5.2.1 *Table Storage*

We first compare three table storage services offered by C_1, C_3, and C_4. C_2 does not provide a table service. Here we only show the results obtained using our Java-based client, as other non-Java clients achieve similar performance, because the table operations are lightweight on the client side. For each table service, we test the performance of three operations: `get`, `put`, and `query` (see Table 2). Each operation runs against two pre-defined data tables: a small one with 1K entries, and a large one with 100K entries. The `get/put` operations operate on one table entry, while the `query` operation returns on average 10 entries. For storage benchmarks, unless otherwise specified, we use instance types that occupy at least one physical core to avoid excessive variation due to CPU time sharing.

Figure 4 shows the distributions of response time for each type of operation on the large table. We repeat each operation several hundred times. The results of using the small table show similar trends and are omitted to save space. From the figure, we can see that all table services exhibit high variations in response time. For example, the median response time of the `get` operation is less than 50ms, while the 95th-percentile is over 100ms for all services. The three services perform similarly for both `get` and `put` operations, with C_3 slightly slower than the other two providers. However, for the `query` operation, C_1's service has significantly shorter response time than the other two. C_4's service has a very long response time, because unlike the other providers, it does not appear to maintain indexes over the non-key fields in a table. In contrast, C_1 appears to have an indexing strategy that is better than the others.

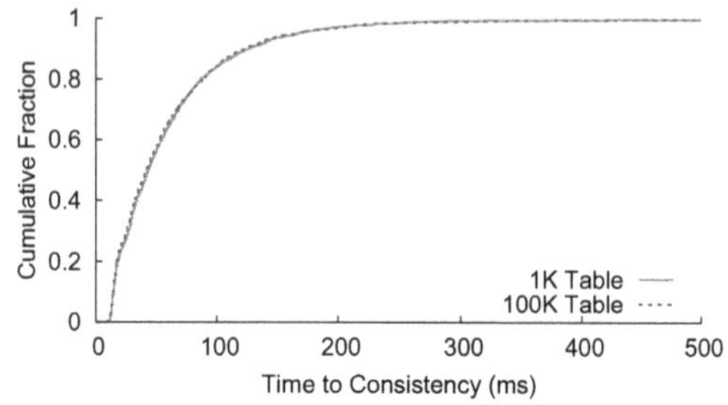

Figure 5: The cumulative distribution of the time to consistency for C_1's table service.

Provider	Cost per Operation (milli-cents)		
	get	put	query
C_1	0.13	0.31	1.47
C_3	0.02	0.23	0.29
C_4	0.10	0.10	0.10

Table 4: The average cost per operation for all three table services. The cost is in the unit of milli-cent, i.e., one-thousandth of a cent.

We also measure how well each table service scales by launching multiple concurrent operations. None of the services show noticeable performance degradation when up to 32 operations are issued at the same time. This suggests that all these table storage services appear to be reasonably well provisioned. Testing at higher scale is deferred to future work.

We then evaluate the time to reach consistency for the table services by using the mechanism described in §4.2. We discover that around 40% of the `get` operations in C_1 see inconsistency when triggered right after a `put`, and do not return the entry just inserted by the `put`. Other providers exhibit no such inconsistency. Figure 5 shows the distribution of the time to reach consistency for C_1. From the figure, we see that over 99% of the inconsistencies are resolved within 500ms, with the median resolved within 80ms. The long duration of the inconsistency opens up a sizable window for race conditions. C_1 does provide an API option to request strong consistency but disables it by default. We confirm that turning on this option eliminates inconsistencies and surprisingly does so without much extra latency for `get` or `put`. We conjecture that the performance overhead of enforcing consistency might be visible only when more users request it or during failure cases because otherwise C_1 would have enabled it by default.

Finally, we compare the cost per operation for different table services in Table 4. We can see that, although the charging models of the providers are different, the costs are comparable. Both C_1 and C_3 charge lower cost for `get/put` than `query`, because the former

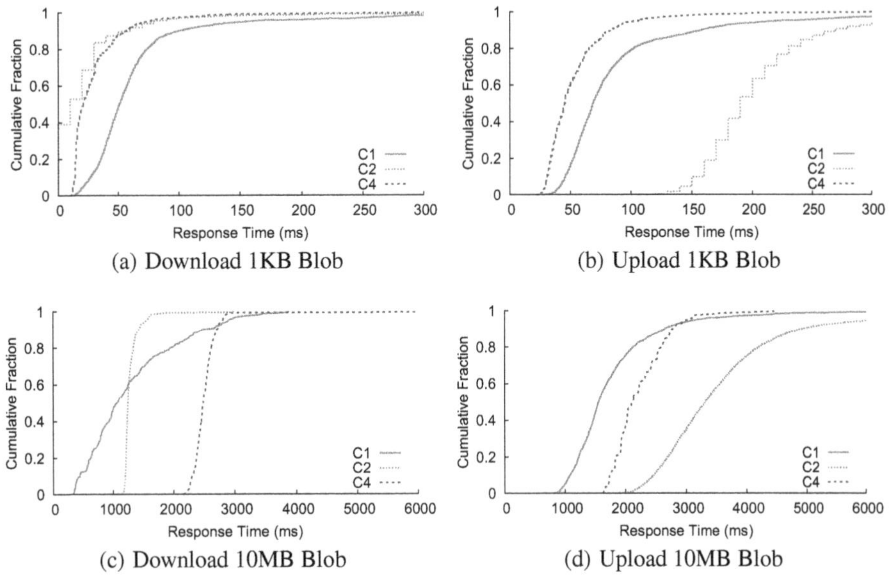

Figure 6: The cumulative distribution of the response time to download or upload a blob using Java-based clients.

operations are simpler and consume less CPU cycles to serve. C_4 charges the same across operations and can improve its charging model by accounting for the complexity of the operation. This is an example of how CloudCmp's benchmarking results can help the providers make better choices.

A comparison with the compute costs in Table 3 indicates that the cost of table storage is comparable to that of compute instances for workloads that trigger about 1000 operations per instance per hour. Applications that use storage at a lower rate can choose their provider based on their computation costs or performance.

5.2.2 *Blob Storage*

We compare the blob storage services provided by C_1, C_2, and C_4. C_3 does not offer a blob store.

Figure 6 shows the response time distributions for uploading and downloading one blob measured by our Java-based clients. We consider two blob sizes, 1KB and 10MB, to measure both latency and throughput of the blob store. The system clock of C_2's instances have a resolution of 10ms, and thus its response time is rounded to multiples of 10ms. We see that the performance of blob services depends on the blob size. When the blob is small, C_4 has the best performance among the three providers. When the blob is large, C_1's average performance is better than the others. This is because blobs of different sizes may stress different bottlenecks – the latency for small blobs can be dominated by one-off costs whereas that for large blobs can be determined by service throughput, network bandwidth, or client-side contention. Uniquely, C_2's storage service exhibits a 2X lower performance for uploads compared to downloads from the blob store. It appears that C_2's store may be tuned for read heavy workload.

Figure 7 illustrates the time to download a 10MB blob measured by non-Java clients. Compared to Figure 6(c), in every provider, non-Java clients perform much better. Markedly C_4's performance improves by nearly 5 times because it turns out that the Java implementation of their API is particularly inefficient.

We then compare the scalability of the blob services by sending multiple concurrent operations. As per above, we use non-Java clients to eliminate overheads due to Java. Figure 8 shows the

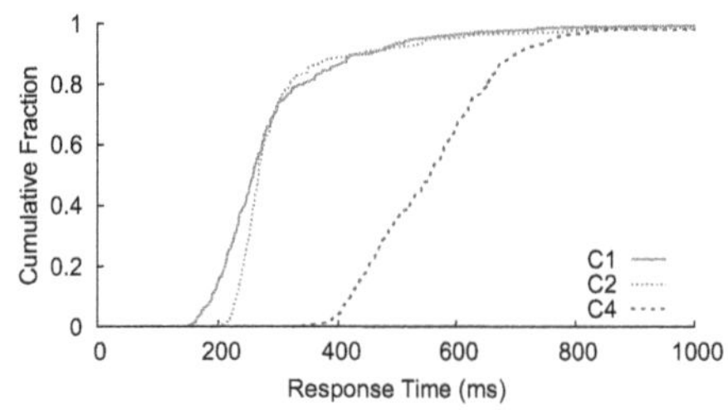

Figure 7: The cumulative distribution of the time to download a 10MB blob using non-Java clients.

Provider	Maximum throughput achieved by one instance (Mbps)	
	Smallest instance with at least one core	Largest instance from a provider
C_1	773.4	782.3
C_2	235.5	265.7
C_4	327.2	763.3

Table 5: The maximum throughput an instance obtains from each blob service when downloading many 10MB blobs concurrently.

downloading time with the number of concurrent operations ranging from 1 to 32. We omit the results for uploading because they are similar in trend. When the blob size is small, all services except for C_2 show good scaling performance. This suggests that C_1 and C_4's blob services are well-provisioned to handle many concurrent operations. When the blob is large, C_4 and C_1 continue to scale better though all three providers show certain scaling bottlenecks. The average time to download increases with the number of concurrent operations, illustrating a throughput bottleneck.

We compute the maximum throughput of the blob service that one instance can obtain by increasing the number of simultaneous operations until the throughput stabilizes. Table 5 shows the results for two types of instances – the smallest instance that has at least one full core and the largest instance from each provider. The former data point eliminates CPU time sharing effects [35] while the latter minimizes contention from colocated VMs. We report

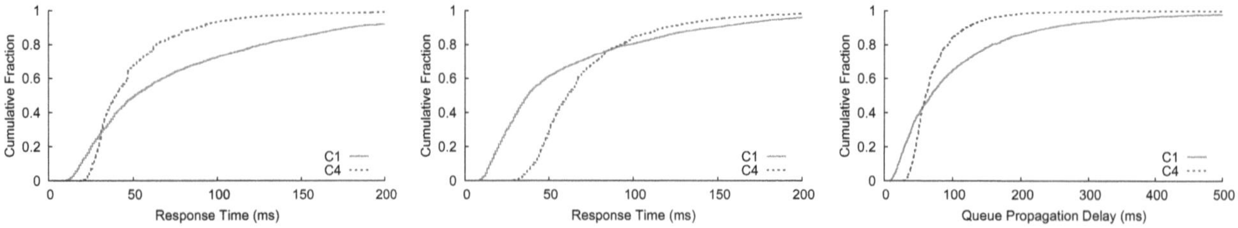

(a) Send (b) Retrieve (c) Propagation delay

Figure 9: The cumulative distributions of the response time to send or retrieve a message from a queue, and the propagation delay of a queue.

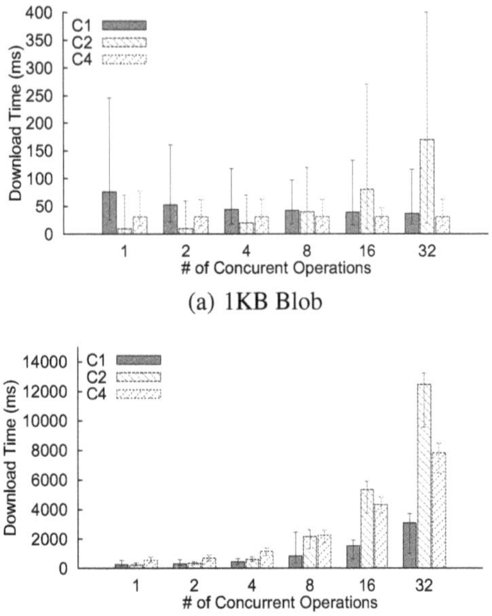

(a) 1KB Blob

(b) 10MB Blob

Figure 8: The blob downloading time from each blob service under multiple concurrent operations. The number of concurrent requests ranges from 1 to 32. Note that the x-axes are on a logarithmic scale.

results with non-Java clients to eliminate overheads due to client side inefficiency. As we will soon show, C_1 and C_2's blob service throughput is close to their intra-datacenter network bandwidth (see Figure 10), suggesting that the bottleneck in throughput is unlikely within the blob service itself. This is also true for C_4's blob service throughput of a large instance, which more than doubles that of the single core instance that we were using earlier. It appears that the impact on an instance's throughput due to other VMs colocated on the machine is non trivial in C_4.

In summary, we observe that client implementation and contention from other VMs or along network paths significantly impact the perceived storage service performance (across the three cloud platforms we study). Therefore, a more efficient client implementation or less contention may improve the results in this paper.

We tested the consistency property of the blob services, and did not find inconsistency problems in the three providers. The charging models are similar for all three providers and are based on the number of operations and the size of the blob. We omit these results for brevity.

5.2.3 Queue Storage

We compare the queue services of C_1 and C_4. Similar to table services, we only show the results from our Java-based client.

Cloud Provider	Data Center Name	Location	Region
C_1	$C_1.DC_1$	North Virginia	US
	$C_1.DC_2$	North California	US
	$C_1.DC_3$	Ireland	Europe
C_2	$C_2.DC_1$	Dallas/Fort Worth, Texas	US
	$C_2.DC_2$	Chicago, Illinois	US
C_4	$C_4.DC_1$	Chicago, Illinois	US
	$C_4.DC_2$	Amsterdam, Netherlands	Europe
	$C_4.DC_3$	San Antonio, Texas	US
	$C_4.DC_4$	Singapore	Asia
	$C_4.DC_5$	Dublin, Ireland	Europe
	$C_4.DC_6$	Hong Kong	Asia

Table 6: The geographical location of the cloud data centers.

Figure 9(a) and 9(b) show the distributions of the response time of sending and retrieving a message. The queue services are designed to transfer only small messages up to 8KB. Thus, we choose a message size of 50B in our measurement. The results show that both services have large variations in response time. C_4 is slightly faster at sending messages while C_1 is faster at retrieving messages. We test the scalability of the queue services, up to 32 concurrent messages, and no significant performance degradation is found, mostly due to the small message size.

It is interesting to note that the response time of the queue service is on the same order of magnitude as that of the table and blob services. This suggests that although the queue service is simpler and designed to be more efficient compared to the other storage services, the performance gain is insignificant. One may use the table or blob service to implement a simple signaling framework with similar functionality as the queue service without much performance degradation.

We then measure the propagation delay of a queue. The delay is defined as the time between when a message is sent to an empty queue and when it is available to be retrieved. A queue with shorter propagation delay can improve the responsiveness of an application. Figure 9(c) shows the distribution of the propagation delay of the two services. We see that roughly 20% of the messages for C_1 take a long time (>200ms) to propagate through the queue, while C_4's queue service has a similar median propagation delay but lower variation. Finally, both services charge similarly–1 cent per 10K operations.

5.3 Intra-cloud Network

In this section, we compare the intra-cloud network performance of different providers. As of April 27th, when we conducted this measurement, we found a total of 11 data center locations from three providers: 6 for C_4, 3 for C_1, and 2 for C_2. Similar to instance types, we name each data center as provider.DC_i. Table 6 summarizes the geographic locations of the data centers. We do not

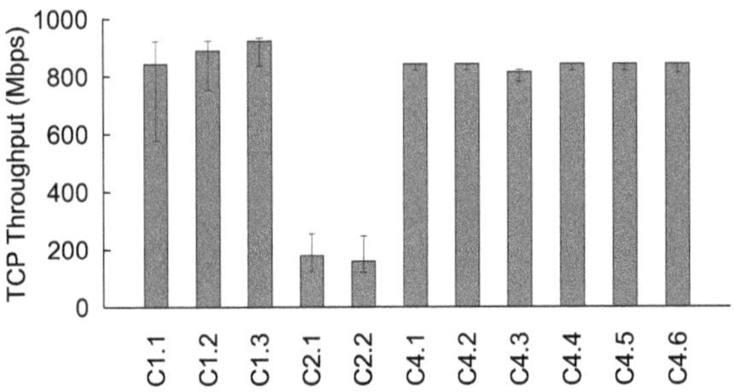

Figure 10: The intra-datacenter TCP throughput between two instances in all data centers we measure.

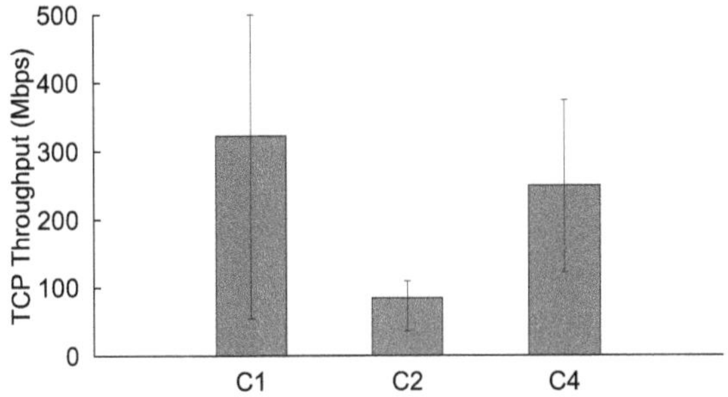

Figure 11: The TCP throughput between two different US data centers of a cloud provider.

consider C_3's intra-cloud network performance because it does not allow direct communication between instances.

When measuring the intra-cloud bandwidth and latency, we choose the instance types that can at least fully occupy one CPU core. This is to avoid the network performance degradation due to CPU time sharing introduced by virtualization [35].

5.3.1 *Intra-datacenter Network*

Figure 10 shows the TCP throughput between two instances in the same data center. In rare cases, a pair of instances are colocated on the same machine and obtain a throughput larger than 1Gbps which is the speed of the NIC. We filter out such pairs as they do not measure actual network performance. We combine the results for intra-zone and inter-zone cases, because the difference between them is not significant. From the figure, we see that the network bandwidth of providers differs significantly. C_1 and C_4 provide very high TCP throughput which is close to the limit of the NIC (1Gbps) and the variation is low. C_2 has much lower throughput, probably due to throttling or under-provisioned network.

In terms of latency, all data centers achieve low round trip time (< 2ms) for all pairs of instances we test. This result is not surprising, because the instances located in the same data center are physically proximate. We omit the results to save space.

5.3.2 *Inter-datacenter Network*

Next, we show the performance of network paths between data centers of the same provider. Because most providers focus on the US market (and some only have US data centers), we only show the results for data centers within the US. Figure 11 shows that the throughput across datacenters is much smaller than that within the datacenter for all providers. Both C_1 and C_4 have their median inter-datacenter TCP throughput higher than 200Mbps, while

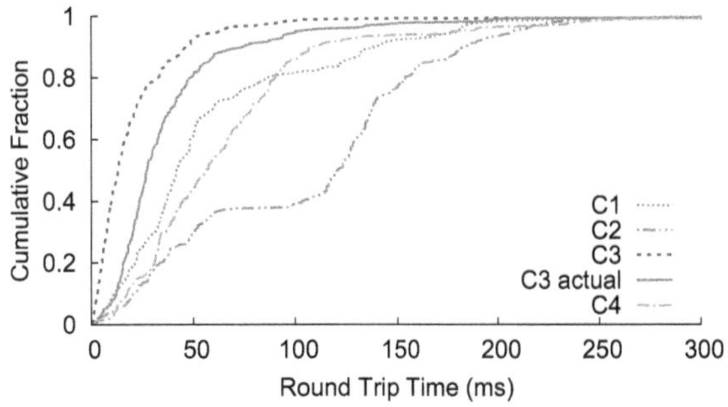

Figure 12: This figure shows the cumulative distribution of the optimal round trip time (RTT) to the instances deployed on a cloud provider from 260 global vantage points. For C_3 we also show the actual RTT from a vantage point to the instance returned by the cloud's DNS load balancing.

C_2's throughput is much lower. Further, the variation in throughput across datacenters is higher since the wide-area traffic may have to compete with much other traffic.

We also compare the above result with the inter-datacenter throughput obtained by a vanilla client that uses one TCP flow with the default send and receive window sizes configured by the provider. All providers see a smaller throughput with this vanilla client. This is because the network paths across data centers have a high bandwidth-delay product (*e.g.*, 50ms $\times$ 800Mbps = 5MB) and the default window sizes are not configured appropriately. We find that the degradation is less with Linux instances, since modern Linux kernels auto-tune the size of the TCP receive buffer [11] which can grow up to 4MB in the default setting. However the degradation is far worse in the non-Linux instances since either auto-tuning is not turned on or is configured poorly.

We find that the latencies between data centers largely correspond to the geographical distance between the data centers. The latencies across providers are incomparable because their data centers are at different locations. Hence, we omit these results.

5.4 Wide-area Network

In this section, we compare the wide area network performance of different providers. Figure 12 shows the distribution of the optimal wide-area latency observed from a diverse set of vantage points. We also show the actual latency of C_3 which is the latency to the instance returned by its DNS load balancing system. From the figure, we can see that both the optimal and actual latency distributions of C_3 are lower than that of other providers. This could be explained by the provider's widely dispersed presence – we observe 48 unique IP addresses simultaneously serving our test application. These IP addresses likely correspond to the virtual IPs of front-end load balancers at distinct locations. Furthermore, the gap between the optimal and actual latency of C_3 is less than 20ms, suggesting that its load balancing algorithm works very well in practice.

C_1 and C_4 have similar latency distributions: they are worse than C_3, but much better than C_2. A main difference is that C_1 has a larger fraction of vantage points that have an optimal latency higher than 100ms. Closer examination of our data reveals that these high latency vantage points are mostly in Asia and South America, where C_1 does not have a presence (Table 6).

C_2 has the worst latency distribution because it has the smallest number of data centers. The flat curve between 50ms and 100ms corresponds to the latency differences between two groups of vantage points: the North American nodes and those in other conti-

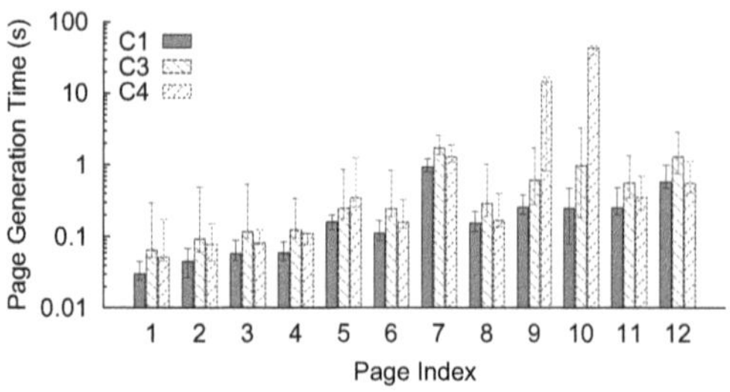

Figure 13: The page generation time of TPC-W when deployed on all three cloud providers that support it. The y-axis is in a logarithm scale.

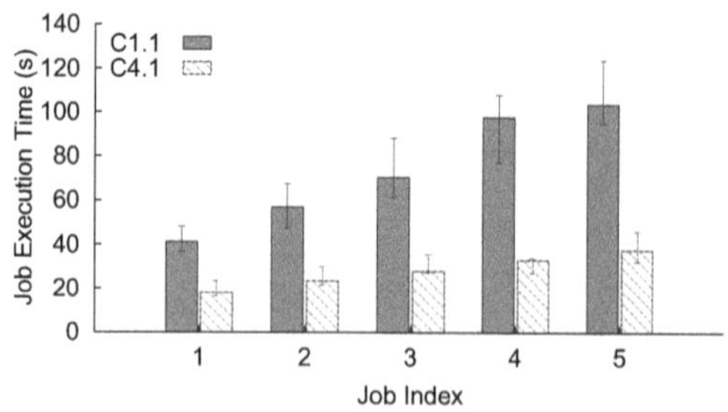

Figure 14: The job execution time of Blast when deployed on both C_1.1 and C_4.1. We show the results for five example jobs.

nents. Because all C_2's data centers reside within the US, there is a latency jump for vantage points outside North America.

6. USING CLOUDCMP: CASE STUDIES

In this section, we deploy three simple applications on the cloud to check whether the benchmark results from CloudCmp are consistent with the performance experienced by real applications. If they are, it validates our conjecture that CloudCmp's results can be used by customers to choose cloud providers in lieu of porting, deploying, and measuring their applications on each cloud. The applications include a storage intensive e-commerce website, a computation intensive application for DNA alignment, and a latency sensitive website that serves static objects. This study is a first step. We do not claim to represent all the existing cloud applications and defer the design of a generic tool for estimating the performance of arbitrary applications to future work (§7).

6.1 E-commerce Website

The first application we choose is TPC-W [20], a standard benchmark for transactional web services. TPC-W itself is a fully functional e-commerce website where customers can browse and purchase books online. It is advantageous for such applications to migrate to a cloud computing utility, because the cloud provides highly scalable and available storage services and free intra-datacenter bandwidth.

We use a Java implementation of TPC-W [10] and port it to various cloud providers by redirecting the database operations to use each cloud's table storage APIs. However, not all database operations used in TPC-W map directly to the APIs offered by the cloud. Specifically, there is no equivalent for JOIN and GROUP BY. We disable pages that use these operations. Out of the original 16 pages in TPC-W, we had to disable four pages. The three operations we benchmarked (`put`, `get`, and `query`) account for over 90% of TPC-W's storage operations. Other operations include `delete` and `count`.

One major performance goal of TPC-W, similar to other dynamic web applications, is to minimize the page generation time. The performance bottleneck lies in accessing table storage. From CloudCmp's comparison results of table storage service, shown in Figure 4, we see that cloud C_1 offers the lowest table service response time among all providers. That benchmark appears relevant because the table size it uses (100K) is on the same order as that of the TPC-W tables (100K - 400K), and because it covers most of the storage operations used by the ported version of TPC-W. Therefore, from the benchmarking results, a customer may guess that C_1 will offer the best performance for TPC-W.

To verify this, we deploy TPC-W on the three providers that offer table storage service: C_1, C_3, and C_4. We use instances that occupy a physical core to avoid interference due to CPU sharing. Figure 13 shows the page generation time for all twelve pages. We see that C_1 indeed has the lowest page generation time among all three providers, consistent with our benchmarking result. Furthermore, C_4 has lower generation time than C_3 for most pages except for pages 9 and 10. These pages contain many `query` operations and are consistent with CloudCmp's results in Figure 4, where C_4 has a much higher `query` response time but lower `get` and `put` response time than C_3.

6.2 Parallel Scientific Computation

We then test Blast, a parallel computation application for DNA alignment. We choose Blast because it represents computation-intensive applications that can take advantage of the cloud computing utility. The application is written in C#, with one instance running a web service to accept job input and return job output, and multiple worker instances responsible for executing the jobs in parallel. Blast instances communicate with each other through the queue storage service, which serves as a global messaging system. The application also leverages the blob storage service to store computation results.

We consider two cloud providers for Blast: C_1 and C_4. The others do not support queue service. The performance goal of Blast is to reduce job execution time given a budget on number of instances. CloudCmp's computational benchmark results shown in Figure 1 suggest that at a similar price point, C_4.1 performs better than C_1.1.

To check this prediction, we deploy Blast on both types of instance (C_1.1 and C_4.1) and compare the real execution time of five example jobs. Figure 14 shows the results. For all five jobs, Blast running on C_4.1 takes only a portion of the time it takes when running on C_1.1. This suggests that C_4.1 indeed offers better performance than C_1.1 for real applications at similar price point, consistent with CloudCmp's benchmarks.

6.3 Latency Sensitive Website

We choose a latency sensitive website for our third case study. We configure a simple web server to serve only static pages, and download the pages from PlanetLab nodes around the world. The performance goal is to minimize the page downloading time from many vantage points, and the main performance bottleneck is the wide area network latency. We choose this application because many existing online services such as web search and online gaming depend critically on network latency [28]. Due to TCP semantics, shorter latency also often leads to higher throughput [30].

We deploy our website on all providers and use `wget` to fetch web pages from PlanetLab nodes. Each vantage point fetches from the instance with the minimum network latency to emulate a perfect load balancing scheme. Figure 15 shows the distributions of

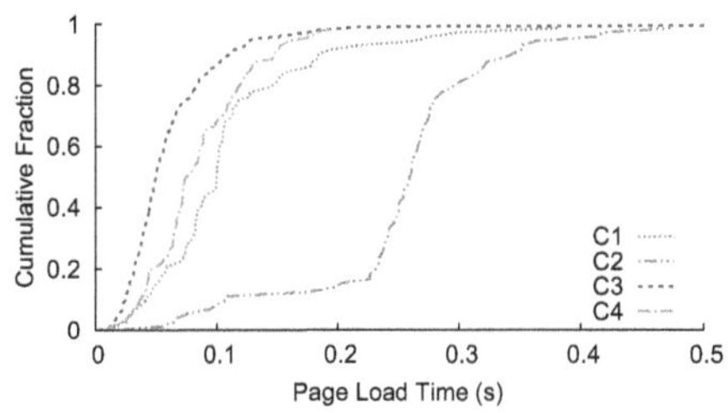

(a) 1KB Page

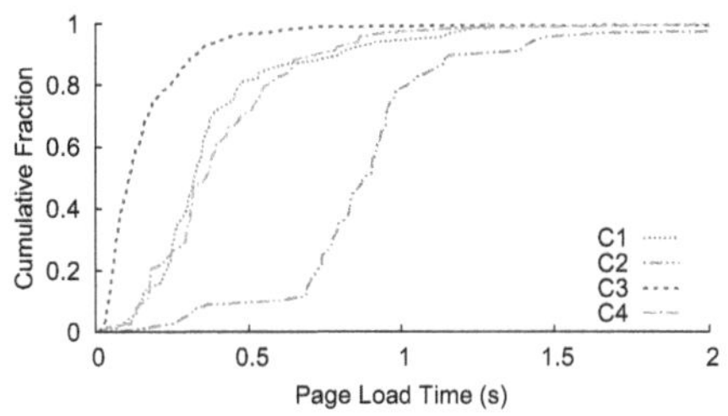

(b) 100KB Page

Figure 15: The distribution of the page downloading time of our website. We show the results for two different page sizes: 1KB and 100KB.

the page downloading time for various providers. We download two web pages of sizes 1KB and 100KB. In both cases, C_3 has the smallest page downloading time, consistent with our benchmarking results in Figure 12 that show C_3 having the lowest wide-area network latency distribution.

7. DISCUSSION

In this section, we discuss CloudCmp's limitations and future research directions.

Breadth vs. depth trade-off. As our main goal is to perform a comprehensive comparison among cloud providers, in several occasions, we sacrifice depth for breadth. For instance, an in-depth study that focuses on the storage service of a particular provider could have used more storage system benchmarks [23] in addition to the metrics we use, to examine factors such as pre-fetching and other query optimization techniques. The results presented in this paper show only the first-order differences among various providers, and can be complemented with more in-depth measurement results on each individual provider.

Snapshot vs. continuous measurement. The results in this paper should be viewed as a snapshot comparison among cloud providers in today's market. As time goes by, providers may upgrade their hardware and software infrastructure, and new providers may enter the market. It is our future work to use CloudCmp to continually update those results.

Future work. CloudCmp opens at least two venues for future research. First, we can use CloudCmp's measurement results to make application-specific performance prediction. A customer who is interested in selecting a cloud provider for its specific application may combine the application's workload traces with CloudCmp's results to predict how the application may perform on each cloud platform. This prediction result will help a customer make an informed decision.

Second, it can be promising to develop a meta-cloud that combines the diverse strengths of various providers. CloudCmp's results show that there is no clear winner on the current market. For instance, C_1 has fast storage service, C_2 has the most cost-effective virtual instances, and C_3 has the smallest wide-area latency. A meta-cloud that uses C_2 for computation, C_1 for storage, and C_3 for front-end request processing may outperform any standalone provider. How to build such a meta-cloud is an interesting future research question.

8. RELATED WORK

Cloud computing has drawn significant attention from researchers in the past several years. Armbrust *et al.* provide a comprehensive overview of cloud computing, including the new opportunities it enables, the potential obstacles to its adoption, and a classification of cloud providers [22]. Their work motivates this study on comparing the cloud providers in today's market.

Wang and Ng show that the virtualization technique in Amazon EC2 can lead to dramatic instabilities in network throughput and latency, even when the data center network is lightly loaded [35]. This is mainly caused by CPU sharing among small virtual instances. To avoid such effects, we carefully design our network measurements to only use virtual instances that can at least fully utilize one CPU core.

Garfinkel studies the performance of Amazon Simple Storage Service (S3) and describes his experience in migrating an application from dedicated hardware into the cloud [24]. Walker investigates the performance of scientific applications on Amazon EC2 using both macro and micro benchmarks [34]. Compared to the work above, CloudCmp evaluates a much more complete set of services offered by cloud providers.

CloudStatus continually monitors the status of Amazon AWS and Google AppEngine [5]. It keeps track of several performance metrics specific to each of the two providers. In contrast, we identify a common set of key performance and cost metrics shared by various providers and conduct a thorough comparison among them to guide provider selection.

Yahoo! Cloud Serving Benchmark (YCSB) [23] is a framework to benchmark distributed data serving systems, such as Cassandra, HBase, and PNUTS. The authors present comparison results from experiments conducted on local clusters. We compare similar types of table storage operations offered by main commercial cloud providers in the wild.

Our earlier work argues for the importance of a comprehensive cloud provider comparison framework, and presents some preliminary results to highlight the wide performance gap among cloud providers [29]. In this paper, we have taken several significant steps further to fulfill our earlier vision. First, we measure and compare more cloud services, such as virtual instance memory and disk I/O, blob and queue storage, and inter-datacenter network transfer. Second, we conduct a more fine-grained study on providers by measuring each data center and virtual instance type separately. Third, we demonstrate that CloudCmp is useful in guiding provider selection by comparing CloudCmp's results with the performance of real applications deployed in the clouds.

Finally, there is much recent work studying other aspects of cloud computing platforms, such as how to make cloud platforms trustworthy and accountable [26, 33], how to enable private cloud computing environment [37], and how to exploit and remedy interference between colocated virtual instances [31, 32]. Our work complements previous work by studying an orthogonal aspect of cloud computing: the cost-performance comparison of today's cloud providers.

9. CONCLUSION

Arguably, the time for computing-as-a-utility has now arrived. It is hard to see a future wherein rapidly growing startups, low footprint "mom and pop" companies that want a presence on the web, and one-off tasks needing large amounts of specialized computation such as document translation and protein sequencing would not benefit from public cloud computing services.

In this context, this work presents the first tool, CloudCmp, to systematically compare the performance and cost of cloud providers along dimensions that matter to customers. We address some key challenges with regards to scoping the problem to one that is manageable given bounded money and time and yet is meaningful to predict the performance of real applications. We observe dramatic performance and cost variations across providers in their virtual instances, storage services, and network transfers. We believe CloudCmp represents a significant first step towards enabling fast and accurate provider selection for the emerging cloud applications and towards an end-to-end benchmark suite that can serve as a progress card for provider's optimizations.

Acknowledgements

This work was funded in part by an NSF CAREER Award CNS-0845858 and Award CNS-0925472. We thank the anonymous reviewers for their helpful feedback and suggestions. We also thank Reza Baghai and Brad Calder for insights that helped improve the methodology and presentation.

10. REFERENCES

[1] Amazon SimpleDB. `http://aws.amazon.com/simpledb/`.

[2] Amazon Web Service. `http://aws.amazon.com`.

[3] AWS SDK for Java. `http://aws.amazon.com/sdkforjava`.

[4] CloudCmp Project Website. `http://cloudcmp.net`.

[5] CloudStatus. `http://www.cloudstatus.com`.

[6] Comparing Amazon EC2 performance with other cloud/VPS hosting options... and real hardware. `http://www.paessler.com/blog/2009/04/14/prtg-7/comparing-amazon-ec2-performance-with-other-cloudvps-hosting-options-and-real-hardware`.

[7] Google AppEngine. `http://code.google.com/appengine`.

[8] Iperf. `http://iperf.sourceforge.net`.

[9] Java binding for Rackspace CloudFiles. `http://github.com/rackspace/java-cloudfiles/tree`.

[10] Java TPC-W Implementation. `http://www.ece.wisc.edu/~pharm/tpcw.shtml`.

[11] Linux TCP Protocol. `http://www.kernel.org/doc/man-pages/online/pages/man7/tcp.7.html`.

[12] Microsoft Windows Azure. `http://www.microsoft.com/windowsazure`.

[13] PlanetLab. `http://www.planet-lab.org`.

[14] Rackspace Cloud. `http://www.rackspacecloud.com`.

[15] Rackspace Cloud Servers versus Amazon EC2: Performance Analysis. `http://www.thebitsource.com/featured-posts/rackspace-cloud-servers-versus-amazon-ec2-performance-analysis/`.

[16] SPEC CPU2006 Benchmark. `http://www.spec.org/cpu2006`.

[17] SPEC Java Virtual Machine Benchmark 2008. `http://www.spec.org/jvm2008/`.

[18] Standard Performance Evaluation Corporation. `http://www.spec.org`.

[19] State of the Cloud, May 2010. `http://www.jackofallclouds.com/2010/05/state-of-the-cloud-may-2010`.

[20] TPC Benchmark W. `http://www.tpcw.org/tpcw`.

[21] Windows Azure SDK for Java. `http://www.windowsazure4j.org/`.

[22] M. Armbrust, A. Fox, R. Griffith, A.D. Joseph, R.H. Katz, A. Konwinski, G. Lee, D. Patterson, A. Rabkin, I. Stoica, and Others. Above the clouds: A berkeley view of cloud computing. *EECS Department, University of California, Berkeley, Tech. Rep. UCB/EECS-2009-28*, 2009.

[23] B.F. Cooper, Adam Silberstein, Erwin Tam, Raghu Ramakrishnan, and Russell Sears. Benchmarking Cloud Serving Systems with YCSB. In *ACM Symposium on Cloud Computing*, 2010.

[24] Simson Garfinkel. An Evaluation of Amazon s Grid Computing Services : EC2 , S3 and SQS. *Harvard University, Tech. Rep. TR-08-07*.

[25] Seth Gilbert and Nancy Lynch. Brewer's conjecture and the feasibility of consistent, available, partition-tolerant web services. In *ACM SIGACT News*, 2002.

[26] Andreas Haeberlen. A Case for the Accountable Cloud. In *ACM SIGOPS LADIS*, 2009.

[27] Mohammad Hajjat, Xin Sun, Yu-Wei Eric Sung, David Maltz, Sanjay Rao, Kunwadee Sripanidkulchai, and Mohit Tawarmalani. Cloudward Bound: Planning for Beneficial Migration of Enterprise Applications to the Cloud. In *ACM SIGCOMM*, 2010.

[28] Ron Kohavi, Randal M. Henne, and Dan Sommerfield. Practical guide to controlled experiments on the web. In *ACM KDD*, volume 2007. ACM Press, 2007.

[29] Ang Li, Xiaowei Yang, Srikanth Kandula, and Ming Zhang. CloudCmp: Shopping for a Cloud Made Easy. In *USENIX HotCloud*, 2010.

[30] Jitendra Padhye, Victor Firoiu, Don Towsley, and Jim Kurose. Modeling TCP Throughput: A Simple Model and its Empirical Validation. In *ACM SIGCOMM*, 1998.

[31] Himanshu Raj, R Nathuji, A Singh, and Paul England. Resource management for isolation enhanced cloud services. In *ACM Workshop on Cloud Computing Security*, pages 77–84, 2009.

[32] Thomas Ristenpart, Eran Tromer, Hovav Shacham, and Stefan Savage. Hey, You, Get Off of My Cloud: Exploring Information Leakage in Third-Party Compute Clouds. In *ACM CCS*, Chicago, 2009.

[33] Nuno Santos, K.P. Gummadi, and Rodrigo Rodrigues. Towards trusted cloud computing. In *HotCloud*, 2009.

[34] E. Walker. Benchmarking amazon EC2 for high-performance scientific computing. *USENIX Login*, 2008.

[35] Guohui Wang and T. S. Eugene Ng. The Impact of Virtualization on Network Performance of Amazon EC2 Data Center. In *IEEE INFOCOM*, 2010.

[36] Jonathan S. Ward. A Performance Comparison of Clouds: Amazon EC2 and Ubuntu Enterprise Cloud. SICSA DemoFEST, 2009.

[37] T. Wood, A. Gerber, KK Ramakrishnan, P. Shenoy, and J. Van Der Merwe. The Case for Enterprise-Ready Virtual Private Clouds. In *USENIX HotCloud*, 2009.

Comparing DNS Resolvers in the Wild

Bernhard Ager
T-Labs/TU Berlin
bernhard@net.t-labs.tu-berlin.de

Wolfgang Mühlbauer
ETH Zurich
muehlbauer@tik.ee.ethz.ch

Georgios Smaragdakis
T-Labs/TU Berlin
georgios@net.t-labs.tu-berlin.de

Steve Uhlig
T-Labs/TU Berlin
steve@net.t-labs.tu-berlin.de

ABSTRACT

The Domain Name System (DNS) is a fundamental building block of the Internet. Today, the performance of more and more applications depend not only on the responsiveness of DNS, but also the exact answer returned by the queried DNS resolver, e. g., for Content Distribution Networks (CDN).

In this paper, we compare local DNS resolvers against GoogleDNS and OpenDNS for a large set of vantage points. Our end-host measurements inside 50 commercial ISPs reveal that two aspects have a significant impact on responsiveness: (1) the latency to the DNS resolver, (2) the content of the DNS cache when the query is issued. We also observe significant diversity, even at the AS-level, among the answers provided by the studied DNS resolvers. We attribute this diversity to the location-awareness of CDNs as well as to the location of DNS resolvers that breaks the assumption made by CDNs about the vicinity of the end-user and its DNS resolver. Our findings pinpoint limitations within the DNS deployment of some ISPs, as well as the way third-party DNS resolvers bias DNS replies.

Categories and Subject Descriptors

C.2.5 [**Computer-Communication Networks**]: Local and Wide-Area Networks—*Internet*

General Terms

Measurement, Performance

Keywords

DNS resolvers, measurement, performance analysis

1. INTRODUCTION

The Domain Name System (DNS) was originally intended to provide a naming service, i. e., one-to-one mappings between a domain name and an IP address. Since then, the popular applications have changed from static content hosting to distributed and dynamic content delivery. As a consequence, DNS is a highly scalable system that fulfills the needs of applications that often have very strong requirements in terms of responsiveness of DNS [9, 10, 12]. The scalability of the DNS system stems from the heavy use of caching by DNS resolvers [8].

Today, the DNS system has become a commodity infrastructure that allows applications to map individual users to specific content. This behavior clearly diverges from the original purpose of deploying DNS, and is sometimes considered as abusing it [17]. Given the importance of DNS for end-user experience and how much the DNS system has changed over the last decade, in this paper we study DNS deployment in commercial ISPs and compare it with widely used third-party DNS resolvers, GoogleDNS and OpenDNS.

Based on active measurements carried out across more than 50 commercial ISPs, spanning 5 continents and 28 countries around the world, we study the responsiveness and the returned IP addresses by the local DNS resolvers as well as GoogleDNS and OpenDNS. Our results show that a surprisingly high number of commercial ISPs suffer from poor latency to the local DNS resolver. In general, our results do not reveal drastic differences between the local DNS resolvers, GoogleDNS, and OpenDNS, in terms of responsiveness. Several ISPs show clear signs of DNS load balancing, that leads to a poor usage of DNS caching.

Our findings also reveal that third-party DNS resolvers do not manage to redirect the users towards content available within the ISP, contrary to the local DNS ones. We conjecture and partly validate that the reason for this behavior of third-party DNS resolvers has to do with their location, typically outside ISPs, in combination with current inability of DNS resolvers to indicate the original IP address of the end-host in the DNS requests [5]. The current advantage of local DNS resolvers is their ability to represent the end-user in terms of geographic location and its vicinity to content.

In spite of the importance of DNS, we are not aware of any work that has performed such an extensive study of the DNS system based on measurements from end-hosts, and compared local DNS resolvers against third-party DNS resolvers.

The remainder of this paper is structured as follows: we start with an overview of the DNS system (Section 2) and describe our data set and how it was collected in Section 3. Then Section 4 analyzes our results before we conclude in Section 5.

IMC'10, November 1–3, 2010, Melbourne, Australia.

2. DOMAIN NAME SYSTEM

In this section we give a brief overview of the design of the Domain Name System (DNS) and how the different DNS components interact. We also take a look at how DNS is being used today.

2.1 DNS Primer

DNS relies on a distributed database with a hierarchical structure. The root zone of the DNS system is centrally administered and serves its *zone* information via a collection of *root servers*. The root servers delegate responsibility for specific parts (zones) of the hierarchy to other *name servers*, which may in turn delegate the responsibility to other name servers. At the end, each site is responsible for its own *domain* and maintains its own database containing its information and operates an *authoritative* name server.

The whole database is usually queried by end-hosts using a local name server called *caching resolver*. If this name server receives a query for information that it does not have, it must fetch this information from another name server. If the server does not know how to contact the authoritative server for a zone, it will query a root server[1]. The root server will *refer* the resolver to another server that is authoritative for the domain that is immediately below the root and of which the zone is a part. The resolver will then query this server, and so forth, stepping down the tree from the root to the desired zone.

For efficiency reasons DNS relies heavily on caching [8]. All information that a name server delivers to a resolver is cached for a duration specified in the TTL field of the *resource records* (RR). Caching today is usually also performed on end-hosts by the operating system's *stub resolver*, as well as applications, e. g., web browsers.

2.2 DNS Today

When DNS was introduced in 1983, its sole purpose was to resolve host names into IP addresses in a more scalable fashion than the until then used `hosts` file. Since then a number of features and new uses have found their way into the omnipresent DNS. In addition to the increasing complexity within the DNS protocol itself [16], new and oftentimes unforeseen (ab)uses have been established. Paul Vixie gives an overview in [17]. The most important points of critique are as follows:

CDN load balancing: Content delivery networks set short TTLs on their DNS answers to allow for short reaction times to load shifts, thus crippling cacheability and scalability of the whole system. In addition, CDNs tailor their reply for the IP address of the requesting resolver using the often misguided assumption that the DNS resolver is close to the client originating the request.

NXDOMAIN catcher: Some ISPs and also OpenDNS mangle a negative reply with the NXDOMAIN status code into a positive one with the IP address of a search website under the control of the ISP. By hosting advertisements along the search results it is easily possible to increase the profit margin. While this may work to some degree for web browsing, applications relying on proper delivery of NXDOMAIN records, e. g., email, are inevitably hampered.

[1]The first query can go to some authoritative server below the root if there exists cached information.

A third-party ecosystem around DNS has evolved over the last couple of years. Players like OpenDNS, AdvantageDNS, UltraDNS, and most recently Google offer open resolvers to anyone with different feature sets. OpenDNS Basic does NXDOMAIN catching but offers phishing and botnet protection for free. Furthermore, OpenDNS increases the service level for payment between 5 dollars a month up to several thousand dollars per year for business customers. When Google Public DNS entered the market, their highest-valued goals were to "speed up your browsing experience" and to "improve your security." To achieve both targets Google advertises an impressive list of optimizations and fine tuning [2], e. g., prefetching, load balancing with shared cache, validity checking, and nonce prepending. Google Public DNS also refrains from utilizing NXDOMAIN to make profit. From an implementation perspective, most if not all of the third-party resolvers host their DNS servers on multiple sites around the globe and use anycast to guide DNS clients to the nearest resolver.

In this open market space a user annoyed by his ISP's DNS can easily choose for cost-free third-party service. Tools like namebench [3] might help him in choosing a well-performing one. The irony however is that a user by choosing a different DNS than the one assigned by his ISP will most likely undermine the traffic matrix optimizations performed by CDNs and ISPs, and can potentially even lower his quality of experience due to longer download times.

3. MEASUREMENTS

Data collection on end-hosts is intrinsically difficult due to lack of willingness to participate or due to privacy concerns [7]. Yet, for this paper we are interested in the DNS performance as perceived by end-users and therefore make efforts to collect data directly from users' computers. This section describes our data and how it was collected.

To achieve our goal of comparing the responsiveness of various DNS resolvers, we wrote code that performs DNS queries for more than 10,000 hosts. Amongst other tasks, the code measures DNS response times and returned TTLs for all queried hosts, relying on different DNS resolvers. We asked friends to run our code in early April 2010, leading to traces from more than 60 vantage points, covering 28 countries and 5 continents. Overall, we have obtained traces for some 50 commercial ISPs. During our measurements, the following information was collected:

1. **Vantage point:** Our code initially determines the public IP address and operating system of the executing machine as well as a current time stamp and the IP address of the local DNS resolver.

2. **Resolver:** Periodically, we determine the RTT[2] towards the local, Google, and OpenDNS resolver and perform traceroutes towards these three resolvers. This reveals potential route changes and the proximity of DNS resolvers to our vantage points.

[2]We rely on the response time reported by `dig` when querying for the root zone NS records, rather than using `ping` or `traceroute`.

3. **Host:** For each of our approximately 10,000 target host names we perform, using the `dig` program, two consecutive DNS queries and measure the response times. Comparing response times between the first and second query gives insights into caching and load balancing, see Section 4.2. Besides response times, we record the returned TTL values and the IP addresses of the DNS responses.

Presumably, the majority of Internet users rely on DNS services that are provided by their ISP. This local DNS resolver is automatically configured during the dial-in handshake or via DHCP (*Local DNS*). Yet, alternative DNS providers claim to speed up the browsing experience (GoogleDNS) [2], and some users think that DNS queries can be processed much more quickly by employing a large cache of domain names (OpenDNS) [4]. To check for potential differences in performance, our code sends the same DNS queries to multiple DNS servers: the locally configured DNS server, to 8.8.8.8, and to 208.67.222.222, whereby the latter two are the DNS IP addresses used by Google and OpenDNS,[3] respectively.

In order to improve its efficiency, DNS heavily relies on caching, i. e., storing DNS query results for a period of time in DNS cache servers provided by ISPs or in home routers that implement DNS caches. As we seek to investigate potential bias in DNS response times for different types of queried hosts (e. g., popular vs. rarely queried hosts), we download from Alexa the list of top 1,000,000 sites [1], and select more than 10,000 hosts to be queried by our code as follows:

top5000: These are the 5,000 most popular hosts according to the Alexa ranking. The answer to many of these DNS queries may already be stored at close-by cache servers. We point out that the top5000 hosts are selected based on a global ranking, and hence are not necessarily the most popular hosts if ranked by country, region, etc.

tail2000: These are 2,000 hosts from the tail of the Alexa ranking and are less likely to be cached in close-by DNS servers.

embedded: Many web-pages include embedded content (e. g., AVI, Flash, or Java) that the browser may have to retrieve separately from different domains. We take the top 1,000 hosts according to the Alexa ranking, download with `wget` the content of all these hosts and compile a list of domains from which such embedded content is retrieved. By doing so, we obtain some 3,500 host domains.

Restricting to 10,000 hosts allows our measurements to finish within a couple of hours, which turned out to be acceptable to our end-users. Resolving the names of our 10,000 hosts reveals that a significant number of them (709) rely on DNS redirection. The set **redirected** contains all host names for which we see a CNAME record to an external domain (such as a CDN). The set **akamaized** is a subset of **redirected**, containing the 434 hosts that are redirected to Akamai. Information about redirection will be used for the CDN study in Section 4.3.

In principle, there can be interactions between two different vantage points in our experiments if the script is run close in time and based on the same list of hosts: for example, OpenDNS or GoogleDNS can cache the answer when vantage point A sends a query. When another vantage point B sends the same query, the response time will be significantly shorter if the reply is already in the cache. However, by inspecting timestamps in our traces and the DNS servers' approximate locations as revealed by traceroute and the RTT, we can infer whether interactions may have happened. The traces presented here are carefully selected and do not show any degree of interaction.

4. EVALUATION OF DNS RESOLVERS

In this section we rely on the measurements explained in the previous section, and analyze the behavior of the different DNS resolvers, with respect to responsiveness (Section 4.1), DNS deployment (Section 4.2) and the returned answers (Section 4.3).

4.1 Responsiveness

Google claims on its website that Google Public DNS speeds up browsing performance [2]. One primary goal of this paper is to understand the impact of the selected DNS resolver on the observed DNS response time. Is it really true that alternative DNS resolvers such as GoogleDNS or OpenDNS offer better performance than the local resolver?

To answer this question, it is crucial to rely on measurements that are carried out directly from end-hosts connected to commercial ISPs, see Section 3. If the DNS deployment within the local ISP is properly done, we would expect very small latencies to the resolvers maintained by the local DNS. Yet, we find cases where GoogleDNS and OpenDNS outperform the local DNS resolver in terms of observed response times.

We select two vantage points that are representative for many other traces. The first is located in Germany and we qualify it as "good ISP". The second is based in the US and we call it "bad ISP". It is not our goal to assess individual ISPs. Rather these terms reflect that the "good ISP" shows better DNS performance in terms of response times, load balancing, caching, etc., compared to the "bad ISP", see Section 4.2. Figure 1 and Figure 2 display the CCDF of the response times, in milliseconds, observed at these two vantage points. The leftmost part of the curves on these two figures shows the minimal latency that has been achieved by the DNS resolvers across all 10,000 queries. This minimal latency can be seen as a metric to characterize the proximity of a DNS resolver to the actual end-host. Figure 1 shows a case where the smallest latency differs significantly between the local ISP, OpenDNS, and GoogleDNS at 11ms, 24ms and 44ms. Although both GoogleDNS and OpenDNS maintain a large set of strategically placed resolvers and rely on anycast to route DNS queries, their latencies are far higher than those of the local resolver. The local resolver appears to be close to the end-host. This underlines the importance of placing a resolver in the proximity of end-hosts.

Surprisingly, there are cases where we observe that GoogleDNS or OpenDNS perform as well if not better than the local ISP resolver, see Figure 2. For our "bad ISP" the network distance towards OpenDNS appears to be especially

[3]Other DNS IP addresses such as 8.8.4.4 for GoogleDNS are generally configured as secondary DNS server.

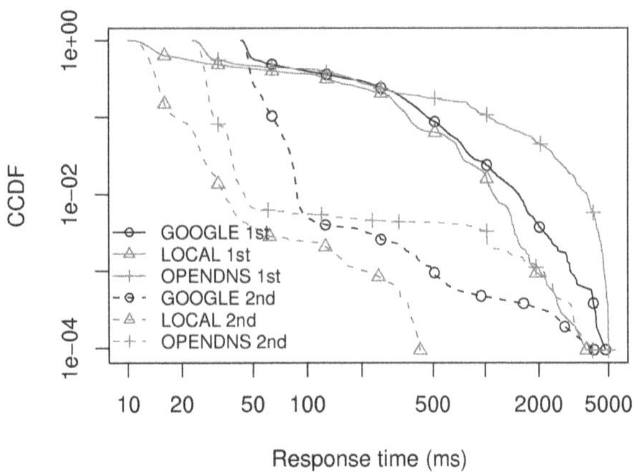

Figure 1: CCDF of response times for "good ISP". The local resolver has significantly lower RTTs than both GoogleDNS and OpenDNS.

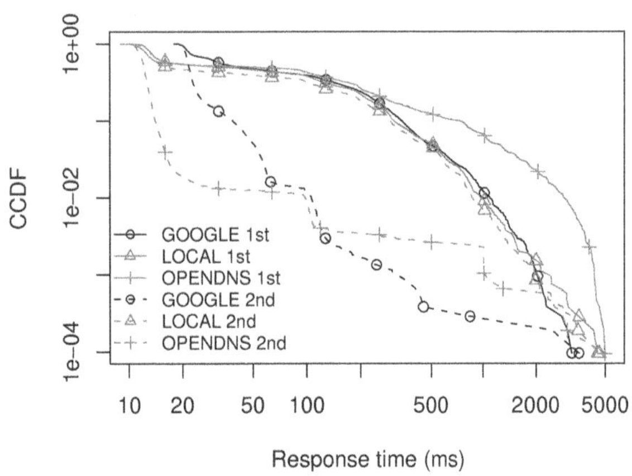

Figure 2: CCDF of response times for "bad ISP". The time for the second query does not improve much.

small. Indeed, the RTT towards OpenDNS is only 10ms while it is 11ms towards the local DNS. In total, we observe 17 vantage points where either GoogleDNS or OpenDNS have in the worst case the same latency as the local DNS. On 21 vantage points, the local DNS is at least 25ms faster than the other two third-party resolvers; for the remaining 29 vantage points the local DNS only marginally outperforms GoogleDNS and OpenDNS.

In addition to deploying resolvers in the proximity of end-hosts, another key aspect to achieve good DNS performance is efficient caching. With respect to caching, Google aims to increase the number of cache hits through load balancing DNS resolvers that avoid cache fragmentation or by actively prefetching names [2]. When the curves for the first query are close to vertical, this shows that the caches are primed. Based on our plots, the three resolvers do not seem to be so well primed. While GoogleDNS performs significantly better on the tail of the curve than OpenDNS for the traces shown, this does not hold in general. Based on our measurements, we can neither confirm nor refute any gains obtained from techniques such as name prefetching or load balancing for shared caching as Google or OpenDNS may use.

To study caching behavior, our measurements always perform two consecutive DNS queries for the same name. Comparing the curves in Figure 1 for the first and second DNS query, we observe considerably faster response times for the second query due to caching of the DNS answers by the resolvers. The differences in the latencies to the resolvers become then even more obvious. Typically over 95% of the second queries are being answered within 100ms.

Overall, the barrier to achieve lower DNS response times seems to be the distance to the local resolver, once the DNS resolver cache is properly populated. GoogleDNS for instance does not seem to achieve their 50ms objective [10] for most of the queries in the case of the "good ISP" (Figure 1). There are still less than 1% of the cases for which all resolvers take more than 100ms to answer, due to non-cacheable records, one-time errors, and measurement artifacts.[4]

4.2 DNS Deployment

The observation from the previous section, that most of the second queries can be answered from the cache, does not hold for the local DNS of the "bad ISP" (Figure 2). In this section, we dig further into the results from Section 4.1, by showing the results from the first query against those of the second query on a scatter plot (see Figure 3 and 4). The x-axis of Figure 3 and 4 show the response time in milliseconds for the first query, while the y-axis the response time in milliseconds for the second query.

In Figure 3, we observe one horizontal line per DNS resolver for the "good ISP", meaning that the response times for the second queries show only small variation and are consistently better than those for the first query. An ISP that has a properly deployed DNS infrastructure should show this kind of pattern. However, several of our vantage points display a behavior like the "bad ISP" (Figure 4), where points are scattered along a horizontal and vertical line, as well as the diagonal. We explain this behavior by a load balancing setup without a shared cache. Sections with a sharp decline in the CCDF for the second query (Figure 1) correspond to the horizontal patterns in Figure 3: the first query primed the cache and the second query could be served from that cache. The diagonal in Figure 4 stems from hostnames for which both queries needed an iterative resolving because the second query was redirected to a different resolver. Finally, the vertical line springs from host names for which the first query could be served from the cache, while the second query was directed to a different resolver where the cache was not primed. Our conjecture is supported by consistent observations in which a significant proportion of the TTLs for the first and the second query differ considerably.

Several ISPs for which we have multiple traces display this behavior in a consistent way. Furthermore, we see this behavior for both OpenDNS and GoogleDNS in several traces. We conjecture that OpenDNS and GoogleDNS also use load balancing for highly loaded sites.

For some ISPs, we observe high RTTs towards the local DNS *and* load balancing. We conjecture that in these cases the DNS infrastructure is centralized and requires load bal-

[4]Typically, the second latency is considerably higher than the first one for at most 10 out of 10,000 hosts. Potential reasons may include fluctuations in routing, links resets, server reconfiguration, etc.

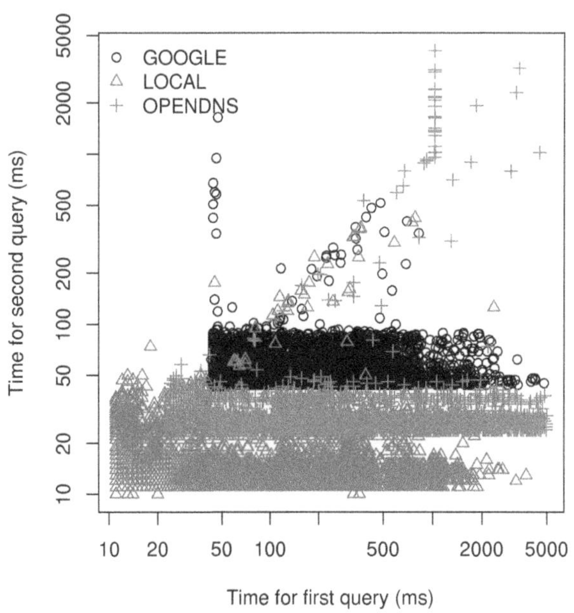

Figure 3: "Good ISP": as expected most of the second queries can be answered significantly faster than the first query due to caching.

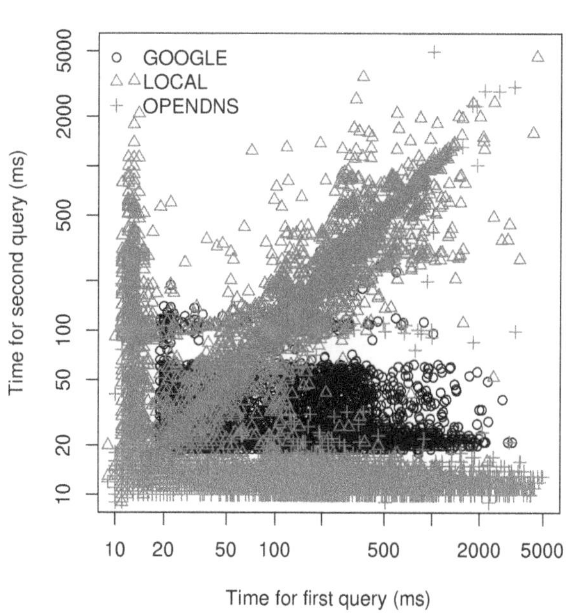

Figure 4: "Bad ISP": the ISP balances load over different DNS resolvers, so the second query cannot always be answered from the cache. A strong diagonal and a vertical line emerge.

ancing to compensate for the high number of queries arriving at a single location.

Although there are valid reasons to rely on DNS load balancing, the way some ISPs are implementing it prevents caching from being properly utilized. A hierarchical DNS infrastructure could improve hit rates while preserving distribution of load to different machines.

4.3 DNS Answers

For good end-user experience, fast DNS response times are important. While this aspect has already been studied in Section 4.1, we now investigate the exact answers that DNS returns, i. e., the resolved IP addresses. Frequently, there is more than one available option from where content can be retrieved. Possible reasons include both the use of load balancing and content distribution networks (CDNs) [9, 15]. The latter replicate content and provide copies near the client to optimize network performance [12]. The goal of this section is to study the observed diversity in resolved DNS names (i. e., IP addresses) across different vantage points and different DNS resolvers. In particular, we examine potential interferences between the choice of the DNS resolver and measurements done by CDNs. After all, CDNs such as Akamai determine which IP to return in the DNS response to the client based on measurements done against the DNS resolver, not against the client. Choosing a DNS resolver that is far from the end-host might vitiate the performance optimizations made by CDNs.

As expected, there is indeed diversity in the IP addresses returned by DNS. While we perform DNS queries for 10,000 unique host names in our experiments, the overall number of unique resolved IP addresses across all traces is 36,000. One reason is that we always perform two DNS queries for the same host name and then even repeat this for three different DNS resolvers. Apart from load balancing, this can be due to CDN content. When repeating queries or when changing between DNS resolvers, the resolved DNS names may be different depending on the mechanisms CDNs use to optimize network performance for the clients.

In Section 4.1 we find that the local DNS resolvers generally provide lower latencies due to their proximity to the end-hosts. Hence, one may speculate that they better represent the location of end-hosts than other resolvers. If possible, it might be more desirable for performance or economic reasons that CDNs be queried by a DNS resolver that is located within the local ISP of the end-host. Figure 5 shows for each vantage point of our study (x-axis), how many IP addresses that belong to the same ISP as the host of the vantage point, were returned by each DNS resolver, across all queried content.

We find that the majority of DNS answers point to content outside the vantage point's network. GoogleDNS and OpenDNS even return IP addresses from different networks for all our traces. One of the reasons is that these resolvers are usually not located inside the ISP. Yet, for approximately 30 vantage points we observe that content is downloaded from at least 100 hosts located within the ISP's network when the local DNS resolver is queried. There even exist vantage points where local access occurs for 926 of our 10,000 host names.

Although this may not appear much, it is significant if we consider that this locally available content completely covers the `akamaized` set[5] (see Section 3). We harvest IP addresses of Akamai servers by sending DNS queries to Akamai content from different Planetlab servers. Interestingly, we find based on manual inspection that the vantage points with local content generally have an Akamai server deployed within the same network.

[5]Additionally, there is strong overlap with `top5000` and `embedded`.

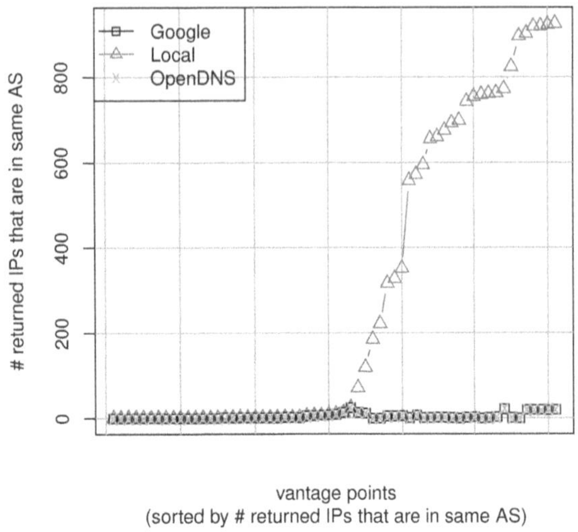

Figure 5: How often do DNS answers point to locally available content?

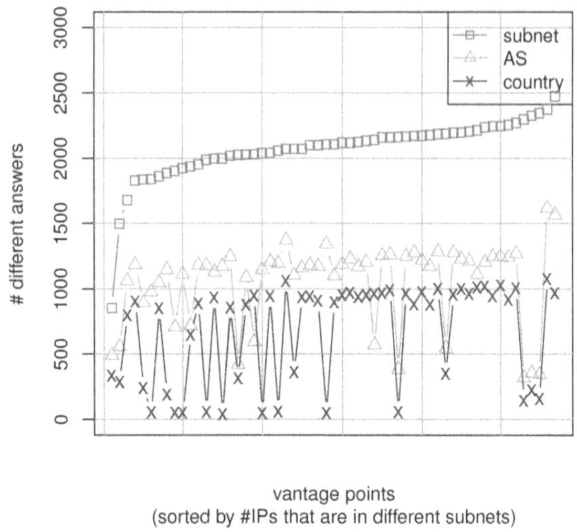

Figure 6: How often do the DNS answers of local resolver and GoogleDNS differ?

From Figure 5 we can infer that only local DNS resolvers direct end-users to content that is locally available in the network of the vantage point. Instead of matching the results of the resolvers against the network of the vantage point, we now directly compare our three DNS resolvers pairwise against each other. More precisely, we count how often the results of the two resolvers are different with respect to the subnet, autonomous system (AS), and country[6] of the DNS answer. Figure 6 presents for each vantage point of our study (x-axis) the number of differences for the comparison local DNS vs. GoogleDNS.

Figure 6 reveals that the answers to the DNS resolvers differ in terms of subnets for approximately 2,000 out of our 10,000 host names. In half of these cases, the returned IP addresses even belong to different ASs and countries. Since the local DNS resolver points to content inside the ISP's network for a significant number of host names (Figure 5), we claim that GoogleDNS and OpenDNS unnecessarily direct end-users to content servers in different ASs or even subnets. Due to space limitations we do not present the plots for the comparisons between Local vs. OpenDNS and Google vs. OpenDNS. Both plots are very similar to Figure 5. Apparently, whenever we change the DNS resolver, there will be different answers from DNS for at least some of the host names. This observation justifies recent activities of the IETF in the direction of standardizing a way to include the IP address of the original end-host in DNS requests [5].

5. CONCLUSION

Based on active measurements from inside more than 50 commercial ISPs, we have studied DNS performance by comparing the ISPs' DNS deployment against widely used third-party DNS resolvers, namely GoogleDNS and OpenDNS.

Typically, end-hosts experience very small latencies to the resolvers maintained by the local ISP, though there exist cases where GoogleDNS and OpenDNS outperform the local DNS resolvers in terms of the observed response times. Moreover, our findings suggest that several ISPs and OpenDNS rely on a load balancing setup without a shared cache, resulting in poor caching efficiency. Even Google Public DNS, despite their claim [2] exhibits the same behavior for a few vantage points. Moreover, we observe that third-party DNS resolvers do not manage to redirect the users towards content available within the ISP, contrary to the local DNS ones. This observation holds for all akamaized content.

Given the increasing share of CDN traffic [11, 13] we aim in the future to fully understand to what degree the choice of DNS resolvers does vitiate the performance optimizations made by CDNs. In this regard, we plan to rerun our experiments based on an enlarged set of vantage points and with an enhanced version of our script, e. g., to scrutinize caching and investigate the role of anycast in DNS performance.

Acknowledgments

The authors wish to thank all volunteers who ran our script on their systems and submitted the results. Moreover, we would like to thank our shepherd, Craig Partridge, and the anonymous reviewers for their constructive comments.

6. REFERENCES

[1] Alexa top sites. http:///www.alexa.com/topsites.

[2] Google Public DNS. http://code.google.com/intl/de-DE/speed/public-dns/.

[3] Namebench—open-source dns benchmark utility. http://code.google.com/p/namebench/.

[4] OpenDNS: What's Your Take? http://www.neowin.net/news/opendns-whats-your-take.

[5] C. Contavalli, W. van der Gaast, S. Leach, and D. Rodden. Client IP information in DNS requests. IETF draft, work in progress, draft-vandergaast-edns-client-ip-00.txt, Jan 2010.

[6] We used geolocation data to map IP addresses to countries [6].

[6] Hexasoft Development Sdn. Bhd. IP Address Geolocation to Identify Website Visitor's Geographical Location. `http://www.ip2location.com`.

[7] D. Joumblatt, R. Teixeira, J. Chandrashekar, and N. Taft. Perspectives on Tracing End-hosts: A Survey Summary. *Computer Communication Review*, 40(2):51–55, 2010.

[8] J. Jung, E. Sit, H. Balakrishnan, and R. Morris. DNS Performance and the Effectiveness of Caching. *IEEE/ACM Trans. Netw.*, 10(5):589–603, 2002.

[9] B. Krishnamurthy, C. Wills, and Y. Zhang. On the Use and Performance of Content Distribution Networks. In *Proc. of ACM IMW '01*, San Francisco, CA, USA.

[10] R. Krishnan, H. Madhyastha, S. Srinivasan, S. Jain, A. Krishnamurthy, T. Anderson, and J. Gao. Moving Beyond End-to-end Path Information to Optimize CDN Performance. In *Proc. of ACM IMC '09*, Chicago, IL, USA.

[11] C. Labovitz, D. McPherson, and S. Iekel-Johnson. Internet observatory report. http://www.nanog.org/meetings/nanog47/.

[12] T. Leighton. Improving Performance on the Internet. *Commun. ACM*, 52(2):44–51, 2009.

[13] Ingmar Poese, Benjamin Frank, Bernhard Ager, Georgios Smaragdakis, and Anja Feldmann. Improving Content Delivery using Provider-aided Distance Information. In *Proc. of ACM IMC '10*, Melbourne, Australia.

[14] A. Su, D. Choffnes, A. Kuzmanovic, and F. Bustamante. Drafting Behind Akamai: Inferring Network Conditions Based on CDN Redirections. *IEEE/ACM Trans. Netw.*, 17(6):1752–1765, 2009.

[15] S. Triukose, Z. Al-Qudah, and M. Rabinovich. Content Delivery Networks: Protection or Threat? In *Proc. of ESORICS '09*, Saint-Malo, France.

[16] P. Vixie. DNS Complexity. *ACM Queue*, 5(3):24–29, 2007.

[17] P. Vixie. What DNS is Not. *Commun. ACM*, 52(12):43–47, 2009.

Improving Content Delivery Using Provider-aided Distance Information

Ingmar Poese
T-Labs/TU Berlin
ingmar@net.t-labs.tu-berlin.de

Benjamin Frank
T-Labs/TU Berlin
bfrank@net.t-labs.tu-berlin.de

Bernhard Ager
T-Labs/TU Berlin
bernhard@net.t-labs.tu-berlin.de

Georgios Smaragdakis
T-Labs/TU Berlin
georgios@net.t-labs.tu-berlin.de

Anja Feldmann
T-Labs/TU Berlin
anja@net.t-labs.tu-berlin.de

ABSTRACT

Content delivery systems constitute a major portion of today's Internet traffic. While they are a good source of revenue for Internet Service Providers (ISPs), the huge volume of content delivery traffic also poses a significant burden and traffic engineering challenge for the ISP. The difficulty is due to the immense volume of transfers, while the traffic engineering challenge stems from the fact that most content delivery systems themselves utilize a distributed infrastructure. They perform their own traffic flow optimization and realize this using the DNS system. While content delivery systems may, to some extent, consider the user's performance within their optimization criteria, they currently have no incentive to consider any of the ISP's constraints. As a consequence, the ISP has "lost control" over a major part of its traffic. To overcome this impairment, we propose a solution where the ISP offers a Provider-aided Distance Information System (PaDIS). PaDIS uses information available only to the ISP to rank any client-host pair based on distance information, such as delay, bandwidth or number of hops.

In this paper we show that the applicability of the system is significant. More than 70% of the HTTP traffic of a major European ISP can be accessed via multiple different locations. Moreover, we show that deploying PaDIS is not only beneficial to ISPs, but also to users. Experiments with different content providers show that improvements in download times of up to a factor of four are possible. Furthermore, we describe a high performance implementation of PaDIS and show how it can be deployed within an ISP.

Categories and Subject Descriptors

C.2.4 [**Distributed Systems**]: Client/Server; C.2.5 [**Local and Wide-Area Networks**]: Internet

General Terms

Measurement, Performance

Keywords

Content Distribution, Host Diversity, Server Selection, DNS Redirection, Residential Traces

IMC'10, November 1–3, 2010, Melbourne, Australia.

1. INTRODUCTION

The Internet has evolved into a system where users can easily share content with friends and/or other users via applications such as online social networks, video portals, One-Click Hosters, Web services, wikis, blogs, or P2P file-sharing applications. In terms of volume, multi-media content, including photos, music, and videos, as well as software downloads and updates, are major contributors and together responsible for most of the Internet traffic [24, 22, 31, 29]. Indeed, HTTP is used to access this information and therefore accounts for more than 50 % of the traffic [2, 22, 24, 31, 29]. Moreover, it is hardly (mis-)used as a transport protocol for other applications [24]. Among the causes for the increase of HTTP traffic are the increase of streaming content, e.g., offered by `youtube.com` and the popularity of the content offered by One-Click Hosters [7] such as `rapidshare.com` or `uploaded.to`.

This content is hosted by the new "Hyper Giants" [22] which include large content providers, such as Google and Yahoo, as well as Content Distribution Networks (CDNs), like Akamai and Limelight. Most of these Hyper Giants are operating not only a substantial number of data centers but are also building up their own network [21]. Some networking researchers are claiming that, due to the phenomenal growth of Hyper Giants, the topological structure of the Internet must be redrawn to include them, together with the Global transit and backbone networks as part of the Internet core, resulting in the topology sketched in Figure 1. This may leave the ISPs as dump pipe providers to the consumer.

To achieve high levels of performance and scalability, most content delivery architectures, including well provisioned hosting and content distribution networks, heavily rely on a distributed infrastructure. Indeed, some of them have deployed hosts in more than 5000 locations throughout the Internet [23]. What's more, the content delivery providers have full control of their transfer process. Therefore, they can optimize the traffic flows so that it minimizes operational costs as long as quality of service agreements with the content producers are met. With the help of the DNS system, they can redirect requests to hosts within their infrastructure and minimize their operational costs. This may result in sub-optimal content delivery performance to the end-users, while imposing a heavy burden on the ISP caused by the pure traffic volume of the content as well as the control loop interactions. If the ISP changes its routing, e.g., for the purpose of traffic engineering, the content delivery network may re-optimize this delivery strategy and change the traffic matrix, which may render the traffic engineering choice of the ISP void [18]. Even though we show in Section 2 that most content is available at multiple locations throughout the Internet, the ISP has no choice regarding where users fetch content from. This decision is, at this point, left to the content delivery network, even though

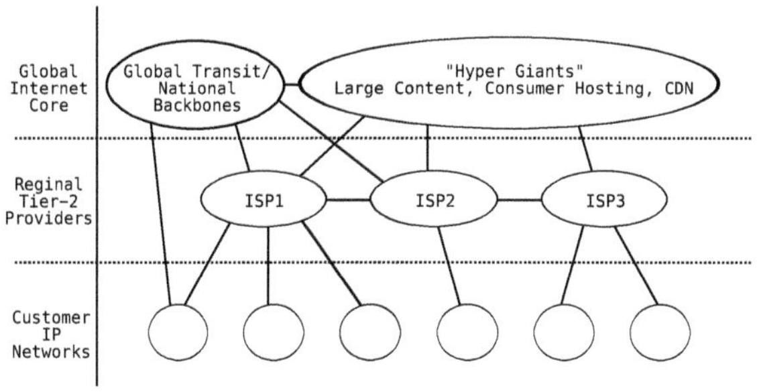

Figure 1: The new Internet Reality [22]?

the content delivery architectures provide a diverse set of hosts for any requested object.

Nevertheless, the ISP has substantial information at its fingertips which can be used to improve overall traffic flow and thus lower network utilization. This, in turn, can increase content delivery performance. However, this information is not readily available to the CDN. Rather, the CDN has to infer such information either via active measurements or client reports. Therefore, we claim that it is possible to improve content delivery using Provider-Aided Distance Information (PaDIS), see Section 3, much in the same way as P2P content delivery can be improved using ISP-P2P collaboration.

Previous work, e.g., [8][19][28] has in principle shown potential for biasing location choices. Indeed, we proposed that each ISP offers a service to the P2P users which explicitly helps them to choose "good" neighbors by ranking possible peers [4, 3]. Such traffic localization mechanism for P2P traffic, as proposed by Aggarwal et al. [4, 3], Xie et al. [36], Choffnes and Bustamante [11], are currently under discussion within the IETF ALTO [32] working group.

Network based information is in particular useful to circumvent bottlenecks, or to handle application flash crowds and other moving targets. Moreover, if an ISP has more control over its traffic flows, it can choose servers more intelligently and thus avoid network bottlenecks or choose closer servers in terms of network hops. This can both reduce overall traffic volume, as well as network utilization, which may further reduce network based congestion and thus improve the overall user performance.

We therefore propose to improve content delivery using PaDIS. Using active measurements, we show that choosing the appropriate server for content delivery can improve the user's download experience by up to a factor of four; see Section 4.

Our contributions in this paper are:

- To show that more than half of the total traffic, including the dominant HTTP traffic, can be delivered in principle from multiple servers at diverse network locations based on observations from passive packet-level monitoring of more than 20,000 residential DSL lines from a major European ISP.
- To capitalize on the diversity of content delivery, we propose to deploy PaDIS as a content location recommendation system, within the ISP. PaDIS can be interfaced with the ISP's DNS to redirect traffic, or it can be contacted directly by the client system.
- To quantify the content delivery performance improvement when using PaDIS in the wild, within a major European ISP. We report on our experience of downloading content from content distribution networks, and show significant potential for performance improvements. More specifically, we report on our experience when downloading content from different content distribution networks as well as One-Click Hosters. Our results clearly show that the end-user download time is significantly improved, while the ISP regains the ability to perform traffic engineering by biasing application layer choices.

To the best of our knowledge, this is the first work that proposes application and ISP collaboration based on the observation that content is usually accessible at multiple locations due to the prevalence of distributed content delivery architectures. However, there is a chance that the content delivery architecture may try to boycott the choice of the ISP by no longer exposing the multiple locations. However, since the ISPs control the access to the eyeballs, they can still use the principle approach as a negotiation tool. Moreover, with the help of the information from the ISP, it is possible to improve user performance substantially.

The remainder of the paper is structured as follows: In Section 2, we provide evidence in support of the potential diversity of hosts from which content can be downloaded. In Section 3, we provide the architecture of PaDIS and we show how it can be deployed within an ISP. In Section 4, we quantify the content delivery performance improvement while using PaDIS in the wild. We put our work in context with previous related research in Section 5 and conclude in Section 6.

2. CONTENT SERVER DIVERSITY

To highlight that a significant amount of traffic can, in principle, be delivered from multiple different servers at diverse network locations, we rely on passive network traces to identify popular services and active measurements to identify server location diversity.

2.1 Residential ISP Traces

We base our study on three sets of anonymized packet-level observations of residential DSL connections collected at aggregation points within a large European ISP. Our monitor, using Endace monitoring cards, allows us to observe the traffic of more than 20,000 DSL lines to the Internet. The data anonymization, classification, as well as application protocol specific header extraction and anonymization is performed immediately on the secured measurement infrastructure using the Bro NIDS [27] with dynamic protocol detection (DPD) [15].

We use an anonymized 24 h packet trace collected in March 2010 (MAR10) for detailed analysis of the protocol behavior. For studying longer term trends, we used Bro's online analysis capabilities to collect an anonymized protocol specific trace summary (HTTP-14d) spanning 2 weeks. Additionally, we collected an anonymized 5 day DNS trace (DNS-5d) in February 2010 to achieve a better understanding of how hostnames are resolved by different sites. Due to the amount of traffic at our vantage point and the resource intensive analysis, we gathered the online trace summaries one at a time. Table 1 summarizes the characteristics of the traces, including their start, duration, size, and protocol volume. It is not possible to determine the exact application mix for the protocol specific traces, as we only focus on the specific protocol. However, we use full traces to cross check the general application mix evolution.

2.1.1 Popular Services

With regards to the application mix, see Table 1, Maier et al. [24] find that HTTP, BitTorrent, and eDonkey each contribute a significant amount of traffic. In MAR10 HTTP alone contributes almost 60 % of the overall traffic at our vantage point, BitTorrent and eDonkey contribute more than 10 %. Similar protocol distributions have been observed at different times and at other locations of the same ISP. Moreover, these observations are consistent with

Table 1: **Summaries of anonymized traces.**

Name	Type	Start date	Dur	Size	Application Volume
MAR10	packet	Thu 04 Mar'10 2am	24 h	>5 TB	> 3 TB HTTP, > 5 GB DNS
HTTP-14d	log file	Wed 09 Sep'09 3am	14 d	> 200 GB	corresponds to > 40 TB HTTP
DNS-5d	packet	Wed 24 Feb'10 4pm	5 d	>25 GB	> 25 GB DNS

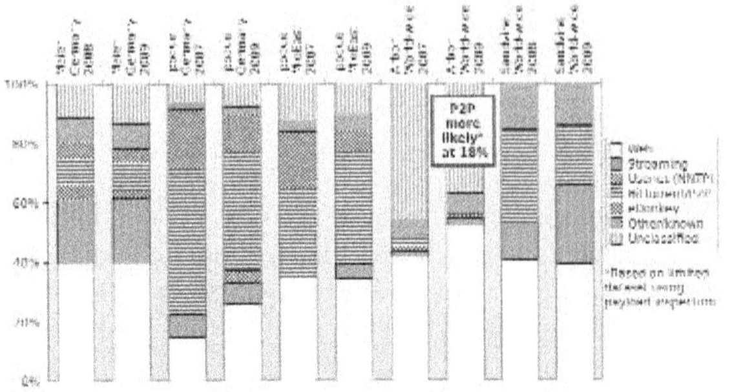

Figure 2: Barplot of Internet Application Mix (unified categories) across years and regions from multiple sources.

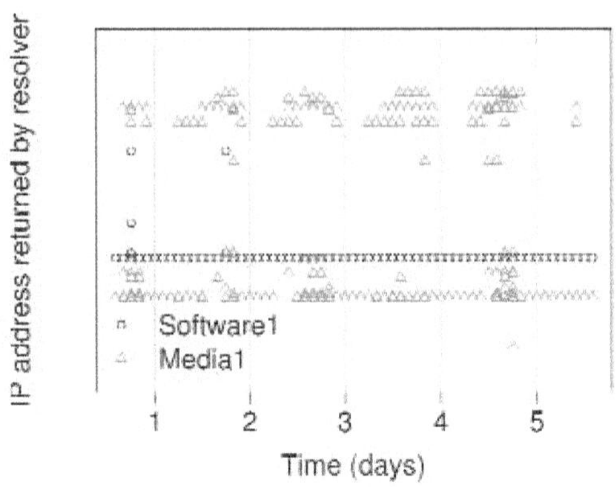

Figure 3: DNS replies for two different CDN-ized sites, in two-hour bins.

other recent Internet application mix studies [24, 22, 31, 29]. Figure 2 [30] summarizes the results of these studies. Note that almost all streaming is done via the Web on top of HTTP. Therefore, we conclude that HTTP is the dominant service.

Analyzing HTTP-14d, we find more than 1.2 billion HTTP requests, or 89 million requests per day on average. This is consistent with 95 million requests in 24 hours in MAR10. The advantage of using click stream data from a large set of residential users is their completeness. We are, e.g., not biased by the content offered *(i)* by a Web service, *(ii)* whether sufficient users installed measurement tools such as the `alexa.com` toolbar, or *(iii)* whether users actually use some kind of Web proxy.

To identify the most popular Web services, we focus on the most popular hosts. As expected, the distribution of host popularity by volume as well as by number of requests is highly skewed and is consistent with a Zipf-like distribution as observed in other studies [24]. The top 10,000 hosts by volume and the top 10,000 hosts by number of requests together result in roughly 17,500 hosts. This indicates that on the one hand, some hosts that are popular by volume may not be popular by number of requests and vice versa. On the other hand, there are some hosts that are popular according to both metrics. The total activity by these hosts accounts for 88.5 % of the overall HTTP volume and more than 84 % of the HTTP requests. Assuming that the HTTP traffic volume accounts for roughly 60 % of the total traffic, similar to the observations made in September 2009 [24, 2] and in MAR10, more than 50 % of the trace's total traffic is captured by these hosts.

2.2 Server Diversity and DNS Load Balancing

To better understand how HTTP requests are handled and assigned to servers, we use DNS-5d to analyze the 20 most heavily queried DNS names to identify typical usage patterns. We consider only the most heavily used resolver. Figure 3 shows two of the typical patterns for two of the DNS names. It also shows how the resolved IP addresses change (y-axis) across time (x-axis) for two hostnames; respectively a software site, labeled Software1, and a media site, labeled Media1. The vertical lines annotate midnight. If two IP addresses are plotted close to each other, this indicates that the longest common prefix of the two addresses is close. We note that the hostname of Software1 is mainly resolved to a single subnet, excepting a few special cases. However, Media1 is load balanced across approximately 16 different sites. For Media1, there appears to be one main site which is almost always available, while the remaining 15 are predominantly used during afternoon and evening peak usage hours.

These results are promising, and show that individual sites do expose a certain degree of server diversity to their users. While our trace (HTTP-14d) includes the queried hostnames, it does not include the resolved IP address, as a HTTP request header contains the hostname but not the IP address of a server. To verify the above behavior and get an up-to-date view of the DNS replies for the hostnames of our trace, we used 3 hosts within the ISP to issue DNS queries to the ISP's DNS resolver for all 17,500 hostnames repeatedly over a fourteen day measurement period starting on Tue Apr 13th 2010. During these two weeks, we received more than 16 million replies. Unless otherwise mentioned, we rely on our active DNS measurements, with augmented statistics concerning volume and requests from HTTP-14d.

2.3 Server Location Diversity

Our analysis of hostnames and their assignment to servers in section 2.2 has shown that content can be served by multiple servers in different locations. In fact, many domains use the service of a *Content Delivery Service* (CDS), which can be seen during the name resolution progress: The original domain name is mapped to the domain of a CDS, which then answers requests on behalf of the requested domain name from one of its caches [34]. Almost all CDSs rely on a distributed infrastructure to handle the expected load, load spikes, flash crowds, and special events. Additionally, this introduces needed redundancy and fail over configurations in their services. Among the most studied CDS' are Content Distribution Networks (CDNs), such as Akamai [23, 34, 17], and Content Delivery Platforms (CDPs), such as Google [21] and their YouTube service [10].

To better understand the DNS resolution process for hostnames hosted on CDS infrastructure, we refer to the machine requesting content as the `DNS client`. Along the same lines, we refer to

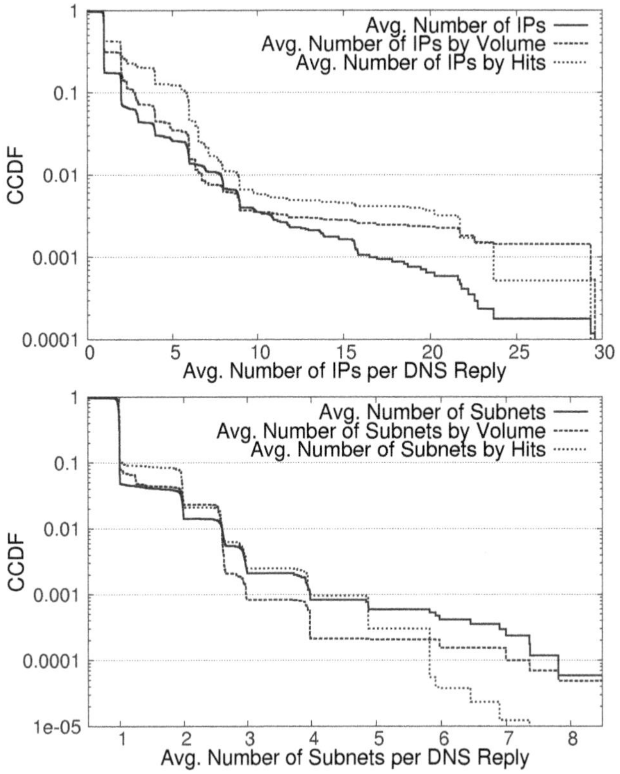

Figure 4: CCDF of mean # of IPs (top) and subnets (bottom) per DNS reply for the ISPs DNS resolver.

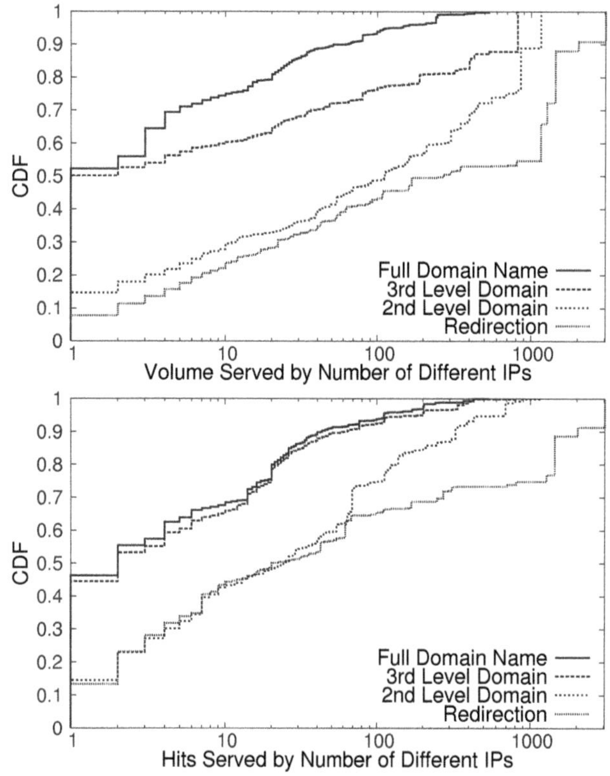

Figure 5: CDF of # of IPs for the ISP DNS resolver normalized by traffic volume (top) and requests (bottom) including aggregation on domain levels. (Logarithmic x-axis.)

the DNS server that receives the query from the client as the `DNS resolver`. This is usually run by the ISP or a third party DNS infrastructure like OpenDNS, also acting as a cache. Lastly, the authoritative DNS server, henceforth referred as `DNS server`, which is usually run by the CDS, replies to the DNS resolver. The DNS resolver caches the reply and hands it back to the DNS client.

The DNS server can choose to return one or more server IP addresses based on the domain name in the request and the IP address of the requesting DNS resolver. For example, it may use a geo-location database [33] to localize the region of the DNS resolver, utilize BGP data to identify the ISP, create a topology map derived via traceroutes, or any combination of these and other topological and geographic localization techniques. A DNS server has, in principle, two methods for load balancing across multiple servers:

MultQuery: Can return multiple IP addresses within a single DNS response

CrossQuery: Can return different IP addresses for repeated queries and thus perform DNS redirection.

In our active DNS measurements, we found that often a mixture of MultQuery and CrossQuery is being used in practice. Furthermore, we used the measurement results to *(i)* map hostnames to sets of IP addresses and *(ii)* check the IP address diversity of these sets for a better understanding of server diversity and their location. We achieved this by aggregating the returned IP addresses into subnets based on BGP information obtained from within the ISP. This allows for detailed information about the different locations within the ISP, while giving an aggregated view of subnets reachable via peering links.

Another issue stems from the fact that the IP address returned by the CDS depends on the IP address of the ISP DNS resolver [5, 26, 34]. Due to this, we used the DNS resolver of the ISP of our vantage point as well as external DNS resolvers (see section 2.3.1). The former reflects the experience of most of the clients at our vantage point[1]. The latter lets us discover additional diversity as well as understand the preference of the CDS for this specific ISP.

Prevalence of MultQuery.

We start our analysis by checking the prevalence of the first form of DNS based load balancing, MultQuery. Figure 4 shows a CCDF plot of the average number of IP addresses (top) and subnets (bottom) per DNS reply. In addition, we included the same data normalized by traffic volume and number of requests.

A first observation is that the number of returned IP addresses per request is rather small. The median is 1, the average is 1.3 and even the 0.9 percentile is 2. We note that even when an answer yields multiple IP addresses, the majority of them are from the same subnet. Therefore, the diversity decreases even further if we aggregate to subnets. From a network perspective, this implies that there is not much choice, neither for the ISP nor for the user, regarding where to download the content from. Both are limited to the information provided by the DNS server. However, when we normalize the hosts by their respective popularity, we see a significant improvement. More than 29% of the volume and 19% of requests have a choice among at least 2 IP addresses.

[1]We verify using the traces that more than 95 % of the clients use the ISP's DNS resolver as their default one.

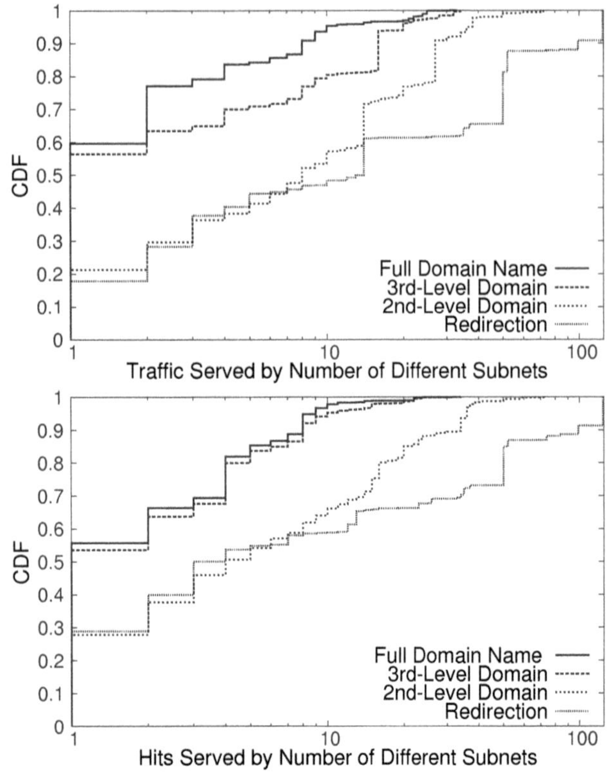

Figure 6: CDF of # of subnets for ISP DNS resolver normalized by traffic volume (top) and by requests (bottom) including aggregation on domain levels. (Logarithmic x-axis.)

Prevalence of CrossQuery.

Next, we check how prevalent CrossQuery, the second form of DNS based load balancing is. Since CrossQuery returns different IP addresses for repeated queries, its potential contribution to server diversity can only be studied by aggregating across time. The lines labeled `Full Domain Name` in Figures 5 and 6 capture this case.

We find that more than 50 % of the volume or requests can be served by more than one IP address. similarly, there is choice between at least two subnets over 40 % of the time across both metrics, see Figure 6. This indicates that there is significant potential for the ISP to bias the location preference of the CDS.

Subdomain Aggregation.

Since some CDSs only use subdomains as hints about the context of the requested URLs or the requested services, we accumulate the answers further regarding the 2nd and 3rd part of the domain names of the hosts, see Figures 5 and 6 at the respective data series called `3rd Level Domain` and `2nd Level Domain`. For example, we might accumulate the IP addresses from DNS replies for `dl1.example.org` and `dl2.example.org` for the statistics on the 2nd level domain, but not the third level domain.

This is a feasible approach, since many hosts respond to all requests that belong to a subset of the subnets returned when accumulating by the second-level domain of DNS resolver answer, including recursive requests and redirections. We verify this behavior with active measurements, see Section 4. We find that at least two major CDNs, a streaming provider and a One-Click Hoster, serve

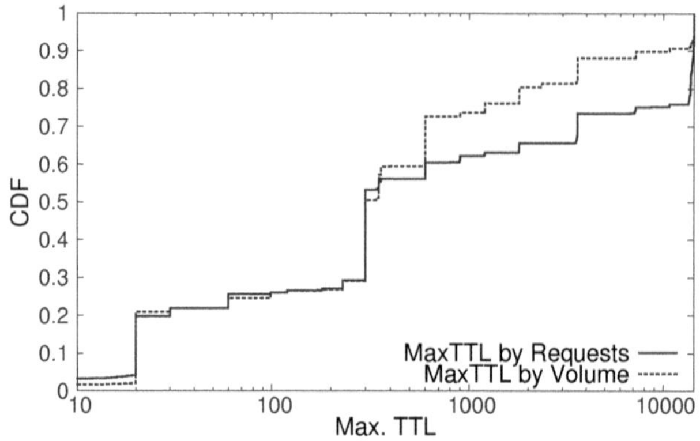

Figure 7: CDF of DNS TTL value by traffic volume and by number of requests.

requested content from servers that match in their second level domain.

We note that the accumulation by third-level domain, and especially by second level domain significantly increases the number of observed subnets per request both normalized by requests as well as by volume. The number of returned subnets further increases when accumulating to the second-level domain of DNS resolver answer. Studying our traces in more detail, we find that this is due to the substantial traffic volume and number of requests that are served by CDNs, some of which are highly distributed within ISPs or located in multihomed datacenters or peer-exchange points.

Infrastructure Redirection Aggregation.

Taking a closer look at the DNS replies [25], we find that some CDSs use CNAME records to map queried hostname to an A record. These A records show the same pattern as the hostnames in the previous section: the second level domain is identical. Similar to the previous approach, we can aggregated by these A records.

For example, at some point in time the hostname `www.bmw.de` is mapped via a CNAME chain to an A record with the name `a1926.b.akamai.net`, while `www.audi.de` is mapped to `a1845.ga.akamai.net`. Since the second level domain on the A records match, these DNS replies will be aggregated. Indeed, it has been shown that both caches will serve the content of either website [35]. On the down side, it is possible that this scheme of aggregation reduces the effectiveness of the CDN's caching strategy. This aggregation is called `Redirection` in Figures 5 and 6.

Turning our attention to the implications of the proposed aggregation schemes, we notice the available diversity increases tremendously. More than 50% of the hits and 70% of the bytes can be served by more than 20 servers. With regards to subnets, the diversity decreases slightly. Nevertheless, more than 5 subnets are available for 45% of the hits and 55% of the bytes.

If we consider aggregation periods in the order of tens of minutes, the numbers do not decrease by much. The reason that most of the diversity is observable even over these short aggregation time periods, is that the typical TTL, see Figure 7, is rather short with a mean of 2, 100 seconds and an median of 300 seconds normalized by volume. When weighted by requests, the mean is 4, 100 seconds and the median is 300 seconds.

2.3.1 *Alternative DNS Resolvers*

So far we have only considered the effect of content diversity when the ISP DNS resolver is used. To understand how much the

DNS load balancing deployed by a CDS is biased by the queried DNS resolver, we repeat the experiment from Section 2.2 using two other DNS resolvers. In particular, we pick the next most popular DNS resolvers found in our traces: GoogleDNS and OpenDNS. Both are third-party resolvers with a global footprint and utilize DNS anycast.

Comparing the results, we find that we attain more IP address diversity and subnet diversity when using the ISP DNS resolver. This is mainly due to the fact that CDSs select the supplied caches based on the source IP address of the querying DNS resolver. Since the CDSs are no longer able to map the request to the AS it originates from, but rather to AS the DNS resolver belongs to, the server selection by the CDS cannot optimize for the location of the DNS client.

2.3.2 Impact on Traffic Localization

Analyzing the three active DNS measurements from the ISP, OpenDNS as well as Google DNS resolver, we find that a significant part of the requests that could have been in principle served by sources within the ISP are directed towards servers that are outside of the ISP. However, before tackling this issue, we need to understand what fraction of the traffic may be served by IP addresses within the ISP's network and what fraction is served by IP addresses outside of the AS. To this end, we analyze each of the three active DNS traces separately. For each trace, we start by classifying all DNS replies regarding the `redirection` aggregation described in section 2.3 and account the volume (or hits) evenly to each of the IP addresses. Next, we classify the IP addresses in two groups - inside and outside of the ISP network. Table 2 summarizes the results of this aggregation regarding the traffic and hits that were kept inside the ISP's network in the columns labeled `observed`.

Turning to the results, we find that there is hardly any difference between those clients that use the external DNS resolvers. Of the returned IP addresses, less than 6 % are within the AS. When weighted by number of requests, this does not change much. However, when normalizing by volume, about 12 % of the traffic stays within the AS.

In contrast, clients that use the ISP's DNS resolver fare better: almost a quarter of the traffic volume is served from servers within the AS. Normalized by requests, we see a three fold increase, and normalized by hits or volume, roughly a two fold increase over using external DNS resolvers. Among the reasons for the "bad" performance of external DNS resolvers is that some CDSs may always return IP addresses outside the ISP, despite the fact that many of its servers are deployed within the ISP. This explains the substantial difference and highlights on the one hand the effectiveness of the CDS optimization, but also points out its limits. As such, it is not surprising that there are efforts under way within the IETF to include the source IP addresses of the DNS client in the DNS requests [12].

However, one can ask if the CDS utilizes the full potential of traffic localization. For this, we check the potential of traffic localization, by changing the volume (or hit) distribution from even to greedy. Thus, as soon as we observe at least one IP address inside the ISP's network, we count all traffic for the entire aggregation to be internal. Table 2 shows the results in the columns labeled `potential` for all three DNS traces.

Note the substantial differences. Our results indicate that a gain of more than a factor of two can be achieved. Furthermore, up to 50 % of the traffic can be delivered from servers within the ISP rather than only 23.4 %. This may not only in itself result in a substantial reduction of costs for the ISP, but it also points out the potential of our proposed approach. While the increase is noticeable for OpenDNS, it is nowhere near that of the ISP's DNS resolver. The potential benefit when relying on GoogleDNS is rather small. A deeper study on our results unveils that content served by highly distributed and redundant infrastructure can be localized the most.

2.4 From Server Diversity to Path Diversity

Next, we ask the question whether the substantial diversity of server locations actually translates to path diversity. For this purpose, we generate a routing topology of the ISP by using data from an IS-IS listener and a BGP listener. However, due to the asymmetry of routing, we have to explore both directions separately. With the same argumentation as in Section 2.3 we choose to aggregate using the `redirection` scheme for calculating path diversity. For the HTTP requests we can determine the path within the ISP using the routing topology. We find that roughly 65 % of the total HTTP requests can be forwarded along at least two different paths. Indeed, roughly 37 % of the HTTP requests can be forwarded along at least four different paths.

In addition, we can use the routing data to determine the paths of all content that is potentially available within the ISP's AS.[2] We find that there is significant path diversity. In some cases, a request can follow up to 20 unique different paths. Moreover, we see that around 70 % of the HTTP traffic volume and requests can be sent along at least two different paths.

2.5 Summary

We see that HTTP is again the dominant traffic source, while the prevalence of P2P traffic decreases. Since most CDSs rely on distributed infrastructure, we not only observe significant server location diversity but also significant path diversity for accessing HTTP based content. Indeed, there is the potential to bias roughly half of the overall traffic by redirecting queries to different content servers.

More precisely, we estimate that around 70 % of the HTTP traffic in a big European ISP can be redirected when taking advantage of the diversity due to MultQuery, CrossQuery and hostname aggregation. Furthermore, we show that current CDS optimizations that approximate the location of end-users based on the location of the local DNS resolvers are more effective than those based on the location of third-party resolvers. Finally, we show that the traffic localization potential within the above mentioned ISP is very high especially when the ISP DNS resolver is utilized.

3. PaDIS ARCHITECTURE AND DEPLOYMENT

Given that a substantial fraction of the overall traffic is available at multiple locations within the ISP and that there is significant path diversity, we now propose a system, named PaDIS, that lets the ISP take advantage of this diversity while improving content delivery to the user.

PaDIS is the abbreviation for *Provider-aided Distance Information System*. PaDIS' task is to act as a location recommendation service and it is operated by an ISP. More specifically, a user, a CDN, a CDP, a DNS resolver [6], or any other entity can query PaDIS by submitting a list of possible IP addresses and a source. Upon receiving such a list, PaDIS will rank the submitted IP addresses according to its metrics such as distance within the Internet topology, path capacity, path congestion, path delay, etc. To be able to issue such a ranking, PaDIS relies on ISP specific network information, e. g., the local topology as well as Internet wide information, e. g., BGP information.

[2] Augmenting the routing topology with flow information may allow us to extend this analysis to all content.

Table 2: **Traffic localization within the network by different DNS resolvers normalized by number of requests and traffic volume together with the potentially available fraction of localized traffic.**

	ISP DNS		OpenDNS		GoogleDNS	
Metric	observed	potential	observed	potential	observed	potential
IPs	12.3 %	24.2 %	5.8 %	16.0 %	6.0 %	9.7 %
requests	14.9 %	33.2 %	4.7 %	18.8 %	4.8 %	6.4 %
volume	23.4 %	50.0 %	12.0 %	27.7 %	12.3 %	13.4 %

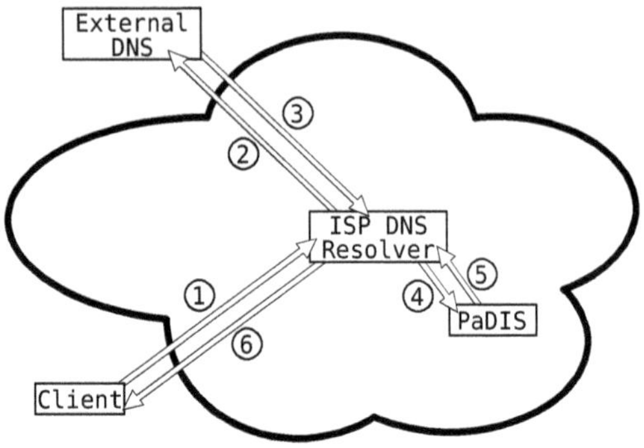

Figure 8: PaDIS use case: Optimizing content delivery transparent to both CDN/CDPs and clients.

We first outline how PaDIS can be used to take advantage of server diversity for content delivery, then outline its architecture, before discussing its scalability and responsiveness properties.

3.1 PaDIS Usage Options

While PaDIS can be used as an ALTO [32] server to offer ISP-aided localization for neighbor or peer selection for P2P users, it offers many more possibilities for optimizing content delivery. PaDIS rankings can either optimize for delay, e. g., for web sites where objects are typically small and the retrieval time is dominated by the round-trip-time (Section 4.1) or bandwidth, e. g., for One-Click Hosters (Section 4.2) offering bulk data.

Assuming that the local ISP runs a PaDIS server much in the same manner as it offers a DNS resolver to clients, CDSs, the ISP itself, etc. can use it in a multitude of different ways as outlined below:

Clients (a): Clients can install a plug-in to their Web browser to send all DNS replies or even summaries of past DNS replies to the PaDIS server for re-ranking the returned IP addresses taking the ISP's preferences into account.

Clients (b): Clients can overwrite the library responsible for DNS lookups with one that adds a PaDIS query and then re-ranks the DNS responses.

Clients (c): Another possibility is to pre-configure the home-router located at the edge of a client's network. Note, these routers also often act as DNS-relay. In this case, the home-router can also send any DNS reply to the PaDIS server and then return a re-ranked DNS reply.

CDNs/CDPs: Content delivery services may collaborate with the ISPs by contacting them before returning their server choices to the DNS resolver. A good heuristic for identifying an appropriate PaDIS server is to contact the ISP where the DNS resolver is located. This use case has the advantage that content delivery networks can take the ISP preferences into account during their optimization process. However, the CDS requires a hint as to the location of the client, e.g., its IP address. This is already under discussion within the IETF [12].

ISP: The ISP can enhance its DNS resolver to contact its PaDIS server and reorder the IP addresses if needed before returning any answer to a client. This is fully transparent to both the clients as well as the CDNs/CDPs. Figure 8 shows this scenario, which involves the following steps:

1. The client sends the DNS query to the ISP operated DNS resolver.
2. The query is recursively resolved using the authoritative DNS servers.
3. The reply is received by the ISP's DNS resolver.
4. The reply is sent to the PaDIS server for ranking.
5. The PaDIS server augments the reply with information from previous ones and ranks them according to its metrics, which takes the current network status into account. This reply is then sent back to the DNS resolver.
6. The ISP's DNS resolver sends the ranked and augmented reply back to the client.

One drawback to most of the above approaches is that most DNS responses are of the type CrossQuery and therefore do not contain a large number of possible server locations. However, as we have seen, DNS TTLs are usually short, so when aggregating across time, server diversity increases.

Let us revisit the DNS TTLs: Originally these were designed to ensure that stale cache entries do not linger forever in the DNS caches and that it is possible to relocate, add, or remove servers and domains within the DNS hierarchy. Today, however, DNS TTLs are significantly shorter than originally envisioned and are mainly used to aid CDSs with their load balancing and traffic flow optimization [34, 23]. Moreover, not all clients adhere to the DNS TTL values. Therefore, even today, a CDS has to add safety margins to the TTL values before they can stop serving specific content from a possible server. We propose to take advantage of this and allow the PaDIS server to keep a history of DNS hostname to IP address mappings. Using these mappings, the DNS replies can be augmented and clients can take full advantage of the server location and path diversity.

However, while the above ISP use case is transparent to the clients as well as the CDSs, we favor the CDN/CDP use case as it gives flexibility and control to both the CDNs/ CDPs as well as the ISP.

3.2 PaDIS Architecture

The designed architecture of PaDIS is shown in Figure 9. It has two main functionalities: to answer client ranking queries according to certain metrics, and to maintain a network information database. The latter includes network information, such as topology, routing, link capacity, link congestion, and link delay. It also needs to keep in sync with the network, e. g., the network has to be monitored for topology changes and changes to the path characteristics. Internally, PaDIS represents the network as an anno-

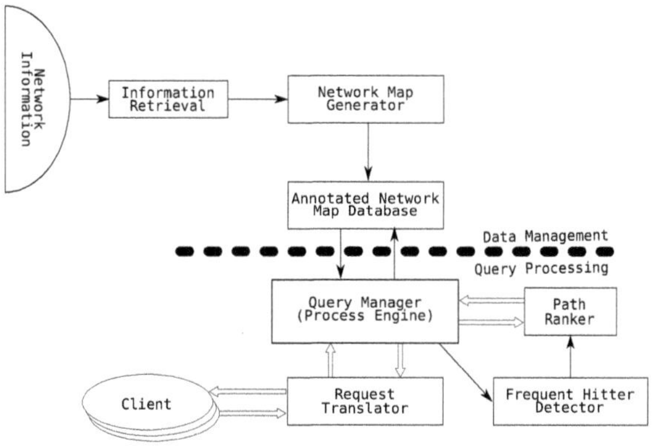

Figure 9: PaDIS architecture: Overview

tated graph. Accordingly, PaDIS is divided into two parts: data management and query processing, which communicate via shared memory.

Data Management Subsystem.

The data management subsystem consists of components for information retrieval, network map generation and the network map database.

The information retrieval component is responsible for continuously collecting network information, e. g., it listens to IGP messages, fetching status information and monitors routes learned via EGP. The ISP in question uses IS-IS as its IGP. The information retrieval component generates a representation of the physical network topology from the IGP messages it receives. In case of topology changes due to failures, addition of new components or scheduled downtime of monitored hardware, the topology is updated online. The information retrieval subsystem also fetches network status information and per link statistics, e. g., utilization and delay. In addition, the operator can assign customized values to links, e. g., related to operational costs or contract specifics.

Moreover, the information retrieval subsystem augments the ISP internal topology with external routing information by incorporating EGP messages. For the ISP in question these are BGP updates. Thus, by combining IGP and EGP information, PaDIS can find network path information, including performance characteristics, for any IP-based connection originating in the ISP. Customers of the ISP are handled in the same manner as EGP messages. However, their position and link characteristics may have to be learned from a data source such as a radius server. In short, the information retrieval subsystem learns as much as possible about the network topology of the ISP to generate a fully annotated network topology from it.

The network map generator is responsible for maintaining an up-to-date view of the topology supplied by the information retrieval subsystem. It pre-calculates the paths within the network and caches them for fast look-up. Since the routing within the ISP is typically more stable than customer and external prefixes, there is a significant benefit to caching the path, as it allows for a constant $O(1)$ look-up of the full path, regardless of the network's diameter, and a $O(1)$ complexity when updating the more volatile EGP information, e. g., BGP and/or radius information. However, recalculating the paths after a topology change costs $O(n^2)$ where n is the number of routers maintained by PaDIS.

Query Processing Subsystem.

The query processing subsystem consists of a request translator, a query manager, a path ranker and a frequent hitter detector.

The request translator component checks whether the query complies with the protocol specification and performs admission control based on the client IP address. Furthermore, PaDIS can be configured to augment requests with additional IP addresses to further enhance the choices presented to the client. If the request is admitted, the request translator reformats it and submits it to the Query Manager.

The query manager fetches all available information about each source-destination pair from the topology. Each pair, together with the path information, is then handed to the path ranker which uses a customized ranking function to calculate a weight representing the preference for this path. Once all pairs have been weighted, the query manager sorts the list by weights, striping all additional information added for ranking. The ordered list is passed back to the request translator and then returned to the client as a sorted list of sources in descending order of preference as seen by this ISP.

PaDIS is able to support a number of customized ranking functions. Each of these can optimize for different aspects of the path, e. g., bandwidth, hops, delay, etc., or a combination thereof. The client can specify its preference regarding the chosen metrics in the query, triggering the usage of an appropriate ranking function. However, the details of the functions are not revealed to the clients and the ranking weights are stripped from the reply. More importantly, no network information is revealed, contrary to other schemes of user-provider collaboration [36]. Note, that it is intractable to extract network properties or topologies from the ranking even when combined with traceroute information [1].

No information about clients is stored within the system, thus it preserves client privacy. However, to prevent abuse, PaDIS includes a frequent heavy hitter detector which can be activated by the ISP operator. The heavy hitter detector in our prototype is based on probabilistic lossy counting [13]. It maintains a list of the most popular IP addresses and sources which can also be utilized by the ranking function to avoid the creation of hot spots.

3.3 Scalability and Responsiveness

To decrease protocol handling overhead, we use UDP as the default protocol. However, TCP is supported for requests that exceed one MTU. Next we quantify the performance and scalability of PaDIS.

We use two identical dual quad-core CPU machines with sixteen gigabytes of memory directly connected via Gigabit Ethernet, one as PaDIS client and one as PaDIS server. We start by sending queries at a slow rate and gradually increase the pace until the PaDIS server is fully utilizing all CPUs, all the while ensuring that the client still receives all replies. Figure 10 shows the resulting number of served queries as well as the average delay for an eight-thread instance of the PaDIS server. Since the overhead depends on the number of IP addresses within the query, we varied this number from 50 to 363 — the maximum number of IP addresses for UDP-based queries which are restricted to one MTU. PaDIS is able to serve roughly 90,000 requests per second while ranking 50 IP addresses. This number drops to about 15,000 per second when ranking 363 IP addresses. Therefore, we conclude that a single PaDIS server offers sufficient throughput to be matched with one DNS resolver of the ISP.

The response time of the PaDIS server ranges from 1 millisecond to a few milliseconds and is dominated by the processing overhead in the hardware rather than the network connection. Moreover,

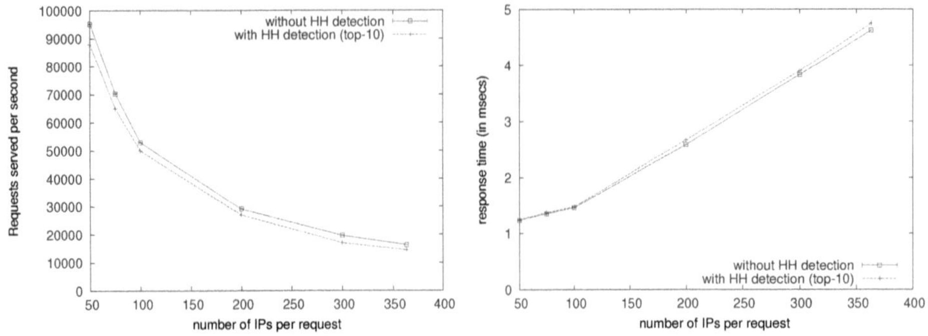

Figure 10: PaDIS performance: # of requests (left) average response time (right) with increasing query sizes.

CDN1		CDN2	
object#	size	file#	size
01	38K	01	36K
02	66K		
03	154K		
04	217K	02	254K
05	385K	03	471K
06	510K	04	599K
07	905K		
08	2.48M	05	3.4M
09	6.16M	06	4.5M
10	17M	07	8.6M

Table 3: CDN performance evaluation: Object sizes.

response time variance was minimal and the software ran stably throughout all experiments.

We repeated the experiment with heavy hitter detection activated and maintained a list of heavy hitters by considering the top ten replies, aggregating them every ten seconds. These were then fed into the ranking function. Our results show that both the number of requests served by PaDIS as well as the average response time decreases only slightly.

4. PERFORMANCE EVALUATION

To highlight that CDSs do not necessarily optimize their DNS load balancing strategies in such a way as to maximize user performance, and to show the potential of application ISP collaboration, which PaDIS enables, we perform extensive active measurements. Using ten vantage points within the ISP at residential locations and selected Web services that are responsible for a significant fraction of the HTTP traffic, we show that the server location diversity leads to different service performance results, and that PaDIS can help realize these. Among the studied Web services are the leading content providers, including the two most popular CDNs, the most popular One-Click Hoster (OCH) and the most popular streaming video provider.

The ten vantage points are deployed within residential locations with DSL connectivity to the ISP. The downstream bandwidth ranges from 1 Mbps to 25 Mbps while the upstream ranges from 0.128 Mbps to 5 Mbps. The measurements started on 1st of May 2010 and lasted for 14 days. Each client accesses the selected services 24 times during each day. In addition, we perform a DNS query for the hostname, in order to determine which IP addresses the service recommends. This methodology allows us to understand the possible end-user performance improvements. Moreover, we can estimate the network distances and thus the network savings. In the following section we show a selected subset of these measurements which represent the entire dataset collected.

4.1 Content Delivery Networks

Using the data sets from the residential ISP, see section 2.1, we identify the two most popular CDNs, referred to as CDN1 and CDN2. These are responsible for roughly 20 % of all HTTP traffic. Using the methodology discussed in Section 2, we identify more than 3,500 unique IP addresses that are caches for CDN1 and more than 700 unique IP addresses for CDN2. Both of these CDNs have more than 300 of their cache IP addresses within the ISP. In addition to CDN services, CDN1 offers an extensive range of service to content producers, including load-balancing and DNS services. If a content producer uses these services, it effectively outsources the DNS load balancing for requests to the CDN. However, the content is still provided by the content producer.

After augmenting each identified CDN IP address with its network path information, see Section 2, we find that the cache diversity translates not only into cache subnet diversity, but also path diversity. Thus, PaDIS can in principle be used to take advantage of both the server and the path diversity. However, at this point, it is still unclear whether the optimization of the CDN can be improved by PaDIS in terms of client download time and/or number of hops traversed within the ISP.

Since recent studies of CDN behavior have shown that any CDNized object is accessible from an arbitrary cache [17, 35], we can bypass the CDN recommendation. Thus, we request the URL directly from each of the identified CDN cache IP addresses regardless of their location. We verify this for all caches of CDN1. In addition, we point out that CDN1 caches also serve content of domains which only use their load balancing or DNS service in the same manner as if the content was supposed to be delivered by CDN1.

However, CDN2 is more restrictive. Our measurements show that CDN2 caches only reply to requests from the same region. In our case, we observe that European caches do serve the content to our European clients. However, when these requested content from North American caches, the delivery was refused.

Since the download performance of Web pages may depend on the size of the object, we select ten different files for CDN1 and seven for CDN2 of different but comparable file sizes ranging from 36 KB to 17 MB, see Table 3. To be able to repeat the measurements multiple times during a small time period while not overwhelming the client DSL lines, we subsample the number of caches of both CDNs. To preserve path diversity, we randomly select one cache from each of CDN1's subnets. This reduces the number of caches to 124 for CDN1. For CDN2 we found five subnets[3] containing caches, yet only two answered our queries with the requested data, as we have already explained. Since we use the raw IP addresses for accessing the various caches and override the CDN's server selection, we also exclude the domain name resolution time for the CDN recommended download.

Figures 11 and 12 show boxplots of the object retrieval time on a typical day (May 12th) of our selected caches across time for CDN1 and CDN2 respectively, for a subset of the objects and one specific client. Inspecting the results from the other clients, and for the other objects, throughout the experiment we see similar results.

[3]Apparently, CDN2 utilizes well provisioned and well connected data centers around the world and thus relies on the redundancy within the data centers and their access to multiple ISPs.

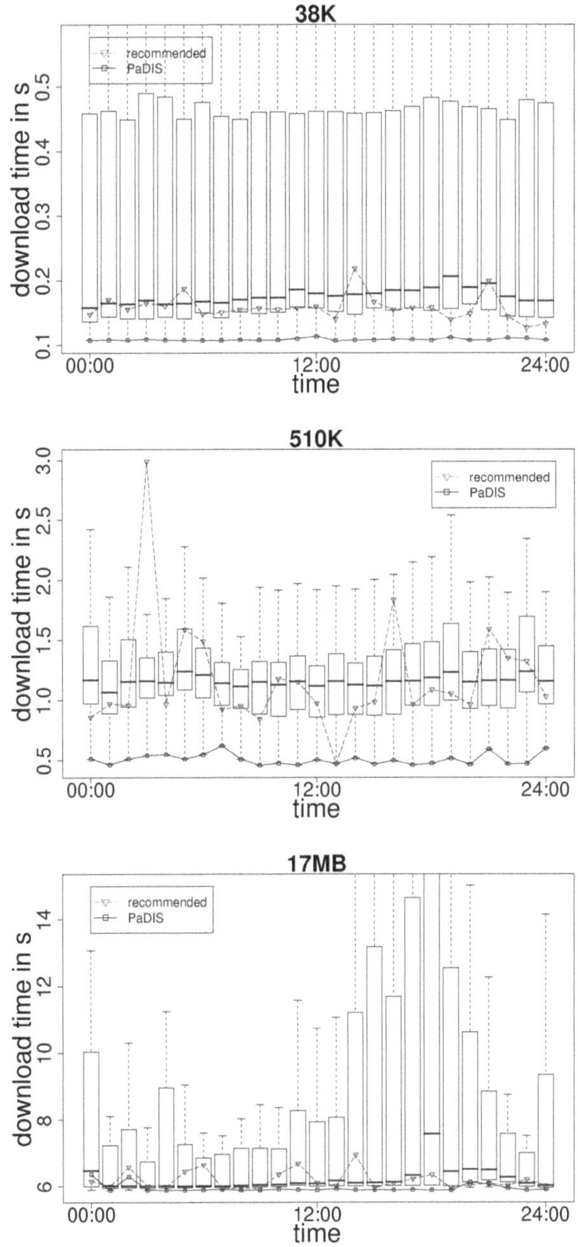

Figure 11: CDN1 performance evaluation: Boxplot of file downloads for the caches across time for objects 01, 06, and 10.

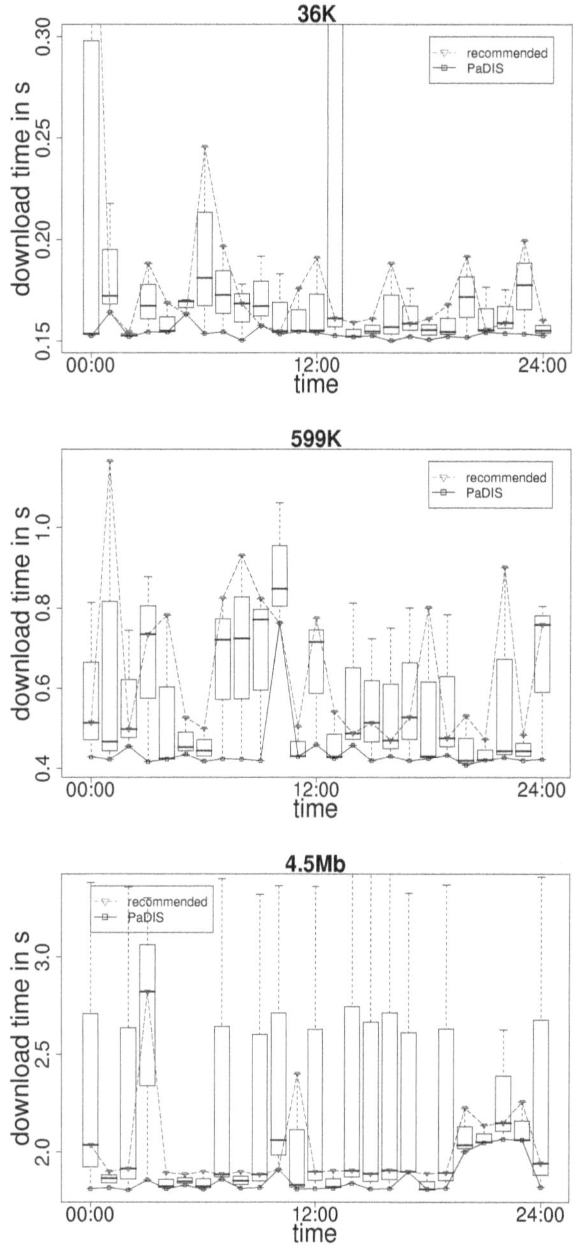

Figure 12: CDN2 performance evaluation: Boxplot of file downloads for the caches across time for objects 01, 04, and 06.

We use box plots because they are a good exploratory tool allowing the visual inspection of typical value ranges, spread, skewness, as well as outliers. Each Box analyzes the results of downloading the selected file at one point in time from one server in each of the subnets, e. g., for CDN1 each box consists of 124 data-points. The Box itself stretches from the 25th to the 75th percentile. The line within the box corresponds to the 50th percentile (the median). The whiskers represent the lowest and highest datum still within 1.5 times the interquartile range of the lower and upper quartile respectively. The dashed lines with triangles corresponds to the object download time for the recommended cache by the CDN. The solid line with squares corresponds to the object download time for the cache that ranked the highest by PaDIS based on delay.

A first observation regarding Figures 11 and 12 is that the download time for the recommended caches by CDN1 and CDN2 are quite good and close to the median download time over all the caches examined. Still, there is significant space from improvement especially during peak hours. Overall, PaDIS is able to improve the download time up to a factor of four.

Our active measurements also highlight typical network effects. For example, when downloading small objects, TCP is typically stuck in slow start. Thus, the round-trip time to the cache is the dominant factor for the retrieval time.

When downloading medium-size objects, both bandwidth and delay matter. For large objects the performance is restricted by the available network bandwidth including the download bandwidth

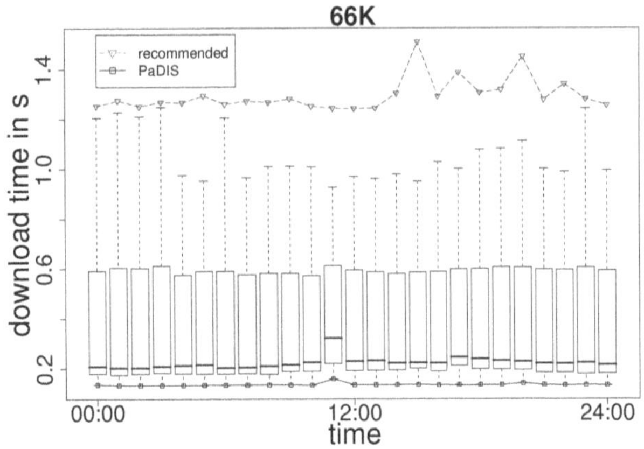

Figure 13: CDN1 load balancer performance evaluation: Boxplot of file downloads across time for object 03.

of the last-hop to the client (25Mbit/s in this experiment). For CDN1 the download time improvement for large objects is less than for small and medium ones, especially during the night, since the achieved download speeds are close to the nominal speed of the vantage points.

Since CDN1 also offers a pure DNS load balancing service, we are interested in examining if PaDIS can be helpful in such a scenario. Thus, we we repeat the experiment of fetching content from CDN1 recommended server as well as from all caches we associated with CDN1. As discussed before, the content of the website is served by all caches from CDN1. Also, CDN1 consistently returns the original server and never any of its own caches. In Figure 13 we plot the download time for objects that are retrieved using the above mentioned DNS load balancing service when following the recommendation by CDN1 and PaDIS. We also use boxplots to summarize the download time for the above mentioned 124 caches. The performance gain is substantial but has to be taken with caution as the recommended server is the original one and no CDN optimization takes place for this content. Nevertheless, we were able to use the CDN infrastructure to improve download time for content that was not distributed by the CDN. We limit the duration of our experiment, as such a behavior may violate the agreement between CDN1 and the site operator.

With respect to the ISP's benefits, we point out that PaDIS is able to localize the content within the ISP and that the average path length within the AS was reduced from 3.8 to 3 when downloading content from CDN1. Due to the small diversity of choices in CDN2, the internal path-length remained unchanged, even when the PaDIS decreased the download time.

4.2 One-Click Hosters

One-Click Hosters (OCH) offer users the ability to share files via a server based infrastructure, typically located within one or several well-provisioned data centers. Recent studies have shown that OCHs can achieve better download time than, e. g., P2P systems such as BitTorrent [7]. Therefore, it is believed that such services may become the leading platform for file sharing and replace P2P systems. Using our data sets from the residential ISP, we identify the most popular OCH, referred to as OCH1, which is responsible for roughly 15 % of all HTTP traffic. OCH1 is located at a multi-homed data center in central Europe. To scale the number of parallel flows, OCH1, like other OCHs, limits the maximum file size to 200 MByte.

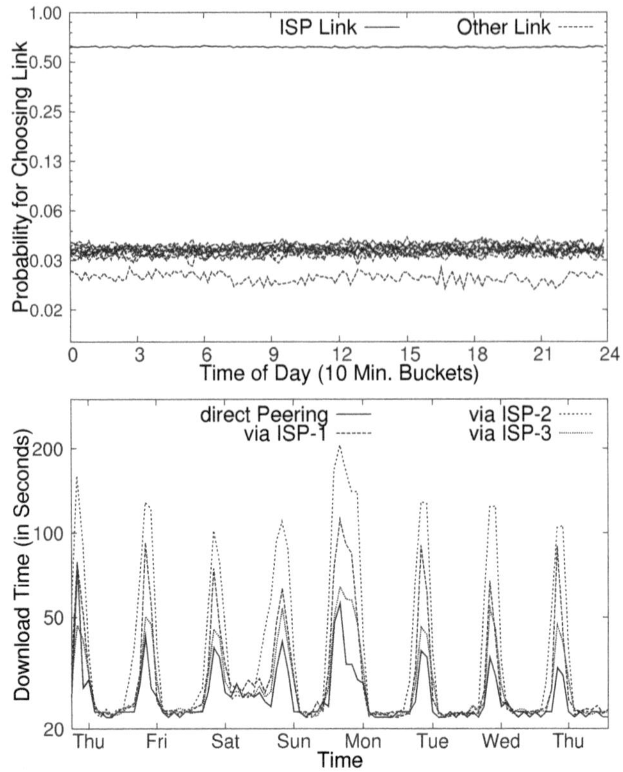

Figure 14: Probability of selecting a link of OCH1 (top) and download time per OCH1 link (bottom).

Using the traces, uploading a 60 Mbyte test file, as well as studying the domain name scheme of the servers, we are able to deduce that OCH1 has twelve uplinks to four different providers. The ISP we are collaborating with is among these providers. To understand how OCH1 does uplink selection, we repeatedly asked the OCH1 for a server to download the file during the one week period starting on the 7th of April 2010. The results, in terms of link selection probabilities for the twelve uplinks, are shown in Figure 14 (top). Roughly 60 % of the requests are shown to be directed to a server that can serve the content via the direct peering with the client's ISP. From the other eleven uplinks, ten uplinks are chosen with equal probability while one is chosen with smaller probability. It is worth noting that there are no time-of-day or time-of-week effects at all, while the HTTP volume of OCH1 in our traces exhibits time-of-day effects. This leads us to believe that the link utilization can be improved by using PaDIS' recommendation when assigning clients to servers.

From the replies of the OCH1, we derive a list of their available servers on a per uplink and provider basis. We validated that it is feasible to download the file from any one of the servers and thus download the content via any of the providers. To quantify the potential benefit, in download time, for the end-user, we repeatedly download the test file from one server per uplink once every two hours for one week. Figure 14 (bottom) shows the resulting download time for the client. For presentation purposes and since the performance was very close, we average over all uplinks on a provider. Our results show that the best download times are possible via the direct peering link which directly connects the ISP to the OCH. While the download speed during the off periods is again close to the nominal speed of the client and does not vary across different ISPs, the download time improvements can be up to a factor of four during peak hours. This together with the observation of static uplink assignment, even during peak hours, shows that there is significant potential for PaDIS to improve end-user experience and enable the collaboration between ISPs and OCHs.

4.3 Video Streaming Providers

Video streaming via HTTP is popular and accounts for more than 20 % of the HTTP traffic. The leading video streaming provider in our trace, VSP1, is responsible for roughly 13 % of the overall HTTP traffic. We identify the architecture of VSP1 by examining our traces to analyze their naming scheme and perform a series of active measurements. We found that VSP1, in contrast to other CDS's, does not employ a DNS based load balancing scheme, but uses application layer redirection, namely HTTP 3xx return codes [16]. Additionally, we found that VSP1 uses a naming scheme that implies a caching hierarchy that organizes the caches of different layers into groups. While we have verified that all servers reply to any valid request, the reply might just be a redirection into the upper caching layer when the content is not available or even in a lower layer if the content is already well distributed. Another interesting observation we made is that VSP1 throttles the speed at which a user can download a video. After a short, but fast burst of data, the bitrate of the connection is throttled to roughly the video-bitrate. This behavior leads to virtually no performance difference of the caches as long as they can retain the video's bitrate. In this case, the PaDIS is not able to improve the perceived performance of an end-user.

Even though we found many unique cache IP addresses in our active measurements, they all belong to prefixes within the VSP1 AS and there seems to be limited path diversity for this provider. Still, we do believe this might be an interesting setting for PaDIS. On the one hand, a single path towards VSP1 is actually not as crucial as the the number of paths from VSP1 to the ISP, since the bulk of the transfered volume is flowing from VSP1 to the ISP. If the number of ingress paths exceeds the number of egress paths, PaDIS can be utilized to recommend caches such that the content is injected from the most appropriate ingress point in the ISP. On the other hand, in a collaborative scheme, VSP1 can utilize PaDIS to redirect clients to its caches taking into consideration network performance characteristics and replicate content in a more efficient manner.

4.4 Summary

We find that PaDIS has potential to substantially improve the end-user experience within an ISP by exploring the existing server and path diversity. We were able to show using active measurements in a big European ISP that PaDIS can significantly improve content delivery of some of the dominant content delivery platforms, including the two major CDNs and the top OCH, that are responsible for roughly 35 % of the overall HTTP traffic.

5. RELATED WORK

Content delivery networks are used to provide fast and scalable commercial-grade Web applications [23]. CDNs rely on large-scale commodity infrastructure to improve application performance. Krishnamurthy et al. [20] and later Huang et al. [17] characterize their performance, i. e., by quantifying the end-user performance, analyzing the DNS redirection overhead, unveiling the CDN server location, and assessing their availability.

Su et al. [34] propose to utilize CDN's redirection to locate high performance paths. Choffnes et al. [11] propose to use information from CDNs to bias neighbor selection in P2P systems without any path monitoring or probing.

Recently, Triukose et al. [35] show that most popular commercial CDNs as well as several community CDNs serve any object from any cache. They then use this insight to show that it is feasible to use the CDN's infrastructure to amplify attacks against CDN costumer web sites. Our work leverages this observation by including ISP information for cache site selection and thus improves end-user performance and enables ISP traffic engineering.

The ideas presented in this paper build upon our previous work on biasing peer selection in P2P systems [4, 3]. Our work also utilizes the insights from previous work [9] which has shown that server selection is important for enhancing the end-user experience.

To the best of our knowledge, this is the first work that proposes and deploys a system for ISP and application collaboration. It is based on the insight that today content is usually accessible from multiple locations. In the past, game-theoretic studies [18, 14] have investigated the principle possibilities of cooperation between ISPs and CDNs as well as the potential of an ISP deploying its own CDN. However, they have not proposed a system that enables this.

6. CONCLUSION

Our study, based on traces from more than 20,000 residential users as well as active DNS measurements, shows that there is significant server location diversity as well as path diversity for accessing HTTP based content. The key insight is that today most content delivery architectures rely on distributed infrastructures. We therefore propose and deploy PaDIS, a novel system that allows ISPs to discover and utilize path diversity. Using extensive active measurements from vantage points within a residential network, we were able to show the benefits that PaDIS can offer to the end-user experience. More specifically, we can show significant improvements in download times of up to a factor of four for content offered by the most popular content providers, including CDNs and OCHs, for users of an ISP. Our results also highlight the benefits for ISPs.

PaDIS may act as a catalyst for ISPs to regain control of their own traffic. PaDIS is a tool that can assist ISPs in performing traffic engineering or in driving up utilization for monetary gain at the application layer by biasing server selection for their customers. Furthermore, it can also serve as a negotiation tool between ISPs or between ISPs and content providers. In addition, it might be used not only as a means of cooperation but also for revenue sharing. Content providers and distributors may also utilize PaDIS to enhance content replication and delivery strategy due to increased access to meta-information.

7. ACKNOWLEDGMENTS

This work was supported in part by a grant from Deutsche Telekom Laboratories and the BMBF project G-Lab. We would also like to thank our shepherd, Robert Beverly, and the anonymous reviewers for their constructive comments.

8. REFERENCES

[1] Hrishikesh B. Acharya and Mohamed G. Gouda. The Theory of Network Tracing. In *Proc. of ACM PODC '09*.

[2] Bernhard Ager, Fabian Schneider, Juhoon Kim, and Anja Feldmann. Revisiting cacheability in times of user generated content. In *Proc. of IEEE Global Internet Symp. '10*.

[3] Vinay Aggarwal, Obi Akonjang, and Anja Feldmann. Improving User and ISP Experience through ISP-aided P2P Locality. In *Proc. of IEEE Global Internet Symp. '08*.

[4] Vinay Aggarwal, Anja Feldmann, and Christian Scheideler. Can ISPs and P2P Users Cooperate for Improved Performance? *SIGCOMM Comput. Commun. Rev.*, 37(3), 2007.

[5] B. Agger, W. Mühlbauer, G. Smaragdakis, and S. Uhlig. Comparing DNS Resolvers in the Wild. In *Proc. of ACM IMC '10.*

[6] Hussein A. Alzoubi, Michael Rabinovich, and Oliver Spatscheck. MyXDNS: A Request Routing DNS Server with Decoupled Server Selection. In *Proc. of WWW '07.*

[7] Demetres Antoniades, Evangelos P. Markatos, and Constantine Dovrolis. One-click Hosting Services: a File-sharing Hideout. In *Proc. of ACM IMC '09.*

[8] Ruchir Bindal, Pei Cao, William Chan, Jan Medved, George Suwala, Tony Bates, and Amy Zhang. Improving Traffic Locality in BitTorrent via Biased Neighbor Selection. In *Proc. of IEEE ICDCS '06.*

[9] Robert L. Carter and Mark E. Crovella. On the Network Impact of Dynamic Server Selection. *Computer Networks*, 31((23-24)):2529–2558, 1999.

[10] Meeyoung Cha, Haewoon Kwak, Pablo Rodriguez, Yong-Yeol Ahn, and Sue Moon. Analyzing the Video Popularity Characteristics of Large-scale User Generated Content Systems. *IEEE/ACM Trans. Networking*, 17(5):1357–1370, 2009.

[11] David R. Choffnes and Fabián E. Bustamante. Taming the Torrent: a Practical Approach to Reducing Cross-ISP Traffic in Peer-to-peer Systems. In *Proc. of ACM SIGCOMM '08.*

[12] C. Contavalli, W. van der Gaast, S. Leach, and D. Rodden. Client IP Information in DNS Requests. IETF draft, work in progress, draft-vandergaast-edns-client-ip-00.txt, Jan 2010.

[13] Graham Cormode and Marios Hadjieleftheriou. Methods for Finding Frequent Items in Data Streams. *The VLDB J.*, 19(1):3–20, 2010.

[14] Dominic DiPalantino and Ramesh Johari. Traffic Engineering versus Content Distribution: A Game-theoretic Perspective. In *Proc. of IEEE INFOCOM '09.*

[15] Holger Dreger, Anja Feldmann, Michael Mai, Vern Paxson, and Robin Sommer. Dynamic Application-Layer Protocol Analysis for Network Intrusion Detection. In *Proc. of USENIX Security Symp. '06.*

[16] Roy Fielding, Jim Gettys, Jeffrey Mogul, Henrik Frystyk, Larry Masinter, Paul Leach, and Tim Berners-Lee. Hypertext Transfer Protocol – HTTP/1.1. RFC 2616, Jun 1999.

[17] Cheng Huang, Angela Wang, Jin Li, and Keith W. Ross. Measuring and Evaluating Large-scale CDNs. In *Proc. of ACM SIGCOMM IMC '08, paper withdrawn.*

[18] Wenjie Jiang, Rui Zhang-Shen, Jennifer Rexford, and Mung Chiang. Cooperative Content Distribution and Traffic Engineering in an ISP Network. In *Proc. of ACM SIGMETRICS '09.*

[19] Thomas Karagiannis, Pablo Rodriguez, and Konstantina Papagiannaki. Should ISPs fear Peer-Assisted Content Distribution? In *Proc. of ACM IMC '05.*

[20] Balachander Krishnamurthy, Craig Wills, and Yin Zhang. On the Use and Performance of Content Distribution Networks. In *Proc. of ACM SIGCOMM IMW '01.*

[21] Rupa Krishnan, Harsha V. Madhyastha, Sridhar Srinivasan, Sushant Jain, Arvind Krishnamurthy, Thomas Anderson, and Jie Gao. Moving Beyond End-to-end Path Information to Optimize CDN Performance. In *Proc. of ACM SIGCOMM IMC '09.*

[22] Craig Labovitz, Scott Iekel Johnson, Danny McPherson, Jon Oberheide, and Farnam Jahanian. Internet Inter-Domain Traffic. In *Proc. of ACM SIGCOMM '10.*

[23] Tom Leighton. Improving Performance on the Internet. *Commun. ACM*, 52(2):44–51, 2009.

[24] Gregor Maier, Anja Feldmann, Vern Paxson, and Mark Allman. On Dominant Characteristics of Residential Broadband Internet Traffic. In *Proc. of ACM SIGCOMM IMC '09.*

[25] P. Mockapetris. Domain Names - Implementation and Specification. RFC 1035, Nov 1987.

[26] Jianping Pan, Y. Thomas Hou, and Bo Li. An Overview of DNS-based Server Selections in Content Distribution Networks. *Comput. Netw.*, 43(6):695–711, 2003.

[27] Vern Paxson. Bro: A System for Detecting Network Intruders in Real-Time. *Computer Networks*, 31(23–24), 1999.

[28] Sylvia Ratnasamy, Mark Handley, Richard Karp, and Scott Shenker. Topologically Aware Overlay Construction and Server Selection. In *Proc. of IEEE INFOCOM '02.*

[29] Sandvine Inc. 2009 global broadband phenomena. `http://www.sandvine.com/news/global_broadband_trends.asp`.

[30] Fabian Schneider. *Analysis of New Trends in the Web from a Network Perspective*. PhD thesis, Technische Universität Berlin, Mar 2010.

[31] Hendrik Schulze and Klaus Mochalski. Internet study 2008-9. `http://www.ipoque.com/resources/internet-studies`.

[32] Jan Seedorf and Eric W. Burger. Application-Layer Traffic Optimization (ALTO) Problem Statement. RFC 5693, Oct 2009.

[33] S. S. Siwpersad, Bamba Gueye, and Steve Uhlig. Assessing the Geographic Resolution of Exhaustive Tabulation for Geolocating Internet Hosts. In *Proc. of PAM '08.*

[34] Ao-Jan Su, David R. Choffnes, Aleksandar Kuzmanovic, and Fabián E. Bustamante. Drafting behind Akamai: Inferring Network Conditions based on CDN Redirections. *IEEE/ACM Trans. Netw.*, 17(6):1752–1765, 2009.

[35] Sipat Triukose, Zakaria Al-Qudah, and Michael Rabinovich. Content Delivery Networks: Protection or Threat? In *Proc. of ESORICS '09.*

[36] Haiyong Xie, Y. Richard Yang, Arvind Krishnamurthy, Yanbin Grace Liu, and Abraham Silberschatz. P4P: Provider Portal for applications. In *Proc. of ACM SIGCOMM '08.*

Detecting and Characterizing Social Spam Campaigns

Hongyu Gao
Northwestern University
Evanston, IL, USA
hygao@u.northwestern.edu

Jun Hu
Huazhong Univ. of Sci. & Tech
and Northwestern University
junehu1210@gmail.com

Christo Wilson
U. C. Santa Barbara
Santa Barbara, CA USA
bowlin@cs.ucsb.edu

Zhichun Li
Northwestern University
Evanston, IL, USA
lizc@cs.northwestern.edu

Yan Chen
Northwestern University
Evanston, IL, USA
ychen@northwestern.edu

Ben Y. Zhao
U. C. Santa Barbara
Santa Barbara, CA USA
ravenben@cs.ucsb.edu

ABSTRACT

Online social networks (OSNs) are popular collaboration and communication tools for millions of users and their friends. Unfortunately, in the wrong hands, they are also effective tools for executing spam campaigns and spreading malware. Intuitively, a user is more likely to respond to a message from a Facebook friend than from a stranger, thus making social spam a more effective distribution mechanism than traditional email. In fact, existing evidence shows malicious entities are already attempting to compromise OSN account credentials to support these "high-return" spam campaigns.

In this paper, we present an initial study to quantify and characterize spam campaigns launched using accounts on online social networks. We study a large anonymized dataset of asynchronous "wall" messages between Facebook users. We analyze all wall messages received by roughly 3.5 million Facebook users (more than 187 million messages in all), and use a set of automated techniques to detect and characterize coordinated spam campaigns. Our system detected roughly 200,000 malicious wall posts with embedded URLs, originating from more than 57,000 user accounts. We find that more than 70% of all malicious wall posts advertise phishing sites. We also study the characteristics of malicious accounts, and see that more than 97% are compromised accounts, rather than "fake" accounts created solely for the purpose of spamming. Finally, we observe that, when adjusted to the local time of the sender, spamming dominates actual wall post activity in the early morning hours, when normal users are asleep.

Categories and Subject Descriptors

J.4 [**Computer Applications**]: Social and behavioral sciences

General Terms

Human Factors, Measurement, Security

Keywords

Online social networks, Spam, Spam Campaigns

1. INTRODUCTION

Online social networks (OSNs) are popular collaboration and communication tools for millions of Internet users. For example, Facebook alone boasts over 500 million users, and has recently surpassed Google as the most visited site on the Internet [22]. As communities built out of friends, family, and acquaintances, the public perception of OSNs is that they provide a more secure environment for online communication, free from the threats prevalent on the rest of the Internet. In fact, a study of a social auction site demonstrated that a social network could indeed provide a protective environment with significantly lower levels of fraud [38].

Unfortunately, recent evidence shows that these trusted communities can become effective mechanisms for spreading malware and phishing attacks. Popular OSNs are increasingly becoming the target of phishing attacks launched from large botnets [8, 10], and OSN account credentials are already being sold online in underground forums [39]. Using compromised or fake accounts, attackers can turn the trusted OSN environment against its users by masquerading spam messages as communications from friends and family members.

In this paper, we present a first of its kind study to measure and analyze attempts to spread malicious content on OSNs. Our work is based on a large dataset of "wall" messages from Facebook. Wall posts are the primary form of communication on Facebook, where a user can leave messages on the public profile of a friend. Wall messages remain on a user's profile unless explicitly removed by the owner. As such, wall messages are the intuitive place to look for attempts to spread malicious content on Facebook since the messages are persistent and public, *i.e.* likely to be viewed by the target user and potentially the target's friends. Through crawls of several Facebook regional networks conducted in 2009, we obtained a large anonymized dataset of Facebook users, their friendship relationships, and 1.5 year-long histories of wall posts for each user [41]. In total, our dataset contains over 187 million wall posts received by 3.5 million users.

Our study of Facebook wall posts contains two key phases. First, we analyze all wall messages and use a number of complementary techniques to identify attempts to spread malicious content (Section 3). We focus our analysis on messages that contain URLs or web addresses in text form. From these messages, we produce correlated subsets of wall posts. We model each post as a node, and create edges connecting any two nodes referring to the same URL, or any two nodes sharing similar text content as defined by an approximate textual fingerprint. This process creates a number of connected subgraphs that partition all suspect wall messages into mutually exclusive subsets, where messages in a set are potentially related. Using dual behavioral hints of bursty activity and distributed communication, we can identify subsets of messages that exhibit properties of malicious spam campaigns. We use several complementary mechanisms to validate the effectiveness of our technique, and show that our approach is highly effective at detecting the spread of malicious content (Section 4).

In our second phase, we analyze the characteristics of the malicious wall posts we have identified (Section 5). Our results provide several interesting observations on the spread of malicious content in OSNs, and the behavior of users that spread it. We find that phishing is by far the most popular attack on Facebook. We also find that users who spread malicious content communicate using very different patterns compared to the average user, and that malicious users stand out by both the bursty nature of their wall posts, as well as their diurnal activity patterns. By studying the time-duration of malicious messages and the lifetimes of users that send them, we conclude that the overwhelming majority of spam messages are sent through compromised accounts, rather than fake accounts specifically created for spam delivery. Finally, we study the largest observed spam campaigns, and make observations about their attack goals and sales pitch.

In summary, we present in this project the first attempt to quantify the prevalence of malicious accounts and spread of malicious content on an OSN. We employ multiple techniques to detect correlation between wall messages and to identify the spread of potentially malicious content. Our results are confirmed by a number of validation mechanisms. Our subsequent analysis provides insights into the operation of malicious accounts, and has significant implications on the design of future mechanisms to detect malicious behavior on OSNs.

2. BACKGROUND

In this section, we provide background information about the Facebook OSN, introduce the dataset used in our work, and clarify the scope of this work before we begin analysis of our data.

2.1 Facebook

Facebook is the most popular OSN in the world, boasting a population of over 500 million users. It is the largest photo hosting service on the web [23], and has recently surpassed Google as the most visited site on the Internet [22].

Like most OSNs, Facebook encourages users to create profiles that contain rich information about themselves, including their name, photo, address, occupation, interests. Users create undirected friendship links with their family and acquaintances in order to stay connected. The most popular ways for users to interact on Facebook are posting status updates to their profile and writing on their friends' "walls." In turn, each of these events can be commented on by other users. All status updates, wall posts, and comments are tagged with the sender, the recipient, and a timestamp.

Facebook includes a set of API's for developers to write applications that can plug in to user's profiles. Applications, especially games, are quite popular among Facebook users. Once installed, applications can generate update messages that appear in a user's profile alongside status updates and wall posts from friends.

Originally, users' default privacy settings on Facebook were tied to the concept of "networks." Each network represented a school, company, or geographic region. Joining school and company networks required providing authentication details in the form of a EDU or company email address. Access to regional networks was unauthenticated. By default, users in the same network could view each other's information. In late 2009, after we completed our measurements, Facebook deprecated the use of networks in their system.

2.2 Crawled Facebook Data

Between April and June of 2009 we crawled Facebook for data. Because access to regional networks is unauthenticated, we chose 8 regional networks of various sizes (from over 1.6 million users down to $\sim$14K users) as targets for data collection. These networks are Egypt, Los Angeles, London, Monterey Bay (California), New York City, Russia, Santa Barbara (California), and Sweden. Each crawl was seeded with 50 random users from the given regional network, and includes a breadth-first search of all users in the region with visible profiles (*i.e.* users with the default privacy settings). We acknowledge that there is about one year time gap between the data collection and our analysis. This time gap poses additional difficulty on our analysis process. We leverage a stringent set of heuristic tests (Section 4) to overcome this difficulty.

For each crawled user we recorded their anonymized userID, friend list, and interaction records going back to January 1, 2008. Interaction records include the complete history of wall posts received by each crawled user within the given time frame. Each crawled interaction record is associated with the timestamp when the event occurs, adjusted to the local time of the crawling machine (Pacific Daylight Time). In this study, we focus on the 187M wall posts crawled from roughly 3.5 million users. Table 1 summarizes the dataset characteristics.

For the purposes of this study, we are interested in studying wall posts that could potentially be spam. This means isolating the set of wall posts that are: i) generated by users, not third-party applications, and ii) include embedded URLs to external websites. Note that we do not limit ourselves to URLs in the form of hypertext links. We also handle wall posts with "hidden" URLs, *i.e.* URLs in plain text or even obfuscated form.

2.3 Scope of This Work

A wide range of attacks exists in today's OSNs. We do not attempt to address all of them in this work. Our focus is solely on detecting and measuring large-scale *spam campaigns* transmitted via Facebook users' *wall messages*. Although spam traditionally refers to massive, unsolicited campaigns to sell goods over email, we do not restrict ourselves to this behavior alone. Rather, we identify and measure multiple types of attacks that are executed via spam wall posts, including but not restricted to: i) *product advertisements*, ii) *phishing attacks* and iii) *drive-by-download attacks*. Although the purpose of each attack varies, they share one common feature: attackers create or compromise a large number of Facebook accounts and use them to spam wall posts to a even larger set of users. The wall posts left by attackers each contain a potentially obfuscated URL and text to convince the recipient to visit the URL. If a recipient is deceived and visits the URL, she will be led to a malicious website associated with the spam campaign. Throughout this paper, we refer to a wall post as "malicious" if it belongs to a spam campaign. In addition, we refer to an account as "malicious" if it has made at least one malicious wall post.

3. SPAM CAMPAIGN DETECTION

To identify malicious wall posts from our large dataset, we use semantic similarity metrics to identify mutually exclusive groups within the total set of wall posts. We then use behavioral cues to identify distinct wall post groups as benign or potentially malicious. In this section, we describe the multi-step process through which we organize, cluster, and identify potentially malicious posts. We begin with an overview of the entire process, followed by a detailed description of each step.

3.1 Overview

The design of our system is guided by intuition about techniques used in spam campaigns to maximize reach and avoid detection. Spammers generate profit from these visits by selling products or services, performing phishing attacks, or installing malware onto victim's machines. Therefore, we assume each spam campaign is focused on convincing a maximum number of users to visit some particular URL(s).

To make a spam campaign effective, spammers are likely to a) customize individual messages towards the targeted user, and b) attempt to avoid detection by hiding the destination URL through obfuscation. Thus, it is possible for messages within the same campaign to look significantly different. This "diversity" makes detection of spam campaigns challenging, since neither the textual description nor the destination URL, or even their combination, can be used as an effective signature to detect a single campaign.

Our intuition is to use complementary techniques to overcome these hurdles, with the goal of grouping messages from the same spam campaign together into clusters. Note that we do not aim to completely aggregate spam wall posts from one campaign into one single group, as this level of precision is unnecessary. First, to overcome *user-customization* techniques, we refer to recent work that shows spamming botnets use templates to generate customized email spam messages [29]. We also observe that there are a large number of malicious posts in our dataset that look similar to each other. From this we hypothesize that spam wall posts are also generated using templates, and posts generated from the same template should contain only small differences. Thus, we propose to group wall posts with "similar" textual description together, where similarity is captured by a probabilistic fingerprint. This probabilistic fingerprint must be more efficient to compute than edit distance, yet accurate enough to reflect similarity between text samples despite attempts by attackers to obfuscate or customize the text.

Second, we reason that all attempts to direct OSN users towards a single destination URL must come from the same spam campaign. Thus, we group together all wall posts that include URLs to the same destination, including those that have been hidden through textual obfuscation (*e.g.* www dot hack dot com) and chains of HTTP redirects.

In summary, our detection approach focuses on two techniques that group together wall posts that share either the same (possibly obfuscated) destination URL, or strong textual similarity. We model all wall posts as nodes in a large graph, and build edges when two posts are connected by one of the above techniques. Intuitively, the resulting connected subgraphs could represent messages within the same spam campaign. The pairwise comparison among wall posts results in $O(n^2)$ time complexity where n is the number of wall posts. Although this time complexity can be significant for large values of n, this approach actually performs reasonably fast in practice. Processing our entire dataset with interactions dating back to January 1, 2008 took a total of 2 days of computation time on a commodity server. While the worst case space complexity is also $O(n^2)$, the graph is very sparse in practice, *i.e.* most wall posts are non-malicious, and thus distinct. One of today's modestly configured servers has sufficient memory (4GB) to handle such computations.

After constructing a clustered graph of wall posts, we leverage two additional assumptions about spam campaigns to separate malicious, spam clusters from the large majority of benign wall posts. These assumptions are: a) any single account is limited in the number of wall posts it can post, thus spammers must leverage a significant number of user accounts for large campaigns, and b) spam campaigns must maximize time efficiency of compromised or fake accounts before detection, thus messages in a single campaign are relatively bursty in time. We apply threshold filters based on the number of user accounts sending wall posts and time correlation within each subgraph to distinguish potentially malicious clusters from benign ones. An overview of the system workflow is shown in Figure 1.

3.2 Modeling and Clustering Wall Posts

We model each wall post as a <*description*, *URL*> pair. The *URL* is the destination the spammer wants the target to visit. The URL may be either of legitimate format or obfuscated. The *description* is the text in the wall post surrounding the URL used to convince the target to visit the URL. We build such a model because *description* and *URL* are the *only* information used in the detection phase. Other information, like the sender's and receiver's unique Facebook IDs, are involved in other phases of this study. It is possible for the description to be an empty string, in which case the wall post contains only an URL. Clearly, while most benign wall posts do not contain any URLs, not all wall posts with URLs are malicious.

Since any wall post without a URL cannot achieve a spammer's goals, we begin by first excluding all wall posts without embedded URLs from further analysis. Next, we use our two assumptions (described above) to connect any two wall posts together if they: point to the same destination URL, or share an approximately similar text description. Thus we define two wall posts as *similar* if they share the same URL *or* similar description. Accordingly, the wall post *similarity graph* is an undirected graph $G = < V, E >$, where each node $v \in V$ represents one wall post, and two nodes u and v are connected with an edge e_{uv} if and only if they are similar.

Building the Wall Post Similarity Graph. Before clustering wall posts into a graph, we first identify wall posts containing URLs and extract their URLs. Locating and extracting well formed, properly marked up hyperlinks from wall posts is a simple process. However, it is non-trivial to recover obfuscated URLs that have been hidden inside plaintext. To detect obfuscated URLs, we first use keyword searches, *e.g.* "click here," to detect the starting location of a potential URL. Next, we scan along the text and remove any characters that are not legal in HTTP URLs (*e.g.* whitespace, *etc.*). We also reverse common techniques used by the spammers to obfuscate URLs, *e.g.* replacing " dot " with ".", during the scan. This reconstruction process continues until we either successfully rebuild the URL, or determine that this chunk of text cannot be a legitimate URL. Locating and recovering obfuscated URLs is only done once in the preprocessing stage and is not repeated when building the wall post similarity graph. Following reconstruction, two URLs are considered the same if they match, ignoring HTTP URL parameters.

To find approximate similarity matches between text descriptions, we compute a fingerprint for each block of the description text. We treat the description as a single string, and compute 128-bit MD5 hashes for each 10-byte long substring. We then sort these hash values and choose the 20 numerically smallest values as our approximate fingerprint. Two descriptions are similar if and only if at least 19 of their fingerprints match. This approach matches descriptions even after some substrings have been modified, and has been shown to be successful against adversarial spammers in our prior work [44]. We experimented with our dataset to determine that 19/20 was an appropriate threshold that yielded the best trade-

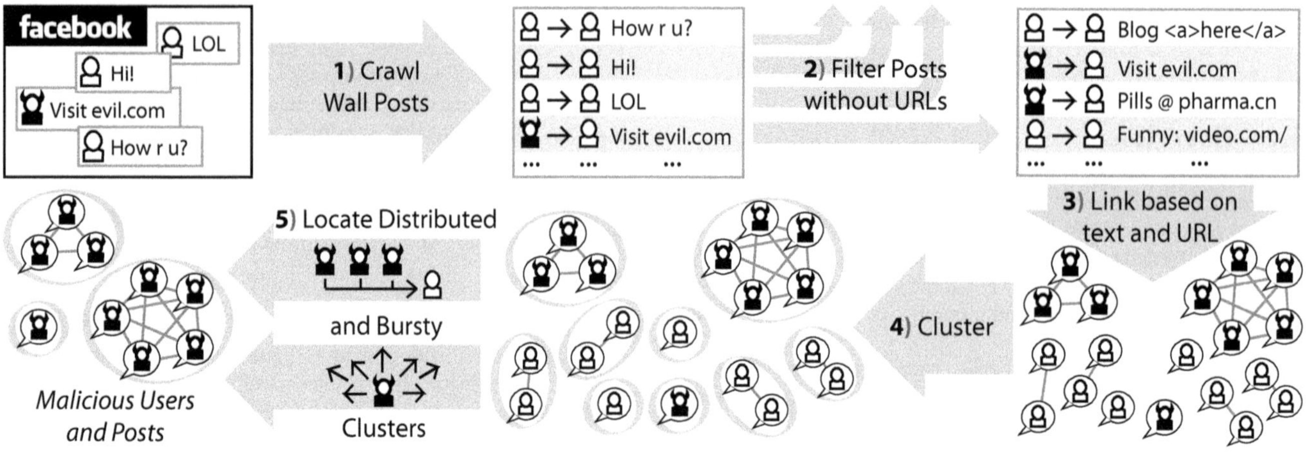

Figure 1: The system design, starting with raw data collection and ending with accurate classification of malicious posts and the users that generating them.

Algorithm 1 **PostSimilarityGraphClustering**($G < V, E >$)

$traversed \leftarrow \emptyset$
$clusters \leftarrow \emptyset$
Foreach $v \in V$
  If $v \in traversed$
    continue
  EndIf
  $one\_cluster \leftarrow BFS(v)$
  $traversed \leftarrow traversed \cup one\_cluster$
  $clusters \leftarrow clusters \cup \{one\_cluster\}$
EndForeach
return $clusters$

off between robustness against obfuscation while avoiding false positives. Additionally, a relatively high absolute threshold implicitly filters out strings shorter than 19 characters, which is useful since it is common for very short text descriptions to have matching content.

Now the problem of identifying spam campaigns reduces to a problem of identifying connected subgraphs inside the similarity graph. Each connected subgraph is equivalent to one component of a potential spam campaign. Identifying connected subgraphs is easily solved by iteratively choosing arbitrary nodes and identifying their transitive closures. We summarize the implementation in Algorithm 1.

As an optimization, we could first cluster together wall posts that share the same URL, then do a pair-wise comparison between the description of wall posts in different clusters. If two wall posts share similar description, their corresponding clusters are merged and the comparison between the remaining wall posts within these two clusters are skipped. This optimization eliminates the redundant computation to compare the descriptions of two wall posts that are already within one cluster, although the total time complexity remains O(n^2).

3.3 Identifying Spam Clusters

Now that we have organized all wall posts into clusters that could represent coordinated spam campaigns, the next step is to identify which clusters are likely to represent the results of active spam campaigns.

To detect spam clusters, we use two widely acknowledged distinguishing features of spam campaigns: their "distributed" coverage and "bursty" nature. The "distributed" property is quantified using the number of users that send wall posts in the cluster. In email spam campaigns, the "distributed" property is usually quantified using the number of IP addresses or ASes of the senders [42]. The analogous identifier in OSNs is each user's unique ID. The "bursty" property is based on the intuition that most spam campaigns involve coordinated action by many accounts within short periods of time [42]. We characterize each cluster of messages by measuring the absolute time interval between consecutive wall post events (using timestamps associated with each wall post), and extracting the median value of all such intervals. The median interval characterizes how fast attackers are generating the wall posts, and is robust to outlier values.

While we use both assumptions of spam's distributed and bursty nature to detect spam campaigns, it is possible that social cascades in the social network might produce similar message clusters. For example, a URL to buy tickets to a highly anticipated concert might be widely propagated throughout Facebook by friends. However, recent studies of social cascades have shown that cascades take significant time to propagate [19], suggesting that false positives from social cascades would be filtered out by our temporal burstiness filter.

Now that we are using the "distributed" and "bursty" properties to identify malicious clusters, we face the problem of identifying the best cutoff threshold value. We can maximize the number of malicious clusters we identify by relaxing the threshold value, but that generally results in the system producing more false alarms on benign clusters. In contrast, using more restrictive threshold can reduce the number of false alarms, but may fail to identify malicious cluster (false negatives).

To solve this dilemma, we first ask ourselves, how many false positives are we willing to tolerate in order to gain one more true positive. Since our system is designed for postmortem analysis, and not detection in real time, we choose this value to be 2. Our goal is to locate as many spam campaigns as possible, and we do not need to guarantee zero false positives, since they can be filtered out using a follow-up validation phase. Instead, we can tolerate a moderate number of false positives at the benefit of reducing false negatives, *i.e.* , the malicious clusters that are missed by the detection process. For example, we can set our thresholds to initial values of (4, 6hr), where 4 is the lower bound of the "distributed" property, and 6 hours is the upper bound of the "bursty" property. If the spammer is

Dataset	Wall Posts	Distinct Senders	Distinct Receivers
All Posts	187.17M	23.73M	3.46M
With URLs	2.08M	1.08M	0.83M

Table 1: Overall statistics of our Facebook dataset.

using less than 4 accounts to send spam with an interval greater than 6 hours, he is likely to generate negligible impact on the system.

In practice, we test different possible threshold values to determine values that maximize our utility as we defined earlier. We present our detailed experimental results in Section 4.3. Our process found that the best threshold values are (5, 1.5hr), but also that a number of possible threshold combinations can work well.

3.4 Dataset and Detection Results

Before we describe our efforts to validate our methodology in detail, we first briefly summarize the outcome of our clustering and classification approach. Table 1 summarizes statistics of our initial wall posts dataset, and lists the total number of wall posts, distinct users that send posts, and distinct users who received wall posts. The first row corresponds to the entire crawled dataset. The second row is restricted to the subset of wall posts that include embedded URLs, which form the basis of our study.

Applying our clustering approach to our corpus of 2.08 million wall posts produces 1,402,028 clusters. As expected, there is a heavy tail in the size of clusters, *i.e.* a small number of very large clusters and a large number of very small clusters. When we apply our chosen detection threshold, which uses 5 as the minimum number of users involved in each cluster and 5400 seconds (1.5 hours) as the maximum median interval between the timestamp of two consecutive wall posts, we produce 297 clusters that are classified as potentially malicious spam campaigns. There are a total of 212,863 wall posts contained in these 297 clusters.

4. EXPERIMENTAL VALIDATION

We have described our methodology for identifying malicious wall posts and users from the general Facebook population. In this section, we delve more deeply into the results of our detection techniques, in an effort to verify that the posts we identified were indeed malicious. We accomplish this using a combination of techniques and tools from both the research community and the commercial sector. These techniques provide independent, third-party verification of our results.

We apply a stringent set of heuristic tests to each URL that has been embedded in one or more wall posts in a potentially malicious cluster. Whether the URL is malicious determines whether the wall posts containing it are malicious. However, none of these techniques are foolproof, since there are no guaranteed foolproof methods to identify malicious content online. In the absence of such tools, we take a best-effort approach to validating our results.

4.1 Validation Methodology

Our validation methodology includes a series of steps, each of which encapsulates a different heuristic or tool and aims to concretely verify some portion of the suspicious wall posts as definitively malicious. Our goal is to investigate the false positive rate of our proposed methodology by reexamining the 212,863 malicious wall posts identified in Section 3.4. Later in Section 4.4, we will try to determine the false negative rate amongst our entire dataset of 2.08 million wall posts.

Step 1: URL De-obfuscation. A common technique among spammers is to obfuscate malicious URLs by adding white spaces and unicode characters into them. This allows the offending message to bypass filters that look for blacklisted URLs by simple string matching. We do observe that a significant number of wall posts on Facebook included obfuscated links of this nature. Since there is no incentive for benign users to obfuscate links in this manner, we mark any wall posts that include such URLs as malicious. We de-obfuscate URLs by reversing the obfuscation process, including removing whitespace padding and canonicalizing URL encoded characters (*e.g.* , “%65%76%69%6C%2E%63%6F%6D” becomes “evil.com”).

Step 2: Redirection Analysis. Another common technique used by spammers to evade detection is to hide malicious sites behind chains of redirects [40]. This serves to obfuscate the true destination of a URL (which may be blacklisted) from users and automated filters. Before proceeding with our validation for a suspicious URL, we use an automated web browser script to detect and follow the chain of redirects, if they exist. More specifically, we use the JSSH extension for Mozilla, which allows us to establish a JavaScript shell connection to a running Mozilla process via TCP/IP [27]. This allowed us to control running Mozilla processes while they traversed through chains of HTTP redirects, eventually retrieving the final destination URL.

Step 3: Third-party tools. We leverage multiple third-party tools from the research community and the private sector to assess the malice of URLs in our dataset. We leverage a number of the most popular URL blacklisting services to determine if URLs are malicious, including: McAfee SiteAdvisor [3], Google's Safe Browsing API [1], SURBL [6], URIBL [7], Spamhaus [4], and SquidGuard [5]. We submit each unique URL from our dataset to each service in order to account for discrepancies between the coverage of different blacklists. If any blacklist returns a positive for a given URL, it is classified as malicious.

In addition to URL blacklists, we leverage the Wepawet [9] tool from UC Santa Barbara. Wepawet is a specialized tool that uses machine learning to identify web pages with characteristics associated with drive-by download attacks [34]. URLs receiving a “malicious” rating from Wepawet are immediately classified as malicious for our purposes as well.

The primary challenge of using automated tools for validation is that our Facebook data was collected during the first half of 2009, roughly one year ago. Given the ephemeral nature of malicious websites, this means that many of the URLs in our dataset point to stale destinations that no longer exist. Blacklists periodically purge old records from their databases, which further complicates matters. Whenever possible, we query the Internet archive service [2] for the content of URLs based on the timestamp of the associated wall post.

Step 4: Wall Post Keyword Search. Certain keywords often appear in spam messages sent over email. The spammed wall posts in our dataset are no exception: many of them attempt to sell the usual assortment of shady merchandise. To capture these wall messages, we built a set of well-known keywords that are indicative of spam, such as “viagra,” “enlargement pill,” and “legal bud.” We then performed full-text searches on the suspicious wall posts from the detection result for these strings, and classify the resulting posts as malicious.

Step 5: URL Grouping. In this point in our validation, we have verified that some portions of the wall posts in our dataset are malicious. However, shortcomings will likely have prevented us from performing full validation. For example, some URLs are too old and stale to be verified by blacklists. Similarly, we may have

# of URLs	Common features
1,895	URL signature: www.facebook.com.profile.id.* Wall post content: Invitation to visit a fake Facebook profile
407	URL signature: domain followed by single folder with obfuscated video as name, *e.g. www.nemr.net/pub1icsh0w/* Wall post content: Either "wow video" or "cool video"
511	URL signature: */imageshack.us/img[0-9]{2-3}/[0-9]{3-4}/mcr[a-z]{2-2}[0-9].swf Wall post content: Invitation to find out about a secret admirer or read a disparaging remark written by a personal enemy
296	URL signature: *ring*.blogspot.com Wall post content: Facebook is giving out ring tones for the user's cell phone via the provided URL
317	URL signature: *mcy[sz]*[0-9]{3-11}.com or (multi|rng)tn[sz]*[0-9]{2-6}.com Wall post content: Invitation to win a free Playstation 3

Table 2: Examples of URL groups and their shared features.

missed variants of spam keywords (*e.g.* "v14gr4" vs. "viagra") in our full-text search. To expand the coverage of our detection techniques beyond positive results using the prior techniques, we will use a grouping strategy to further detect relationships between posts.

We manually construct groups of URLs that exhibit highly uniform features, which is a strong indicator that the whole group is under the control of a single attacker and is typical of many well-organized spam campaigns. Benign URLs are more random in nature, and highly unlikely to exhibit such clustering. The features we leverage include signatures that characterize the URL group [42] and similarity of textual content of the associated wall posts. For each group, if any of its constituent URLs has been identified as malicious in a previous validation step, then all URLs in the group are classified as malicious. We identify 8 such groups in total and list examples with their features in Table 2.

Step 6: Manual Analysis. Even after all five previous validation steps, a small portion of suspicious wall posts still remain unclassified. Since widespread spam campaigns are likely to be reported and discussed by people on the web, we can manually validate these URLs by searching for them on Google. Because this task is highly time-intensive, we only use this approach on URLs that each appear in at least four hundred wall posts.

4.2 Validation Results

We use the multi-step validation process outlined above to confirm the malice of each wall post identified in our detection process. We assume that all wall posts whose malice cannot be confirmed are false positives. Table 3 summarizes the number of URLs and wall posts confirmed as malicious following each validation step, as well as the number of false positives. We see that our heuristic verification mechanisms are surprisingly successful at confirming the large majority of our detected spam messages. Only a very small portion of URLs (roughly 3.9%) remains unconfirmed.

The bulk of true positive URLs are either blacklisted, redirect to a blacklisted site, or grouped together with other blacklisted URLs/wall posts. In contrast, when viewed in terms of total wall posts, Table 3 shows that obfuscated and manually verified URLs account for a significant proportion of wall posts. This demonstrates that some URLs are spammed a disproportionally large number of times, while other spam campaigns spread their traffic across a long tail of unique URLs.

4.3 Burst and Distribution Thresholds

Our detection mechanism relies heavily on the bursty and distributed nature of spam messages. In order to choose a good cutoff threshold between normal and aberrant behavior, we define a desired tradeoff between false positives and true positives: we are

Reason for Classification	# of URLs	# of Wall Posts
Obfuscated URL	1,003 (6.3%)	45,655 (21.4%)
Blacklisted URL	4,485 (28.0%)	55,957 (26.3%)
Redirects to blacklisted URL	4,473 (27.9%)	29,365 (13.8%)
Contains spam keywords	196 (1.2%)	19,018 (8.9%)
Grouped with malicious URL	5,300 (32.5%)	33,407 (15.7%)
Manual confirmation	27 (<0.1%)	16,380 (7.7%)
Malicious, True Positives	15,484 (96.1%)	199,782 (93.9%)
Benign, False Positives	616 (3.9%)	13,081 (6.1%)

Table 3: Validation results. Each row provides the number of confirmed malicious URLs and wall posts in a given validation step. All URLs that have not been validated after all steps are assumed to be benign.

willing to tolerate two false positives if we can gain at least one true positive. We then choose the threshold value with the best utility (Section 3.3). In order to find the optimal threshold, we vary our filtering threshold for the "distributed" property of wall posts from 4 to 10, and for the "bursty" property from 0.5 to 6 hours, varied in increments of 0.5 hour. Every combination of these two properties is tested to examine the resulting false positives and true positives, with the results plotted in Figure 2. The resulting points roughly form a convex curve. We choose a straight line with slope of 0.5, which represents the desired tradeoff, to approach the curve from above. The straight line and the curve intersect at the point representing the threshold (5, 1.5hr). Thus we choose (5, 1.5hr) as the threshold for our detection system. Note that, as Figure 2 shows, a number of alternative threshold value combinations would also have yielded good results.

4.4 False Negative Rate Estimation

In addition to estimating the rate of false positives resulting from our detection methodology, it would also be desirable to characterize the amount of false negatives it can produce, *i.e.* the number of malicious wall posts that go undetected. Unfortunately, computing the false negative rate is not feasible in practice for a number of reasons. Given the sheer size of our dataset (2.08 million wall posts with URLs), none of our validation techniques, third-party or manual, would scale. While we cannot compute a real false negative rate, we can offer some numbers on the effectiveness of some of our mechanisms, as rough indicators of how many potential malicious posts could be missed.

Obfuscated URLs. As mentioned in Section 4.1, we believe that all obfuscated URLs are indicative of malicious activity. Hence, any obfuscated URL that is not included in the detection results should be viewed as a false negative. We searched our entire dataset

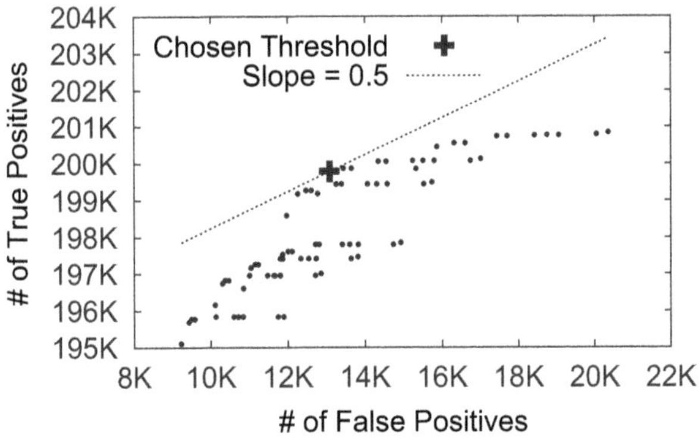

Figure 2: Number of true positives and false positives for each tested combination of threshold values. The dotted line represents our assumed best trade-off between the two (1:2). The highlighted point (cross) represents the threshold we chose for our use.

for obfuscated URLs and identified 1,012 total URLs, of which 1,003 were found in our detection results. These 9 missed URLs are only used in 141 wall posts. In contrast, the 1,003 correctly identified obfuscated URLs appear in 45,655 wall posts. Thus using the pool of obfuscated URLs as ground truth, our detection mechanisms are more than 99% effective.

Blogger Pages. We notice that Blogger pages are frequently used by attackers in our dataset to host malicious content. We took all the *blogspot.com* pages from our full dataset, and applied our validation process to them. This generated a total of 8,162 Blogger pages identified as malicious. Using this set as ground truth, only 406 of these URLs were not detected by our detection mechanism, for a false negative rate of 5%.

5. ANALYSIS OF SPAM ACTIVITY

After going through the detection (Section 3) and the validation (Section 4) steps, we arrive at a set of true positive malicious wall posts. In this section, we analyze the detected malicious users and wall posts to understand their characteristics and their impact on the OSN. Wherever possible, we compare the behavior of malicious accounts using corresponding characteristics of benign users as points for comparison.

Because of the way default privacy settings are configured on Facebook, we have more complete information on users within the crawled regional networks than outside users. Thus we prepare two datasets. The first contains the full set of detected malicious posts and users. We refer to it as the *full set*. The second excludes all malicious users outside the crawled regional network, and all wall posts they generated. We refer to it as the *local set*. The full set contains 199,782 posts from 56,922 users, while the local set includes 37,924 posts from 6,285 users. In the following analyses, we present results from the more appropriate dataset, depending on whether completeness is necessary for the metric.

5.1 URL Characteristics

We categorize malicious URLs by URL format and by domain name, and measure the prevalence of each category. We use the *full set* for this analysis.

Type	# of URLs	# of Wall Posts
Obfuscated	1,003	50,459
Plaintext	583	13,361
Hypertextlink	13,898	135,962

Table 4: Number of malicious URLs of each format type, tabulated over distinct URLs and all wall posts.

5.1.1 *Categorized by Format*

Throughout this study, we identified three different formats used to embed URLs in wall posts: *hyperlinks*, *plain text* and *obfuscated text*. A hyperlink, *e.g.* <a href="..."> http://2url.org/?67592 </a>, is a standard link embedded in the wall posts. It is the easiest format for victims to visit, but is also easily recognized by automated detection techniques. A plain text URL, *e.g.* mynewcrsh.com, is not as easy to use. The victim must copy and paste the URL to the browser's address bar to visit the site. An obfuscated URL, *e.g.* nevasubevu\t. blogs pot\t.\tco\tm (take out spaces), is the most sophisticated. It describes the actual URL to the victim in a human decipherable way. The victim must comprehend and reconstruct the URL by hand before she can visit. It is the most inconvenient to traverse, but is also the most difficult to detect.

Table 4 shows the number of distinct URLs and the number of malicious posts that contain URLs of each format. Normal hyperlinks are the dominant format when counting either the number of distinct URLs or the number of wall posts. They make up 89.8% of all distinct destinations and 68.1% of all malicious posts. However, the other two formats still account for a non-negligible fraction of the overall results. 25.2% of malicious posts contain plain text URLs, while 6.7% contain obfuscated text URLs.

Interestingly, non-hyperlink format URLs are repeated in more total wall posts. On average, each hyperlink URL appears in 9.8 malicious posts. In contrast, an average plain text URL is used in 22.9 malicious posts, while each obfuscated URL is observed on average in 50.3 wall posts.

These results convey two takeaways. First, attackers are willing to embed URLs in a way that is relatively difficult for the target user to visit, potentially for the sole purpose of evading detection. Second, obfuscated URLs are much more likely to be used repeatedly in many wall posts. One cause might be that human effort is required to construct each obfuscated URL, thus reducing the likelihood of mass-producing those URLs.

5.1.2 *Categorized by Domain*

We extract the domain names of malicious URLs and categorize them into four general types: *content sharing services*, *URL shortening services*, *blogs* and *others*. The first three types demonstrate attackers misusing legitimate services. For content sharing domains, the attacker puts the malicious content into a file and uploads it to the content sharing service, *e.g.* imageshack. For URL shortening domains, the attacker uses the URL shortening service, *e.g.* tinyurl, to hide the real (malicious) destination website. For blog domains, the attacker registers an account on the blog service, *e.g.* blogspot, and uses it to host malicious content. Finally, the *other* category contains domain names that do not appear to have any systematic or contextual similarities.

Table 5 shows the number of distinct domains in each category, as well as the the number of malicious posts that contain domains in each category. The *blog* category dominates in terms of distinct domains. We conjecture that the ease of registering new accounts is the main reason why blogs are popular. However, since all major blog services are administered centrally, it is also easy to identify

Type	# of Domains	# of Wall Posts
URL-short	110	10,041
Blogs	8,609	31,488
ContentShare	440	9,506
Other	6,325	148,747

Table 5: Number of malicious domain names in each group, tabulated over distinct domains and all wall posts.

Campaign	Summary of wall post	Clusters	Posts
Crush	Someone has a crush on you	21	51,082
Ringtone	Get free ringtones	23	31,329
Pharma	Pharmaceutical products like viagra	20	17,614
Narcotics	Sell illegal drugs	11	16,668
Love-calc	Test love compatibility	5	16,354
Macy-gift	Get free Macy's giftcard	4	14,092
Fake-video	Checkout this cool video	114	11,464
Pic-misuse	Someone is misusing your photo	1	10,683
Iphone	Get a free iPhone	4	6,317
Blog	You're mentioned in a blog	2	3,948
Fake-fbid	View a (fake) Facebook profile	1	3,556
Fake-news	View (fake) breaking news	1	2,707
Is-that-you	Is this webpage about you?	4	2,620
IPod-touch	Get a free iTouch	1	2,125
Denigration	Someone is disparaging you	2	1,440
PS3	Get a free PlayStation 3	2	1,131
Webcam	Invitation to video chat	4	1,127
Luxury	Get cheap luxury item	1	981
Online-job	Work online and earn big money	5	502
Others	No common patterns	64	4,042

Table 6: A summary of spam campaigns encountered in our study. Spammers use wall posts to entice the target to visit an embedded malicious URL. Clusters is the number of clusters involved in the campaign. Posts is the number of malicious posts in the campaign.

and remove malicious users and their pages. This potentially explains the high turnover in blog domains: on average, each individual blog is used in only 3.7 malicious posts, while domains in other categories are observed in 20 malicious posts on average.

5.2 Spam Campaign Analysis

A spam "campaign" refers to a set of malicious wall posts that all strive towards a common goal, *e.g.* selling back-door pharmaceuticals. We use the description of each wall post to distinguish between campaigns, without considering the destination URL.

5.2.1 Campaign Identification

To isolate individual spam campaigns out of the full set of malicious posts, we iteratively classify wall posts by identifying characteristic strings in each campaign. Human input is used to aid this process. For example, any wall post containing words like "viagra" or "enlarge pill" are classified into the "pharmaceutical" campaign. If the wall post contains words like "crush on you" or "someone admires you," we classify it into the "crush" campaign. Overall, we identified 19 unique campaigns. They represent 19 common ways that spammers entice targets to visit malicious URLs. Malicious wall posts that cannot be grouped into any campaign are put into an additional "other" group for statistical purposes. We present all campaigns along with a summary of their characteristics in Table 6.

At a high level, three major types of campaigns appear most popular amongst OSN spammers. First, spammers may promise free gifts, *e.g.*, free iPhones, free ringtones, *etc.* Second, spammers may trigger the target's curiosity by saying that someone likes them, is disparaging them, or has written about them on a blog. Finally, spammers may simply describe a product for sale (usually drugs). These three types of campaigns account for roughly 88.2% of all malicious posts.

We associate each campaign with the clusters produced by the detection mechanism. The "fake-video" campaign appears in an exceptionally large number of clusters. The reason is that the description in these wall posts is very short, thus the detection mechanism does not merge the clusters.

For most campaigns, the corresponding clusters form mutually exclusive groups. There are only two instances where one cluster is shared by multiple campaigns. The "crush" campaign shares one cluster with the "love-calc" campaign and the "PS3" campaign. This overlap occurs because both the "crush" and "love-calc" campaigns use a single common URL in the same period of time. The "crush" campaign also shares 400 URLs with the "PS3" campaign. The wall posts containing these shared URLs are naturally grouped into one cluster. This suggests that there is likely a single entity controlling all three of these campaigns.

5.2.2 Phishing and Malware

We turn our focus to spam campaigns that attempt to lure victims to phishing and drive-by download sites. To determine which malicious URLs in our dataset link to sites of these types, we rely on McAfee SiteAdvisor's [3] user review feature, which allows users to collaboratively mark websites as malicious and categorize their misbehavior. We discard reported sites for which the number of benign reports exceeds the number of reports of malicious behavior. If multiple malicious behaviors are reported, *i.e.* phishing and malware propagation, we count all of them.

Our results demonstrate that phishing is an extremely common practice among OSN spammers. Approximately 70.3% of malicious wall posts direct the victim to a phishing site. We encountered two different types of phishing attacks during our investigation. In the first case, spammers target confidential information. Instead of bank account credentials, the OSN account credentials are the primary targets. For instance, the spammer posts wall messages saying Facebook is giving out free ringtones to its users. When the victim visits the provided URL, he is led to a page identical to the Facebook login page and prompted to "log in" again. In the second case, the spammer is after monetary gain. For example, the spammer leaves wall posts asking victims to take a love compatibility test. Clicking the malicious link directs the victim to a site that asks them to provide their cellphone number and agree to a "terms of service" before they can see the results of the love compatibility test. If the victim proceeds, she is automatically signed up for a service and charged a monthly fee.

Malware propagation is the second most common attack associated with malicious URLs in our dataset. About 35.1% of malicious wall posts direct victims to sites laced with malware.

The high percentage of phishing and malware attacks likely stems from the social context of OSNs. It has been shown in prior work [25] that adding a bit of personal information to spam greatly increases the effectiveness of phishing attacks. Intuitively, OSN spam messages appear to come directly from trustworthy friends, and are thus more likely to successfully trick their victims. The same argument holds for malware propagating messages, which effectively turn legitimate users into "bots" controlled by attackers. They are used to send out more phishing and malware propagating wall posts.

5.2.3 Temporal Behavior

We study the temporal characteristics of the identified spam campaigns, and plot the result in Figure 3. The x-axis represents the

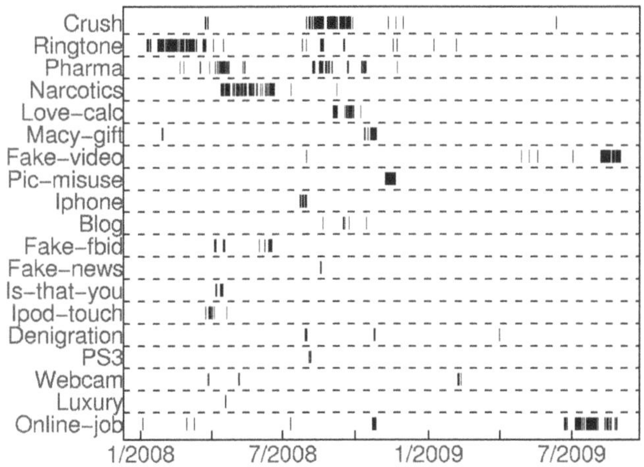

Figure 3: The timeline of each campaign.

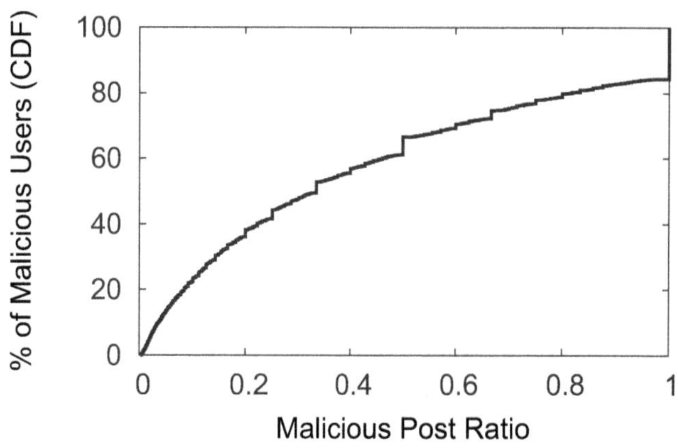

Figure 4: The malicious wall post ratio.

time period between January 1, 2008 and September 1, 2009, which corresponds to the timeframe of wall posts from our dataset. Each spam campaign is represented by a different horizontal strip. A short, thin vertical line within the strip corresponds to one malicious post within the campaign. A block in the strip reflects a burst of messages in the campaign.

Figure 3 shows the bursty nature of all the campaigns. The majority of malicious posts within each campaign are densely packed into a small number of short time bursts, while the entire campaign may span a much longer time period. As stated earlier, URL overlap seems to indicate that the "crush", "love-calc" and "PS3" campaigns are correlated. This is consistent with the observation that active time periods of the "crush" campaign overlaps with the active times of the "love-calc" and "PS3" campaigns.

5.3 Malicious Account Analysis

We now examine characteristics of accounts where malicious wall posts originated. We use our data to study the possible origins of these accounts, their impact on their social circles, temporal characteristics of their wall post activity, and whether malicious activity dominates the accounts they originate from.

5.3.1 Are Malicious Accounts Compromised?

Spammers can obtain their malicious accounts in one of two ways: *compromising* existing accounts and creating *fake* or Sybil accounts [20]. In the first case, the spammer takes control of a legitimate account following a successful phishing or password-cracking attack. This method is attractive, because legitimate accounts already have a significant number of friends (or potential targets). Plus, since these accounts are trusted or at least known to their friends, spam messages sent from these accounts are be more likely to succeed. However, the downside of this approach is that it is a non-trivial task for the spammer to compromise such accounts. Additionally, they may lose control over these accounts at any time, *i.e.* the original owners may detect the account compromise and change the password. Alternatively, spammers may create brand new Sybil accounts. These Sybil accounts are "fake" in the sense that they do not represent a real person. Despite the use of mechanisms like CAPTCHAs, account registration is still relatively easy to automate, and attackers can potentially create a large number of accounts [15]. However, they have to establish friendship with potential victims before they can post spam messages to the victims' walls.

To distinguish between the two types of malicious accounts, we analyze the overall behavior of malicious accounts to determine if they have ever exhibited characteristics of a benign user. In particular, we study each account's *application usage* and number of *received benign wall posts*. Application usage includes uploading photos and video, as well as using third-party social applications. All of these activities are indicative of "normal" account behavior, since it is highly unlikely that attackers would expend time and effort to perform these activities on fake Sybil accounts. We find that 33.9% of malicious accounts exhibit application usage, while 84.5% of accounts received benign wall posts from their friends. Only 11% of malicious accounts do not use applications or receive benign wall posts.

Simply receiving benign wall posts may not be enough to prove that a malicious account is a compromised legitimate account. First, the received posts may be complaints from other accounts. Second, a sophisticated attacker may create Sybil accounts to post messages on each others' walls, making them look like normal user accounts. Unfortunately, it is very difficult to use automateds tool to identify these cases. Instead, we chose uniformly at random a sample of 200 malicious accounts, approximately 5% of the local malicious accounts, and manually inspect the wall posts they received. The key property that we look for is the diversity of the topic and the context of offline events. For example, if the friends are talking about the party last week, the college they go to, *etc.* , it strongly suggests that this conversation involved two real human users. For 5 accounts in the sampled set, users conversed in a foreign language we were unable to reliably translate. For the remaining 195 accounts, we only suspect one account to be a fake Sybil account created by attackers. This user only received complaints and wall posts asking who he is. In addition, the corresponding user account has been suspended. The other 194 (97%) accounts exhibited normal communication patterns with their friends, despite their posting of spam-like content. This sampled result, while not representative, strongly suggests that compromised accounts are the prevailing source of malicious accounts for OSN spammers.

5.3.2 Malicious Post Ratio

We now study the ratio of malicious wall posts to the total number of wall posts made by the detected malicious accounts. This ratio indicates how dominant the malicious posting activity is. A compromised account is expected to exhibit mixed behaviors, *i.e.* they post benign wall messages before the account compromise and (potentially) after the compromise is detected and the account re-secured.

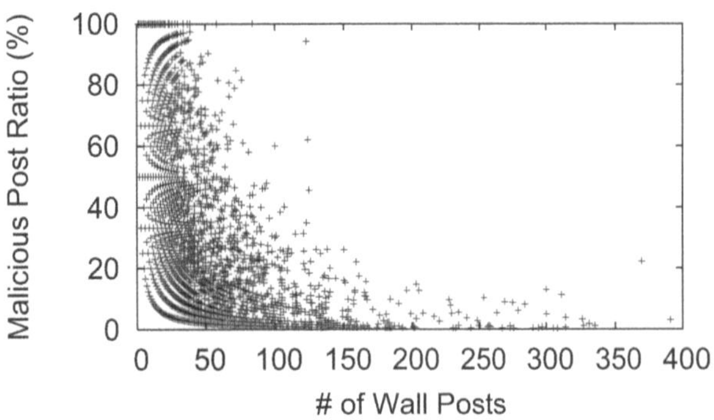

Figure 5: The malicious wall post ratio as a function of number of wall posts made by the user.

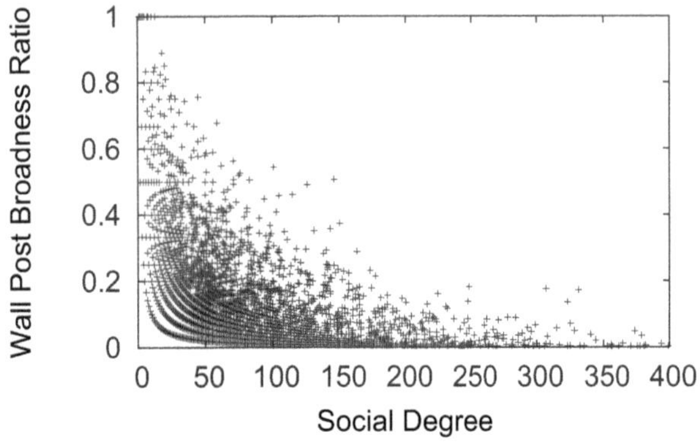

Figure 6: The wall post broadness ratio for malicious users, as a function of their social degree.

Figure 4 plots the CDF of this ratio for all malicious accounts. Less than 20% of the malicious accounts only post malicious wall messages. The remaining 80% of accounts post a mixture of malicious and benign wall posts. Among these accounts, the ratio of malicious wall posts distributes quite evenly. If we make the assumption that fake Sybil accounts would not post non-malicious messages to friends' walls, then this result means that at most 20% of all malicious accounts were created by attackers as Sybil accounts.

Figure 5 considers the malicious post ratio relative to the total number of wall posts. Most malicious users have less than 100 total wall posts. Within this range, the malicious post ratio is distributed relatively evenly. For users with larger number of wall posts, the malicious post ratio decreases. It suggests that attackers might be avoiding excessive malicious wall posts, possibly to avoid detection.

5.3.3 The Impact of Malicious Accounts

We now measure the extent of influence of malicious accounts over their friends, *i.e.* how many of their friends receive spam messages. We quantify this using the "broadness ratio," defined as *the portion of friends that receive wall posts from a user*. Since this measurement requires us to know a user's social degree (total number friends), we use the local data set and extract the social degree from the measured social graph.

Figure 6 plots the broadness ratio of malicious accounts as a function of the user's social degree. Surprisingly, malicious accounts are not posting malicious messages all of their friends' walls. Instead, broadness ratio values are most concentrated around the

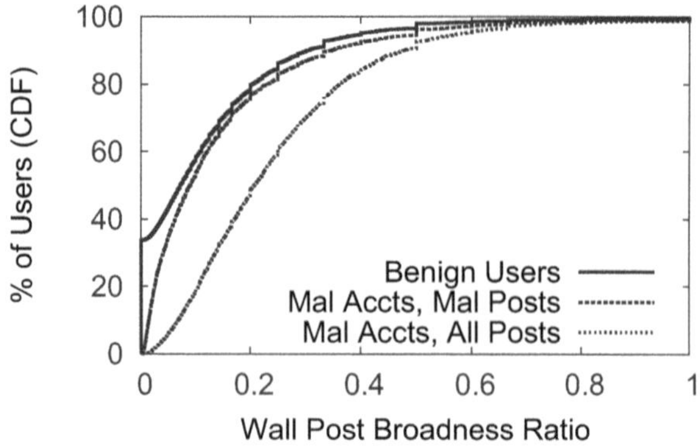

Figure 7: The post broadness ratio of both malicious and benign accounts.

20% range. As social degree increases, the trend is that the broadness ratio decreases. The result is consistent with Figure 5. Note that there are striped, round patterns towards the lower end of the x-axis in both Figures 6 and 5. This is due to the fact that we are dividing two integers to compute the percentage value. For example, the bottom left curve is formed when the numerator is one while the denominator increases. This is a numerical artifact, and represents no underlying trends in the dataset.

Figure 7 shows the CDF of the broadness ratio of both malicious and benign accounts. For malicious accounts, we plot two broadness ratio curves. One curve represents the broadness or coverage of malicious wall posts sent by the account, and the other represents the broadness of all wall posts (malicious and benign) sent by the account. The broadness of benign accounts reflects how broadly each user actually interacts with its friends on Facebook, and the results match prior work from [41] that most users interact with a small portion of their friends. About 60% of benign accounts have broadness value less than 0.1, meaning they interact with less than 10% of their friends. In addition, more than 30% of users have not posted any wall messages.

Overall, malicious accounts tend to interact with a broader portion of their friends than benign users. However, if we only consider malicious wall posts, the results are similar: spammers tend to spam the same distribution of friends as normal users post to their friends. If we consider both malicious and benign posts for malicious accounts, however, the broadness value becomes considerably larger, indicating that the friends that the accounts normally interact with are disparate from the friends receiving the malicious wall posts. Note that the our data only reveals the lower bound of the broadness of malicious accounts, since recipients of spam wall posts will often delete them from their wall, making it impossible for us to find those posts through measurement.

5.4 Temporal Properties of Malicious Activity

We now turn our attention to analyzing the temporal activity patterns of malicious accounts. Specifically, we examine the length of time that accounts are actively under the control of malicious attackers, and the diurnal activity patterns of malicious accounts.

5.4.1 Malicious Account Active Times

We define a malicious account's "active time" to be the time span between the posting time of its first and last *malicious* wall posts. We ignore benign wall posts made by the malicious account when computing its active time. Since most malicious accounts are actually compromised accounts, the active time is also a conservative estimate of the length of time it took for the account owner to detect

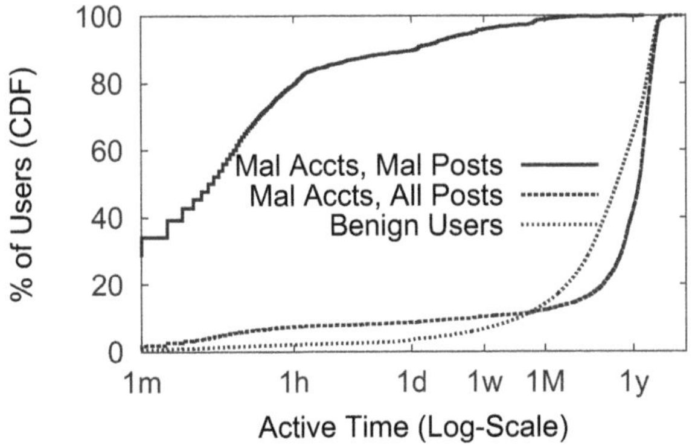

Figure 8: The active time of malicious and benign accounts.

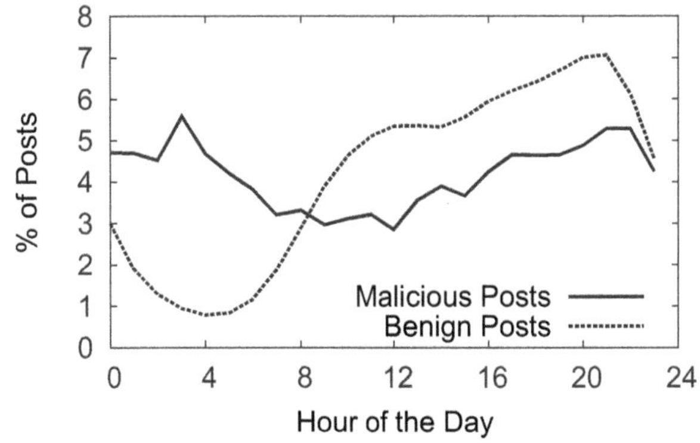

Figure 9: The hourly distribution of malicious and benign wall posts. The time has been adjusted to the local time corresponding to the regional network.

the account compromise and fix the problem. Similarly, we define a benign account's "active time" to be the time span between its first and last wall posts.

Figure 8 plots the CDF of the active time of both malicious accounts and benign accounts. Note that we have again plotted two curves representing malicious accounts. One shows active time as defined above, the other captures the time between the first and last wall posts (benign and malicious) of a malicious account. In all cases, only the accounts that have made at least 2 wall posts are included. To show greater detail on the curve, we plot the x-axis using log-scale, and mark ticks for 1 minute, 1 hour, 1 day, 1 week, 1 month and 1 year.

Clearly, most malicious accounts are actively under control of the attacker for only a short period of time. Roughly 30% of all malicious accounts are active for only a single moment in time, when it posts a single burst of spam to its friends, and never behaves maliciously again. Roughly 80% of the malicious accounts are active for less than 1 hour, and only about 10% of them are active for longer than 1 day. The reason for this phenomenon may be that when an account starts to post malicious wall messages, its friends will immediately complain, and the account owner will quickly realize that their account has been compromised. We observe a considerable number of such complaints in our wall post dataset. Once account owners recognize the attack, they can quickly reclaim control by contacting Facebook and changing the password. Nevertheless, a small portion of malicious accounts continues to post malicious wall messages for a longer period of time (1 month or more), perhaps exploiting accounts of users who rarely log in to Facebook.

In contrast, the benign accounts exhibit a drastically different pattern. More than 80% of benign accounts are active for more than 1 month, and about 35% of them remain active for more than 1 year. However, if we count all wall posts made by the malicious accounts, *i.e.* including benign messages, the curve for malicious accounts shifts drastically and becomes quite similar to the curve for benign users. This is further support for the belief that most malicious accounts are actually compromised legitimate accounts, rather than those created by the attackers.

5.4.2 *Diurnal Patterns in Malicious Activity*

Finally, we study diurnal activity patterns in the malicious wall posts. We extract the Unix timestamps attached to both malicious and benign wall posts. Since timestamps correspond to the local time where our crawling machines reside, (see Section 2.2), we adjust them to the local time zone based on the location of the regional network. For example, to compute local timestamps of events in the New York City regional network, we add an offset of 3 hours to timestamps to account for the 3-hour time difference between New York City and U. C. Santa Barbara (California). Next, we group the wall posts by the hour of day, *e.g.*, all wall posts that are made between 8am and 9am are grouped together. After that, we aggregate events based on local time, and plot the results in Figure 9. For readability, we normalize the y-value based on the total number of wall posts.

The curve for the benign wall posts clearly reflects the typical diurnal pattern. Few posts are made between 1am and 7am. After the morning, people become active, and more wall posts are made. Wall activity increases steadily over the day, peaking at 9PM and dropping quickly afterwards. However, the hourly distribution of malicious wall posts shows a much different pattern. Malicious wall posts peak at 3am, when most users are asleep and away from their accounts. This is one possible reason for the attackers to pick this time to post messages, so that they avoid immediate detection by the account owners. This suggests that mechanisms for detecting spam activity can prove the most useful in the early morning of each time zone.

6. RELATED WORK

We discuss prior related work by organizing them into three general areas: measurement studies of online social networks, studies of spam on social sites, and design of security and privacy mechanisms for online social networks.

OSN Measurements. A rich corpus of research work lies in measuring and understanding online social networks. Schneider *et al.* use clickstreams to study how users actually use OSNs [36]. Benevenuto *et al.* studied how users interact with friends, like how frequently users visit their friends' pages [18]. They discovered that browsing is actually the dominant behavior on OSNs. Jiang *et al.* studied user browsing behavior in the context of a 42 million user measurement of the Renren social network, through detailed OSN logs of user profile visits [26]. Wilson *et al.* also studied user interactions on OSNs and found that users only interact with small portion of their online friends [41]. There are other works focusing on studying the topological characteristics of OSN graphs [11, 30, 33]. They confirm that OSNs obey approximately power-law scaling characteristics [16], and are small-world networks [12].

Spam Studies. There is a large body of prior work on email spam measurements [13, 28, 29, 42]. However, to our knowledge, little work focuses on understanding the behavior of spam on OSNs. Benevenuto *et al.* propose a supervised learning approach [17] for detecting spammers in the user feedbacks of Youtube videos. However, due to the difficulty of creating a training set for Facebook, we do not adopt this detection approach. Markines *et al.* proposed to detect spam on social bookmarking sites [32]. Webb *et al.* place honeypot accounts on MySpace and study the captured social spammers [40]. At the beginning of 2010, Facebook launched a new feature to combat unknown friend requests, giving users the ability to reject friend requests as "don't know." Facebook collects this information in order to identify and remove spamming users leveraging fake accounts [21]. It is not yet reported how well this feature works in practice. Finally, Yardi *et al.* proposed to detect spam in the Twitter network [43] using techniques from the traditional email spam detection domain.

OSN Security. Given the overwhelming popularity of OSNs, a significant number of studies have focused on security mechanisms to protect OSN users. A. Felt *et al.* propose a privacy-by-proxy design for third-party OSN applications [24]. They suggest that OSNs hide actual user information from social applications and replace it with tags that represent the information. Other systems, such as xBook [37], require third-party applications to specify how they will use personal information and leverage information flow control to enforce the specification. Persona [14] lets users define fine-grained data access policies; FaceCloak [31] hides personal information from the OSN itself; and StarClique [35] provides strong user privacy guarantees in social applications by modifying the underlying social graph.

7. CONCLUSION

In this paper, we describe our work on detecting and characterizing spam campaigns performed using asynchronous wall messages on the Facebook social network. We analyze a large dataset composed of over 187 million wall posts written to the profile walls of 3.5 million Facebook users. From this dataset, we use automated techniques to group together wall posts that show strong similarities in advertised URL destination or text description. Using clustering techniques based on text similarity and URL destination matching, we build large subgraphs to represent potential social spam campaigns.

Using threshold-based techniques for spam detection, we identify over 200,000 malicious wall posts attributable to 57,000 malicious accounts. Over 70% of these attacks are phishing attacks, and the overwhelming majority of malicious accounts are compromised accounts, not "fake" accounts created for spamming. Our results show that attackers are actively leveraging the "ready-made" friend links of compromised accounts for spam.

To the best of our knowledge, our study is the first to quantify the extent of malicious content and compromised accounts in a large online social network. While we cannot determine how effective these posts are at soliciting user visits and spreading malware, our results clearly show that online social networks are now a major delivery platform targeted for spam and malware delivery. In addition, our work demonstrates that automated detection techniques and heuristics can be successfully used to detect online social spam.

Acknowledgments

We express our sincere thanks to Christian Kreibich and the anonymous reviewers for their valuable feedback. We would also like to give special thanks to Marco Cova, Christopher Kruegel and the Wepawet team at UCSB, without whose help this work would not be possible. The UCSB team is supported by the National Science Foundation under IIS-0916307, CNS-0546216, and IIS-0847925. Any opinions, findings, and conclusions or recommendations expressed in this material are those of the authors and do not necessarily reflect the views of the National Science Foundation.

8. REFERENCES

[1] Google safe browsing API. http://code.google.com/apis/safebrowsing/.

[2] Internet archive: Wayback machine. http://www.archive.org/web/web.php.

[3] McAfee SiteAdvisor. http://www.siteadvisor.com/.

[4] The SPAMHAUS domain block list. http://www.spamhaus.org/dbl/.

[5] SquidGuard. http://www.squidguard.org/.

[6] SURBL. http://www.surbl.org/.

[7] URIBL. http://www.uribl.com/gold.shtml.

[8] Users of social networking websites face malware and phishing attacks. Symantec.com Blog.

[9] Wepawet (alpha). http://wepawet.iseclab.org/.

[10] Zeus botnet targets facebook. http://blog.appriver.com/2009/10/zeus-botnet-targets-facebook.html.

[11] AHN, Y.-Y., HAN, S., KWAK, H., MOON, S., AND JEONG, H. Analysis of topological characteristics of huge online social networking services. In *Proceedings of the 16th World Wide Web Conference* (2007).

[12] AMARAL, L., SCALA, A., AND BARTHELEMY, M. Classes of small-world networks. *Proc. of National Academy of Sciences 97*, 21 (2000), 11149–11152.

[13] ANDERSON, D. S., ET AL. Spamscatter: Characterizing internet scam hosting infrastructure. In *Proc. of the USENIX Security Symposium* (August 2007).

[14] BADEN, R., BENDER, A., SPRING, N., BHATTACHARJEE, B., AND STARIN, D. Persona: an online social network with user-defined privacy. In *Proc. of SIGCOMM* (2009).

[15] BAJAJ, V. Spammers pay others to answer security tests. NY Times, April 2010. http://www.nytimes.com/2010/04/26/technology/26captcha.html.

[16] BARABASI, A.-L., AND ALBERT, R. Emergence of scaling in random networks. *Science 286*, 5439 (1999), 509–512.

[17] BENEVENUTO, F., RODRIGUES, T., AND ALMEIDA, V. Detecting spammers and content promoters in online video social networks. In *Proc. of SIGIR* (Boston, Massachusetts, USA, July 2009).

[18] BENEVENUTO, F., RODRIGUES, T., CHA, M., AND ALMEIDA, V. Characterizing user behavior in online social networks. In *Proc. of IMC* (2009).

[19] CHA, M., MISLOVE, A., ADAMS, B., AND GUMMADI, K. P. Characterizing social cascades in flickr. In *Proc. of SIGCOMM Workshop on Online Social Networks* (Seattle, WA, August 2008).

[20] DOUCEUR, J. R. The Sybil attack. In *Proc. of IPTPS* (Cambridge, MA, March 2002).

[21] EHRLICH, B. New facebook feature combats dodgy friend requests. http://mashable.com/2010/01/11/facebook-fights-dodgy-friend-requests-with-mark-you-dont-know-feature/.

[22] Facebook traffic tops google for the week. CNN Money.com, March 2010.

[23] FACEBOOK PRESS ROOM. Statistics, 2009. http://www.facebook.com/press/info.php?statistics.

[24] FELT, A., AND D., E. Privacy protection for social networking platforms. In *Workshop on Web 2.0 Security and Privacy, Oakland, CA* (May 2008).

[25] JAGATIC, T. N., JOHNSON, N. A., JAKOBSSON, M., AND MENCZER, F. Social phishing. *Communications of the ACM 50*, 10 (2007), 94–100.

[26] JIANG, J., WILSON, C., WANG, X., HUANG, P., SHA, W., DAI, Y., AND ZHAO, B. Y. Understanding latent interactions in online social networks. In *Proc. of the ACM SIGCOMM Internet Measurement Conference* (Melbourne, Australia, November 2010).

[27] JSSh - a TCP/IP javascript shell server for mozilla. `http://www.croczilla.com/bits_and_pieces/jssh/`.

[28] KANICH, C., KREIBICH, C., LEVCHENKO, K., ENRIGHT, B., VOELKER, G. M., PAXSON, V., AND SAVAGE, S. Spamalytics: An empirical analysis of spam marketing conversion. In *Proc. of the ACM Conference on Computer and Communications Security* (October 2008).

[29] KREIBICH, C., KANICH, C., LEVCHENKO, K., ENRIGHT, B., VOELKER, G., PAXSON, V., AND SAVAGE, S. Spamcraft: An inside look at spam campaign orchestration. In *Proc. of LEET* (2009).

[30] KUMAR, R., NOVAK, J., AND TOMKINS, A. Structure and evolution of online social networks. In *Proceedings of KDD* (2006).

[31] LUO, W., XIE, Q., AND HENGARTNER, U. Facecloak: An architecture for user privacy on social networking sites. In *Proc. of IEEE Conference on Privacy, Security, Risk and Trust* (2009).

[32] MARKINES, B., CATTUTO, C., AND MENCZER, F. Social spam detection. In *Proc. of AIRWeb* (2009).

[33] MISLOVE, A., MARCON, M., GUMMADI, K. P., DRUSCHEL, P., AND BHATTACHARJEE, B. Measurement and analysis of online social networks. In *Proc. of ACM SIGCOMM Internet Measurement Conference* (2007).

[34] PROVOS, N., MAVROMMATIS, P., RAJAB, M. A., AND MONROSE, F. All your iframes point to us. In *Proc. of Usenix Security* (San Jose, CA, July 2008).

[35] PUTTASWAMY, K. P. N., SALA, A., AND ZHAO, B. Y. Starclique: Guaranteeing user privacy in social networks against intersection attacks. In *Proc. of ACM CoNEXT* (Rome, Italy, December 2009).

[36] SCHNEIDER, F., FELDMANN, A., KRISHNAMURTHY, B., AND WILLINGER, W. Understanding online social network usage from a network perspective. In *Proc. of the ACM SIGCOMM Internet Measurement Conference* (2009).

[37] SINGH, K., BHOLA, S., AND LEE, W. xbook: Redesigning privacy control in social networking platforms. In *Proc. of USENIX Security* (August 2009).

[38] SWAMYNATHAN, G., WILSON, C., BOE, B., ALMEROTH, K. C., AND ZHAO, B. Y. Do social networks improve e-commerce: a study on social marketplaces. In *Proc. of SIGCOMM Workshop on Online Social Networks* (August 2008).

[39] Verisign: 1.5m facebook accounts for sale in web forum. PC Magazine, April 2010.

[40] WEBB, S., CAVERLEE, J., AND PU, C. Social honeypots: Making friends with a spammer near you. In *Proc. of CEAS* (2008).

[41] WILSON, C., BOE, B., SALA, A., PUTTASWAMY, K. P., AND ZHAO, B. Y. User interactions in social networks and their implications. In *Proceedings of the ACM European conference on Computer systems* (2009).

[42] XIE, Y., YU, F., ACHAN, K., PANIGRAHY, R., HULTEN, G., AND OSIPKOV, I. Spamming botnets: signatures and characteristics. In *Proc. of SIGCOMM* (2008).

[43] YARDI, S., ROMERO, D., SCHOENEBECK, G., AND BOYD, D. Detecting spam in a twitter network. *First Monday 15*, 1 (2010).

[44] ZHOU, F., ZHUANG, L., ZHAO, B. Y., HUANG, L., JOSEPH, A. D., AND KUBIATOWICZ, J. D. Approximate object location and spam filtering on peer-to-peer systems. In *Proc. of Middleware* (Rio de Janeiro, Brazil, June 2003).

Detecting Algorithmically Generated Malicious Domain Names

Sandeep Yadav, Ashwath K.K. Reddy, and A.L. Narasimha Reddy
Department of Electrical and Computer Engineering
Texas A&M University
College Station, TX 77843, USA
{sandeepy@, kashwathkumar@, reddy@ece.}tamu.edu

Supranamaya Ranjan
Narus Inc.
Sunnyvale, CA 94085, USA
soups@narus.com

ABSTRACT

Recent Botnets such as Conficker, Kraken and Torpig have used DNS based "domain fluxing" for command-and-control, where each Bot queries for existence of a series of domain names and the owner has to register only one such domain name. In this paper, we develop a methodology to detect such "domain fluxes" in DNS traffic by looking for patterns inherent to domain names that are generated algorithmically, in contrast to those generated by humans. In particular, we look at distribution of alphanumeric characters as well as bigrams in all domains that are mapped to the same set of IP-addresses. We present and compare the performance of several distance metrics, including KL-distance, Edit distance and Jaccard measure. We train by using a good data set of domains obtained via a crawl of domains mapped to all IPv4 address space and modeling bad data sets based on behaviors seen so far and expected. We also apply our methodology to packet traces collected at a Tier-1 ISP and show we can automatically detect domain fluxing as used by Conficker botnet with minimal false positives.

Categories and Subject Descriptors

C.2.0 [**Computer-Communication Networks**]: Security and protection; K.6.5 [**Management of Computing and Information Systems**]: Security and Protection

General Terms

Measurement, Security, Verification

Keywords

Components, Domain flux, Domain names, Edit distance, Entropy, IP Fast Flux, Jaccard Index, Malicious

1. INTRODUCTION

Recent botnets such as Conficker, Kraken and Torpig have brought in vogue a new method for botnet operators to control their bots: DNS "domain fluxing". In this method, each bot algorithmically generates a large set of domain names and queries each of them until one of them is resolved and then the bot contacts the corresponding IP-address obtained that is typically used to host the command-and-control (C&C) server. Besides for command-and-control, spammers also routinely generate random domain names in order to avoid detection. For instance, spammers advertise randomly generated domain names in their spam emails to avoid detection by regular expression based domain blacklists that maintain signatures for recently 'spamvertised' domain names.

The botnets that have used random domain name generation vary widely in the random word generation algorithm as well as the way it is seeded. For instance, Conficker-A [27] bots generate 250 domains every three hours while using the current date and time at UTC (in seconds) as the seed, which in turn is obtained by sending empty HTTP GET queries to a few legitimate sites such as *google.com*, *baidu.com*, *answers.com etc.* This way, all bots would generate the same domain names every day. In order to make it harder for a security vendor to pre-register the domain names, the next version, Conficker-C [28] increased the number of randomly generated domain names per bot to 50K. Torpig [30, 6] bots employ an interesting trick where the seed for the random string generator is based on one of the most popular trending topics in Twitter. Kraken employs a much more sophisticated random word generator and constructs English-language alike words with properly matched vowels and consonants. Moreover, the randomly generated word is combined with a suffix chosen randomly from a pool of common English nouns, verbs, adjective and adverb suffixes, such as -able, -dom, -hood, -ment, -ship, or -ly.

From the point of view of botnet owner, the economics work out quite well. They only have to register one or a few domains out of the several domains that each bot would query every day. Whereas, security vendors would have to pre-register *all* the domains that a bot queries every day, even before the botnet owner registers them. In all the cases above, the security vendors had to reverse engineer the bot executable to derive the exact algorithm being used for generating domain names. In some cases, their algorithm would predict domains successfully until the botnet owner would patch all his bots with a repurposed executable with a different domain generation algorithm [30].

We argue that reverse engineering of botnet executables is resource- and time-intensive and precious time may be lost before the domain generation algorithm is cracked and consequently before such domain name queries generated by bots are detected. In this regards, we raise the following question: *can we detect algorithmically generated domain names while monitoring DNS traffic even when a reverse engineered domain generation algorithm may not be available?*

Hence, we propose a methodology that analyzes DNS traffic to detect *if* and *when* domain names are being generated algorithmically as a line of first defense. In this regards, our proposed methodology can point to the presence of bots within a network and the network administrator can disconnect bots from their C&C server by filtering out DNS queries to such algorithmically generated domain names.

Our proposed methodology is based on the following observation: current botnets do not use well formed and pronounceable language words since the likelihood that such a word is already registered at a domain registrar is very high; which could be self-defeating as the botnet owner would then not be able to control his bots. In turn this means that such algorithmically generated domain names can be expected to exhibit characteristics vastly different from legitimate domain names. Hence, we develop metrics using techniques from signal detection theory and statistical learning which can detect algorithmically generated domain names that may be generated via a myriad of techniques: (*i*) those generated via pseudo-random string generation algorithms as well as (*ii*) dictionary-based generators, for instance the one used by Kraken[5, 3, 4] as well as a publicly available tool, Kwyjibo [12] which can generate words that are pronounceable yet not in the english dictionary.

Our method of detection comprises of two parts. First, we propose several ways to group together DNS queries: (*i*) either by the Top Level Domain (TLD) they all correspond to or; (*ii*) the IP-address that they are mapped to or; (*iii*) the connected component that they belong to, as determined via connected component analysis of the IP-domain bipartite graph. Second, for each such group, we compute metrics that characterize the distribution of the alphanumeric characters or bigrams (two consecutive alphanumeric characters) within the set of domain names. Specifically, we propose the following metrics to quickly differentiate a set of legitimate domain names from malicious ones: (*i*) Information entropy of the distribution of alphanumerics (unigrams and bigrams) within a group of domains; (*ii*) Jaccard index to compare the set of bigrams between a malicious domain name with good domains and; (*iii*) Edit-distance which measures the number of character changes needed to convert one domain name to another.

We apply our methodology to a variety of data sets. First, we obtain a set of legitimate domain names via reverse DNS crawl of the entire IPv4 address space. Next, we obtain a set of malicious domain names as generated by Conficker, Kraken and Torpig as well as model a much more sophisticated domain name generation algorithm: Kwyjibo [12]. Finally, we apply our methodology to one day of network traffic from one of the largest Tier-1 ISPs in Asia and South America and show how we can detect Conficker as well as a botnet hitherto unknown, which we call *Mjuyh* (details in Section 5).

Our extensive experiments allow us to characterize the effectiveness of each metric in detecting algorithmically generated domain names in different attack scenarios. We model different attack intensities as number of domain names that an algorithm generates. For instance, in the extreme scenario that a botnet generates 50 domains mapped to the same TLD, we show that KL-divergence over unigrams achieves 100% detection accuracy albeit at 15% false positive rate (legitimate domain groups classified as algorithmic). We show how our detection improves significantly with much lower false positives as the number of words generated per TLD increases, *e.g.*, when 200 domains are generated per TLD, then Edit distance achieves 100% detection accuracy with 8% false positives and when 500 domains are generated per TLD, Jaccard Index achieves 100% detection with 0% false positives.

Finally, our methodology of grouping together domains via connected components allows us to detect not only "domain fluxing" but also if it was used in combination with "IP fluxing". Moreover, computing the metrics over components yields better and faster detection than other grouping methods. Intuitively, even if botnets were to generate random words and combine them with multiple TLDs in order to spread the domain names thus generated (potentially to evade detection), as long as they map these domains such that at least one IP-address is shared in common, then they reveal a group structure that can be exploited by our methodology for quick detection. We show that per-component analysis detects 26.32% more IP addresses than using per-IP analysis and 16.13% more hostnames than using per-domain analysis when we applied our methodology to detect Conficker in a Tier-1 ISP trace.

The rest of this paper is organized as follows. In Section 2, we compare our work against related literature. In Section 3, we present our detection methodology and introduce the metrics we have developed. In Section 4, we present the various ways by which domains can be grouped in order to compute the different metrics over them. Next, in Section 5, we present results to compare each metric as applied to different data sets and trace data. Further, in Section 6, we present the detection of malicious domains in a supervised learning framework, in particular, L1-regularized linear regression. We present a discussion over the relative computational complexity of each metric and the usefulness of component analysis in Section 7. Finally, in Section 8 we conclude.

2. RELATED WORK

Characteristics, such as IP addresses, whois records and lexical features of phishing and non-phishing URLs have been analyzed by McGrath and Gupta [22]. They observed that the different URLs exhibited different alphabet distributions. Our work builds on this earlier work and develops techniques for identifying domains employing algorithmically generated names, potentially for "domain fluxing". Ma, et al [17], employ statistical learning techniques based on lexical features (length of domain names, host names, number of dots in the URL *etc.*) and other features of URLs to automatically determine if a URL is malicious, *i.e.*, used for phishing or advertising spam. While they classify each URL independently, our work is focused on classifying a group of URLs as algorithmically generated or not, solely by making use of the set of alphanumeric characters used.

In addition, we experimentally compare against their lexical features in Section 5 and show that our alphanumeric distribution based features can detect algorithmically generated domain names with lower false positives than lexical features. Overall, we consider our work as complimentary and synergistic to the approach in [17].

With reference to the practice of "IP fast fluxing", *e.g.*, where the botnet owner constantly keeps changing the IP-addresses mapped to a C&C server, [24] implements a detection mechanism based on passive DNS traffic analysis. In our work, we present a methodology to detect cases where botnet owners may use a combination of both domain fluxing with IP fluxing, by having bots query a series of domain names and at the same time map a few of those domain names to an evolving set of IP-addresses. Also earlier papers [23, 20] have analyzed the inner-working of IP fast flux networks for hiding spam and scam infrastructure. With regards to botnet detection, [14, 15] perform correlation of network activity in time and space at campus network edges, and Xie et al in [33] focus on detecting spamming botnets by developing regular expression based signatures from a dataset of spam URLs .

We find that graph analysis of IP addresses and domain names embedded in DNS queries and replies reveal interesting macro relationships between different entities and enable identification of bot networks (Conficker) that seemed to span many domains and TLDs. With reference to graph based analysis, [34] utilizes rapid changes in user-bot graphs structure to detect botnet accounts.

Statistical and learning techniques have been employed by various studies for prediction [10, 25, 13]. We employed results from detection theory in designing our strategies for classification [31, 11].

Several studies have looked at understanding and reverse-engineering the inner workings of botnets [5, 3, 4, 16, 30, 26, 29]. Botlab has carried out an extensive analysis of several bot networks through active participation [19] and provided us with many example datasets for malicious domains.

3. DETECTION METRICS

In this section, we present our detection methodology that is based on computing the distribution of alphanumeric characters for groups of domains. First, we motivate our metrics by showing how algorithmically generated domain names differ from legitimate ones in terms of distribution of alphanumeric characters. Next, we present our three metrics, namely Kullback-Leibler (KL) distance, Jaccard Index (JI) measure and Edit distance. Finally, in Section 4 we present the methodology to group domain names.

3.1 Data Sets

We first describe the data sets and how we obtained them: (*i*) **Non-malicious ISP Dataset:** We use network traffic trace collected from across 100+ router links at a Tier-1 ISP in Asia. The trace is one day long and provides details of DNS requests and corresponding replies. There are about 270,000 DNS name server replies. (*ii*) **Non-malicious DNS Dataset:** We performed a reverse DNS crawl of the entire IPv4 address space to obtain a list of domain names and their corresponding IP-addresses. We further divided this data set in to several parts, each comprising of domains which had 500, 200, 100 and 50 domain labels. The DNS Dataset is considered as non-malicious for the following reasons. Botnets may own only a limited number of IP addresses. Based on our study, we find that a DNS PTR request maps an IP address to only one domain name. The dataset thus obtained will contain very few malicious domain names per analyzed group. In the event that the bots exhibit IP fluxing, it is noteworthy that the botnet owners cannot change the PTR DNS mapping for IP addresses not owned. Although, the malicious name servers may point to any IP address. (*iii*) **Malicious datasets:** We obtained the list of domain names that were known to have been generated by recent Botnets: Conficker [27, 28], Torpig [30] and Kraken [5, 3]. As described earlier in the Introduction, Kraken exhibits the most sophisticated domain generator by carefully matching the frequency of occurrence of vowels and consonants as well as concatenating the resulting word with common suffixes in the end such as -able, -dom, *etc.* (*iv*) **Kwyjibo**: We model a much more sophisticated algorithmic domain name generation algorithm by using a publicly available tool, Kwyjibo [12] which generates domain names that are pronounceable yet not in the English language dictionary and hence much more likely to be available for registration at a domain registrar. The algorithm uses a syllable generator, where they first learn the frequency of one syllable following another in words in English dictionary and then automatically generate pronounceable words by modeling it as a Markov process.

3.2 Motivation

Our detection methodology is based on the observation that algorithmically generated domains differ significantly from legitimate (human) generated ones in terms of the distribution of alphanumeric characters. Figure 1(a) shows the distribution of alphanumeric characters, defined as the set of English alphabets (*a-z*) and digits (0-9) for both legitimate as well as malicious domains [1]. We derive the following points: (*i*) First, note that both the non-malicious data sets exhibit a non-uniform frequency distribution, *e.g.*, letters 'm' and 'o' appear most frequently in the non-malicious ISP data set whereas the letter 's' appears most frequently in the non-malicious DNS data set. (*ii*) Even the most sophisticated algorithmic domain generator seen in the wild for Kraken botnet has a fairly uniform distribution, albeit with higher frequencies at the vowels: 'a', 'e' and 'i'. (*iii*) If botnets of future were to evolve and construct words that are pronounceable yet not in the dictionary, then they would not exhibit a uniform distribution as expected. For instance, Kwyjibo exhibits higher frequencies at alphabets, 'e', 'g', 'i', 'l', 'n', *etc.* In this regards, techniques that are based on only the distribution of unigrams (single alphanumeric characters) may not be sufficient, as we will show through the rest of this section.

The terminology used in this and the following sections is as follows. For a hostname such as *physics.university.edu*, we refer to *university* as the second-level domain label, *edu* as the first-level domain, and *university.edu* as the second-level domain. Similarly, *physics.university.edu* is referred to as the third-level domain and *physics* is the third-level domain label. The ccTLDs such as *co.uk* are effectively considered as first-level domains.

[1]Even though domain names may contain characters such as '-', we currently limit our study to alphanumeric characters only.

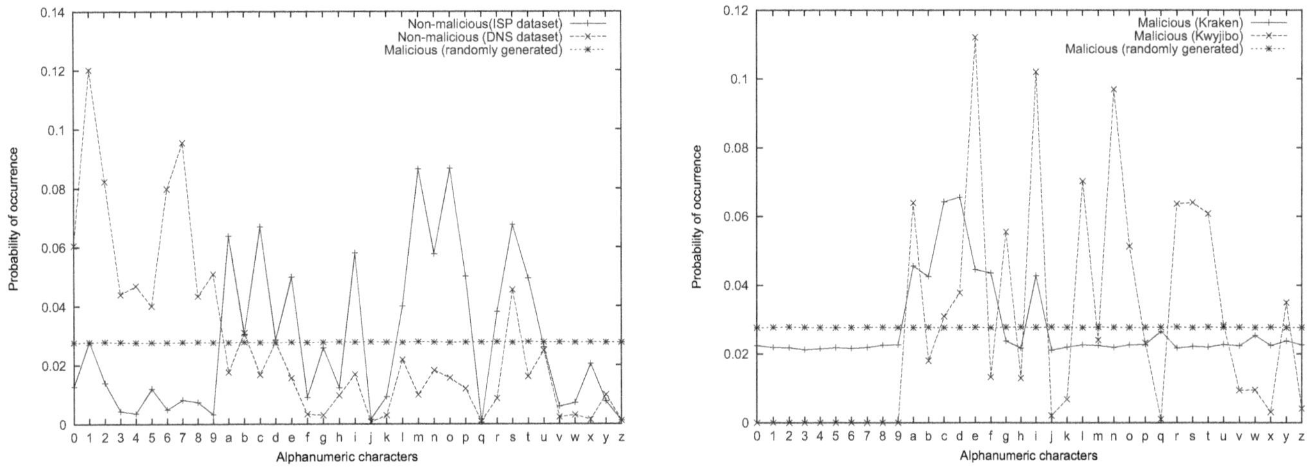

(a) Non-malicious and malicious domains.

(b) Only malicious entities

Figure 1: Probability distributions of malicious and non-malicious domains

3.3 Metrics for anomaly detection

The K-L(Kullback-Leibler) divergence metric is a non-symmetric measure of "distance" between two probability distributions. The divergence (or distance) between two discretized distributions P and Q is given by: $D_{KL}(P||Q) = \sum_{i=1}^{n} P(i) log \frac{P(i)}{Q(i)}$.

where n is the number of possible values for a discrete random variable. The probability distribution P represents the test distribution and the distribution Q represents the base distribution from which the metric is computed.

Since the K-L measure is asymmetric, we use a symmetric form of the metric, which helps us deal with the possibility of singular probabilities in either distribution. The modified K-L metric is computed using the formula: $D_{sym}(PQ) = \frac{1}{2}(D_{KL}(P||Q) + D_{KL}(Q||P))$.

Given a test distribution $\underline{q}$ computed for the domain to be tested, and non-malicious and malicious probability distribution over the alphanumerics as $\underline{g}$ and $\underline{b}$ respectively, we characterize the distribution as malicious or not via the following optimal classifier (for proof see appendix):

$$D_{sym}(\underline{qb}) - D_{sym}(\underline{qg}) \underset{b}{\overset{g}{\gtrless}} 0 \quad (1)$$

For the test distribution $\underline{q}$ to be classified as non-malicious, we expect $D_{sym}(\underline{qg})$ to be less than $D_{sym}(\underline{qb})$. However, if $D_{sym}(\underline{qg})$ is greater than $D_{sym}(\underline{qb})$, the distribution is classified as malicious.

3.3.1 *Measuring K-L divergence with unigrams*

The first metric we design measures the KL-divergence of unigrams by considering all domain names that belong to the same group, *e.g.* all domains that map to the same IP-address or those that belong to the same top-level domain. We postpone discussion of groups to Section 4. Given a group of domains for which we want to establish whether they were generated algorithmically or not, we first compute the distribution of alphanumeric characters to obtain the test distribution. Next, we compute the KL-divergence with a good distribution obtained from the non-malicious data sets (ISP or DNS crawl) and a malicious distribution obtained by modeling a botnet that uses generates alphanumerics uniformly. As expected, a simple unigram based technique may not suffice, especially to detect Kraken or Kwyjibo generated domains. Hence, we consider bigrams in our next metric.

3.3.2 *Measuring K-L divergence with bigrams*

A simple obfuscation technique that can be employed by algorithmically generated malicious domain names could be to generate domain names by using the same distribution of alphanumerics as commonly seen for legitimate domains. Hence, in our next metric, we consider distribution of bigrams, *i.e.*, two consecutive characters. We argue that it would be harder for an algorithm to generate domain names that exactly preserve a bigram distribution similar to legitimate domains since the algorithm would need to consider the previous character already generated while generating the current character. The choices for the current character will be hence more restrictive than when choosing characters based on unigram distributions. Thus, the probability of test bigrams matching a non-malicious bigram distribution, becomes smaller.

Analogous to the case above, given a group of domains, we extract the set of bigrams present in it to form a bigram distribution. Note that for the set of alphanumeric characters that we consider [*a-z*, 0-9], the total number of bigrams possible are 36x36, *i.e.*, 1,296. Our improved hypothesis now involves validating a given test bigram distribution against the bigram distribution of non-malicious and malicious domain labels. We use the database of non-malicious words to determine a non-malicious probability distribution. For a sample malicious distribution, we generate bigrams randomly. Here as well, we use KL-divergence over the bigram distribution to determine if a test distribution is malicious or legitimate.

3.3.3 *Using Jaccard Index between bigrams*

We present the second metric to measure the similarity

between a known set of components and a test distribution, namely the *Jaccard index* measure. The metric is defined as

$$JI = \frac{A \cap B}{A \cup B}$$

where, A and B each represent the set of random variables. For our particular case, the set comprises of bigrams that compose a domain label or a hostname. Note that Jaccard index (JI) measure based on bigrams is a commonly used technique for web search engine spell-checking [21].

The core motivation behind using the JI measure is same as that for KL-divergence. We expect that bigrams occurring in randomized (or malicious) hostnames to be mostly different when compared with the set of non-malicious bigrams. To elaborate, we construct a database of bigrams which point to lists of non-malicious words, domain labels or hostnames, as the case may be. Now for each sub-domain present in a test set, we determine all non-malicious words that contain at least 75% of the bigrams present in the test word. Such a threshold helps us discard words with less similarity. However, longer test words may implicitly satisfy this criteria and may yield ambiguous JI value. As observed in section 5, the word sizes for 95% of non-malicious words do not exceed 24 characters, and hence we divide all test words into units of 24 character strings. Figure 2 presents the CDF of domain label sizes as observed in our DNS PTR dataset (described in section 5).

Calculating the JI measure is best explained with an example. Considering a randomized hostname such as *ickoxjsov.botnet.com*, we determine the JI value of the domain label *ickoxjsov* by first computing all bigrams (eight, in this case). Next, we examine each bigram's queue of non-malicious domain labels, and short list words with at least 75% of bigrams, *i.e.*, six of the eight bigrams. Words satisfying this criteria may include thequ*ick*brownf*oxj*ump*sov*erthelazydog (35 bigrams). However, such a word still has a low JI value owing to the large number of bigrams in it. Therefore, the JI value is thus computed as 6/(8 + 35 - 6) = 0.16. The low value indicates that the randomized test word does not match too well with the word from the non-malicious bigram database.

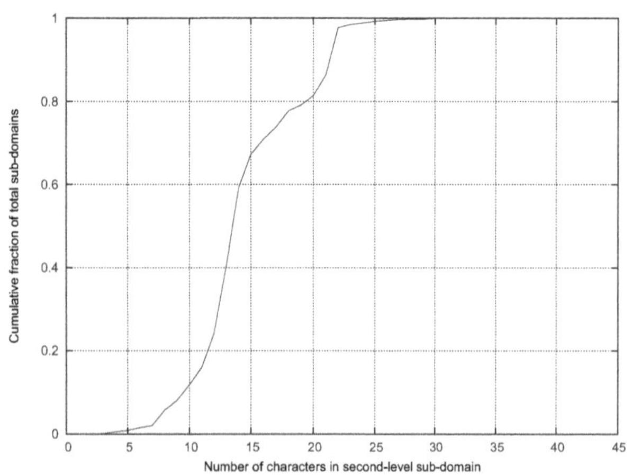

Figure 2: CDF of domain label sizes for DNS PTR dataset.

The JI measure is thus computed for the remaining words. The test words might comprise of a large number of bigrams and therefore do not always ensure a high JI value. We compute the JI measure using the equation described above and average it for all test words belonging to a particular group being analyzed. The averaged JI value for a non-malicious domain is expected to be higher than those for malicious groups.

As observed via our experiments in Section 5, the JI measure is better at determining domain based anomalies. However, it is also computationally expensive as the database of non-malicious bigrams needs to be maintained in the memory. Also, classifying a non-malicious hosts will take more CPU cycles as we would obtain and compare a large set of words consisting of test word's bigrams. Section 7 examines the computational complexity of various metrics that we use.

3.3.4 *Edit distance*

Note that the two metrics described earlier, rely on definition of a "good" distribution (KL-divergence) or database (JI measure). Hence, we define a third metric, Edit distance, which classifies a group of domains as malicious or legitimate by only looking at the domains within the group, and is hence not reliant on definition of a good database or distribution. The Edit distance between two strings represents an integral value identifying the number of transformations required to transform one string to another. It is a symmetric measure and provides a measure of intra-domain entropy. The type of eligible transformations are addition, deletion, and modification. For instance, to convert the word *cat* to *dog*, the edit distance is three as it requires all three characters to be replaced. With reference to determining anomalous domains, we expect that all domain labels (or hostnames) which are randomized, will, on an average, have higher edit distance value. We use the Levenshtein edit distance dynamic algorithm for determining anomalies. The algorithm for computing the Levenshtein edit distance has been shown in Algorithm 1 [21].

Algorithm 1 Dynamic programming algorithm for finding the edit distance

EditDist(s_1,s_2)

int $m[i,j] = 0$
for $i \leftarrow 1$ **to** $|s_1|$
do $m[i,0] = i$
for $j \leftarrow 1$ **to** $|s_2|$
do $m[0,j] = j$
for $i \leftarrow 1$ **to** $|s_1|$
do for $j \leftarrow 1$ **to** $|s_2|$
do $m[i,j] = \min\{m[[i-1,j-1] + \text{if}(s_1[i] = s_2[j])$ then 0 else 1 fi,
$m[i-1,j] + 1$
$m[i,j-1] + 1\}$
return $m[|s_1|,|s_2|]$

4. GROUPING DOMAIN NAMES

In this section, we present ways by which we group together domain names in order to compute metrics that were defined in Section 3 earlier.

4.1 Per-domain analysis

Note that several botnets use several second-level domain names to generate algorithmic sub-domains. Hence, one way by which we group together domain names is via the second-level domain name. The intention is that if we begin seeing several algorithmically generated domain names being queried such that all of them correspond to the same second-level domain, then this may be reflective of a few favorite domains being exploited. Hence for all sub-domains, *e.g.*, *abc.examplesite.org, def.examplesite.org, etc.*, that have the same second-level domain name *examplesite.org*, we compute all the metrics over the alphanumeric characters and bigrams of the corresponding domain labels. Since domain fluxing involves a botnet generating a large number of domain names, we consider only domains which contain a sufficient number of third-level domain labels, *e.g.*, 50, 100, 200 and 500 sub-domains.

4.2 Per-IP analysis

As a second method of grouping, we consider all domains that are mapped to the same IP-address. This would be reflective of a scenario where a botnet has registered several of the algorithmic domain names to the same IP-address of a command-and-control server. Determining if an IP address is mapped to several such malicious domains is useful as such an IP-address or its corresponding prefix can be quickly blacklisted in order to sever the traffic between a command-and-control server and its bots. We use the dataset from a Tier-1 ISP to determine all IP-addresses which have multiple hostnames mapped to it. For a large number of hostnames representing one IP address, we explore the above described metrics, and thus identify whether the IP address is malicious or not.

4.3 Component analysis

A few botnets have taken the idea of domain fluxing further and generate names that span multiple TLDs, *e.g.*, Conficker-C generates domain names in 110 TLDs. At the same time domain fluxing can be combined with another technique, namely "IP fluxing" [24] where each domain name is mapped to an ever changing set of IP-addresses in an attempt to evade IP blacklists. Indeed, a combination of the two is even harder to detect. Hence, we propose the third method for grouping domain names into connected components.

We first construct a bipartite graph G with IP-addresses on one side and domain names on the other. An edge is constructed between a domain name and an IP-address if that IP-address was ever returned as one of the responses in a DNS query. When multiple IP addresses are returned, we draw edges between all the returned IP addresses and the queried host name.

First, we determine the connected components of the bipartite graph G, where a connected component is defined as one which does not have any edges with any other components. Next, we compute the various metrics (KL-divergence for unigrams and bigrams, JI measure for bigrams, Edit distance) for each component by considering all the domain names within a component.

Component extraction separates the IP-domain graph into components which can be classified in to the following classes: (*i*) **IP fan**: these have one IP-address which is mapped to several domain names. Besides the case where one IP-address is mapped to several algorithmic domains, there are several legitimate scenarios possible. First, this class could include domain hosting services where one IP-address is used to provide hosting to several domains, *e.g.* Google Sites, *etc.* Other examples could be mail relay service where one mail server is used to provide mail relay for several MX domains. Another example could be when domain registrars provide domain parking services, *i.e.*, someone can purchase a domain name while asking the registrar to host it temporarily. (*ii*) **Domain fan**: these consist of one domain name connected to multiple IPs. This class will contain components belonging to the legitimate content providers such as Google, Yahoo!, *etc.* (*iii*)**Many-to-many component**: these are components that have multiple IP addresses and multiple domain names, *e.g.*, Content Distribution Networks (CDNs) such as Akamai.

In section 6, we briefly explain the classification algorithm that we use to classify test components as malicious or not.

5. RESULTS

In this section, we present results of employing various metrics across different groups, as described in section 3 and 4. We briefly describe the data set used for each experiment.

With all our experiments, we present the results based on the consideration of increasing number of domain labels. In general, we observe that using a larger test data set yields better results.

5.1 Per-domain analysis

5.1.1 Data set

The analysis in this sub-section is based only on the domain labels belonging to a domain. The non-malicious distribution $\underline{g}$ may be obtained from various sources. For our analysis, we use a database of DNS PTR records corresponding to all IPv4 addresses. The database contains 659 second-level domains with at least 50 third-level sub-domains, while there are 103 second-level domains with at least 500 third-level sub-domains. From the database, we extract all second-level domains which have at least 50 third-level sub-domains. All third-level domain labels corresponding to such domains are used to generate the distribution $\underline{g}$. For instance, a second-level domain such as *university.edu* may have many third-level domain labels such as *physics*, *cse*, *humanities* etc. We use all such labels that belong to trusted domains, for determining $\underline{g}$.

To generate a malicious base distribution $\underline{b}$, we randomly generate as many characters as present in the non-malicious distribution. We use domain labels belonging to well-known malware based domains identified by Botlab, and also a publicly available webspam database, as malicious domains [1, 9] for verification using our metrics. Botlab provides us with various domains used by Kraken, Pushdo, Storm, MegaD, and Srizbi [1]. For *per-domain* analysis, the test words used are the third-level domain labels.

Figure 1(a) shows how malicious/non-malicious distributions appear for the DNS PTR dataset as well as the ISP dataset described in the following sections.

We will present the results for all the four measures de-

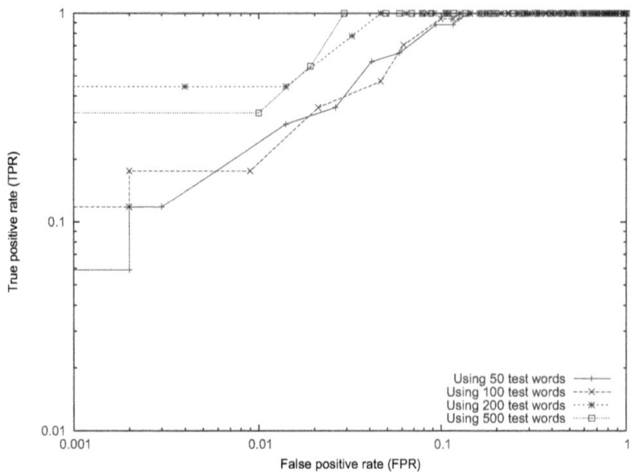

(a) K-L metric with unigram distribution (Per-domain).

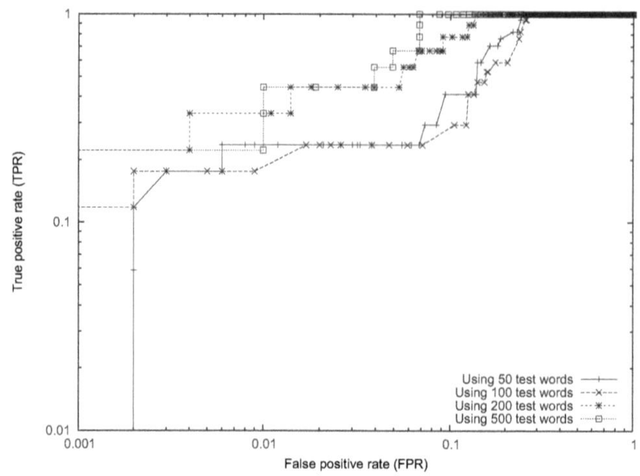

(b) K-L metric with bigram distribution (Per-domain).

Figure 3: ROC curves for Per-domain analysis

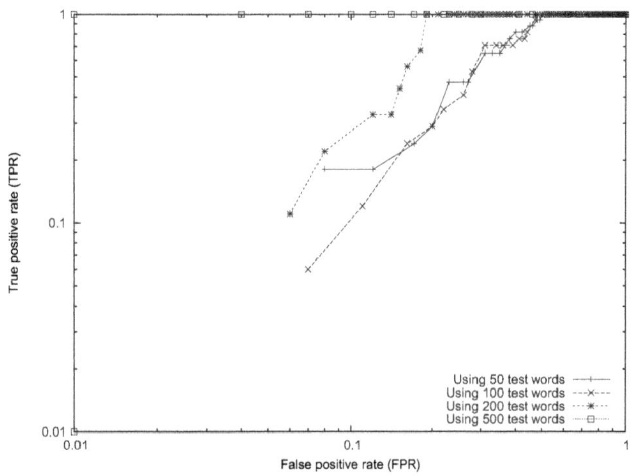

(a) Jaccard measure for bigrams (Per-domain).

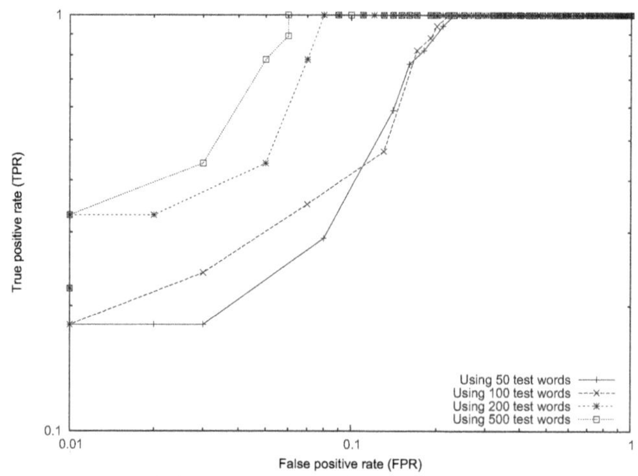

(b) Edit distance (Per-domain).

Figure 4: ROC curves for Per-domain analysis

scribed earlier, for domain-based analysis. In later sections, we will only present data from one of the measures for brevity.

5.1.2 *K-L divergence with unigram distribution*

We measure the symmetrized K-L distance metric from the test domain to the malicious/non-malicious alphabet distributions. We classify the test domain as malicious or non-malicious based on equation (10) in Appendix A. Figure 3(a) shows the results from our experiment presented as an ROC curve.

The figure shows that the different sizes of test data sets produce relatively different results. The area under the ROC is a measure of the goodness of the metric. We observe that with 200 or 500 domain labels, we cover a relatively greater area, implying that using many domain labels helps obtain accurate results. For example, using 500 labels, we obtain 100% detection rate with only 2.5% false positive rate. Note that with a larger data set, we indeed expect higher true positive rates for small false positive rates, as larger samples will stabilize the evaluated metrics.

The number of domain labels required for accurate detection corresponds to the latency of accurately classifying a previously unseen domain. The results suggest that a domain-fluxing domain can be accurately characterized by the time it generates around 500 names.

5.1.3 *K-L divergence with bigram distribution*

Figure 3(b) presents the results of employing K-L distance metric over bigram distributions. We observe again that using 200 or 500 domain labels does better than using smaller number of labels, with 500 labels doing the best. Experiments with 50/100 domain labels yield similar results.

We note that the performance with unigram distributions is slightly better than using bigram distributions. However, when botnets employ counter measures to our techniques, the bigram distributions may provide better defense compared to unigram distributions as they require more effort to match the good distribution ($\underline{g}$).

5.1.4 *Jaccard measure of bigrams*

The Jaccard Index measure does significantly better in

comparison to the previous metrics. From figure 4(a), it is evident that using 500 domain labels gives us a clear separation for classification of test domains (and hence an area of 1). Using 50 or 100 labels is fairly equivalent with 200 labels doing comparatively better. The JI measure produces higher false positives for smaller number of domains (50/100/200) than K-L distance measures.

5.1.5 Edit distance of domain labels

Figure 4(b) shows the performance using edit distance as the evaluation metric. The detection rate for 50/100 test words reaches 1 only for high false positive rates, indicating that a larger test word set should be used. For 200/500 domain labels, 100% detection rate is achieved at false positive rates of 5-7%.

5.1.6 Kwyjibo domain label analysis

Kwyjibo is a tool to generate random words which can be used as domain labels [12]. The generated words are seemingly closer to pronounceable words of the english language, in addition to being random. Thus many such words can be created in a short time. We anticipate that such a tool can be used by attackers to generate domain labels or domain names quickly with the aim of defeating our scheme. Therefore, we analyze Kwyjibo based words, considering them as domain labels belonging to a particular domain.

The names generated by Kwyjibo tool could be accurately characterized by our measures given sufficient names. Example results are presented in Fig. 5 with K-L distances over unigram distributions. From figure 5, we observe that verification with unigram frequency can lead to a high detection rate with very low false positive rate. Again, the performance using 500 labels is the best. We also observe a very steep rise in detection rates for all the cases. The Kwyjibo domains could be accurately characterized with false positive rates of 6% or less.

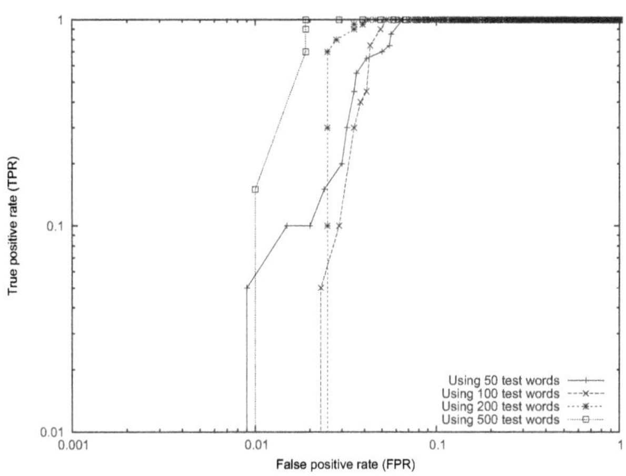

Figure 5: ROC curve : K-L metric with unigram distribution (Kwyjibo).

The initial detection rate for Kwyjibo is low as compared to the per-domain analysis. This is because the presence of highly probable non-malicious unigrams in Kwyjibo based domains makes detection difficult at lower false positive rates. The results with other measures (K-L distance over bigram distributions, JI and edit distances) were similar: kwyjibo domains could be accurately characterized at false positive rates in the range of 10-12%, but detection rates were nearly zero at false positive rates of 10% or less.

The scatter plot presented in Fig. 6 indicates the clear separation obtained between non-malicious and malicious domains. The plot represents the Jaccard measure using 500 test words. We highlight the detection of botnet based malicious domains such as *Kraken*, *MegaD*, *Pushdo*, *Srizbi*, and *Storm*. A few well-known non-malicious domains such as *apple.com*, *cisco.com*, *stanford.edu*, *mit.edu*, and *yahoo.com* have also been indicated for comparison purposes.

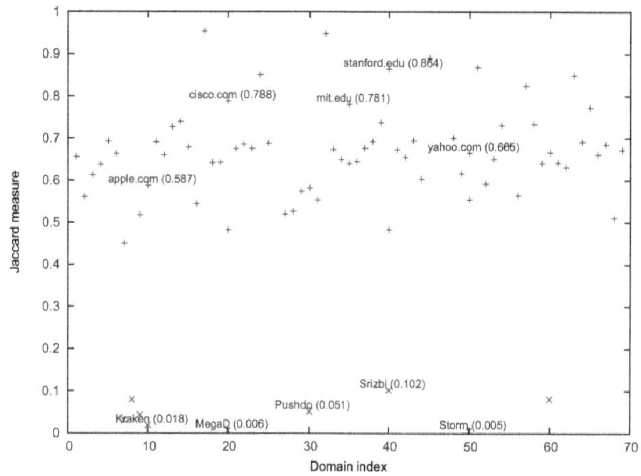

Figure 6: Scatter plot with Jaccard Index for bigrams (500 test words).

5.1.7 Progressive demarcation

The earlier results have showed that very high good detection rates can be obtained at low false positive rates once we have 500 or more hostnames of a test domain. As discussed earlier, the number of hostnames required for our analysis corresponds to latency of accurately characterizing a previously unseen domain. During our experiments, not all the test domains required 500 hostnames for accurate characterization since the distributions were either very close to the good distribution $\underline{g}$ or bad distribution $\underline{b}$. These test domains could be characterized with a smaller latency (or smaller number of hostnames).

In order to reduce the latency for such domains, we tried an experiment at progressive demarcation or characterization of the test domains. Intuitively, the idea is to draw two thresholds above one there are clearly good domains, below the second threshold there are clearly bad domains and the domains between the two thresholds require more data (or hostnames) for accurate characterization. These thresholds are progressively brought closer (or made tighter) as more hostnames become available, allowing more domains to be accurately characterized until we get 500 or more hostnames for each domain. The results of such an experiment using the JI measure are shown in Fig. 7.

We establish the lower bound using the formula $\mu_b + \sigma_b$ where μ_b is the mean of JI values observed for bad or malicious domains and σ_b is the standard deviation. Similarly, the upper bound is obtained using the expression $\mu_g - \sigma_g$ where the subscript g implies good domains. Figure 7 shows the detection rate for the considered domains.

We see a monotonically increasing detection rate for both good and bad domains. It is observed that 85% of bad domains could be so characterized accurately with only 100 hostnames while only about 23% of good domains can be so characterized with 100 hostnames. In addition, our experiments indicate that only a small percentage of domains require 200 or more hostnames for their characterization.

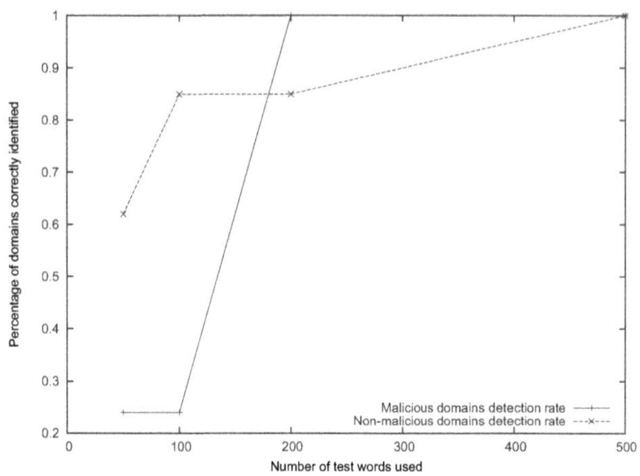

Figure 7: Illustrating benefits of progressive demarcation with JI measure.

5.2 Per-IP analysis

5.2.1 Data set

Here, we present the evaluation of domain names that map to an IP address. For analyzing the per-IP group, for all hostnames mapping to an IP-address, we use the domain labels except the top-level domain TLD as the test word. For instance, for hostnames *physics.university.edu* and *cse.university.edu* mapping to an IP address, say *6.6.6.6*, we use *physicsuniversity* and *cseuniversity* as test words. However, we only consider IP addresses with at least 50 hostnames mapping to it. We found 341 such IP addresses, of which 53 were found to be malicious, and 288 were considered non-malicious. The data is obtained from DNS traces of a Tier-1 ISP in Asia.

Many hostnames may map to the same IP address. Such a mapping holds for botnets or other malicious entities utilizing a large set of hostnames mapping to fewer C&C(Command and Control) servers. It may also be valid for legitimate internet service such as for Content Delivery Networks (CDNs). We first classify the IPs obtained into two classes of malicious and non-malicious IPs. The classification is done based on manual checking, using blacklists, or publicly available Web of Trust information [7]. We manually confirm the presence of *Conficker* based IP addresses and domain names [28]. The ground truth thus obtained may be used to verify the accuracy of classification. Figure 1 shows the distribution of non-malicious test words and the randomized distribution is generated as described previously.

We discuss the results of per-IP analysis below. For the sake of brevity, we present results based on K-L distances of bigram distributions only. Summary of results from other metrics is also provided.

The ROC curve for K-L metric shows that bigram distribution can be effective in accurately characterizing the domain names belonging to different IP addresses. We observe a very clear separation between malicious and non-malicious IPs with 500, and even with 200 test words. With a low false positive rate of 1%, high detection rates of 90% or more are obtained with 100 or greater number of test words.

The bigram analysis was found to perform better than unigram distributions. The per-IP bigram analysis performed better than per-domain bigram analysis. We believe that the bigrams obtained from the ISP dataset provide a comprehensive non-malicious distribution. The second-level domain labels also assist in discarding false anomalies, and therefore provide better accuracy.

The JI measure performed very well, even for small set of test words. The area covered under the ROC curve was 1 for 200/500 test words. For the experiment with 100 test words, we achieved the detection rates of 100% with false positive rate of only 2%.

Edit distance with domains mapping to an IP, results in a good performance in general. The experiments with 100 test words results in a low false positive rate of about 10% for a 100% detection rate. However for using only 50 test words, the detection rate reaches about 80% for a high false positive rate of 20%. Thus, we conclude that for per-IP based analysis, the JI measure performs relatively better than previous measures applied to this group. However, as highlighted in section 7, the time complexity for computing jaccard index is higher.

Table 2: Summary of interesting networks discovered through component analysis

Comp. type	#Comps.	#domains	#IPs
Conficker botnet	1	1.9K	19
Helldark botnet	1	28	5
Mjuyh botnet	1	121	1.2K
Misspelt Domains	5	215	17
Domain Parking	15	630	15
Adult content	4	349	13

Table 3: Domain names used by bots

Type of group	Domain names
Conficker botnet	vddxnvzqjks.ws gcvwknnxz.biz joftvvtvmx.org
Mjuyh bot	935c4fe[0-9a-z]+.6.mjuyh.com c2d026e[0-9a-z]+.6.mjuyh.com
Helldark Trojan	may.helldark.biz X0R.ircdevils.net www.BALDMANPOWER.ORG

5.3 Summary

For a larger set of test words, the relative order of efficacy of different measures decreases from JI, to edit distance to

Table 1: **Different types of classes**

Type of class	**# of components**	**# of IP addresses**	**# of domain names**	**Types of components found**
Many-to-many	440	11K	35K	Legitimate services (Google, Yahoo), CDNs, Cookie tracking, Mail service, Conficker botnet
IP fans	1.6K	1.6K	44K	Domain Parking, Adult content, Blogs, small websites
Domain fans	930	8.9K	9.3K	CDNs (Akamai), Ebay, Yahoo, Mjuyh botnet

K-L distances over bigrams and unigrams. However, interestingly, we observe the exact opposite order when using a small set of test words. For instance, with 50 test words used for the per-domain analysis, the false positive rates at which we obtain 100% detection rates, are approximately 50% (JI), 20% (ED), 25% (K-L with bigram distribution), and 15% (K-L with unigram distribution). Even though the proof in the Appendix indicates that K-L divergence is an optimal metric for classification, in practice, it does not hold as the proof is based on the assumption that it is equally likely to draw a test distribution from a good or a bad distribution.

6. DETECTION VIA SUPERVISED LEARNING

As discussed in Section 5.3 immediately above, the relative merits of each measure vary depending, for instance, on the number of subdomains present in a domain being tested. In this section, we formulate detection of malicious domains (algorithmically generated) as a supervised learning problem such that we can combine the benefits afforded by each measure while learning the relative weights of each measure during a training phase. We divide the one-day long trace from the South Asian Tier-1 ISP in to two halves such that the first one of 10 hours duration is used for training. We test the learnt model on the remainder of the trace from South Asian ISP as well as over a different trace from a Tier-1 ISP in South America. In this section, we use the grouping methodology of connected components, where all "domain name, response IP-address" pairs present during a time window (either during training or test phases) are grouped in to connected components.

6.1 L1-regularized Linear Regression

We formulate the problem of classifying a component as malicious (algorithmically generated) or legitimate in a supervised learning setting as a linear regression or classification problem. We first label all domains within the components found in the training data set by querying against domain reputation sites such as McAfee Site Advisor [2] and Web of Trust [7] as well as by searching for the URLs on search-engines [32]. Next, we label a component as good or bad depending on a simple majority count, *i.e.*, if more than 50% of domains in a component are classified as malicious (adware, malware, spyware, *etc.*) by any of the reputation engines, then we label that component as malicious.

Define the set of features as F which includes the following metrics computed for each component: KL-distance on unigrams, JI measure on bigrams and Edit distance. Also define the set of Training examples as T and its size in terms of number of components as $|T|$. Further, define the output value for each component $y_i = 1$ if it was labeled malicious or $= 0$ if legitimate. We model the output value y_i for any component $i \in T$ as a linear weighted sum of the values attained by each feature where the weights are given by β_j for each feature $j \in F$: $y_i = \sum_{j \in F} \beta_j x_j + \beta_0$

In particular, we use the LASSO, also known as L1-regularized Linear Regression [18], where an additional constraint on each feature allows us to obtain a model with lower test prediction errors than the non-regularized linear regression since some variables can be adaptively shrunk towards lower values. We use 10-fold cross validation to choose the value of the regularization parameter $\lambda \in [0\text{-}1]$ that provides the minimum training error (equation below) and then use that λ value in our tests:

$$arg \min_{\beta} \sum_{i=1}^{|T|} (y_i - \beta_0 - \sum_{j \in F} \beta_j x_j)^2 + \lambda \sum_{j \in F} |\beta_j|. \quad (2)$$

6.2 Results

First, note the various connected components present in the South Asian trace as classified in to three classes: IP fans, Domain fans and Many-to-many components in Table 1. During the training phase, while learning the LASSO model, we mark 128 components as good (these consist of CDNs, mail service providers, large networks such as Google) and one component belonging to the Conficker botnet as malicious. For each component, we compute the features of KL-divergence, Jaccard Index measure and Edit distance. We train the regression model using glmnet tool [18] in statistical package R, and obtain the value for the regularization parameter λ as $1e-4$, that minimizes training error during the training phase. We then test the model on the remaining portion of the one day long trace. In this regard, our goal is to check if our regression model can not only detect Conficker botnet but whether it can also detect other malicious domain groups during the testing phase over the trace. During the testing stage, if a particular component is flagged as suspicious then we check against Web of Trust [7], McAfee Site Advisor [2] as well as via Whois queries, search engines, to ascertain the exact behavior of the component. Next, we explain the results of each of the classes individually.

On applying our model to the rest of the trace, 29 components (out of a total of 3K components) are classified as malicious, and we find 27 of them to be malicious after cross checking with external sources (Web of Trust, McAfee, *etc.*) while two components (99 domains) are false positives and comprise of Google and domains belonging to news blogs.

Note that here we use a broad definition of malicious domains as those that could be used for any nefarious purposes on the web, *i.e.*, we do not necessarily restrict the definition to only include botnet domain generation algorithm. Out of the 27 components that were classified as malicious, one of them corresponds to the Conficker botnet, which is as expected since our training incorporated features learnt from Conficker. We next provide details on the remaining 26 components that were determined as malicious (see Table 2).

Mjuyh Botnet: The most interesting discovery from our component analysis is that of another Botnet, which we call Mjuyh, since they use the domain name *mjuyh.com* (see Table 3). The fourth-level domain label is generated randomly and is 57 characters long. Each of the 121 domain names belonging to this bot network return 10 different IP addresses on a DNS query for a total of 1.2K IP-addresses. Also, in some replies, there are invalid IP addresses like 0.116.157.148. All the 10 IP addresses returned for a given domain name, belong to different network prefixes. Furthermore, there is no intersection in the network prefixes between the different domain names of the mjuyh bot. We strongly suspect that this is a case of "domain fluxing" along with "IP fast fluxing", where each bot generated a different randomized query which was resolved to a different set of IP-addresses.

Helldark Trojan: We discovered a component containing five different third-level domains (a few sample domain names are as shown in Table 3) The component comprises of 28 different domain names which were all found to be spreading multiple Trojans. One such Trojan spread by these domains is Win32/Hamweq.CW that spreads via removable drives, such as USB memory sticks. They also have an IRC-based backdoor, which may be used by a remote attacker directing the affected machine to participate in Distributed Denial of Service attacks, or to download and execute arbitrary files [8].

Mis-spelt component: There are about five components (comprising 220 domain names) which used tricked (mis-spelt or slightly different spelling) names of reputed domain names. For example, these components use domain names such as uahoo.co.uk to trick users trying to visit yahoo.co.uk (since the alphabet 'u' is next to the alphabet 'y', they expect users to enter this domain name by mistake). Dizneyland.com is used to misdirect users trying to visit Disneyland.com (which replaces the alphabet 's' with alphabet 'z'). We still consider these components as malicious since they comprise of domains that exhibit unusual alphanumeric features.

Domain Parking: We found 15 components (630 domain names) that were being used for domain parking, *i.e.*, a practice where users register for a domain name without actually using it, in which case the registrar's IP-address is returned as the DNS response. In these 15 components, one belongs to GoDaddy (66 domain names), 13 of them belong to Sedo domain parking (510 domain names) and one component belongs to OpenDNS (57 domain names). Clearly these components represent something abnormal as there are many domains with widely disparate algorithmic features clustered together on account of the same IP-address they are mapped to.

Adult Content: We find four components that comprise of 349 domains primarily used for hosting adult content sites. Clearly this matches the well known fact, that in the world of adult site hosting, the same set of IP-addresses are used to host a vast number of domains, each of which in turn may use very different words in an attempt to drive traffic.

In addition, for comparison purposes, we used the lexical features of the domain names such as the length of the domain names, number of dots and the length of the second-level domain name (for example, *xyz.com*) for training on the same ISP trace, instead of using the KL-divergence, JI measure and Edit distance measures used in our study. These lexical features were found to be useful in an earlier study in identifying malicious URLs [17]. The model trained on these lexical features correctly labeled four components as malicious (Conficker bot network, three adult content components and one component containing mis-spelt domain names) during the testing phase, but it also resulted in 30 components which were legitimate as being labeled incorrectly; compare this against 27 components that were correctly classified as malicious and two that were false positives on using our alphanumeric features.

We also test our model on a trace obtained from a South America based Tier-1 ISP. This trace is about 20 hours long and is collected on a smaller scale as compared to the ISP trace from Asia. The time lag between the capture of S. American Tier-1 ISP trace and the previously used ISP trace from Asia, is about 15 days. We use the same training set for the prediction model as we use for the ISP trace from Asia. In the prediction stage, we successfully detect the Conficker component with no false positives. The Conficker component has 185 domain names and 10 IP addresses. Of the 10 IP addresses determined for the Conficker component of the South American trace, nine are common with the Asia ISP trace's Conficker component. We conclude that Conficker based C&C servers have relatively large TTLs. However, out of the 185 domain names only five domains are common from this component and the component from the ISP trace from Asia. Clearly, the Conficker botnet exhibits rapid domain fluxing. Overall, this experiment shows that a training model learnt in one network can be applied to a completely different network and still successfully detect malicious domain groups.

7. DISCUSSION

7.1 Usefulness of component analysis

Conficker botnet, present in our ISP trace, employs domain fluxing across TLDs, that became directly visible after IP-domain components were extracted and analyzed from the trace. The component analysis allowed the application of our detection methods across several different domains, which otherwise would have been separated from each other. In addition, component analysis allowed us to detect Conficker domains that would not have been detectable with our approach when applied to domain names alone since some of these domains contained fewer than 50 names needed for accurate analysis. Similarly, some of the IP addresses in the component hosted fewer than 50 names and would not have been detected with the IP address based analysis either. However, these domains will be included in the component analysis as long as the component has altogether more than 50 names.

Let D_c be the number of hostnames and I_c be the number of IP addresses in the component. If D_d, I_d are the number of hostnames and corresponding IP addresses detected through domain level analysis, we define domain level completeness ratios as D_d/D_c and I_d/I_c. Similarly, we can define the completeness ratios for IP-based analysis as D_i/D_c and I_i/I_c, where D_i and I_i correspond to the total number of hostnames and IP addresses of the Conficker botnet detected by the IP-based analysis.

For the Conficker botnet, these completeness ratios for IP-based analysis were 73.68% for IP addresses and 98.56% for hostnames. This implies that we are able to detect an additional 26.32% of IP addresses and a relatively small fraction of 1.44% of hostnames for those IP addresses. The completeness ratios for domain based analysis were found to be 100% for IP addresses and 83.87% for the hostnames. Therefore, we do 16.13% better in terms of determining the hostnames using the per-domain analysis. This shows that the component level analysis provides additional value in analyzing the trace for malicious domains.

7.2 Complexity of various measures

Table 4 identifies the computational complexity for every metric, and for all groups that we use. We observe that K-L metrics analyzing unigram and bigram distributions can be computed fairly efficiently. However, for the JI measure, the size of the non-malicious database largely influences the time taken to compute the measure. A good database size results in a higher accuracy, at the cost of increased time taken for analysis. Similarly, edit distance takes longer for large word lengths, and the number of test words. However, it is independent of any database, hence the space requirements are smaller.

Notation	
A	Alphabet size
W	Maximum word size
K	Number of test words
K'	Number of test words in a component
S_g	Number of words in non-malicious database

Table 4: Computational complexity

Grp.	K-L unigram	K-L bigram	JI	ED
dom.	$O(KW+A)$	$O(KW+A^2)$	$O(KW^2S_g)$	$O(K^2W^2)$
IP	$O(KW+A)$	$O(KW+A^2)$	$O(KW^2S_g)$	$O(K^2W^2)$
Com.	$O(K'W+A)$	$O(K'W+A^2)$	$O(K'W^2S_g)$	$O(K'^2W^2)$

We briefly describe how we determine the bounds as expressed in table 4 for the per-domain group. For the K-L unigram analysis since we examine every character of every test word, the complexity is bounded by KW. We then compute, for every character in the alphabet A, the divergence values. Therefore, we obtain the complexity as $O(KW+A)$. Bigram distribution based K-L divergence is calculated similarly except that the new alphabet size is A^2. While calculating the Jaccard index, note that the number of bigrams obtained is $O(W-1)$. For each bigram, we examine the queues pointing to words from the non-malicious database. Thus, for each bigram, we examine $O(WS_g)$ bigrams. Since we do it for K test words, we obtain $O(KW^2S_g)$. For every test word used while obtaining the edit distance, we examine it against the K - 1 test words. Therefore, the total complexity is simply $O(K^2W^2)$. The expressions for *per-IP* and *per-component* groups are obtained analogously.

It is interesting to note that A is of the size 36 (0-9, a-z characters). K used in our analysis varies as 50/100/200/500. However, the average value for K' is higher in comparison. The DNS PTR dataset considered for *per-domain* analysis has approximately 469,000 words used for training purposes. This helps us estimate S_g. For the ISP dataset, S_g is of the order of 11522 words. An estimate of W for the DNS PTR dataset is obtained from figure 2.

8. CONCLUSIONS

In this paper, we propose a methodology for detecting algorithmically generated domain names as used for "domain fluxing" by several recent Botnets. We propose statistical measures such as Kullback-Leibler divergence, Jaccard index, and Levenshtein edit distance for classifying a group of domains as malicious (algorithmically generated) or not. We perform a comprehensive analysis on several data sets including a set of legitimate domain names obtained via a crawl of IPv4 address space as well as DNS traffic from a Tier-1 ISP in Asia. One of our key contributions is the relative performance characterization of each metric in different scenarios. In general, the Jaccard measure performs the best, followed by the Edit distance measure, and finally the KL divergence. Furthermore, we show how our methodology when applied to the Tier-1 ISP's trace was able to detect Conficker as well as a botnet yet unknown and unclassified, which we call as *Mjuyh*. In this regards, our methodology can be used as a first alarm to indicate the presence of domain fluxing in a network, and thereafter a network security analyst can perform additional forensics to infer the exact algorithm being used to generate the domain names. As future work, we plan to generalize our metrics to work on n-grams for values of $n > 2$.

9. ACKNOWLEDGMENTS

This work is supported in part by a Qatar National Research Foundation grant, Qatar Telecom, and NSF grants 0702012 and 0621410. We thank Prof. K.R.Narayanan, Department of Electrical and Computer Engineering, Texas A&M University, for helping us with the proof as provided in the appendix. Part of this work was done while Narasimha Reddy was on a sabbatical at the University of Carlos III and Imdea Networks in Madrid, Spain.

10. REFERENCES

[1] Botlab. http://botlab.cs.washington.edu/.

[2] Mcafee site advisor. http://www.siteadvisor.com.

[3] On kraken and bobax botnets. http://www.damballa.com/downloads/r_pubs/Kraken_Response.pdf.

[4] On the kraken and bobax botnets. http://www.damballa.com/downloads/r_pubs/Kraken_Response.pdf.

[5] Pc tools experts crack new kraken. http://www.pctools.com/news/view/id/202/.

[6] Twitter api still attracts hackers. http://blog.unmaskparasites.com/2009/12/09/twitter-api-still-attracts-hackers/.

[7] Web of trust. http://mywot.com.
[8] Win32/hamewq. http://www.microsoft.com/security/portal/Threat/Encyclopedia/Entry.aspx?Name=Win32/Hamweq.
[9] Yahoo webspam database. http://barcelona.research.yahoo.net/webspam/datasets/uk2007/.
[10] A. Bratko, G. V. Cormack, B. Filipic, T. R. Lynam, and B. Zupan. Spam filtering using statistical data compression models. *Journal of Machine Learning Research 7*, 2006.
[11] T. Cover and J. Thomas. Elements of information theory. *Wiley*, 2006.
[12] H. Crawford and J. Aycock. Kwyjibo: Automatic Domain Name Generation. In *Software Practice and Experience, John Wiley & Sons, Ltd.*, 2008.
[13] S. Gianvecchio, M. Xie, Z. Wu, and H. Wang. Measurement and Classification of Humans and Bots in Internet Chat. *In Proceedings of the 17th USENIX Security Symposium (Security '08)*, 2008.
[14] G. Gu, R. Perdisci, J. Zhang, and W. Lee. BotMiner: Clustering Analysis of Network Traffic for Protocol- and Structure-independent Botnet Detection. *Proceedings of the 17th USENIX Security Symposium (Security'08)*, 2008.
[15] G. Gu, J. Zhang, and W. Lee. BotSniffer: Detecting Botnet Command and Control Channels in Network Traffic. *Proc. of the 15th Annual Network and Distributed System Security Symposium (NDSS'08)*, Feb. 2008.
[16] T. Holz, M. Steiner, F. Dahl, E. W. Biersack, and F. Freiling. Measurements and Mitigation of Peer-to-peer-based Botnets: A Case Study on Storm Worm. *In First Usenix Workshop on Large-scale Exploits and Emergent Threats (LEET)*, April 2008.
[17] S. S. J. Ma, L.K. Saul and G. Voelker. Beyond Blacklists: Learning to Detect Malicious Web Sites from Suspicious URLs. *Proc. of ACM KDD*, July 2009.
[18] R. T. Jerome Friedman, Trevor Hastie. glmnet: Lasso and Elastic-net Regularized Generalized Linear Models. Technical report.
[19] J. P. John, A. MoshChuck, S. D. Gribble, and A. Krishnamurthy. Studying Spamming Botnets Using Botlab. *Proc. of NSDI*, 2009.
[20] M. Konte, N. Feamster, and J. Jung. Dynamics of Online Scam Hosting Infrastructure. *Passive and Active Measurement Conference*, 2009.
[21] C. D. Manning, P. Raghavan, and H. Schutze. An Information to Information Retrieval. *Cambridge University Press*, 2009.
[22] D. K. McGrath and M. Gupta. Behind Phishing: An Examination of Phisher Modi Operandi. *Proc. of USENIX workshop on Large-scale Exploits and Emergent Threats (LEET)*, Apr. 2008.
[23] E. Passerini, R. Paleari, L. Martignoni, and D. Bruschi. Fluxor : Detecting and Monitoring Fast-flux Service Networks. *Detection of Intrusions and Malware, and Vulnerability Assessment*, 2008.
[24] R. Perdisci, I. Corona, D. Dagon, and W. Lee. Detecting Malicious Flux Service Networks Through Passive Analysis of Recursive DNS Traces. In *Annual Computer Society Security Applications Conference (ACSAC)*, dec 2009.
[25] R. Perdisci, G. Gu, and W. Lee. Using an Ensemble of One-class SVM Classifiers to Harden Payload-based Anomaly Detection Systems. *In Proceedings of the IEEE International Conference on Data Mining (ICDM '06)*, 2006.
[26] P. Porras, H.Saidi, and V. Yegneswaran. Conflicker C P2P Protocol and Implementation. *SRI International Tech. Report*, Sep. 2009.
[27] P. Porras, H. Saidi, and V. Yegneswaran. An Analysis of Conficker's Logic and Rendezvous Points. Technical report, mar 2009.
[28] P. Porras, H. Saidi, and V. Yegneswaran. Conficker C Analysis. Technical report, apr 2009.
[29] J. Stewart. Inside the Storm: Protocols and Encryption of the Storm Botnet. *Black Hat Technical Security Conference, USA*, 2008.
[30] B. Stone-Gross, M. Cova, L. Cavallaro, B. Gilbert, M. Szydlowski, R. Kemmerer, C. Kruegel, and G. Vigna. Your Botnet is my Botnet: Analysis of a Botnet Takeover. In *ACM Conference on Computer and Communications Security (CCS)*, nov 2009.
[31] H. L. V. Trees. Detection, Estimation and Modulation Theory. *Wiley*, 2001.
[32] I. Trestian, S. Ranjan, A. Kuzmanovic, and A. Nucci. Unconstrained Endpoint Profiling: Googling the Internet. In *ACM SIGCOMM*, aug 2008.
[33] Y. Xie, F. Yu, K. Achan, R. Panigrahy, G. Hulten, and I. Osipkov. Spamming Botnets: Signatures and Characteristics. *ACM SIGCOMM Computer Communication Review*, 2008.
[34] Y. Zhao, Y. Xie, F. Yu, Q. Ke, Y. Yu, Y. Chen, and E. Gillum. Botgraph: Large Scale Spamming Botnet Detection. *USENIX Symposium on Networked Systems and Design Implementation (NSDI '09)*, 2009.

APPENDIX

Let $\mathcal{A} = \{a_1, a_2, \ldots, a_M\}$ denote M the letters of the alphabet from which the domain names are chosen (in our case, this is English alphabet with spaces and special characters). Let $\underline{g} = [g_1, g_2, \ldots, g_M]$ and $\underline{b} = [b_1, b_2, \ldots, b_M]$ be the distribution of the letters in the good and bad domains, respectively. Let $\underline{x}$ be the actual domain name of length N, that has to be classified as being good or bad. Let the letter a_i appear n_i times in $\underline{x}$ such that $\sum_i n_i = N$. Let $\underline{q} = [q_1, q_2, \ldots, q_M]$ be the distribution of the different letters in $\underline{x}$, i.e., $q_i = n_i/N$.

Under the assumption that *a priori*, $\underline{x}$ can belong to a good or bad domain with equal probability, the classifier that minimizes the probability of error (wrong classification) is given by the maximum-likelihood classifier which classifies $\underline{x}$ according to

$$P(\underline{x}|\underline{g}) \underset{b}{\overset{g}{\gtrless}} P(\underline{x}|\underline{b}) \qquad (3)$$

Intuitively, $\underline{x}$ is classified as good, if it is more likely to have resulted from the good distribution than from the bad distribution. The above classifier can be specified in terms of the likelihood ratio given by

$$\lambda(\underline{x}) = \frac{P(\underline{x}|\underline{g})}{P(\underline{x}|\underline{b})} \underset{b}{\overset{g}{\gtrless}} 1 \tag{4}$$

As we will see later, it is easier to work with an equivalent quantity $\frac{1}{N}\log\lambda(x)$. The classifier is then given according to

$$\frac{1}{N}\log\lambda(x) = \frac{1}{N}\log\frac{P(\underline{x}|\underline{g})}{P(\underline{x}|\underline{b})} \underset{b}{\overset{g}{\gtrless}} 0 \tag{5}$$

Under the assumption that the letters in $\underline{x}$ have been generated independently from the same distribution, $P(\underline{x}|\underline{g})$ is given by

$$P(\underline{x}|\underline{g}) = \prod_{k=1}^{N} P(x_k|\underline{g}) = \prod_{i=1}^{M} P(a_i|\underline{g})^{n_i} = \prod_{i=1}^{M} g_i^{n_i} = \prod_{i=1}^{M} g_i^{q_i N}. \tag{6}$$

The second equality follows by grouping all the occurrences of the letters a_i together and recall that there are n_i such occurrences. Similarly,

$$P(\underline{x}|\underline{b}) = \prod_{k=1}^{N} P(x_k|\underline{b}) = \prod_{i=1}^{M} P(a_i|\underline{b})^{n_i} = \prod_{i=1}^{M} b_i^{n_i} = \prod_{i=1}^{M} b_i^{q_i N}. \tag{7}$$

Using (6) and (7) in (5), the log-likelihood ratio can be seen to be

$$\frac{1}{N}\log\lambda(x) = \frac{1}{N}\log\frac{P(\underline{x}|\underline{g})}{P(\underline{x}|\underline{b})} = \log\frac{\prod_{i=1}^{M} g_i^{q_i}}{\prod_{i=1}^{M} b_i^{q_i}} \tag{8}$$

Dividing the numerator and the denominator by $\prod_i {q_i}^{q_i}$, we get

$$\frac{1}{N}\log\lambda(x) = \log\frac{\prod_{i=1}^{M}\left(\frac{g_i}{q_i}\right)^{q_i}}{\prod_{i=1}^{M}\left(\frac{b_i}{q_i}\right)^{q_i}} \tag{9}$$

$$= \sum_i q_i \log\frac{g_i}{q_i} - \sum_i q_i \log\frac{b_i}{q_i} \tag{10}$$

$$= D(\underline{q}|\underline{b}) - D(\underline{q}|\underline{g}) \tag{11}$$

where $D(\underline{q}|\underline{b})$ is the Kullback-Liebler (KL) distance between the two distributions. Thus, the optimal classifier given in (5) is equivalent to

$$D(\underline{q}|\underline{b}) - D(\underline{q}|\underline{g}) \underset{b}{\overset{g}{\gtrless}} 0 \tag{12}$$

This result is intuitively pleasing since the classifier essentially computes the KL "distance" between $\underline{q}$ and the two distributions and chooses the one that is 'closer'.

Internet Background Radiation Revisited

Eric Wustrow
Networking Research and Development
Merit Network Inc.
Ann Arbor, MI 48104 USA
ewust@merit.edu

Manish Karir
Networking Research and Development
Merit Network Inc.
Ann Arbor, MI 48104 USA
mkarir@merit.edu

Michael Bailey
Department of EECS
University of Michigan
Ann Arbor, MI 48109 USA
mibailey@eecs.umich.edu

Farnam Jahanian
Department of EECS
University of Michigan
Ann Arbor, MI 48109 USA
farnam@eecs.umich.edu

Geoff Huston
Asia Pacific Network Information Centre
Brisbane QLD 4064 Australia
gih@apnic.net

ABSTRACT

The monitoring of packets destined for routeable, yet unused, Internet addresses has proved to be a useful technique for measuring a variety of specific Internet phenomenon (e.g., worms, DDoS). In 2004, Pang et al. stepped beyond these targeted uses and provided one of the first generic characterizations of this non-productive traffic, demonstrating both its significant size and diversity. However, the six years that followed this study have seen tremendous changes in both the types of malicious activity on the Internet and the quantity and quality of unused address space. In this paper, we revisit the state of Internet "background radiation" through the lens of two unique data-sets: a five-year collection from a single unused /8 network block, and week-long collections from three recently allocated /8 network blocks. Through the longitudinal study of the long-lived block, comparisons between blocks, and extensive case studies of traffic in these blocks, we characterize the current state of background radiation specifically highlighting those features that remain invariant from previous measurements and those which exhibit significant differences. Of particular interest in this work is the exploration of address space pollution, in which significant non uniform behavior is observed. However, unlike previous observations of differences between unused blocks, we show that increasingly these differences are the result of environmental factors (e.g., misconfiguration, location), rather than algorithmic factors. Where feasible, we offer suggestions for clean up of these polluted blocks and identify those blocks whose allocations should be withheld.

IMC'10, November 1–3, 2010, Melbourne, Australia.

Categories and Subject Descriptors

C.2 [**Information Systems Applications**]: Network Operations

General Terms

Measurement

Keywords

Darknet, Internet background traffic, Network pollution

1. INTRODUCTION

The monitoring of allocated, globally routeable, but unused Internet address blocks has been widely used by the security, operations, and research communities to study a wide range of interesting Internet phenomenon. As there are no active hosts in these unused blocks, packets destined to these IP addresses must be the result of worm propagation[1, 2, 3], DDoS attacks[4], misconfiguration, or other unsolicited activity. Systems that monitor unused address spaces have a variety of names, including darknets [5], network telescopes [6], blackhole monitors [7], network sinks[8], and network motion sensors [9].

While this monitoring technique had seen heavy use in the measurement of specific phenomena, it wasn't until 2004 when Pang et. al [10] published their seminal paper "Characteristics of Internet Background Radiation" that a detailed characterization of this incessant non-productive traffic was available. Through passive measurement and active elicitation of connection payloads over several large unused blocks, the authors characterized the behavior of sources and the activities prevalent in Internet background radiation. Most notable in their analysis was the ubiquity of Internet background radiation, its scale, its rich variegation in targeted services, and the extreme dynamism in many aspects of the observed traffic.

The six years since this landmark paper have seen significant changes both in the size, shape, and traffic carried by the Internet as well as the methods and motivations of malicious traffic that makes up Internet background radiation. While both scanning as a reconnaissance activity and as a propagation method are both alive and well, the emergence and growth of botnets [11, 12] have changed the threat landscape significantly for most operators. This view of compromised hosts as a resource worth protecting highlights a tension in botnet design between the degree of detection as evidenced by how noisy malicious behaviors are, and the desire to maintain the useful resource and avoid detection. As with any design tradeoff, there are malicious botnets that continue to be noisy in how they use and acquire hosts (e.g., Conficker), nevertheless, the last six years has seen a marked change in how malicious code behaves [13].

Additionally, today's Internet continues to witness tremendous year over year growth, fueled in large part by demand for video [14]. The role of new content delivery mechanisms have changed how traffic flows and user demands continue to change the applications of interest. These changes impact the behaviors observed in background radiation as new services become more desirable to discover and new network services offer new ways to misconfigure themselves.

Our study is primarily motivated by the dramatic shifts in attack behaviors and the Internet as as whole since the original 2004 Internet background radiation study [10], Additionally, as IPv4 address exhaustion nears [15] and dirty network blocks can no longer be returned for newer allocations, there is an increasing need to both identify and quantify *address pollution* to determine the quality of a network address block and to determine the utility of any cleanup effort. The purpose of this paper is to revisit Internet background radiation in order to determine any evolution in the nature of this traffic and to explore any new features that might have emerged. To provide as broad and detailed a characterization as possible, we draw on two unique sources of data for our analysis. First, we examine five week-long datasets taken from the same routed /8 unused address block, representing the first week in February over the last five years. Second, we examine three week-long datasets built by announcing and capturing traffic to three separate /8 networks recently allocated to APNIC and ARIN from IANA. These three datasets are compared with each other, as well as with three matching week-long collections from the /8 used in the longitudinal study.

To summarize, the value of our work is threefold:

- **Revisiting Internet Background Radiation** In this paper we present the first thorough study of Internet background radiation since 2004. We study and characterize this traffic in an attempt to answer two specific questions:
  - *Temporal Analysis of Internet Background Radiation* The first question is an attempt to understand how this traffic has evolved over a 5 year time-period.
  - *Spatial Analysis of Internet Background Radiation* The second question attempts to answer the question of how this traffic might vary based on the specific darknet address block under observation.
- **A study of Internet Address Pollution** Our spatial analysis of background radiation shows significant differences between large blocks of unused address space. We argue these differences are distinct from previously reported diversity measurements as they are the result of significant volumes of non-uniform environmental factors—a class of behaviors we collectively label as *address space pollution.*
- **Availability of these Traces**. We will make all 11 datasets, nearly 10 TB of compressed PCAP data, available through the Protected Repository for the Defense of Infrastructure Against Cyber Threats (PREDICT) [16] dataset archive in an effort to further expand our knowledge of these interesting phenomena and encourage additional exploration.

The rest of this paper is organized as follows; in Section 2 we describe some directly related work; Section 3 provides an overview of our data collection methodology and describes our datasets; Section 4 we revisit Internet background radiation, providing both temporal and spatial studies of this traffic; Section 5 outlines our study of address pollution; Section 6 summarizes our results and offers some conclusions and future work.

2. RELATED WORK

Directly related work in this area can generally be categorized into two related areas. The first area is concerned with the design, operation and scalability of monitoring Internet background radiation, while the second focuses on the analysis of the data collected via these systems.

There have been several attempts at building Internet background radiation monitoring systems; here we describe the three most popular systems. In [6] the authors discuss perhaps the most popular and visible monitor at CAIDA. They describe how the size of the monitored address space can influence its ability to detect events. They also present several alternative models for building distributed network monitors. Data from this monitor has been made available to the broad network research community which has served to increase its visibility. The iSink monitor at the University of Wisconsin was first published in [8], where the authors describe their experience in building this system as well as using it for both active and passive monitoring for detection of possible network abuse activity. One of the chief characteristics of the system was its ability to filter the traffic as well as incorporate application level responders. The Internet Motion Sensor (IMS) system at the University of Michigan has been described in [9]. The IMS system was perhaps the most distributed and extensive system of the three we have described here. A main finding of this work was the value in a distributed monitoring system, as different blocks in different networks reported significantly different behaviors. The spatial analysis in our study re-confirms these differences, both in space and time, but highlights a growing trend toward pollution as the cause of these differences.

A wide variety of work based on improving these techniques and systems has followed. A non-exhaustive list of examples includes: practical techniques for deploying these sensors [5], how to build scalable filters in distributed darknets [17], where to place distributed sensors [7], how to configure services in these sensors [18], the security and anonymity of these sensor blocks [19], and the effectiveness of distributed sensors in various domains such as worm detection [20]. One relevant body of work is that of Cooke et. al [21] in which we examined observed non uniformity across monitors and showed that this non uniformity was the result of algorithmic factors in worm propagation and

Data Set	Start Date	End Date	Size (gz'd)
A-1: 1/8	2/23/2010	3/1/2010	4134 GB
A-2: 35/8	2/23/2010	3/1/2010	739 GB
B-1: 50/8	3/12/2010	3/19/2010	1067 GB
B-2: 35/8	3/12/2010	3/19/2010	770 GB
C-1: 107/8	3/25/2010	3/31/2010	1230 GB
C-2: 35/8	3/25/2010	3/31/2010	770 GB

Table 1: Datasets used in Darknet Traffic Spatial Analysis

Data Set	Start Date	End Date	Size (gz'd)
D-1: 35/8	2/13/2006	2/19/2006	113 GB
D-2: 35/8	2/5/2007	2/11/2007	95 GB
D-3: 35/8	2/4/2008	2/10/2008	119 GB
D-4: 35/8	2/2/2009	2/8/2009	386 GB
D-5: 35/8	2/8/2010	2/14/2010	630 GB

Table 2: Datasets used in Darknet Traffic Evolution Analysis

environmental factors such as misconfiguration. While our study shows that both of these factors continue to play a role, the increase in importance of environmental factors is a striking addition of our study.

The systems described above have led to multiple studies regarding the nature and characteristics of traffic observed in these darknets. Darknet traffic has been used for specific analysis of malicious activity such as: propagation [22, 1, 2, 3], DDoS attacks [4], misconfiguration, or other unsolicited activity [23]. The most relevant work to this paper, of course, is [10] in which the authors present an extremely detailed analysis of Internet background radiation as observed in 2004 at four unused IPv4 network blocks. They performed both active and passive characterization of the background traffic and concluded that there is significant diversity in this traffic both in terms of the address blocks monitored as well as over time. There are three main distinctions between this work and the collection methodology in this paper in addition to the freshness of the data being examined. First, due to the availability of a large computation and storage infrastructure, we do not need to filter or sample the traffic being analyzed in any way (both were done in the previous work). In spite of the large increases in volume over time, we find fairly robust processing scripts able to process weeks of data on the order of hours. Second, due to the transient nature and sensitive nature of the blocks being studied (see Section 3) we do not utilize any active responders to solicit traffic to the block. As a result, we are unable to differentiate traffic based on payload, except in the cases of UDP. Finally, we make use of substantially larger amounts of space and over longer scales than the previous study.

3. METHODOLOGY

In this section we describe the datasets used in our experiments as well as our long term collection methodology for the study of Internet address space pollution.

3.1 Data Collection

For our analysis we used two datasets. The first set of six distinct sub-datasets we used for studying the spatial properties of darknet traffic, and the second set of five distinct sub-datasets was used for studying the temporal properties of darknet traffic.

The six spatial sub-datasets were constructed by obtaining permission from ARIN and APNIC to announce previously unallocated /8 network blocks to the Internet via BGP. This resulted in all darknet data destined for these networks to be routed to our data collection infrastructure at Merit. Each of the 1.0.0.0/8, 50.0.0.0/8 and 107.0.0.0/8 networks were announced over a period of one week. The resulting three datasets were then paired with data from our ongoing data collection on the unused portion of the 35.0.0.0/8 network block for the same time period. The 35.0.0.0/8 network block is unused except for a /13 block of addresses that is routed internally at Merit for its customers (96.8% unused). For each dataset we performed a full packet capture using a customized packet capture utility based on libpcap. Table 1 lists these datasets.

Though we actively worked with our upstream provider AT&T to ensure that our BGP route announcements would be propagated into the Internet core, it is possible that local or regional policies and configuration differences could have impacted the global visibility of our darknet route announcements. This in turn would have an impact on what data is actually routed to our data collectors. Using publicly available BGP routing data from routeviews.org [24] and RIPE [25] we were able to confirm that our BGP route announcement for 1.0.0.0/8 was visible to 31 out of 41 active routeviews peers and 9 out of 16 active RIPE peers. The 50.0.0.0/8 route announcement was visible to 31 out of 41 routeviews peers and 9 out of 14 RIPE peers. The 107.0.0.0/8 BGP route announcement was visible to 28 out of 41 routeviews peers and 10 out of 16 RIPE peers. Though we cannot claim to have collected *all* the network pollution directed at these network blocks we believe our data is fairly representative of the overall trends and data patterns.

The second set of five datasets were used for the temporal analysis section of this paper and were extracted from our ongoing continuous data collection of packets directed towards the unused portions of 35/8 network block. We extracted week-long datasets for the first week of February for each year since 2006. Table 2 lists these datasets. We used 3 additional days of data for each of the 5 years to verify that the volume of traffic and pollution type distribution was relatively stable throughout the year. From this, we find that our week-long datasets are representative of their respective years. A total of 11 datasets were created representing roughly 10TB of compressed packet captures.

3.2 Internet Pollution and Data Archiving

This data collection is a part of an ongoing research activity in which we are working with IP address registries such as ARIN and APNIC in order to collect and archive samples from newly allocated network blocks for the broad Internet research community. These datasets will then be published via PREDICT [16] dataset archive. Any research activity which interacts with critical Internet infrastructure must carefully balance the need for informing relevant parties as well as ensuring that such a process does not result in a dirty dataset. For each new allocation we obtain a clear Letter of Authorization (LOA) from the RIR whose network block we wish to monitor. This LOA outlines the research activity and the duration for which we are authorized

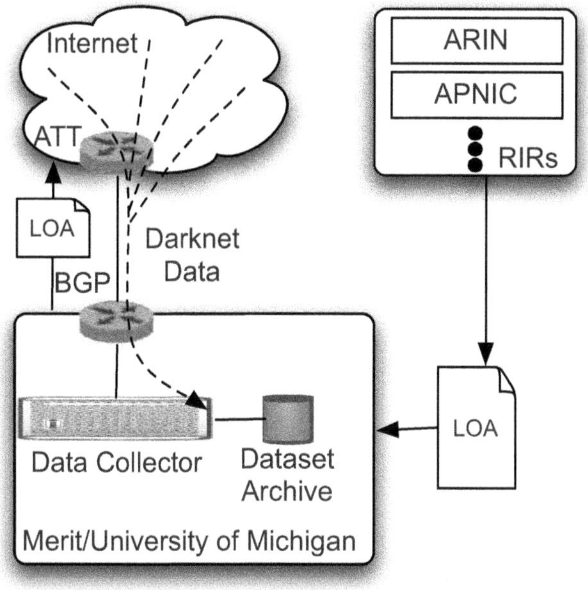

Figure 1: Cooperative Internet background radiation data collection

to announce this network block. This is then presented to our primary upstream provider, AT&T, which then removes any filters that would prevent our BGP announcement from propagating to the Internet. We also take care to publish information regarding our proposed announcement in the RADB [26] in the case the network operator community has some concerns regarding our BGP announcements. We do not actively announce our experiments on the network operator mailing lists as it might result in tampering with our data collection; though we are prompt to answer any specific queries that might arise as a result of our experiment. Figure 1 summarizes this process.

4. REVISITING INTERNET BACKGROUND RADIATION

At a high level, Internet background radiation can be classified into three distinct types based on different root causes of these activities. *Scanning* is largely the result of infected hosts on the Internet attempting to find other vulnerable targets, *backscatter* is most often the result of Denial of Service attacks, and finally *misconfiguration*, which is a result of software or hardware errors. Table 4 shows the contribution of the these three main types of background radiation to each of 1/8, 50/8, 107/8 and 35/8. We classify TCP SYN packets as scanning traffic. We define backscatter traffic as TCP SYN+ACK, RST, RST+ACK, and ACK packets, as these packets are likely to be generated by hosts attempting to respond to communication from a forged source in the darknet. Finally, we classify the remaining traffic as misconfiguration. When comparing /8s to the baseline 35/8 captured during the same time interval, we observe that backscatter traffic volumes (in billions of packets per week) are nearly identical. Likewise, scanning is of similar magnitudes, despite slightly increased volumes in 50/8 and 107/8. Misconfiguration traffic contains the most variance between /8s, due to its directed nature. In the following subsections,

Protocol	2006	2007	2008	2009	2010
TCP(%pkts)	76.5	85.7	45.8	87.8	87.2
UDP(%pkts)	19.1	6.8	49.9	11.4	12.3
ICMP(%pkts)	4.2	5.0	3.8	0.6	0.4
other(%pkts)	0.2	2.5	0.5	0.2	0.1
TCP(%bytes)	22.5	75.6	16.3	82.5	82.2
UDP(%bytes)	75.3	13.4	81.6	16.6	17.2
ICMP(%bytes)	2.1	8.3	1.8	0.7	0.4
other(%bytes)	0.1	2.7	0.3	0.2	0.2

Table 3: Traffic Distribution by protocol over time in terms of total packets as well as bytes, for 35/8 2006-2010 (D1-D5).

Dataset	Scanning	Backscatter	Misconfiguration
1/8 (A1)	12.5 B	1.7 B	55.9 B
35/8 (A2)	15.5 B	1.6 B	5.2 B
50/8 (B1)	17.7 B	2.4 B	10.2 B
35/8 (B2)	15.2 B	2.5 B	5.6 B
107/8(C1)	18.9 B	2.2 B	14.8 B
35/8 (C2)	14.8 B	2.2 B	6.0 B
2006 (D1)	1.7 B	1.0 B	0.8 B
2007 (D2)	1.8 B	0.8 B	0.5 B
2008 (D3)	1.1 B	0.4 B	1.8 B
2009 (D4)	9.5 B	1.4 B	1.5 B
2010 (D5)	15.5 B	1.6 B	5.2 B

Table 4: Billions of packets received per week for each pollution type in Upper: 1/8 (A1), 50/8 (B1), 107/8 (C1) and 35/8 (A2,B2,C2); Lower: 35/8 2006-2010 (D1-D5).

we investigate background radiation in the context of its temporal and spacial properties.

4.1 Temporal Analysis of Internet Background Radiation

Figure 2 shows the overall traffic rate observed at the 35/8 darknet during the first week of February for each year starting from 2006. There is an almost 4 fold increase in the observed traffic volume to the address space over this 5 year observation window. While the observed traffic rate in 2006 is less than 5Mbps it does have a significant number of extremely large spikes which can reach as high as 60Mbps. These spikes are largely the result of traffic on UDP port 1026, which represents Windows Messenger popup spam campaigns and are consistent with similar increases in activity seen in the second half of 2005 and the first half of 2006 (e.g., `http://www.dshield.org/`). 2007 demonstrates only a modest increase over 2006, but this traffic rate increases steadily to almost 20 Mbps by Feb 2010. This translates into roughly 100% growth over each of the last four years. It is interesting to note that this rate of growth is nearly twice that of productive Internet traffic which is currently exhibiting 50% year over year growth rates [14].

Table 3 shows the relative composition of the darknet traffic over time in terms of packets and bytes. The percentage of UDP traffic increases dramatically in 2008 in terms of both packets and bytes. It is particularly interesting to note that there appears to be a significant outbreak of SQL Slammer worm scanning in 2008, initially evidenced by the spike in the volume of traffic observed on UDP port 1434. Recall that the SQL Slammer worm spread over the course of

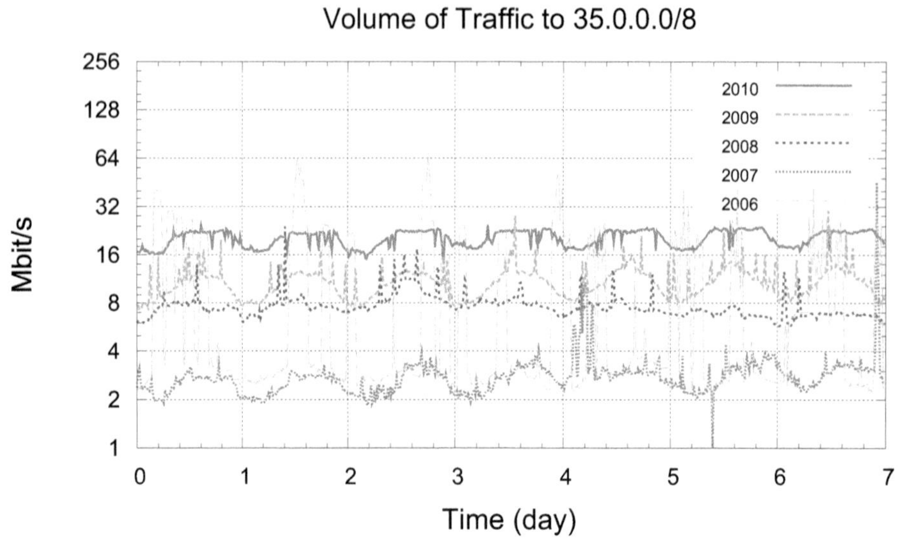

Figure 2: Temporal analysis of Internet Background Radiation. Overall measured traffic is shown from 2006-2010 using datasets D-1, D-2, D-3, D-4, D-5.

TCP Port	2006	2007	2008	2009	2010
445	23.1	8.8	7.2	70.8	83.1
139	12.9	4.2	3.5	0.9	0.6
4662	-	17.1	8.3	-	-
80	2.6	-	-	0.6	0.2
135	6.9	3.4	12.9	1.3	-

Table 5: Most popular TCP destination ports over time in terms of percentage of total TCP packets, 2006-2010 (D1-D5).

TCP Flags	2006	2007	2008	2009	2010
syn	62.7	66.7	74.2	87.5	93.9
syn+ack	26.1	28.9	21.2	8.6	5.2
rst+ack	8.5	3.3	3.0	2.9	0.3
rst	2.3	0.8	1.4	0.4	0.3
ack	0.1	-	-	0.3	0.1

Table 6: Most popular TCP flags over time in terms of percentage of total TCP packets, 2006-2010 (D1-D5).

10 minutes in 2003, infecting thousands of hosts. We were able to manually verify that this spike was indeed Slammer exploits and not some other exploit by verifying the payload and comparing it with the well known SQL Slammer payload. Whether the re-emergence of the worm or other scanning efforts, its occurrence at scale five years after the initial outbreak is puzzling. It should be noted that when compared to the results reported in [10] the percentages of TCP traffic in terms of packets appears very similar.

Table 5 shows the most popular TCP ports in terms of the total percentage of TCP traffic. When compared to the results reported in [10] in 2004 by the time of dataset D1 in 2006 we notice only a minor up-tick in port 445 activity and a general decrease in the fraction of the reported popular ports (i.e., 80, 135, 139) in the study. We do, however, witness the same dynamism as reported in that study, with ports such as 4662 shown in Table 5 appearing and disappearing in popularity. While most of these shifts are short lived and seemingly without explanation, several major events stand out. It is particularly interesting to note the dramatic increase in traffic on port 445 in 2009-2010. This is consistent with the emergence of the Conficker botnet in October 2008. Another interesting artifact visible in the data is the emergence of ssh scanning as a significant percentage of background radiation traffic starting in 2007. Scans on TCP port 23 also begin to emerge starting 2007 which indicates a significant up-tick in attempts to locate backdoors installed by various worms.

Table 6 shows the most commonly used flags in TCP packets over time as a percentage of total number of packets. A very clear trend is visible from this data which is the steady increase in packets which have only the SYN flag set. From 2006 to 2010 the total percentage of TCP packets with SYN flag increases from 63% to almost 94% at the same time the percentage of packets with SYN-ACK flags set decreases dramatically from 26.1% in 2006 to 5.2% in 2010. It is unclear if this indicates an increase in scanning activity and a decline in DDoS activity.

The emergence of Conficker also accounts for perhaps the most significant shift in the nature of Internet background radiation. Figure 3 shows the Cumulative Distribution Function (CDF) of all destinations for which traffic was received in the 35/8 darknet. The 2006 CDF is virtually a straight line, indicating no significant hot-spot activity in this traffic. However, starting in 2008 a knee starts to form in the CDF which indicates the emergence of hot-spot activity. Finally, in 2009 and 2010 we are able to observe a very pronounced kink in the CDF.

This is congruent with a bug in Conficker's pseudo-random propagation algorithm [27]. This bug causes it to fix bits 8 and 24 (most-significant bits of octets 2 and 4, respectively) as 0, resulting in Conficker propagation scans being limited to only 1/4 of the Internet address space. In all observed /8s

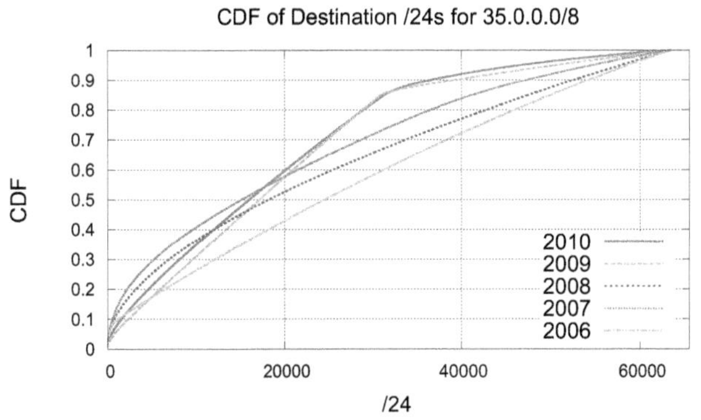

(a) The distribution of destination /24s targeted in the unused address block.

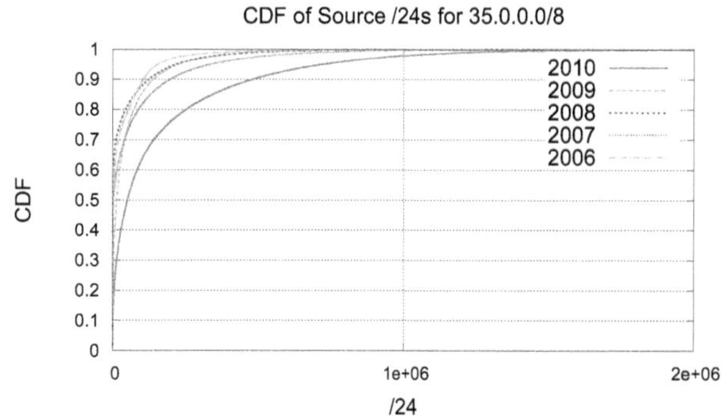

(b) The distribution of source /24s targeted in the unused address block.

Figure 3: Changes in source and destination behavior from 2006-2010 using datasets D-1, D-2, D-3, D-4, D-5.

TCP Port	A1 - A2	B1 - B2	C1 - C2
21	40.3	—	—
25	1.7	—	—
80	8.7	—	—
443	1.6	—	—
445	-75.0	-2.0	-7.5
143	32.5	—	—
1024	—	—	-1.1
5022	1.6	—	—
6112	2.2	—	—

Table 7: The most significant changes in the contribution of a TCP destination port when compared between blocks. Only those ports whose contribution to total traffic at a block that were different by more than %1 are shown.

after 2008, we observe roughly 3 times less traffic for destination IPs with a second or fourth octet of 128 or greater.

4.2 Spatial Analysis of Internet Background Radiation

Figures 4, 6, 8, 9, and 7 represent our analysis of datasets A-[1,2], B-[1,2], and C-[1,2]. The stacked graphs represent data collected from the 35/8 darknet (A2, B2, and C2) on the top row, while the bottom row of graphs represents data collected from 1/8(A1), 50/8(B1), and 107/8(C1).

The overall traffic volume in bytes and packets is shown in Figure 4. One of the most dramatic features is the enormous volume of traffic in 1/8. The 1/8 network sees Internet Background Radiation rates as high as 150Mbps. As we discuss in the following section, most of this traffic is directed toward a small number of destinations in 1/8, due to misconfiguration in a wide range of Internet devices. Both 50/8 and 107/8 traffic rates show a significant diurnal pattern with almost similar data rates. The overall darknet traffic volume ranges from 20-40Mbps or 40-60Kps. One puzzling feature visible in these figures is the clipped nature of the 35/8 graphs. We believe this is caused by a rate limit on a device that is present in the path of our data collector. While we have been able to verify that such a limit is not present in oCDFown collection network, we have so far not been able to verify that there is no such setting at our upstream provider. The traffic volume by protocol is shown in Figure 5. The traffic volume in Figures 5 and 4 shows a sharp dip on day 7 of the A-1 dataset. This was caused by a temporary duplicate BGP announcement by APNIC.

The first column of Figures 6 and 7 show the cumulative distribution function (CDF) of the cumulative contributions of traffic with destination and source in each /24 network. The 1/8 graphs show extremely high hotspot activity in both these figures as evidenced by the extremely sharp knee in these graphs. The second and third columns correspond with datasets B-1 and C-1 respectively. Both of these display moderate hotspot activity in the destination CDF but the source CDF graphs are virtually identical across A-2, B-1, B2, C-1, C-2. We describe some of this hotspot activity in detail in the next section.

Datasets A-2, B-1, B-2, C-1, and C-2 all display remarkable similarity in the TCP destination port distributions. Table 7 summarizes the differences between these datasets. It shows ports whose contribution was different by more than 1% when compared to the A2, B2, and C2. The most interesting features that we discovered during our analysis of the UDP destination ports was some unusual activity on port 514 in dataset B-1, which is the port associated with syslog, as well as activity on port 15206, which represents SIP traffic in dataset A-1. Figure 8 shows the traffic volume contributed by these features and we discuss some of them in the following section.

The source Operating System estimate obtained by observing the TTL values in the TCP packets shows that the relative volume of traffic generated from the various sources appears to be the same for 35/8, 50/8, and 107/8 (datasets A-2, B-1, B-2, C-1, C-2). Recall that the default TTL values for Windows, Linux and Solaris are 128, 64 and 255 respectively. Windows hosts tend to dominate the total traffic volume by various sources in all except the 1/8 darknet block, where Linux sources are responsible for a majority of the traffic. Analysis of the UDP TTL values displays similar distribution for all darknets except once again the 1/8 where we see Windows, Linux, Solaris and perhaps some embedded devices as possible contributors to the pollution. We were, for example, able to identify some pollution at this network

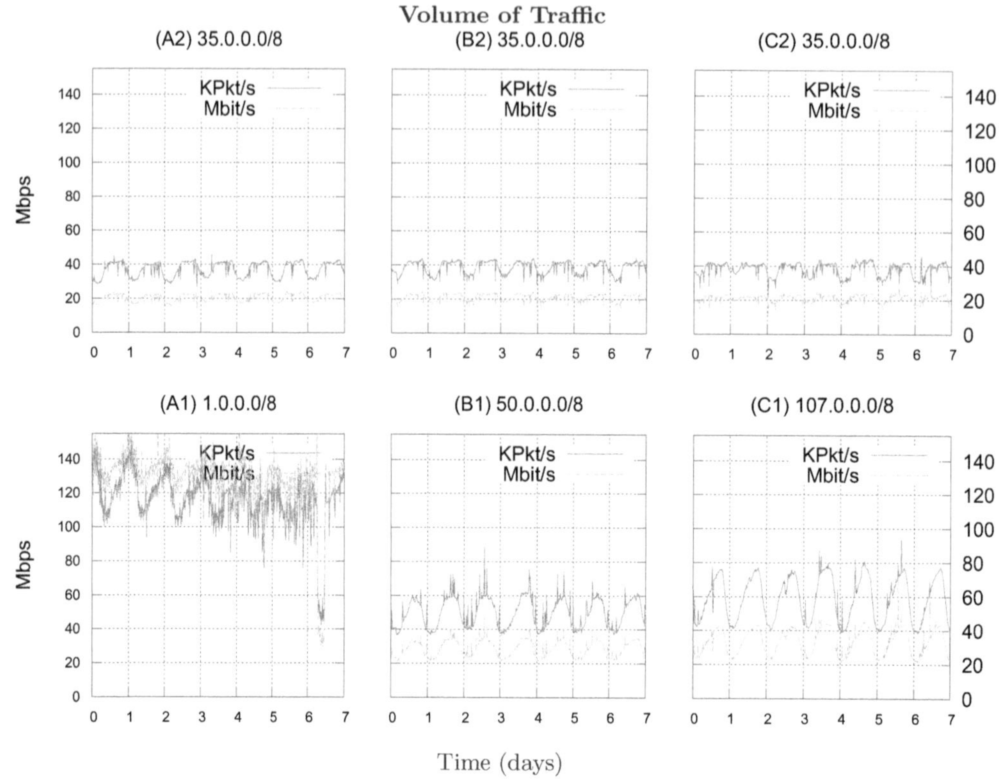

Figure 4: Spatial analysis of Internet Background Radiation. Overall measured traffic (bytes and packets) is shown for datasets A-1, A-2, B-1, B-2, C-1, C-2

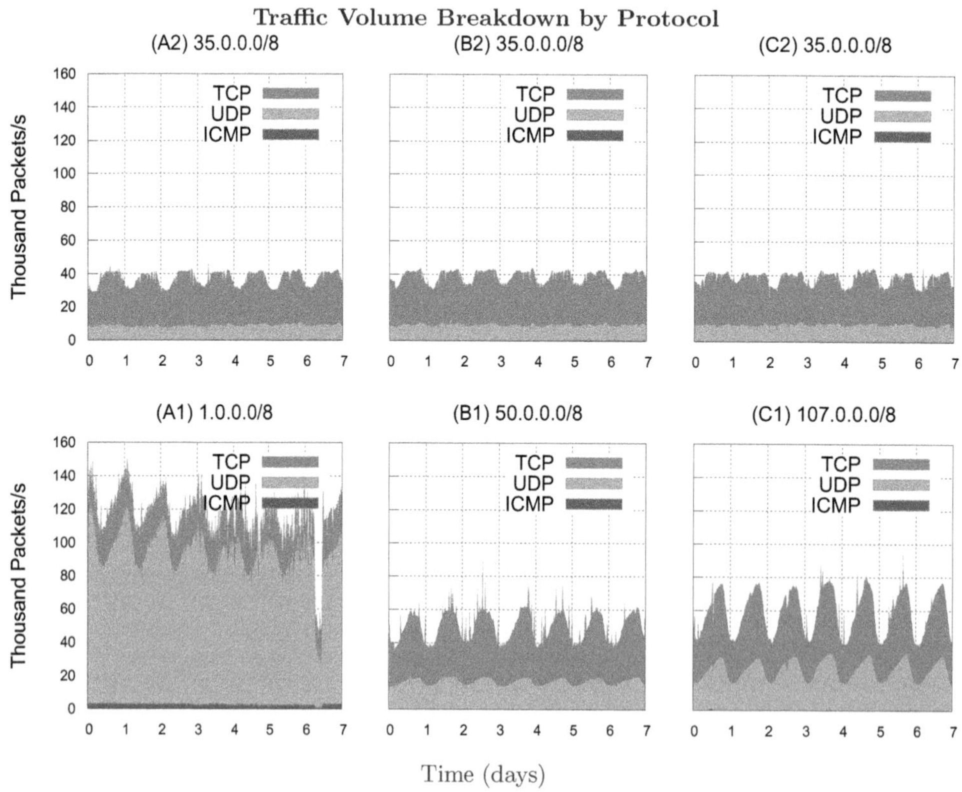

Figure 5: Spatial analysis of Internet Background Radiation. Overall measured traffic by protocols is shown for datasets A-1, A-2, B-1, B-2, C-1, C-2

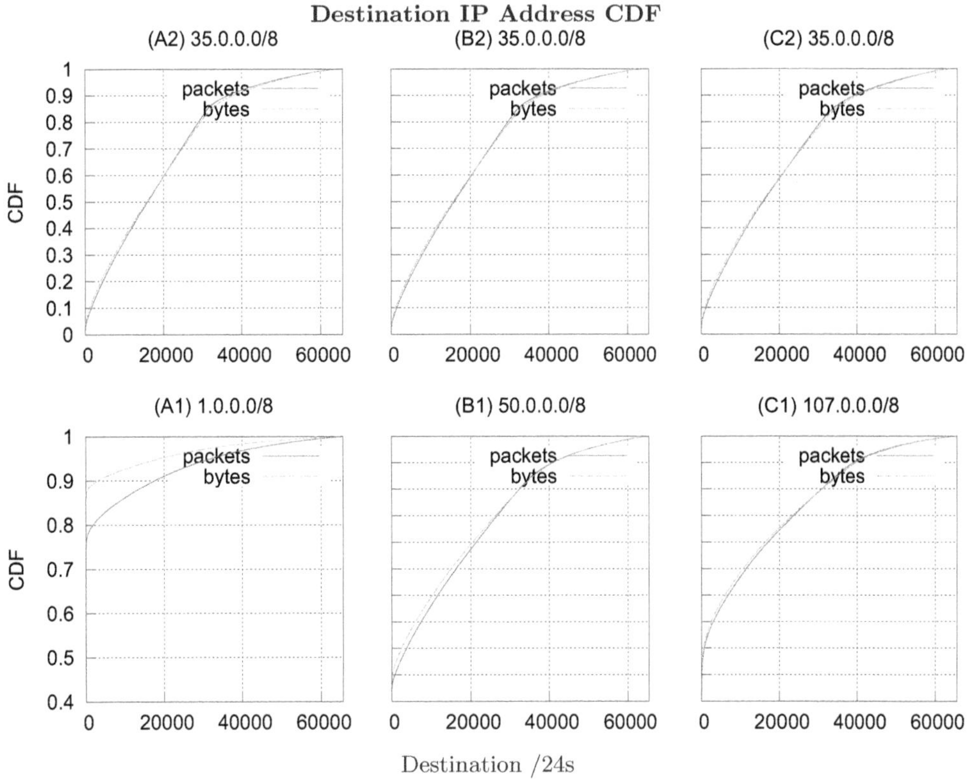

Figure 6: Spatial analysis of Internet Background Radiation. The CDF representing the cumulative contribution of individual /24 destination using datasets A-[1,2], B-[1,2], C-[1,2].

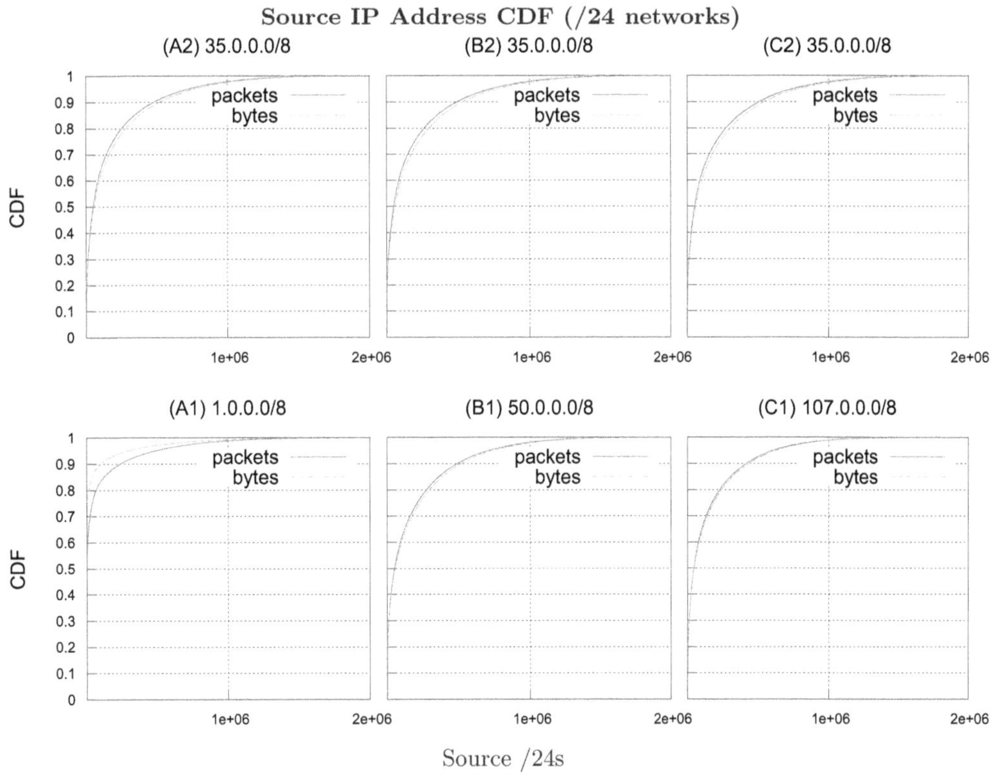

Figure 7: Spatial analysis of Internet Background Radiation. The cumulative distribution function (CDF) representing cumulative contribution of individual /24 source network blocks for both total packets and bytes are shown using datasets A-[1,2], B-[1,2], C-[1,2]. Sorted with highest contributors on the left.

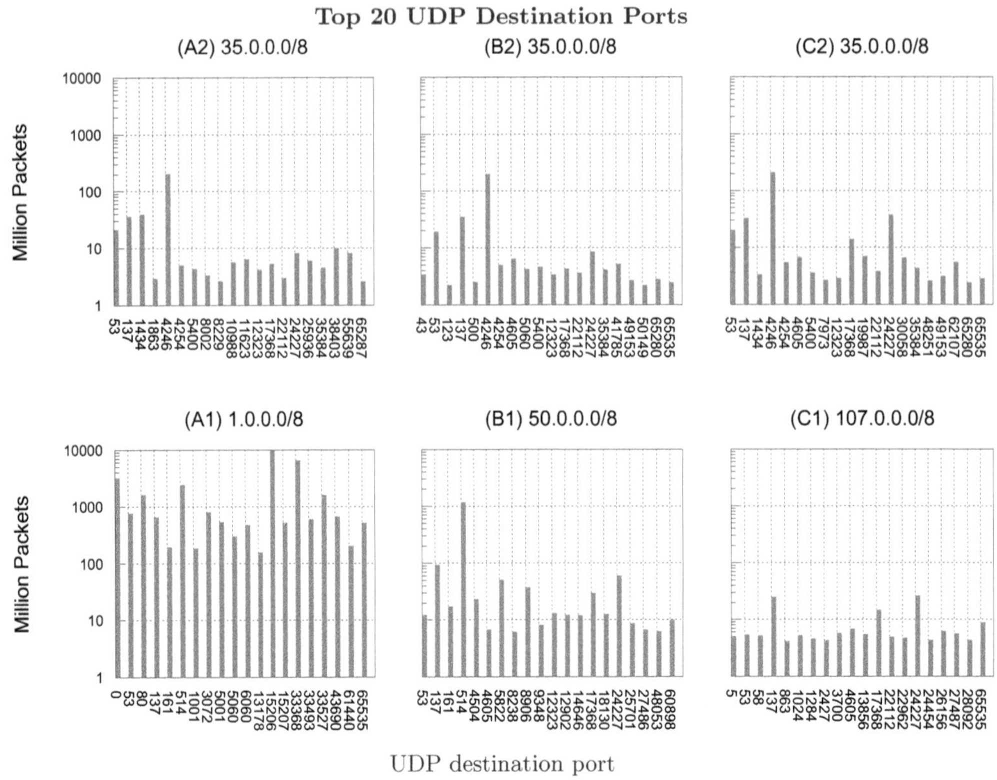

Figure 8: Spatial analysis of Internet Background Radiation. The top 20 UDP destination ports are shown using datasets A-[1,2], B-[1,2], C-[1,2].

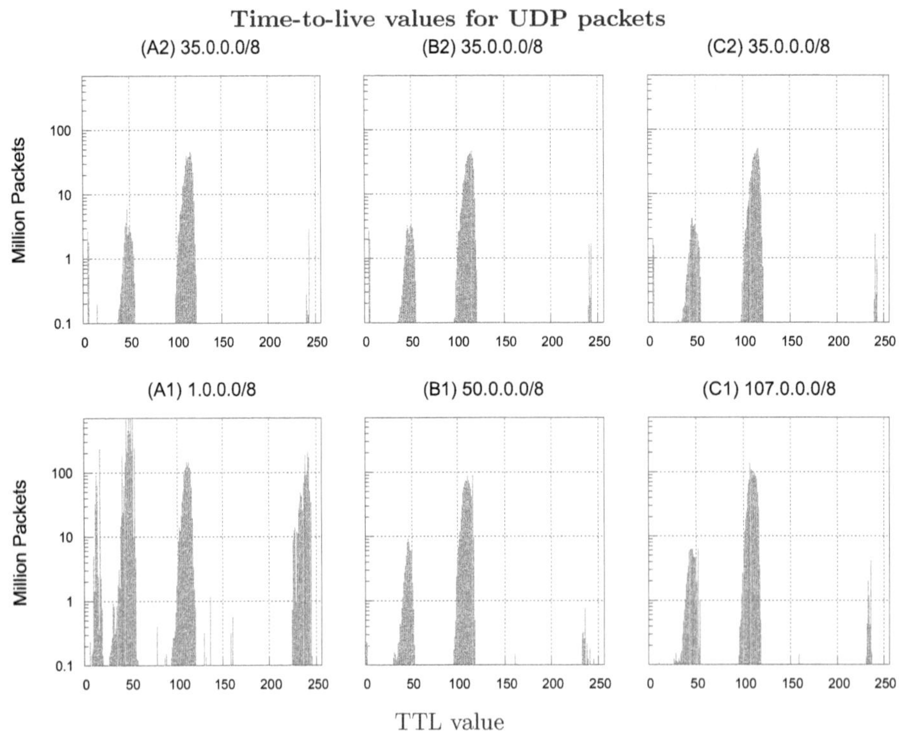

Figure 9: Spatial analysis of Internet Background Radiation. The distribution of TTL values for UDP traffic is shown using datasets A-[1,2], B-[1,2], C-[1,2].

subnet (/24)	%pkts	%bytes
1.1.1.0	44.0	58.7
1.4.0.0	16.7	9.4
1.0.0.0	10.6	6.2
1.2.3.0	2.0	8.6
1.1.168.0	0.6	0.3
1.10.10.0	0.3	2.4
1.1.0.0	0.2	0.1
1.0.168.0	0.2	0.1
1.0.1.0	0.1	0.1
1.2.168.0	0.1	0.1
total	74.8	86.0

Table 8: Top 10 /24 destinations in 1.0.0.0/8

block due to a specific model of a DSL modem. Figure 9 shows this source OS distribution.

5. POLLUTION

In the previous section we discussed that many of the large scale differences observed between announced blocks and our reference unused block were clustered in a small portion of destination or source address space. We call this significant nonuniform behavior *address space pollution*. Unlike previous observations of differences between unused blocks [21] we show that increasingly these differences are the result of environmental factors (e.g., misconfiguration, location), rather than algorithmic factors.

For example, in analyzing the significant difference between A-1 and A-2 we find that the top 10 /24 destinations receive 75% of the total packets. Table 8 shows the 10 /24 destination subnets that received the most packets in 1.0.0.0/8. These blocks observe significant non uniform traffic that is primarily the result of misconfiguration. Example classes of these misconfigurations include: network protocol vulnerabilities, misconfigured network servers, services, and devices, misconfigured attack tools, misconfigured peer-to-peer network software, and various other software programming bugs. In the following sections we explore these interesting sources of pollution in more depth.

5.1 UDP SIP Traffic to 1.1.1.1

In analyzing the destination IP addresses of traffic to 1/8, we discovered a relatively high amount of hot-spots, compared to other /8s we analyzed during roughly the same time. We found that packets with a destination address in the 1.1.1.0/24 subnet made up 44.0% of packets and 58.7% of bytes in the 1.0.0.0/8 traffic over the entire week analyzed. Further analysis of this traffic showed that the vast majority of this traffic was UDP packets to 1.1.1.1, port 15206. This highly specific subset of traffic made up 34.2% of packets and 49.3% of bytes to the entire 1.0.0.0/8 subnet. We found that 71.0% of packets (75.8% of bytes) of traffic to UDP 1.1.1.1:15206 started with a payload of 0x8000. An additional 17.5% of packets (18.6% of bytes) started with 0x8008, and 7.4% of packets (2.8% of bytes) started with 0x8004. Previous analysis by RIPE suggested that this traffic was a trojan, however a couple of SIP blogs [28] [29] revealed that this traffic was likely RTP streams resulting from malicious SIP INVITE packets sent to vulnerable servers. These INVITE packets request that the server dial a telephone number, and send the resulting audio stream back to an IP address and port specified in the INVITE packet. In

2-byte prefix	packets(M)	bytes(M)	% pkts	%bytes
0x8000	17093	3658152	71.0	75.8
0x8008	4213	901639	17.5	18.6
0x8004	1791	138671	7.4	2.8
0x8012	605	51917	2.5	1.0
0x8080	334	71540	1.3	1.4
0x8088	5	1283	0.0	0.0
0x8003	2	232	0.0	0.0
0xa012	0.5	28	0.0	0.0

Table 9: Top 8 RTP Payloads

dport	packets(M)	bytes(M)	%pkts	%bytes
33368	6511	515323	55.7	55.8
514	2114	165388	18.0	17.9
33527	1582	124775	13.5	13.5
3072	803	63827	6.8	6.9
33493	588	46752	5.0	5.0
721	50	3974	0.4	0.4
17055	18	1418	0.1	0.1
33437	7	517	0.0	0.0
570	4	303	0.0	0.0
58689	3	232	0.0	0.0

Table 10: Top 10 destination ports for UDP traffic to 1.4.0.0

this case, the packets were created to have the stream sent to 1.1.1.1:15206. Since these RTP streams are done over connectionless UDP, no response from 1.1.1.1 was necessary for us to receive these RTP streams in our capture.

We were able to isolate a handful of these streams, and using Wireshark, extract the unencrypted audio encoded in these streams. The audio file consists of a series of reorder tones (fast busy), followed by an automated voice stating: "The number you have dialed is not in service. Please check the number and try again." Each RTP stream contributes about 40-50 packets per second (80kbit/s), with an average of more than 5000 streams sending to 1.1.1.1:15206 simultaneously at any time.

Analysis of the TTL values for this traffic reveals 4 separate default TTL values that appear to be the original TTL for the packet. Due to the nature of TTL values decreasing at every hop on its way from the source to our darknet, we expect the received TTL value to be approximately 10-20 less than the starting value. From this, we infer 4 distinct starting values, of 32, 64, 128 and 255. As different operating systems choose different default TTL values, we can conclude that this traffic is likely coming from a cross-platform software application.

5.2 DNS Traffic to 1.4.0.0

The second highest hot-spot in 1.0.0.0/8 is 1.4.0.0/24, receiving 16.6% of packets and 9.4% of bytes over the week-long capture. We observed that almost all of this traffic was UDP packets to 1.4.0.0, on a handful of destination ports.

Inspection of these packets reveals them to be validly constructed DNS queries. Over the week-long capture, 6,536,254 unique source IPs contributed to this traffic, mostly from a handful of ASNs. Using nmap, we were able to determine that most of these hosts were in fact ASUS DSL modems. We suspect that these modems have either a hardware or software misconfiguration that causes them to use 1.4.0.0 on certain non-standard ports as a DNS server. We are un-

Domains
hotelnikkohimeji.co.jp
x.myspacecdn.com
wirelessdigest.typepad.com
th411.photobucket.com
www.google.com

Table 11: Example A record lookups to 1.4.0.0

sure why these modems would send DNS queries on such non-standard, yet concentrated few ports. Analysis of the domains that are being looked up to 1.4.0.0 shows a mix of domains that users are not likely to look up directly — for example, content distribution network domains from popular sites like myspace or youtube. This suggests that 1.4.0.0 is not the sole DNS server for the misconfigured box, as these CDN domains are looked up upon retrieval of the main site — which requires a successful DNS resolution in the first place.

5.3 Iperf Traffic to 1.2.3.4

Roughly 1.8% of all packets measured to the 1.0.0.0/8 network were UDP packets with a destination port of 5001. This port is the default port commonly used by the network testing application *iperf*. These packets were all sent to the 1.2.3.4 destination IP address. This pollution by itself accounted for roughly 10Mbps of traffic and was observed to be originating from fewer than 100 unique sources.

5.4 IP Address Byte-Order Misconfiguration

Though not singly a high contributor of packets, there are three seemingly out-of-place /24s in the top 10 destination subnets for traffic captured to 1.0.0.0/8. These are 1.1.168.0/24, 1.0.168.0/24 and 1.2.168.0/24. Further analysis of packets with 168 in the third octet reveals almost all of these packets to be to 1.x.168.192. Interestingly, this is the popular RFC1918-space gateway address 192.168.x.1 in host-byte order for little-endian machines. Furthermore, these packets are UDP to destination port 80, and contain the same data. The UDP length field specifies 1 byte of payload data (9 bytes - 8 byte UDP header), and the data that follows the UDP packet is always 0x31. While we do not know of a specific device or program that would produce such packets, it is possible a program is sending raw packets, and not doing a proper htonl() on its destination IP. Another explanation is an embedded device (or other platform) using a big-endian architecture is running an incorrectly ported network application from a little-endian system, and could still be performing the byte-ordering switch. We also see the same UDP packets (destination port 80, same payload data) sent to 1.1.0.10, and 1.0.0.10, which are 10.0.1.1 and 10.0.0.1 (other popular RFC1918 gateway addresses) in little endian.

5.5 Syslog to 50.153.199.194

In dataset B-1 (50/8), an interesting hotspot on UDP destination port 514 caught our attention. Subsequent analysis revealed that the hotspot destination /24 is 50.153.199.0/24, receiving 3.8% of packets, and 6.7% of bytes for the entire 1 week capture. Almost all of these were to a single IP, 50.153.199.194, UDP port 514. Closer examination revealed that these packets are all syslog messages originating mainly from IPs in the .de (Germany) TLD. Many of these messages contain combinations of the strings "david", "tobit" and "cosynus".

```
<31>Mar 11 23:59:57 Muck-TS.CheckUserDir -
check snapshot in
\\muck-ts\david\archive\user\
10088000\todo
<31>Mar 11 23:59:59 srv-tobit Creating
Watchdog (C:\Programme\COSYNUS\
BlackBerry4Dv\TXEngine4BB.
watchdog.txt)
<31>Mar 12 00:02:01 vm-eco_cosynus
archive \\eco-online-serv\david\
archive\system\cosynus\bb4dv\bcc\
archive.dat is empty
```

Table 12: Three example syslog messages received on 50.153.199.194 UDP/514. The PRI part (<31>) corresponds to security/authorization messages with a debug (lowest) level severity.

We contacted Cosynus, a German software publishing company, that owns the Cosynus Blackberry connector, to verify the source of this traffic. This software allows Tobit software's David to run on the blackberry. Tobit's David software is a multimedia application available for Windows that consists of E-mail, speech, fax, RSS and instant messaging.

Cosynus confirmed that some of their customers entered "062" as the first octet of an IP address during configuration. This is interpreted as octal, resulting in the traffic being sent to 50.153.199.194 instead of 62.153.199.194. Cosynus offered to firewall the victim IP address in future client updates, which should allow this /24 netblock to become useable. Table 12 shown an example of the messages received.

5.6 eMule to 35.206.63.212

In each week-long capture of 35/8 (datasets A-2, B-2, C-2), 1.0% of packets and 0.9% of bytes were for a specific destination IP 35.206.63.212. Of this, roughly 83% was UDP packets, mostly with 18 bytes of data. The first two bytes of these packets are the same (e3 9a), followed by 16 bytes of varied data. These packets, when interpreted with the eDonkey protocol, a peer-to-peer file sharing protocol, indicate that these are "Get Sources" packets, used to fetch a seed-list for a given file hash.

We found that 35.206.63.212 was listed as a fake server on the official eMule forum [30], confirming that this traffic is in fact peer-to-peer traffic using the eDonkey protocol.

5.7 μTorrent traffic

Recently, newer versions of the popular bittrorrent client μTorrent have implemented a new protocol called Micro Transport Protocol (μTP), to provide better congestion control for bittorrent connections. μTP runs on top of UDP, allowing the μTorrent application to perform congestion control on its bittorrent streams independent of TCP congestion control.

In each of our datasets we were able to observe approximately 4 MBit/s of μTP traffic. This traffic consists primarily of 33 byte packets, to various UDP ports. The destination IPs seem to be varied as well, though the source IP for a given destination IP appears to send packets only to that destination IP. In other words, each source IP sends several packets to only a single destination IP.

Each 33 byte UDP packet starts with 12 bytes of changing

data, followed by 21 bytes of data that is the same in all packets: 7f ff ff ff ab 02 04 00 01 00 00 00 08 00 00 00 00 00 00 00 00. We were able to confirm that this 21 byte sequence occurs in packets generated during a torrent download with a recent version of μTorrent.

5.8 Responding to Pollution

In responding to these unique forms of pollution, we adopt the philosophy of the original authors of [10] to build classifiers for the removal of the unwanted traffic. Our purpose, however, is different. Unlike [10], we are not attempting to reduce traffic in order to build a scalable active responder, our goal instead is to determine the usability of a network block and the utility of any cleanup effort. Given the concentrated nature of much of this pollution, these classifiers need not be complicated and may often simply filter based on net-blocks. Table 8 lists the top 10 most polluted /24 network blocks in 1/8. Together these account for 75% of all packets and 85% of all bytes of pollution traffic to the 1/8 network block. Based on this, APNIC has already proposed the following filters for one of their recently allocated blocks based on this philosophy: "The following /24s should be withheld from general allocation by APNIC: 1.0.0.0/24, 1.1.1.0/24, 1.2.3.0/24, 1.4.0.0/24, 1.10.10.0/24. If further investigation reveals that the traffic to any of these /24s abates to a normal background level in the future, then these addresses would be returned to the APNIC unallocated address pool at that time."

We also know that a cleanup of some of the pollution to 50/8 is possible, as we have contacted the software vendors responsible for the misconfiguration. Their response was helpful in eliminating the pollution being caused by their software. The pollution traffic which we were able to identify as SIP was originating from only a few thousands of sources and the iperf pollution traffic was originating from only a few tens of unique sources. These as well as other similar types of pollution can likely be minimized with a sustained cleanup effort.

6. CONCLUSIONS AND FUTURE WORK

In this paper we have taken a fresh look at Internet background radiation. While today's Internet radiation continues to be as ubiquitous, variegated, and dynamic as was uncovered in the initial study [10], we note several important changes since the last study including: rapid growth outpacing the growth in productive network traffic, reduced contribution from the exploit ports reported in previous work, and trends toward increasing SYN and decreasing SYN-ACK traffic. In examining traffic across address blocks, we note that significant differences exist, but often these differences are clustered in a handful of network blocks. We use the term *Internet address pollution* to refer to this significant nonuniform behavior that is primarily the result of environmental rather than algorithmic factors. We examine several case studies in Internet address pollution and offer some specific suggestions for filtering the most egregious of these blocks.

We would like to develop a more systematic process that passes all newly allocated network blocks through an evaluation phase, where potential usability of the block is assessed. Any recipient of a tainted network block will be unfairly penalized in terms of bandwidth costs and actual usability of their address space. Therefore, it is important that any such network blocks that are found be placed on a well-known temporary watch list, publicized to the network operator community. Furthermore, address block tainting is not simply a result of Internet background radiation, but can also occur when address space is re-allocated from one user to another. Prior ownership of an address block might have resulted in that network block being placed on various spam or botnet blacklists, thereby affecting its usability. We would like to work with the RIRs and the Internet operator community to understand how a simple process can be put in place which attempts to mitigate the affect of address block pollution, either via the dissemination of widespread filters or via a sustained cleanup effort. A related issue is of the study address pollution beyond unallocated or re-allocated blocks, including the problem of discovering and removing pollution in already allocated and routed blocks. While some work has been done on examining what is normal for background radiation [7] and how to maximize visibility to unused space within a network [31], we believe this is a very interesting future area of study.

We view this work as yet another step in understanding the interesting phenomenon of Internet background radiation. As such, we hope to encourage follow-on work in this area by making the datasets used here available via the PREDICT [16] dataset archive. We acknowledge that the current policy for PREDICT limits the use of these datasets to research carried out at US institutions. We will continue to work with existing internal PREDICT efforts to broaden participation beyond its initial scope. Until these efforts bear fruit, the authors encourage interested non-US researchers to contact them directly to investigate alternative paths to data sharing, including jointly seeking institutionally approved research studies (e.g., via research oversight organizations such as the US institutional review board system and similar systems abroad) and/or through entering into researcher-specific data sharing agreements.

Acknowledgments

The authors wish to thank the anonymous reviewers for their helpful comments and suggestions. Furthermore, we wish to thank the IMS team, especially Evan Cooke, without whom the longitudinal collections would not have been possible. We would also like to thank Jakub Czyz and Michael Milliken at Merit for their help in the collection and archiving of the data used in this paper. This work was supported in part by the Department of Homeland Security (DHS) under contract numbers NBCHC080037, NBCHC060090, and FA8750-08-2-0147, the National Science Foundation (NSF) under contract numbers CNS 091639, CNS 08311174, CNS 0627445, and CNS 0751116, and the Department of the Navy under contract N000.14-09-1-1042.

7. REFERENCES

[1] D. Moore, V. Paxon, S. Savage, and Shannon C. Inside the Slammer Worm. *In Proceedings of IEEE Security and Privacy*, Jun 2003.

[2] D. Moore, C. Shannon, and J. Brown. A Case Study on the Spread and Victims of an Internet Worm. *In Proceedings of ACM SIGCOMM Internet Measurement Workshop*, Nov 2002.

[3] Michael Bailey, Evan Cooke, David Watson, Farnam

Jahanian, and Jose Nazario. The Blaster Worm: Then and Now. *IEEE Security & Privacy*, 3(4):26–31, 2005.

[4] D. Moore, G. Voelker, and S. Savage. Inferring Internet Denial of Service Activity. *In Proceedings of the 2001 USENIX Security Symposium*, Aug 2001.

[5] M. Bailey, E. Cooke, D. Watson, F. Jahanian, and N. Provos. Practical Darknet Measurement. *In Proceedings of the 40th Annual Conference on Information Sciences and Systems (CISS)*, Mar 2006.

[6] D. Moore, C. Shannon, G.M. Voelker, and S. Savage. Network Telescopes. *Cooperative Association for Internet Data Analysis - Technical Report*, 2004.

[7] M. Bailey, E. Cooke, D. Watson, F. Jahanian, and N. Provos. Towards Understanding Distributed Blackhole Placement. *In Proceedings of the 2nd Workshop on Rapid Malcode (WORM)*, Oct 2004.

[8] V. Yegneswaran, P. Barford, and D. Plonka. On the Design and Use of Internet Sinks for Network Abuse Monitoring. *In Proceedings of the Symposium on Recent Advances in Intrusion Detection*, Sep 2004.

[9] M. Bailey, E. Cooke, D. Watson, F. Jahanian, and N. Provos. The Internet Motion Sensor - A Distributed Blackhole Monitoring System. *In Proceedings of the 12th Annual Network and Distributed System Security Symposium (NDSS)*, Feb 2005.

[10] R. Pang, V. Yegneswaran, P. Barford, V. Paxson, and L. Peterson. Characteristics of Internet Background Radiation. *In Proceedings of the 4th ACM SIGCOMM Conference on Internet Measurement*, Oct 2004.

[11] Moheeb Abu Rajab, Jay Zarfoss, Fabian Monrose, and Andreas Terzis. A multifaceted approach to understanding the botnet phenomenon. In *IMC '06: Proceedings of the 6th ACM SIGCOMM on Internet measurement*, pages 41–52, New York, NY, USA, 2006. ACM Press.

[12] Evan Cooke, Farnam Jahanian, and Danny McPherson. The Zombie roundup: Understanding, detecting, and disrupting botnets. In *Proceedings of the Steps to Reducing Unwanted Traffic on the Internet (SRUTI 2005 Workshop)*, Cambridge, MA, July 2005.

[13] E. Eugene Schultz. Where have the worms and viruses gone?–new trends in malware. *Computer Fraud & Security*, 2006(7):4–8, 2006.

[14] Craig Labovitz, Scott Iekel-Johnson, Danny McPherson, Jon Oberheide, and Farnam Jahanian. Internet Inter-Domain Traffic. In *Proc. ACM SIGCOMM (To Appear)*, 2010.

[15] Geoff Huston. The changing Foundation of the Internet: confronting IPv4 Address Exhaustion. *The Internet Protocol Journal*, September 2008.

[16] Protected Repository for the Defense of Infrastructure Against Cyber Threats. `http://www.predict.org`.

[17] Michael Bailey, Evan Cooke, Farnam Jahanian, Niels Provos, Karl Rosaen, and David Watson. Data Reduction for the Scalable Automated Analysis of Distributed Darknet Traffic. *Proceedings of the USENIX/ACM Internet Measurement Conference*, October 2005.

[18] Sushant Sinha, Michael Bailey, and Farnam Jahanian. Shedding light on the configuration of dark addresses. In *Proceedings of Network and Distributed System Security Symposium (NDSS '07)*, February 2007.

[19] John Bethencourt, Jason Franklin, and Mary Vernon. Mapping Internet sensors with probe response attacks. In *Proceedings of the 14th USENIX Security Symposium*, Baltimore, MD, August 2005.

[20] Moheeb Abu Rajab, Fabian Monrose, and Andreas Terzis. On the effectiveness of distributed worm monitoring. In *Proceedings of the 14th USENIX Security Symposium*, Baltimore, MD, August 2005.

[21] Evan Cooke, Z. Morley Mao, and Farnam Jahanian. Hotspots: The root causes of non-uniformity in self-propagating malware. In *Proceedings of the International Conference on Dependable Systems and Networks (DSN'2006)*, June 2006.

[22] Abhishek Kumar, Vern Paxson, and Nicholas Weaver. Exploiting underlying structure for detailed reconstruction of an internet-scale event. *Proceedings of the USENIX/ACM Internet Measurement Conference*, October 2005.

[23] Mark Allman, Vern Paxson, and Jeff Terrell. A brief history of scanning. In *IMC '07: Proceedings of the 7th ACM SIGCOMM conference on Internet measurement*, New York, NY, USA, 2007.

[24] Route Views Project. University of Oregon Route Views Project. *http://archive.routeviews.org/*, Aug 2010.

[25] RIPE (RÃľseaux IP EuropÃľens). RIS Raw Data. *http://www.ripe.net/projects/ris/rawdata.html*, Aug 2010.

[26] RADb: Merit network inc. routing assets database. `http://www.radb.net/`.

[27] B. Kantor, S. Savage, R. Wesson, B. Enright, P. Porras, V. Yegneswaran, J. Wolfgang, and Castro S. Conficker/Conflicker/Downadup as seen from the UCSD Network Telescope - Feb 2009. *http://www.caida.org/research/security/ms08-067/conficker.xml.*

[28] S. Gauci. RTP Traffic to 1.1.1.1 - Feb 2010. *http://blog.sipvicious.org/2010/02/rtp-traffic-to-1111.html.*

[29] S. Eivind. usken.no - VoIP news! - Feb 2010. *http://www.usken.no/2010/02/sip-scanning-causes-ddos-on-ip-1-1-1-1/.*

[30] Adrian MariÃšo. Fake Servers List - Official eMule-Board - Apr 2010. *http://forum.emule-project.net/index.php?showtopic=139609&st=60.*

[31] Evan Cooke, Michael Bailey, Farnam Jahanian, and Richard Mortier. The Dark Oracle: Perspective-Aware Unused and Unreachable Address Discovery. In *Proceedings of the 3rd Symposium on Networked Systems Design & Implementation (NSDI '06)*, pages 101–114, San Jose, California, USA, May 2006.

On Economic Heavy Hitters: Shapley value analysis of 95th-percentile pricing

Rade Stanojevic
Telefonica Research

Nikolaos Laoutaris
Telefonica Research

Pablo Rodriguez
Telefonica Research

ABSTRACT

Cost control for the Internet *access providers* (AP) influences not only the nominal speeds offered to the customers, but also other, more controversial, policies related to traffic shaping and discrimination. Given that the cost for the AP is determined by the peak-hour traffic (e.g. through the 95th-percentile), the individual user contribution towards the aggregate cost is not a linear function of its byte usage. In this paper we propose a metric for evaluating the contribution each individual user has on the peak demand, that is based on Shapley value, a well known game-theoretic concept. Given the computational complexity of calculating the Shapley value, we use a Monte Carlo method for approximating it with reasonable accuracy. We employ our methodology to study a dataset that logs per-subscriber temporal usage patterns over one month period for 10K broadband subscribers of a European AP and report observed results.

Categories and Subject Descriptors

C.2.3 [**Computer-Communications networks**]: Network Operations; Network monitoring; C.4 [**Performance of systems**]: Measurement techniques

General Terms

Measurement, Economics

Keywords

Heavy-hitters, Network economics, Net-neutrality, Shapley value, Monte-Carlo method

1. INTRODUCTION

A large number of Internet Access Provider (AP) adopted flat-rate pricing as a de-facto standard for charging of broadband services as such pricing appears to be preferred by the customers [18]. This creates many difficulties for the APs as it does not allow APs to transparently control the uplinking (transit + infrastructure) costs and forced many APs to create nontransparent rules for traffic shaping and violate net-neutrality as a means for control of their costs [9]. Using the terminology of [22], uplinking costs are the single most expensive component of the costs for broadband connectivity for a majority of currently used technologies, including DSL, cable and WiFi (mash and access point). An important property of the uplinking costs (influenced by the transit costs and the cost of infrastructure) is that they are determined by the peak demand (e.g. through the 95th-percentile) rather than average demand, which makes it hard to assess per-customer contribution towards these costs.

Flight ticket prices typically depend on the time of travel and hotel rooms in tourist resorts are less expensive during off-season. Similarly, a byte downloaded in peak-hour costs more (for the provider) than a byte of traffic in off-peak hours. In this paper we study per-user contribution in the AP peak hour demand. More precisely, we measure per-customer contribution towards the 95th-percentile of the aggregate demand series[1]. For the purpose of quantifying per-user contribution to the 95th-percentile, we use Shapley value, an intuitive concept from coalitional game theory that characterizes fair cost sharing among involved players (customers). Shapley value framework allows us to: (1) accurately quantify the contribution of each customer towards the peak-hour traffic, (2) analyze the relationship between the aggregate usage (in bytes) and the peak-hour contribution and (3) formally measure how cost of bandwidth is related to the demand pattern. We validate our methodology over a dataset that logs temporal usage of 10K broadband customers of a European AP.

Note that we talk about costs customers generate for the AP rather than the price they pay; retail prices are often strongly impacted by other market, competition and social factors [22]. For various mechanisms for pricing the communication services in the context of revenue (or social welfare) maximization, see [6].

1.1 Toy example

For measuring the peak demand we use the 95th-percentile of the aggregate demand, the most standard measure for billing of the transit traffic and an indicator of the network utilization, used for the dimensioning of the infrastructure; see Appendix A for a brief description. To understand the concept of Shapley value and how it applies to the 95th-

[1]We stress, however, that the framework is general enough to accommodate any other metric that measures the peak demand.

percentile billing let us consider a synthetic example of an AP ISP providing service to only two users that have demand patterns that are depicted in Figure 1. The user 1 generates a demand of $1Mbps$ during the whole day except for the four-hour period [15-19h]. The user 2 is idle for 22 hours and generates $3Mbps$ traffic during two hours: [16-18h]. The 95-th percentile of the aggregate user demand is the peak-hour traffic $v_{95th} = 3Mbps$ and the price the ISP would need to pay to its transit provider is $v_{95th} \cdot A_0$ (where A_0 is the price in USD per $Mbps$). The following question arises: What is the fair cost sharing among the two involved users? The Shapley value concept gives an answer to this question and the intuition behind it is described bellow.

If there was only user 1 or only user 2 in the system, the 95th percentile would have been:

$$v_{95th}(\{1\}) = 1Mbps \quad \text{and} \quad v_{95th}(\{2\}) = 3Mbps$$

respectively. As we already observed, the 95th percentile of the union of these two users is

$$v_{95th}(\{1,2\}) = 3Mbps.$$

The Shapley value of user i, ϕ_i is now the average marginal contribution that user i imposes to the coalition cost. In other words:

$$\phi_i = \frac{1}{2}\left(v_{95th}(\{i\}) + (v_{95th}(\{i,i'\}) - v_{95th}(\{i'\}))\right),$$

where $\{i'\} = \{1,2\} \setminus \{i\}$. In our example the per user Shapley values are:

$$\phi_1 = 0.5Mbps \quad \text{and} \quad \phi_2 = 2.5Mbps.$$

Thus by entering the coalition, the fair cost sharing of the 95th-percentile $v_{95th}(\{1,2\}) = 3Mbps$ would be the one in which the user 1 is accounted for $\phi_1 = 0.5Mbps$ and the user 2 for $\phi_2 = 2.5Mbps$. The nature of the 95th-percentile pricing is such that even though the user 1 generates in total 3.3 times more traffic than user 2, its contribution to the 95th-percentile is 5 times lower.

COMMENT 1. *We can learn two lessons from the above example: firstly, the user that sends/receives more data does not necessarily have higher impact on the 95th-percentile; and secondly, even if a user does not generate any traffic in the peak hours that does not imply that its impact towards the 95th-percentile is zero. Shapley value balances between these two extremes (aggregate usage and peak-only usage) by evaluating the average marginal contribution of each user (eq. 1).*

1.2 Summary of contributions

Briefly, the main contributions of this paper are the following:

- We develop a new methodology for studying heavy users in an operational ISP. We use the standard concept from cooperational game theory, known as Shapley value, to quantify per-user cost contribution in the context of 95th-percentile pricing.

- Using the Shapley value methodology, we study a month-long dataset that tracks temporal usage patterns from 10K broadband users of a European ISP. We quantify several relevant metrics over this dataset. In particular

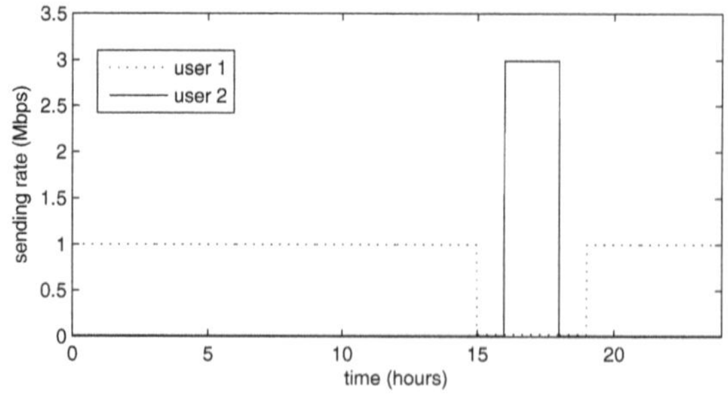

Figure 1: Toy example. Two users with different demand pattern.

we find that for approximately 10% of users, the relative cost contribution (Shapley value) is less than half of the relative byte usage (off-peak users), and that for additional 10% of users the relative cost contribution is more than twice of their relative byte usage (peak users). Finally, we use the Shapley value framework to formalize the intuitive wisdom "a byte in the peak-hour has a higher value/cost than an off-peak byte" by quantifying the hourly per-byte bandwidth prices that approximate best the measured Shapley value.

2. APPROXIMATING SHAPLEY VALUE

In this section we will briefly introduce the Shapley value concept for general cooperative games, relate it to our framework in which the cost of a user coalition is determined by the 95th-percentile of the traffic they generate and propose a randomized method for efficiently computing SV for large number of players.

2.1 Shapley value: definition

Consider a set $\mathcal{N}$ of N players[2]. For each subset (coalition) $S \subset \mathcal{N}$ let $v(S)$ be the cost of coalition S. In other words if S is a coalition of players which agree to cooperate, then $v(S)$ determines the total cost from this cooperation.

For given cost function v, the Shapley value is a (uniquely determined) vector $(\phi_1(v), \ldots, \phi_N(v))$ defined bellow that is "fair" in that it satisfies four intuitive properties (see [20, 23]) for sharing the cost $v(\mathcal{N})$ that exhibits the coalition of all players. It can be shown that Shapley value of player i is determined by

$$\phi_i(v) = \frac{1}{N!}\sum_{\pi \in S_N}\left(v(S(\pi,i)) - v(S(\pi,i) \setminus i)\right) \qquad (1)$$

where π is a permutation or arrival order of set $\mathcal{N}$ and $S(\pi, i)$ is the set of players arrived in the system not later than i. In other words, player i is responsible for its marginal contribution $v(S(\pi,i)) - v(S(\pi,i) \setminus i)$ averaged across all $N!$ arrival orders π. Note that the Shapley value defined by (1) satisfies (so called efficiency) property:

$$\sum_{i \in \mathcal{N}} \phi_i(v) = v(\mathcal{N}).$$

2.2 The 95th-percentile cost

The 95th-percentile billing is a method of measuring bandwidth usage based on peak utilization, defined in Appendix

[2]We interchangeably use terms player, user, customer and subscriber.

A. Informally it measures close-to-peak demand but it also allows usage to exceed a specified threshold for brief periods of time without the financial penalty.

The setup over which we apply the Shapley value framework is the following. We have the set $\mathcal{N}$ of N users that generate traffic over a charging period, say one month. The charging period is split into T sampling intervals, and at time $t \in [1, T]$, user i generates the traffic $Z_i(t)$ (measured in bytes). For a time series $D = (D(1), \ldots, D(T))$, the 95th-percentile $P_{95th}(D)$ is defined as the $\lceil \frac{T}{20} \rceil$-th largest number of the time series. For a coalition S of users the cost they generate is determined by the 95th-percentile of the aggregate demand pattern they generate:

$$v(S) = P_{95th}(\sum_{i \in S} Z_i(1), \ldots, \sum_{i \in S} Z_i(T)).$$

Given the cost function $v(\cdot)$, the contribution of each user to the 95th-percentile of the aggregate traffic $v(\mathcal{N})$ is defined by the Shapley value defined by (1). From the definition, one can notice that the 95th-percentile does not decrease by adding new users to the coalition, therefore implying that the cost function v is monotone:

$$(\forall S \subset \mathcal{N})(\forall i \in \mathcal{N}) \quad v(S \cup i) \geq v(S).$$

The monotonicity of the cost function v implies that the Shapley value of each user is indeed nonnegative.

2.3 Approximating Shapley value

Brute force application of formula (1) is computationally unfeasible once N becomes greater than 100. For APs with thousands (or millions) of subscribers such exact computation is not possible. In this Section we describe a simple randomized method for approximating the Shapley, that can scale with datasets of tens of thousands (if not millions) of subscribers.

The idea of the method is simple. The Shapley value of user i defined by (1) can be seen as the marginal cost increase by user i, averaged over all $N!$ arrival orders. In the example from Section 1.1, $N = 2$ and there are 2 arrival orders: $\pi_1 = (1, 2)$ and $\pi_2 = (2, 1)$ and the user 1 and user 2 Shapley values are

$$\phi_1 = \frac{1}{2}((v(\{1\}) - v(\emptyset)) + (v(\{1,2\}) - v(\{2\}))) =$$

$$= \frac{1}{2}((1 - 0) + (3 - 3))) = 0.5.$$

$$\phi_2 = \frac{1}{2}((v(\{1,2\}) - v(\{1\})) + (v(\{2\}) - v(\emptyset))) =$$

$$= \frac{1}{2}((3 - 1) + (3 - 0))) = 2.5.$$

While computing the exact Shapley value through the formula (1) is straightforward for small N, it becomes unfeasible for $N > 50$, as the number of different permutation orders grows with $N!$. However, the computational complexity can be significantly reduced by using the Monte Carlo method.

Instead of calculating the exact Shapley value as the average cost contribution across all $N!$ arrival orders, we estimate the Shapley value as the average cost contribution over a set Π_k of k randomly sampled arrival orders (permutations).

$$\hat{\phi}_i(v) = \frac{1}{k} \sum_{\pi \in \Pi_k} (v(S(\pi, i)) - v(S(\pi, i) \setminus i)) \qquad (2)$$

The parameter k determines the error between the real Shapley value and its estimate: the higher k the lower the error. So basically, one can control the accuracy of the estimators by increasing the number of sample permutation orders (see Section 3.2).

PROPOSITION 1. *The estimator $\hat{\phi}_i(v)$ is an unbiased estimator of the real Shapley value $\phi_i(v)$.*

PROOF. See [21]. □

Thus the Shapley value estimator (2) is unbiased. However the variance of the estimator is hard to model and in Section 3.2 we present empirical evidence that for reasonably small sample size (say, $k = 1000$) the estimator exhibits small variance, especially for the top users.

PROPOSITION 2. *The estimated Shapley values satisfy the efficiency property:*

$$\sum_{i \in \mathcal{N}} \hat{\phi}_i(v) = v(\mathcal{N}).$$

PROOF. See [21]. □

3. EMPIRICAL RESULTS

In this section we present the empirical results obtained by analyzing the dataset of around 10K broadband users of a major European ISP. In Section 3.1 we describe the dataset, then in Section 3.2 we analyze the accuracy of the randomized method for calculating Shapley value. We proceed by analyzing the correlation between per-user aggregate usage and its Shapley value in Section 3.3 and then in Section 3.4 we quantify the relative cost of bandwidth in time that would best approximate the Shapley value. Additional empirical results, related to the consistency of the Shapley value over time, as well as additional discussion on the relative cost of bandwidth, can be found in the Technical report [21].

3.1 Dataset description

The dataset consists of around 10K ADSL users of a major access provider in one European country. For each customer, its downstream and upstream consumption (in bytes) is captured during each hour for 30 days (thus spanning 720 hours). These users represent a random sample of ADSL users of the ISP and have diverse uplink/downlink capacities in the ranges of 256Kbps–10Mbps, and 1Mbps–20Mbps, respectively. The downstream traffic dominates the upstream traffic in the ratio 4 : 1, which is consistent with the recent findings from another European access provider ISP [15]. Virtually all ADSL users from the dataset pay flat-fee, without incentives to shift their traffic to the off-peak hours[11]. We stress that the empirical results derived from this dataset are mainly qualitative, used for the purpose of validating the Shapley value methodology and basic properties of Shapley value, and results derived here should not be generalized for other types of environments such as campus, backbone or enterprize networks.

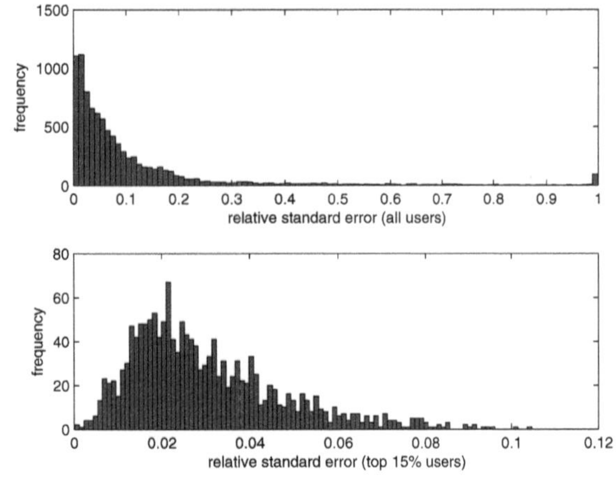

Figure 2: Relative standard errors of the Shapley value estimator (2). Top: all users (top); bottom: users with estimated Shapley value higher than the mean (approx top 15%).

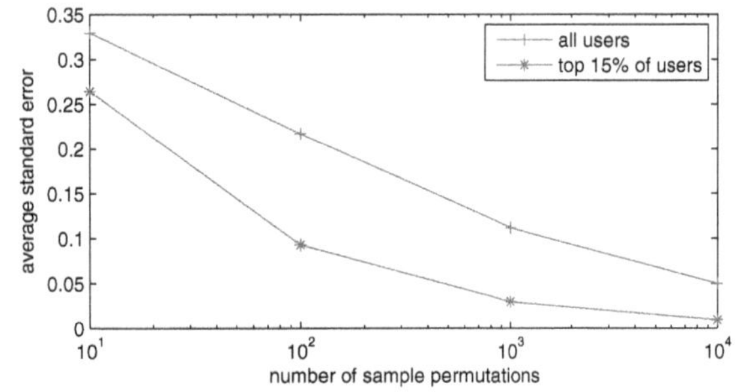

Figure 3: Standard error as a function of number of sample permutations (parameter k).

For the computation of 95th-percentile we use 1-hour bins, as this is the granularity of our dataset. Given that we consider large traffic volumes and large number of users, using different bin sizes (e.g. 5 minutes) would have minor effects on the 95th-percentile [8].

As we said, the downstream traffic dominates the upstream and in the following analysis we will therefore focus on the downstream traffic, as it is the direction that determines the 95th-percentile (see Appendix A). The dataset does not distinguish the per-user share of transit/nontransit traffic, so for the evaluation purposes we assume that all the traffic contributes to the 95th-percentile.

3.2 Accuracy of the Shapley value estimator

Our first step is the evaluation of the accuracy of the Shapley value estimator (2). Given that we do not have the ground truth measurement, to evaluate the error that the estimator exhibits, we use the standard statistical method as follows. Recall that the Shapley value estimator (2) of user i is a mean of k samples of marginal cost contributions $v(S(\pi, i)) - v(S(\pi, i) \setminus i)$. If we denote by $\hat{\sigma}_i$ the estimated standard deviation of the same k marginal cost samples. Then the relative standard error of the estimator (2) is $\frac{\hat{\sigma}_i}{\sqrt{k}\hat{\phi}_i(v)}$. In Figure 2 we plot the histograms of these standard errors when the sample size is $k = 1000$ permutations[3] for all users as well as the users with Shapley value estimate higher than the mean Shapley value $1/N \cdot v(\mathcal{N})$. One can observe that the relative standard errors are moderately small across all users and are consistently under 10% for top users. In Figure 3 we vary the number of sample permutation orders (parameter k) and evaluate the relative standard errors averaged across all the users and also the top 15% users.

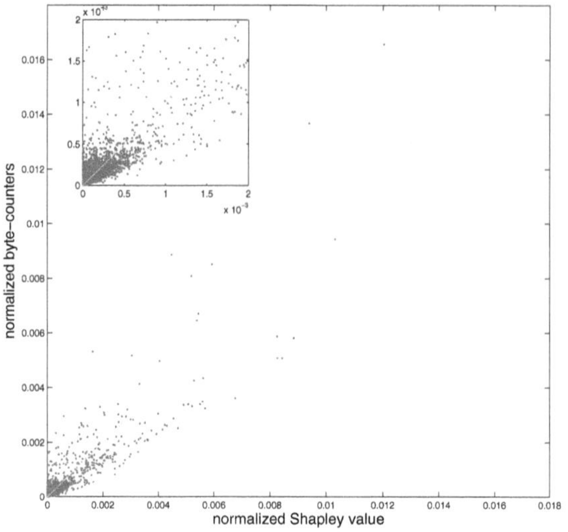

Figure 4: Normalized byte-counters vs. normalized Shapley value.

3.3 Aggregate usage vs. Shapley value

Now, that we established the accuracy of Shapley value estimates, we will compare it with the time-oblivious usage measure: bytes downloaded over the whole 30-day period (byte-counters). In Figure 4 we plot the normalized[4] Shapley value (x-axis) against the normalized byte-counters (y-axis) for each user from our dataset. Users with relatively high off-peak usage correspond to datapoints that are far above $x - y = 0$ line. Conversely, users with modest off-peak usage and heavy "peak-hour" usage correspond to datapoints close to x-axis. Finally, the more similar the usage activity of a user is to the aggregate usage pattern, the closer its datapoint is to the $x - y = 0$ line. To measure how different the user's Shapley value and byte-count are we introduce the following metric that basically measures the discrepancy between the user's relative aggregate usage and its relative contribution to the 95th-percentile:

$$\rho_i = \frac{\text{normalized Shapley value of user } i}{\text{normalized byte-count of user } i}, \; i \in \mathcal{N}.$$

As we said above, the users with high off-peak usage (compared to their peak-usage) have low ρ_i and vice versa. In Figure 5 we plot the histogram of ρ_i for all users i with Shapley value greater than the mean (approx 15% of the users) as we have a high confidence in the measured Shapley value for those users (see Figure 2). We see that there are ap-

[3]The computation took under 5 minutes on a PC running Intel Core 2 Duo CPU, 2.33GHz and 2GB of RAM.

[4]Scaled down proportionally to have the sum equal to 1.

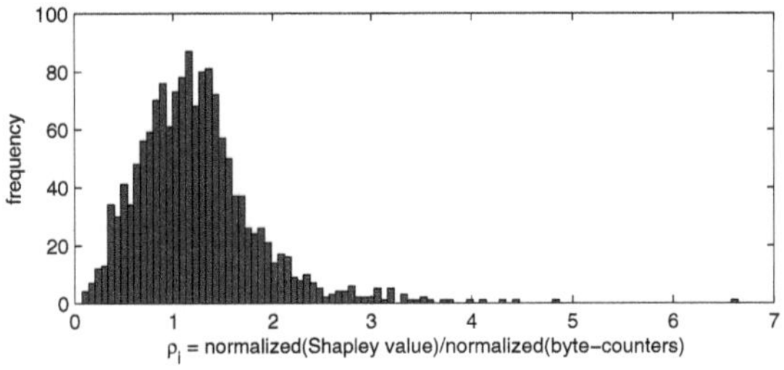

Figure 5: Normalized byte-counters vs. normalized Shapley value.

proximately 10% of users whose relative cost contribution is more than twice the relative byte counters ($\rho_i > 2$) and another 10% of users with relative cost contribution less than half of its relative byte count ($\rho_i < 0.5$). The proportion of users with very large or very small ρ_i is even higher for low-Shapley-value users (the remaining 85% of the dataset), but we avoid reporting these numbers because of the accuracy issues for the low-Shapley-value users (see Section 3.2).

Another interesting statistics is that around 30% of top-1% (and around 25% of top-10%) Shapley value users are not in the corresponding top-1% (top-10%) byte-count list.

3.4 Relative cost of bandwidth

As we already mentioned in the Introduction, the consequence of the 95th-percentile pricing of the transit traffic is that the bandwidth is "more expensive" in the peak hours than in the off-peak hours. Here we use the Shapley value framework to quantify how the value of bandwidth changes in time. Namely we seek to find the hourly per-byte prices $c_1, \ldots, c_{24}$, such that if a user i is charged c_h monetary units for each byte downloaded during hour h, then the monthly bill is (approximately) equal to its Shapley value. More formally, if $Z_i(t)$ is the usage of user i at time $t = 1, ..., 720$, we seek for $c_1, \ldots, c_{24} \geq 0$ such that

$$\sum_{h=1}^{24} c_h \sum_{d=1}^{30} Z_i(h + 24(d-1)) \approx \phi_i, \quad \forall i \in \mathcal{N}.$$

Given that the above system of equations is overdetermined (it has 24 variables and 10K equations), we need to seek a fit that matches some optimization criteria. A well know method for approximating solution of the overdetermined linear systems is the nonnegative least square (nnls) method that seeks to minimize

$$\sum_{i=1}^{N} \left(\sum_{h=1}^{24} c_h \sum_{d=1}^{30} Z_i(h + 24(d-1)) - \phi_i \right)^2 .$$

Very efficient solutions for nnls problem have been proposed recently and we use [10] to solve our problem. Running nnls over our dataset, we derive time series $c_1, \ldots, c_{24}$ depicted in Figure 6. One can observe that (for the dataset analyzed here) in the 95th-percentile setup, the bandwidth is "free" (has virtually zero impact on the 95th-percentile) for some 18 hours per day and has strictly positive cost during 6 hours per day. Note that even though the monthly 95th-percentile is crossed during only one or two hours per day, the cost of bandwidth is still non-zero for 6 (near-peak) hours.

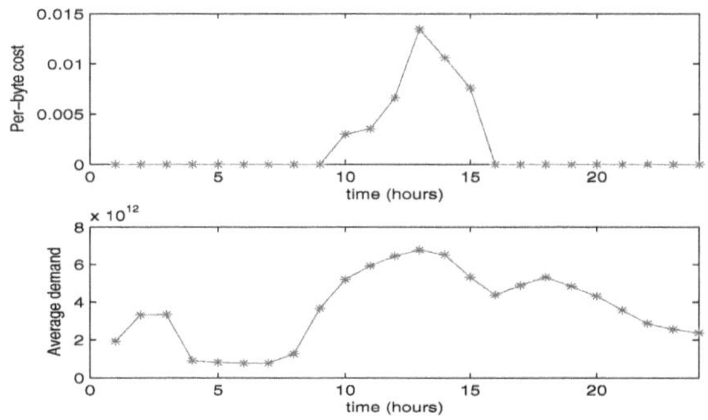

Figure 6: Top: hourly per-byte cost (nonnegative least squares). Bottom: average hourly utilization.

4. RELATED WORK

Per user analysis of broadband internet traffic was a subject of several recent studies. Cho et al. analyzes broadband traffic from several Japanese ISPs in [4, 5]. They analyze the per-user traffic usage and they show that it is highly skewed[5] (can be modeled with a log-normal distribution). With the duration of the dataset they analyzed, they were able to track upload/download traffic trends over multiple years and quantify the effects different applications have on the traffic aggregates. In [15] Maier et al. perform a measurement study of residential broadband users in one European ISP and analyze several relevant metrics: per-application usage, DSL session duration, and observable round trip-times. Here we take a different look at the broadband traffic by analyzing per-user temporal usage patterns and how they impact the costs for the access provider.

One of the key reasons that influence traffic shaping (also known as traffic discrimination) of Internet traffic is the fact that by throttling some traffic, ISPs control (reduce) their costs [16]. Dhamdhere and Dovrolis [7] and Biczok et al [1] analyze several broadband pricing models that aim to offer a solution that obey the net neutrality rules by discriminating the price of the heavy-hitters (based on the total bytes downloaded/uploaded). In this work we empirically show that the heavy-hitters are not necessarily expensive for the ISP and that temporal usage effects should be taken into account when designing pricing models in the context of net neutrality.

Briscoe [2, 3] argues that fairness mechanisms in computer networks should be judged on "how they share out the 'cost' of each user's action on others" and he offers several heuristics (e.g. he suggests that the number of dropped packets over a billing circle is a good indicator of a customer's cost contribution) for evaluating the 'cost'. The Shapley value framework we introduced here can be seen as a formal way to measure user's cost contribution.

Pricing of communication networks has been extensively studied in the past; see [6] and references therein. These efforts mainly focus on how to use pricing to achieve some form of social welfare (or revenue) maximization. We stress that we do not aim to propose a new pricing scheme in this paper, but rather set to measure the diversity of the broadband usage behavior patterns and their effect on the peak hour consumption.

[5]The fact that we also observe in our dataset.

Recently, several research efforts suggested using Shapley value as a means for providing incentives for optimal resource control. Ma et al. promote use of Shapley value for ISP settlement by proposing revenue sharing among ISPs based on the importance each ISP has on the Internet ecosystem [13, 14]. In the context of peer-to-peer systems, Misra et al. [17] propose using Shapley value to incentivize cooperation in p2p systems.

The 95th-percentile pricing has been analyzed recently by Dimitropoulos et al. [8]. They quantify the dependence between the size of measurement slot and the observed 95th-percentile and show that this dependence becomes weak for large volumes of traffic. Laoutaris et al. [12] use the 95th-percentile pricing to propose ISP-friendly bulk transfers that explicitly avoid to use bandwidth that could increase the 95th-percentile.

5. SUMMARY

Days in which the technological reasons were impacting the performance of the residential Internet users are coming to an end and in the near future, the performance offered to the end users will be predominantly shaped by the economic factors rather than physical bottlenecks. In such environments it is crucial to determine the cost contribution of each individual user to the operation of ISP, as it would be a key metric for evaluating the consumption and accounting in such an ecosystem. Our study is a step towards the fairer usage of the Internet in which economic aspects dominate the per-user performance as it formally quantifies the individual per-user cost contributions in the specific context of burstable (95th-percentile) billing.

In the future we plan to investigate the effects the traffic shaping (e.g. p2p throttling [9]) has on the customers' Shapley value, as well as the relationship between the operational parameters (oversubscription rate, nominal capacities, etc.) and the Shapley value. Finally, in light of the fact that the Shapley value is an off-line (and somewhat complex) metric, it would be useful to find a simpler online metric that accurately approximates the Shapley value (one possible way would be along the lines discussed in Section 3.4).

6. ACKNOWLEDGEMENTS

R.S. would like to thank Tianbai (Richard) Ma for introducing him to the concept of Shapley value and many valuable discussions. Authors also thank Alberto Lopez for his assistance in obtaining the dataset.

APPENDIX

A. THE 95TH-PERCENTILE PRICING

The 95th-percentile pricing is the most prevalent method that transit ISPs use for charging their customers. A billing cycle, typically one month, is split in constant-size intervals (e.g. 5-min or 1-hour) and number of bytes transferred in each interval is recorded, and the 95th-percentile of the distribution of recorded samples is used for billing. Thus, in a billing cycle of 30 days, 36 hours (5% of time) of the heaviest traffic is filtered out, and then the maximal traffic of the remaining 684 hours is used for billing. Usually, the downstream and upstream 95th-percentile are computed independently, and the lower value is neglected.

The 95th-percentile is also a good measure of how utilized the network is, and is often used as an indicator for dimensioning of infrastructure, whose cost is determined by the peak hour demand.

B. REFERENCES

[1] G. Biczok, S. Kardos, T. A. Trinh. "Pricing internet access for disloyal users: a game-theoretic analysis". In Proceedings of NetEcon 2008.

[2] B. Briscoe. "A Fairer, Faster Internet Protocol". IEEE Spectrum, Dec 2008.

[3] B. Briscoe. "Flow Rate Fairness: Dismantling a Religion". ACM Computer Communication Review vol. 37(2), 2007.

[4] K. Cho, K. Fukuda, H. Esaki, A. Kato. "The impact and implications of the growth in residential user-to-user traffic". In Proceedings of SIGCOMM 2006.

[5] K. Cho, K. Fukuda, H. Esaki, A. Kato. "Observing slow crustal movement in residential user traffic". In Proceedings of CoNEXT 2008.

[6] C. Courcoubetis, R. Weber. "Pricing communication networks". John Wiley and Sons, 2003.

[7] A. Dhamdhere, C. Dovrolis. "Can ISPs be profitable without violating "netwotk neutrality"?". In Proceedings of NetEcon 2008.

[8] X. Dimitropoulos, P. Hurley, A. Kind. M. Stoecklin "On the 95-percentile billing method". In Proceedings of PAM 2009.

[9] M. Dischinger et al. "Glasnost: Enabling End Users to Detect Traffic Differentiation". In Proceedings of NSDI 2010.

[10] D. Kim, S. Sra, I. S. Dhillon. "Fast Projection-Based Methods for the Least Squares Nonnegative Matrix Approximation Problem". Statistical Analysis and Data Mining, vol. 1(1), 2008.

[11] N. Laoutaris, P. Rodriguez. "Good Things Come to Those Who (Can) Wait – or how to handle Delay Tolerant traffic and make peace on the Internet". In Proceedings of ACM HotNets 2008.

[12] N. Laoutaris, G. Smaragdakis, P. Rodriguez, R. Sundaram. "Delay Tolerant Bulk Data Transfers on the Internet". In Proceedings of ACM SIGMETRICS 2009.

[13] R. T. B. Ma, D.M. Chiu, J. C. S. Lui, V. Misra, D. Rubenstein. "Internet economics: the use of Shapley value for ISP settlement". In Proceeding of CoNEXT 2007.

[14] R. T. B. Ma, D.M. Chiu, J. C. S. Lui, V. Misra, D. Rubenstein. "On cooperative settlement between content, transit and eyeball internet service providers.". In Proceeding of CoNEXT 2008.

[15] G. Maier, A. Feldmann, V. Paxson, M. Allman. "On dominant characteristics of residential broadband internet traffic". In Proceedings of IMC 2009.

[16] M.Marcon, M. Dischinger, K. P. Gummadi, A. Vahdat. "The Local and Global Effects of Traffic Shaping in the Internet". In Proceedings of SIGCOMM 2008.

[17] V. Misra, S. Ioannidis, A. Chaintreau, L. Massoulié. "Incentivizing Peer-Assisted Services: A Fluid Shapley Value Approach". In Proceedings of SIGMETRICS 2010.

[18] A. Odlyzko. "Internet pricing and the history of communications". Computer Networks, vol. 36, 2001.

[19] S.Shakkottai, R. Srikant, A. E. Ozdaglar, D. Acemoglu. "The Price of Simplicity". IEEE Journal on Selected Areas in Communications, vol 26(7), 2008.

[20] L. S. Shapley. "A Value for n-person Games". Annals of Mathematical Studies vol. 28, 1953.

[21] R. Stanojevic, N. Laoutaris, P. Rodriguez. "On Economic Heavy Hitters: Shapley value analysis of the 95th-percentile pricing. Technical report, available online: http://www.hamilton.ie/person/rade/TREHH.eps.

[22] R. Tongia. "Why is connectivity in developing regions expensive: policy challenges more than technical limitations?". In Proceedings of WWW 2006.

[23] E. Winter. "The Shapley Value". The Handbook of Game Theory, North-Holland, 2002.

Challenges in Measuring Online Advertising Systems

Saikat Guha
Microsoft Research India
Bangalore, India
saikat@microsoft.com

Bin Cheng, Paul Francis
Max Planck Institute for Software Systems
Kaiserslautern-Saarbruecken, Germany
{bcheng,francis}@mpi-sws.org

ABSTRACT

Online advertising supports many Internet services, such as search, email, and social networks. At the same time, there are widespread concerns about the privacy loss associated with user targeting. Yet, very little is publicly known about how ad networks operate, especially with regard to how they use user information to target users. This paper takes a first principled look at measurement methodologies for ad networks. It proposes new metrics that are robust to the high levels of noise inherent in ad distribution, identifies measurement pitfalls and artifacts, and provides mitigation strategies. It also presents an analysis of how three different classes of advertising — search, contextual, and social networks, use user profile information today.

Categories and Subject Descriptors

C.4 [**Performance of Systems**]: Measurement techniques; K.4.1 [**Computers and Society**]: Public Policy Issues—*Privacy*

General Terms

Experimentation, Measurement

Keywords

Advertising, Privacy, Behavioral Targeting, Contextual, Churn, Similarity, Google, Facebook

1. INTRODUCTION

Online advertising is a key economic driver in the Internet economy, funding a wide variety of websites and services. At the same time, ad networks gather a great deal of user information, for instance users' search histories, web browsing behaviors, online social networking profiles, and mobile locations [6–8]. As a result, there are widespread concerns about loss of user privacy. In spite of all this, very little is publicly known about how ad networks use user information to target ads to users. For instance, Google recently started allowing advertisers to target ads based not just on keywords and demographics, but on user interests as well [9]. Knowing how well Google and others are able to determine user characteristics is an important consideration in the ongoing public debate about user privacy.

If an ad network is able to accurately target users, we can deduce that the ad network is able to determine user characteristics (though the inverse does not follow). Given then the goal of determining how well ad networks can target users, the high-level methodology is straightforward. Create two clients that emulate different values of a given user characteristic (i.e. location or gender), and then measure whether the two clients receive different sets of ads as a result. If the ads are identical, we can trivially conclude the ad network doesn't use that user characteristic for targeting (although it might still be storing the data). But the outcome is unclear if the two sets are different: the difference may genuinely be due to the difference in characteristic, or it may be due to noise.

As it turns out, the level of noise in measuring ads is extremely high. Even queries launched simultaneously from two identically configured clients on the same subnet can produce wildly different ads over multiple timescales. As we show later, some of this noise is systemic (e.g. DNS load-balancing), and can therefore be eliminated through proper experiment design. Other noise has a temporal component, which likely reflects ad churn, the constant process of old ads being deactivated and new ads being activated. We design a metric that mitigates the noise from churn.

Overall this paper makes two contributions. First, we present the detailed design of a measurement methodology for measuring online advertising that is robust to the high levels of noise inherent in today's systems. We present a set of guidelines for researchers that wish to study advertising systems. Second, we present an analysis of the key factors that determine ad targeting on Google and on Facebook.

2. MEASUREMENT METHODOLOGY

In this section we present the detailed design of our measurement methodology. We face four key challenges: 1) comparing individual ads, 2) collecting a representative snapshot of ads, 3) quantifying differences between snapshots while being robust to noise, and 4) avoiding measurement artifacts arising from the experiment design.We present our design decisions and justify each using measurement data. The methodology we design applies to text-ads in any context including ads in search results, contextual ads on webpages

IMC'10, November 1–3, 2010, Melbourne, Australia.

Instance A:
Red Prom Dresses
Win a Free Dress for Prom 2010.
Find New Trends; Great Prices!
`DavidsProm.com`
MD5(RedirURL): 8ebc...45dc
Dest: ...detail.jsp?i=2462

Instance B:
Red Prom Dresses
Beautiful Designer Prom Dresses
to Fit Every Figure; Price Range.
`DavidsProm.com`
MD5(RedirURL): 3646...85d3
Dest: ...detail.jsp?i=2462

Instance C:
Baby Doll Prom Dresses
Win a Free Dress for Prom 2010.
Find New Trends; Great Prices!
`DavidsProm.com`
MD5(RedirURL): 99d0...f0bf
Dest: ...detail.jsp?i=2203

Instance D:
Red Prom Dresses
Shop JCPenney For Colorful Prom
Gowns; Dresses From Top Designers.
`JCPenney.com/dresses`
MD5(RedirURL): c12d...ce2c
Dest: ...X6.aspx?ItemId=17bd2fb

Table 1: Examples that complicate uniquely identifying ads.

and webmail systems, and ads on online social networking pages; additionally, many qualitative aspects of our design may also apply to banner ads.

2.1 Comparing Individual Ads

Before we can compare sets of ads, we first need the ability to identify the same ad in different scenarios. The problem is hard because ad networks typically do not reveal the unique ID for the ad (except for Facebook), and some (like Bing) even go so far as to obfuscate or encrypt parameters in the click URL denying scraping based measurement approaches any visibility into internal parameters. The only data available consistently across ad networks is the content of the ad, and even there the extensive abilities to customize it (e.g. for Google), makes it hard to identify different instances of the same ad. Since slight variations of the same ad defeat simple equality tests, heuristics must be used and their false positive and false negative behavior must be understood.

Consider, for example, the four ads illustrated in Table 1. Instances A and B are semantically equivalent, mutually exclusive (i.e. never both served for the same request), and lead to the same page on the advertiser's website (despite having different redirect URLs[1]). Instances A and C appear to be from the same template, but are semantically different and lead to different pages. Instances A and D are from different advertisers altogether.

Ideally, instances A and B would be considered equivalent, and different from both C and D. This cannot be achieved with simple equality tests on any single ad attribute (title, summary, display URL[1], redirect URL); other examples not presented here demonstrate the presence of false positives or false negatives for equality tests on combinations of attributes.

Experiment 1: Since comparison errors are unavoidable, we analyze false positives and false negatives of different approaches to comparing ads in order to pick the best approach as well as provide a bound on analysis errors. We consider 4 approaches: 1) equality of the redirect URL, 2) equality of the display URL, 3) equality of the ad title and display URL, and 4) equality of the ad title and summary text with all occurrences of the search keywords masked. Note: we cannot consider the destination URL for the ad since that is revealed only after the ad is clicked (and clicking on the ad in an automated matter constitutes fraud). We apply each approach to all pairs of ads in two datasets of ads scraped from Google search results. For estimating false positives, we manually check a sampling of pairs flagged as equal by the comparison approach. For false negatives, we manually check pairs flagged as different by the comparison approach; to focus manual analysis on pairs likely to be false negatives, we examine those flagged as equal by one of the other approaches, thus providing a lower bound. The first dataset contains ads for search queries related to fashion in general (clothing, shoes, accessories, etc.), while the second dataset restricts the queries to only dress-related.

[1]Display URL (e.g. `DavidsProm.com`) is the URL displayed to the user. Redirect URL (RedirURL), is the URL the user is actually redirected to when he clicks the ad. The redirect URL is longer and less user-friendly, containing deep path information and URL parameters. The destination URL (Dest) where the user is eventually taken to may be different from the redirect URL when multiple redirects are involved.

	All Fashion		Dresses only	
Approach	% FP	% FN	% FP	% FN
RedirURL	0	38	1	52
DisplayURL	7	13	12	10
Title + DisplayURL	0	45	0	50
Title + Summary	0	68	0	69

Table 2: False positives (FP) and false negatives (FN) of various approaches for uniquely identifying ads.

Table 2 summarizes the false positives and false negatives for each comparison approach based on manual analysis of 100 ad-pairs flagged by each approach. Except when comparing display URLs, there are (almost) no false positives. The false positives for display URLs arise from some stores using the same display URL for a wide range of products (e.g. `target.com` instead of `target.com/mens`). The display URL does, however, have significantly lower false negatives in both datasets. This is because advertisers often have multiple variations of the same ad. This includes different title, summary, and a different redirect URL to measure how each variation performs; comparing ads based on these is therefore more error prone. The display URL, in contrast, is more stable across variations of the same ad.

False negatives have the effect of over-counting the number of unique ads and in the process, increasing noise. False positives, on the other hand do not increase noise, but under-count the number of unique ads. In this paper we perform all analysis relative to a control experiment (affected equally by false positives or negatives) to mitigate the effect of over-counting or under-counting. This leaves added noise (for false negatives) as the only differentiating factor. In this paper we therefore use the display URL, which has significantly lower false negatives and slightly higher false positives, to compute uniqueness of ads.

2.2 Taking a Snapshot

There typically are more ads than can be displayed on a single page (search result, or adbox in a webpage). A single query therefore reveals incomplete information. The actual subset returned depends on the ad network, but likely takes into account the ad value (based on auctions), and frequency capping (not showing the same ad to the same user too often). Reloading the page multiple times typically reveals more ads, but runs the risk of capturing inaccurate snapshots in the presence of ad churn.

Experiment 2: To determine how many times the page should be reloaded to capture accurate and complete snapshots we perform the following experiment. We reload the Google search results for a given query every 5 seconds for 5 minutes; the experiment is repeated for over 200 different

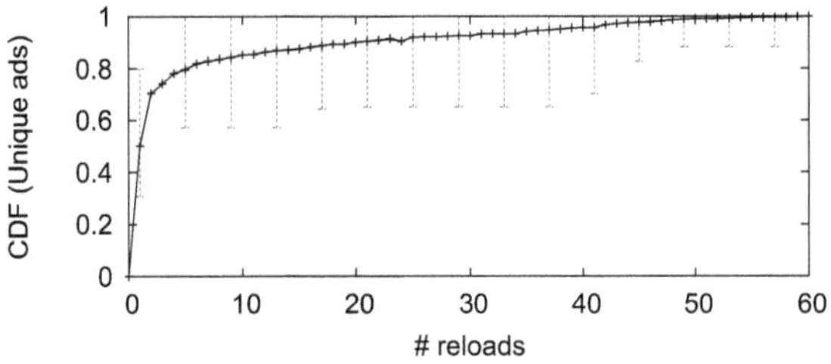

Figure 1: Reloading the page initially reveals more ads that didn't originally fit. Beyond a point, however, ad churn overtakes diminishing returns of reloading the page. 95-5 error bars.

search queries (chosen randomly from a set of 5000 keywords scraped from Google Product Search[2]).

Figure 1 plots the CDF of unique ads for the median search query, with error bars marking off the 95th and 5th percentiles. The graph comprises a steep increase (5 reloads) where we discover most ads that didn't fit the first time, after which point diminishing return kicks in. Instead of flattening out, however, beyond 10 requests the graph becomes linear. This gradual linear increase, we believe, is evidence of a constant rate of ad churn where new ads are constantly activated and old ones deactivated. The high rate of churn (1–4% per minute depending on the search keyword) is consistent with [5] where we found that roughly only 60% of ads are stable (hour-to-hour, and day-to-day) while the rest change rapidly. The knee of the graph (around 10 reloads) represents the point at which the diminishing returns of reloading the page is overtaken by ad churn.

In our experiments we therefore balance completeness and churn by reloading the page 10 times when collecting snapshots. We also keep track of the number of times each ad was seen (if multiple reloads contain the ad) and the positions where the ad was seen.

2.3 Quantifying Change

The simplest approach to comparing two snapshots is to compute the set overlap. The Jaccard index quantifies this overlap as $\frac{|A \cap B|}{|A \cup B|}$ where A and B are the sets of unique ads in the two snapshots; 0 implies no overlap and 1 implies identical snapshots. While simple, the Jaccard index is highly susceptible to noise (fleeting ads); each unique ad is weighed equally whether it was seen only once or seen many times. The typical way of dealing with noise is to look at aggregate behavior. Taking the union of multiple snapshots, however, makes the situation worse by also aggregating the noise.

The extended Jaccard index (also called cosine similarity) addresses this limitation by interpreting the two sets as vectors in n-dimensional space (where each set element defines one dimension), and the coefficient of the vector in that dimension is some weight function (w) based on the element. The metric is defined as $\frac{\bar{A} \cdot \bar{B}}{\|\bar{A}\| \|\bar{B}\|}$ where $\bar{A} = [w_{A,e}]$; $w_{A,e}$ is some non-zero weight if ad e exists in A, or 0 if it doesn't. As before, the metric evaluates to 0 for dissimilar snapshots, and to 1 for identical snapshots. We explore three approaches to picking the non-zero weight: 1) the number of page reloads containing the ad, 2) the logarithm of the same, and 3) the number of page reloads scaled by the "value" of the ad; the value, defined in [4], is based on the ad's position with ads near the top of the page getting more weight than those near the bottom. By taking the number of times the ad was seen into account, each weight function also effectively attenuates noise when snapshots are aggregated together.

[2] `http://www.google.com/products`

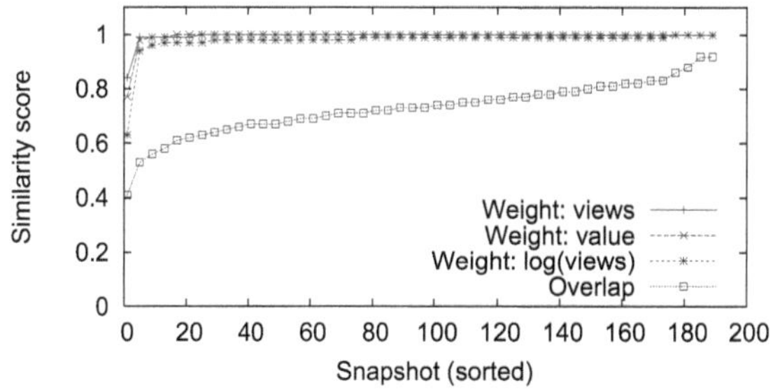

(a) Identical setup (higher is better)

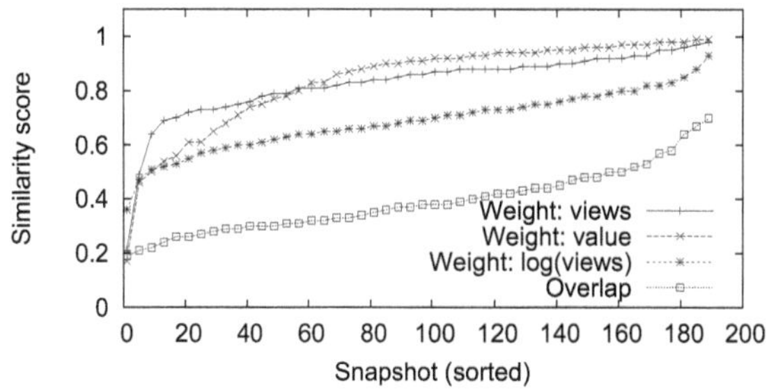

(b) Different setup (lower is better)

Figure 2: CDF of similarity scores computed by the four metrics tracked over 8 days.

Experiment 3: To determine which approach performs the best we conducted the following experiment. We simultaneously collect snapshots from two browser instances configured identically and on the same machine (in New York); we expect the snapshots to be substantially the same. We also simultaneously collect snapshots from a machine set up at a remote location (in San Francisco) where we expect to see some differences in the set of ads. Snapshots (for 15 queries) are collected every 5 minutes for a period of 8 days. We then aggregate 1 hour's worth of data (12 snapshots) and compare the performance of all four metrics: the Jaccard index, and the extended Jaccard index with the three weight functions.

Figure 2(a) plots the CDF of the computed metric value for the case where we expect snapshots to be identical; the closer to $y = 1$ the better. As expected, the plain Jaccard index performs poorly. The other three perform quite well, with the logarithmic weight function trailing slightly due to the reduced influence of highly-stable ads. Figure 2(b) plots the CDF for the case where we expect snapshots to be different; the greater the difference between the corresponding lines between 2(a) and 2(b) the better. The logarithmic weight clearly outperforms the other two here. This is because for the other two weight functions, and especially so for weights based on the ad value, the long tail of ads is drowned out by a handful of highly-stable highly-ranked ads, which tend to be from large companies (e.g. eBay, Amazon) that target broadly across many demographics, interests, and locations.

In our analysis we use the extended Jaccard index with logarithmic weights to quantify the similarity or difference between snapshots. The metric in practice is both robust to

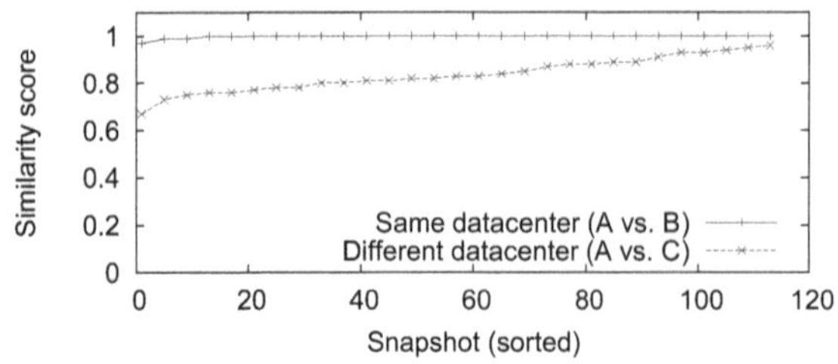

Figure 3: Artifact of DNS load-balancing by ad network.

noise, as well as sensitive to changes in the underlying set of ads.

2.4 Avoiding Artifacts

During the course of our experiments we identified several measurement artifacts that stemmed from poor interactions between lower level protocols and the operational architecture of the ad network. We discuss two artifacts and how they can be eliminated: the first pertains to DNS load-balancing, and the second to distributed data collection from multiple machines.

In one case we observed discrepancies between data collected by three identically configured browser instances all running on the same machine. Snapshots for the first two browser instances (A and B) are virtually identical, while that for the third instance (C) is very different (Figure 3). We discovered the ad network domain is DNS load-balanced and the browsers did not share a DNS cache (and therefore each queried DNS independently). Instance A and B were communicating with different IP addresses in the same /24 (same city), while C was communicating with an IP address in the same /16 but different /24 (different nearby city), which we take to mean two different datacenters. Thus even for identical requests from the same source, the choice of datacenter, we found, dramatically affects the ads served. This artifact is, of course, easily avoided by configuring a static entry in the hosts file so all instances reach the same datacenter.

Even with static DNS entries, we sometimes (but not always) observed discrepancies when running identical browser instances on different machines. The 5th percentile similarity score dropped to 0.87 for different machines (compared to 0.99 in the same-machine case). We noticed the cookies assigned to the two instances were different; when we synchronized the cookie values, the noise disappeared. In another case, we measured similar levels of noise when we added a HTTP proxy in front of the two machines (which downgraded HTTP/1.1 to 1.0). We believe these artifacts are because of black-box frontend load-balancer behavior at the ad network that, based on at least the IP address, HTTP version, and cookies, we suspect, directs the requests to different backend servers, each of which has a slightly different cache of ads. The only way to mitigate this source of noise, we believe, is to ensure as many header fields are held constant as possible. Ideally, traces for an experiment are all collected from a single IP address, not behind a proxy, with cookies synchronized across browser instances.

Applying these techniques significantly reduces the base noise level, but does not eliminate it. We therefore measure the noise during our experiments to detect anomalies and to establish a level of confidence in our results.

3. ANALYSIS

In this section we use the above methodology to explore specific questions regarding how ads are targeted in three different contexts: search, websites, and online social networks. These questions include, among others, whether behavioral targeting affects search ads, whether past searches affect ads on websites, and what profile data affects social network ads. That said, since ad targeting is a black-box where we can reliably control only a small set of inputs, we are restricted in the questions we can answer. An example of a question we cannot answer is whether Google learns the user's gender by observing which search results the user clicks and then uses it to target ads; this is because we cannot reliably affect or verify the gender learned by Google's (black-box) algorithm if it indeed does so at all.

For questions where we can reliably affect the inputs to the ad selection algorithm, our experimental methodology is as follows. For each experiment we configure two (or more) measurement instances to differ by exactly one input parameter, and configure two measurement instances identically to serve as the noise-level control. If the similarity score between the control pair is high (i.e. low noise) but that between two differently configured instances is low, we conclude that the input parameter in which the two instances differ affects the choice of ads. For scalability and repeatability, all experiments are scripted using the Chickenfoot browser automation framework [2].

3.1 Search Ads

Search ads have typically been targeted based on keywords in the search query. It is therefore expected that keyword based targeting dominates search. The question we ask is: to what extent does behavioral targeting affect search ads? Behavioral targeting refers to using the user's browsing habits to influence ad selection.

Experiment 4: We set up four browser instances: the first two (A and B), which also serve as our control, disable DoubleClick's DART cookie [3] that Google uses for behavioral targeting. The third (C) and fourth (D) have cookies enabled, but are seeded with different user personae[3]. C was seeded with long-term interests in 'Autos & Vehicles', while D was seeded with interests in 'Shopping'. We then perform Google searches for 730 random product-related queries for a period of 5 days.

Figure 4(a) illustrates to what extent behavioral targeting affected search ads. As is evident from the figure, for keywords where the data is not too noisy (i.e. control score is high), there is no appreciable difference in the ads served whether the behavioral targeting cookie is disabled or enabled (A vs. C), or for two users with different interests (C vs. D). To understand why, we looked at the ads served. 73% of them contained the whole search query somewhere in the ad, and 97% of them contained at least one word from the search query. It is therefore clear that ads are selected primarily based on keywords. Furthermore the average number of unique ads for our search queries is 8. Since all the ads matching the keyword can be shown to the user in a

[3]Google normally learns short-term and long-term user interests completely automatically. It also allows users to view and modify the learned interests (`http://www.google.com/ads/preferences`), which we use to create (or verify Google learned) different personae.

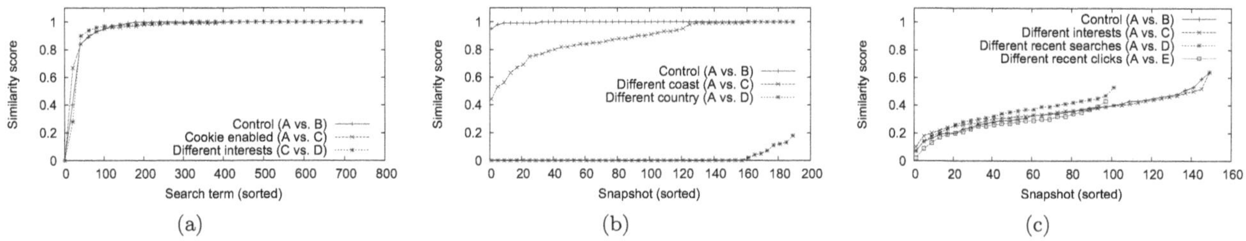

Figure 4: (a) Behavioral targeting doesn't appear to affect search ads. (b) Location affects website ads. (c) The affect of user behavior (browsing, search, clicks) on website ads is indistinguishable from noise in the system.

short period, there may be little reason to pick and choose any further.

3.2 Website Ads

Website ads have typically been based on the context of the page and are hence also known as contextual advertising. We ask here to what extent the user's location affects the choice of ads, and to what extent the user's behavior (browsing behavior, recent searches, and recent clicks on products) affects website ads. We measure a set of 15 websites that show Google ads; the websites are picked randomly from the set of websites visited by CoDeeN [1] users. While we are able to answer the location question, we are able to present only weak evidence towards the lack of use of behavioral data due to noise.

Experiment 5: To understand the impact of user location, we set up four browsers: A and B, the control pair, in the same city in the US (New York), C in a different city on the other coast (San Francisco), and E in a different country (Germany).

Figure 4(b) plots the similarity scores between the different instances. As one might expect, location affects the set of ads, but interestingly, there is (relatively) little difference between cities on opposite coasts (median similarity of 0.9). This is higher than we expected given the long-tail of ads appears to contain local mom-and-pop retailers, although in retrospect, these retailers may nevertheless conduct business nation wide.

Experiment 6: To understand the effect of user behavior, we set up five browsers: instance A and B, the control pair, are configured identically except for the cookie that is needed for tracking user behavior. For C we browse 3 out of the 15 websites in the query set until Google learns the set of long-interests associated with those websites (which we verified[3]). For D and E we additionally browse random websites and perform Google searches on 50 product-related keywords shortly before collecting each snapshot (but don't click any result for D); we verified[3] that Google learned short-term interests for the random websites visited. Finally, for E we additionally click on product results before collecting each snapshot.

Figure 4(c) plots the similarity score between A and the other instances. While at first glance it might appear that browsing behavior, recent searches, and recent product clicks all result in different sets of ads, the problem is that even for the control pair similarity is very low — indicative of high levels of noise. We compared the fraction of ads shown to A and D that contained one or more of the search query terms and found no difference. The same held for ads containing the interests associated with instance C, and product names or categories used for instance E. We therefore believe that Google does not currently use recent browsing, search, or click behavior in picking website ads, but due to the high noise cannot definitively make the case for it.

That said, the measurement methodology developed here will allow us to monitor the evolution of these systems. As to the origin of the noise, we speculate this is because contextual ad systems have not yet been optimized for relevancy to the same extent as search ad systems, especially considering Google started collecting this data only since 2009 [9]. As contextual ad targeting improves over time, we expect the similarity score of the control pair to increase, and depending on whether the score for various user behaviors stay the same or increase in the future, we hope to conclude with certainty whether or not they are used.

3.3 Online Social Network Ads

We next turn our attention to ads on online social networking sites, specifically Facebook. We seek to understand which pieces of profile information (gender, age, education, sexual-preference, etc.) Facebook uses today.

Experiment 7: We set up three (or more) Facebook profiles: profile A and B are set up identically (control), while profile C onwards differ from A in the value of the profile parameter of interest; the number of unique profiles depends on the number of values that parameter can take (e.g. 2 for gender, 5 for education, etc.) When not being varied, the gender was set to female, the age was set to 30, the location was set to New York, and the remaining fields were left empty.

Figure 5 plots the time-series of similarity scores for six different profile parameters. In short, Facebook uses all profile elements we checked. All the plots show some sort of diurnal behavior where around midnight US east-coast time the similarity score changes abruptly. Similar diurnal artifacts were observed in [5], and as in that paper, we believe the cause is the daily reactivation of ads that exhausted their daily budget the previous day. On the issue of profile elements, it appears that the two primary factors affecting ads are the user's age and their gender. While there exist values for education and relationship status that affect ads shown, not all values affect ads equally. For instance, there is little difference between ads targeted to users without any listed education and users in high-school. Similarly, if the gender is male, or the relationship-status is married, relationship-status has only a small impact on ads; the greatest impact of relationship-status on ads is seen for women who are engaged.

Experiment 8: Lastly, we set up six Facebook profiles to check the impact of sexual-preference: a highly-sensitive personal attribute. Two profiles (male control) are for males interested in females, two (female control) for females inter-

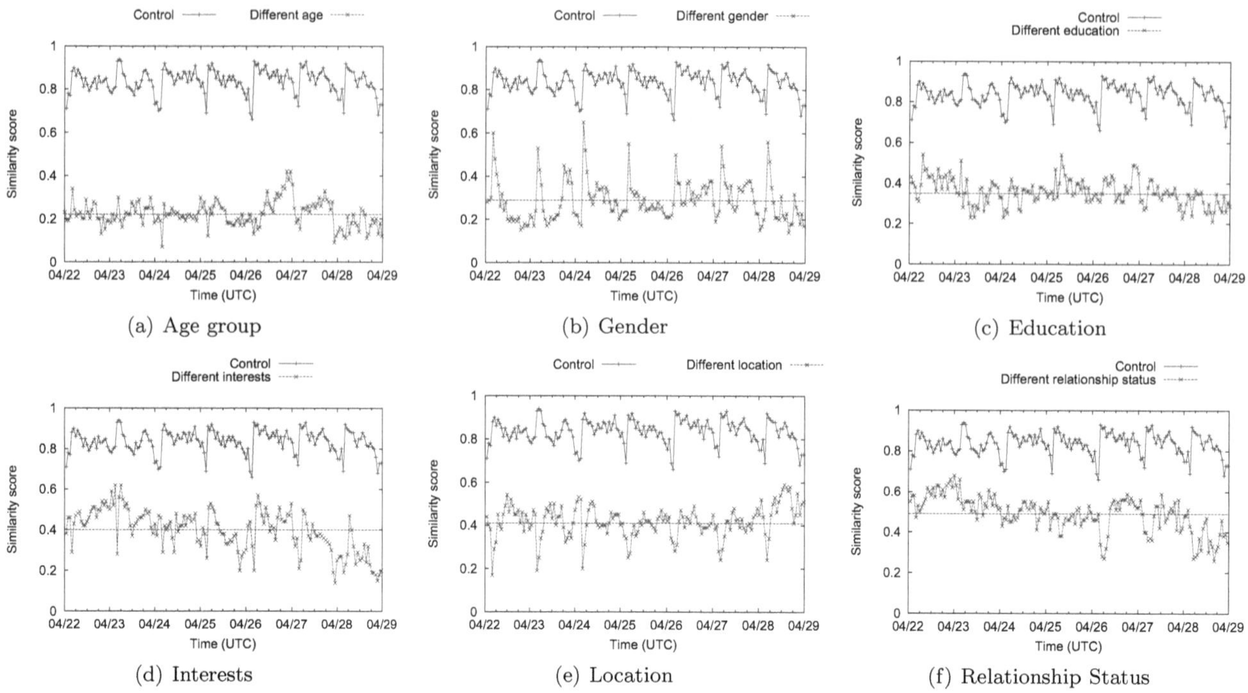

(a) Age group (b) Gender (c) Education

(d) Interests (e) Location (f) Relationship Status

Figure 5: Age group, gender, education, interests, location and relationship-status all appear to affect ads on Facebook

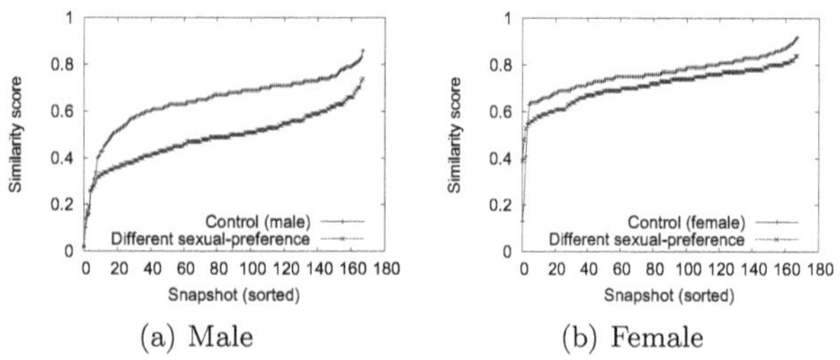

(a) Male (b) Female

Figure 6: Sexual-preference affects ads on Facebook, but more so for males than females.

ested in males, and one test profile of a male interested in males and one of a female interested in females. The age and location were set to 25 and Washington D.C. respectively.

Figure 6 plots the similarity scores for 1 week of data. While there is more noise in general, unlike in 4(c) there is a measurable difference between the control and test pairs; we further manually verified based on ad content that this difference is qualitative in nature (e.g. ads for gay bars were never shown for the control profiles, but shown often for the test profiles). The median similarity score for gay women was 0.15 higher than for gay men, indicating that advertisers target more strongly to the latter demographic.

Alarmingly, we found ads where the ad text was completely neutral to sexual-preference (e.g. for a nursing degree in a medical college in Florida) that was targeted *exclusively* to gay men. The danger with such ads, unlike the gay bar ad where the target demographic is blatantly obvious, is that the user reading the ad text would have *no idea* that by clicking it he would reveal to the advertiser both his sexual-preference and a unique identifier (cookie, IP address, or email address if he signs up on the advertiser's site). Furthermore, such deceptive ads are not uncommon; indeed exactly half of the 66 ads shown exclusively to gay men (more than 50 times) during our experiment did not mention "gay" anywhere in the ad text.

Overall we find that while location affects Google ads, behavioral targeting does not today appear to significantly affect either search or website ads on Google. Location, user demographics and interests, and sexual-preference all affect Facebook ads. As these systems evolve, our methodology can track changes in their use of user data. We thus inform, and hope to keep informed, the ongoing public debate about user privacy.

4. RELATED WORK

There is little past work in studying ad networks through measurement. In [5] we presented an ad hoc measurement result for Google ads, however, based on our experience presented here, we now believe that result significantly underestimated the number of ads and didn't properly account for noise.

5. SUMMARY

We have presented the first principled and robust methodology for measurement-based studies of online ad networks. We also inform the ongoing privacy debate regarding what user data is used today for targeting search ads, contextual ads, and ads on online social networks. Like most measurement studies, however, this analysis is a snapshot in time. Moving forwards, we hope that the methodology we have developed can continue to be used to broaden our knowledge of online advertising as well as to track trends in the future.

6. REFERENCES

[1] CoDeeN: A Content Distribution Network for PlanetLab. `http://codeen.cs.princeton.edu/`.

[2] M. Bolin, M. Webber, P. Rha, T. Wilson, and R. C. Miller. Automation and Customization of Rendered Web Pages. In *Proceedings of The Eighteenth Annual ACM Symposium on User Interface Software and Technology (UIST '05)*, Seattle, WA, Oct. 2005.

[3] DoubleClick. DART for Advertisers. `http://www.doubleclick.com/products/dfa/index.aspx`, 2009.

[4] J. Feng, H. K. Bhargava, and D. M. Pennock. Implementing Sponsored Search in Web Search Engines: Computational Evaluation of Alternative Mechanisms. *INFORMS Journal on Computing*, 19(1):137–148, Jan. 2007.

[5] S. Guha, A. Reznichenko, K. Tang, H. Haddadi, and P. Francis. Serving Ads from `localhost` for Performance, Privacy, and Profit. In *Proceedings of the 8th Workshop on Hot Topics in Networks (HotNets '09)*, New York, NY, Oct. 2009.

[6] B. Krishnamurthy and C. Wills. On the Leakage of Personally Identifiable Information Via Online Social Networks. In *Proceedings of The Seconds ACM SIGCOMM Workshop on Online Social Networks (WOSN '09)*, Barcelona, Spain, Aug. 2009.

[7] B. Krishnamurthy and C. Wills. Privacy Leakage in Mobile Online Social Networks. In *Proceedings of The Third Workshop on Online Social Networks (WOSN '10)*, Boston, MA, June 2010.

[8] B. Krishnamurthy and C. E. Wills. Cat and Mouse: Content Delivery Tradeoffs in Web Access. In *Proceedings of the 15th international conference on World Wide Web (WWW '06)*, Edinburgh, Scotland, 2006.

[9] Kurt Opsahl. Google Begins Behavioral Targeting Ad Program. `http://www.eff.org/deeplinks/2009/03/google-begins-behavioral-targeting-ad-program`, Mar. 2009.

Measurement of Loss Pairs in Network Paths

Edmond W. W. Chan[‡], Xiapu Luo[§], Weichao Li[‡], Waiting W. T. Fok[‡], and Rocky K. C. Chang[‡]
Department of Computing[‡]
The Hong Kong Polytechnic University
{cswwchan|cswcicli|cswtfok|csrchang}@comp.polyu.edu.hk
College of Computing[§]
Georgia Institute of Technology
csxpluo@cc.gatech.edu

ABSTRACT

Loss-pair measurement was proposed a decade ago for discovering network path properties, such as a router's buffer size. A packet pair is regarded as a loss pair if exactly one packet is lost. Therefore, the residual packet's delay can be used to infer the lost packet's delay. Despite this unique advantage shared by no other methods, no loss-pair measurement in actual networks has ever been reported. In this paper, we further develop the loss-pair measurement and make the following contributions. First, we characterize the residual packet's delay by including other important factors (such as the impact of the first packet in the pair) which were ignored before. Second, we employ a novel TCP-based probing method to measure from a single endpoint all four possible loss pairs for a round-trip network path. Third, we conducted loss-pair measurement for 88 round-trip paths continuously for almost three weeks. Being the first set of loss-pair measurement, we obtained a number of original results, such as prevalence of loss pairs, distribution of different types of loss pairs, and effect of route change on the paths' congestion state.

Categories and Subject Descriptors

C.2.3 [**Computer-Communication Networks**]: Network Operations; C.4 [**Performance of Systems**]: Measurement Techniques

General Terms

Experimentation, Measurement, Performance

Keywords

Loss pair, Packet pair, Non-cooperative, Delay

1. INTRODUCTION

Packet loss behavior in network paths has been extensively studied for the last twenty years. Most of the efforts focus on packet losses as a result of router congestion. The packet loss behavior has been characterized by loss rates, loss stationarity [53], loss episodes [53, 47], and loss correlation [52, 37]. Both active (e.g., ZING [4], Sting [44], Badabing [46, 47], OneProbe [33], and Queen [50]) and passive (e.g., [5, 39]) measurement methods have been proposed for measuring losses on end-to-end paths. For active methods, the probing process is an important consideration for minimizing measurement errors [6, 48, 7]. Moreover, various tomography techniques have been proposed for measuring packet losses on the link level [13, 17, 15].

Besides the packet loss measurement, it is also useful to study the correlation between loss and other important metrics. However, the correlation problem has so far received much less attention. A notable exception is using a packet pair to correlate a packet loss event and the delay that would have been experienced by the lost packet. A *packet pair* is referred to as a *loss pair* [31, 30] if exactly one packet (the first or second) in the pair is lost. If the two packets traverse the path close to each other, then the residual packet's delay can be used to infer the lost packet's delay. The loss-pair analysis was originally motivated by the problem of estimating buffer size of the congested node responsible for dropping the packet. Other possible applications of the lost-pair measurement include characterizing packet dropping behavior [31], classifying the type of packet loss [32], detecting dominant congestion links [51], and detecting common congestion points [21, 41].

Although loss pairs could be considered rare events in typical network paths, they can be detected by many existing measurement methods without extra cost. For example, the path capacity measurement methods, such as [42, 16, 26, 11], send a sequence of packet pairs to capture the packet dispersion from the bottleneck link. But they usually discard the loss pairs, which fail to provide the dispersion information. Other measurement methods for packet loss (e.g., [44, 35]), packet reordering (e.g., [34, 8]), Internet traffic characterization (e.g., [12]), and path fingerprinting (e.g., [45]) also send packet pairs for their measurement. Therefore, loss-pair measurement is considered a bonus feature for these tools, and the previously regarded useless probes can now be exploited for discovering additional path properties.

However, loss pairs have not been reported in actual network path measurement. In [31, 32, 30], only ns-2 simulation and emulated testbed experiments were performed to evaluate the effectiveness of using loss pairs to measure path properties. As a result, the behavior of loss pairs in Internet paths is largely unknown. Moreover, some important delay components, such as the impact of the first packet on the second, have not been taken into consideration. In this paper, we revisit the loss-pair measurement method and make three main contributions:

1. Delay characterization We conducted a more detailed analysis for the residual packets' delays by including the impacts of cross traffic and the first packet. The new analysis invalidates the previous claim that the first and second residual packets give the same result [31, 30]. We instead show that using the first packet's delay is generally more accurate than the second packet's delay on inferring the congested router's queueing delay upon packet loss. Moreover, we show that the delay variation of the first and second residual packets can be used to estimate the link capacity of a hop preceding the congested router.

2. Method for measuring loss pairs We exploited OneProbe's capability [33] of detecting path events from a single endpoint to measure all four possible loss pairs on a round-trip path: two for the forward path and the other two for the reverse path. To the best of our knowledge, OneProbe is the first non-cooperative method capable of performing comprehensive loss-pair measurement. Previous loss-pair measurement considered only two possible loss pairs on a round-trip path [31, 30]. We also utilized OneProbe's facility of packet size configuration to validate that a smaller packet size generally increases the accuracy of delay inference.

3. Loss-pair measurement in the Internet We conducted loss-pair measurement using HTTP/OneProbe (an OneProbe implementation based on HTTP/1.1 [19]) for 88 round-trip paths between eight universities in Hong Kong and 11 PlanetLab nodes located at eight countries. Our measurement shows that loss pairs were prevalent in the packet pairs that suffered packet loss, and a loss-pair analysis can help infer additional properties about the lossy paths. Besides, we show that loss pairs' delays provide path signatures for correlating multiple path measurements.

In §2, we first discuss previous works related to this paper. In §3, we review the loss-pair measurement method and describe how OneProbe detects the loss-pair events. In §4, we analyze the residual packets' delays and relate the results to the problem of estimating the queueing delay at the congested router upon packet drop. In §5, we report our findings of measuring 88 paths continuously for almost three weeks. In §6, we conclude this paper with a few potential directions to extend this work.

2. RELATED WORK

The notion of packet pair was first defined in [24] as a pair of back-to-back packets of the same size dispatched by a source to a destination. Each packet arrived at the destination is acknowledged by an acknowledgement packet, which travels along a returning path back to the source. Assuming that the pair traverses the path close to each other, they may observe similar states of the congested hop before a packet is discarded. Therefore, the residual packet in the loss pair has been used to estimate the packet dropping mechanism of the congested hop governed by various active queue management schemes (e.g., droptail, RED [20], and BLUE [18]) and a droptail queue's buffer size [31], and to classify the causes for packet loss [32]. In this paper, we analyze the accuracy of two possible residual packets' delays for inferring the network path properties.

Previous studies used packet pairs to measure various path performance metrics, including packet reordering [34, 8], packet loss [44, 35], available bandwidth [36, 23], and capacity [10, 43, 16, 26]. The pioneer work by Keshav [28] exploited the dispersion of a packet pair to measure the capacity of rate allocating servers. The packet-pair dispersion observed from the destination contains the latency of the packet pair after leaving the bottleneck link. Pásztor and Veitch [38] analyzed several types of components embedded in the packet-pair dispersion. On the other hand, Bolot [9] relied on the queueing of the first packet in a packet pair at the bottleneck hop to measure the bottleneck link's capacity. MultiQ [27] exploited the congestion experienced by packet pairs to infer the capacity of congested links. In this paper, we propose a method of estimating the capacity of a network link preceding the congested hop based on the two residual packets' delays.

A number of methods were proposed for monitoring congested network links, including Pathload [25] and Pong [14] that detect network congestions by observing increasing queueing delays of its probe packets. Besides, various methods [41, 21, 51] were proposed to detect the shared network congestion point in the paths. However, these methods were evaluated based on either simulation or cooperative measurement. In this paper, by using OneProbe's probing technique [33], our loss-pair measurement and analysis can infer the packet loss behavior for both forward and reverse paths in a non-cooperative manner and identify artifacts, such as packet reordering, that may affect the measurement results.

3. ACTIVE LOSS-PAIR MEASUREMENT

In loss-pair measurement, a source node sends a sequence of *probe pairs*, each pair consisting of two back-to-back probe packets, to a destination node. The possible delivery statuses of a probe pair are `00` (both received), `01` (only the first is received), `10` (only the second is received), or `11` (none is received). The cases of `01` and `10` are referred to as *loss pairs* in [31]. Moreover, the destination node may be induced to send a sequence of *response pairs*, each pair consisting of two back-to-back response packets, to the source node. There are four similar delivery statuses for each response pair. As a result, there are generally four possible loss pairs for a round-trip path: `P10` and `P01` for a probe pair, and `R10` and `R01` for a response pair.

Both passive and active methods could be used for measuring loss pairs. An active loss-pair measurement of a path can be performed on both endpoints of the path or from only a single endpoint. In this section, we use OneProbe [33] to illustrate how the four types of loss pairs can be measured from only one endpoint. We also deployed HTTP/OneProbe [33] to measure loss pairs on Internet paths, and the results will be presented in §5.

OneProbe sends a sequence of probe pairs, each consisting of two TCP data packets, to a remote server. If both packets are received in the same order, each packet elicits a response TCP packet, thus returning a response pair. Even if one or more probe packets is lost, at least one response TCP packet will be elicited immediately. Moreover, by predetermining the number, types, and order of the response packets elicited under each delivery status (`00`, `01`, `10`, or `11`) of the probe pair, OneProbe can distinguish the delivery statuses for both probe and response pairs just based on the elicited response packets. Figure 1(a) shows two cases. For those marked by '✓', OneProbe can simultaneously detect the probe pair's

	R00	R10	R01	R11
P00	✓	✓	✓	✓
P10	✓	✓	✓	✓
P01	–	–	–	–
P11	–	–	–	–

(a) The delivery statuses.

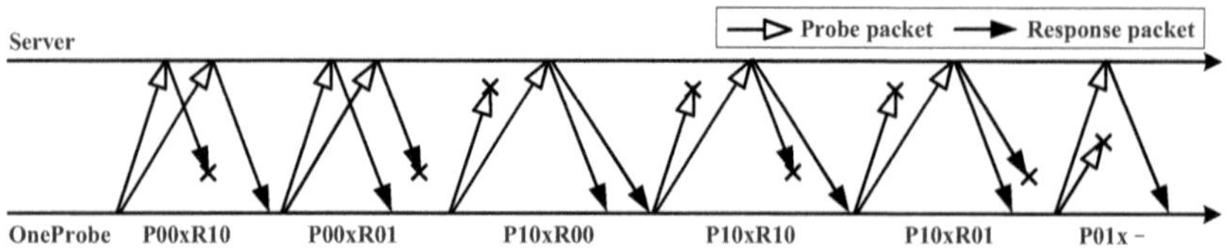

(b) The six loss-pair events.

Figure 1: The delivery statuses of probe and response pairs and six loss-pair events measured by OneProbe.

and response pair's delivery statuses. For those marked by '–', OneProbe can only detect the probe pair's status, because at most one response packet can be elicited for those cases.

Six cases in Figure 1(a) involve at least one loss pair, and they are illustrated in Figure 1(b). For P00 and P10, two response packets can be elicited from the server. As a result, OneProbe can detect the forward-path and reverse-path loss pairs at the same time. However, in the absence of a response pair, OneProbe can detect only the forward-path loss pair for P01. Furthermore, packet reordering does not affect the loss-pair measurement, because OneProbe can also identify from the response packets end-to-end packet ordering events for the probe and response pairs.

4. ANALYSIS OF LOSS PAIRS' DELAYS

Since a packet pair's delay is used for inferring path properties, in this section we analyze the first and second packets' delay, and their difference. In the following analysis, we consider the four loss-pair events (P10xR00, P01x–, P00xR10, and P00xR01) for which a loss pair exists in only one unidirectional path, and a similar analysis can be performed for the other events. To simplify the notations, we also use LP_{10} to denote a loss pair with the delivery status 10 (i.e., P10xR00 and P00xR10), and LP_{01} to denote that with the status 01 (i.e., P01x– and P00xR01).

After presenting the network models in §4.1, we first derive in §4.2 the residual packets' delays in the LP_{10} and LP_{01}, taking into consideration the queueing delay at all hops. In §4.3, we then extend the analysis to the problem of using the delay to characterize the congested node's queueing delay upon packet drops. Finally in §4.4, we show that the LP_{10}'s and LP_{01}'s delays can be utilized to estimate the capacity of a link preceding the congested node.

4.1 Network models

Consider a sequence of probe pairs dispatched on a network path of n hops (where $n \geq 1$) which also admits other cross traffic. The network path is assumed unchanged throughout the measurement. Each hop in the path consists of a store-and-forward node and its outgoing link connecting to the next hop. We use $H^{(h)}$ to denote the hth hop that transmits (i.e., serializes) packets to the outgoing link with capacity of $C^{(h)}$ bits/s. Each node is configured with a drop-tail queue which is modeled as a single-server queue with a buffer size of $B^{(h)}$ bits for $H^{(h)}$ and a First-Come-First-Serve (FCFS) queueing discipline. For convenience, we label the hops on the path sequentially, starting from 1 at the source node. The n-hop network path can be either a one-way path (forward path) depicted in Figure 2(a) or a round-trip path (forward path and reverse path) in Figure 2(b) in which the destination node is located at $H^{(m+1)}$, $1 \leq m < n$.

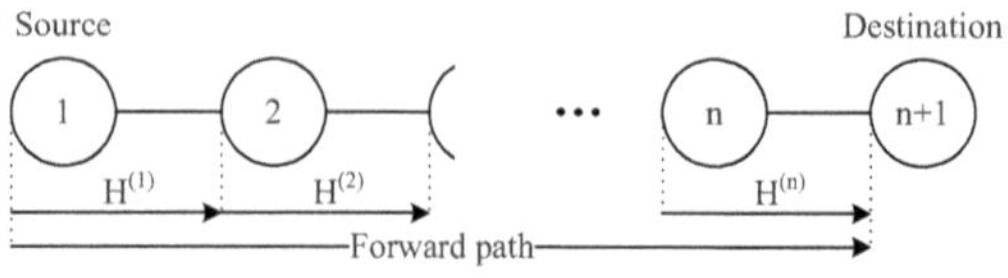

(a) One-way path.

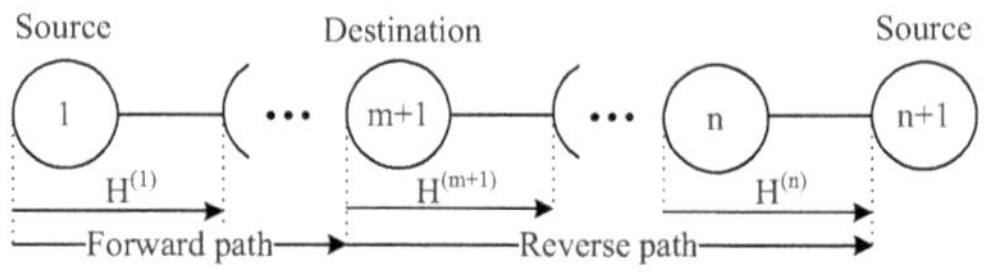

(b) Round-trip path.

Figure 2: Two models for the loss-pair analysis.

We use $\{p_{j-1}, p_j\}$, $j = 2i, i = 1, 2, \ldots$, to denote the ith probe pair with p_{j-1} being the first packet in the pair. Each probe packet is of S bits long, including the IP header. Therefore, sending a probe packet on $H^{(h)}$ incurs at least a packet transmission delay of $X^{(h)}$ $(= S/C^{(h)})$ and a constant propagation delay denoted by $T^{(h)}$. Besides, adjacent probe pairs are assumed to be sufficiently spaced out, so that a packet is never queued behind the preceding packet pair, and the probe packets are not out-of-ordered due to the FCFS queueing discipline. In the case of round-trip path, we also make similar assumptions for the response packet pairs. Moreover, we use the same notations and packet size for the response pairs to simplify our ensuing discussion. However, the analysis can be easily adapted to different probe and response packet sizes.

We start the analysis by considering the total delay for p_j to traverse the first h hops of the path, denoted by $d_j^{(h)}$, $h = 0, 1, \ldots, n$, and $d_j^{(0)} = 0$. We also let $t_j^{(h)}$, $h = 1, \ldots, n+1$, be the time for p_j's to fully arrive (including the last bit of the packet) at $H^{(h)}$. Therefore,

$$\begin{aligned} d_j^{(h)} &= t_j^{(h+1)} - t_j^{(1)}, \\ &= d_j^{(h-1)} + \left(w_j^{(h)} + X^{(h)} + T^{(h)}\right), \end{aligned} \qquad (1)$$

where $w_j^{(h)}$ is the queueing delay experienced at $H^{(h)}$. The recursive expression in Eqn. (1) also applies to p_{j-1} after updating the subscripts.

Moreover, we can relate $d_j^{(h)}$ and $d_{j-1}^{(h)}$ as

$$\begin{aligned} d_j^{(h)} &= \left(t_j^{(h+1)} - t_{j-1}^{(h+1)}\right) + \left(t_{j-1}^{(h+1)} - t_{j-1}^{(1)}\right), \\ &= \tau_{j-1,j}^{(h+1)} + d_{j-1}^{(h)}. \end{aligned} \qquad (2)$$

where $\tau_{j-1,j}^{(h+1)}$ is the $\{p_{j-1}, p_j\}$'s inter-arrival time at $H^{(h+1)}$.

4.2 Analyzing the residual packets' delays

In the following, we consider a packet in $\{p_{j-1}, p_j\}$ being dropped at $H^{(h')}$ and the other packet delivered successfully. Thus, the loss pair is either an LP_{10} or LP_{01}. We also assume that the packet losses are due to node congestion. We obtain their residual packets' delays by including the queueing delay incurred from each hop. For the LP_{10}, it is also important to include p_{j-1}'s delay on the first $h'-1$ hops.

4.2.1 LP_{10}

To obtain p_j's delay for the LP_{10}, we first apply Eqn. (1) recursively until reaching the $(h'-1)^{th}$ node (since p_{j-1} is discarded at the h'^{th} node):

$$d_j^{(n)} = d_j^{(h'-1)} + \sum_{h=h'}^{n} \left(w_j^{(h)} + X^{(h)} + T^{(h)} \right). \quad (3)$$

By using Eqn. (2) for $d_j^{(h'-1)}$ and then applying Eqn. (1) recursively for $d_{j-1}^{(h'-1)}$, we obtain

$$\begin{aligned} d_j^{(n)} &= d_{j-1}^{(h'-1)} + \tau_{j-1,j}^{(h')} + \sum_{h=h'}^{n} \left(w_j^{(h)} + X^{(h)} + T^{(h)} \right), \\ &= \sum_{h=1}^{h'-1} w_{j-1}^{(h)} + \sum_{h=h'}^{n} w_j^{(h)} + \tau_{j-1,j}^{(h')} + \\ & \sum_{h=1}^{n} \left(X^{(h)} + T^{(h)} \right). \quad (4) \end{aligned}$$

In addition to the queueing delay at all the nodes [31], Eqn. (4) also shows that the residual packet's delay contains $\tau_{j-1,j}^{(h')}$ which, as will be seen shortly, depends on a number of delay components in the preceding hops.

4.2.2 LP_{01}

To obtain p_{j-1}'s delay for the LP_{01}, we apply Eqn. (1) recursively for $d_{j-1}^{(h)}$ to obtain

$$d_{j-1}^{(n)} = \sum_{h=1}^{n} w_{j-1}^{(h)} + \sum_{h=1}^{n} \left(X^{(h)} + T^{(h)} \right). \quad (5)$$

Since the first packet is the residual packet, its delay is not affected by the second packet and does not contain $\tau_{j-1,j}^{(h')}$.

4.2.3 Testbed experiments

We conducted testbed experiments to evaluate the impact of $\tau_{j-1,j}^{(h')}$ on the residual packet's delay. The testbed, shown in Figure 3, was configured with a 12-hop round-trip path ($n = 12$), consisting of a probe sender, a web server running Apache v2.2.3 as the destination node, three cross-traffic clients $\mathbb{X}_1 - \mathbb{X}_3$, and five forwarding devices: two Linux 2.6.26 routers $\mathbb{R}_1 - \mathbb{R}_2$ and three 100 Mbits/s Ethernet switches $\mathbb{S}_1 - \mathbb{S}_3$. We designated $H^{(5)}$ ($\mathbb{R}_2$ and its link to $\mathbb{S}_3$) to be the only congested node on the path (i.e., $h' = 5$). We achieved this by running TC/Netem [22] in $\mathbb{R}_2$ to emulate $C^{(5)} = 50$ Mbits/s and a FCFS queue to accommodate approximately 100 ms of packets, and generating forward-path cross traffic (from $\mathbb{X}_2$ to $\mathbb{X}_3$) to congest $H^{(5)}$. Moreover, we designated $H^{(3)}$ ($\mathbb{R}_1$ and its link to $\mathbb{S}_2$) to be a bottleneck link by configuring Click v1.8 [29] in $\mathbb{R}_1$ to emulate $C^{(3)} = 1$ Mbit/s. The Click router was also configured to set the RTT between the probe sender and web server to 200 ms.

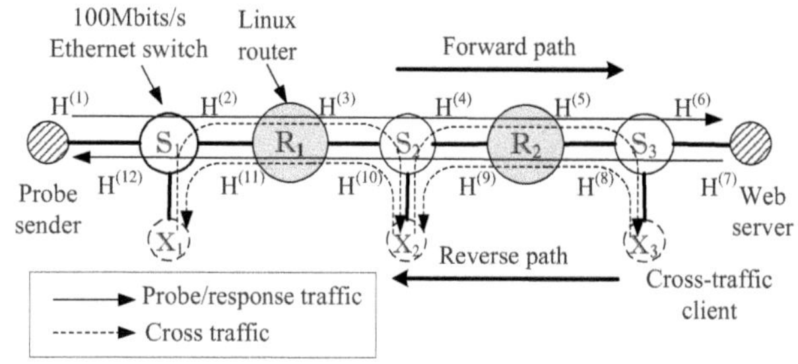

Figure 3: The testbed for the loss-pair experiments.

For this set of experiments, except for $H^{(5)}$, we did not generate cross traffic for other hops (i.e., $w_j^{(h)} = 0$, $\forall h \neq h'$, in Eqns. (4) and (5)). We ran HTTP/OneProbe from the probe sender to dispatch a sequence of 5000 Poisson-modulated probe pairs with a mean probing rate of 5 Hz. The probe sender was equipped with a DAG 4.5 passive network monitoring card [1] to obtain the RTT samples in microsecond resolution which is limited by the `pcap` header structure [2]. Similar to [26], the cross-traffic sources entered Pareto-distributed `ON` and `OFF` states with a shape $\alpha = 1.9$ and had a fixed packet size of 1500 bytes.

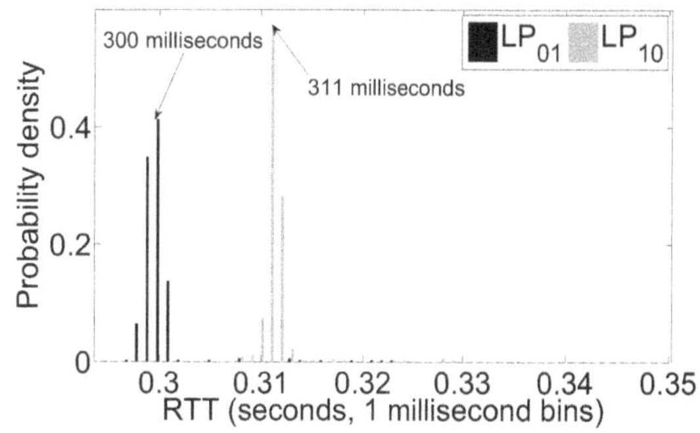

Figure 4: Residual packets' delays for LP_{10} and LP_{01} with $S = 1500$ bytes on the testbed for which $C^{(3)} = 1$ Mbit/s, $C^{(h')} = 50$ Mbits/s, and $h' = 5$.

Figure 4 shows the distributions of the residual packets' delays for the LP_{10} (i.e., P10xR00) and LP_{01} (i.e., P01x–) with $S = 1500$ bytes. Similar to [31], we applied a small bin size of 1 ms to mitigate the noise introduced by the non-congested hops. The figure shows that the residual packets' delays are dominated by the congested node's queueing delay of 100 ms, because most of them center around 300 ms and 311 ms for the LP_{01} and LP_{10}, respectively. We also note that many delay samples for the LP_{10} include an additional quantity of 11 ms which, according to Eqn. (4), came from $\tau_{j-1,j}^{(h')}$. Unlike other noises, this quantity cannot be filtered out by choosing a small bin size.

4.3 Characterizing the congested node's state

4.3.1 LP_{10}

A packet is dropped at $H^{(h')}$ when the node's buffer is full after the instantaneous input traffic rate exceeds $C^{(h')}$ for some time. We let $\{Q^{(h)}(t),\ t \geq 0\}$ be the continuous-time process of its queue length in terms of bits, and $\mathbb{Q}_j^{(h)} = Q^{(h)}(t_j^{(h)-})$ (i.e., the queue length just prior to the arrival of p_j). When $\{p_{j-1}, p_j\}$ is an LP_{10}, we have

$$\mathbb{Q}_{j-1}^{(h')} + S \;>\; B^{(h')}, \text{ and} \tag{6}$$

$$\mathbb{Q}_{j}^{(h')} + S \;\leq\; B^{(h')}, \tag{7}$$

where

$$\mathbb{Q}_j^{(h')} = \left(\mathbb{Q}_{j-1}^{(h')} + A_{j-1,j}^{(h')} - D_{j-1,j}^{(h')}\right)^+, \tag{8}$$

and $(x)^+ = \max\{0, x\}$. $A_{j-1,j}^{(h')}$ is the amount of packets (in bits) arriving to and buffered at the queue during $(t_{j-1}^{(h')}, t_j^{(h')})$, and $D_{j-1,j}^{(h')}$ is the total amount of packets (in bits) departed from the node during $[t_{j-1}^{(h')}, t_j^{(h')})$. Therefore, the queueing delay of p_j at $H^{(h')}$ can be expressed as

$$w_j^{(h')} \;=\; \frac{\mathbb{Q}_j^{(h')}}{C^{(h')}} + R_j^{(h')}, \tag{9}$$

where $R_j^{(h')}$ is the residual service time upon p_j's arrival.

Moreover, $\tau_{j-1,j}^{(h')}$, $h' > 1$, can be expressed as [38]:

$$\tau_{j-1,j}^{(h')} = X^{(h^*)} + q_{j-1,j}^{(h^*)} + \sum_{h=h^*+1}^{h'-1}\left(w_j^{(h)} - w_{j-1}^{(h)}\right), \tag{10}$$

where $H^{(h^*)}$, $1 \leq h^* \leq h'-1$, is the last hop preceding $H^{(h')}$ for which p_j arrives before p_{j-1}'s full departure from the node. That is, both belong to the same busy period of the queue at $H^{(h^*)}$ [38]. Moreover, $q_{j-1,j}^{(h^*)}$ is p_j's queueing delay at $H^{(h^*)}$ due to intervening cross traffic arriving between p_{j-1} and p_j, and $X^{(h^*)}$ is the time for transmitting p_j at $H^{(h^*)}$.

For the purpose of estimating $\mathbb{Q}_j^{(h')}/C^{(h')}$, it is useful to consider p_j's *path queueing delay* defined by $\Theta_j = d_j^{(n)} - \min_{\forall i,\ j=2i}\{d_{j-1}^{(n)}\}$. Assuming that the minimum observable delay of p_{j-1}, $j = 2i$, $i = 1, 2, \ldots$, precludes the cross-traffic-induced queueing delay and using Eqns. (4), (9), and (10), we have

$$\begin{aligned}\Theta_j \;&=\; d_j^{(n)} - \sum_{h=1}^{n}\left(X^{(h)} + T^{(h)}\right), \\ &=\; \frac{\mathbb{Q}_j^{(h')}}{C^{(h')}} + R_j^{(h')} + X^{(h^*)} + \zeta_j, \end{aligned} \tag{11}$$

where $\zeta_j (= \sum_{h=1}^{h^*} w_{j-1}^{(h)} + q_{j-1,j}^{(h^*)} + \sum_{h=h^*+1}^{h'-1} w_j^{(h)} + \sum_{h=h'+1}^{n} w_j^{(h)})$ is the queueing delay contributed by the cross traffic present at $H^{(h')}$'s upstream and downstream hops.

From Eqn. (11), Θ_j can be used to estimate $\mathbb{Q}_j^{(h')}/C^{(h')}$, and the estimation is biased by the residual service time, $X^{(h^*)}$, and cross traffic. Furthermore, $\mathbb{Q}_j^{(h')}/C^{(h')}$ is a good approximation for $\mathbb{Q}_{j-1}^{(h')}/C^{(h')}$ under certain conditions. For instance, when $\tau_{j-1,j}^{(h')}$ is small enough and Eqn. (7) still holds, $\mathbb{Q}_j^{(h')}$ is expected to be very close to $\mathbb{Q}_{j-1}^{(h')}$, thus making $\mathbb{Q}_j^{(h')}$ a tight lower bound for $B^{(h')} - S$. As a result, if $\mathbb{Q}_j^{(h')}/C^{(h')} \gg R_j^{(h')} + X^{(h^*)} + \zeta_j$ and $B^{(h')} \gg S$, then $\Theta_j \approx B^{(h')}/C^{(h')}$ which was first given in [31]. On the other hand, according to Eqn. (8), $\mathbb{Q}_j^{(h')}$ could be dampened when $A_{j-1,j}^{(h')} \ll D_{j-1,j}^{(h')}$ and $\tau_{j-1,j}^{(h')}$ becomes large, because the congestion may be relieved by the time p_j arrives.

4.3.2 LP$_{01}$

The analysis for the LP_{01} is similar to the above. When $\{p_{j-1}, p_j\}$ is an LP_{01}, we have

$$\mathbb{Q}_{j-1}^{(h')} + S \;\leq\; B^{(h')}, \text{ and} \tag{12}$$

$$\mathbb{Q}_{j}^{(h')} + S \;>\; B^{(h')}, \tag{13}$$

where

$$\mathbb{Q}_j^{(h')} = \left(\mathbb{Q}_{j-1}^{(h')} + S + A_{j-1,j}^{(h')} - D_{j-1,j}^{(h')}\right)^+. \tag{14}$$

By replacing $w_{j-1}^{(h')}$ with a similar expression as Eqn. (9), we obtain p_{j-1}'s path queueing delay, defined by $\Theta_{j-1} = d_{j-1}^{(n)} - \min_{\forall i,\ j=2i}\{d_{j-1}^{(n)}\}$:

$$\Theta_{j-1} = \frac{\mathbb{Q}_{j-1}^{(h')}}{C^{(h')}} + R_{j-1}^{(h')} + \zeta_{j-1}, \tag{15}$$

where $\zeta_{j-1} = \sum_{h=1}^{h'-1} w_{j-1}^{(h)} + \sum_{h=h'+1}^{n} w_{j-1}^{(h)}$ and $R_{j-1}^{(h')}$ is the residual service time upon p_{j-1}'s arrival. Unlike the LP_{10}, the LP_{01}'s path queueing delay does not contain $X^{(h^*)}$, and ζ_{j-1} contains fewer components.

To estimate $B^{(h')}/C^{(h')}$ by the LP_{01}, note that $\mathbb{Q}_{j-1}^{(h')}$ serves as a tight lower bound for $\mathbb{Q}_j^{(h')}$ if $A_{j-1,j}^{(h')}$ is close to $D_{j-1,j}^{(h')}$ or $\tau_{j-1,j}^{(h')}$ is small enough. If p_{j-1} arrives at $H^{(h')}$ with its queue length not close to $B^{(h')}$ and $\tau_{j-1,j}^{(h')}$ is small, then Eqn. (13) will not hold with a high probability. However, if p_{j-1} arrives at an almost full queue and $\tau_{j-1,j}^{(h')}$ is small, it is more likely that Eqn. (13) will hold. As a result, if $\mathbb{Q}_{j-1}^{(h')}/C^{(h')} \gg R_{j-1}^{(h')} + \zeta_{j-1}$, $\tau_{j-1,j}^{(h')}$ is small enough, and $B^{(h')} \gg S$, then $\Theta_{j-1} \approx B^{(h')}/C^{(h')}$.

4.3.3 Testbed results

Figure 5(a) plots the path queueing delays for the LP_{10} and LP_{01} with $S = 1500$ bytes which are obtained from the previous set of testbed experiments. Notice that $B^{(h')}/C^{(h')}$ ($= 100$ ms) is much greater than $S/C^{(h')}$ ($= 240$ μs). We denote the bin with the highest count for the LP_{10} as $\hat{\Theta}_j$ and that for the LP_{01} as $\hat{\Theta}_{j-1}$. As shown, $\hat{\Theta}_{j-1}$ is the same as $B^{(h')}/C^{(h')}$. However, $\hat{\Theta}_j$ deviates from $B^{(h')}/C^{(h')}$ by about 11 ms, which is close to $X^{(h^*)}$ ($= 1500$ bytes/1 Mbit/s $= 12$ ms). Therefore, the results validate the contribution of $X^{(h^*)}$ to Θ_j, as modeled in Eqn. (11).

We also repeated the experiments by using a small probe packet size $S = 240$ bytes (with the same bottleneck link capacity $C^{(h^*)} = 1$ Mbit/s) and a larger bottleneck link capacity $C^{(h^*)} = 10$ Mbits/s (with the same probe packet size $S = 1500$ bytes), where $B^{(h')}/C^{(h')} \gg S/C^{(h')}$ for both cases. As shown in Figures 5(b) and 5(c), $\hat{\Theta}_{j-1}$ remains very close to $B^{(h')}/C^{(h')}$. Although $\hat{\Theta}_j$ may still deviate from $B^{(h')}/C^{(h')}$, the degree of the deviation becomes smaller, because of the decrease in $X^{(h^*)}$.

The estimates of $B^{(h')}/C^{(h')}$ made by the LP_{10} and LP_{01} are both prone to queueing delay at the non-congested nodes. However, the effect on the LP_{10}'s estimate is generally more

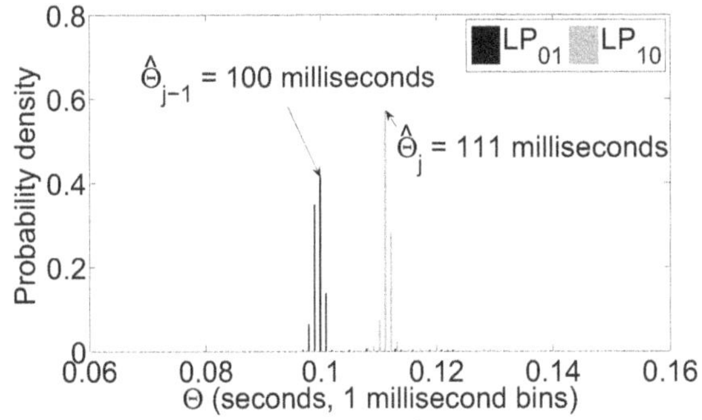

(a) $S = 1500$ bytes, $C^{(h^*)} = 1$ Mbit/s.

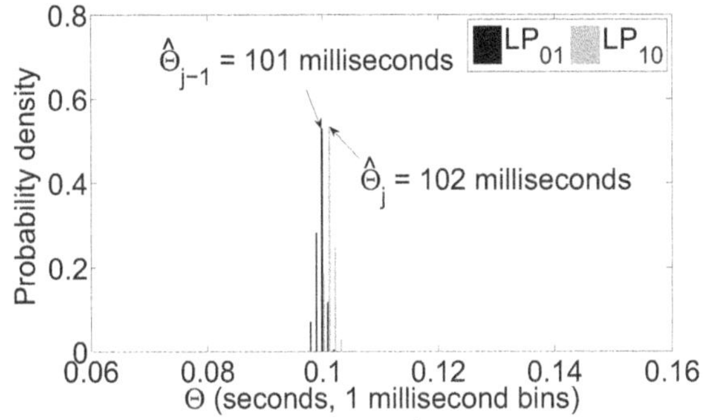

(b) $S = 240$ bytes, $C^{(h^*)} = 1$ Mbit/s.

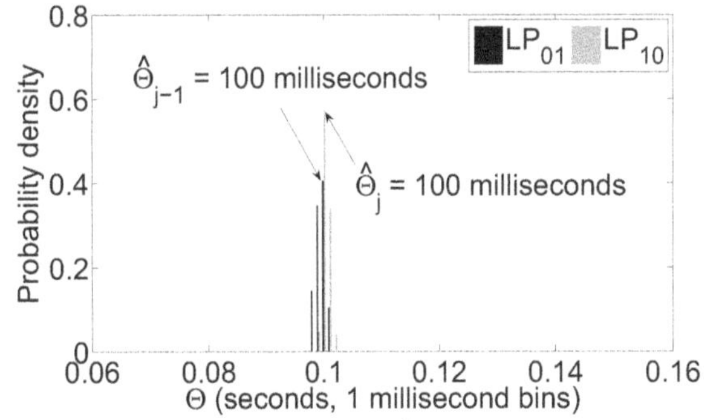

(c) $S = 1500$ bytes, $C^{(h^*)} = 10$ Mbits/s.

Figure 5: Path queueing delays for the LP_{10} and LP_{01} on the testbed for which $C^{(h^*)} = \{1, 10\}$ Mbits/s, $C^{(h')} = 50$ Mbits/s, $h^* = 3$, and $h' = 5$.

significant than the LP_{01}'s, because the LP_{10}'s delay always contains $X^{(h^*)}$ which cannot be eliminated. Note that $X^{(h^*)}$ could be significant if the measurement is conducted using a low-bandwidth residential link. Though the impact of $X^{(h^*)}$ can be mitigated by choosing a smaller packet size for active loss-pair measurement, this is not feasible for passive loss-pair measurement. Whenever the packet size is not configurable, the LP_{01} should be used to avoid the bias.

4.4 Estimating $H^{(h^*)}$'s link capacity

In this section, we show that another benefit of the loss-pair analysis is estimating $H^{(h^*)}$'s link capacity from both LP_{10}'s delay and LP_{01}'s delay, assuming that both LP_{10} and LP_{01} observe the same congested hop $H^{(h')}$. Subtracting Eqn. (15) from Eqn. (11) gives

$$\Delta_{j-1,j} = \Theta_j - \Theta_{j-1} \quad = \quad X^{(h^*)} + \epsilon, \qquad (16)$$

where $\epsilon = \frac{\mathbb{Q}_j^{(h')}}{C^{(h')}} - \frac{\mathbb{Q}_{j-1}^{(h')}}{C^{(h')}} + \zeta_j - \zeta_{j-1} + R_j^{(h')} - R_{j-1}^{(h')}$. Eqn. (16) shows that $\Delta_{j-1,j}$ includes a signature for $X^{(h^*)}$ and a noise term ϵ. Since the queueing delay and residual service times of p_{j-1} and p_j are contributed from different busy periods of the nodes, ϵ can be reasonably regarded as a random noise.

4.4.1 *Testbed results*

We conducted a new set of testbed experiments to evaluate this capability by configuring $\mathbb{R}_1$ to emulate $C^{(3)} = C^{(11)} = 10$ Mbits/s, and keeping $C^{(5)} = 50$ Mbits/s and $B^{(5)}/C^{(5)} = 100$ ms unchanged. Besides $H^{(5)}$, we also introduced the Pareto `On/Off` cross traffic between $\mathbb{X}_1$ and $\mathbb{X}_2$ in the forward and reverse paths. Other configuration settings were unchanged. As a result, $h^* = 3$ and $h' = 5$. We obtain the distribution of $\Delta_{j-1,j}$ by a mutual subtraction between Θ_{j-1} and Θ_j measured from `P01x-` and `P10xR00`, respectively, with $S = 1500$ bytes.

As shown in Figure 6(a), although $\hat{\Theta}_{j-1}$ and $\hat{\Theta}_j$ are relatively close to $B^{(h')}/C^{(h')} = 100$ ms, they also experience a higher variation due to the more significant cross traffic throughout the round-trip path. On the other hand, the probability density distribution of $\Delta_{j-1,j}$, shown in Figure 6(b), is symmetric about the peak at around 1.2 ms, which corresponds to the transmission delay of $H^{(h^*)}$ (i.e., $X^{(h^*)} = 1500$ bytes/10 Mbits/s). Thus, the peak of the distribution, together with the packet size, gives an accurate estimation of $H^{(h^*)}$'s link capacity. We also note from other testbed results (which are not shown in the paper) that $\Delta_{j-1,j}$ diminishes with the $H^{(h^*)}$'s link capacity and increases with the probe packet size. For example, for $S = 40$ bytes, we expect to use a microsecond bin size to make the transmission delay stand out in the distribution of $\Delta_{j-1,j}$.

We also include the results for the reverse-path loss pairs based on `P00xR10` and `P00xR01` in Figures 6(c)-6(d), and they are obtained by configuring $C^{(9)} = 50$ Mbits/s and $B^{(9)}/C^{(9)} = 100$ ms in the same testbed, and restoring the link capacity of $H^{(5)}$ to 100 Mbits/s with unlimited buffer. As a result, $h^* = 3$ remains unchanged, but $h' = 9$. Figure 6(c) shows that the corresponding $\hat{\Theta}_{j-1}$ and $\hat{\Theta}_j$ are still relatively close to $B^{(h')}/C^{(h')}$ and experience a similar variation due to the significant cross traffic introduced by $\mathbb{X}_1$ and $\mathbb{X}_2$. Moreover, as shown in Figure 6(d), $\Delta_{j-1,j}$ is quite similar to the forward-path results.

5. LOSS PAIRS IN THE INTERNET

We conducted end-to-end Internet path measurement between 26 February 2010 20:00 UTC and 17 March 2010 09:00 UTC, inclusively, using HTTP/OneProbe. The measurement covered a total of 112 (= 8×14) network paths between eight local universities in Hong Kong, denoted by UA–UH, as the sources of the paths and the 14 PlanetLab nodes listed in Table 1 as the destinations. Since HTTP/OneProbe performs measurement in a legitimate web session, we installed a `mini_httpd` (a web server) [40] at each PlanetLab node.

To monitor the path measurement from multiple sources to multiple destinations, we deployed a management system to dispatch the measurement tasks to the measurement

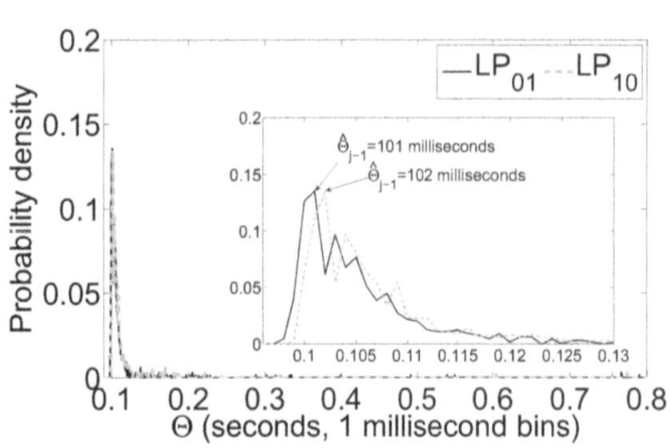

(a) Θ_{j-1} and Θ_j for $h' = 5$.

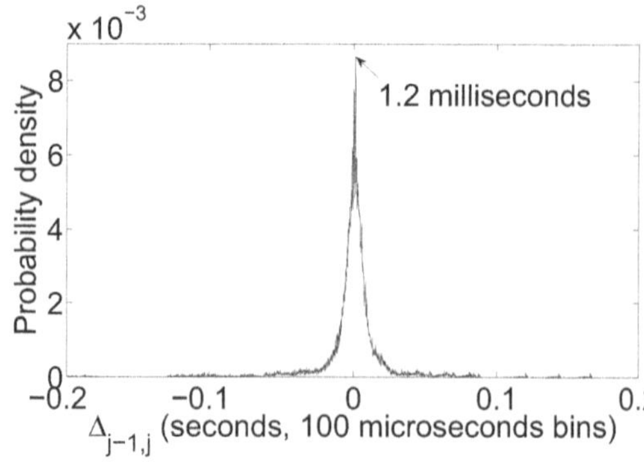

(b) $\Delta_{j-1,j}$ for $h' = 5$.

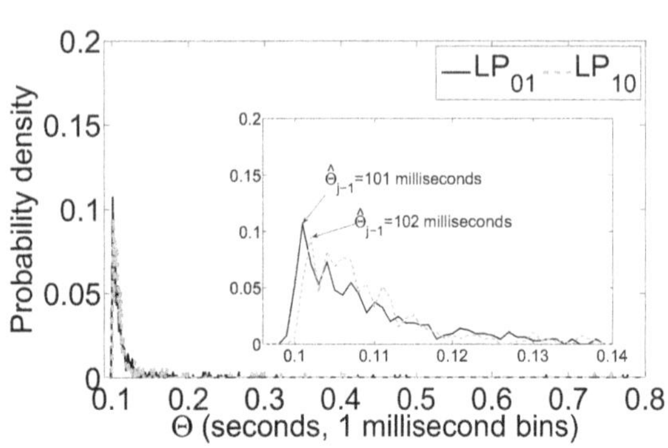

(c) Θ_{j-1} and Θ_j for $h' = 9$.

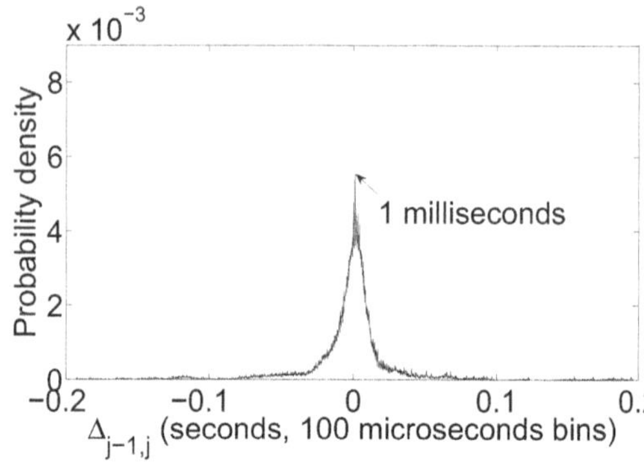

(d) $\Delta_{j-1,j}$ for $h' = 9$.

Figure 6: Path queueing delays and their differences for LP_{10} and LP_{01} with $S = 1500$ bytes on the testbed for which $C^{(h^*)} = 10$ Mbits/s, $C^{(h')} = 50$ Mbits/s, $h^* = 3$, and $h' = \{5, 9\}$.

Table 1: PlanetLab nodes used for the Internet path measurements.

Aliases	IP addresses	Locations	Average RTTs
PL001	212.235.18.114	Israel	308.24 ms
PL002	216.48.80.14	Canada	244.31 ms
PL003	202.112.28.98	China	83.67 ms
PL004	131.179.50.70	United States	–
PL005	128.143.6.134	United States	–
PL006	165.91.83.23	United States	229.55 ms
PL007	132.72.23.10	Israel	358.54 ms
PL008	210.123.39.168	Korea	53.34 ms
PL009	140.123.230.248	Taiwan	50.54 ms
PL010	134.151.255.181	UK	273.62 ms
PL011	142.104.21.241	Canada	248.99 ms
PL012	194.117.20.214	Portugal	–
PL013	198.82.160.239	United States	237.59 ms
PL014	137.132.80.110	Singapore	38.30 ms

nodes, monitor the resource usages in the nodes, and retrieve measurement data from the nodes. Each measurement node executed the measurement tasks to measure the network paths to the 14 destinations. To avoid self-induced network congestion, the destinations were evenly divided into two groups. The sources performed concurrent measurement for the paths in a group for one minute. Specifically, the sources launched HTTP/OneProbe to dispatch a sequence of Poisson-modulated probe pairs with a mean rate of 5 Hz and $S = 576$ bytes to each destination. To augment the path measurement with route information, tcptraceroute [49] was performed at both the sources and destinations. At the end of the minute, the nodes switched to the other group and repeated the same process. As a result, the average measurement traffic generated by each source was less than 48 KB/s (and less than 7 KB/s for each destination).

The measurement was conducted in the period during which HARNET [3]—a network through which the eight universities peered with one another—changed the service provider. In the switch-over process, the eight universities' networks were first switched to a temporary network one by one between 24 February 2010 14:00 UTC and 27 February 2010 23:00 UTC. They were then migrated back to the new service provider's network between 5 March 2010 11:00 UTC and 7 March 2010 2:00 UTC. As a result of these changes, we observed diverse network path characteristics even for the same source-destination pair.

In the stage of pre-processing the measurement data, we identified and removed a number of measurement artifacts. In particular, we identified artifacts associated with each source by correlating its measurement results. If there is a consistent pattern, such as persistent packet reordering, appearing in all the results, we conclude that the pattern is originated from the source or the path segment close to the source. This diverse-path-correlation method reveals the following measurement artifacts:

1. Forward-path and reverse-path reordering for UF between 27 February 2010 and 05 March 2010, and

2. Forward-path and reverse-path reordering for UH during the entire period.

Besides the artifacts, we observed system failures in three PlanetLab nodes PL004, PL005, and PL012 during the measurement period. After eliminating the paths to these destinations, we analyzed the remaining 88 paths for general packet loss statistics and loss-pair measurement.

5.1 Packet loss behavior: An overview

In this section, we present the overview results on the packet loss behavior, particularly the loss pairs, observed from the network paths. We consider the forward and reverse paths separately, because HTTP/OneProbe can distinguish the two paths for loss measurement. For the forward path, we define a *loss frequency* $f_{FL} = \sum_{i=1}^{M} \mathbf{1}_{\{L_i>0\}}/M$, where L_i represents the delivery status (i.e., 00, 01, 10, or 11) of the ith probe pair, $\mathbf{1}$ is the indicator function, and M is the total number of packet pairs dispatched during a given time period. $L_i > 0$ if there is at least a packet loss in the pair, and $L_i = 0$, otherwise. For the reverse path, we apply a similar procedure to compute the loss frequency denoted by f_{RL}.

5.1.1 *Prevalence of packet losses and loss pairs*

We summarize in Table 2 the packet-loss and loss-pair statistics measured from all the paths for the entire measurement period. The table is organized based on the destinations. That is, the statistics for each destination is computed based on an aggregation of the path measurement from the eight sources to the destination. The statistics are also separated into forward and reverse paths. Besides the f_{FL} and f_{RL}, we also report f_{P10}, f_{P01}, and f_{P11} which give the respective percentages of P10, P01, and P11 in the set of lossy probe pairs. The columns for f_{R10}, f_{R01}, and f_{R11} give similar statistics for the reverse path.

We observe the following results from Table 2:

1. Both f_{PL} and f_{RL} were less than 1% for most of the paths, and the highest loss frequency was 2.2% (i.e., PL003's f_{RL}).
2. Except for PL008 and PL011, the reverse paths suffered from more severe packet loss than the corresponding forward paths according to the loss frequencies. This result, however, is most likely location dependent.
3. Loss pairs were prevalent in the lossy packet pairs, because f_{P11} and f_{R11} were generally below 50% (except for PL007's f_{P11}). The frequencies for some of the paths were even below 10%.
4. The LP_{01} dominated the LP_{10} in both forward paths and reverse paths, because f_{P01} (f_{R01}) was consistently higher than f_{P10} (f_{R10}).

5.1.2 *Time series for packet loss events*

To analyze the packet loss statistics as a function of time, we divide the entire measurement period into one-hour bins for each path. Each bin's value is set to 1 if there exists at least a one-minute session with loss frequency greater than 1%; otherwise, the bin value is set to 0. As a result, we obtain a time series of bin values for each path. We can combine the eight sources' time series for a given destination by adding their bin values. Alternatively, we can combine the 11 destinations' time series for a given source by also adding their bin values.

Table 2: Packet loss and loss pair statistics (in %) grouped by destinations.

	Forward Paths				Reverse Paths			
	f_{FL}	f_{P10}	f_{P01}	f_{P11}	f_{RL}	f_{R10}	f_{R01}	f_{R11}
PL001	0.04	29.01	33.02	37.97	0.13	24.19	33.60	42.21
PL002	0.16	13.09	57.52	29.39	0.35	19.41	42.53	38.06
PL003	0.23	47.72	51.03	1.25	2.22	41.73	41.76	16.51
PL006	0.01	20.56	43.89	35.55	0.10	30.84	38.10	31.06
PL007	0.07	23.08	25.73	51.19	0.15	25.86	33.86	40.28
PL008	0.67	15.25	34.80	49.95	0.33	25.56	31.26	43.18
PL009	0.29	44.41	44.97	10.62	0.69	44.50	45.80	9.71
PL010	0.01	21.72	36.55	41.73	0.16	29.03	37.38	33.59
PL011	0.17	44.75	49.62	5.62	0.09	36.05	41.61	22.34
PL013	0.04	33.15	40.08	26.77	0.11	29.06	36.78	34.16
PL014	0.93	44.46	47.06	8.49	1.93	47.38	48.02	4.59

To effectively visualize the time series, we resort to heat-map diagrams. Figures 7(a) and 7(b) show the heat-map time series for the packet loss events in the forward paths grouped by the sources and destinations, respectively. Since there are 11 paths per source, the possible values in Figure 7(a) are $0, 1, \ldots 11$. A darker color corresponds to a higher value. We also grey out all the bins with no measurement data. Similarly, the possible values in Figure 7(b) are $0, 1, \ldots 8$. Moreover, there are three vertical dash lines: the first indicates the completion time for the transition to the temporary network, the second the beginning of the transition to the new service provider, and the third the completion time for the transition to the new service provider. We also show the diagrams for the reverse paths in Figures 7(c) and 7(d).

The heat-map diagrams enable us to effectively evaluate the loss behavior in the spatial and temporal domains:

1. (Loss patterns) The heat maps can quickly identify loss patterns for a set of paths. In our case, the set of paths share either the same source or the same destination for forward/reverse paths. Figure 7(a) shows that there is no clear loss pattern for all the eight sets of source-identical forward paths. However, Figure 7(c) shows intense loss for some of the reverse paths during the network transition (between the first two dotted lines). On the other hand, Figures 7(b) and 7(d) depict that the loss is much more prevalent for some destination-identical paths.
2. (Loss correlations) The heat maps also reveal strong correlation among different sets of source/destination-identical paths. The most notable one is the periodic, intense losses for the UE, UF, UG, and UH paths in Figure 7(c). The similar pattern suggests that they probably shared the same loss origins. Moreover, Figure 7(d) shows that all 11 sets of destination-identical paths share similar reverse-path loss patterns during the network transition, but they are no longer similar after migrating to the new service provider's network.
3. (Loss diagnosis) We use heat maps to further diagnose the loss behavior by correlating the source-identical paths and destination-identical paths. Going back to the intense losses for the UE, UF, UG, and UH paths in Figure 7(c), we can obtain more insights by comparing Figure 7(c) and Figure 7(d) in the same five periods of heavy losses. Figure 7(d) shows that some destinations contributed losses to most of the reverse paths

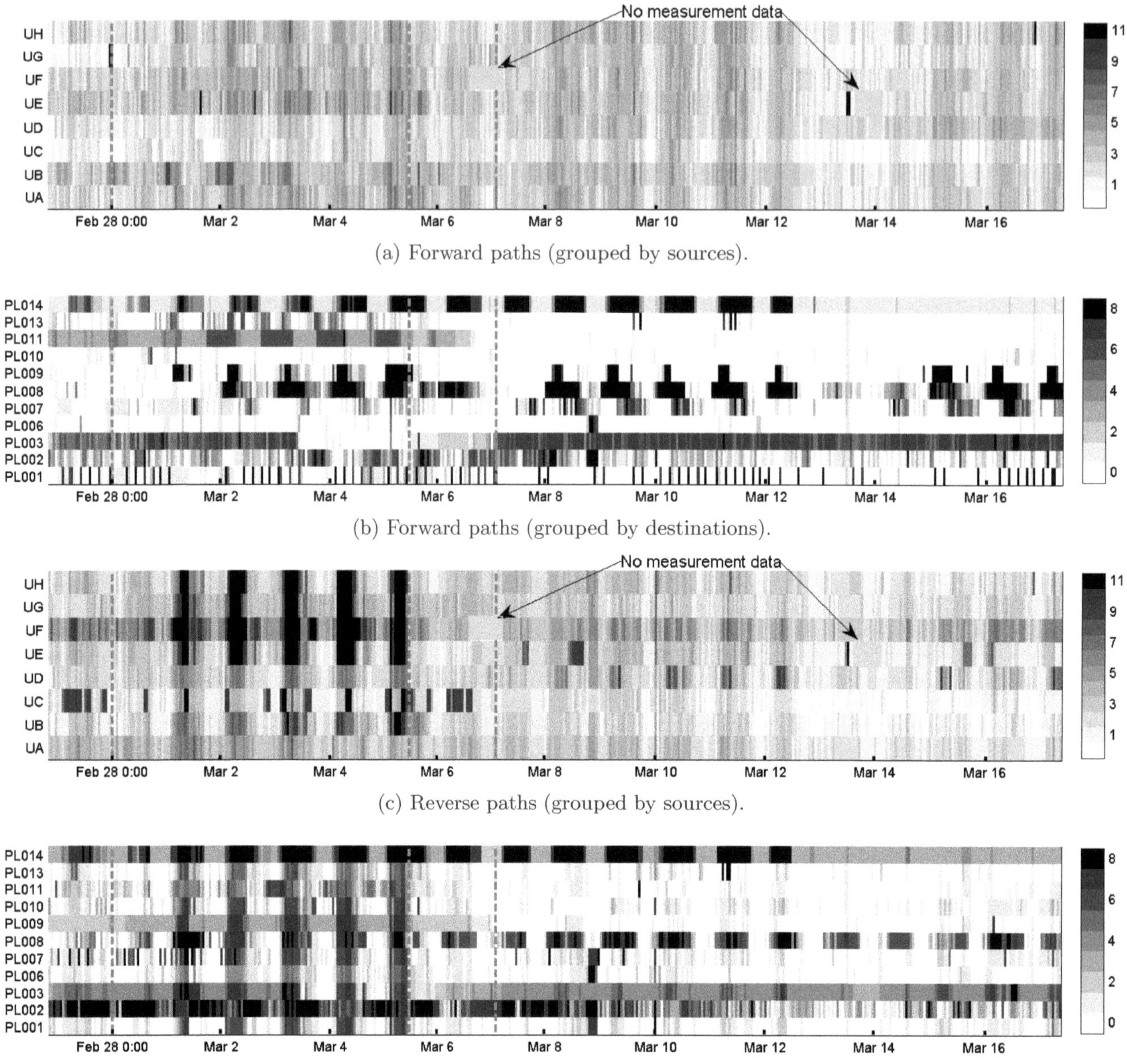

(a) Forward paths (grouped by sources).

(b) Forward paths (grouped by destinations).

(c) Reverse paths (grouped by sources).

(d) Reverse paths (grouped by destinations).

Figure 7: Heat-map time series for the packet loss events in the forward and reverse paths.

(notably PL014). Therefore, the losses for the four paths actually occurred on multiple locations: some on the destination side and others on the source side.

4. (Loss anomalies) The heat maps also help reveal loss anomalies. A time-correlation of the forward-path and reverse-path measurements based on the destinations shows that PL014 is a "congested" node. The paths to and from this node experienced high loss for all paths in a diurnal pattern until 13 March 2010. The loss could occur as a result of congestion at the node or the node's network. Since this path's loss measurement is heavily biased by the destination, a more useful path measurement can be obtained by replacing this with another node in the same vicinity. The forward paths to PL008 and PL009 also experienced periodic high losses. Unlike PL014, the loss patterns continued to the end of the measurement period.

5.2 Loss-pair analysis of the paths to PL009

In this section, we use the eight forward paths to PL009 as a case study of loss-pair analysis. Figure 8 shows the heat-map time series for the frequency of event P01x– obtained from the eight paths. We do not give the time series for the event P10xR00, because it exhibits a similar pattern shown in Figure 8. We compute the frequency for each path using one-hour bins and grey out all the bins with no measurement data. The loss-pair frequencies of the forward paths were 1-3%, and they distributed in several loss episodes, each of which lasted for several hours. In the ensuing discussion, we zoom into two loss episodes e_1 and e_2 in Figure 8 observed

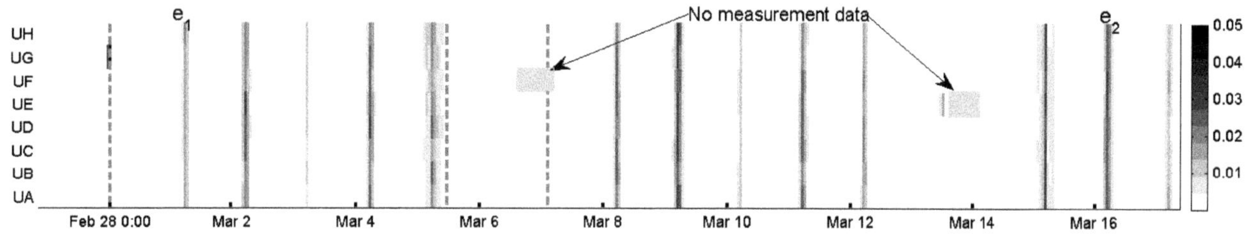

Figure 8: Heat-map time series for the frequency of event P01x– from UA–UH to PL009.

on 1 March 2010 (during the period of the temporary network operation) and 16 March 2010 (after the transition to the new service provider), respectively, with the same time period between 02:00 and 11:00 UTC on each day.

5.2.1 The loss episode e_1

Figure 9 shows the RTT time series for the first packets (i.e., p_{j-1}) for the paths from UA, UB, UD, and UE during e_1. In each time series, we also superimpose the residual packets' RTTs for events P01x– and P10xR00 observed from the corresponding path. We do not show the time series for UC, UF, UG, and UH, because the time series for UC is similar to that for UB, and UF–UH to UE. The following highlights the main observations from Figure 9:

1. A minimum RTT (minRTT) of 30 ms was found for the path from UD and 32 ms for the others. Most of the RTTs were found below 100 ms for each path.
2. Except for the UA path, other paths experienced two RTT surges at around 02:15 and 06:15 UTC.
3. Forward-path loss pairs were observed between 03:00 and 07:45 UTC from all the paths.
4. Forward-path loss pairs were observed between 07:45 and 11:00 UTC only from the UD–UH paths.
5. The first packets' RTTs remained low and relatively stable between 02:35 and 06:15 UTC for all the paths. The loss pairs' RTTs clustered around the peaks and most of residual packets' RTTs for event P10xR00 were higher than that for event P01x– (which is consistent with our analysis in §4).
6. The first packets' RTTs became high and unstable after 06:15 UTC (especially between 06:15 and 09:45 UTC) except for the UD path. A significant variation was also observed from the loss pairs' RTTs, and many residual packets' RTTs for event P10xR00 were found lower than that for event P01x–.

Since diverse RTT characteristics were observed among the eight paths, we further analyze the tcptraceroute results for both the forward and reverse paths between the eight sources and the destination, and find that the sources actually used different IP routes to reach the destination. The tcptraceroute results also reveal that no IP route change occurred during e_1.

Figure 10(a) shows the eight forward paths to PL009. As shown, while the forward paths from UB–UH went through the peering of HKIX towards ASNET, the path from UA actually went through the new service provider to ASNET. As a result, the two RTT surges (point 2 above) were probably introduced by the HKIX network. Besides, we observe that only ASNET and TANET were involved in all the eight forward paths. Therefore, the loss pairs observed between 03:00 and 07:45 UTC (point 3) were probably introduced by a congestion point near the destination. However, since only UD–UH went through the temporary network to HKIX during e_1, the loss pairs observed between 07:45 and 11:00 UTC from their paths (point 4) were likely due to the congestion in this temporary network.

On the other hand, the tcptraceroute for the reverse paths provide additional information to reveal the effect of the reverse-path networks on the observed first packets' and loss pairs' RTTs. Figure 10(b) shows the reverse paths to the eight sources. As shown, only the reverse path to UD went through the ASGCNET network (with at least three router hops shorter). This observation suggests that the shorter minRTT observed from the UD path (point 1) was probably due to the shorter IP reverse route. While the other reverse paths from PL009 went through ASNET, the new service provider, and then HARNET to the sources, these paths actually shared only three common router hops in ASNET. Therefore, the RTT fluctuation after 06:15 UTC observed from most of the paths, except for the UD path (point 6), was introduced by another common congestion point in the ASNET network on the reverse paths.

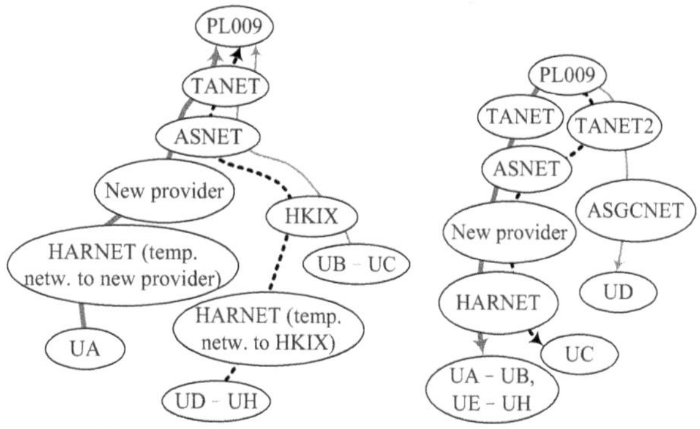

(a) Forward paths. (b) Reverse paths.

Figure 10: A comparison of forward and reverse paths between UA–UH and PL009 during e_1.

The observations above indicate that the eight paths exhibit relative stable RTTs and similar loss pairs' patterns between 02:35 and 06:15 UTC. To further characterize the properties for the eight forward paths, we compute the distributions of the residual packets' path queueing delays for events P01x– (i.e., Θ_{j-1}) and P10xR00 (i.e., Θ_j) in Figures 11(a)–11(b). Figure 11(a) shows that the modes of the path queueing delays for event P01x– were around 2 ms for the eight sources; therefore, the sources probably shared the same congestion point on their forward paths (which further supports our above findings). Moreover, by studying the

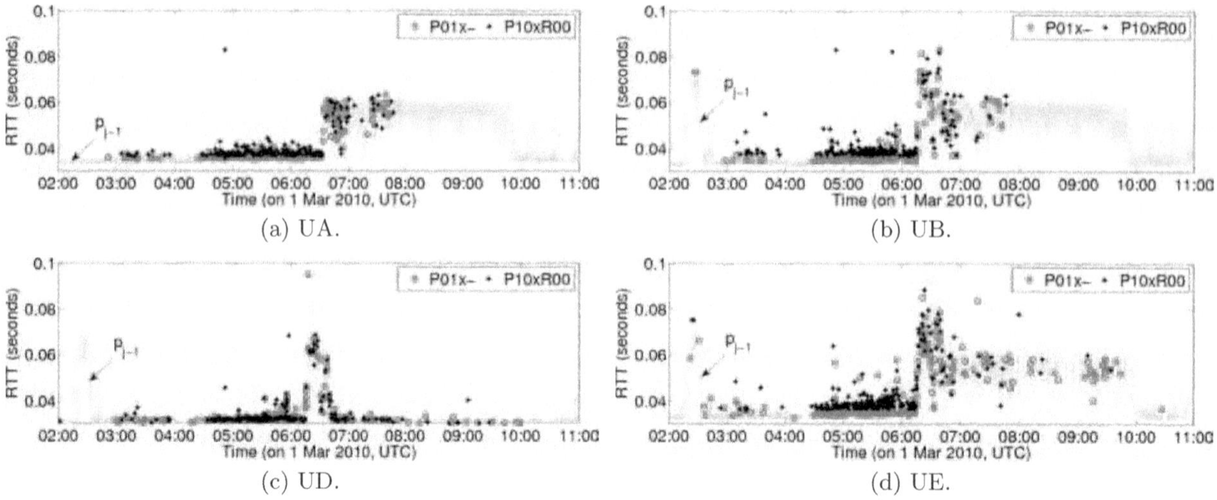

(a) UA. (b) UB. (c) UD. (d) UE.

Figure 9: RTT time series for the paths from UA, UB, UD, and UE to PL009 during e_1.

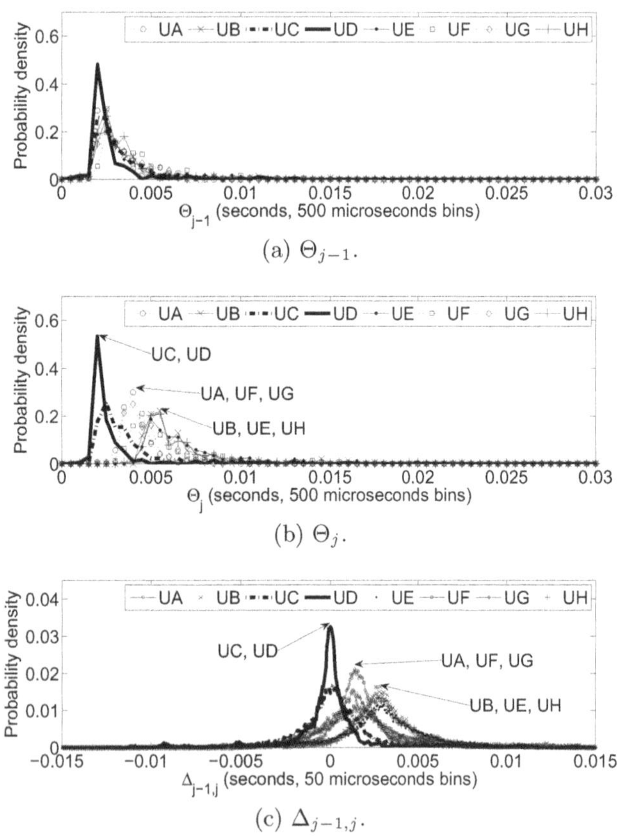

(a) Θ_{j-1}. (b) Θ_j. (c) $\Delta_{j-1,j}$.

Figure 11: Path queueing delays for loss-pair events P01x– and P10xR00 and their differences between 02:35 and 06:15 UTC during the loss episode e_1.

distributions of the path queueing delays for event P10xR00 shown in Figure 11(b), we obtain additional fingerprints for the eight paths and can further classify the sources into three groups: (i) UC and UD; (ii) UA, UF, and UG; and (iii) UB, UE, and UH.

Figure 11(c) shows the $\Delta_{j-1,j}$ distribution for each path based on the mutual differences between the corresponding residual packets' path queueing delays for events P01x– and P10xR00. As shown, the $\Delta_{j-1,j}$ distributions for the three groups are distinct from each other, meaning that they experienced different $H^{(h^*)}$'s configurations during the time period. For group (i), the figure shows that the corresponding link capacity was at least greater than 100 Mbits/s. However, we are unable to determine the exact value due to the coarse packet timestamp resolution. For groups (ii) and (iii), the estimated link capacities were at least 3 Mbits/s and 1.5 Mbits/s, respectively. Overall, the loss-pair analysis provides more comprehensive comparison of the eight paths and their characteristics which would not be easily discovered by considering only the loss frequencies (Figures 7(a) and 8) or the packet-pair RTTs (Figure 9).

5.2.2 *The loss episode e_2*

Figure 12 plots the time series of the first packets' RTTs observed from the UF's path to PL009 during e_2. Similarly, we superimpose the residual packets' RTTs for events P01x– and P10xR00 on the first packets' RTTs. Since this loss episode was located after the transition to the new service provider, it gives different path characteristics as compared with e_1. The figure shows that the minRTT for the UF path was around 65 ms, and most of the RTTs fell below 75 ms. We also observe similar RTT ranges for the other paths, except for the UC path whose RTTs ranged between 101 ms and 119 ms. Since all the eight paths exhibit very similar RTT time series patterns as in Figure 12, including two RTT surges at 04:50 and 05:30 UTC, we omit the time series for other paths.

Moreover, forward-path loss pairs were observed from the eight paths between 03:00 and 07:45 UTC. It is interesting to note that this time period is exactly the same as that in e_1 when forward-path loss pairs also existed in all the paths, although the loss pairs' RTTs found in e_2 mostly hit the highest values. This observation suggests that the transition event did *not* affect the congestion point in the forward path. Our tcptraceroute results for the forward paths obtained in e_2 also show that the forward paths still went through the same hops in ASNET and TANET observed during e_1.

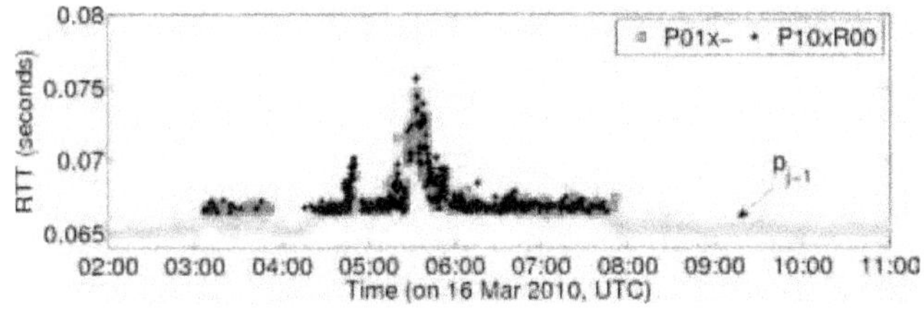

Figure 12: RTT time series for the path from UF to PL009 during the loss episode e_2.

We obtain the path queueing delays to further examine the impact of the transition to the new service provider. Figure 13 plots the distributions of the path queueing delays for events P01x– and P10xR00, and their differences obtained from the eight paths between 02:35 and 06:15 UTC during e_2. Figure 13(a) shows that the modes of the path queueing delays for event P01x– were still around 2 ms. Therefore, the transition probably had no impact on the congestion point encountered by the eight paths. However, Figures 13(b) and 13(c) show that the transition affected the configuration of $H^{(h^*)}$ for the eight paths (comparing with Figures 11(b) and 11(c)), where the distributions for both $\Delta_{j-1,j}$ and path queueing delays for event P10xR00 are very similar among the eight sources. As a result, the sources likely shared the same hop at $H^{(h^*)}$ after the transition.

5.3 Loss-pair analysis of the paths to PL014

In this section, we apply the loss-pair analysis to the eight sources' reverse paths from PL014. Recall from Figure 7(d) that the reverse paths from PL014 exhibited significant packet loss during the measurement period. Figure 14 shows the heat-map time series for the frequency of event P00xR01. Similarly, the grey areas indicate the periods with no measurement data. We also note that the time series for the event P00xR10 (not shown in the figure) shows a similar pattern. Figure 14 shows that the frequency for each path was less than 4%. The reverse paths to UD, UF, and UG suffered a long-term loss episode for the entire measurement period, and the paths to others encountered several loss episodes before 13 March 2010.

5.3.1 *The loss episode* e_3

We analyze a reverse-path loss episode (labeled as e_3 in Figure 14) between 00:00 and 23:59 UTC on 8 March 2010. Figure 15 plots the RTT time series of the first packets and the residual packets' RTTs for events P00xR01 and P00xR10 obtained from the paths for UC and UF to PL014 during e_3. Figure 15(a) shows an RTT inflation period between 03:00 and 18:00 UTC. Note that most of the loss pairs were found within this RTT inflation period. Figure 15(b), on the other hand, also shows an RTT inflation period, but the loss pairs can be found throughout the measurement period. For other paths, the RTT time series for UA, UB, UE, and UH exhibit similar patterns as that for UC, whereas the time series for UD and UG are similar to that for UF. Therefore, we classify the eight sources into two groups: (i) UA, UB, UC, UE, and UH; and (ii) UD, UF, and UG. Moreover, we observe a minRTT of 50 ms for the UD path, and 35 ms for the other paths.

To characterize the congestion node's state encountered by the two groups of paths, we plot the path queueing delays

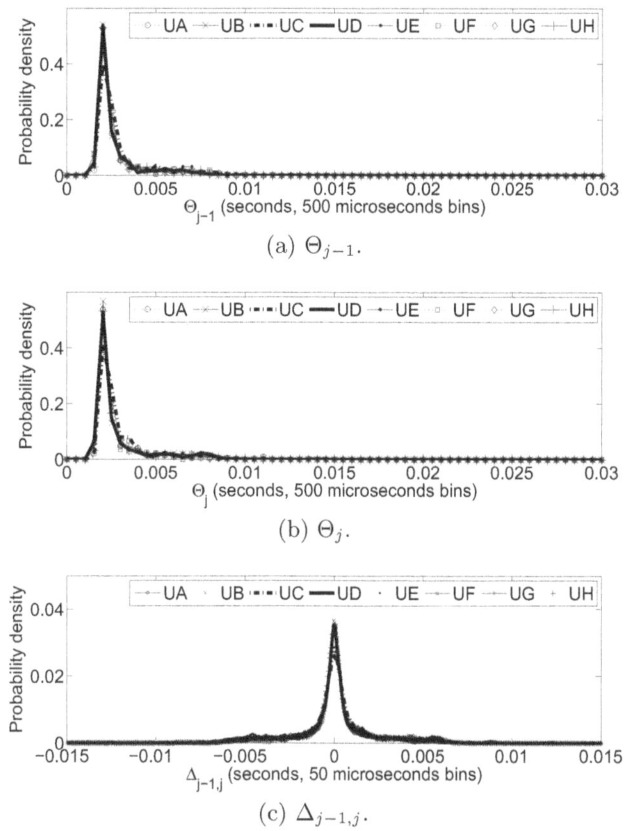

Figure 13: Path queueing delays for loss-pair events P01x– and P10xR00 and their differences obtained from UA–UH to PL009 between 02:35 and 06:15 UTC during the loss episode e_2.

for events P00xR01 and P00xR10 and their differences during e_3 in Figures 16(a)-16(c). In particular, Figures 16(a)-16(b) show that group (i) exhibits a single mode at around 4 ms for the path queueing delays for both events P00xR01 and P00xR10. According to Figure 15(a), the path queueing delays represent the congestion experienced by the group of sources during the RTT inflation period, during which almost all the loss pairs were found. We also notice that group (ii) exhibits a similar (but weaker) mode at around 3.5 ms, but the mode vanishes if we only consider the loss pairs outside the RTT inflation period. Consequently, it seems that all eight sources suffered from the same congestion point during the RTT inflation. Based on the tcptraceroute results, the congestion point was very likely a router hop in the destination's network which was the only one present in all eight reverse routes.

Figures 16(a)-16(b) also show that group (ii) exhibits another stronger mode at around 500 μs. A further investigation finds that the mode was contributed by the loss pairs across the loss episode e_3 (instead of only outside the RTT inflation period). This observation suggests that multiple congestion points existed across e_3 for the paths in group (ii). Moreover, it is interesting to note from Figure 16(c) that the two groups experienced a similar $H^{(h^*)}$'s link capacity estimate of at least 100 Mbits/s.

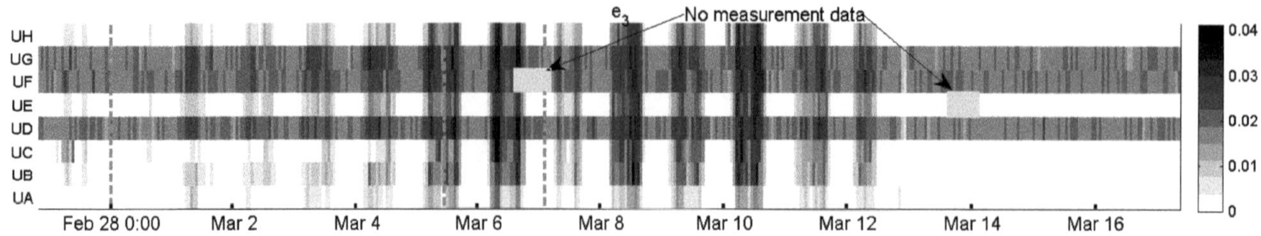

Figure 14: Heat-map time series for the frequency of event P00xR01 from UA–UH to PL014.

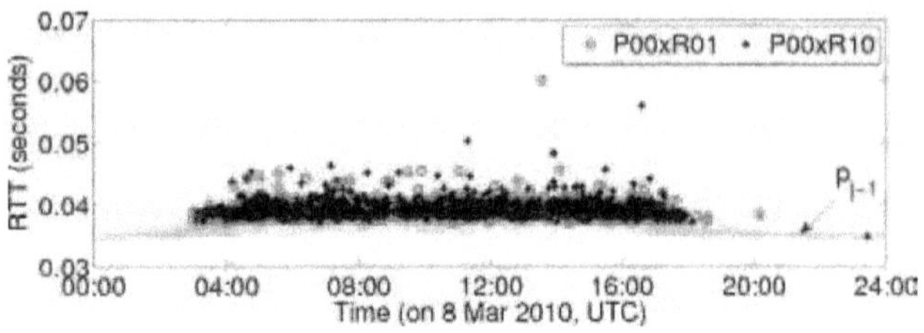

(a) UC.

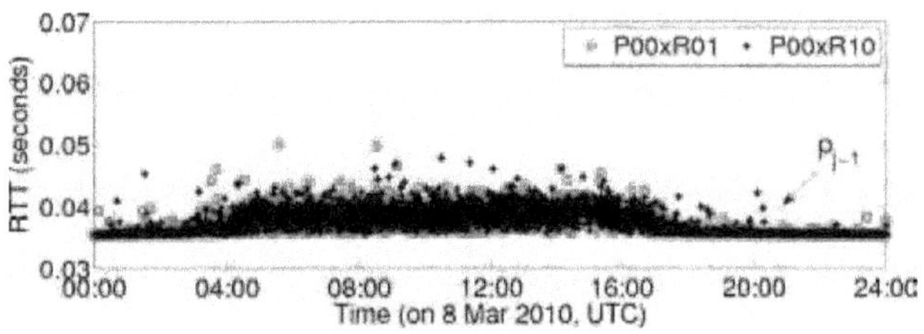

(b) UF.

Figure 15: RTT time series for the paths from UC and UF to PL014 during the loss episode e_3.

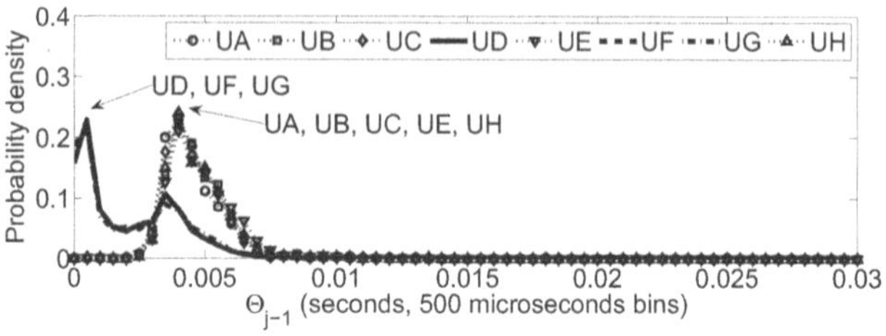

(a) Θ_{j-1}.

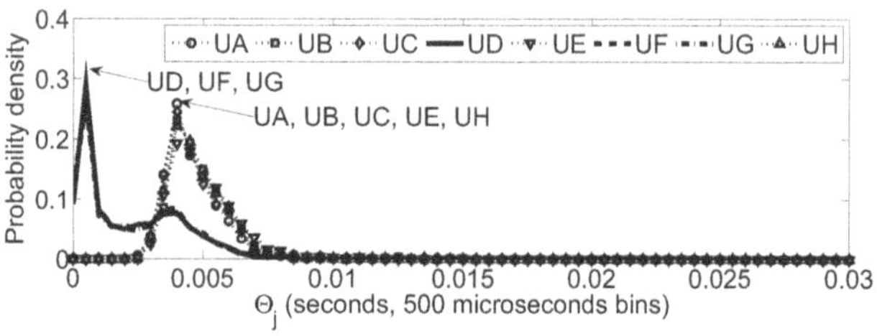

(b) Θ_j.

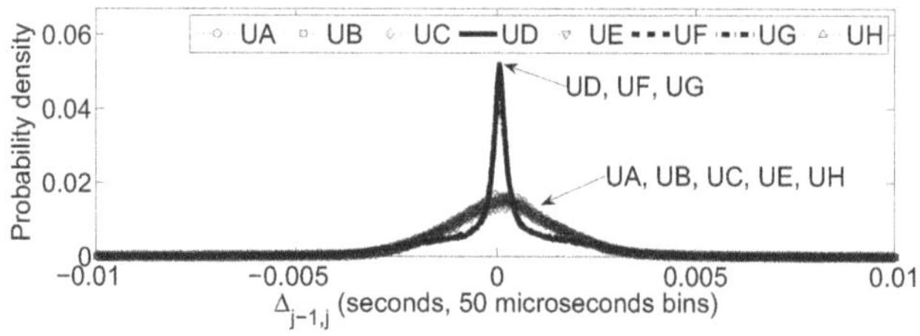

(c) $\Delta_{j-1,j}$.

Figure 16: Path queueing delays for loss-pair events P00xR01 and P00xR10 and their differences obtained from UA–UH to PL014 during the loss episode e_3.

6. CONCLUSIONS

In this paper, we revisited the loss-pair measurement method proposed a decade ago. Based on our new analysis and Internet measurement results, we concluded that the loss-pair measurement is a very useful method for correlating a packet loss event and the delay that would be experienced by the lost packet. This correlation provides insight into, for example, the congested node's state upon packet drop, capacity of a link preceding the congested node, and loss asymmetry. Moreover, the loss-pair measurement could be incorporated in the existing measurement tools, such as capacity measurement based on packet-pair dispersion. A possible direction to extending this work is to integrate the loss-pair measurement with capacity measurement, and the other is to obtain useful path signatures for path fingerprinting and detecting common congestion points for multiple paths.

Acknowledgments

This work is partially supported by a grant (ref. no. ITS/355 /09) from the Innovation Technology Fund in Hong Kong and a grant (ref. no. H-ZL17) from the Joint Universities Computer Centre of Hong Kong.

7. REFERENCES

[1] endace. http://www.endace.com/.

[2] TCPDUMP/LIBPCAP public repository. http://www.tcpdump.org/.

[3] The Joint Universities Computer Centre (JUCC). http://www.jucc.edu.hk/jucc/harnet.html, May 2010.

[4] A. Adams, J. Mahdavi, M. Mathis, and V. Paxson. Creating a scalable architecture for Internet measurement. In *Proc. INET*, 1998.

[5] M. Allman, W. Eddy, and S. Ostermann. Estimating loss rates with TCP. *ACM SIGMETRICS Perform. Eval. Rev.*, 31(3):12–24, 2003.

[6] F. Baccelli, S. Machiraju, D. Veitch, and J. Bolot. The role of PASTA in network measurement. In *Proc. ACM SIGCOMM*, 2006.

[7] F. Baccelli, S. Machiraju, D. Veitch, and J. Bolot. On optimal probing for delay and loss measurement. In *Proc. ACM/USENIX IMC*, 2007.

[8] J. Bellardo and S. Savage. Measuring packet reordering. In *Proc. ACM SIGCOMM IMW*, 2002.

[9] J. Bolot. End-to-end packet delay and loss behavior in the Internet. In *Proc. ACM SIGCOMM*, 1993.
[10] R. Carter and M. Crovella. Measuring bottleneck link speed in packet-switched networks. *Performance Evaluation*, 27-28:297–318, 1996.
[11] E. Chan, X. Luo, and R. Chang. A minimum-delay-difference method for mitigating cross-traffic impact on capacity measurement. In *Proc. ACM CoNEXT*, 2009.
[12] Y. Cheng, V. Ravindran, and A. Leon-Garcia. Internet traffic characterization using packet-pair probing. In *Proc. IEEE INFOCOM*, 2007.
[13] M. Coates and R. Nowak. Network loss inference using unicast end-to-end measurement. In *Proc. ITC Conf. IP Traffic, Modeling and Management*, 2000.
[14] L. Deng and A. Kuzmanovic. Monitoring persistently congested Internet links. In *Proc. IEEE ICNP*, 2008.
[15] G. Denisa, H. Nguyen, M. Kurant, K. Argyraki, and P. Thiran. Netscope: Practical network loss tomography. In *Proc. IEEE INFOCOM*, 2010.
[16] C. Dovrolis, P. Ramanathan, and D. Moore. Packet dispersion techniques and a capacity-estimation methodology. *IEEE/ACM Trans. Netw.*, 12(6):963–977, 2004.
[17] N. Duffield, L. Presti, V. Paxson, and D. Towsley. Network loss tomography using striped unicast probes. *IEEE/ACM Trans. Netw.*, 14(4):697–710, 2006.
[18] W. Feng, K. Shin, D. Kandlur, and D. Saha. The BLUE active queue management algorithms. *IEEE/ACM Trans. Netw.*, 10(4):513–528, 2002.
[19] R. Fielding, J. Gettys, J. Mogul, H. Frystyk, L. Masinter, P. Leach, and T. Berners-Lee. Hypertext transfer protocol – HTTP/1.1. RFC 2616, IETF, June 1999.
[20] S. Floyd and V. Jacobson. Random early detection gateways for congestion avoidance. *IEEE/ACM Trans. Netw.*, 1(4):397–413, 1993.
[21] K. Harfoush, A. Bestavros, and J. Byers. Robust identification of shared losses using end-to-end unicast probes. In *IEEE ICNP*, 2000.
[22] S. Hemminger. Network emulation with NetEm. In *Proc. Australia's National Linux Conference*, 2005.
[23] N. Hu and P. Steenkiste. Evaluation and characterization of available bandwidth probing techniques. *IEEE Journal on Selected Areas in Communications*, 21(6):879–894, 2003.
[24] V. Jacobson. Congestion avoidance and control. In *Proc. ACM SIGCOMM*, 1988.
[25] M. Jain and C. Dovrolis. End-to-end available bandwidth: Measurement methodology, dynamics, and relation with TCP throughput. *IEEE/ACM Trans. Netw.*, 11(4):537–549, 2003.
[26] R. Kapoor, L. Chen, L. Lao, M. Gerla, and M. Sanadidi. CapProbe: A simple and accurate capacity estimation technique. In *Proc. ACM SIGCOMM*, 2004.
[27] S. Katti, D. Katabi, C. Blake, E. Kohler, and J. Strauss. MultiQ: Automated detection of multiple bottleneck capacities along a path. In *Proc. ACM/USENIX IMC*, 2004.
[28] S. Keshav. A control-theoretic approach to flow control. In *Proc. ACM SIGCOMM*, 1991.
[29] E. Kohler. The Click Modular Router Project. http://read.cs.ucla.edu/click/.
[30] J. Liu. *Characterizing Network Elements and Paths Using Packet Loss Behavior.* PhD dissertation, Boston University, 2003.
[31] J. Liu and M. Crovella. Using loss pairs to discover network properties. In *Proc. ACM SIGCOMM IMW*, 2001.
[32] J. Liu, I. Matta, and M. Crovella. End-to-end inference of loss nature in a hybrid wired/wireless environment. In *Proc. WiOpt*, 2003.
[33] X. Luo, E. Chan, and R. Chang. Design and implementation of TCP data probes for reliable and metric-rich network path monitoring. In *Proc. USENIX Annual Tech. Conf.*, 2009.
[34] X. Luo and R. Chang. Novel approaches to end-to-end packet reordering measurement. In *Proc. ACM/USENIX IMC*, 2005.
[35] R. Mahajan, N. Spring, D. Wetherall, and T. Anderson. User-level Internet path diagnosis. In *Proc. ACM SOSP*, 2003.
[36] B. Melander, M. Bjorkman, and P. Gunningberg. A new end-to-end probing and analysis method for estimating bandwidth bottlenecks. In *Proc. IEEE GLOBECOM*, 2000.
[37] H. Nguyen and M. Roughan. On the correlation of Internet packet losses. In *Proc. ATNAC*, 2008.
[38] A. Pásztor and D. Veitch. The packet size dependence of packet-pair like methods. In *Proc. IWQoS*, 2002.
[39] K. Papagiannaki, R. Cruz, and C. Diot. Network performance monitoring at small time scales. In *Proc. ACM/USENIX IMC*, 2003.
[40] J. Poskanzer. mini_httpd: small HTTP server. http://www.acme.com/software/mini_httpd/.
[41] D. Rubenstein, J. Kurose, and D. Towsley. Detecting shared congestion of flows via end-to-end measurement. *IEEE/ACM Trans. Netw.*, 10(3):381–395, 2002.
[42] S. Saroiu, P. Gummadi, and S. Gribble. A measurement study of peer-to-peer file sharing systems. In *Proc. MMCN*, 2002.
[43] S. Saroiu, P. Gummadi, and S. Gribble. SProbe: A fast technique for measuring bottleneck bandwidth in uncooperative environments. In *Proc. IEEE INFOCOM*, 2002.
[44] S. Savage. Sting: A TCP-based network measurement tool. In *Proc. USENIX Symp. Internet Tech. and Sys.*, 1999.
[45] R. Sinha, C. Papadopoulos, and J. Heidemann. Fingerprinting Internet paths using packet pair dispersion. Technical Report 06-876, USC, Computer Science Dept., 2005.
[46] J. Sommers, P. Barford, N. Duffield, and A. Ron. Improving accuracy in end-to-end packet loss measurement. In *Proc. ACM SIGCOMM*, 2005.
[47] J. Sommers, P. Barford, N. Duffield, and A. Ron. A geometric approach to improving active packet loss measurement. *IEEE/ACM Trans. Netw.*, 16(2):307–320, 2008.
[48] M. Tariq, A. Dhamdhere, C. Dovrolis, and M. Ammar. Poisson versus periodic path probing (or, does PASTA matter?). In *Proc. ACM/USENIX IMC*, pages 10–10, 2005.
[49] M. Toren. tcptraceroute. http://michael.toren.net/code/tcptraceroute/.
[50] Y. Wang, C. Huang, J. Li, and K. Ross. Queen: Estimating packet loss rate between arbitrary Internet host. In *Proc. PAM*, 2009.
[51] W. Wei, B. Wang, D. Towsley, and J. Kurose. Model-based identification of dominant congested links. In *Proc. ACM/USENIX IMC*, 2003.
[52] M. Yajni, S. Moon, J. Kurose, and D. Towsley. Measurement and modelling of the temporal dependence in packet loss. In *Proc. IEEE INFOCOM*, 1999.
[53] Y. Zhang and N. Duffield. On the constancy of Internet path properties. In *Proc. ACM SIGCOMM IMW*, 2001.

Measuring Path MTU Discovery Behaviour

Matthew Luckie
Department of Computer Science
University of Waikato
Hamilton, New Zealand
mjl@wand.net.nz

Ben Stasiewicz
Department of Computer Science
University of Waikato
Hamilton, New Zealand
ben@wand.net.nz

ABSTRACT

Path MTU Discovery (PMTUD) is widely believed to be unreliable because of firewalls that discard ICMP "Packet Too Big" messages. This paper measures PMTUD behaviour for 50,000 popular websites and finds the failure rate in IPv4 is much less than previous studies. We measure the overall failure rate between 5% and 18%, depending on the MTU of the constraining link. We explore methods webserver operators are using to reduce their dependence on PMTUD, and find 11% limit themselves to sending packets no larger than 1380 bytes. We identify a number of common behaviours that seem to be software bugs rather than filtering by firewalls. If these are corrected PMTUD failures could be reduced by 63%. We further find the IPv6 failure rate is less than the IPv4 rate even with more scope for failure in IPv6.

Categories and Subject Descriptors

C.4 [**Performance of Systems**]: Measurement techniques

General Terms

Measurement

Keywords

TCP, Path MTU Discovery, IPv6, IPv4, middleboxes

1. INTRODUCTION

Path MTU Discovery (PMTUD) is widely believed to be unreliable because of firewalls that discard ICMP "Packet Too Big" (PTB) messages. Previous work by Medina, *et al.* in 2004 [1] reported 17% of the IPv4 webservers they tested failed PMTUD by not reducing their packet size when requested. They reason this is likely due to firewalls discarding PTB messages. IPv4 hosts may choose whether or not they use PMTUD, but IPv6 hosts do not have a choice and are required to act on PTB messages. This paper investigates PMTUD behaviour for IPv4 and IPv6 webservers.

IMC'10, November 1–3, 2010, Melbourne, Australia.

The PMTUD mechanism is similar for both IPv4 [2] and IPv6 [3]. When a router receives a packet that is too big for it to forward, it discards the packet and sends a PTB message telling the host the maximum transmission unit (MTU) it can forward. The host should then reduce its packet size to the size advised. Using the largest packet size that can be forwarded intact through a network is optimal, as "much of the cost of packetized communication is per-packet rather than per-byte" [4].

Unfortunately, there are many causes of PMTUD failure [5]. When PMTUD does not work, it causes Internet communications to fail in a way that is difficult to diagnose [6]. The most well-known cause is the firewall that discards all ICMP messages, including the PTB. Similarly, some routers are configured to not send ICMP destination unreachable messages; in IPv4, this also suppresses the PTB message. IPv6 separates PTB messages from the destination unreachable message so disabling destination unreachable messages should not also cause PTB messages to be suppressed. Finally, a router will not send a PTB message if it believes the network is capable of forwarding a larger packet than it actually can; this failure mode is known as an MTU mismatch.

Based on experiences with IPv4 and the IPv6 requirement for PTB messages to be delivered and acted on, there is concern PMTUD will fail more often when IPv6 is used, hampering end-user experience and thus IPv6 adoption. Some have recommended operators configure the MTU of interfaces on end-hosts to 1280 bytes [7, 8, 9]. The rationale behind this advice is the IPv6 minimum MTU is 1280 bytes so a host will never have to send a smaller packet or rely on a server accepting PTB messages. If this advice is taken, the host no longer has to use PMTUD as it will never send a packet larger than 1280 bytes, and it will also advertise a TCP Maximum Segment Size (MSS) that should cause the remote host to never send a packet larger than 1280 bytes over the TCP connection. This advice has the downside of not using the capabilities of paths which are able to forward larger packets. In addition, RFC 2460 requires a host to act on a PTB message with an MTU smaller than 1280 bytes by sending all packets with an IPv6 fragmentation header regardless of size [10].

This paper investigates PMTUD behaviour for IPv4 and IPv6 webservers. The method we use is similar to that used by Medina, *et al.* [1]. Our contributions are: (1) measurements of IPv4 webserver response to PTB messages containing different MTU values, (2) longitudinal measurement of IPv4 PMTUD behaviour from a packet trace, (3) a method to measure IPv6 webserver PMTUD behaviour and comparison with IPv4 behaviour for those webservers, and (4) identification of apparent software flaws responsible for more than half of the failures. The rest of this paper begins with a survey of related work. Section 3 describes the methodology, the hosts surveyed, and the vantage points we use. Section 4 presents the data collected for a set of 50,000 popular websites reachable with IPv4, analysis of the effect of popularity on ICMP filtering behaviour, and comparison with the results of Medina, *et al.* Section 5 presents the data collected for all webservers with globally routable IPv6 addresses in the Alexa top 1 million list [11]. Finally, section 6 concludes.

2. RELATED WORK

Medina, *et al.* [1] characterised the TCP behaviour of webservers in 2004 using TBIT [12]. Overall, 17% of 81,776 targets they tested and 35% of the top 500 webservers as reported by Alexa at the time did not send smaller packets when requested to reduce their packet size to 256 bytes. They hypothesise this behaviour is caused by firewalls that discard PTB messages. We derive our methodology from theirs; we measure the response to PTB messages containing different MTU values, separately classify hosts that respond to a PTB message by clearing the DF bit, add reassembly support for fragmented packets, and add IPv6 support.

Luckie, *et al.* [13] characterised PMTUD failures for hosts that are able to send 9000 byte packets towards hosts that can only receive 1500 byte packets. In this situation, routers in the path are required to send PTB messages for PMTUD to work. In total, 30% of the paths tested to 136 hosts failed PMTUD. Many are caused by operators configuring their routers to not send ICMP destination unreachable messages, but some are also caused by MTU mismatches where a router believed it could forward larger packets than the network could carry. The tests in this work measure the ability of hosts to receive and act on PTB messages, rather than the ability of routers to send PTB messages.

The IETF PMTUD working group released an alternative PMTUD method known as Packetization Layer Path MTU Discovery (PLPMTUD) [14]. PLPMTUD does not rely on the delivery of PTB messages, but requires the use of a reliable transport protocol. For TCP, the PLPMTUD technique causes a large segment designed to test the network's ability to carry that packet-size to be inserted before a sequence of smaller segments that are known to be able to be forwarded. If the large segment is discarded because it is too big, the smaller segments that follow will cause duplicate acknowledgements to be returned by the remote TCP; the sender will then break the data into smaller segments and retransmit, avoiding a delay waiting for the TCP retransmission timer to be activated, and in future try a smaller maximum segment size. Implementation of PLPMTUD is complicated as it is difficult to determine if a large segment is lost due to congestion or MTU issues. The only deployed implementation is found in the Linux kernel from version 2.6.17, and it is off by default [15].

Microsoft Windows implements PMTUD blackhole detection for TCP, which is disabled by default [16]. If a system does not receive an acknowledgement after two retransmissions, it will either clear the DF bit, or lower its MSS value for the connection to 536 bytes, depending on the version of Windows. If acknowledgements are then forthcoming, it will send 536 byte packets for the lifetime of the connection.

3. METHOD

3.1 Measuring PMTUD Behaviour

We use an approach derived from the TCP Behaviour Inference Tool (TBIT) work in [1] to measure PMTUD behaviour. Briefly, PMTUD behaviour is inferred by the behaviour of a remote TCP after a PTB is sent asking it to send smaller packets. If the host reduces the packet size as requested, we infer the PTB message was received and acted on. If the host does not reduce the segment size and retransmits the data, another PTB is sent requesting it do so. We infer failure if the host retransmits the data in question three times and does not reduce the segment size or clear the DF bit.

3.1.1 An IPv4 PMTUD test

We test the PMTUD behaviour of webservers with four different MTU values; 1480, 1280, 576, and 256 bytes. A 1480 byte MTU corresponds to an IP tunnel over Ethernet, 1280 is a popular choice for tunnel software, 576 is the minimum size packet a host is required to reassemble, and 256 bytes is the MTU value tested in [1]. We send PTB messages if the DF bit is set in a packet larger than the MTU we are testing. We advertise an MSS of 1460 bytes to each webserver for all IPv4 tests.

If we do not receive any packet larger than the MTU value we are testing, we classify the test as such. If we receive data packets larger than the MTU value we are testing but the DF bit is not set, we classify these hosts as not attempting PMTUD. A host that supports PMTUD might react to a PTB message by clearing the DF bit in subsequent packets; we classify these hosts as clearing the DF bit. This behaviour is a defence against an adversary sending a PTB message with a small MTU which could then lead to the host sending many small data packets [17].

3.1.2 An IPv6 PMTUD test

An IPv6 host must accept and process PTB messages, but does not have to reduce its packet size below 1280 bytes [10]. Tunnelled connectivity is common in IPv6, so our ability to directly test PMTUD is limited if a tunnel with a 1280 byte MTU is in the path. Similarly, if the webserver sends segments that are too big for the network to carry to the vantage point and the webserver does not receive a PTB message, the vantage point will not see any data packets that can be used to test for PMTUD behaviour. Therefore we begin by advertising an MSS of 1440 bytes to the webserver, sending a PTB with an MTU of 1480 bytes if a data packet larger than this is received. Then, we test a connection with an MSS of 1380 bytes and an MTU of 1280 bytes. Finally, we test a connection with an MSS of 1220 bytes and an MTU of 576 bytes. For the last test, we expect subsequent packets to arrive with an IPv6 fragmentation header, even if the packet is smaller than 1280 bytes. The last test also allows us to infer PMTUD failure for earlier tests where no data packets are received as an MSS of 1220 bytes should be small enough in practice that packets could be carried.

3.2 Vantage Points

For our IPv4 tests we use two vantage points: a host located in San Diego, USA, and another in Hamilton, New Zealand. We use two hosts to reduce the chance that some aspect of the network they are hosted on or their service

MTU tested	Hamilton, NZ, 2010 1480	1280	576	256	San Diego, USA, 2010 1480	1280	576	256	2004 [1] 256
No TCP connection	1.7%	2.4%	1.6%	1.5%	0.7%	1.5%	0.7%	0.6%	2.5%
Early TCP reset	0.4%	0.3%	0.3%	0.3%	0.4%	0.2%	0.2%	0.2%	0.6%
No data packets	0.2%	0.2%	0.2%	0.3%	0.2%	0.2%	0.2%	0.2%	–
Data packets too small	18.0%	6.1%	3.9%	0.3%	17.2%	5.2%	3.2%	0.1%	–
DF not set on data packets	1.5%	2.0%	2.2%	3.3%	1.5%	2.0%	2.2%	3.3%	29.6%
Cleared DF after PTB	1.6%	2.7%	4.5%	70.8%	1.6%	2.7%	4.6%	72.1%	–
PMTUD success	71.1%	77.4%	78.0%	5.2%	72.6%	79.1%	79.5%	5.3%	40.8%
PMTUD failure	5.7%	8.9%	9.4%	18.3%	6.0%	9.1%	9.5%	18.3%	17.3%

Table 1: Results of our experiments and the earlier work of Medina, *et al.* [1]. The portion of webservers that failed at PMTUD increases from 6% for an MTU of 1480 to 18% for an MTU of 256. Few webservers will reduce their packet size to 256 bytes; instead, most reduce their packet size to 552 bytes, and most send these packets with the DF bit cleared.

providers influencing the result; for example, by setting or clearing the DF bit on received packets, or by re-writing the MSS option contained in our SYN packets. For our IPv6 tests we use five vantage points in geographically and topologically diverse locations. We use the same San Diego vantage point, as well as hosts in Amsterdam, Tokyo, New York, and Christchurch, New Zealand. More vantage points are required for the IPv6 tests owing to the belief that tunnelled paths are widespread; because PMTUD relies on a tunnel sending a PTB message if it reduces the Path MTU, they provide an additional failure mode.

3.3 Targets

We derive our targets from the Alexa Top 1,000,000 websites list [11]. For our IPv4 tests, each vantage point independently derives its list of IP addresses to probe from the first 50,000 entries. We do this so the appropriate addresses for each vantage point will be tested if the location of the vantage point influences the addresses supplied. We test all IPv4 addresses the domain resolves to. We use wget [18] to determine a suitable URL to use in our tests. If the default page for the domain is at least 1600 bytes in size, we ask for it when we test PMTUD behaviour. Otherwise, we use wget to obtain all objects required to display the default page that are on that webserver, and select the first object that is at least 1600 bytes in size, or the largest object available. The San Diego vantage point tests the behaviour of 45,752 addresses, the Hamilton vantage point tests 45,990 addresses, and 54,008 addresses in total are tested with an intersection of 70% across 5,492 ASes.

For our IPv6 tests, we resolve the domains for the million websites in the list for IPv6 addresses. For those with IPv6 addresses, we resolve the domain for IPv4 addresses as well to enable PMTUD behaviour comparison for these dual-stacked webservers. The same 1,067 IPv6 addresses are tested by all five vantage points.

3.4 Implementation

We implemented a TBIT-style PMTUD test in scamper, a parallelised packet-prober [19]. For each measurement made our tool records, in a single data unit, meta-data about the test such as the URL, the server MSS seen and the MTU value used, as well as all packets sent and received for that test. It is simple to ensure inferences are valid given the packets recorded. We also implemented a driver to coordinate scamper's measurements. For each IP address, the driver begins by sending up to four ping packets to see if the network allows any ICMP through. Then, it does the sequence of PMTUD tests towards the webserver one at a time, testing the MTU values from highest to lowest. The driver waits at least one minute between PMTUD tests to each unique IP address to avoid being a nuisance.

Server MSS	Portion	Fail rate (1280)
1460	86.5%	6.7%
1380	10.8%	27.1%
1400	0.4%	6.8%
1414	0.3%	6.9%
536	0.2%	–
other	1.8%	–

Table 2: Top five server MSS values advertised and their corresponding failure rate. 10.8% of the population advertise an MSS of 1380, and these are four times more likely to fail at PMTUD.

4. IPV4 PMTUD BEHAVIOUR

Table 1 shows the overall results of our IPv4 tests, with the final column containing corresponding classifications from [1]. We see a similar failure rate in 2010 for the tests with a 256 byte MTU as was seen in the 2004 study. However, the failure rate is much lower for the other MTU values tested. Compared with the 2004 study we measure a success rate of 78–80% which is nearly double the 2004 result, and the number of servers we measure that do not set the DF bit on data packets is nearly an order of magnitude less than the 2004 result. We believe the results are different in the 2004 study because of a bug in TBIT that classifies hosts that clear the DF bit as not attempting PMTUD, and because of the choice of 256 as the MTU value to use in PTB messages. Figure 1 shows the fraction of webservers that always set the DF bit in a long-term packet header trace collected at the border of the University of Waikato network [20]. In 2004, 94% of webservers always set the DF bit, and is independent of the website population changing when students are on campus. This is consistent with the behaviour of most operating systems to enable PMTUD by default.

The proportions of classifications are similar for the two vantage points, so the following analyses will use the data obtained from Hamilton. The proportion of webservers that

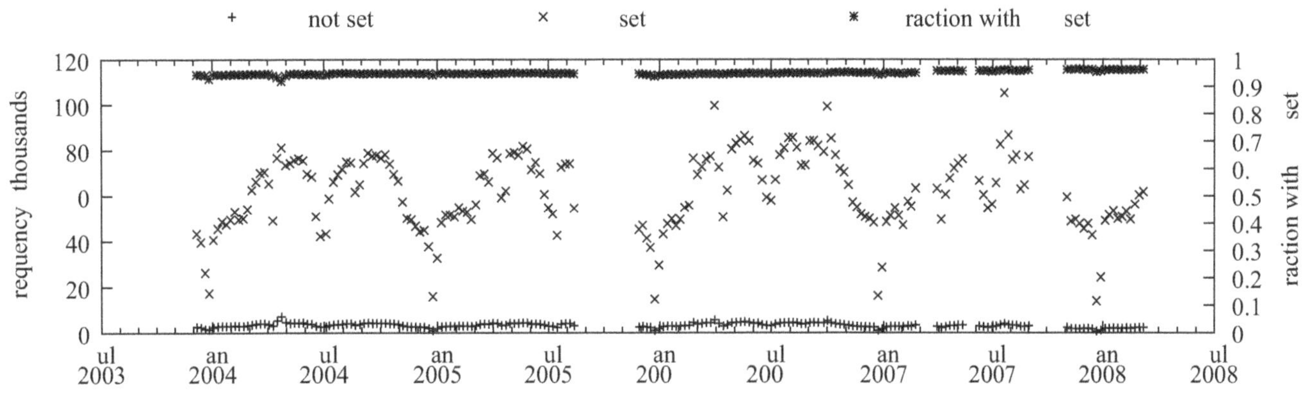

Figure 1: IPv4 webservers that send data packets with the DF bit set over time as measured by packet traces at the edge of the University of Waikato network. Each point represents one week. The bottom series is the number of webservers that never set the DF bit on any data packet. The middle series is the number of webservers that set the DF bit on all data packets. The top series is the fraction of these webservers that always set the DF bit; the fraction grows from 94% in 2004 to 96% by 2008.

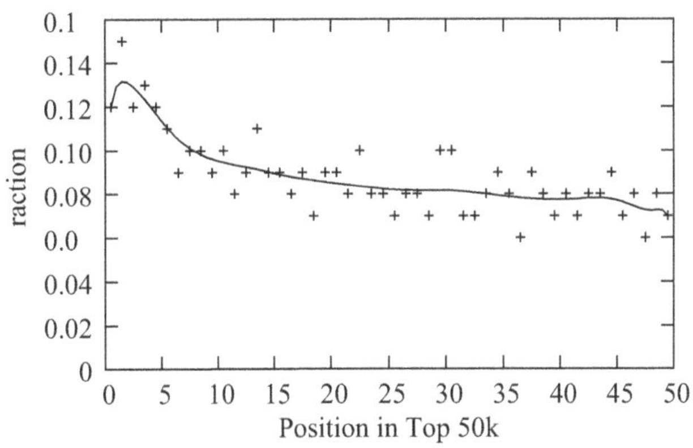

Figure 2: Fraction of IPv4 webservers that fail at PMTUD with a 1280 byte MTU in buckets of 1000, by popularity. The line is a Bézier curve showing the trend that the more popular a webserver is the more likely it is to fail at PMTUD.

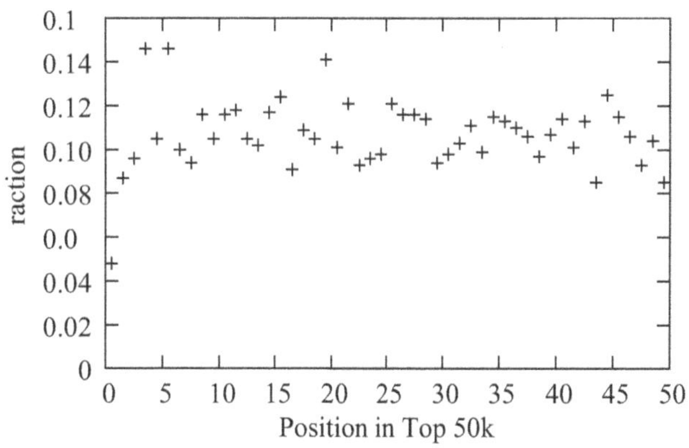

Figure 3: Fraction of IPv4 webservers that advertise an MSS of 1380, ordered by popularity in buckets of 1000. There is no correlation evident between the popularity of a webserver and the advertisement of 1380.

do not send packets large enough to allow for a test using an MTU of 1480 is 18%, compared with 6% for an MTU of 1280. Table 2 shows why: 10.8% of servers in our population advertise an MSS of 1380 bytes and send packets no larger than 1420 bytes. This MSS is associated with middleboxes that clamp the MSS of TCP connections they pass to avoid PMTUD problems when the client is behind a tunnel. Table 2 also shows the PMTUD fail rate associated with these servers, which is 4 times higher than the fail rate of the other MSS values listed. It seems worthwhile to identify the manufacturers of the middleboxes involved to determine if there is a bug involved, as if these webservers had a failure rate of 6.7% like most of the rest of the population the overall failure rate would drop 25%.

Figure 2 shows how the popularity of a webserver corresponds with the probability it will fail PMTUD with an MTU of 1280 bytes. As with Medina [1], we find the most popular webservers are much more likely to filter PTB messages than webservers that are less popular, but the failure rate for the most popular 500 we measure is half the rate reported in 2004. Because servers that advertise an MSS of 1380 are more likely to fail at PMTUD, we wondered if this was more likely to be a feature of the popular webservers. Figure 3 shows there is no correlation evident; in fact the most popular 1000 webservers have the lowest fraction of 1380 MSS.

As noted in section 3.4, before we commenced each PMTUD test, we tested the webserver's responsiveness to ping. Overall, 85% of the webservers that succeeded at PMTUD are responsive, but only 33% of those which failed PMTUD are, suggesting the presence of firewalls configured to deny by default. Of the systems that did not set the DF bit on any data packet, 50% are responsive, indicating a deliberate choice to disable PMTUD because of the presence of a firewall. Figure 4 shows how the popularity of a webserver influences the probability it will be responsive to ping. More popular webservers are more likely to be unresponsive.

Figure 5 shows the size of a segment observed after a PTB message is sent regardless of the PMTUD classification made. For the 576, 1280, and 1480 MTU tests, at least

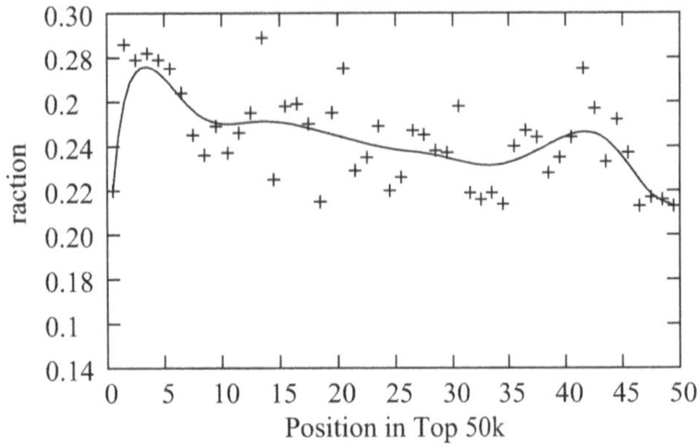

Figure 4: Fraction of IPv4 webservers that are not responsive to ping, ordered by popularity in buckets of 1000. The line is a Bézier curve showing the trend that the more popular webservers are more likely to be unresponsive to ping.

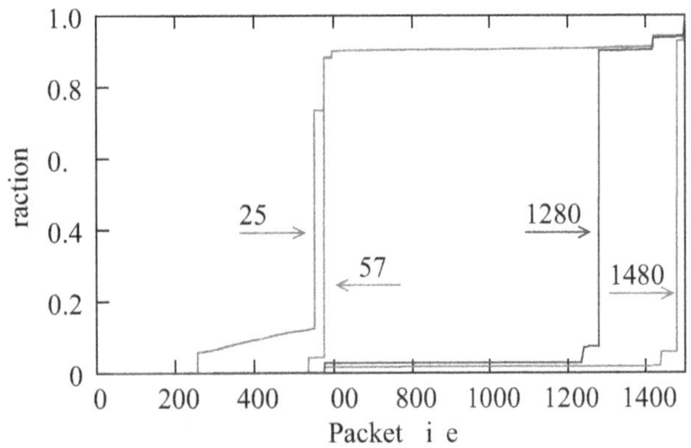

Figure 5: The subsequent size of a segment after a PTB message is sent, for each MTU tested. Most webservers behave as expected and reduce their packet size to the size advised, although most webservers will not reduce their packet size below 552 bytes if asked.

70% of the population behave as expected and reduce their packet size to the MTU advised. 5% reduce their packet size 40 bytes further, perhaps to ensure they send packets that will easily clear the link concerned. Few servers will reduce their packet size below 552 bytes in response to a PTB with MTU 256. Instead, most clear the DF bit to allow packets to be fragmented. The TBIT tool used in [1] classifies these systems as not attempting PMTUD, though it is clear from tests with other MTUs that most will attempt and successfully complete PMTUD. Systems that reduce their packet size to 552 bytes but do not clear the DF bit are failing PMTUD due to a bug in the operating system of the webserver; FreeBSD is one operating system with this bug [21]. Correcting these bugs will cut the failure rate for MTU 256 in half. The choice of 256 as an MTU value is not optimal for measuring the impact of middleboxes filtering PTB messages, because (1) most operating systems disable PMTUD when a PTB with this MTU is received, and (2) some reduce their packet size to a threshold but do not clear the DF bit.

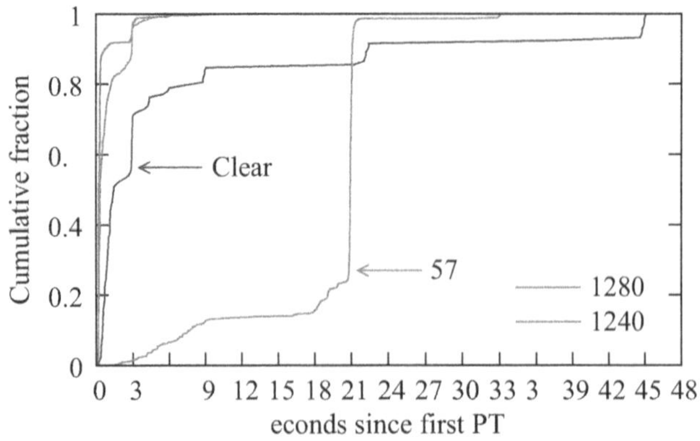

Figure 6: The delay between the first PTB sent and the action by the host. The delays measured in reducing to 576 bytes suggest the reductions are due to the hosts filtering PTB messages but having PMTUD blackhole detection enabled.

For the 1280 MTU test, 2.7% reduce their segment size to 576 bytes, and 91% of these reductions also clear the DF bit. This behaviour indicates the use of blackhole detection by the webserver, such as that done by Windows [16], in the presence of a firewall that discards PTB messages. Figure 6 shows the delay between the first PTB sent and the webserver transmitting packets that will pass a link with a 1280 byte MTU. 91% of the webservers that reduce their packet size to 1280 do so within one second. In addition, 94% of all webservers that appear to take action based on receiving a PTB message also do so within three seconds. However, 77% of the webservers that reduce their packet size to 576 do so at least 20 seconds after the first PTB is sent, and are likely to be Windows hosts that have inferred a PMTUD blackhole; 74% of these webservers are unresponsive to ping. The Clear DF line represents 118 webservers that cleared the DF bit but did not reduce their packet size so it would clear a link with a 1280 byte MTU. 71% of these webservers respond within three seconds, though the tail is long, with 8% waiting 43 seconds to take their action.

We searched the data for evidence of other webservers using techniques to avoid PMTUD failures if they do not receive a PTB message when they should. Linux implements two techniques, neither of which are enabled by default. The first technique begins by sending large packets, and if the first large packet is lost twice and no PTB message is received, then after nine seconds the host will revert to sending 552 byte packets with the DF bit cleared. The second technique is PLPMTUD [14]; Linux begins by sending 552 byte packets by default, and after the window size has grown to 11 segments it will try sending a 1064 byte segment with the DF bit set. MacOS since 10.6 also implements blackhole detection; it begins by sending a small segment followed by a flight of several large packets. If the large packets do not cause acknowledgements, and the retransmission of the first large packet is not acknowledged either, it will lower its packet size to 1240 bytes and clear the DF bit. We observed no evidence of any of these in our data, though the tests are unlikely to find evidence of the first or third techniques unless a middlebox discards our PTB messages before they reach the destination.

MTU tested	Tokyo 1480	1280	576	New York 1480	1280	San Diego 1480	1280	Amsterdam 1480	1280	Christchurch 1480	1280
Early TCP reset	0.1%	0.1%	nil	0.1%	0.1%	0.2%	0.1%	0.2%	0.1%	0.2%	0.1%
No data packets	0.3%	0.1%	0.1%	0.1%	nil	0.3%	nil	0.6%	0.4%	0.6%	0.2%
Too small	35.9%	16.8%	–	32.9%	17.0%	32.7%	17.6%	33.4%	17.2%	34.2%	17.3%
PMTUD success	62.7%	80.5%	44.1%	66.0%	80.7%	65.9%	80.1%	64.9%	80.0%	64.1%	79.9%
PMTUD failure	1.0%	2.4%	55.7%	0.9%	2.2%	0.9%	2.2%	1.0%	2.2%	0.9%	2.4%

Table 3: Results of our IPv6 experiments. The results across vantage points are similar. At least 80% of the webservers we measure will reduce their packet size when asked, but less than half will include a fragmentation header as RFC 2460 requires when the MTU supplied is 576 bytes.

Server MSS	Portion	Fail rate (1280)
1440	83.6%	1.6%
1220	5.3%	–
1420	5.0%	2.2%
1380	3.8%	23.5%
other	1.8%	–

Table 4: Top four MSS values advertised for IPv6 and their corresponding failure rate. As with IPv4, IPv6 systems that advertise an MSS of 1380 are much more likely to fail PMTUD.

5. IPV6 PMTUD BEHAVIOUR

As noted in section 3.3, there are only 1,067 unique IPv6 addresses that are globally routable in the Alexa list of the top million websites [11]. We could not establish a connection to 15%, which we exclude from the following results so the summary statistics for PMTUD behaviour are not underestimated. However, the results are encouraging for the 910 websites for which we could test PMTUD behaviour.

Table 3 shows the results of our IPv6 experiments. The proportion of servers that fail at PMTUD for 1280 bytes is 2.4%. The corresponding failure rate for the IPv4 servers for this population is 4.4%. This may be due to fewer webservers having an IPv6 firewall enabled where they currently have an IPv4 firewall. As with the IPv4 tests, we assessed the responsiveness of each IPv6 webserver to ping. For the systems where PMTUD is successful 96% respond to ping, but for the failures 50% do so. Table 4 shows the top four server MSS values seen, and their corresponding failure rates. As with IPv4, systems that advertise an MSS of 1380 are much more likely to fail PMTUD.

Less than half of the webservers successfully complete PMTUD when sent a PTB message with an MTU of 576. In this scenario, we expect to receive all packets with an IPv6 fragmentation header even if the packets are not sent in fragments. This restricts our ability to directly test if a webserver receives and acts on a PTB message if it sends packets too small to test with an MTU of 1280 bytes. Table 3 contains results for Tokyo; we saw nearly identical results and behaviour with the other vantage points. We did not observe many TCP retransmissions in these tests; 72% of the failures saw just one retransmission, usually at least 45 seconds after the PTB was sent, before the TCP connection timed out. It is possible that another software bug is behind this result; some firewalls discard IPv6 packets with a fragmentation header if they are not part of a fragmented series [22], even if their only rule is to accept all IPv6 packets.

For 32% of 1480 MTU tests and 17% of 1280 MTU tests, we are not able to measure PMTUD behaviour because the packets we receive are too small. Because this figure is relatively large compared with the IPv4 population of section 4, we examined the packet traces for further evidence of PMTUD behaviour related to tunnelled IPv6 connectivity between our vantage points and the webservers. We filtered TCP connections where the maximum packet size received was less than the maximum packet size suggested by the server's MSS advertisement, and then looked for clusters of maximum packet size values. For all vantage points, we see clusters at 1480 and 1280, and for Tokyo we also see a cluster at 1476 corresponding to GRE [23]. However, the proportion of hosts that send packets smaller than their MSS is only 20%, and these clusters account for half of the maximum packet sizes we see. This indicates 10% of TCP sessions in our tests were carried over a tunnel, suggesting that tunnelled IPv6 connectivity is not very prevalent. This result is consistent with other measurements of the prevalence of IPv6 tunnelling [24], which have shown the percentage of tunnelled IPv6 reducing from 40% in 2004 to 10% in 2010.

6. CONCLUSION

Path MTU Discovery is a relatively simple algorithm to implement, but it depends on packet too big messages being generated by routers, forwarded by middleboxes, and correct action being taken by end-hosts. This paper shows the proportion of webservers that receive and correctly act on PTB messages is at least 80% for both IPv4 and IPv6. We identified two strategies to significantly cut the IPv4 failure rate. First, operating systems that refuse to lower their packet size below a threshold must be modified to not set the DF bit if the Path MTU is lower than the threshold. Second, the middleboxes that rewrite the TCP MSS to 1380 bytes should be debugged to ensure they correctly forward PTB messages, if it is possible to identify their manufacturers. A third strategy, which is arguably the most challenging, is to educate system administrators about the necessity of forwarding PTB messages.

Acknowledgements

This work was supported by New Zealand Foundation for Research Science and Technology (FRST) contract UOW-X0705. The following provided data or access to hosts to conduct experiments from: Emile Aben (RIPE NCC), Daniel Andersen (CAIDA), Kenjiro Cho (IIJ), Bill Owens (NYSERNet) and Bill Walker (SNAP Internet).

7. REFERENCES

[1] Alberto Medina, Mark Allman, and Sally Floyd. Measuring interactions between transport protocols and middleboxes. In *IMC '04*, pages 336–341, Taormina, Sicily, Italy, October 2004.

[2] J. Mogul and S. Deering. Path MTU Discovery. RFC 1191, IETF, November 1990.

[3] J. McCann, S. Deering, and J. Mogul. Path MTU Discovery for IP version 6. RFC 1981, IETF, August 1996.

[4] C.A. Kent and J.C. Mogul. Fragmentation considered harmful. *ACM SIGCOMM Computer Communication Review*, 17(5):390–401, 1987.

[5] K. Lahey. TCP problems with path MTU discovery. RFC 2923, IETF, September 2000.

[6] Richard van den Berg and Phil Dibowitz. Over-zealous security administrators are breaking the Internet. In *Proceedings of LISA '02: Sixteenth Systems Administration Conference*, pages 213–218, Berkeley, CA, November 2002.

[7] Geoff Huston. A tale of two protocols: IPv4, IPv6, MTUs and fragmentation. `http://www.potaroo.net/ispcol/2009-01/mtu6.html`

[8] Geoff Huston. Mutterings on MTUs. `http://www.potaroo.net/ispcol/2009-02/mtu.html`

[9] Iljitsch van Beijnum. IPv6 and path MTU discovery black holes. `http://www.bgpexpert.com/article.php?article=117`

[10] S. Deering and R. Hinden. Internet protocol, version 6 (IPv6) specification. RFC 2460, IETF, December 1998.

[11] Alexa. Top 1,000,000 sites. `http://www.alexa.com/topsites`.

[12] TBIT: TCP behaviour inference tool. `http://www.icir.org/tbit/`.

[13] Matthew Luckie, Kenjiro Cho, and Bill Owens. Inferring and debugging path MTU discovery failures. In *IMC '05*, pages 193–198, San Francisco, CA, USA, October 2005.

[14] M. Mathis and J. Heffner. Packetization layer path MTU discovery. RFC 4821, IETF, March 2007.

[15] Matt Mathis. Raising the Internet MTU. `http://staff.psc.edu/mathis/MTU/`.

[16] Microsoft. Documentation for EnablePMTUDBHDetect registry key.

[17] F. Gont. ICMP attacks against TCP. RFC 5927, IETF, July 2010.

[18] Wget 1.12. `http://www.gnu.org/software/wget/`.

[19] Matthew Luckie. Scamper. `http://www.wand.net.nz/scamper/`.

[20] WITS: Waikato Internet traffic storage. `http://www.wand.net.nz/wits/waikato/`.

[21] Matthew Luckie. kern/146628: [patch] TCP does not clear DF when MTU is below a threshold. `http://www.freebsd.org/cgi/query-pr.cgi?pr=146628`.

[22] Matthew Luckie. kern/145733: [patch] ipfw flaws with IPv6 fragments. `http://www.freebsd.org/cgi/query-pr.cgi?pr=145733`.

[23] S. Hanks, T. Li, D. Farinacci, and P. Traina. Generic routing encapsulation (GRE). RFC 1701, IETF, October 1994.

[24] RIPE Labs. Untunneling IPv6. `http://labs.ripe.net/content/untunneling-ipv6`.

Demystifying Service Discovery: Implementing an Internet-Wide Scanner

Derek Leonard and Dmitri Loguinov
Department of Computer Science and Engineering
Texas A&M University, College Station, TX 77843 USA
{dleonard,dmitri}@cse.tamu.edu

ABSTRACT

This paper develops a high-performance, Internet-wide service discovery tool, which we call IRLscanner, whose main design objectives have been to maximize politeness at remote networks, allow scanning rates that achieve coverage of the Internet in minutes/hours (rather than weeks/months), and significantly reduce administrator complaints. Using IRLscanner and 24-hour scans, we perform 21 Internet-wide experiments using 6 different protocols (i.e., DNS, HTTP, SMTP, EPMAP, ICMP and UDP ECHO), demonstrate the usefulness of ACK scans in detecting live hosts behind stateless firewalls, and undertake the first Internet-wide OS fingerprinting. In addition, we analyze the feedback generated (e.g., complaints, IDS alarms) and suggest novel approaches for reducing the amount of blowback during similar studies, which should enable researchers to collect valuable experimental data in the future with significantly fewer hurdles.

Categories and Subject Descriptors

C.4 [**Performance of Systems**]: Measurement Techniques

General Terms

Design, Measurement, Performance

Keywords

Horizontal Scanning, Service Discovery

1. INTRODUCTION

Characterizing visible services in the Internet (e.g., web sites [5], [16], [28], end-hosts [17], [18],[23]), discovering and patching servers with critical security vulnerabilities (e.g., SSH [42], DNS [13]), and understanding how Internet worms create massive botnets [10], [25], [31], [53] are important research topics that directly benefit from efficient and scalable scanning techniques that can quickly discover available services in the Internet.

IMC'10, November 1–3, 2010, Melbourne, Australia.

Our focus in this paper is on *horizontal scanning* [52], which is a method for enumerating (in some set $\mathcal{S}$) all remote hosts that support a given protocol/service p. This is accomplished by sending packets to destinations in $\mathcal{S}$ and counting positive responses within some time interval. We call a scan *complete* if each address in $\mathcal{S}$ is probed and *partial* otherwise. The latter type of scan significantly reduces the burden on remote networks and is useful when an estimate of the number of responsive hosts (rather than their IP addresses) is sufficient.

While several large-scale measurements have been conducted in the past [5], [13], [17], [43], researchers initially considering a similar project are often faced with delays on the order of months for individual tests to run [5], [43]. During this time, computational resources of potentially dozens [5] of local machines that could be put to other uses are tied up. Further complicating the issue is the possibility of facing a significant number of complaints from hostile network administrators [5], [8], [11], [13], [15], [17], [42], [43], even for partial measurements. Given these issues, questions arise about the feasibility of service discovery [9], especially on sensitive TCP ports. Evidence suggests that sometimes [17] researchers are even forced to abort planned activities due to the negative publicity generated by scan traffic.

Since previous work has not explicitly aimed to design a high-performance scanner and/or maximize its politeness, there is no standard by which to judge the quality or intrusiveness of a scanner. Our first step then is to propose three main objectives that a good Internet-wide scanning solution must satisfy: 1) efficient usage of resources (i.e., bandwidth, CPU, memory) in complete scans; 2) accuracy of extrapolation in partial scans; and 3) maximum politeness at remote networks. The first objective ensures that the implementation scales well when scan duration T is reduced to hours or even minutes. The second objective delivers a platform for extremely fast partial scans with accurate extrapolation of metrics of interest. The last objective maximally reduces the instantaneous load (i.e., burstiness) applied to target subnets and controls the rate of IDS activity (i.e., false-positive alarms, wasted investigation effort, and dynamic firewall blocks against the scanner network) in response to scan traffic.

We next build a scanner that satisfies these goals and evaluate its performance in real scans.

1.1 Our Contributions

The first part of the paper analyzes the approaches exposed in the literature to understand whether they can be used to optimize performance, politeness, and extrapolation ability of an Internet-wide scanner. In addition to realizing that prior work was not driven by any particular objectives in designing their scanners (besides obtaining the data of interest in some finite amount of time), we also reach the conclusion that there is no consensus on such important parameters as scan scope, permutation, split among source IPs, implementation, timeouts, handling of complaints, and monitoring of the scan's intrusiveness at remote networks.

To overcome this problem, the second part of the paper presents our design of IRLscanner, which is a high-performance and source-IP scalable framework for service discovery in the Internet. The central element of the scanner is a novel permutation/split algorithm, which we show is optimally polite at each CIDR subnet s as it spaces probes arriving to s equally throughout scan duration $[0, T]$, even with multiple source IPs. Extrapolation results with IRLscanner running at its default rate r (at which it covers the Internet in $T = 24$ hours) demonstrate that partial scans of our approach are unbiased, leading to 1% estimation error in the number of live hosts in just 10 seconds.

Due to the goal of allowing faster scan durations (i.e., minutes/hours) and politeness concerns, IRLscanner incorporates additional features that help it achieve our objectives. These include a significantly reduced scope of measurements (i.e., one billion packets fewer) compared to previous scanners, absence of largely ineffective retransmissions, ability to run with any number of IPs aliased to the same server, capture of all back-scan and bogus traffic (e.g., from hackers and buggy implementations), and significantly higher timeouts for unresponsive targets, which allows it to capture a wider variety of busy/slow hosts in the Internet than was possible before.

Armed with IRLscanner, the third part of the paper highlights 21 Internet-wide scans across a wide range of protocols and ports, including DNS (port 53), HTTP (port 80), SMTP (port 25), EPMAP (port 135), and UDP ECHO (port 7). In addition to running over 20 times faster than any prior scanner and probing ports that have never been scanned in the literature (i.e., SMTP, ECHO, EPMAP), we experiment with several techniques never achieved on an Internet-wide scale in previous work (e.g., ACK scanning, testing ECN and TCP option support) and perform the first large-scale OS fingerprinting study of 44M hosts responding to port 80.

We finish the paper by analyzing the feedback generated from our experiments. This includes a detailed complaint analysis, techniques for monitoring the impact of scan traffic on IDS activity in the Internet, approaches for a-priori predicting the amount of blowback in response to scanning a particular port, and various ways for reducing the perceived maliciousness of the scan.

1.2 Ethical Implications

Over the last two years, we have closely worked with university officials and taken numerous steps (see below) in an effort to reduce investigation effort and aggravation for remote administrators. While our interest in this paper is purely to expose the underlying issues of service discovery and make it more accessible to researchers without damaging remote networks, one concern might be that our scan techniques are not only maximally polite, but also optimally stealthy against popular IDS packages. As a result, one could argue that attackers could benefit from our work and thus inflict certain damage that would not otherwise be possible.

However, we do not believe this to be the case. First, stealthier scanning by itself does not compromise hosts; in contrast, intrusion using malicious payload (e.g., delivered through unsolicited packets or email) does. As a result, many networks with patched hosts and up-to-date IDS signatures of various malware should remain well protected despite the findings of this paper. Second, botnets afford hackers such a diverse pool of IPs that they often do not care to remain stealthy and rely on the most basic sequential scanning [2], which apparently is sufficient for their purposes. Instead, we believe that the discussion and techniques exposed in this paper might be useful in building future defenses against scanning worms, should they choose to deploy similar techniques.

Another concern might be that we are collecting information about remote networks that their administrators do not wish to make public. We contend that such information is well-protected by firewalls, and this paper makes no attempt to trick or confuse network monitoring devices to gather sensitive data. Further, given the constant background scanning performed by attackers [41], any data (and likely much more) we collect is already available to them. However, to ensure privacy, we do not publicize any information about individual networks collected during our scans and instead rely only on summary statistics.

2. SCANNER DESIGN

Beyond the experiment-specific choice of the protocol/port pair that uniquely characterize a service, every researcher considering a horizontal scan must answer a common set of questions before proceeding. In this section, we turn to several recent studies [5], [13], [17], [43] that have performed large-scale service discovery to determine whether these design questions have been definitively answered and our objectives met.

2.1 Scan Scope

We start with the issue of which IP addresses to target when scanning. Define $\mathcal{F}$ to be the Internet IPv4 address space, which consists of $n = 2^{32}$ addresses available for scanning. While intuition may suggest to probe the entire space to ensure completeness, certain IPs may not be suitable for scanning. Before delving into details, define set $\mathcal{NR} \subseteq \mathcal{F}$ to be all non-reserved destinations [20], $\mathcal{I} \subseteq \mathcal{NR}$ to be all IANA-allocated blocks [19], and $\mathcal{B} \subseteq \mathcal{I}$ to be the set of IPs advertised in BGP prefixes [59] at the border router of the scanner network. Note that $\mathcal{B}$ must be verified against $\mathcal{I}$ to ensure that invalid advertisements are not included.

To capture the choice of which destinations to target, we define scan *scope* $\mathcal{S}$ to be the subset of $\mathcal{F}$ probed during measurement. As shown in the second column of Table 1, all previous Internet-wide service discovery projects scanned at least the IANA allocated space $\mathcal{I}$, which is justified [17], [34] by churn in BGP routing tables and desire to avoid losing responses during the period of the experiment (i.e., 30+ days in Table 1). In [5], however, no reason is given for scanning unallocated space, although there is a slight possibility of new blocks being allocated by IANA during the measurement.

As we discuss later, sets $\mathcal{I}$ and $\mathcal{NR}$ may be appropriate for slow scans; however, faster scanners have little incentive

Scanner	Scope	Permutation	Servers	Protocol	Port	Timeout	Duration	Blacklist	.0/.255	Exclude
Pryadkin [43]	$\mathcal{I}$	uniform	3	ICMP/TCP	–	10s	123d	yes	no	no
Benoit [5]	$\mathcal{NR}$	uniform	25	TCP	80	30s	92d	no	yes	no
Dagon [13]	$\mathcal{I}$	uniform	–	UDP	53	–	30d	–	yes	US Gov
Heidemann [17]	$\mathcal{I}$	RIS	8	ICMP	echo	5s	52d	yes	no	no

Table 1: Large-scale service discovery in the literature (dashes represent unreported values).

to utilize sets larger than $\mathcal{B}$ in the current Internet since performance concerns (i.e., volume of sent traffic) usually outweigh completeness of scan results.

2.2 Scan Order

The next factor we consider is the order in which IP addresses are scanned. This is determined by the *permutation* [53] of space $\mathcal{S}$, which is simply a reordering of target addresses to achieve some desired result. The chosen permutation controls the burstiness of traffic seen by remote networks and is a significant factor in both the perceived politeness of scan traffic and estimation accuracy of Internet-wide metrics from partial scans. For all discussion below, we assume that target subnets s are full CIDR blocks (i.e., given in the $/b$ notation).

The most basic approach, which we call *IP-sequential*, does not shuffle the address space and probes it in numerical order (e.g., 10.0.0.1, 10.0.0.2, 10.0.0.3, etc.). It is not only simple to implement, but also routinely used in the Internet [2], [22], [30] and measurement studies [3], [16]. IP-sequential targets individual subnets s with a burst of $|s|$ consecutive packets at the rate of n/T before moving on to another network. Besides extremely high sending rates to s regardless of its size (e.g., 37 Kpps for $\mathcal{S} = \mathcal{I}$ and $T = 24$ hours), IP-sequential also suffers from poor extrapolation ability.

The main alternative to IP-sequential is the *uniform* permutation [53] also extensively used in the literature [5], [13], [42], [43]. This approach draws targets uniformly randomly from the full address space $\mathcal{S}$ and intermingles probes to many subnets, which reduces instantaneous load on individual networks and produces unbiased random sampling during partial scans. In the literature, the uniform permutation is usually accomplished by either an LCG (linear congruential generator) [29] or some encryption algorithm applied sequentially to each element of $\mathcal{S}$ (e.g., TEA [42]), both of which ensure that no IP is probed twice.

The final approach proposed in [17] we call *Reverse IP-sequential* (RIS) due to its reversal of the bits in the IP-sequential permutation and targeting the same address in each subnet (e.g., *.*.127.10, *.*.8.10, *.*.248.10, etc.) before moving on to another address. Intuition suggests that RIS is poorly suited for extrapolation (which we confirm below), while the uniform permutation fails to deliver packets with maximum spacing to each subnet. Since no analysis exists to further evaluate the differences between these three permutation algorithms, making an informed choice remains an open problem.

2.3 Scan Origin

In a bid to obtain multiple vantage points [17] and decrease the time required to complete the scan [5], past measurement studies have often distributed the burden of scanning amongst several hosts. We call this process a *split*, which in the literature parcels blocks of either contiguous [3], [5] or permuted [17], [43] IP addresses to m scanning nodes. Column four of Table 1 contains values for m used previously, with [17] being the only study that used multiple hosts residing on two different networks (four at each location).

The current consensus in the literature is that multiple scanning hosts on a single network are necessary only if the full assigned scanning bandwidth cannot be utilized by one host, a condition that is implied in [43] and mentioned explicitly in [3], [5], [17]. However, it is not clear from these studies how many hosts are needed to efficiently utilize a link or provide reasonably short scan durations. Further, the literature does not consider the split's impact on the perceived politeness of the scan, which we tackle later in the paper.

2.4 Extrapolation

In many research applications, especially those that monitor growth of the Internet [17], [23], it is sufficient to obtain the number of live hosts or estimate their characteristics (e.g., mean uptime) rather than a list of their exact IPs. The best approach in such cases is a partial scan, which produces a tiny footprint at remote networks and in many cases allows accurate extrapolation of metrics of interest. This requires that targets within each subnet be randomly selected, without any bias being given to certain parts of $\mathcal{S}$ or particular patterns within probed IP addresses (because the density of live hosts varies both across the Internet and the last $1-2$ bytes of the IP). In addition, non-random probing is often seen by administrators as purposefully malicious, which in turn leads to unnecessary investigation overhead, firewall blocks, and complaints.

2.5 Implementation

The next pressing issue of service discovery is the method used to send/receive packets, which significantly impacts the efficiency of the scanner. The easiest implementation method uses scripts that execute pre-written utilities [16], [43] or existing scanners [3]. An alternative is to write a custom scanner for a particular measurement, which opens the possibility of using connectionless sockets [13], [17] for ICMP or UDP-based scans, connection-oriented TCP sockets [5], and finally raw IP sockets for TCP SYN scans [42], [43]. While there is no consensus in the scanning literature on what method to use, [14] suggests that software limitations on packet sending rates can be overcome using a network subsystem that bypasses the default network stack.

2.6 Timeouts and Duration

The next two issues are when to mark a host as unresponsive and what aspects should determine scan duration T. The former issue comes down to two choices: 1) waiting a "safe" amount of time before retransmitting [5], [42], [43]; and 2) when to finally time out and declare targets dead [17]. Note that both incur substantial overhead due to the need to remember all covered destinations and to maintain numerous timers. Furthermore, it is unclear what benefit retransmission carries given the low packet loss on the backbone and whether the increased overhead (i.e., doubling or tripling the number of sent packets) justifies the potentially minuscule accuracy gains.

Table 1 lists timeout values that range from 5 to 30 seconds for previous measurements studies. Given the limited number of outstanding sockets, finite bandwidth and CPU power, and a wide range of possible choices, it remains unclear how to choose timeouts to simultaneously allow for efficiency and accuracy (e.g., certain busy servers respond with a 60-second delay, but should they be captured by the scanner?).

After settling the above problems, it is important to ensure that the scan will complete in such amount of time T that produces the most relevant data without overburdening local/remote network resources. Of the measurement studies listed in Table 1, only [13] was unencumbered by software/hardware restrictions, while for others these issues dominated the choice of T. As such, previous measurement studies have generally been limited to a tradeoff between small T, few servers m, large timeouts, and large scan scope. Instead, our goal is to develop a scanner in which the researcher can control T independently of all other listed parameters.

2.7 Negative Feedback

Due to the unsolicited nature of the packets sent by service discovery measurement studies and the diversity of networks in the Internet, it is inevitable that some targeted hosts will take offense. This often manifests itself in the form of email/phone complaints from network administrators [5], [11], [13], [17], [42], [43], though the literature is lacking in details on the exact nature of complaints (e.g., frequency of legal threats) and specific techniques for dealing with them.

In Table 1, we list three of the methods used by previous studies to mitigate complaints. The first is the use of a blacklist by [17], [42], [43] to exclude the networks of sensitive/suspicious administrators, which generally avoids repeated complaints from the same network. The other two approaches boil down to a further reduction in scope by the omission of network/broadcast IP addresses (i.e., *.*.*.0 and *.*.*.255) [17], [43] and preemptively blacklisting networks before they complain (e.g., U.S. government) [13]. While blacklisting complaining parties is undoubtedly a sound approach, no reasoning or motivating factors have been provided for the other two methods and it is unclear whether they are indeed necessary.

3. IRLscanner

Based on our analysis of scanning literature in the last section, it appears that researchers interested in service discovery projects are faced with scan durations on the order of months, tying up several machines that could be dedicated to other projects, and the likelihood of significant negative feedback that could easily lead to the measurement being terminated. For example, [17] reports that TCP scans produce 30 times more complaints than ICMP scans, which has precluded the authors from conducting them after the first attempt.

Assuming a fixed amount of bandwidth available for scanning, in this section we seek to alleviate these concerns by designing a service discovery tool we call IRLscanner that allows for very small scan durations T, originates from a single inexpensive host, and minimizes aggravation of network administrators (both remote and local) by scanning as politely as possible for a given T.

Set $\mathcal{S}$	Size	Reduction	Rate (Mbps)	Rate (Kpps)
$\mathcal{F}$	4.29B	–	33.4	49.7
$\mathcal{NR}$	3.7B	14%	28.8	42.8
$\mathcal{I}$	3.27B	24%	25.4	37.8
$\mathcal{B}$	2.11B	51%	16.4	24.4

Table 2: Scan set size, Ethernet bandwidth requirement, and pps rate in a 24 hour TCP SYN scan.

3.1 Scan Scope

We start by determining the scope of IRLscanner. While firewalls and routers routinely use the Bogons list [12] to filter nonsensical traffic (i.e., reserved and unallocated blocks), packets destined to unadvertised BGP networks are also dropped by the scanner's border router, but only after unnecessarily increasing router load and wasting scanner resources. Therefore, one expects that only set $\mathcal{B}$ should normally produce valid results or be used for discovering hosts responsive to unicast traffic. However, given that BGP tables change dramatically in the long-term [34], restricting the scope to only routable addresses either requires a live BGP feed or potentially allows for inaccurate representation of the Internet in the resulting measurement.

While this is definitely a concern for slow scanners (i.e., T is weeks or months), our goal is to complete measurements in much shorter periods (i.e., hours) during which BGP changes can often be neglected. For fast scans, updates pulled from RouteViews [46] at start time sufficiently approximate the routable space during the entire experiment. Our analysis of BGP tables during August 2009 discovered less than 0.1% difference in advertised prefixes over a 10-day period, with proportionally fewer changes during $T = 24$ hours used in our experiments. While for IRLscanner it makes sense to only probe $\mathcal{B}$, the tradeoff between scope, duration T, and BGP table accuracy must be determined on a case-by-case basis.

To gauge the potential gains from restricting the scope to routable destinations, we determine [19], [46] the current state of sets $\mathcal{B}$, $\mathcal{NR}$, and $\mathcal{I}$ in late August 2009 and list them in Table 2. While previous scanners achieve a significant reduction (i.e., by 24%) in the number of sent packets by omitting the reserved/unallocated space, probing only set $\mathcal{B}$ removes almost one billion *additional* targets and doubles the performance gains of previous work to 51%. The table also shows the bandwidth necessary to complete the scan in 24 hours, where all 40-byte SYN packets are padded to 84-byte minimum-size Ethernet frames, and the corresponding pps (packets per second) rate.

To implement a scanner with scope $\mathcal{B}$, it is necessary to obtain a timely BGP dump from either the RouteViews project [46] or the local border router. Given the desire for small scan durations on inexpensive hardware, checking individual IP addresses against a list of roughly 300,000 prefixes must be very efficient. While IP checking can be accomplished with a balanced binary tree [13] with logarithmic lookup complexity, IRLscanner uses a 512 MB hash table, where each bit indicates whether the corresponding IP is allowed

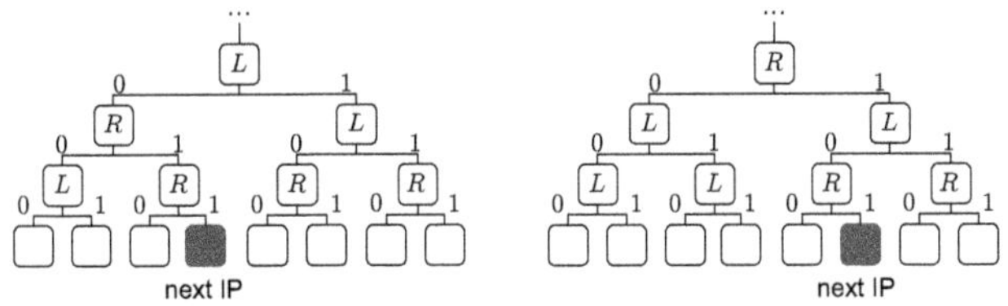

(a) IP ends with 011 (b) IP ends with 101

Figure 1: Illustration of AGT.

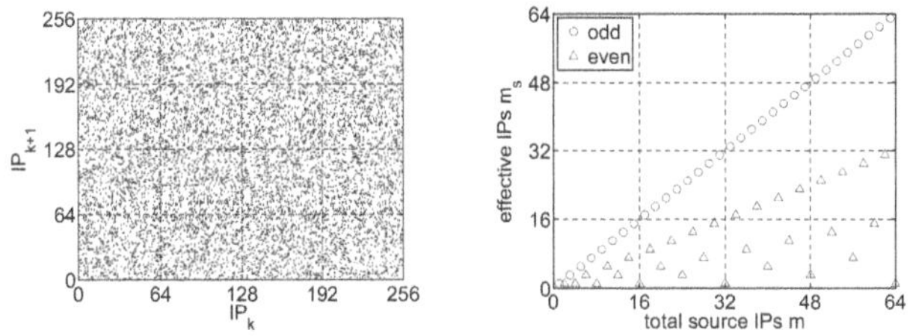

(a) last-octet correlation (b) m_s in (1)

Figure 2: Randomness of RLCG and effectiveness of the GIW/RR split.

or not. This ensures that checks are accomplished in $O(1)$ time and improves lookup speed from 923 Kpps (balanced tree) to 11 Mpps (using a single core of a 2.2 GHz Opteron). Given that most commodity machines have at least 1 GB of RAM and the rest of our scanner requires only 2 MB of main memory, this tradeoff allows us to dedicate more computational power to sending packets and performing other processing as needed.

3.2 Scan Order

Despite the constant volume of scanning traffic in the Internet [41], network administrators generally view this activity as malicious and periodically complain to networks that originate such traffic [13], [17] [42]. Furthermore, many IDS tools [7], [51], [58] automatically generate firewall rules against scanning hosts, whether detected locally or through distributed collaborative systems [36], [47]. With this perception in mind, researchers must first weigh the benefit gained from performing a service discovery measurement with the possibility of negative publicity for their institution and/or its address space being blacklisted at remote networks.

Upon determining to proceed, these negative effects can be reduced for all involved parties by using an address permutation that avoids targeting individual subnets with large bursts of traffic, which often triggers Intrusion Detection Systems (IDS) and raises concerns of malicious/illegal activity. Since IDS predominantly operates on a per-IP basis, additional reduction in false-alarms is possible by using multiple source IPs at the scanner host, which we discuss later in this section. While the uniform permutation [53] is routinely used in scanning applications, no previous paper has examined the issue of achieving maximal politeness and whether such methods could be implemented in practice. We address this open problem next.

For a given CIDR subnet s in the Internet, our goal is to maximally reduce the burstiness of scan traffic seen by s, which is equivalent to maximizing inter-packet delays for *all* probes arriving to s. Recalling that $n = 2^{32}$, we define permutations that return to s with a period $n/|s|$ to be *IP-wide* at s and those that achieve this simultaneously for all possible CIDR subnets to be *globally IP-wide* (GIW). Note that GIW permutations spread probes to each s evenly throughout $[0, T]$, which ensures that all networks are probed at a constant rate $|s|/T$ proportional to their size and that no s can be scanned slower for a given value of T. This makes GIW optimally polite[1] across the entire Internet.

The simplest GIW technique, which we call an *alternating gateway tree* (AGT), is a binary tree of depth 32 where target IPs reside in leaves and all edges are labeled with 0/1 bits. Traversing the tree, the scanner accumulates individual bits along the edges into the next IP. Decisions to move left or right at internal nodes (gateways) v depend on their states θ_v, which are flipped during each visit to ensure that no IP is probed twice and that packets alternate between left/right children of each gateway. Figure 1 shows the bottom four levels of some random AGT, where the tree in part (a) generates an IP address ending with bits 011. Part (b) of the figure illustrates the next IP generated when the scanner returns to this portion of the AGT, which results in the address ending with bits 101.

Since balanced binary trees have well-defined rules for calculating the offset of each internal node, AGTs do not require storing child pointers. Thus, their RAM overhead is $(n-1)/8 = 512$ MB needed to store tuple $(\theta_1, \dots, \theta_{n-1})$ and their computational complexity is 26 memory reads/writes (i.e., 52 total) per generated IP (assuming depth-31 traversal and 64-bit lookups that yield the first 5 levels of the tree in one RAM access).

Note that AGT provides the scanner with 2^{n-1} possible GIW permutations, which is enormous. In practice, one does not require this much diversity and other GIW algorithms may be sufficient. One reason to seek alternatives is that AGT requires saving 512 MB during checkpointing and transmission of the same amount of seed data to other scanner hosts in distributed implementations. Another reason is that AGT's CPU complexity is quite high, which we reduce in our next method.

Let ${}_bx$ be the lower b bits of an integer x and $\mathcal{R}(x)$ be the bit-reversal function. Then, we have the following result.

THEOREM 1. *Given a sequence of integers $\{x_k\}_{k=1}^n$, suppose $\{_b(x_k)\}_{k=1}^n$ has a full period for all $b = 1, 2, \dots, 32$. Then, sequence $\{\mathcal{R}(_{32}x_k)\}_k$ is GIW.*

PROOF. Assume that subnet s has depth b in the AGT (i.e., $n/|s| = 2^b$) and observe that GIW patterns must visit all remaining $2^b - 1$ subnets at depth b before returning to s. In practice, this means that the permutation must exhibit a full period in the upper b bits. Since for GIW this holds for all s, the full period must be simultaneously maintained at all depths $1 \le b \le 32$. Reversing the bits in each IP, we can replace this condition with a much simpler one – the full period must hold in the lower b bits. □

While there are many possible ways to construct $\{x_k\}_k$, an LCG of the form $x_k = ax_{k-1} + c$ is a natural choice due to its computational efficiency and need for only a single integer of state. To establish its suitability for Theorem 1, we note

[1]While completely refraining from scanning is even more polite, it does not produce any useful service-discovery results.

Type	Bit reversal	Rate (IP/sec)	State & seed
AGT	–	661,247	512 MB
LCG	Bit shifts	10,729,920	4 bytes
	Two-byte hash	21,263,889	4 bytes

Table 3: Benchmark of GIW address generation.

that the conditions for achieving a full period in $\{x_k\}_k$ with an LCG are well-known and require that $a-1$ be divisible by 4 and c be odd [26]. We call the resulting algorithm *Reversed LCG* (RLCG) and use it with $a = 214,013, c = 2,531,011$, which are well-known constants that produce an uncorrelated sequence of random variables (shown in Figure 2(a) for the last byte of generated IPs). Initial seed x_0 can then be used to change the scan order across multiple runs.

To efficiently reverse the bits, we use a 2-byte hash table that flips the order of bits in 16-bit integers. Therefore, any 32-bit IP can be processed in two memory lookups (i.e., 26 times faster than AGT); however, the CPU cache often makes this operation run even faster in practice. Table 3 benchmarks IP generation of AGT, naive bit-shifts (32 shifts down and 32 up), and the hash table technique. Observe that RLCG with a hash table runs at double the speed of bit-shifts and beats AGT by a factor of 32, which is slightly faster than 26 predicted by the analysis above. In more practical terms, AGT constrains the scanner to $T \geq 108$ minutes, while hash-based RLCG generates the entire permutation in just 3.4 minutes.

3.3 Scan Origin

While previous work has split the scan burden among m nodes to decrease total duration [3], [5], [17], [43] or obtain multiple vantage points [17], no apparent consideration has been given to the possible effect it has on the perceived politeness of the measurement. The main objective of a polite split in this paper is to maintain the GIW pattern across scanner IPs, which requires a mechanism for not only parceling the address space to m scanning hosts without burdensome message-passing, but also ensuring that each subnet s sees scanner IPs in a *perfectly alternating and equally-spaced fashion* (e.g., IP1, IP2, IP3, IP1, IP2, IP3, ...).

The rationale for using all m sources to scan each s lies in the fact that IDS (both open-source [7], [51] and commercial [24], [38]) detect scan traffic and throw alarms in response to perceived malicious activity based on individual source IPs. Therefore, a particular IP address sending its packets to s faster than other IPs is more readily detected as it simply stands out from the others. The reason for maximally spacing probes from different IPs is the same as before – reducing the overall burstiness at remote subnets – which for large m (i.e., hundreds or thousands) may become non-trivial. One example of an extremely impolite split is IP-sequential, which scans each s from a *single* source IP at rates similar to those in Table 2 (i.e., megabits per second and thousands of pps), regardless of subnet size.

Analysis shows that GIW split does not require a new permutation; however, individual source IPs must now return to s every $mn/|s|$ packets (i.e., alternating in some order with a full period m). Synchronizing m hosts using the block-split algorithms of previous work [3], [5], [17], [43], while sustaining the GIW split is a difficult problem. We instead introduce a new split algorithm that satisfies our conditions and requires low overhead/state.

Algorithm 1 RLCG/RR at host $i \in \mathcal{M}$

```
x_0 = rand()                          ▷ Set initial seed x_0
for k = 1 to n do                     ▷ Iterate through all IPs
    ip = k mod m                      ▷ Assigned source IP
    x_k = a x_{k-1} + c               ▷ Advance LCG
    if (ip == i) then                 ▷ Our IP?
        target = R(x_k)               ▷ Reverse bits
        if (BGP[target]==VALID) then  ▷ In BGP?
            probe(target)             ▷ Hit destination
        end if
    end if
    sleep(T/n)                        ▷ Wait for next packet
end for
```

The intuition behind our split, which we call *round-robin* (RR), is to generate a single RLCG permutation $\{z_k\}$ and assign target z_k to host k mod m. Assuming $\mathcal{M}$ is the set of scanning hosts, RR sends the initial seed x_0 to every host $i \in \mathcal{M}$, its position i, and the number of sources m. Each host then generates the entire sequence $\{z_k\}_k$ locally and hits target z_{i+jm} at time $(i+jm)T/n$ for $j = 0, 1, \ldots, n/m$, the simplicity of which is demonstrated in Algorithm 1. Even with $T = 24$ hours, subnets are visited so infrequently (e.g., every 337 seconds for a /24) that perfect synchronization of start times is not necessary. Furthermore, in scanners running from a single location, all m IPs can be aliased to the same host and RR-split can be used locally to ensure perfect synchronization, which is the approach taken by IRLscanner later in the paper.

From the well-known properties of LCGs [4], we immediately obtain the following crucial result.

THEOREM 2. *RR-split with any GIW permutation scans s with $\min(|s|, m_s)$ sources, where*

$$m_s = \frac{m}{\gcd(\frac{n}{|s|}, m)} \quad (1)$$

and $\gcd(a, b)$ is the greatest common divisor of (a, b).

PROOF. Examine $\{z_k\}_k$ and assume it is GIW. For a given subnet s, observe that its IPs appear in this list with a period $n/|s|$, which follows from the definition of GIW. Assuming $w_j \in \mathcal{M}$ is the j-th IP that hits s, we have

$$w_j = \left(w_{j-1} + \frac{n}{|s|}\right) \bmod m, \quad j = 1, 2, \ldots \quad (2)$$

This recurrence is an additive-only LCG whose period [4] is given by (1), which means that the number of sources scanning s is the smaller of its size and m_s. □

To better understand this result, examine Figure 2(b) that shows one example of (1) for $|s| = 65536$ (i.e., a /16 target subnet). Notice that even values of m lead to $m_s \leq m/2$ (triangles in the figure), which reduces the effective number of IPs seen by each subnet at least by half. The worst choice of m is a power of two, in which case $m_s = 1$ regardless of m. On the other hand, odd values of m produce the ideal $m_s = m$ (circles in the figure) and thus achieve a GIW split. We rely on this fact later in Section 4.

3.4 Extrapolation

Given the goal of being able to extrapolate the number of responsive hosts and other properties of open ports from a severely abbreviated scan (e.g., $1-10$ seconds instead of 24

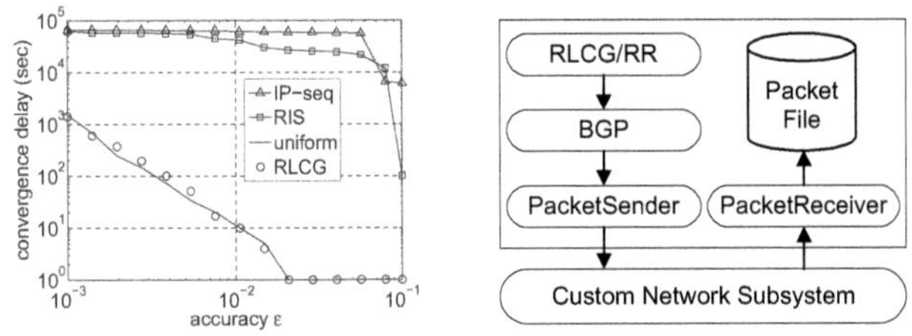

(a) extrapolation delay (b) implementation

Figure 3: Extrapolation delay and IRLscanner implementation.

hours), we next examine how the existing and proposed approaches handle this problem. We split the allocated IANA space into three blocks (i.e., ARIN, RIPE, and APNIC), roughly corresponding to different geographical zones, and build three distributions of live IPs from our Internet measurements. Specifically, PMF function $p_j(x_3, x_4)$ specifies the probability that IP $x_1.x_2.x_3.x_4$ is alive in geographical zone $j \in \{1, 2, 3\}$. We then generate a Bernoulli random variable for each IP in the IANA space and make it alive using the corresponding probability $p_j(x_3, x_4)$.

Using a simulation with $T = 24$ hours, we scan the assigned distribution of live/dead hosts using four approaches – uniform, RLCG, IP-sequential, and RIS. Assuming A is the true number of live hosts in the assignment and $\tilde{A}(t)$ is an estimate at time t, define the relative extrapolation error $e(t) = |1 - \tilde{A}(t)/A|$. Convergence to threshold ϵ is established at such time t_ϵ when estimates for all $t \geq t_\epsilon$ have error smaller than ϵ.

Figure 3(a) plots the expected convergence delay t_ϵ averaged over 100 iterations. Observe that both RLCG and uniform converge to 1% error in 10 seconds, while RIS and IP-sequential take 11 and 16 hours, respectively. This result is easy to explain since IP-sequential gets trapped in certain CIDR blocks for an extended period and RIS hits the same last octet 16M times in a row. Furthermore, 0.1% error in Figure 3(a) can be achieved in 23 minutes for both uniform and RLCG, while the other two methods require 17+ hours. Even to arrive at 5% accuracy, which takes RLCG less than a second, RIS requires 6 hours, which makes this method unsuitable for all but most crude extrapolations.

3.5 Implementation

Figure 3(b) shows the general structure of IRLscanner. IPs generated by RLCG/RR are first checked against BGP prefixes and then delivered to the sending module, which forms raw Ethernet frames and transmits them to a custom network driver [49], which can transmit SYN packets at 5.25 Mpps using a modern quad-core CPU. Assuming 3.5 Gbps of available bandwidth, IRLscanner can cover the entire BGP space in 6.7 minutes from a single server.

The custom stack also allows us to intercept arbitrary incoming/outgoing packets and suppress RSTs from the OS TCP/IP stack, which we utilize later in the paper when profiling remote operating systems. All received packets are saved to disk without inspection and are processed offline. After completing each run, IRLscanner continues to listen for incoming packets for several hours to capture extremely slow hosts and record back-scanning packets from hackers and other potentially interesting entities.

3.6 Timeouts and Duration

Previous measurement studies [5], [42], [43] used retransmissions to the unresponsive set of target hosts to minimize false negatives, which we now evaluate in light of politeness and efficiency. Cursory inspection shows that retransmitting probes to unresponsive hosts is the violation of the GIW pattern, which is undesirable. Combining this with the likelihood that many false negatives in the unresponsive set are likely to be from persistently congested links or over-burdened servers [1], politeness concerns suggest that retransmission is not generally advisable.

From an efficiency standpoint, it should also be noted that the unresponsive set accounts for $90 - 99\%$ of $\mathcal{S}$ (depending on the protocol), which means that a single timeout-based retransmission would require almost doubling the number of sent packets. Our experiments show that retransmission not only yields a negligible increase in found hosts (i.e., by $0.3 - 1.7\%$ depending on the port and time of day), but also introduces bias by capturing hosts that come online within the retransmission timeout.

We next turn to the issue of *when* the status of an IP address can be determined, which in related work [5], [17], [42], [43] has occurred at some timeout after the initial probe was sent. Considerable effort has been spent deciding on appropriate timeout values [5], the choice of which affects the number of false negatives due to slowly responding hosts and the overhead of keeping large amounts of state for outstanding targets. Given that retransmissions are not required, we avoid this tradeoff entirely by delaying the classification of IP addresses until *after* the scan completes.

In practice, we accomplish this by saving all received packets (i.e., 25 GB per scan) to disk for later analysis. As there are many packets that are not relevant to the scan, we note that certain information can be embedded in the packets themselves to correlate responses with hosts scanned. This option has been used by encoding the target IP address in ICMP ID fields [17] and DNS queries [13]. For TCP scans, we take advantage of the sequence number field to encode the target IP, which allows us to detect invalid and/or malicious replies. Concerns about I/O speed do not arise until scan duration T drops below 60 seconds (i.e., assuming modest RAID write speed of 400 MB/s).

3.7 Negative Feedback

Throughout this section, we have explored and implemented several techniques to reduce the sending rate (i.e., BGP scope reduction), minimize the burden on remote networks (i.e., GIW), lower IDS false-alarm rates (i.e., RR-split), and avoid probing busy/firewalled/non-existent hosts with repeat packets (i.e., no retransmission).

In addition to technical solutions outlined above, a political strategy for reducing complaints and dealing with their aftermath is beneficial. Our general approach in this pursuit is to make the non-malicious purpose of our scans as transparent as possible to those remotely investigating our traffic. This includes providing scanning IPs with descriptive names (i.e., indicating their research purpose) in the forward/reverse DNS tree, as well as creation of TXT DNS records pointing to the project web-page with instructions on how to opt out. With over 123 IPs participating in this endeavor, special scripts have been written to manipulate IP assignment to various NIC interfaces and modify DNS records in our authoritative server.

Name	Protocol	Port	Type	Date	T	m	$\lvert\mathcal{O}\rvert$	$\lvert\mathcal{C}\rvert$	$\lvert\mathcal{U}\rvert$	pps	Mbps
DNS_1	UDP	53	DNS A	2-21-08	30d	1	15.2M	–	148M	709	0.48
DNS_2		53	DNS A	3-25-08	6d	5	15.2M	–	155M	3.5K	2.38
DNS_3		53	DNS A	5-07-08	1d	31	14.7M	–	168M	21.2K	14.28
DNS_4		53	DNS A	5-19-08	1d	31	14.5M	–	169M	21.2K	14.28
DNS_5		53	DNS A	5-20-08	1d	31	14.6M	–	168M	21.2K	14.28
DNS_6		53	DNS A	5-21-08	1d	31	14.5M	–	167M	21.2K	14.28
DNS_7		53	DNS A	5-22-08	1d	31	14.5M	–	169M	21.2K	14.28
ECHO		7	–	7-01-08	1d	31	322K	–	170M	22.1K	21.03
PING	ICMP	–	echo	6-24-08	1d	31	139M	–	99M	22.1K	14.85
$SMTP_S$	TCP	25	SYN	7-30-08	2d	61	17M	87.1M	119M	11.2K	7.55
$SMTP_A$		25	ACK	7-30-08	2d	61	–	116M		11.2K	7.55
$EPMAP_S$		135	SYN	8-05-08	2d	61	4.9M	40.2M	127M	11.3K	7.58
$EPMAP_A$		135	ACK	8-05-08	2d	61	–	68.4M		11.3K	7.58
$HTTP_1$		80	SYN	7-17-08	1d	123	30.3M	49.1M	78M	22.6K	15.19
$HTTP_2$		80	SYN	8-05-09	1d	61	44.3M	61.3M	97.1M	24.4K	16.39
$HTTP_3$		80	SYN	8-06-09	1d	61	44.0M	61.2M	85.1M	24.2K	16.26
$HTTP_4$		80	SYN	8-10-09	1d	123	44.2M	61.5M	94.7M	24.4K	16.39
$HTTP_5$		80	SYN	8-24-09	2d	123	44.5M	61.7M	96.4M	12.1K	8.15
$HTTP_6$		80	SYN	8-27-09	1d	61	44.1M	61.4M	80.7M	24.4K	16.37
$HTTP_{AS}$		80	ACK→SYN	9-02-09	1d	61	31.7M	49.6M	92M	25.8K	17.35
$HTTP_{OPT}$		80	SYN+OPT	7-15-10	1d	121	37.8M	48.1M	71.3M	26.3K	20.70

Table 4: Summary of scans performed.

However, the most widely-used means of investigation is through a whois lookup on offending IP addresses, followed by a direct email to the party listed therein. In the event a complaint is received, our policy is to reply as quickly as possible with an explanation of our traffic, a link to the project web-page, and an offer to blacklist the network. Dynamic blacklisting in IRLscanner is implemented through periodic reading of a flat file of blocked networks and simply removing them from the BGP hash table. Under the assumption that network administrators who complain will do so again later, blacklisted networks are maintained across scans. However, given that no analysis was provided in prior work [13], [17], [43] to justify preemptively removing subnets or addresses, our initial scan started with an empty blacklist.

The final issue one must also be aware of is that significant care should be taken to avoid negatively impacting the *local* network, where internal stateful firewalls and IDS are particularly vulnerable (from the load perspective) to large volumes of traffic destined to billions of unique destinations. We have experienced a number of issues with department and campus-wide IDS/firewall installations at our institution, which all had to be manually bypassed for this project to proceed.

4. EXPERIMENTS

In this section, we test our design decisions by performing several Internet-wide scans. We defer in-depth analysis of the actual scan data to a later paper, instead focusing on high-level observations and results.

4.1 Overview

As the goal of scanning is to produce the set of hosts offering a given service, each targeted IP address must eventually be classified into one of four categories. Define *open* set $\mathcal{O}$ to contain all hosts that responded positively to a scan packet (e.g., a SYN-ACK to a TCP SYN), *closed* set $\mathcal{C}$ to represent IPs responding negatively using the same protocol (e.g., a TCP RST to a SYN packet), *unreachable* set $\mathcal{U}$ to consist of IPs that return ICMP unreachable or TTL expired errors, and *dead* set $\mathcal{D}$ to designate hosts from which no reply was received at all. Note that excluding bogus responses and strange firewall/NAT behavior, $\mathcal{O} \cup \mathcal{C} \cup \mathcal{U} \cup \mathcal{D} = \mathcal{S}$ and the individual sets do not overlap.

Through development of IRLscanner and in the course of other projects, we have performed 21 Internet-wide scans since February 2008. To test a wide range of possibilities and demonstrate the general feasibility of service discovery, we targeted UDP, TCP, and ICMP protocols on both popular services (e.g., HTTP, DNS) and those often used for nefarious purposes (e.g., SMTP, EPMAP). Table 4 summarizes our scanning activity. We initially started slowly with a 30-day scan duration from a single source IP to gauge the feedback, then increased the sending rate over subsequent scans until we achieved a duration of 24 hours, which is over 20 times faster than any documented scan [17]. The number of source IPs m varied based on their availability in our subnet and specific goals of the measurement, generally ranging from 31 to 123. In comparison, the highest IP diversity in related work was $m = 25$ in [5], followed by $m = 8$ in [17].

4.2 UDP/ICMP Scans

We started with seven DNS scans due to an interest in public recursive DNS servers. These scans produced between 14.5M and 15.2M responses in each run, which represents a 30% growth from the 10.5M found in [13] less than 9 months prior. We discovered a stable set of 4.4M servers that responded to every DNS scan over a period of three months, which indicates that the number of consistently available hosts is far fewer than might be expected from the responses to a single scan.

Of further interest is the reduction in found hosts from 15.2M to 14.7M when scan duration reduced to 24 hours in DNS_3. This suggests that faster scan durations produce a lower cumulative response among the targets, which in part may be attributed to the lower possibility of counting the same host multiple times under different DHCP'ed IPs. To investigate whether previous scanning activity in some immediate past influences the response rate in subsequent scans, we probed DNS on four consecutive days in May 2008 (i.e., 96 hours of continuous scanning) and received roughly

Year	Data Source	IPs	ECN	MSS	TS	SACK	WS	EOL
2000	Padhye [40]	4.55K	1.15%	93.71%	–	40.75%	–	–
2004	Medina [33]	84.4K	2.09%	–	85%	67.79%	–	–
2005	Veal [54]	475	–	–	76.4%	–	–	–
2008	Langley [27]	1.35M	1.07%	–	–	–	–	–
2010	HTTP_{OPT}	37.8M	2.32%	99.47%	74.77%	60.94%	83.08%	6.21%

Table 5: Prevalence of TCP options in the Internet (dashes represent unreported values).

the same number of responses in each case, which indicates that the Internet is memoryless (at least at our scan rates).

Our last UDP scan was on ECHO port 7, which simply replies with a verbatim copy of the received packet and to our knowledge has never been scanned in the literature. We chose this port as a representative of a sensitive UDP service largely because of its notoriety for broadcast amplification attacks [32]. Later in the paper, we deal with the huge volume of complaints and speculation that ensued in the co-operative intrusion-detection community, but note that even though best practice is to disable this service, we nevertheless received replies from 321,675 unique IP addresses.

Our lone ICMP scan was a simple echo request [17], [43] that garnered 139M replies, representing a 20% gain over a similar scan performed in June 2007 [17].

4.3 TCP Scans

Our experiments targeted TCP with 12 scans using three target ports, two combinations of TCP flags, and one set of TCP options. TCP has not been scanned in the literature with T less than three months [5] and has not included any options or flags other than SYN [5], [17], [42], [43].

We start by describing the performed scans in an increasing order of their sensitivity. We initially scanned HTTP with a duration more than 90 times shorter than the only previous attempt [5], discovering 30.3M hosts in July 2008 and 44.5M in August 2009, the latter of which is a 140% increase compared to 18.5M IPs found in 2006 [5]. The other two services we targeted with SYN scans were SMTP, which is frequently probed by spammers searching for open relays, and EPMAP, which is heavily scanned for network reconnaissance prior to attack [32], discovering 17M and 4.9M hosts respectively. Given the large number of Windows hosts in the Internet, the EPMAP result seems low, which suggests that many ISPs filter SYN traffic on port 135.

To determine the feasibility of scanning with other types of TCP packets, we performed three measurements with ACK packets (i.e., SMTP_A, EPMAP_A, and HTTP_{AS}), which can be used not only to determine a host's liveness (i.e., an ACK normally elicits a RST from non-firewalled stacks), but also to bypass stateless firewalls. Both SMTP_A and EPMAP_A were executed *concurrently* with the corresponding SYN scan (i.e., two packets were sent to each IP) in order to allow us to detect and characterize firewalls. Observe in the table that SMTP_A found 12M more hosts (i.e., 116M total) than SMTP_S whose $|\mathcal{O}| + |\mathcal{C}|$ is only 104.1M. Without firewalls, the two sets should be identical. Similarly, EPMAP_A elicited 23M more responses (i.e., 68M total) compared to EPMAP_S (i.e., 45.1M). The EPMAP_A scan also suggests that filtering is heavily applied on port 135 not only for SYN packets, but for ACKs as well.

For HTTP_{AS}, we scanned the entire BGP space with ACK packets, then immediately followed the resulting RST responses with a SYN packet. We present our motivation and the results from this approach in a later section.

4.4 TCP Options

Over the last decade there has been an interest in the literature [27], [33], [40], [54] regarding the deployment of various extensions to TCP (e.g., SACK, ECN) in network stacks of both end-systems and intermediate network devices (e.g., routers, NATs, firewalls). While our first 20 scans did not utilize any options, the last scan HTTP_{OPT} not only attempted to negotiate ECN [45], but also transmitted four TCP options – MSS (maximum segment size), WS (window scaling), SACK (selective acknowledgments), and TS (timestamps), which are normally echoed in the SYN-ACK if the corresponding target supports it. The order of options transmitted by the scanner followed that in Windows Server 2008 (i.e., MSS, NOP, WS, SACK, TS).

Observe in Table 4 that in July 2010 HTTP_{OPT} yielded only 37.8M responses, which represents a nearly 15% reduction from HTTP scans a year earlier. This does not align well with the 30% annual growth rate during 2006-2009 and suggests that option-heavy packets indeed produce a dramatically lower response rate in the Internet.[2] While this single scan is insufficient to conclusively pinpoint which options are responsible for the dropped SYN packets, the most likely culprit is ECN. A similar result was found in [33], [40], where between 1 and 8% of the tested web servers were unable to accept ECN connections due to various protocol issues in end-systems and interference from ECN-challenged intermediate devices [33]. The larger percentage of ECN failures in our dataset is likely caused by the broader range of sampled embedded stacks (e.g., printers, cameras, modems).

Our next task is to analyze the number of responsive hosts that support each of the options. Prior work [27], [33], [40], [54] has examined this problem on a smaller scale using traditional (i.e., non-embedded) web servers and found that ECN support ranged from 1 to 2%, while each of SACK, MSS, and TS was enabled in at least 40% of the hosts. Table 5 summarizes these findings and shows our results, including two new fields – window scaling (WS) and end-of-options-list (EOL). Excluding a few nonsensical replies, the percentage of hosts that accept ECN still remains small (i.e., 2.32%), having grown by only 1.3% over the last 10 years.

As shown in the next column of the table, MSS is now included in almost all connections, up from 94% in 2000. While in our earlier experiments the source port remained constant for the duration of each scan, HTTP_{OPT} randomly varied the source port of each connection (using a separate 2-byte LCG that skipped reserved ports), which was encoded in the TCP timestamp of the outgoing SYN packet and later checked against the destination port of the SYN-ACK. As

[2]Other reasons include increased deployment of ISP firewalls, new OS patches that block port 80, and fewer hosts on the Internet, none of which is historically probable.

Device	Found	%
Linux (2.4 or 2.6 kernel)	13.0M	32.9
Windows XP/Server 2003	6.3M	15.8
Windows Vista/7/Server 2008	5.6M	14.0
Windows Server 2003 SP2	3.5M	8.9
FreeBSD	1.5M	3.8

Table 6: Top 5 devices.

Device Type	Found	%
General purpose	32.4M	81.8
Network device	2.7M	6.8
Printer	1.8M	4.6
Networked storage	1.5M	3.7
Media	929K	2.3
Other embedded	287K	0.7
Total	39.6M	

Table 7: Summary of fingerprinted devices.

OS Class	Found	% of GP
Windows	16.3M	50.2
Linux	13.0M	40.2
BSD/Unix	2.2M	6.7
Mac	862K	2.7

Table 8: General purpose (GP) devices.

the table shows, approximately 75% of the responsive IPs returned the correct timestamp. Ignoring a handful of bogus replies, the remaining 25% of the hosts did not support TS.

Next, SACK results suggest a 20% increase from 2000 and a 6% decrease from 2004, though our numbers are again affected by the wider coverage of embedded devices than in prior work. While WS is often used to enable high-speed transfers in networks with large bandwidth-delay products, a surprising 83% of hosts support it. Finally, over 6% of Internet devices are compelled to use EOL, even though this optional field typically serves no practical purpose.

4.5 Remote OS Fingerprinting

While service discovery projects usually focus on enumerating open set $\mathcal{O}$, further information about the hosts themselves is often critical to the depth and usefulness of measurement studies [5], [13]. With the goals of resource efficiency and maximal politeness at remote networks, in this section we focus on determining the operating system of discovered hosts in $\mathcal{O}$, which could be used to estimate the global impact of known security vulnerabilities [35], approximate Internet-wide market share [37], or track hosts with dynamic IP addresses [13]. The main difficulty in executing such a study is that most existing tools [39], [57] not only trip IDS alarms and crash older end-hosts with unusual combinations of TCP/IP flags, but also require substantial overhead (e.g., 16 packets for Nmap) in Internet-wide use [50], [55]. It is thus not surprising that large-scale OS profiling has not been attempted in the literature.

Instead of traditional fingerprinting methods, we utilize a single-packet technique called Snacktime [50], which exploits OS-dependent features in SYN-ACKs such as the TCP window, IP time-to-live, and the sequence of RTOs (retransmission timeouts) of the SYN-ACK during TCP handshakes. While initial results on accuracy were promising [50], [55], Snacktime's requirement that outgoing TCP RST packets be dropped, long period needed to produce an answer (e.g., several minutes), and limited database (i.e., 25 signatures last updated in 2003) has previously restricted its usefulness. Given that we must already send a TCP SYN packet to every host in $\mathcal{O}$, modifying the Snacktime technique for use on an Internet-wide scale would result in *no additional sent packets* to enumerate remote OSes.

To implement a scalable Snacktime, we take advantage of our custom network driver to block outgoing TCP RST packets in response to arriving SYN-ACKs. Since IRLscanner already captures all incoming packets (including delayed retransmissions), it is a perfect platform for massively parallelizing the Snacktime technique. After a scan completes, we generate the RTOs of each target from the packet dump, then run a custom implementation of the Snacktime matching algorithm that gives preference to general classes of operating system in the case of ambiguity and reduces the microsecond precision of RTOs to manage random queuing delays in the Internet. To make the technique more useful, we processed almost 7K responsive hosts at a large university to manually verify and increase the database to 98 signatures, including the latest Windows versions (e.g., Vista, 7, Server 2008, Server 2003 SP2), webcams, switches, printers, and various other devices.

We applied the modified Snacktime technique to $HTTP_2$, which consisted of $|\mathcal{O}| = 44.3$M web servers that responded with at least one SYN-ACK on port 80. We achieved a Snacktime fingerprint for 39.6M hosts, with 2.3M being excluded due to insufficient retransmissions (i.e., none) and the remaining difference attributable to gaps in our signature database (the algorithm, signatures, and dataset are available [21]). According to Snacktime, the top 5 profiled OSes are given in Table 6, with Linux contributing 32.9% of the total and various Windows implementations consisting of the next several slots, which is indicative of their co-dominance in the web-server market. We provide more detail in Table 7, where we classified each signature into one of six categories and calculated summary statistics. Note that general-purpose systems (e.g., Linux, Windows) are responsible for nearly 82% of the total, with network devices (e.g., switches, routers, NAT boxes), networked storage (e.g., NAS, tape drives), and printers showing up with more than 1M devices each. The media category is comprised mainly of webcams and presentation devices (e.g., TVs, DVRs, projectors).

To finish this section, we present in Table 8 the total number of devices and their percentage attributed to each class of OS in the general-purpose category. Snacktime results suggest that approximately half of the total consists of Microsoft OSes (5.6% of which belong to Windows 2000 or older), which is likely due at least partially to individuals hosting personal web-sites on their home machines. It also shows that Linux hosts are responsible for 40%, which combined with the various related forms of BSD (e.g., OpenBSD, FreeBSD), SunOS, and Unix results in nearly 47% of the total and rivals Microsoft.

4.6 Service Lifetime

Another interesting property of Internet services is their average *lifetime* (uptime) $E[L]$, which is the mean duration of time a port stays active on a given IP. One technique [17] is to first estimate the CDF of lifetime L and then compute its mean $E[L]$. However, avoiding round-off errors and CDF

Service	Scans	Emails	Avg	IPs excluded	Avg
DNS	7	45	6.4	3.7M	530K
Echo	1	22	22	752K	752K
Ping	1	4	4	1K	1K
HTTP	8	27	3.4	459K	57K
SMTP	2	6	3	262K	131K
EPMAP	2	2	1	65K	32K
Total	21	106	5.05	5.3M	250K

Table 9: Emails and IPs excluded by service.

Source	Cease		FYI		Total
	Human	Script	Human	Script	
Individual	14	14	7	8	43
Government	6	2	6	2	16
Corporation	11	5	8	0	24
University	6	3	10	4	23
Total	37	24	31	14	106

Table 10: Email notices by complainant type.

tail cut-off often requires monitoring the pool of target IPs at frequent intervals (i.e., minutes) and for extended periods of time (i.e., days), all which contributes not only to higher bandwidth overhead, but also to more likely aggravation of remote network administrators.

We offer an alternative method that can estimate $E[L]$ using much lower overhead and overall delay. Modeling each host as an alternating ON/OFF process [56], a set $\mathcal{K}$ of uniformly selected live hosts exhibits a departure rate $\lambda = |\mathcal{K}|/E[L]$ hosts/sec (a similar result follows from Little's Theorem). Thus, by probing $\mathcal{K}$ twice at time t and $t + \Delta$, one can estimate λ as $p(\Delta)|\mathcal{K}|/\Delta$, where $p(\Delta)$ is the fraction of hosts that have disappeared in this interval. Solving $p(\Delta)|\mathcal{K}|/\Delta = |\mathcal{K}|/E[L]$, we obtain $E[L] = \Delta/p(\Delta)$.

The key to this technique is to uniformly randomly select $\mathcal{K}$ and simultaneously ensure maximal politeness of the scan. Leveraging the findings of Section 3.4 aimed exactly at this issue, we first use RLCG to scan the Internet for Δ time units at some constant rate r. We then re-generate the same sequence of IPs at the same rate, but actually send packets only to those targets that have responded in the first scan. Due to limited space, we omit simulations confirming the accuracy of this method and discuss only one extrapolation using port 80 and $\Delta = 45$ seconds. This experiment covered 1M targets, found $|\mathcal{K}| = 23.7$K live hosts, and yielded $E[L] = 50$ minutes (i.e., $p(\Delta) = 1.5\%$).

5. ANALYSIS

While it would be ideal to scan the Internet using different techniques (e.g., IP-sequential, uniform, GIW) and then assess the collected feedback as a measure of intrusiveness of each scan, certain practical limitations typically prevent one from doing so (e.g., our network administrators have explicitly prohibited scanning activity using certain non-optimal permutations). Thus, comparison is often only possible through feedback analysis exposed in publications, which unfortunately is very scarce in the existing literature. To overcome this limitation, this section introduces a number of novel metrics related to the perceived intrusiveness of Internet-wide scans, studies them in detail, and unveils certain simple, yet effective, techniques for reducing the blowback.

5.1 Email Complaints

One of the uncertainties we encountered when initially considering a service discovery project was the number of complaints to expect, particularly as they related to serious threats or resulted in widespread blacklisting of the scanner to the point of making Internet-wide measurements impossible. In this section, we attempt to clarify the issue by detailing the complaints we received and the effect they had on our measurements.

Table 9 contains a summary of email complaints broken down by service type. Over all 21 scans, we received 106 complaints for an average of 5.05 per scan. Our initial run (i.e., DNS_1) resulted in 10 complaints and more than 2.5M IP addresses blocked, which is nearly half the total of 5.3M blacklisted over the course of the project. Most of this initial number came from a single large ISP asking us to block several /16 residential networks. However, even with the initial burst removed from the calculation, DNS scans resulted in an average of 172K blacklisted IPs per scan. The most significant backlash we received was for the ECHO scan (UDP port 7), which led to 22 complaints and more than 750K blocked IP addresses. In the next section we provide an explanation for this significant increase, but note here that UDP scans account for 65% of all complaints, while being responsible for only 40% of the packets sent.

In contrast to the experience of [17], where the authors received 30 times more complaints for a TCP scan than ICMP pings, our TCP measurements produced a *total* of 35 complaints over 12 scans, or about three per scan. This is an even more remarkable result given that we scanned two sensitive ports, used ACK packets that penetrate stateless firewalls, and clustered six scans in less than a month. While we cannot explain this discrepancy, our numbers do not support the notion that TCP scans are more invasive than the other protocols.

We next categorize the received emails in Table 10 to show the severity and type of each complaint. Out of 106 complaints, 61 were demands to cease the activity, while the other 45 were FYI notifications about a possible virus with no expectation that the measurement stop. The first row of the table shows that individual users who monitor a single IP address with a personal firewall (e.g., ZoneAlarm, Norton) represented 41% of the total complaints (i.e., 43 out of 106), which indicates that a large portion of these emails cannot be avoided by any means. The remaining three rows of the table represent complaints received from large network entities, with universities being the most likely to send an FYI notification and worldwide government entities comprising only 15% of the total complaints.

In contrast to [13], we received only four cease demands from U.S. Federal Government entities, none of which were defense-related. Another point of interest is the number of threats to pursue legal action, though of the three received none of them turned out to be legitimate. Finally, analysis of emails generated by an automated script suggests that a large chunk of all received complaints (i.e., 36% in our case) are seldom reviewed by an actual human given the large amount of background scan traffic their networks receive [41].

We now determine the impact of email complaints on the scope of subsequent measurements (i.e., size of $\mathcal{S}$ after removing blacklisted networks) by studying the progres-

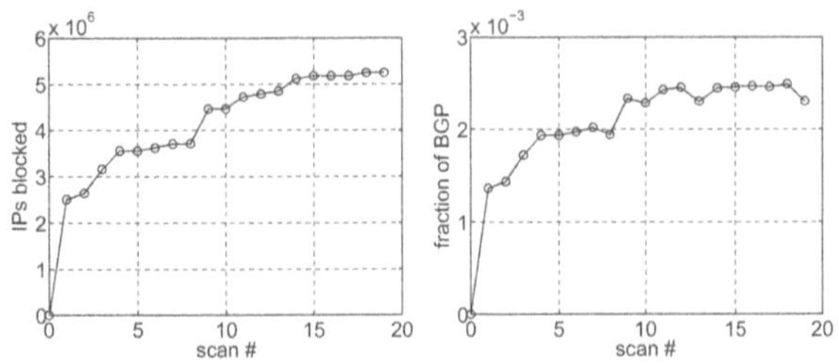

(a) total (b) fraction of BGP

Figure 4: Progression of blacklisted IPs.

sion of blacklisted IP addresses in Figure 4, where scans are assigned numbers in chronological order. Note that the complaints for the two simultaneous scans (i.e., SMTP and EPMAP) are encompassed in a single data point due to our inability to tell whether the SYN or the ACK portion caused the complaint. Part (a) of the figure contains the raw number of blacklisted addresses, which did not increase significantly after we stopped scanning UDP. Part (b) shows the blocked addresses as a percentage of BGP, where the total number of 5.3M represents only 0.23% of the current space (the curve is non-monotonic due to the constant expansion of BGP).

5.2 Firewall Log Correlation

To gain a broader view of the Internet and decrease the amount of time required to detect large-scale attacks, online collaborative systems [36], [47] have been developed to pool data from strategically placed Internet sensors and firewall/IDS logs of various networks. We focus on the SANS Internet Storm Center (ISC) [47] due to its relatively large size of 500K monitored IP addresses and detailed publicly available data. An ISC report consists of an IP address detected as a scanner, its source port, and the target's (IP, port) pair. These reports are often shared publicly, although certain fields (e.g., destination IP) are obscured to protect the identity of subnets that submit their logs. Given that these reports represent information about unwanted traffic, they can be used to gain insight into how our scans are perceived by remote networks.

We examine ISC report summaries for several scans from Table 4. These summaries are compiled daily for each service (e.g., HTTP) and consist of the number of scanned targets, scanning hosts that targeted that service, and the ratio of packets that are TCP. We are particularly interested in the first metric as *all* reports related to our 24-hour scans should be contained in a single data point.

We downloaded summary data from ISC for one month surrounding a sample of our HTTP, EPMAP, DNS, and ECHO scans (i.e., 15 days prior and after). The result is plotted in Figure 5, where the x-axis labels days in the 30-day window surrounding each scan and the highlighted points represent the days our scanner was actively probing that particular port. We happened to scan both HTTP in part (a) and EPMAP in part (b) on days when ISC experienced roughly a third of its peak number of daily reports (i.e., 27K compared to $80-90$K), which is nevertheless an huge number. The figure also shows that EPMAP clearly stands out as being scanned with a consistently high amount of daily traffic.

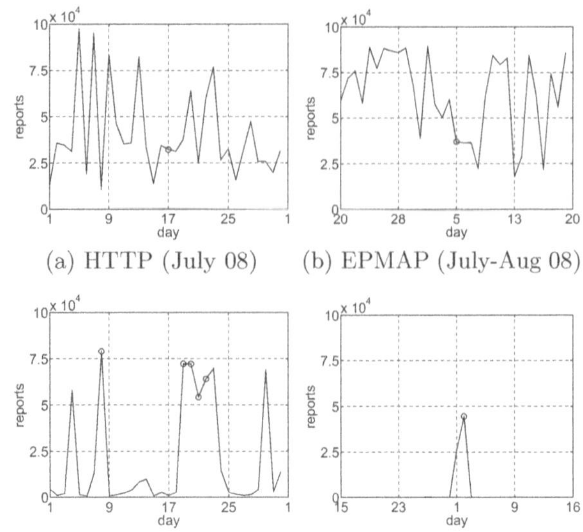

(a) HTTP (July 08) (b) EPMAP (July-Aug 08)

(c) DNS (May 08) (d) ECHO (June-July 08)

Figure 5: ISC reports with our scans marked.

In contrast, parts (c) and (d) for DNS and ECHO show that IRLscanner spiked report levels well above those of surrounding days. In fact, in the case of ECHO we produced an extremely anomalous event, raising the total from almost zero to 50K. Our activity on that port created concerns among network administrators that a new exploit was under way and/or a virus outbreak was in progress. All this eventually drew the attention of one of the traffic monitors at ISC, who wrote an explanatory blog post to calm down the ISC community.

Given the large amount of background noise from many scanning sources (whose totals ISC also makes available) in parts (a) and (b) of Figure 5, we conjecture that network administrators are more likely to react only to traffic that clearly stands out (i.e., makes its presence known by its high signal-to-noise ratio) rather than to scans on sensitive ports. This is confirmed by the fact that attack-reconnaissance port 135 generated the *least* number of complaints and that the ECHO port, which inherently represents little real threat to administrators due to the lack of hosts offering this service and heavy firewall filtering, produced an unusually strong blowback. This relationship where higher background scan traffic seems to imply fewer complaints might benefit researchers considering scans on sensitive/popular ports in the future.

5.3 Enumerating Contributors

It is well-known [6], [48] that the contributors to ISC and other firewall log correlation systems are vulnerable to losing their anonymity due to the nearly real-time public display of firewall reports with only the destination IP address omitted. Several techniques for correlating reports with targeted subnets (which is called *contributor enumeration*) have been proposed [6]; however, they require tens of billions of packets, allow for false positives, and consume multiple days during full enumeration.

Given our high-performance scanner that is capable of locally using multiple IP addresses, a much simpler attack preys on the source port, destination port, and source IP address reported in detailed ISC logs, which are displayed for all scanning hosts that ISC tracks. Probing each address in BGP set $\mathcal{B}$ with a unique combination of source/destination ports and source IP eliminates the possibility of false positives and the need to send any extra packets beyond those in $\mathcal{B}$. This can be accomplished for the current 2.1B hosts with 128 source IPs by simply rotating through all 64K source ports and roughly 250 destination ports, which can be handpicked from the most-scanned lists to minimize the likelihood of raising suspicion. However, by removing the source port from the public report, ISC can render this technique largely ineffective.

5.4 ACK Scans

To prepare their subnet's data for submission to ISC, many network administrators rely on firewall log analyzers such as psad [44] to separate scan traffic from innocuous packets dropped by the firewall. During our analysis, we discovered that many such tools ignore ACK packets, which suggests that network administrators often do not consider them to be particularly dangerous. To leverage this intuition, we propose a scan technique for cases where finding the majority of hosts in open set $\mathcal{O}$, while significantly reducing IDS detection, is beneficial (e.g., for rarely scanned ports).

The first phase of the technique is a simple ACK scan to every host in $\mathcal{B}$, which effectively discovers the subset of hosts that are not heavily protected by stateful firewalls. For every RST received, we verify that it has not been previously probed using a hash table and then immediately send it a SYN packet to establish whether the service is open or not. By only targeting hosts that previously responded, this type of scan reduces the SYN footprint by 94% for HTTP. We performed a single test measurement ($HTTP_{AS}$ in Table 4), which discovered 31.7M of the 44M total responsive hosts, while requiring only 125M SYN packets to be sent. ISC data shows only $4,746$ reports for our IPs during $HTTP_{AS}$ compared to $29,869$ reports collected for $HTTP_2$, which used the same T and m. This is significant as it amounts to an 84% decrease in the perceived intrusiveness of the scan.

5.5 DNS Lookups

We now turn to the last form of feedback we consider in this paper. While whois lookups seem to be the predominate form of reconnaissance performed by remote network administrators and individuals when they detect a scan, many specialized tools augment IDS reports and firewalls logs with DNS lookups on offending IPs to provide more information on the scanning host to the user. While for large networks this functionality should be disabled (as it allows remote hosts to DoS the network by loading it up with billions of useless DNS lookups), many personal firewalls and small subnets implement some form of it.

We tested the frequency of these additional lookups by collecting all incoming requests for IP addresses and hostnames at our locally controlled authoritative DNS server. To ensure that each request initiated by a remote entity contacted our nameserver, we set the DNS TTL to zero for both the reverse and forward lookups on scanner IPs/hostnames. After doing so, no RFC compliant nameserver should maintain our records in their cache.

The result of this collection process for three HTTP scans is contained in Table 11, which lists the number of reverse

Scan	Reverse	Forward	Req/sec	Servers
$HTTP_2$	3.03M	85.4K	36	47.8K
$HTTP_3$	2.89M	80.1K	34	48.2K
$HTTP_6$	2.85M	66.3K	33	49.2K

Table 11: DNS lookups on scanner source IPs.

lookups for the IP addresses themselves and forward lookups on the names returned by those queries. We made sure that these IP addresses were not used for any other purpose but scanning and their names were not publicized beyond the project web-site. Therefore, forward lookups are almost certainly due to the common verification technique of determining the consistency between the forward and the reverse response. While the number of requests slightly declined for each subsequent scan, the last column shows that the number of unique servers in each dataset had the opposite trend. The decline in lookup rates can be attributed to random noise, long-term caching at non-compliant DNS servers, and users growing tired of looking up our IPs.

It should be noted that performing DNS queries on scanner IPs potentially reveals the location of the IDS tool unless steps are taken to increase anonymity (e.g., using a DNS forwarding service at some distant location). The three scans in Table 11 have identified 64K unique DNS servers, out of which 35K were present in each dataset. Further analysis of this data is deferred to future work.

6. CONCLUSION

In this paper, we designed novel algorithms for maximally polite Internet scanning and documented our experience through extensive service-discovery statistics based on our implementation of the proposed methods. Future work involves exploring methods for reducing $\mathcal{B}$ to avoid scanning unproductive networks, expanding RLCG/RR to provide optimal spacing for multiple destination ports (i.e., in hybrid vertical/horizontal scanning), and more in-depth analysis of scan data.

7. ACKNOWLEDGMENT

We are grateful to the Network Security team at Texas A&M University for their helpful discussions and professional handling of network administrator complaints.

8. REFERENCES

[1] M. Allman, W. M. Eddy, and S. Ostermann, "Estimating loss rates with TCP," *ACM Performance Evaluation Review*, vol. 31, pp. 12–24, 2003.

[2] M. Allman, V. Paxson, and J. Terrell, "A Brief History of Scanning," in *Proc. ACM IMC*, Oct. 2007, pp. 77–82.

[3] G. Bartlett, J. Heidemann, and C. Papadopoulos, "Understanding Passive and Active Service Discovery," in *Proc. ACM IMC*, Oct. 2007, pp. 57–70.

[4] H. Bauke and S. Mertens, "Random numbers for large-scale distributed Monte Carlo simulations," *Phys. Rev. E*, vol. 75, no. 6, p. 066701, 2007.

[5] D. Benoit and A. Trudel, "World's First Web Census," *Intl. Journal of Web Information Systems*, vol. 3, no. 4, pp. 378–389, 2007.

[6] J. Bethencourt, J. Franklin, and M. Vernon, "Mapping Internet Sensors with Probe Response Attacks," in *Proc. USENIX Security*, Jul. 2005, pp. 193–208.

[7] Bro IDS. [Online]. Available: http://bro-ids.org/.

[8] H. Burch and B. Cheswick, "Mapping the Internet," *IEEE Computer*, vol. 32, no. 4, pp. 97–98,102, 1999.

[9] M. Casado, T. Garfinkel, W. Cui, V. Paxson, and S. Savage, "Opportunistic Measurement: Extracting Insight from Spurious Traffic," in *Proc. HOTNETS*, Nov. 2005.

[10] Z. Chen and C. Ji, "Optimal Worm-Scanning Method using Vulnerable-Host Distributions," *ACM IJSN*, vol. 2, no. 1/2, pp. 71–80, Mar. 2007.

[11] B. Cheswick, H. Burch, and S. Branigan, "Mapping and Visualizing the Internet," in *Proc. USENIX Annual Technical Conference*, Jun. 2000, pp. 1–12.

[12] Team Cymru. [Online]. Available: http://www.team-cymru.org/Services/Bogons/.

[13] D. Dagon, N. Provos, C. P. Lee, and W. Lee, "Corrupted DNS Resolution Paths: The Rise of a Malicious Resolution Authority," in *Proc. NDSS*, Feb. 2008.

[14] L. Deri and F. Fusco, "Exploiting Commodity Multicore Systems for Network Traffic Analysis," Jul. 2009. [Online]. Available: http://ethereal.ntop.org/MulticorePacketCapture.pdf.

[15] R. Govindan and H. Tangmunarunkit, "Heuristics for Internet Map Discovery," in *Proc. IEEE INFOCOM*, Mar. 2000.

[16] B. He, M. Patel, Z. Zhang, and K. C.-C. Chang, "Accessing the Deep Web," *Comm. of the ACM*, vol. 50, no. 5, pp. 94–101, 2007.

[17] J. Heidemann, Y. Pradkin, R. Govindan, C. Papadopoulos, G. Bartlett, and J. Bannister, "Census and Survey of the Visible Internet," in *Proc. ACM IMC*, Oct. 2008, pp. 169–182.

[18] Geoff Huston. [Online]. Available: http://bgp.potaroo.net.

[19] IANA, "IPv4 Global Unicast Address Assignments." [Online]. Available: http://www.iana.org/assignments/ipv4-address-space/.

[20] IANA, "Special-Use IPv4 Addresses," *IETF RFC 3330*, Sep. 2002.

[21] IRL Internet-Wide Fingerprinting Dataset. [Online]. Available: http://irl.cs.tamu.edu/projects/sampling/.

[22] B. Irwin and J. P. van Riel, "Using InetVis to Evaluate Snort and Bro Scan Detection on a Network Telescope," in *Proc. IEEE VizSEC*, Oct. 2007, pp. 255–273.

[23] ISC Internet Domain Survey. [Online]. Available: http://www.isc.org/index.pl?/ops/ds/.

[24] Juniper IDP. [Online]. Available: http://www.juniper.net/.

[25] M. G. Kang, J. Caballero, and D. Song, "Distributed Evasive Scan Techniques and Countermeasures," in *Proc. DIMVA*, Jul. 2007, pp. 157–174.

[26] D. Knuth, *The Art of Computer Programming, Vol. II*, 2nd ed. Addison-Wesley, 1981.

[27] A. Langley, "Probing the Viability of TCP Extensions," Google, Inc., Tech. Rep., Sep. 2008.

[28] S. Lawrence and C. L. Giles, "Accessibility of Information on the Web," *Intelligence*, vol. 11, no. 1, pp. 32Ű–39, 2000.

[29] D. H. Lehmer, "Mathematical Methods in Large-Scale Computing Units," in *Proc. Large-Scale Digital Calculating Machinery*, 1949, pp. 141–146.

[30] Z. Li, A. Goyal, Y. Chen, and V. Paxson, "Automating Analysis of Large-Scale Botnet Probing Events," in *Proc. ACM ASIACCS*, Mar. 2009, pp. 11–22.

[31] P. K. Manna, S. Chen, and S. Ranka, "Exact Modeling of Propagation for Permutation-Scanning Worms," in *Proc. IEEE INFOCOM*, Apr. 2008, pp. 1696–1704.

[32] S. McClure, J. Scambray, and G. Kurtz, *Hacking Exposed: Network Security Secrets & Solutions*, 5th ed. McGraw-Hill/Osborne, 2005.

[33] A. Medina, M. Allman, and S. Floyd, "Measuring the Evolution of Transport Protocols in the Internet," *ACM SIGCOMM Comp. Comm. Rev.*, vol. 35, no. 2, pp. 37–52, Apr. 2005.

[34] X. Meng, Z. Xu, B. Zhang, G. Huston, S. Lu, and L. Zhang, "IPv4 Address Allocation and the BGP Routing Table Evolution," *ACM SIGCOMM Comp. Comm. Rev.*, vol. 35, no. 1, pp. 71–80, 2005.

[35] D. Moore, V. Paxson, S. Savage, C. Shannon, S. Staniford, and N. Weaver, "Inside the Slammer Worm," *IEEE S&P*, vol. 1, no. 4, pp. 33–39, 2003.

[36] myNetWatchman – Network Intrusion Detection and Reporting. [Online]. Available: http://www.mynetwatchman.com/.

[37] Netcraft Web Server Survey. [Online]. Available: http://news.netcraft.com/.

[38] NetVCR. [Online]. Available: http://www.niksun.com/.

[39] Nmap. [Online]. Available: http://nmap.org/.

[40] J. Padhye and S. Floyd, "On Inferring TCP Behavior," in *Proc. ACM SIGCOMM*, Aug. 2001, pp. 287–298.

[41] R. Pang, V. Yegneswaran, P. Barford, V. Paxson, and L. Peterson, "Characteristics of Internet Background Radiation," in *Proc. ACM IMC*, Oct. 2004, pp. 27–40.

[42] N. Provos and P. Honeyman, "ScanSSH - Scanning the Internet for SSH Servers," in *Proc. USENIX LISA*, Dec. 2001, pp. 25–30.

[43] Y. Pryadkin, R. Lindell, J. Bannister, and R. Govindan, "An Empirical Evaluation of IP Address Space Occupancy," USC/ISI, Tech. Rep. ISI-TR-2004-598, Nov. 2004.

[44] Psad: Intrusion Detection and Log Analysis with Iptables. [Online]. Available: http://www.cipherdyne.org/psad/.

[45] K. K. Ramakrishnan, S. Floyd, and D. Black, "The Addition of Explicit Congestion Notification (ECN) to IP," *IETF RFC 3168*, Sep. 2001.

[46] Route Views Project. [Online]. Available: http://www.routeviews.org/.

[47] SANS Internet Storm Center – Cooperative Network Security Community. [Online]. Available: http://isc.sans.org/.

[48] Y. Shinoda, K. Ikai, and M. Itoh, "Vulnerabilities of Passive Internet Threat Monitors," in *Proc. USENIX Security*, Jul. 2005, pp. 209–224.

[49] M. Smith and D. Loguinov, "Enabling High-Performance Internet-Wide Measurements on Windows," in *Proc. PAM*, Apr. 2010, pp. 121–130.

[50] Snacktime: A Perl Solution for Remote OS Fingerprinting. [Online]. Available: http://www.planb-security.net/wp/snacktime.html.

[51] Snort IDS. [Online]. Available: http://www.snort.org/.

[52] S. Staniford, J. A. Hoagland, and J. M. McAlerney, "Practical Automated Detection of Stealthy Portscans," *Computer Security*, vol. 10, no. 1–2, pp. 105–136, 2002.

[53] S. Staniford, V. Paxson, and N. Weaver, "How to 0wn the Internet in Your Spare Time," in *Proc. USENIX Security*, Aug. 2002.

[54] B. Veal, K. Li, and D. Lowenthal, "New Methods for Passive Estimation of TCP Round-Trip Times," in *Proc. PAM*, Mar. 2005, pp. 121–134.

[55] F. Veysset, O. Courtay, and O. Heen, "New Tool And Technique For Remote Operating System Fingerprinting," Intranode Software Technologies, Tech. Rep., Apr. 2002.

[56] Z. Yao, D. Leonard, X. Wang, and D. Loguinov, "Modeling Heterogeneous User Churn and Local Resilience of Unstructured P2P Networks," in *Proc. IEEE ICNP*, Nov. 2006, pp. 32–41.

[57] F. V. Yarochkin, O. Arkin, M. Kydyraliev, S.-Y. Dai, Y. Huang, and S.-Y. Kuo, "Xprobe2++: Low Volume Remote Network Information Gathering Tool," in *Proc. IEEE/IFIP DSN*, Jun. 2009, pp. 205–210.

[58] J. Zhang, P. Porras, and J. Ullrich, "Highly Predictive Blacklisting," in *Proc. USENIX Security*, Jul. 2008, pp. 107–122.

[59] C. C. Zou, D. Towsley, W. Gong, and S. Cai, "Routing Worm: A Fast, Selective Attack Worm based on IP Address Information," in *Proc. IEEE PADS*, Jun. 2005, pp. 199–206.

Measurement and Analysis of Real-World 802.11 Mesh Networks

Katrina LaCurts and Hari Balakrishnan
MIT Computer Science and Artificial Intelligence Lab
Cambridge, Massachusetts, U.S.A.
{katrina, hari}@csail.mit.edu

ABSTRACT

Despite many years of work in wireless mesh networks built using 802.11 radios, the performance and behavior of these networks in the wild is not well-understood. This lack of understanding is due in part to the lack of access to data from a wide range of these networks; most researchers have access to only one or two testbeds at any time. In recent years, however, 802.11 mesh networks networks have been deployed commercially and have real users who use the networks in a wide range of conditions. This paper analyzes data collected from 1407 access points in 110 different commercially deployed Meraki [28] wireless mesh networks, constituting perhaps the largest study of real-world 802.11 networks to date.

After analyzing a 24-hour snapshot of data collected from these networks, we answer questions from a variety of active research topics, such as the accuracy of SNR-based bit rate adaptation, the impact of opportunistic routing, and the prevalence of hidden terminals. The size and diversity of our data set allows us to analyze claims previously only made in small-scale studies. In particular, we find that the SNR of a link is a good indicator of the optimal bit rate for that link, but that one could not make an SNR-to-bit rate look-up table that was accurate for an entire network. We also find that an ideal opportunistic routing protocol provides little to no benefit on most paths, and that "hidden triples"—network topologies that can lead to hidden terminals—are more common than suggested in previous work, and increase in proportion as the bit rate increases.

Categories and Subject Descriptors

C.4 [**Performance of Systems**]: Measurement techniques

General Terms

Measurement, Performance

Keywords

802.11, Bit Rate Adaptation, Hidden Terminals, Measurement, Mesh, Opportunistic Routing, Wireless

IMC'10, November 1–3, 2010, Melbourne, Australia.

1. INTRODUCTION

Despite the popularity of 802.11 networks, very little has been published about their performance in production settings. One of the main challenges has been the lack of a network provider with a large and diverse footprint, who has taken the care to provide a significant amount of instrumentation and logging. The data set analyzed in this paper (discussed in detail in Section 3) includes measurements collected from 110 different production Meraki [28] wireless mesh networks located around the world (see Figure 1). These networks are used by real clients; they are not testbeds, and do not suffer from researchers setting up the nodes in particular ways, inadvertently introducing biases. It is an "in situ" study, and as such, it is larger in scale and diversity than any previous study of which we are aware.

Although there are many interesting topics worthy of investigation, we study three that have seen a great deal of activity in recent years: bit rate adaptation protocols [4, 21, 38], opportunistic mesh network routing protocols [7, 9], and MAC protocols to cope with hidden terminals [17]. We investigate the following questions, with the intent of utilizing our data set to answer them on a larger scale than previous work.

1. How does the optimal bit rate depend on the SNR across a range of networks? A good bit rate adaptation scheme is the most significant contributor to high throughput in 802.11 networks. Because the APs in our data set are stationary, one might expect the SNR to be a good determinant of the optimal bit rate. If that were the case, one could streamline bit rate adaptation within the mesh by either eliminating the need for probing to find the best bit rate, or using the SNR to determine the bit rates that are most likely to be the best and only probing this set. Limiting the number of probes would be particularly beneficial for 802.11n, which has several dozen bit rate configurations.

   Indeed, results from small testbeds have indicated that the SNR can be used effectively in bit rate adaptation [10, 13, 18, 21, 33, 39]. We seek to confirm this finding on a larger scale, as well as to determine how specific the training environment needs to be. For example, is the SNR-to-best-bit-rate mapping the same for an entire network, or must we train on each link individually?

2. How well are opportunistic routing schemes likely to work in practice? What benefit would they observe over traditional single-path routing using the expected number of transmissions [12] or expected transmission time [6] metrics? Opportunistic routing has been shown to be beneficial on certain topologies [7, 9], but how often do such configurations arise in production deployments?

Figure 1: Approximate locations of networks in our data set (some are co-located). This data set exhibits more geographic diversity than any previous study of which we are aware.

3. How common are *hidden triples*—topologies that can lead to hidden terminals—in these diverse real-world deployments? Interference caused by hidden terminals can affect even an ideal rate adaptation protocol, however previous studies have not provided conclusive answers as to how frequently hidden terminals occur. For instance, [11], [17], [23], [25], and [29], report proportions of hidden terminals ranging from 10% to 50% in a particular testbed or network. The disagreements among these previous studies suggest that the prevalence of hidden terminals depends heavily on the relative positions of the nodes and the peculiarities of each network. We measure how much variation there is in the proportion of hidden triples across different topologies and how it changes with the transmit bit rate.

After analyzing a 24-hour snapshot of data from 1407 APs in 110 networks, our main findings are as follows:

1. When trained on a particular link in a static setting, the SNR is a very good indicator of the optimal bit rate for 802.11b/g and a surprisingly good indicator for 802.11n, given the number of bit rates present. For 802.11b/g networks, we find that when trained on each link, the SNR can frequently predict the best bit rate over 95% of the time. In 802.11n, we find that a trained look-up table keyed by SNR, while not perfect, can substantially reduce the number of bit rates that need to be probed. However, in both 802.11b/g and 802.11n, using other links in the network to train provides little benefit, indicating that it would not be possible to build one SNR-to-bit-rate look-up table that worked well for an entire network.

2. Analyzing all networks with at least five access points, we find that the expected number of transmissions incurred by an idealized opportunistic routing protocol (such as ExOR [7] or MORE [9] without overheads) would be rather small, even if an almost-perfect bit rate adaptation algorithm were used: there is no improvement for at least 13% of node pairs, and the median improvement is frequently less than 7%.

3. The prevalence of hidden triples—topologies where nodes A and B cannot hear each other, but node C can hear both of them—depends on the bit rate. At the lowest bit rate of 1 Mbit/s, and thresholding on a very low success probability of 10% (i.e., considering two nodes to be neighbors if they can hear each other at least 10% of the time), we find that the median number of hidden triples is over 13%. Hidden triples occur with far greater frequency at higher bit rates.

   We also find that, as the bit rates increase, the probability of nodes hearing each other decreases. This result is hardly surprising, but what is noteworthy is that there is a high variance: the mean number of nodes that can hear each other reduces, but the standard deviation is large. This variance implies that there are node pairs that are able to hear each other at a higher bit rate but not at a lower one at around the same time, most likely because of differences in modulation and coding (e.g., spread spectrum vs. OFDM). As a result, one cannot always conclude that higher bit rates have poorer reception properties than lower ones under similar conditions.

The rest of this paper is organized as follows. After discussing related work in the next section, we describe the relevant features of our data set in Section 3. Section 4 analyzes the performance of various bit rates and how it relates to SNR, Section 5 discusses the performance of opportunistic routing vs. traditional routing, and Section 6 analyzes the frequency of hidden triples. We conclude in Section 7.

2. RELATED WORK

We break related work into four sections. First, we discuss general wireless measurement studies. Then we address each of the topics of our study—SNR-based bit rate adaptation, opportunistic routing, and hidden terminals—in turn.

2.1 Wireless Measurement Studies

Unlike this paper, most previous measurement studies focus on results from single testbeds in fairly specific locations, such as universities or corporate campuses. For example, Jigsaw [11] studies a campus network with 39 APs. Their focus is merging traces of packet-level data. As such, they are able to calculate packet-level statistics that we cannot, but must employ complicated merging techniques. [14], [15], and [37] also deal with packet-level characteristics, again for only one network.

Henderson and Kotz [19] study the use of a campus network with over 550 APs and 7000 users. They focus on what types of devices are most prevalent on the network and the types of data being transferred. Though they have a fairly large testbed, they cannot capture inter-network diversity. Other campus studies address questions of traffic load [20, 34] and mobility [27, 35].

Other wireless measurement papers focus on single testbeds in more diverse locations. Rodrig et al. measure wireless in a hotspot setting [31]. They study overhead, retransmissions, and the dynamics of bit rate adaptation in 802.11b/g. [2] studies user behavior and network performance in a conference setting, as does [22].

Though the aforementioned studies make important contributions toward understanding the behavior of wireless networks, they are all limited by the scope of their testbeds. It is not possible to determine which characteristics of 802.11 are invariant across networks with access to only one network. Our data set, however, gives us this capability.

2.2 SNR-based Bit Rate Adaptation

Most bit rate adaptation algorithms can be divided into two types: those that adapt based on loss rates from probes, and those that adapt based on a estimate of channel quality. In algorithms in the first category, for example SampleRate [4], nodes send occasional probes at different bit rates, and switch to the rate that provides the highest throughput (throughput being a function of the loss rate and the bit rate). Algorithms in the second category measure the channel quality in some way (e.g., by sampling the SNR), and react based on the results of this measurement. In general, poor channel quality results in decreasing the bit rate, and vice versa. Here we take a closer look at studies which use the SNR as an estimate of channel quality in adaptation algorithms, as this is the approach we examine in Section 4.

SGRA [39] uses estimates of the SNR on a link to calculate thresholds for each bit rate, which define the range of SNRs for which a particular bit rate will work well. The authors find that the SNR can overestimate channel quality in the presence of interference. RBAR [21] uses the SNR to derive thresholds, similar to SGRA. Here, however, it is the SNR at the receiver that is used to determine these thresholds. The receiver's desired rate is communicated via RTS/CTS packets. RBAR also depends on a theoretical estimate of the BER to select a bit rate. Although using the SNR at the receiver is likely more accurate than using the SNR at the sender, this scheme incurs relatively high overhead. OAR [33] is similar to RBAR in the way in which it uses the SNR, but it maintains the temporal fairness of 802.11. Other threshold-based SNR schemes include [10], [13], and [18].

Though all of these schemes report positive results from SNR-based rate adaptation, they are all evaluated on research testbeds or in simulation. None of them have been validated on real networks, much less across networks. In Section 4, we evaluate the accuracy of SNR-based bit rate adaptation across many networks. We also attempt to quantify the losses that are seen when a sub-optimal bit rate is selected (a sub-optimal bit rate being one that was not the best for a particular SNR).

Other studies have explored using the SNR for a predictor in a mobile setting [8, 24]. Because of the nature of our data, we are only able to make conclusive claims for static environments. Though we find that a per-link SNR works well in these cases, we make no claims that this finding would hold in a mobile setting.

Finally, other studies examine using measures of channel quality other than the SNR for adaptation algorithms, for instance [3], [16], and [30]. Though potentially more accurate, these measures can be complicated or difficult to obtain. We focus our efforts in Section 4 towards using the SNR, as we find that it is simple to determine and performs well enough for our needs.

2.3 Opportunistic Routing

In Section 5, we measure the possible improvements that could be seen in our networks using opportunistic routing. Here, we provide a brief summary of how opportunistic routing differs from standard routing. In particular, we focus on the opportunistic routing protocol ExOR [7] and the contrasting shortest-path routing algorithms using ETX [12] and ETT [6].

The ETX of a path is the expected number of transmissions it will take to send a packet along that path, based on the delivery probability of the forward and reverse paths. Unless all links are perfect, the ETX of a path will be higher than the number of hops in the path, and it is possible for a path with a large number of hops to have a smaller ETX metric than a path with fewer hops.

The ETT metric is similar to the ETX metric, except that it allows for varying bit rates. The ETT of a path is the expected amount of *time* it will take to send a packet along that path, based on the delivery probability of the forward and reverse paths, as well as the bit rate chosen by each node along the path.

A potential shortcoming of this type of shortest-path routing in wireless networks is that it does not take into account the broadcast nature of wireless [7]. When the source sends a packet to the first hop in the path, the packet may in fact reach the second hop since it was broadcasted. In this case, it is redundant to send the packet from the first hop to the second. Opportunistic routing exploits this scenario.

ExOR [7], in particular, works as follows. The source node broadcasts a packet, and a subset of nodes between it and the destination receive it. These nodes coordinate amongst themselves, and the node in that subset that is closest to the destination broadcasts the packet. A subset of nodes receive that broadcast, and so on until the packet reaches its destination. Note that it is unlikely that short paths would see much improvement due to opportunistic routing, as there are not as many hops in the path to skip. It is also important to point out that the overhead required by ExOR to coordinate packet broadcasts is not inherent to opportunistic routing. Indeed, there are opportunistic routing protocols that operate without this type of coordination [9]. In Section 5.4 we quantify the improvements that an ideal opportunistic routing protocol (one with no overhead) could incur over shortest-path routing via ETX or ETT.

2.4 Hidden Terminals

Hidden terminals occur when two nodes, A and B, are within range of a third node, C, but not within range of each other. Because A and B cannot sense each other, they may send packets to C simultaneously, and those packets will collide. Different studies find different numbers of hidden terminals in practice: Zigzag [17] assumes that 10% of node pairs are part of hidden terminals, while Jigsaw [11] finds that up to 50% of nodes in their networks could be part of hidden terminals. Both of these studies, as well as others [23, 25, 29], only study hidden terminals in one network or testbed. In Section 6, we examine how frequently hidden terminals can occur across many networks, as well as how this frequency changes with the transmit bit rate.

3. DATA

Our data set contains anonymized measurements collected from 110 geographically disperse Meraki [28] networks. These networks include a total of 1407 APs, and range in size from three APs to 203 APs, with a median of 7 and a mean of about 13. Of these networks, 77 used only 802.11b/g radios, 31 used only 802.11n APs, and two contained a mix of both kinds of radios. 802.11n traffic used the 20MHz channel. 72 of these networks were indoor networks, 17 were outdoor, and 21 included both indoor and outdoor nodes.[1] All radios are made by Atheros, which makes it possible for us to conduct meaningful inter-network comparisons when dealing with the SNR (the way in which the SNR is reported can vary across vendors; see Section 3.1.1). Our data is made up of measurements from controlled probes sent periodically between APs in the mesh at varying bit rates. Though these probes are controlled, they are sent while the network is being used by real users.

3.1 Probe Data

The probe data contains loss rates and SNRs from broadcast probes sent by each AP every 40 seconds (this is the default reporting rate used in Meraki networks [5]). These probes are very similar to those used in Roofnet [32] to calculate the ETX metric [12]. The loss rate between AP_1 and AP_2 at a particular bit rate b is calculated as the average of the loss rates of each probe sent at rate b between AP_1 and AP_2 over the past 800 seconds, an interval used to make bit rate adaptation decisions in the production networks. We collect data from each node every 300 seconds; the reported loss rate data is for the past 800 seconds, so one should think of the data as a sliding window of the inter-AP loss rate at different bit rates.

We refer to each collection of inter-AP loss rates at a set of measured bit rates as a *probe set*. Note that one probe set represents aggregate data from roughly $800/40 = 20$ probes for each bit rate.

[1] We ignore these networks when classifying by environment.

We refer to the set of bit rates present in probe set P as P_{rates}. Each bit rate b in P_{rates} is associated with a loss rate, b_{loss}.

We use the loss rates and SNRs of these probes to measure the accuracy of SNR-based bit rate adaptation algorithms in Section 4, to measure the potential improvements from opportunistic routing in Section 5, and to determine the frequency of hidden terminals in Section 6. Before delving into these problems, we discuss two properties of our data set in more detail.

3.1.1 SNR

Each received probe has an SNR value associated with it, reported by the Atheros chip and logged on the Meraki device. The MadWiFi driver reports an "RSSI" quantity on each packet reception. The 802.11 standard does not specify how this information should be calculated, so different chipsets and drivers behave differently. The behavior of MadWiFi on the Atheros chipset is well-documented on the MadWiFi web site[2] and has been verified by various researchers (including us in the past). The MadWiFi documentation describes the RSSI it reports as follows:

> "In MadWiFi, the reported RSSI for each packet is actually equivalent to the Signal-to-Noise Ratio (SNR) and hence we can use the terms interchangeably. This does not necessarily hold for other drivers though. This is because the RSSI reported by the MadWiFi HAL is a value in dB that specifies the difference between the signal level and noise level for each packet. Hence the driver calculates a packet's absolute signal level by adding the RSSI to the absolute noise level."

In this paper, we use the term SNR rather than RSSI because the former is a precise term while the latter varies between vendors.

The SNR for a given probe set is not always the same because wireless channel properties vary with time. As mentioned, each probe set contains data from about 20 probes per each bit rate, which are averaged to produce tuples of the form

$$\langle \textit{Sender, Bit rate, Mean loss rate, Most recent SNR} \rangle$$

There is one such entry for each probed bit rate from each sender AP, and the means are calculated using the number of probes received at each bit rate from the neighbor. The transmissions at the different bit rates are interspersed, and the SNR at each bit rate may be different for each bit rate because of channel variations. We use the median of these SNRs as the "SNR of the probe set". We find that this way of estimating the receiver SNR over the duration of these probes is robust, as the SNR values within a probe set do not value significantly; see Figure 2, explained below.

Figure 2 presents a CDF of the standard deviations of SNRs within each probe set as well as over each link. The standard deviation within each probe set is small (less than 5 dB approximately 97.5% of the time). The bulk of the observed SNRs in our data set lie between 0 and 70 dB. We also present the standard deviations of the SNRs on each link and within each network over time, to illustrate the diverse range of SNRs present in each network. Not pictured is the standard deviation of the k most recent SNR values on a link, which we found to be comparable to the standard deviation within a probe set for small values of k; i.e., the SNR on a link does not vary significantly on short time scales.

3.1.2 Throughput

A word on the definition of throughput is in order. What really matters in practice is the performance observed by applications that

[2]`http://madwifi-project.org/wiki/UserDocs/RSSI`

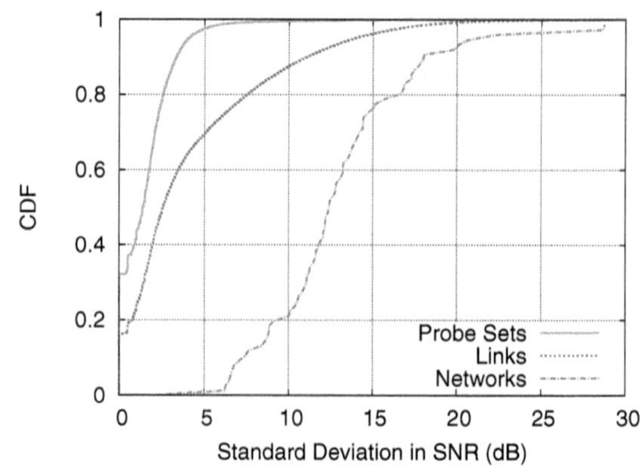

Figure 2: CDF of the standard deviation of SNR values within a probe set, for individual links, and for the network at large. The standard deviation of the SNR within a probe set is less than 5 dB over 97.5% of the time. The standard deviations taken over all the links of each network are quite a bit larger, indicating each network has links with a diverse range of SNRs.

run over transport protocols like TCP. Unfortunately, using link-layer measurements to predict the application-perceived throughput and latency of data transfers is difficult, if not impossible, with the data set we have (for instance, we don't have information about the burst loss patterns or over short time scales). We do know, however, that with a good link-layer error recovery scheme and a good transport protocol, the throughput should track the product of the bit rate and the packet success rate. In this paper, we use the product of the bit rate and packet success rate as the definition of throughput. This metric is what some bit rate adaptation schemes like RRAA [38] seek to optimize.

4. SNR-BASED BIT RATE ADAPTATION

We begin by using our inter-AP probe data to determine how accurate an indicator the SNR is of the optimal bit rate. By "optimal" bit rate, we mean the bit rate that results in the highest throughput between two nodes. There are two reasons for investigating this question:

1. Dynamically selecting a suitable bit rate is a significant factor in achieving high throughput in wireless network.
2. For bit rate adaptation schemes that use frame-level information, such as [4] and [38], it takes a non-negligible amount of probe traffic and time to pick the best rate. As networks move from 802.11b/g to 802.11n, there are many more bit rate configurations to pick from. It is possible that the SNR can be used as a hint to narrow down the set of bit rates to consider, especially in relatively static settings involving fixed mesh APs, saving much of the current overhead of probes.

Our main finding in this section is that the SNR is not an accurate indicator when trained over an entire network (i.e., when one SNR-to-bit-rate look-up table is used for an entire network), but as the specificity of the training environment increases (from per-network to per-link), the SNR begins to work quite well. For a given link, it is possible to train the nodes to develop a simple look-up method keyed by SNR to pick the optimal bit rate almost all the time. This result implies that one could not use the SNR to select the optimal bit rate between two APs without knowing anything about the condition of the link between them. However, with knowledge of a link's condition, a simple bit rate selection algorithm using the SNR would likely work very well. The caveat is that this result holds in our data set for inter-AP communication. It is probable that it would hold for static clients, but not as likely to hold for mobile ones (see Section 4.6).

4.1 Bit Rate Selection Using SNR

Recall that the SNR is a measure of how much a signal has been corrupted by noise. Intuitively, a higher SNR indicates a "better" link, and one would expect to be able to send more information, i.e., use a higher bit rate on that link. Similarly, a low SNR indicates a poor link, and one would expect to need a lower bit rate. It is this intuition that motivates SNR-based bit rate adaptation. Indeed, the throughput and optimal bit rate clearly depend on the SNR according to Shannon's theorem, but the question is whether our relatively coarsely-sampled SNR can be used as an accurate hint for determining the correct bit rate. Our bit rate adaptation algorithm works as follows: To select the bit rate for a link between AP_1 and AP_2, measure the SNR s on this link. Then, using a look-up table that maps SNR values to bit rates, look up s and use the corresponding bit rate.

The key question in this method is how to create the look-up table from SNR to bit rate. For a probe set between AP_1 and AP_2, we define P_{opt} as the bit rate that maximized the throughput for a particular probe set, i.e.,

$$P_{opt} = max\{b \times (1 - b_{loss}) : b \in P_{rates}\}$$

Given the SNR and P_{opt} values from every probe set P in our data set, we consider three options for creating the look-up table:

1. **Network:** For each network n and each SNR s represented in our data for n, assign bit rate b to s, where b is the most frequent value of P_{opt} for SNR s (i.e., the bit rate that was most frequently the optimal bit rate for the probe sets with SNR s). For links in network n, select the bit rates by using n's look-up table.

2. **AP:** Instead of creating one look-up table per network, create one per AP. For a particular link, the source will use its own look-up table to select the bit rate, but this table will not vary with the destination.

3. **Link:** Instead of creating one look-up table per AP, create one per link. Use a link's own table to select its bit rates. This approach differs from the AP approach in that each AP now has one table per neighbor.

As listed, each of these methods uses a more specific environment than the last. As a result, each would have a different start-up cost. With the first, training needs to be done on the network as a whole, but not per-link. If one were to add a link to the network, the same look-up table could still be used (though it may be beneficial to re-train if the network changed drastically). With the second, training would need to occur when a new node was added, but only at that node. With the third, training would need to occur every time a new link was added, at both the source and destination of the link; this is discussed more in Section 4.5.

Note that we could also make a global look-up table, where the same look-up table was used for every link in every network. This strategy would have virtually no start-up cost. However, it would also only work well if P_{opt} never changed (i.e., if it were the case that, for a particular SNR value, the optimal bit rate was always the same regardless of the network or link that we were using). Figure 3 shows the unique values of P_{opt} for each SNR in our 802.11b/g networks (a similar result holds for 802.11n, which we do not show separately here). Note that each probe set contains data for each bit rate, so on any link all bit rates have a chance of being optimal.

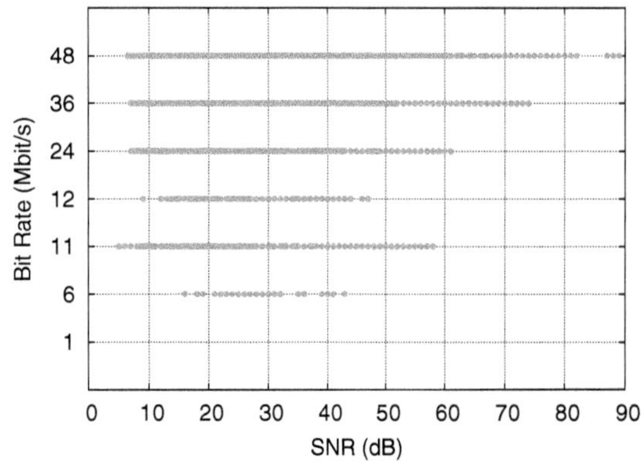

Figure 3: Optimal bit rates for an SNR at a particular time, over our entire data set. Many SNRs see different optimal bit rates at different times, which motivates the need for a better method than a global SNR look-up table.

We find that one bit rate is *not* always optimal for a particular SNR in most cases, indicated by the fact that many SNRs have points at multiple bit rates. Occasionally there is a clear winner: for SNRs above 80 dB, the optimal bit rate is 48 Mbit/s in our data set (we don't evaluate the performance of 54 Mbit/s because Meraki does not probe that rate as frequently [5]). However, for the majority of SNRs, at least two bit rates, and in some cases as many as six, could be the best. Thus, for most of this section, we do not present results for the global look-up table, as Figure 3 indicates that it is not a viable bit rate-selection strategy (and indeed, we have verified that it is not with our own analysis).

As an aside, note that in Figure 3, 1Mbit/s is *never* the optimal bit rate; each link always performed better with a higher bit rate. This result leads us to believe that ACKs, which are sent at 1Mbit/s in 802.11b/g, could possibly be sent at a higher bit rate, at least for static nodes. This is the approach taken in 802.11a.

4.2 Distribution of Optimal Bit Rate with SNR

Though Figure 3 shows that one SNR can have multiple optimal bit rates over time, it does not give us any information about the frequency with which each bit rate is optimal. It may be the case that, for each SNR, one bit rate is the best 99% of the time over all networks, in which case even a global look-up table would work 99% of the time.

To understand this notion better, we consider the following: Given a particular percentile p, what is the smallest number of unique bit rates needed to select the optimal bit rate p% of the time? For example, if one bit rate was the best 67% of the time for a given SNR and another was the best 30% of the time, then it would take two bit rates to select the optimal bit rate 95% of the time, but only one to select it 50% of the time.

Figure 4 shows this result for varying percentiles in each of our three cases (per-network, per-AP, and per-link), for 802.11b/g networks. We can see from Figure 4(a) that a network-centric approach can still require more than three unique bit rates before it is able to predict the optimal one with 95% accuracy. This implies that a network-based look-up table would not be able to be at least 95% accurate in all cases. However, as we move to the per-AP

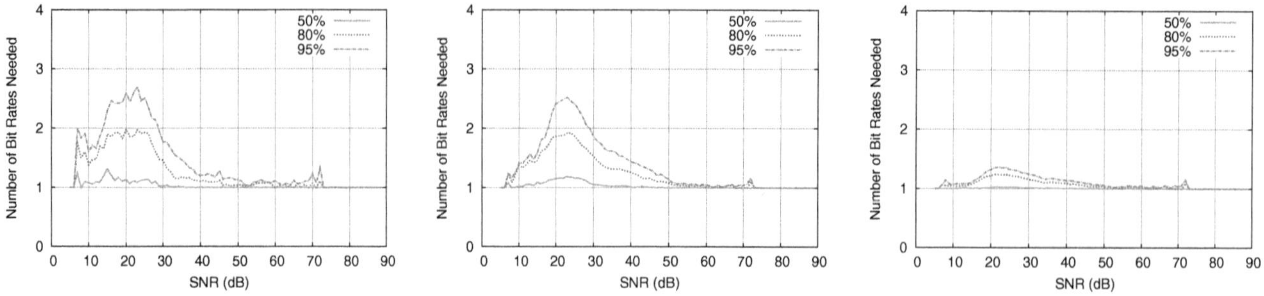

(a) Network-specific (b) AP-specific (c) Link-specific

Figure 4: Number of unique bit rates needed to achieve the optimal bit rate various percentages of the time, for 802.11b/g. As the specificity of our look-up table increases (from being aggregated over all networks to using per-link data), the number of unique bit rates needed decreases.

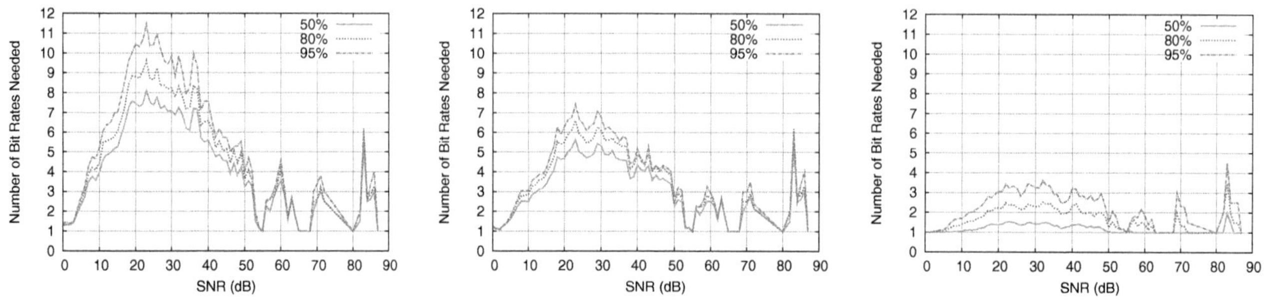

(a) Network-specific (b) AP-specific (c) Link-specific

Figure 5: Number of unique bit rates needed to achieve the optimal bit rate various percentages of the time, for 802.11n.

method (Figure 4(b)), the situation improves; fewer bit rates are needed before we can select the optimal one with 95% accuracy. In the per-link case (Figure 4(c)), for each SNR, it is common for one bit rate to be the best more than 95% of the time (note that these results do not imply that the *same* bit rate is best 95% of the time for all SNRs).

Figure 5 shows the percentile results for 802.11n networks. Similar to the results for 802.11b/g networks, we see that performance improves as we use a more specific look-up table. However, *unlike* the 802.11b/g networks, we see that, even in a link-specific setting, the SNR does not frequently predict the optimal bit rate at least 95% of the time. This is not particularly surprising, as 802.11n has significantly more bit rates than 802.11b/g. Although it may not be possible to use only SNR data for 802.11n bit rate adaptation, it is likely that the SNR could be used to reduce the number of probes used in probe-based bit rate adaptation; we discuss this more in Section 4.5.

4.3 Consequences of Selecting a Suboptimal Bit Rate

In the previous section, we discussed how frequently our bit rate selection scheme could select the optimal bit rate. Here, we examine the penalty of selecting a suboptimal bit rate. Recall that because the throughput depends on the loss rate as well as the bit rate, it is possible for a low bit rate that sees little loss to have throughput comparable to a higher bit rate that sees more loss. If it is the case that the throughput of the optimal bit rate is comparable to that of other bit rates, then the more coarsely-grained look-up tables would still be effective (since selecting a suboptimal bit rate would not affect performance significantly).

In this section, we are concerned with quantifying the potential loss in throughput that occurs from using our simple bit rate selection method versus using the optimal bit rate every time (i.e., using a scheme with perfect knowledge). Because our throughput measurements are upper bounds on the actual throughput, it is possible that we would see higher losses in practice. Nonetheless, we expect these results to be indicative of the differences we would see between each of our methods in practice.

To determine this loss, for each of our three strategies, we create the appropriate look-up table. Then, for every probe set P, we calculate two quantities: the throughput of the probe in P sent at the optimal bit rate, and the throughput of the probe in P sent at the rate that we would have selected using the look-up table. Figure 6(a) shows the CDF of these differences for 802.11b/g, for each of the three cases. In addition to the link-, AP-, and network-based approaches, we also show the results for a global look-up table (discussed previously) for comparison. We choose to show absolute differences instead of relative differences as we find these values to be more instructive. For instance, a 100% loss in throughput could be from 2Mbit/s to 1Mbit/s, or 40Mbit/s to 20Mbit/s; we consider the latter case to be much worse.

The most interesting conclusion from this graph is that there is very little difference between network-wide and global training, but that link-specific and AP-specific training are considerably better. These findings suggest that many individual networks may well exhibit the degree of variation that one might only expect across a range of different networks, insofar as throughput results are concerned. On the other hand, it generally takes far more bit rates to achieve the 95th-percentile using a global lookup table than it does

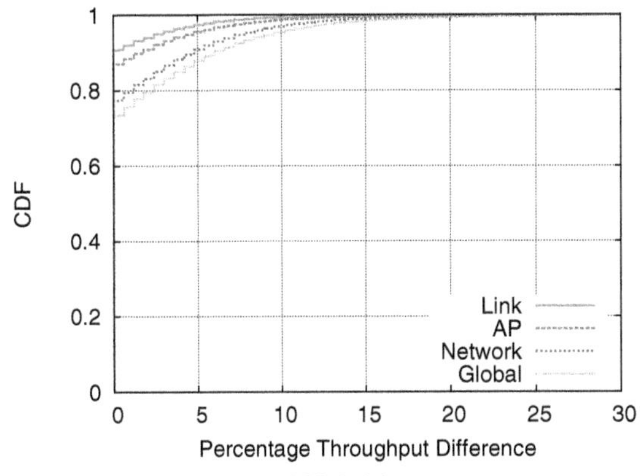

(a) 802.11b/g

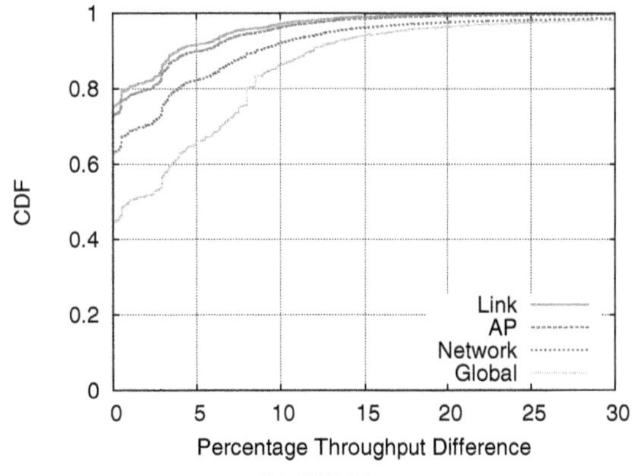

(b) 802.11n

Figure 6: CDF of the throughput differences using the simple bit rate selection method vs. the best bit rate for each probe set for 802.11b/g and 802.11n.

using a network-based lookup table (this graph was not shown in the previous section).

Figure 6(b) shows the CDF of the corresponding throughput differences for 802.11n. Here, the difference between network-wide training and global training is more substantial, and both approaches are inferior to link-specific training to produce the look-up table. The absolute throughput difference that we see is generally much higher than in the 802.11b/g networks. There are two reasons for this: first, 802.11n is capable of much higher throughput than 802.11b/g, so we can see throughput differences in 802.11n that are simply not possible in 802.11b/g. Second, as we have seen in Figure 5, the SNR is not as good a predictor in 802.11n networks as it is in 802.11b/g networks, and thus we are more likely to see errors between the throughput achieved from our simple lookup method and the optimal throughput. Still, it is worth noting that link-specific training gets the right answer about 75% of the time even in 802.11n networks (the equivalent number for 802.11b/g is 90%). Further work is required to identify when link-specific training works well and when it does not.

4.4 Correlation of SNR and Throughput

We also investigate the variation in throughput for a given SNR. This is different from the previous question; here we are interested in how much the throughput can vary for a particular SNR, not the potential loss in throughput that we expect to see from our simple bit rate selection method.

Figure 7 shows the SNR vs. the median throughput seen by probes with that SNR in 802.11b/g networks. The mean throughput increases with the SNR until an SNR of about 30 dB, and then levels off. These curves track the theoretical SNR-vs-throughput curves calculated in [13] and [18]. A similar result holds for 802.11n, which we do not show here. Not surprisingly, 802.11n networks see a higher peak value than the 802.11b/g networks. In 802.11n, the throughput tends to level off around 15dB instead of 30dB. In both cases, the variation (measured in Figure 7 by the upper and lower quartiles) is largest in the steepest part of the curves.

4.5 Practical Considerations

Though our primary goal in this section was to examine how well the SNR could be used in bit rate adaptation algorithms, we briefly touch on some of the practical considerations of using our SNR-based look-up tables in the link-specific case.

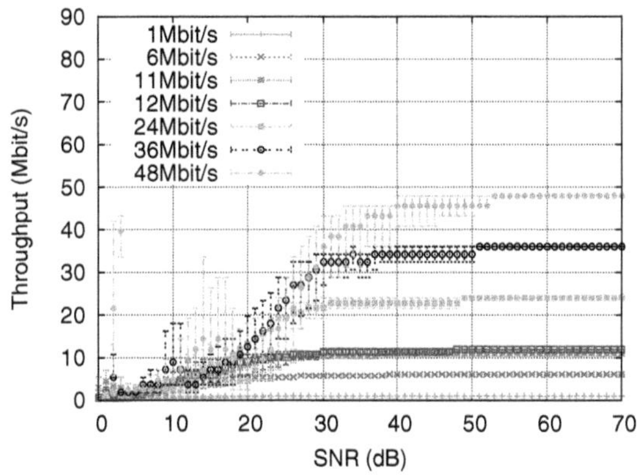

Figure 7: Median throughput versus SNR aggregated across all links in all 802.11b/g networks. Error bars indicate the upper and lower quartiles.

4.5.1 802.11b/g

For 802.11b/g, Figure 4 indicates that one bit rate can be used for each SNR with high accuracy. Because of this result, for each SNR on a link, only one probe set per day ever needs to be sent[3]. Algorithm 1 presents a viable strategy for source *s* to select a bit rate to use to send to destination *d*.

Since we see standard deviation of <10dB for the SNRs on 90% of links (Figure 2), we do not expect to see many different SNR values, and thus not to need many different probe sets. Also note that since each source uses its own look-up tables, there is no need for coordination amongst nodes.

4.5.2 802.11n

For 802.11n, we envision making a look-up table as described above, but keeping track of the *k* best bit rates for each SNR (where *k* is small; perhaps two or three). A standard probing algorithm (for example, SampleRate [4]) could be used in conjunction with this augmented table, restricting its probes to the bit rates present for each SNR. This strategy effectively divides bit rate selection

[3]We say "per day" because we only have one day's worth of data. Additionally, it may be worthwhile to send probes more frequently (e.g., once every hour), in case conditions change drastically.

Algorithm 1 Bit rate selection for source s sending to destination d, for 802.11b/g. $lookup\_table[snr, d]$ holds the best bit rate for an SNR snr measured on the link $s \rightarrow d$. This algorithm returns the bit rate for s to use when sending to d.

```
Measure the SNR snr to d
if lookup_table[snr, d] exists then
    r = lookup_table[snr, d]
else
    Send a probe set to d
    Determine b_opt for this probe set
    lookup_table[snr, d] = b_opt
    r = b_opt
end if
Return r
```

into two phases: Finding the k best bit rates for each SNR, which involves probing at all bit rates, and probing at that restricted set of bit rates once the k best are found. Algorithm 2 presents a possible strategy. We refer to *full* probe sets as ones that send probes at all bit rates; these are the types probe sets we have discussed thus far. We refer to *restricted* probe sets as those that send probes only at certain bit rates.

Algorithm 2 Bit rate selection for source s sending to destination d, for 802.11n. $lookup\_table[snr, d]$ holds the k best bit rates for an SNR snr measured on the link $s \rightarrow d$. This algorithm returns the bit rate for s to use when sending to d.

```
Measure the SNR snr to d
if lookup_table[snr, d] exists then
    Let C = lookup_table[snr, d]
    Send a restricted probe set to the bit rates in C
    Let b_opt be the best bit rate in this restricted probe set
    r = lookup_table[snr, d]
else
    Send a full probe set to d
    Determine the k best bit rates in this probe set. Let C be this
    set, and let b_opt be the best bit rate in this probe set (as before)
    lookup_table[snr, d] = C
    r = b_opt
end if
Return r
```

The key concern with this algorithm is whether the k best bit rates in the first full probe set are indeed the k bit rates to which we should restrict future probes. Recall that Figure 5(c) implies that four bit rates are enough, i.e., that there are no more than four different values of b_{opt} for each link. However, this does *not* imply that the top four bit rates in one probe set comprise the same set as the four distinct values of b_{opt}

However, we find that it *is* sufficient to send only one full probe set for each $\langle$SNR, link$\rangle$ pair; the above algorithm performed with 91% accuracy on our data set, for $k = 4$. Note that this substantially decreases the overhead of probing. Currently, Meraki sends probes at 29 of the 802.11n bit rates, and could one day send as many as 64 (the number of bit rates in 802.11n for a particular channel). Algorithm 2 decreases this number by over 86%.

4.6 Key Take-Aways and Caveats

The results that we have presented in this section are from inter-AP measurements taken in a static setting with stationary APs. In these situations, across a wide range of networks, we find that per-link SNR-based training can narrow down the optimal bit rate a large fraction of the time for both 802.11b/g and 802.11n, verifying the claims of previous small-scale studies. We also found that the penalty for picking a suboptimal bit rate is small much of the time for 802.11b/g. It is also important to note that links vary substantially in the same network and between networks, so training the SNR-to-rate look-up table on a different link in the same network will be less accurate.

That said, we should note that these findings regarding per-link training will not necessarily translate directly for communication to a client or between two clients, particularly if they are mobile. Here, link conditions change more frequently and depend on speed, as previous work has shown. Our results may translate to clients that are mostly static, but even so one has to consider the fact that movement in the environment may render even per-link training less effective than in the inter-AP setting within a mesh network.

5. OPPORTUNISTIC ROUTING

Having studied the performance of bit rate adaptation protocols in mesh networks, we now turn our attention to the performance of recently-developed mesh routing protocols. Like bit rate adaptation, routing is a significant factor affecting throughput of mesh networks. Traditional mesh routing involves finding a single path between any source and destination, using a metric like the expected number of transmissions (ETX) to pick next-hops to each destination [12]. With ExOR [7] and MORE [9] researchers have proposed using packet-level opportunistic routing protocols that take advantage of broadcast transmissions and probabilistic receptions to reduce the number of transmissions needed to transfer packets between a source and destination (a more detailed description of these protocols is given in Section 2.3).

To date, these protocols have been evaluated only on relatively small lab testbeds. With the inter-AP data we have, we can evaluate these protocols and compare them to traditional routing. The reason is that the reduction in the number of transmitted packets due to opportunistic routing, to first order, depends only on the packet loss rates between nodes.

For opportunistic routing, we are interested in the performance of an ideal scheme that incurs no overhead; in this sense, it models MORE, not ExOR, because of the absence of explicit coordination in the former. We are interested in quantifying the following: given each $\langle AP_1, AP_2\rangle$ pair in our data, what is the expected number of transmissions to send a packet from AP_1 to AP_2 using opportunistic routing (ExOR) vs. using a standard routing protocol (ETX). In this section, we restrict ourselves to data from our 802.11b/g networks, and use a snapshot of our data, due to processing time.

5.1 Expected Improvements from Opportunistic Routing

The right comparison should use a bit rate adaptation method for traditional routing. However, we also need to consider the bit rate at which the opportunistic routing protocol operates. This question is a difficult one because there is no satisfactory bit rate adaptation protocol available for opportunistic routing. In this section, adopt a simple approach and calculate the improvements as if the entire network were operating at the same bit rate; we present the results for each bit rate separately. In Section 5.4, we turn our attention to allowing variable bit rates. Though it is likely that different bit rate adaptation algorithms will affect the throughput of opportunistic routing in different ways, we still expect our results to be highly instructive and likely to reflect the gains one might observe in practice.

We now have, for each bit rate, a matrix of packet success rates for each network (one success rate for each link). Given this ma-

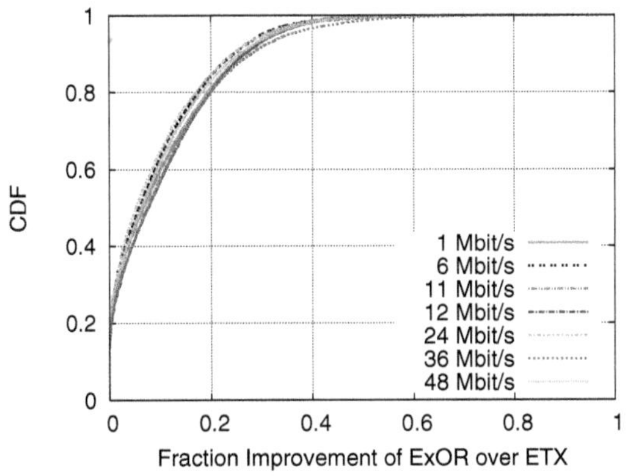

Figure 8: Improvement (in terms of expected number of transmissions needed to send one packet) of opportunistic routing (ExOR) over one-way ETX (ETX1)

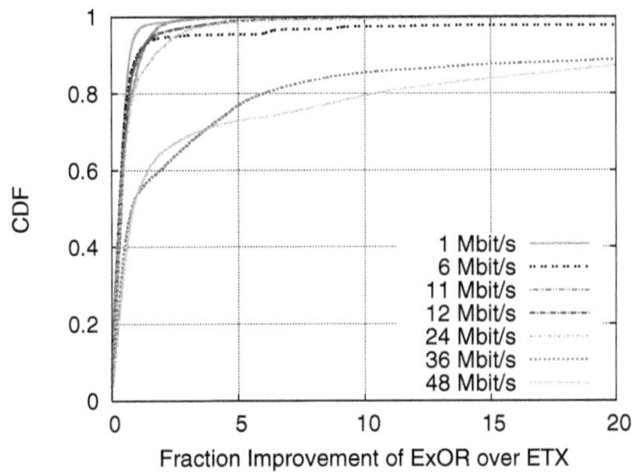

Figure 9: Improvement (in terms of expected number of transmissions needed to send one packet) of opportunistic routing (ExOR) over two-way ETX (ETX2)

trix, we can compute the ETX cost for each link (explained below). With this cost, our standard routing protocol is simply shortest-path routing using ETX as the metric, and the ETX cost between s and d under this routing protocol is the sum of the ETX metrics for each link on the resulting path from s to d.

Calculating the ExOR cost from s to d is only slightly more complicated. First, we determine the set C of neighbors of s that are closer to d under the ETX metric. If there is no node closer to d, then $ExOR(s \rightarrow d)$ is simply $ETX(s \rightarrow d)$. Otherwise, imagining that s broadcasts the packet to these nodes, for each node $n \in C$, we calculate $r(n)$ = the probability that n received the packet and that no node closer to d also received it. Then,

$$ExOR(s \rightarrow d) = \frac{1 + \sum_{n \in C} r(n) \cdot ExOR(n \rightarrow d)}{1 - r(s)} \qquad (1)$$

The 1 in the numerator accounts for the one transmission that s made to broadcast the packet in the first place, and the denominator accounts for the fact that there is a small probability that the packet will not leave s.

To calculate the ETX metric of a link, we consider two approaches. ETX1 uses a probability of 1 for the link-layer ACK, which is sent at the lowest bit rate and usually has a much higher probability of arriving than a packet. This means that, under the

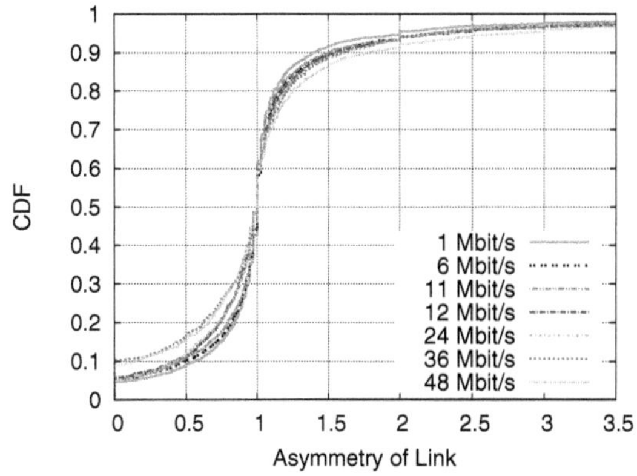

Figure 10: CDF of packet success rate of a link to the packet success rate on the reverse link. There is some asymmetry, but not an egregious amount; however, this amount is enough to lead to a noticeable difference in the expected number of transmissions for ETX1 (perfect ACK channel) and ETX2. The asymmetry does not change significantly with the bit rate.

ETX1 metric, the cost of sending from s to d is $\frac{1}{\mathbb{P}(s \rightarrow d)}$, where $\mathbb{P}(s \rightarrow d)$ is the delivery probability on the link $s \rightarrow d$. ETX2 uses the packet success rate on the reverse link, which is along the lines of the metric suggested in the original ETX paper. Under the ETX2 metric, the cost of sending from s to d is $\frac{1}{\mathbb{P}(s \rightarrow d) \cdot \mathbb{P}(d \rightarrow s)}$. It is almost certainly the case that ETX1 is what networks should use, not ETX2, but we compare against both ETX1 and ETX2 here. Finally, we restrict our attention to networks with at least five nodes, as smaller networks are unlikely to show significant differences.

Figures 8 and 9 show the fraction improvement of ExOR over ETX for each source-destination pair in all of our networks with at least five nodes. This fraction is in terms of the expected number of transmissions needed to send a packet. An improvement of x means ETX1 requires $(x * 100)\%$ *more* transmissions than opportunistic routing (for example, an ExOR cost of 1.2 and an ETX cost of 1.5 is an improvement of .25). The mean of the ETX1 to opportunistic routing ratio of the expected number of packets sent ranges from .09 to .11 depending on the bit rate (that is, roughly a 9-11% improvement); the median ranges from .05 to .08 for all bit rates. For between 13% and 20% of pairs, there is no improvement, regardless of bit rate. With ETX2, the improvement is more substantive: a mean ratio of between .39 and 1.3 for the five lowest bit rates, and between 7.26 and 9.25 for the two highest. The median is between .30 and .86 for the five lowest bit rates, and .80 and .86 for the two highest. If we restrict our analysis to the 20% of source-destination pairs with the most improvement, we see a slight improvement for ETX1. In this case, the mean ranges from .25 to .29, and the median from .24 to .27.

5.2 Causes of Improvement

In this section, we examine the factors that can cause a path to see improvement (or not) with ExOR. In particular, we find that the differences between the improvements over ETX1 and ETX2 arise due to link asymmetry, the overall lack of improvement of ExOR over ETX1 is a result of many paths being short, and he average improvement from ExOR roughly increases as path length increases.

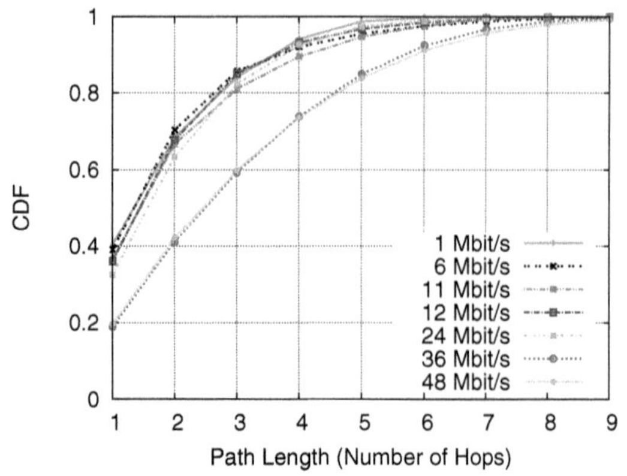

Figure 11: CDF of path lengths in our networks, for each bit rate.

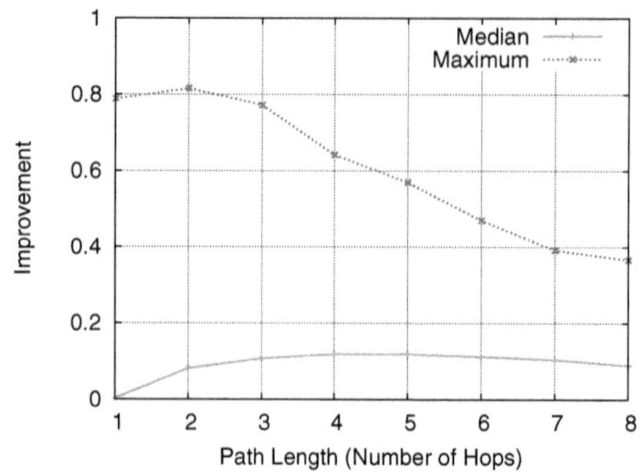

Figure 12: The median and maximum improvement from opportunistic routing vs. path length. Note that while the median improvement increases with path length—as expected—the maximum in fact decreases.

5.2.1 *Impact of Link Asymmetry*

The reason that ETX1 and ETX2 have such different performance is that link delivery rates are asymmetric. Figure 10 shows the CDF of the link asymmetries: the x-axis is the ratio of the packet success rate at the optimal bit rate between A and B, and the packet success rate at the optimal bit rate between B and A, for each link AB. Although the degree of asymmetry is not as pronounced as in some previous smaller-scale studies, it exists, and is the reason why the gains of opportunistic routing are more significant with ETX2 (recall that ETX2 assumes a lossy ACK-channel whereas ETX1 does not).

5.2.2 *Impact of Path Length and Diversity*

As discussed in Section 2.3, short paths are unlikely to see much benefit when using ExOR. Figure 11 shows that, indeed, most paths are short. For the five lowest bit rates, between 30 and 40% of paths are only one hop, and around 80% are fewer than three hops. However, for the two highest bit rates, roughly 40% of the paths are *more* than three hops. These long paths are the ones on which ETX2 sees the greatest improvement. The lack of improvement of ExOR over ETX1 supports the recent work of Afanasyev and Snoeren, who found that ExOR sees most of its improvement due to its bulk-acknowledgment scheme rather than because of opportunistic receptions [1].

In Figure 12 we plot the path length vs. the median and maximum improvement. Because the trends for each bit rate are the same, Figure 12 presents these quantities averaged over all bit rates. The median improvement almost always increases with the path length. This result is expected, and is what is indicated in [7]. However, the maximum improvement tends to *decrease* with the path length. We also see a similar result with path diversity (not pictured): the median improvement increases as the number of diverse paths from the source to the destination increases, but the maximum improvement tends to decrease. The fact that the median improvement increases in both of these cases makes sense; more nodes in between the source and destination means more nodes with forwarding potential.

Non-intuitively, the paths with the maximum proportional improvements tend to be short paths. For instance, consider the path $A \rightarrow B \rightarrow C$, with link probabilities of .9 on the links $A \rightarrow B$ and $B \rightarrow C$, and also a probability of .3 that the packet goes from A to C directly when broadcasted. We expect to need roughly 2.2 transmission for each packet (the shortest ETX1 path is $A \rightarrow B \rightarrow C$, but there is a probability of .3 that ExOR will reduce this to 1 transmission). Hence, the high proportional improvement. However, these types of paths are somewhat rare, which is why the median path improvement still increases with path length.

5.3 Network Variability

Having discussed what types of links see see the best ExOR improvements, we now turn our attention to the types of networks that do. Given our conclusions in the previous section, we might expect that larger networks (with the potential for longer paths) would see the good improvements, as the median improvement increases with path length.

In Figure 13 we plot the mean improvement over all links in a network vs. the number of nodes in the network (for readability, we leave out our largest networks, but the result is consistent), at 1Mbit/s (the results are similar at other bit rates; we do not present them here). We also include standard deviation bars to indicate the variability of improvement. Counter-intuitively, the mean improvement *does not* increase with network size; in fact, it remains relatively constant. Similarly, the variability in improvement is about the same regardless of size. The reason for this constancy is that even though large networks have more long paths—and thus paths that tend to see greater improvements with ExOR—they also have many more shorter paths than small networks. These short paths see less improvement, keeping the mean low, as well as the variance.

5.4 Bit Rate Selection for Opportunistic Routing

In Section 5.1, we examined the benefits of opportunistic routing when the entire network was operating at the same bit rate. In this section, we allow APs to send at different bit rates. Because bit rate adaptation in opportunistic routing is an open question, we do not adapt a particular rate adaptation strategy. Instead, we examine the improvements in a network with perfect knowledge about which bit rate each AP should use.

Because we allow for variable bit rates, our definition of $ExOR(s \rightarrow d)$ changes slightly; we refer to this new definition as $ExOR'(s \rightarrow d)$. Before calculating $ExOR(s \rightarrow d)$, we must calculate $ExOR'(s \rightarrow d, rate)$ for each bit rate that s can use. s's bit rate of choice will be the one that minimizes this value.

For a bit rate r, we first determine the set C of neighbors of s that are closer to d, but instead of using the ETX metric, we use the ETT

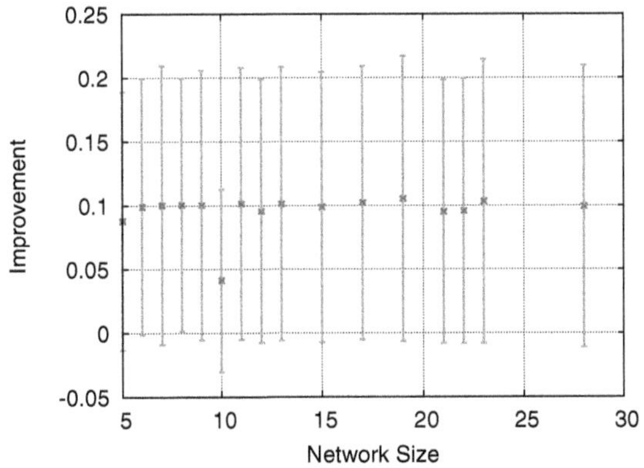

Figure 13: Mean improvement over the entire network from opportunistic routing vs. the network size, for 1Mbit/s (error bars indicate standard deviations). The mean and standard deviation remain relatively constant as size increases, indicating that neither larger nor smaller networks are more likely to see benefits from opportunistic routing.

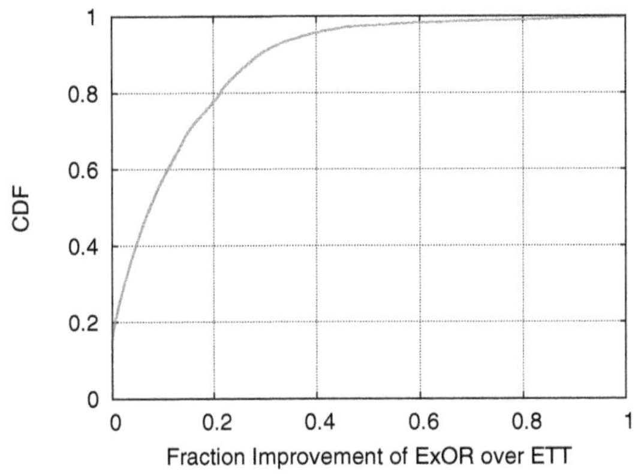

Figure 14: Improvement (in terms of expected transmission time) of opportunistic routing (ExOR) over ETT.

metric [6][4]. Recall that the difference between the two is that ETT takes into account the bit rate; thus, it reflects the expected amount of *time* it will take to transmit a packet, not the expected number of transmissions. Even though we are concentrating on a particular bit rate r, we use ETT here, not ETX, to allow for the possibility of the nodes in C sending at rates other than r. After all, r need not be the bit rate for the entire path.

Then,

$$ExOR'(s \rightarrow d, rate) = \frac{\frac{1}{rate} + \sum_{n \in C} r(n) \cdot ExOR'(n \rightarrow d)}{1 - r(s)} \quad (2)$$

where $r(n)$ is the same as in Equation 1: the probability that node n received the packet and that no node closer to d also received it. Note that because we are concerned with the expected transmission time, not the expected number of transmissions, we use $\frac{1}{rate}$ in the numerator, rather than 1. Then,

$$ExOR'(s \rightarrow d) = argmin\{ExOR'(s \rightarrow d, rate)\} \quad (3)$$

and s would use the corresponding bit rate when sending to d.

[4]specifically we are using one-way ETT, i.e., considering only the probability of the forward link, analogous to ETX1

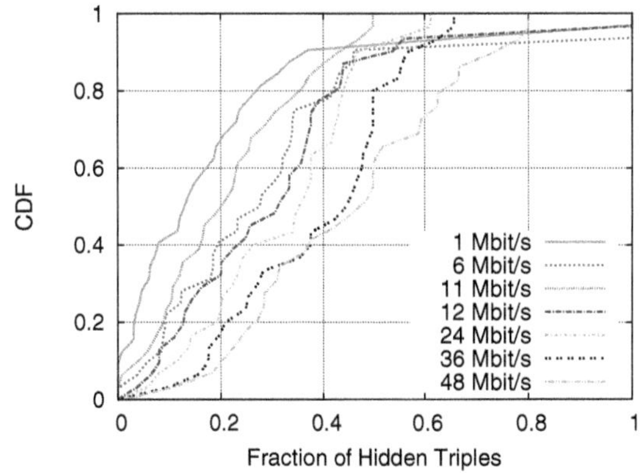

Figure 15: Fraction of hidden triples to relevant triples at a threshold of 10%.

Figure 14 shows the results using this method. The CDF is comparable to that in Figure 8; even with perfect knowledge of bit rates, opportunistic routing offers little benefit on most paths.

6. HIDDEN TRIPLES

Our next set of results relates to the likelihood of interference from concurrent transmissions and how frequent hidden terminals are at each bit rate. In Section 4 we examined the performance of various bit rate adaptation schemes. Even with an ideal rate adaptation algorithm, throughput can still be affected by interference from hidden terminals. We estimate the frequency of hidden terminals in this section, using networks with at least 10 APs.

Since a hidden terminal is a property of the MAC protocol, which in turn depends on how the carrier sense thresholds are picked and the method used for carrier sense, we investigate the occurrence of *hidden triples*. We define a hidden triple as follows. A triple of APs, $\langle AP_1, AP_2, AP_3 \rangle$, in a network is a hidden triple at a bit rate b if AP_2 can hear both AP_1 and AP_3 at bit rate b, but *neither* AP_1 nor AP_3 can hear each other when sending at bit rate b. We define AP_1's and AP_2's ability to hear one another at bit rate b based on a threshold t: if we observe that AP_1 and AP_2 could hear more than t percent of the probes sent between them at bit rate b, then AP_1 and AP_2 can hear each other; otherwise, they cannot.

We are interested in what fraction of triples in a network are hidden triples at each bit rate. It is not particularly interesting to determine what fraction of *all* triples are hidden triples, since three APs that are far from each other are not likely to become hidden terminals or interfere appreciably with one another. Instead, we want to know what fraction of *relevant* triples are hidden triples. We define a relevant triple $\langle AP_1, AP_2, AP_3 \rangle$ as one where AP_1 and AP_3 can both hear AP_2; AP_1 and AP_3 may or may not be able to hear each other. If they cannot, we have a hidden triple.

6.1 Frequency of Hidden Triples

Figure 15 shows the CDF of the fraction of hidden triples to relevant triples for a threshold of 10% (our results don't change significantly as the threshold varies). For each of our 802.11b/g networks, we used the probe data to determine the number of relevant triples at each bit rate, and then the proportion of those that were hidden triples. The CDF is taken over all networks; for example, roughly 13% of networks had fewer than 50% hidden triples at 1Mbit/s.

For the most part, as the bit rate increases, the fraction of hidden triples to relevant triples also increases. One exception is the results for 6Mbit/s and 11Mbit/s; there are almost always fewer hidden

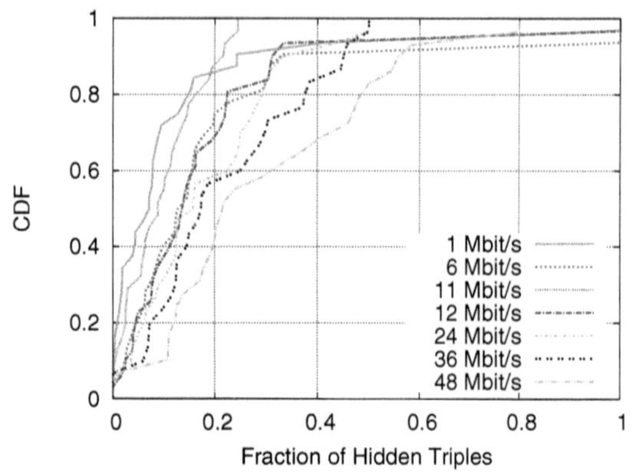

Figure 16: Hidden triples at a threshold of 10%, taking into account the capture effect with a threshold of 10dB.

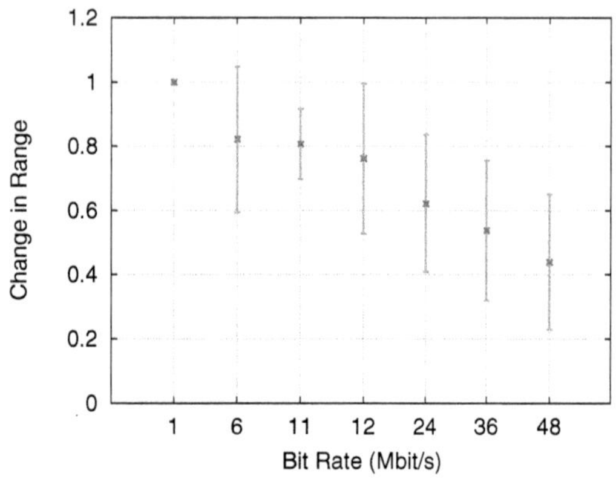

Figure 17: Change in range of APs at different bit rates. The change is calculated with respect to the range at 1Mbit/s, thus by definition the change in range at 1Mbit/s is 1.

triples at 11Mbit/s than at 6Mbit/s. We believe that this exception is because the 11Mbit/s rate uses DSSS rather than OFDM, which is known to have better reception in 802.11 at lower SNR values. (1Mbit/s also uses spread spectrum; all other bit rates use OFDM).

6.1.1 The Capture Effect

In the previous section, we gave a rough upper bound on the number of hidden terminals that could be present in a network. Here, we estimate how many of those could potentially be saved by the capture effect. The capture effect [36] is the property of 802.11 radios where a strong signal can be decoded even when a weak signal is received at the same time. In the context of our hidden terminal example, if AP_1 and AP_2 both sent to AP_3 at the same time, but AP_1 had a much stronger signal, it is possible that AP_1's communication would not be disrupted by the signal from AP_2.

Whether the stronger of the two signals is captured depends on the difference in their SNRs; if this difference is below a certain threshold, the stronger signal will not be captured. This threshold can vary. Ware et al. find that under certain conditions a difference of 5dB is sufficient [36], while others report larger values of over 20dB [26]. In Figure 16, using a relatively conservative estimate of 10dB, we again estimate the number of hidden triples at each bit rate (as in Figure 15).

Here, we see that roughly 7% of networks had fewer than 50% hidden triples at 1Mbit/s, and again, we see the percentage of hidden triples increases with the bit rate, with the exception of 6Mbit/s and 11Mbit/s.

6.1.2 Discussion

Our results show that hidden triples are quite common; the median value over all the networks even at the lowest 1Mbit/s bit rate is about 7% of triples when there is only a 10% chance of successfully receiving a packet and we consider the capture effect, and 13% of hidden triples when we do not. However, these percentages do not necessarily translate into the percentage of APs in a network that are involved in hidden triples (i.e., 13% of relevant triples being hidden triples does not mean that 13% of the APs in the network are involved in hidden triples). In fact, for each bit rate, when considering the capture effect, we find that a median value of between 65% and 81% of APs are involved in a hidden triple in any given network, with between 46% and 63% of APs acting as AP_1 or AP_2 at some point (i.e., sending data in a hidden triple). When not considering the capture effect, between 81% and 90% of APs are involved in a hidden triple, with between 62% and 75% of APs acting as AP_1 or AP_2.

We also note that this result is an upper bound on the percentage of hidden terminals that could occur in these networks, as a hidden triple may not always result in a hidden terminal. Of course, it might be possible to eliminate hidden terminal occurrences altogether by using carrier sensing parameters that are conservative, but that would reduce transmission opportunities. We note that a 10% chance of receiving packets at 1Mbit/s is actually symptomatic of a very low SNR; frame preambles are sent at this bit rate, which means that in these cases the preamble isn't being detected 90% of the time.

As such, this result suggests to us that hidden terminals in real-world 802.11b/g mesh networks with static APs using current MAC protocols probably occur in around 7% of triples or more, and involve at least 65% of APs. These values are higher than those assumed by [17], and in some networks, we even see values higher than those reported by [11]. This knowledge is helpful for systems like ZigZag [17], which require an accurate model of hidden terminals in a network for their analysis, and also for estimating the loss in throughput that could be incurred using a perfect bit rate adaptation scheme. The caveat is that, since our data is for static APs, it is possible that clients experience hidden terminals at higher or lower rates.

6.2 Range

People colloquially refer to the "range" of radio communication, but this is an ill-formed notion because receptions are probabilistic and depend on the bit rate. We formally define and estimate this notion as follows: the *range* of a network at a particular bit rate b is the number of node pairs that can hear each other at that bit rate.

Because our networks differ in size (in terms of number of APs), comparing the absolute range across networks is not interesting. Instead, we measure the *change* in range of a network. To do this, we define R to be the range of the network at a bit rate of 1Mbit/s. For every other bit rate, we look at how the range differs from R by plotting the ratio of the range at bit rate b to R. (By definition, the change in range for 1Mbit/s is 1.)

This result is plotted in Figure 17. The error bars represent the standard deviation across all networks. Two important points stand out. First, as expected, the mean change in range reduces as the bit rate increases in a steady way. This property has been noted anecdotally before, but the way in which it drops has not been well-understood. Second, there is a tremendous variation in the drop-off, suggesting that one cannot always conclude that higher bit rates have poorer reception properties than lower ones under similar conditions. Indeed, we find that roughly 26% of networks experience at least one pair of bit rates $b_1 < b_2$ where the range at b_2 is higher than that at b_1. The majority of these cases (73%) occur with bit rates of 6Mbit/s and 11Mbit/s, again perhaps a result of 11Mbit/s using DSSS instead of OFDM.

6.3 Impact of Environment

Figures 15 and 16 indicate that not all networks have similar proportions of hidden terminals; if they did, we would see much steeper curves in the CDFs. Here we briefly examine the impact of the environment—indoor or outdoor—on the number of hidden triples, as well as the range.

We have found that outdoor networks, not surprisingly, have a larger range than indoor networks (because the absolute range depends on the size of the network, we measured the quantity $range/size^2$, where *size* is the number of APs in the network.) Indoor networks also tend to see a higher percentage of hidden triples than outdoor networks, most likely due to their density (indoor networks are more likely to have nodes closer to each other). In indoor networks (most of our data set), when taking into account the capture effect, we see a median of about 7% hidden triples at a 10% threshold, at 1Mbit/s. When not considering the capture effect, we see a median of 14%. However, when restricting ourselves to only outdoor networks, these percentages drop to less than 1% and 2%, respectively.

7. CONCLUSION

This paper analyzed data collected from over 1407 access points in 110 commercially deployed Meraki wireless mesh networks, constituting perhaps the largest published study of real-world 802.11 networks to date. We found that the SNR is not a sufficient determinant of the optimal bit rate within a same network, but on a given link with static nodes (APs), the SNR can be a good indicator with sufficient training. We found that an ideal opportunistic routing protocol does not reduce the number of transmissions on the majority of paths as compared to traditional unicast routing. We also found that "hidden triple" situations, where a triple of nodes A, B, C have the property that AB and BC can communicate with each other, but AC cannot are more common than suggested in previous work (a median of 13% of all triples in our results), and increase in proportion as the bit rate increases.

These findings, and others in the paper, shed light on three critical areas that have seen a great deal of activity in recent years: bit rate adaptation, mesh network routing, and MAC protocols to overcome interference. Bit rate adaptation and mesh routing both significantly affect throughput, while interference from hidden terminals can be detrimental to even an ideal bit rate adaptation algorithm. This paper provided more conclusive answers to questions in all of these areas, using a data set that is larger in scale and diversity than any other of which we are aware.

8. ACKNOWLEDGMENTS

We are indebted to Cliff Frey, John Bicket, and Sanjit Biswas at Meraki Networks for their generous help with the data collection and for several discussions. We thank Mythili Vutukuru, Lenin Ravindranath, and the anonymous reviewers for their insightful comments. This work was supported by the National Science Foundation under grant CNS-0721702 and in part by Foxconn Corporation.

9. REFERENCES

[1] M. Afanasyev and A. Snoeren. The Importance of Being Overheard: Throughput Gains in Wireless Mesh Networks. In *Internet Measurement Conference*, 2009.

[2] A. Balachandran, G. M. Voelker, P. Bahl, and P. V. Rangan. Characterizing User Behavior and Network Performance in a Public Wireless LAN. In *ACM SIGMETRICS*, 2002.

[3] K. Balachandran, S. R. Kadaba, and S. Nanda. Channel Quality Estimation and Rate Adaptation for Cellular Mobile Radio. *IEEE Journal on Selected Areas in Communications*, 17(7), 1999.

[4] J. Bicket. Bit-rate Selection in Wireless Networks. Master's thesis, Massachusetts Institute of Technology, February 2005.

[5] J. Bicket. personal communication, 2009.

[6] J. Bicket, D. Aguayo, S. Biswas, and R. Morris. Architecture and Evaluation of an Unplanned 802.11b Mesh Network. In *MobiCom*, 2005.

[7] S. Biswas and R. Morris. ExOR: Opportunistic Multi-hop Routing for Wireless Networks. *ACM SIGCOMM*, 2005.

[8] J. Camp and E. Knightly. Modulation Rate Adaptation in Urban and Vehicular Environments: Cross-layer Implementation and Experimental Evaluation. In *MobiCom*, 2008.

[9] S. Chachulski, M. Jennings, S. Katti, and D. Katabi. Trading Structure for Randomness in Wireless Opportunistic Routing. In *ACM SIGCOMM*, 2007.

[10] C. Chen, E. Seo, H. Luo, and N. H. Vaidya. Rate-adaptive Framing for Interfered Wireless Networks. In *IEEE INFOCOM*, 2007.

[11] Y. Cheng, J. Bellardo, P. Benkö, A. C. Snoeren, G. M. Voelker, and S. Savage. Jigsaw: Solving the Puzzle of Enterprise 802.11 Analysis. In *ACM SIGCOMM*, 2006.

[12] D. S. J. De Couto, D. Aguayo, J. Bicket, and R. Morris. A High-throughput Path Metric for Multi-hop Wireless Routing. In *MobiCom*, 2003.

[13] J. del Prado Pavon and S. Choi. Link Adaptation Strategy for IEEE 802.11 WLAN via Received Signal Strength Measurement. In *IEEE International Conference on Communications*, 2003.

[14] D. Duchamp and N. F. Reynolds. Measured Performance of a Wireless LAN. In *IEEE Conference on Local Computer Networks*, 1992.

[15] D. Eckhardt and P. Steenkiste. Measurement and Analysis of the Error Characteristics of an In-Building Wireless Network. In *ACM SIGCOMM*, 1996.

[16] D. L. Goeckel. Adaptive Coding for Time-Varying Channels Using Outdated Fading Estimates. *IEEE Transactions on Communications*, 47(6), 1999.

[17] S. Gollakota and D. Katabi. Zigzag Decoding: Combating Hidden Terminals in Wireless Networks. In *ACM SIGCOMM*, 2008.

[18] I. Haratcherev, K. Langendoen, R. Lagendijk, and H. Sips. Hybrid Rate Control for IEEE 802.11. In *MOBIWAC*, 2004.

[19] T. Henderson, D. Kotz, and I. Abyzov. The Changing Usage of a Mature Campus-wide Wireless Network. In *MobiCom*, 2004.

[20] F. Hernández-Campos and M. Papadopouli. A Comparative Measurement Study of the Workload of Wireless Access Points in Campus Networks. In *IEEE International Symposium on Personal, Indoor and Mobile Radio Communications*, 2005.

[21] G. Holland, N. Vaidya, and P. Bahl. A Rate-adaptive MAC Protocol for Multi-Hop Wireless Networks. In *MobiCom*, 2001.

[22] A. P. Jardosh, K. N. Ramachandran, K. C. Almeroth, and E. M. Belding-Royer. Understanding Link-Layer Behavior in Highly Congested IEEE 802.11b Wireless Networks. In *E-WIND*, 2005.

[23] G. Judd and P. Steenkiste. Using Emulation to Understand and Improve Wireless Networks and Applications. In *USENIX NSDI*, 2005.

[24] G. Judd, X. Wang, and P. Steenkiste. Efficient Channel-aware Rate Adaptation in Dynamic Environments. In *MobiSys*, 2008.

[25] S. Khurana, A. Kahol, and A. P. Jayasumana. Effect of Hidden Terminals on the Performance of IEEE 802.11 MAC Protocol. In *IEEE Conference on Local Computer Networks*, 1998.

[26] J. Lee, W. Kim, S.-J. Lee, D. Jo, J. Ryu, T. Kwon, and Y. Choi. An Experimental Study on the Capture Effect in 802.11a Networks. In *WiNTECH*, 2007.

[27] M. McNett and G. M. Voelker. Access and Mobility of Wireless PDA Users. In *SIGMOBILE*, 2005.

[28] Meraki Networks. `http://meraki.com`.

[29] P. C. Ng, S. C. Liew, K. C. Sha, and W. T. To. Experimental Study of Hidden-node Problem in IEEE 802.11 Wireless Networks. In *ACM SIGCOMM Poster Session*, 2005.

[30] M. B. Pursley and C. S. Wilkins. Adaptive Transmission for Direct-Sequence Spread-Spectrum Communications over Multipath Channels. *International Journal of Wireless Information Networks*, 7(2):69–77, 2004.

[31] M. Rodrig, C. Reis, R. Mahajan, D. Wetherall, and J. Zahorjan. Measurement-based Characterization of 802.11 in a Hotspot Setting. In *E-WIND*, 2005.

[32] Roofnet. `http://pdos.csail.mit.edu/roofnet`.

[33] B. Sadeghi, V. Kanodia, A. Sabharwal, and E. W. Knightly. Opportunistic Media Access for Multirate Ad Hoc Networks. In *MobiCom*, 2002.

[34] D. Schwab and R. Bunt. Characterising the Use of a Campus Wireless Network. In *IEEE INFOCOM*, 2004.

[35] D. Tang and M. Baker. Analysis of a Local-Area Wireless Network. In *MobiCom*, 2000.

[36] C. Ware, J. Judge, J. Chicharo, and E. Dutkiewicz. Unfairness and Capture Behaviour in 802.11 Adhoc Networks. In *IEEE International Conference on Communications*, 2000.

[37] A. Willig, M. Kubisch, C. Hoene, and A. Wolisz. Measurements of a Wireless Link in an Industrial Environment Using an IEEE 802.11-Compliant Physical Layer. *IEEE Transactions on Industrial Electronics*, 49(6), 2002.

[38] S. H. Y. Wong, H. Yang, S. Lu, and V. Bharghavan. Robust Rate Adaptation for 802.11 Wireless Networks. In *MobiCom*, 2006.

[39] J. Zhang, K. Tan, J. Zhao, H. Wu, and Y. Zhang. A Practical SNR-Guided Rate Adaptation. In *IEEE INFOCOM*, 2008.

Characterizing Radio Resource Allocation for 3G Networks

Feng Qian
University of Michigan

Zhaoguang Wang
University of Michigan

Alexandre Gerber
AT&T Labs Research

Z. Morley Mao
University of Michigan

Subhabrata Sen
AT&T Labs Research

Oliver Spatscheck
AT&T Labs Research

ABSTRACT

3G cellular data networks have recently witnessed explosive growth. In this work, we focus on UMTS, one of the most popular 3G mobile communication technologies. Our work is the first to accurately infer, for any UMTS network, the state machine (both transitions and timer values) that guides the radio resource allocation policy through a light-weight probing scheme. We systematically characterize the impact of operational state machine settings by analyzing traces collected from a commercial UMTS network, and pinpoint the inefficiencies caused by the interplay between smartphone applications and the state machine behavior. Besides basic characterizations, we explore the optimal state machine settings in terms of several critical timer values evaluated using real network traces. Our findings suggest that the fundamental limitation of the current state machine design is its *static* nature of treating all traffic according to the same inactivity timers, making it difficult to balance tradeoffs among radio resource usage efficiency, network management overhead, device radio energy consumption, and performance. To the best of our knowledge, our work is the first empirical study that employs real cellular traces to investigate the optimality of UMTS state machine configurations. Our analysis also demonstrates that traffic patterns impose significant impact on radio resource and energy consumption. In particular, We propose a simple improvement that reduces YouTube streaming energy by 80% by leveraging an existing feature called *fast dormancy* supported by the 3GPP specifications.

Categories and Subject Descriptors

C.2.1 [**Computer-Communication Networks**]: Network Architecture and Design – Wireless Communication; C.4 [**Performance of Systems**]: Measurement Techniques

General Terms

Measurement, Algorithms

IMC'10, November 1–3, 2010, Melbourne, Australia.

Keywords

UMTS, 3G Networks, RRC state machine, Inactivity timers, Tail effects, Smartphones, Multimedia streaming

1. INTRODUCTION

3G cellular data networks have recently witnessed rapid growth, especially due to the emergence of smartphones. In this paper, we focus on the UMTS (the Universal Mobile Telecommunications System) 3G network, which is among the most popular 3G mobile communication technologies. As evidence of this popularity, in Q3 2008, among the 400 million of worldwide 3G users, 300 million were UMTS subscribers [1].

Compared to WiFi, 3G systems operate under more radio resource constraints. To efficiently utilize the limited radio resources, UMTS introduces for each *user equipment* (UE, *i.e.,* a smartphone) a *radio resource control* (RRC) state machine that determines radio resource usage affecting device energy consumption and user experience. Usually a UE (user equipment) can be in one of three states, each with different amount of allocated radio resources. The transitions between states also have significant impact on the UMTS system. Frequent state promotions (resource allocation) may lead to unacceptably long delays for the UE, as well as additional processing overheads for the radio access network [10, 21]. State demotions (resource release) are controlled by critical inactivity timers affecting radio resource utilization and UE energy consumption.

The current design of the RRC state machine appears to be ad-hoc with statically configured parameters. Our work systematically studies its design using real cellular traces from a large cellular ISP and analyzes the effect on important factors from both the network operator's perspectives, namely radio resource usage efficiency and management overhead, and from end-user's perspective, namely device energy consumption and application performance. We examine tradeoffs among these factors. In particular, we focus on settings of critical inactivity timer values that determine when to release radio resources after a period of inactivity.

As an example of the challenge in balancing the tradeoffs, using real UMTS cellular traces we observe that decreasing one inactivity timer by three seconds can reduce the overall radio resource usage by 40%, but increasing the number of state promotions by 31%. On the other hand, increasing the inactivity timer effectively enhances end user experience and reduces the management overhead, however at the expense of low efficiency in radio resource utilization and energy consumption. Intuitively, the optimal timer settings heavily depend on application traffic patterns and thus can benefit from *traffic awareness* via trace-driven tuning.

In this paper, we undertake a detailed exploration of the RRC state machine and its optimizations using real traces from a large cellular ISP. In particular, we make the following contributions.

1. Accurate inference of the RRC state machine. Different carriers may adopt different state machine models with varied parameters. Accurate inference is therefore the very first necessary step towards characterizing and improving the RRC state machine. We propose a novel inference technique purely based on probing from the user device. It systematically discovers the state transitions by strategically adjusting the packet dynamics. We applied our algorithm to two UMTS carriers and validated its accuracy by measuring the device power consumption.

2. Characterization of state machine behaviors. The current RRC state machine parameters are either empirically configured in an ad-hoc manner [7], or determined using analytical traffic models [20, 32]. The latter approach, however, suffers from several limitations. *(i)* The expressiveness of an analytical model is quite limited and is unlikely to capture, using a statistical distribution with a few parameters, the characteristics of real-world traffic patterns generated by millions of cellular users. *(ii)* The existence of concurrent applications accessing the network further increases the difficulty of modeling the packet dynamics.

We systematically characterize the impact of existing operational state machines by analyzing traces collected from a commercial UMTS network. We found that short data transfers severely suffer from the state promotion delay, and significant portions (up to 45.3%) of the occupation time of the high-speed dedicated transmission channel is wasted on the idle time period matching the inactivity timer value before a state demotion, which is called *tail* time [14]. We explore the optimal timer values by replaying the trace against different state machine settings with varying parameters. Our findings suggest that the fundamental limitation of the current state machine design is its *static* nature of treating all packets according to the same inactivity timer, making it difficult to balance the aforementioned tradeoffs. We also observe that applications exhibit different sensitivities to the change of inactivity timers due to their different traffic patterns. To the best of our knowledge, our work is the first empirical study that employs real cellular traces to investigate the optimality of RRC state machine configurations.

3. Analysis of multimedia streaming strategies. We study the streaming approaches employed by Pandora audio [5] and YouTube video streaming, the two most popular smartphone multimedia streaming applications contributing large traffic volume. Our analysis demonstrates that traffic patterns impose significant impact on the radio resource and energy consumption, again due to the interplay between the UE application and the RRC state machine. The current Pandora approach incurs long tail periods, which waste 50% of the dedicated channel time and 59% of the radio energy, while the YouTube strategy suffers from long dedicated channel occupation time due to bandwidth underutilization. We propose a simple improvement that saves the YouTube streaming energy by 80% by leveraging an existing feature called *fast dormancy* supported by 3GPP specifications [8, 9].

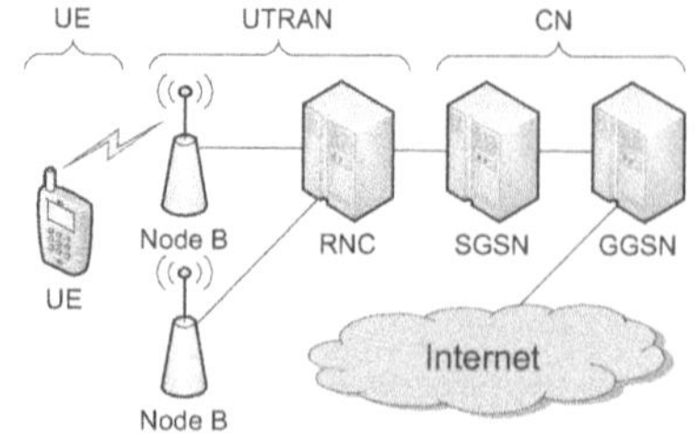

Figure 1: The UMTS architecture

4. Data preprocessing scheme for cellular data traces. We are the first to highlight the need and address the challenge of preprocessing cellular network traces, which differ from Internet traffic data in that cellular data can reflect significant delays imposed by state promotions transitioning from low power to higher power state due to radio resource allocation overhead. To extract the actual traffic patterns, *e.g.*, for the purpose of evaluating alternate designs of the RRC state machine, such delays must be eliminated.

2. BACKGROUND

This section provides sufficient background for further discussions of this paper.

2.1 The UMTS Network

As illustrated in Figure 1, the UMTS network consists of three subsystems: User Equipments (UE), UMTS Terrestrial Radio Access Network (UTRAN), and the Core Network (CN). UEs are essentially mobile handsets carried by end users. The UTRAN allows connectivity between a UE and the CN. It consists of two components: base stations, called Node-Bs, and Radio Network Controllers (RNC), which control multiple Node-Bs. Most UTRAN features such as packet scheduling, radio resource control, and handover control are implemented at the RNC. The centralized CN is the backbone of the cellular network. In particular the GGSN (Gateway GPRS Support Node) within the CN serves as a gateway hiding UMTS internal infrastructures from the external network.

2.2 The RRC State Machine

In the context of UMTS, the *radio resource* refers to WCDMA codes that are potential bottleneck resources of the network. To efficiently utilize the limited radio resources, the UMTS radio resource control (RRC) protocol introduces a state machine associated with each UE. There are typically three RRC states as described below [25, 19].

IDLE. This is the default state when a UE is turned on. The UE has not yet established an RRC connection with the RNC, thus no radio resource is allocated, and the UE cannot transfer any user data (as opposed to control data).

CELL_DCH. The RRC connection is established and a UE is usually allocated dedicated transport channels in both downlink (DL, RNC to UE) and uplink (UL, UE to RNC) direction. This state allows a UE to fully utilize radio resources for user data transmission. We refer to CELL_DCH as DCH henceforth. A UE can access HSDPA/HSUPA (High Speed Downlink/Uplink Packet Access) mode, if supported by the infrastructure, at DCH state. For HSDPA, the high speed transport channel is not dedicated, but shared by a limited number (*e.g.*, 32) of users [19]. Further, when a large

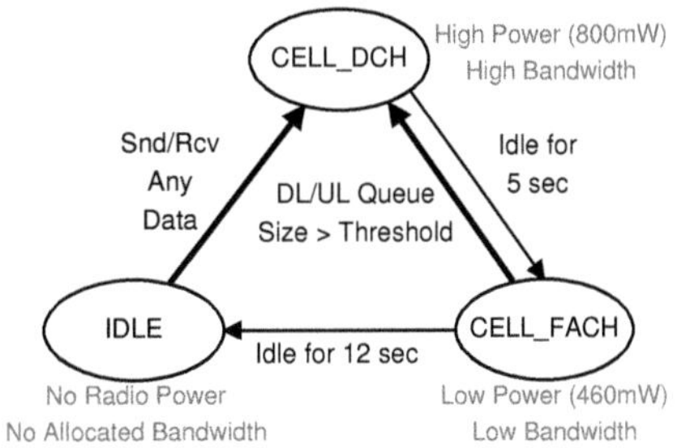

Figure 2: The RRC state machine for the 3G UMTS network of Carrier 1

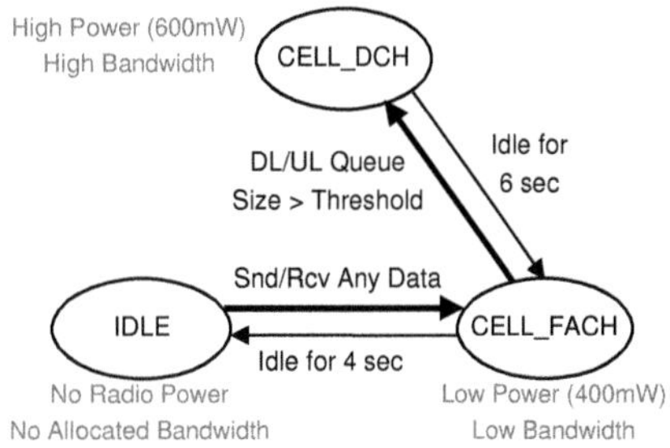

Figure 3: The RRC state machine for the 3G UMTS network of Carrier 2

Table 1: Inferred parameters for two carriers

Inactivity timer	Carrier 1	Carrier 2
α: DCH→FACH	5 sec	6 sec
β: FACH→IDLE	12 sec	4 sec
Promotion time	Carrier 1	Carrier 2
IDLE→FACH	N/A	0.6 sec
IDLE→DCH	2 sec	N/A
FACH→DCH	1.5 sec	1.3 sec
RLC Buffer threshold	Carrier 1	Carrier 2
FACH→DCH(UL)	543 ± 25 B	151 ± 14 B
FACH→DCH(DL)	475 ± 23 B	119 ± 17 B
State radio power	Carrier 1	Carrier 2
DCH/FACH/IDLE	800/460/0 mW	600/400/0 mW
Promotion radio power	Carrier 1	Carrier 2
IDLE→FACH	N/A	410 mW
IDLE→DCH	550 mW	N/A
FACH→DCH	700 mW	480 mW

number of UEs are in DCH state, the radio resources may be exhausted due to the lack of channelization codes in the cell. Then some UEs have to use low-speed shared channels although their RRC states are still DCH.

CELL_FACH. The RRC connection is established but there is no dedicated channel allocated to a UE. Instead, the UE can only transmit user data through shared low-speed channels that are typically less than 15kbps. We refer to CELL_FACH as FACH from this point on. FACH is designed for applications requiring very low data throughput rate. It consumes much less radio resources than DCH does.

RRC states impact a UE's energy consumption. A UE at IDLE consumes almost no energy from its radio interface. The radio power consumption for DCH is 50% to 100% higher than that for FACH (Table 1). While within the same state, the radio power is fairly stable regardless of the data throughput when the signal strength is stable. Further, the RRC state machine is maintained at both the UE and the RNC. The two peer entities are always synchronized via control channels except during transient and error situations. Also note that both the downlink (DL) and the uplink (UL) use the same state machine.

In the RRC state machine, there are two types of state transitions. *State promotions*, including IDLE→FACH, IDLE→DCH, and FACH→DCH, switch from a state with lower radio resource and UE energy utilization to another state consuming more resources and UE energy. *State demotions*, consisting of DCH→FACH, FACH→IDLE, and DCH→IDLE, go in the reverse direction. Depending on the starting state, a state promotion is triggered by either any user data transmission activity, if the UE is at IDLE, or the per-UE queue

Table 2: Optimize radio resources: the key tradeoff

Increase α or β timers	**Decrease α or β timers**
ΔD increases *Increase* tail time (§5.2) *Waste* radio resources	ΔD decreases *Decrease* tail time *Save* radio resources
ΔS decreases *Reduce* state promotions *Reduce* RNC overhead *Improve* user experiences	ΔS increases *Increase* state promotions *Increase* RNC overhead *Degrade* user experiences
ΔE increases *Waste* UE radio energy	ΔE decreases *Save* UE radio energy

size, called Radio Link Controller (RLC) buffer size, exceeding a threshold in either direction, if the UE is at FACH.

The state demotions are triggered by two inactivity timers maintained by the RNC. We denote the DCH→FACH timer as α, and the FACH→IDLE timer as β. At DCH, the RNC resets the α timer to T seconds, a fixed threshold, whenever it observes any UL/DL data frame. If there is no user data transmission activity for T seconds, the α timer times out and the state is demoted to FACH. A similar scheme is used for the β timer for the FACH→IDLE demotion.

Promotions involve more work than demotions do. In particular, state promotions incur a long "ramp-up" latency of up to 2 seconds during which tens of control messages are exchanged between a UE and the RNC for resource allocation (*e.g.*, radio bearer reconfiguration and RRC connection setup). Excessive state promotions increase the management overhead at the RNC and degrade user experience [10, 21, 28], especially for short data transfers, which we investigate in §5.1.

Figures 2 and 3 depict our inferred state machine models for two large UMTS carriers, based on our inference methodology described in §3. Their difference naturally introduces the problem of seeking the optimal state machine configuration to better balance radio resource utilization and performance. We quantitatively compare both carriers in §6.4.

2.3 Tradeoff Considerations to Optimize Resource Allocation

As discussed in §1, the RRC state machine introduces tradeoffs among radio resource utilization, UE energy consumption, end user experience, and management overheads at the RNC. We need to quantify these factors to analyze the tradeoff. Given a cellular trace and a state machine configuration C, we compute three metrics to characterize the above factors. Previous work either consider only one factor [20, 32] or focus on other metrics (*e.g.*, dropping rate due to congestion [22] and web page response time [31]), using analytical models. We detail our methodology for computing the three metrics in §6.

- The DCH state occupation time, denoted by $D(C)$, quantifies the overall radio resources consumed by UEs on dedicated channels in DCH state. We ignore the relatively low radio resources allocated for shared low-speed channels on FACH.
- The number of state promotions, denoted by $S(C)$, is the total number of IDLE→DCH, IDLE→FACH, and FACH→DCH promotions. $S(C)$ quantifies the overhead brought by state promotions that worsen user experience and increase the management overhead at the RNC. We ignore the state demotion overhead as it is significantly smaller compared with the state promotion overhead.
- The energy consumption, denoted by $E(C)$, is the total energy consumed by radio interfaces of all UEs in the trace.

We are interested in relative changes of D, S, E when we switch to a new state machine using the same trace. Let C be the default state machine used as the comparison baseline, and let C' be a new state machine configuration. The relative change of D, denoted as ΔD, is computed by $\Delta D(C') = (D(C') - D(C))/D(C)$. We have similar definitions for ΔS and ΔE.

As we shall see throughout this paper, the key tradeoff expressed in our notations is that, for any state machine setting, increasing ΔS causes both ΔD and ΔE to decrease (there may exist exceptions when ΔS is too large). In other words, if more state promotions are allowed, then we can save more radio resources and UE energy. Ideally, we want to find a state machine configuration C' such that $\Delta D(C')$ and $\Delta E(C')$ are significantly negative, while $\Delta S(C')$ is reasonably small. This important tradeoff is summarized in Table 2.

3. INFERRING THE STATE MACHINE

We describe an end-host based probing technique for inferring the state machine, which we validate using power measurements. Accurate inference of the state machine and its parameters is the first necessary step towards characterizing and improving the RRC state machine. We study two large 3G carriers with results presented in Figures 2, 3, and Table 1, which will be used in our simulation program described in §4.

3.1 Methodology

We make the following assumptions for the inference algorithm. *(i)* There are at most three states: IDLE, FACH, and DCH. DCH is the state allowing high data rate transfer. *(ii)* The time granularity for inactivity timers is assumed to be seconds. Our algorithms can easily adapt to finer granularities. *(iii)* The state promotion delay is significantly longer than (at least two times as) a normal RTT for both DCH and FACH (less than 300 ms based on our measurements). This is reasonable due to the promotion overhead explained earlier. *(iv)* We roughly know the range of RLC buffer thresholds (64B–1KB) that trigger the FACH→DCH promotion. We detail our methodology below.

State promotion inference determines one of the two promotion procedures adopted by UMTS:
$P1$: IDLE→FACH→DCH, or $P2$: IDLE→DCH. Algorithm 1 illustrates how we distinguish between $P1$ and $P2$, where min and max denote RLC buffer sizes that does not trigger, and does trigger, the FACH→DCH promotion, respectively. Note that IDLE→DCH or IDLE→FACH always happens regardless of the RLC buffer size. The idea is to distinguish $P1$ and $P2$ by detecting the presence of the FACH→DCH promotion. We set min and max to 28 bytes (an empty UDP packet plus an IP header) and 1K bytes, respectively. If $P1$ holds, then the state is promoted to FACH after Step 2, and then further promoted to DCH at Step 3. Thus Δt includes an additional FACH→DCH promotion delay. Otherwise, for $P2$, Δt does not include the promotion delay since the state is already DCH after Step 2.

Algorithm 1 State promotion inference

1: Keep UE on IDLE.
2: UE sends min bytes. Server echoes min bytes.
3: UE sends max bytes. Server echoes min bytes.
4: UE records the RTT Δt for Step 3.
5: Report $P1$ iff $\Delta t \gg$ normal RTT. Otherwise report $P2$.

Algorithm 2 State demotion inference

1: **for** $n = 0$ to 30 **do**
2: UE sends max bytes. Server echoes min bytes.
3: UE sleeps for n sec.
4: UE sends min bytes. Server echoes min bytes.
5: UE records the RTT $\Delta t_1(i)$ for Step 4.
6: **end for**
7: **for** $n = 0$ to 30 **do**
8: UE sends max bytes. Server echoes min bytes
9: UE sleeps for n sec.
10: UE sends max bytes. Server echoes min bytes.
11: UE records the RTT $\Delta t_2(i)$ for Step 10.
12: **end for**
13: Report $D1$ iff $\Delta t_1(\cdot)$ and $\Delta t_2(\cdot)$ are similar, else report $D2$.

State demotion inference determines whether UMTS uses $D1$: DCH→IDLE or $D2$: DCH→FACH→IDLE. The inference method is shown in Algorithm 2, which consists of two experiments. The first experiment (Steps 1 to 6) comprises of 30 runs. In each run, the UE goes to DCH by sending max bytes (Step 2), sleeps for n seconds (Step 3), then sends min bytes (Step 4). Recall that min and max denote RLC buffer sizes that does not trigger, and does trigger, the FACH→DCH promotion, respectively. By increasing n from 0 to 30, we fully exercise all the states experienced by the UE at the beginning of Step 4 due to the inactivity timer effects. The second experiment (Step 7 to 12) is similar to the first one except that after Step 10, the UE always promotes to DCH. In contrast, after Step 4, if there exists a DCH→FACH demotion, the UE will be in FACH. Therefore, for $D1$ the observed RTTs for two experiments, $\Delta t_1(0..30)$ and $\Delta t_2(0..30)$, will be similar. On the other hand, for $D2$, *i.e.*, the state is demoted to FACH (the α timer), then back to IDLE (the β timer), then for $\lfloor\alpha\rfloor < i \leq \lfloor\alpha+\beta\rfloor$, the difference between $\Delta t_1(i)$ and $\Delta t_2(i)$ is roughly the FACH→DCH promotion delay.

Inferring other parameters. Given the process of inferring the state transitions, it is easy to infer related parameters. First, the inactivity timers can be directly obtained from $\Delta t_1(\cdot)$ and $\Delta t_2(\cdot)$ computed by Algorithm 2. For the case where the demotion is DCH→FACH→IDLE, we can deduce α and β from the fact that $\Delta t_1(0...\lfloor\alpha+\beta\rfloor)$ are smaller than $\Delta t_1(\lceil\alpha+\beta\rceil...30)$, and $\Delta t_2(0...\lfloor\alpha\rfloor)$ are smaller than

$\Delta t_2(\lceil\alpha\rceil...30)$. This is because in the first experiment in Algorithm 2, a state promotion (IDLE→FACH or IDLE→DCH) will not happen until $n \geq \lceil\alpha+\beta\rceil$, while in the second experiment, a state promotion from IDLE or FACH happens when $n \geq \lceil\alpha\rceil$. Similarly, for the case where the demotion is DCH→IDLE, let the only inactivity timer be γ. Then we will observe that $\Delta t_1(0...\lfloor\gamma\rfloor)$ are much smaller than $\Delta t_1(\lceil\gamma\rceil...30)$. Second, to infer the promotion delay X→Y, we measure the entire RTT including the promotion, then subtract from it the normal RTT (*i.e.,* the RTT not including the promotion) on state Y. Finally, using the promotion delay as an indicator, we infer the RLC buffer threshold by performing binary search for the packet size that exactly triggers the FACH→DCH promotion, in each direction.

3.2 Results on State Machine Inference

We present the inference results for state machines used by two large UMTS carriers: Carrier 1 and 2. For each carrier, we repeat Algorithm 1 and Algorithm 2 for three times, ensuring that in each experiment *(i)* the server does not experience a timeout; *(ii)* in tcpdump trace, we never observe other user data transmission that may trigger a state transition; *(iii)* the 3G connection is never dropped. The entire experiment is discarded if any of these conditions is violated.

For the state promotion inference, the normal RTTs for Carrier 1 and 2 are less than 0.3 sec, and the measured Δt values in Algorithm 1 are 0.2 sec for Carrier 1, and 1.5 sec for Carrier 2, for all three trials. Based on Algorithm 1, we conclude that the promotion procedures for Carrier 1 and Carrier 2 are IDLE→DCH and IDLE→FACH→DCH, respectively. For the state demotion inference, we notice the qualitative difference between $\Delta t_1(5...16)$ in Figure 4(a) and $\Delta t_2(5...16)$ in Figure 4(b), indicating that the state demotion procedure for Carrier 1 is DCH→FACH→IDLE. Similarly, Figure 5(a) and Figure 5(b) imply that Carrier 2 also uses DCH→FACH→IDLE, due to the obvious difference between $\Delta t_1(6..9)$ and $\Delta t_2(6..9)$.

We note that for Carrier 1, $\Delta t_1(17...30)$ and $\Delta t_2(17...30)$ are roughly the same, because in Algorithm 2, for $17 \leq n \leq 30$, either sending *min* bytes (Step 4) or sending *max* bytes (Step 10) triggers an IDLE→DCH promotion, which is the only promotion transition for Carrier 1. In contrast, for Carrier 2, $\Delta t_1(10...30)$ is smaller than $\Delta t_2(10...30)$. Carrier 2 may perform two types of promotions depending on the RLC buffer size, therefore for $10 \leq n \leq 30$ in Algorithm 2, sending *min* bytes in Step 4 and sending *max* bytes in Step 10 will trigger IDLE→FACH and IDLE→FACH→DCH, respectively, resulting in different promotion delays. This observation does not affect the inference results of Algorithm 2 for either carrier.

Given the $\Delta t_1(\cdot)$ and $\Delta t_2(\cdot)$ values computed by Algorithm 2, it is easy to infer α and β by following the logic described in §3.1. The inference results are $(\alpha,\beta) = (5sec, 12sec)$ for Carrier 1 and $(\alpha,\beta) = (6sec, 4sec)$ for Carrier 2. To infer the RLC buffer thresholds, we repeat the experiments 30 times and summarize the results in Table 1[1]. Although their variances are higher than those of other parameters, we found that they have very small impact on our measurement results described later.

We investigated the stability of the state machine and found that the state transitions and timer values do not change over the four months of our study (July to November 2009). They are also independent of the time of the day, the Access Point Name (APN), or the location[2]. Also the state promotion delays are largely static.

[1]Results in Table 1 were measured in November 2009.

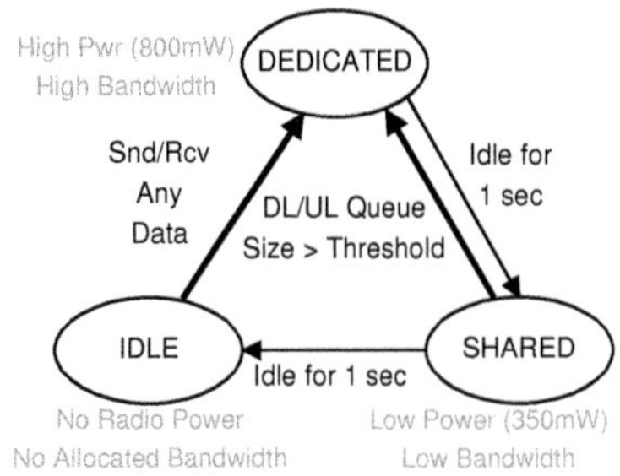

Figure 6: The RRC state machine for the 2G GPRS/EDGE network of Carrier 2

For 2G (GPRS/EDGE) networks, there exists a similar RRC state machine model. The three RRC states are "IDLE", "CELL_SHARED", and "CELL_DEDICATED" [6], corresponding to IDLE, FACH, and DCH in the 3G case, respectively. We applied our inference methodology (using a smaller increment of n in Algorithm 2) on Carrier 2's 2G network, and show the inference results in Figure 6. We observe that the inactivity timers (1 sec) are much shorter, therefore resulting in better efficiency of radio resource utilization and UE energy consumption. The negative impact of short timers is more frequent state transitions. The state promotion delays of IDLE→DEDICATED and SHARED→DEDICATED are both 0.5 sec.

3.3 Validation using Energy Consumption

As described in §2, a UE's radio energy consumption differs for each state, a property we may use to infer the state machine. However, accurately measuring energy consumption requires special monitoring equipments. So we use it as validation for our inference algorithms, which only require UE-based probing.

We set up experiments to confirm the inactivity timers and state promotion delays for Carrier 1 by monitoring UE's energy consumption as follows. The battery of an HTC TyTN II smartphone is attached to a hardware power meter [4], which is also connected via USB to a PC that records fine-grained power measurements by sampling the current drawn from the battery at a frequency of 500 Hz. Figure 7 shows one representative experimental run of the validation. During probing, we keep the UE's LCD at the same brightness level, turn off GPS and WiFi, and disable all network activities. After keeping the smartphone in this inactive state for 20 sec, we send a UDP packet at $t = 23.8s$ thus triggering an IDLE→DCH promotion that takes approximately 2 sec as inferred in §3.1. From $t = 26.1s$, the phone remains at the high-power DCH state for about 5 sec, then switches to the low-power FACH state at $t = 31.5s$. Finally at $t = 44.1s$, the phone returns to the IDLE state. The measured inactivity timer values are longer than the inferred ones by about 10%, likely due to the synchronization overhead between the RNC and the UE. We similarly verified

[2]We did probing at two locations that are 600 miles apart in the U.S., using an HTC TyTN II smartphone and a Sierra 3G Air card to perform our experiment.

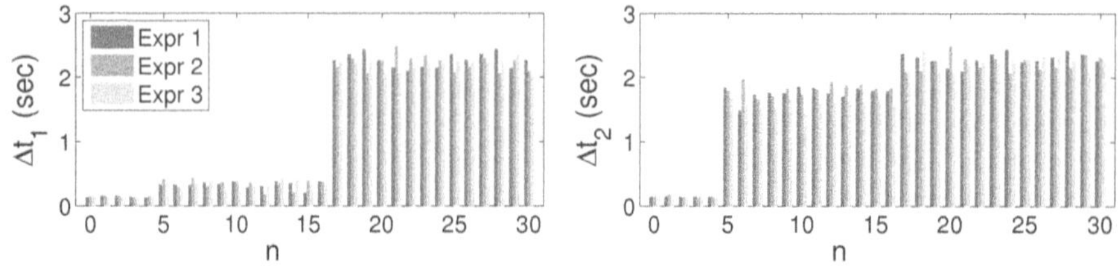

(a) Algorithm 2 ($\Delta t_1(\cdot)$) (b) Algorithm 2 ($\Delta t_2(\cdot)$)

Figure 4: State machine inference results for Carrier 1

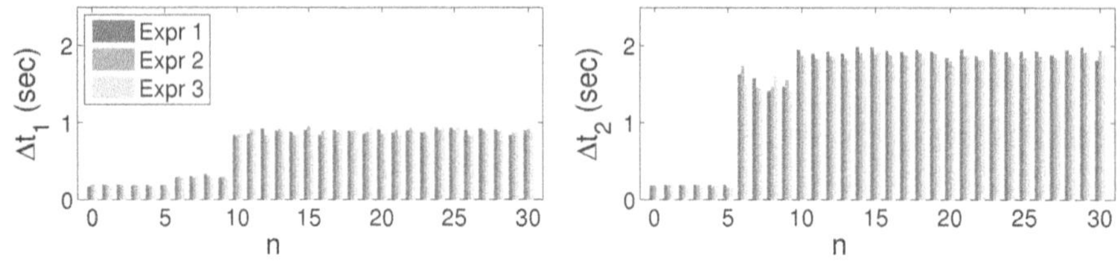

(a) Algorithm 2 ($\Delta t_1(\cdot)$) (b) Algorithm 2 ($\Delta t_2(\cdot)$)

Figure 5: State machine inference results for Carrier 2

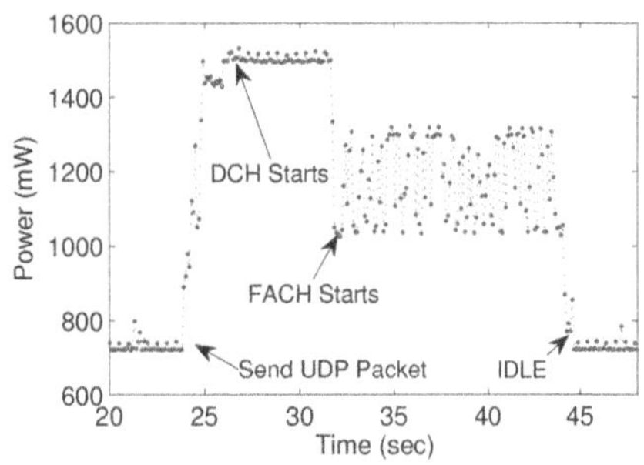

Figure 7: Validation using power measurements

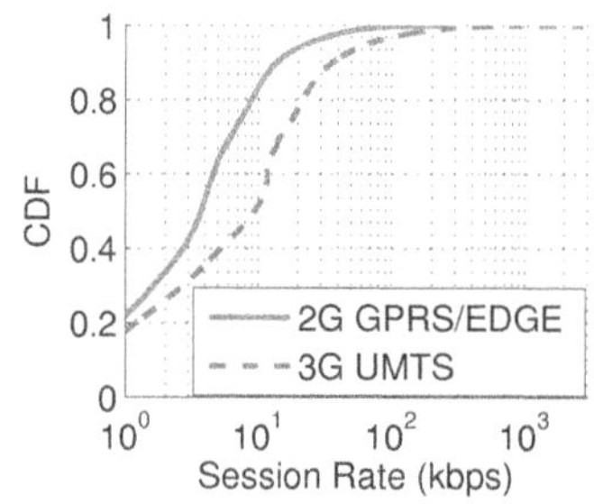

Figure 10: Session rate distribution over sessions longer than 100ms for 2G and 3G data

the FACH→DCH promotion delay, and validated Carrier 2's state machines for both 2G and 3G.

Using the IDLE power as baseline, we compute the power consumption of the 3G radio interface as shown in Table 1[3]. We also infer the RLC buffer thresholds for the FACH→DCH promotion by performing binary search. Instead of using the promotion delay as described in §3.1, we use energy as an indicator to search for the RLC buffer threshold that exactly triggers the promotion, for each direction. The validation results are consistent with our inference results.

4. 3G MEASUREMENT DATA

This section discusses the traffic data used in our study (§5 and §6). We first describe the raw dataset in §4.1, then in §4.2, we explain our preprocessing methodology to eliminate the side effects brought by the RRC state machine on the dataset. This enables us to use the preprocessed trace to experiment with different state machine configurations. In §4.3, we describe the extraction procedure for application-specific data for further analysis.

[3]The power values in Table 1 were measured in good signal strength conditions. [29] shows that signal strength may have significant impact on a UE's radio power consumption.

4.1 The Raw Dataset

Our dataset is a large TCP header packet trace collected from Carrier 1 on January 29, 2010 in the normal course of operations. The collection point is one GGSN that primarily serves 3G UMTS users but also 2G GPRS users. Non-3G traffic are filtered by excluding SGSNs that exclusively serve 2G users. Sampling was performed on a per GTP (GPRS Tunneling Protocol) session basis with a sampling rate of 1:16, so that all packets in both directions from a sampled GTP session were captured. Our trace contains 278 million TCP packets (162 GB data) of 3G traffic continuously captured in 3 hours. Due to concerns of large traffic volume and user privacy issues, we only recorded TCP/IP headers and a 64-bit timestamp for each packet, but no subscriber IDs or phone numbers.

Subsequently, we extract *sessions* (they are different from GTP sessions) from the trace, with each session consisting of all packets transferred by the same UE identified through the private client IP address present in the trace. It is known that cellular public IPs change very quickly [12]. But private IPs of Carrier 1 are much less dynamic, changing only at the interval of tens of minutes. Multiple TCP flows from concurrent applications may be mixed in the same session. We use a threshold of 60 sec of idle time to decide that a session has terminated. Changing this value to other values such as 45 or 75 sec does not qualitatively affect the anal-

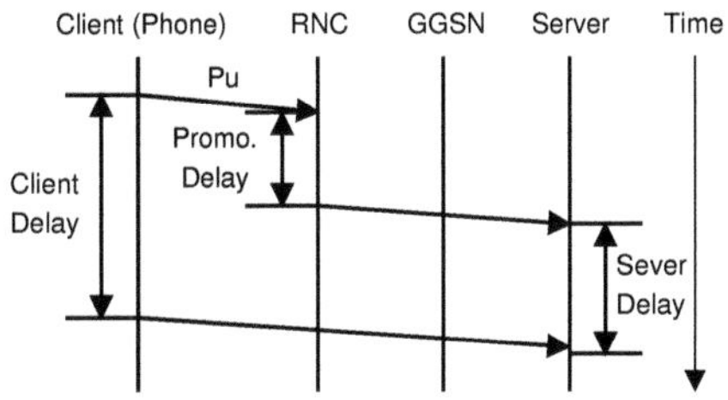

Figure 8: State promotion triggered by an UL packet

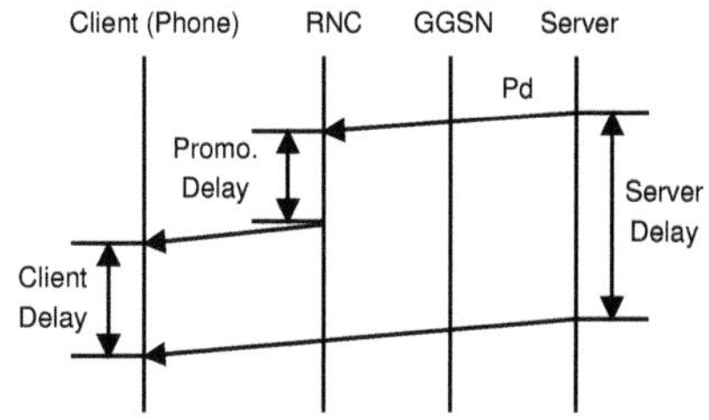

Figure 9: State promotion triggered by a DL packet

ysis results. Besides, as shown in Figure 10, we do observe qualitative difference of session rate (total bytes divided by the duration of a session) between 3G and 2G. Finally, we extracted about 1.0 million 3G sessions from the raw trace.

We discuss three limitations of our dataset. First, similar to previous measurements of wired network using passive trace [33, 26], the finite duration (3 hours) may influence distributions of state machine characteristics. Second, the dataset does not contain UDP traffic. A recent study [26] indicates that UDP accounts for less than 8% of the traffic volume for a wired VPN link. We expect the percentage of UDP traffic for cellular networks to be even smaller because currently UDP-based streaming and gaming applications on smartphones are not as popular as those on PCs. The third limitation relates to the data collection location (GGSN). We address this issue next in §4.2. Overall, we believe that the above limitations do not qualitatively affect our state machine analysis results.

4.2 Data Preprocessing

One issue regarding our cellular dataset is that the packet timestamps recorded by the GGSN are affected by delays introduced by RRC state promotions that may take up to 2 seconds to finish. Ideally we would like to capture traffic traces directly at the RNC to understand the network interaction between UEs and the radio access network so that we can use the trace to experiment with different state machine configurations. However, the data collection point, GGSN, is at the upstream from the RNC where state promotions take place. There are two scenarios for this impact. First, if an uplink packet P_u from client (UE) to the server triggers a state promotion, *e.g.*, from IDLE to DCH, which happens *before* P_u is captured by the GGSN. Thus, the GGSN records a later timestamp than the actual arrival time of P_u as shown in Figure 8. In this case, we need to shift backward in time for packet P_u and all its subsequent packets within this session by the promotion delay to preserve the correct time spacing among packets. This case is detected by simulating the state machine for each session.

The second case depicted in Figure 9 is similar except that the state promotion is triggered by a downlink packet P_d from the server to the client, so that the promotion takes place *after* the GGSN observes P_d. The packet P_d received by the client will be delayed by the state promotion, therefore the echoing uplink packet from the client and any other subsequent packets should have their timestamps shifted back by the promotion delay to exclude the effect of the promotion delay on the inter-packet time spacing.

To verify the accuracy of this preprocessing procedure, we performed controlled experiments shown in Figures 8 and 9. From the UE (client), starting from IDLE, we send two UDP packets P_1 and P_2 (two uplink packets sent in a row in Figure 8, their interval observed at the client is less than α) where P_1 triggers a state promotion, then the difference between the latency between P_1 and P_2 of the client and that of the server is approximately the state promotion delay. Similarly we verified the downlink case.

Table 3: Cellular traces of five applications

Application	Sessions	Bytes	Description
Email-1	15K	1.4 GB	Email provider 1
Email-2	11K	536 MB	Email provider 2
Sync	4.9K	62 MB	Synchronization service
Stream	2.7K	395 MB	Pandora audio streaming [5]
Map	1.8K	60 MB	Interactive mapping

The main purpose of this data preprocessing is to eliminate the effects brought by the non-trivial promotion time while keeping other packet dynamics unchanged. It enables us to experiment with different state machine parameters or to apply a different state machine on the preprocessed trace in our further analysis. Given a session extracted in §4.1, we replay it against the original state machine of Carrier 1. If a state promotion is detected, then we shift relevant packets accordingly to remove the promotion delay. The preprocessing also detects sessions that violate the state machine. For example, we assume the state is FACH after P_k is transmitted. An uplink packet P_{k+1} triggers a FACH→DCH promotion, but the inter-arrival time between P_k and P_{k+1} is less than the FACH→DCH promotion delay. We expect that such violations are mostly caused by the variation of the RLC buffer thresholds (our simulation program assumes that they have fixed values). Sessions violating the state machine account for only 3% of the total sessions, and are not used in our subsequent data analysis.

4.3 Application-specific Data Extraction

From the preprocessed trace, we select five traffic types each corresponding to a particular application as shown in Table 3. For each application, we extract sessions in which at least 95% of the packets have either the source or the destination as one fixed server IP, thus eliminating coexistence of other applications as one session may contain multiple TCP flows of concurrent applications. For example, "Sync" consists of 4.9K sessions of a popular synchronization service. All its sessions access the same server that synchronizes emails, calendar events, contacts *etc.* between PCs and a UE using push-based notification mechanism. We use the five datasets for per-application analysis in §5.2 and §6.3 to study how application traffic patterns affect the tradeoff described in §2.3.

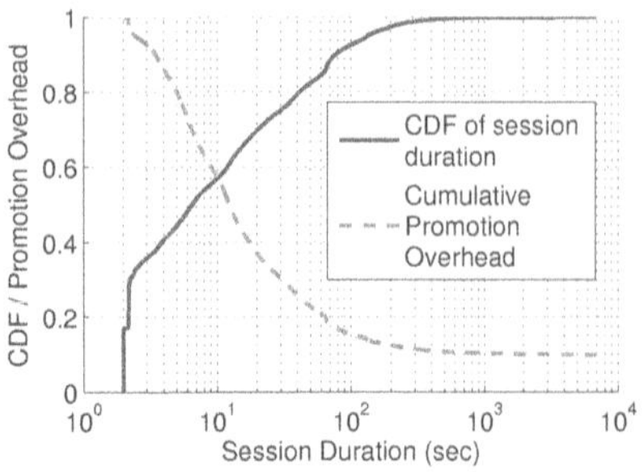

Figure 11: Cumulative promotion overhead

5. IMPACT OF RRC STATE MACHINE

In this section, we study two main negative effects of the RRC state machine, and quantify them using our datasets provided by Carrier 1. As far as we know, this is the first study that uses real cellular traces to understand how the two factors of the RRC state machine, the state promotion overhead (§5.1) and the tail effects (§5.2), impact performance, energy efficiency, and radio resource utilization. These two factors pose key tradeoffs that we attempt to balance in this paper. We investigate how multimedia streaming traffic pattern affects radio resource utilization in §5.3.

5.1 State Promotion Overhead

As discussed in §2 and §3, the RRC state promotion may incur a long latency due to control message exchanges for resource allocation at the RNC. A large number of state promotions increase management overheads at the RNC and worsen user experience [10]. They have particularly negative performance impact on short sessions. For example, starting from the IDLE state, usually it takes less than 10 sec to transfer a 200KB file under normal signal strength conditions. In such a scenario, the constant overhead of 2 sec (the IDLE→DCH promotion delay) accounts for at least 20% of the total transfer time. In other UMTS networks with 3.4kbps SRB (Signalling Radio Bearer), such a promotion time for packet session setup may take even longer, up to 4 seconds [19]. It is also known that signaling DoS attacks that maliciously trigger frequent state transitions can potentially overload the control plane and detrimentally affect the 3G infrastructure [21].

We statistically quantify the state promotion overhead using our dataset. Given Σ, the set of sessions extracted in §4.1 and preprocessed in §4.2, we compute its *average promotion overhead* $R(\Sigma)$, defined as the fraction of the total promotion delay relative to the total duration of all sessions. The duration of a session is defined as the timestamp difference between the first and the last packet in that session.

$$R(\Sigma) = \frac{\sum_{s\in\Sigma}\{2.0N_{\text{Idle-DCH}}(s) + 1.5N_{\text{FACH-DCH}}(s)\}}{\sum_{s\in\Sigma}\{T(s) + 2.0N_{\text{Idle-DCH}}(s) + 1.5N_{\text{FACH-DCH}}(s)\}}$$

Here 1.5 sec and 2.0 sec are the two promotion delays described in Table 1, $N_{\text{Idle-DCH}}(s)$ and $N_{\text{FACH-DCH}}(s)$ denote for session s the number of IDLE→DCH and FACH→DCH promotions, respectively. And $T(s)$ is the session duration after preprocessing (excluding promotion delays). Then in Figure 11, we plot the CDF of total session duration (including promotion delays) and the cumulative promotion overhead function $CP(x)$, defined as $R(\Sigma')$ where Σ' contains all sessions whose session durations (including promotion delays) are less than x. For example, we have CDF(10) = 0.57 and $CP(10) = 0.57$. They indicate that within the dataset, 57% of the sessions are at most 10 sec, and their average promotion overhead $R(\Sigma')$ is 57%. Clearly, Figure 11 indicates that shorter sessions, which contribute to the vast majority of sessions observed, suffer more severely from the promotion delay, as $CP(x)$ is a monotonically decreasing function of x.

Table 4: Duplicated DNS queries and responses due to an IDLE→DCH promotion in Windows XP

Time (s)	Direction	Details of DNS query/response
0.000	Uplink	Std. query A www.eecs.umich.edu
0.989	Uplink	Std. query A www.eecs.umich.edu
1.989	Uplink	Std. query A www.eecs.umich.edu
2.111	Downlink	Std. query response A 141.212.113.110
2.112	Downlink	Std. query response A 141.212.113.110
2.121	Downlink	Std. query response A 141.212.113.110

Our second observation is that, the RRC state promotion delay may be longer than application-specific timeout values, thus causing unnecessary timeouts leading to increased traffic volume and server overhead. For example, by default, Windows uses $t = 1, 2, 4, 8$ sec as timeout values for DNS queries [2]. Whenever a DNS query triggers an IDLE→DCH promotion that takes 2 seconds, the UE always experiences the first two timeouts. Therefore, two additional identical DNS queries are unnecessarily transmitted, and three identical responses simultaneously return to the UE, as shown in Table 4. This often happens in web browsing when a user clicks a link (triggering a DNS query) after an idle period. The problem can be addressed by using a large timeout value after a long idle period for UMTS 3G connection.

5.2 The Tail Effects

One straightforward way to alleviate the state promotion overhead is to increase inactivity timer values. For example, consider two sessions that transfer data on DCH during time=0 to time=3 sec and from $t = 10s$ to $t = 14s$. We can eliminate the state promotion at $t = 10s$ by increasing α to at least 7 sec. However, this decreases the DCH utilization efficiency as the UE occupies the dedicated channel from $t = 3s$ to $t = 10s$ without any data transmission activity. Furthermore, this worsens the negative impact of *tail effects*, which waste radio resources and UE's radio energy.

We define a *tail* as the idle time period matching the inactivity timer value before a state demotion [14]. It can never be used to transfer any data. In the above example, if $\alpha < 7sec$, then there exists a DCH tail from $t = 3$ to $t = 3 + \alpha$. Otherwise the period between $t = 3$ and $t = 10$ does not belong to a tail since there is no state demotion.

During a tail time, a UE still occupies transmission channels and WCDMA codes, and its radio power consumption is kept at the corresponding level of the state. In typical UMTS networks, each UE is allocated dedicated channels whose radio resources are completely wasted during the tail time. For HSDPA [19] described in §2, although the high speed transport channel is shared by a limited number of UEs, occupying it during the tail time can potentially prevent other UEs from using the high speed channel. More importantly, tail time wastes considerable amount of UE radio energy regardless of whether the channel is shared or dedicated. Reducing tail time incurs more frequent state transitions, a key tradeoff we explored in §2.3.

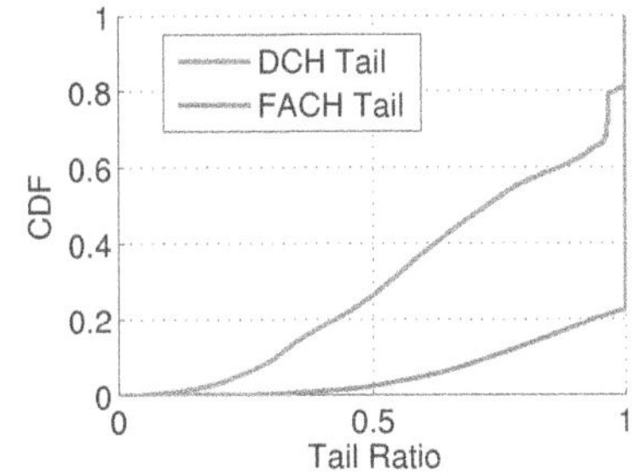

Figure 12: Distribution of $P_{\text{DCH-Tail}}$ and $P_{\text{FACH-Tail}}$ across all sessions

Table 5: Breakdown of RRC state occupation / transition time and the tail ratios

Occupation/Trans. Time	
P_{DCH}	44.5%
P_{FACH}	48.0%
$P_{\text{IDLE}\rightarrow\text{DCH}}$	6.8%
$P_{\text{FACH}\rightarrow\text{DCH}}$	0.7%
Tail Ratios	
$P_{\text{DCH-Tail}}$	45.3%
$P_{\text{FACH-Tail}}$	86.1%

Overall measurement. Table 5 provides overall statistics for all sessions. The first four rows in Table 5 break down state occupation/transition time of all sessions into four categories (they add up to 100%): on DCH/FACH states, or in IDLE→DCH/ FACH→DCH promotions. In the other two rows, $P_{\text{DCH-Tail}}$ is the DCH tail ratio, defined as the total DCH tail time as a percentage of the total DCH time. We define $P_{\text{FACH-Tail}}$, the FACH tail ratio, in a similar way. Figure 12 plots the CDFs of $P_{\text{DCH-Tail}}$ and $P_{\text{FACH-Tail}}$ on a per-session basis. The results indicate that tail time wastes considerable radio resources and hence UE's radio energy. It is surprising that the overall tail ratio for DCH and FACH are 45% and 86% respectively, and that more than 70% of the sessions have $P_{\text{DCH-Tail}}$ higher than 50%.

We also found that although the state occupation time of FACH is 48%, it transfers only 0.29% of the total traffic volume. The vast majority of the bytes (99.71%) are transferred in DCH. In other words, due to its low RLC buffer thresholds (§2), low throughput, and long tail, the efficiency of FACH is extremely low.

There exists strong correlations between session size (*i.e.*, the number of bytes of a session) and state machine characteristics. In particular, Figure 13 indicates that large sessions tend to have high fraction of DCH occupation time (P_{DCH}) as well as low P_{FACH} and $P_{\text{PROMO}} = P_{\text{IDLE}\rightarrow\text{DCH}} + P_{\text{FACH}\rightarrow\text{DCH}}$ values. Also as shown in Figure 14, as session size increases, both DCH and FACH tail ratios statistically decrease. In fact, small sessions are short. Their tail time periods, which are at least 5 sec and 12 sec for DCH and FACH, respectively, are comparable to or even longer than the total session duration, thus causing high $P_{\text{DCH-Tail}}$ and $P_{\text{FACH-Tail}}$ values. Another reason is that, we observe large sessions are more likely to perform continuous data transfers (*e.g.*, file downloading and multimedia streaming) that constantly occupy DCH, while small sessions tend to transfer data intermittently.

Per-application measurement. Figure 15 plots the per-session DCH tail distributions for the five applications

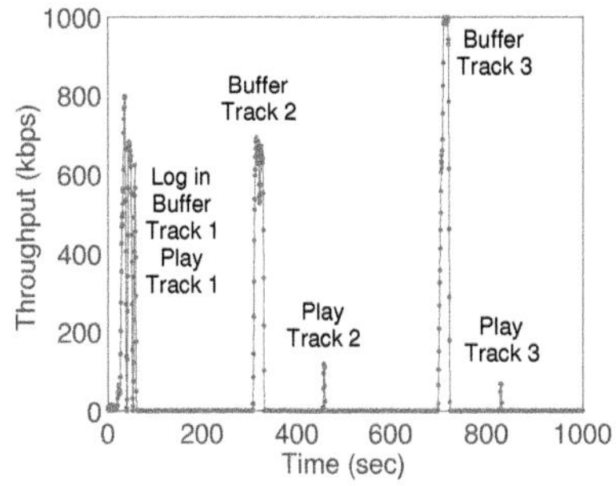

Figure 16: Pandora streaming (first 1k sec)

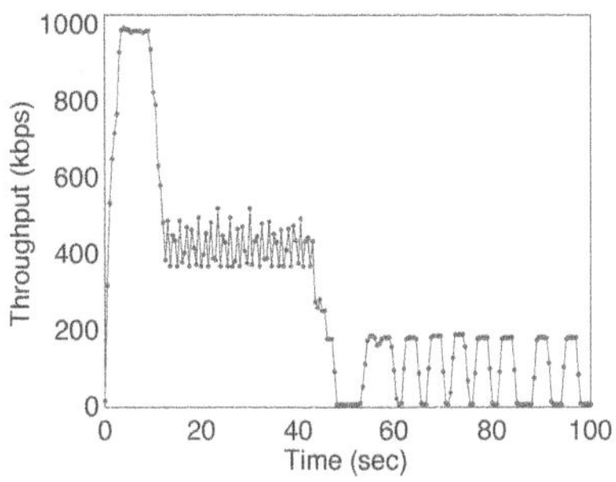

Figure 17: YouTube streaming (first 100 sec)

shown in Table 3. The map application has low DCH tail ratios as its traffic patterns are non-consecutive data bursts interleaved with short pauses that are usually shorter than the α timer, so a UE always occupies DCH. On the other hand, the Sync application has inefficient DCH utilizations indicated by high $P_{\text{DCH-Tail}}$ values, since most of its sessions are very short. Usually a Sync session consists of a single data burst incurring a 5-sec DCH tail and a 12-sec FACH tail.

5.3 Streaming Traffic Pattern and Tails

To investigate streaming traffic tails, we use an Android G2 phone of Carrier 2 to collect tcpdump traces for Pandora audio streaming [5], which is the "Streaming" application in Table 3, and YouTube video streaming[4]. They are the two most popular smartphone multimedia streaming applications. Both of them use TCP.

Pandora [5] is a music recommendation and Internet radio service. A user enter her favorite song or artist (called a "radio station"), then Pandora automatically streams similar music. We collected a 30-min Pandora trace by logging onto one author's Pandora account, selecting a pre-defined station, and then listening to seven tracks (songs). The traffic pattern is shown in Figure 16. Before a track is over, the content of the next track is buffered in one burst utilizing the maximal bandwidth (indicated by "Buffer Track x" in Figure 16). Then at the exact moment of switching to the next track, a small traffic burst is generated (indicated by "Play Track x" in Figure 16). This explains why Pandora has high tail ratios as each short burst incurs a tail. Based on our measurement, in the example shown in Figure 16, 50.1% of the DCH time and 59.2% of the radio energy are wasted on tails.

[4]The two applications' streaming behaviors may be different on other platforms (*e.g.*, iPhone).

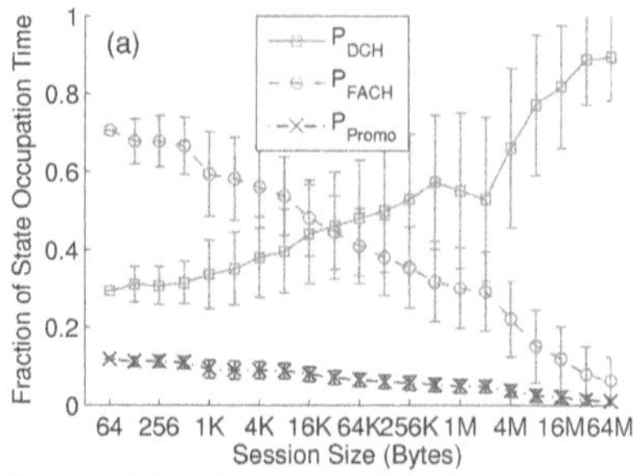

Figure 13: Session size vs. state occupation time

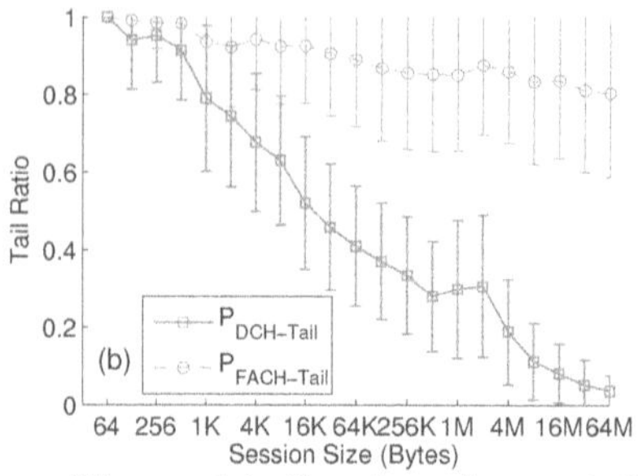

Figure 14: Session size vs.tail ratios

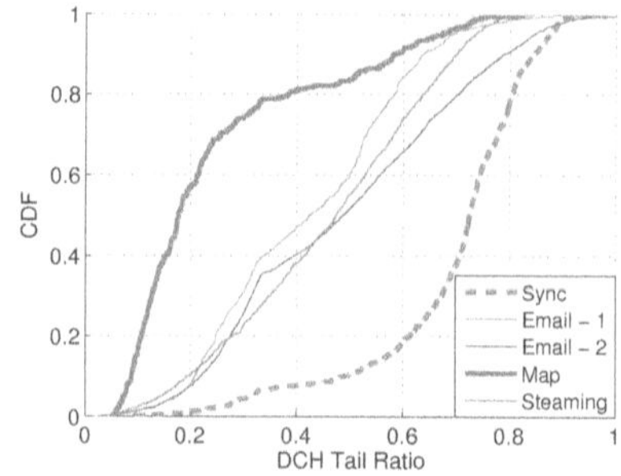

Figure 15: CDF of DCH tail ratios for different apps

YouTube employs a different streaming procedure consisting of three phases shown in Figure 17. *(i)* For the first 10 sec, the maximal bandwidth is utilized for data transmission. *(ii)* The throughput is kept at around 400kbps in the next 30 sec. *(iii)* The remaining content is transmitted intermittently with the inter-burst time between 3 to 5 sec and the throughput for each burst of 200 kbps. Shorter video clips may only experience the first one or two phases. We found that YouTube traffic incurs almost no tail (except for one tail in the end) since nearly all packet inter-arrival times (IATs) are less than the α timer value. However, its drawback is under-utilization of network bandwidth causing its long DCH occupation time. Further, sending data slowly may significantly waste UE's energy since on DCH a UE's radio power is relatively stable ($\pm$ 50mW as measured by a power meter) regardless of the bit rate when the signal strength is stable.

In summary, our analysis of Figure 16 and Figure 17 again implies that application traffic patterns can cause significant impact on radio resource and energy consumptions. The Pandora's approach incurs long tail periods while the YouTube streaming strategy suffers from long DCH occupation time and low energy efficiency due to bandwidth under-utilization. We propose a more energy-efficient approach for YouTube streaming in §7.

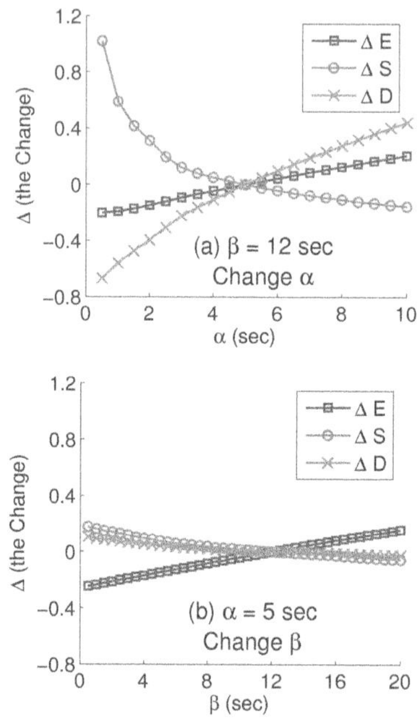

Figure 21: Impact of changing one timer (α or β). The other timer (β or α) is set to the default value

6. TUNING INACTIVITY TIMERS

Given the earlier observation that the inactivity timer values determine the key tradeoff (§2.3), we discuss how to optimize inactivity timers by trace-driven tuning. We describe our methodology and evaluation metrics in §6.1, followed by the results in §6.2 and for different applications in §6.3. We mainly focus on Carrier 1, with Carrier 2's findings briefly covered in §6.4.

6.1 Methodology and Evaluation Metrics

Given the moderate size of the search space for both inactivity timers, we exhaustively enumerate all combinations of the α (DCH$\rightarrow$FACH) timer, and the β (FACH$\rightarrow$IDLE) timer and evaluate each combination empirically by replaying all sessions for the corresponding RRC state machine. This is similar to, but simpler than, the simulation procedure described in §4.2 as the trace is state machine independent after preprocessing. As described in §2.3, we use three metrics to characterize the tradeoff.

- $\Delta E(\alpha,\beta) = (E(\alpha,\beta) - E(A,B))/E(A,B)$: the relative change in UE radio energy consumption relative to that of the default timer setting.
- $\Delta S(\alpha,\beta) = (S(\alpha,\beta) - S(A,B))/S(A,B)$: the relative change in the number of state promotions.
- $\Delta D(\alpha,\beta) = (D(\alpha,\beta) - D(A,B))/D(A,B)$: the relative change in the total DCH time.

where $A = 5sec$ and $B = 12sec$ correspond to the default inactivity timer values for Carrier 1 (Table 1).

6.2 Overall Results

We visualize the distributions of ΔE, ΔS, ΔD in Figure 18, Figure 19, and Figure 20, respectively. Each plot contains $|\{0.5s, 1s, ..., 10s\} \times \{0.5s, 1s, ..., 20s\}| = 800$ samples of (α,β) pairs. We first fit them to quadratic functions for $\alpha,\beta \geq 1$ using multi-linear regression, with the residuals of less than 0.01, 0.08 (for $\alpha,\beta > 2sec$), and 0.03 for ΔE, ΔS, and ΔD, respectively. Clearly, the regression model is traffic-dependent.

$$\Delta E(\alpha,\beta) = -0.544 + 0.061\alpha + 0.026\beta - 0.001\alpha^2$$
$$\Delta S(\alpha,\beta) = 0.652 - 0.123\alpha - 0.023\beta + 0.005\alpha^2 + 0.001\alpha\beta$$
$$\Delta D(\alpha,\beta) = -0.618 + 0.171\alpha - 0.011\beta - 0.006\alpha^2$$

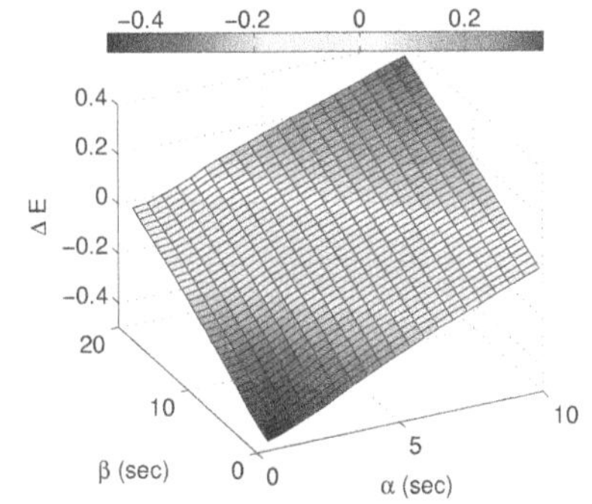

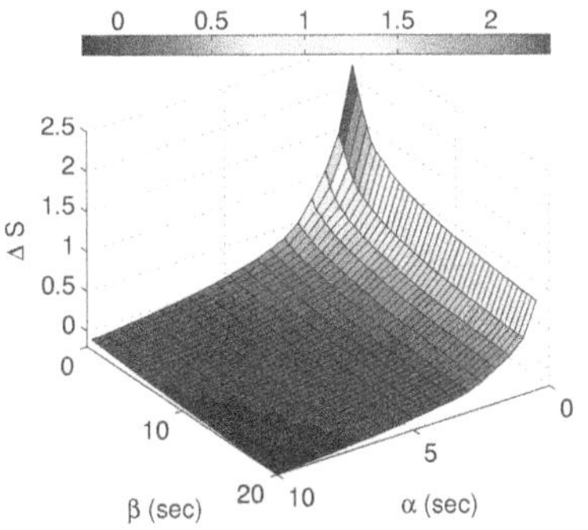

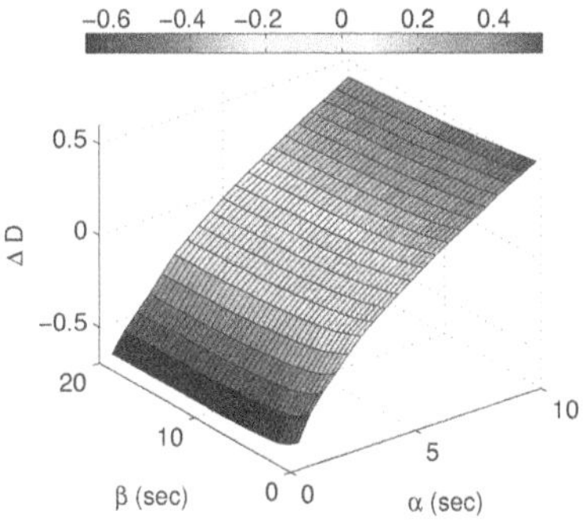

Figure 18: Impact of (α, β) on ΔE **Figure 19: Impact of (α, β) on ΔS** **Figure 20: Impact of (α, β) on ΔD**

We observe that ΔE is close to a linear function of α and β. Clearly, decreasing inactivity timer values reduces tail time, thus cutting a UE's energy consumption. Usually a UE is at DCH after transferring some data. Assuming this, the UE will *first* experience the α and then the β tail. Therefore α contributes more than β does in determining ΔE. For ΔS and ΔD, they can also be approximately regarded as linear functions of α and β when $\alpha, \beta > 2sec$, and the contribution of α is much larger than that of β as well. This is visualized in the 2D plots of Figure 21(a) and (b), where we fix one timer to the default value and change the other timer, then study its impact on the three metrics.

The linear fitting for ΔS does not hold when α is small ($< 2sec$) due to skewed distribution of packet inter-arrival times. Aggressively decreasing α causes excessive number of state promotions, which increase processing overheads at the RNC, worsen the application performance, and cause additional energy overhead since a promotion may consume as much as 87.5% of the power of the DCH state. We observe in Figure 21(a) that $|d\Delta S/d\alpha| > |d\Delta D/d\alpha|$ and $|d\Delta S/d\alpha| > |d\Delta E/d\alpha|$ for $\alpha < 5sec$, meaning that as we reduce α, the incurred state promotion overhead grows faster than the saved DCH time and energy do. This implies the fundamental limitation of current timeout scheme: it is difficult to well balance the tradeoff among ΔD, ΔE, and ΔS as timers are globally and statically set to constant values.

6.3 Per-application Results

Applications exhibit traffic patterns with application-specific packet dynamics, thus with different responses to changes in inactivity timer values. We next study the impact of the α timer on ΔE, ΔS, and ΔD for the five applications described in §4.3. We vary α and fix β at the default value of 12 sec given the relatively small impact of β.

Figures 22, 23, and 24 illustrate the effect of α on ΔE, ΔS, and ΔD, respectively, for the four applications (the curves for "Email-2" are very similar to those for "Email-1"). For the interactive map application, when α is small, decreasing α causes considerable increase of ΔS up to 470% (Figure 23). Accordingly, its ΔE increases as α decreases due to additional energy consumed by state promotions (Figure 22). As described in §5.2, the map traffic pattern consists of non-consecutive data bursts interleaved with short user-injected pauses. Therefore a small value of α comparable to or shorter than most pause durations will trigger a tremendous increase of FACH→DCH promotions. Figures 22 and 24 also indicate that short sessions with a single data burst (the Sync application) benefit more from small α values in terms of energy and radio resource savings. Our observations suggest that dynamically setting timers according to application traffic patterns may better balance the tradeoff.

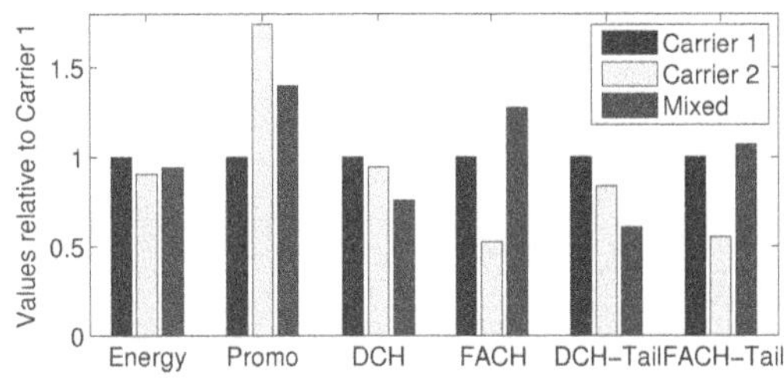

Figure 25: Compare state machines for two carriers

6.4 Comparing to Carrier 2's State Machine

Recall that the major difference between the state machine for Carrier 1 (Figure 2) and that for Carrier 2 (Figure 3) is the state promotion from IDLE, from which upon any user triggered network activity, Carrier 1 directly enters into DCH while Carrier 2 may do either IDLE→FACH or IDLE→FACH→DCH, depending on the packet size. By employing the same simulation approach described in §6.1 for Carrier 2 we observe qualitatively similar trends in terms of the way ΔE, ΔS, and ΔD response to changes of α and β. Also α plays a more important role than β does in controlling the three metrics.

Figure 25 quantitatively compares both carriers. "Carrier 1" and "Carrier 2" are the real state machine settings adopted by both carriers as described in Table 1. "Mixed" corresponds to an artificial scheme using Carrier 2's state transition model but Carrier 1's parameters. We characterize each scheme using six metrics with Carrier 1 serving as the comparison baseline (its Y values are always 1).

The results in Figure 25 verify again the tradeoff discussed in §2.3. First, by comparing "Carrier 1" and "Mixed", we find that changing IDLE→DCH to IDLE→FACH→DCH decreases DCH and DCH tail time by 24% and 39%, respectively, but at the cost of increased number of state promotions by 40%, since for Carrier 2, when a UE at IDLE has non-trivial amount of data (greater than the RLC buffer threshold) to transfer, it always experiences two state promotions to DCH. Our second observation is derived by comparing "Carrier 2" and "Mixed". Their FACH→IDLE timers are significantly different (4 sec for "Carrier 2" and 12 sec for "Mix"), resulting in considerable disparities of their FACH (and FACH tail) times.

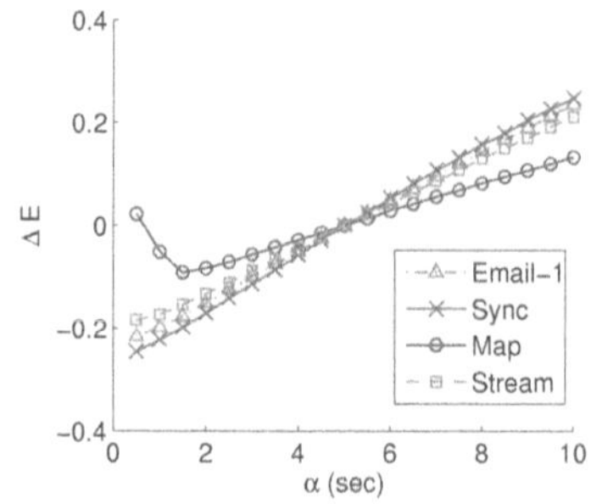

Figure 22: Impact of α on ΔE (β is set to the default) for four apps.

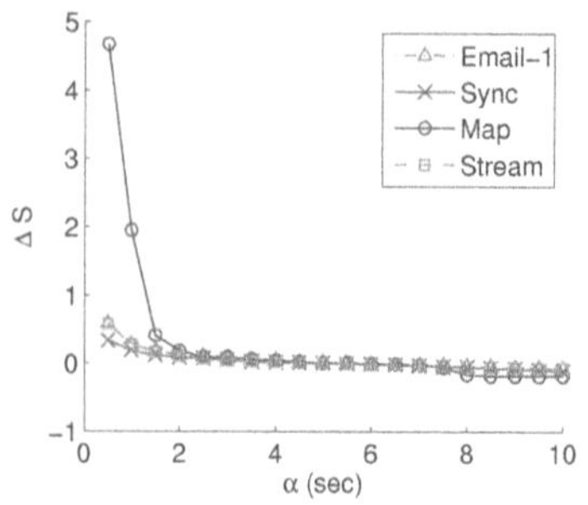

Figure 23: Impact of α on ΔS (β is set to the default) for four apps.

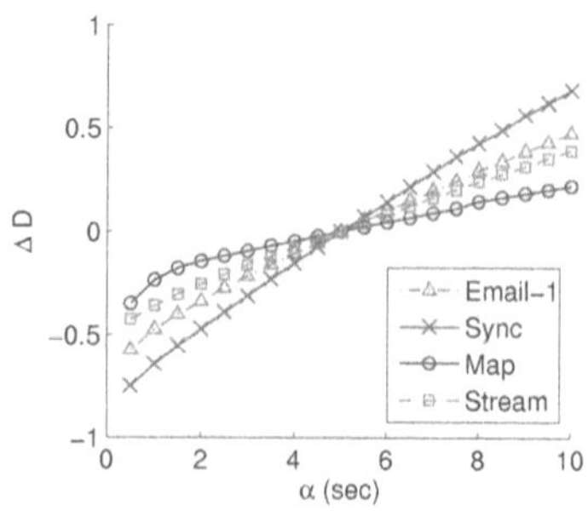

Figure 24: Impact of α on ΔD (β is set to the default) for four apps.

6.5 Summary

We tune the two inactivity timer values for the RRC state machine of Carrier 1. Table 6 summarizes our derived timer values under different constraints of ΔS. Column 2 to 4 correspond to three optimization objectives: energy-saving biased (minimize $0.75\Delta E + 0.25\Delta D$), no bias (minimize $0.5\Delta E + 0.5\Delta D$), and radio-resource-saving biased (minimize $0.25\Delta E + 0.75\Delta D$). The coefficients are empirically chosen to weight the energy and/or the radio resource consumption.

We highlight our findings in this section as follows. *(i)* ΔE, ΔS, and ΔD are approximately linear functions of α and β when they are not very small. The α timer imposes much higher impact on the three metrics than the β timer does. *(ii)* Very small α timer values ($< 2sec$) cause significant increase of the state promotion overhead. *(iii)* Applications have different sensitivities to changes of inactivity timers due to their different traffic patterns. *(iv)* It is difficult to well balance the tradeoff among ΔD, ΔE, and ΔS since the state promotion overhead grows faster than saved DCH time and energy do when we reduce the timers. The fundamental reason is that timers are globally and statically set to constant values.

7. IMPROVE CURRENT TIMER SCHEME

We explore approaches that improve the current inactivity timer scheme whose limitations are revealed in §6.

7.1 Shaping Traffic Patterns

UE applications alter traffic patterns based on the state machine behavior in order to reduce the tail time. We describe two such approaches.

Batching and Prefetching. In [14], the authors discuss two traffic shaping techniques: batching and prefetching. For delay-tolerant applications such as Email and RSS feeds, their transfers can be *batched* to reduce the tail time. In the scenario of web searching, a UE can avoid tails caused by a user's idle time with high probability by *prefetching* the top search results. [14] proposes an algorithm called *TailEnder* that schedules transfers to minimize the energy consumption while meeting user-specified deadlines by batching or prefetching. Their simulation indicates that TailEnder can transfer 60% more RSS feed updates and download search results for more than 50% of web queries, compared to using the default scheme. Similar schemes for delay-tolerant applications in cellular environment were proposed for, for example, offloading 3G data transfers to WiFi [13] and scheduling communication during periods of strong signal strength [29].

Proposed Traffic shaping scheme for YouTube. Recall that in §5.3, we pinpoint the energy inefficiency of YouTube traffic caused by under-utilizing the available bandwidth (Figure 17). To overcome such inefficiency, we reshape the traffic using a hypothetical streaming scheme called *chunk mode*, as illustrated in Figure 26(a). The video content is split into n chunks $C_1, ..., C_n$, each transmitted at the highest bit rate. We model the traffic pattern of chunk mode transfer as follows. Let $L = 9.7MB$ be the size of a 10-minute video and let $M = 800kbps$ be the maximal throughput. For each chunk, it takes T_{SS} seconds for the TCP slow start[5] to ramp up to the throughput of M. By considering delayed ACKs and letting the RTT be 250ms (as measured by the ping latency to YouTube), we compute T_{SS} at 1.3 sec during which $L_{SS} = 60KB$ of data is transferred. The total transfer time for the n chunks (excluding tails) is $T = (T_{SS} + (\frac{L}{n} - L_{SS})/M)n$, and the DCH tail and FACH tail time are $n\alpha$ and $n\beta$, respectively. The whole transfer incurs n IDLE→FACH promotions and n FACH→DCH promotions for Carrier 2's UMTS network.

Based on the above parameters, we compute ΔD and ΔE and plot them in Figure 26(b) and (c), respectively. Note that the energy E consists of three components: the state promotion energy, the DCH non-tail energy, and the tail energy of DCH/FACH. In each plot, the two curves "YouTube" and "Chunk Mode" correspond to streaming schemes of current YouTube and the chunk mode, respectively. We describe the "Chunk + FD" curve in §7.2.

As indicated by Figure 26, compared to current YouTube streaming strategy, the chunk mode saves DCH time and energy by up to 80%. Transferring the whole video in one chunk ($n = 1$) is the most effective. However, measurement results show that users often do not watch the entire video [18]. Therefore when n is small, it may cause unnecessary data transfers if a user only watches part of the video. This problem can be addressed by increasing n and transferring data chunks according to the playing progress of the video. However, resources saved by the chunk mode decrease as n increases due to the tail effect.

To summarize, for some applications, shaping their traffic patterns based on the prior knowledge of the RRC state machine brings significant savings of radio resources and UE

[5] A slow start is necessary since the interval between consecutive chunks is longer than one TCP retransmission timeout [11]. Using TCP keep alive can avoid slow starts but it consumes more energy due to the tail effect.

Table 6: Optimal timer values under constraints of ΔS and different objective functions

Constraint	Obj: $\min\{0.75\Delta E + 0.25\Delta D\}$ $(\alpha, \beta, \Delta E, \Delta D)$	Obj: $\min\{0.50\Delta E + 0.50\Delta D\}$ $(\alpha, \beta, \Delta E, \Delta D)$	Obj: $\min\{0.25\Delta E + 0.75\Delta D\}$ $(\alpha, \beta, \Delta E, \Delta D)$
$\Delta S < -0.1$	(8.0, 11.5, +0.12, +0.28)	(6.5, 18.0, +0.18, +0.12)	(6.5, 18.0, +0.18, +0.12)
$\Delta S < 0.0$	(6.0, 7.0, −0.06, +0.13)	(4.0, 19.0, +0.10, −0.13)	(4.0, 19.0, +0.10, −0.13)
$\Delta S < 0.1$	(4.0, 8.0, −0.13, −0.09)	(3.0, 14.5, −0.04, −0.23)	(3.0, 14.5, −0.04, −0.23)
$\Delta S < 0.2$	(3.5, 4.5, −0.23, −0.11)	(2.5, 11.5, −0.13, −0.31)	(2.5, 11.5, −0.13, −0.31)
$\Delta S < 0.3$	(3.0, 3.0, −0.30, −0.16)	(2.5, 6.0, −0.26, −0.28)	(2.0, 13.5, −0.11, −0.40)
$\Delta S < 0.4$	(2.5, 3.0, −0.33, −0.25)	(2.0, 7.5, −0.25, −0.38)	(1.5, 13.5, −0.14, −0.48)
$\Delta S < 0.5$	(2.0, 4.0, −0.34, −0.35)	(1.5, 8.0, −0.26, −0.46)	(1.5, 8.0, −0.26, −0.46)

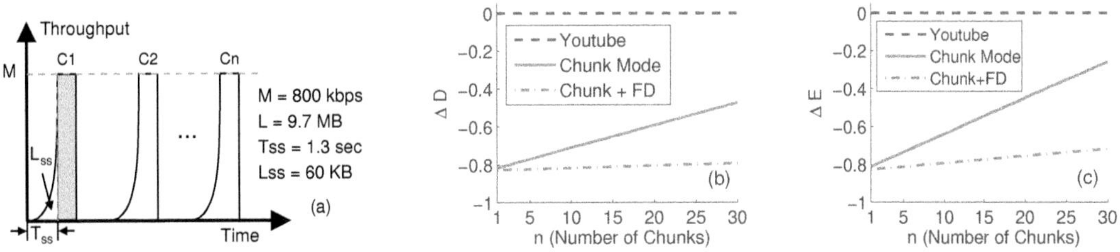

Figure 26: (a) Streaming in chunk mode and its evaluations of (b) ΔD and (c) ΔE

energy. However, this technique has limited applicability. For example, it is difficult to be applied to delay-sensitive applications such as web browsing.

7.2 Dynamic Timers and Fast Dormancy

Dynamic Timer Scheme. Our per-application study in §5.2 and §6.3 suggests that *dynamically* changing timers can potentially better balance the tradeoff. Ideally, this can be achieved by the RNC that adjusts timers at a per-UE basis according to observed traffic patterns. However, such an approach requires significant changes to the RNC, which currently does not recognize IP and its upper layers. The computational overhead is also a concern as the RNC has to identify traffic patterns and compute the appropriate timer values for all connected UEs. The third challenge is that for each UE, the traffic observed by the RNC may originate from multiple applications that concurrently access the network, thus making identifying traffic patterns even harder.

Fast Dormancy. Let us revisit the fundamental reason why inactivity timers are necessary. Since the RNC has no easy way of predicting a UE's network idle time, it conservatively appends a tail to every network usage period. This naturally gives rise to the idea of letting UE applications determine the end of a network usage period (*i.e.*, predicting a tail) by leveraging detailed application-specific knowledge. Applications try to *predict* tails. Once an imminent tail is predicted, a UE notifies the RNC, which then immediately releases the allocated resources. Based on this simple intuition, a feature called *fast dormancy* has been proposed to be included in 3GPP Release 7 [8] and Release 8 [9]. A UE sends a special RRC message to the RNC through the control channel. Upon receiving the message, the RNC releases the RRC connection and lets the UE go to IDLE (or a hibernating PCH state with a lower promotion delay). This feature is currently supported by several handsets [9].

We use the YouTube example to demonstrate a typical scenario where fast dormancy can be applied. Recall the chunk mode streaming scheme shown in Figure 26. In order to eliminate tails, the YouTube application would invoke fast dormancy to demote the state to IDLE immediately after a chunk is received (assuming no concurrent network activity exists). This corresponds to the "Chunk + FD" curve in Figure 26(b) and (c), which indicate that by eliminating the tails, fast dormancy can keep ΔD and ΔE almost constant regardless of n, the number of chunks. Recall that a large n prevents unnecessary data transfers in common cases [18] where a user watches part of the video.

Based on measuring the device power consumption, we do observe that Google Nexus One [3], one of the newly released phones in 2010, adopts fast dormancy in an *application-agnostic* manner: the UE goes to IDLE faster than normal phones do for the same carrier. Or equivalently, the Nexus One uses shorter inactivity timers controlled by the device in order to improve the battery life. The incurred drawbacks, again, are the extra state promotions that cause additional RNC processing overhead and worsen user experience [10, 21].

To the best of our knowledge, however, no individual smartphone application today can invoke fast dormancy based on its traffic pattern, partly due to two reasons. First, for user-interactive applications (*e.g.*, web browsing), accurately predicting a long idle period is non-trivial as user behavior injects randomness to the packet timing. Second, there lacks OS support that provides a simple programming interface for invoking fast dormancy. In particular, the concurrency problem presents a challenge. It is not feasible that applications independently predict the tail and invoke fast dormancy since state transitions are determined by the aggregated traffic of all applications. The OS should schedule concurrent applications and invoke fast dormancy only if the combined idle period predicted by all applications is long enough. Bridging the gap between the application and the fast dormancy support is our on-going work [27].

8. RELATED WORK

To the best of our knowledge, our work is the first comprehensive study that characterizes the RRC state machine and optimizes radio resource allocation using realistic traffic patterns. We have discussed related work of improving current timeout scheme (TailEnder and fast dormancy) in §7.

The problem of choosing the optimal inactivity timer values has also been studied in several previous work. Among them, Chuah *et al.* [16] studied the impact of inactivity timers on UMTS network capacity by simulating the performance of web browsing. Some [20, 32] proposed analytical models to measure the energy consumption of user devices under different timer values. In addition, some [22, 31] also discussed the influence of different timeout values on both service quality and energy consumption. Several other projects also studied network resource management [17, 30]. However, all this prior work was evaluated based on simulation using particular traffic models. In fact, real traffic patterns depend highly on user behavior among other factors and are not easily captured using analytic models. We therefore use real traffic traces for evaluation to ensure the applicability of our work to real network settings.

Researchers also proposed ideas on setting timeout values dynamically. In [23] timeouts for the inactivity timers are decided dynamically for radio resources and computation resources. However, they only addressed the problem from the perspective of network capacity as to reducing the call blocking and dropping rate. In their scenario, the same timer values are applied *globally* to all UEs at any given time. The dynamic timer scheme described in §7.2, however, is to save radio resources and UE's energy. Therefore the timer is customized for each UE.

Inferring the state machine used in radio resource control is another interesting topic. Previous work [15, 24] introduced 3G Transition Triggering Tool to infer RRC state machine parameters and to measure one-way delays in different RRC states. But their approach is based on a fixed state transition model and only infers the corresponding parameters (*e.g.,* inactivity timers). Beyond their work, we also considered and inferred different state transition models configured by two commercial UMTS carriers.

9. CONCLUDING REMARKS

In this paper, we undertook a detailed exploration of the RRC state machine, which guides the radio resource allocation policy in 3G UMTS network, by analyzing real cellular traces and measuring from real smartphones. We found that the RRC state machine may cause considerable performance inefficiency due to the state promotion overhead, as well as cause significant radio resource and UE energy inefficiency due to the tail effects. These two factors form the key tradeoff that is difficult to balance by the current inactivity timer designs. The fundamental reason is that the timers are globally and statically set to constant values that cannot adapt to the diversity of traffic patterns generated by different applications. We believe that addressing this problem requires the knowledge of UE applications, which can proactively alter traffic patterns based on the state machine behavior, or cooperate with the radio access network in allocating radio resources (*i.e.,* the fast dormancy approach). We will explore both approaches in our future work.

10. REFERENCES

[1] 300 Million UMTS Subscribers. http://www.3gpp.org/300-million-UMTS-subscribers.

[2] DNSQueryTimeouts. http://technet.microsoft.com/en-us/library/cc977482.aspx.

[3] Google Nexus One Phone. http://www.google.com/phone/static/en_US-nexusone_tech_specs.html.

[4] Monsoon power monitor. http://www.msoon.com/.

[5] Pandora Radio. http://www.pandora.com.

[6] GERAN RRC state-machine. 3GPP GAHW-000027, 2000.

[7] System Parameter Recommendations to Optimize PS Data User Experience and UE Battery Life. Engineering Services Group, Qualcomm, 2007.

[8] UE "Fast Dormancy" behavior. 3GPP discussion and decision notes R2-075251, 2007.

[9] Configuration of fast dormancy in release 8. 3GPP discussion and decision notes RP-090960, 2009.

[10] System impact of poor proprietary fast dormancy. 3GPP discussion and decision notes RP-090941, 2009.

[11] M. Allman, V. Paxson, and W. R. Stevens. TCP Congestion Control. RFC 2581, 1999.

[12] M. Balakrishnan, I. Mohomed, and V. Ramasubramanian. Where's That Phone?: Geolocating IP Addresses on 3G Networks. In *IMC*, 2009.

[13] A. Balasubramanian, R. Mahajan, and A. Venkataramani. Augmenting Mobile 3G Using WiFi. In *Mobisys*, 2010.

[14] N. Balasubramanian, A. Balasubramanian, and A. Venkataramani. Energy Consumption in Mobile Phones: A Measurement Study and Implications for Network Applications. In *IMC*, 2009.

[15] A. Barbuzzi, F. Ricciato, and G. Boggia. Discovering Parameter Setting in 3G Networks via Active Measurements. *Communications Letters, IEEE*, 12(10), 2008.

[16] M. Chuah, W. Luo, and X. Zhang. Impacts of Inactivity Timer Values on UMTS System Capacity. In *Wireless Communications and Networking Conference*, 2002.

[17] M. Ghaderi, A. Sridharan, H. Zang, D. Towsley, and R. Cruz. Tcp-aware resource allocation in cdma networks. In *Proceedings of ACM MOBICOM*, Los Angeles, CA, USA, September 2006.

[18] L. Guo, E. Tan, S. Chen, Z. Xiao, O. Spatscheck, and X. Zhang. Delving into Internet Streaming Media Delivery: A Quality and Resource Utilization Perspective. In *IMC*, 2006.

[19] H. Holma and A. Toskala. HSDPA/HSUPA for UMTS: High Speed Radio Access for Mobile Communications. John Wiley and Sons, Inc., 2006.

[20] C.-C. Lee, J.-H. Yeh, and J.-C. Chen. Impact of inactivity timer on energy consumption in WCDMA and cdma2000. In *Wireless Telecommunications Symposium*, 2004.

[21] P. P. C. Lee, T. Bu, and T. Woo. On the Detection of Signaling DoS Attacks on 3G Wireless Networks. In *INFOCOM*, 2007.

[22] F. Liers, C. Burkhardt, and A. Mitschele-Thiel. Static RRC Timeouts for Various Traffic Scenarios. In *PIMRC*, 2007.

[23] F. Liers and A. Mitschele-Thiel. UMTS data capacity improvements employing dynamic RRC timeouts. In *PIMRC*, 2005.

[24] P. Perala, A. Barbuzzi, G. Boggia, and K. Pentikousis. Theory and Practice of RRC State Transitions in UMTS Networks. In *Proc. of IEEE Broadband Wireless Access Workshop*, 2009.

[25] J. Perez-Romero, O. Sallent, R. Agusti, and M. Diaz-Guerra. Radio resource management strategies in UMTS. John Wiley and Sons, Inc., 2005.

[26] F. Qian, A. Gerber, Z. M. Mao, S. Sen, O. Spatscheck, and W. Willinger. TCP Revisited: A Fresh Look at TCP in the Wild. In *IMC*, 2009.

[27] F. Qian, Z. Wang, A. Gerber, Z. M. Mao, S. Sen, and O. Spatscheck. TOP: Tail Optimization Protocol for Cellular Radio Resource Allocation. In *ICNP*, 2010.

[28] P. Rodriguez and V. Fridman. Performance of PEPs in CellularWireless Networks. In *WCW*, 2003.

[29] A. Schulman, V. Navda, R. Ramjee, N. Spring, P. Deshpande, C. Grunewald, K. Jain, and V. Padmanabhan. Bartendr: A Practical Approach to Energy-aware Cellular Data Scheduling. In *Mobicom*, 2010.

[30] A. Sridharan, R. Subbaraman, and R. Guerin. Distributed Uplink Scheduling in CDMA Networks. In *Proceedings of IFIP-Networking 2007*, May 2007.

[31] A. Talukdar and M. Cudak. Radio resource control protocol configuration for optimum Web browsing. In *IEEE VTC*, 2002.

[32] J.-H. Yeh, J.-C. Chen, and C.-C. Lee. Comparative Analysis of Energy-Saving Techniques in 3GPP and 3GPP2 Systems. *IEEE transactions on vehicular technology*, 58(1), 2009.

[33] Y. Zhang, L. Breslau, V. Paxson, and S. Shenker. On the Characteristics and Origins of Internet Flow Rates. In *SIGCOMM*, 2002.

On the Feasibility of Effective Opportunistic Spectrum Access

Vinod Kone
U. C. Santa Barbara
Santa Barbara, CA USA
vinod@cs.ucsb.edu

Lei Yang
U. C. Santa Barbara
Santa Barbara, CA USA
leiyang@cs.ucsb.edu

Xue Yang
Intel Labs
Hillsboro, OR, USA
xue.yang@intel.com

Ben Y. Zhao
U. C. Santa Barbara
Santa Barbara, CA USA
ravenben@cs.ucsb.edu

Haitao Zheng
U. C. Santa Barbara
Santa Barbara, CA USA
htzheng@cs.ucsb.edu

ABSTRACT

Dynamic spectrum access networks are designed to allow today's bandwidth hungry "secondary devices" to share spectrum allocated to legacy devices, or "primary users." The success of this wireless communication model relies on the availability of unused spectrum, and the ability of secondary devices to utilize spectrum without disrupting transmissions of primary users. While recent measurement studies have shown that there is sufficient underutilized spectrum available, little is known about whether secondary devices can efficiently make use of available spectrum while minimizing disruptions to primary users.

In this paper, we present the first comprehensive study on the presence of "usable" spectrum in opportunistic spectrum access systems, and whether sufficient spectrum can be extracted by secondary devices to support traditional networking applications. We use for our study fine-grain usage traces of a wide spectrum range (20MHz–6GHz) taken at 4 locations in Germany, the Netherlands, and Santa Barbara, California. Our study shows that on average, 54% of spectrum is never used and 26% is only partially used. Surprisingly, in this 26% of partially used spectrum, secondary devices can utilize very little spectrum using conservative access policies to minimize interference with primary users. Even assuming an optimal access scheme and extensive statistical knowledge of primary user access patterns, a user can only extract between 20-30% of the total available spectrum. To provide better spectrum availability, we propose *frequency bundling*, where secondary devices build reliable channels by combining multiple unreliable frequencies into virtual frequency bundles. Analyzing our traces, we find that there is little correlation of spectrum availability across channels, and that bundling random channels together can provide sustained periods of reliable transmission with only short interruptions.

Categories and Subject Descriptors

C.4 [**Performance of Systems**]: Reliability, availability, and serviceability

General Terms

Measurement, Performance, Reliability

Keywords

Opportunistic spectrum access, Channel bundling, Measurement

1. INTRODUCTION

Radio spectrum is perhaps the wireless industry's most valuable asset. The deployment and growth of any wireless network depend on the amount of spectrum it can access. Despite its recognized value, current policies on spectrum distribution are highly inefficient. Spectrum frequency ranges are assigned statically to wireless carriers in long-term leases, generally ignoring market demands that vary significantly over time. Over the years, the large majority of frequency ranges have been assigned, leaving little room for new technologies or growth. Meanwhile, demands for previously assigned frequencies have dropped significantly, leaving most ranges woefully underutilized at an average of 5% of capacity [16].

Opportunistic and dynamic spectrum access is a new access model designed to "extract" unused spectrum from allocated but underutilized frequencies, supporting newcomer traffic without affecting existing owners. In this model, wireless devices that need spectrum locate and "opportunistically (re)use" unused frequencies ranges. These "secondary" devices take great precaution to avoid disrupting original or "primary" users, and immediately exit the frequency whenever they detect traffic from primary users. Through this carefully planned access model, secondary devices can increase spectrum utilization with zero or bounded disruptions to existing owners. Note that compared to more liberal spectrum access rules [11], this "conservative" access model is easier to implement and much more likely to gain acceptance with regulators and primary users.

The success of the dynamic spectrum access model depends heavily on both the availability of unused spectrum, and whether secondary devices can efficiently extract and utilize them. While a number of measurement studies have measured and modeled the availability of unused spectrum [1, 5, 7, 13, 23, 24], the community has generally overlooked the second factor, and optimistically assumed that secondary devices can always efficiently utilize available spectrum. Despite its importance, little is known about whether secondary devices can efficiently make use of available spectrum, given the hard constraints of avoiding disruptions to primary users. This is understandable, since such a study requires access to a fine-grained measurement trace of spectrum usage, which has not been available until recently.

In this paper, we present the first comprehensive study of performance in opportunistic spectrum access systems that limit disruptions to unpredictable primary users. Our goal is to understand whether dynamic spectrum access can provide reliable spectrum to secondary users, while respecting hard disruption limits that protect primary user transmissions. Our study can address key concerns about the feasibility of supporting traditional network applications in this new model. We answer questions in three key areas:

(1) *How much usable spectrum is available at different frequency ranges? How does this availability change across time and spectrum frequency?*

(2) *How much spectrum is accessible by conservative secondary users who must avoid disrupting spectrum owners at all costs?*

(3) *Can we design novel spectrum access methods that allow us to build a reliable wireless channel using unreliable dynamic spectrum channels?*

We answer these questions by performing a deep analysis of a large collection of spectrum usage measurements. These measurements are taken from four locations across the globe: two in Germany, one in the Netherlands, and one in Santa Barbara, USA. Each measurement uses a spectrum analyzer to sweep a range of radio frequencies between 20MHz and 6GHz for a period of 2–7 days, capturing the raw energy level observed on each of the 200kHz frequency channels at a periodic interval of 0.65 or 1.8 seconds. These results capture, at a very fine granularity, when specific radio frequencies are occupied by primary users in the measurement area. This dataset is unique in its combination of wide frequency coverage (20MHz to 6GHz), measurement length (one week for 3 of the locations), and measurement frequency (one sweep per 1.8 or 0.65 seconds compared to 75 seconds of prior studies [7]). We extract from them spectrum occupancy traces (occupied or free) across a large set of frequencies, covering 5922 wireless channels and a total of more than 5 billion data points for analysis. While four locations are in no way representative of spectrum usage in general, these measurements do provide initial insights into whether opportunistic spectrum access has the potential to support traditional networking applications.

Our analysis of spectrum availability (Section 3) confirms that most assigned frequencies are heavily underutilized. Out of 5922 channels analyzed, an average of 26% (or 1267 channels) were partially occupied (5%–95% occupancy). We are primarily interested in evaluating dynamic spectrum access on these channels, since other channels are either fully occupied (20% of our dataset, or 1317 channels), or can be statically allocated as free channels (54%) of our dataset, or 3338 channels. We also observe that spectrum availability varies significantly based on the frequency range and measurement location. More importantly, short term availability varies significantly across time, and both idle duration and busy periods show high variance. This highly variable spectrum availability poses significant challenges to secondary devices, making it harder to access and utilize a channel while respecting a fixed limit of disruptions to primary users.

In Section 4, we use these spectrum traces to compare the performance of two "optimal" opportunistic access mechanisms: one scheme where secondary devices have zero knowledge of primary user patterns, and one where secondary devices have accurate statistical knowledge of the primary user accesses [14]. We are shocked to find that, even with accurate statistical knowledge of primary user accesses, secondary devices can only extract 20–30% of the available spectrum under a reasonable disruption limit of 10%, and less than 10% of spectrum if the disruption limit drops to 1%. In addition, spectrum extracted from each channel is heavily fragmented and scattered across time. As a result, the equivalent channels available to secondary devices are highly unreliable – spectrum access on each channel is frequently interrupted, and often takes 10–100 seconds before being restored.

But there is hope. We propose and evaluate *frequency bundling*, where secondary devices build reliable transmission channels by combining together multiple unreliable frequencies, essentially utilizing frequency diversity to compensate for the lack of reliability on individual channels. To evaluate different bundling strategies, we analyze correlation between availability patterns of different 200kHz channels, and find little or no correlation (Section 5). This availability independence means that we can significantly improve overall reliability by simply bundling random channel pairs together. Experimental results from our datasets are promising. Using a random bundling strategy, the improvement in channel reliability scales exponentially with the size of the bundle. For example, bundling 5–10 randomly selected channels together will reduce the secondary device's blocking time by two orders of magnitude. The resulting new channel enjoys average transmission periods of 120–1300s while being occasionally interrupted by 2-4s.

Finally, we wish to understand the impact of the sweeping frequency parameter in our conclusions. Are our datasets sufficiently fine grain to capture the variability in primary user access patterns? If so, then secondary devices can improve their spectrum utilization simply by sensing and utilizing the channel at a finer granularity. We use the 2nd component of our dataset (collected locally by us for this project) to test this theory. We find that the variations in channel availability continue at finer time scales, meaning secondary devices cannot simply improve performance by working at finer time scales (Section 6). Using this dataset, we also examine potential artifacts of using coarse time scale for opportunistic access.

In summary, our study provides a first look into the feasibility of accessing spectrum opportunistically while respecting hard limits to disruptions to primary users. We show that given the unpredictable nature of primary user access, current spectrum access methods cannot provide usable channels to secondary devices. Only by bundling multiple unreliable channels together can we provide reasonable levels of reliability to network applications on these devices. We also make several other observations:

- The performance of opportunistic spectrum access cannot be determined solely from average spectrum availability, *i.e.* higher availability does not necessarily mean more usable spectrum.
- Statistical knowledge of spectrum occupancy can improve the performance of opportunistic access by a factor of 2–3.
- Frequency channels (200kHz) are mostly uncorrelated, unless they are frequency-adjacent. This conflicts with a prior measurement study [7]. The difference could be attributed to the use of different energy detection methods, measurement location and time granularity.

2. OVERVIEW

In this section, we first provide background information on opportunistic spectrum access. We then describe the objectives of our investigation and the datasets we use.

2.1 Opportunistic Spectrum Access

Opportunistic spectrum access involves two entities: primary users or original owners of allocated but underutilized frequencies, and secondary users who seek to make use of unused spectrum, under the hard constraints of avoiding disruptions to primary users at all costs [3, 27, 14].

Figure 1 shows a representative example of opportunistic spectrum access on a partially used primary user channel. A secondary user x accesses the channel using a slotted sensing-then-access mechanism. At the start of each slot, x senses the channel to detect whether any primary user is present, often using a RF energy detection [10]. If the channel is occupied, x does nothing and waits till the next slot. If the channel appears to be unused, x will decide whether to access the channel in the current slot. In order to satisfy hard primary user disruption limits, x must carefully access the risk of using the channel because the primary user can potentially return in the middle of its transmission slot. When necessary, x will give up using an idle channel to avoid disrupting the original owner.

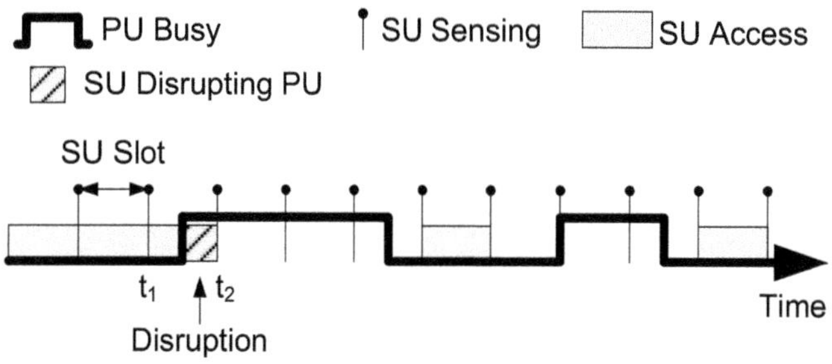

Figure 1: An illustrative example of opportunistic spectrum access. The bold line shows the primary user (PU)'s channel occupancy. A secondary user (SU) periodically senses channel to detect primary user and determine whether to access the channel. A disruption occurs if the primary user returns in the middle of secondary user transmissions.

2.2 Goals

By analyzing real world measurements on primary user spectrum usage patterns, we have three key goals. First, we wish to understand the feasibility and effectiveness of opportunistic spectrum access. More specifically, we seek to examine the availability of both completely unused and intermittently used spectrum. For intermittently used channels, we also seek to examine the amount of spectrum actually accessible to secondary devices, given the hard constraints of avoiding disruptions to primary users.

Second, we seek to examine the role of various design decisions and network factors in opportunistic spectrum access, including the disruption limit set by the original owners, the time granularity of spectrum access, and the type of information available to secondary devices about the original owners.

Finally, we are interested to examine practical issues in utilizing extracted spectrum to support today's wireless services. Because the extracted spectrum is fragmented across time and frequency, we seek to identify ways to build reliable wireless transmission from scattered spectrum pieces.

2.3 Datasets

We use two datasets in our analysis. They are unique in their combination of wide frequency coverage, extensive measurement length, and fine-grained measurement frequency.

The first dataset, used for most of the analysis, records the received signal strength across 20MHz to 6GHz at three locations over a period of one week. Table 1 lists some of the original owners and their frequency ranges. The measurement was performed by the Mobnets group of RWTH Aachen University, Germany [2]. The three measurement sites were i) on a balcony of a residential building in Germany (GER1), ii) inside an office building in Germany (GER2) and iii) on a roof top in Netherlands (NED). At each location, a spectrum analyzer repeatedly swept the 20MHz–6GHz frequency range, measuring signal energy on each of the 200kHz frequency channels. The measurement uses a 1.8 seconds sweep time. That is, any two subsequent measurements on a single channel were 1.8 seconds apart. Using this dataset, we analyzed 5622 channels corresponding to the service bands listed in Table 1.

The second dataset came from our own measurements at UC Santa Barbara, California, USA over a period of two weekdays in April 2010 when school was in session. The goal of these measurements is to sample primary user access patterns at a finer-granularity than the first dataset. It contains the received energy strength in the 1925-1995MHz GSM frequency band, observed in an office trailer. We configured a GSM1900 digital receiver (Agilent E6454C) as a spectrum analyzer which swept the GSM frequency with a resolution of 200kHz. Unlike a wide-band spectrum analyzer, our digital analyzer only tunes to GSM frequencies. But since it covers a much smaller frequency range, we can increase the sweep frequency to once every 0.65 seconds. This dataset covers 300 channels, which we use in Section 6 to study the impact of time granularity on opportunistic spectrum access.

Preprocessing. We preprocess our datasets to convert the received signal strength traces to spectrum occupancy patterns (busy or idle) on each measurement channel. To do so, we use the energy-detection method [7, 23] and select (for each 200kHz measurement channel) an energy threshold of -107dBm that is specified by the IEEE 802.22 standard for TV bands [20]. We declare a frequency channel as occupied (or busy) at a given time if its measured signal strength is above the threshold. While service bands could use different thresholds to protect their transmissions, there are no reasonable guides on what those individual thresholds should be. Thus we apply this known threshold uniformly across different service bands. For the NED location in the RWTH measurement as well as our own UCSB measurement, we use a slightly higher threshold of -100dBm. This is to compensate for the presence of stronger noise floor, due to the proximity to a railway station in the case of NED (also recommended by [23]), and the presence of metal walls and obstacles in the case of UCSB measurements.

In addition to using a fixed threshold, we also consider using dynamic thresholds as suggested by [7]. This is to set the threshold for a frequency channel to be 3dBm higher than the minimum energy recorded on this channel. We found that this method, however, is highly sensitive to the variance in the noise floor. It also marks the majority of frequency channels as heavily occupied. Therefore, we choose to use the fixed threshold for our analysis, but adjust the threshold based on local noise characteristics, as discussed in the above.

2.4 Assumptions

We make a few assumptions in order to perform analysis on the measurement datasets.

First, because both measurements sweep the frequency band sequentially to measure a wide frequency range, they do not capture usage activities at time granularity smaller than the sweeping time. Thus we set secondary user's access slot size to be the same as

Original owner	TV1	Aviation	Marine	TV2	TV3	GSM900 UL	GSM900 DL	DAB
Freq. Range (MHz)	41-67	109-136	157-173	175-229	471-861	890-915	935-960	1453-1491
Original owner	Meteo	GSM1800 UL	GSM1800 DL	DECT	UMTS UL	UMTS DL	ISM	
Freq. Range (MHz)	1675-1710	1710-1785	1805-1880	1882-1897	1920-1980	2110-2170	2400-2500	

Table 1: The 15 original spectrum owners and their frequency ranges (MHz) measured by the RWTH dataset.

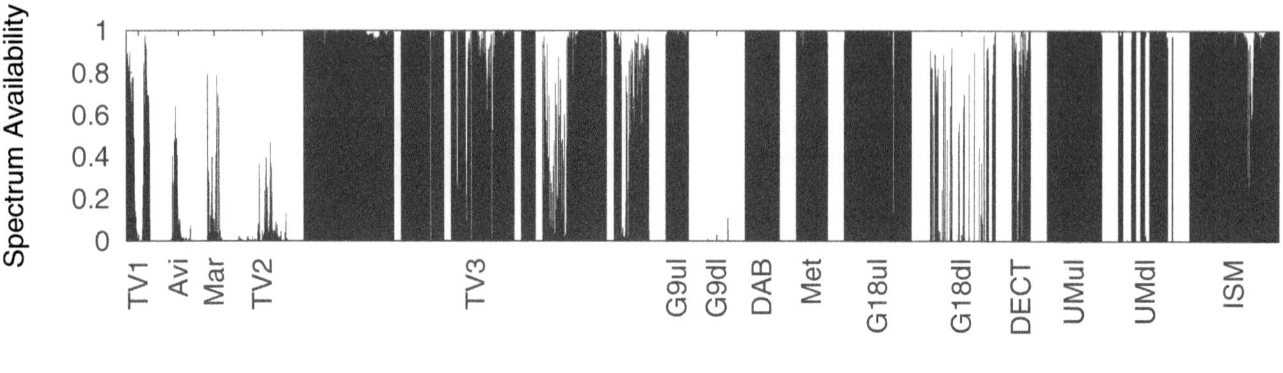

Figure 2: Spectrum availability of the 5622 frequency channels measured at the NED location, averaged over a period of one week. The channels are ordered in the ascending order of their operating frequencies. Each vertical line corresponds to the spectrum availability of a 200 KHz channel within each of the 15 service bands.

the sweeping time. Note that the sweeping times of our datasets (1.8 seconds for the RWTH dataset and 0.65 seconds for the UCSB dataset) are two orders of magnitude smaller than previous measurements of 75 seconds [7]. We show in Section 6 that such fine-grained measurement is required to capture useful statistics of spectrum availability and usability.

Second, we capture the effect where a primary user returns to the channel in the middle of a slot in our calculations of the primary user disruption rate. Specifically, if an idle slot is followed by an occupied slot, then the primary user is likely to arrive in the middle of the first slot. If the secondary user decides to transmit in the first slot, we flag this slot as creating a disruption to the primary user. We compute the primary user disruption rate as the ratio of primary user busy blocks that suffer any disruption [14].

Finally, we assume that secondary users' sensing is accurate, and that multiple secondary users coordinate their access to avoid transmission collision. Since our focus is on studying the impact of spectrum usage patterns of original owners, we abstract multiple coexisting secondary users into a single secondary link. The design and overhead of optimal spectrum sensing and coordination protocols, although important, are out of the scope of this paper. We refer the reader to [3, 6, 18, 26, 27] for more details on cooperative spectrum sensing and sharing.

3. SPECTRUM AVAILABILITY ANALYSIS

The performance of opportunistic spectrum access depends heavily on the sustained availability of unused spectrum. In this section, using the RWTH data set, we examine in detail the availability of spectrum, its dependency on frequencies and locations, as well as its temporal dynamics. In total, we analyzed a one-week spectrum usage patterns (busy or idle) on each of the 5622 frequency channels. In the following, we first describe our findings on overall spectrum availability across frequencies and locations, and then present observed temporal dynamics on instantaneous spectrum availability.

3.1 Overall Spectrum Availability

We define *Spectrum Availability* (SA) as the percentage of measured intervals where a channel is not occupied by existing owners in a given time frame. While each service has its own operating channel width, in this study we treat each 200kHz measurement band as a single spectrum channel.

Figure 2 plots the spectrum availability measured at the NED location, for each of 5622 spectrum channels corresponding to the 15 selected service bands listed in Table 1, averaged over a period of one week. It shows that many spectrum channels are either completely free or partially-used. Interestingly, for some of the services (*e.g.* TV3, GSM1800DL and UMTSDL), the spectrum availability varies significantly across channels within the same service. To further examine the impact of measurement location, Figure 3(a) shows the spectrum availability measured at the three locations (NED, GER1, and GER2), averaged over a period of one week and across channels within each service band.

We make two key observations from these results. First, for all three locations, a significant portion of allocated spectrum is available for secondary devices. Second, the availability varies significantly across frequencies. Very low frequencies (TV1, Aviation, Marine, TV2) are heavily occupied, while others experience only light and moderate usage. The cellular uplink bands (GSM900UL, GSM1800UL, UMTSUL) are mostly idle because their signals are significantly weaker than those of downlink transmissions, and are thus harder to detect even using high-end spectrum analyzers. Nevertheless, we use these uplink measurements to examine opportunistic access, assuming that secondary users take extra precautions on these bands to avoid disrupting primary users, *e.g.* by lowering their transmit power.

After examining each channel in detail, we found that out of 5622 channels analyzed, 1176 channels are *partially occupied, i.e.* whose average spectrum availability is within [0.05, 0.95], and 3181 channels are idle, *i.e.* whose availability is greater than 0.95. In Figure 3(b), we plot the cumulative distribution of the spectrum availability across these partially occupied channels, and see that

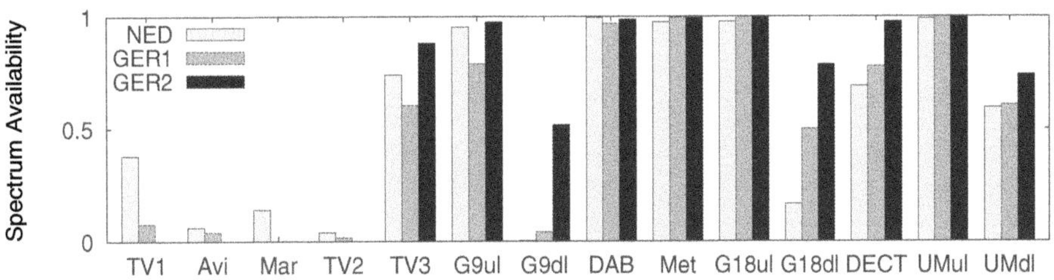

(a) Average Spectrum Availability of Each Service

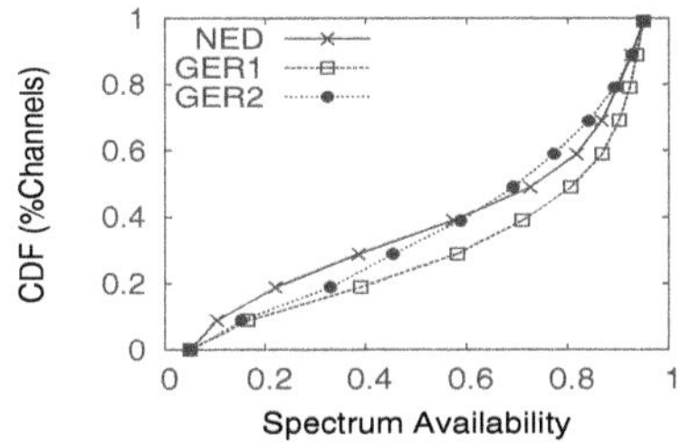

(b) Distribution of Spectrum Availability of Partially-used Channels

Figure 3: (a) The average spectrum availability of various service bands over the entire measurement period. The services are ordered in the ascending order of their operating frequencies. Ample unused spectrum exists at all three locations but the availability varies across locations and frequencies. (b) Cumulative distribution of spectrum availability of all partially used spectrum channels, which is evenly distributed between [0.05, 0.95].

their availability is evenly distributed between 0.05 and 0.95. In the rest of the paper, we will focus on these partially occupied channels for which we must rely on opportunistic spectrum access to extract unused spectrum.

3.2 Dynamics of Available Spectrum

In this section, we investigate the temporal dynamics of spectrum availability. To understand both long- and short-term trends, we analyze the dynamics at two different granularity levels. To understand day-to-day trends, we start from dividing traces into half-hour segments and compute for each segment the average spectrum availability. Figure 4(a) plots the resulting spectrum availability observed over 6 days on three selected GSM1800DL channels with intermediate spectrum availability, one for each location. In this case, spectrum availability varies significantly over time, and displays a weak 1-day periodicity.

Next we investigate the availability dynamics at the granularity of the measurement interval (1.8s). Figure 4(b) shows a 1 minute snapshot of the spectrum occupancy on all the partially available GSM1800DL channels. A white strip in the figure indicates that the corresponding channel during this time period is idle. This result clearly demonstrates that the available spectrum is fragmented and scattered across time. A more precise view of the channel idle/busy durations is shown in Figure 5, for NED and GER1. It represents a randomly selected GSM1800DL channel for a period of 1 hour between 11AM and noon. In this example, the channel busy duration varies between 1.8 seconds and 20 seconds, while the idle duration varies significantly between 1.8 seconds to 100 seconds. The large variance in idle durations, however, poses significant challenges to secondary devices, making it harder to access and utilize a channel while respecting a fixed limit of disruption to original owners. We examine this challenge and its impact in greater detail next in Section 4.

4. PERFORMANCE OF OPPORTUNISTIC SPECTRUM ACCESS

Our analysis of real world measurements has demonstrated the ample scope for opportunistic spectrum access. In this section, we investigate its performance in terms of "extracting" the unused spectrum without disrupting original owners. As illustrated in Figure 1, secondary devices sense and access spectrum in a slotted manner. Without knowing exactly when the primary user will return, secondary devices must take great precaution and occasionally give up using an idle channel. As a result, they cannot extract all the available spectrum. Using the RWTH dataset, we seek to understand how much spectrum a secondary device can actually obtain.

Specifically, our analysis answers three key questions:

- What is the rate of spectrum extraction? Can statistical knowledge on primary user spectrum usage patterns improve the performance, and if so, by how much?
- Is the average spectrum availability a reliable predictor of the amount of spectrum extracted?
- What is the usability of the extracted spectrum? How long must a secondary user wait to access a channel and how long does the access last?

In the following, we first describe the access strategies used in our analysis, and then address these questions.

4.1 Access Strategies

Given the primary user disruption limit η and the probability density function of primary user idle duration, prior work has developed optimal access strategies for opportunistic spectrum access [14]. A secondary user x senses the channel at the start of an access slot t. If the channel is busy, x does nothing and waits till the next slot. If the channel is idle, x estimates the risk of accessing the current slot, using its past channel observations, the primary user idle duration statistics $f(\cdot)$ and the primary user disruption limit η. Based on this risk factor, x computes $q^*(t)$, the probability of accessing the channel at time t. Formally, $q^*(t)$ can be derived as follows:

$$q^*(t) = \begin{cases} 1 & \text{if } g(t) > \gamma^* \ \& \ \Phi(t) = \text{Idle} \\ p^*, & \text{if } g(t) = \gamma^* \ \& \ \Phi(t) = \text{Idle} \\ 0, & \text{otherwise} \end{cases} \quad (1)$$

In this formula, $\Phi(t)$ is the sensing result at the beginning of time slot t (idle/busy), $1/g(t)$ is the conditional probability that the primary user will return during time slot t given that $\Phi(t)$=Idle. γ^* is the risk threshold derived from the primary user idle time distribution $f(\cdot)$ and the primary user disruption limit η [14]. If the risk is small ($g(t) > \gamma^*$), x uses the channel. If the risk is close to the collision probability ($g(t) = \gamma^*$), x uses the channel with probability p^* derived from $f(\cdot)$ and η [14], otherwise, x does not access the channel. It has been proved that using small access slots, the above strategy is optimal and satisfies the primary user disruption limit. The detailed derivations and proof can be found from [14].

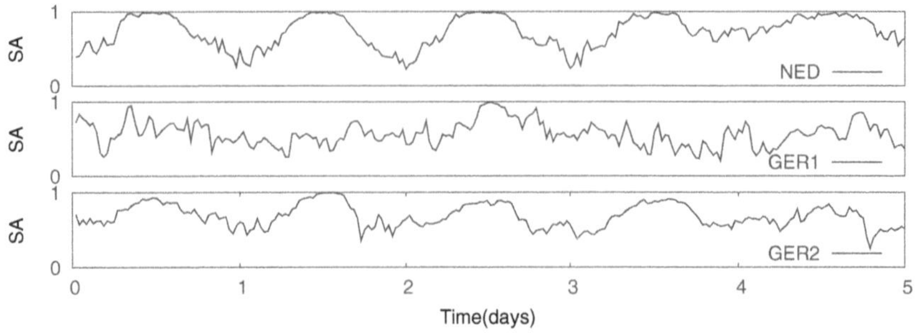

(a) Long-term Dynamics of Spectrum Availability over 5 days

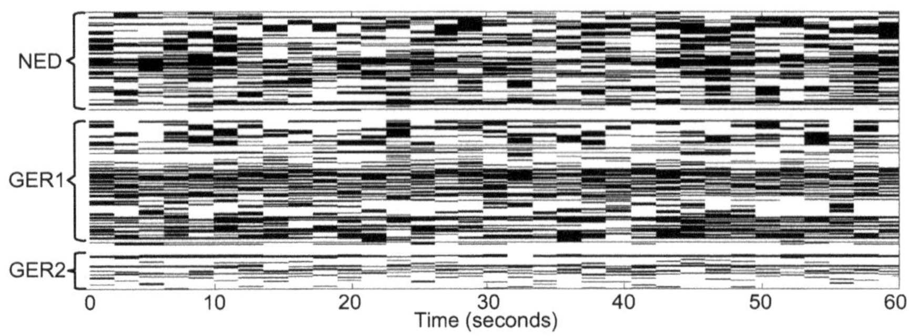

(b) Short-term Dynamics of Spectrum Availability over 1 minute

Figure 4: Long- and short-term dynamics of spectrum availability. (a) The availability (averaged over 30 minutes) varies significantly over 5 weekdays, on randomly selected GSM1800DL channels (one per location). (b) The per 1.8s availability of a 1-minute snapshot, for all the partially-used GSM1800DL channels. The availability, shown as various white strips, is scattered randomly across time.

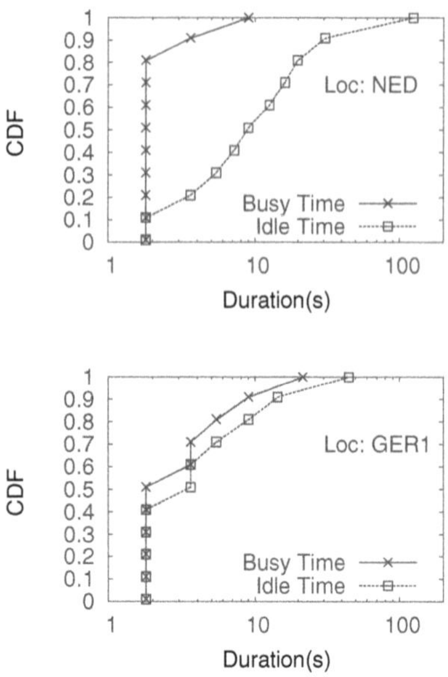

Figure 5: Cumulative distributions of channel idle and busy period on a randomly selected channel in an one hour period. Large variation in idle duration poses significant challenges for opportunistic access. The GER2 result is similar to the NED result and thus omitted.

We apply this optimal strategy to create two practical opportunistic access schemes:

- *No knowledge-based Access (NKA).* This scheme requires no knowledge about primary user usage patterns. Secondary devices will access a channel with a probability η (the primary user disruption limit) when sensing it idle, leading to an extraction rate around η. This is the optimal result if the primary user idle time follows the exponential distribution [14].

- *Statistical knowledge-based Access (SKA).* It assumes that secondary devices have the exact statistical distribution of primary user idle time, $f(\cdot)$. Such knowledge is either provided by original owners or 3rd party or built by secondary devices via online/offline learning.

We note that secondary users can schedule channel access to utilize all available spectrum if and only if they can completely predict each primary user's spectrum usage events. This ideal scheme, however, is only feasible when the primary user displays a deterministic access pattern, which we did not find in our measurement datasets. Thus we did not consider it in our analysis.

The SKA scheme requires an accurate statistical distribution of primary user idle time. Results in Section 3 show that the distribution varies significantly over time, especially within the same day. To make a fair evaluation, we apply time-series analysis to segment traces of each frequency channel into multiple time segments, each displaying stable availability [15]. The results show that most segments are roughly 1-2 hours in length. We then extract the statistical distribution $f(\cdot)$ of primary user idle time in each segment and use it to implement and evaluate SKA in the same segment.

4.2 Spectrum Extraction Rate

For each partially-used channel, we measure the spectrum extraction rate as the ratio between the amount of spectrum actually obtained by secondary devices and the amount of available spectrum. By default, the primary user disruption limit η=0.1.

SKA vs. NKA. Figure 6 plots, for each of the 15 services, the one-week average of the spectrum extraction rate. Without any knowledge on primary user idle time, NKA's extraction rate is roughly 10% (due to $\eta = 0.1$). SKA, on the other hand, improves the extraction rate by 2–3 times. This demonstrates the benefits of having statistical knowledge of the primary user access patterns.

A disappointing observation is that even with accurate statistical knowledge on primary user access patterns, the average extraction rate is only 15–35%. To further explore this problem, we also plot in Figure 7 the cumulative distribution of SKA's extraction rate among all the segments of partially occupied channels. Across all locations, the median extraction rate is 19%, and 80% of the segments can produce no more than 37% extraction rate.

The low effectiveness can be attributed to two factors. 1) The spectrum usage patterns are highly random and hard to predict, so without a reliable estimation on channel idle duration, secondary devices are forced to be overly conservative; or 2) the access slot used by secondary devices is too large, forcing them to being overly conservative. The first reason has been confirmed by the highly random distribution of primary user idle time, shown in Figure 5. A related study has also confirmed the difficulty in predicting primary user access patterns [23]. The second reason, however, is impossible to verify without the ground truth on primary user spectrum usage patterns – the RWTH dataset is measured at the same 1.8s intervals, preventing us from pinpointing the exact primary user

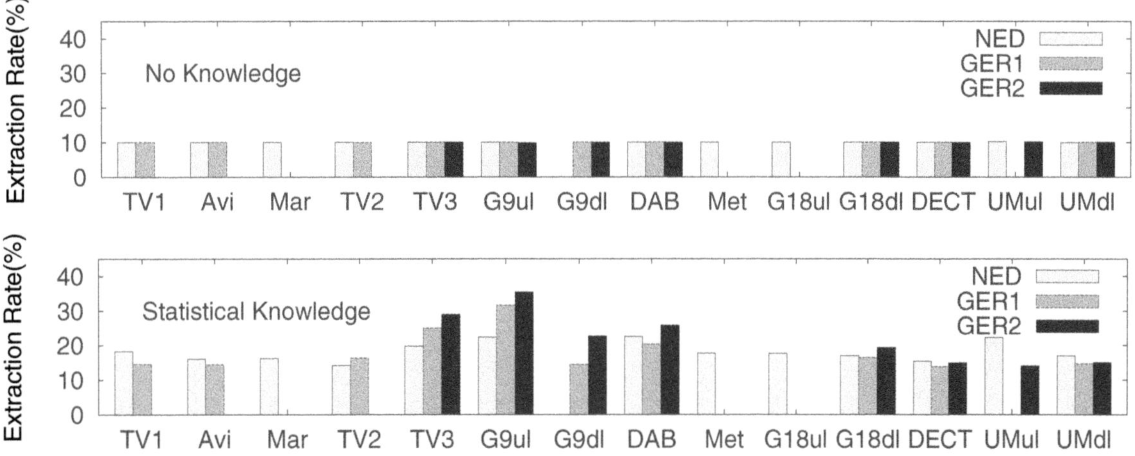

Figure 6: Spectrum extraction rate with no knowledge (NKA) and statistical knowledge(SKA). The results are averaged over all segments for each service over a week. For GER1 and GER2, some services have no data because they do not have any partially-available frequency channels. NKA only extracts 10% of available spectrum due to the 0.1 primary user disruption limit. SKA increases the extraction rate to 15-35%.

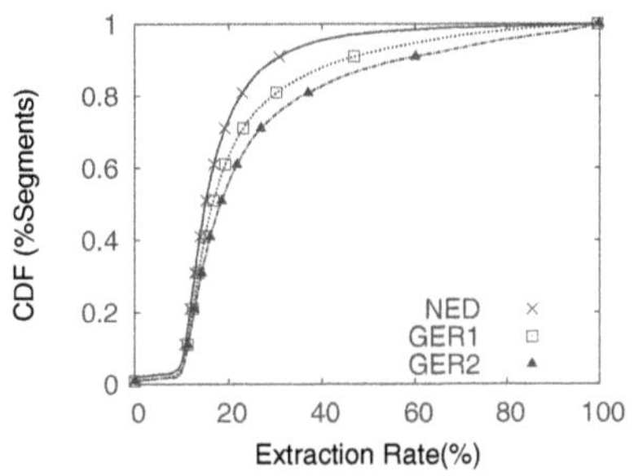

Figure 7: CDF of extraction rate of the SKA scheme for all segments across all services. For all locations, 80% of segments only get up to 37% extraction rate despite accurate statistical knowledge.

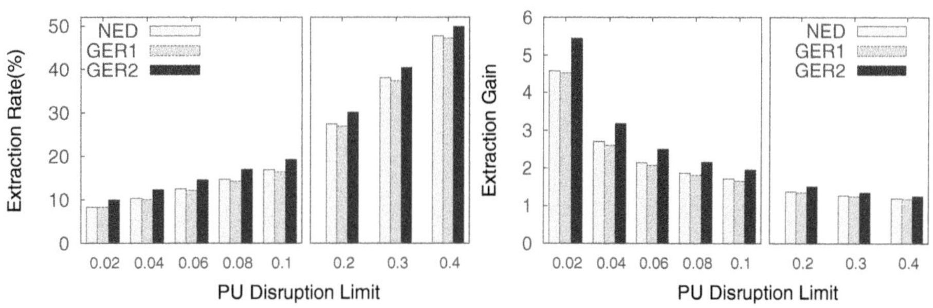

(a) SKA's Extraction Rate

(b) Gain of SKA over NKA

Figure 8: Impact of primary user disruption limit on spectrum extraction rate of the SKA scheme for GSM1800 DL (a) The extraction rate increases non-linearly with the disruption limit. (b) The gain of SKA over NKA decreases as we relax the primary user disruption limit.

arrival and departure time that are required to evaluate the performance of systems using smaller slot sizes.

We revisit this issue in Section 6 using our own UCSB dataset with a 0.65s sweeping time. We show that because original owners display highly random access patterns, reducing slot sizes helps but does not eliminate the need for conservative spectrum access. Thus the problem of low extraction rate still remains.

Impact of Primary User Disruption Limit. The design of access strategies implies that the primary user disruption limit has a significant impact on the extraction rate. For example, the extraction rate of NKA scales linearly with the disruption limit. To understand this dependency for SKA, we plot in Figure 8(a) the average extraction rate as a function of the primary user disruption limit. As expected, relaxing the disruption limit improves the spectrum extraction rate. On the other hand, the relationship between the two is non-linear. In fact, it can be proved that when the probability of primary user returning to a channel increases monotonically with existing channel idle time, SKA's spectrum extraction rate is a monotonically increasing and concave function of the primary user disruption limit. We omit the proof due to the space limitation. Because of such non-linearity, we can show that the gain of SKA over NKA shrinks as the primary user disruption limit increases, which is also confirmed by Figure 8(b).

4.3 Available vs. Extracted Spectrum

Our second question is whether the average spectrum availability is a reliable predictor of the amount of spectrum extracted. Answering this question is particularly important because many existing studies have been using the average spectrum availability to evaluate opportunistic access. Using the RWTH dataset, we re-evaluate this claim by examining the relationship between the amount of spectrum extracted and the amount of spectrum available.

We first plot the extraction rate as a function of the average spectrum availability. Using the segments discussed in Section 4.2, Figure 9(a) and (b) show the spectrum extraction rate for all the GSM1800DL segments at NED, as a function of the average spectrum availability of each segment. As expected, NKA extracts about 10% available spectrum due to the 0.1 primary user disruption limit. The results display some small variations, especially at

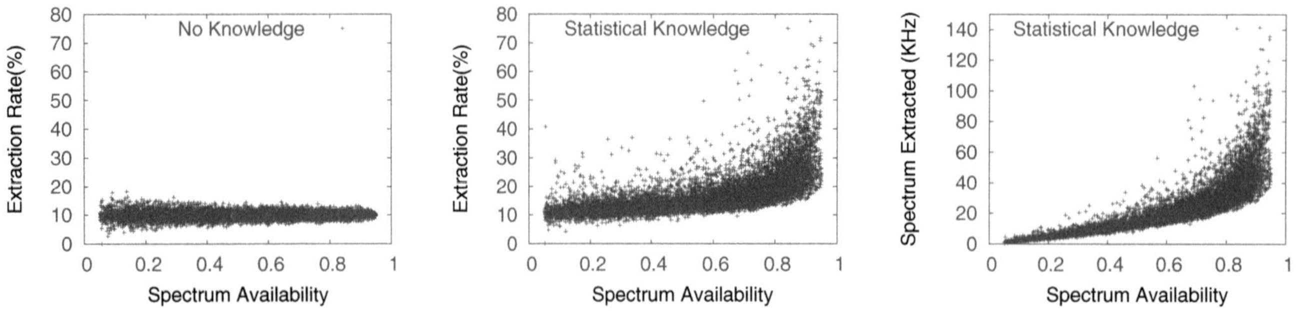

(a) Extraction Rate, NKA (b) Extraction Rate, SKA (c) Spectrum Extracted, SKA

Figure 9: Scatter plots of spectrum extraction rates of GSM1800DL at NED with 0.1 primary user disruption limit. (a) NKA leads to roughly 10% extraction rate. (b) SKA becomes more effective when the spectrum availability increases, although there is significant variance at higher availability values. (c) But, the spectrum availability is no longer an accurate indicator of the spectrum extracted, due to the large variance at high availability values.

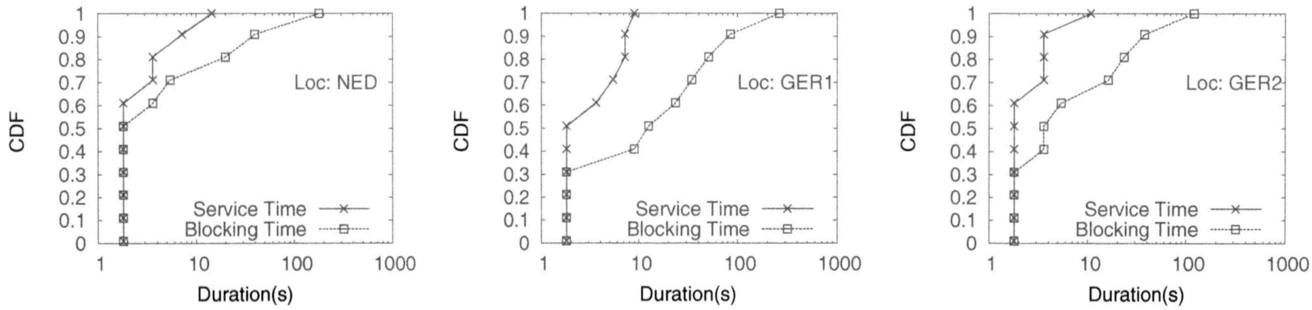

Figure 10: Cumulative distributions of secondary user's blocking and service time, measured on all three locations, using a 2-hour segment of randomly selected channels (same as the channels used in Figure 5), using SKA and 0.1 primary user disruption limit. We see that the median blocking time is an order of magnitude higher than the primary user busy time in Figure 5, while the median service time is an order of magnitude smaller than the primary user idle time.

low availability values. This is because some segments have fewer idle periods where the performance of a random access scheme like NKA does not converge to its expected value of 10%. Nevertheless, the extraction rate remains stable for all the availability values.

SKA's extraction rate, however, shows significant variance, especially at high spectrum availability regions. This is not triggered by the lack of idle instances, but the large variations in the distribution of primary user idle time. While many segments display similar average availability, their primary user idle time distributions and access strategies are significantly different, leading to notably large difference in their extraction rates. Overall, we observe a weak relationship between the extraction rate and the average availability.

Next, we compare the amount of spectrum extracted to the amount of spectrum available. Intuitively, a channel with larger availability will produce more usable spectrum using opportunistic access, which has been widely used to evaluate opportunistic access [8, 5]. Our results in Figure 9(c) show that such claim can be problematic. Again we observe significant variance in terms of the actual amount of spectrum extracted, particularly at high availability values. For example, for GSM1800DL at NED, the uncertainty (standard deviation/mean) of using the availability to predict the extracted spectrum is 36%. Therefore, an important conclusion from our analysis is that spectrum availability is no longer a sole metric to evaluate opportunistic spectrum access. One must also examine the access strategy as well as the primary user idle time distribution when comparing two frequency channels.

4.4 Usability of Extracted Spectrum

We also wish to understand the feasibility of using extracted spectrum channels to serve traditional wireless applications. To do so, we examine the statistical patterns of the channel service and blocking time experienced by secondary devices. For each frequency channel, the service time defines the time a secondary user can continuously access the channel while the blocking time defines the amount of time a secondary user must wait before accessing the channel.

Figure 10 shows the cumulative distribution of both metrics using the same set of channels in Figure 5 and the SKA scheme. Comparing this result to that of Figure 5 (the raw idle and busy duration of the channel), we see that the service time is one order of magnitude smaller than the primary user idle time, while the blocking time is one order of magnitude larger than the primary user busy time! While disappointing, this result is somewhat expected, given that the extraction rate of SKA is <30%.

The absolute values are not promising. Secondary users experience prolonged blocking (2-200 seconds) and short service time (2-10 seconds). This means that secondary users have a very lim-

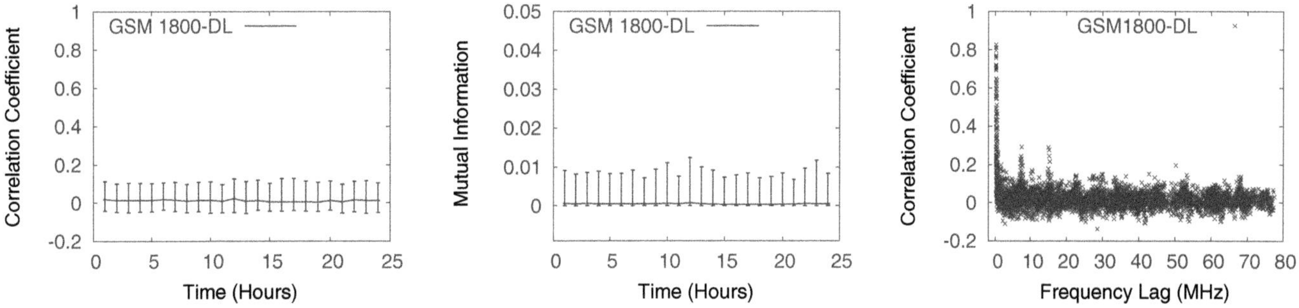

(a) Correlation Coefficient (b) Mutual Information (c) Impact of Frequency Separation

Figure 11: (a)-(b) Pair-wise correlation of GSM1800DL channels at NED across different hours of the day. Both correlation coefficient and mutual information are close to 0. (c) Correlation coefficient as a function of frequency separation. Adjacent channels are highly correlated due to imperfect alignment between measurement and service channels.

ited window for transmissions and face frequent interruptions. This type of access is unable to serve many of today's applications.

5. FREQUENCY BUNDLING

The results in Section 4 demonstrate that despite the abundant availability of partially used spectrum, the amount of spectrum actually accessible is much smaller than expected. More importantly, the extracted spectrum is heavily fragmented and scattered across time. Thus the equivalent channels available to secondary devices are highly unreliable.

In this section, we examine the feasibility of building reliable transmission channels by combining together multiple unreliable frequencies, utilizing frequency diversity to compensate for the lack of reliability on individual channels. We refer to this method as *frequency bundling*.

Frequency bundling is both feasible in practice and attractive to primary and secondary users. Recent advances in radio hardware design make frequency bundling practical for secondary users. New frequency-agile radios can combine non-contiguous frequency channels to form a single transmission [25]. This bundling can be performed either before allocation by a primary user or spectrum regulator, or after allocation by the secondary users themselves. In the second case, care must be taken to avoid bundling contention between secondary users.

Challenges. Frequency bundling faces two key challenges. First, how should secondary users choose and group channels? To reduce blocking time, one should group channels that complement each other in time, *i.e.* negatively correlated in their spectrum usage patterns. This motivates us to examine the correlation across channels using our measurement dataset. Second, given a bundle of frequency channels, how should we design multi-channel secondary access mechanisms that effectively utilize these channels? We address these questions in Section 5.1 and 5.2, respectively, and examine the bundling performance in Section 5.3.

5.1 Correlation among Frequency Channels

In searching for bundling strategies, we start by examining the correlation among frequency channels in terms of their primary user spectrum usage patterns. For this task, we again use the RWTH dataset because of its extensive coverage of frequency channels. We divide each channel trace into multiple 1-hour segments and compute pair-wise correlation among the channels by individual segments. We do not use our segmentation mechanism from Section 3 and 4 here, because it produces variable-length segments among channels that cannot be used to calculate time-domain correlation. We study correlation between channels within the same service as well as across adjacent services, considering that frequency-agile radios are likely to combine channels in close proximity.

We use two metrics to quantify correlation: *Pearson's correlation coefficient* [17] and *mutual information* [12].

Metric 1: Correlation Coefficient. For any two binary sequences, X and Y, the correlation coefficient is defined as:

$$\rho_{x,y} = \frac{E[(X-\mu_X)(Y-\mu_Y)]}{\sigma_X \sigma_Y}$$

where μ_X and μ_Y are the mean, σ_X and σ_Y are the standard deviation of X and Y, respectively. The value of $\rho_{x,y}$ ranges from -1 to 1, where -1 indicates strong negative correlation, 1 indicates strong positive correlation, and 0 indicates independency when X and Y are jointly normal [17]. While capturing both positive and negative correlation, this metric can only detect linear dependency.

Metric 2: Mutual Information. It is an entropy-based quantity for measuring the mutual dependency between any two sequences:

$$I(X;Y) = \sum_{x \in X} \sum_{y \in Y} p(x,y) \cdot log \frac{p(x,y)}{p(x)p(y)}$$

where $p(x,y)$ is the joint probability distribution function of X and Y, and $p(x)$ and $p(y)$ are the marginal probability distribution functions of X and Y, respectively. $I(X;Y)$ ranges from 0 to 1, where it is 0 if and only if X and Y are independent. Unlike correlation coefficient, this metric detects general dependency.

Results. Our analysis on the RWTH dataset shows that channels display little dependency unless they are adjacent in frequency. As an illustrative example, Figures 11(a) and (b) plot both correlation metrics over a day using all the GSM1800DL channels at NED. We segment the 24-hour duration into 24 1-hour segments, and for each hour calculate the pair-wise correlation among all the channel pairs. We show our results by the median, 5% and 95% values of the channel pairs. We see that all these values are close to 0, indicating minimum correlation between channels.

Figure 11(c) shows a detailed trace of the correlation coefficient as a function of frequency separation. Again it shows that unless the two channels are adjacent to each other, there is no sign

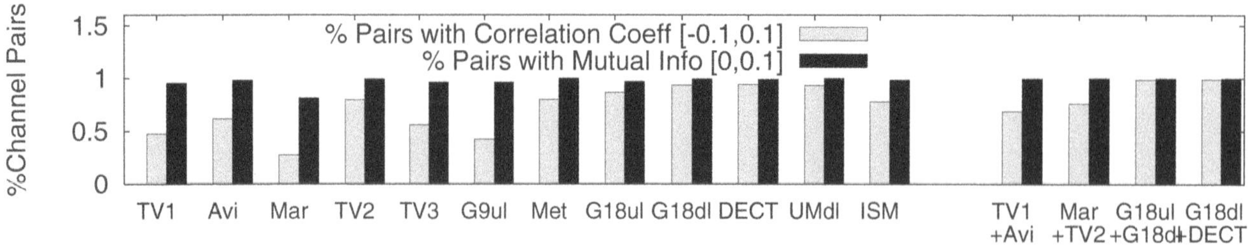

Figure 12: Percentage of pairs with correlation coefficient between [-0.1,0.1] and mutual information between [0,0.1] at NED. A high percentage of channel pairs have very low correlation both within a service and across services.

of strong correlation. The strong correlation among close pairs (those separated by less than 400KHz) can be explained by two reasons. First, while the RWTH measurement channels are of the same width as the GSM1800 service channels (200kHz), they are, however, not perfectly aligned with the GSM1800 service channels. Thus, adjacent measurement channels may map to the same service channel and hence appear heavily correlated. Second, adjacent channels can produce cross-band interference to each other, which makes them inherently correlated. The same was found from our UCSB GSM measurement results.

We have examined other services over different time periods and the results show very similar trends. To illustrate the general trend across all the services, in Figure 12 we show the portion of channel pairs with correlation coefficient between [-0.1,0.1] and mutual information between [0.0.1]. In addition to considering channel pairs within each service, we also include the result of channel pairs across adjacent services. We see that the majority of channel pairs, either within the same or adjacent services, display very little correlation. The correlation result is service-dependent because each service has different transmission properties and service channel width.

Summary of Findings. Our analysis on pair-wise channel correlation leads to two key findings:

- Most of the channel pairs, either within a service or between adjacent services, display little correlation.
- Frequency channel pairs that are adjacent in frequency display relatively high correlation.

These results imply that opportunistic spectrum access across a frequency range will produce multiple channels with little correlation in their available spectrum patterns.

5.2 Bundling Frequency Channels

The availability independency across channels means that we can significantly improve overall reliability by simply bundling random channel pairs together. In the following, we first describe three candidate methods to access channels in a bundle, and then present our method for forming channel bundles.

Using Frequency Bundles. We propose three usage models, each mapping to a specific radio configuration and application type.

- *Channel Switching* (for simplified hardware) – We consider secondary users with WiFi-like radios that can only access a single channel, but can switch between channels on the fly. In this model, each user switches to another channel in the bundle when the current channel becomes busy or too risky to access. One artifact of this model is that because secondary users cannot monitor each channel continuously, they cannot use SKA which requires the channel usage history. Instead, they can only use NKA and extract less spectrum.
- *Channel Redundancy* (for maximum reliability) – In this model, secondary users can sense and communicate on multiple channels simultaneously. To maximize transmission reliability and minimize blocking time, this model sends the same data stream on all the idle channels in the bundle. When a channel becomes blocked, it skips the data stream. Because secondary users can sense and monitor each channel, they use SKA to access each channel independently. This model focuses on maximizing reliability – unless all the channels are inaccessible, secondary users can communicate continuously.
- *Channel Multiplexing* (for maximum bandwidth) – This model also accesses multiple channels simultaneously using individual SKA, but multiplexes the data stream across current idle channels without any redundancy. Different from the Redundancy model, the effective transmission bandwidth varies over time.

Forming Frequency Bundles. We choose a random bundling method. It takes as input, k, the bundle size, and randomly selects k channels from the channel pool to form a bundle. We choose this method because of two reasons. First, the best strategy to minimize blocking time for all three models is to combine channels that complement each other, *i.e.* negatively correlated. Yet because the majority of channel pairs show no sign of correlation, random bundling wins due to its simplicity. Second, we use random bundling to understand the performance trend of opportunistic access with different bundle sizes, and to evaluate practical situations where secondary users have a small pool of channels for bundling. We only consider partially used channels for bundling, since adding idle channels simply increases the bundle capacity by a fixed amount.

5.3 Bundling Performance

Using the RWTH data set, we evaluate the effectiveness of frequency bundling by combining channels from the same services. We divide an one-day trace into one-hour segments, randomly bundle channels together, and simulate the three usage models on each segment. As usual, we only consider channels with daily average availability within [0.05,0.95], and assume a primary user disruption limit of η=0.1.

We evaluate frequency bundling by the resulting channel's blocking time and extracted spectrum. In this case, the blocking time of a frequency bundle is the duration where all the channels are busy

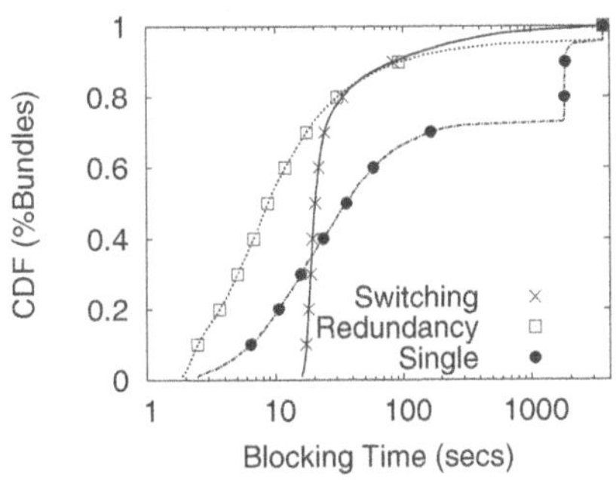

(a) Blocking Time

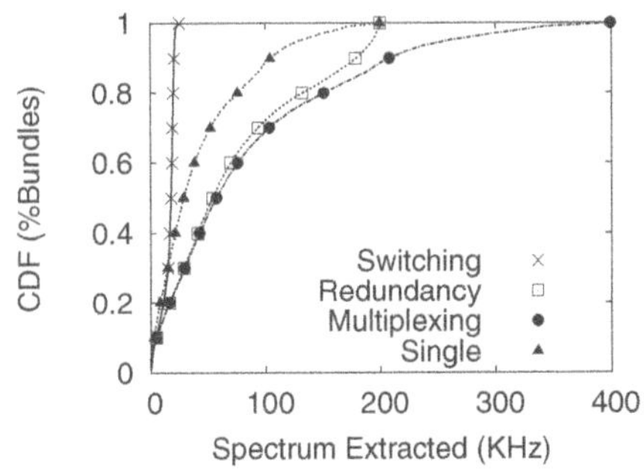

(b) Extracted Spectrum

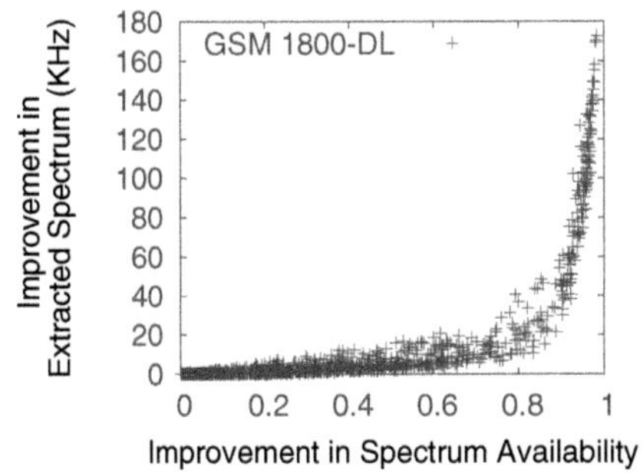

(c) Extracted Spectrum vs Availability

Figure 13: The performance of 2-channel frequency bundling from all the 15 services at the NED location. Redundancy experiences the lowest blocking time, and Multiplexing enjoys the highest extracted spectrum. Yet for 70+% of bundles, Redundancy has similar extracted spectrum as Multiplexing. This is because of (c) the non-linearity between the improvement in available spectrum and those in effective spectrum availability.

or too risky to access. The extracted spectrum defines the amount of spectrum used to send unique information. For Multiplexing, this is the sum of those from each channel in the bundle, while for Redundancy, it must discount periods where both channels simultaneously extract their spectrum (but use them to send the same information).

2-Channel Bundling. Figures 13(a)-(b) plot the cumulative distribution of secondary user's blocking time and extracted spectrum using 2-channel bundles. We compare the performance of Single-channel, Switching, Redundancy and Multiplexing. The performance of Single-channel is the mean of the two channels bundled together. Figure 13(a) shows that Redundancy has the least blocking time by utilizing every available channel to avoid blockage. On the other hand, Switching experiences 16+ seconds blocking time. This is because Switching uses NKA due to lack of continuous channel monitoring. With a 0.1 primary user disruption limit, in average its users will be blocked by 90% of time, or a blocking time of $9 * 1.8 = 16.2s$. On the other hand, if we extend Switching to monitor each channel continuously, its performance will approach that of Redundancy for the 2-channel case.

Figure 13(b) examines the actual spectrum extracted from these bundles. As expected, Multiplexing extracts the largest amount of spectrum by avoiding redundancy across channels. Yet surprisingly, Redundancy performs similar to Multiplexing for 70% of the bundles. This is due to the non-linear mapping between spectrum available and spectrum extracted (discussed in Section 4, Figure 9(c)). While Multiplexing improves the effective spectrum availability, its improvement in the spectrum extracted is limited. We confirm this hypothesis in Figure 13(c), plotting the improvement in extracted spectrum as a function of the improvement in the effective spectrum availability. Even after adding 0.8 (or a raw 160KHz) to the effective availability, the actual extraction improvement is only 20-30KHz.

Impact of Bundle Size. Next we investigate how the performance of frequency bundling scales with the size of the bundle. Using the same pool of channels, we vary the bundle size k between 2 and 10, and measure the resulting secondary user blocking time, service time as well as extracted spectrum. Results for the Redundancy model in Figure 14 (a)-(c) show that bundling can effectively reduce blocking time and increase service time. In fact, a linear increase in the bundling size k leads to one order of magnitude reduction in blocking time and improvement in service time. As k increases beyond 5, the performance quickly converges because additional channels do not offer any new availability. These results clearly demonstrate the effectiveness of frequency bundling.

The absolute values of average blocking and service times look very promising. For the 6 services shown in this result, bundling k=10 channels randomly creates a pseudo single channel that enjoys in average a prolonged service time of 120–1300 seconds and occasionally 2–4 seconds interruptions. These numbers are almost two orders of magnitude better than the single channel performance.

Figure 14(d) plots extracted spectrum for various bundle sizes using the Multiplexing model. Like the Redundancy model, the spectrum extracted increases exponentially with bundle size. The improvement is much higher than that of the redundancy model because multiplexing transmits different data on each channel to maximize spectrum utilization. Unlike the Redundancy model, however, the amount of usable spectrum varies across time depending on the availability of each channel in the bundle.

5.4 Summary of Findings

Our analysis in this section leads to two key findings:

- In terms of their spectrum availability patterns, the majority of frequency channel pairs in our dataset (200kHz in size) display little correlation, unless they are adjacent in frequency.
- Frequency bundling can effectively build reliable and high performance frequency channels from multiple unreliable channels. Even with random bundling, the improvement in secondary user's service and blocking time scales exponentially with the bundle size.

6. IMPACT OF TIME GRANULARITY

Finally, we wish to understand the impact of the sweeping interval in our conclusions. In particular, are the measurements sufficiently fine grain to capture the variability in primary user access patterns? If so, then secondary devices can improve their spectrum usage by simply sensing and accessing channels at a finer time granularity. If not, then what are the potential artifacts when secondary devices sense and access channels at a coarser granularity than the variability in primary user access patterns?

We use the 2nd dataset (collected locally by us for this project) to answer these questions. It only covers the GSM1900 downlink

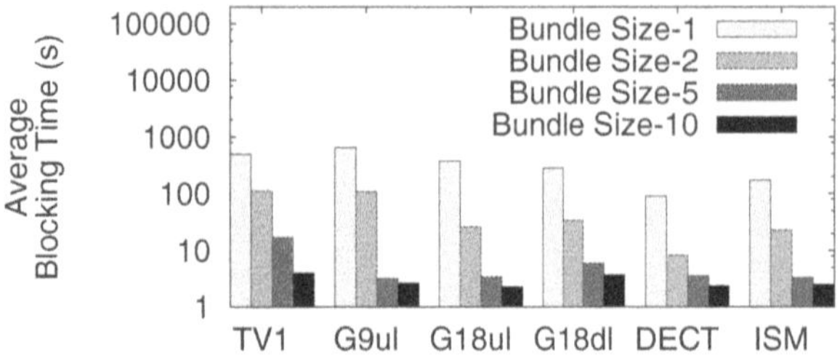

(a) Blocking Time, Redundancy Model

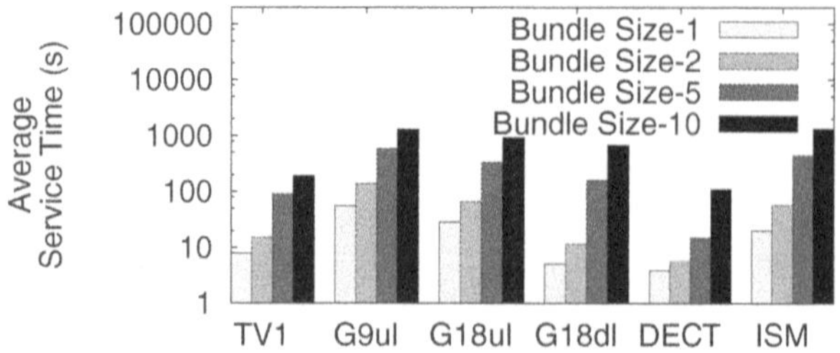

(b) Service Time, Redundancy Model

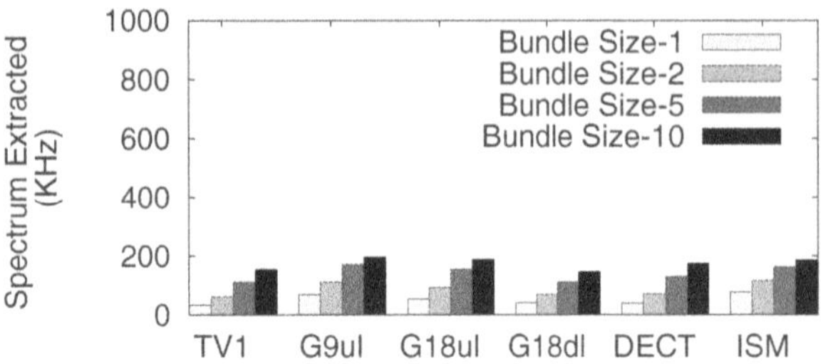

(c) Extracted Spectrum, Redundancy Model

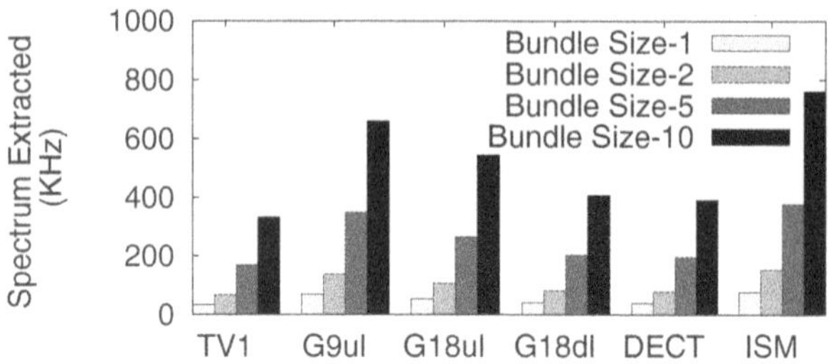

(d) Extracted Spectrum, Multiplexing Model

Figure 14: (a-c) Impact of bundle size on average blocking time, service time and extracted spectrum, using random bundling and the Redundancy model, for 6 services over a period of one day. The improvement in both blocking time and service time scales exponentially with the bundle size k. (d) Impact of bundle size on extracted spectrum, using random bundling and the Multiplexing model, for 6 services over a period of one day.

frequency band (1925MHz-1995MHz), but uses a sweep interval of 0.65s. Out of 300 channels we measured, 91 were partially used and thus considered in our analysis.

The Need for Fine Grained Measurements. Figure 15 compares the distribution of the spectrum availability and channel idle time on each of the 91 channels. We segment traces into one-hour segments. To examine the impact of sweep time, we compare the results by using 0.65, 1.3 and 1.95 seconds sweep time. The measurement results of the latter two were obtained by downsampling the original measurement traces. We see that while their average availabilities appear similar, the measurement results using different sweep times display different idle duration distributions. This means that the variations in channel availability continue at finer time scales, and secondary devices cannot simply improve performance by working at finer time scales.

Artifacts of Using Coarse Granularity. The above results show that the current measurement granularity (1.8 seconds and even 0.65 seconds) is unable to capture variations in primary user spectrum access. With this in mind, we wish to understand the potential artifacts when secondary devices use coarse access granularity than that of channel availability variations.

We use the measured traces (with slot size of τ) to approximate true primary user access patterns. To implement coarse access granularity, we consider opportunistic access with slot size of $k\tau$ by subsampling the traces by a factor of k. This means that secondary users sense the channel at the start of each $k\tau$ interval, and make access decision for the entire $k\tau$ interval. For a fair comparison, we evaluate all the access systems using the same primary user access patterns and the same, exact statistical knowledge on primary user access patterns.

We examine the artifacts of using k=2 and 3 (1.3s and 1.95s access slots) and the SKA scheme. Figure 16(a)-(b) show the cumulative distribution of the normalized change in extraction rate and the actual primary user disruption rate, across all channel segments. Using coarser access granularity leads to both overly conservative and aggressive access decisions – the normalized change of extraction rate is between 0.6 and 1.4. These suboptimal decisions lead to 0–0.4 primary user disruptions. On 45+% of channel segments, they violate the primary user disruption limit (0.1). This shows that only if secondary user's access granularity is no coarser than that of variations in primary user access patterns, can SKA defined in (1) fully satisfy the primary user disruption limit. When using a coarser access granularity, secondary users must modify their SKA scheme in order to avoid disrupting primary users.

These improper access decisions occur because secondary users must round the optimal fine-grained access decision by the coarser time granularity, either stop transmission too earlier or too late. Intuitively, the impact of such rounding effect is most severe when primary user access patterns display small idle durations. This is further confirmed by the results in Figure 16(c), which plot the normalized difference in extraction rate vs. the average primary user idle duration.

7. RELATED WORK

We classify the related work into spectrum measurement studies and opportunistic spectrum access.

Spectrum Measurements. Several measurement campaigns have studied spectrum occupancy across the globe [1, 5, 7, 13, 23, 24]. All of them have discovered significant opportunities for opportunistic spectrum access. An extensive measurement on 30MHz-3GHz frequency bands at six US locations [1] identified a maxi-

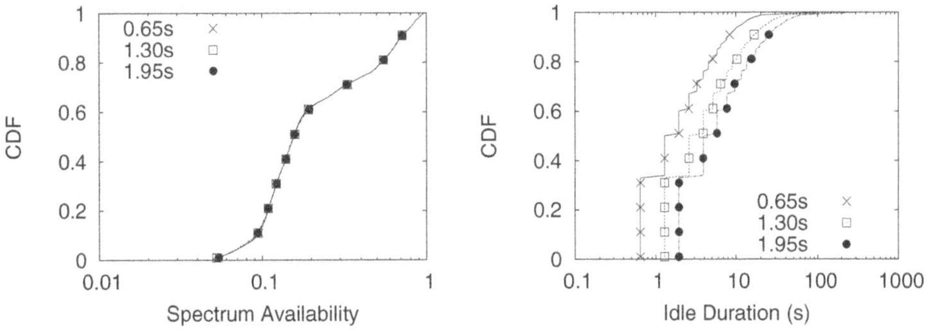

Figure 15: Statistics of observed spectrum availability using different measurement sweep times. Changes in sweeping time have little impact on the availability distribution, but significantly affect the idle time distribution.

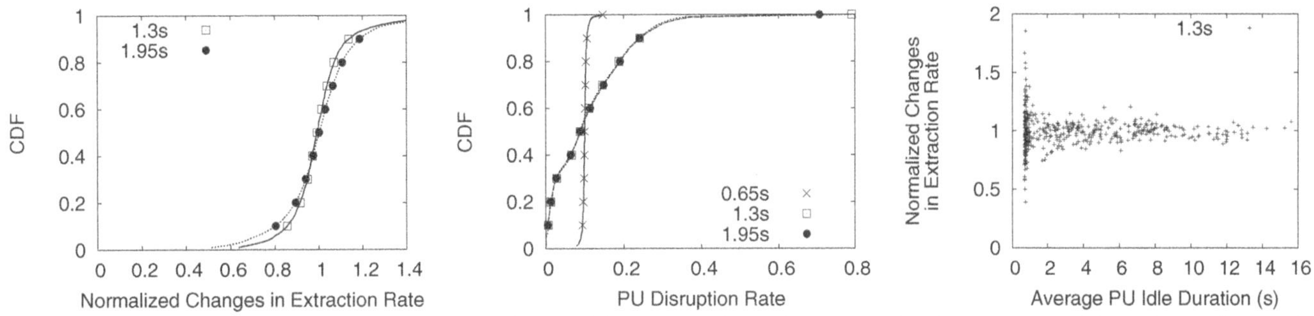

(a) CDF of Norm. Change in Extraction Rate (b) CDF of Primary User Disruption Rate (c) Dependency on Primary User Idle Duration

Figure 16: Artifacts of using coarser access granularity. (a) The cumulative distribution of the normalized difference in extraction rate (the extraction rate of systems using $k\tau$ slots divided by that of systems using τ). The value ranges between 0.6 and 1.4, implying both overly conservative and aggressive access decisions. (b) Using the original SKA scheme under coarser access granularity can violate the primary user disruption limit. It must be modified to include additional conservativeness. (c) The artifacts amplify on channels with small average primary user idle duration.

mum 13% spectrum occupancy. Measurements on 2006 Football World Cup at two Germany locations shows significant variations in spectrum usage before, during and after the match. Significant variance was also found on cellular network's spectrum usage, using call logs over three weeks [24]. Recent measurement study at four Chinese locations detects strong dependency across frequency channels and applies a pattern matching algorithm to predict channel state from past observations [7]. Finally, the Mobnets group from RWTH performed extensive measurements at three European locations [23].

Our work differs from existing works by examining the actual spectrum accessible to secondary users without violating the primary user disruption limit. Even with accurate knowledge of primary user access statistics, we show that the accessible spectrum is significantly less than the available spectrum. We then propose and evaluate frequency bundling that builds high-quality transmissions out of many scattered spectrum fragments. Different from [7], our analysis shows that channels are mostly independent in their spectrum occupancy patterns. These differences might be attributed to two factors: 1) differences in usage at different measurement sites and 2) inclusion of completely busy and idle channels in [7] during correlation calculation.

Opportunistic Spectrum Access. Research efforts in this area have developed both analytical access strategies and models [14, 21, 19, 28] as well as practical algorithms and systems [4, 9, 22]. They have motivated us to consider practical opportunistic access systems and to quantify the actual accessible spectrum. While most of these works either assume analytical models on primary user access patterns or focus on realizing sensing and accessing in real systems, our work offers a complementary study that uses real world measurement traces to understand the feasibility and effectiveness of opportunistic spectrum access.

8. CONCLUSION

Little is known about how well secondary devices in dynamic spectrum networks can make use of the partially utilized channels occupied by primary users. We present in this paper the first comprehensive study on the level of "usable" spectrum available to secondary devices while respecting hard limits on disruptions to primary users. Our analysis of extensive fine-grain spectrum usage traces shows that even with extensive statistical knowledge on primary user access patterns, and while running optimal algorithms, secondary devices can only extract 20–30% of available spectrum in a channel. While this means current access schemes cannot provide usable channels to support traditional applications, we can regain reasonable levels of reliability by bundling multiple unreliable channels together. Our analysis shows very little to no correlation in spectrum usage patterns across channels, which leads us to choose a simple random frequency bundling scheme. We also show that performing fine-grain extensive spectrum measurement is critical to understanding the performance and limitations of opportunistic spectrum access, and that the granularity of current measurements is not enough to fully capture original owner's spectrum usage variations.

Acknowledgments

We express our sincere thanks to the RWTH Mobnets group for sharing their spectrum measurement dataset. We also thank the anonymous reviewers for their valuable feedback. This work is supported by the National Science Foundation under CNS-0832090, CNS-0905667, CNS-0546216, and IIS-0847925, a research grant from Intel Corporation, and an equipment gift from Agilent. Any opinions, findings, and conclusions or recommendations expressed in this material are those of the authors and do not necessarily reflect the views of the National Science Foundation.

9. REFERENCES

[1] `http://sharedspectrum.com/measurements.`

[2] `http://download.mobnets.rwth-aachen.de.`

[3] AKYILDIZ, I. F., LEE, W.-Y., VURAN, M. C., AND MOHANTY, S. NeXt generation/dynamic spectrum access/cognitive radio wireless networks: A survey. *Computer Networks 50* (May 2006), 2127–2159.

[4] BAHL, P., CHANDRA, R., MOSCIBRODA, T., MURTY, R., AND WELSH, M. White space networking with Wi-Fi like connectivity. In *Proc. of SIGCOMM* (2009).

[5] BLASCHKE, V., JAEKEL, H., RENK, T., KLOECK, C., AND JONDRAL, F. K. Occupation Measurements Supporting Dynamic Spectrum Allocation for Cognitive Radio Design. In *Proc. of CrownCom* (2007).

[6] CAO, L., AND ZHENG, H. Spectrum allocation in ad hoc networks via local bargaining. In *Proc. of SECON* (2005).

[7] CHEN, D., YIN, S., ZHANG, Q., LIU, M., AND LI, S. Mining Spectrum Usage Data: a Large-scale Spectrum Measurement Study. In *Proc. of MobiCom* (2009).

[8] DATLA, D., RAJBANSHI, R., WYGLINSKI, A. M., AND MINDEN, G. J. Parametric Adaptive Spectrum Sensing Framework for Dynamic Spectrum Access Networks. In *Proc. of IEEE DySPAN* (2007).

[9] DEB, S., SRINIVASAN, V., AND MAHESHWARI, R. Dynamic spectrum access in DTV whitespaces: design rules, architecture and algorithms. In *Proc. of MobiCom* (2009).

[10] DIGHAM, F. F., ALOUINI, M. S., AND SIMON, M. K. On the energy detection of unknown signals over fading channels. In *Proc. of ICC* (2003).

[11] DOPPLER, K., RINNE, M., WIJTING, C., RIBEIRO, C. B., AND HUGL, K. Device-to-Device Communication as an Underlay to LTE-Advanced Networks. *IEEE Communications Magazine 47* (December 2009), 42–49.

[12] FANO, R. Transmission of Information: A Statistical Theory of Communication. *MIT Press* (March 1961).

[13] HOLLAND, O., CORDIER, P., MUCK, M., MAZET, L., KLOCK, C., AND RENK, T. Spectrum Power Measurements in 2G and 3G Cellular Phone Bands During the 2006 Football World Cup in Germany. In *Proc. of IEEE DySPAN* (2007).

[14] HUANG, S., LIU, X., AND DING, Z. Optimal Transmission Strategies for Dynamic Spectrum Access in Cognitive Radio Networks. *IEEE Transactions on Mobile Computing 8* (December 2009), 1636–1648.

[15] KEOGH, E., CHU, S., HART, D., AND PAZZANI, M. Segmenting Time Series: A Survey and Novel Approach. *Data mining in time series databases* (1993), 1–21.

[16] MCHENRY, M. NSF Spectrum Occupancy Measurements Project Summary. Shared Spectrum Company Report, 2005.

[17] PEARSON, K. Contributions to the mathematical theory of evolution, II: Skew variation in homogeneous material. *Philosophical Transactions of the Royal Society of London 186* (January 1895), 343–414.

[18] PENG, C., ZHENG, H., AND ZHAO, B. Y. Utilization and fairness in spectrum assignemnt for opportunistic spectrum access. *Mobile Networks and Applications (MONET) 11* (May 2006), 555–576.

[19] SAHAI, A., HOVEN, N., AND TANDRA, R. Some Fundamental Limits on Cognitive Radio. In *Proc. of Allerton Conference* (2004).

[20] SHELLHAMMER, S., AND CHOUINARD, G. Spectrum sensing requirements summary. IEEE 802.22-05/22-06-0089-05-0000, 2006.

[21] SRINIVASA, S., AND JAFAR, S. The Throughput Potential of Cognitive Radio: A Theoretical Perspective. In *Proc. of Asilomar Conference on Signals, Systems and Computers* (2006).

[22] WELLENS, M., DE BAYNAST, A., AND MÄHÖNEN, P. Performance of dynamic spectrum access based on spectrum occupancy statistics. *IET Communications 2* (July 2008), 772–782.

[23] WELLENS, M., RIIHIJÄRVI, J., AND MÄHÖNEN, P. Empirical time and frequency domain models of spectrum use. *Physical Communications 2* (May 2009), 10–32.

[24] WILLKOMM, D., MACHIRAJU, S., BOLOT, J., AND WOLISZ, A. Primary Users in Cellular Networks: A Large-Scale Measurement Study. In *Proc. of IEEE DySPAN* (2008).

[25] YANG, L., HOU, W., CAO, L., ZHAO, B. Y., AND ZHENG, H. Supporting Demanding Wireless Applications with Frequency-agile Radios. In *Proc. of NSDI* (2010).

[26] ZHANG, W., MALLIK, R., AND LETAIEF, K. Cooperative Spectrum Sensing Optimization in Cognitive Radio Networks. In *Proc. of ICC* (2008).

[27] ZHAO, Q., AND SWAMI, A. A Survey of Dynamic Spectrum Access: Signal Processing and Networking Perspectives. In *Proc. of ICASSP* (2007).

[28] ZHAO, Q., TONG, L., SWAMI, A., AND CHEN, Y. Decentralized cognitive MAC for opportunistic spectrum access in ad hoc networks: A POMDP framework. *IEEE JSAC 25* (April 2007), 589–600.

Primitives for Active Internet Topology Mapping: Toward High-Frequency Characterization

Robert Beverly
Naval Postgraduate School
rbeverly@nps.edu

Arthur Berger
MIT CSAIL / Akamai
awberger@csail.mit.edu

Geoffrey G. Xie
Naval Postgraduate School
xie@nps.edu

ABSTRACT

Current large-scale topology mapping systems require multiple days to characterize the Internet due to the large amount of probing traffic they incur. The accuracy of maps from existing systems is unknown, yet empirical evidence suggests that additional fine-grained probing exposes hidden links and temporal dynamics. Through longitudinal analysis of data from the Archipelago and iPlane systems, in conjunction with our own active probing, we examine how to shorten Internet topology mapping cycle time. In particular, this work develops discriminatory primitives that maximize topological fidelity while being efficient.

We propose and evaluate adaptive probing techniques that leverage external knowledge (e.g., common subnetting structures) and data from prior cycle(s) to guide the selection of probed destinations and the assignment of destinations to vantage points. Our *Interface Set Cover* (ISC) algorithm generalizes previous dynamic probing work. Crucially, ISC runs across probing cycles to minimize probing while detecting load balancing and reacting to topological changes. To maximize the information gain of each trace, our *Subnet Centric Probing* technique selects destinations more likely to expose their network's internal structure. Finally, the *Vantage Point Spreading* algorithm uses network knowledge to increase path diversity to destination ingress points.

Categories and Subject Descriptors

C.2.3 [**Computer Communication Networks**]: Network Operations—*network monitoring*; C.2.1 [**Computer Communication Networks**]: Network Architecture and Design

General Terms

Measurement, Experimentation

Keywords

Internet Topology, Network Topology, Adaptive Probing

IMC'10, November 1–3, 2010, Melbourne, Australia.

1. INTRODUCTION

The scale of the Internet makes obtaining representative metrics and characteristics challenging. Compounding this challenge, the Internet is poorly instrumented, lacks measurement and management mechanisms [5], and providers hide information. Researchers therefore must frequently make inferences over limited available data, and may form false conclusions [15].

Understanding the complex structure of the Internet is vital for network research including routing, protocol validation, developing new architectures, etc. More importantly, building robust networks, and protecting critical infrastructure, depends on accurate topology mapping.

While dedicated platforms exist to perform topology measurements, e.g. [11, 19], these must balance induced measurement load against model fidelity. Unfortunately, in practice, such balancing results in multiple days worth of measurement to capture even an incomplete portion of the Internet. Employing more vantage points is an effective technique to improve topological recall [23], but does not reduce total load or cycle time.

This work proposes primitives toward the eventual goal of performing *high-frequency* active Internet topology measurement. Measurement load hinders the ability to capture small-scale dynamics and transient effects that occur at frequencies higher than the measurement period; effectively creating Nyquist aliasing loss. For example, recent work [20] shows fewer than 50% of Internet paths remain stationary across consecutive days. Our own analysis of set cover techniques [10] finds that the rate of missed interfaces increases in proportion to the time since the covering set was created: implying that "train-then-test" methodologies are insufficient.

Our work therefore focuses on two separable problems via a unified methodology, how to: i) *select destinations* in the network to probe; and ii) *perform the probe*. We examine the hypothesis that by leveraging external network knowledge, e.g. routing, address structure, etc., and adaptive probing, the active traffic load can be significantly reduced without sacrificing the inferred topology fidelity. Our methodology extends prior schemes, e.g. [8] which attempt to reduce measurement overhead, but are artificially parametrized, lossy, and ignore temporal effects across measurement periods. Toward high-frequency Internet topology mapping, we:

1. Quantify unnecessary probing performed by production topology measurement platforms.
2. Develop three algorithms that use network knowledge to intelligently drive adaptive probing.

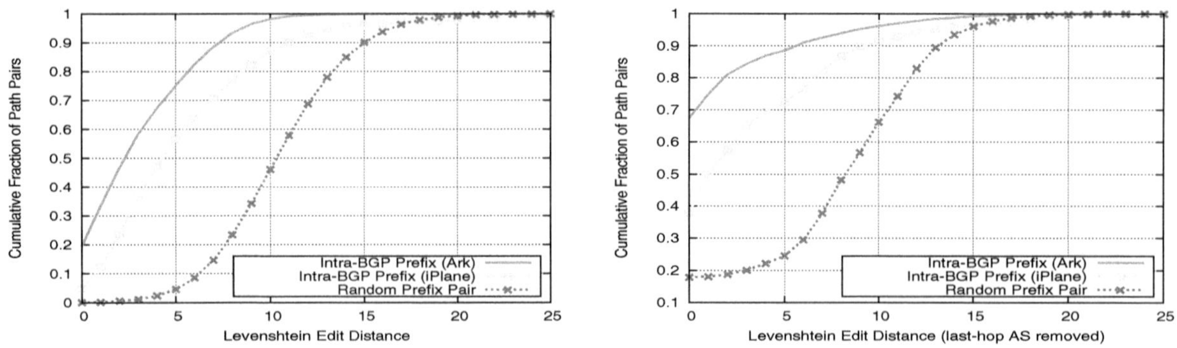

(a) Unnecessary probing: > 60% of intra-BGP traces have $ED \leq 3$; fewer than 50% of random traces have $ED \leq 10$.

(b) Contribution of last-hop AS to path variance: $\sim$ 70% of probes to same prefix yield no information gain beyond the leaf AS.

Figure 1: Edit distance (ED) distribution of Ark ($\simeq 260k$) and iPlane ($\simeq 150k$) traces to *different* addresses within the *same* BGP prefix compared to baseline ED between random trace pairs.

2. UNNECESSARY PROBING

Several large topology measurement experiments have been deployed, including CAIDA's Skitter/Archipelago project (Ark) [11, 13], iPlane [19], and DIMES [22]. To better understand the challenges in topology mapping, this section focuses on the existing practice of Ark and iPlane which infer interface-level topologies via traceroute-like [1, 17] probing.

So that measurement is tractable, production systems often follow common assumptions over the Internet's structure, for instance by probing a target in each subnetwork of size 2^8 (herein referred to via common /24 prefix notation). Ark subdivides all routed prefixes (i.e. visible in BGP) into /24's. A "cycle" of probing is a complete set of measurements to one destination address within each routed /24. The probe target for a given /24 is randomly selected from the 2^8 possible addresses.

With approximately half of all IP addresses globally routable, a cycle consists of $\sim 2^{31-8}$ /24s. Due to this large number of /24's to be probed in a cycle, approximately 9M, Ark divides the probing work among multiple vantage points (measurement sites). Probing at a /24 granularity requires significant time, and load. With asynchronous, distributed probing to mitigate per-path RTT variance, a full cycle requires multiple days to partially characterize the Internet.

Traces can be distilled into an interface-level representation of the Internet graph. Some traces yield more information than others based on the choice of prior probes. For instance, we expect traces to different addresses within the same BGP prefix to be similar, while probes to very different destination addresses are likely to have a higher information gain.

2.1 A Path Pair Distance Metric

To quantify the information gain of intra-BGP traces, we use the Levenshtein, or edit, distance which is a measure of the minimum number of insert, delete or modify operations required to equate two strings.

Let the alphabet of symbols be the unsigned 32-bit integer space, $\Sigma = \{0, \ldots, 2^{32} - 1\}$. We compute the edit distance (ED) between trace pairs using each IP address along the path. An ED of zero implies that the two paths are identical, whereas an ED of one implies that the two traces differ by a single interface addition, subtraction, or replacement. For example, for the following two interface paths, $ED(t_1, t_2) = 2$:

$t_1 =$ 1.2.6.1, 1.186.254.13, 2.245.179.52, 4.53.34.1

$t_2 =$ 1.2.6.1, 2.245.179.52, 4.69.15.1

We use data from a single Ark and single iPlane monitor in a January, 2010 cycle for ED analysis. As a comparative baseline, we also compute ED over an equal number of random trace pairs.

2.2 Quantifying Unnecessary Probing

Figure 1(a) shows the cumulative fraction of path pairs in Ark and iPlane as a function of ED. The ED is larger for the randomly selected traceroute path pairs than the pairs from within the same BGP prefix, as determined by a contemporaneous Routeviews [21] BGP routing table. Approximately 60% of traces to destination in the same BGP prefix have $ED \leq 3$ while fewer than 50% of random traces have $ED \leq 10$. Thus, as we intuitively expect, there is value to using the BGP structure to drive the probe target selection in order to maximize the information gain.

Next, we wish to quantify the contribution of the last hop autonomous system (AS) to the edit distance of traces to the same BGP prefix, i.e. path difference attributable to subnetting within an AS. For example, Figure 2 depicts the sources of path diversity observed as an "hourglass" with multiple vantage points contributing to diversity into an AS's ingress points, and the degree of subnetting within the destination AS contributing to the remaining diversity. The "waist" is the set of ingress points for a prefix which may be common to multiple traces or require distributed vantage points in order to be discovered (§4.3 discusses the diminishing return of additional vantage points).

Figure 1(b) is the result of an ED analysis after removing interface hops belonging to the destination AS, as determined by the Routeviews BGP table. We observe that for $\sim$ 70% of the probe pairs to the same prefix, there is zero additional information gain beyond the leaf-AS. Therefore, from this off-line analysis of traces from two important

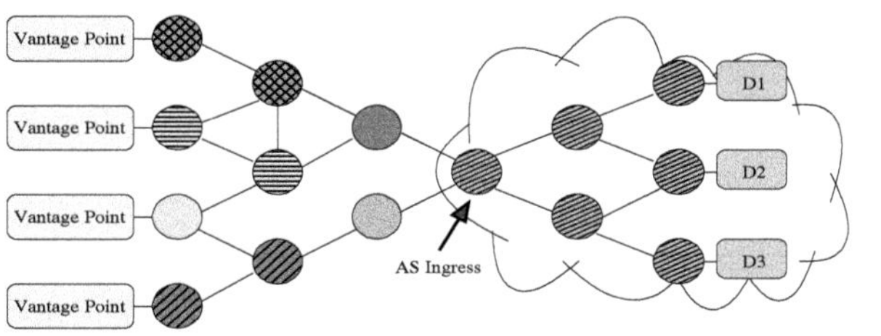

Figure 2: Topology information gain hourglass: path diversity comes via multiple vantage points and via multiple destinations in a prefix. The hourglass "waist" is the AS ingress point(s).

topology platforms, we conclude that there exist *significant possible packet savings* by intelligently tuning, e.g. via time-to-live (TTL), the set of hops each trace interrogates. For instance, a basic tracing strategy might start with a TTL suitable to reach the destination and iteratively decrement the TTL until a previously discovered hop, i.e. at the AS ingress, is found.

Moreover, in analyzing pairs of traceroutes to the same destination prefix, but from different vantage points, we find that in $\sim 30\%$ of the cases, entirely new paths are discovered. Only approximately 10% of the probes from a new vantage point yield less than four previously undiscovered interfaces. Thus, there exists *significant information gain from additional vantage points.*

These potential efficiencies have been recognized, most prominently by the DoubleTree method [8, 7]. Unfortunately, DoubleTree relies on heuristics to tune its probing. In §3 we detail non-parameterized primitives designed to address the low-gain we find here and provide efficiency without sacrificing inference power.

Note that the ED's for iPlane are higher than for Ark due a non-uniform distribution of traces to prefixes as part of the iPlane logic [18]. Since iPlane provides significantly fewer instances of multiple probes to the same prefix as compared with Ark, we can more readily test our primitives against the latter. We therefore use historic Ark data, as well as our own active probing, for the remainder of this paper.

3. ADAPTIVE PROBING METHODOLOGY

This section presents three strategies to illustrate the potential power of adaptive probing in reducing unnecessary probing: 1) *subnet centric probing*; 2) *interface set cover*; and 3) *vantage point spreading.*

3.1 Subnet Centric Probing

A naïve strategy of leveraging BGP knowledge is to probe exactly one destination within each advertised prefix. The potential for using BGP routing information was first recognized by Krishnamurty and Wang [14]. While we show that such an approach incurs approximately one-fifth of the normal amount of probing packets sent by Ark, it is too aggressive and misses significant topology information of networks with a rich subnetting structure.

Intuitively, we expect two numerically consecutive IP addresses to be more likely to share paths (and, hence, have a low *ED*) than two distant addresses. But simply employing address distance is too simplistic and does not capture typical network subnetting structure [4]. For example, the two IP addresses 18.255.255.254 and 19.1.1.1 have a numerical distance of 2, but they would belong to different networks unless both belonged to a single 18.0.0.0/7 subnetwork.

Instead, we propose to use the knowledge of how networks are subnetted (the preceding example illustrating an example where subnetting is much more probable than no subnetting) to select addresses to probe within each BGP advertised prefix. The motivation is to adapt the number of probes to the degree of subnetting within the prefix to avoid wasted probing. We term this strategy "subnet centric." The current Ark strategy assumes a fixed subnetting boundary, which may be too granular (wasted probing) or too coarse (missing information). In contrast, we ensure that subsequent destinations in a prefix are as distinct as possible in their most significant bits, i.e., likely part of distinct subnet prefixes. We term this selection of destination the *least common prefix* principle. For example, to choose four probes for prefix 192.168.0.0/16, our algorithm initially picks four addresses from the distinct prefixes: 192.168.0.0/18, 192.168.64.0/18, 192.168.128.0/18, and 192.168.192.0/18.

As probing progresses, we use our pair-wise ED measure to determine whether finer-grained destinations within a prefix are yielding useful additional information. The prefix is continually probed until the ED value of the paths returned by a pair falls within an empirically derived pre-determined threshold $\tau = 3$.

3.2 Interface Set Cover

DoubleTree [8] explores a method to adapt probing in real-time as a measurement cycle progresses. By beginning at a heuristically chosen mid-point and working both back to the vantage point (decreasing TTL) and toward the destination (increasing TTL), DoubleTree achieves packets savings by preempting a trace when a previously discovered interface is observed – the inherent assumption is that subsequent probes along the path will be duplicates of previous traces.

While DoubleTree's technique partially addresses our findings in §2, it must determine a path's mid-point and does not cope well with load balancing. More importantly, it treats each cycle independently and is agnostic to information learned in previous probing cycles. Our goal is to leverage this knowledge to reduce the number of trace packets in subsequent cycles.

We hypothesize a greedy *Interface Set Cover* (ISC) scheme that always selects a subset of probing packets based on the interface-level topology of the previous cycle. More specifically, the interface-level topology includes directed edges where the direction of the edge records the direction of a probe. (It is not a problem if an edge is bi-directional, which for the interface-level graph should occur only as outliers.) The ISC scheme iteratively selects paths, and sub-paths, from the directed interface-level topology of the previous round, such that packets would probe interfaces that are not yet accounted for by the paths already selected. The initial "bootstrap" set of destinations may be chosen using our subnet centric probing algorithm. We note that the optimization problem of identifying a *minimum subset* of paths to cover the interfaces discovered is an instance of the well-known NP-complete "Min Set Cover" problem. However, efficient greedy solutions have been shown to be $ln\ n$ approximate of optimal [9].

Formally, let $\mathbf{P}$ be a set of paths from vantage points to destinations. Each $\vec{p_i} \in \mathbf{P}$ is a vector of router interfaces

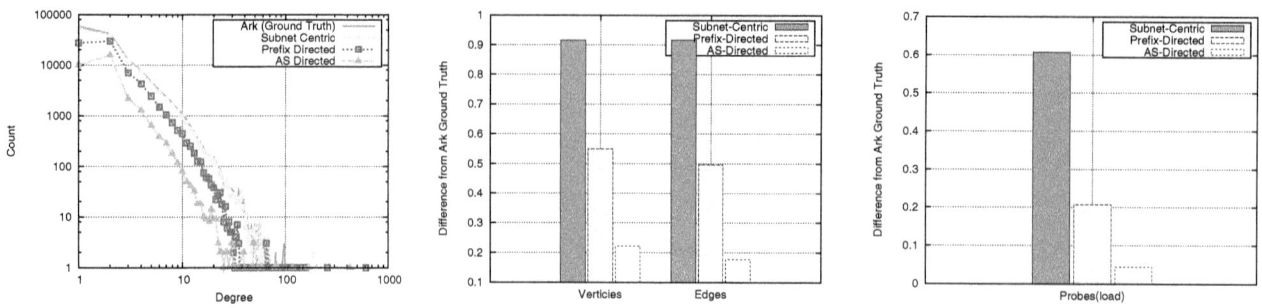

(a) Inferred degree distribution: subnet centric probing well approximates Ark ground truth.

(b) Model fidelity: Subnet centric probing captures $\geq 90\%$ of the vertices and edges.

(c) Induced load: Subnet centric uses $\simeq 60\%$ of the ground truth load.

Figure 3: Subnet Centric directed probing performance.

corresponding to the i'th path. Let the universe of interfaces be $\mathbf{I} = \bigcup_{i,j} p_i[j]$. A sub-path, $p_i[n : m]$, is the n through m'th hops of $\vec{p_i}$, and includes the case of a full path[1]. The *size* of sub-path $|p_i[n : m]|$ is $m - n + 1$, i.e. the number of packets to probe hops n through m. The ISC problem is to find the set of sub-paths from $\mathbf{P}$ with minimum total size among all subsets of paths covering $\mathbf{I}$. We thus contrast ISC with the full set cover problem that finds a covering set of paths $\vec{p_i}$ from $\mathbf{P}$ of minimum size.

We observe that a tension exists between the two conflicting goals of reducing probing traffic and capturing dynamic forwarding paths. Many networks deploy traffic engineering and load balancing. Thus, regardless of whether only full paths or sub-paths are used, we expect that probes will reveal deviations from the prior cycle. When this occurs, we augment ISC with a "change driven" logic: during the interface verification phase, if an interface other than expected is found, ISC begins a DoubleTree-like strategy probing outward in both directions from the unexpected interface. This allows ISC to not only learn of load balancing over multiple cycles, but also adapt to underlying topological changes.

3.3 Vantage Point Spreading

Internet-scale mapping involves probing from dozens of different vantage points (VPs). How to divide the probing among VPs presents another opportunity for an adaptive strategy to reduce the probing traffic. However, as our preceding analysis in §2 shows, additional vantage points yield more interface information. Further, in the next section we find that the information gain of additional VPs to the same destination decays slowly. Therefore, due to large value in any additional vantage points, we adopt a simple strategy for assigning destinations to VPs.

Our *vantage point spreading* algorithm simply uses as many distinct VPs as possible for the set of destinations within a given BGP prefix. When combined with *subnet centric probing*, as additional destinations are chosen from determined subnet prefixes, *vantage point spreading* will assign them, if possible, to VPs not yet used for the original BGP prefix, or otherwise distribute them as uniformly as possible when there are more destinations to be probed than VPs.

[1]In practice then, a trace sub-path has the same origin and destination IP addresses, but uses TTL=n to m.

4. RESULTS

Having defined our three intelligent topology measurement primitives, this section examines their individual performance through a series of Ark experiments.

4.1 Subnet Centric Probing

We evaluate the subnet centric probing strategy against a full cycle of Ark probing, which for the sake of this exercise we will consider to be the known ground-truth. Note that this ground-truth is a relative measure, rather than the actual topology which remains unknown. We simulate various strategies by filtering the full Ark probe data from a cycle, i.e. we simulate different resulting topologies by selectively using different available Ark paths. Our performance measures examine the balance between probing load and the topological structure resulting from the probes.

To gain intuition over using external BGP data to drive probe selection, we first follow a naïve strategy similar to [14]. We select a single destination per BGP prefix at random from the available Ark traces; effectively assuming that this single destination is representative of the entire cluster of destinations that fall within its prefix. Similarly, we experiment with an even coarser technique whereby trace destinations are clustered according to their AS and a single destination in the AS is deemed representative of the AS.

We build the interface-level graph as inferred by the raw Ark data as well as using a single destination per prefix and a single destination per AS. The degree distribution of the resulting inferred graphs is given Figure 3(a). While both naïve strategies capture a structure that appears similar to ground-truth from the full Ark data, there are large numbers of missing interfaces and edges (40-80% of total as shown in Figure 3(b)). However, as shown in Figure 3(c), the prefix clustering method requires approximately one-fifth of the full probing load while the AS clustering method results in even greater probe savings.

Armed with this intuition over the potential probe savings, we ask whether the subnet centric probing algorithm can strike a better balance between consumed probing load and the fidelity of the resulting topology. We observe no qualitative difference[2] in the topology resulting from the

[2]We omit other graph-theoretic measures [24, 16] for brevity, but note that such metrics show similarity to ground truth.

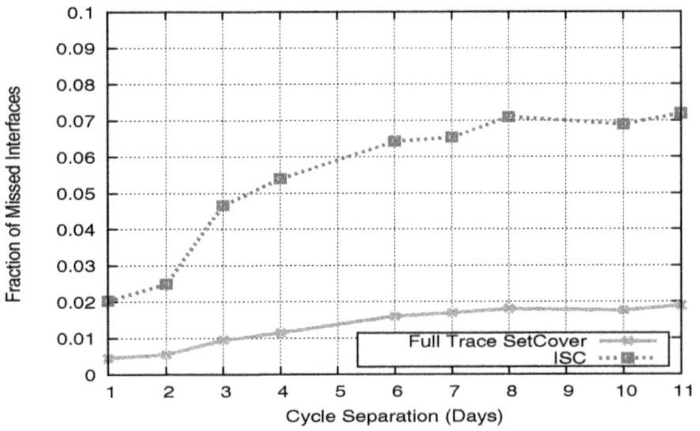

(a) Set cover performance (model interface fidelity relative to traceroute baseline).

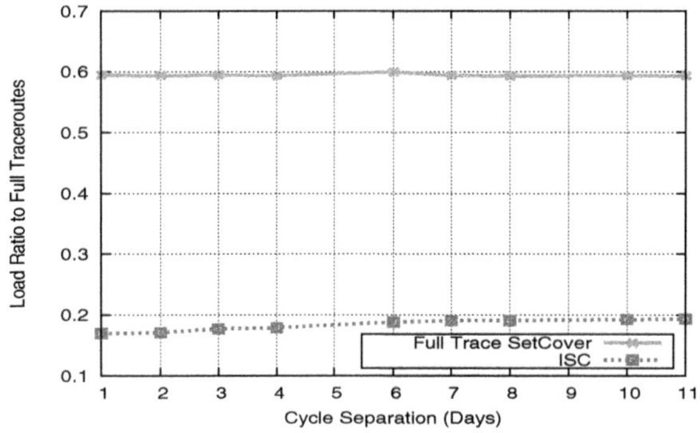

(b) Set cover efficiency (induced packet load relative to traceroute baseline).

Figure 4: Comparing full trace topology set covering and ISC techniques over time.

subnet centric approach versus the ground-truth in Figure 3(a). The subnet centric algorithm is able to capture $\geq 90\%$ of the ground truth vertices and edges while using less than 60% of the ground truth full probing load.

4.2 Interface Set Cover

Next, we examine the performance of the Interface Set Cover algorithm, but excluding the "change driven" logic (§3.2). In particular, we are concerned with how the performance of ISC compares with full trace set cover, the degradation of performance over time as the topology changes, and comparative load metrics.

We select 20,000 routed IP destinations at random for these experiments. Each day over a two-week period, we probe the same set of destinations from the same vantage point. The results from the first probing cycle are used to "train" the full set cover and ISC. Figure 4(a) show the fraction of missing interfaces using each set cover technique relative to the interfaces discovered from the full set of traces in that cycle.

We see that after a single day, the full trace set cover misses less than 1% of the interfaces while ISC misses approximately 2%. However, while the full trace set cover uses approximately 60% of the ground-truth probing load, ISC uses less than 20% – a huge savings. Note that for this comparison, we omit consideration of the last hop, the destination. If the destination were included and given that just one vantage point traces to a given destination (as is the case with Ark), then the full trace set cover yields no savings.

The performance of both set cover techniques degrades over time, with ISC degrading faster to 7% interfaces missing relative to ground-truth after 11 cycles. Thus, while set cover techniques can provide a significant savings in probe traffic, they alone do not suffice, as the topology changes over time. Thus, we augment ISC with "change driven" logic. Our expectation, to be tested in future experiments, is that the substantial additional savings in probe traffic with ISC, as compared with full traces, will dominate the amount of additional probing stimulated by the discovered deviations (new and absent interfaces) from the prior cycle.

4.3 Vantage Point Influence

To gain intuition over how to assign destinations to vantage points, we first perform a tightly controlled experiment where 2000 randomly selected destinations were each probed from 38 different vantage points. We wish to understand whether adding additional vantage points to probe the same destination increases the discovered topology, and at what point the gain in adding additional vantage points (VPs) diminishes. Figure 5(a) shows the average number of discovered interfaces for each probed destination as a function of the number of vantage points. In addition, the standard deviation error bars shows that the variance in discovered interfaces increases as the number of probing vantage points increases. We find that up to approximately ten vantage points, the number of discovered interfaces is linear, after which the influence of additional vantage points decreases. Yet, the decrease is quite slow – suggesting again that there is significant value in each additional vantage point. This finding contrasts with earlier results [2], suggesting that AS-level peering and interconnections have become richer [6].

Next, we examine vantage point spreading in the context of two other strategies: "random" which models Ark's current methodology and "single" which uses a single VP to probe all /24's within a prefix. Figures 5(b) and 5(c) show the number of vertices and edges in the inferred topology using each strategy. As expected, the "single" strategy performs poorly. And while the "random" assignment strategy performs well, we achieve approximately 6% gain in leveraging network knowledge via our VP spreading algorithm.

A reasonable goal for our primitives is substantial savings in probing traffic while attaining as rich or almost as rich interface topology. For the latter, if we consider the criterion of being within 1% the number of discovered interfaces as with full traces, then the above 6% gain in interfaces is well within the scope of concern.

Analytically, for random assignment of /24's to VPs, and for a prefix with a mask of m ($k = 2^{24-m}$ /24's in the prefix), and for N vantage points, where $k \leq N$, then the probability that all k /24's are probed by a unique VP is:

$$P = \prod_{i=0}^{k-1} \frac{N-i}{N}$$

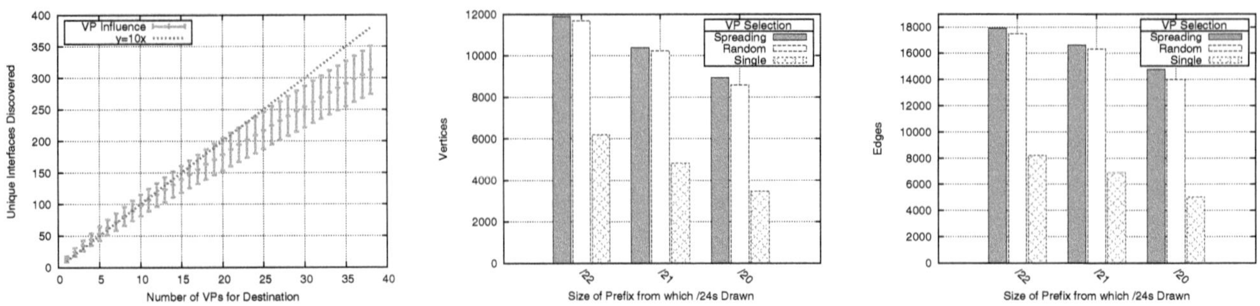

(a) Diminishing return of vantage point influence

(b) Vertices in Discovered Graph

(c) Edges in Discovered Graph

Figure 5: Vantage Point spreading algorithm performance.

Given 23 vantage points, there is only a 25% chance that the 8 /24's in a /21 would be assigned to distinct vantage points. The chance for the 16 /24's in a /20 is 0.1%. Empirically, our experiments find, on average, each of the 16 /24's in a /20 prefix is hit by approximately 12 unique VPs, when performing assignment at random. In summary, vantage point spreading is simple and imposes no additional probing load, and yet the resulting use of additional vantage points attains worthwhile improvement in the estimated topology.

5. DISCUSSION

Reducing the number of measurements required to infer network topologies has been explored in the past, notably in DoubleTree [8]. However, our primitives are the first to exploit structural knowledge of the network to reduce measurement cost, while the ISC algorithm is the logical extension of DoubleTree to the multiple-round tracing scenario.

Prior work [12] examines using externally generated and collected synthetic network coordinates to iteratively select probe destinations where the topological distance is most different from the inferred euclidean distance. While their ultimate goal of reducing measurement cost is the same as ours, their problem formulation entails constructing efficient overlay topologies among a known set of nodes by inferring their underlay connectivity. In contrast, we leverage external network knowledge to guide the selection of destinations for topology characterization of an entire AS.

In the big picture, we view the preceding techniques as important building blocks for a new generation of "Internet-scopes" capable of performing one complete round of probing within a day. With the substantial load savings of these primitives, our hope is to utilize the resulting probing budget gain to more completely characterize the Internet – capturing small-scale dynamics and previously hidden structure.

One challenge in combining these primitives into a single system design is that the ISC technique, by nature, has its search space constrained by historical views. To capture the changes in Internet topology, the supplemental "change driven" logic needs to be integrated into ISC and will likely need further refinement.

We also note the complimentary interaction between subnet-centric probing and vantage point spreading. In isolation, VP spreading probes discover the network ingress points while subnet centric probing finds internal network subnetting structure. Used together, however, both goals can be accomplished without exhausting probing budgets. Subnet centric probing is used for stub networks that have a limited number of ingress points whereas vantage point spreading is designed for exploring path diversity of transit networks that have many peering points but not many internal subnets. In other words, we do not need to perform subnet centric probing per vantage point; we can use the same set of probes to accomplish both objectives, by independently choosing their source and destination addresses.

Our abstraction of the narrow waist in Figure 2, and its impact on topology measurement strategy and vantage point selection, is less relevant for core networks. A top-tier network peers with the other top-tiers, in multiple cities, and provides transit for its many downstream networks. Since these interconnections often occur at inter-exchange points, the number of border router interfaces of a top-tier network, though more than for an edge network, is less than the number of its connections to other AS's. Thus, discovering the topology of a core network, for which additional vantage points is key, has less opportunity for reduction in probing than does edge networks. We intend to quantify the extent of probe reduction possible in measuring core topologies in future work.

Finally, this paper only targets an interface-level graph. An additional alias resolution [3] step, with more probing, is required to reduce an interface-level graph to a router-level graph. We leave the question of how to efficiently perform alias resolution to future work.

Acknowledgments

The authors would like to thank Young Hyun, k. claffy and CAIDA for measurement infrastructure support, Joel Young, Nick Feamster and Steve Bauer for early feedback, and the anonymous reviewers for their constructive comments. This research was partially supported by the NSF under grants ANI-0520210 and CNS-0721574. Views and conclusions contained in this document are those of the authors and should not be interpreted as representing the official policies, either expressed or implied, of NSF or the U.S. government.

6. REFERENCES

[1] B. Augustin, X. Cuvellier, B. Orgogozo, F. Viger, T. Friedman, M. Latapy, C. Magnien, and R. Teixeira. Avoiding traceroute anomalies with paris traceroute. In *Proceedings of the 6th ACM Conference on Internet measurement*, 2006.

[2] P. Barford, A. Bestavros, J. Byers, and M. Crovella. On the marginal utility of network topology measurements. In *Proceedings of the 1st ACM SIGCOMM Workshop on Internet Measurement*, 2001.

[3] A. Bender, R. Sherwood, and N. Spring. Fixing ally's growing pains with velocity modeling. In *Proceedings of the 8th ACM SIGCOMM conference on Internet measurement*' 2008.

[4] R. Beverly and K. Sollins. An internet protocol address clustering algorithm. In *Proceedings of the 3rd Tackling Computer Systems Problems with Machine Learning Techniques Workshop*, Dec. 2008.

[5] D. D. Clark. The design philosophy of the DARPA internet protocols. In *Proceedings of ACM SIGCOMM*, pages 102–111, 1988.

[6] A. Dhamdhere and C. Dovrolis. Ten years in the evolution of the internet ecosystem. In *Proceedings of the 8th ACM SIGCOMM conference on Internet measurement*, 2008.

[7] B. Donnet, T. Friedman, and M. Crovella. Improved algorithms for network topology discovery. In *Proceedings of the 6th Passive and Active Measurement Conference*' volume 3431, 2005.

[8] B. Donnet, P. Raoult, T. Friedman, and M. Crovella. Efficient algorithms for large-scale topology discovery. In *Proceedings of the 2005 ACM SIGMETRICS*, 2005.

[9] U. Feige. A threshold of ln n for approximating set cover. *Journal of the ACM*, 45(4), July 1998.

[10] M. Gonen and Y. Shavitt. An o(logn)-approximation for the set cover problem with set ownership. *Inf. Process. Lett.*, 109(3), 2009.

[11] Y. Hyun and k. claffy. Archipelago measurement infrastructure, 2009. `http://www.caida.org/projects/ark/`.

[12] X. Jin, W.-P. Yiu, S.-H. CHan, and Y. Wang. Network topology inference based on end-to-end measurements. *IEEE Selected Areas in Communications*, 24(12), Dec. 2006.

[13] k. claffy, Y. Hyun, K. Keys, and M. Fomenkov. Internet mapping: from art to science. In *Proceedings of IEEE Cybersecurity Applications and Technologies Conference for Homeland Security*, Mar. 2009.

[14] B. Krishnamurthy and J. Wang. On network-aware clustering of web clients. In *ACM SIGCOMM*, pages 97–110, 2000.

[15] B. Krishnamurthy and W. Willinger. What are our standards for validation of measurement-based networking research? *SIGMETRICS Perform. Eval. Rev.*, 36(2), 2008.

[16] L. Li, D. Alderson, W. Willinger, and J. Doyle. A first-principles approach to understanding the internet's router-level topology. In *Proceedings of the 2004 ACM SIGCOMM conference*, 2004.

[17] M. Luckie, Y. Hyun, and B. Huffaker. Traceroute probe method and forward IP path inference. In *Proceedings of the ACM Internet Measurement Conference*, 2008.

[18] H. Madhyastha. Private communication with iplane author, Mar. 2010.

[19] H. V. Madhyastha, T. Isdal, M. Piatek, C. Dixon, T. Anderson, A. Krishnamurthy, and A. Venkataramani. iPlane: An information plane for distributed services. In *Proceedings of USENIX OSDI*, Nov. 2006.

[20] H. V. Madhyastha, E. Katz-Bassett, T. Anderson, A. Krishnamurthy, and A. Venkataramani. iplane nano: path prediction for peer-to-peer applications. In *Proceedings of the 6th USENIX NSDI*, 2009.

[21] D. Meyer. University of Oregon RouteViews, 2010. `http://www.routeviews.org`.

[22] Y. Shavitt and E. Shir. Dimes: let the internet measure itself. *SIGCOMM Comput. Commun. Rev.*, 35(5), 2005.

[23] Y. Shavitt and U. Weinsberg. Quantifying the importance of vantage points distribution in internet topology measurements. In *Proceedings of IEEE INFOCOM*, Mar. 2009.

[24] H. Tangmunarunkit, R. Govindan, S. Jamin, S. Shenker, and W. Willinger. Network topology generators: degree-based vs. structural. In *Proceedings of the 2002 SIGCOMM Conference*, 2002.

Resolving IP Aliases with Prespecified Timestamps

Justine Sherry* Ethan Katz-Bassett* Mary Pimenova*
Harsha V. Madhyastha† Thomas Anderson* Arvind Krishnamurthy*
*University of Washington †University of California, San Diego

ABSTRACT

Operators and researchers want accurate router-level views of the Internet for purposes including troubleshooting and modeling. However, tools such as traceroute return IP addresses. Because routers may have dozens of IP addresses, or *aliases*, multiple measurements may return different addresses, obscuring whether they represent the same machine. While many techniques exist to address this issue by identifying some IP aliases, these techniques, even in combination, find only a subset of alias pairs.

To improve this state, we design and evaluate a new alias resolution technique using the IP prespecified timestamp option. This option allows a sender to request timestamp values from multiple IP addresses in the same probe. By careful arrangement of these IP addresses, we show that we can infer aliases in many cases.

In this paper, we conduct a measurement study of how many routers support IP timestamps, demonstrating that enough honor the option to base our technique on it. Using our technique, and compared to the most accurate alias information available, we find that 94.7% of the aliases identified by our technique are true positives. Further, we show that our IP timestamp-based technique complements existing alias resolution techniques, providing significant gains by discovering previously unidentifiable aliases.

Categories and Subject Descriptors

C.2.3 [**Computer Communication Networks**]: Network Operations—*Network Monitoring*; C.2.1 [**Computer Communication Networks**]: Network Architecture and Design—*Network topology*

General Terms

Measurement, Experimentation

Keywords

Alias resolution, IP timestamp, IP options

1. INTRODUCTION

Internet topology measurements from tools like traceroute serve numerous purposes. Network operators and researchers use them to pinpoint outages or failures [22, 12, 26]. Measurements can reveal the underlying structure and evolution of the Internet [7, 21, 23, 24]. Researchers use them as the basis for performance comparisons between ISPs [18], Internet latency estimates [6, 4, 16], and IP geolocation [25, 12].

Because each router has more than one IP address, multiple measurements of the same router can appear disjoint to IP-level tools, making it more difficult to draw conclusions from those measurements. To correct this, one must accurately map from IP addresses to routers. We refer to the multiple IP addresses of a router as its aliases, and the process of mapping from IP addresses to routers as alias resolution.

While considerable progress has been made in building better tools [3, 8, 9, 20, 21] for alias resolution, existing techniques are still limited in scope. For example, RadarGun leverages the fact that, on some routers, the multiple interfaces share a single linearly increasing IPID counter. However, the authors of RadarGun observed only 31% of addresses exhibiting such a counter [3]. Mercator, another technique, relies on the fact that some routers respond to certain probes with a response sourced from an address different from the original destination of the probe, implying the two addresses both belong to the router [8]. However, most routers do not respond in this way: only 66% of addresses respond to such probes at all, and only 23% of those respond from an address other than the original destination [10].

In this paper, we present a new technique for IP alias resolution that uses the IP prespecified timestamp option. This option allows a sender to request timestamp values from up to four IP addresses along the path, all in a single packet. Our technique identifies alias pairs by constructing a single probe with timestamp requests for two suspected aliases. By careful interleaving of the alias addresses, and a small amount of repeated probing, we show that we can very reliably identify aliases. Our technique potentially applies to any router capable of providing multiple timestamps in the same probe; we find 32.4% of IP addresses in our measurements respond in this way. Compared to a set of the most accurate alias information, 94.7% of aliases declared by our technique are true positives, and of those we declare non-aliases only 2.4% are misclassified. Further, we find that our technique complements existing techniques: 76.7% aliases we discover were unidentifiable using previous techniques.

The rest of the paper is organized as follows. In Section 2, we describe the timestamp option and quantify the degree of router support for the option. In Section 3 we describe our alias resolution technique. Section 4 includes evaluations of our alias resolution technique for accuracy and coverage. We discuss related work in Section 5 before concluding in Section 6.

IMC'10, November 1–3, 2010, Melbourne, Australia.

2. PRESPECIFIED TIMESTAMP OPTION

We next describe the timestamp option, and we provide a measurement study to discover how often routers respond to the timestamp option in ways that we can exploit for alias resolution.

2.1 Background

Timestamp requests are an optional extension to any packet that traverses the Internet [1]. Three 'flags' specify different behaviors of the IP timestamp option; we make use of only one, 'prespecified timestamps.' For a packet with the prespecified timestamp option, the sender lists up to four IP addresses in the options header. As a shorthand, we describe timestamp requests in the following format: $(A|BCDE)$, where A is the destination of the probe, and B, C, D, and E are the ordered list of prespecified addresses. Each machine which forwards the packet will check to see if the first unstamped IP address is one of its own, and, if so, it will record a timestamp in the packet header before forwarding the packet. The order is important: if C receives the packet, it will only record a timestamp if B has already done so.

2.2 Measurement Study of Support

Although timestamps are a standard option in the IP specification, many routers do not honor them and some ISPs filter them. Further, the protocol specification does not dictate a behavior for routers to follow upon encountering their own IP address multiple times in the same probe. Our technique, described in detail in Section 3, relies on a single router providing multiple timestamps for multiple addresses in the same probe. Hence, our technique is only applicable to the subset of routers whose implementation provides multiple stamps in this case.

To assess how many routers honor such requests, we performed a measurement study of all IP addresses discovered by iPlane on May 10, 2010 [15]. iPlane issues daily traceroutes from all PlanetLab sites [2] to approximately 140,000 prefixes. To generate our data set, we gathered all 351,214 IP addresses observed in iPlane traceroutes from May 10, then removed all private addresses and addresses in prefixes whose operators opted out of our experiments. We then issued ICMP echo requests (pings) to each remaining address and report on the 267,736 addresses that responded.

For these 267,736 addresses, we first sent each address D an ICMP echo request with the timestamp option enabled requesting $(D|DXXX)$. X is an address at the University of Washington known not to be on the path, to ensure that extra, invalid stamps were not being introduced into the responses we received. In our previous work, we found that some PlanetLab sites receive few or no timestamp responses, presumably due to filters [11]. To attempt to avoid such filters, we sent the probes from multiple PlanetLab vantage points. Further, to account for packet loss, we sent each measurement five times redundantly from each vantage point. As seen in Table 1, we did not receive any responses from 31% of addresses. An additional 15.5% of addresses responded to our probes without recording a timestamp value. We also identified a common faulty implementation, exhibited by 5.8% of addresses, in which the router recorded two stamps on encountering its address, even though the second prespecified address did not belong to it. The table lists this as *Extra Stamp* behavior.

The remaining 47.7% of addresses correctly responded to these probes with a single timestamp. To characterize their behavior in response to multiple requests for their own address, we next sent each of them a probe request $(D|DDDD)$; the table indicates how many stamps the addresses responded with. The most common stamping behavior was to provide two stamps; 22.2% of addresses demonstrated this behavior. A further 10.2% of addresses provided four stamps. Since our alias technique will require a router to record multiple stamps in a single probe, it potentially applies to the 32.4% of ping-responsive addresses in our dataset that responded with two or more timestamps. This is an upper bound on the applicability of our technique; we show later that some routers that stamp twice do not always stamp for queries involving different interfaces.

Classification	IP Addresses	%
Unresponsive	83002	31.0%
Extra Stamp	15606	5.8%
Zero Stamps	41422	15.5%
One Stamp	40886	15.3%
Two Stamps	59450	22.2%
Three Stamps	40	0%
Four Stamps	27330	10.2%
Total	267736	100%

Table 1: Responsiveness to timestamp probes for the set of 267,736 public, ICMP-responsive addresses discovered by iPlane on May 10, 2010. Each address D was sent probes requesting $(D|DXXX)$ and $(D|DDDD)$. The classifications reflect the number of timestamps provided in D's responses. Our alias resolution technique potentially works for targets responding with 2-4 stamps.

3. ALIAS CONFIRMATION

The prespecified timestamp option allows a single packet to request timestamps from multiple IP addresses. Our technique nests requests for pairs of IP addresses. To check if A and B are aliases, we send two ICMP echo requests, with the timestamp options set to $(A|ABAB)$ and $(B|BABA)$. If they are aliases of the same router and the router stamps multiple times, the router should record timestamps for both addresses at a single point along the path, with consistent timestamp values. To identify this, we look for timestamp replies whose ordering constrains A and B to reside on the same router, and whose timestamp values are identical.

3.1 Timestamp Values as a Fingerprint

Timestamp values allow us to identify whether two IP addresses are likely to share a common clock. A single host recording multiple timestamps at once into a single packet should provide the same value for each stamp.

Making use of this observation, when we receive a response containing timestamps for candidates A and B, we check the difference between the timestamp values. However, in our study in Section 2.2, we observed rare cases when timestamp values incremented between stamps, although the timestamps are provided by the same host (in response to $(D|DDDD)$). To account for this, we allow some leeway. We send duplicates of our probes to generate multiple timestamped responses. If fewer than 90% of the responses received for a pair have all timestamps equal or

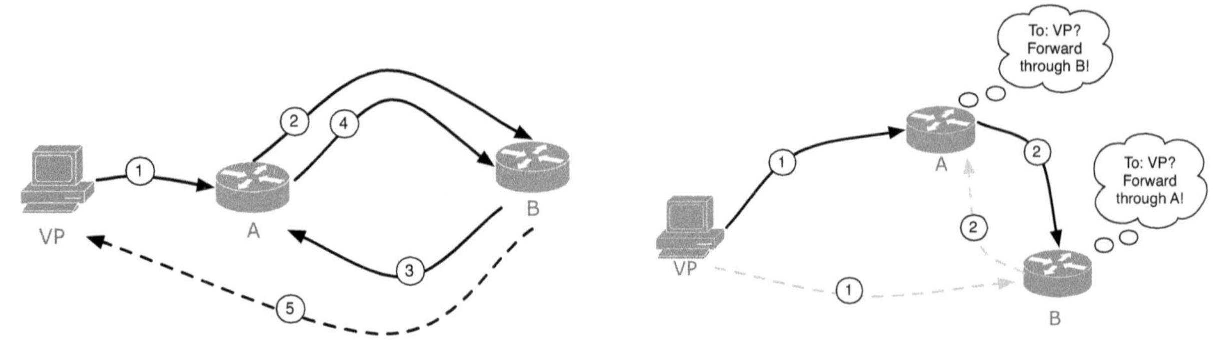

(a) Configuration of two distinct routers providing four stamps to the request $(A|ABAB)$.

(b) Configuration of two distinct routers providing two stamps to both the request $(A|ABAB)$ (solid line) and the request $(B|BABA)$ (dashed).

Figure 1: Two configurations of looped routing implied by certain timestamp responses. These cases can only be transient. Thus, repeatedly receiving these responses implies that the IP pairs are likely to be aliases.

if we observe decrements between stamps, we eliminate the pair and declare it to be a non-alias. If the timestamps are consistent, however, we require further evidence.

3.2 Topological Constraints

Because a prespecified address will only be stamped after all previous addresses have been stamped, the ordering of the timestamps recorded must be consistent with the path the packet traverses. By carefully arranging the IP addresses in the timestamp request, we can make it highly likely that only true aliases will respond with a given pattern. The absence of the pattern does not necessarily mean that the addresses are not aliases, just that we cannot determine their relationship.

Loops. While it is possible for a packet to encounter a transient loop, such cases should be rare and can be accounted for via redundant measurements over time. If a packet encounters a persistent loop, we should not receive an echo reply for our probe. Hence, if we receive multiple replies each of which implies a loop, we can conclude that the packets (in all likelihood) did not travel back and forth between two routers, but rather that a single router stamped multiple times for its multiple interfaces.

There are two separate scenarios in which we can infer aliases because the alternative would be a persistent loop. The first occurs when we receive four stamps in response to any of our queries. Figure 1(a) illustrates the route taken by a timestamp request $(A|ABAB)$, assuming A and B are not aliases. Timestamp values for all four prespecified addresses suggest that the packet reached the destination A, then went to B, to A, and to B again. These stamps mean that B must be configured to forward the return traffic en route to S through A, and A must be configured to forward the return traffic en route to S through B. This is a loop, or, if we see this pattern repeated for multiple probes over time, it is more likely that A and B are aliases.

The second scenario, demonstrated in Figure 1(b), occurs when a single vantage point S receives responses with two stamps for both the request $(A|ABAB)$ and the request $(B|BABA)$. If A and B are not aliases, these responses imply that B routes traffic to S through A, and A routes traffic to S through B. Because this explanation is once again a loop, if we see this pattern repeated over multiple probes,

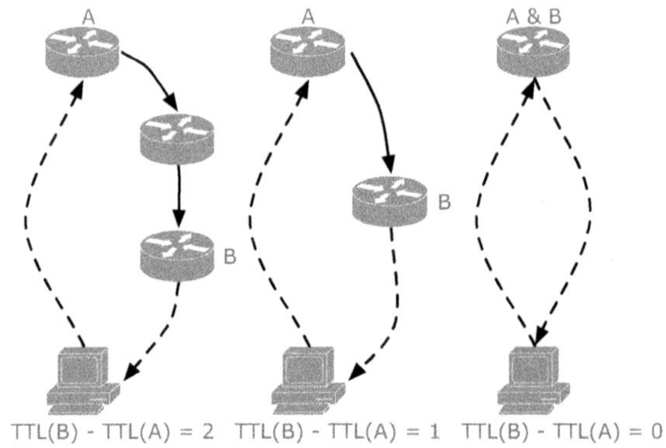

Figure 2: Because TTL values are initialized to a small number of standard values, we can estimate the reverse path length to S from routers A and B. If we know that the reverse path from A traverses B and we assume that the routers are distinct, B's reverse path length to S must be shorter than A's. If their reverse path lengths are the same, A and B likely reside on the same router.

we can conclude that A and B are likely to be aliases on the same machine.

Distance. In our measurements, a single vantage point will often receive two timestamps for $(A|ABAB)$, but not receive any for $(B|BABA)$. In this situation, we are able to infer aliases by coupling the topological relationship implied by the timestamps with reasoning about the relative distance of A and B from the vantage point.

Given that the vantage point S received the first two timestamps in the request $(A|ABAB)$, we know that either A and B are aliases, or that B is on the reverse path from A back to S. A's reverse path length should be equal to B's reverse path length, plus some difference δ representing the number of hops in between A and B along the reverse path. If this δ value is 0, it suggests that there are no hops between A and B, and A and B are likely to reside on the same router. By sending extra pings to A and B, we can acquire TTL values from the response packets that allow us

	Total	True aliases	Non-aliases
Classified as aliases			
Four Stamps	14810	14025 (94.7%)	785 (5.3%)
Two Stamps (Loop)	354	349 (98.6%)	5 (1.4%)
Two Stamps (Distance)	2580	2422 (93.9%)	158 (6.1%)
→ Total classified as aliases	17744	**16796 (94.7%)**	**948 (5.3%)**
Classified as non-aliases			
Bad Clock	17046	**412 (2.4%)**	16634 (97.6%)
Unclassified			
Two Stamps (Unclassified)	8440	729 (8.6%)	7711 (91.4%)
Overall			
All pairs with multiple stamps	43230	17937 (41.5%)	25293 (58.5%)

Table 2: Results and accuracy of timestamp confirmed alias pairs from the `mrinfo` dataset. The candidate pairs included 43,230 two stamping pairs, 17,937 of which were true aliases. We report the accuracy of our categorizations, showing the true positives (16,796), false positives (948), and false negatives (412) in bold.

to estimate the length of the paths taken from A and B back to the source. This inference can be confounded if A and B use different initial TTL values; however, most routers choose their initial value from a small set of standard values. One other source of inaccuracy may arise from 'hidden routers' [20], which do not decrement the TTL value when forwarding the packet, thus violating our TTL argument described in Section 3.2.

Figure 2 shows the relationship between A and B given a δ value of 2, 1, or 0.

3.3 Algorithm

To take advantage of the previously described aliasing characteristics, we perform the following steps to confirm alias pairs.

First, we send a preliminary $(A|AXXX)$ probe to all IP addresses A involved in any candidate pair, and we remove any addresses which display the *Extra Stamp* behavior described in Section 2.

Then, for each candidate pair we send probes $(A|ABAB)$ and $(B|BABA)$ redundantly five times each from several vantage points. We require the redundancy in order to generate enough responses for our 90% shared-clock threshold, as well as to compensate in case some packets are dropped or filtered. Next, we trim our candidates to the set of pairs which responded to our measurements at least five times with two or more timestamps.

Then, we split the candidates by stamp count. We classify those which stamp four times as aliases. For those which stamp twice, we trim the set to those which pass our shared clock test: those which never display a decrement between stamps, and for which at least 90% of the timestamp values are the same. We declare non-aliases those which do not pass this test.

Finally, for those which pass the clock test we identify pairs which exhibit either two stamp (loop) or two stamp (distance) configurations to any single vantage point. To evaluate the 'distance' configuration, we require TTL values from addresses which may not have responded to our timestamp probes, hence we send extra pings to the candidate addresses. Those which display these configurations, we declare aliases. Those which do not, we characterize as unknown.

4. EVALUATION

To assess the accuracy of our technique, we use a dataset of known aliases generated by `mrinfo` measurements on December 30th, 2009 [19]. `mrinfo` identifies aliases by issuing IGMP `ASK_NEIGHBORS` requests to multicast-enabled routers. Multicast-enabled routers respond to such requests with a list of their interfaces, associated IP addresses, and neighboring routers. Assuming the configuration on the router is correct and up-to-date, the alias information should be correct. However, the resulting datasets are limited in several ways: they only include multicast-enabled routers, they are limited to routers which are connected across Mbone to the vantage point used to initiate the requests, and they are restricted to networks which do not filter IGMP traffic. After removing private and blacklisted addresses, the December 30th set contains 9,130 addresses over 1,635 routers. Because of the dataset's limited size and biases introduced by its limitations, it has a different distribution of aliasing behaviors than the iPlane dataset in Section 2.2. More specifically, 21% of addresses in it provide four stamps, while only 14.4% provide two.

4.1 Accuracy

Timestamp-based alias resolution requires candidate alias pairs as inputs. We generated candidate pairs by clustering together IP addresses with a similar vector of TTL values observed in pings from several hundred PlanetLab vantage points, a technique borrowed from iPlane [15]. The intuition for this heuristic is that we only need to consider addresses as potential aliases if they are at similar distances from most locations. By only considering pairs that clustered together, we eliminated roughly 99% of the potential pairs from consideration.

After clustering, we were left with 874,699 candidate pairs. Within those candidate pairs were 32,853 alias pairs. Of these actual aliases, 18,939 included at least one IP address which had previously responded to timestamp requests with multiple stamps, as we described in section 2.2. These 18,939 pairs are an upper bound on the number of aliases our technique could potentially discover.

To each of the 874,699 candidate pairs we sent two probes: $(A|ABAB)$ and $(B|ABAB)$. Of the candidates pairs that we probed, 576,068 pairs responded to at least one probe, 43,230 with two or more stamps. Note that many of the pairs respond with fewer than two stamps because they are not aliases: a response to $(A|ABAB)$ might include only a stamp for A because B is not an alias and is not on the reverse path. Within those 43,230 responsive pairs were 17,937 true alias pairs, 94.7% of the 18,939 pairs we could potentially address. Table 2 displays the categorization and accuracy of pairs which provided two or more stamps.

We classified 17,744 of the pairs as aliases. Overall 16,796 of the 17,744 aliases (94.7%) we found are true positives, according to the `mrinfo` data. It is possible that some of the 5.3% false positives are due to out-of-date `mrinfo` configurations or changes in configuration between the generation of the `mrinfo` data in December 2009 and our experiments in May 2010.

The 16,796 true alias pairs we identified represent 88.7% of the original 18,939 alias pairs our technique could potentially find. We note that we had much more success in identifying alias pairs for addresses which stamped four times than for those that stamped twice. Of those pairs for which one of the addresses stamped four times (when queried with its own address four times), we correctly identified 94.3% of them as aliases. However, for those pairs for which neither address stamped four times, but at least one of the addresses stamped twice, we only identified 63.4% of the pairs as aliases.

Of the 17,046 pairs our technique declares to not be aliases, 412 are classified as aliases by `mrinfo`, only 2.4% false negatives. Over half of these false negatives included a clock decrement between stamps.

4.2 Coverage

To further evaluate our technique, we assess whether it identifies aliases not found by RadarGun [3] and Mercator [8], two existing, widely-used techniques. Similar to how our technique relies on routers stamping multiple times, these techniques also rely on specific router behaviors, limiting their applicability. We look to the overlap of the aliases discovered by each technique, to assess whether by combining techniques we may be able to do better than any single technique on its own. We discuss combined techniques further in related work.

For our evaluation, we again use `mrinfo` as a basis for comparison. It is possible that the selection bias of this data influences the relative effectiveness of the different techniques. For example, RadarGun relies on routers using linear IPID counters, and we found that a higher proportion of addresses in the `mrinfo` dataset returned random IPID values compared to the RadarGun study (also of just over 9000 addresses) [3]. Similarly, as we noted above, a higher proportion of addresses in this dataset will stamp four times, compared to the broader dataset used in Section 2.2, increasing our relative effectiveness.

We evaluate each technique under the condition where all true pairs are included as candidates. Thus, we provided each technique all of the IP addresses as inputs (for those which take addresses as input) or all of the true alias pairs as candidates (for those which require candidate pairs). Because some techniques may not find all combinations of pairs (identifying (A, B) and (B, C) as pairs, but not (A, C)), we take the transitive closure of all pairs confirmed, providing us with a complete set of implied aliases for each technique.

Figure 3 shows a CCDF demonstrating the per-router coverage provided by the techniques individually and by all

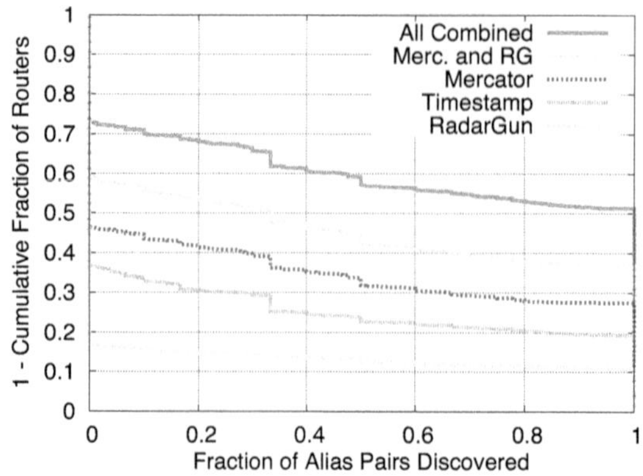

Figure 3: Comparison of coverage of alias resolution techniques over `mrinfo` dataset. Graph is a CCDF showing the fraction of routers for which the techniques identify a given fraction of alias pairs. Merging successive techniques improves the proportion of identifiable alias pairs, for this dataset.

techniques merged. The metric evaluates how completely the techniques identify all alias pairs for the routers in the dataset. The vertical axis provides a complementary cumulative fraction of the 1,635 `mrinfo` routers, and the horizontal axis provides the fraction of alias pairs per router successfully identified by the alias resolution technique. A given (x, y) point shows that a technique identified at least x fraction of pairs for y fraction of the routers. Some routers in the dataset had many more interfaces than others: 75% had six or fewer addresses, and the largest had 70 addresses.

The merger of the three techniques provides much greater coverage than any technique in isolation for this dataset. With all techniques merged together, 52.3% of routers have their aliases resolved entirely (100% of pairs identified) and 72.9% are resolved partially (some, but not all of their alias pairs are identified by the alias resolution). In aggregate, 68.3% of all alias pairs within the dataset are identified by one or more technique. Furthermore, the gains provided by including each successive technique are large. In particular, adding our technique to the merger of RadarGun and Mercator increases the number of routers that are completely resolved from 36.9% to 52.3%. In fact, 76.7% of the pairs discovered by our technique are unidentified by either RadarGun or Mercator.

5. RELATED WORK

We next discuss related work which has dealt with alias resolution or measurements using timestamps.

5.1 Alias Resolution

Many techniques exist to address the IP alias resolution problem, but none have complete coverage or offer a complete solution.

Mercator sends a UDP probe to a high numbered port, generating an ICMP Port Unreachable error message. On some routers, the error message is sourced from an address different from the destination of the original UDP probe, revealing that the two addresses reside on the same router [8]. Mercator cannot discover aliases for routers that respond from the original destination address.

Ally sends a succession of probes to suspected aliases and analyzes the IPID value in response packets. Since some routers use a common counter to set IPID values, Ally declares a pair of addresses aliases if subsequent probes interleaved between the two addresses remain in the same range [21]. RadarGun borrows Ally's IPID insight and improves on its technique to reduce measurements from $O(n^2)$ probes to $O(n)$ probes. RadarGun does this by probing each IP address several times to generate a 'velocity model' of how the address's IPID values change over time. It then compares the velocity models between all pairs of addresses to identify aliases [3]. However, many routers do not have well-behaved linear counters, leaving both Ally and RadarGun unable to identify their aliases.

Whereas our technique, as well as the others discussed so far, classify aliases by probing the IP addresses in question and inspecting the replies, DisCarte [20] and APAR [9] base their techniques on topological relationships observed in traceroute and similar probes. The IP record route option often discovers different IP addresses than traceroute, even along the same path, and DisCarte attempts to align the two types of probes to resolve aliases [20]. APAR (Analytic and Probe-based Alias Resolver) uses common IP address assignment schemes to analyze traceroutes and infer aliases. The developers of APAR found that approximately half of the alias pairs they discovered were also found by Ally [9], whereas we found that 76.7% of the pairs we discovered in the `mrinfo` dataset were not found by the Ally-based RadarGun or by Mercator. An interesting question for the future is how well DisCarte and APAR combine with our technique.

We are not the first to suggest combining techniques. While we showed in Section 4.2 that combining techniques can provide more complete alias information, challenges remain for such a technique to be successful. Efficient probing, resolving conflicts between techniques, and limiting the impact of false positives all remain unresolved questions for a complete aliasing system [13].

5.2 IP Timestamps

Fonseca et al. investigated whether packets with timestamp or other IP options were dropped on paths between PlanetLab sites. They found that approximately half the paths dropped options packets, but that most of the drops were at the edge of the network, concentrated in a small number of ASes [5]. We measure from multiple vantage points to counteract this, an approach we also used in earlier work [11]. Since we are targeting routers, rather than end hosts, many of our destinations are in the core, where Fonseca et al. found little filtering. Still, our technique will not work for destinations that do not provide timestamps or that are completely behind filters.

In earlier work, we used prespecified timestamps as part of our reverse traceroute [11] and iPlane [14] systems. Neither system used timestamps for alias resolution.

In addition to the IP timestamp option that we use, there is an ICMP Timestamp request message. With this message, a sender can request the timestamp of the destination, but not of other IP addresses, so it cannot be used for our alias resolution technique. Tulip uses ICMP Timestamp messages to help diagnose performance problems [17].

6. CONCLUSION

Despite numerous efforts to develop alias resolution techniques, comprehensive IP alias resolution remains a challenge. We have demonstrated a new technique for IP alias resolution using IP prespecified timestamp measurements, a standard IP option. Our technique requests timestamps from both addresses in a candidate alias pair in a single probe. We have shown that many routers honor IP timestamp requests, and 32.4% of routers in our dataset will provide two or more timestamps in response to a request for their own IP address multiple times in the same probe. We found that timestamp-based alias resolution provides accurate results for routers that support it: in our study, 94.7% of alias pairs identified were true positives. In addition, timestamp alias resolution provides gains in overall coverage by discovering alias pairs which existing techniques failed to identify.

Acknowledgments

We would like to thank the anonymous IMC reviewers for their valuable comments and feedback. We would also like to thank Adam Bender for modifying the RadarGun tool for our use and Colin Scott for comments on an early draft of this paper.

7. REFERENCES

[1] RFC 791: Internet Protocol, September 1981.

[2] Bavier, A., Bowman, M., Chun, B., Karlin, D. C. S., Muir, S., Peterson, L., Roscoe, T., Spalink, T., and Wawrzoniak, M. Operating system support for planetary-scale network services. In *Network Systems Design and Implementation* (2004).

[3] Bender, A., Sherwood, R., and Spring, N. Fixing Ally's growing pains with velocity modeling. In *Internet Measurement Conference* (2008).

[4] Costa, M., Castro, M., Rowstron, A., and Key, P. PIC: Practical Internet Coordinates for distance estimation. In *International Conference on Distributed Computing Systems* (2004).

[5] Fonseca, R., Porter, G., Katz, R., Shenker, S., and Stoica, I. IP options are not an option. Tech. rep., EECS Department, University of California, Berkeley, 2005.

[6] Francis, P., Jamin, S., Jin, C., Jin, Y., Paxson, V., Raz, D., Shavitt, Y., and Zhang, L. IDMaps: A global Internet host distance estimation service. In *INFOCOM* (2000).

[7] Gao, L. On inferring autonomous system relationships in the Internet. *IEEE/ACM Transactions on Networking* (2000).

[8] Govindan, R., and Tangmunarunkit, H. Heuristics for Internet map discovery. In *INFOCOM* (2000).

[9] Gunes, M., and Sarac, K. Resolving IP aliases in building traceroute-based Internet maps. *IEEE/ACM Transactions on Networking* (2009).

[10] Hyun, Y. Personal Communication, May 2010.

[11] Katz-Bassett, E., Madhyastha, H. V., Adhikari, V., Scott, C., Sherry, J., van Wesep, P., Anderson, T., and Krishnamurthy, A. Reverse traceroute. In *Network Systems Design and Implementation* (2010).

[12] KATZ-BASSETT, E., MADHYASTHA, H. V., JOHN, J. P., KRISHNAMURTHY, A., AND ANDERSON, T. Studying black holes in the Internet with Hubble. In *Network Systems Design and Implementation* (2008).

[13] KEYS, K. Internet-scale IP alias resolution techniques. *ACM SIGCOMM Computer Communication Review (CCR)* (2009).

[14] MADHYASTHA, H. V. *An Information Plane for Internet Applications*. PhD thesis, Univ. of Washington, 2008.

[15] MADHYASTHA, H. V., ISDAL, T., PIATEK, M., DIXON, C., ANDERSON, T., KRISHNAMURTHY, A., AND VENKATARAMANI, A. iPlane: An information plane for distributed services. In *Operating Systems Design and Implementation* (2006).

[16] MADHYASTHA, H. V., KATZ-BASSETT, E., ANDERSON, T., KRISHNAMURTHY, A., AND VENKATARAMANI, A. iPlane Nano: Path prediction for peer-to-peer applications. In *Network Systems Design and Implementation* (2009).

[17] MAHAJAN, R., SPRING, N., WETHERALL, D., AND ANDERSON, T. User-level Internet path diagnosis. In *Symposium on Operating Systems Principles* (2003).

[18] MAHAJAN, R., ZHANG, M., POOLE, L., AND PAI, V. Uncovering performance differences among backbone ISPs with Netdiff. In *Network Systems Design and Implementation* (2008).

[19] MÉRINDOL, P., DEN SCHRIECK, V. V., DONNET, B., BONAVENTURE, O., AND PANSIOT, J.-J. Quantifying ASes multiconnectivity using multicast information. In *Internet Measurement Conference* (2009).

[20] SHERWOOD, R., BENDER, A., AND SPRING, N. DisCarte: A disjunctive Internet cartographer. In *SIGCOMM* (2008).

[21] SPRING, N., MAHAJAN, R., AND WETHERALL, D. Measuring ISP topologies with Rocketfuel. In *SIGCOMM* (2002).

[22] STEENBERGEN, R. A. A practical guide to (correctly) troubleshooting with traceroute. In *NANOG 45* (2009).

[23] SUBRAMANIAN, L., AGARWAL, S., REXFORD, J., AND KATZ, Y. H. Characterizing the Internet hierarchy from multiple vantage points. In *INFOCOM* (2002).

[24] TANGMUNARUNKIT, H., GOVINDAN, R., JAMIN, S., SHENKER, S., AND WILLINGER, W. Network topology generators: Degree-based vs. structural. In *SIGCOMM* (2002).

[25] WONG, B., STOYANOV, I., AND SIRER, E. G. Octant: A comprehensive framework for the geolocalization of Internet hosts. In *Network Systems Design and Implementation* (2007).

[26] ZHANG, Y., MAO, Z. M., AND ZHANG, M. Effective diagnosis of routing disruptions from end systems. In *Network Systems Design and Implementation* (2008).

On the Impact of Layer-2 on Node Degree Distribution

Pascal Mérindol, Benoit Donnet,
Olivier Bonaventure
Université catholique de Louvain – ICTEAM
Louvain-la-Neuve – Belgium
firstname.name@uclouvain.be

Jean-Jacques Pansiot
LSIIT, Université de Strasbourg
Strasbourg – France
pansiot@unistra.fr

ABSTRACT

The Internet topology data collected through traceroute exploration has been extensively studied in the past. In particular, a remarkable property of the Internet, the power-law shape of node degree distribution, drew the attention of the research community. Several studies have since questioned this property.

In this paper, based on a large dataset collected using `mrinfo`, we show that the node degree distribution is strongly impacted by the presence of layer-2 (L2) networks, such as switches. L2 devices interconnect a large number of routers, themselves being also involved in multiple L2 interconnections. Such a situation induces nodes with very high degree when analyzing the layer-3 (L3) graph with traceroute probing. Considering the physical design of a network, our analysis provides a lower bound on the bias generated by using only an L3 view. We also provide a model that can be a first step towards L2 aware topology generation.

Categories and Subject Descriptors

C.2.1 [**Network Architecture and Design**]: Network topology

General Terms

Measurement

Keywords

network topology, mrinfo, degree distribution, layer-2

1. INTRODUCTION

Several measurement systems aim at eliciting the Internet topology. CAIDA's *Archipelago* [1] uses 41 monitors tracing towards roughly 8.25 millions destinations. *iPlane* [2] constructs an annotated map of the Internet and evaluates end-to-end performances (latency, bandwidth, capacity, etc). *DIMES* [3] is publicly released as a daemon running on endhosts that traces a set of targets obtained from a central server. The recently introduced *Scamper* is able to conduct Internet measurement to large numbers of IPv4 and IPv6 addresses, in parallel, to fill a specified packets-per-second rate [4]. All of these efforts are based on one of the most common probing tool: *traceroute* [5].

The collected traceroute data is used for various purposes [6]. Among others, from a scientific point of view, the results underlie efforts to model the network [7]. In particular, the node degree distribution fascinates the research community, specially since the Faloutsos et al. seminal paper highlighting the power law shape of this distribution [8].

However, this power law distribution has been extensively questioned. Lakhina et al. [9] showed that, in simulations of a network in which the degree distribution does not at all follow a power law, traceroutes conducted from a small number of monitors can induce a subgraph in which the node degree distribution does follow a power law. Clauset and Moore [10] have since demonstrated analytically that such a phenomenon is to be expected for the specific case of the Erdös-Rényi random graphs [11].

Another potential reason influencing the node degree distribution are layer-2 (L2) clouds (such as Ethernet switches) and how they are used to interconnect layer-3 (L3) routers. A simple scenario involving one L2 device is illustrated on Fig. 1. Fig. 1(a) shows the real topology where four routers are interconnected through an L2 device. Each router on Fig. 1(a) has an L2 degree of 1. On the contrary, Fig. 1(b) provides a view of the same topology as it can be seen through a traceroute exploration: since the L2 device is not discovered (even not suggested), the topology appears as a full mesh and each router has an L3 degree of three. The impact of L2 devices on the node degree distribution has never been deeply investigated, mainly due to the difficulty of iden-

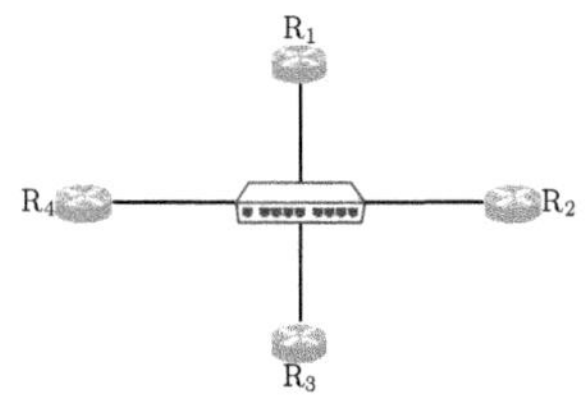

(a) L2 topology

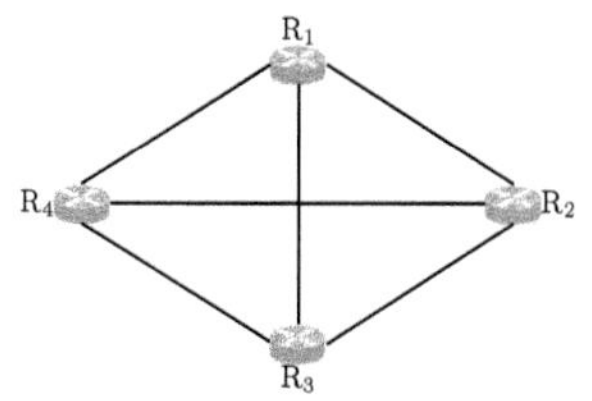

(b) L3 topology

Figure 1: From star to clique: the effect of L2 device using a logical L3 vision

IMC'10, November 1–3, 2010, Melbourne, Australia.

tifying those systems in a traceroute exploration. However, Pansiot and Grad [12], Clauset and Moore [10], and Willinger et al. [13] as well have already pointed the potential impact of L2 networks on the degree analysis.

In this paper, we propose several contributions in order to demonstrate and quantify the impact of L2 devices on node degree distribution. We base our work on a large dataset collected using `mrinfo` [14]. `mrinfo` is a tool that silently discovers all multicast enabled links belonging to an IPv4 router. It has been recently used for Internet topology discovery [15, 16]. One of the key advantages of `mrinfo` is that it allows one to infer the presence of an L2 network between routers. We demonstrate that our inference of broadcast L2 networks is coherent in 90% of the cases and seems to reveal Ethernet L2 devices such as switches. Considering the L3 view of the topology provided by our dataset, on average, 70% of the connections between routers can be classified as *point-to-multipoint* connections (i.e., three or more L3 routers connected through an L2 network). In contrast, a *point-to-point* connection refers to a direct link involving two routers.

Our first contribution is an analysis of the impact of L2 devices on the node degree distribution considering the whole network graph discovered by our `mrinfo` campaign. In particular, we show that the tail of the node degree distribution is heavier when using an L2 agnostic view than when distinguishing L2 and L3 layers. Our results also question the scale free property and the shape of such a distribution considering the physical topology of the Internet.

Second, we refine our view of the problem by focusing on several large Tier-1 and Transit autonomous systems (ASes). Our results show that, although each AS is topologically engineered in a different way, in all cases, the impact of L2 networks is really significant. We notice a great shift in the node degree distribution but specific to each AS. We analyze several key distributions to understand this property in each AS. Among others, we observe three phenomena:

1. the degree of L2 devices is generally greater than the one of routers,
2. routers are frequently connected to several L2 devices,
3. large access routers are involved in even more L2 connections.

To highlight the correlation implied by the third point[1], we provide a first analytical model that captures the heavy tail distribution of the L3 view. We also believe that this model can be a first step towards L2 aware topology generation.

Generally speaking, our results indicate that L2 networks must be carefully taken into account when analyzing physical topology properties such as path redundancy. The huge difference between the physical graph of the Internet and its L3 view can introduce a large bias in a path diversity analysis. Our L2 based topology extraction allows one to analyze a lower bound on such a bias.

The remainder of this paper is organized as follows: Sec. 2 describes our dataset, the methodology we follow for preprocessing the data, and our L2 inference mechanism; Sec. 3 provides a global view of the L2 impact on the node degree distribution; Sec. 4 refines this view by focusing on large Tier-1 and Transit ISPs; Sec. 5 provides a first analytical model capturing the dependence between L2 and L3 degrees; Sec. 6 positions our work regarding the state of the art; finally, Sec. 7 concludes this paper by summarizing its main results.

[1]There exists a strong correlation between the router point-to-point degree and the number of its L2 neighbors.

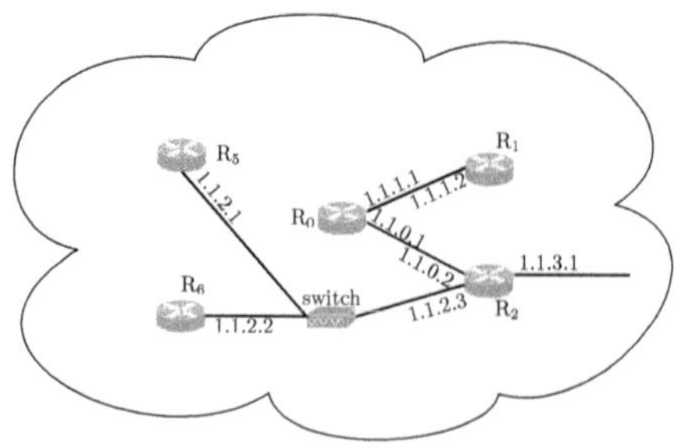

1.1.0.2 [version 12.4]
1.1.0.2 → 1.1.0.1 [1/0/pim/querier]
1.1.2.3 → 1.1.2.1 [1/0/pim/querier]
1.1.2.3 → 1.1.2.2 [1/0/pim/querier]
1.1.3.1 → 0.0.0.0 [1/0/pim/leaf]

Figure 2: `mrinfo` example

2. DATASET

In this section, we discuss the dataset used throughout this paper and how data was collected. We first present `mrinfo` (Sec. 2.1), a tool that is able to silently discover all the multicast interfaces of a router, and how we used it for gathering topology data. Next, we discuss how our dataset was preprocessed (Sec. 2.2). Finally, we explain how we can infer L2 networks from `mrinfo` data and how confident we are in our inference technique (Sec. 2.3).

2.1 `mrinfo`

`mrinfo` messages use the Internet Group Management Protocol (IGMP [17]). IGMP was initially designed to allow hosts to report their active multicast groups to a multicast router on their LAN. Most IGMP messages are sent with a Time-to-Live of 1. However, the Distance Vector Multicast Routing Protocol, DVMRP, has defined two special types of IGMP messages that can be used to monitor routers [18]. Although current IPv4 multicast routers do not use DVMRP anymore, they still support these special IGMP messages. Upon reception of an IGMP `ASK_NEIGHBORS` message, an IPv4 multicast router replies by sending an IGMP `NEIGHBORS_REPLY` message that lists all its multicast enabled local interfaces with some information about their state. Cisco and Juniper routers also report in the IGMP `NEIGHBORS_REPLY` message the version of their operating system. Fig. 2 shows an example of the usage of `mrinfo` to query the router R_2, `1.1.0.2` being the responding interface of R_2. `mrinfo` reports that this router is directly connected to R_0 (through interface `1.1.0.1`). We can also notice that R_2 is connected to routers R_5 and R_6 through an L2 network (labeled "switch" in Fig. 2) because interface `1.1.2.3` appears twice in the `mrinfo` reply (see bold text in Fig. 2). Finally, `mrinfo` reports that interface `1.1.3.1` has no multicast neighbor because the right IP address is equal to 0.0.0.0 (or is directly connected to a LAN, as indicated by the "leaf" keyword). All this information is obtained by sending a single IGMP message. In practice, `mrinfo` provides information similar to the output of a `show` command on the router's command line interface.

Our approach in probing the network with `mrinfo` is recursive and we call such a probing scheme `mrinfo-rec`. Initially, `mrinfo-rec` is fed with a single IP address corresponding to the first router attached to the `mrinfo-rec` vantage point. `mrinfo-rec` probes this router and recursively applies its probing mechanism on all the collected IP addresses. These recursive queries stop at unresponsive routers or when all discovered routers have been queried. The same process is run every day. It is worth to notice that an address not replying to an `mrinfo` probe during a given day will not be queried the days after except if it appears again in a list of captured addresses.

To illustrate this behavior, let us apply it on the topology depicted in Fig. 2. `mrinfo-rec` receives, as input, an IP address belonging to router R_0. From R_0, `mrinfo-rec` collects a set of neighbor IP addresses, i.e., {1.1.1.2, 1.1.0.2}. For all IP addresses in this set that were not previously probed, `mrinfo-rec` sends an IGMP `ASK_NEIGHBORS` message and, if the probed router replied, it again runs through the set of neighbor IP addresses collected.

This recursive probing scheme comes with the strong advantage of being very easy to setup as it initially requires only a single IP address as input. However, it has the drawback of limiting the `mrinfo-rec` probing spectrum. If the address set specified as input for a given day corresponds to non-responding routers (because, simply, the ISP filters IGMP messages), `mrinfo-rec` will not be able to discover any topological information. To overcome this limitation, the set of responding router addresses of a given day is given as input of `mrinfo-rec` the next day.

2.2 Data Processing

Since May 1st, 2004, we have been collecting topology data from a host located at the University of Strasbourg, France. In this paper, we consider the data collected until the end of December 2008. The entire dataset is publicly available [19] and has been collected using `mrinfo-rec`.

During the whole probing period, on average, `mrinfo-rec` daily discovered roughly 10,000 different routers while scanning 100,000 interfaces. For the remainder of this paper, we remove interfaces with non-publicly routable IP addresses or marked as down or disabled. The addresses that we consider as non-publicly routable are the special-use IPv4 addresses described in [20]. Specifically, we eliminate the private IP address blocks 10.0.0.0/8, 172.16.0.0/12, and 192.168.0.0/16. We also remove the loopback address block 127.0.0.0/8 and the 0.0.0.0 address. On average, 25% of the interfaces collected by `mrinfo-rec` are categorized as non-publicly routable. We also remove all multicast tunnel interfaces detected with the keyword "tunnel" in the `mrinfo` raw output.

From our four year daily dataset, we arbitrarily select, each month, the largest `mrinfo-rec` output file, leading thus to 56 global topologies. Those 56 graphs form the dataset analyzed in this paper.

In the analysis provided in this paper, the inference of *L2 networks* is critical. In our context, by L2 network, we mean a technology allowing a router to transmit IP packets to several other IP routers through the same interface, i.e., a multi-access network. One often distinguishes between *Non Broadcast Multiple Access* (NBMA) networks (ATM, Frame Relay, X25), and *broadcast networks* such as most LAN networks (Ethernet, token ring, FDDI).

These two kinds of networks behave differently as far as IP multicast is concerned. In particular, when using *Protocol Independent Multicast* (PIM) as a routing protocol in a broadcast network, each router is a PIM neighbor of each other, and only one of them is elected as the *querier* [21]. These properties can be easily checked with the `mrinfo` raw output (see the symmetry and querier rules in Sec. 2.3). In NBMA networks, IP packets are usually transmitted via circuits that behave as a collection of point-to-point or point-to-multipoint connections (which does not imply the rules defined in Sec. 2.3). Note that if these circuits locally use different subinterfaces and IP addresses, they cannot be discovered by `mrinfo`.

Furthermore, we can also study the specific case of MPLS networks [22]. Notice first that an MPLS network is not an actual L2 network since MPLS routers are usually IP routers, and MPLS signalling (LDP [23], RSVP [24], BGP [25]) uses IP. On the one hand, most techniques to transmit multicast packets over MPLS (for traffic engineering or multicast L3 VPN) use some sort of tunnels (Traffic engineering tunnels, or GRE encapsulation for PIM in L3 VPN), and since we discard tunnel interfaces from `mrinfo` output in our analysis, such MPLS networks should not introduce artifacts. On the other hand, in the case of basic MPLS, multicast packets are not sent through Label Switch Paths (LSP), contrary to unicast packets. Therefore, although `traceroute` may infer a false link between the two endpoints of an LSP, `mrinfo` will correctly provide the direct IP neighbor. However, the case of *L2 multicast VPN* (VPLS [26, 27]) is different since IP multicast routers (if any) of each customer site will see each other through a virtual L2 switch instead of the provider MPLS network. The `mrinfo` analysis will correctly discover this L2 network, but will not detect that it is an L2 VPN through the provider network. However this can happen only in customer ASes and will be seen only if `mrinfo` queries are not filtered between the VPN and Internet which is not very likely. In the following, we only study the impact of broadcast L2 networks: in practice, *ethernet networks* such as switches.

Among all interfaces discovered in our selected dataset (i.e., 56 global topologies), more than a million has a fully qualified domain name that allows us to determine the physical interface type (i.e., ge0, tunnel0, vlan500, pos0, ..., are typical naming conventions used by network administrators). About 42% of these names allow us to infer the interface type. Focusing on multi-access networks, we notice that about 99% of discovered interfaces seem to be Ethernet links of various data rates (from 10M to 10G) or VLAN interfaces (probably on top of Ethernet interfaces too).

2.3 L2 Inference

In Sec. 2.1, we have seen how an L2 network is suggested from the raw `mrinfo` output. However, this inference comes with two limitations. First, we are only able to detect L2 networks involving at least three routers. Second, the inferred presence of an L2 network may hide a "cascade" of L2 networks. However, the nature of the router degree distribution (i.e., the actual number of devices directly connected to it) is not impacted by those limitations. Only the degree of L2 networks might suffer from this. In this paper, we

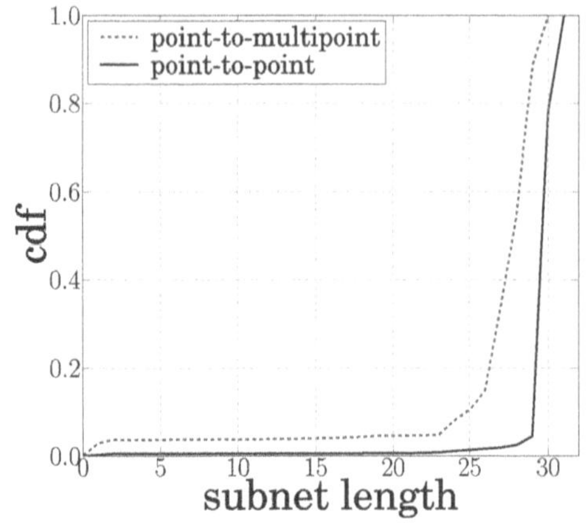

Figure 3: Subnet length distribution for point-to-point and point-to-multipoint connections

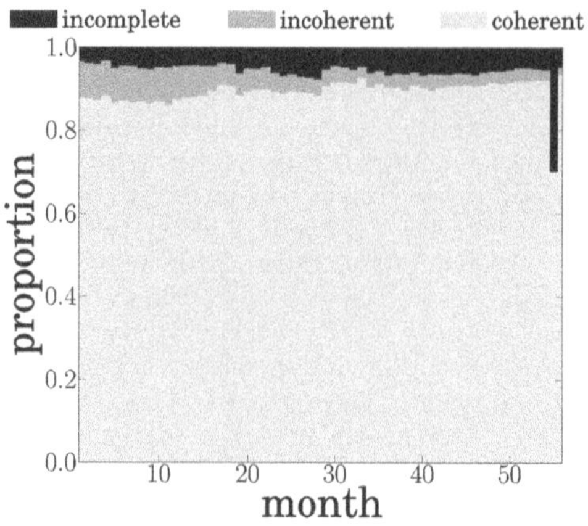

Figure 4: L2 inference rule verification with a /16 threshold for the subnet mask rule

focus on the degree distribution of routers considering the difference between the L2 and L3 visions.

Here, we verify whether our inference technique is accurate and what kind of technology it seems to reveal. Indeed, there are several kinds of L2 networks such ATM clouds or simple Ethernet switches. In our analysis, we particularly focus on broadcast L2 networks such as Ethernet.

There are several ways to validate our L2 inference technique. First, one could use small testbeds and access networks whose administrators give us the physical map. We performed such tests in our local AS in Strasbourg and found that our inference is correct in revealing L2 networks.

Second, the validation can be done "theoretically" based on three rules:

- *symmetry rule.* We verify that all the routers attached to a given potential L2 network have the same view. For instance, on Fig. 2, we are able to detect that router R_2 is connected to R_5 and R_6 through an L2 network. When probing R_5 and R_6 with `mrinfo`, the L2 connection to R_2 must also be visible in their `mrinfo` output as well as the connection between them. Such a symmetry rule suggests the detection of broadcast L2 network.

- *querier rule.* In a normal case, only one router per L2 network must be tagged as the IGMP "querier" (i.e., it won the querier election on the subnet [21]: it has the greatest IP address on the subnet). In the case depicted in Fig. 2, as interface `1.1.2.3` is tagged as "querier", interfaces `1.1.2.1` of R_5 and `1.1.2.2` of R_6 should not be tagged as such.

- *subnet mask rule.* We verify the validity of the minimum subnet mask covering all IPs involved in the L2 network. Fig. 3 provides the cumulative distribution of the subnet lengths for point-to-point (i.e., a direct connection involving two routers) and point-to-multipoint (i.e., three or more L3 routers connected through an L2 network) connections. We notice that roughly 90% of the prefix lengths are very long: usually longer than /24 for point-to-multipoint and using a /30 or /31 prefix for point-to-point connections.

  Fig. 3 shows that more than 99% of the point-to-point connections (plain line) use a subnet mask longer than /24 and more than 95% uses a subnet mask longer than /28. In a few cases the minimal subnet mask may yield a prefix shorter that /24 or even /16 (less than 5% for point-to-multipoint connections). This is probably an anomaly, possibly explained by the use of tunneling or a NBMA L2 WAN technology (ATM, frame relay, ...). We consider a /16 threshold for the minimal subnet mask rule applied to an L2 network.

Note that the symmetry and the querier rule need at least two responding L3 nodes connected to the same L2 network to be verified. Based on those three rules, we classify an L2 inference in one of three categories:

- *coherent.* In this case, the three rules are verified and we are sure that our L2 inference technique is accurate and suggests a traditional L2 broadcast network. This is the best case.

- *incoherent.* In this case, at least one of the three rules is not verified. This category gathers L2 networks that we are not able to accurately reveal (such as NBMA L2 WAN technology).

- *incomplete.* In this case, the L2 component is only seen by a single L3 device (the symmetry and querier rules cannot be verified).

Fig. 4 shows how our L2 inference technique verifies the three prescribed rules over the 56 months. Note that L2 inferred networks falling in the *coherent* category are typically "broadcast L2 network" such as Ethernet switches (thanks to the symmetry and querier rules).

Over the whole period and on average, we have the following results: 90.16% of the L2 inferred nodes are coherent and suggest broadcast capable L2 networks such as Ethernet switches. 5.84% of the inferred nodes are incomplete, meaning that only 4% are incoherent. Thus, in the vast majority of the cases, our L2 inference algorithm seems to be verified and coherent. In the remainder of our analysis, we ignore L2 components falling into incoherent or incomplete categories. Note that those problematic cases are not uniformly

Notation	Meaning
S	set of L2 nodes
R	set of L3 nodes
$N = R \bigcup S$	set of nodes (including L2 inferred ones)
$succ(a)$	set of neighbors of node a
$deg(a) = \|succ(a)\|$	degree of node a in the L2 graph
$r(x)$	number of L3 nodes of degree x
$s(x)$	number of L2 nodes of degree x
$t(x) = r(x) + s(x)$	number of nodes of degree x
$p(x)$	number of L3 nodes having a degree of x and at least one neighbor in S
$b(x)$	number of L3 nodes having x neighbors in S
$r'(x)$	number of routers having a logical L3 degree of x in the L3 graph

Table 1: Notations

distributed across the domains and time: for example, we notice that a large proportion of those cases comes from AS680 and AS5400 and seem to progressively and slightly disappear. We suppose that those cases correspond to "L2 circuits technologies" such as ATM.

Finally, note that the drop observed on Fig. 4 during the week 55 is due to a stronger filtering policy applied by the French National Research Network leading to a strong decrease in the amount of routers discovered by `mrinfo`.

3. HOW L2 NETWORKS IMPACT THE L3 NODE DEGREE DISTRIBUTION

In the remainder of the paper, we focus on the relative difference between an L3 and an L2 vision of the network. We do not claim to provide the actual degree distribution: our goal is rather to emphasize the difference in the apparent connectivity when adopting a vision of the network at a given layer.

Hence, using the same set of IP addresses, we construct two graphs, one corresponding to a `traceroute` like view and the other to the L2-aware view inferred thanks to `mrinfo`. Obviously, our analysis is based on a partial view of the Internet graph. Furthermore, we restrict the two constructed topologies to their connected and responding components, i.e., we remove all links connected to a router that does not respond to `mrinfo` so that we guarantee a set of active and existing links and routers. We assume that this partial vision does not impact the relative comparison although it may introduce some non coherent results in an absolute analysis, e.g., a large proportion of leaf routers. In practice, these routers might be located at the boundary of the multicast part of the probed network. Indeed, if their neighbors not already discovered are not multicast enabled, `mrinfo` will only report one active link per multicast border router: the one allowing `mrinfo-rec` to reach it.

3.1 Notations

In an L2-aware graph, there are two types of connections: L3 point-to-point connections that are correctly interpreted by traceroute, and L2 point-to-multipoint connections that are seen as a full mesh of point-to-point connections using traceroute. Our goal is to measure the importance of this confusion using the node degree distribution as an indicator to understand the difference between the L3 and L2 graphs. Note that one may also use other indicators such as the clustering coefficient, the assortativity, or a path diversity indicator.

Table 1 provides the basic definitions and notations used in the remainder of this paper. In our analysis, the notion of *degree* is related to the L2 graph. In contrast, we use the term *layer-3 degree* to refer to the number of edges discovered by an L3 tool such as traceroute. A node n has a logical L3 degree of x if and only if

$$deg_r(n) + deg_s(n) = x. \quad (1)$$

Notations $deg_r(a)$ and $deg_s(a)$ respectively refer to the L3 point-to-point degree of node a, and to the L3 point-to-multipoint degree of a such that:

$$deg_s(a) = \sum_{\forall v \in succ(a) \ \mid \ v \in S} (deg(v) - 1). \quad (2)$$

Furthermore, we consider the IP multigraph issue: there might exist several links or IP address pairs connecting the same two nodes. In our analysis, the degree of a node is the number of the neighboring IP addresses, e.g., the number of active and replying IP addresses seen on the right part of the raw `mrinfo` output. Typically, an L2 node refers to a broadcast network such as an Ethernet switch, while an L3 node corresponds to an IP router.

Eqn. 2 is the key point of our analysis: L2 point-to-multipoint connections between a node a and its neighbors are seen as a full mesh using an L2 agnostic view, whereas using `mrinfo`, we can infer a star centered on L2 nodes instead of cliques.

In order to reveal the underlying L2 topology, when parsing our dataset, we generate an L2 aware graph containing inferred L2 nodes and links. The set of nodes in this L2 inferred graph is denoted N. Except considering the use of technologies such as VLAN, we can assume that this vision describes the L2 topology. Let us assume an L2 network connected to m routers ($2m$ directed links in the L2 graph), then it induces $m \times (m-1)$ directed links in the L3 graph. With the use of VLAN, let us now consider k VLANs deployed on a L2 node connecting m routers (at most $2km$ directed links in the L2 graph instead of $2m$ in the physical topology), then, in the worst case, it can induce $km \times (m-1)$ directed links in the L3 graph. Note that we provide a lower bound on the bias resulting from a L3 graph when considering the physical topology: $2m < 2km \leq km \times (m-1)$, $\forall k > 1$, $m \geq 3$. Moreover, our analysis is conservative because `mrinfo` may underestimate the number of active IP interfaces: the probing view is restricted to multicast enabled links and `mrinfo` replies may be fragmented and then only partially interpreted. See the technical report [28] for details.

3.2 Results

In this section, we focus on the node degree distribution considering two points of view: the logical L3 graph and the underlying L2 graph. In particular, we would like to know how L2 devices might impact the degree distribution. The purpose of our study is to: (1) highlight the huge difference between graphs describing L2 and L3 connections, and (2) explain why there exist nodes with very high degree in a L3 graph.

Using our L2 inference technique, we can easily compute $r(x)$ (i.e., the number of L3 nodes of degree x - see Table 1) and $s(x)$ (i.e., the number of L2 nodes of degree x - see Table 1). In contrast, with an L2 agnostic view such as with traceroute, the global degree distribution is purely logical: we can only compute $r'(x)$ (i.e., the number of routers having a logical L3 degree of x - see Table 1). Hence, using our `mrinfo` dataset, we can easily emphasize the difference between $t(x)$ (i.e., the sum of $r(x)$ and $s(x)$ - see Table 1) and $r'(x)$ because we are able to compute all key distributions defined in Table 1.

Fig. 5 shows the difference between those two distributions.[2] The horizontal axis gives the degree, while the vertical axis shows the proportion distribution. The shaded area represents the $t(x)$ distribution while the line refers to the $r'(x)$ distribution. Note that the maximum degree for $r'(x)$ is 115 but it is too tight (0.01%) to appear on the plot.

The degree distribution is strongly impacted using only an L3 perspective: the L2 agnostic distribution has a much more heavy tail than the one considering both L2 and L3 nodes. For example, using the L2 view ($t(x)$), we observe that there do not exist routers having a degree greater than 45 whereas the L3 views ($r'(x)$) suggests routers having degree larger than 100. This means that there are more nodes having large degree when L2 interconnections are translated to full mesh connections. Consequently, it also means that the shape parameter used to model the power law distribution of the node degree and the degree of connectivity in general are strongly biased if one wants to consider a physical view of a given network (which is generally the case when measuring path diversity characteristics for example).

This result is of the highest interest since many studies use L3 topologies such as those provided by *Rocketfuel* [29] to perform path redundancy analysis and to evaluate the quality of the re-routing protocol offered by link protection schemes [30, 31]. However, Rocketfuel topologies do not model the specific *Shared Risk Link Groups* (SRLG) [32, 33] of L2 networks. This leads to nodes with overestimated degree and thus more path diversity and redundancy than in the actual underlying graph.

A first attempt to model the high degree shifting of an L3 view is to consider that a router connected to an L2 network "will increase" its logical L3 degree by the number of neighbors connected to that L2 network. With a naive model considering that, in the vast majority of cases, L2 networks interconnect leaf routers (e.g., routers of degree 1, so that distributions $p(x)$ and $b(x)$ -see Table 1- are meaningless), we may obtain:

$$r'(x) \approx \begin{cases} r(x) + s(x+1) \times x & \text{if } x > 1, \\ r(1) - \sum_{s \in S} deg(s) & \text{otherwise.} \end{cases} \quad (3)$$

However, we can easily notice that this model is not sufficient to explain the heavy tail of the L3 distribution. Indeed, we can observe that obtaining such an amount of nodes having such a high degree requires point-to-multipoint connections through multiple L2 nodes. We will detail this issue in the next section considering a closer look at each key distribution (e.g., the L2 nodes degree distribution and the number of L2 neighbors) and according to the specifics of several routing domains.

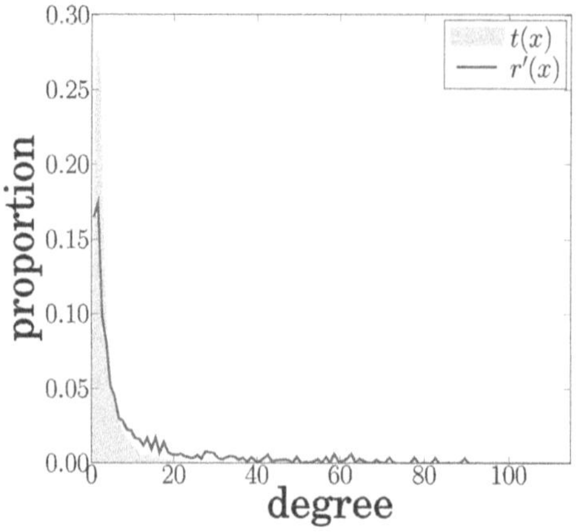

Figure 5: L2 ($t(x)$) vs. L3 ($r'(x)$) Node Degree Distribution Comparison

4. DOMAIN SPECIFICITY

In Sec. 3, we have seen that the impact of L2 networks on the node degree distribution is considerable. This analysis was done on our entire dataset, without considering the potential particularities of domains. In this section, we refine our analysis, focusing on several ASes of interest: we want to know whether there exist some common patterns between domains.

We first discuss our methodology in extracting and selecting particular domains from the raw `mrinfo` dataset (Sec. 4.1) and, next, analyze the impact of L2 networks on the node degree distribution of selected ASes (Sec. 4.2).

4.1 Methodology

From our four year daily dataset, we arbitrarily select, each month, the largest `mrinfo-rec` output file, leading thus to 56 global topologies. For each of these 56 selected `mrinfo-rec` files, we extract the topologies of four particular ASes. This extraction is made possible with our *router-to-AS* mapping algorithm [16]. This algorithm assigns a unique AS number to each router and identifies AS border routers (ASBRs). Our algorithm is based on a set of rules using common IP address allocation guidelines and probabilistic methods. To reenforce our mapping, it verifies, at each step, the consistency of the assignment returned by each rule. A subset of those rules are also used in [34].

Using this router-to-AS mapping, we have extracted a set of intra-domain topologies that can be classified as follows: *Tier-1* (such as Sprint), *Transit* (such as IUnet), and *Stub* networks (such as UNINETT). Those one-per-month topologies are freely available in various formats.[3]

Due to space limitations, we only consider four ASes taken from the set of extracted topologies, two being Tier-1 (AS1239

[2]For the sake of clarity, we select only one of our 56 global topologies, the one being the most connected (i.e., with the maximum number of edges). The general behavior is roughly identical across our whole set of global topologies.

[3]See `http://inl.info.ucl.ac.be/content/mrinfo`.

Level	ASN	Name	$\|R\|$		$\|S\|$		α		$\beta - L3$		$\beta - L2$	
Global	-	-	8,670	±448	1,100	±63	0.38	±0.01	0.69	±0.01	0.34	±0.01
Tier-1	1239	Sprint	649	±7	63	±0	0.58	±0.01	0.70	±0.01	0.34	±0.01
	3356	Level-3	254	±6	123	±7	0.67	±0.03	0.87	±0.01	0.69	±0.01
Transit	1267	IUnet	517	±16	225	±10	0.77	±0.04	0.85	±0.03	0.74	±0.03
	3269	Telecom Italia	822	±28	73	±2	0.69	±0.02	0.95	±0.01	0.67	±0.01

Table 2: Selected ASes global overview

and AS3356) and two being Transit (AS1267 and AS3269). We select those ASes because they are the largest topologies in our dataset. Furthermore, they are very well connected and seem more impacted by the presence of L2 networks compared to the global vision provided by the whole dataset (see Table 2). We performed the same analysis for other domains, results can be found in [28]. Note that we remove inter-domain links from those topologies reducing so the degree of connectivity of the routers in those ASes.

Table 2 provides an overview of the amount of L3 and L2 nodes in our dataset. Values have been averaged over the 56 considered `mrinfo` files. The confidence intervals are also given. In addition, Table 2 provides three ratios: (α) the proportion of routers connected to at least one L2 node in the L2 graph, and ($\beta - L3$ and $\beta - L2$) the proportion of connections using an L2 node. Note that $\beta - L3$ refers to the quantity of connections using an L2 point-to-multipoint network in the L3 graph whereas $\beta - L2$ refers to the same quantity in the L2 graph.

For the remainder of the analysis and for the sake of clarity, we select only one probing day per AS according to the size of the largest connected component inside each AS. [28, Sec. V] details this process: intuitively, we simply extract the *best topology* for each AS.

4.2 Experimental results

First, as shown in Table 2, the proportion of L2 nodes (i.e., $\frac{S}{N}$) is generally quite significant. On the whole dataset, approximately 11.2% of the nodes are inferred as L2 nodes. It is worth to notice that this proportion is not uniformly distributed across ASes. For instance, some large ASes, such as AS1267 or AS3356, verify: $|S| \approx 0.3 \times |N|$. This high proportion can obviously lead to an important difference when considering the connectivity degree in L2 and L3 graphs. However, another aspect impacts this difference: if the degree of L2 nodes is high, it means that a large number of routers are involved in L2 connections. For example, we can notice that, although less than 10% of the nodes in AS3269 are L2 networks, about 97% of the connections between routers modeled by a L3 graph actually involve L2 nodes. This phenomenon is due to the fact that L2 nodes interconnect a large number of routers. It is worth to notice that the number of logical links is much more important in the L3 graph than the number of "physical " links in the L2 one when most of L2 nodes involve more than three routers.

In the fashion of Fig. 5, and for the four considered ASes, Fig. 6 compares the node degree distribution when L2 nodes are taken into account ($t(x)$ - see Table 1) and when L2 nodes are ignored by an L3 only vision ($r'(x)$).

As mentioned in Sec. 3, we notice a great shift in the distribution of large degrees. However, we observe that this difference significantly varies from one AS to another. For example, Level 3 is much more impacted than Sprint. In all cases, we can notice that the model given in Eqn. 3 cannot describe such a degree shifting. For instance, even for Sprint, the maximum router degree in the topology is 21 (see Fig. 7(a)). And if we assume that this router is connected to the largest L2 node of degree 21 (see Fig. 7(b)), we may obtain a L3 logical degree of $21 + 21 - 1 = 41$ whereas there exists a router having 47 neighbors in the L3 topology. Note that the Sprint topology given in the Rocketfuel dataset [29] presents approximatively the same degree distribution as the L3 one ($r'(x)$) given in Fig. 6(a): there also exists routers having a degree greater than 40. However, note that it is likely that this bias is also due to alias resolution limitations.

The bias resulting from an L2 agnostic view obviously depends on the $s(x)$ distribution, but also on the way L2 and L3 nodes are interconnected. Indeed, we can notice that the ratio $\frac{S}{N}$ is not the only factor explaining this bias. Fig. 6 shows completely different $t(x)$ and $r'(x)$ distributions even for topologies with less than 10% of L2 nodes, such as Sprint and Telecom Italia.

In practice, two other distributions could emphasize the influence of L2 nodes: $p(x)$ (i.e., the number of L3 nodes n having a degree of $x \mid deg_s(n) > 0$ - see Table 1), and $b(x)$ (i.e., number of L3 nodes having x L2 neighbors - see Table 1). Fig. 7(a), Fig. 7(b), Fig. 7(c), and Fig. 7(d) illustrate some key patterns useful to understand the difference between $t(x)$ and $r'(x)$.

First of all, we can notice among our set of selected ASes illustrated on Fig. 7 that network administrators do not seem to use a common engineering way to construct and deploy their topology. It highly depends on economic and technological factors not captured by classical models. Compared to the global analysis depicted in Fig. 5, we can highlight the difficulty of providing a model capturing the particularities of each domain.

Second, focusing on common properties, we can observe that r and p are slightly different distributions: keeping in mind that most routers counted in the r distribution also fall in p, we can emphasize the fact that peak values in r become still more important in p such that routers connected to L2 networks may strongly influence those peaks values. For example, in AS1239, it means that globally 40% of its routers have a degree of 1 while focusing on routers connected to L2 nodes, this proportion grows to almost 70%. In practice, on AS1239, we can conclude that the majority of the routers connected to L2 nodes are leaf nodes. However, this observation is highly topology dependent. The only common characteristic is the increase of the same peak values for each AS. Those results explain why the difference between the t and r' distributions shown in Fig. 6 is so high for most representative degree values.

Fig. 7(b) and Fig. 7(d) plot the degree distribution of L2

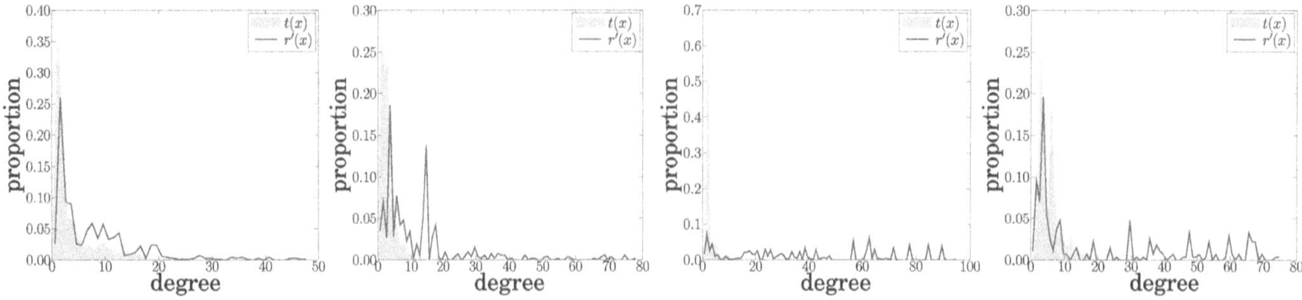

(a) AS 1239: Sprint (b) AS 1267: IUnet (c) AS 3269: Telecom Italia (d) AS 3356: Level-3

Figure 6: L2 ($t(x)$) vs. L3 ($r'(x)$) Degree distribution comparison for our set of selected ASes

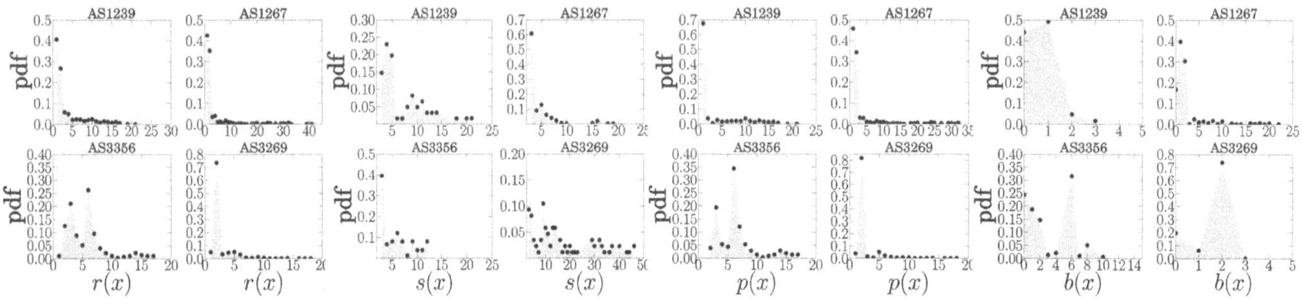

(a) L3 node degree distribution (b) L2 node degree distribution (c) Routers having L2 neighbors (d) Number of L2 neighbors

Figure 7: Key distributions for our selected ASes

nodes, $s(x)$, and the distribution of the number of L2 neighbors of routers, $b(x)$. First, we can notice on Fig. 7(d) that the power law modeling the L2 node degree distribution is again highly dependent on the topology and not equivalent to the one modeling $r(x)$ for each given topology. The maximum degree of $s(x)$ plays a critical role in the absolute difference between $t(x)$ and $r'(x)$ but Fig. 7(c) highlights the higher importance of $b(x)$. First, we can see on Fig. 7(d) that most routers are connected to L2 nodes. Only 10% for AS3356 and 40% for AS1239 of routers are only connected through point-to-point links. Moreover, we observe that, for topologies such as AS1267 and AS3269, most routers are not connected to a single L2 node but to several ones: two for AS3269 and six for AS3356. Generally speaking, the number of L2 neighbors is an important factor explaining the heavy tail distribution of $r'(x)$. In practice, it means that a significant subset of the routers are connected to several high degree L2 nodes. Surprisingly, this experimental analysis shows that, for topologies such as AS3356 and AS3269, more than half of the routers are connected to more than two L2 nodes. We also notice that there exists routers connected to more than 20 L2 nodes in AS1267: in that case, it probably means that those routers are involved in VLANs crossing one or several switches.

Fig. 8 illustrates two practical cases leading to a large difference between $r'(x)$ and $t(x)$ distributions. Those scenarios are common in our dataset and may explain why the impact of L2 networks is so significant:

(a) MAN access routers are generally connected to multiple metropolitan locations to distribute the access. The use of L2 networks is very common in order to facilitate and reduce the cost of small deployments.

(b) The use of redundant access connections for load balancing purposes can increase of this effect.

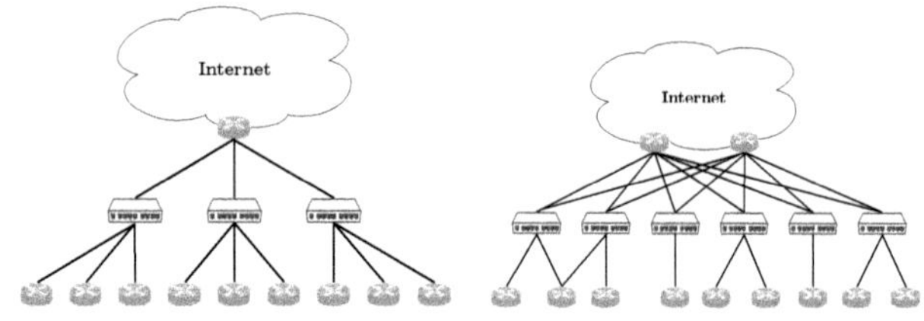

(a) access (b) redundancy

Figure 8: Examples of L2 configuration

On Fig. 8(a), the Internet access router has a logical L3 degree of nine while it has actually only three physical links. On Fig. 8(b), the two access routers are logically connected to each other router in order to ensure load balancing and resiliency. Note that a further analysis is necessary to understand the difference in terms of L2 usage between core and access part of a network. Indeed, the pure backbone part is probably differently impacted than the border of a network. To mitigate this effect, we need to characterize the core and access parts in order to divide networks in multiple areas. The use of traceroute probes may help us to perform such a mapping. However, this is a huge challenge that is outside the scope of this paper.

5. WHY SUCH A GREAT SHIFT IN THE NODE DEGREE DISTRIBUTION?

The goal of this section is to model the relationships between the key L2 and L3 distributions explaining such an heavy tail distribution when considering a L3 view. We focus on the correlation between L2 and L3 devices that generates routers having a very high degree. In Sec. 4.2, we have seen that the degree distribution of L2 nodes ($s(x)$) and the distribution of the number of L2 neighbors ($b(x)$) are the first impacting factors.

5.1 L2 and L3 Correlations

In order to provide an accurate model, correlations between keys distributions should be considered. For routers involved in L2 interconnections, we denote p their maximum degree and b their maximum number of L2 neighbors. Using $r(x)$, $p(x)$ and normalizing $b(x)$ and $s(x)$[6], we are able to propose a probabilistic model. For that purpose, we also need to quantify the nature of the dependence between the $p(x)$, $b(x)$ and $s(x)$ distributions.

Fig. 9 shows the normalized $p(x) \times b(x)$ dependence distribution (in practice, we have also plotted the distribution of routers which are not connected to L2 nodes). It allows us to understand the relationship between the $p(x)$ and $b(x)$ distributions. Obviously, $b(x)$ depends on $p(x)$ because a router cannot have more L2 neighbors than its total degree, as indicated by empty portions in upper triangles of Fig. 9. We further notice that large degree routers generally have a great number of their neighborhood being L2 nodes.

We thus observe a strong correlation between those two distributions meaning that $b(x)$ is not uniformly distributed among routers and their degree: a router having a large number of neighbors has a higher likelihood to be connected to a large number of L2 nodes. This correlation seems quite linear on most of the ASes that we analyzed.

We do not find any other linear dependency between other relationships: Figs. 10 and 11 do not suggest any kind of obvious dependence in relationships[7]. However, we cannot argue that there does not exist any kind of non linear dependence. Figs. 10 and 11 may also help to understand some specific behaviors seen in Fig. 6. Indeed, one can argue that $s(x)$ may be the main factor explaining the shift in the degree distribution. Potentially, if there exist some particular relations between $p(x)$ and $s(x)$, it may explain several shifting details in the degree distribution. For example, looking at the peak value at $x = 14$ in Fig. 6(b), we can explain this phenomenon with Fig. 11(b): we observe that a great number of routers having a degree of 1 ($p(1)$ values) are connected to L2 nodes of degree 15 resulting in a large value of routers having a logical L3 degree of $15 - 1 = 14$. However, this kind of behavior is highly topology dependent and do not seem to follow any particular rule. Taking this kind of exceptions into account leads to lose the model generality. Here, we propose a high level model trying to capture global properties.

In this section, we investigate whether the $p(x) \times b(x)$ dependence seems sufficient to explain the large tail of the L2-agnostic degree distribution. To study this question, we decide to only model the linear correlation between $p(x)$ and $b(x)$.

5.2 Model

In this section, we only model the relationship between the number of L2 neighbors and the total number of neighbors of a router. Our goal is to highlight the fact that this relationship conditions the L2-agnostic degree distribution. Our model works as follows: considering a router having i neighbors with j being L2 ones ($j \leq i$), its L3 logical degree may become $x = i - j + \eta$ where η denotes the sum of the degrees (minus one) of its L2 neighbors. Because we do not model any relationship between s and the other distributions, we consider that the degree of its L2 neighbors only depends on $s(x)$. Generalizing this idea, the set of routers having an L3 logical degree of x is composed by all routers having a lower degree that may reach this degree thanks to their L2 neighbors. Our model is probabilistic in the sense that we consider the probability that a router having a degree of i connected to a set of j L2 nodes will increase its L3 logical degree by a certain amount, $x - i$, to appear directly connected to x neighbors.

In the following, the notation $bp(i, j)$ refers to the probability to have a router having a degree of i and j L2 neighbors ($0 < j \leq i$). In other words, $bp(i, j)$ corresponds to the probability distribution function given in Fig. 9 without considering cases where $j = 0$. Hence, our probabilistic model verifies:

$$r'(x) \approx \begin{cases} r(x) + \chi(x) - p(x) & \text{if } x > 1 \\ r(x) - p(x) & \text{otherwise.} \end{cases} \quad (4)$$

with $\chi(x)$ referring to the probability that L3 nodes with a lower degree than x reach a degree of x because of their connections to L2 nodes, such that:

$$\chi(x) = \sum_{i=1}^{min(x-1,p)} \left[p(i) \times \sum_{j=1}^{min(i,b)} bp(i,j) \times c_j^i(x) \right] \quad (5)$$

where $c_j^i(x)$ denotes the sum of all possible product combinations between a set of j elements $\{s(a_1), \ldots, s(a_k), \ldots, s(a_j)\}$, with $2 < a_k \leq x - i - j + 3 \; \forall k \in [1, j]$, and such that:

$$\begin{aligned} \sum_{k=1}^{j} a_k &= x - i + 2j \\ &= \omega. \end{aligned} \quad (6)$$

We denote δ the set containing a_k's j-tuple, $\delta = [3, x - i - j + 3]^j$. Thus, it comes:

[5] Here, we also provide the degree distribution for routers which are not connected to L2 networks, i.e, $r(x)$ in general.
[6] Note that for $s(x)$, it implies to take into account the fact that large degree L2 nodes impact a greater number of routers than L2 nodes with small degree. For $b(x)$, we decide to model the dependence between this distribution and the one of $p(x)$.
[7] For these two figures we list the degree of L2 networks connected to routers and then analyze the potential dependence. Note that those distributions have been normalized according to the proportion of routers having a given x-axis value. Furthermore, one may also analyze the three dimensional relationship between p, s, and b distributions.

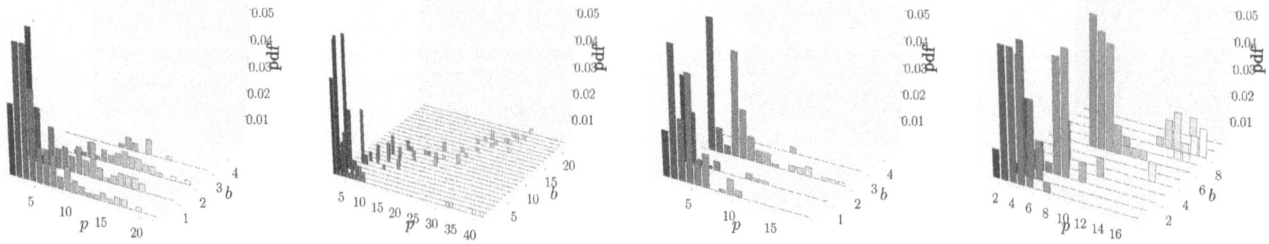

(a) AS 1239: Sprint (b) AS 1267: IUnet (c) AS 3269: Telecom Italia (d) AS 3356: Level-3

Figure 9: Dependence between p (degree of routers having L2 neighbors[5]) and b (number of L2 neighbors) distributions

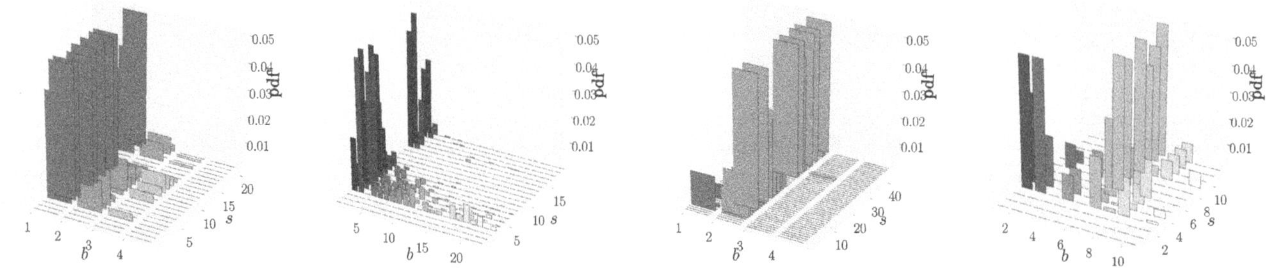

(a) AS 1239: Sprint (b) AS 1267: IUnet (c) AS 3269: Telecom Italia (d) AS 3356: Level-3

Figure 10: Dependence between b (number of L2 neighbors) and s (degree of L2 nodes) distributions

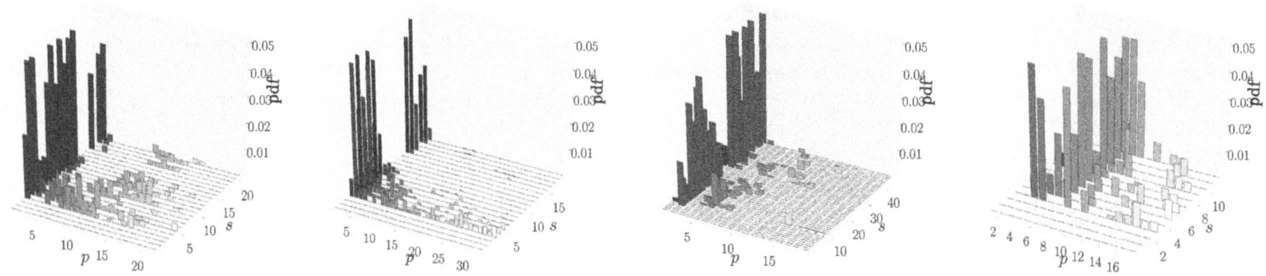

(a) AS 1239: Sprint (b) AS 1267: IUnet (c) AS 3269: Telecom Italia (d) AS 3356: Level-3

Figure 11: Dependence between p (degree of routers having L2 neighbors) and s (degree of L2 nodes) distributions

$$c_j^i(x) = \sum_{\forall \text{j-tuple}\{a_1,\ldots,a_j\}\in\delta \;|\; \sum_{k=1}^{j} a_k = \omega} \prod_{k=1}^{j} s(a_k) \quad (7)$$

Note that in practice we do not have to explore all possible combinations in the space δ to perform the computation of $c_j^i(x)$. Indeed, we do not care about the degree apparition order because $c_j^i(x)$ is a sum of products, so the j terms are permutable in each sub-product. Let us denote Δ the set of j-tuple $\{a_1,\ldots,a_j\} \in \delta$ verifying Eqn. 6. In practice, we then just need to compute:

$$c_j^i(x) = \sum_{\substack{\forall\{a_1,\ldots,a_l,\ldots,a_j\}\in\Delta \\ \text{such that } a_l \leq a_{l+1} \forall 0<l\leq j}} \prod_{k=1}^{j} s(a_k) \times \frac{k!}{\prod_{z=1}^{w} \sigma_z!} \quad (8)$$

where $\sigma_{z,1\leq\sigma_z\leq j}$, denotes the number of occurrence of each integer in the set Δ such that $\sum_{z=1}^{w} \sigma_z = j$. Thus, using this computation optimization, it is possible to compute $c_j^i(x)$ in a reasonable time, on the order of a few minutes

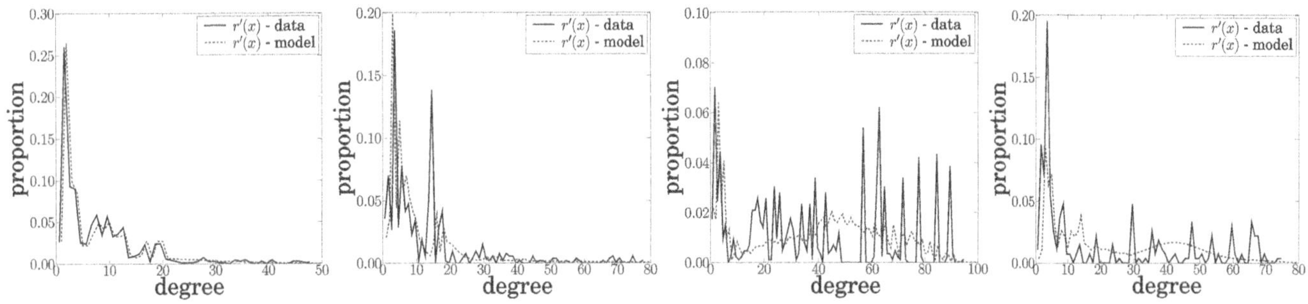

(a) AS 1239: Sprint (b) AS 1267: IUnet (c) AS 3269: Telecom Italia (d) AS 3356: Level-3

Figure 12: Degree distribution for real data and generated by our model using an L3 view ($r'(x)$)

even for $(i, j) \approx (40, 20)$ such as with AS1267. Results are given in Fig. 12: the lines labeled "$r'(x)$−model" correspond to the application of our model on our set of four ASes while the lines labeled "$r'(x)$−data" result from the experimental analysis. Depending on the AS, our model is more or less accurate to simulate the L3 view: it performs very well on Sprint but it is less accurate on Level-3. Indeed, the probabilistic nature of our model cannot capture sparse discrete values at the tail of the degree distribution. This values may be explained with some specific behavior of the $p \times s$ dependence. However, in all cases, our model captures the significant probability to generate a great shift in the node degree distribution. Considering a high level view of service providers networks using power laws shape to model their properties, we argue that our model is sufficient to provide a first step in the L2 aware topology generation. We claim that a probabilistic generation model taking into account parameters such that the similarity between r and p, the fact that s has a different shape than r and the linear correlation between p and b is able to provide the first step of the generation of L2 aware graphs. The second step consists in analyzing the connectivity nature of relationships between nodes: does it often exist a similar pattern (e.g., the degree) or some sort of correlation between directly connected nodes? This question implies the study of other graph properties such as the clustering coefficient in L2 aware networks.

5.3 Summary

Using the model given in Eqn. 4, we implicitly assume the independence between $s(x)$ and the two other distributions: $p(x)$ and $b(x)$. However, as shown in Fig. 12, our model captures the heavy tailed distribution $r'(x)$ on each AS. Although it does not integrate all stochastic details (Fig. 10 and 11 may help to solve peak values at the tail or differences at the head), it captures the significant probability to generate nodes with high degree. This result emphasizes the importance of the correlation between L2 and L3 degree properties and tends to show that the main critical relationship between key distributions is the one linking $p(x)$ and $b(x)$.

Thus, the answer to the question "Why such a great shift in the node degree distribution?" is: "*Because a large proportion of the links of large degree routers are usually connected to L2 nodes*". In practice, on Fig. 9(a), we can interpret this answer like this: the largest router seen in Sprint has 21 neighbors with two being L2 networks. Then, considering the L3 view, this router may reach, in theory (i.e., following the general idea of Eqn. 4), a degree of $21-2+2\times(21-1) = 59$ (21 also being the maximum degree of L2 nodes). This phenomenon is exacerbated for topologies such as Level-3 (AS3356) because most large degree routers have many L2 neighbors (≥ 6). Note that, in the worst theoretical case, we might observe routers having a L3 logical degree of roughly 100 in this L3 topology.

Although there does not exist a common model describing all topologies, we have shown that the heavy tail of the node degree distribution using a pure L3 view is due to multiple factors (in particular $s(x)$ and $b(x)$ distributions), and the correlation between $p(x)$ and $b(x)$ helps to understand the shift in the degree distribution generated by an L3 view.

In order to generate L2-aware topologies, it is necessary to carefully consider several distributions, e.g., $r(x)$, $p(x)$, $s(x)$, $b(x)$, and their relationships to produce realistic models. Our model is a first basis for L2-aware graphs generation. According to the set of keys distributions and their similarities, it may allow for generating L2 topologies focusing on particular relationships between $p(x)$, $b(x)$, and $s(x)$ distributions. The next step being to model other properties, such as the assortativity, in order to capture the connectivity nature between nodes.

Finally, using L3 traces such as those obtained by traceroute campaigns and minimal L2 information, one may analytically refine our model to produce L2 aware topologies verifying several L2-L3 connectivity constraints. For example, it is possible to simplify the model and so reduce the number of distributions taken into account by considering some relationships between key them (e.g, the one between $r(x)$ and $p(x)$) and modeling them with specific power laws.

6. RELATED WORK

Modeling Internet topology has been a large subject of research since Faloutsos et al. seminal paper [8] in which they discuss the existence of power law relationships between several properties of the Internet graph.

If this work has been extended by others [35, 36, 37, 38, 39], it has also been strongly questioned. In particular, Lakhina et al. [9] show that if a graph has a node degree distribution that is very different from a power law, sampling from a small set of vantage points will yield a picture of a graph with a node degree distribution that follows a power law. One of the reasons evoked by Lakhina et al. is that the sampled graph has fewer edges than the genuine graph. Clauset and Moore [10] explain analytically this bias. They demonstrate that, for sparse random graphs of large average degree, the apparent degree distribution displays a power law.

These biases have been further studied by Petermann and De Los Rios [40], and Dall'Asta et al. [41]. Guillaume and Latapy [42] have extended these studies to include the trade-off between the number of monitors and the number of destinations.

Li et al. have shown that the node degree distribution is not sufficient to describe network topology [43, 44]. They point out that there exist many different graphs having the same distribution of node degree. Some of them might be considered opposites from the point of view of network engineering. Instead, Li et al. propose models that incorporate technological constraints on router and link bandwidth and connectivity, together with abstract models of user demand and network performance.

Prior to our study, Pansiot and Grad already mentioned the influence of L2 networks on node degree as seen by traceroute [12]. Further, Clauset and Moore proposed another explanation for the emergence of power law degree distributions: the complex interaction of routers with the link-level topology (identical to our "L2 networks"). However, on the contrary to our work, they do not quantify the influence of L2 clouds. They further do not provide any model. Willinger et al. [13] also mention opaque L2 clouds as a source of potential bias when using traceroute based probing. In this paper, we go further by quantifying, on a large dataset, the impact of broadcast L2 networks, making them less opaque.

7. CONCLUSION

In this paper, we analyzed how layer-2 (L2) networks impact the node degree distribution resulting from a pure layer-3 (L3) vision (such as with data collected by traceroute). Our analysis is based on a large dataset collected using `mrinfo`, a tool that silently discovers all multicast enabled IPv4 interfaces of a given router and that allows one to infer L2 networks interconnecting routers.

Our analysis showed that the power law shape usually describing the node degree distribution of IP networks is strongly impacted when considering the presence of L2 devices. In particular, the tail of the degree distribution is much less heavy when L2 networks are taken into account. Our results show that, unfortunately, there does not exist obvious common patterns between domains. However, for the ISP topologies studied in this paper, L2 networks play an important role in the network connectivity: it is very likely that large degree routers are connected to multiple L2 nodes having themselves a large degree. Considering the physical topology, this implies that the actual degree of connectivity (e.g., the number of redundant physical paths) is generally lower than the one discovered by a pure L3 campaign using traceroute.

In addition, we proposed a first probabilistic model capturing the interaction between L2 and L3 topological properties. Among others, we highlighted that the degree of L2 networks is generally higher than the degree of L3 nodes and large degree routers are involved in many L2 connections.

In a near future, we plan to investigate the impact of L2 devices in IP networks according to their access and core backbone parts. More generally, our dataset also questions the power law nature of the node degree distribution. Using another probing methodology than traceroute, we might observe that the scale free property of the Internet may result from artifacts of a traceroute campaign.

Acknowledgements

This work has been partially supported by the European funded 216372 Trilogy project and the European funded 223936 ECODE project. Mr. Donnet's work is supported by the FNRS (Fonds National de la Recherche Scientifique, rue d'Egmont 5 – 1000 Bruxelles, Belgium).

8. REFERENCES

[1] k. claffy, Y. Hyun, K. Keys, M. Fomenkov, and D. Krioukov, "Internet mapping: from art to science," in *Proc. IEEE Cybersecurity Applications and Technologies Conference for Homeland Security (CATCH)*, March 2009.

[2] H. V. Madhyastha, T. Isdal, M. Piatek, C. Dixon, T. Anderson, A. Krishnamurthy, and A. Venkataramani, "iPlane: An information plane for distributed services," in *Proc. USENIX Symposium on Operating Systems Design and Implementation (OSDI)*, November 2006.

[3] Y. Shavitt and E. Shir, "DIMES: Let the internet measure itself," *ACM SIGCOMM Computer Communication Review*, vol. 35, no. 5, October 2005.

[4] M. Luckie, "Scamper: a scalable and extensible packet probet for active measurement of the Internet," in *Proc. USENIX/ACM Internet Measurement Conference (IMC)*, November 2010.

[5] V. Jacobson et al., "traceroute," UNIX," man page, 1989, see source code: ftp://ftp.ee.lbl.gov/traceroute.tar.gz.

[6] B. Donnet and T. Friedman, "Internet topology discovery: a survey," *IEEE Communications Surveys and Tutorials*, vol. 9, no. 4, pp. 2–15, December 2007.

[7] R. Pastor-Satorras and A. Vespignani, *Evolution and Structure of the Internet: a Statistical Physics Approach.* Cambridge University Press, February 2004.

[8] M. Faloutsos, P. Faloutsos, and C. Faloutsos, "On power-law relationships of the internet topology," in *Proc. ACM SIGCOMM*, September 1999.

[9] A. Lakhina, J. Byers, M. Crovella, and P. Xie, "Sampling biases in IP topology measurements," in *Proc. IEEE INFOCOM*, April 2003.

[10] A. Clauset and C. Moore, "Traceroute sampling makes random graphs appear to have power law degree distributions," arXiv, cond-mat 0312674, February 2004.

[11] P. Erdös and A. Rényi, "On the evolution of random graphs," *Publ. Math. Inst. Hung. Acad. Sci.*, vol. 5, pp. 17–61, 1960.

[12] J.-J. Pansiot and D. Grad, "On routes and multicast trees in the Internet," *ACM SIGCOMM Computer Communication Review*, vol. 28, no. 1, pp. 41–50, January 1998.

[13] W. Willinger, D. Alderson, and J. Doyle, "Mathematics and the Internet: a source of enormous confusion and great potential," *Notices of the*

American Mathematical Society, vol. 56, no. 5, pp. 586–599, May 2009.

[14] V. Jacobson, "`mrinfo` ," 1995, see http://cvsweb.netbsd.org/bsdweb.cgi/src/usr.sbin/mrinfo/?only_with_tag=MAIN.

[15] P. Mérindol, V. Van den Schriek, B. Donnet, O. Bonaventure, and J.-J. Pansiot, "Quantifying ASes multiconnectivity using multicast information," in *Proc. ACM USENIX Internet Measurement Conference (IMC)*, November 2009.

[16] J.-J. Pansiot, P. Mérindol, B. Donnet, and O. Bonaventure, "Extracting intra-domain topology from `mrinfo` probing," in *Proc. Passive and Active Measurement Conference (PAM)*, April 2010.

[17] S. Deering, "Host extensions for IP multicasting," Internet Engineering Task Force, RFC 1112, August 1989.

[18] T. Pusateri, "Distance vector multicast routing protocol version 3 (DVMRP)," Internet Engineering Task Force, Internet Draft (Work in Progress) draft-ietf-idmr-dvmrp-v3-11, October 2003.

[19] J.-J. Pansiot, "`mrinfo` dataset," see http://svnet.u-strasbg.fr/mrinfo/.

[20] IANA, "Special-use IPv4 addresses," Internet Engineering Task Force, RFC 3330, September 2002.

[21] W. Fenner, "Internet group management protocol (IGMP), version 2," Internet Engineering Task Force, RFC 2236, November 1997.

[22] E. Rosen, A. Viswanathan, and R. Callon, "Multiprotocol label switching architecture," Internet Engineering Task Force, RFC 3031, January 2001.

[23] L. Andersson, P. Doolan, N. Feldman, A. Fredette, and B. Thomas, "LDP specification," Internet Engineering Task Force, RFC 3036, January 2001.

[24] D. Awduche, L. Berger, D. Gan, T. Li, V. Srinivasan, and G. Swallow, "RSVP-TE: Extensions to RSVP for LSP tunnels," Internet Engineering Task Force, RFC 3209, December 2001.

[25] Y. Rekhter and E. Rosen, "Carrying label information in BGP-4," Internet Engineering Task Force, RFC 3107, May 2001.

[26] K. Kompella and Y. Rekhter, "Virtual private LAN service (VPLS) using BGP for auto-discovery and signaling," Internet Engineering Task Force, RFC 4761, January 2007.

[27] M. Lasserre and V. Kompella, "Virtual private LAN service (VPLS) using label distribution protocol (LDP) signaling," Internet Engineering Task Force, RFC 4762, January 2007.

[28] J.-J. Pansiot, P. Mérindol, B. Donnet, and O. Bonaventure, "Internet topology discovery through `mrinfo` probing," Université catholique de Louvain (UCL), Tech. Rep., October 2009, see http://inl.info.ucl.ac.be/content/mrinfo.

[29] N. Spring, R. Mahajan, and D. Wetherall, "Measuring ISP topologies with Rocketfuel," in *Proc. ACM SIGCOMM*, August 2002.

[30] Y. Ohara, S. Imahori, and R. Van Meter, "MARA: Maximum alternative routing algorithm," in *Proc. IEEE INFOCOM*, April 2009.

[31] K.-W. Kwong, L. Gao, R. Guérin, and Z.-L. Zhang, "On the feasibility and efficacy of protection routing in IP networks," in *Proc. IEEE INFOCOM*, March 2010.

[32] B. Rajagopalan, J. Luciani, and D. Awduche, "IP over optical networks: a framework," Internet Engineering Task Force, RFC 3717, March 2004.

[33] Network Protection, "Shared risk link group (SRLG)," February 2010, http://www.network-protection.net/shared-risk-link-group-srlg/.

[34] B. Huffaker, A. Dhamdhere, M. Fomenkov, and k. caffy, "Toward topology dualism: Improving the accuracy of AS annotations for routers," in *Proc. Passive and Active Measurement Conference (PAM)*, April 2010.

[35] D. Magoni and J. J. Pansiot, "Analysis of the autonomous system network topology," *ACM SIGCOMM Computer Communication Review*, vol. 31, no. 3, pp. 26 – 37, July 2001.

[36] A. Broido and k. claffy, "Internet topology: Connectivity of IP graphs," in *Proc. SPIE International Symposium on Convergence of IT and Communication (ITCom)*, August 2001.

[37] A. L. Barabási and R. Albert, "Emergence of scaling in random networks," *Science*, vol. 286, pp. 509–512, October 1999.

[38] A. Medina, I. Matta, and J. Byers, "On the origin of power laws in internet topologies," *ACM SIGCOMM Computer Communications Review*, vol. 30, no. 2, pp. 18–28, April 2000.

[39] Q. Chen, H. Chang, R. Govindan, S. Jamin, S. Shenker, and W. Willinger, "The origin of power laws in internet topologies revisited," in *Proc. IEEE INFOCOM*, June 2002.

[40] T. Petermann and P. De Los Rios, "Exploration of scale-free networks," *The European Physical Journal B*, vol. 38, p. 201, 2004.

[41] L. Dall'Asta, I. Alvarez-Hamelin, A. Barrat, A. Vásquez, and A. Vespignani, "A statistical approach to the traceroute-like exploration of networks: Theory and simulations," in *Proc. Combinatorial and Algorithmic Aspects of Networking (CAAN) Workshop*, August 2004.

[42] J. L. Guillaume and M. Latapy, "Relevance of massively distributed explorations of the internet topology: Simulation results," in *Proc. IEEE INFOCOM*, March 2005.

[43] L. Li, D. Alderson, W. Willinger, and J. Doyle, "A first-principles approach to understanding the Internet's router-level topology," in *Proc. ACM SIGCOMM*, August 2004.

[44] D. Alderson, L. Li, W. Willinger, and J. Doyle, "Understanding Internet topology: Principles, models, and validation," *IEEE/ACM Transactions on Networking*, vol. 13, no. 6, pp. 1205–1218, December 2005.

Eyeball ASes: From Geography to Connectivity

Amir H. Rasti
University of Oregon
amir@cs.uoregon.edu

Nazanin Magharei
University of Oregon
nazanin@cs.uoregon.edu

Reza Rejaie
University of Oregon
reza@cs.uoregon.edu

Walter Willinger
AT&T Labs—Research
walter@research.att.com

ABSTRACT

This paper presents a new approach to determine the geographical footprint of individual Autonomous Systems that directly provide service to end-users, *i.e.,eyeball ASes*. The key idea is to leverage the geo-location of end-users associated with an eyeball AS to identify its geographical footprint. We leverage the kernel density estimation method to estimate the density of users across individual eyeball ASes. This method enables us to cope with the potential error associated with the location of individual end-users while controlling the level of aggregation among data points to capture a geo-footprint at the desired resolution. We use the resulting geo-footprint of individual eyeball ASes to identify their likely Point-of-Presence (PoP) locations.

To demonstrate our proposed technique, we use the inferred geo-locations of 48 million users from three popular P2P applications and assess the geo- and PoP-level footprints of 1233 eyeball ASes. The validation of the identified PoP locations by our technique against online information and prior results by a commonly-used technique based on traceroute shows a very high accuracy. Leveraging the acquired PoP locations, we examine the implications of geo-footprint of eyeball ASes on their connectivity to the rest of the Internet. In particular, we present a case study that reveals a much more complex picture of AS-level connectivity as compared to what the more traditional but geography-agnostic BGP- or traceroute-based approaches depict.

Categories and Subject Descriptors

C.2.1 [**Computer-Communication Networks**]: Network Architecture and Design—*Network topology, Distributed networks*

General Terms

Measurement, Algorithms

Keywords

Autonomous System (AS), AS geography, Point-of-Presence (PoP), Eyeball AS

1. INTRODUCTION

As a network of networks, the Internet consists of some 30,000 inter-connected Autonomous Systems (ASes). This AS-level topology has been the focus of much research in the past decade, with studies that range from measurements and inference [15] to modeling and analysis [13] and the development of synthetic topology generators [14]. In fact, much of the research in this area has been fueled by large-scale data collection projects (*e.g.*, [10, 18, 20]) that have resulted in a high volume of readily available BGP-based or traceroute-based measurements. These datasets have been used to infer the Internet's AS-level topology as a graph where nodes are ASes and edges indicate business relationships (*e.g.*, customer-provider, peer-to-peer) between ASes.

More recently, this graph view of the AS-level Internet has been questioned. First, there has been an increasing awareness that the available BGP- or traceroute-based measurements are of limited quality to obtain an accurate and complete picture of the AS-level connectivity structure of today's Internet (*e.g.*, see [1, 19] and references therein). Second, the models that this graph view has motivated are largely descriptive in nature and essentially agnostic to the main forces responsible for shaping the structure and causing the evolution of this inherently virtual rather than physical topology of the Internet.

Partly in response to this criticism, alternative approaches to study the AS-level Internet have been advocated that align more closely with the real-world business relationships and practices encountered in the logical fabric of the Internet (see for example [4] and [6] and references therein). These recent efforts often start with the realization that ASes are not generic nodes but are entire networks that operate for a purpose and have a rich internal structure. Depending on an AS's size, its network interconnects a number of geographically dispersed points-of-presence (PoPs), where it connects to its customers or interconnects with other networks, either directly or via Internet eXchange Points (IXPs). The importance of AS geography (*i.e.*, geographic coverage or reach, number and location of PoPs, presence at IXPS) is further highlighted by the fact that the peering contracts of many ASes list explicit and geography-specific requirements for potential peering partners. For example, AS X will only peer with AS Y if Y's geographic reach is sufficiently large, or X and Y have a certain number of overlapping PoP locations, or X and Y are both present at a certain number of IXPs. Unfortunately, little is known in general about the geography of most ASes, with the possible exception of their presence at IXPs that was specifically examined [1].

In this paper, we outline a promising approach to tackle the problem of AS geography; that is, inferring an AS's geographic coverage (*geo-footprint*) and identifying its likely PoP locations. Our approach is complementary to the traditional BGP- or traceroute-based method of inferring AS-level connectivity, in both perspective and type of data used. First the traditional approach is known to perform in general increasingly worse the closer to the "edge" of the network (*i.e.*, end users) the measurements are made [5]. However, our approach starts at the "edge" (*i.e.*, "eyeballs") and experiences increasingly more difficulties as we move away from the edge towards the core of the Internet. In terms of data, instead of using BGP or traceroute data, our approach relies on the geographical location of end users or "eyeballs" (*i.e.*,, IP addresses) that are associated with an AS. In particular, the starting point of our work is a dataset consisting of the IP addresses of about 48 million users of three popular P2P applications that map to a total of 1233 "eyeball" ASes. Our main contributions are:

- We present a general methodology for determining the geo-footprint of eyeball ASes by leveraging the geo-location of their end users (Sections 2, 3).
- We use the above method to identify the likely PoP locations of an eyeball AS by associating areas with high user concentration with close-by cities in its geo-footprint (Section 4). We validate our approach using published PoP data from a number of ASes that make this information available on their websites.
- Using the PoP locations identified by our method and the AS-level connectivity resulting from a state-of-the-art inference approach, we show that the world of peering relationship at the "edge" of the network is highly diverse and complex. For example, even simple eyeball ASes tend to peer very actively at local and remote IXPs, especially in Europe, and also maintain rich upstream connectivity

The question of how to leverage the geo-properties of an eyeball AS to predict likely scenarios of how the AS connects to the rest of the Internet is left for future work. In view of our preliminary findings, a major challenge will be to explain the observed rich connectivity structure of eyeball ASes and characterize it in a quantitative manner.

2. OUR APPROACH: AN OVERVIEW

The basic idea of our approach is to use the location of end-users (*i.e.*, customers) of an AS to infer the AS's geographical reach (geo-footprint) as well as its PoP locations. To achieve this goal, our method consists of the following four steps:

- *Sampling end-users*: We collect a large number of IP addresses associated with Internet users.
- *Mapping end-users to locations*: We map individual IP addresses (or users) to their geo-location.
- *Grouping end-users by AS*: We use BGP information to group users to their corresponding ASes.
- *Estimating AS geo-footprints*: We leverage the collection of geo-locations of end-users associated with an eyeball AS to determine the geo- and PoP-level footprint of that AS.

There are three main reasons for our focus on eyeball ASes. First, the geo-features and connectivity of eyeball ASes indicate how end-users connect to the rest of the Internet. These eyeball ASes are not adequately visible to traceroute- or BGP-based approaches. Second, the accuracy of IP-geo mapping tools is significantly higher for IP addresses associated with end-users compared to infrastructure nodes [22]. Lastly, it is feasible to obtain a collection of IP addresses associated with end-users from eyeball ASes. Next, we provide further details for the first three steps of our approach. The last step, estimating geo- and PoP-level footprints, is described in Sections 3 and 4.

Sampling End-users: We crawl three large-scale P2P applications (*i.e.*, Kad, BitTorrent and Gnutella) during the months of January to June of 2009 to obtain more than 89.1 million unique IP addresses associated with end-users (peers) of these applications.

Mapping Users to Locations: To estimate the geo-location of each IP address, we examined several IP geo-location tools and databases and selected *GeoIP City from Maxmind* [16] and *IP2Location DB-15 from Hexasoft* [9] because of their reputation and coverage. Each of these databases map any IP address to a geo-location record with the following format *(city, state, country, longitude, latitude)*. The resolution of the provided coordinates is zip codes in each city, *i.e.*, all users in a given zip code are mapped to the same coordinates. We eliminated roughly 2.4M peers for which at least one of the databases did not provide city-level location. Since the two IP-geo mapping databases are from independent sources, we use the difference between their reported locations for each peer as a measure of error in IP-geo mapping [1]. We use GeoIP City as the main reference for IP-geo mapping in our analysis and use IP2Location as a second reference to estimate the error in IP-geo mapping. Using this notion of error, we remove all IP addresses whose error is larger than the diameter of typical metropolitan area, around 100km. We further elaborate on the selection of this threshold in Section 3.

Grouping Users by AS: We also group the users based on their AS affiliation using archived BGP tables from the routeviews[18] database collected during the same time period that our P2P data was gathered. To ensure a minimum density of samples in each AS, we eliminate all ASes with less than 1000 peers.

Target Dataset: Conditioning our dataset based on error in geo-location and density of sampled peers per AS significantly decreases any noise that could affect our analysis. However, it also reduces the total number of peers to 48 million and the corresponding number of eligible eyeball ASes to 1233. We call this set of ASes our *target dataset*. Given the location of all peers associated with an AS, we can broadly classify all ASes in this target dataset into city-, state-, country-, continent-level, or global ASes by identifying the smallest geographical region that contains a large

[1]While this measure of error may not be accurate, it provides a first-order approximation of geo error and could be useful to conservatively remove problematic peers with potentially large error in their geo-location.

Table 1: Profile of the target eyeball ASes.

Region	#Peers by source(k)			#ASes by level		
	Kad	Gnu	BT	City	State	Country
NA	1218	8984	1761	36	162	129
EU	18004	2519	2529	60	76	292
AS	17865	1606	1016	117	35	134

majority (>95%) of the associated peers. Table 1 summarizes the number and level of our target ASes in North America(NA), Europe (EU) and Asia (AS).

3. ESTIMATING GEO-FOOTPRINT

Given the locations of peers associated with an eyeball AS, our first goal is to infer the geographical region(s) where the AS offers service to end-users (*i.e.*, its geo-footprint) and estimate the density of users throughout the identified regions. We use a Kernel Density Estimation (KDE) [2] method with a Gaussian kernel function to estimate the probability density of customer population for an eyeball AS based on the locations of peers associated with that AS. More precisely, we place a bivariate kernel function with a predefined bandwidth at the geo-location of individual users of the AS. The aggregation of these kernel functions forms a function that estimates the overall user density over the map for each AS as shown in Figure 1. The largest contour of the aggregate density represents the geo-footprint of the AS at certain levels of resolution and may consist of one or multiple partitions. The geo-footprint of an AS clearly highlights the area within a state, country, or continent where an AS offers service, and its pronounced peaks indicate the main places with high user concentration throughout the covered region. This geo-footprint provides useful information about the services offered (*e.g.*, residential vs. retail) and connectivity provided (many vs. a few peaks) by individual eyeball ASes.

The KDE method presents a weighted average across close-by peers that serves two purposes. First, averaging smooths out the effect of error in IP-geo mapping across close-by users and provides a more reliable estimation of user density. Second, averaging offers a more aggregate (lower resolution) view (city- or state-level) of the users that is typically more useful than a detailed user-level view for assessing the geo-footprint of an AS.

3.1 Setting the Kernel Bandwidth:

The level of smoothing (*i.e.*, scope of averaging) performed by the KDE method is directly controlled by the bandwidth of the kernel function. Increasing the bandwidth leads to aggregation over a larger geographical region that has two important effects. First, it results in a coarser resolution and thus less accurate estimation of the geo-footprint for an AS. In fact, the bandwidth of the kernel function can be viewed as a tuning parameter that offers a multi-resolution view of an eyeball AS's geo-footprint. Figure 1 clearly demonstrates how increasing bandwidth can change the resolution of the geo-footprint from city- to region- and finally country-level. Second, averaging smooths out the variations in user density which makes the distinction of (smaller) peaks more difficult. It is therefore desirable to set the bandwidth so that the following two conditions are satisfied: *(i)* the resulting geo-footprint should have the desired resolution, and *(ii)* the expected geo-location error across the provided users should be filtered out. In summary, the larger value of the minimum bandwidth required by each one of these conditions determines the proper bandwidth value for the kernel function. For example, samples with a large *geographical mapping error (geo error)* cannot provide reliable city-level resolution of an AS's geo-footprint.

In our analysis, we focus on the *city-level* resolution because it provides the most useful view for detecting the main concentration point of users in order to infer likely PoP locations for each eyeball AS. To achieve this goal, the bandwidth should be larger than the average radius of a city which is around 30-35km. We set the bandwidth of the kernel function to 40km to achieve aggregation over a slightly larger region and avoid multiple peaks over a single city (*e.g.*, a separate peak for each zip code).

To determine a lower bound for the bandwidth based on geo error, we could set the bandwidth for each AS to the 90th percentile of geo error across all peers in that AS. This would result in an AS-dependent bandwidth selection. Instead, we remove all the ASes whose 90th percentile of geo error is larger than 80km. This is the main justification for removing all peers with geo error larger than 80km from our initial dataset. This strategy allows us to set the bandwidth to 40km for all ASes to obtain a city-level resolution. This choice simplifies the comparison of geo-footprints across different eyeball ASes

For a different application of the KDE method to IP geolocation, see the recent paper by Eriksson *et al.* [7] that casts the problem as a machine-learning-based classification. Their approach is relevant for fusing information from different datasets so that areas with low information content from one dataset can be compensated with information from other datasets.

4. ESTIMATING POP-LEVEL FOOTPRINT

A geo-footprint of an eyeball AS can be summarized or represented by the list of major cities where significant portions of its customers are located. Intuitively, each AS must have a proportional level of presence (*e.g.*, PoP) in areas where there is a high concentration of customers. Therefore, this representation of an AS geo-footprint offers a reasonably reliable view of its PoP-level infrastructure that we call *PoP-level footprint*. Since eyeball ASes usually connect to their provider, peering and customer ASes at their PoPs, the PoP-level footprint also reveals valuable information about the location(s) of connections between related ASes.

4.1 Estimating PoP Coordinates

To extract the PoP-level footprint of an eyeball AS from its geo-footprint, we proceed as follows. First, we identify the geo-coordinates of all the local maxima $D(i)$ (*i.e.*, peaks) in the estimated density function and determine the density value of the highest peak (D_{max}). Next we select all the peaks $D(i)$ with a relatively large density compared to the highest peak, *i.e.*, ($D(i) > \alpha * D_{max}$), where α is a threshold that determines the range of density values that are considered for PoP identification. We set α to 0.01 to conservatively select peaks with a density of at least two orders of magnitude below D_{max}.

4.2 Mapping PoPs to Cities

The coordinates of identified major peaks may not directly map to a city due to the combined effects of selected

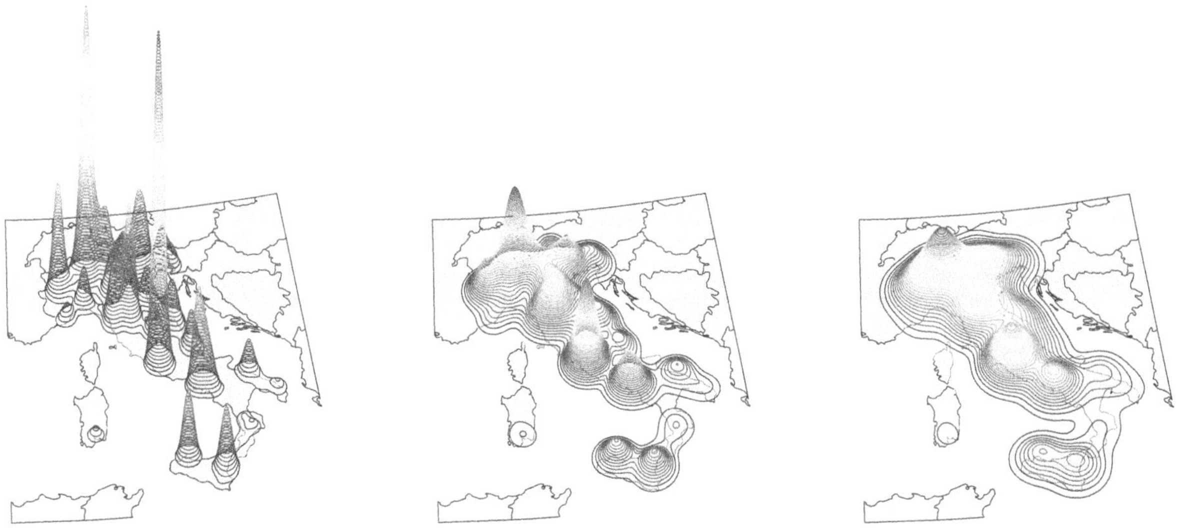

(a) Kernel bandwidth = 20km (b) Kernel bandwidth = 40km (c) Kernel bandwidth = 60km

Figure 1: 3D visualization of user density using KDE method for AS 3269 (in Italy) using 2.2M samples with different values for kernel bandwidth.

bandwidth, threshold for peak selection (*i.e.*, α), and the distribution of user population around each city. To address this issue, we map identified peaks to a particular city in a "loose" fashion as follows: we assume that PoPs are more likely to be located in the most populated city of a given region. For each identified peak, we examine a circular region with a radius equal to the selected kernel bandwidth around the location of the peak and map the peak to the city with the largest population in that circular region. Otherwise, we report "no city" for a peak. Using small values for α may result in an error whereby minor peaks of user density get selected at locations where a small number of users are randomly clustered due to their geo error.Using a proper α threshold, we can filter out such peaks if the selected location is not in the required vicinity of any city with sufficiently large population. The resulting PoP-level footprint obtained by this process consists of a list of cities sorted by their associated user density where PoPs of an eyeball AS are likely to be located. The user density of each PoP quantifies the level of presence of an AS in that city. For example, PoP-level footprint of AS 3269 using kernel bandwidth of 40km, as depicted in Figure 1(b), is as follows: [Milan (.130), Rome (.122), Florence (.061), Venice (.054), Naples (.051), Turin (.047), Ancona (.027), Catania (.027), Palermo (.026), Pescara (.017), Bari (.015), Catanzaro (.007), Cagliari (.005), Sassari (.001)].

4.3 Bias in Sampling Different Locations

We crawl peers in major P2P applications to sample customers of eyeball ASes from different geo-locations. Uneven penetration of P2P applications among Internet users in different ASes and locations could introduce bias to our samples. However, it is generally difficult to clearly distinguish the small market share of an AS from low penetration of a P2P application in a particular city. This potential bias can be qualitatively considered at two different levels.

1) Mild Bias: This scenario occurs when the fraction of sampled peers for an AS A in city C has a noticeable density ($D_A(C) > \alpha \cdot Max(D_A)$) but is disproportional with respect to the total number of AS customers in C. In this case, the derived PoP-level footprint of the AS includes city C as a PoP but the density value associated with C is inaccurate.
2) Significant Bias: A significant bias in collected samples could result from having a negligible (or zero) fraction of samples from a particular PoP location for a given eyeball AS. In this case, our approach does not discover that PoP location. However, for an AS with a sufficiently large number of samples, the probability of not capturing a major PoP (with a large number of customers) should be rather small. We do not examine sampling bias in this study and leave this for future work.

Another issue is whether the strategy for IP-geo mapping leverages the location of PoPs for each AS to estimate the location of end-users in that AS. In this case, our approach simply identifies the PoP locations that were used for IP-geo mapping. Our private communication with maxmind.com confirmed that the IP-geo mapping strategy relies on the information provided by users through online surveys, and information from Internet registries and ISPs. Since the actual location of PoPs for each ISP is unknown and thus not considered for determining the geo location of users in an ISP, the identified PoP locations by our approach are not affected by the mapping strategy used for each dataset.

5. EVALUATION

This section summarizes the preliminary evaluation of our proposed technique. Towards this end, we collect the reported PoP information of some eyeball ASes on the Web as the ground truth for validation. Unfortunately, collecting this information is a rather tedious task since many ISPs do not post this information online or do not use a consistent terminology or approach for listing these PoPs. For exam-

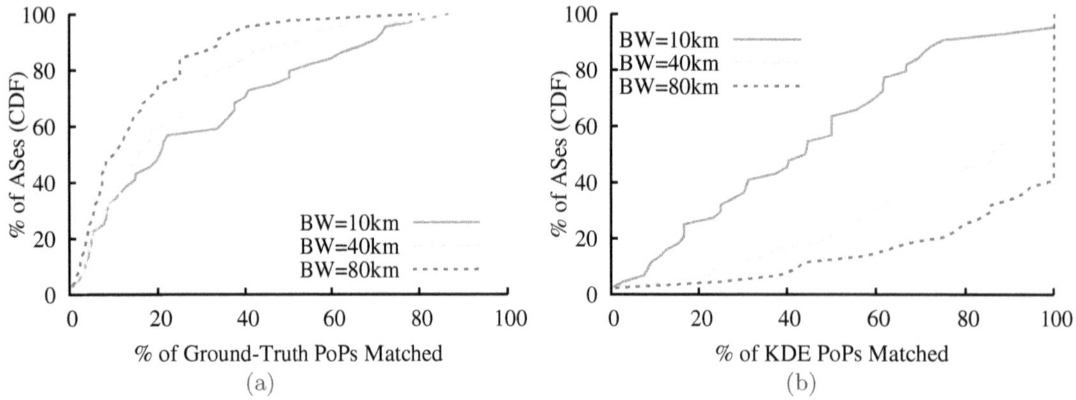

Figure 2: Validation of our technique with the reported PoP information online. (a) Percentage of ground-truth PoPs found by our method. (b) Percentage of PoPs reported by our method that match a ground-truth PoP.

ple, some ISPs may consider their access points as a PoP or list their PoPs of their peering ISPs as their own.

We focused on 672 state- or country-level ASes in our target dataset and searched the Web for their PoP information. We were able to identify PoP information for a total of 45 eyeball ASes (10 state-, 33 country-, and 2 continent-level) across North America and Europe [2]. We consider this information as ground truth and call this our reference dataset. Overall, our approach on average identified 31.9, 13.6 and 7.3 PoPs per AS with kernel bandwidth of 10km, 40km and 80km, respectively. The average number of reported PoPs per AS in our reference dataset is 43.7. We match a discovered PoP location by our technique for each AS with a reported PoP locations in the reference dataset if their relative distance is less than the radius of a city (*i.e.*, 40 km), *i.e.*, matching PoPs at the city level. Figure 2(a) depicts the distribution of the percentage of PoPs in the reference dataset that are matched with the identified PoPs by our techniques using different bandwidth values. When kernel bandwidth is 40km, for the bottom 60% of ASes, the fraction of matched PoP locations in the reference dataset is less than 20%. However, this ratio is larger than 50% for the top 10% of ASes. Furthermore, this figure suggests that using lower bandwidth generally results in mapping a larger number of PoPs in the reference dataset.

Figure 2(b) illustrates the opposite view by showing the distribution of the percentage of discovered PoP locations by our technique for each AS that match a reported PoP in the reference dataset. This figure reveals that with the bandwidth of 80km, 60% of ASes exhibit perfect match. Interestingly, decreasing the value of kernel bandwidth to 40km and 10km rapidly drops the percentage of perfect match to 41% and 5%, respectively. *Collectively, these results indicate that using larger kernel bandwidth leads to a smaller but more reliable set of PoP locations for most ASes.*

Our preliminary examination revealed that the following factors appear to cause the mismatched PoPs: First, some eyeball ASes seem to use certain PoPs in locations away from their regular customers to connect to provider (or peering) ASes. Since these ASes do not serve end-users, our approach is not able to identify them. Second, some eyeball ASes have a few PoPs within a relatively short distance. Using the KDE approach especially with moderate to large bandwidth does not distinguish these PoPs. As part of our future work, we plan to use different kernel bandwidth and determine these PoPs based on the relative distance and user density of associated peaks with different bandwidths. Third, we might have mis-interpreted a non-IP PoP as valid PoP from the obtained information online or a PoP location might be missing due to the obsolete online information. We plan to explore these issues in our future work

We have also compared our discovered PoP locations with the PoP coordinates reported in a recent traceroute-based study by the DIMES project [21]. The overlap between the two datasets consists of 226 eyeball ASes across EU and NA. While for those common eyeball ASes, our approach identified 7.14 PoPs per AS on average (with bandwidth=40km), DIMES reports only 1.54 PoPs per AS. We match a discovered PoP location by our technique for an AS with a reported PoP coordinates in the DIMES dataset within 40km distance. Our results show that for 80% of eyeball ASes our identified PoPs are a clear superset of reported PoPs by the DIMES project.

6. AS CONNECTIVITY AT THE "EDGE": A CASE STUDY

Having derived the geo-footprint and PoP locations of eyeball ASes, we next examine what this information may enable us to say about how these eyeball ASes connect to the rest of the Internet. Our comparisons are made against the current state-of-the-art "best effort" ground truth for AS-level Internet connectivity and is provided by two different datasets. For customer-provider relationships, we rely on the CAIDA AS relationships data set [3] and for peer-to-peer relationships at IXPs, we consult the dataset produced by the IXP mapping project [1].

To illustrate the challenges of making any claims about real-world AS-level connectivity at the "edge" of the network, we present a case study involving a metropolitan-area eyeball AS in Europe. Specifically, we consider AS8234 (RAI - Radiotelevisione Italiana). Based on our data, this AS has 3,000 P2P users whose geo-locations are all mapped to the

[2] This information is posted online at http://mirage.cs.uoregon.edu/AS2PoP

city of Rome. As a city-level eyeball AS, we expect it to have one or two regional or country-wide upstream providers. Examining the geo-footprints of some of our Italy-wide eyeball ASes, a natural choice of such a provider is AS1267 (Infostrada) for which we observe 1470K P2P users and obtain PoP locations across Italy, including Rome. The large number of P2P users for this ISP suggests that its major business is selling Internet connectivity to residential customers across Italy, and examining the company's website confirms this. Expecting at least one alternative connection of RAI to the rest of the Internet, plausible options include another upstream provider (possibly with more global reach than Infostrada) or peering at the Rome IXP NaMEX with a selected number of tier-2 ISPs.

However, when comparing against the best effort ground truth which we validated by performing a set of selective traceroute experiments, we encounter a substantially more complex AS-level connectivity picture for RAI. For one, this Rome-based eyeball AS has a total of five upstream providers: Infostrada (as expected) and Fastweb, two Italy-wide ISPs; Easynet and Colt, two service providers with global reach; and BT-Italia, Italy's legacy ISP. Moreover, while RAI is not present at the Rome IXP, it is a member of the Milan IXP MIX and peers there with three other ASes (*i.e.*, GARR - the Italian academic and research network, ASDASD - an Italian network provider, and ITGate - an Italian Internet service company). The two unexpected findings are the richness of upstream connectivity of this eyeball AS and its decision to peer remotely at MIX rather than locally at NaMEX.

Thus, when trying to determine the actual upstream connectivity of eyeball ASes such as RAI, one may quickly run into a bewildering web of real-world peering relationships [17, 8, 12, 11]. In some cases, a partial explanation of this richness in AS connectivity may be the separate treatment of residential and business customer traffic; *e.g.*, residential traffic is carried by one upstream provider, while commercial traffic is sent on to a different provider. In the case of RAI, having the legacy ISP BT-Italia as an additional provider may be more a historical artifact than a strategic business decision. Dual connectivity to upstream providers with global reach may again be a strategic decision based on the eyeball's business model. With respect to RAI's remote peering at MIX, it is worth pointing out that while one of its peering partners there (*i.e.*, GARR) is also present at the Rome IXP, the two other networks (*i.e.*, ASDASD and ITGate) are not members of NaMEX. This suggests that the ability for RAI to peer with the latter two networks is important enough to forgo a cheaper local solution over a more expensive remote peering arrangement.

This example of a simple eyeball AS illustrates the challenges associated with trying to leverage the geo-properties of eyeball ASes to predict and ultimately explain their connectivity to the rest of the Internet.

7. CONCLUSION

The work described in this paper has demonstrated the potential of obtaining the geographic footprints of eyeball ASes, which in turn can be used to infer infrastructure-related properties (*e.g.*, PoP locations, AS connectivity) or business-specific features (*e.g.*, serving residential vs. business customers) of these ASes. Doing so by relying solely on measurements at the "edge" of the Internet (*i.e.*, eyeball IP addresses) provides a complementary approach to the more traditional methods for studying the AS-level Internet that exploit exclusively BGP- or traceroute-based measurements. It also suggests a possible fusion of the two approaches whereby the former is augmented with tracerouting capabilities **from** the "edge" and the latter is empowered with performing targeted tracerouting **towards** the edge of the Internet (*i.e.*, eyeballs). Such a combined approach holds the promise to unearth much of what has remained invisible in the AS-level Internet and reveal a maze of real-world peering relationships whose solution will require substantial future research efforts.

Acknowledgments

The authors are grateful to Matthew Roughan for his invaluable contributions to this project and to the anonymous reviewers for their helpful feedback. Kad and BitTorrent datasets are kindly provided by Ghulam Memon and Ruben Cuevas. We acknowledge Kaveh Kazemi for extracting PoP information for a large number of ASes from the web. We also thank Maxmind and IP2Location for providing their geo-IP mapping databases. This material is based upon work supported in part by the NSF Award Nets-NBD-0627202.

8. REFERENCES

[1] B. Augustin, B. Krishnamurthy, and W. Willinger. IXPs: Mapped? In *ACM SIGCOMM conference on Internet measurement conference*, Nov. 2009.

[2] Z. Botev, J. Grotowski, and D. Kroese. Kernel Density Estimation via Diffusion. *Annals of Statistics*, 2010.

[3] The Cooperative Association for Internet Data Analysis (CAIDA). AS relationships. *http://www.caida.org/data/active/as-relationships.*

[4] H. Chang, S. Jamin, and W. Willinger. Internet connectivity at the as-level: An optimization-driven modeling approach. In *ACM SIGCOMM MoMeTools Workshop*, Aug. 2003.

[5] K. Chen, D. Choffnes, R. Potharaju, Y. Chen, F. Bustamante, D. Pei, and Y. Zhao. Where the Sidewalk Ends: Extending the Internet AS Graph Using Traceroutes From P2P Users. In *ACM CoNEXT*, Dec. 2009.

[6] A. Dhamdhere and C. Dovrolis. An agent-based model for the evolution of the internet ecosystem. In *COMmunication Systems And NETworks*, July 2009.

[7] B. Eriksson, P. Barford, J. Sommers and R. Nowak. A Learning-based Approach to IP Geolocation. In *Passive and Active Measurement conference*, Apr. 2010.

[8] P. Faratin, D. Clark, P. Gilmore, and A. Berger. Complexity of internet interconnections: Technology, incentives and implications for policy. In *Telecommunications Policy Research Conference*, Sept. 2007.

[9] Hexasoft. IP2Location. *http://www.ip2location.com/aboutus.aspx.*

[10] Y. Hyun. Archipelago Infrastructure. *http://www.caida.org/projects/ark.*

[11] R. Ma, D. Chiu, J. Lui, V. Misra, and D. Rubenstein. Interconnecting eyeballs to content: a shapley value perspective on isp peering and settlement. In *ACM*

SIGCOMM workshop on Economics of networked systems, Aug. 2008.

[12] R. Ma, D. Chiu, J. Lui, V. Misra, and D. Rubenstein. On cooperative settlement between content, transit and eyeball internet service providers. In *ACM CoNEXT*, Dec. 2008.

[13] P. Mahadevan, C. Hubble, B. Huffaker, D. Krioukov, and A. Vahdat. Orbis: Rescaling Degree Correlations to Generate Annotated Internet Topologies. In *ACM SIGCOMM*, Aug. 2007.

[14] P. Mahadevan, D. Krioukov, K. Fall, and A. Vahdat. Systematic Topology Analysis and Generation Using Degree Correlations,. In *ACM SIGCOMM*, Sept. 2006.

[15] P. Mahadevan, D. Krioukov, M. Fomenkov, B. Huffaker, and X. Dimitropoulos. The Internet AS-level topology: Three data sources and one definitive metric. *Computer Communication Review*, 36(1):17–26, 2006.

[16] Maxmind. GeoIP. *http://www.maxmind.com/app/ip-locate.*

[17] W. B. Norton. The Evolution of the U.S. Internet Peering Ecosystem. *http://tinyurl.com/39rwjwc*, 2003.

[18] U. of Oregon. RouteViews Project. *http://www.routeviews.org/.*

[19] R. Oliveira, D. Pei, W. Willinger, B. Zhang, and L. Zhang. The (in)completeness of the observed internet as-level structure. *IEEE/ACM Transactions on Networking*, 18(1):109 –122, Feb. 2010.

[20] Y. Shavitt. The DIMES Project. *http://www.netdimes.org.*

[21] Y. Shavitt and N. Zilberman. A Structural Approach for PoP Geo-Location. In *IEEE Workshop on Network Science For Communication Networks*, Mar. 2010.

[22] S. Siwpersad, B. Gueye, and S. Uhlig. Assessing the geographic resolution of exhaustive tabulation for geolocating Internet hosts. In *Passive and Active Measurement conference*, Apr. 2008.

Towards an AS-to-Organization Map*

Xue Cai[1] John Heidemann[1] Balachander Krishnamurthy[2] Walter Willinger[2]
[1] USC/ISI, Marina del Rey, CA [2] AT&T Labs Research, Florham Park, NJ
{xuecai,johnh}@isi.edu, {bala,walter}@research.att.com

ABSTRACT

An understanding of Internet topology is central to answer various questions ranging from network resilience to peer selection or data center location. While much of prior work has examined AS-level connectivity, meaningful and relevant results from such an abstract view of Internet topology have been limited. For one, semantically, AS relationships capture business relationships and not physical connectivity. Additionally, many organizations often use multiple ASes, either to implement different routing policies, or as legacies from mergers and acquisitions. In this paper, we move beyond the traditional AS graph view of the Internet to define the problem of *AS-to-organization mapping*. We describe our initial steps at automating the capture of the rich semantics inherent in the AS-level ecosystem where routing and connectivity intersect with organizations. We discuss preliminary methods that identify multi-AS organizations from WHOIS data and illustrate the challenges posed by the quality of the available data and the complexity of real-world organizational relationships.

Categories and Subject Descriptors

C.2.1 [**Computer-Communication Networks**]: Network Architecture and Design—*Network topology*; C.2.3 [**Computer-Communication Networks**]: Network Operations—*Network management*

General Terms

Measurement

*Xue Cai and John Heidemann are partially supported by the US DHS, contract number NBCHC080035, and by the NSF, grant number CNS-0626696. The conclusions of this work are those of the authors and do not necessarily reflect the views of DHS or NSF.
This work was begun when Xue Cai was an intern at AT&T Labs-Research.

IMC'10, November 1–3, 2010, Melbourne, Australia.

Keywords

Autonomous System (AS), organization, mapping, clustering, WHOIS, Regional Internet Registry (RIR)

1. INTRODUCTION

The Internet is of great importance to millions of people and businesses today, as a source of information, entertainment, and commerce. Thus resilience of the Internet to various threats has been the topic of a large number of research papers [1,6,13–15]. This resilience has also been extensively discussed in the popular press, especially in cases of actual outages of popular services, such as the 2008 YouTube routing problem [16,24], service interruptions for large user groups [29], loss of connectivity due to peering disputes [25] or routing errors [22,23], and catastrophic events [5,10,28].

To study Internet resilience, many analyses focus on the Internet's *AS-level topology*. Autonomous systems (ASes) appear in BGP Internet routing [21] and are defined to represent a network or group of networks that operate with a common routing policy [11]. More than 30,000 ASes in the Internet today form a logical fabric that reflects the policy and business relationships necessary to manage the flow of Internet traffic. ASes and their relationships are an attractive target for analysis because paths through the AS topology are often visible in public routing tables, implying that the resulting data can be readily mined to obtain the Internet *AS-graph* [7]. Given the apparent ease with which the Internet AS-graph can be obtained, it is not surprising that it features prominently in studies of Internet resilience since Albert et al. [1]. These studies typically treat the Internet AS topology as an abstract graph and change it, perhaps by deleting nodes or removing edges, on the assumption that these changes predict the outcome of threats to the actual Internet.

In this paper, we provide evidence that the relationship between the AS graph and the organizations that make up the Internet is much richer than previously thought, making it difficult to justify conclusions based only on modifications to the AS graph. Abstracting the Internet to a simple graph and treating it as a collection of generic nodes and links ignores much of the rich semantic content inherent in the key components that make up the AS-level Internet. This semantic content is critical to its understanding and its proper use in experiments. Another basic problem that has been gradually recognized is that obtaining a reasonably accurate AS-graph from available measurements is quite challenging. Recent work has suggested that presently available AS graphs are of questionable quality [27], limiting their use in careful studies of many Internet connectivity-related problems.

Motivated by these questions about current approaches, the first contribution of this paper (Section 2) is to move beyond the traditional AS-graph view, towards a structure we call *AS-level ecosystem*. This structure aims to capture the organizations and their ASes that make up the Internet, along with the realities of router-level connectivity in Internet Exchange Points (IXPs). Consider the frequently raised questions such as: what damage to the Internet results from the outage of a particular IXP, or legal action in a particular country, or a business dispute between organizations? Answering these requires a deeper understanding of Internet semantics than simply evaluating deletion of a node or edge in an AS graph, because such prior work omits the fact that many important organizations operate multiple ASes. To our knowledge, the only prior recognition of this fact was in differences between AS paths derived from traceroute and BGP routing [12], and PCH's manually generated AS/organization directory for network operator assistance [19].

In Section 3 we present our second contribution, a number of automated methods for extracting organization-level relationships from information in the Regional Internet Registry (RIR) WHOIS databases. This work builds on prior work [12] to provide a step towards automatic identification of the mapping of ASes to the organization to which they belong.

A final, more indirect, contribution of our work results from the validation efforts (Section 4). As part of evaluating our methods, we also characterize the quality and timeliness of the WHOIS data itself, suggesting opportunities for both operators, as contributors to and users of this data, and researchers, as users of the data, to improve the data for their mutual benefits.

2. THE INTERNET AS ECOSYSTEM

Our goal is to move towards models of the Internet AS ecosystem, so we consider ASes and organizations, how they connect, and how we can use this information to improve performance and evaluate risk.

2.1 ASes and Organizations

Central to our work are ASes and organizations. An *Autonomous System (AS)* is defined in RFC1930 [11] as "a connected group of one or more IP prefixes run by one or more network operators which has *a single and clearly defined routing policy*". While this definition is prescriptive, routing policies are not necessarily enforced or even written down. A practical, descriptive definition of an AS would be whatever is identified by an AS number in BGP routing messages.

A precise definition of *organization* is more elusive, since organizations are fundamentally socio-economic arrangements with many gradations of collaboration or independence. It is difficult to adopt a formal definition that is neither too loose, joining what should be logically separate, nor too strict, separating business units or subsidiaries that should be joined. Here we define *an organization is an entity which has control over itself and is not a subsidiary of any other organization.* (A subsidiary is majority-owned by another organization.) We adopt this definition since our emphasis is to join entities that share common, Internet-relevant business decisions.

2.2 Types of Connectivity

AS relationships can reflect a number of different contractual relationships between organizations. Common relationships are peers, customers, providers, and siblings (mutual transit providers) [9]. Single organizations can use multiple ASes to facilitate other, more complex arrangements, including creating non-uniform routing policies over one organization. Note that by their very definition, AS relationships are logical or virtual in nature and say little about the physical connectivity between the ASes in question.

This many-to-one mapping of ASes to organizations motivates an organization-level view of the AS ecosystem; another explicitly logical graph structure that is coarser-grained than the traditional AS-graph. Here nodes represent organizations and two organizations are connected if there exists an AS relationship between at least one affiliated AS in each of the two organizations. Although such an organization-level view has not attracted much prior attention in the networking literature, it is of critical importance for understanding organization-level routing.

When considering ASes by themselves, it is important to recognize that they have a rich internal structure. Depending on their size, an AS's physical infrastructure interconnects a number of different, geographically dispersed Points-of-Presence (PoPs). It is generally at these PoPs where the network connects to its customers and interconnects with other networks, either directly through Private Network Interconnects (PNIs) or via public Internet eXchange Points (IXPs). IXPs are physical infrastructure managed by third parties where members (ASes) choose to exchange traffic directly by peering with each other, rather than via upstream service providers (for a cost) [3]. It is this combination of physical, AS-level, and organization-level connectivity that makes the proposed AS ecosystem an ideal candidate for careful analyses of, for example, threats to and resilience of the Internet.

2.3 Future Applications from Understanding

An understanding of the AS ecosystem can be applied to improve performance and manage risk.

Analysis and Planning: An organization-level topology can assist in Internet analysis. For example, the accuracy of prior work in AS-peering inference [9] may be improved by considering AS/organization relationships. These peering relationships and a direct understanding of organizations can also inform what-if projections of performance and reliability and so help guide selection of additional peering agreements, or build-outs to new IXPs, or siting of content provisioning or caches.

Threat Analysis: The centrality of the Internet to everyday life raises the importance of threat assessment due to accidental or malicious damage. Goals of attackers or risks of accidents may vary from partitioning to increased latency or reduced cross-section bandwidth, or may be more subtle, such as sending unauthorized traffic (e.g., spam) or eavesdropping.

Defining threats is aided by what we believe is a *non-threat*. It is mathematically true that graphs with power-law distributions of node degree are extremely robust to random node removal, yet highly vulnerable to removal of high-degree nodes. Yet we believe application of this result to Internet AS-graphs to predict Internet stability is specious, because *there is no threat corresponding to "delete a node in*

	All	OrgID	Phone	Email
ARIN	21k (100%)	20K (95%)	20K (94%)	20K (93%)
RIPE	19k (100%)	11K (59%)	*unavail.*	13K (68%)
APNIC	6k (100%)	*unavail.*	4K (67%)	5K (78%)
LACNIC	1.5K (100%)	*unavail.*	*unavail.*	*unavail.*
AfriNIC	0.5K (100%)	0.4K (82%)	0.5K (96%)	*unavail.*
All	*48K (100%)*	*31K (65%)*	*25K (51%)*	*38K (79%)*

Table 1: Data availability (AS count) for three fields across the 5 RIRs.

the AS graph". Simply put, high-degree ASes cannot simply "disappear"; even in cases of major bankruptcies (such as WorldCom in 2004), the affected networks provided service throughout reorganization. Instead, we must consider models and mutations that reflect Internet semantics.

As for realizable threats to the Internet's AS ecosystem, prefix hijacking, organization disputes, and IXP outage are examples that *have actually occurred* multiple times in the past. In *route prefix hijacking*, one AS mistakenly overrides another AS's route. Prefix hijacking has been both accidental and intentional [8, 22–24]. A *de-peering* is an intentional choice by one network to refuse to route traffic from a prior peer [4, 26]. *IXP outage* refers to the fact that IXPs are physical locations and as such are vulnerable to correlated physical problems including power outages [5, 17], natural disasters [10], or human-induced problems [28]. While prefix hijacking may appear similar to "deleting an AS", a careful analysis of this as well as the other two threats shows that they are *not well described* by operations on the traditional AS graphs, but become substantially more complex problems when networks can connect in multiple locations, run their business using different ASes, or use these different ASes to interconnect at multiple IXPs.

3. DISCOVERING ORGANIZATIONS

The goals of our methodology described next is modest: we want to understand how effective simple automated clustering is at discovering an AS-to-organization mapping. Our goal here is to obtain an initial lower bound on accuracy, and to identify challenges and trade-offs for future methods. We expect that better results are possible, but will require more sophisticated information extraction and clustering methods.

3.1 Data Sources

We depend on AS registration data (i.e., WHOIS data) to discover AS-to-organization relationships. Unfortunately, this data is neither complete, nor up-to-date, nor in a common, simple format. There are five regional Internet registries [20] that provide WHOIS data, with RIPE, APNIC, LACNIC and AfriNIC relying on the Routing Policy Specification Language (RPSL) [18], and with ARIN using its own format [2]. However, given the similarity of the two formats, we can generally merge them into one.

Our work is concerned with three types of records: those corresponding to **Autonomous Systems** (ASes), **organizations** (orgs, for short), and **points-of-contact** (contact, for short). To illustrate the potential of the three types of records for performing an AS-to-organization mapping, note that ASes are identified by *ASHandle* records in ARIN and *aut-num* records in other RIRs (48K AS records, see Table 1). Some AS records are associated with an org record (via the *OrgID* or *org* fields) or administrative/technical contact information. Org records are intended to facilitate the common management of an organization's multiple records and are clearly relevant when trying to map ASes to organizations. Unfortunately, their direct use is complicated by the fact that RIR policies explicitly allow organizations to use multiple OrgID records, possibly with different OrgID's. However, org records often include administrative/technical points-of-contact information that can provide further clues about belonging to the same organization. In fact, contact records refer to individuals and can include information such as name of individual or role, a contact address, telephone numbers, and e-mail addresses. Given the role these individuals are supposed to play in managing an organization's network operations and responding to inquiries, we view telephone numbers and e-mail addresses as supporting important every-day business interactions and focus on them as providing promising clues for associating individual ASes with their parent organization.

The challenges posed by using the OrgID, telephone number, and e-mail address information buried in the AS, organization, and contact records are many. For example, only 65% of all AS records contain OrgID information, with APNIC and LACNIC providing none whatsoever; other ASes provide OrgIDs for the majority of records (59% for RIPE, 82% and 95% for AfriNIC and ARIN). However, even when coverage is good, many organizations use a number of different OrgIDs making OrgID clustering difficult. With respect to telephone numbers, they are unavailable for RIPE due to European privacy laws, and are also missing for LACNIC. Similarly, e-mail addresses are unavailable for LACNIC and AfriNIC, and partially missing for ARIN, RIPE, and APNIC (see Table 1). Clearly, the performance of any AS-to-org mapping method that relies exclusively on WHOIS data will necessarily suffer from such missing data issues and may further be impacted by the largely unknown quality of the existing WHOIS data.

3.2 Basic Clustering to Identify Organizations

Our mapping method consists of performing basic clustering on one or a number of different (canonicalized) attributes.

1. Extract (raw attributes, AS) pairs from the source data.
2. Canonicalize to (simple attribute, AS) pairs.
3. Discard *generic* attributes common to many organizations.
4. Cluster all ASes with related simple, non-generic attributes: (a) Start a new cluster c_i with some unclustered AS a_i. Then repeat until no more merges into c_i: (b) Identify c_i by the union of attributes of all its ASes, (c) Merge some other AS a_j with some matching attribute.
5. Label the cluster (Section 3.2.5).

3.2.1 Clustering by organization IDs

Clustering by OrgID is the simplest method and is included here as "baseline" and because it is essentially the method described in the only prior work [12] on this topic.

OrgIDs are designed to group ASes into organizations. They require no canonicalization, but we discard 8 "generic" OrgIDs belonging to 5 RIRs, IANA and 2 Network Information Centers (NIC). Given that OrgID information is not widely available and not unique (when available), we expect OrgID clustering to have poor coverage but *no* false positives.

3.2.2 Clustering by telephone numbers

When clustering by telephone numbers, we associate them with ASes by following three paths through WHOIS: AS-record → org-record, AS-record → contact-record, or AS-record → org-record → contact-record. We observe multiple telephone numbers with each AS (for administrative, or technical purposes), so the many-to-many telephone-to-AS relationship can cluster otherwise separate ASes.

Telephone numbers require both canonicalization (e.g., inferring country code and stripping extensions) and generic filtering. We manually build a blacklist of 11 generic telephone numbers that includes RIR, IANA, ICANN, and NIC contact numbers, as well as a few outsourcing companies. Since only 51% of ASes provide telephone numbers (see Table 1), we expect the telephone clustering method to have relatively poor performance.

3.2.3 Clustering by e-mail domains

To cluster based on e-mail addresses, we associate them with ASes using the same two- or three-step paths through WHOIS we relied on for telephone number-based clustering. In addition, we exploit the fact that many RIPE and APNIC records provide an additional source of administrative-pertinent e-mail addresses in the *changed* and *notify* fields. In particular, we retain the e-mail addresses in all *notify* fields and the most recent *changed* fields, providing e-mail coverage in spite of missing point-of-contact records.

Like telephone numbers, e-mail also requires careful canonicalization (e.g., discarding the user portion and keeping only the distinguishing, right-most part of the domain address) and generic filtering. Since there is no universal number of distinguishing components, we compare against a manually-built list of more than 6K suffixes with longest-suffix matching. We build a blacklist of about 50 generic e-mail domains that takes care of generic e-mail addresses in use by RIRs, NICs, outsourcing companies, and public e-mail services like Gmail and Hotmail.

While e-mail addresses capture many relationships inside organizations, their flexibility has the potential of causing many false positives. To avoid some of the more obvious misclassifications of ASes, we adjust the above basic method by implementing a simple rule designed to ensure that two clusters are not merged into one because of an e-mail address or domain used by a single individual, associated with an outsourcing effort, or affiliated with an isolated joint venture.

Given the ubiquity of e-mail in today's Internet and the critical role e-mail plays in communication between network operators within an organization or across different companies, we expect the email clustering to outperform clustering by OrgID and clustering by telephone numbers.

3.2.4 Hybrid clustering

While each of the above-mentioned (single-attribute) clustering methods has its strengths and weaknesses, we can combine the different types of attributes and develop two- or three-attributes clustering method to improve coverage. Our preferred method is hybrid clustering with all three attributes: OrgID, phone number, and e-mail address.

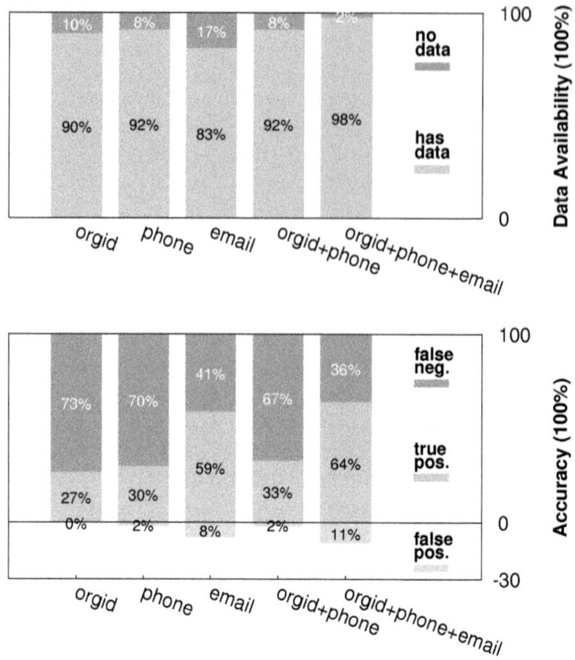

Figure 1: Validation from real ground truth of a Tier-1 ISP, data availability (top), biggest-cluster accuracy (bottom).

3.2.5 Cluster Labeling and Selection

While our basic mapping methods generate clusters, they are arbitrarily grouped, without human-friendly names. To label clusters, we extract the text names in AS and OrgID records, including *ASName*, *OrgName*, *as-name*, *descr*, and *owner* fields. Since a cluster will have many such names, often with minor variations (Org, Org Inc., Org Europe, Nippon-Org, etc.), we split these names on word boundaries to form keywords and rank keywords by their frequency in the cluster.

Finally, when comparing the accuracy of our methods against a candidate set of ASes (e.g., ground truth of all ASes belonging to an organization), we have to decide with which cluster to compare among the typically many clusters produced by a given method. For the sake of simplicity, we always compare to the *largest* cluster produced by the particular method, biasing in favor of both better coverage and larger number of false-positives (see also Section 4).

4. VALIDATION

We next evaluate accuracy and false positives and negatives of each approach. We first consider *real* ground truth from one organization's operator, then *inferred* ground truth of nine organizations as determined by manual inspection of public records.

4.1 Validation with Organization Input

We first compare our approaches against real ground truth obtained from network operators of a Tier-1 ISP. We caution that, while we have good confidence in the ground truth we were able to obtain, even operations staff suggest that this data may be incomplete.

Figure 1 shows the results of our analysis with each of our methods for the Tier-1 ISP. As a baseline, we take the ground truth of 213 ASes provided to us by the network operators. Of these 213 (100%), the top part of the figure shows that we have data of only 177 (83%) to 195 (92%) ASes for the non-hybrid methods, depending on attribute; one AS is simply missing from our bulk WHOIS data, with others omitting attributes in the data or using only generic attributes. However, by combining all three attributes together (OrgID+phone+email), the data availability rises to 98%. Thus missing or generic data leads to 8–17% of the undercount (false negatives) for the non-hybrid methods and 2%–8% for the hybrid methods.

Our automated clustering methods produce 21–50 clusters that overlap with the Tier-1 ISP, many with relevant keywords.

Selecting the largest cluster (see Section 3.2.5), we first compare the completeness (true-positive rate) of our several approaches. We see that e-mail has significantly better coverage than other approaches, finding 71% of ASes with records and 59% of ground truth, compared to 30% for telephone number and 27% for OrgID. E-mail provides better coverage because, unlike OrgID and phone numbers, e-mail addresses for different contacts can be loosely matched to cluster disparate ASes.

We next consider false positives: ASes mis-matched into the Tier-1 ISP. While our e-mail method gives better coverage, it also allows false positives. Examination of the AS record details shows 3 due to stale or incorrect data, 7 due to technical setup help, 5 due to former customer relationship, and 3 wrongly clustered because they share related attributes with 2 of these 5 ASes.

The main reason for false positives is therefore the *spectrum of relationships* between organizations—with technical support, outsourcing and joint ventures, there often is no clean organizational boundary. In 7 of 18 false positives due to e-mail clustering, we see examples of ASes acquired for customers. A secondary reason is outdated information in WHOIS, accounting for 3 of the 18 e-mail false positives.

Finally, we examine why we miss clusters (false negatives). For e-mail, 17% is due to missing or generic data, and most of these (30 of 36) are registration records using generic e-mail addresses. Clustering is *difficult when operational and customer e-mail use the same domain.* For the 52 with WHOIS data that do link to the main cluster, the dominant cause (35 of 52) is due to mergers where all WHOIS data remains in the original company's identity, with a few (5) due to independent business units not obviously linked to the parent, and some more (9) with outdated records. Three records indicate outsourced WHOIS handling, which may be related to agreements made prior to organizational changes.

Overall, we find the main clustering problem is due to registration with generic e-mail addresses and mergers that maintain all aspects of original identity, and apparently independent business units, together accounting for 33% of our missing ground truth (70 of 213) and 80% of what is missing from our cluster.

We speculate that loose matching on the names of ASes may help correct these errors. Technical support, outsourcing, both as a service offered by the Tier-1 ISP and by acquisitions cause many false positives (7 of 18) and a few false negatives (3 of 213). Stale/incorrect data and organizational churn account for a handful of the remaining (3 and 9 false positives and negatives).

Hybrid methods combine different types of attributes together to achieve a higher true-positive rate with the potential sacrifice of false-positive rate. We first start from the OrgID method with 27% coverage, then gradually add phone and email attributes. The coverage rises from 27% to 33% then to 64%, but also with a 2% and 11% increase on false-positive rate.

4.2 Validation with External Observation

We next compare our methods against manually collected estimates of clusters for nine different organizations (each with multiple ASes): four telecommunications companies, Verizon (234 ASes), Comcast (48), Time Warner (35), and China Mobile (CN Mobile) (10); four content providers, Yahoo (76), Akamai (32), Google (21), and Limelight (11); and a root-DNS provider, Internet Systems Consortium (ISC, 55). Unlike Section 4.1, the ground truth here is weaker: for each of the organizations we did our best to determine their ASes based on examination of public documents, routing data, and WHOIS data. Given the difficultly in getting strong ground truth even with operator cooperation, we know of no better way to confirm our results.

We first consider data availability (Figure 2, top). Just as the Tier-1 ISP was missing 8–17% of each kind of attribute, we see that most cases are missing up to 30% of attributes. In about half the cases (CN Mobile, Yahoo, Akamai, Limelight, ISC), many or all OrgIDs are missing; this deficit is due to poor or no OrgID coverage in APNIC/LACNIC and RIPE. We conclude that use of multiple attributes is important to provide good coverage.

Turning to coverage (Figure 2, bottom), we see that in most cases, coverage (true positives) is as good or better for these organizations compared to the Tier-1 ISP, particularly for e-mail and hybrid methods. However, for Google and Limelight, they are consistently worse, and OrgID coverage is very bad for these and Verizon, CN Mobile, and Yahoo. Coverage problems with OrgID are mainly due to attribute availability, and because some organizations such as Verizon use many (48) OrgIDs. Limelight's 11 inferred ground truth ASes break into two parts, one containing its 7 North American ASes and the other containing its 4 Asian ASes, each with separate contact information and so resulting in low coverage by all methods. Finally, Google is an unusual case because, while it has acquired other companies like YouTube, DoubleClick, GrandCentral and Picnik, to date it has done little consolidation of its RIR data.

We see a wider range of false positives for these organizations. Several show none (CN Mobile, Comcast, Google, Yahoo, Akamai) or a few, similar to the Tier-1 ISP (Verizon, TW Cable, Limelight). However, ISC shows a large number of false positives with phone or phone-related hybrid clustering. For ISC, these errors are due to outsourcing arrangements by individuals at ISC with other organizations.

Overall, we find this broader study confirms our main observations seen in the Tier-1 ISP, although they show a broader range of reactions.

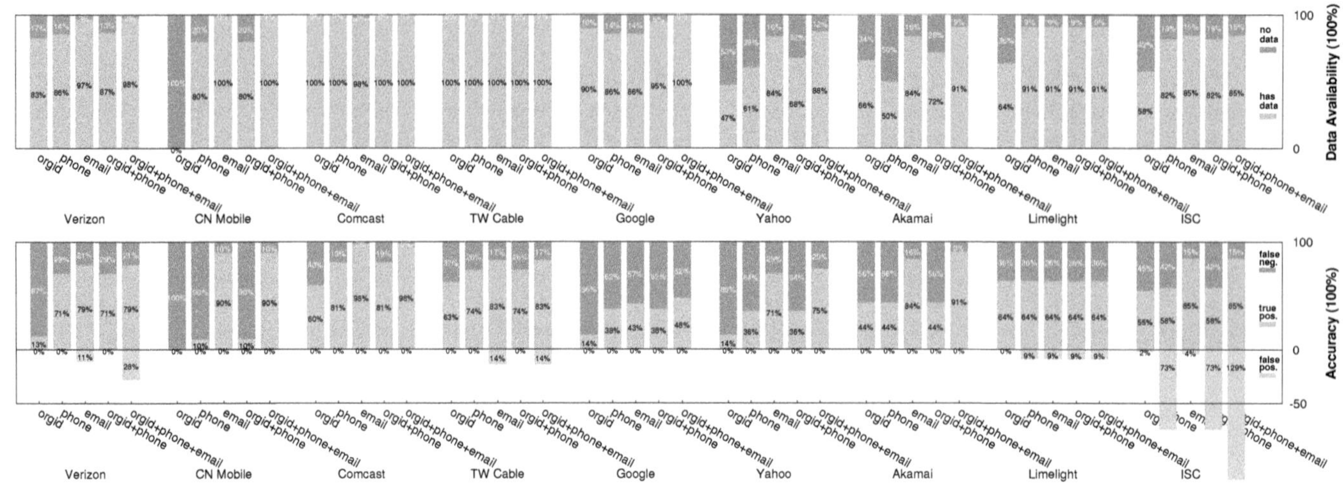

Figure 2: Validation based on inferred ground truth of 9 organizations data coverage (top) accuracy (bottom). Comparison between inferred ground truth and the biggest cluster by each method.

5. CONCLUSIONS

This paper has defined the problem and challenges of associating ASes with organizations and has described our first approach that uses WHOIS data from the RIRs. Although the WHOIS database has incorrect, missing, and outdated entries, it also has valuable information. However, relying on this data turns tasks such as clustering ASes by organization into hard problems. While the ad-hoc clustering method described in this paper shows promise, a proper AS clustering mechanism will (i) require incorporating methods for giving higher importance to attributes that are more critical to the business of running an AS, and (ii) necessitate ways to bring in additional ambient information for associating existing ASes with their parent organization. Developing a more *informed* AS clustering algorithm and running it on the nearly 30,000 ASes in the Internet is part of our future work and we hope it will lay the groundwork to better understand the characteristics of the Internet ecosystem.

Acknowledgments

We thank all those who contributed valuable information regarding ASes in the Tier-1 ISP. We also thank Myra Agostino for her considerable help in answering our questions. We also thank Yuri Pradkin for managing our RIR datasets.

6. REFERENCES

[1] Réka Albert, Hawoong Jeong, and Albert-László Barabási. Error and attack tolerance in complex networks. *Nature*, 406:378–382, July 27 2000.

[2] ARIN. Introduction to ARIN's database. `https://www.arin.net/knowledge/database.html`, March 2010.

[3] Brice Augustin, Balachander Krishnamurthy, and Walter Willinger. IXPs: mapped? In *IMC '09: Proceedings of the 9th ACM Internet measurement conference*, pages 336–349, New York, NY, USA, 2009. ACM.

[4] Martin Brown, Alin Popescu, and Earl Zmijewski. Peering Wars: Lessons Learned from the Cogent-Telia De-peering. `http://www.renesys.com/tech/presentations/pdf/nanog43-peeringwars.pdf`, June 2008.

[5] James H. Cowie, Andy T. Ogielski, BJ Premore, Eric A. Smith, and Todd Underwood. Impact of the 2003 Blackouts on Internet Communications. `https://www.renesys.com/tech/presentations/pdf/Renesys_BlackoutReport.pdf`, November 2003.

[6] Danny Dolev, Sugih Jamin, Osnat Mokryn, and Yuval Shavitt. Internet resiliency to attacks and failures under BGP policy routing. *Computer Networks*, 50(16):3183–3196, 2006.

[7] Michalis Faloutsos, Petros Faloutsos, and Christos Faloutsos. On power-law relationships of the Internet topology. In *Proc. of ACM SIGCOMM*, pages 251–262, Cambridge, MA, USA, September 1999. ACM.

[8] Avi Freedman. 7007: From the horse's mouth. NANOG mailing list, April 1997.

[9] Lixin Gao. On inferring autonomous system relationships in the Internet. *ACM/IEEE Transactions on Networking*, 9(6):733–745, December 2001.

[10] Donald Greenlees and Wayne Arnold. Asia scrambles to restore communications after quake. International Herald Tribune, `http://www.nytimes.com/2006/12/28/business/worldbusiness/28iht-connect.4042439.html?_r=1`, December 2006.

[11] J. Hawkinson and T. Bates. Guidelines for creation, selection, and registration of an autonomous system (AS). RFC 1930, Internet Request For Comments, March 1996.

[12] Young Hyun, Andre Broido, and k. c. claffy. Traceroute and BGP AS path incongruities. Technical report, UCSD CAIDA, 2003. Published as web page `http://www.caida.org/publications/papers/2003/ASP/`.

[13] Z.M. Morley J. Wu, Y. Zhang and K.G. Shin. Internet routing resilience to failures: Analysis and implications. In *Proc. ACM CoNEXT'07*, New York, US, 2007.

[14] A.-L. Barabási M. Newman and D.J. Watts. *The Structure and Dynamics of Networks*. Princeton University Press, 2006.

[15] R. Nilchiani M. Omer and A. Mostashari. Measuring the resilience of the global Internet infrastructure system. In *Proc. of the 2009 IEEE International Systems Conference*, Vancouver, Canada, 2009.

[16] Danny McPherson. Internet routing insecurity: Pakistan nukes YouTube? Security to the Core: the Arbor Networks Security Blog, February 2008.

[17] Rich Miller. Car crash triggers Amazon power outage. *DataCenter Knowledge*, May 2010. `http://www.datacenterknowledge.com/archives/2010/05/13/car-crash-triggers-amazon-power-outage/`.

[18] RIPE NCC. Ripe database query reference manual. `http://www.ripe.net/db/support/query-reference-manual.pdf`, November 2009.

[19] Packet Clearing House. PCH INOC-DBA. `https://www.pch.net/inoc-dba/`, April 2010.

[20] Regional Internet Registry. `http://www.afrinic.net/`, `http://www.apnic.net/`, `http://www.arin.net/`, `http://www.lacnic.net/`, `http://www.ripe.net/`, November 2009.

[21] Y. Rekhter and T. Li. A border gateway protocol 4 (BGP-4). RFC 1771, Internet Request For Comments, March 1995.

[22] Renesys. Internet-Wide Catastrophe–Last Year. `http://www.renesys.com/blog/2005/12/internetwide_nearcatastrophela.shtml`, December 2005.

[23] Renesys. Con-Ed Steals the 'Net. `http://www.renesys.com/blog/2006/01/coned_steals_the_net.shtml`, January 2006.

[24] Renesys. Pakistan hijacks YouTube. `http://www.renesys.com/blog/2008/02/pakistan_hijacks_youtube_1.shtml`, February 2008.

[25] Renesys Blog. Sprint and Cogent Peer. `http://www.renesys.com/blog/2006/11/sprint-and-cogent-peer.shtml`, November 2006.

[26] Mikael Ricknas. Sprint-Cogent Dispute Puts Small Rip in Fabric of Internet. `http://www.pcworld.com/businesscenter/article/153123/sprintcogent_dispute_puts_small_rip_in_fabric_of_internet.html`, October 2008.

[27] Matthew Roughan, Jonanthan Tuke, and Olaf Maennel. Bigfoot, Sasquatch, the Yeti and other missing links: what we don't know about the AS graph. In *Proc. of 8th ACM Internet Measurement Conf.*, pages 325–330, Vouliagmeni, Greece, October 2008. ACM.

[28] The National Academic Press. The Internet under crisis conditions: Learning from the impact of September 11. `http://books.nap.edu/openbook.php?isbn=0309087023`, 2003.

[29] WIRED. Oops! AT&T Blackhole Was 4Chan's Fault. `http://www.wired.com/threatlevel/2009/07/4chan/`, July 2009.

Comparing and Improving Current Packet Capturing Solutions based on Commodity Hardware

Lothar Braun, Alexander Didebulidze, Nils Kammenhuber, Georg Carle
Technische Universität München
Institute for Informatics
Chair for Network Architectures and Services
{braun,didebuli,kammenhuber,carle}@net.in.tum.de

ABSTRACT

Capturing network traffic with commodity hardware has become a feasible task: Advances in hardware as well as software have boosted off-the-shelf hardware to performance levels that some years ago were the domain of expensive special-purpose hardware. However, the capturing hardware still needs to be driven by a well-performing software stack in order to minimise or avoid packet loss. Improving the capturing stack of Linux and FreeBSD has been an extensively covered research topic in the past years. Although the majority of the proposed enhancements have been backed by evaluations, these have mostly been conducted on different hardware platforms and software versions, which renders a comparative assessment of the various approaches difficult, if not impossible.

This paper summarises and evaluates the performance of current packet capturing solutions based on commodity hardware. We identify bottlenecks and pitfalls within the capturing stack of FreeBSD and Linux, and give explanations for the observed effects. Based on our experiments, we provide guidelines for users on how to configure their capturing systems for optimal performance and we also give hints on debugging bad performance. Furthermore, we propose improvements to the operating system's capturing processes that reduce packet loss, and evaluate their impact on capturing performance.

Categories and Subject Descriptors

C.2.3 [Network Operation]: Network Monitoring

General Terms

Measurement, Performance

1. INTRODUCTION

Packet capture is an essential part of most network monitoring and analysing systems. A few years ago, using specialised hardware—e.g., network monitoring cards manufactured by Endace [1]—was mandatory for capturing Gigabit or Multi-gigabit network traffic, if little or no packet loss was a requirement. With recent development progresses in bus systems, multi-core CPUs and commodity network cards, nowadays off-the-shelf hardware can be used to capture network traffic at near wire-speed with little or no packet loss in 1 GE networks, too [2, 3]. People are even building monitoring devices based on commodity hardware that can be used to capture traffic in 10 GE networks [4, 5]

However, this is not an easy task, since it requires careful configuration and optimization of the hardware and software components involved—even the best hardware will suffer packet loss if its driving software stack is not able to handle the huge amount of network packets. Several subsystems including the network card driver, the capturing stack of the operating system and the monitoring application are involved in packet processing. If only one of these subsystems faces performance problems, packet loss will occur, and the whole process of packet capturing will yield bad results.

Previous work analysed [2, 4, 6] and improved [5, 7, 8] packet capturing solutions. Comparing these work is quite difficult because the evaluations have been performed on different hardware platforms and with different software versions. In addition, operating systems like Linux and FreeBSD are subject to constant changes and improvements. Comparisons that have been performed years ago therefore might today not be valid any longer. In fact, when we started our capturing experiments, we were not able to reproduce the results presented in several papers. When we dug deeper into the operating systems' capturing processes, we found that some of our results can be explained by improved drivers and general operating systems improvements. Other differences can be explained by the type of traffic we analysed and by the way our capturing software works on the application layer. While it is not a problem to find comparisons that state the superiority of a specific capturing solution, we had difficulties to find statements on why one solution is superior to another solution. Information about this topic is scattered throughout different papers and web pages. Worse yet, some information proved to be highly inconsistent, especially when from Web sources outside academia. We therefore encountered many difficulties when debugging the performance problems we ran into.

This paper tries to fill the gap that we needed to step over when we set up our packet capturing environment with Linux and FreeBSD. We evaluate and compare different capturing solutions for both operating systems, and try to summarise the pitfalls that can lead to bad capturing perfor-

IMC'10, November 1–3, 2010, Melbourne, Australia.

mance. The paper aims at future developers and users of capture systems and serves as a resource helping them not to repeat the pitfalls we and other researchers have encountered.

A special focus of this paper is on explaining our findings. We try to identify the major factors that influence the performance of a capturing solution, providing users of packet capture systems with guidelines on where to search for performance problems in their systems. Our paper also targets developers of capturing and monitoring solutions: We identify potential bottlenecks that can lead to performance bottlenecks and thus packet loss. Finally, we propose a modification that can be applied to popular capturing solutions. It improves capturing performance in a number of situations.

The remainder of this paper is organised as follows: Section 2 introduces the capturing mechanisms in Linux and FreeBSD that are in use when performing network monitoring, and presents related improvements and evaluations of packet capturing systems. Section 3 presents the test setup that we used for our evaluation in Section 4. Our capturing analysis covers scheduling issues in Section 4.1 and focuses on the application and operating system layer with low application load in Section 4.2. Subsequently, we analyse application scenarios that pose higher load on the system in Section 4.3, where we furthermore present our modifications to the capturing processes and evaluate their influence on capturing performance. In Section 4.4, we move downwards within the capturing stack and discuss driver issues. Our experiments result in recommendations for developers and users of capturing solutions, which are presented in Section 5. Finally, Section 6 concludes the paper with a summary of our findings.

2. BACKGROUND AND RELATED WORK

Various mechanisms are involved in the process of network packet capturing. The performance of a capturing process thus depends on each of them to some extent. On the one hand, there is the hardware that needs to capture and copy all packets from the network to memory before the analysis can start. On the other hand, there is the driver, the operating system and monitoring applications that need to carefully handle the available hardware in order to achieve the best possible packet capturing performance. In the following, we will introduce popular capturing solutions on Linux and FreeBSD in 2.1. Afterwards, we will summarise comparisons and evaluations that have been performed on the different solutions in Section 2.2.

2.1 Solutions on Linux and FreeBSD

Advances made in hardware development in recent years such as high speed bus systems, multi-core systems or network cards with multiple independent reception (RX) queues offer performance that has only been offered by special purpose hardware some years ago. Meanwhile, operating systems and hardware drivers have come to take advantage of these new technologies, thus allowing higher capturing rates.

Hardware:

The importance of carefully selecting suitable capturing hardware is well-known, as research showed that different hardware platforms can lead to different capturing performance.

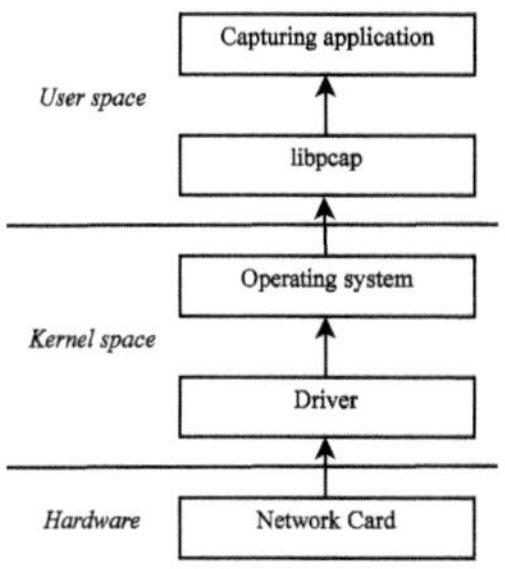

Figure 1: Subsystems involved in the capturing process

Schneider et al. [4] compared capturing hardware based on Intel Xeon and AMD Opteron CPUs with otherwise similar components. Assessing an AMD and an Intel platform of comparable computing power, they found the AMD platform to yield better capturing results. AMD's superior memory management and bus contention handling mechanism was identified to be the most reasonable explanation. Since then, Intel has introduced Quick Path Interconnect [9] in its recent processor families, which has improved the performance of the Intel platform; however, we are not able to compare new AMD and Intel platforms at this time due to lack of hardware. In any case, users of packet capturing solutions should carefully choose the CPU platform, and should conduct performance tests before buying a particular hardware platform.

Apart from the CPU, another important hardware aspect is the speed of the bus system and the used memory. Current PCI-E buses and current memory banks allow high-speed transfer of packets from the capturing network card into the memory and the analysing CPUs. These hardware advances thus have shifted the bottlenecks, which were previously located at the hardware layer, into the software stacks.

Software stack:

There are several software subsystems involved in packet capture, as shown in Figure 1. Passing data between and within the involved subsystems can be a very important performance bottleneck that can impair capturing performance and thus lead to packet loss during capturing. We will discuss and analyse this topic in Section 4.3.

A packet's journey through the capturing system begins at the network interface card (NIC). Modern cards copy the packets into the operating systems kernel memory using Direct Memory Access (DMA), which reduces the work the driver and thus the CPU has to perform in order to transfer the data into memory. The driver is responsible for allocating and assigning memory pages to the card that can be used for DMA transfer. After the card has copied the captured packets into memory, the driver has to be informed about the new packets through an hardware interrupt. Raising an interrupt for each incoming packet will result in packet loss, as the system gets busy handling the interrupts (also known as an *interrupt storm*). This well-known issue has lead to the development of techniques like interrupt moderation or device polling, which have been proposed several years ago [7, 10, 11]. However, even today hardware interrupts can be a problem because some drivers are not able to use the hardware features or do not use polling—actually, when we used the igb driver in FreeBSD 8.0, which was released in late 2009, we experienced bad performance due to interrupt storms. Hence, bad capturing performance can be explained by bad drivers; therefore, users should check the number of generated interrupts if high packet loss rates are observed.[1]

The driver's hardware interrupt handler is called immediately upon the reception of an interrupt, which interrupts the normal operation of the system. An interrupt handler is supposed to fulfill its tasks as fast as possible. It therefore usually doesn't pass on the captured packets to the operating systems capturing stack by himself, because this operation would take to long. Instead, the packet handling is deferred by the interrupt handler. In order to do this, a kernel thread is scheduled to perform the packet handling in a later point in time. The system scheduler chooses a kernel thread to perform the further processing of the captured packets according to the system scheduling rules. Packet processing is deferred until there is a free thread that can continue the packet handling.

As soon as the chosen kernel thread is running, it passes the received packets into the network stack of the operating system. From there on, packets need to be passed to the monitoring application that wants to perform some kind of analysis. The standard Linux capturing path leads to a subsystem called PF_PACKET; the corresponding system in FreeBSD is called BPF (Berkeley Packet Filter). Improvements for both subsystems have been proposed.

Software improvements:

The most prominent replacement for PF_PACKET on Linux is called PF_RING and was introduced in 2004 by Luca Deri [8]. Deri found that the standard Linux networking stack at that time introduced some bottlenecks, which lead to packet loss during packet capture. His capturing infrastructure was developed to remove these bottlenecks. He showed to achieve a higher capturing rate with PF_RING when small packets are to be captured. PF_RING ships with several modified drivers. These are modified to directly copy packets into PF_RING and therefore completely circumvent the standard Linux networking stack. This modification further boosts the performance for network cards with a modified driver.

Figure 2 shows the difference between the two capturing systems. One important feature of PF_RING is the way it exchanges packets between user space and kernel: Monitoring applications usually access a library like libpcap [12] to retrieve captured packets from the kernel. Libpcap is an abstraction from the operating systems' capturing mechanisms and allows to run a capturing application on several operating systems without porting it to the special capturing architecture. Back in 2004, the then current libpcap version 0.9.8 used a copy operation to pass packets from the kernel to the user space on Linux. An unofficial patch against that libpcap version from Phil Woods existed, which replaced the copy operation by a shared memory area that was used to exchange packets between kernel and application [13]. This modification will be called MMAP throughout the rest of the paper. PF_RING uses a similar structure to exchange packets by default. Libpcap version 1.0.0, which was released in late 2008, is the first version that ships built-in shared memory (SHM) exchange support; hence the patch from Phil Woods is not longer necessary. We will analyse the performance of these different solutions in Section 4.2.

[1]FreeBSD will report interrupt storms via kernel messages. Linux exposes the number of interrupts via the proc file system in */proc/interrupts*.

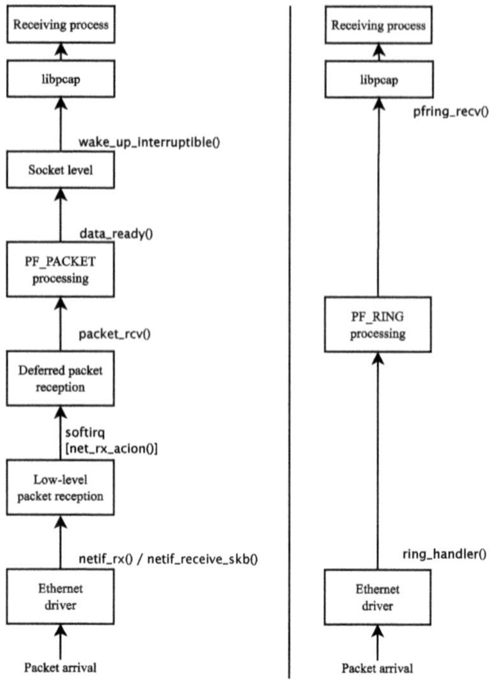

Figure 2: PF_RING and PF_PACKET under Linux

All capturing mechanisms on Linux have something in common: They handle individual packets, meaning that each operation between user space and kernel is performed on a per-packet basis. FreeBSD packet handling differs in this point by exchanging buffers containing potentially several packets, as shown in Figure 3.

Both BPF as well as its improvement Zero-Copy BPF (ZCBPF) use buffers that contain multiple packets for storing and exchanging packets between kernel and monitoring application. BPF and ZCBPF use two buffers: The first, called HOLD buffer, is used by the application to read packets, usually via libpcap. The other buffer, the STORE buffer, is used by the kernel to store new incoming packets. If the application (i.e., via libpcap) has emptied the HOLD buffer, the buffers are switched, and the STORE buffer is copied into user space. BPF uses a copy operation to switch the buffers whereas ZCBPF has both buffers memory-mapped between the application and the kernel. Zero-Copy BPF is expected to perform better than BPF as it removes the copy operation between kernel and application. However, as there are fewer copy operations in FreeBSD than in non-shared-memory packet exchange on Linux, the benefits between ZCBPF and normal BPF in FreeBSD are expected to be smaller than in Linux with shared memory support.

TNAPI is very recent development by Luca Deri [5]. It improves standard Linux network card drivers and can be used in conjunction with PF_RING. Usually, Linux drivers assign new memory pages to network cards for DMA after the card copied new packets to old memory pages. The driver allo-

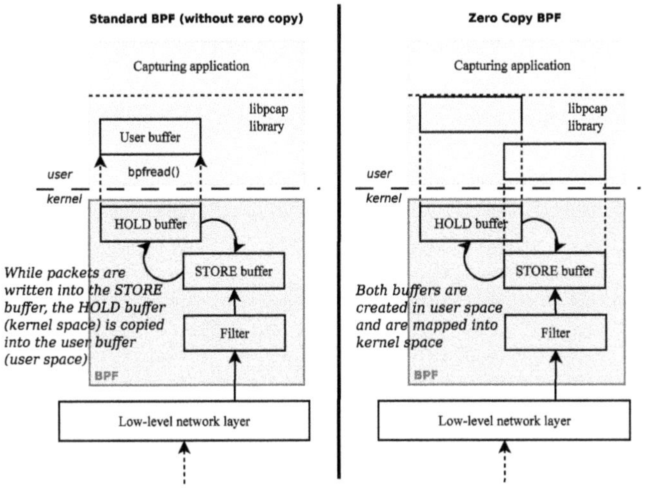

Figure 3: Berkeley Packet Filter and Zero Copy Berkeley Packet Filter

cates new pages and assign them to the card for DMA. Deri changed this behaviour in two ways: Non-TNAPI drivers receive an interrupt for received packets and schedule a kernel thread to perform the packet processing. The processing is performed by a kernel thread that is not busy doing other work and is chosen according to the scheduling rules of the operating system. Deri's driver creates a separate kernel thread that is only used to perform this processing. Hence, there is always a free kernel thread that can continue, and packet processing can almost immediately start.

The second major change is the memory handling within the driver: As soon as the thread is notified about a new packet arrival, the new packet is copied from the DMA memory area into the PF_RING ring buffer. Usually, network drivers would allocate new memory for DMA transfer for new packets. Deri's drivers tell the card to reuse the old memory page, thus eliminating the necessity of allocating and assigning new memory.

Furthermore, his drivers may take advantage of multiple RX queues and multi-core systems. This is done by creating a kernel thread for each RX queue of the card. Each kernel thread is bound to a specific CPU core in the case of multicore systems. The RX queues are made accessible to the user space, so that users can run monitoring applications that read from the RX queues in parallel.

A rather non-standard solution for wire-speed packet capture is *ncap*. Instead of using the operating system's standard packet processing software, it uses special drivers and a special capturing library. The library allows an application to read packets from the network card directly [3].

2.2 Previous Comparisons

Previous work compared the different approaches to each other. We will now summarise the previous findings and determine which experiments we need to repeat with our hardware platforms and new software versions. Results from related work can also give hints on further experiments we need to conduct in order to achieve a better understanding of the involved processes.

Capturing traffic in 1 GE networks is seen as something that today's off-the-shelf hardware is able to do, whereas it remains a very challenging task in 10 GE networks [4]. Apart from the ten-fold increased throughput, the difficulties also lie in the ten-fold increased packet rate, as the number of packets to be captured per time unit is a factor that is even more important than the overall bandwidth. As an example, capturing a 1 GE stream that consists entirely of large packets, e.g., 1500 bytes, is easy; whereas capturing a 1 GE stream consisting entirely of small packets, e.g., 64 bytes, is a very difficult task [8, 4]. This is due to the fact that each packet, regardless of its size, introduces a significant handling overhead.

Driver issues that arise with a high number of packets have been studied very well [7, 10, 11]. Problems concerning interrupt storms are well understood and most network cards and drivers support mechanisms to avoid them. Such mechanisms include polling or interrupt moderation.

In 2007, Schneider et al. compared FreeBSD and Linux on Intel and AMD platforms [4]. They determined that device polling on Linux reduces the CPU cycles within the kernel and therefore helps to improve capturing performance. On FreeBSD however, device polling actually reduced the performance of the capturing and furthermore reduced the stability of the system. Hence, they recommend using the interrupt moderation facilities of the cards instead of polling on FreeBSD. In their comparison, FreeBSD using BPF and no device polling had a better capturing performance than Linux with PF_PACKET and device polling. This trend is enforced if multiple capturing processes are simultaneously deployed; in this case, the performance of Linux drops dramatically due to the additional load. Schneider et al. find that capturing 1 GE in their setup is possible with the standard facilities because they capture traffic that contains packets originated from a realistic size distribution. However, they do not capture the maximum possible packet rate, which is about 1.488 million packets per second with 64 bytes packets [5]. Another important aspect about the workload of Schneider et al. is that during each measurement, they send only one million packets (repeating each measurement for 7 times). This is a very low number of packets, considering that using 64 byte packets, it is possible to send 1.488 million packets within one second. Some of the effects we could observe are only visible if more packets are captured. Based on their measurement results, they recommend a huge buffer size in the kernel buffers, e.g., for the HOLD and STORE buffers in FreeBSD, to achieve good capturing performance. We can see a clear correlation between their recommendation and the number of packets they send per measurement and will come back to this in Section 4.2.

Deri validated his PF_RING capturing system against the standard Linux capturing PF_PACKET in 2004 [8]. He finds PF_RING to really improve the capturing of small (64 bytes) and medium (512 bytes) packets compared to the capturing with PF_PACKET and libpcap-mmap. His findings were reproduced by Cascallana and Lizarrondo in 2006 [6] who also found significant performance improvements with PF_RING. In contrast to Schneider et al., neither of the PF_RING comparisons consider more than one capturing process.

Using TNAPI and the PF_RING extensions, Deri claims to be able to capture 1 GE packet streams with small packet sizes at wire-speed (1.488 million packets) [5].

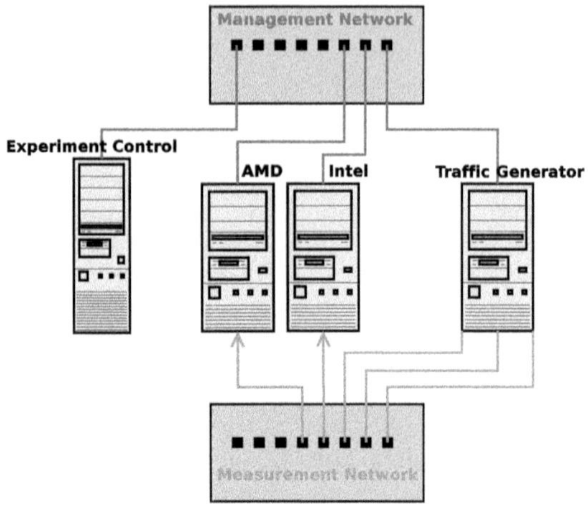

Figure 4: Evaluation Setup

3. TEST SETUP

In this section, we describe the hardware and software setup that we used for our evaluation. Our test setup (see Figure 4) consists of three PCs, one for traffic generation, the other two for capturing.

The traffic generator is equipped with several network interface cards (NICs) and uses the Linux Kernel Packet Generator [14] to generate a uniform 1 GE packet stream. It was necessary to generate the traffic using several NICs simultaneously because the deployed cards were not able to send out packets at maximum speed when generating small packets. Even this setup was only able to generate 1.27 million packets per seconds (pps) with the smallest packet size. However, this packet rate was sufficient to show the bottlenecks of all analysed systems. We had to deploy a second generator for our experiments in Section 4.4, where we actually needed wire-speed packet generation (1.488 million pps).

In contrast to [4], we where did not produce a packet stream with a packet size distribution that is common in real networks. Our goal is explicitly to study the behaviour of the capturing software stacks at high packet rates. As we do not have 10 GE hardware for our tests available, we have to create 64 bytes packets in order to achieve a high packet rate for our 1 GE setup.

Each of our test runs is configured to produce a packet stream with a fixed number of packets per seconds and runs over a time period of 100 seconds and repeated for five times. As our traffic generator is software based and has to handle several NICs, the number of packets per second is not completely stable and can vary to some extend. Hence, we measure the variations in our measurements and plot them where appropriate.

Capturing is performed with two different machines with different hardware in order to check whether we can reproduce any special events we may observe with different processor, bus systems and network card, too. The first capturing PC is operated by two Intel Xeon CPUs with 2.8 GHz each. It has several network cards including an Intel Pro/1000 (82540EM), an Intel Pro /1000 (82546EB) and a Broadcom BCM5701 all connected via a PCI-X bus. In our experiments, we only use one NIC at a time.

The second capturing PC has an AMD Athlon 64 X2 5200+ CPU and is also equipped with several network cards, including an Intel Pro/1000 (82541PI) and a nVidia Corporation CK804 onboard controller. Both cards are connected via a slow PCI bus to the system. Furthermore, there are two PCI-E based network cards connected to the system. One is an Intel Pro/1000 PT (82572EI), the other is a Dual Port Intel Pro/1000 ET(82576). It should be noted that the AMD platform is significantly faster than the Xeon platform.

Using different network cards and different architectures, we can check if an observed phenomenon emerges due to a general software problem or if it is caused by a specific hardware or driver. Both machines are built from a few years old and therefore cheap hardware, thus our machines are not high end systems. We decided not to use more modern hardware for our testing because of the following reasons:

- We did not have 10 GE hardware.
- We want to identify problems in the software stack that appear when the hardware is fully utilised. This is quite difficult to achieve with modern hardware on a 1 GE stream.
- Software problems that exist on old hardware which monitors 1 GE packet streams still exist on newer hardware that monitors a 10 GE packet stream.

Both machines are installed with Ubuntu Jaunty Jackalope (9.04) with a vanilla Linux kernel version 2.6.32. Additionally, they have an installation of FreeBSD 8.0-RELEASE for comparison with Linux.

We perform tests with varying load at the capturing machines' application layer in order to simulate the CPU load of different capturing applications during monitoring. Two tools are used for our experiments:

First, we use tcpdump 4.0.0 [15] for capturing packets and writing them to `/dev/null`. This scenario emulates a simple one-threaded capturing process with very simple computations, which thus poses almost no load on the application layer. Similar load can be expected on the capturing thread of multi-threaded applications that have a separate thread that performs capturing only. Examples for such multi-threaded applications are the Time Machine [16, 17] or the network monitor VERMONT [18].

The second application was developed by us and is called *packzip*. It poses variable load onto the thread that performs the capturing. Every captured packet is copied once within the application and is then passed to `libz` [19] for compression. The compression mode can be configured by the user from 0 (no compression) to 9 (highest compression level). Increasing the compression level increases CPU usage and thus can be used to emulate an increased CPU load for the application processing the packets. Such packet handling has been performed before in [2] and [4]. We used this tool in order to make our results comparable to the results presented in this related work.

4. EVALUATION

This section presents our analysis results of various packet capture setups involving Linux and FreeBSD, including a performance analysis of our own proposed improvements to the Linux capturing stack. As multi-core and multi-processor architectures are common trends, we focus in particular on this kind of architecture. On these hardware platforms, scheduling issues arise when multiple processes involved in packed capturing need to be distributed over several processors or cores. We discuss this topic in Section 4.1. Afterwards, we focus on capturing with low application load in Section 4.2 and see if we can reproduce the effects that have been observed in the related work. In Section 4.3, we proceed to capturing with higher application load. We identify bottlenecks and provide solutions that lead to improvements to the capturing process. Finally, in Section 4.4 we present issues and improvements at the driver level and discuss how driver improvements can influence and improve the capturing performance.

4.1 Scheduling and packet capturing performance

On multi-core systems, scheduling is an important factor for packet capturing: If several threads, such as kernel threads of the operating system and a multi-threaded capturing application in user space are involved, distributing them among the available cores in a clever way is crucial for the performance.

Obviously, if two processes are scheduled to run on a single core, they have to share the available CPU time. This can lead to shortage of CPU time in one or both of the processes, and results in packet loss if one of them cannot cope with the network speed. Additionally, the processes then do not run simultaneously but alternately. As Schneider et al. [4] already found in their analysis, packet loss occurs if the CPU processing limit is reached. If the kernel capturing and user space analysis are performed on the same CPU, the following effect can be observed: The kernel thread that handles the network card dominates the user space application because it has a higher priority. The application has therefore only little time to process the packets; this leads to the kernel buffers filling up. If the buffers are filled, the kernel thread will take captured packets from the card and will throw them away because there is no more space to store them. Hence, the CPU gets busy capturing packets that will be immediately thrown away instead of being busy processing the already captured packets, which would empty the buffers.

Conversely, if the processes are scheduled to run on two cores, they have more available CPU power to each one of them and furthermore can truly run in parallel, instead of interleaving the CPU. However, sharing data between two cores or CPUs requires memory synchronisation between both of the threads, which can lead to severe performance penalties.

Scheduling can be done in two ways: Processes can either be scheduled dynamically by the operating system's scheduler, or they can be statically pinned to a specific core by the user. Manual pinning involves two necessary operations, as described in [5, 20]:

- Interrupt affinity of the network card interrupts have to be bound to one core.
- The application process must be bound to another core.

We check the influence of automatic vs. manually pinned scheduling in nearly all our experiments.

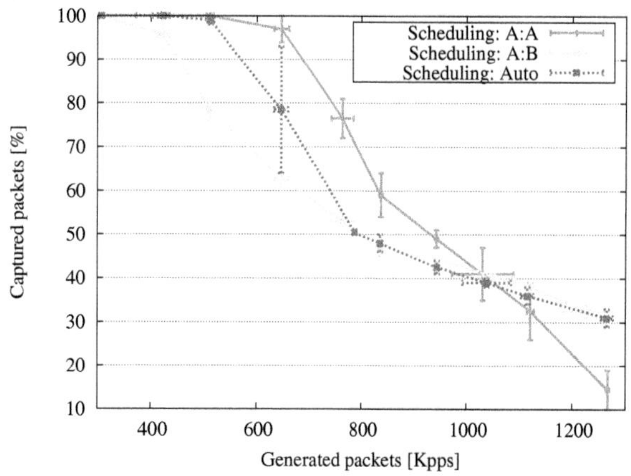

Figure 5: Scheduling effects

Figure 5 presents a measurement with 64 byte packets with varying numbers of packets per seconds and low application load.

Experiments were run where the kernel and user space application are processed on the same core (A:A), are pinned to run on different cores (A:B), or are scheduled automatically by the operating system's scheduler. Figure 5 shows that scheduling both processes on a single CPU results in more captured packets compared to running both processes on different cores, when packet rates are low. This can be explained by the small application and kernel load at these packet rates. Here, the penalties of cache invalidation and synchronisation are worse than the penalties of the involved threads being run alternately instead of parallel. With increasing packet rate, the capturing performance in case A:A drops significantly below that of A:B.

Another interesting observation can be made if automatic scheduling is used. One would expect the scheduler to place a process on the core where it performs best, depending on system load and other factors. However, the scheduler is not informed about the load on the application and is therefore not able to make the right decision. As can be seen on the error bars in Figure 5, the decision is not consistent over the repetitions of our experiments in all cases, as the scheduler tries to move the processes to different cores and sometimes sticks with the wrong decision whereas sometimes it makes a good decision.

Real capturing scenarios will almost always have a higher application load than the ones we have shown so far. In our experiments with higher application load which we will show in Section 4.3, we can almost always see that running the processes in A:B configuration results in better capturing performance. Static pinning always outperformed automatic scheduling as the schedulers on Linux and FreeBSD almost make wrong decisions very frequently.

4.2 Comparing packet capture setups under low application load

Applications that capture network traffic usually build on `libpcap` [12] as presented in Section 2.1. FreeBSD ships libpcap version 1.0.0 in its base system, and most Linux

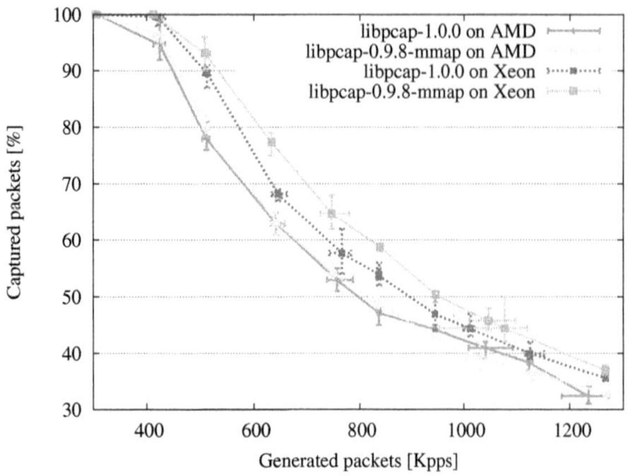

Figure 6: Comparison of different libpcap versions on Linux

distributions use the same version today[2]. Not long ago, libpcap version 0.9.8 was the commonly used version on Linux based systems and FreeBSD. As already explained in Section 2, libpcap-0.9.8 or libpcap-0.9.8-mmap were used in most earlier evaluations.

In this paper, we want to use the standard libpcap-1.0.0, which ships with a shared-memory support. As the shared-memory extensions in libpcap 0.9.8 and 1.0.0 where developed by different people, we first want to compare both versions. The results of this comparison are plotted in Figure 6 for the AMD and Xeon platforms. We can see that libpcap-0.9.8 performs slightly better on Xeon than libpcap 1.0.0 while 1.0.0 performs better on AMD. However, both differences are rather small, so that we decided to use the now standard 1.0.0 version for our experiments.

Having a closer look at the figure, one can see that the Xeon platform performs better than the AMD platform. This is very surprising as the AMD system's hardware performance is otherwise much faster than the aged Xeon platform. Things get even more weird if we include libpcap-0.9.8 without MMAP into our comparison (not shown in our plot): As the copy operation is way more expensive than the MMAP, one would expect MMAP to perform better than the copy operation. This assumption is true on the Xeon platform. On the AMD platform however, we can observe that libpcap-0.9.8 *without* MMAP performs better than libpcap-0.9.8-mmap or libpcap-1.0.0. This points to some unknown performance problems which prevents the AMD system from showing its superior hardware performance.

The next comparison is between standard Linux capturing with PF_PACKET and capturing on Linux using the PF_RING extension from Deri [8]. We therefore use Deri's patches to libpcap-1.0.0 which enables libpcap to read packets from PF_RING. Two important PF_RING parameters can be configured. The first one is the size of the ring buffer, which can be configured in number of packets that can be stored in the ring. Our experiments with different ring sizes reveal that in our setup, the size of the memory mapped area is not of much influence. We conducted similar experiments with the sizes of Berkeley Packet Filter on FreeBSD and other buffer sizes on Linux. All these experiments showed that increasing the buffer size beyond a certain limit does not boost capturing performance measurably. Instead, we found evidence that too large buffers have a negative impact on capturing performance. These findings are contrary to the findings from Schneider et al. [4], who found large buffers to increase the capturing performance.

The biggest factor regarding the performance is our capturing application—since our hardware, at least the AMD platform, is able to transfer all packets from the network card into memory. If the software is able to consume and process incoming packets faster than wire-speed, the in-kernel buffers will never fill up and there will be no packet loss. However, if the application is not able to process the packets as fast as they come in, increasing the buffer will not help much—rather, it will only reduce the packet loss by the number of elements that can be stored in the buffer, until the buffer is filled.

Schneider et al. sent only 1,000,000 packets per measurement run, whereas we produce packets with 1 GE speed (i.e., more than 100 Megabytes per second), which usually amounts to much more than 1,000,000 packets *per second*, over a time interval of 100 seconds. Increasing kernel buffer sizes to 20 megabytes, as recommended by Schneider et al., allows them to buffer a great share of their total number of packets, but does not help much on the long term. If we increase the buffers to the recommended size, we cannot see any significant improvements in our experiments.

Buffer size can be crucial, though: This is the case when the monitoring is not able to process packets at wire-speed, e.g., it can consume up to N packets per second (pps), and bursty Internet traffic is captured. If this traffic transports less or equal than N pps on average but has bursts with a higher pps rate, then having a sufficient dimensioned buffer to store the burst packets is obviously very important.

The second important parameter is a configuration option called `transparent_mode`. It configures how PF_RING handles packets:

- Transparent mode 0: Captured packets are inserted into the ring via the standard Linux socket API.
- Transparent mode 1: The network card driver inserts the packets directly into the ring (which requires an adopted network driver). Packets are also inserted into the standard Linux network stack.
- Transparent mode 2: Same as mode 1, but received packets are not copied into the standard Linux network stack (for capturing with PF_RING only).

It is obvious that *transparent_mode* 2 performs best as it is optimised for capturing. We conducted some comparisons using different packet sizes and packets rates and indeed found PF_RING to perform best in this mode.

We expected PF_RING to outperform the standard Linux capturing due to the evaluations performed in [8] and [6] when using small packet sizes. This performance benefit should be seen with small packets (64 bytes) and a high number of packets per second, and disappear with bigger packet sizes. According to Deri's evaluation, capturing small packet

[2]An exception is the current stable version of Debian 5.0 "Lenny", which still contains libpcap version 0.9.8-5 at the time this paper was written.

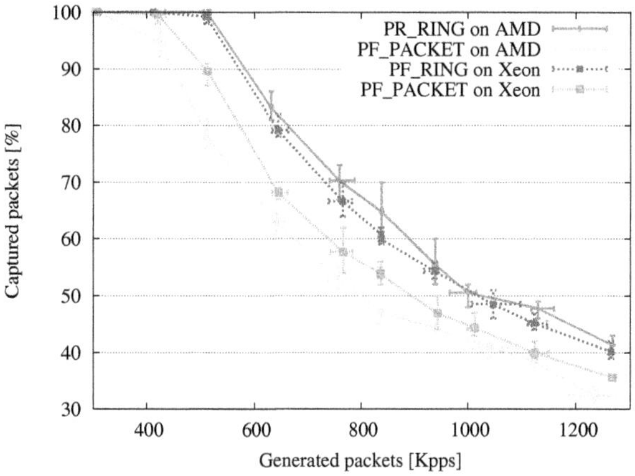

Figure 7: PF_PACKET vs. PF_RING

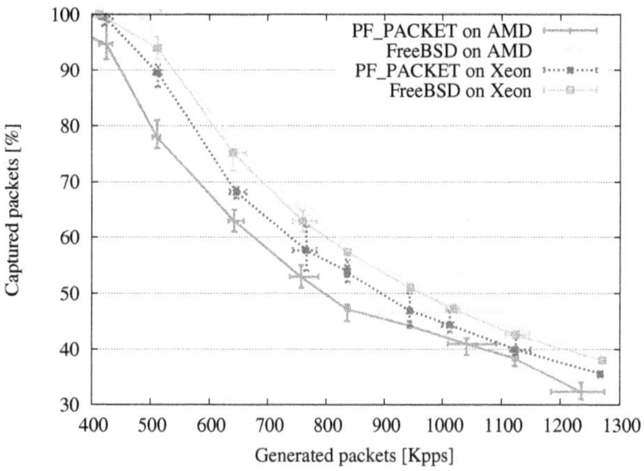

Figure 8: Linux vs. FreeBSD

streams using PF_PACKET in Linux 2.6.1 with libpcap-mmap only captured 14.9% of all packets while PF_RING within the same kernel version was able to capture 75.7% of all packets. Our comparison confirms that PF_RING indeed performs better than PF_PACKET, as can be seen in Figure 7. We can also see that PF_RING is better than PF_PACKET on both systems. Furthermore, PF_RING on the faster AMD hardware performs better than PF_RING on Xeon. However, the performance difference is small if one considers the significant differences in hardware, which again points to some performance problems which we pointed out before. One more observation concerns the difference between PF_PACKET and PF_RING within the same platform. Although there is some difference, it is not as pronounced as in previous comparisons. We explain this by the improvements that have been made in the capturing code of PF_PACKET and within libpcap since Deri's and Cascallana's evaluations in 2004 and 2006.

We now compare the measurement results of FreeBSD against the Linux measurements. FreeBSD has two capturing mechanisms: Berkeley Packet Filter (BPF) and Zero Copy Berkeley Packet Filter (ZCBPF) as described in Section 2.1. At first, we compared both against each other, but

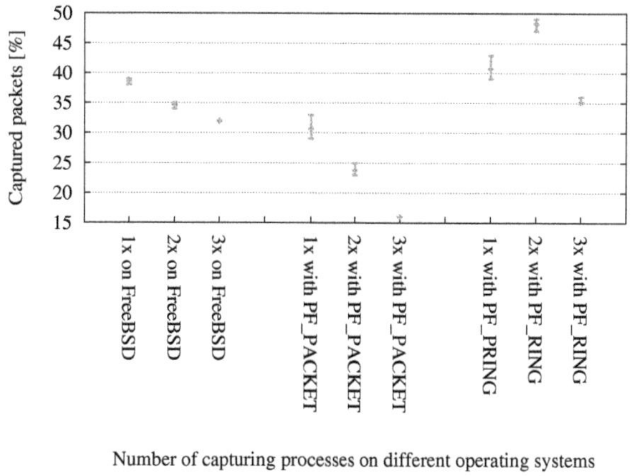

Figure 9: Capturing with multiple processes

we could not find any significant differences in any of our tests. Schneider et al. found FreeBSD to perform amazingly good even though FreeBSD employed this packet copy operation. This might indicate that the copy operation is indeed not a significant factor that influences the performance of the FreeBSD capturing system. We are uncertain about the true reason for Zero Copy BPF not performing better than BPF; therefore, we do not include ZCBPF into our further comparisons.

Our comparison with the standard BPF is shown in Figure 8 and presents the differences between PF_PACKET and FreeBSD. We can see some differences between capturing with PF_PACKET on Linux and capturing with BPF on FreeBSD. FreeBSD performs slightly better on both platforms, which confirms the findings of Schneider et al. [2, 4].

Differences increase if more than one capturing process in running on the systems, as shown in Figure 9. This figure shows the capturing performance of FreeBSD, Linux with PF_PACKET and Linux with PF_RING capturing a packet stream of 1270 kpps on the AMD system with one, two and three capturing processes running simultaneously.

Capturing performance on both systems decreases due to the higher CPU load due to the multiple capturing processes. This is an obvious effect and has also been observed in [4]. Linux suffers more from the additional capturing processes compared to FreeBSD, which has also been observed in related work. Amazingly, Linux with PF_RING does not suffer much from these performance problems and is better than FreeBSD and Linux with PF_PACKET. A strange effect can be seen if two capturing processes are run with PF_PACKET: Although system load increases due to the second capturing process, the overall capturing performances increases. This effect is only visible on the AMD system and not on the Xeon platform and also points to the same strange effect we have seen before and which we will explain in Section 4.3.

If we compare our analysis results of the different capturing solutions on FreeBSD and Linux with the results of earlier evaluations, we can see that our results confirm several prior findings: We can reproduce the results of Deri [8] and Cascallana [6] who found PF_RING to perform better than PF_PACKET on Linux. However, we see that the difference between both capturing solutions is not as strong

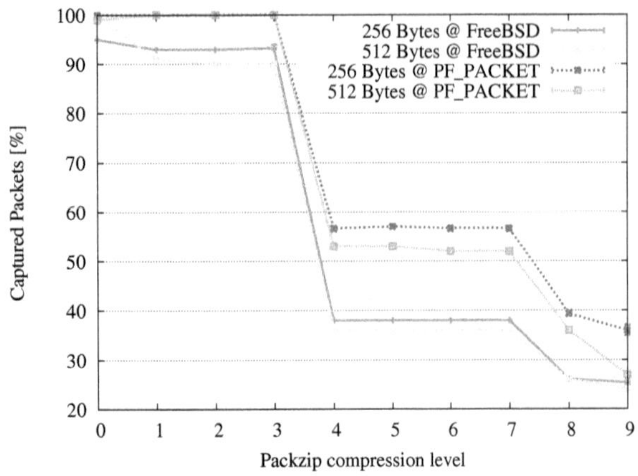

Figure 10: Packzip on 256 and 512 byte packets

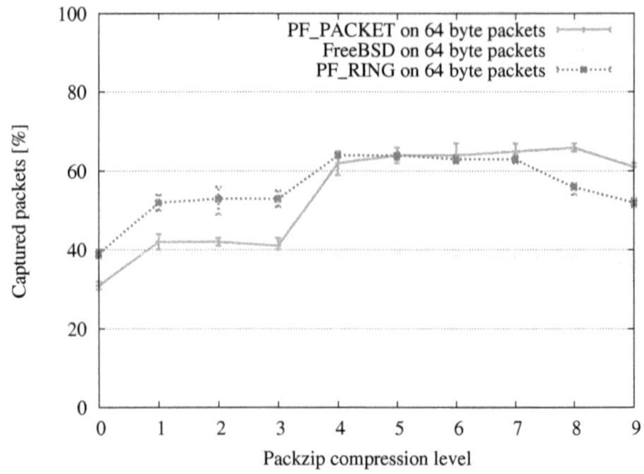

Figure 11: Packzip on 64 byte packets

as it used to be in 2004 and 2006 due to general improvements in the standard Linux software stack. Furthermore, we can confirm the findings of Schneider et al. [4] who found that FreeBSD outperforms Linux (with PF_PACKET), especially when more than one capturing process is involved. In contrast, our own analyses reveal that PF_RING on Linux outperforms both PF_PACKET and FreeBSD. PF_RING is even better than FreeBSD when more than one capturing process is deployed, which was the strength of FreeBSD in Schneiders' analysis [4]. We are now comparing the capturing solutions with increased application load and check whether our findings are still valid in such setups.

4.3 Comparing packet capture setups under high application load

So far, we analysed the capturing performance with very low load on the application by writing captured packets to `/dev/null`. We now increase the application load by performing more computational work for each packet by using the tool *packzip*, which compresses the captured packets using `libz` [19]. The application load can be configured by changing the compression level libz uses. Higher compression levels result in higher application load; however, the load does not increase linearly. This can be seen at the packet drop rates in Figure 10.

The figure presents the results of the capturing process on various systems when capturing a stream consisting of 512 and 256 bytes sized packets at maximum wire-speed at the AMD platform. It can clearly be seen that a higher application load leads to higher packet loss. This happens on both operating system with every capturing solution presented in Section 2.1, and is expected due to our findings and the findings in related work. Packet loss kicks in as soon as the available CPU processing power is not sufficient to process all packets. We note that FreeBSD performs worse on our AMD platform compared to Linux with PF_PACKET with higher application load. This observation can be made throughout all our measurements in this section.

However, if we look at a packet stream that consists of 64 byte packets, we can see an amazing effect, shown in Figure 11. At first, we see that the overall capturing performance is worse when no application load (compression level 0) compared to the capturing results with 256 and 512 byte packets. This was expected because capturing a large number of (small) packets is more difficult than small number of (big) packets. However, if application load increases, the capturing performance increases as well. This effect is quite paradox and points to the same strange effect as seen in the experiments before. It can be observed with PF_PACKET and with PF_RING but is limited to Linux. FreeBSD is not affected by this weird effect; instead, capturing performance is nearly constant with increasing application load but almost always below Linux' performance.

In order to better understand what is causing this bewildering phenomenon, we have to take a closer look at the capturing process in Linux. An important task within the capturing chain is the passing of a captured packet from the kernel to the application. This is done via a shared memory area between the kernel and application within libpcap. The shared memory area is associated with a socket, in order to allow signaling between the kernel and the application, if this is desired. We will call this memory area SHM in the remainder of this section.

Packets are sent from kernel to user space using the following algorithm:

- The user application is ready to fetch a new packet.
- It checks SHM for new packets. If a new packet is found, it is processed.
- If no new packet is found, the system call `poll()` is issued in order to wait for new packets.
- The kernel receives a packet and copies it into SHM.
- The kernel "informs" the socket about the available packet; subsequently, `poll()` returns, and the user application will process the packet.

This algorithm is problematic because it involves many systems calls if the application consumes packets very quickly, which has already been found to be problematic in Deri's prior work [8]. A system call is a quite expensive operation as it results in a context switch, cache invalidation, new scheduling of the process, etc. When we increase the compression level, the time spent consuming the packets increases as well, thus less system calls are performed[3]. Obviously, reducing the number of system calls is beneficial to the performance of the packet capture system.

There are several ways to achieve such a reduction. The most obvious solution to this problem is to skip the call to `poll()` and to perform an active wait instead. However, this solution can pose problems to the system: If capturing and analysis are scheduled to run on the same processor (which is not recommended, as we pointed before), polling in a user space process eats valuable CPU time, which the capturing thread within the kernel would need. If capturing and analysis run on different cores, there still are penalties: The kernel and the user space application are trying to access the same memory page, which the kernel wants to write and the user space application wants to read. Hence, both cores or CPUs need to synchronise their memory access, continuously leading to cache invalidations and therefore to bad performance. We patched libpcap to perform the active wait and found some, but only little, improvement due to the reasons discussed above.

Hence, we searched for ways to reduce the number of calls to `poll()` that do not increase the load on the CPU. The first one was already proposed by Deri [8]. The basic idea is to perform a sleep operation for several nano seconds if the SHM is found to be empty. Although the sleep operations still implies a system call, it is way better than multiple calls to `poll()`, as the kernel capturing gets some time to copy several packets into the SHM. Deri proposed an adaptive sleep interval that is changed according to the incoming packet rate. We implemented this modification into the libpcap which used PF_PACKET. We found that it is not an easy task to choose a proper sleep interval, because sleeping too long will result in filled buffers, whereas a sleep interval that is too short will result in too many system calls and therefore does not solve the problem. Unfortunately, the optimal sleep interval depends on the hardware, the performed analysis and, even worse, on the observed traffic. Hence, a good value has to be found through the end-user by experiments, which requires quite some effort. Deri's user space code that uses PF_RING does not implement his proposed adaptive sleep, probably due to the same reasons. Instead, poll() avoidance is achieved by calls to sched_yield(), which interrupts the application and allows the scheduler to schedule another process. A call to pool() is only performed if several sched_yield() was called for several times and still no packets arrived. Figure 11 shows that the algorithm used by PF_RING yield better performance compared to the simple call to poll() with PF_PACKET. However, we can also see negative effects of calling sched_yield() often.

We therefore propose a new third solution that works without the necessity to estimate a timeout and works better than calling sched_yield(): We propose to change the signalling of new incoming packets within `poll()`. As of now, PF_PACKET signals the arrival of every packet into the user space. We recommend to only signal packet arrival if one of the two following conditions are true:

- N packets are ready for consuming.
- A timeout of m microseconds has elapsed.

Using these conditions, the number of system calls to `poll()` is reduced dramatically. The timeout is only necessary if less than N packets arrive within m, e.g. if the incoming packet rate is low. In contrast to the sleep timeout discussed before, choosing m properly is not necessary to achieve good capturing performance.

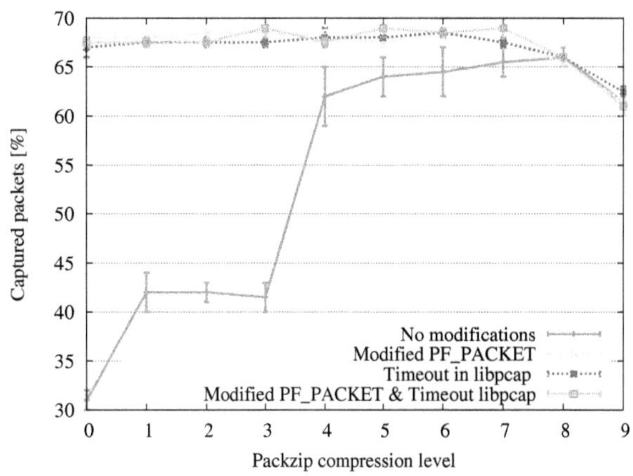

Figure 12: Capturing 64 byte packets with and without modifications

We implemented all the solutions into PF_PACKET and libpcap and compared their implications on the performance. For the sleep solutions, we determined a good timeout value by manual experiments. The results are summarised in Figure 12. As we can see, the reduced number of system calls yields a large performance boost. We can see that both timeout and our proposed modification to PF_PACKET yield about the same performance boost. Combining both is possible, but does not result in any significant further improvements. We did not have the time to include and evaluate the same measurements with PF_RING, but we are confident that PF_RING will also benefit from our proposed modification.

4.4 Driver Improvements

In the experiments presented up to now, we were not able to process small packets at wire-speed, even with our previous improvements. We now move further down the capturing software stack and test driver improvements.

Deri proposed to use modified drivers in order to improve the capturing performance [5]. His driver modifications focus on changing two things previously described:

- Create a dedicated thread for the packet consumption in the driver (respectively for every RX queue of the card).
- Reuse DMA memory pages instead of allocating new pages for the card.

His driver modifications hence help to use the power of multi-core CPUs by spawning a kernel thread that handles the card. This implies that no other thread is scheduled to perform the driver tasks and ensures that there is always a free thread to handle the packets, which is good for the overall performance. Additionally, if interrupts are bound to a given core, the driver thread will run on the same core. It is unclear to us which of the modifications has

[3] We confirmed this by measuring the number of calls to `poll()`.

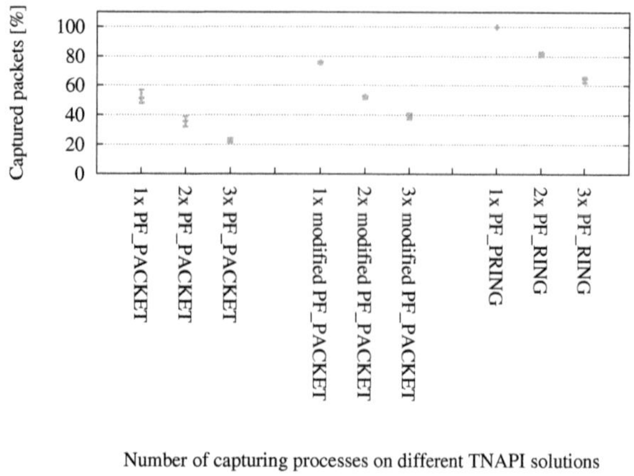

Figure 13: TNAPI with different capturing solutions on Linux

a bigger influence on the performance. If TNAPI is used with PF_PACKET instead of PF_RING, an additional copy operation is performed to copy the packet from the DMA memory area into a new memory area. The DMA area is reused afterwards.

We tested these improvements with different solutions on Linux but could not consider FreeBSD as there where no modified drivers at the time this paper was written. Our comparison is plotted in Figure 13. In contrast to our previous experiment, we deployed one more traffic generator, which allowed us to generate traffic at real wire-speed (i.e., 1.488 million packets). The plot shows results on the AMD system and compares PF_PACKET against our modified PF_PACKET and PF_RING. As can be seen, the TNAPI-aware drivers result in improvements compared to normal drivers. PF_PACKET capturing also benefits from TNAPI, but the improvements are not very significant.

Using TNAPI with our modified PF_PACKET results in good capturing results which are better than the results with standard drivers and also better than the results with standard FreeBSD. The best performance, however, can be found when TNAPI is combined with PF_RING, resulting in a capturing process that is able to capture 64 byte packets at wire-speed.

5. RECOMMENDATIONS

This section summarises our findings and gives recommendations to users as well as system developers. Our recommendations for developers of monitoring applications, drivers and operating systems are listed in subsection 5.1. Users of capturing solutions can find advices on how to configure their systems in subsection 5.2.

5.1 For Developers

During our evaluation and comparison, we found some bottlenecks within the software which can be avoided with careful programming. Developers of monitoring applications, operating systems or drivers should consider these hints in order to increase the performance their systems provide.

Our first advice is targeted at developers of network card drivers. We were able to determine that having a separate kernel thread that is only responsible for the network card can really help to improve performance. This is especially useful if more than multi-core or multi-CPU systems are available. With current hardware platforms tending to be multi-core systems and the ongoing trend of increasing the number of cores in a system, this feature can be expected to become even more important in the future. In addition, reusing memory pages as DMA areas and working with statically allocated memory blocks should be preferred over using dynamically allocated pages. However, it is unclear to us which of this two recommendations results in the greatest performance boosts.

Signalling between different subsystems, especially if they are driven by another thread, should always be done for accumulated packets. This assumption is valid for all subsystems, ranging from the driver, over the general operating system stacks, up to the user space applications. We therefore recommend the integration of our modifications to PF_PACKET into Linux.

Other areas besides packet capturing may also benefit from our modification: A generic system call that allows to wait for one or more sockets until N elements can be read or a timeout is seen, whichever happens first, would be a generalised interface for our modifications to PF_PACKET. Such system calls could be of use in other applications that need to process data on-line as fast as the data arrives.

5.2 For Users

Configuring a capture system for optimal performance is still challenging task. It is important to choose proper hardware that is capable of capturing the amount of traffic in high-speed networks.

The software that drives the hardware is very important for capture as well, since it highly influences the performance of the capturing process. Our findings conclude that *all* parts of the software stack have great influence on the performance—and that, unfortunately, a user has to check *all* of them in order to debug performance problems.

Performance pitfalls can start at the network card drivers, if interrupt handling does not work as expected, which we found to be true with one of the drivers we used. Checking for an unexpectedly high number of interrupts should one of the first performance debugging steps. Here, enabling polling on the driver could help to solve the issue. However, we found that the POLLING option, a static compile time options for many drivers, did not improve the performance in our tests.

We also recommend to use PF_RING with TNAPI, as its performance is superior to the standard capturing stack of FreeBSD or Linux. If using TNAPI or PF_RING is not an option, e.g., because there is no TNAPI-aware driver for the desired network interface card, we recommend to use Linux with our modifications to PF_PACKET.

Regardless of the capturing solution used, pinning all the involved threads and processes to different cores is highly recommended in most of the application cases. Using the default scheduler is only recommended when low packet rates are to be captured with low load at the application layer. Kernel and driver threads should also be pinned to a given core if possible. This can be achieved by explicitly setting the interrupt affinity of a network cards' interrupt.

Finally, if it is not an option to apply one of our proposed techniques for reducing the number of system calls (cf. Sections 4.3 and 5.1), the user should check if performance improves if he puts a higher load on the application capturing process. As we have seen in 4.3, a higher application can reduce the number of calls to poll() and therefore improve the performance. This holds especially for applications that do not involve much CPU workload, e.g., writing a libpcap stream to disk.

6. CONCLUSION

This paper summarised and compared different capturing solutions on Linux and FreeBSD, including some improvements proposed by researchers. We compared the standard capturing solutions of Linux and FreeBSD to each other, leading to a reappraisal of past work from Schneider et al [4] with newer versions of the operating systems and capturing software. The evaluation revealed that FreeBSD still outperforms standard Linux PF_PACKET under low application load. FreeBSD is especially good when multiple capturing processes are run.

Our comparison between standard Linux capturing with PF_PACKET and PF_RING confirmed that performance with PF_RING is still better when small packets are to be captured. However, differences are not as big as they where in 2004 or 2006, when the last evaluations were published. Further analyses showed that PF_RING performs better than PF_PACKET if multiple capturing processes are run on the system, and that performance with PF_RING is even better than FreeBSD. During our work, we found a performance bottleneck within the standard Linux capturing facility PF_PACKET and proposed a fix for this problem. Our fix greatly improves the performance of PF_PACKET with small packets. Using our improvements, PF_PACKET performs nearly as good as PF_RING.

Finally, we evaluated Luca Deri's TNAPI driver extension for Linux and found increased performance with all Linux capturing solutions. Best performance can be achieved if TNAPI is combined with PF_RING.

Acknowledgements

We gratefully acknowledge support from the German Research Foundation (DFG) funding the LUPUS project in the scope of which this research work has been conducted. Additional work was funded through ResumeNet, an EU FP7 project within the FIRE initiative.

The authors would like to thank Luca Deri and Gerhard Münz for their valuable support throughout our research.

7. REFERENCES

[1] Endace Measurement Systems, http://www.endace.com/.

[2] F. Schneider and J. Wallerich, "Performance evaluation of packet capturing systems for high-speed networks," in *CoNEXT'05: Proceedings of the 2005 ACM conference on Emerging network experiment and technology*. New York, NY, USA: ACM Press, Oct. 2005, pp. 284–285.

[3] L. Deri, "ncap: Wire-speed packet capture and transmission," in *In Proceedings of the IEEE/IFIP Workshop on End-to-End Monitoring Techniques and Services (E2EMON)*, May 2005.

[4] F. Schneider, J. Wallerich, and A. Feldmann, "Packet capture in 10-gigabit ethernet environments using contemporary commodity hardware," in *In Proceedings of the 8th International Conference on Passive and Active Network Measurement*, Apr. 2007.

[5] L. Deri and F. Fusco, "Exploiting commodity multi-core systems for network traffic analysis," http://luca.ntop.org/MulticorePacketCapture.pdf, July 2009.

[6] G. A. Cascallana and E. M. Lizarrondo, "Collecting packet traces at high speed," in *Proc. of Workshop on Monitoring, Attack Detection and Mitigation (MonAM) 2006*, Tübingen, Germany, Sep. 2006.

[7] J. Mogul and K. K. Ramakrishnan, "Eliminating receive livelock in an interrupt-driven kernel," *ACM Transactions on Computer Systems*, vol. 15, no. 3, pp. 217–252, 1997.

[8] L. Deri, "Improving passive packet capture: Beyond device polling," in *In Proceedings of the Foruth International System Adminstration and Network Engineering Conference (SANE 2004)*, Sep. 2004.

[9] Intel Corporation, "An Introduction to the Intel QuickPath Interconnect," http://www.intel.com/technology/quickpath-/introduction.pdf, 2009.

[10] I. Kim, J. Moon, and H. Y. Yeom, "Timer-based interrupt mitigation for high performance packet processing," in *5th International Conference on High-Performance Computing in the Asia-Pacific Region*, 2001.

[11] Luigi Rizzo, "Device Polling Support for FreeBSD," in *BSDCon Europe Conference 2001*, 2001.

[12] V. Jacobson, C. Leres, and S. McCanne, "libpcap," http://www.tcpdump.org.

[13] Phil Woods, "libpcap MMAP mode on linux," http://public.lanl.gov/cpw/.

[14] R. Olsson, "pktgen the linux packet generator."

[15] tcpdump, http://www.tcpdump.org.

[16] S. Kornexl, V. Paxson, H. Dreger, A. Feldmann, and R. Sommer, "Building a Time Machine for Efficient Recording and Retrieval of High-Volume Network Traffic," in *Proc. of ACM SIGCOMM Internet Measurement Conference (IMC) 2005*, Berkeley, CA, USA, Oct. 2005.

[17] G. Maier, R. Sommer, H. Dreger, A. Feldmann, V. Paxson, and F. Schneider, "Enriching Network Security Analysis with Time Travel," in *Proc. of ACM SIGCOMM 2008 Conference on Applications, Technologies, Architectures, and Protocols for Computer Communication*, Seattle, WA, USA, Aug. 2008.

[18] R. T. Lampert, C. Sommer, G. Münz, and F. Dressler, "Vermont - A Versatile Monitoring Toolkit for IPFIX and PSAMP," in *Proceedings of Workshop on Monitoring, Attack Detection and Mitigation (MonAM) 2006*, Tuebingen, Germany, Sep. 2006.

[19] Homepage of the zlib project, http://www.zlib.net/.

[20] C. Satten, "Lossless gigabit remote packet capture with linux," http://staff.washington.edu/corey/gulp/, University of Washington Network Systems, Mar. 2008.

High Speed Network Traffic Analysis with Commodity Multi-core Systems

Francesco Fusco
IBM Research - Zurich
ETH Zurich
ffu@zurich.ibm.com

Deri Luca
ntop
deri@ntop.org

ABSTRACT

Multi-core systems are the current dominant trend in computer processors. However, kernel network layers often do not fully exploit multi-core architectures. This is due to issues such as legacy code, resource competition of the RX-queues in network interfaces, as well as unnecessary memory copies between the OS layers. The result is that packet capture, the core operation in every network monitoring application, may even experience performance penalties when adapted to multi-core architectures. This work presents common pitfalls of network monitoring applications when used with multi-core systems, and presents solutions to these issues. We describe the design and implementation of a novel multi-core aware packet capture kernel module that enables monitoring applications to scale with the number of cores. We showcase that we can achieve high packet capture performance on modern commodity hardware.

Categories and Subject Descriptors

D.4.4 [**Operating Systems**]: Communications Management; C.2.3 [**Network Operations**]: Network monitoring

General Terms

Measurement, Performance

Keywords

Linux kernel, network packet capture, multi-core systems

1. INTRODUCTION

The heterogeneity of Internet-based services and advances in interconnection technologies raised the demand for advanced passive monitoring applications. In particular analyzing high-speed networks by means of software applications running on commodity off-the-shelf hardware presents major performance challenges.

IMC'10, November 1–3, 2010, Melbourne, Australia.

Researchers have demonstrated that packet capture, the cornerstone of the majority of passive monitoring applications, can be substantially improved by enhancing general purpose operating systems for traffic analysis [11, 12, 26]. These results are encouraging because today's commodity hardware offers features and performance that just a few years ago were only provided by costly custom hardware design. Modern network interface cards offer multiple TX/RX queues and advanced hardware mechanisms able to balance traffic across queues. Desktop-class machines are becoming advanced multi-core and even multi-processor parallel architectures capable of executing multiple threads at the same time.

Unfortunately, packet capture technologies do not properly exploit this increased parallelism and, as we show in our experiments, packet capture performance may be reduced when monitoring applications instantiate several packet capture threads or multi-queues adapters are used. This is due to three major reasons: a) resource competition of threads on the network interfaces RX queues, b) unnecessary packet copies, and c) improper scheduling and interrupt balancing.

In this work, we mitigate the above issues by introducing a novel packet capture technology designed for exploiting the parallelism offered by modern architectures and network interface cards, and we evaluate its performance using hardware traffic generators. The evaluation shows that thanks to our technology a commodity server can process more than *4 Gbps* per physical processor, which is more than *four* times higher than what we can achieve on the same hardware with previous generation packet capture technologies.

Our work makes several important contributions:

- We successfully exploit traffic balancing features offered by modern network adapters and make each RX queue visible to the monitoring applications by means of *virtual capture devices*. To the best of our knowledge, this work describes the first packet capture technology specifically tailored for modern multi-queue adapters.
- We propose a solution that substantially simplifies the development of highly scalable multi-threaded traffic analysis applications and we released it under an open-source license. Since compatibility with the popular libpcap [5] library is preserved, we believe that it can smooth the transition toward efficient parallel packet processing.
- We minimize the memory bandwidth footprint by reducing the per-packet cost to a single packet copy, and

optimize the cache hierarchy utilization by combining lock-less buffers together with optimal scheduling settings.

2. MOTIVATION AND SCOPE OF WORK

Modern multi-core-aware network adapters are logically partitioned into several RX/TX queues where packets are flow-balanced across queues using hardware-based facilities such as RSS (Receive-side Scaling) part of Intel™ I/O Acceleration Technology (I/O AT) [17, 18]. By splitting a single RX queue into several smaller queues, the load, both in terms of packets and interrupts, can be balanced across cores to improve the overall performance. Modern interface cards (NICs) support static or even dynamically configurable [13] balancing policies. The number of available queues depends on the NIC chipset, and it is limited by the number of available system cores.[1]

However, in most operating systems, packets are fetched using packet polling [23, 25] techniques that have been designed in the pre-multi-core age, when network adapters were equipped with a single RX queue. From the operating system point of view, there is no difference between a legacy 100 Mbit card and a modern 10 Gbit card as the driver hides all card, media and network speed details. As shown in Figure 1, device drivers must merge all queues into one as it used to happen with legacy adapters featuring a single queue. This design limitation is the cause of a major performance bottleneck, because even if a user space application spawns several threads to consume packets, they all have to compete for receiving packets from the same socket. Competition is costly as semaphores or similar techniques have to be used in order to serialize this work instead of carrying it out in parallel.

Even if multi-core architectures, such as the one depicted in Figure 2, are equipped with cache levels dynamically shared among different cores within a CPU, integrated memory controllers and multi-channel memories, memory bandwidth has been identified as a limiting factor for the scalability of current and future multi-core processors [7, 24]. In fact, technology projections suggest that off-chip memory bandwidth is going to increase slowly compared to the desired growth in the number of cores. The *memory wall* problem represents a serious issue for memory intensive applications such as traffic analysis software tailored for high-speed networks. Reducing the memory bandwidth by minimizing the number of packet copies is a key requirement to exploit parallel architectures.

To reduce the number of packet copies, most capture packet technologies [11] use memory mapping based zero-copy techniques (instead of standard system calls) to carry packets from the kernel level to the user space. The packet journey inside the kernel starts at the NIC driver layer, where incoming packets are copied into a temporary memory area, the socket buffer [8, 21], that holds the packet until it gets processed by the networking stack. In network monitoring, since packets are often received on dedicated adapters not used for routing or management, socket buffers' allocations and deallocations are unnecessary and zero-copy could start directly at the driver layer and not just at the networking layer.

[1]For example on a quad-core machine we can have up to four queues per port.

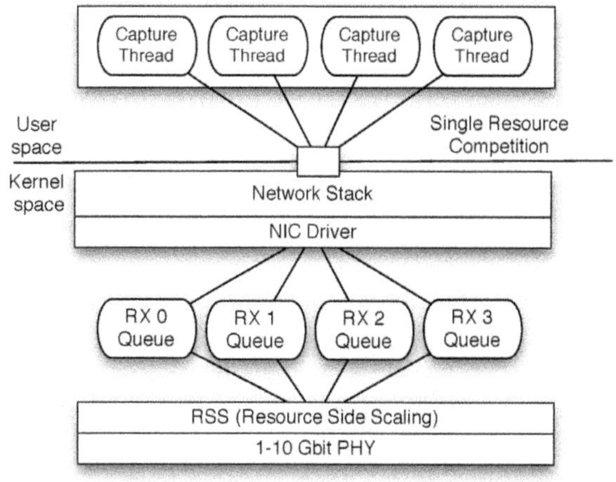

Figure 1: Design limitation in Network Monitoring Architectures.

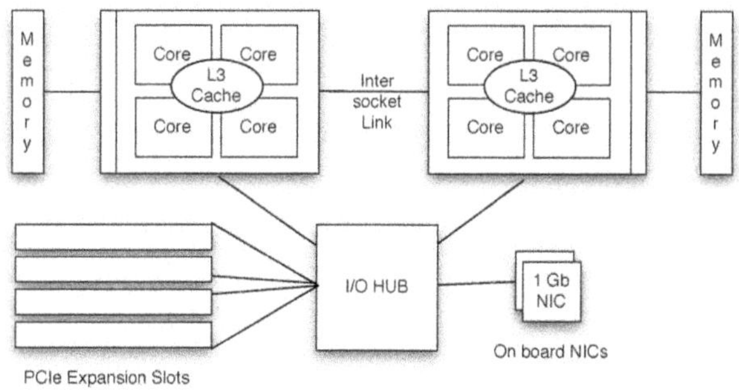

Figure 2: Commodity parallel architecture.

Memory bandwidth can be wasted when cache hierarchies are poorly exploited. Improperly balancing interrupt requests (IRQs) may lead to the excessive cache misses phenomena usually referred to as cache-trashing. In order to avoid this problem, the interrupt request handler and the capture thread that consumes such a packet must be executed on the same processor (to share the L3 level cache) or on the same core with Hyper-Threaded processors. Unfortunately, most operating systems uniformly balance interrupt requests across cores and schedule threads without considering architectural differences between cores. This is, in practice, a common case of packet losses. Modern operating systems allow users to tune IRQ balancing strategy and override the scheduling policy by means of CPU affinity manipulation [20]. Unfortunately, since current operating systems do not deliver queue identifiers up to the user space, applications do not have enough information to properly set the CPU affinity.

In summary, we identified two main issues that prevent parallelism from being exploited:

- There is a single resource competition by multi-threaded applications willing to concurrently consume packets coming from the same socket. This prevents multi-queue adapters being fully exploited.
- Unnecessary packet copies, improper scheduling and interrupt balancing cause a sub-optimal memory bandwidth utilization.

The following section describes a packet capture architecture that addresses the identified limitations.

3. TOWARDS MULTI-CORE MONITORING ARCHITECTURES

We designed a high performance packet capture technology able to exploit multi-queue adapters and modern multi-core processors. We achieve our high performance by introducing virtual capture devices, with multi-threaded polling and zero-copy mechanisms. Linux is used as the target operating system, as it represents the de-facto reference platform for the evaluation of novel packet capture technologies. However, the exploited concepts are general and can also be adapted to other operating systems.

Our technology natively supports multi-queues and exposes them to the users as *virtual capture devices* (see Figure 3). Virtual packet capture devices allow applications to be easily split into several independent threads of execution, each receiving and analyzing a portion of the traffic. In fact monitoring applications can either bind to a physical device (e.g., eth1) for receiving packets from all RX queues, or to a virtual device (e.g., eth1@2) for consuming packets from a specific queue only. The RSS hardware facility is responsible for balancing the traffic across RX queues, with no CPU intervention.

The concept of virtual capture device has been implemented in PF_RING [11], a kernel level network layer designed for improving Linux packet capture performance. It also provides an extensible mechanism for analyzing packets at the kernel-level. PF_RING provides a zero-copy mechanism based on memory mapping to transfer packets from the kernel space to the user space without using expensive system calls (such as *read()*). However, since it sits on top of the standard network interface card drivers, it is affected by the same problems identified in the previous section. In particular, for each incoming packet a temporary memory area, called socket buffer [8, 21], is allocated by the network driver, and then copied to the PF_RING ring buffer which is memory mapped to user space.

TNAPI drivers: For avoiding the aforementioned issue, PF_RING features a zero-copy ring buffer for each RX queue and it supports a new NIC driver model optimized for packet capture applications called TNAPI (Threaded NAPI[2]).

TNAPI drivers, when used with PF_RING completely avoid socket buffers' allocations. In particular, packets are copied directly from the RX queue to the associated PF_RING ring buffer for user space delivery. This process does not require any memory allocation because both the RX queue and the corresponding PF_RING ring are allocated statically. Moreover, since PF_RING ring buffers are memory-mapped to the user-space, moving packets from the RX queue ring to the user space requires a *single* packet copy. In this way, the driver does not deliver packets to the legacy networking stack so that *the kernel overhead is completely avoided.* If desired, users can configure the driver to push packets into the standard networking stack as well, but this configuration is not recommended as it is the cause of a substantial performance drop as packets have to cross legacy networking stack layers.

[2]NAPI is the driver model that introduced polling in the Linux kernel

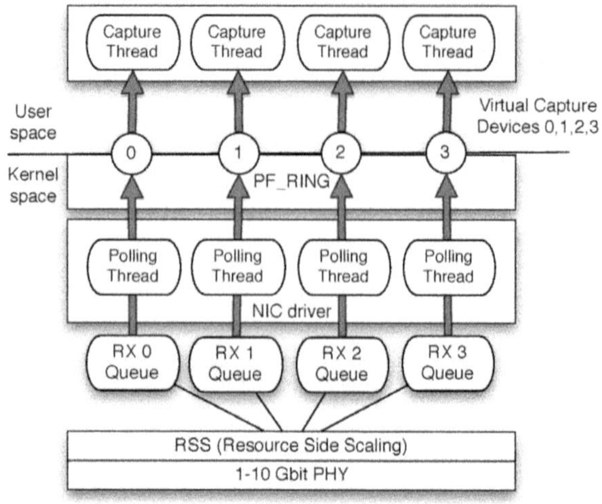

Figure 3: Multi-queue aware packet capture design. Each capture thread fetches packets from a single Virtual Capture Device.

Instead of relying on the standard kernel polling mechanisms to fetch packets from each queue, TNAPI features in-driver *multi-threaded packet polling.* TNAPI drivers spawn one polling thread for each RX queue (see Figure 3). Each polling thread fetches incoming packet(s) from the corresponding RX queue, and, passes the packet to PF_RING. Inside PF_RING, packet processing involves packet parsing and, depending on the configuration, may include packet filtering using the popular BPF filters [5] or even more complex application level filtering mechanisms [16]. Kernel level packet processing is performed by polling threads in *parallel.*

TNAPI drivers spawn polling threads and bind them to a specific core by means of CPU affinity manipulation. In this way the entire traffic coming from a single RX queue is always handled by the same core at the kernel level. The obvious advantage is the increased cache locality for poller threads. However, there is another big gain that depends on interrupt mitigation. Modern network cards and their respective drivers do not raise an interrupt for every packet under high-rate traffic conditions. Instead, drivers disable interrupts and switch to polling mode in such situations. If the traffic is not properly balanced across multi-queues, or if simply the traffic is bursty, we can expect to have busy queues working in polling mode and queues generating interrupts. By binding the polling threads to the same core where interrupts for this queue are received we prevent threads polling busy queues being interrupted by other queues processing low-rate incoming traffic.

The architecture depicted in Figure 3 and implemented in TNAPI, solves the single resource competition problem identified in the previous section. In fact, users can instantiate one packet consumer thread at the user space level for each virtual packet capture device (RX queue). Having a single packet consumer per virtual packet capture device does not require any locking primitive such as semaphores that, as a side effect, invalidate processor caches. In fact, for each RX queue the polling thread at the kernel level and the packet consumer thread at the user space level exchange packets through a lock-less Single Reader Single Writer (SRSW) buffer.

In order to avoid cache invalidation due to improper

scheduling, users can manipulate the CPU affinity to make sure that both threads are executed on cores or Hyper-Threads sharing levels of caches. In this way, multi-core architectures can be fully exploited by leveraging high bandwidth and low-latency inter-core communications. We decided not to impose specific affinity settings for the consumer threads, meaning that the user level packet capture library does not set affinity. Users are responsible for performing fine grained tuning of the CPU affinity depending on how CPU intensive the traffic analysis task is. This is straightforward and under Linux requires a single function call.[3] It is worth noting, that fine-grained tuning of the system is simply not feasible if queue information is not exported up to the user space.

Compatibility and Development Issues: Our packet capture tecnology comes with a set of kernel modules and a user-space library called libpring. A detailed description of the API can be found in the user guide [1]. For compatibility reasons we also ported the popular libpcap [5] library on top of our packet capture technology. In this way, already existing monitoring applications can be easily ported onto it. As of today, we have implemented packet capture optimized drivers for popular multi-queue Intel™ 1 and 10 Gbit adapters (82575/6 and 82598/9 chips).

4. EVALUATION

We evaluated the work using two different parallel architectures belonging to different market segments (low-end and high-end) equipped with the same Intel multi-queue network card. Details of the platforms are listed in Table 1. An IXIA 400 [4] traffic generator was used to inject the network traffic for experiments. For 10 Gbit traffic generation, several IXIA-generated 1 Gbit streams were merged into a 10 Gbit link using a HP ProCurve switch. In order to exploit balancing across RX queues, the IXIA was configured to generate 64 byte TCP packets (minimum packet size) originated from a single IP address towards a rotating set of 4096 IP destination addresses. With 64 bytes packets, a full Gbit link can carry up to 1.48 Million packets per second (Mpps).

Table 1: Evaluation platforms

	low-end	high-end
motherboard	Supermicro PSDBE	Supermicro X8DTL-iF
CPU	Core2Duo 1.86 Ghz 2 cores 0 HyperThreads	2x Xeon 5520 2.26 Ghz 8 cores 8 HyperThreads
Ram	4 GB	4 GB
NIC	Intel ET (1 Gbps)	Intel ET (1 Gbps)

In order to perform performance measurements we used *pfcount*, a simple traffic monitoring application that counts the number of captured packets. Depending on the configuration, pfcount spawns multiple packet capture threads per network interface and even concurrently captures from multiple network devices, including *virtual capture devices.*

In all tests we enabled multi-queues in drivers, and modified the driver's code so that queue information is propagated up to PF_RING; this driver does not spawn any poller thread at the kernel level, and does not avoid socket buffer allocation. We call this driver MQ (multi-queue) and TNAPI the one described in Section 3.

[3]See pthread_setaffinity_np().

Table 2: Packet capture performance (kpps) at 1 Gbps with different two-thread configurations.

		Setup A	Setup B	Setup C
Platform	SQ	SQ	MQ	TNAPI
	Threads Userspace/Kernel space			
	1/0	2/0	2/0	11
low-end	721 Kpps	640 Kpps	610 Kpps	1264 Kpps
high-end	1326 Kpps	1100 Kpps	708 Kpps	1488 Kpps

Comparing Different Approaches: As a first test, we evaluated the packet capture performance when using multi-threaded packet capture applications with and without multi-queue enabled. To do so, we measured the maximum loss free rate when pfcount uses three different two-threaded setups:

- *Setup A*: multiple queues are disabled and therefore capture threads read packets from the same interface (single queue, SQ). Threads are synchronized using a r/w semaphore. This setup corresponds to the default Linux configuration shown in Figure 1.
- *Setup B*: two queues are enabled (MQ) and there are two capture threads consuming packets from them. No synchronization is needed.
- *Setup C*: there is one capture thread at the user level and a polling thread at the kernel level (TNAPI).

Table 2 shows the performance results on the multi-threaded setups, and also shows as a reference point the single-threaded application. The test confirmed the issues we described in Section 2. When pfcount spawns two threads at the user level, the packet capture performance is actually worse than the single-threaded one. This is expected in both cases (setup A and B). In the case of setup A, the cause of the drop compared to the single-threaded setup is cache invalidations due to locking (semaphore), whereas for B the cause is the round robin IRQ balancing. On the other hand, our approach consisting of using a kernel thread and a thread at the user level (setup C) is indeed effective and allows the low-end platform to almost double its single-thread performance. Moreover, the high-end machine can capture 1 Gbps (1488 kpps) with no loss.

CPU Affinity and Scalability: We now turn our attention to evaluating our solution at higher packet rates with the high-end platform. We are interested in understanding if by properly setting the CPU affinity it is possible to effectively partition the computing resources and therefore increase the maximum loss-free rate.

2 NICs: To test the packet capture technology with more traffic, we plug another Intel ET NIC into the high-end systems and we inject with the IXIA traffic generator 1.488 Mpps for each interface (wire-rate at 1 Gbit with 64 bytes packets). We want to see if it is possible to handle 2 full Gbit links with two cores and two queues per NIC only. To do so, we set the CPU affinity to make sure that for every NIC the two polling threads at the kernel level are executed on different Hyper-Threads belonging to the same core (e.g. 0 and 8 from Figure 4 belong to Core 0 of the first physical processor[4]). We use the pfcount application to spawn

[4]Under Linux, */proc/cpuinfo* lists the available processing

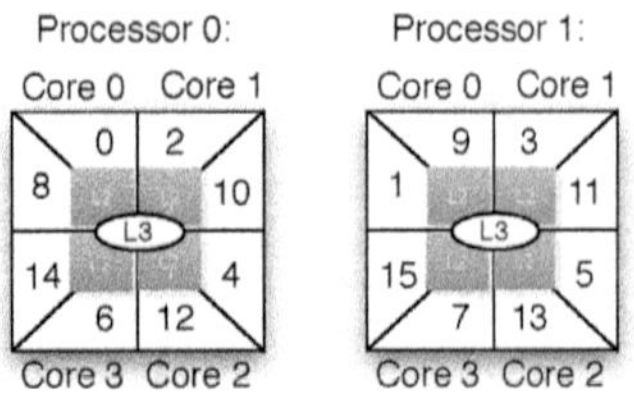

Figure 4: Core Mapping on Linux with the Dual Xeon. Hyper-Threads on the same core (e.g. 0 and 8) share the L2 cache.

Table 3: Packet capture performance (kpps) when capturing concurrently from two 1 Gbit links.

Test	Capture threads affinity	Polling threads affinity	NIC1 Kpps	NIC2 Kpps
1	not set	not set	1158	1032
2	NIC1@0 on 0 NIC1@1 on 8 NIC2@0 on 2 NIC2@1 on 10	NIC1@0 on 0 NIC1@1 on 8 NIC2@0 on 2 NIC2@1 on 10	1122	1290
3	NIC1 on 0,8 NIC2 on 2,10	NIC1@0 on 0 NIC1@1 on 8 NIC2@0 on 2 NIC2@1 on 10	1488	1488

capture threads and we perform measurements with three configurations. First of all, we measure the packet capture rate when one capture thread and one polling thread per queue are spawn (8 threads in total) without setting the CPU affinity (Test 1). Then (Test 2), we repeat the test by binding each capture thread to the same Hyper-Thread where the polling thread for that queue is executed (e.g. for the queue NIC1@0 both polling and capture thread run on Hyper-Thread 0). Finally, in Test 3, we reduce the number of capture threads to one for each interface. For each NIC, the capture thread and the polling threads associated to that interface run on the same core.

Table 3 reports the maximum loss-free rate when capturing from two NIC simultaneously using the configurations previously described. As shown in Test 1, without properly tuning the system by means of CPU affinity, our test platform is not capable of capturing, at wire-rate, from two adapters simultaneously. Test 2 and Test 3 show that the performance can be substantially improved by setting the affinity and wire-rate is achieved. In fact, by using a single capture thread for each interface (Test 3) all incoming packets are captured with no loss (1488 kpps per NIC).

In principle, we would expect to achieve the wire-rate with the configuration in Test 2 rather than the one used in Test 3. However, splitting the load on two RX queues means that capture threads are idle most of the time, at least on high-end processors such as the Xeons we used and a dummy application that only counts packets. As a consequence, capture threads must call *poll()* very often as they have no packet to process and therefore go to sleep until a new packet arrives; this may lead to packet losses. As system calls are slow, it is better to keep capture threads busy so that poll() calls are reduced. The best way of doing so is to capture from two RX queues, in order to increase the number of incoming packets. It is worth noting that, since monitoring applications are more complex than pfcount, the configuration used for Test 2 may provide better performance in practice.

units and reports for each of them the core identifier and the physical CPU. Processing units sharing the same physical CPU and core identifier are Hyper-Threads.

4 NICs: We decided to plug two extra NICs to the system to check if it was possible to reach the wire-rate with 4 NICs at the same time (4 Gbps of aggregated bandwidth with minimum sized packets). The third and fourth NIC were configured using the same tuning parameters as in Test 3 and the measurements repeated. *The system can capture 4 Gbps of traffic per physical processor without losing any packet.*

Due to lack of NICs at the traffic generator we could not evaluate the performance at more than 4 Gbps with synthetic streams of minimum size packets representing *the worst-case scenario for a packet capture technology.* However, preliminary tests conducted on a 10 Gbit production network (where the average packet size was close to 300 bytes and the used bandwidth around 6 Gbps) confirmed that this setup is effective in practice.

The conclusion of the validation is that when CPU affinity is properly tuned, our packet technology allows:

- Packet capture rate to scale linearly with the number of NICs.
- Multi-core computers to be partitioned processor-by-processor. This means that load on each processor does not affect the load on other processors.

5. RELATED WORK

The industry followed three paths for accelerating network monitoring applications by means of specialized hardware while keeping the software flexibility. Smart traffic balancers, such as cPacket[2], are special purpose devices used to filter and balance the traffic according to rules, so that multiple monitoring stations receive and analyze a portion of the traffic. Programmable network cards [6] are massively parallel architectures on a network card. They are suitable for accelerating both packet capture and traffic analysis, since monitoring software written in C can be compiled for that special purpose architecture and run on the card and not on the main host. Unfortunately, porting applications on those expensive devices is not trivial. Capture accelerators [3] completely offload monitoring workstations from the packet capturing task leaving more CPU cycles to perform analysis. The card is responsible for coping the traffic directly to the address space of the monitoring application and thus the operating system is completely bypassed.

Degiovanni and others [10] show that first generation packet capture accelerators are not able to exploit the parallelism of multi-processor architectures and propose the adoption of a software scheduler to increase the scalability. The scalability issue has been solved by modern capture accelerators that provide facilities to balance the traffic among several threads of execution. The balancing policy is implemented by their firmware and it is not meant to be changed at run-time as it takes seconds if not minutes to reconfigure.

The work described in [19] highlights the effects of cache coherence protocols in multi-processor architectures in the context of traffic monitoring. Papadogiannakis and others

[22] show how to preserve cache locality for improving traffic analysis performance by means of traffic reordering.

Multi-core architectures and multi-queue adapters have been exploited to increase the forwarding performance of software routers [14, 15]. Dashtbozorgi and others [9] propose a traffic analysis architecture for exploiting multi-core processors. Their work is orthogonal to ours, as they do not tackle the problem of enhancing packet capture through parallelism exploitation.

Several research efforts show that packet capture can be substantially improved by customizing general purpose operating systems. nCap [12] is a driver that maps the card memory in user-space, so that packets can be fetched from user-space without any kernel intervention. The work described in [26] proposes the adoption of large buffers containing a long queue of packets to amortize the cost of system calls under Windows. PF_RING [11] reduces the number of packet copies, and thus, increases the packet capture performance, by introducing a memory-mapped channel to carry packets from the kernel to the user space.

6. OPEN ISSUES AND FUTURE WORK

This work represents a first step toward our goal of exploiting the parallelism of modern multi-core architectures for packet analysis. There are several important steps we intend to address in future work. The first step is to introduce a software layer capable of automatically tuning the CPU affinity settings, which is crucial for achieving high performance. Currently, choosing the correct CPU affinity settings is not a straightforward process for non-expert users.

In addition, one of the basic assumption of our technology is that the hardware-based balancing mechanism (RSS in our case) is capable of evenly distributing the incoming traffic among cores. This is often, but not always, true in practice. In the future, we plan to exploit mainstream network adapters supporting hardware-based and dynamically configurable balancing policies [13] to implement an adaptive hardware-assisted software packet scheduler that is able to dynamically distribute the workload among cores.

7. CONCLUSIONS

This paper highlighted several challenges when using multi-core systems for network monitoring applications: resource competition of threads on network buffer queues, unnecessary packet copies, interrupt and scheduling imbalances. We proposed a novel approach to overcome the existing limitations and showed solutions for exploiting multi-cores and multi-queue adapters for network monitoring. The validation process has demonstrated that by using TNAPI it is possible to capture packets very efficiently both at 1 and 10 Gbit. Therefore, our results present the first software-only solution to show promise towards offering scalability with respect to the number of processors for packet capturing applications.

8. ACKNOWLEDGEMENT

The authors would like to thank J. Gasparakis and P. Waskiewicz Jr from Intel™ for the insightful discussions about 10 Gbit on multi-core systems, as well M. Vlachos, and X. Dimitropoulos for their suggestions while writing this paper.

9. CODE AVAILABILITY

This work is distributed under the GNU GPL license and is available at no cost from the ntop home page http://www.ntop.org/.

10. REFERENCES

[1] PF_RING User Guide. http://www.ntop.org/pfring_userguide.pdf.

[2] cpacket networks - complete packet inspection on a chip. http://www.cpacket.com.

[3] Endace ltd. http://www.endace.com.

[4] Ixia leader in converged ip testing. Homepage http://www.ixiacom.com.

[5] Libpcap. Homepage http://www.tcpdump.org.

[6] A. Agarwal. The tile processor: A 64-core multicore for embedded processing. Proc. of HPEC Workshop, 2007.

[7] K. Asanovic et al. The landscape of parallel computing research: A view from berkeley. Technical Report UCB/EECS-2006-183, EECS Department, University of California, Berkeley, Dec 2006.

[8] A. Cox. Network buffers and memory management. The Linux Journal, Issue 30,(1996).

[9] M. Dashtbozorgi and M. Abdollahi Azgomi. A scalable multi-core aware software architecture for high-performance network monitoring. In *SIN '09: Proc. of the 2nd Int. conference on Security of information and networks*, pages 117–122, 2009.

[10] L. Degioanni and G. Varenni. Introducing scalability in network measurement: toward 10 gbps with commodity hardware. In *IMC '04: Proc. of the 4th ACM SIGCOMM conference on Internet measurement*, pages 233–238, 2004.

[11] L. Deri. Improving passive packet capture: beyond device polling. Proc. of SANE, 2004.

[12] L. Deri. ncap: Wire-speed packet capture and transmission. In *E2EMON '05: Proc. of the End-to-End Monitoring Techniques and Services*, pages 47–55, 2005.

[13] L. Deri, J. Gasparakis, P. Waskiewicz Jr, and F. Fusco. Wire-Speed Hardware-Assisted Traffic Filtering with Mainstream Network Adapters. In *NEMA'10: Proc. of the First Int. Workshop on Network Embedded Management and Applications*, page to appear, 2010.

[14] N. Egi, A. Greenhalgh, M. Handley, M. Hoerdt, F. Huici, L. Mathy, and P. Papadimitriou. A platform for high performance and flexible virtual routers on commodity hardware. *SIGCOMM Comput. Commun. Rev.*, 40(1):127–128, 2010.

[15] N. Egi, A. Greenhalgh, M. Handley, G. Iannaccone, M. Manesh, L. Mathy, and S. Ratnasamy. Improved forwarding architecture and resource management for multi-core software routers. In *NPC '09: Proc. of the 2009 Sixth IFIP Int. Conference on Network and Parallel Computing*, pages 117–124, 2009.

[16] F. Fusco, F. Huici, L. Deri, S. Niccolini, and T. Ewald. Enabling high-speed and extensible real-time communications monitoring. In *IM'09: Proc. of the 11th IFIP/IEEE Int. Symposium on Integrated Network Management*, pages 343–350, 2009.

[17] Intel. Accelerating high-speed networking with intel i/o acceleration technology. White Paper, 2006.

[18] Intel. Intelligent queuing technologies for virtualization. White Paper, 2008.

[19] A. Kumar and R. Huggahalli. Impact of cache coherence protocols on the processing of network traffic. In *MICRO '07: Proc. of the 40th Annual IEEE/ACM Int. Symposium on Microarchitecture*, pages 161–171, 2007.

[20] R. Love. Cpu affinity. Linux Journal, Issue 111,(July 2003).

[21] B. Milekic. Network buffer allocation in the freebsd operating system. Proc. of BSDCan, 2004.

[22] A. Papadogiannakis, D. Antoniades, M. Polychronakis, and E. P. Markatos. Improving the performance of passive network monitoring applications using locality buffering. In *MASCOTS '07: Proc. of the 2007 15th Int. Symposium on Modeling, Analysis, and Simulation of Computer and Telecommunication Systems*, pages 151–157, 2007.

[23] L. Rizzo. Device polling support for freebsd. BSDConEurope Conference, 2001.

[24] B. M. Rogers, A. Krishna, G. B. Bell, K. Vu, X. Jiang, and Y. Solihin. Scaling the bandwidth wall: challenges in and avenues for cmp scaling. *SIGARCH Comput. Archit. News*, 37(3):371–382, 2009.

[25] J. H. Salim, R. Olsson, and A. Kuznetsov. Beyond softnet. In *ALS '01: Proc. of the 5th annual Linux Showcase & Conference*, pages 18–18, Berkeley, CA, USA, 2001. USENIX Association.

[26] M. Smith and D. Loguinov. Enabling high-performance internet-wide measurements on windows. In *PAM'10: Proc. of Passive and Active Measurement Conference*, pages 121–130, Zurich, Switzerland, 2010.

Network Tomography on Correlated Links

Denisa Ghita, Katerina Argyraki, Patrick Thiran
School of Computer and Communication Sciences
École Polytechnique Fédérale de Lausanne (EPFL), Switzerland

ABSTRACT

Network tomography establishes linear relationships between the characteristics of individual links and those of end-to-end paths. It has been proved that these relationships can be used to infer the characteristics of links from end-to-end measurements, provided that links are not correlated, i.e., the status of one link is independent from the status of other links.

In this paper, we consider the problem of identifying link characteristics from end-to-end measurements when links are "correlated," i.e., the status of one link may depend on the status of other links. There are several practical scenarios in which this can happen; for instance, if we know the network topology at the IP-link or at the domain-link level, then links from the same local-area network or the same administrative domain are potentially correlated, since they may be sharing physical links, network equipment, even management processes.

We formally prove that, under certain well defined conditions, network tomography works when links are correlated, in particular, it is possible to identify the probability that each link is congested from end-to-end measurements. We also present a practical algorithm that computes these probabilities. We evaluate our algorithm through extensive simulations and show that it is accurate in a variety of realistic congestion scenarios.

Categories and Subject Descriptors

C.2.3 [**Computer-Communication Networks**]: Network Operations—*network monitoring*

General Terms

Algorithms, Measurement, Performance

Keywords

network performance tomography, link correlation

IMC'10, November 1–3, 2010, Melbourne, Australia.

1. INTRODUCTION

Network performance tomography infers the characteristics of network links from end-to-end path measurements. Such inference can be a powerful monitoring tool in situations where explicitly measuring the characteristics of each link is impractical or is not an option. For instance, consider the scenario where the operator of an Internet service provider (ISP) wants to estimate the quality of service offered by a peer. In this case, the operator needs to estimate the quality of the peer's links without having direct access to these links. Alternatively, consider the scenario where an operator wants to monitor the quality of a link in her own domain. With conventional network equipment, this can be done with the help of test traffic, e.g., traceroute probes or custom probes explicitly exchanged between the two end-points of the link; such probes, however, are typically generated and processed by the general-purpose processor that handles the control plane of the corresponding network equipment (as opposed to the specialized hardware that handles the data plane), hence, can meet a different fate (e.g., significantly different latency) than the one met by the rest of the traffic.

Network performance tomography formulates the problem of inferring link characteristics from end-to-end path measurements as a system of linear equations, where the known entities are the available path measurements and the network topology, while the link characteristics constitute the unknowns. There exist different tomographic algorithms, depending on which link characteristics we are interested in (e.g., latency, loss, congestion status) and how we conduct the end-to-end measurements (e.g., using multicast probes, packet trains, or normal traffic). Existing algorithms, however, form their linear equations assuming that links are not correlated, i.e., that the latency, loss, or congestion status of one link is independent from that of other links.

There exist at least two practical scenarios in which ignoring link correlation is not reasonable. (i) Consider the scenario where an operator uses network tomography to monitor the quality of links in her domain in a non-intrusive manner and relies on traceroute to discover the domain's topology. As a result, she misses all nodes that do not respond to traceroute, necessarily including all network elements operating below layer 3. In the resulting network graph, nodes represent layer-3 elements; hence, links between nodes located in the same local-area network are potentially correlated, because they may be sharing physical links. (ii) Consider the scenario where the operator of one administrative domain wants to monitor a set of neighboring domains at the granularity of domain-level (as opposed to physical or IP-level) links; this may be because the operator does not have visibility into the internals of other domains, e.g., because they use multi-protocol label switching (MPLS) for internal routing; it may also be because the operator does not *care* to have such visibility—she is only trying to determine whether the neighbors are honoring a service-level agreement (SLA). In the resulting network graph, intermediate nodes represent border routers; hence, links between nodes located in the same administrative domain are potentially correlated, because they may be sharing physical links, as well as management processes.

In this paper, we take the first step toward applying network tomography on correlated links. We consider a network model where we know the network topology and which links are potentially correlated, but not to what extent (i.e., we do not assume that we know the degree of correlation between links). For instance, we can use our model to describe the fact that all links that are located in the same local-area network and/or all links that are managed by the same administrative entity are potentially correlated. Assuming this model and that we can perform unicast end-to-end path measurements, we seek to characterize the congestion behavior of each link, in particular, how frequently each link is congested (we formally define "congestion" in Section 2).

We make two contributions. First, we formally prove that, under certain well defined conditions, by using end-to-end measurements, it is feasible to identify, for each link, the probability that the link is congested, even in the presence of correlated links (Section 3). Second, we show how to actually compute these probabilities, i.e., we present an algorithm that takes as input (i) the network topology, (ii) which links may be correlated, and (iii) end-to-end path measurements, and outputs, for each link, the probability that the link is congested (Section 4). We evaluate our algorithm through extensive simulations and show that it is accurate in a variety of congestion scenarios (Section 5).

2. SETUP

2.1 Network Model

Links and Paths. We model the network as a directed graph $\mathcal{G} = (\mathcal{V}, \mathcal{E})$. Each node $v_i \in \mathcal{V}$ represents a network element that generates, receives, and/or relays network traffic, e.g., an end-host, an Ethernet switch, or an IP router. Each edge $e_k \in \mathcal{E}$ represents a logical link between two network elements. We use the term "logical" to emphasize the fact that an edge does not necessarily represent a physical link; it may also represent an IP-level or domain-level link—in general, a sequence of physical links between two network elements.

The underlying nature of each node and edge depends on the method used for building the network graph. For instance, if an operator relies on traceroute to build the network graph, and all layer-3 elements in her network respond to traceroute, then each node in the resulting graph represents a layer-3 network element, while each edge represents an IP-level link. In the rest of the paper, unless otherwise specified, we will use the term "link" to refer to an edge in the network graph, i.e., a logical link between two network elements.

We define a "path" as a sequence of links whose congestion status (defined below) can be determined through end-to-end measurements. We denote the set of paths in the network by $\mathcal{P}$. If a path $P_i \in \mathcal{P}$ traverses a link $e_k \in \mathcal{E}$, then we write $e_k \in P_i$. A path never crosses a link more than once, i.e., there are no loops. All links participate in at least one path, i.e., there are no unused links.

We also define the "path coverage" function ψ, which maps a set of links $A \subseteq \mathcal{E}$ to the set of paths that they "cover," i.e., the set of paths that traverse at least one of these links:

$$\psi(A) = \{\ P_i \in \mathcal{P} \mid P_i \ni e_k \text{ for some } e_k \in A\ \}. \quad (1)$$

We denote by $|\psi(A)|$ the number of paths in $\psi(A)$. For example, in Figure 1(a), we have: $\psi(\{e_1, e_2\}) = \{P_1, P_2, P_3\}$.

Congestion. We divide time into even slots called "snapshots," such that each experiment involves a finite sequence of N snapshots.

We model the congestion behavior of link e_k during an experiment as a stationary random process: We define e_k's "packet-loss rate" during the n-th snapshot of the experiment as the fraction of packets that are not delivered to their next link out of all the packets that arrive at e_k during the snapshot. We say that e_k is "congested" (resp. "good") during the n-th snapshot, if its packet-loss rate is above (resp. below or equal to) a threshold t_l (we follow the model proposed in [10], where all links have the same link-congestion threshold t_l). For each link e_k and each snapshot n, we define a random variable $X_{e_k}(n)$ as follows:

$$X_{e_k}(n) = \begin{cases} 1, & \text{if } e_k \text{ is congested during the } n\text{-th snapshot} \\ 0, & \text{otherwise.} \end{cases}$$

For a given link e_k, all random variables $X_{e_k}(n), n = 1..N$, are identically distributed; hence, for simplicity, we use X_{e_k} to denote any of them. This implies that the congestion probability of each link remains the same throughout the experiment. The scenario in which link e_k is always congested (resp. good) is a special, degenerate case of our model, where X_{e_k} is always 1 (resp. 0).

Similarly, we model the congestion behavior of path P_i during an experiment as a stationary random process: We define P_i's "packet-loss rate" during the n-th snapshot of the experiment as the fraction of packets that are not delivered to their destination out of all packets sent on P_i during that snapshot. We say that P_i is "congested" (resp. "good") during the n-th snapshot, if its packet-loss rate is above (resp. below or equal to) a threshold $t_p = 1 - (1 - t_l)^d$, where d is the number of links traversed by P_i. For each path P_i and each snapshot n, we define a random variable $Y_{P_i}(n)$ as follows:

$$Y_{P_i}(n) = \begin{cases} 1, & \text{if } P_i \text{ is congested during the } n\text{-th snapshot} \\ 0, & \text{otherwise.} \end{cases}$$

For a given path P_i, all random variables $Y_{P_i}(n), n = 1..N$, are identically distributed; hence, for simplicity, we use Y_{P_i} to denote any of them. Finally, Y_{P_i} has expected value $E(Y_{P_i}) = \mathbb{P}(Y_{P_i} = 1)$, equal to the fraction of snapshots during which P_i is congested. In other words, if, during the experiment, we observe that P_i is congested during half of the snapshots, we model this by saying that $\mathbb{P}(Y_{P_i} = 1) = 0.5$. The scenario in which path P_i is always congested (resp. good) is a special, degenerate case of our model, where Y_{P_i} is always 1 (resp. 0).

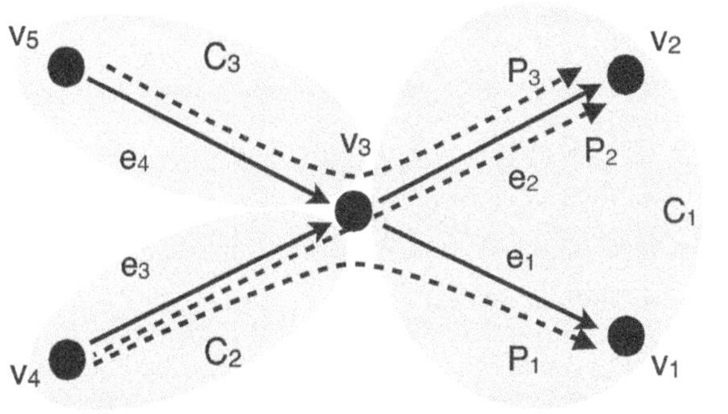

(a) A topology where Assumption 4 holds, i.e., each correlation subset covers a distinct set of paths. Links $\mathcal{E} = \{e_1, e_2, e_3, e_4\}$. Paths $\mathcal{P} = \{P_1, P_2, P_3\}$. Correlation sets $\mathcal{C} = \{\{e_1, e_2\}, \{e_3\}, \{e_4\}\}$. Correlation subsets $\tilde{\mathcal{C}} = \{\{e_1\}, \{e_2\}, \{e_1, e_2\}, \{e_3\}, \{e_4\}\}$.

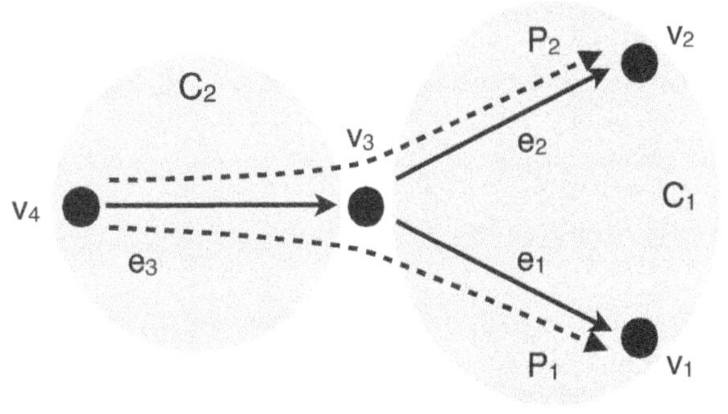

(b) A topology where Assumption 4 does not hold, because correlation subsets $\{e_1, e_2\}$ and $\{e_3\}$ cover the same set of paths $\{P_1, P_2\}$. Links $\mathcal{E} = \{e_1, e_2, e_3\}$. Paths $\mathcal{P} = \{P_1, P_2\}$. Correlation sets $\mathcal{C} = \{\{e_1, e_2\}, \{e_3\}\}$. Correlation subsets $\tilde{\mathcal{C}} = \{\{e_1\}, \{e_2\}, \{e_1, e_2\}, \{e_3\}\}$.

Figure 1: Two toy topologies, where Assumption 4 holds (on the left) and does not hold (on the right).

Link Correlation. We say that two links e_k and e_l are "independent" or "uncorrelated" when the random variables X_{e_k} and X_{e_l} are independent (or, equivalently, since they are Bernoulli random variables, uncorrelated) from one another; this corresponds to the situation where e_k's congestion status during a snapshot cannot affect e_l's congestion status during the same or any other snapshot. Otherwise, we say that the two links are "correlated."

Previous work has generally assumed that links are uncorrelated. More precisely, the algorithm from [13] requires that any two links that participate in at least one common path are uncorrelated with one another, while the algorithms from [10, 12] explicitly require that any link is uncorrelated with any other link.

Instead, we assume that each link may be correlated with a specific set of other links, and we assume that we know which links may be correlated with one another. Based on this knowledge, we group links into "correlation sets," such that two links from the same correlation set may be correlated with one another, but not with links from other correlation sets. For instance, in Figure 1(a), we know that links e_1 and e_2 may be correlated (e.g., because they are sharing a physical link), whereas each of links e_3 and e_4 may not be correlated with any other link; hence, we assign links e_1 and e_2 to the same correlation set C_1, link e_3 to correlation set C_2, and link e_4 to correlation set C_3.

More formally, consider a partition $\mathcal{C} = \{C_1, C_2, ... C_{|\mathcal{C}|}\}$ of $\mathcal{E}$, such that:

$$\forall e_k, e_l, \; k \neq l, \quad \text{s.t.} \quad e_k \in C_p, \; e_l \in C_q, \; p \neq q,$$
$$e_k \text{ is uncorrelated with } e_l;$$

we call each set of links $C_p \in \mathcal{C}$ a "correlation set." In the scenario where each link in the network is uncorrelated with any other, there are $|\mathcal{E}|$ correlation sets, one for each link in the network, i.e., $\mathcal{C} = \{\{e_1\}, \{e_2\}, ...\{e_{|\mathcal{E}|}\}\}$. At the other extreme, if all links in the network are correlated with one another, there is only one correlation set that consists of all links in the network, i.e., $\mathcal{C} = \{\{e_1, e_2, ... e_{|\mathcal{E}|}\}\}$.

In our analysis, we will often refer to a "correlation subset" $A \subseteq C_p$, $A \neq \emptyset$, i.e., a non-empty subset of a correlation set. We will also refer to the set of all possible correlation subsets:

$$\tilde{\mathcal{C}} = \{ \; A \subseteq \mathcal{E} \mid A \neq \emptyset \text{ and } A \subseteq C_p \text{ for some } C_p \in \mathcal{C} \; \}.$$

For instance, in Figure 1(a), we have $\mathcal{C} = \{\{e_1, e_2\}, \{e_3\}, \{e_4\}\}$ and $\tilde{\mathcal{C}} = \{\{e_1\}, \{e_2\}, \{e_1, e_2\}, \{e_3\}, \{e_4\}\}$.

2.2 Assumptions

We make four assumptions. The first three are inherited from previous work on tomography, whereas the fourth assumption is new—and key to the contribution of this paper.

Assumption 1. *Stability: The set of paths $\mathcal{P}$ remains unchanged during each experiment.*

This assumption is common in all tomographic algorithms. In practice, if a path changes during a certain snapshot, we discard the measurements collected during that snapshot and stop the current experiment, i.e., we apply our algorithms only on sequences of snapshots during which $\mathcal{P}$ remains unchanged.

Assumption 2. *Separability: A path is good if and only if all the links it traverses are good. A path is congested if and only if at least one of the links it traverses is congested.*

This assumption is common in Boolean-tomography algorithms [10, 12]. It is closely related to the problem of setting the link-congestion threshold t_l, defined in Section 2.1. We use $t_l = 0.01$, which has been shown to work well for mesh topologies and introduce negligible error [10].

Assumption 3. *Stationarity: The congestion behavior of any link during an experiment can be modeled as a stationary random process.*

This assumption is inherent in our congestion model (inherited from [12]), since we use the identically distributed random variables $X_{e_k}(n), n = 1..N$, to represent link e_k's congestion status during subsequent snapshots. We would like to clarify that this does not mean that the congestion status of link e_k remains the same during the experiment, only that the *probability* of link e_k being congested remains the same. We need this assumption in order to keep the theoretical analysis (Section 3) simple—to model e_k's congestion status as a non-stationary random process, we would need to assume that each of the random variables $X_{e_k}(n), n = 1..N$, has a potentially different probability distribution.

ASSUMPTION 4. *Identifiability: Given any two correlation subsets $A, B \in \tilde{\mathcal{C}}$, $A \neq B$, it holds true that $\psi(A) \neq \psi(B)$, i.e., A and B are not traversed by exactly the same paths.*

This generalizes a fundamental assumption of network tomography, that any two *links* are not traversed by exactly the same paths [18]. Intuitively, this earlier assumption captured the fact that, when two links participate in exactly the same paths, there is no way to differentiate between the two links based on end-to-end observations. We are generalizing this to say that, when two *groups of correlated links* participate in exactly the same paths (and assuming we know nothing about the nature of the correlation), there is no way to differentiate between the two groups based on end-to-end observations. Indeed, in the extreme case where each link in the network is uncorrelated with any other, our assumption becomes exactly the earlier assumption.

3. FEASIBILITY

3.1 Problem Statement and Result

Suppose we can perform unicast end-to-end path measurements, i.e., measure the probability that any path or combination of paths is congested. We want to determine whether, given this information, it is feasible to identify the probability that a particular set of links (or a particular link) is congested.

THEOREM 1. *If Assumptions 1, 2, 3 and 4 hold, the probability that any set of links is congested is identifiable for all possible sets of links.*

PROOF. In the Appendix, Section A. □

To illustrate this result, we first consider the scenario depicted in Figure 1(a), where Assumption 4 holds. Here is the set of paths $\psi(A)$ covered by each correlation subset $A \in \tilde{\mathcal{C}}$:

$A \in \tilde{\mathcal{C}}$	$\psi(A)$
$\{e_1\}$	$\{P_1\}$
$\{e_2\}$	$\{P_2, P_3\}$
$\{e_1, e_2\}$	$\{P_1, P_2, P_3\}$
$\{e_3\}$	$\{P_1, P_2\}$
$\{e_4\}$	$\{P_3\}$

Indeed, each correlation subset A covers a distinct set of paths $\psi(A)$. Intuitively, this allows us to measure the probability that the paths covered by each correlation subset are congested and infer, from that, the probability that the links in each correlation subset are congested.

To illustrate the challenge introduced by link correlation, we also consider the scenario depicted in Figure 1(b), where Assumption 4 does not hold. In this case, we have:

$A \in \tilde{\mathcal{C}}$	$\psi(A)$
$\{e_1\}$	$\{P_1\}$
$\{e_2\}$	$\{P_2\}$
$\{e_1, e_2\}$	$\{P_1, P_2\}$
$\{e_3\}$	$\{P_1, P_2\}$

i.e., correlation subsets $\{e_3\}$ and $\{e_1, e_2\}$ cover the same set of paths $\{P_1, P_2\}$. As a result, we cannot distinguish between the probability that e_3 is congested and the probability that e_1 and e_2 are both congested.

If links e_1 and e_2 were uncorrelated, we would not have this problem. We could do the following: (i) Measure the probability that P_1 is the only congested path, which is equal to the probability that e_1 is the only congested link; from that, compute the probability that e_1 is congested, as shown in [12]. (ii) Repeat for P_2 and e_2. (iii) *Using the fact that e_1 and e_2 are uncorrelated*, compute the probability that e_1 and e_2 are both congested as the product of the probability that link e_1 is congested and of the probability that link e_2 is congested. (iv) Measure the probability that P_1 and P_2 are both congested, which is a function of the probability that e_3 is congested and the probability that e_1 and e_2 are both congested. Since we have already computed the latter, we could now compute the probability that e_3 is congested. This is, at a high level, the algorithm followed in [12].

The problem is that, in our setup, e_1 and e_2 are correlated, which means that we cannot perform step (iii). We can go directly to step (iv) and measure the probability that P_1 and P_2 are both congested; however, since we do not know the probability that e_1 and e_2 are both congested, we cannot draw any conclusions about e_3.

3.2 Proof Illustration

We now illustrate how our proof works using the example of Figure 1(a). Again, we assume that we can measure the probability that any set of paths is congested and we want to identify the probability that each set of links is congested, i.e., $\mathbb{P}(X_{e_{1..4}} = 1)$, $\mathbb{P}(X_{e_1} = 1, X_{e_2} = 1)$, etc.

As already hinted, the challenge in proving Theorem 1 comes from the fact that links may be correlated. As a result, we cannot easily compute joint probabilities, e.g., we cannot compute $\mathbb{P}(X_{e_k} = 1, X_{e_l} = 1)$ simply by multiplying $\mathbb{P}(X_{e_k} = 1)$ and $\mathbb{P}(X_{e_l} = 1)$. Yet to prove that we can identify $\mathbb{P}(X_{e_k} = 1)$ for all links e_k, we do need to compute many such joint probabilities. In fact, we need to compute the probability that all the links in A are congested *for every possible correlation subset $A \in \tilde{\mathcal{C}}$*. Hence, the core of our proof—and a key contribution of this work—consists of showing that we can, indeed, compute all these $|\tilde{\mathcal{C}}|$ probabilities.

Definitions and Notation. We start by defining and providing compact notation for certain terms that appear frequently in our illustration. All defined symbols are summarized in Table 1 in the Appendix.

▷ S^p is a random set equal to the set of all congested links in correlation set C_p during a snapshot:

$$S^p \equiv \{ e_k \in C_p \mid X_{e_k} = 1 \}.$$

Since $X_{e_k} \in C_p$ and $X_{e_l} \in C_q \neq C_p$ are independent, it is also the case that S^p and $S^q \neq S^p$ are independent. In the example of Figure 1(a), we have three such independent random sets, S^1, S^2, and S^3.

▷ The "network state," denoted by $\mathcal{S}$, is a random set equal to the set of all congested links during a snapshot:

$$\mathcal{S} \equiv \bigcup_{p=1..|\mathcal{C}|} S^p.$$

E.g., in Figure 1(a), $\mathcal{S} \equiv S^1 \cup S^2 \cup S^3$.

▷ $\psi(\mathcal{S})$ is a random set equal to the set of congested paths during a snapshot:

$$\psi(\mathcal{S}) \equiv \bigcup_{p=1..|\mathcal{C}|} \psi(S^p).$$

Given these definitions, we will refer to the following events, given a correlation subset $A \subseteq C_p$:

▷ $(S^p = A)$ is the event that the links in A are the only congested links in $C_p \supseteq A$. E.g., in Figure 1(a), $(S^1 = \{e_1\})$ is the event that e_1 is congested and e_2 is good.

▷ $(\psi(\mathcal{S}) = \psi(A))$ is the event that the paths covered by A are the only congested paths in the network. E.g., in Figure 1(a), $(\psi(\mathcal{S}) = \psi(\{e_1\}))$ is the event that P_1 is congested, while P_2 and P_3 are good.

▷ Finally, for each correlation subset $A \subseteq C_p$, we define its "congestion factor" α_A as follows:

$$\alpha_A = \mathbb{P}(S^p = A) \;/\; \mathbb{P}(S^p = \emptyset). \qquad (2)$$

This expresses how often the links in $A \subseteq C_p$ are congested compared to how often *all* links in the correlation set C_p are good.

Setup. Through end-to-end measurements, we can measure the probability that all paths are good, i.e.,

$$\mathbb{P}(\psi(\mathcal{S}) = \emptyset) = \mathbb{P}(S^1 = \emptyset)\,\mathbb{P}(S^2 = \emptyset)\,\mathbb{P}(S^3 = \emptyset). \qquad (3)$$

Moreover, given a correlation subset A, we can measure the probability that the paths in $\psi(A)$ are the *only* congested paths in the network, i.e., $\mathbb{P}(\psi(\mathcal{S}) = \psi(A))$.

Step 1. Consider correlation subset $\{e_1\}$ and the set of paths it covers, $\psi(\{e_1\}) = \{P_1\}$. Consider the event that P_1 is the only congested path in the network. If this is the case, then e_1 must be the only congested link, i.e, the network can only be in state $\mathcal{S} = \{e_1\}$:

S^1	S^2	S^3	$\mathcal{S}$	$\psi(\mathcal{S})$
$\{e_1\}$	$\emptyset$	$\emptyset$	$\{e_1\}$	$\{P_1\}$

Hence, we can write:

$$\mathbb{P}(\psi(\mathcal{S}) = \psi(\{e_1\})) = \mathbb{P}(S^1 = \{e_1\})\,\mathbb{P}(S^2 = \emptyset)\,\mathbb{P}(S^3 = \emptyset).$$

If we divide this by Eq. 3, we get

$$\frac{\mathbb{P}(\psi(\mathcal{S}) = \psi(\{e_1\}))}{\mathbb{P}(\psi(\mathcal{S}) = \emptyset)} = \frac{\mathbb{P}(S^1 = \{e_1\})}{\mathbb{P}(S^1 = \emptyset)} = \alpha_{\{e_1\}}.$$

Since both the numerator and denominator of the left-most term can be measured, we can compute $\alpha_{\{e_1\}}$.

Step 2. Consider correlation subset $\{e_3\}$ and the set of paths it covers, $\psi(\{e_3\}) = \{P_1, P_2\}$. Consider the event that P_1 and P_2 are the only congested paths in the network. If this is the case, either e_3 is the only congested link, or e_1 and e_3 are the only congested links, i.e., the network can only be in state $\mathcal{S} = \{e_3\}$ or in state $\mathcal{S} = \{e_1, e_3\}$:

S^1	S^2	S^3	$\mathcal{S}$	$\psi(\mathcal{S})$
$\emptyset$	$\{e_3\}$	$\emptyset$	$\{e_3\}$	$\{P_1, P_2\}$
$\{e_1\}$	$\{e_3\}$	$\emptyset$	$\{e_1, e_3\}$	$\{P_1, P_2\}$

Hence, we can write:

$$\mathbb{P}(\psi(\mathcal{S}) = \psi(\{e_3\})) = \mathbb{P}(S^1 = \emptyset)\,\mathbb{P}(S^2 = \{e_3\})\,\mathbb{P}(S^3 = \emptyset) + \mathbb{P}(S^1 = \{e_1\})\,\mathbb{P}(S^2 = \{e_3\})\,\mathbb{P}(S^3 = \emptyset).$$

If we divide this by Eq. 3, we get

$$\frac{\mathbb{P}(\psi(\mathcal{S}) = \psi(\{e_3\}))}{\mathbb{P}(\psi(\mathcal{S}) = \emptyset)} = (1 + \alpha_{\{e_1\}})\,\alpha_{\{e_3\}}.$$

Since both the numerator and denominator of the left-most term can be measured, and we have already computed $\alpha_{\{e_1\}}$, we can now compute $\alpha_{\{e_3\}}$.

Step 3. With the same rationale, we compute all congestion factors α_A, $\forall A \in \tilde{\mathcal{C}}$. The gist is that, thanks to Assumption 4, we can *order* the correlation subsets and compute their congestion factors such that each factor depends only on terms that can be measured or have already been computed. In our particular example, the ordering we follow is $\langle \{e_1\}, \{e_4\}, \{e_3\}, \{e_2\}, \{e_1, e_2\} \rangle$.

Step 4. According to Lemma 3 (Appendix, Section A.3), once we have computed all congestion factors, we can derive $\mathbb{P}(X_{e_{1..4}} = 1)$ and $\mathbb{P}(X_{e_1} = 1, X_{e_2} = 1)$. Once we know these 5 probabilities, we can easily compute the rest, e.g., $\mathbb{P}(X_{e_1} = 1, X_{e_3} = 1) = \mathbb{P}(X_{e_1} = 1)\,\mathbb{P}(X_{e_3} = 1)$.

3.3 Practical Significance

We now answer certain questions regarding the practical significance of our result.

▷**In what kind of scenarios are links correlated?** There are at least two situations that can lead to link correlation: (i) a congested network resource is shared by multiple links; (ii) congestion is caused by a traffic pattern that involves a particular set of links.

The first situation can occur when an operator is using network tomography to monitor the quality of links in a network and relies on traceroute to discover the network topology. As a result, she misses all nodes that do not respond to traceroute, e.g., all Ethernet and MPLS switches. In the resulting network graph, each node represents a layer-3 element, while each edge represents a sequence of physical links between two layer-3 elements. Hence, two distinct edges in the network graph (i.e., two distinct logical links) may share physical links; when one of these shared physical links is congested, both logical links are congested, which means that the two logical links are correlated.

The second situation can occur when a badly written network protocol, a distributed application, or even a denial-of-service attack causes a particular set of source nodes to generate high-rate traffic to a particular set of destination nodes. For instance, consider a group of end-hosts participating in a distributed game, which causes them to periodically exchange high-rate traffic; or, a botnet master commanding a group of compromised end-hosts to periodically send high-rate traffic to a group of public-access sites. Either scenario can result in a particular set of links becoming congested and de-congested at the same times, i.e., becoming correlated.

▷**In which of these scenarios is our result useful?** In the scenarios where the operator knows which links are most likely to be correlated.

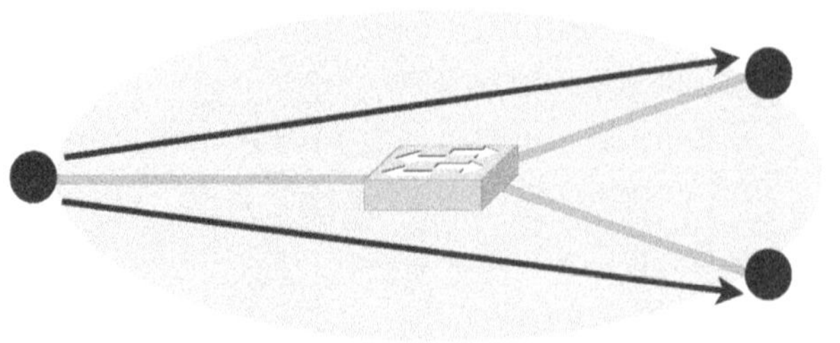

(a) A local-area network. The undiscovered node in the middle is an Ethernet switch.

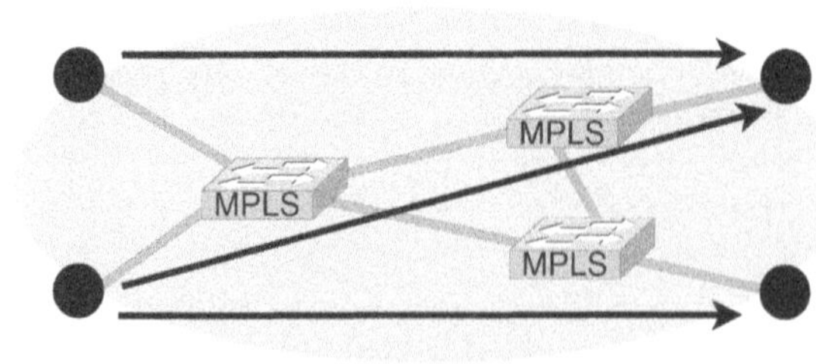

(b) An administrative domain. The undiscovered nodes in the middle are MPLS switches.

Figure 2: Two scenarios where logical links are correlated because they are sharing physical links. Each figure shows a part of a network graph. Black nodes (circles) represent IP routers discovered with traceroute, while black arrows represent logical links between discovered IP routers. Gray nodes represent undiscovered network elements (that do not respond to traceroute), while gray lines represent physical links.

For instance, consider the scenario where an operator uses network tomography to monitor the quality of links in her domain and relies on traceroute to discover the domain's topology. This may seem unreasonable at first—one would assume that an operator already knows the topology of her own domain. Yet, in practice, the operator of a large network (e.g., a university-campus network) does not always have access to all areas and equipment of the network. Moreover, given that paths change in response to network conditions, the operator does not always know which links compose each path. In this context, it makes sense for the operator to map each local-area network discovered through traceroute to one correlation set (Figure 2(a)). The links in each correlation set are potentially correlated, because they may be sharing physical links and/or management processes.

Alternatively, consider the scenario where the operator of one administrative domain uses network tomography to determine whether a set of neighboring domains are honoring their SLA, but does not have visibility into the internals of these domains, because they use MPLS for internal routing. In this context, it makes sense for the operator to map each administrative domain to one correlation set (Figure 2(b)). As above, the links in each correlation set are potentially correlated, because they may be sharing physical links and/or management processes.

Our result is not useful in scenarios where the operator does not know which links may be correlated, e.g., when an unpredictable traffic pattern affects the congestion status of multiple otherwise uncorrelated links. For instance, consider the denial-of-service scenario mentioned above. Unless the botnet's structure and targets are known, there is no way to guess the link-correlation pattern caused by the attack. Hence, an operator using our algorithm to identify the links affected by the attack would mislabel these links as uncorrelated, causing the algorithm to yield inaccurate results.

▷In what topologies does Assumption 4 hold?

In topologies where each intermediate node touches multiple correlation sets, like the one depicted in Figure 1(a).

Assumption 4 does not hold when there exists an intermediate node that has all its ingress links in one correlation set and all its egress links also in one (the same or different) correlation set; this causes the correlation subset formed by its ingress links and the correlation subset formed by its egress links to cover exactly the same paths (all the paths that traverse the node). This situation occurs when an intermediate node touches one correlation set and sometimes even when it touches two correlation sets, as in Figure 1(b). In contrast, in Figure 1(a), there is no intermediate node that touches one or two correlation sets, and Assumption 4 holds.

▷What happens when Assumption 4 does not hold?

Our algorithm cannot accurately compute the congestion probability of those links that belong to correlation subsets for which the assumption does not hold—we will refer to these links as "unidentifiable."

One way to deal with this situation is to try to alter the topology, i.e., add nodes and paths to the system, such that Assumption 4 holds. For instance, consider the topology of Figure 1(b), where the assumption does not hold; by adding node v_5 and path P_3 we get the topology of Figure 1(a), where the assumption does hold. If altering the topology is not an option (e.g., because the operator does not have access to additional nodes for performing end-to-end measurements from/to them), we can act as if the unidentifiable links were uncorrelated; as a result, we compute their congestion probability inaccurately, but, at least, we can still compute the congestion probability of the remaining links accurately. We will look at this effect in Section 5.

Moreover, in certain cases, when Assumption 4 does not hold, we can apply a transformation to the network topology (merge certain consecutive links) so that it does. This is akin to the merging of consecutive links traversed by the same paths in the context of traditional network performance tomography. We will now outline how our transformation relates to traditional tomography and how it works, however, for lack of space, we will not provide here a formal description and analysis.

A fundamental assumption of network performance tomography is that any two links are not traversed by exactly the same paths. However, if two such "indistinguishable" links occur *consecutively* in the network, they can be elegantly abstracted away into a single "merged" link, such that the above fundamental assumption holds. This transformation enables tomographic algorithms to work, albeit at decreased granularity, i.e., they can characterize each link in the transformed network graph (including the merged links), but not the original links that were merged.

We are in a similar situation: According to our Assumption 4, any two correlation subsets must not be traversed by exactly the same paths. However, if two such subsets occur consecutively in the network, we can abstract them away into a single subset of merged links, such that the assumption 4 holds. This transformation enables our algorithm to work, albeit at decreased granularity, i.e., it can accurately characterize each link in the transformed network graph, but not the original links that were merged.

The transformation works as follows: If intermediate node v has all its ingress links in one correlation set and all its egress links also in one correlation set, we remove v and all its adjacent links from the network graph; if, in the original network graph, there was a path that went consecutively through nodes v_{last}, v, and v_{next}, then we draw a merged link from v_{last} to v_{next}. For instance, to transform the topology of Figure 1(b), we remove node v_3 and its adjacent links (links e_1, e_2, and e_3) and draw, in their place, two merged links, one from v_4 to v_1 and one from v_4 to v_2; as a result, we end up with a single correlation set that contains two (merged) links.

▷Why not assign all links to one correlation set?

If we do that, Assumption 4 does not hold for any part of the network graph, hence, our algorithm does not yield any useful results.

If we assign all links in the network graph to the same correlation set, Assumption 4 does not hold. If we apply the transformation described above, we end up with a transformed network graph where each link corresponds to an end-to-end path. At that point, we can compute the congestion probability of each link (in the transformed network graph) through end-to-end measurements—network tomography cannot provide any additional information. For instance, consider a topology that consists of the nodes and links depicted in Figure 1(a), but where all four links belong to the same correlation set. In that topology, Assumption 4 does not hold, because node v_3 has all its ingress and egress links in the same correlation set. To apply our transformation, we remove v_3 and all its adjacent links (i.e., all four links), and draw three merged links in their place: from v_4 to v_1, from v_4 to v_2, and from v_5 to v_2. As a result, we get a transformed network graph like the one of Figure 2(b), where each link corresponds to an end-to-end path, which means that we can measure its congestion probability through end-to-end measurements.

▷Can our result help determine whether a link was congested or not?

Yes. Our result states that it is feasible to compute the probability that any set of links is congested. Obtaining this information is the first step toward accurately computing which particular set of links were congested during each snapshot.

There exist several tomographic algorithms that observe which set of paths were congested during each snapshot and try to determine which set of links were congested during the last snapshot [13, 10, 12]. This is an "ill-posed inverse problem," i.e., there are typically multiple sets of links that, if congested, would have led to the observed outcome. Each algorithm uses its own technique to choose which of all the feasible solutions is the most likely: the first two algorithms favor solutions that involve a small number of congested links, whereas the last one explicitly computes which of the feasible solutions is the most likely (albeit assuming no link correlation).

Our result implies that the last approach (explicitly computing which feasible solution is the most likely) can also work in the presence of link correlations (as long as we have observed the network long enough to have computed the probability of each solution). As part of our future work, we plan to build an algorithm that determines which particular set of links were congested during each snapshot using this approach.

4. ALGORITHM

In this section, we present an algorithm that takes as input unicast end-to-end measurements and outputs, for each link, the probability that the link is congested, i.e., $\mathbb{P}(X_{e_k} = 1)$ for all links e_k in $\mathcal{E}$.

We already know that such an algorithm exists from Theorem 1 (which tells us that we can identify the probability that any set of links is congested, hence, also the probability that any individual link is congested). Moreover, we already have such an algorithm from the proof of Theorem 1, which is a proof by construction (we will refer to it as the "theorem algorithm"). Unfortunately, the theorem algorithm is impractical, because it requires an amount of computation that depends on the number of correlation subsets in the network, which grows exponentially with the size of correlation sets. For instance, if a correlation set consists of 100 links—a plausible number, if the correlation set represents an Autonomous System (AS), it introduces more than 10^{30} correlation subsets.

We now describe a more practical algorithm, which requires an amount of computation that depends only on the number of links in the network. Our algorithm achieves this by leveraging the following observation: The theorem algorithm takes long, because it computes the probability of congestion of every possible combination of links. However, we are not interested in all these probabilities; we are only interested in the probability of congestion of every *individual* link. Hence, our algorithm tries to form just enough equations to solve for these unknowns.

We first illustrate through the example of Figure 1(a):

▷ Consider the case where path P_1 is good. Using Assumption 2 (when a path is good, all its links are necessarily good), we can write:

$$\begin{aligned} \mathbb{P}(Y_{P_1} = 0) &= \mathbb{P}(X_{e_1} = 0)\,\mathbb{P}(X_{e_3} = 0) \Leftrightarrow \\ \log(\mathbb{P}(Y_{P_1} = 0)) &= \log(\mathbb{P}(X_{e_1} = 0)\,\mathbb{P}(X_{e_3} = 0)) \\ &= \log(\mathbb{P}(X_{e_1} = 0)) + \log(\mathbb{P}(X_{e_3} = 0)) \\ \Leftrightarrow y_1 &= x_1 + x_3 \end{aligned} \tag{4}$$

where $y_i = \log(\mathbb{P}(Y_{P_i} = 0))$ and $x_k = \log(\mathbb{P}(X_{e_k} = 0))$.

▷ Similarly, if we consider the cases where paths P_2 and P_3 are good, we can write:

$$y_2 = x_2 + x_3 \tag{5}$$

$$y_3 = x_2 + x_4 \tag{6}$$

▷ Finally, if we consider the case where paths P_2 and P_3 are both good, we can write:

$$\begin{aligned} \mathbb{P}(Y_{P_2} = 0,\ Y_{P_3} = 0) &= \\ \mathbb{P}(X_{e_2} = 0)\,\mathbb{P}(X_{e_3} = 0)\,\mathbb{P}(X_{e_4} = 0) & \\ \Leftrightarrow y_{23} &= x_2 + x_3 + x_4 \end{aligned} \tag{7}$$

where $y_{ij} = \log(\mathbb{P}(Y_{P_i} = 0,\ Y_{P_j} = 0))$.

▷ Equations 4, 5, 6, 7 form a system of 4 linearly independent equations, from which we can compute $x_{1..4}$ and, consequently, $\mathbb{P}(X_{e_{1..4}} = 0)$ and $\mathbb{P}(X_{e_{1..4}} = 1)$.

There are two things to note about the above example. First, we used not only single-path observations ($y_{1..3}$), but also two-path observations (y_{23}), which allowed us to form 4 linear equations, exactly as many as we needed to solve for our unknowns. Second, to form our fourth equation, we used paths P_2 and P_3. What is special about these two paths is that they do not involve any correlated links. If, instead, we had used paths P_1 and P_2, our fourth equation would have been:

$$\mathbb{P}(Y_{P_1} = 0,\ Y_{P_2} = 0) = \mathbb{P}(X_{e_1} = 0,\ X_{e_2} = 0)\ \mathbb{P}(X_{e_3} = 0)$$
$$\Leftrightarrow y_{12} = x_{12} + x_3 \qquad (8)$$

which introduces a new unknown, $x_{12} = \log(\ \mathbb{P}(X_{e_1} = 0,\ X_{e_2} = 0\ )$. So, by considering paths and combinations of paths that do not involve any correlated links, we can form equations that do not introduce new unknowns beyond x_k for all links.

Our algorithm, then, consists of the following steps:

▷ Identify all paths P_i that do not involve correlated links and form a set of $N_1 \leq |\mathcal{P}|$ linearly independent equations

$$y_i = \sum_{k \text{ s.t. } e_k \in P_i} x_k \qquad (9)$$

▷ Identify all pairs of paths that do not involve correlated links, and form a set of N_2 linearly independent equations

$$y_{ij} = \sum_{\substack{k \text{ s.t. } e_k \in P_i \\ \text{or } e_k \in P_j}} x_k \qquad (10)$$

▷ If $N_1 + N_2 = |\mathcal{E}|$, we compute x_k for all links $e_k \in \mathcal{E}$ by solving the system of $|\mathcal{E}|$ equations that we have formed. If $N_1 + N_2 < |\mathcal{E}|$, there are multiple solutions that satisfy our system of equations; we pick the one that minimizes the L1 norm error.

In all topologies we experimented with, by considering paths and pairs of paths that did not involve correlated links, we were able to gather close to $|\mathcal{E}|$ linearly independent equations; thanks to L1 norm minimization, the error introduced by the (few) missing equations was negligible.

5. EVALUATION

Simulator. We built a simulator, in which the network is represented as a graph, with vertices corresponding to nodes and edges corresponding to links. In the beginning of each experiment, we determine which links belong to each correlation set, the probability of congestion of each link, and the joint probability of congestion of each set of correlated links.

An experiment consists of multiple rounds. In each round, we take the following actions:

▷ For each link, we determine whether it will be congested in this round or not, such that we respect the individual and joint probabilities of congestion determined in the beginning of the experiment.

▷ To each link, we assign a packet-loss rate according to the loss model from [13] (also similar to the models from [11, 16]), which assigns packet-loss rates between 0 and 0.01 to good links and between 0.01 and 1 to congested links.

▷ We simulate the scenario in which a given number of packets are sent along each path, hence, along each link. For each packet that arrives at a given link, we flip a coin to determine whether it will be dropped or not, such that we respect the packet-loss rate of the link determined in the previous step.

▷ We measure the packet-loss rate of each path as the fraction of packets sent along the path that were lost. If the packet-loss rate of a path is above the congestion threshold $t_p = 1-(1-t_l)^d$, we identify the path as congested; $t_l = 0.01$, as proposed in [10].

Topologies. We experimented with two types of topologies.

(i) **Brite topologies**: We used the Brite topology generator [1] to obtain pairs of AS-level and router-level topologies. From each pair, we used the AS-level topology to derive a network graph for our simulator and the router-level topology to determine the degree of correlation between each pair of links in the network graph; the point was to simulate scenarios where each correlation set corresponds to an administrative domain. More specifically, we mapped each link in the AS-level topology to a sequence of links in the router-level topology. We assumed that any two links in the router-level topology are uncorrelated; and that two links in the AS-level topology are correlated if and only if they share at least one link in the underlying router-level topology. In the beginning of the experiment, we assigned a probability of congestion to each link in the router-level topology, then derived the probability of congestion of each AS-level link and each set of correlated AS-level links accordingly. We show results for topologies consisting of 1500 paths.

(ii) **PlanetLab topologies**: To obtain each of these topologies, we got hold of several PlanetLab nodes and ran traceroute between them to identify the sequence of routers on each path; we discarded all paths with incomplete traceroute results. We assigned links to correlation sets, such that each correlation set consisted of a contiguous cluster of links; the point was to simulate scenarios where each correlation set corresponds to a local-area network or an administrative domain. We show results for topologies consisting of roughly 2000 links and 1500 paths.

Simulated Algorithms. We compare the algorithm presented in Section 4 (we will call this "correlation algorithm") against the algorithm presented in [12], which assumes that all links are independent (we will call this "independence algorithm"). To the best of our knowledge, this is the only tomographic algorithm that computes the congestion probabilities of links. The fact that our algorithm performs better is not surprising, since we consider scenarios where links are correlated. The point of the comparison is to show that, when links are correlated, ignoring this correlation leads to significant error, even when congestion and correlation are limited.

Metrics. To evaluate the performance of each algorithm, we look at the absolute error between the actual congestion probability of a link and its congestion probability as computed by the algorithm. For instance, if the actual congestion probability of a link is 0.5, but the algorithm thinks it is 0.1, then the absolute error is 0.4.

We use three ways to illustrate the performance of each algorithm for a given experiment: (i) We plot the cumulative distribution function (CDF) of the absolute error for all the *potentially congested links*, i.e., all links that participate in at least one congested path. For a perfect algorithm, this CDF would be a single point at $x = 0$, $y = 100\%$, i.e., the algorithm would compute the congestion probability of

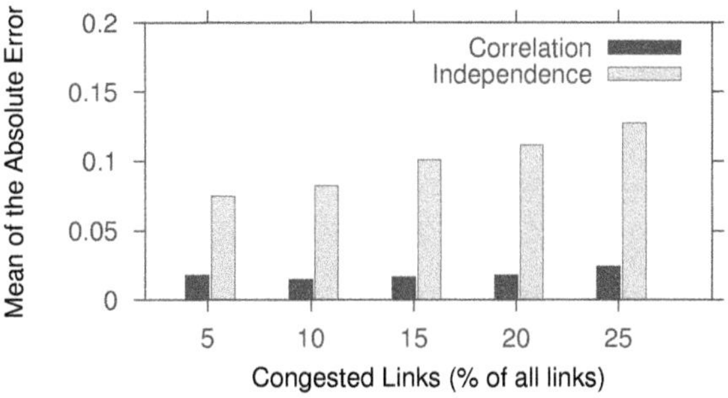

(a) Mean of the absolute error when congested links are highly correlated (more than 2 congested links per correlation set). Brite topology.

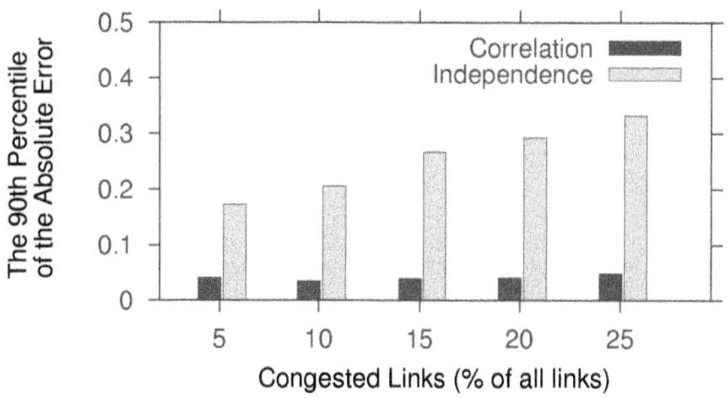

(b) The 90th percentile of the absolute error when congested links are highly correlated (more than 2 congested links per correlation set). Brite topology.

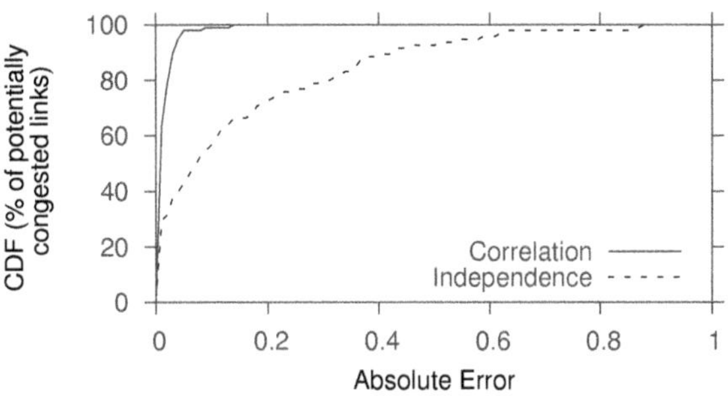

(c) CDF of the absolute error when 10% of the links are congested. Congested links are highly correlated (more than 2 congested links per correlation set). Brite topology.

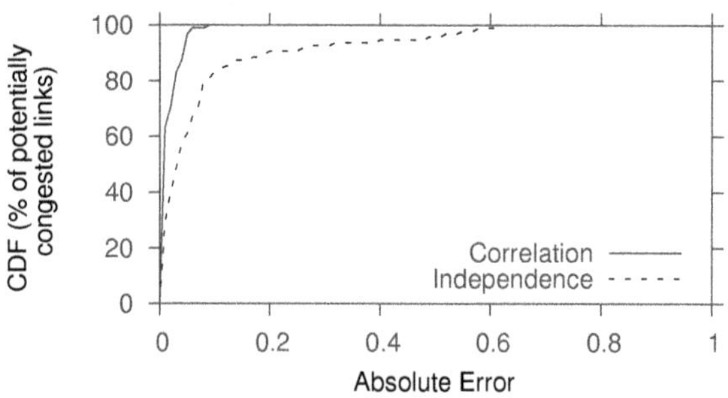

(d) CDF of the absolute error when 10% of the links are congested. Congested links are loosely correlated (up to 2 congested links per correlation set). Brite topology.

Figure 3: Performance of the two algorithms under ideal conditions, when different fractions of the links are congested.

all the potentially congested links with an absolute error of 0. In general, the earlier the CDF hits the $y = 100\%$ line, the better the performance of the corresponding algorithm. (ii) For a more compact illustration, we show the 90th percentile of the absolute error for all the potentially congested links, i.e., the absolute error that corresponds to a value of $y = 90\%$ of the CDF. For instance, if the 90th percentile of the absolute error is 0.1, this means that the corresponding algorithm computed the congestion probability of 90% of the potentially congested links with an absolute error below 0.1. (iii) We show the mean of the absolute error for all the potentially congested links.

Performance Under Ideal Conditions. We first look at the performance of the two algorithms when the congestion probabilities of all links are identifiable (i.e., Assumption 4 holds) and there are no unknown correlation patterns in the network (i.e., links from different correlation sets are never correlated). Figure 3 shows the results for a Brite topology and various congestion scenarios.

First, we observe that our algorithm performs well even when congested links are highly correlated. As the percentage of congested links in the network increases from 5% to 25%, the mean of the absolute error stays below 0.03 (Figure 3(a)), while the 90th percentile of the absolute error stays below 0.1 (Figure 3(b)). For the independence algorithm, the mean and the 90th percentile of the absolute error increase with the percentage of congested links, because more congestion in the network implies that more correlated links are congested. When 10% of the links are congested, our algorithm computes the congestion probability of 95% of the links with an error below 0.1; the independence algorithm computes the congestion probability of only 50% of the links with this error (Figure 3(c)).

Second, we observe that taking correlation into account matters, even when the congested links are (very) loosely correlated. For instance, when 10% of the links are congested, and there are only up to 2 congested links per correlation set, our algorithm computes the congestion probability of 95% of the links with an error below 0.1; the independence algorithm computes the congestion probability of only 80% of the links with this error (Figure 3(d)).

Unidentifiable Links. Next, we look at the performance of the two algorithms when Assumption 4 does not hold, i.e., there exist correlation subsets whose congestion probability is unidentifiable; for brevity, we refer to links that belong to such subsets as "unidentifiable links." Figure 4 shows the results for a Brite and a PlanetLab topology, when 10% of the links in the network are congested.

We observe that our algorithm performs well (and better than the independence algorithm), even when *half* of the congested links are unidentifiable. This is true both for the Brite (Figure 4(b)) and the PlanetLab topology (Fig. 4(d)). Interestingly, in certain cases, we outperform the independence algorithm *even with respect to the unidentifiable links* (we do not show the corresponding graphs for lack of space). This may seem counter-intuitive at first—why

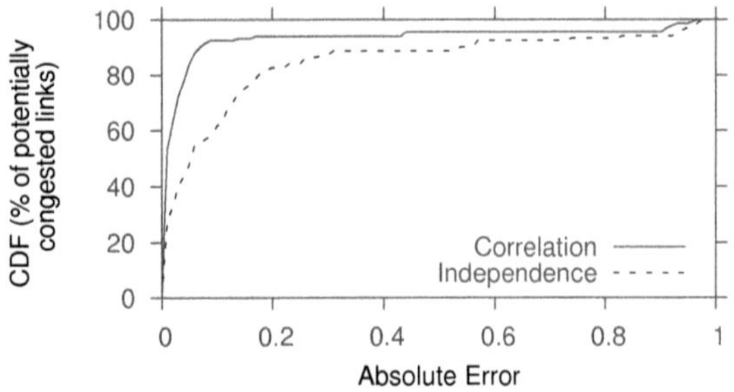

(a) CDF of the absolute error when 25% of the congested links are unindentifiable. Brite topology.

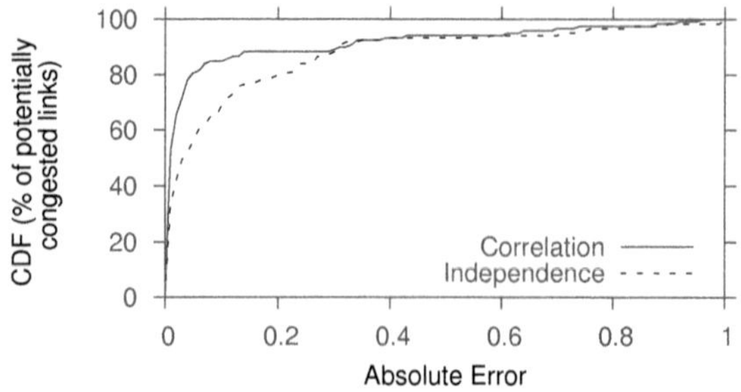

(b) CDF of the absolute error when 50% of the congested links are unindentifiable. Brite topology.

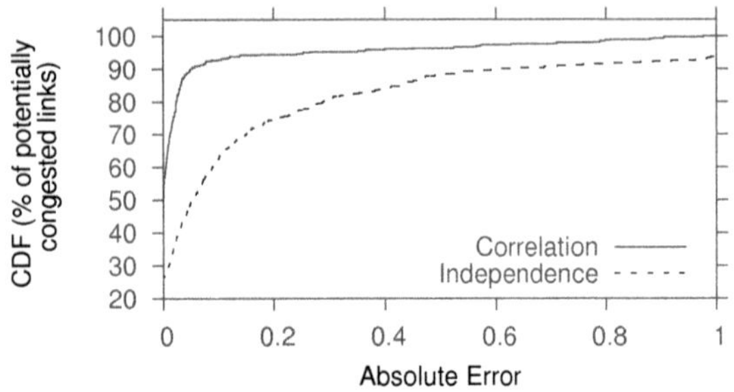

(c) CDF of the absolute error when 25% of the congested links are unindentifiable. PlanetLab topology.

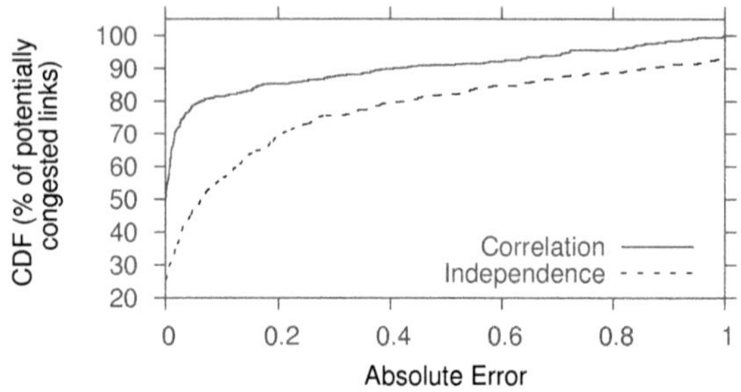

(d) CDF of the absolute error when 50% of the congested links are unindentifiable. PlanetLab topology.

Figure 4: Performance of the two algorithms, when different fractions of congested links are unidentifiable. In all cases, 10% of the links are congested.

should the independence algorithm be any worse in characterizing unidentifiable links? The reason is that, in tomographic algorithms, mistakes "propagate," i.e., mischaracterizing one link leads to a cascade of link mischaracterizations; this effect is stronger when problematic links are concentrated in the same few paths. Our algorithm characterizes the identifiable links accurately, which means that it makes fewer mistakes, hence suffers less from this cascading effect, which improves its accuracy with the rest of the links as well.

Unknown Correlation Patterns. Finally, we look at the performance of the two algorithms when Assumption 4 does not hold *and* there are unknown correlation patterns in the network. In particular, we consider the scenario where a worm has infected a large number of end-hosts and periodically orders them to flood a set of otherwise uncorrelated links; as a result, these links become correlated, i.e., they get congested at about the same time. Since there is no practical way for an operator to know of this correlation pattern, we assume that it is unknown, i.e., our algorithm treats the targeted links as uncorrelated; for brevity, we refer to these links that are incorrectly labeled as uncorrelated with one another as "mislabeled." Figure 5 shows the results for a Brite and a PlanetLab topology, when 10% of the links in the network are congested.

We observe that our algorithm still performs well (and better than the independence algorithm), even when *half* of the congested links participate in unknown correlation patterns (Figures 5(b) and 5(d)). Moreover, we significantly outperform the independence algorithm, even with respect to the links that are affected by the unknown correlation patterns (graphs omitted for lack of space). The reason is that we ignore one correlation pattern, whereas the independence algorithm ignores *all* correlation patterns in the network, which is compounded by the cascading effect mentioned above.

Ongoing Work: PlanetLab Tomographer. We are in the process of building a network tomographer that runs on PlanetLab nodes and infers the congestion probabilities of the links between them (we measure its accuracy through the indirect validation method proposed in [13]). Our tomographer uses traceroute to identify the sequence of routers between each pair of PlanetLab nodes, then tries to map each router to an AS number. Our plan is to run our tomographer (i) assuming that all links are uncorrelated and (ii) assuming that all links in the same AS are correlated, and compare the results; such a comparison would provide evidence regarding the effect of link correlation on network tomography in practice.

6. RELATED WORK

Network performance tomography, which infers the characteristics of links from end-to-end path measurements, is an ill-posed inverse problem well studied in the last decade. A number of methods have been proposed and validated, which differ on the assumptions made about the network and on the characteristics of links they provide.

In order to infer the characteristics of links, the initial methods rely on temporal correlation, either by sending multicast packets (which are perfectly correlated) [5, 4, 2, 3], or

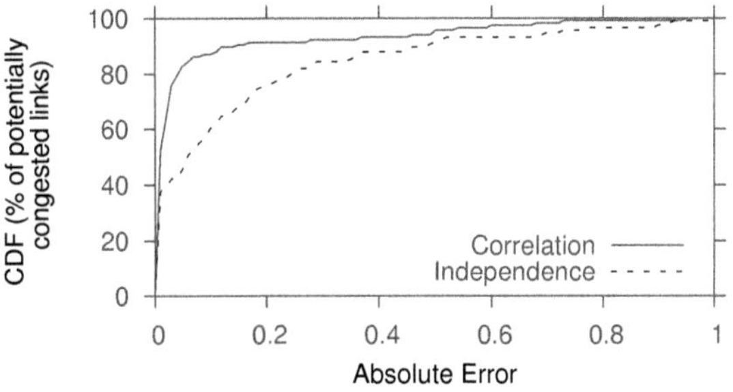

(a) CDF of the absolute error when 25% of the congested links are mislabeled. Brite topology.

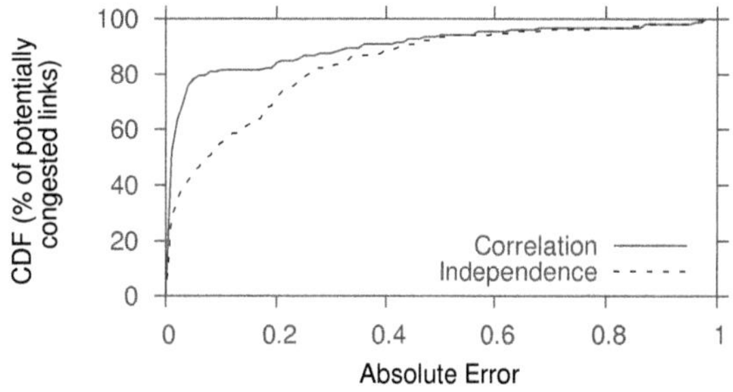

(b) CDF of the absolute error when 50% of the congested links are mislabeled. Brite topology.

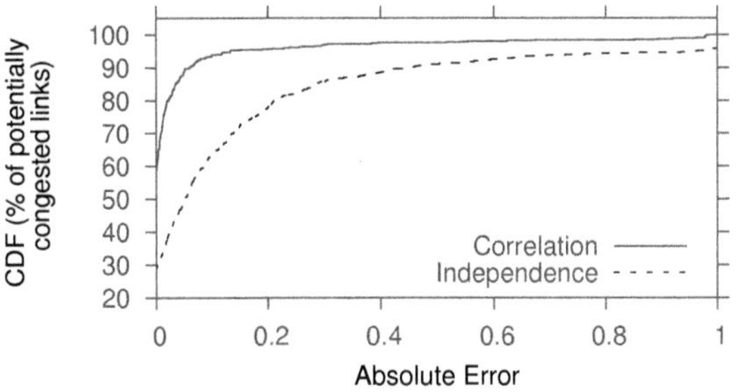

(c) CDF of the absolute error when 25% of the congested links are mislabeled. PlanetLab topology.

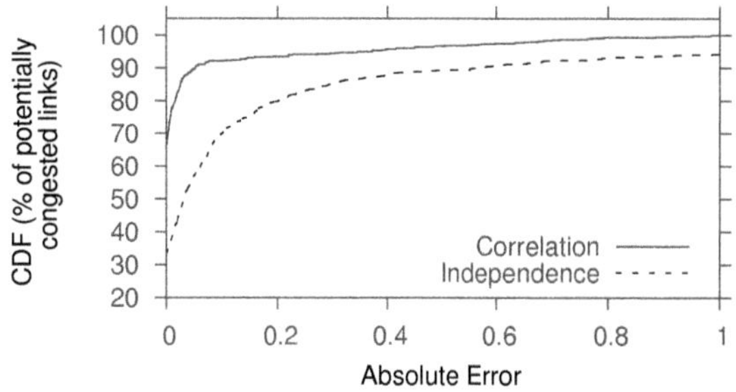

(d) CDF of the absolute error when 50% of the congested links are mislabeled. PlanetLab topology.

Figure 5: Performance of the two algorithms, when different fractions of the links are mislabeled, i.e., participate in unknown correlation patterns. In all cases, 10% of the links are congested.

emulating multicast by sending unicast back to back packets (which are strongly correlated on shared links) [8, 9, 17]. All moments of link loss rates and delays (except first moments) are statistically identifiable in a multicast tree topology [7]. However, multicast is not widely deployed, and groups of unicast packets require substantial development and administrative costs, hence, it is not easy to rely on temporal correlations.

The set of methods that followed [13, 10, 19, 15], use only unicast end-to-end measurements for the simpler goal of identifying the congested links (i.e. identifying if the link loss rate or delay exceeds some threshold, instead of computing their actual value). These "Boolean" network tomographic methods use additional information or assumptions. For example, the methods in [13, 10] identify the congested links by finding the smallest set of links whose congestion can explain the observed measurements. These methods essentially use three assumptions: (i) network links are independent, (ii) links are equally likely to be congested, and (iii) the number of congested links is small.

Assumption (ii) holds for homogeneous networks, but the Internet is a heterogeneous network, and some links such as access links or peering links are often more congested than core links. Fortunately, the congestion probabilities of links can be identified from end-to-end measurements if the links are independent (i.e. if Assumption (i) holds) [12]. These probabilities can be learned from multiple network measurements, and used to locate the congested links with higher accuracy [12]. In addition, they correct the bias towards the (usually non congested) core links, since these links are shared by many more paths than access links, and therefore, by Assumption (iii) they are the smallest number of links that explains the end-to-end performance.

However, all the previous methods strongly rely on Assumption (i), that is, links are independent. This paper shows that one can lift this assumption in part, allow for some local link correlation, and still identify correctly the congestion probabilities of links. Our goal is not to determine the link correlations, we want to eliminate them as to identify the first-order marginal distribution of congested link probabilities.

Another network tomography problem that has received a lot of attention is traffic matrix estimation, which infers the volumes of end-to-end flows from link measurements [18, 6]. Here, the unknown variables are the flow volumes, and are assumed to follow a certain parametric distribution. Flow correlations have been studied by Singhal and Michailidis [14], who showed that under some classes of dependencies, the order n moments of the flow volumes are identifiable from link measurements for $n \geq 2$. Our approach differs in three aspects. First, we are interested in the "dual" problem of inferring link properties given the end-to-end measurements, whereas in [18, 6, 14] link measurements are known, but end-to-end traffic counts need to be inferred. Second, we are interested in Boolean variables, and we do not need a parametrization of the continuous distribution of the variables at stake. The different nature of the relation between the unknown quantities of interest and the measurements restrain us to extend the theoretical results in [14]. Finally, we prove identifiability of the first order moments of the quantities of interest, while the authors in [14] prove identifiability of order $n \geq 2$ moments.

7. CONCLUSION

We considered the problem of identifying the probability that each link in a network is congested from end-to-end path measurements. The key characteristic that sets our work apart from related work is that it takes into account link correlations. In particular, we considered the model where we know which links are most likely to be correlated (e.g., links from the same local-area network or the same administrative domain), however, we do not know the exact nature of the correlation (i.e., we do not assume knowledge of any correlation coefficients). We formally proved that, under certain well defined conditions, it is feasible to identify the probability that each link is congested from end-to-end path measurements, even in the presence of link correlations. We also presented an algorithm that computes these probabilities. We showed through simulations that our algorithm is accurate in a variety of congestion scenarios, even when we do not know all the correlation patterns in the network. Moreover, by comparing with a similar algorithm that does not take link correlation into account, we showed that considering link correlation matters, even when there is a low level of congestion in the network and congested links are only loosely correlated.

Acknowledgments

This work was supported by grant ManCom 2110 of the Hasler Foundation, Bern, Switzerland, and by an Ambizone grant from the Swiss National Science Foundation. We would like to thank the anonymous reviewers for their constructive feedback.

8. REFERENCES

[1] Boston University Representative Internet Topology Generator. http://www.cs.bu.edu/brite/.

[2] A. Adams, T. Bu, T. Friedman, J. Horowitz, D. Towstey, R. Caceres, N. Duffield, F. L. Presti, S. B. Moon, and V. Paxson. The Use of End-to-end Multicast Measurements for Characterizing Internal Network Behavior. *IEEE Communications Magazine*, May 2000.

[3] V. Arya, N. Duffield, and D. Veitch. Temporal Delay Tomography. In *Proceedings of the IEEE INFOCOM Conference*, 2008.

[4] T. Bu, N. Duffield, F. L. Presti, and D. Towsley. Network Tomography on General Topologies. In *Proceedings of the ACM SIGMETRICS Conference*, 2002.

[5] R. Caceres, N. G. Duffield, J. Horowitz, and D. Towsley. Multicast-based Inference of Network-Internal Loss Characteristics. *IEEE Transactions on Information Theory*, 45:2462–2480, 1999.

[6] J. Cao, D. Davis, S. V. Wiel, and B. Yu. Time-Varying Network Tomography: Router Link Data. *Journal of the American Statistical Association*, 95(452):1063–1075, Dec. 2000.

[7] A. Chen, J. Cao, and T. Bu. Network Tomography: Identifiability and Fourier Domain Estimation. In *Proceedings of the IEEE INFOCOM Conference*, 2007.

[8] M. Coates and R. Nowak. Network Loss Inference Using Unicast End-to-End Measurement. In *Proceedings of the ITC Specialist Seminar on IP Traffic Measurement, Modeling and Management*, 2000.

[9] N. Duffield, F. L. Presti, V. Paxson, and D. Towsley. Inferring Link Loss Using Striped Unicast Probes. In *Proceedings of the IEEE INFOCOM Conference*, 2001.

[10] N. G. Duffield. Network Tomography of Binary Network Performance Characteristics. *IEEE Transactions on Information Theory*, 52(12):5373–5388, December 2006.

[11] H. X. Nguyen and P. Thiran. Network Loss Inference with Second Order Statistics of End-to-End Flows. In *Proceedings of the IEEE Internet Measurement Conference (IMC)*, 2007.

[12] H. X. Nguyen and P. Thiran. The Boolean Solution to the Congested IP Link Location Problem: Theory and Practice. In *Proceedings of the IEEE INFOCOM Conference*, 2007.

[13] V. N. Padmanabhan, L. Qiu, and H. J. Wang. Server-based Inference of Internet Performance. In *Proceedings of the IEEE INFOCOM Conference*, 2003.

[14] H. Singhal and G. Michailidis. Identifiability of Flow Distributions from Link Measurements with Applications to Computer Networks. *Inverse Problems*, 23:1821–1850, 2007.

[15] J. Sommers, P. Barford, N. Duffield, and A. Ron. Accurate and Efficient SLA Compliance Monitoring. In *Proceedings of the ACM SIGCOMM Conference*, 2007.

[16] H. H. Song, L. Qiu, and Y. Zhang. NetQuest: A Flexible Framework for Large-Scale Network Measurement. In *Proceedings of the ACM SIGMETRICS Conference*, 2006.

[17] Y. Tsang, M. Coates, and R. Nowak. Passive Network Tomography Using the EM Algorithms. In *Proceedings of the IEEE International Conference on Acoustics, Speech and Signal Processing (ICASSP)*, 2001.

[18] Y. Vardi. Network Tomography: Estimating Source-Destination Traffic Intensities. *Journal of the American Statistical Association*, 91:365–377, 1996.

[19] Y. Zhao, Y. Chen, and D. Bindel. Toward Unbiased End-to-End Network Diagnosis. In *Proceedings of the ACM SIGCOMM Conference*, 2006.

APPENDIX

A. PROOF OF THEOREM 1

A.1 Definitions and Notation

We introduce three more symbols. All our symbols are summarized in Table 1.

Network States. We denote by $\mathcal{S}_n$ a particular value of $\mathcal{S}$ and by $S_n^p \subseteq C_p$ the corresponding value of S^p (i.e., the set of congested links in correlation set C_p when $\mathcal{S} = \mathcal{S}_n$). We can write:

$$\mathcal{S}_n \equiv \bigcup_{p=1..|\mathcal{C}|} S_n^p. \qquad (11)$$

During any particular snapshot, each correlation set (as well as the entire network) can only be in one state, hence, any two states $S_n^p, S_m^p, n \neq m$, (as well as $\mathcal{S}_n, \mathcal{S}_m, n \neq m$,) are mutually exclusive.

Ordering of Path Sets. Consider two correlation subsets $A, B \in \tilde{\mathcal{C}}$. We define the precedence property as:

$$A \prec B \quad \equiv \quad |\psi(A)| < |\psi(B)| \qquad (12)$$

that is, the edges in B are traversed by more paths than the edges in A. Using this definition, we can determine a partial ordering $\mathcal{T}$ of all the correlation subsets in $\tilde{\mathcal{C}}$, i.e., order them by the number of paths that traverse them.

$\mathcal{G}$	the network graph
$\mathcal{V}$	the set of all nodes
$\mathcal{E}$	the set of all links
$\mathcal{P}$	the set of all paths
$e_k \in \mathcal{E}$	a link
$P_i \in \mathcal{P}$	a path
$e_k \in P_i$	link e_k is traversed by path P_i
$\psi(A)$	the paths "covered" by the set of links A
$\lvert\psi(A)\rvert$	the number of paths in $\psi(A)$
X_{e_k}	(r.v.) the state of link e_k
Y_{P_i}	(r.v.) the state of path P_i
$\mathcal{C}$	partition of $\mathcal{E}$ into correlation sets
$C_p \in \mathcal{C}$	a correlation set
$\tilde{\mathcal{C}}$	the set of all correlation subsets
$A, B \in \tilde{\mathcal{C}}$	two correlation subsets
S^p	(r.v.) the set of congested links in C_p
$\mathcal{S}$	(r.v.) the set of all congested links
$\psi(\mathcal{S})$	(r.v.) the set of all congested paths
α_A	congestion factor of $A \in \tilde{\mathcal{C}}$
$\mathcal{S}_n$	a value of the random set $\mathcal{S}$
S^p_n	a value of the random set S^p
$A \prec B$	$\lvert\psi(A)\rvert < \lvert\psi(B)\rvert$

Table 1: List of defined symbols. "r.v." = "random variable."

A.2 Some Basic Probabilities

Network State Probability. We will first express the probability that the network is in state $\mathcal{S}_n$. We will use Eq. 11 and the fact that S^p and $S^q, p \neq q$, are independent.

$$\mathbb{P}(\ \mathcal{S} = \mathcal{S}_n\ ) = \mathbb{P}\left(\bigcap_{p=1..|\mathcal{C}|} (\ S^p = S^p_n\ ) \right) = \prod_{p=1..|\mathcal{C}|} \mathbb{P}(\ S^p = S^p_n\ ). \quad (13)$$

All Paths Are Good. Next, we will express the probability that all paths in $\mathcal{P}$ are good. We will use Assumption 2, in particular, its implication that, if all paths in $\mathcal{P}$ are good, then necessarily all links in $\mathcal{E}$ are good.

$$\mathbb{P}(\ \psi(\mathcal{S}) = \emptyset\ ) = \mathbb{P}(\ \mathcal{S} = \emptyset\ ) = \prod_{p=1..|\mathcal{C}|} \mathbb{P}(\ S^p = \emptyset\ ). \quad (14)$$

Some Paths Are Congested. Next, we will express the probability of event $\psi(\mathcal{S}) = \psi(A)$, i.e., that the paths covered by correlation subset A are the only congested paths in the network.

$$\mathbb{P}(\ \psi(\mathcal{S}) = \psi(A)\ ) = \sum_{\substack{n \text{ s.t.} \\ \psi(\mathcal{S}_n)=\psi(A)}} \mathbb{P}(\ \mathcal{S} = \mathcal{S}_n\ ). \quad (15)$$

Eq. 15 expresses the fact that, when the paths in $\psi(A)$ are the only congested paths, it must be true that a set of links that cover exactly these paths (for which $\psi(\mathcal{S}_n) = \psi(A)$) are the only congested links. One such set of links is A, but there may be other sets that consist of multiple correlation subsets.

We will now develop Eq. 15 further by considering the following: Since $A \in \tilde{\mathcal{C}}$, there exists one correlation set $C_q \in \mathcal{C}$, which contains A. In the following, we denote by q the index of the correlation set C_q such that $A \subseteq C_q$. We partition the possible network states in two sets: the states where $A = S^q_n$ (the only congested links in C_q are the links in A) and the states where $A \neq S^q_n$:

$$\mathbb{P}(\ \psi(\mathcal{S}) = \psi(A)\ ) = \sum_{\substack{n \text{ s.t. } S^q_n=A, \\ \psi(\mathcal{S}_n)=\psi(A)}} \mathbb{P}(\ \mathcal{S} = \mathcal{S}_n\ ) + \sum_{\substack{n \text{ s.t. } S^q_n\neq A, \\ \psi(\mathcal{S}_n)=\psi(A)}} \mathbb{P}(\ \mathcal{S} = \mathcal{S}_n\ ). \quad (16)$$

Finally, if we combine Eq. 16 with Eq. 13, we get:

$$\mathbb{P}(\ \psi(\mathcal{S}) = \psi(A)\ ) = \mathbb{P}(\ S^q = A\ ) \sum_{\substack{n \text{ s.t. } S^q_n=A, \\ \psi(\mathcal{S}_n)=\psi(A)}} \left(\prod_{\substack{p=1..|\mathcal{C}|, \\ p\neq q}} \mathbb{P}(\ S^p = S^p_n\ ) \right) + \sum_{\substack{n \text{ s.t. } S^q_n\neq A, \\ \psi(\mathcal{S}_n)=\psi(A)}} \left(\prod_{p=1..|\mathcal{C}|} \mathbb{P}(\ S^p = S^p_n\ ) \right). \quad (17)$$

Illustration. Consider Figure 1(a), correlation subset $A = \{e_1, e_2\}$, and the event $(\psi(\mathcal{S}) = \psi(A) = \{P_1, P_2, P_3\})$, i.e., that all paths are congested. This means that the network is in one of the following states:

$\mathcal{S}_n$	S^1_n	$\cup$	S^2_n	$\cup$	S^3_n
$\mathcal{S}_1$	$\{e_1, e_2\}$	$\cup$	$\emptyset$	$\cup$	$\emptyset$
$\mathcal{S}_2$	$\{e_1, e_2\}$	$\cup$	$\{e_3\}$	$\cup$	$\emptyset$
$\mathcal{S}_3$	$\{e_1, e_2\}$	$\cup$	$\emptyset$	$\cup$	$\{e_4\}$
$\mathcal{S}_4$	$\{e_1, e_2\}$	$\cup$	$\{e_3\}$	$\cup$	$\{e_4\}$
$\mathcal{S}_5$	$\emptyset$	$\cup$	$\{e_3\}$	$\cup$	$\{e_4\}$
$\mathcal{S}_6$	$\{e_1\}$	$\cup$	$\{e_3\}$	$\cup$	$\{e_4\}$
$\mathcal{S}_7$	$\{e_2\}$	$\cup$	$\{e_3\}$	$\cup$	$\{e_4\}$
$\mathcal{S}_8$	$\{e_2\}$	$\cup$	$\{e_3\}$	$\cup$	$\emptyset$

In this particular case, $A \subseteq C_1$, i.e., $q = 1$. For the first four states, $S^1_n = A$, whereas for the rest, $S^1_n \neq A$. Hence, if we apply Equations 16 and 17, we get:

$$\mathbb{P}(\ \psi(\mathcal{S}) = \psi(\{e_1, e_2\})\ ) = \sum_{n=1}^{4} \mathbb{P}(\ \mathcal{S} = \mathcal{S}_n\ ) + \sum_{n=5}^{8} \mathcal{S} = \mathcal{S}_n\ ) =$$

$$\begin{array}{lll}
\mathbb{P}(\ S^1 = \{e_1, e_2\}\ ) & \mathbb{P}(\ S^2 = \emptyset\ ) & \mathbb{P}(\ S^3 = \emptyset\ ) + \\
\mathbb{P}(\ S^1 = \{e_1, e_2\}\ ) & \mathbb{P}(\ S^2 = \{e_3\}\ ) & \mathbb{P}(\ S^3 = \emptyset\ ) + \\
\mathbb{P}(\ S^1 = \{e_1, e_2\}\ ) & \mathbb{P}(\ S^2 = \emptyset\ ) & \mathbb{P}(\ S^3 = \{e_4\}\ ) + \\
\mathbb{P}(\ S^1 = \{e_1, e_2\}\ ) & \mathbb{P}(\ S^2 = \{e_3\}\ ) & \mathbb{P}(\ S^3 = \{e_4\})\ ) + \\
\mathbb{P}(\ S^1 = \emptyset\ ) & \mathbb{P}(\ S^2 = \{e_3\}\ ) & \mathbb{P}(\ S^3 = \{e_4\}\ ) + \\
\mathbb{P}(\ S^1 = \{e_1\}\ ) & \mathbb{P}(\ S^2 = \{e_3\}\ ) & \mathbb{P}(\ S^3 = \{e_4\}\ ) + \\
\mathbb{P}(\ S^1 = \{e_2\}\ ) & \mathbb{P}(\ S^2 = \{e_3\}\ ) & \mathbb{P}(\ S^3 = \{e_4\}\ ) + \\
\mathbb{P}(\ S^1 = \{e_2\}\ ) & \mathbb{P}(\ S^2 = \{e_3\}\ ) & \mathbb{P}(\ S^3 = \emptyset\ ).
\end{array}$$

A.3 Proof

If we divide Eq. 17 by Eq. 14, we obtain:

$$\frac{\mathbb{P}(\ \psi(\mathcal{S}) = \psi(A)\ )}{\mathbb{P}(\ \psi(\mathcal{S}) = \emptyset\ )} = \alpha_A\, \Gamma_A + \Gamma_{\bar{A}} \qquad (18)$$

where

$$\Gamma_A = \sum_{\substack{n \text{ s.t. } S_n^q = A,\\ \psi(\mathcal{S}_n) = \psi(A)}} \left(\prod_{\substack{p=1..|\mathcal{C}|,\\ p \neq q}} \alpha_{S_n^p} \right)$$

and

$$\Gamma_{\bar{A}} = \sum_{\substack{n \text{ s.t. } S_n^q \neq A,\\ \psi(\mathcal{S}_n) = \psi(A)}} \left(\prod_{p=1..|\mathcal{C}|} \alpha_{S_n^p} \right).$$

Lemma 1. *The terms Γ_A and $\Gamma_{\bar{A}}$ depend on congestion factors $\alpha_{S_n^p}$, where n and p are such that $S_n^p = \emptyset$ or $S_n^p \prec A$.*

Proof. We know that Γ_A and $\Gamma_{\bar{A}}$ depend on congestion factors $\alpha_{S_n^p}$, where n and p are such that $S_n^p \neq A$. This is because: Γ_A depends on congestion factors $\alpha_{S_n^p}$, where n is such that $S_n^q = A$ and $p \neq q$. $\Gamma_{\bar{A}}$ depends on congestion factors $\alpha_{S_n^p}$, where n is such that $S_n^q \neq A$.

Moreover, Γ_A and $\Gamma_{\bar{A}}$ depend on congestion factors $\alpha_{S_n^p}$, where n is such that $\psi(\mathcal{S}_n) = \psi(A)$. Since $\psi(S_n^p) \subseteq \psi(\mathcal{S}_n)$, it implies that $\psi(S_n^p) \subseteq \psi(A)$. We distinguish two cases:

1. $\psi(S_n^p) = \psi(A)$. Correlation subsets S_n^p and A cover exactly the same paths. From Assumption 4, it follows that $S_n^p = A$, which contradicts the fact that $S_n^p \neq A$.
2. $\psi(S_n^p) \subset \psi(A)$. Correlation subset S_n^p covers fewer paths than A, i.e., $|\psi(S_n^p)| < |\psi(A)|$. Thus, either $S_n^p = \emptyset$ or, by definition, $S_n^p \prec A$.

□

Lemma 2. *The congestion factors α_A are identifiable, for all $A \in \tilde{\mathcal{C}}$.*

Proof. We prove the lemma by induction on the partial ordering $\mathcal{T}$.

Initial Step. Let A be the first element from the partial ordering $\mathcal{T}$ defined by Eq 12. We will prove that we can compute α_A from Eq. 18.

Γ_A and $\Gamma_{\bar{A}}$ consist of terms $\alpha_{S_n^p}$, where n is such that $\psi(\mathcal{S}_n) = \psi(A)$ (call this Condition 1). Moreover, from Lemma 1, we know that n and p are such that $S_n^p = \emptyset$ or $S_n^p \prec A$; since A is the first element in $\mathcal{T}$, it cannot be that $S_n^p \prec A$, hence, $S_n^p = \emptyset$ (call this Condition 2). The only network state that satisfies Conditions 1 and 2 is $\mathcal{S}_n = S_n^q = A$.

Hence, we have:

$$\Gamma_A = \sum_{\substack{n \text{ s.t. } S_n^q = A\\ \mathcal{S}_n = A}} \left(\prod_{\substack{p=1..|\mathcal{C}|,\\ p \neq q}} \alpha_{S_n^p} \right) = \prod_{\substack{p=1..|\mathcal{C}|,\\ p \neq q}} \frac{\mathbb{P}(\ S^p = \emptyset\ )}{\mathbb{P}(\ S^p = \emptyset\ )} = 1$$

and

$$\Gamma_{\bar{A}} = \sum_{\substack{n \text{ s.t. } S_n^q \neq A\\ \mathcal{S}_n = A}} \left(\prod_{p=1..|\mathcal{C}|} \alpha_{S_n^p} \right) = 0.$$

Thus, we can compute α_A from Eq. 18, where the term on the left hand side is obtained through end-to-end measurements.

Induction Step. We assume that we know α_B, for all $B \prec A$. We will prove that we can compute α_A.

Let us recast Eq. 18 as

$$\alpha_A = \frac{\frac{\mathbb{P}(\ \psi(\mathcal{S}) = \psi(A)\ )}{\mathbb{P}(\ \psi(\mathcal{S}) = \emptyset\ )} - \Gamma_{\bar{A}}}{\Gamma_A}.$$

Note that the denominator Γ_A is never 0, because for any correlation subset A, there always exists at least one state $\mathcal{S}_n$ such that $\psi(\mathcal{S}_n) = \psi(A)$ and $S_n^q = A$, which is $\mathcal{S}_n = A$.

According to Lemma 1, Γ_A and $\Gamma_{\bar{A}}$ depend on congestion factors $\alpha_{S_n^p}$, where n and p are such that either $S_n^p = \emptyset$ or $S_n^p \prec A$. If $S_n^p = \emptyset$, then by definition, $\alpha_{S_n^p} = \frac{\mathbb{P}(\ S^p = \emptyset\ )}{\mathbb{P}(\ S^p = \emptyset\ )} = 1$. If $S_n^p \prec A$ with $S_n^p \neq \emptyset$, from the induction hypothesis, we know $\alpha_{S_n^p}$. Thus, we can compute α_A from Eq. 18, where the term on the left is obtained through end-to-end measurements. □

Lemma 3. *If the congestion factors α_A are known for all $A \subseteq C_p$, then the probability $\mathbb{P}(\ X_{e_k} = 1\ )$ is identifiable for all $e_k \in C_p$.*

Proof. As

$$\begin{aligned}\mathbb{P}(\ S^p = \emptyset\ ) &= 1 - \mathbb{P}(\ S^p \neq \emptyset\ ) \\ &= 1 - \sum_{A \subseteq C_p, A \neq \emptyset} \mathbb{P}(\ S^p = A\ ) \\ &= 1 - \sum_{A \subseteq C_p, A \neq \emptyset} \alpha_A\, \mathbb{P}(\ S^p = \emptyset\ )\end{aligned}$$

we have that

$$\mathbb{P}(\ S^p = \emptyset\ ) = \frac{1}{1 + \sum_{A \subseteq C_p, A \neq \emptyset} \alpha_A}.$$

Since α_A is known for all $A \in C_p$, we can compute $\mathbb{P}(\ S^p = \emptyset\ )$ from the above equation.

Furthermore, we can compute $\mathbb{P}(\ S^p = A\ )$ for all $A \subseteq C_p, A \neq \emptyset$:

$$\mathbb{P}(\ S^p = A\ ) = \alpha_A \cdot \mathbb{P}(\ S^p = \emptyset\ )$$

and $\mathbb{P}(\ X_{e_k} = 1\ )$ for all $e_k \in C_p$:

$$\mathbb{P}(\ X_{e_k} = 1\ ) = \sum_{\substack{A \subseteq C_p\\ e_k \in A}} \mathbb{P}(\ S^p = A).$$

□

We have proved that the congestion factors α_A are identifiable for all correlation subsets $A \in \tilde{\mathcal{C}}$ (Lemma 2). We have also proved that, if the congestion factors α_A are known for all $A \subseteq C_p$, the probability that all the links in A are congested is identifiable for all $A \subseteq C_p$ (Lemma 3), which proves Theorem 1.

Scamper: a Scalable and Extensible Packet Prober for Active Measurement of the Internet

Matthew Luckie
Department of Computer Science
University of Waikato
Hamilton, New Zealand
mjl@wand.net.nz

ABSTRACT

Large scale active measurement of the Internet requires appropriate software support. The better tools that we have for executing consistent and systematic measurements, the more confidence we can have in the results. This paper presents scamper, a powerful open-source packet-prober for active measurement of the Internet designed to stand alone from coordination mechanisms. We built scamper and populated it with specific measurement techniques, making design decisions aimed at allowing Internet researchers to focus on scientific experiments rather than building accurate instrumentation.

Categories and Subject Descriptors

C.4 [**Performance of Systems**]: Measurement techniques

General Terms

Measurement

Keywords

Active measurement, Software, Tools

1. INTRODUCTION

Packet probing experiments capture relatively simple measurements – typically delay, loss, reordering, and topology – that yield surprising insights into the structure and behaviour of the Internet. An early measurement experiment investigating the effect of packet size on delay suggested that TCP implementers should refine the algorithm used to compute the TCP RTO value [1]. The massive scale and continuing growth of the Internet has increased the complexity of measuring it, both technically and methodologically. In the past decade, researchers have built and operated many large-scale active Internet measurement platforms [2, 3, 4, 5, 6, 7, 8, 9] where each typically reproduces a tremendous amount of supporting software development. Faced with continuing funding constraints, members of the Internet measurement community organised a workshop in 2005 to strategise a way to collaborate on creating and operating a community-oriented network measurement infrastructure; the workshop report [10] presents many goals and desires, including the need for better ways to organise large-scale measurements.

This paper focuses on a small part of this problem; building a packet-prober that makes it easy to conduct large-scale measurements and archive collected data in a well-defined format. A packet-prober should abstract away problems of coordinating individual measurements on a host, provide APIs that deal with operating system differences, provide APIs for obtaining accurate timing information, and produce output that is more detailed and easier to process than that produced by existing system tools. By building a packet-prober with these goals in mind we can help the experimental researcher avoid the system programming and administration problems of coordinating individual measurements on a single host. Rather than suffering the overhead associated with parallelisation of a single instance of a given measurement process, a researcher can rapidly implement a new measurement technique and focus on the analysis and validation of results.

Such community software infrastructure will also improve the capability of researchers to leverage measurements from volunteers across the global Internet. At present researchers need to be careful when soliciting volunteers to do a measurement that uses the system's included traceroute as the implementation included in each operating system differs remarkably in operation and utility, even though most are based on Van Jacobson's implementation [11]. For instance, none support Paris traceroute [12], FreeBSD's implementation supports TCP probing but does not process TCP responses, and Ubuntu's implementation can trigger rate limiting because it sends bursts of probes.

This paper presents scamper, a powerful packet-prober designed to support large-scale Internet measurement. Included in the contribution to the measurement community are feature-rich implementations of traceroute, ping, MDA traceroute, four alias resolution techniques, Sting, and parts of TBIT. We begin in section 2 by first establishing a set of design objectives. Sections 3, 4, 5, and 6 present a technical overview of scamper, detailing its implementation, features, performance, and use. Section 7 shows how scamper has been useful in conducting research, including both our experiences and those of others. Finally, section 8 outlines related work and section 9 concludes.

2. DESIGN OBJECTIVES

Precise: promote good science by ensuring details found in a response packet are easily available to measurement techniques, easily stored, and then easily read by analysis routines. A researcher should be able to annotate both individual measurements and a collection of measurements describing the purpose and specifics of the data collection. Packet timestamps should be recorded from the best available source – whether it be from user-space or the network interface. Decoding a chain of packet headers can be tedious and error prone; therefore, the packet-prober should present decoded packet headers to a measurement technique so that the implementer can easily use them. Finally, the details found in a packet header should be preserved in a data file even if the need to do so has not yet been established.

To motivate this last point, consider macroscopic Internet topology mapping using traceroute; traditionally, the data recorded per-hop is an IP address, the RTT measured, and the TTL used in the probe packet. However, Augustin *et al.* recently brought to the community's attention the problem of routers that forward traceroute probes with a TTL of zero, which results in a subsequent router appearing twice in a path and therefore a false link inference [12]. Unfortunately, few topology mapping projects record the TTL found in the ICMP quotation, preventing the correction of link inferences made using topology data archived years earlier.

Parallelised: efficiently manage the several hundred concurrent measurements that are a reality of macroscopic Internet measurement. For Internet-scale experiments to complete in a reasonable length of time requires concurrent measurements. Active measurements can spend a lot of time waiting, for example, for a reply to a TTL-limited probe in traceroute, or for a reply to a TCP SYN probe. The period of time where productive work is done is when sending a probe and receiving a reply, so measurement is most productive when we are able to probe at a constant rate. However, an architecture that allocates a thread per measurement does not scale as well as an event-based system. A packet-prober should provide APIs that allow resources such as sockets to be shared amongst measurements. Doing so improves performance by reducing the number of file descriptors that the operating system has to service when multiplexing synchronous I/O.

Portable: support a wide range of operating systems and computer architectures. The requirements of some active measurement techniques are not well catered for by the Berkeley sockets API, which is designed for general-purpose Internet software. The methods available to bypass the sockets API differ amongst operating systems, so a significant volume of code has to be implemented for any one technique to be portable across systems. The experimental researcher would benefit from an API that is operating system agnostic and reduces the code required to create and send a packet and then receive and decode a response.

Flexible: each experiment has different motivations and requirements; a packet-prober should be flexible enough to support them. While some experiments can be specified as a one-shot measurement where the order in which a measurement is conducted is not important, some measurements are conducted in reaction to a previous measurement [13], or require some amount of coordination and control. These requirements call for the packet-prober to be flexible in the ways it allows a researcher to specify measurements.

Volunteer friendly: some measurements are made by volunteers that run experiments on behalf of researchers. A packet-prober should therefore be easily compiled on systems for which a pre-compiled binary is unavailable; easily operated by a volunteer; lightweight enough to run in a resource constrained environment such as an embedded system; and self-contained so that a potential volunteer will not need to install a suite of dependencies.

Modular: support multiple measurement techniques, and be easily extended to include techniques that have not yet been devised.

3. SCAMPER

Guided by the design objectives listed in section 2 we implemented scamper, a parallelised packet-prober capable of large-scale Internet measurement using many different measurement techniques. Figure 1 illustrates the overall architecture of scamper. Briefly, scamper obtains a sequence of measurement tasks from the input sources and probes each in parallel as needed to meet a packets-per-second rate specified on the command line. Tasks currently being probed are held centrally by scamper in a set of queues – the probe queue if the task is ready to probe, the wait queue if it is waiting for time to elapse, and the done queue if the task has completed and is ready to be written out to disk. Each measurement technique is implemented in a separate module that includes the logic for conducting the measurement as well as the input/output routines for reading and writing measurement results, allowing measurement techniques to be implemented independently of each other. When a new measurement task is instantiated, the task attaches a set of callback routines to itself that scamper then uses to direct the measurement as events occur, such as when it is time to probe, when a response is received, or when a time-out elapses. Sockets required as part of a measurement are held centrally by scamper in order to share them amongst tasks where possible so that resource requirements are reduced. Finally, scamper centrally maintains a collection of output files where completed measurements are written.

Output: scamper provides two output file formats; an ASCII text option, and a binary file format known as *warts*. The text option produces low-fidelity output similar to the ping and traceroute utilities and is suitable for interactive use. The binary option is an extensible format designed for use by researchers because of its ability to record detail and provide archival features. Scamper includes a library that allows its binary output files to be easily read, and CAIDA have created a Ruby library [14] which allows researchers to develop analysis programs in Ruby. Scamper supplies an API to assist a researcher implementing a new measurement technique to create a record which can then be stored in the binary file format. To promote precision and discourage researchers from recording results in the text option, the library provides no ability to read results from a text file.

Portability layer: scamper provides a portability layer that shields a researcher implementing a measurement technique from the differences in the APIs of each operating system. An author of a measurement technique uses scamper's portability layer to define the details of a probe packet and to transmit it, and has the corresponding responses decoded and passed to the task by its specified callback routines. The portability layer hides, for example, the details of which byte order the system expects packet headers to be supplied in,

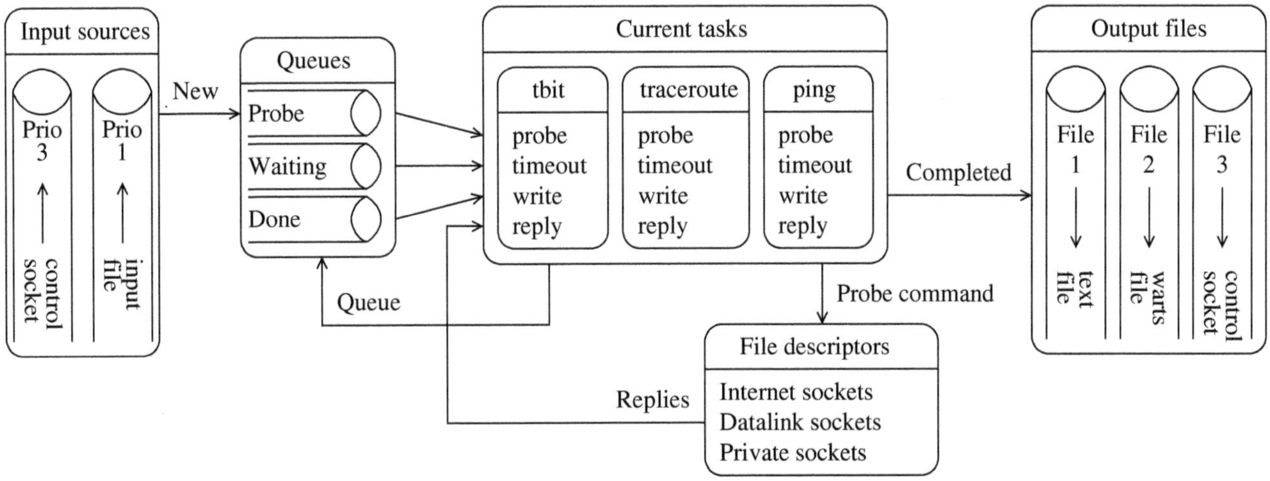

Figure 1: The architecture of scamper. Measurement tasks are supplied from one or more input sources, including from an input file, from the command line, or from a control socket. A scamper task is abstract; the exact behaviour is determined by a set of implementer-provided callback functions. Current tasks can be in one of three states; waiting to probe, waiting for a response or to timeout, or waiting to be written to disk. Completed tasks can be written to a text file or a binary file, or over a control socket for interpretation.

and the byte order that values in packet headers in response packets are returned in. If the system would interfere in transmitting a packet – e.g. by silently fragmenting a probe or re-writing packet header fields, scamper allows a technique to use the datalink sockets instead. Because datalink sockets expect a complete frame including layer-2 headers, scamper provides an API to obtain the layer-2 addresses dynamically using neighbour discovery protocols. Similarly, a technique can use a datalink socket if the system does not provide the ability to read particular types of packets from an Internet socket, such as raw TCP frames. Finally, some techniques that use TCP as their probe method, such as Sting [15] and TBIT [16], require the ability to prevent the operating system's TCP stack from interfering in a measurement by responding to unexpected packets; scamper provides the ability to install a temporary firewall rule for some firewall types. Scamper runs on BSD, Linux, MacOS X, Solaris, and Windows systems; however, not all portions of the portability layer work on all systems.

Operation: scamper can run either as a one-shot measurement or as a daemon that is externally controlled. Scamper receives instructions in two ways. One, it accepts a list of IP addresses to probe, either in a file or on the command line itself, along with a measurement technique to use with each address specified on the command line. When all addresses have been probed, scamper has completed all required work and exits. The second way is to start scamper as a daemon and then connect to scamper's control socket and issue measurement instructions dynamically. This can be done either by specifying a measurement technique and a file with IP addresses to use, or by specifying individual measurement instructions interactively. The latter approach is powerful because it allows a macroscopic Internet measurement infrastructure to rapidly begin collecting data without implementing its own parallelised measurement tools and data collection system.

Event driven: there are no threads in scamper, so authors of new measurement techniques do not have to be concerned about reentrancy of their functions. To achieve parallelism, scamper uses non-blocking file descriptors in conjunction with the select system call. The main limitation with select is there is no guarantee that it will return exactly when the timeout expires. However, the finer resolution of the modern operating system scheduling clock has reduced the scale of this problem. Also, some techniques are self-clocking; for example, traceroute usually sends the next probe immediately after the last has been received, rather than waiting for a timeout.

Parallelism: scamper has two parameters that control its parallelism. The first is the minimum inter-packet transmit delay permitted, defined in packets per second (PPS). The default value of 20 means that scamper will send packets spaced 50ms apart. The second, a window parameter, defines the maximum number of active tasks permitted at any one time. The default value of zero means the window is unrestricted and the parallelism is defined solely by the PPS value. Scamper has been observed to probe at 1000 PPS on modest hardware, suggesting the event driven model scales well. Scamper aims to reach the desired rate by adding new tasks as required. As scamper can have multiple input sources supplying tasks concurrently, the user can specify the priority of each source. A priority value defines the ratio of new tasks it contributes overall in weighted round robin. If a source is not ready to supply a command and scamper has room in its probing budget, it obtains a new task from the next ready input source to maximise work done.

Stand-alone: as one design objective is to make scamper easy for volunteers to install and operate, scamper has no dependencies on external libraries or a configuration file, and has a small number of parameters configurable on the command line. These features make scamper easy to compile, install, and run. We considered using external libraries such as libpcap and libdnet, but not all operating systems contain a recent version of these libraries, and these libraries presently do not contain all required features.

4. MEASUREMENT TECHNIQUES

Traceroute: scamper began with a desire to conduct IPv6 traceroute in parallel to a large number of target addresses in support of CAIDA's macroscopic Internet topology discovery project [5]. The traceroute included in scamper is feature-rich: it supports IPv4 and IPv6; probe methods based on UDP, ICMP, and TCP, including Paris traceroute [12]; path MTU discovery (PMTUD) to infer the presence of tunnels [17]; a method to infer the hops in a path that do not send an ICMP packet too big message which is required for PMTUD to work [18]; and doubletree [19] to reduce redundant probing. It is optimised for macroscopic Internet topology discovery by halting if a sequence of unresponsive hops is encountered.

Ping: ping is useful to measure end-to-end delay and loss, search for responsive IP addresses, and classify the behaviour of hosts by examining how they respond to probes. In addition to the traditional ICMP echo method, scamper supports UDP, TCP, and TTL-limited probing, which can be used if directed ICMP echo probes do not obtain a response. Scamper includes the ability to spoof the source address of probes, as well as include IP options for record route and timestamps; these features are useful for implementing reverse traceroute [20].

MDA traceroute: scamper implements the multipath detection algorithm described in [21] to infer all interfaces visited between a source and destination in a per-flow load-balanced Internet path. It does this by deliberately varying the flow-identifier that a router may compute when load balancing. Probes with different flow-identifiers may take different paths and thus reveal different parts of the forward IP path. In addition to the ICMP and UDP methods originally implemented by Augustin *et. al* which vary the ICMP checksum and UDP destination port values, scamper implements a UDP method which varies the source port instead of the destination port so that the probes do not appear to be a port scan. This method also provides the ability to probe past a firewall that blocks UDP probes to ports above the usual range used by traceroute [22]. Scamper also implements TCP methods that vary the flow-id by changing the source or destination port, depending on the user's choice.

Alias resolution: scamper implements four techniques for inferring which IP addresses observed in the Internet topology are aliases. First, it implements Mercator probing [23] which infers aliases when a common source IP address is observed in ICMP port unreachable responses to probes sent to different destination IP addresses. Second, it implements Ally probing [24] which infers aliases by observing a sequence of increasing IP-ID values in response to probes interleaved to two different targets. Third, it implements RadarGun probing [25] where all candidates are tested simultaneously and aliases are then inferred by observing different IP addresses with the same IP-ID velocity. Finally, it implements a prefix scan method which infers a router's outgoing interface by finding an alias in the same subnet as the next interface in the forward path. As with the traceroute and ping implementations, scamper supports UDP, ICMP, and TCP probe methods. It also supports sending TTL-limited probes with a specific 5-tuple of values to solicit ICMP time exceeded messages from routers in a path; the 5-tuple can be obtained from the data recorded by scamper with traceroute data. This is useful for mapping router-level topologies when operators firewall probes directed at their routers, or do not announce prefixes used to number router interfaces.

Sting: scamper implements Savage's [15] TCP-based algorithm to infer one-way loss by making use of algorithms used by TCP receivers when they receive out-of-sequence packets. The technique is challenging to implement because a firewall rule must be inserted to prevent the host's operating system from interfering in the measurement by sending a TCP reset in response to a packet it does not expect. There is no standardised method across operating systems for an application to request particular packets be ignored. The original implementation of Sting no longer runs on a modern operating system due to the firewall interfaces changing substantially in the past ten years.

TBIT: scamper implements two of the techniques described in [16]: measurement of behaviour in response to an ICMP packet too big message, and measurement of behaviour in response to ECN negotiation and notification. As with Sting, a firewall rule is required with each measurement to prevent the host operating system from interfering. These techniques are well suited to being implemented in scamper because the probes are not time critical and fit with scamper's method of probing at a constant rate defined in PPS. However, sometimes bursts of packets are required, such as when ramping up a TCP connection through slow start so that the server response to a dropped packet can be measured. We are investigating methods to support parallelised measurement of this class of measurement.

5. EVALUATION OF SCALABILITY

This section demonstrates the performance of scamper measured by memory and CPU usage when run with different PPS rates on modest hardware. In particular, we explore the impact of increased parallelism on performance. We test performance using scamper's implementation of Paris traceroute with UDP probes [12]. Our experiment uses traceroute in the style of macroscopic Internet topology discovery [5]; traceroutes are launched to a randomly generated set of destination Internet addresses. This experiment tests multiple dimensions of scamper. Most traceroute measurements to randomly selected addresses are long-lived because most destinations are unresponsive to probes, requiring scamper to use memory to store information about tasks in progress. Even though most destinations are unresponsive, most probes are responded to by intermediate routers that send time exceeded messages. This requires scamper to efficiently use the CPU to receive and decode responses, determine the appropriate task that requires the response, store the response, and then take an appropriate action.

Our probing host is a Pentium 3 800Mhz with 128MB of RAM and a 100Mbps Ethernet interface, running FreeBSD 8.0. We compiled scamper with gcc's default settings on FreeBSD to build with compiler optimisations at level two. We instrumented scamper using the getrusage system call, recording the total amount of user and system CPU time consumed, as well as the maximum resident set size (RSS) which defines the maximum amount of RAM used by a process. We also recorded the percentage of CPU consumed by scamper at five second intervals because scamper is likely to be idle for a fixed amount of time towards the end of its workload while tasks timeout due to three consecutive unresponsive hops. We tested scamper at rates between 100 and 1000 PPS, in random order. For each probe rate, we used

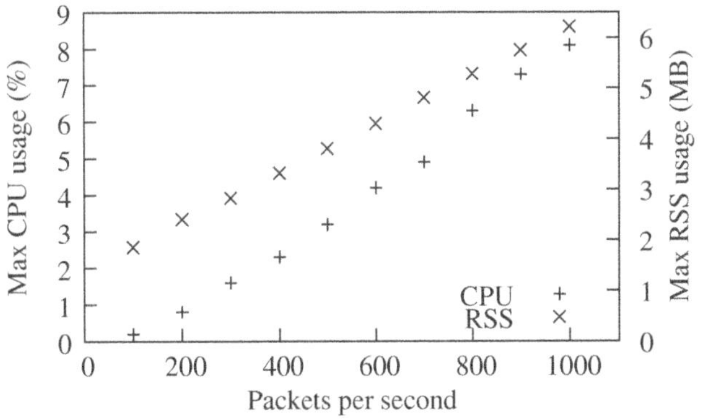

Figure 2: Maximum CPU and RSS usage observed for different packets per second rates. With traceroute, scamper's CPU and memory requirements grow linearly with probing speed, but neither requires significant computing resources.

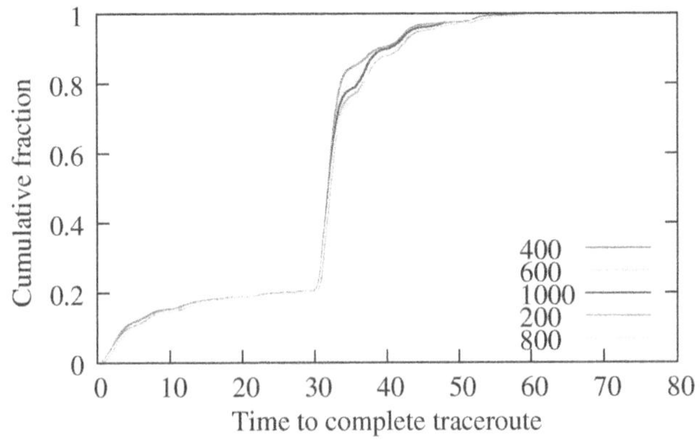

Figure 3: Time required to complete tasks at different PPS rates. The time elapsed for each traceroute is almost identical. The separation at 32 seconds is caused by some tasks waiting an additional timeout.

the same list of 10,000 randomly selected IP addresses from prefixes observed at Route Views [26]. We did not probe beyond 1000 PPS because of measurement etiquette considerations, as most probes in this experiment solicit a response from an intermediate router. The machine is otherwise idle.

CPU consumption: All of our tests consumed nearly the same total amount of CPU time regardless of PPS rate, between 25.3 seconds and 26.9 seconds. This can be explained by the use of efficient data structures that scale in $O(logn)$ and sharing sockets amongst tasks so that only a few sockets need to be monitored. The total CPU time consumed is greatest for the tests with the lowest PPS rates, because the scamper process accounts for more wall and therefore system CPU time. Figure 2 plots the maximum CPU usage observed for scamper when configured with different PPS rates. CPU requirements grow linearly with probing speed. This experiment is well within system capabilities of our Pentium 3 800Mhz, requiring 8.1% of the CPU at peak when probing at 1000pps.

Memory consumption: In order to meet a specified PPS rate, scamper adds new tasks as necessary, each requiring additional memory for maintaining state. Figure 2 also plots the maximum RSS reported by the operating system for each test. At 100pps, scamper requires 1.9MB at peak, and memory requirements grow linearly to 6.2MB at 1000pps. The memory and CPU requirements to run scamper are modest.

Effect on data collected: Overall, summary statistics for the data collected are almost identical for each PPS rate; 5.2% of destination were reachable, 10.0% received an ICMP destination unreachable code, 5.9% halted because of an apparent forwarding loop, and 78.9% halted after three consecutive unresponsive hops. In addition, the number of packets sent for all data sets is between 232k and 234k, and the number of IP-level links is between 29.2k and 29.3k. Figure 3 plots the time required to complete each traceroute for selected PPS values; the lines for other PPS rates fall between the PPS values that are plotted. For this workload, the distribution of time required to complete task is also almost identical for all PPS rates; however, 10% of tasks take up to five seconds more to complete in some experiments – the time that traceroute waits before timing out and sending another probe. There is no correlation between the probing rate and these variations; our experience with experiments at other times leads us to believe that the differences are due to network conditions at the time of this sample.

6. USING SCAMPER

As described in Section 3, scamper provides the ability to be run as a daemon and then controlled using a Unix domain socket or a TCP socket bound to the loop-back interface. As a simple example, consider a researcher who wishes to dynamically collect data about router-level connectivity available towards a set of destinations. To do so, the researcher requires the ability to collect the interface graph using MDA traceroute, determine the utility of probing each interface with TCP, ICMP, and UDP probes with ping to determine which probe types are able to solicit responses with incrementing IP-ID values, and then the ability to collapse the graph using an alias resolution technique such as RadarGun. The driver program the researcher would write to support this collection follows from the data requirements.

Briefly, the driver is responsible for remembering the list of targets to probe with MDA traceroute, the list of interfaces to probe with ping, and the utility of each ping method for soliciting an incrementing IP-ID so that repeated ping measurements are unnecessary. While there are targets to probe, the driver communicates to scamper the measurement tasks for it to traceroute and ping. As each measurement completes, scamper sends the results back to the driver across the control socket. The data arrives in a binary form, so to decode it the driver could use a socketpair, writing the binary data in one end and then reading the decoded measurements from the other using the provided API for doing so. At the same time, the driver can record the binary data to disk to archive the raw data for later use. When the list of targets to probe has become empty and all results are back from scamper, the final step is to provide scamper with a RadarGun probing specification containing the interfaces to probe paired with the appropriate probe method it should use, be it ICMP, UDP, or TCP. When the data collection is complete, the final step required is process the data collected to infer which interfaces are aliases, and then produce the router-level graph from it.

7. EXPERIENCES

Identifying IPv6 network problems in the dual-stack world: the first use of scamper was a 2004 study that compared the forward paths of IPv4 and IPv6 addresses believed to belong to the same host [17]. The goal was to use the data to find IPv6 paths that performed poorly compared to their IPv4 counterpart, and to provide operators with suggestions on where IPv6 routing could be improved. The work used scamper's one-shot measurement functionality; a list of IPv4 and IPv6 addresses were provided to scamper which then probed addresses in parallel until the list was completed. The main findings of this work were (1) only a small proportion of targets have a much larger delay with IPv6 than with IPv4, and (2) the impact of IPv6 tunnels, inferred by changes in Path-MTU, depends heavily on the upstream connectivity of the vantage point. With the IANA pool of remaining IPv4 addresses rapidly running out, it is important that the worst of the indirect IPv6 routes be identified and mechanisms created to make operators aware of them. Future work will look into automating data collection and procedures to communicate problems to operators.

CAIDA's macroscopic Internet topology project: scamper is used in CAIDA's macroscopic Internet topology discovery project to collect forward-IP path data on a continuous basis, beginning in September 2007. As of August 2010, there are 48 vantage points distributed across the globe, divided into three teams. Members of each team collectively probe a randomly generated address in all /24 prefixes routed on the Internet. Work is coordinated amongst vantage points using the Marinda tuple-space system [9]. An external measurement process monitors scamper's progress; when a unit of work is complete, a new set of random IP addresses is written to a file and passed to scamper using its control socket. Scamper is configured to probe at 100pps; a team of 12 vantage points requires approximately two and a half days to probe all routed /24 prefixes. The data collected is made available to researchers as the IPv4 Routed /24 Topology dataset [27]. There is substantial work to be done to translate the data into a router-level graph of the Internet using alias resolution, and the development of techniques to correctly filter AS-level links from it.

IPv6 AS-core poster: one of CAIDA's widely recognised visualisations is the IPv4 AS core poster showing the geographic connectivity and importance of ASes. In 2008, CAIDA had few vantage points with IPv6 connectivity with which to collect the raw IP topology data required, so volunteers were solicited on the NANOG mailing list. Each volunteer downloaded the scamper source code, compiled it, and then ran scamper using a supplied address list. Contributors from 53 different cities running varied operating systems supplied data, demonstrating scamper's portability and ease of volunteer use. The data was used to support a geographic comparison of the IPv4 and IPv6 AS-level graphs [28].

Traceroute probe method comparison: in 2008, we compared the utility of five different methods and found that ICMP-Paris traceroute reaches the most destinations and infers the most AS links when destinations are chosen randomly [29]. To collect the data required, we wrote a driver that connected to a running scamper process and issued a series of traceroute commands for each destination; the next method to use was chosen randomly by the driver, and it waited at least five seconds between traceroutes to any single destination. Using scamper's support for external drivers allowed us to focus on the data collection and analysis aspects of the work, rather than implementing our own complicated probing loops and algorithms.

Quantifying the pitfalls of traceroute: in 2009, researchers at Harbin Institute of Technology and UCLA examined the limitations of using traceroute data and the corresponding longest BGP prefix matches to infer AS connectivity [30]. To do so requires the ability to collect traceroutes from a vantage point where a BGP feed is also available. CAIDA's Ark topology project has three such vantage points; a fourth was created in UCLA by using scamper to collect traceroute data from their campus network where they were also able to procure a BGP feed.

8. RELATED WORK

Spring *et al.* built scriptroute with a goal of allowing implementations of measurement techniques to be portable and able to be used on a public general purpose measurement facility [6]. Both scriptroute and scamper include a portability layer so researchers can focus on the logic of their technique, and include implementations of common measurement techniques. Scriptroute provides researchers with a distributed set of machines from which to run experiments; with scamper, we focused on building a parallelised packet-prober that can be used easily in both measurement infrastructure and stand-alone contexts.

fping [31], hping [32], and nmap [33] have portable and parallelised implementations of ping, traceroute, and network security tests respectively, allowing networks to be rapidly tested. Scamper is built with the Internet researcher in mind; it provides an extensible file-format that records the detail of a measurement to provide a researcher with sound data, and provides flexibility in the control of the measurement process making it suited for use in Internet measurement infrastructure.

9. CONCLUSION

Internet researchers are faced with many challenges when building and designing experiments; overcoming technical limitations of operating systems, recording results and data in a way that allows sound analysis to take place, parallelising their implementation so it can scale to meet the size of the Internet, and finding enough vantage points to be confident their results are representative of the Internet. Scamper provides a flexible and reusable packet-probing architecture that allows researchers to focus on scientific experiments rather than building accurate and scalable instrumentation. Scamper's architecture has been shown to be useful to a community-oriented network measurement infrastructure, as it is currently used in CAIDA's Archipelago system [9]. The source code to scamper is freely available at `http://www.wand.net.nz/scamper/`.

Acknowledgements

We thank WIDE and CAIDA for funding and supporting the initial development of scamper. This work is currently supported by New Zealand Foundation for Research Science and Technology (FRST) contract UOWX0705.

10. REFERENCES

[1] David Mills. Internet delay experiments. RFC 889, December 1983.

[2] V. Paxson, J. Mahdavi, A. Adams, and M. Mathis. An architecture for large-scale Internet measurement. *IEEE Communications Magazine*, 36(8):48–54, 1998.

[3] Sunil Kalidindi and Matthew J. Zekauskas. Surveyor: An infrastructure for Internet performance measurements. In *INET'99*, San Jose, CA, June 1999.

[4] Tony McGregor and Hans-Werner Braun. Balancing cost and utility in active monitoring: The AMP example. In *INET 2000*, Yokohama, Japan, July 2000.

[5] Bradley Huffaker, Daniel Plummer, David Moore, and k claffy. Topology discovery by active probing. In *SAINT 2002*, pages 90–96, Nara City, Japan, January 2002.

[6] Neil Spring, David Wetherall, and Tom Anderson. Scriptroute: A public Internet measurement facility. In *USITS '03*, pages 225–238, Seattle, WA, March 2003.

[7] Yavul Shavitt and Eran Shir. DIMES: let the Internet measure itself. *Computer Communication Review*, 35(5):71–74, 2005.

[8] Harsha Madhyastha, Tomas Isdal, Michael Piatek, Colin Dixon, Thomas Anderson, Arvind Krishnamurthy, and Arun Venkataramani. iPlane: An information plane for distributed services. In *OSDI '06*, pages 367–380, Seattle, WA, November 2006.

[9] Young Hyun. Archipelago measurement infrastructure. `http://www.caida.org/projects/ark/`.

[10] kc claffy, Mark Crovella, Timur Friedman, Colleen Shannon, and Neil Spring. Community-oriented network measurement infrastructure (CONMI) workshop report. *ACM/SIGCOMM Computer Communication Review*, 36(2):41–48, April 2006.

[11] Van Jacobson. traceroute. `ftp://ftp.ee.lbl.gov/traceroute.tar.gz`.

[12] Brice Augustin, Xavier Cuvellier, Benjamin Orgogozo, Fabien Viger, Timur Friedman, Matthieu Latapy, Clémence Magnien, and Renata Teixeira. Avoiding traceroute anomalies with Paris traceroute. In *IMC '06*, pages 153–158, Rio de Janeiro, Brazil, October 2006.

[13] Mark Allman and Vern Paxson. A reactive measurement framework. In *PAM 2008*, pages 92–101, Cleveland, OH, April 2008.

[14] Young Hyun. rb-wartslib: ruby warts library. `http://rb-wartslib.rubyforge.org/`.

[15] Stefan Savage. Sting: a TCP-based network measurement tool. In *USITS '99*, pages 71–79, Boulder, CO, October 1999.

[16] A. Medina, M. Allman, and S. Floyd. Measuring the evolution of transport protocols in the Internet. *Computer Communication Review*, 35(2):37–52, April 2005.

[17] Kenjiro Cho, Matthew Luckie, and Bradley Huffaker. Identifying IPv6 network problems in the dual-stack world. In *ACM SIGCOMM workshop on Network Troubleshooting*, pages 283–288, Portland, OR, August 2004.

[18] Matthew Luckie, Kenjiro Cho, and Bill Owens. Inferring and debugging path MTU discovery failures. In *IMC '05*, pages 193–198, Berkeley, CA, October 2005.

[19] Benoit Donnet, Timur Friedman, and Mark Crovella. Improved algorithms for network topology discovery. In *PAM 2005*, pages 149–162, Boston, MA, March 2005.

[20] Ethan Katz-Bassett, Harsha V. Madhyastha, Vijay Kumar Adhikari, Colin Scott, Justine Sherry, Peter van Wesep, Thomas Anderson, and Arvind Krishnamurthy. Reverse traceroute. In *NSDI '10*, pages 219–234, San Jose, CA, April 2010.

[21] Brice Augustin, Timur Friedman, and Renata Teixeira. Measuring load-balanced paths in the Internet. In *IMC '07*, pages 149–160, San Diego, CA, October 2007.

[22] R-fx Networks. Advanced policy firewall (APF). `http://www.r-fx.ca/downloads/apf-0.9.6-3.tar.gz`.

[23] Ramesh Govindan and Hongsuda Tangmunarunkit. Heuristics for Internet map discovery. In *INFOCOM*, pages 1371–1380, Tel-Aviv, Israel, March 2000.

[24] N. Spring, R. Mahajan, and D. Wetherall. Measuring ISP topologies with Rocketfuel. In *SIGCOMM '02*, pages 133–145, Pittsburgh, PA, August 2002.

[25] Adam Bender, Rob Sherwood, and Neil Spring. Fixing Ally's growing pains with velocity modeling. In *IMC '08*, pages 337–342, Vouliagmeni, Greece, October 2008.

[26] University of Oregon. Route Views. `http://www.routeviews.org/`.

[27] Young Hyun, Bradley Huffaker, Dan Andersen, Emile Aben, Matthew Luckie, and kc claffy. The CAIDA IPv4 routed /24 topology dataset. `http://www.caida.org/data/active/ipv4_routed_24_topology_dataset.xml`.

[28] CAIDA. Visualizing IPv6 AS-level internet topology 2008. `http://www.caida.org/research/topology/as_core_network/ipv6.xml`.

[29] Matthew Luckie, Young Hyun, and Brad Huffaker. Traceroute probe method and forward IP path inference. In *IMC '08*, pages 311–323, Vouliagmeni, Greece, October 2008.

[30] Yu Zhang, Ricardo Oliveira, Hongli Zhang, and Lixia Zhang. Quantifying the pitfalls of traceroute in AS connectivity inference. In *PAM '10*, Zurich, Switzerland, April 2010.

[31] fping - a program to ping hosts in parallel. `http://fping.sourceforge.net/`.

[32] hping - active network security tool. `http://www.hping.org/`.

[33] Gordon Lyon. nmap. `http://nmap.org/`.

Netalyzr: Illuminating The Edge Network

Christian Kreibich
ICSI
1947 Center Street
Berkeley, CA, 94704, USA
christian@icir.org

Nicholas Weaver
ICSI
1947 Center Street
Berkeley, CA, 94704, USA
nweaver@icsi.berkeley.edu

Boris Nechaev
HIIT & Aalto University
PO Box 19800
00076 Aalto, Finland
boris.nechaev@hiit.fi

Vern Paxson
ICSI & UC Berkeley
1947 Center Street
Berkeley, CA, 94704, USA
vern@cs.berkeley.edu

ABSTRACT

In this paper we present *Netalyzr*, a network measurement and debugging service that evaluates the functionality provided by people's Internet connectivity. The design aims to prove both comprehensive in terms of the properties we measure and easy to employ and understand for users with little technical background. We structure *Netalyzr* as a signed Java applet (which users access via their Web browser) that communicates with a suite of measurement-specific servers. Traffic between the two then probes for a diverse set of network properties, including outbound port filtering, hidden in-network HTTP caches, DNS manipulations, NAT behavior, path MTU issues, IPv6 support, and access-modem buffer capacity. In addition to reporting results to the user, *Netalyzr* also forms the foundation for an extensive measurement of edge-network properties. To this end, along with describing *Netalyzr*'s architecture and system implementation, we present a detailed study of 130,000 measurement sessions that the service has recorded since we made it publicly available in June 2009.

Categories and Subject Descriptors

C.4 [**Performance of Systems**]: MEASUREMENT TECHNIQUES

General Terms

Measurement, Performance, Reliability, Security

Keywords

Network troubleshooting, network performance, network measurement, network neutrality

1. INTRODUCTION

For most Internet users, their network experience—perceived service availability, connectivity constraints, responsiveness, and reliability—is largely determined by the configuration and management of their *edge network*, i.e., the specifics of what their Internet Service Provider (ISP) gives them in terms of Internet access. While conceptually we often think of users receiving a straightforward "bit pipe" service that transports traffic transparently, in reality a myriad of factors affect the fate of their traffic.

It then comes as no surprise that this proliferation of complexity constantly leads to troubleshooting headaches for novice users and technical experts alike, leaving providers of web-based services uncertain regarding what caliber of connectivity their clients possess. Only a few tools exist to analyze even specific facets of these problems, and fewer still that people with limited technical understanding of the Internet will find usable. Similarly, the lack of such tools has resulted in the literature containing few measurement studies that characterize in a comprehensive fashion the prevalence and nature of such problems in the Internet.

In this work we seek to close this gap. We present the design, implementation, and evaluation of *Netalyzr*,[1] a publicly available service that lets any Internet user obtain a detailed analysis of the operational envelope of their Internet connectivity, serving both as a source of information for the curious as well as an extensive troubleshooting diagnostic should users find anything amiss with their network experience. *Netalyzr* tests a wide array of properties of users' Internet access, starting at the network layer, including IP address use and translation, IPv6 support, DNS resolver fidelity and security, TCP/UDP service reachability, proxying and firewalling, antivirus intervention, content-based download restrictions, content manipulation, HTTP caching prevalence and correctness, latencies, and access-link buffering.

We believe the breadth and depth of analysis *Netalyzr* provides is unique among tools available for such measurement. In addition, as of this writing we have recorded 130,000 runs of the system from 99,000 different public IP addresses, allowing us both to construct a large-scale picture of many facets of Internet edge behavior as well as to track this behavior's technological evolution over time. The measurements have found a wide range of behavior, on occasion even revealing traffic manipulation unknown to the network operators themselves. More broadly, we find chronic over-buffering of links, a significant inability to handle fragmentation, numerous incorrectly operating HTTP caches, common NXDOMAIN wildcarding, impediments to DNSSEC deployment, poor DNS performance, and deliberate manipulation of DNS results.

IMC'10, November 1–3, 2010, Melbourne, Australia.

[1] `http://netalyzr.icsi.berkeley.edu`

We begin by presenting *Netalyzr*'s architecture and implementation (§ 2) and the specifics of the different types of measurements it conducts (§ 3). We have been operating *Netalyzr* publicly and continuously since June 2009, and in § 4 report on the resulting data collection, including flash crowds, their resulting measurement biases, and our extensive calibration tests to assess the correct operation of *Netalyzr*'s test suite. In § 5 we present a detailed analysis of the resulting dataset and some consequences of our findings. We defer our main discussion of related work to § 6 in order to have the context of the details of our measurement analysis to compare against. § 7 discusses our plans for future tests and development. Finally, we summarize in § 8.

2. SYSTEM DESIGN

When designing *Netalyzr* we had to strike a balance between a tool with sufficient flexibility to conduct a wide range of measurement tests, yet with a simple enough interface that unsophisticated users would run it—giving us access to a much larger (and less biased towards "techies") end-system population than possible if the measurements required the user to install privileged software. To this end, we decided to base our approach on using a Java applet ($\approx$ 5,000 lines of code) to drive the bulk of the test communication with our servers ($\approx$ 12,000 lines of code), since *(i)* Java applets run automatically within most major web browsers, *(ii)* applets can engage in raw TCP and UDP flows to arbitrary ports (though not with altered IP headers), and, if the user approves trusting the applet, contact hosts outside the same-origin policy, *(iii)* Java applets come with intrinsic security guarantees for users (e.g., no host-level file system access allowed by default runtime policies), *(iv)* Java's fine-grained permissions model allows us to adapt gracefully if a user declines to fully trust our applet, and *(v)* no alternative technology matches this level of functionality, security, and convenience. Figure 1 shows the conceptual *Netalyzr* architecture, whose components we now discuss in turn.

Application Flow. Users initiate a test session by visiting the *Netalyzr* website and clicking **Start Analysis** on the webpage with the embedded Java test applet. Once loaded, the applet conducts a large set of measurement probes, indicating test progress to the user. When testing completes, the applet redirects to a summary page that shows the results of the tests in detail and with explanations (Figure 2). The users can later revisit a session's results via a permanent link associated with each session. We also save the session state (and server-side packet traces) for subsequent analysis.

Front- and Back-end Hosts. The *Netalyzr* system involves three distinct locations: *(i)* the user's machine running the test applet in a browser, *(ii)* the *front-end* machine responsible for dispatching users and providing DNS service, and *(iii)* multiple *back-end* machines that each hosts both a copy of the applet and a full set of test servers. All back-end machines run identical configurations and *Netalyzr* conducts all tests in a given client's session using the same back-end machine. We use Amazon's EC2 service (`http://aws.amazon.com/ec2/`) to facilitate scalability, employing 20 back-end hosts during times of peak load. Given a conservative, hard-wired maximum number of 12 parallel sessions per minute, this allows *Netalyzr* to serve up to 240 sessions per minute.[2]

Front-end Web Server. Running on the front-end machine, this server provides the main website, including a landing/dispatch page, documentation, FAQs, an example report, and access to reports from previous sessions. The front page also includes an applet that ensures that the user has Java installed and then directs the user to a randomly selected back-end server to load-balance the actual testing process. Finally, the front page rate-limits visitors to a fixed number of measurements per minute per back-end server.

[2]We limited each node to conducting 12 sessions per minute to prevent the UDP-based network bandwidth/buffer stress test from interfering with other tests.

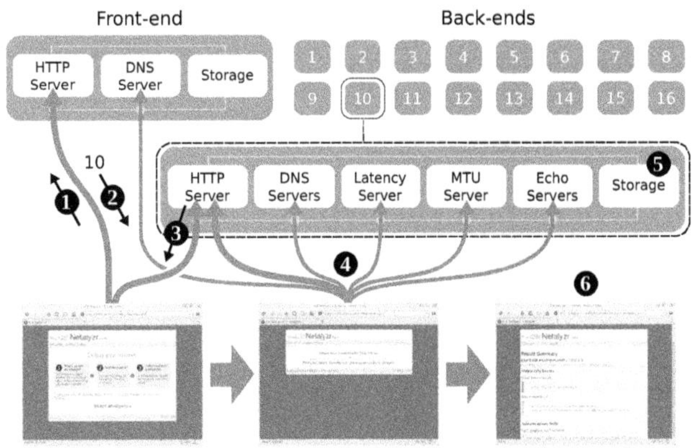

Figure 1: *Netalyzr*'s conceptual architecture. ❶ The user visits the *Netalyzr* website. ❷ When starting the test, the front-end redirects the session to a randomly selected back-end node. ❸ The browser downloads and executes the applet. ❹ The applet conducts test connections to various *Netalyzr* servers on the back-end, as well as DNS requests which are eventually received by the main *Netalyzr* DNS server on the front-end. ❺ We store the test results and raw network traffic for later analysis. ❻ *Netalyzr* presents a summary of the test results to the user.

Back-end Web Servers. The back-end web servers host the actual measurement applet (so that its probe connections to the server accord with the same-origin policy) and perform HTTP testing and overall session management. When sending the measurement applet, the server includes a set of configuration parameters, including a globally unique session ID.

Measurement Applet. The Java applet implements 38 types of tests, some with a number of subtests. We describe them in detail in Section 3. The applet conducts the test cases sequentially, but also employs multithreading to ensure that test sessions cannot stall the entire process, and to speed up some parallelizable tasks. As tests complete, the applet transmits detailed test results to the back-end server; it also sends a continuously recorded client-side transcript of the session. Note that we sign our applet with a certificate from a trusted authority so that browsers indicate a valid signature.

DNS Servers. These run on the front-end as well as the back-end machines. On the front-end, it acts as the authoritative resolver for the two subdomains employed by *Netalyzr*, `netalyzr.icsi.berkeley.edu` and `netalyzr.icir.org`. (In the following, we abbreviate these to `netalyzr.edu` and `netalyzr.org`, respectively.) On the back-ends, the server receives DNS test queries generated directly from the applet rather than through the user's DNS resolver library. The server interprets queries for specific names as commands, generating replies that encode values in A and CNAME records. For example, requesting `has_edns.netalyzr.edu` will return an A record reflecting whether the query message indicated EDNS support. The server also accepts names with arbitrary interior padding to act as a cache-busting nonce, ensuring that queries reach our server.

Echo Servers. An array of simple TCP and UDP echo servers allow us to test service-level reachability and content modifica-

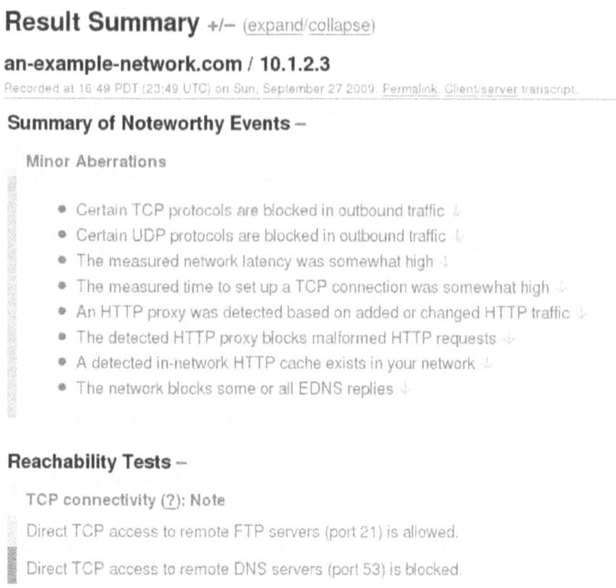

Figure 2: A partial screen capture of *Netalyzr*'s results page as seen by the user upon completion of all tests. The full report is 4–10 times this size, depending on whether the user expands the different sections.

tion of traffic on various ports. The servers mostly run on well-known ports but do not implement the associated application protocol. Rather, they use their own simple payload schema to convey timing, sequencing, and the requester's IP address and source port back to the client. An additional server can direct a DNS request to the user's public address to check if the user's NAT or gateway acts as a proxy for external DNS requests.

Bandwidth Measurement Servers. To assess bandwidth, latency, buffer sizing, and packet dynamics (loss, reordering, duplication), we employ dedicated UDP-based measurement servers. Like the echo servers, these use a custom payload schema that includes timing information, sequence numbers, instructions regarding future sending, and aggregate counters.

Path MTU Measurement Server. To measure directional path MTUs, we use a server that can capture and transmit raw packets, giving us full access to and control over all packet headers.

Storage. To maintain a complete record of server-side session activity, we record all relevant network traffic on the front- and back-end machines, except for the relatively high-volume bandwidth tests. Since Java applets do not have the ability to record packets, we cannot record such traces on the client side.

Session Management. The back-end web servers establish and maintain session state as test sessions progress, identifying sessions via RFC 4122 UUIDs. We serialize completed session state to disk on the back-end hosts and periodically archive it on the front-end where it can still be accessed by the web browser. Thus, the URL summarizing the results can be subsequently refetched when desired, which enables third-party debugging where an individual runs *Netalyzr* but others can interpret the results.[3]

[3]The "League of Legends" online game community regularly uses *Netalyzr* in this way, as part of their Internet connection troubleshooting instructions.

3. MEASUREMENTS CONDUCTED

We now describe the types of measurements *Netalyzr* conducts and the particular methodology used, beginning with layer-3 measurements and then progressing to higher layers, and obtaining user feedback.

3.1 Network-layer Information

Addressing. We obtain the client's local IP address via the Java API, and use a set of raw TCP connections and UDP flows to our echo servers to learn the client's public address. From this set of connections we can identify the presence of NAT, and if so how it renumbers addresses and ports. If across multiple flows we observe more than one public address, then we assess whether the address flipped from one to another—indicating the client changed networks while the test was in progress—or alternates back and forth. This latter implies either the use of load-balancing, or that the NAT does not attempt to associate local systems with a single consistent public address but simply assigns new flows out of a public address block as convenient. (Only 1% of sessions included an address change from any source.)

IP Fragmentation. We test for proper support of IP fragmentation (and also for MTU measurement; see below) by sending UDP payloads to our test servers. We first check for the ability to send and receive fragmented UDP datagrams. In the applet → server direction, we send a 2 KB datagram which, if received, generates a small confirmation response. Due to the prevalence of Ethernet framing, we would expect most clients to send this packet in fragments, but it will always be fragmented by the time it reaches the server. We likewise test the server → applet direction by our server transmitting (in response to a small query from the client) a 2 KB message to the client. This direction will definitely fragment, as the back-end nodes have an interface MTU of 1500 bytes.

If either of the directional tests fails, the applet performs binary search to find the maximum packet size that it can successfully send/receive unfragmented.

Path MTU. A related set of tests conducts path MTU probing. The back-end server for this test supports two modes, one for each direction. In the applet → server direction, the applet sends a large UDP datagram, resulting in fragmentation. The server monitors arriving packets and reports the IP datagram size of the entire original message (if received unfragmented) or of the original message's initial resulting fragment. This represents a lower bound on MTU in the applet → server direction, since the first fragment's size is not necessarily the full path MTU. (Such "runts" occurred in only a handful of sessions). Additionally, the applet tests for a path MTU hole in the applet → server direction by sending a 1499 B packet using the default system parameters.

In the server → applet direction, the applet conducts a binary search beginning with a request for 1500 bytes. The server responds by sending datagrams of the requested size with `DF` set. In each iteration one of three cases occurs. First, if the applet receives the `DF`-enabled response, its size is no more than the path MTU. Second, if the response exceeds the path MTU, the server processes any resulting ICMP "fragmentation required" messages and sends to the applet the attempted message size, the offending location's IP address, and the next-hop MTU conveyed in the ICMP message. Finally, if no messages arrive at the client, the applet infers that the ICMP "fragmentation required" message was not generated or did not reach the server, and thus a path MTU problem exists.

Latency, Bandwidth, and Buffering. We measure packet delivery performance in terms of round-trip latencies, directional bandwidth limits, and buffer sizing. With these, our primary goal is not to measure capacity itself (which numerous test sites already address), but as a means to measure the sizing of bottleneck buffers, which can significantly affect user-perceived latency. We do so by measuring the increase in latency between quiescence and that experienced during the bandwidth test, which in most cases will briefly saturate the path capacity in one direction and thus fill the buffer at the bottleneck.

Netalyzr conducts these measurements in two basic ways. First, early in the measurement process it starts sending in the background small packets at a rate of 5 Hz. We use this test to detect transient outages, such as those due to a poor wireless signal.

Second, it conducts an explicit latency and bandwidth test. The test begins with a 10 Hz train of 200 small UDP packets, for which the back-end's responses provide the baseline mean latency used when estimating buffer sizing effects. The test next sends a train of small UDP packets that elicit 1000-byte replies, with exponentially ramping up (over 10 seconds) the volume in slow-start fashion: for each packet received, the applet sends two more. In the second half of the interval, the applet measures the sustained rate at which it receives packets, as well as the average latency. (It also notes duplicated and reordered packets over the entire run.) After waiting 5 seconds for queues to drain, it repeats with sizes reversed, sending large packets to the server that trigger small responses. Note that most Java implementations will throttle sending rates to $\leq$ 20 Mbps, imposing an upper bound on the speed we can measure.[4]

IPv6 Adoption. To measure IPv6 connectivity we have to rely on an approximation because neither our institution nor Amazon EC2 supports IPv6. However, on JavaScript-enabled hosts the analysis page requests a small logo from `ipv6.google.com`, reachable only over IPv6. We report the outcome of this request to our HTTP server. Since we cannot prevent this test from possibly fetching a cached image, we could overcount IPv6 connectivity if the user's system earlier requested the same resource (perhaps due to a previous *Netalyzr* run from an IPv6-enabled network).

3.2 Service Reachability

To assess any restrictions the user's connectivity may impose on the types of services they can access, we attempt to connect to 25 well-known services along with a few additional ports on the back-end. For `80/tcp` and `53/udp` connectivity, the applet speaks proper HTTP and DNS, respectively. We test all other services using our echo server protocol as described in Section 2.

In addition to detecting static blocking, these probes also allow us to measure the prevalence of proxying. In the absence of a proxy, our traffic will flow unaltered and the response will include our public IP address as expected. On the other hand, protocol-specific proxies will often transform the echo servers' non-protocol-compliant responses into errors, or simply abort the connection. For HTTP and DNS, we include both compliant and non-compliant requests, which will likewise expose proxies. Further protocol content such as banners or headers often conveys additional information, such as whether a proxy resides on the end host (e.g., as part of an AV system) or in the network.

3.3 DNS Measurements

Netalyzr performs extensive measurements of DNS behavior, since DNS performance, manipulations, and subtle errors can have a major impact on a user's network experience. We implement two levels of measurement, *restricted* and *unrestricted*. The former complies with Java's default same-origin policy, which for most JVMs allows the lookup of arbitrary names but only ever returns the IP address of the origin server, or throws an exception if the result is not the origin server's address, while the latter (which runs if the user trusts the applet) can look up arbitrary names, allowing us to conduct much more comprehensive testing. Also, our DNS authority server interprets requests for specific names as commands telling it what sort of response to generate. We encode Boolean results by returning distinct IP addresses (or hostnames) to represent *true* and *false*, with *true* corresponding to the origin server's address. For brevity in the following discussion, we abbreviate fully qualified hostnames that we actually look up by only referring to the part of the name relevant for a given test. The actual names also have embedded in them the back-end node number. When we employ a nonce value to ensure cache penetration, we refer using "*nonce*" in the name.

Glue Policy. One important but subtle aspect of the DNS resolution process concerns the acceptance and promotion of response data in the Authoritative or Additional records of a response, commonly referred to as *"glue"* records. Acceptance of such records can boost performance by avoiding future lookups, but also risks cache poisoning attacks [5]. Assessing the acceptance of these records is commonly referred to as "bailiwick checking," but the guidelines on the procedure allow latitude in how to conduct it [10]. *Netalyzr* leverages glue acceptance to enable tests of the DNS resolver itself.

We first check acceptance of arbitrary A records in the Additional section by sending lookups of special names (made distinct with nonces) that return particular additional A records. We then look up those additional names directly to see whether the resolver issues new queries for the names (which would return *false* when those names are queried directly) or answers them from its cache (returning *true*), indicating that the resolver accepted the glue. We check for arbitrary glue records as well as for those that indicate nameservers. We then likewise check for caching of Authority A records. Finally, we check whether the server will automatically follow CNAME aliases by returning one value for the alias in an Additional record, but a different value for any query for the alias made directly to our server.

DNS Server Identification and Properties. We next probe more general DNS properties, including resolver identity, IPv6 support, `0x20` support [7], respect for short TTLs, port randomization for DNS requests, and whether the user's NAT, if present, acts as a DNS proxy on its external IP address.

When able to conduct unrestricted DNS measurements, we identify the resolver's IP address (as seen by our server) by returning it in an A record in response to a query for `server.`*`nonce`*`.netalyzr.edu`. This represents the address of the final server sending the request, not necessarily the one the client uses to generate the request. During our beta-testing we changed the applet code to conduct this query multiple times because we observed that some hosts will shift between DNS resolvers, and some DNS resolvers actually operate as clusters.

We test IPv6 AAAA support by resolving `ipv6_set.`*`nonce`*. This test is slightly tricky because the resolver will often first request an A record for the name prior to requesting a AAAA record. Thus, the back-end server remembers whether it saw a AAAA record and returns *true/false* indicating if it did in response to a *follow-on* query that our client makes.

Queries for the name `0x20` return *true* if the capitalization in a mix-cased request retains the original mix of casing.

If the DNS resolver accepts glue records for nameservers (NS responses in Authority or Additional), we leverage this to check whether the resolver respects short TTLs. Responses to the name `ttl0` or `ttl1` place a glue record for `return_false` in the

[4] This is the only significant performance limitation we faced using Java compared with other programming languages.

Authoritative section with a TTL of 0 or 1 seconds, respectively. A subsequent fetch of `return_false` reveals whether the short TTLs were respected. (We can't simply use A records for this test because both the browser and end host may cache these records independently.)

We also use lookups of `glue_ns`.*nonce* to measure request latency. If the DNS resolver accepts glue records, it then also looks up `return_false`.*nonce* to check the latency for a cached lookup. We repeat this process ten times and report the mean value to the server, and also validate that `return_false`.*nonce* was fetched from the resolver's cache rather than generating a new lookup.

Finally, we test DNS port randomization. For unrestricted measurements, we perform queries for `port`.*nonce*, which the server answers by encoding in an A record the source port of the UDP datagram that delivered the request. For restricted measurements, the applet sends several queries for `dns_rand_set` and then checks the result using a follow-on query that returns *true* if the ports seen by our DNS server appeared non-monotone.

EDNS, DNSSEC, and actual DNS MTU. DNS resolvers can advertise the ability to receive large responses using EDNS [25], though they might not actually be capable of doing so. For example, some firewalls will not pass IP fragments, creating a de-facto DNS MTU of 1478 bytes for Ethernet framing. Other firewall devices may block all DNS replies greater than 512 bytes under the out-of-date assumption that DNS replies cannot be larger. While today small replies predominate, a lack of support for large replies poses a significant concern for DNSSEC deployment.

We measure the prevalence of this limitation by issuing lookups (*i*) to determine whether requests arrive indicating EDNS support, (*ii*) to measure the DNS MTU (for unrestricted measurements), and (*iii*) to check whether the resolver requests DNSSEC records. As usual, the client returns the results for these via follow-on lookup requests.

That a DNS resolver advertises (via EDNS) the ability to receive large responses does not guarantee that it can actually do so. We test its ability by requesting names `edns_medium` and `edns_large`, padded to 1300 and 1700 bytes, respectively. (We pad the replies to those sizes by adding Additional CNAME records that are removed by the user's DNS resolver before being returned to the client, so that this test only uses large packets on the path between our DNS authority and the DNS resolver.) Their arrival at the client indicates the resolver can indeed receive larger DNS replies. Later releases of the client also then employ binary search to determine the actual maximum supported by the resolver (whether or not it advertises EDNS).

NXDOMAIN Wildcarding. Some DNS operators configure their resolvers to perform "NXDOMAIN wildcarding", where they rewrite hostname lookups that fail with a "no such domain" error to instead return an A record for the IP address of a web server. The presumption of such blanket rewriting is that the original lookup reflected web surfing, and therefore returning the impostor address will lead to the subsequent HTTP traffic coming to the operator's web server, which then typically offers suggestions related to the presumed intended name. Such rewriting—often motivated by selling advertisements on the landing page—corrupts the web browsers' URL auto-complete features, and, worse, breaks protocol semantics for any non-HTTP application looking a hostname.

If unrestricted, the applet checks for this behavior by querying for a series of names in our own domain namespace, and which do not exist. We first look up `www`.*nonce*.`com`. If this yields an IP address, we have detected NXDOMAIN wildcarding, and proceed to probe the behavior in more detail, including simple transpositions (`www.yahoo.cmo`), other top-level domains (`www`.*nonce*.`org`), non-web domains (`fubar`.*nonce*.`com`), and a domain internal to our site (`nxdomain.netalyzr.edu`). The applet also attempts to contact the host returned for `www`.*nonce*.`com` on `80/tcp` to obtain the imposed web content, which we log.

DNS proxies, NATs, and Firewalls. Another set of DNS problems arise not due to ISP interference but misconfigured or misguided NATs and firewalls. If the applet operates unrestrictedly, it conducts the following tests to probe for these behaviors. First, it measures DNS awareness and proxying. Our servers answer requests for `entropy.netalyzr.edu` with a CNAME encoding the response's parameters, including the public address, UDP port, DNS transaction ID, and presence of `0x20` encoding. The applet sends such DNS requests directly to the back-end server, bypassing the configured resolver. If it observes any change in the response (e.g., a different transaction ID or public address), then we have found in-path DNS proxying. The applet makes another request directly to the back-end server, now with deliberately invalid format, to which our server generates a similarly broken reply. If blocked, we have detected a DNS-aware middlebox that prohibits non-DNS traffic on `53/udp`.

During beta-testing we added a series of tests for the presence of DNS proxies in NAT devices. NATs often include such a proxy, returning via DHCP its local address to clients as the DNS resolver location if the NAT has not yet itself acquired an external DNS resolver.[5] Upon detecting the presence of a NAT, the applet assumes the gateway's local address is the *a.b.c.*`1` address in the same `/24` as the local IP address and sends it a query for `entropy.netalyzr.edu`. Any reply indicates with high probability that the NAT implements a DNS proxy. In addition, we can observe to where it forwards the request based on the client IP address seen by our server.

During our beta-testing we became aware of the possibility that some in-gateway DNS resolvers act as open relays *for the outside* (i.e., for queries coming from external sources), enabling amplification attacks [19] and other mischief. We thus added a test in which the the applet instructs the back-end measurement server to send a UDP datagram containing a DNS request for `entropy.netalyzr.edu` to the public IP address of the client to see if it elicits a resulting response at our DNS server.

Name Lookup Test. Finally, if unrestricted the applet looks up a list of 70+ common names, including major search engines, advertisement providers, financial institutions, email providers, and e-commerce sites. It uploads the results to our server, which then performs reverse lookups on the resulting IP addresses to check the forward lookups for consistency. This testing unearthed numerous aberrations, as discussed below.

3.4 HTTP Proxying and Caching

For analyzing HTTP behavior, the applet employs two different methods: using Java's *high-level API*, or its *low-level TCP sockets* (for which we implement our own HTTP logic). The first allows us to assess behavior imposed on the user by their browser (such as proxy settings), while the latter reflects behavior imposed by their access connectivity. (For the latter we take care to achieve the same HTTP "personality" as the browser by having our server mirror the browser's HTTP request headers to the applet so it can emulate them in subsequent low-level requests.) In general, the applet coordinates measurement tasks with the server using URL-encoded commands that instruct the server to deliver specific kinds of content (such as cache-sensitive images), report on properties of

[5] Once the NAT obtains its external DHCP lease, it then forwards all DNS requests to the remote resolver.

the request (e.g., specific header values), and establish and store session state.

HTTP Proxy Detection. We detect HTTP proxy configuration settings by monitoring request and result headers, as well as the server-perceived client address of a test connection. Differences when using the high-level API versus the socket API indicate the presence of a configured proxy. We first send a low-level message with specific headers to the web server. The server mirrors the headers back to the applet, allowing the applet to conduct a comparison. Added, deleted, or modified headers flag the presence of an in-path proxy. To improve the detectability of such proxies, we use eccentric capitalization of header names (e.g. `User-AgEnt`) and observe whether these arrive with the same casing. We observe that some proxies regenerate headers, which will change the case of any header generated even if the value is unchanged. A second test relies on sending an invalid request method (as opposed to `GET` or `POST`). This can confuse proxies and cause them to terminate the connection. A final test sets the `Host` request header to `www.google.com` instead of *Netalyzr*'s domain. Some proxies use this header's value to direct the outgoing connection [12], which the applet detects by monitoring for unexpected content.

Caching policies, Content Transcoding, and File-type Blocking. We next test for in-network HTTP caching. For this testing, our server provides two test images of identical size (67 KB) and dimensions (512·512 pixels), but each the color-inverse of the other. Consecutive requests for the image result in alternating images returned to the applet. We can thus reliably infer when the applet receives a cached image based on the unchanged contents (or an HTTP 304 status code, "Not Modified"). We conduct four such request pairs, varying the cacheability of the images via various request and response headers, and including a unique identifier in each request URL to ensure each session starts uncached.

The applet can also identify image transcoding or blocking by comparing the received image's size to the expected one.

Finally, we test for content-based filtering. The applet downloads (*i*) an innocuous Windows PE executable (notepad.exe), (*ii*) a small MP3 file, (*iii*) a bencoded BitTorrent download file (for a Linux distribution's DVD image), and (*iv*) the EICAR test "virus",[6] a benign file that AV vendors recognize as malicious for testing purposes.

3.5 User Feedback

Because we cannot readily measure the physical context in which the user runs *Netalyzr*, we include a small, optional questionnaire in the results page. Some 19% of the users provided feedback. Of those, 56% reported using a wired rather than a wireless network; 16% reported running *Netalyzr* at work, 79% from home, 2% on public networks, and 2% on "other" networks.

3.6 Intentional Omissions

We considered several tests for inclusion but in the end decided not to do so, for three main reasons.

First, some tests can result in potentially destructive or abusive effects on network infrastructure, particularly if run frequently or by multiple users. In this regard we decided against tests to measure the NAT's connection table size (which could disrupt unrelated network connections purged from the table), fingerprint NAT and access devices by connecting to internal administration interfaces (which might expose sensitive information), general scanning either locally or remotely, and sustained high-bandwidth tests (for detecting BitTorrent throttling or other differential traffic management, for which alternative, bandwidth-intensive tests exist [9]).

[6]`http://www.eicar.org/anti_virus_test_file.htm`

Second, some tests can inflict potential long-term side-effects on the users themselves. These could occur for technical reasons (e.g., we contribute towards possible upload/download volume caps) or legal/political ones (e.g., tests that attempt to determine whether access to certain sites suffer from censorship).

Finally, we do not store per-user HTTP tracking cookies in the user's browsers, since we do not aim to collect mobility profiles. We do however employ user-invariant HTTP cookies to test for modifications and to manage state machines in our testsuite.

4. DATA COLLECTION

We began running *Netalyzr* publicly in June 2009 and have kept it available continuously. We initially offered the service as a "beta" release (termed BETA), and for the most part did not change the operational codebase until January 2010, when we rolled out a substantial set of adjustments and additional tests (RELEASE). These comprise about 58% and 42% of the measurements, respectively. Unless otherwise specified, discussion refers to the combination of both datasets.

Website Operation. To date we have collected 130,436 sessions from 99,513 public IP addresses. The peak rate of data acquisition occurred during the June roll-out, with a maximum of 1,452 sessions in one hour. This spike resulted from mention of our service on several web sites. A similar but smaller spike occurred during the January relaunch, resulting in a peak load of 373 sessions in one hour.

Calibration. We emphasize the importance of capturing subtle flaws in the data and uncovering inconsistencies that would otherwise skew the analysis results or deflate the scientific value of the data. Accordingly, we undertook extensive calibration of the measurement results to build up confidence in the coherence and meaningfulness of our data. A particular challenge in realizing *Netalyzr* has been that it must operate correctly in the presence of a wide range of failure modes. While we put extensive effort into anticipating these problems during development, subsequent calibration served as a key technique to validate our assumptions and learn how the tests actually work on a large scale. In addition, it proved highly beneficial to employ someone for this task who was not involved in developing the tests (coauthor Nechaev), as doing so avoided incorporating numerous assumptions implicitly present in the code.

We based our calibration efforts on the BETA dataset, using it to identify and remedy sources of errors before beginning the RELEASE data collection. To do so, we assessed data-consistency individually for each of the tests mentioned in § 3. We emphasized finding missing or ambiguous values in test results, checking value ranges, investigating outliers, confirming that each test's set of result variables exhibited consistency (e.g., examining that mutual exclusiveness was honored, or that fractions added up to a correct total), ensuring that particular variable values complied with corresponding preconditions (e.g., availability of raw UDP capability reliably enabling certain DNS tests), and searching for systematic errors in the data.

To our relief, this process did not uncover any major flaws in the codebase or the data. The most common problems we uncovered were ambiguity (for example, in distinguishing silent test failures from cases when a test did not execute at all) and inaccuracies in the process of importing the data into our session database. The RELEASE codebase only differs from BETA in the presence of more unambiguous and extensive result reporting (and the addition of new tests).

Figure 3: Global locations of *Netalyzr* runs.

Identified Measurement Biases. A disadvantage of website-driven data collection is vulnerability to sudden referral surges from specific websites—in particular if these entail a technologically biased user population that can skew our dataset. In addition, our Java runtime requirement could discourage non-technical users whose systems do not have the runtime installed by default. It also precludes the use of *Netalyzr* on many smartphone platforms. We now analyze the extent to which our dataset contains such bias.

The five sites referring the most users to *Netalyzr* are: stumbleupon.com (30%), lifehacker.com (11%), slashdot.org (10%), google.com (7%), and heise.de (6%). The context of these referrals affects the number of sessions we record for various ISPs. For example, most users arriving from slashdot.org did so in the context of an article on alleged misbehavior by Comcast's DNS servers, likely contributing to making their customers the biggest share of our users (10.3% of our sessions originate from Comcast's IP address ranges). Coverage in Germany via heise.de likely drove visits from customers of Deutsche Telekom, accounting for 2.4% of the sessions. We show a summary of the dominant ISPs in our dataset in Table 3 below.

The technical nature of our service introduced a "geek bias" in our dataset, which we can partially assess by using the `User-Agent` HTTP request headers of our users to infer browser type and operating system. Here we compare against published "typical" numbers [26, 27], which we give in parentheses. 37.4% (90%) of our users ran Windows, 7.9% (1.0%) used Linux, and 13.8% (5.9%) used MacOS. We find Firefox over-represented with 59.9% (28.3%) of sessions, followed by 18.7% (59.2%) for Internet Explorer, 16.9% (4.5%) for Safari, and 2.9% (1.7%) for Opera. This bias also extends to the choice of DNS resolver, with 12% of users selecting OpenDNS as their DNS provider.

While such bias is undesirable, it can be difficult to avoid in a study that requires user participation. We can at least ameliorate distortions from it because we can identify its presence. Its primary effect concerns our characterizations across ISPs, where we endeavor to normalize accordingly, as discussed below. We also note that technically savvy users may be more likely to select ISPs with fewer connectivity deficiencies, which would mean the prevalence of problems we observe may reflect underestimates.

5. DATA ANALYSIS

We now turn to an assessment of the data gathered from *Netalyzr* measurements to date. In our discussion we follow the presentation of the different types of tests above, beginning with layer 3 measurements and then progressing to general service reachability and specifics regarding DNS and HTTP behavior.

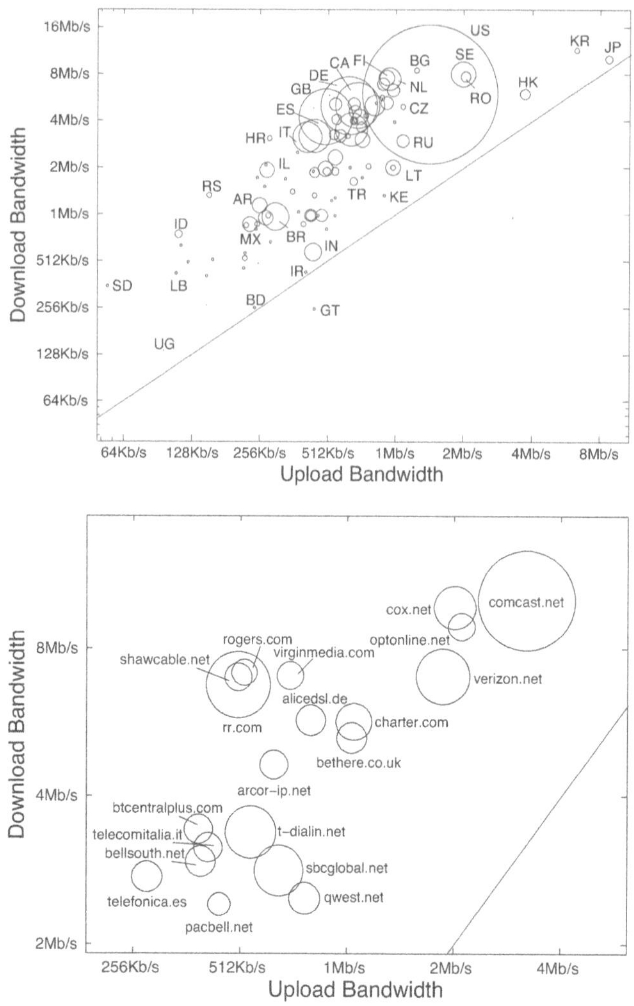

Figure 4: Average up/downstream bandwidths for countries with ≥ 10 sessions (top) and the 20 most prevalent ISPs (bottom). Circle areas are proportional to prevalence in the dataset; diagonals mark symmetric up/download capacity.

5.1 ISP and Geographic Diversity

We estimate the ISP and location of *Netalyzr* users by inspecting reverse (PTR) lookups of their public IP address, if available; or else the final Start-of-Authority record in the DNS when attempting the PTR lookup. We found these results available for 96% of our sessions.

To extract a meaningful organizational name, we started with a database of "effective TLDs," i.e., domains for which the parent is a broad, undifferentiated domain such as `gouv.fr` [17], to identify the relevant name preceding these TLDs. Given this approach, our dataset consists of sessions from 6,884 organizations (see Table 3 below for the 15 most frequent) across 186 countries, as shown in Figure 3. Activity however was dominated by users in the USA (46.1%), the EU (31.7%, with Germany accounting for 8.8% and Great Britain for 8.0%), and Canada (5.3%). 11 countries contributed sessions from more than 1,000 addresses, 50 from more than 100, and 101 from more than 10.

5.2 Network-Layer Information

Network Address Translation. Unsurprisingly, we find NATs very prevalent among *Netalyzr* users (90% of all sessions). 79% of these sessions used the `192.168/16` range, 15% used `10/8`, and 4% used `172.16/12`. 2% of the address-translated sessions employed some form of non-private address. We did not discern any particular pattern in these sessions or their addresses; some were quite bizarre.

Port sequencing behavior. Of 57,510 sessions examined, 30% exhibit port renumbering, where the NAT does not preserve the TCP source port number for connections. Of these, 8.3% appear random (using a Wald-Wolfowitz test with sequence threshold 4), while 90% renumber monotonically, most in a strictly incremental fashion. However, some exhibit jumps of varying size. Identifying the causes of these would then enable us to estimate the level of multiplexing apparently present in the user's access link.

IPv6. We found IPv6 support to be rare but non-negligible: 4.8% of sessions fetched the logo from `ipv6.google.com`. This represents an upper bound due to possible caching effects (as well as "geek bias").

Fragmentation. Overall, we find that fragmentation is not as reliable as desired [14, 23]. In the RELEASE we found 8% of the sessions unable to send 2 KB UDP packets, and likewise 8% unable to receive them.

We also found that 3% of the sessions which *could* send 2 KB packets could *not* send 1500 B packets. We find that 87% of these sessions come from Linux systems, strongly suggesting the likely cause to be Linux's arguably incorrect application of Path MTU discovery to UDP traffic. Java does not appear to retransmit in the face of ICMP feedback, instead raising an exception which *Netalyzr* reports as a failure.

From our server to the client, 79% of the sessions exhibited a path MTU of 1500 B, followed by 1492 B (16%) which suggests a prevalence of PPP over Ethernet (PPPoE). We also observe small clusters at 1480 B, 1476 B, 1460 B, and 1458 B, but these are rare. Only 2% reported an MTU less than 1450 bytes.

For sessions with an MTU $<$ 1500 B, only 59% had a path that successfully sent a proper "fragmentation required" ICMP message back to our server, reinforcing that systems should avoid PMTU for UDP, and for TCP should provide robustness in the presence of MTU black holes [16].

Latency and Bandwidth. Figure 4 illustrates the balance of upstream vs. downstream capacities for countries and ISPs, while Figure 5 shows the distribution of download bandwidths for the three most prominent ISPs in our dataset: Comcast, RoadRunner, and Verizon. Two years after the study by Dischinger et al. [8] our results still partially match theirs, particularly for RoadRunner.

From the most aggregated perspective, we observed an average download bandwidth of 6.7 Mbps and, for upload, 2.7 Mbps. We find far more symmetric bandwidths for sessions that users self-reported as at work (10 Mbps/8.1 Mbps), and reported home connections exhibited far more asymmetry and lower bandwidth (6.2 Mbps/1.6 Mbps). Public networks exhibited less download bandwidth but more symmetry (3.5 Mbps/2.3 Mbps).

We saw less variation in the aggregate perspective for quiescent latency. Sessions reported as run at work had an average latency of 110 ms, while home networks experienced 120 ms and public networks 180 ms of latency.

Network Uplink Buffering. A known problem [8] confirmed by *Netalyzr* is the substantial over-buffering present in the network, especially in end-user access devices such as DSL or DOCSIS cable modems. This can cause significant problems since a single full-rate TCP flow can fill the bottleneck buffer, which, in the absence of advanced queue management, will induce substantial latency to all traffic through the bottleneck.[7]

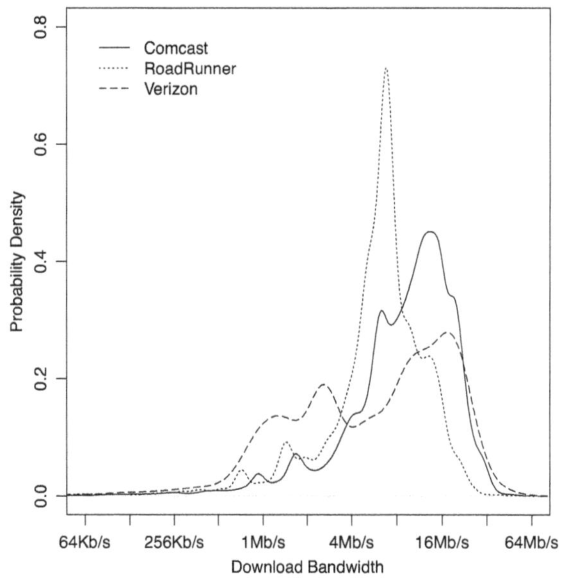

Figure 5: PDF of download bandwidths for the three most prominent ISPs in our dataset.

Netalyzr attempts to measure this by recording the amount of delay induced by the high-bandwidth burst of traffic once it exceeds the actual bandwidth obtained. We then infer the buffer capacity as equal to the sustained sending rate multiplied by the additional delay induced by this test. Since the test uses UDP, no back-off comes into play to keep the buffer from completely filling, though we note that *Netalyzr* cannot determine whether the buffer did indeed actually fill to capacity.

When plotting measured upload bandwidth vs. inferred upload buffer capacity (Figure 6, top), several features stand out. First, we note that because we keep the test short in order to not unduly load the user's link, sometimes *Netalyzr* cannot completely fill the buffer, leading to noise, which also occurs when the bandwidth is quite small (so we do not have a good "quiescence" baseline). Next, horizontal banding reflects commonly provided levels of service and/or access network characteristics (such as 802.11b network speeds).

Most strikingly, we observe frequent instances of very large buffers. Vertical bands reflect common buffer sizes, which we find fall into powers of two, particularly 128 KB or 256 KB. Even with a fast 8 Mbps uplink, such buffers can easily induce 250 ms of additional latency during file transfers, and for 1 Mbps uplinks, well over 1 sec.

We can leverage the biases in our data to partially validate these results. By examining only Comcast customers (Figure 6, bottom), we would naturally expect only one or two buffer sizes to predominate, due to more homogeneous hardware deployments—and indeed the plot shows dominant buffer sizes at 128 KB and 256 KB. In this figure, another more subtle feature stands out with the small cluster that lies along a diagonal. Its presence suggests that a small

[7] A major reason for overly large buffers is the lack of device configurability in the presence of a wide range of access-link bandwidths. For example, a DOCSIS cable modem designed to operate with an uplink between 1 and 50 Mbps might have a buffer perfectly sized for 50 Mbps operation, yet 50 times too large for a 1 Mbps uplink.

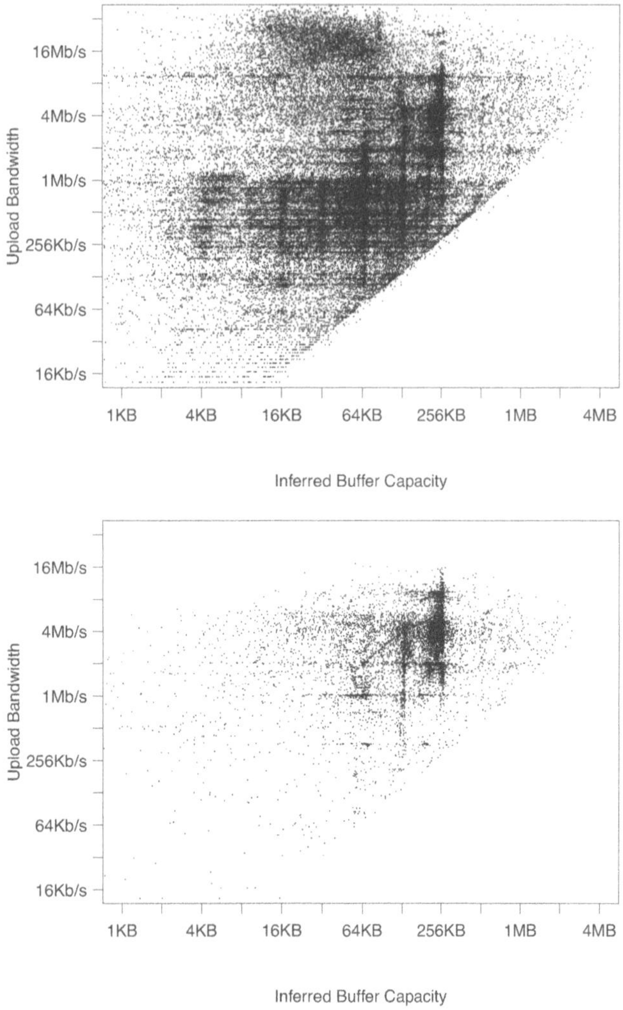

Figure 6: Inferred upload packet-buffer capacity (x-axis) vs. bandwidth (y-axis), for all sessions (top) and Comcast (bottom).

number of customers have access modems that size their buffers directly in terms of time, rather than memory.

In both plots, the scattered values above 256 KB that lack any particular power-of-two alignment suggest the possible existence of other buffering processes in effect for large UDP transfers. For example, we have observed that some of our notebook wireless connections occasionally experience larger delays during this test apparently because the notebook buffers packets at the wireless interface (perhaps due to use of ARQ) to recover from wireless congestion.

Clearly, over-buffering is endemic in access devices. Simply sizing the active buffer dynamically, considering the queue full if the head-of-line packet is more than 200 ms old, would alleviate this problem substantially. While the task of fixing millions of such devices is daunting, one could also consider implementing Remote Active Queue Management [1] elsewhere in the network in order to mitigate the effects of these large buffers.

Packet Replication, Reordering, Outages, and Corruption. The bandwidth tests also provide an opportunity to observe replication or reordering. For these tests, the bottleneck point receives 1000 B packets at up to 2x the maximum rate of the bottleneck. 1% of the uplink tests exhibited packet replication, while 16% included some reordering. For downlink tests, 2% exhibited replication and 33% included reordering. The prevalence of reordering qualitatively matches considerably older results [2]; more direct comparisons are difficult because the inter-packet spacing in our tests varies, and reordering rates fundamentally depend on this spacing.

For the RELEASE data we also check for transient outages, defined as a period losing ≥ 3 background test packets (sent at 5 Hz) in a row. We find fairly frequent outages, with 10% of sessions experiencing one or more such events (44% of these reflect only a single outage event, while 29% included ≥ 5 loss events). These bursts of packet loss are generally short, with 48% of sessions with losses having outages ≤ 1 sec. 10% of wireless sessions exhibited at least one outage, vs. only 5% for wired ones. (The wired/wireless determination is here based on user feedback, per § 3.5.)

Finally, analysis of the server-side packet traces finds no instances of TCP or IP checksum errors. We do see UDP checksum errors at an overall rate of about $1.6 \cdot 10^{-5}$, but these are heavily dominated by bursts experienced by just a few systems. 0.12% of UDP datagrams have checksumming disabled, likewise typically in packet trains from individual systems, with no obvious commonality. The presence of UDP errors but not TCP might suggest use of selective link-layer checksum schemes such as UDP Lite.

		Interference (%)		
Service	Port	Blocked	Closed	Proxied
NetBIOS	139 T	50.6	1.0	
SMB	445 T	49.8	0.9	
RPC	135 T	45.8	1.1	
SMTP	25 T	26.0	8.0	1.0
FTP	21 T	19.4	3.7	0.1
MSSQL	1434 U	11.3		
SNMP	161 T	7.1	0.2	
BitTorrent	6881 T	6.5	0.5	
AuthSMTP	587 T	6.3	0.2	0.7
SecureIMAP	585 T	5.9	0.2	
Netalyzr Echo	1947 T	5.9		
SIP	5060 T	5.5	4.6	
SecureSMTP	465 T	5.4	0.3	<0.1
PPTP Control	1723 T	5.1	5.1	<0.1
DNS	53 T	5.0	0.8	
IMAP/SSL	993 T	4.8	0.2	<0.1
OpenVPN	1194 T	4.8	0.2	
TOR	9001 T	4.7	0.2	
POP3/SSL	995 T	4.7	0.3	<0.1
IMAP	143 T	4.7	6.3	0.2
POP3	110 T	3.8	6.9	6.4
SSH	22 T	3.5	0.1	<0.1
HTTPS	443 T	2.1	0.5	<0.1
HTTP	80 T		3.6	5.3

Table 1: Reachability for services examined by *Netalyzr*. "Blocked" reflects failure to connect to the servers, "Closed" are cases where an in-path proxy or firewall terminated the established connection after the request was sent. "Proxied" indicates cases where a proxy revealed its presence through its response. Omitted values reflect zero occurrences.

5.3 Service Reachability

Table 1 summarizes the prevalence of service reachability for the application ports *Netalyzr* measures. As explained above, for TCP services we can distinguish between blocking (no successful connection), application-aware connectivity (established connection terminated when our server's reply violates the protocol), and proxying (we directly observe altered requests/responses). For

UDP services we cannot in general distinguish the second case due to the lack of explicit connection establishment.

The first four entries likely reflect ISP security policies in terms of limiting exposure to services well-known for vulnerabilities and not significantly used across the wide-area (first three) or to prevent spam. That the fraction of blocking appears low suggests that many ISPs employ other methods to thwart spam, rather than wholesale blocking of all SMTP.[8]

The prevalence of blocking and termination for FTP, however, likely arises as an artifact of NAT usage: in order to support FTP's separate control and data connections, many NATs implement FTP proxies. These presumably terminate our FTP probing when observing a protocol violation in the response from our server. A NAT's FTP proxy causes *Netalyzr* to report a "blocked" response if the proxy checks the server's response for FTP conformance before generating a SYN/ACK to the client, while it causes a "closed" response if it completes the TCP handshake with the client before terminating the connection after failing to validate the server's response format.

Somewhat surprising is the prevalence of blocking for `1434/udp`, used by the Slammer worm of 2003. Likely these blocks reflect legacy countermeasures that have remained in place for years even though Slammer no longer poses a significant threat.

The large fraction of terminated or proxied POP3 connections appears due to in-host antivirus software that attempts to relay all email requests. In particular, we can identify almost all of the proxying as due to AVG antivirus because it alters the banner in the POP3 dialog. We expect that the large number of terminated IMAP connections has a similar explanation.

We found the prevalence of terminated SIP connections surprising. Apparently a number of NATs and Firewalls are SIP-aware and take umbrage at our echo server's protocol violation. We learned that this blocking can even occur without the knowledge of the network administrators—a *Netalyzr* run at a large university flagged the blockage, which came as a surprise to the operators, who removed the restriction once we reported it.

Finally, services over TLS (particularly HTTPS, `443/tcp`) are generally unmolested in the network, as expected given the end-to-end security properties that TLS provides. Thus, clearly if one wishes to construct a network service resistant to network disruption, tunneling it over HTTPS should prove effective.

5.4 DNS Measurements

Selected DNS Server Properties. We measured several DNS server properties of interest, including glue policy, IPv6 queries, EDNS, and MTU. Regarding the first, most resolvers behave conservatively, with only 21% of sessions accepting any glue records present in the Additional field, and those only doing so for records for subdomains of the authoritative server. (The proportion is essentially the same when weighted by distinct resolvers.) Similarly, only 25% accept A records corresponding to CNAMEs contained in the reply. On the other hand, resolvers much more readily (61%) accept glue records when the glue records refer to authoritative nameservers.

We find `0x20` usage scarce amongst resolvers (2.3% of sessions). However, only 4% removed capitalizations from requests, which bodes well for `0x20`'s deployability. Similarly, only a minuscule number of sessions incorrectly cached a 0-TTL record, and none cached a 1 sec TTL record for two seconds.

We quite commonly observe requests for AAAA (IPv6) records (13% of sessions), largely due to a common Linux default to request AAAA records even if the host lacks a routable IPv6 address rather than a resolver property, as 42% of sessions with a Linux-related User-Agent requested AAAA records. (10% of non-Linux systems requested AAAAs.)

The prevalence of EDNS and DNSSEC in requests is significant but not universal, due to BIND's default behavior of requesting DNSSEC data in replies even in the absence of a configured root of trust.[9] 52% of sessions used EDNS-aware DNS resolvers, with 49% DNSSEC-enabled. Most cases where we observe an advertised MTU show the BIND default of 4096 B (94%), but some other MTUs also occur, notably 512 B (3.1%), 2048 B (1.6%) and 1280 B (0.3%).

The prevalence of DNSSEC-enabled resolvers does not mean transition to broad use of DNSSEC will prove painless, however. For EDNS sessions with an advertised MTU of $\geq$ 1800 B, 13% failed to fetch the large EDNS-enabled reply and 1.9% for the medium-sized one. This finding suggests a common failure where the DNS resolver is connected through a network that either won't carry fragmented UDP traffic or assumes that DNS replies never exceed 1500 B (since `edns_medium` is unlikely to be fragmented). Since DNSSEC replies will likely exceed 1500 B, the prevalence of this problem suggests a potentially serious deployment issue that will require changes to the resolver logic.

The RELEASE data includes a full validation of DNS MTU up to 4 KB. We find that despite not advertising a large MTU, almost all sessions (95%) used a resolver capable of receiving messages over 512 B. However, a significant number of sessions (15%) exhibited a measured DNS MTU of 1472 B (equivalent to an IP MTU of 1500 B), suggesting an inability to receive fragmented traffic. This even occurred for 11% of sessions that explicitly advertised an explicit EDNS MTU > 1472 B. This can cause unpredictable timeouts and failures if DNS replies (particularly the potentially large records involved in DNSSEC) exceed the actual 1472 B MTU.

A similar problem exists in the clients themselves, but often due to a different cause. When the client directly requests `edns_large`, `edns_medium`, and `edns_small` from the server, 14.1%/4.3%/1.3% failed, respectively. This suggests two additional difficulties: network devices assuming DNS replies do not exceed 512 B (both `edns_large` and `edns_medium` fail) or networks that do not handle EDNS at all (all three fail).[10] We find this high failure rate quite problematic, as sound DNSSEC validation requires implementation on the end host's stub resolver to achieve end-to-end security, which requires that end hosts can receive large, EDNS-enabled DNS messages.

Another concern comes from the continued lack of DNS port randomization [5]. This widely publicized vulnerability was over a year old when we first released *Netalyzr*, but 5% of sessions used monotone or fixed ports in DNS requests, However, no major ISP showed significant problems with this test.

In terms of DNS performance, it appears that DNS resolvers may constitute a bottleneck for many users. 9% of the sessions required 300 ms more time to look up a name within our domain versus the base round-trip time to our server, and 4.6% required more than 600 ms. (We can attribute up to 100 ms of the increase to the fact that our DNS server resides within our own institution, while the back-end servers are hosted at Amazon EC2's East Coast location.)

[8] Some ISPs publicly disclose that they use dynamic blocking [6].

[9] 32% of sessions exhibit BIND's default handling of glue, CNAMEs, 0x20, EDNS, and DNSSEC.

[10] The failures we observe could instead be due to heavy packet loss. However such failures should not particularly favor one type of query over another, yet we observe only 0.09% of sessions for which `edns_medium` succeeded while `edns_small` failed.

Domain	All Lookups (%) Failed	All Lookups (%) Blocked	OpenDNS (%) Failed	OpenDNS (%) Changed
www.nationwide.co.uk	2.3	<0.01	1.6	0.01
ad.doubleclick.net	1.6	1.88	1.6	1.30
www.citibank.com	1.3	0.01	0.8	0.03
windowsupdate.microsoft.com	0.8	0.02	0.5	0.01
www.microsoft.com	0.8	<0.01	0.4	0.01
mail.yahoo.com	0.7	0.02	0.4	0.17
mail.google.com	0.4	0.02	0.3	0.13
www.paypal.com	0.4	0.04	0.2	0.03
www.google.com	0.3	0.01	0.2	76.45
www.meebo.com	0.4	0.03	0.2	0.87

Table 2: Reliability of DNS lookups for 10 selected names (125,000 sessions total, 11,800 OpenDNS).

When the user's resolver accepted glue records (52% of sessions) we could directly measure the performance of DNS requests answered from the resolver's cache. Surprisingly, 11% of such sessions required over 200 ms to look up *cached* items, and 3.9% required over 500 ms. Such high latency suggests a considerable distance between the client and the resolver. For example, we found 16% of sessions that used OpenDNS required over 200 ms for cached answers compared to 9% for non-OpenDNS sessions.

NXDOMAIN Wildcarding. We find NXDOMAIN wildcarding quite prevalent among *Netalyzr* users. 29% performing this test found NXDOMAIN wildcarding for `www.`*nonce*`.com`. Even excluding users of both OpenDNS (which wildcards by default) and Comcast (which started wildcarding during the course of our measurements), 22% show NXDOMAIN wildcarding. This wildcarding will disrupt features such as Firefox's address bar, which prepends `www.` onto failed DNS lookups before defaulting to a Google search. Finally, excluding Comcast and OpenDNS users, 43% of sessions with NXDOMAIN wildcarding also showed wildcarding for non-`www` names. Wildcarding all addresses mistakenly assumes that only web browsers will generate name lookups.

DNS Proxies, NATs, and Firewalls. Many NATs and firewalls are DNS-aware. Although we find 99% able to perform direct DNS queries, 11% of these sessions show evidence of a DNS-aware network device, where a non-DNS test message destined for `53/udp` failed (but proper DNS messages succeeded). Far fewer networks contain in-path DNS proxies, with only 1.3% of DNS-capable sessions manifesting a changed DNS transaction ID.

Although most NATs don't automatically proxy DNS, most contain DNS proxies. We found 69% of the NATs would forward a DNS request to the server (with this measurement restricted to the cases where *Netalyzr* correctly guessed the gateway IP address). Of these, only 1.6% of the sessions contained their own recursive resolver, rather than forwarding the request to a different recursive resolver. Finally, although rare, the number of NATs providing open DNS resolution *externally* accessible is still significant. When queried by our server, 4.8% of the NATed sessions forwarded the query to our DNS servers. Such systems can be used both for DNS amplification attacks and to probe the ISP's resolver.

DNS Reliability of Important Names. DNS lookups can fail for a variety of reasons, including an unreliable local network, problems in the DNS resolver infrastructure, and failures in the DNS authorities or paths between the resolver and authority. Table 2 characterizes some failure modes for 10 common domain names. For general lookups, "failure" reflects a negative result or an exception returned to the applet by `InetAddress.getByName()`, or a 20 sec timeout expiring. "Blocked" denotes the return of an obviously invalid address (such as a loopback address).

Some behavior immediately stands out. First, regardless of resolver, we observe significant unreliability of DNS to the client, due to packet loss and other issues. Caching also helps, as highly popular names have a failure rate substantially less than that for less common names. For example, compare the failure rate of `www.nationwide.co.uk` to that of `mail.google.com`, for which we presume resolvers or end-hosts will have cached the latter significantly more often.

Second, we observe high reliability for the DNS authorities of the names we tested. Only 14 sessions had OpenDNS returning the SERVFAIL wildcard in response to a legitimate query. (One such session showed many names failing to resolve, obviously due to a problem with OpenDNS's resolver rather than the authority servers.)

Third, we can see the acceptance of DNS as a tool for network management and control. All but the `www.google.com` case for OpenDNS represent user or site-admin configured redirections. For domains like `mail.yahoo.com`, the common change is to return a private Internet address, most likely configured in the institution's DNS server, while blocking of `ad.doubleclick.net` commonly uses nonsense addresses (such as `0.0.0.0`), which may reflect resolution directly from the user's hosts file (as suggested on some forum discussions on blocking `ad.doubleclick.net`).

The DNS results also included two strains of maliciousness. The first concerns an ISP (Wide Open West) that commonly returned their own proxy's IP address as an answer for `www.google.com`, `search.yahoo.com`, and `www.bing.com`, but not for sites such as `mail.google.com` or `www.yahoo.com`. Deliberately invalid requests to these proxies return a reference to `phishing-warning-site.com`, a domain parked with GoDaddy. The proxy seems to have been modified between February and July 2010, as later probing revealed that it was based on Squid 2.6. For SSL-encrypted Google searches, it will forward the request to Google unmolested. We contacted Wide Open West regarding the matter but received no response. We observed similarly divergent lookup behavior for customers of sigecom.net, cavtel.net, rcn.net, fuse.net, and o1.com.

Second, in a few dozen sessions we observed malicious DNS resolvers due to malcode having reconfigured an infected user's system settings. These servers exhibit two signatures: (*i*) malicious resolution for windowsupdate.microsoft.com, which instead returns an arbitrary Google server to disable Windows Update, and (*ii*) sometimes a malicious result for ad.doubleclick.net. In these latter (less frequent) instances, these ad servers insert malicious advertisements that replace the normal ads a user sees with ones for items like "ViMax Male Enhancement" [11].

5.5 HTTP Proxying and Caching

8.4% of all sessions show evidence of HTTP proxying. Of these, 32.5% had the browser explicitly configured to use an HTTP proxy, as the server recorded a different client-side IP address only for HTTP connections made via Java's HTTP API. More interestingly, 91.2% of proxied sessions showed evidence of in-path proxies for all HTTP traffic. (These are not mutually exclusive—the overlap is explained by users that are double-proxied.) We detect such proxies by changes to headers or expected content, requests from a different IP address, or in-network caching. A proxy may announce its location through `Via` or `X-Cache-Lookup` response headers. The applet follows such clues by attempting a direct connection to such potential proxies with instructions to connect to our back-end server, which succeeded in 10.9% of proxied sessions.

We rarely observed caching of our 67 KB image (5.1% of sessions cached at least one version of it). Manual examination reveals that such caching most commonly occurred in wireless hotspots and corporate networks. Two South African ISPs used in-path caching throughout, presumably to reduce bandwidth costs and improve latency.

The infrequency of such caches perhaps represents a blessing in disguise, as they often get it wrong. A minor instance concerns the 55.1% of caches that cached the image when we specified it as weakly uncacheable (no cache-specific HTTP headers). More problematic are the 35.6% that cached the image despite strong uncacheability (use of headers such as `Cache-control: no-cache, no-store`, a fresh `Last-Modified` timestamp expiring immediately). Finally, 5.0% of these broken caches failed to cache a highly cacheable version of the image (those with `Last-Modified` well in the past and `Expires` well into the future, or with an `ETag` identifier). Considering that 42.7% of all HTTP-proxied connections did not gain the benefits of caching legitimately cacheable content, we identify considerable unrealized savings.

Network proxies seldom transcode the raw images during this test, but 0.06% of the sessions did, detected as a returned result smaller than the original length but > 10 KB. Manual examination of a few cases verified that the applet received a proper HTTP response for the image with a reduced `Content-Length` header, and thus the network did indeed change the image (presumably to save bandwidth by re-encoding the `.jpg` with a higher loss rate) rather than merely truncate the request.

In-path processes also only rarely interrupt file transfers. Only 0.7% of all sessions failed to correctly fetch the `.mp3` file and 0.9% for the `.exe`. Slightly more, 1.2%, failed to fetch the `.torrent` file, suggesting that some networks filter on file type. However, 10% filtered the EICAR test "virus", suggesting significant deployment of either in-network or host-based AV. As only 0.36% failed to fetch all four test-files, these results do not reflect proxies that block all of the tests.

5.6 ISP Profiles

Table 3 illustrates some of the policies that *Netalyzr* observed for the 15 most common ISPs. We already discussed the relative lack of SMTP blocking above. A few ISPs do not appear to filter Windows traffic; however, they might block these ports inbound, which we cannot determine since *Netalyzr* does not perform inbound scanning.

Another characteristic we see reflects early design decisions still in place today: many DSL providers initially offered PPPoE connections rather than IP over Ethernet, while DOCSIS-based cable-modems always used IP-over-Ethernet. For Verizon, only 9% of Verizon customers whose reverse name suggests FiOS (fiber to the home) manifest the PPPoE MTU, while 68% of the others do.

A final trend concerns the growth of NXDOMAIN wildcarding, especially ISPs wildcarding all names rather than just `www` names. During *Netalyzr*'s initial release, Comcast had yet to implement NXDOMAIN wildcarding, but began wildcarding during Fall 2009.

We also confirmed that the observed policies for Comcast match their stated policies. Comcast has publicly stated that they will block outbound traffic on the Windows ports, and may block outbound SMTP with dynamic techniques [6]. When they began widespread deployment of their wildcarding, they also stated that they would only wildcard `www` addresses, but we did observe the results of an early test deployment that wildcarded all addresses for a short period of time.

6. RELATED WORK

There is a substantial existing body of work on approaches for measuring various aspects of the Internet. Here we focus on those related to our study in the nature of the measurements conducted or how data collection occurred.

Network performance. Dischinger et al. studied network-level performance characteristics, including link capacities, latencies, jitter, loss, and packet queue management [8]. They used measurement packet trains similar to ours, but picked the client machines by scanning ISP address ranges for responding hosts, subsequently probing 1,894 such hosts autonomously. In 2002 Saroiu et al. studied similar access link properties as well as P2P-specific aspects of 17,000 Napster file-sharing nodes and 7,000 Gnutella peers [22]. They identified probe targets by crawling the P2P overlays, and identified a large diversity in bandwidth (only 35% of hosts exceeded an upload bandwidth of 100Kb/s, 8% exceeded 10Mbps, between 8% and 25% used dial-up modems, and at least 30% had more than 3Mb/s downstream bandwidth) and latency (the fastest 20% of hosts exhibited latencies under 70ms, the slowest 20% exceeded 280ms). Maier et al. analyzed residential broadband traffic of a major European ISP [15], finding that round-trip latencies between users and the ISP's border gateway often exceed that between the gateway and the remote destination (due to DSL interleaving), and that most of the observed DSL lines used only a small fraction of the available bandwidth. Ritacco et al. [21] developed a network testsuite that like *Netalyzr* is driven by a Java applet. Their work is intended as an exploratory study, focusing more on performance in general and wireless networks and their device populations in particular. (While numerous techniques have been developed for measuring network performance, we do not discuss these further in keeping with our main focus on ways that users have their connectivity restricted or shaped, rather than end-to-end performance.)

Network neutrality. Several studies have looked at the degree to which network operators provide different service to different types of traffic. Dischinger et al. studied 47,000 sessions conducted using a downloadable tool, finding that around 8% of the users experienced BitTorrent blocking [9]. Bin Tariq et al. devised NANO, a distributed measurement platform, to detect whether a given ISP induces degraded performance for specific classes of service [24]. They evaluate their system in Emulab, using Click configurations to synthesize "ISP" discrimination, and source synthetic traffic from PlanetLab nodes. Beverly et al. leveraged the "referral" feature of Gnutella to conduct TCP port reachability tests from 72,000 unique Gnutella clients, finding that Microsoft's network filesharing ports are frequently blocked, and that email-related ports are more than twice as likely to be blocked as other ports [3]. Reis et al. used JavaScript-based "web tripwires" to detect modifications to HTTP-borne HTML documents [20]. Of the 50,000 unique IP addresses from which users visited their test website, approximately 0.1% experienced content modifications. Nottingham provided a cache fidelity test for XMLHttpRequest implementations [18], analyzing a large variety of caching properties including HTTP header values, content validation and freshness, caching freshness, and variant treatment. NetPolice [28] measured traffic differentiation in 18 large ISPs for several popular services in terms of packet loss, using multiple end points inside a given ISP to transmit application-layer traffic to destinations using the same ISP egress points. They found clear indications of preferential treatments for different kinds of service. Finally, subsequent to *Netalyzr*'s release, Huang et al. released a network tester for smartphones to detect hidden proxies and service blocks using methodology inspired by *Netalyzr* [13].

ISP	Sessions	Country	Blocked (%) Win	Blocked (%) SMTP	Blocked (%) MSSQL	DNS Wildcarding Type	DNS Wildcarding %	PPPoE (%)	Medium
Comcast	14,765	US	99	8		www	37		Cable
RoadRunner	6,321	US				www	64		Cable
Verizon	4,341	US	7	21		www	84	33	DSL/Fiber
SBC	3,363	US	52	74					DSL
Deutsche Telekom	2,694	DE	76			all	49	55	DSL
Cox Cable	2,524	US	93	77	88	all	30		Cable
Charter Comm.	1,888	US	95	22	36	all	63		Cable
Qwest	1,502	US	18	6		all	50	69	DSL
BE Un Limited	1,439	UK		49					DSL
BellSouth	1,257	US	59	69	96			19	DSL
Telefonica	1,206	ES		7				80	DSL
Arcor	1,206	DE	32					5	DSL
Shaw Cable	1,198	US	5	59					Cable
British Telecom	1,098	UK	10					5	DSL
Alice DSL	1,080	DE	30			www	62	74	DSL
Telecom Italia	1,075	IT	8	5	13	all	63	67	DSL
Virgin Media	1,028	UK	90			www	66		Fiber
Rogers Cable	994	CA	95	79		all	77		Cable
Optimum Online	983	US	98	79		www	79		Cable
Comcast Business	847	US	93	10					Cable

Table 3: Policies detected for the top 20 ISPs. We indicate blocking when > 5% of sessions manifested outbound filtering, with WIN corresponding to Windows services (TCP 135/139/445). We infer PPPoE from path MTUs of 1492 B.

Address fidelity. Casado and Freeman investigated the reliability of using a client's IP address—as seen by a public server—in order to identify the client [4]. Their basic methodology somewhat resembles ours in that they used active web content to record and measure various connection properties, but also differs significantly with regard to the process of users running the measurements. They instrumented several websites to serve an `iframe` "web bug", leading to narrow data collection—users had to coincidentally visit those sites, and remained oblivious to the fact that measurement was occurring opportunistically. They found that 60% of the observed clients reside behind NATs, which typically translated no more than seven clients, while 15% of the clients arrived via HTTP proxies, often originating from a diverse geographical region. Finally, Maier et al. [15] found that DHCP-based address reuse is frequent, with 50% of all addresses being assigned at least twice per day.

7. FUTURE WORK

The main goal of *Netalyzr* is to provide a comprehensive suite of network functionality tests to a wide range of users. To this end, we are currently enhancing the test reports to become more accessible for non-technical users, and have partnered with websites in Germany, Poland, the UK, and the US to bring *Netalyzr* to an increasingly diverse audience.

Additionally, we are developing several additional tests we expect to deploy in the near future, including a command-line client to enable *Netalyzr*'s inclusion in large test suites, a path MTU traceroute to find the location of path MTU failures, advanced DNS probing of the DNS proxies provided by NATs, and an IPv6 test suite, including IPv6 differential latency, path MTU, traceroute, and service reachability.

8. SUMMARY

The *Netalyzr* system demonstrates the possibility of developing a browser-based tool that provides detailed diagnostics, discovery, and debugging for end-user network connectivity. Visitors who ran the *Netalyzr* applet conducted 130,000 measurement sessions from 99,000 public IP Addresses. *Netalyzr* reveals specific problems to individual users in a detailed report that enables them to understand and potentially fix the trouble, and forms the foundation for a broad, longitudinal survey of edge-network behavior. Some systemic problems revealed include difficulties with fragmentation, the unreliability of path MTU discovery, restrictions on DNSSEC deployment, legacy network blocks, frequent over-buffering of access devices, poor DNS performance for many clients, and deliberate manipulations of DNS results. We believe these results to be of significant interest to implementors and operators, and have to date been approached by several organizations with specific inquiries about our findings.

Netalyzr remains in active use and we aim to support it indefinitely as an ongoing service for illuminating edge network neutrality, security, and performance.

9. ACKNOWLEDGEMENTS

We are deeply grateful to the *Netalyzr* users for enabling this study and to our beta testers for the insightful comments and feedback. We would particularly like to thank Mark Allman, Paul Barford, Scott Bradner, John Brzozowski, Randy Bush, Niels Bakker, Richard Clayton, Chris Cowart, Keith Dawson, Adrian Dimcev, Holger Dreger, Brandon Enright, Kevin Fall, Carrie Gates, Andrei Gurtov, Mark Handley, Theodore Hong, Kelly Kane, Matthew Kogan, Keith Medcalf, Thomas Narten, Michael Ross, Chris Switzer, Wooter Wijngaards, and Richard Woundy. We thank Amazon.com for supporting our EC2 deployment. This work was supported by the National Science Foundation under grants NSF CNS-0722035, NSF-0433702, and CNS-0905631, with additional support from Google.

10. REFERENCES

[1] D. Ardelean, E. Blanton, and M. Martynov. Remote active queue management. In *NOSSDAV '08: Proceedings of the 18th International Workshop on Network and Operating Systems Support for Digital Audio and Video*, pages 21–26, New York, NY, USA, 2008. ACM.

[2] J. Bennett, C. Partridge, and N. Shectman. Packet reordering is not pathological network behavior. *IEEE/ACM Transactions on Networking (TON)*, 7:789–798, 1999.

[3] R. Beverly, S. Bauer, and A. Berger. The Internet's Not a Big Truck: Toward Quantifying Network Neutrality. In *Proc. PAM*, 2007.

[4] M. Casado and M. Freedman. Peering through the Shroud: The Effect of Edge Opacity on IP-based Client Identification. In *Proc. NSDI*, 2007.

[5] Chad R. Dougherty. CERT Vulnerability Note VU 800113: Multiple DNS implementations vulnerable to cache poisoning, July 2008.

[6] What ports are blocked by Comcast High-Speed Internet? `http://lite.help.comcast.net/content/faq/What-ports-are-blocked-by-Comcast-High-Speed-Internet`.

[7] D. Dagon, M. Antonakakis, P. Vixie, T. Jinmei, and W. Lee. Increased DNS Forgery Resistance Through 0x20-bit Encoding. In *Proc. CCS*, 2008.

[8] M. Dischinger, A. Haeberlen, K. P. Gummadi, and S. Saroiu. Characterizing Residential Broadband Networks. In *Proc. IMC*, 2007.

[9] M. Dischinger, A. Mislove, A. Haeberlen, and K. Gummadi. Detecting BitTorrent Blocking. In *Proc. IMC*, 2008.

[10] R. Erzs and R. Bush. Clarifications to the DNS Specification. RFC 2181, IETF, July 1997.

[11] M. Fauenfelder. How to get rid of Vimax ads. `http://boingboing.net/2009/01/16/how-to-get-rid-of-vi.html`, January 2009.

[12] R. Giobbi. CERT Vulnerability Note VU 435052: Intercepting proxy servers may incorrectly rely on HTTP headers to make connections, February 2009.

[13] J. Huang, Q. Xu, B. Tiwana, and M. Mao. The UMich Smartphone 3G Test. `http://www.eecs.umich.edu/3gtest/`.

[14] C. Kent and J. Mogul. Fragmentation considered harmful. *ACM SIGCOMM Computer Communication Review*, 25(1):87, 1995.

[15] G. Maier, A. Feldmann, V. Paxson, and M. Allman. On dominant characteristics of residential broadband internet traffic. In *Proc. IMC*, 2009.

[16] M. Mathis and J. Heffner. Packetization Layer Path MTU Discovery. RFC 4821, IETF, March 2007.

[17] Mozilla. Effective TLD names. `http://mxr.mozilla.org/mozilla-central/source/netwerk/dns/src/effective_tld_names.dat`.

[18] M. Nottingham. XMLHttpRequest Caching Tests. `http://www.mnot.net/javascript/xmlhttprequest/cache.html`, December 2008.

[19] V. Paxson. An analysis of using reflectors for distributed denial-of-service attacks. *ACM SIGCOMM Computer Communication Review*, 31(3):38–47, 2001.

[20] C. Reis, S. Gribble, T. Kohno, and N. Weaver. Detecting In-Flight Page Changes with Web Tripwires. In *Proc. NSDI*, 2008.

[21] A. Ritacco, C. Wills, and M. Claypool. How's My Network? A Java Approach to Home Network Measurement. In *ICCCN 2009*, pages 1–7. IEEE, 2009.

[22] S. Saroiu, P. Gummadi, S. Gribble, et al. A measurement study of peer-to-peer file sharing systems. In *Proceedings of Multimedia Computing and Networking*, volume 2002, page 152, 2002.

[23] P. Savola. MTU and Fragmentation Issues with In-the-Network Tunneling. RFC 4459, 2006.

[24] M. Tariq, M. Motiwala, N. Feamster, and M. Ammar. Detecting network neutrality violations with causal inference. In *Proc. Emerging Networking Experiments and Technologies*, 2009.

[25] P. Vixie. Extension Mechanisms for DNS (EDNS0). RFC 2671, IETF, August 1999.

[26] Wikipedia. `http://en.wikipedia.org/wiki/Usage_share_of_operating_systems`, January 2010.

[27] Wikipedia. `http://en.wikipedia.org/wiki/Usage_share_of_web_browsers`, January 2010.

[28] Y. Zhang, Z. M. Mao, and M. Zhang. Detecting traffic differentiation in backbone ISPs with NetPolice. In *Proc. IMC*, 2009.

An Experimental Study of Home Gateway Characteristics

Seppo Hätönen
University of Helsinki
shatonen@cs.helsinki.fi

Aki Nyrhinen
University of Helsinki
anyrhine@cs.helsinki.fi

Lars Eggert
Nokia Research Center
lars.eggert@nokia.com

Stephen Strowes
University of Glasgow
sds@dcs.gla.ac.uk

Pasi Sarolahti
HIIT / Aalto University
pasi.sarolahti@iki.fi

Markku Kojo
University of Helsinki
kojo@cs.helsinki.fi

ABSTRACT

Many residential and small business users connect to the Internet via home gateways, such as DSL and cable modems. The characteristics of these devices heavily influence the quality and performance of the Internet service that these users receive. Anecdotal evidence suggests that an extremely diverse set of behaviors exists in the deployed base, forcing application developers to design for the lowest common denominator. This paper experimentally analyzes some characteristics of a substantial number of different home gateways: binding timeouts, queuing delays, throughput, protocol support and others.

Categories and Subject Descriptors

C.4 [**Performance of Systems**]: Performance Attributes; C.2.6 [**Computer Communication Networks**]: Internetworking

General Terms

Experimentation, Measurement, Performance

Keywords

Home Gateways, Behavior, Characteristics, Measurements

1. INTRODUCTION

Many residential and small business users connect to the Internet through "home gateways" – a colloquial term for customer-premises equipment (CPE) that includes DSL and cable modems, WLAN access points and even some kinds of (wired) Ethernet switches. The common defining characteristic of home gateways is that they do *not* just perform Ethernet switching or basic IP forwarding over various link-layer technologies. They also perform higher-layer operations, such as network address translation (NAT) or, more often, network address and port translation (NAPT). Usually, they include traffic filtering "firewall" functions, act as DHCP servers, and proxy DNS traffic. Many models offer other advanced features, including traffic prioritization, shaping, web and email virus and "phishing" protection, etc.

IMC'10, November 1–3, 2010, Melbourne, Australia.

Despite their wide deployment, few standards exist that regulate what functions home gateways should perform and how they should perform them. The relevant standards bodies have ignored home gateways in the past, and only recently begun to document best current practices for some of the functions they perform, such as translating various protocols [3, 11, 29] or DNS proxying [4].

The result is that the performance and the behavior of the network service that applications in residential and small-business deployments experience depends significantly on the specific home gateway model that provides Internet connectivity. Different home gateway models differ in many application-observable aspect, including NAT schemes [28], NAT binding timeouts, ICMP [23] handling, traffic filtering, queuing, buffer sizes, etc. Incomplete support – or buggy implementation – of common functions, *e.g.*, DNS or DHCP, is another significant source of behavioral variability.

The experimental study in this paper measures and analyzes the behavior of a substantial number of home gateways, including NAT binding timeouts, queuing delay, throughput, and protocol support, to characterize typical behaviors found in many home gateway models. This allows applications to understand the kinds of practices they can expect to encounter in the deployed base.

2. RELATED WORK

A few previous studies have focused on measuring NAT binding timeouts. In a study of UDP binding timeouts in a peer-to-peer network of ca. 3,500 peers, the majority (62%) of bindings were found to time out between 2 and 2.5 min [7]. In the context of investigating energy efficiency of mobile handsets, timeout behavior is important to throttle keepalives and minimize battery usage. The default connection timeout values documented by vendors [13] are approximately in line with these observations.

Other studies have looked at the inbound packet filtering behavior of NATs in the presence of valid bindings created by outbound traffic. An experimental analysis of this behavior on a small set of NATs is documented in [14] using the terminology defined in [28]; other tests focus on hair-pinning and ICMP forwarding. The memo highlights that NAT behavior depends on whether a NAT attempts to preserve port numbers for external mappings: a NAT can exhibit different behaviors for different mappings. Also highlighted are techniques to systematically investigate binding timeout behavior, but no binding timeout results are presented.

Peer-to-peer NAT traversal for UDP and TCP is covered in [10], with a focus on "hole-punching" techniques to make peer-to-peer applications work through NATs. The paper gives a useful characterization of different types of NATs, and describes the properties of a "well-behaving" NAT that supports hole-punching.

The success rates of various NAT traversal techniques for establishing direct TCP connections between two hosts located behind NATs are not as good as those for UDP [12]. The study performed in [12] looks at only a small set of NATs, but none of the techniques presented guarantee the successful creation of an operational TCP connection, the best was a variant of STUNT [21] with a success rate of 89%. Some of the traversal techniques would benefit from a better understanding of how NATs handle unusual packet sequences (for TCP connection negotiation) or ICMP packets.

Another measurement study on NAT behavior [19] determines the applicability of primarily TCP-based NAT traversal techniques to cellular networks. The study treats the network as a "black box" and does not identify NAT manufacturers and models, or if routing policies for different classes of subscribers were in place, which leaves it open whether the reported behaviors are only due to NATs.

Various aspects of TCP interactions with the network are measured in [21]. The results suggest that different TCP options do not appear to cause problems for a TCP connection, except in certain rare cases. One example is middleboxes that shift TCP sequence numbers in the header without considering that certain TCP options also contain them (*e.g.*, SACK [20].) Slightly more problematic are the use of ECN [24] or PMTU discovery [22], which may cause loss of TCP SYN segments and therefore failed connection attempts. The results also indicate that the use of IP options leads to failure in most cases. Because the experiments were conducted end-to-end, the results do not identify whether buggy host implementations or intermediaries along the path caused these issues. Our study does not currently replicate these measurements, but we plan to expand it in the future to confirm their results.

Several studies evaluate the support of DNSSEC [2] in home gateways [1, 5, 9]. This includes testing for support of DNS over TCP, which our study also measures, but we do not currently perform exhaustive tests for DNSSEC support.

Vendor	Model	Firmware	Tag
A-Link	WNAP	e2.0.9A	*al*
Apple	Airport Express	7.4.2	*ap*
Asus	RT-N15	2.0.1.1	*as1*
Belkin	Wireless N Router	F5D8236-4_WW_3.00.02	*be1*
	Enhanced N150	F6D4230-4_WW_1.00.03	*be2*
Buffalo	WZR-AGL300NH	R1.06/B1.05	*bu1*
D-Link	DIR-300	1.03	*dl1*
	DIR-300	1.04	*dl2*
	DI-524up	v1.06	*dl3*
	DI-524	v2.0.4	*dl4*
	DIR-100	v1.12	*dl5*
	DIR-600	v2.01	*dl6*
	DIR-615	v4.00	*dl7*
	DIR-635	v2.33EU	*dl8*
	DI-604	v3.09	*dl9*
	DI-713P	2.60 build 6a	*dl10*
Edimax	6104WG	2.63	*ed*
Jensen	Air:Link 59300	1.15	*je*
Linksys	BEFSR41c2	1.45.11	*ls1*
	WR54G	v7.00.1	*ls2*
	WRT54GL v1.1	v4.30.7	*ls3*
	WRT54GL-EU	v4.30.7	*ls5*
	WRT54G	OpenWRT RC5	*owrt*
	WRT54GL v1.1	tomato 1.27	*to*
Netgear	RP614 v4	V1.0.2_06.29	*ng1*
	WGR614 v7	(1.0.13_1.0.13)	*ng2*
	WGR614 v9	V1.2.6_18.0.17	*ng3*
	WNR2000-100PES	v.1.0.0.34_29.0.45	*ng4*
	WGR614 v4	V5.0_07	*ng5*
Netwjork	54M	Ver 1.2.6	*nw1*
SMC Barricade	SMC7004VBR	R1.07	*smc*
Telewell	TW-3G	V7.04b3	*te*
Webee	Wireless N Router	e2.0.9D	*we*
ZyXel	P-335U	V3.60(AMB.2)C0	*zy1*

Table 1: Home gateway models included in the study, with the shorthand "tags" used throughout this paper.

3. EXPERIMENTAL METHODOLOGY

This section describes the testbed used for the experiments presented in this paper and describes how each measurement result presented in Section 4 was obtained.

3.1 Testbed Setup

Figure 1 illustrates the experimental testbed used for this study, which consists of a test server and a test client, both running Linux 2.6.26 kernels, the *hiit.fi* DNS server, several HP-2524 VLAN switches and the different home gateway models listed in Table 1. Table 1 also defines a unique "tag" for each home gateway, which is used in the remainder of this paper as a shorthand to identify each specific device. All network links are using 100Mb/sec Ethernet.

The "WAN" uplink port of each home gateway connects to the test server through a switch on a separate VLAN. The test server runs a DHCP service that provides information about the global DNS server and leases a different private address block [25] on each VLAN, which the home gateways use to configure their uplink "WAN" interfaces and DNS proxies.

The "LAN" port of each home gateway connects to the test client through a second switch, again on a separate VLAN. The test client runs a separate DHCP client to set up each VLAN interface with the information that each home gateway provides via its DHCP server. The DHCP client is modified to configure only interface-specific routes.

The test server and test client are also directly connected through a management link, which is used to coordinate the measurements. Client and server run an instance of the *testrund* daemon, which is responsible for setting up and performing each measurement, as well as exporting all captured measurement data afterwards. A given measurement is run in parallel across all home gateways in the testbed, except for the throughput test, which measures each home gateway separately to avoid overloading the test network.

3.2 Measurement Methodology

Using the testbed described above, several different measurements were performed across the set of home gateways listed in Table 1, including determining the timeout values used for UDP and TCP bindings under various conditions, testing TCP throughput, and determining whether UDP- and TCP-related ICMP messages are translated correctly, among other measurements.

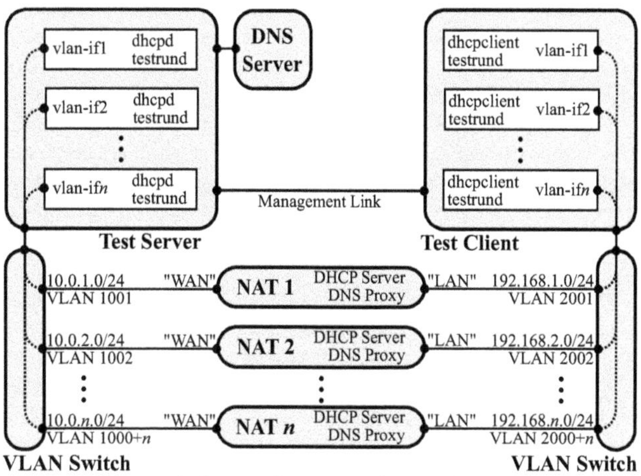

Figure 1: Setup of the experimental testbed.

3.2.1 UDP Binding Timeouts

UDP is a connectionless protocol without explicit connection startup or teardown handshakes. NATs therefore create UDP bindings when they observe a packet exchange, and remove bindings some period of time after the last observed packet on a flow – the *binding timeout*. A few critical services such as DNS use UDP, and it is becoming increasingly common to encapsulate other traffic inside UDP. Consequently, understanding the binding timeouts home gateways apply to UDP traffic is important, *e.g.*, to determine at which rate keepalives need to be sent.

To explore this question, we define several experiments to measure UDP binding timeouts under different conditions. In each case, the client sends UDP packets on a specific source/destination port pair to the server to create a binding, and has a modifiable "sleep timer". When the sleep timer expires, the client uses the management link to instruct the server to send a response packet back via the home gateway. Depending on whether the client receives this response packet, it knows whether the NAT binding is still active or not. Binding timeouts are determined through a modified binary search: The client retains the longest observed binding lifetime and shortest binding expiration, and on the next iteration sets the sleep timer to be their midpoint. The modification to the binary search allows the start of each search iteration to be identical to the first search. The test stops when it has converged to within one second. We define the following five UDP tests:

UDP-1: *Solitary outbound packet.* This test measures how long a NAT maintains a UDP binding after the test client sends a single UDP packet to the server. The server does not send traffic to the client, apart from the packet triggered by the sleep timer, and the client does not send any further traffic.

UDP-2: *Solitary outbound packet, multiple inbound packets.* The intent of this test is to determine if inbound traffic refreshes a binding, compared to *UDP-1*. The test client sends a solitary UDP packet to the test server and then remains silent. The server sends a stream of responses across the binding, and increases the delay between each response packet until the binding times out.

UDP-3: *Multiple outbound and inbound packets.* The intent is to determine whether outbound traffic refreshes a binding. This test is similar to *UDP-2*, except that the client sends another packet to the server whenever it receives a response packet from it.

UDP-4: *Binding and port-pair reuse behavior.* This test determines if a home gateway prefers to use the original source port as the external port for a binding, and if it waits before it reuses an expired binding for the same flow (*i.e.*, the same 5-tuple). This is observed from the *UDP-1* test. The port-pair reuse behavior is determined from the behavior of the binding created in the binary search iteration that follows immediately after a previous binding expires. If the device creates a new binding, as indicated by a changed source port, it is likely that the device prevents immediate binding reuse for the same flow.

UDP-5: *Binding timeout variations for different services.* A NAT might use different binding timeouts for different services, *i.e.*, different well-known destination port numbers. This test is identical to *UDP-2*, but tests different well-known server ports.

3.2.2 TCP Handling

TCP connections involve an explicit creation and tear-down phase, and NATs can observe the tear-down handshake to remove bindings immediately. However, TCP connections may idle for long periods of time (if no TCP or application keepalives are used) and endpoints may silently fail. A NAT therefore cannot assume that it will always be able to observe a tear-down handshake. Also, the number of bindings on a NAT is limited by the available ports.

The following TCP tests are carried out using Linux 2.6.26 on both the client and server, with the congestion control algorithm set to *Reno* and the Linux TCP options – SACK, timestamps, window scaling, F-RTO, D-SACK and control block interdependence (CBI) – disabled.

TCP-1: *TCP binding timeouts.* Although a NAT does not necessarily need to remove TCP bindings before it becomes overloaded, anecdotal evidence suggests that many devices time out idle bindings after a certain amount of time. This test determines the existence of a static timeout similar to *UDP-1*, except that the client opens a TCP connection with the server. The connection is left idle with no TCP keepalives in use. TCP binding timeouts are often much longer than UDP ones. To speed up the test, the binary search technique therefore uses multiple parallel connections, and stops if binding timeouts are longer than 24 hours.

TCP-2: *TCP throughput.* To test if home gateways can limit TCP throughput, we measure the performance of a 100 MB bulk transfer. A first test measures client-to-server upload throughput, a second measures server-to-client download throughput, and a third measures the throughputs of simultaneous up- and downloads.

TCP-3: *Queuing and processing delay.* Anecdotal evidence suggests that many home gateways have over-dimensioned transmission buffers, which can add significantly to the end-to-end delay experienced by TCP. We measure this delay by embedding evenly spaced timestamps (every 2 KB) into the payload of the throughput tests in *TCP-2*. Delay is determined by the difference between the received timestamps and the local system clock. Clocks are synchronized using NTP and the tests are short enough that any error introduced by clock drift stays well below 1 msec. The output is normalized, so that the minimum difference is zero. The maximum delay is the median of the normalized differences, to prevent TCP retransmissions from skewing the results. Since the measured round-trip delay across each device is below 2 msec, it is safe to assume that the results are accurate to about 1 msec.

TCP-4: *Maximum number of TCP bindings.* The recommended behavior for a NAT is to retain a TCP binding for 124 min [11] in the absence of an explicit connection tear-down. When serving many connections, it is likely that a NAT reaches its maximum number of bindings. This test measures the maximum number of TCP bindings a NAT supports, by systematically creating connections to the same server port and periodically passing messages over each, to prevent binding timeouts. When a new connection fails to be created or messages can no longer be passed on an existing one, the maximum number of bindings has been reached.

3.2.3 Other Tests

ICMP: *TCP- and UDP-related ICMP forwarding.* Many NATs attempt to translate ICMP messages related to TCP and UDP bindings, because this can improve application performance. The most important ICMP messages to translate are *Destination Unreachable* messages indicating that fragmentation is needed, which TCP uses for PMTU discovery [22]. If they are not translated properly, PMTU "black hole" issues can occur [17]. For UDP, even detection of port reachability depends on ICMP messages. We test whether ICMP messages are correctly translated by hijacking packets coming from the NAT, generating ICMP messages of the desired kind that are sent back to the NAT, and inspecting packet traces to determine what the NAT actually did.

SCTP and **DCCP**: *Support for SCTP and DCCP.* Deployment of these transport protocols is said to be hindered by middleboxes that do not support them. We therefore determine the level of support for SCTP [30] and DCCP [15,16] among the home gateways in our testbed. For each of these transport protocols, we attempt to create

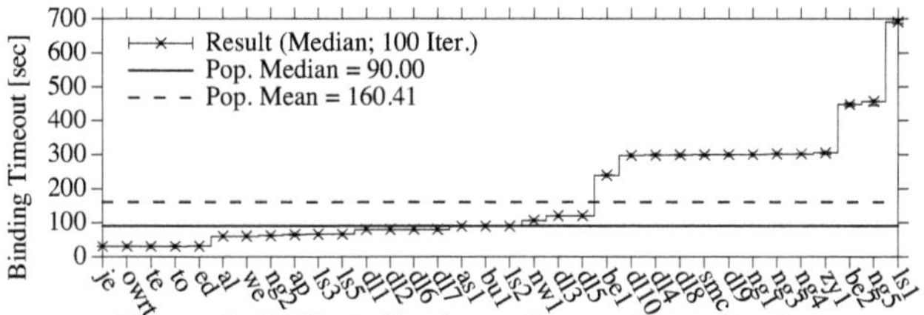

Figure 3: UDP-1: Single packet, outbound only.

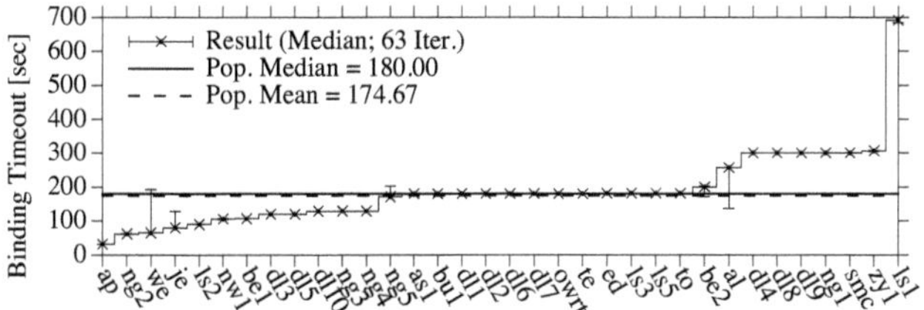

Figure 4: UDP-2: Single packet out, multiple packets in.

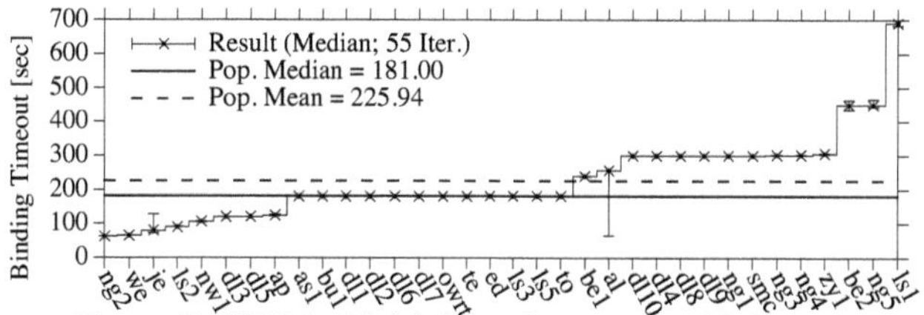

Figure 5: UDP-3: Multiple packets out- and inbound.

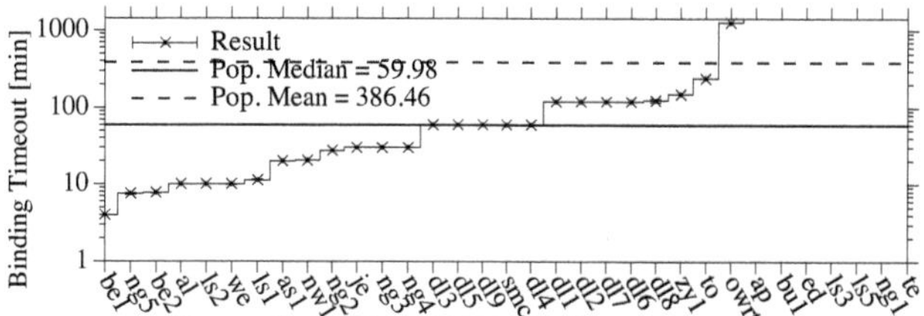

Figure 7: TCP-1: TCP binding timeouts.

a single connection and exchange data. If this succeeds, a home gateway supports the respective transport.

DNS: *DNS over TCP.* The DNS proxy on each NAT is tested for support of DNS-over-TCP by querying it using *dig* from the Berkeley Internet Name Daemon (BIND) suite.

4. EXPERIMENTAL RESULTS

This section presents the measurement results for the experiments described in Section 3. All plots show the measured results across the entire population of studied home gateways, arranged on the x-axis by increasing value. Each data point shown is the median of many repetitions of a measurement, as indicated in the plot legend. Quartiles for each data point are plotted as error bars, but the inter-quartile gap is usually too narrow for them to become visible.

4.1 UDP Timeout Results

Section 3.2.1 described a measurement method for determining UDP binding timeouts as well as several binding usage scenarios. This section presents the experimental results obtained from applying this method in these different scenarios. From Figure 2, it is apparent that home gateways do not behave consistently in the different UDP tests. While it is clear that many devices do not vary their timeout behavior between tests *UDP-2* and *UDP-3*, the timeouts do vary with manufacturers and firmware versions. Most devices retain UDP bindings for the 120 sec required in [3], at least while there is inbound traffic over the binding. *UDP-1* presents a more unusual case, where the binding is often removed much sooner. The next paragraphs discuss the detailed results.

UDP-1: Figure 3 plots the medians of measured binding timeouts for the *UDP-1* case, where the client sends only a single packet to the server. Quartiles are plotted as error bars but the inter-quartile range is too narrow to become visible, indicating stable results for all devices. One obvious result is that UDP binding timeouts vary by an order of magnitude across the measured set of home gateways. The *je* device is among those with the shortest timeout (30 sec), whereas *ls1* has a timeout that is more than twenty times longer (691 sec). The median timeout across the entire set is 90 sec, the mean is 160 sec. Note that more than half of the tested devices do not conform to the IETF specification [3] that requires timeouts of more than 120 sec; and only a single device (*ls1*) complies with the longer 600 sec timeout that the IETF recommends.

UDP-2: Figure 4 shows the measurements for the case where the server sends a stream of response packets to the client. The intent of this measurement was to determine whether inbound traffic affects the binding timeout, and for many devices, it does. Most devices here tend to use longer timeouts; the minimum is now 54 sec, the median is 180 sec and the mean 175 sec. For example, *ed, owrt, to,* and *te*, which shared the shortest timeout (30 sec) in the *UDP-1* case, now use a median timeout of 180 sec. Other devices, however, shorten their timeouts now, *e.g.*, *be2*, which had a timeout of ca. 450 sec previously, now reduces its timeout to ca. 202 sec. The inter-quartile range for *we* and *al* as well as, to a lesser degree, *je* and *ng5* is substantial, because these boxes seem to use very coarse-grained binding timers.

UDP-3: Figure 5 plots the measurements for the case where a received server response triggers the client to send another packet. The intent of this test is to check whether outbound traffic on a binding affects the timeout. The difference to *UDP-2* is less pronounced; the median timeout remains almost unchanged, although the mean increases to 226 sec. This is mostly due to a few devices (*be1*, *dl10*, *ng3 ng4*, and esp. *be2* and *ng5*) lengthening their timeouts as outbound packets are now also present, reaching the same level as in the *UDP-1* test; no devices shorten them.

UDP-4: The results show that different behaviors exist for how NATs choose external port numbers and how they reuse port pairs. Most of the devices (27 out of 34) prefer to use the original source port as the external port for a binding. 23 of these devices seem to also reuse an expired binding, while 4 devices create a new binding. 7 devices do not attempt to use the original source port and seem to always create a new binding after an old one expired.

UDP-5: Figure 6 shows the median measured binding timeouts to different well-known server ports. The results indicate that most devices use a timeout scheme that is independent of the server port. Notable exception is *dl8*, which uses a shorter timeout for the DNS port.

4.2 TCP Results

This section discusses the results of the TCP tests described in Section 3.2.2.

TCP-1: Figure 7 shows the measured TCP binding timeouts. Because the measured timeouts are highly variable, the plot uses a log scale to highlight the differences. *be1* has the shortest timeout; it consistently times out TCP bindings after 239 sec – less than 4 min. More than half the devices fail to meet the IETF recommended timeout of 124 min [11]. Some of the NATs retain TCP bindings for considerably longer – the seven devices on the right in Figure 7 still had not timed out their bindings after 24 h (1,440 min), which was the cutoff for this test.

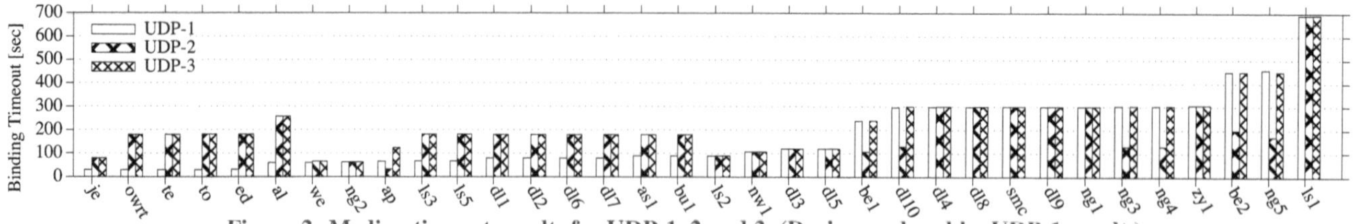

Figure 2: Median timeout results for UDP-1, 2 and 3. (Devices ordered by UDP-1 result.)

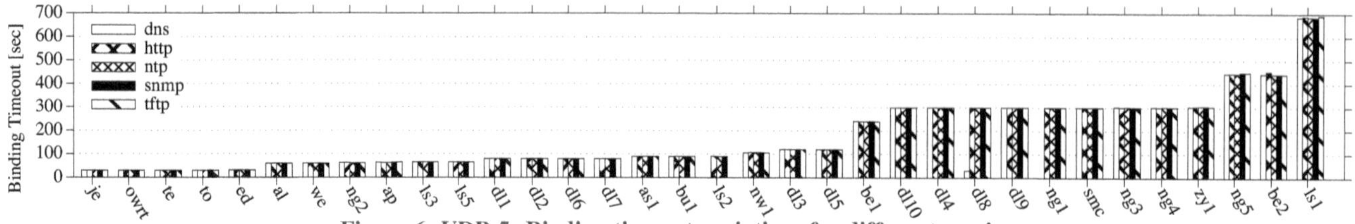

Figure 6: UDP-5: Binding timeout variations for different services.

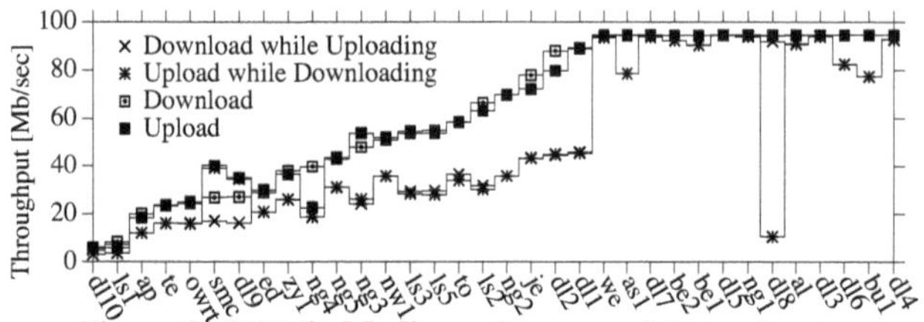

Figure 8: TCP-2: Medians of measured throughputs.

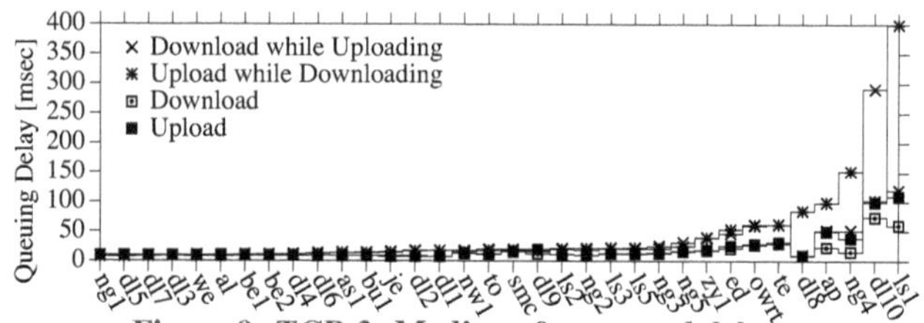

Figure 9: TCP-3: Median of measured delays.

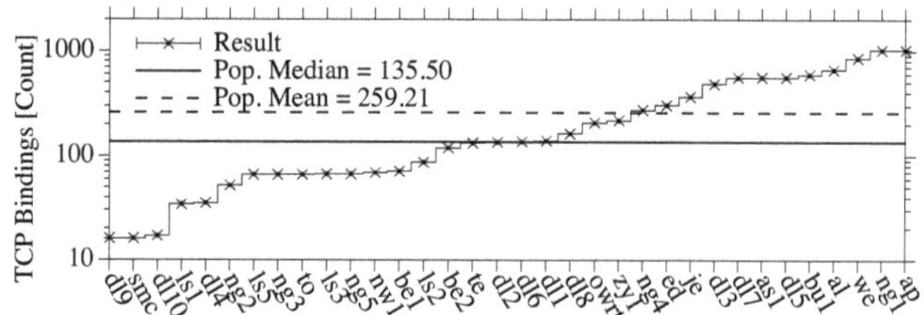

Figure 10: TCP-4: Max. bindings to a single server port.

TCP-2: Figure 8 shows the medians of the measured TCP throughputs for each device. Thirteen devices can sustain the maximum possible throughput of 100 Mb/sec for uploads and downloads, but other devices fail to do so: The median throughput across the device set is roughly 59 Mb/sec for unidirectional uploads and downloads.

For the bidirectional tests, the devices that achieve the best performance in the unidirectional tests continue to demonstrate higher throughputs, though not all reach 100 Mb/sec in both directions. There is a marked distinction in the performance of some devices: many are incapable of handling more than 50 Mb/sec of traffic in either direction. Further, the median in the bidirectional case is ca. 35 Mb/sec, which is much lower than the 68 Mb/sec in the unidirectional case. There are extremely poor performers in this test, *dl10* and *ls1* being the worst performers *dl10* and *ls1* can only sustain unidirectional throughput of around 6 Mb/sec and 8 Mb/sec respectively for download and 6 Mb/sec each for upload. Some other devices also demonstrate a distinct difference in upload and download throughputs: *smc*, for example, can sustain 41 Mb/sec for upload, but only 27 Mb/sec for download.

The poor throughput of many devices may normally go unnoticed: the WAN port will generally connect to the user's ISP over a link with a much lower capacity than 100 Mb/sec.

TCP-3: Figure 9 shows the results for queuing and processing delays introduced by the devices. Perhaps not surprisingly, the devices that perform well in the throughput tests (*TCP-2*) also perform well in the latency test. Bidirectional traffic increases latencies slightly for most of the devices, more significantly so for the poorest performers, which are *ls1* and *dl10*. The median latency for *dl10* is 74 msec when downloading only but jumps to 291 msec when uploading at the same time, whereas the median latency for *ls1* is 110 msec when uploading only but reaches 400 msec when downloading at the same time. Even the best-performing boxes see minor delay increases of ca. 2 msec.

TCP-4: Figure 10 shows the maximum number of bindings a NAT allows to a single server port. *dl9* and *smc* support only 16 bindings, whereas *ng1* and *ap* allow ca. 1024 bindings; the median is 135.

4.3 Other Results

Table 2 shows pass/fail results for the tests described in Section 3.2.3 related to SCTP and DCCP support, DNS-over-TCP support, and ICMP handling.

ICMP: The "TCP" and "UDP" columns in Table 2 indicate which home gateways correctly translate various ICMP messages related to flows of the respective transport protocol. *nw1* does not translate *any* transport-related ICMP messages; all others translate at least "Port Unreachable" and "TTL Exceeded". *ls2* translates all TCP-related ICMP messages into (invalid) TCP resets. About half of the devices (16 out of 34) do not correctly translate transport headers contained in ICMP payloads, and *zy1* and *ls1* do not correctly translate IP checksums in ICMP payloads.

SCTP and **DCCP**: It is possible to establish an SCTP connection through 18 of the 34 devices – an astounding result, since the general belief has been that even single-homed SCTP connections do not usually work across NATs. None of the devices allowed establishing a DCCP connection. *dl4*, *dl9*, *dl10* and *ls1* pass SCTP and DCCP packets entirely untranslated, 20 others attempt to simply translate the IP source address. Among those 20 devices are all those that work with SCTP – which raises the question if they actually fully support SCTP, or whether a single SCTP connection

Tag	DCCP: Conn.	DNS over TCP	DNS over UDP	ICMP: Host Unreach.	SCTP: Conn.	TCP: Reass. Time. Ex.	TCP: Frag. Needed	TCP: Param. Prob.	TCP: Src. Route Fail.	TCP: Source Quench	TCP: TTL Exceeded	TCP: Host Unreach.	TCP: Net Unreach.	TCP: Port Unreach.	TCP: Proto. Unreach.	UDP: Reass. Time Ex.	UDP: Frag. Needed	UDP: Param. Prob.	UDP: Src. Route Fail	UDP: Source Quench	UDP: TTL Exceeded	UDP: Host Unreach.	UDP: Net Unreach.	UDP: Port Unreach.	UDP: Proto. Unreach.
al		●	●	●	●	●	●	●	●	●	●	●	●	●	●	●	●	●	●	●	●	●	●	●	●
ap		●	●	●	●	●	●	●	●	●	●	●	●	●	●	●	●	●	●	●	●	●	●	●	●
as1			●	●	●	●	●	●	●	●	●	●	●	●	●	●	●	●	●	●	●	●	●	●	●
be1			●													●	●		●		●	●	●	●	●
be2			●													●	●		●		●	●	●	●	●
bu1		●	●	●	●	●	●	●	●	●	●	●	●	●	●	●	●	●	●	●	●	●	●	●	●
dl1			●	●	●	●	●	●	●	●	●	●	●	●	●	●	●	●	●	●	●	●	●	●	●
dl10			●								●			●							●			●	
dl2		●	●	●	●	●	●	●	●	●	●	●	●	●	●	●	●	●	●	●	●	●	●	●	●
dl3			●	●		●	●	●	●	●	●	●	●	●	●	●	●	●	●	●	●	●	●	●	●
dl4			●								●			●							●			●	
dl5			●	●		●	●	●	●	●	●	●	●	●	●	●	●	●	●	●	●	●	●	●	●
dl6		●	●	●	●	●	●	●	●	●	●	●	●	●	●	●	●	●	●	●	●	●	●	●	●
dl7		●	●	●	●	●	●	●	●	●	●	●	●	●	●	●	●	●	●	●	●	●	●	●	●
dl8			●	●	●	●	●	●	●	●	●	●	●	●	●	●	●	●	●	●	●	●	●	●	●
dl9			●								●			●							●			●	
ed		●	●	●	●	●	●	●	●	●	●	●	●	●	●	●	●	●	●	●	●	●	●	●	●
je		●	●	●	●	●	●	●	●	●	●	●	●	●	●	●	●	●	●	●	●	●	●	●	●
ls1			●	●			●									●	●	●	●	●	●	●	●	●	●
ls2			●	●												●	●		●	●	●	●	●	●	●
ls3			●	●	●	●	●	●	●	●	●	●	●	●	●	●	●	●	●	●	●	●	●	●	●
ls5			●	●	●	●	●	●	●	●	●	●	●	●	●	●	●	●	●	●	●	●	●	●	●
ng1			●	●		●	●	●	●	●	●	●	●	●	●	●	●	●	●	●	●	●	●	●	●
ng2			●	●		●	●	●	●	●	●	●	●	●	●	●	●	●	●	●	●	●	●	●	●
ng3		●	●	●		●	●	●	●	●	●	●	●	●	●	●	●	●	●	●	●	●	●	●	●
ng4		●	●	●		●	●	●	●	●	●	●	●	●	●	●	●	●	●	●	●	●	●	●	●
ng5			●	●												●			●		●	●	●	●	●
nw1			●																						
owrt		●	●	●	●	●	●	●	●	●	●	●	●	●	●	●	●	●	●	●	●	●	●	●	●
smc			●								●			●							●			●	
te			●	●	●	●	●	●	●	●	●	●	●	●	●	●	●	●	●	●	●	●	●	●	●
to		●	●	●	●	●	●	●	●	●	●	●	●	●	●	●	●	●	●	●	●	●	●	●	●
we		●	●	●	●	●	●	●	●	●	●	●	●	●	●	●	●	●	●	●	●	●	●	●	●
zy1			●	●		●	●	●	●	●	●	●	●	●	●	●	●	●	●	●	●	●	●	●	●

Table 2: Summary of the results of other tests.

works because only IP headers are translated (the SCTP checksum does not cover the network-layer pseudo header). Further experiments are needed to better characterize the nature of SCTP support in these devices, for example, whether SCTP multihoming works over those devices that do support a single-homed connection.

DNS: 14 of the tested devices accept connections on TCP port 53 (DNS), and 10 of them accept and respond to DNS queries on that TCP port; this roughly agrees with [9]. *ap* forwards DNS queries arriving via TCP over UDP, the others forward over TCP.

4.4 Observations and Discussion

The results in Section 4.1 indicate that although UDP binding timeouts are relatively low for bindings that see little use (*UDP-1*), bindings that see some bidirectional traffic (*UDP-2*) and especially bindings that see repeated bidirectional traffic (*UDP-3*) are being granted longer timeouts. (Although no device uses the IETF recommended 600 sec.) In this light, UDP keepalive intervals as short as 15 sec, which are used by some applications, are perhaps overly aggressive: the lowest measured timeout when a binding has seen bidirectional traffic is 54 sec. It is clear that there are a variety of different behaviors among the tested devices, and that the timeout applied to a binding depends more on what traffic pattern is seen than on what port numbers are used.

In Section 4.2, the lowest measured number of parallel TCP bindings to a single server port is 16, and even the "best" devices imposed a limit of ca. 1024, which is much smaller than the 16-bit port number space. A low number of permitted parallel bindings can interfere with important applications, such as web browsing: modern browsers impose a limit on the number of concurrent connections to a DNS name, which has caused content providers to use multiple DNS names for a web server with one IP address. The intent of this practice is to circumvent this browser limit in an attempt to improve performance.

TCP binding timeouts vary much more widely than UDP timeouts. Half the devices time out TCP bindings after less than 1 h, which is much less than the IETF-recommended minimum of 124 min. This also means that TCP stacks that implement the standardized minimum TCP keepalive interval of 2 h [6] will not be able to reliably refresh TCP connections in many cases.

In addition to the specific results reported in this paper, our experiments also exposed a few other interesting behaviors: First, some devices use the same Ethernet MAC address for both their WAN and LAN ports. In a typical configuration, this should make no difference, but it required us to connect the WAN and LAN ports to physically different VLAN switches. Second, some devices do not decrement the IP time-to-live (TTL) field and few honor a "Record Route" IP option, which can interfere with network diagnostics and other uses of the TTL field. Third, it was unexpected to find that some boxes fall back to only translating the IP header when they encounter an unknown transport protocol.

Discovering that this "fallback" behavior is not uncommon raises an interesting question for future transport protocol design. Would it be possible to leverage this behavior, by avoiding dependencies on the IP layer (such as the pseudo-headers for checksum calculation) in order to improve the chances for un-encapsulated and un-relayed NAT traversal?

Finally, it is worth noting that no single home gateway consistently performs better than others across all tests, which makes it difficult for application designers to target a "better" subset of devices.

5. CONCLUSIONS AND FUTURE WORK

The results presented in this paper are a snapshot of an ongoing study, but already present some interesting variations in home gateway behavior. The results cover 34 different home gateway models, but do not necessarily reflect how frequent the observed behaviors are in the deployed device base. We are planning to expand the range of tests to investigate handling of TCP and IP options, to measure the rate at which NATs are capable of creating new bindings, more extensive DNSSEC, queuing and SCTP tests, measuring the success rates of STUN [27], TURN [18] and ICE [26], investigate the support for ECN [24], IPv6 [8] and various IP and TCP options, and more.

We are also continuing to expand the range of home gateways in the testbed. All home gateways measured in this paper use an Ethernet interface for their uplink. We plan to extend this study to include already-donated DSL and cable modems, once a DSLAM (DSL access multiplexer) and a CMTS (cable modem termination system), which also have been donated after preliminary versions of this study were presented, have been added to the testbed.

6. ACKNOWLEDGMENTS

Many of the home gateway devices were donated to the testbed, and we would like to sincerely thank all donors. The results presented in this paper are a snapshot of a study that is continuously being extended. Please contact the authors if you have suggestions for additional or improved tests, or if you can donate a spare, unused home gateway to the testbed – we will cover shipping.

L. Eggert is in part funded by *Trilogy*, a research project supported by the European Commission under its 7th Framework Program.

7. REFERENCES

[1] J. Åhlund and P. Wallström. DNSSEC Tests of Consumer Broadband Routers. Technical Report, .SE Internet Infrastructure Foundation, Feb. 2008.

[2] R. Arends, R. Austein, M. Larson, D. Massey, and S. Rose. DNS Security Introduction and Requirements. RFC 4033 (Proposed Standard), Mar. 2005.

[3] F. Audet and C. Jennings. Network Address Translation (NAT) Behavioral Requirements for Unicast UDP. RFC 4787 (Best Current Practice), Jan. 2007.

[4] R. Bellis. DNS Proxy Implementation Guidelines. RFC 5625 (Best Current Practice), Aug. 2009.

[5] R. Bellis and L. Phifer. Test Report: DNSSEC Impact on Broadband Routers and Firewalls. Technical Report, Nominet, Sept. 2008.

[6] R. Braden. Requirements for Internet Hosts - Communication Layers. RFC 1122 (Standard), Oct. 1989.

[7] L. D'Acunto, J. Pouwelse, and H. Sips. A Measurement of NAT & Firewall Characteristics in Peer to Peer Systems. In *Proc. ASCI Conference*, 2009.

[8] S. Deering and R. Hinden. Internet Protocol, Version 6 (IPv6) Specification. RFC 2460 (Draft Standard), Dec. 1998.

[9] T. Dietrich. DNSSEC Support by Home Routers in Germany. In *Proc. 60th Réseaux IP Européens (RIPE) Meeting*, May 2010.

[10] B. Ford, P. Srisuresh, and D. Kegel. Peer-to-Peer Communication Across Network Address Translators. In *Proc. USENIX Annual Technical Conference*, pages 13–13, 2005.

[11] S. Guha, K. Biswas, B. Ford, S. Sivakumar, and P. Srisuresh. NAT Behavioral Requirements for TCP. RFC 5382 (Best Current Practice), Oct. 2008.

[12] S. Guha and P. Francis. Characterization and Measurement of TCP Traversal through NATs and Firewalls. In *Proc. ACM SIGCOMM IMC*, pages 199–211, 2005.

[13] H. Haverinen, J. Siren, and P. Eronen. Energy Consumption of Always-On Applications in WCDMA Networks. In *Proc. IEEE Vehicular Technology Conference*, pages 964–968, Apr. 2007.

[14] C. Jennings. NAT Classification Test Results. Internet-Draft draft-jennings-behave-test-results-04, Internet Engineering Task Force, July 2007. Work in Progress.

[15] E. Kohler, M. Handley, and S. Floyd. Datagram Congestion Control Protocol (DCCP). RFC 4340 (Proposed Standard), Mar. 2006.

[16] E. Kohler, M. Handley, and S. Floyd. Designing DCCP: Congestion Control Without Reliability. *ACM SIGCOMM CCR*, 36(4):27–38, 2006.

[17] K. Lahey. TCP Problems with Path MTU Discovery. RFC 2923 (Informational), Sept. 2000.

[18] R. Mahy, P. Matthews, and J. Rosenberg. Traversal Using Relays around NAT (TURN): Relay Extensions to Session Traversal Utilities for NAT (STUN). RFC 5766 (Proposed Standard), Apr. 2010.

[19] L. Mäkinen and J. Nurminen. Measurements on the Feasibility of TCP NAT Traversal in Cellular Networks. In *Proc. Conference on Next Generation Internet Networks*, pages 261–267, 2008.

[20] M. Mathis, J. Mahdavi, S. Floyd, and A. Romanow. TCP Selective Acknowledgment Options. RFC 2018 (Proposed Standard), Oct. 1996.

[21] A. Medina, M. Allman, and S. Floyd. Measuring the Evolution of Transport Protocols in the Internet. *ACM SIGCOMM CCR*, 35(2):37–52, 2005.

[22] J. Mogul and S. Deering. Path MTU Discovery. RFC 1191 (Draft Standard), Nov. 1990.

[23] J. Postel. Internet Control Message Protocol. RFC 792 (Standard), Sept. 1981.

[24] K. Ramakrishnan, S. Floyd, and D. Black. The Addition of Explicit Congestion Notification (ECN) to IP. RFC 3168 (Proposed Standard), Sept. 2001.

[25] Y. Rekhter, B. Moskowitz, D. Karrenberg, G. J. de Groot, and E. Lear. Address Allocation for Private Internets. RFC 1918 (Best Current Practice), Feb. 1996.

[26] J. Rosenberg. Interactive Connectivity Establishment (ICE): A Protocol for Network Address Translator (NAT) Traversal for Offer/Answer Protocols. RFC 5245 (Proposed Standard), Apr. 2010.

[27] J. Rosenberg, R. Mahy, P. Matthews, and D. Wing. Session Traversal Utilities for NAT (STUN). RFC 5389 (Proposed Standard), Oct. 2008.

[28] J. Rosenberg, J. Weinberger, C. Huitema, and R. Mahy. STUN - Simple Traversal of User Datagram Protocol (UDP) Through Network Address Translators (NATs). RFC 3489 (Proposed Standard), Mar. 2003.

[29] P. Srisuresh, B. Ford, S. Sivakumar, and S. Guha. NAT Behavioral Requirements for ICMP. RFC 5508 (Best Current Practice), Apr. 2009.

[30] R. Stewart. Stream Control Transmission Protocol. RFC 4960 (Proposed Standard), Sept. 2007.

Network Traffic Characteristics of Data Centers in the Wild

Theophilus Benson*, Aditya Akella* and David A. Maltz†
*University of Wisconsin–Madison
†Microsoft Research–Redmond

ABSTRACT

Although there is tremendous interest in designing improved networks for data centers, very little is known about the network-level traffic characteristics of current data centers. In this paper, we conduct an empirical study of the network traffic in 10 data centers belonging to three different types of organizations, including university, enterprise, and cloud data centers. Our definition of cloud data centers includes not only data centers employed by large online service providers offering Internet-facing applications, but also data centers used to host data-intensive (MapReduce style) applications. We collect and analyze SNMP statistics, topology, and packet-level traces. We examine the range of applications deployed in these data centers and their placement, the flow-level and packet-level transmission properties of these applications, and their impact on network utilization, link utilization, congestion, and packet drops. We describe the implications of the observed traffic patterns for data center internal traffic engineering as well as for recently-proposed architectures for data center networks.

Categories and Subject Descriptors

C.4 [**Performance of Systems**]: Design studies; Performance attributes

General Terms

Design, Measurement, Performance

Keywords

Data center traffic, characterization

1. INTRODUCTION

A *data center* (DC) refers to any large, dedicated cluster of computers that is owned and operated by a single organization. Data centers of various sizes are being built and employed for a diverse set of purposes today. On the one hand, large universities and private enterprises are increasingly consolidating their IT services within on-site data centers containing a few hundred to a few thousand servers. On the other hand, large online service providers, such as Google, Microsoft, and Amazon, are rapidly building geographically diverse cloud data centers, often containing more than 10K servers, to offer a variety of cloud-based services such as E-mail, Web servers, storage, search, gaming, and Instant Messaging. These service providers also employ some of their data centers to run large-scale data-intensive tasks, such as indexing Web pages or analyzing large data-sets, often using variations of the MapReduce paradigm [6].

Despite the growing applicability of data centers in a wide variety of scenarios, there are very few systematic measurement studies [19, 3] of data center usage to guide practical issues in data center operations. Crucially, little is known about the key differences between different *classes* of data centers, specifically university campus data centers, private enterprise data centers, and cloud data centers (both those used for customer-facing applications and those used for large-scale data-intensives tasks).

While several aspects of data centers still need substantial empirical analysis, the specific focus of our work is on issues pertaining to a data center network's operation. We examine the sending/receiving patterns of applications running in data centers and the resulting link-level and network-level performance. A better understanding of these issues can lead to a variety of advancements, including traffic engineering mechanisms tailored to improve available capacity and reduce loss rates within data centers, mechanisms for improved quality-of-service, and even techniques for managing other crucial data center resources, such as energy consumption. Unfortunately, the few recent empirical studies [19, 3] of data center networks are quite limited in their scope, making their observations difficult to generalize and employ in practice.

In this paper, we study data collected from *ten data centers* to shed light on their network design and usage and to identify properties that can help improve operation of their networking substrate. The data centers we study include *three university campus data centers, two private enterprise data centers, and five cloud data centers*, three of which run a variety of Internet-facing applications while the remaining two predominantly run MapReduce workloads. Some of the data centers we study have been in operation for over 10 years, while others were commissioned much more recently. Our data includes SNMP link statistics for all data centers, fine-grained packet traces from select switches in four of the data centers, and detailed topology for five data centers. By studying different classes of data centers, we are able to shed light on the question of how similar or different they are in terms of their network usage, whether results taken from one class can be applied to the others, and whether different solutions will be needed for designing and managing the data centers' internal networks.

We perform a top-down analysis of the data centers, starting with

IMC'10, November 1–3, 2010, Melbourne, Australia.

the applications run in each data center and then drilling down to the applications' send and receive patterns and their network-level impact. Using packet traces, we first examine the type of applications running in each data center and their relative contribution to network traffic. We then examine the fine-grained sending patterns as captured by data transmission behavior at the packet and flow levels. We examine these patterns both in aggregate and at a per-application level. Finally, we use SNMP traces to examine the network-level impact in terms of link utilization, congestion, and packet drops, and the dependence of these properties on the location of the links in the network topology and on the time of day.

Our key empirical findings are the following:

- We see a wide variety of applications across the data centers, ranging from customer-facing applications, such as Web services, file stores, authentication services, Line-of-Business applications, and custom enterprise applications to data intensive applications, such as MapReduce and search indexing. We find that application placement is non-uniform across racks.

- Most flows in the data centers are small in size ($\leq 10KB$), a significant fraction of which last under a few hundreds of milliseconds, and the number of active flows per second is under 10,000 per rack across all data centers.

- Despite the differences in the size and usage of the data centers, traffic originating from a rack in a data center is ON/OFF in nature with properties that fit heavy-tailed distributions.

- In the cloud data centers, a majority of traffic originated by servers (80%) stays within the rack. For the university and private enterprise data centers, most of the traffic (40-90%) leaves the rack and traverses the network's interconnect.

- Irrespective of the type, in most data centers, link utilizations are rather low in all layers but the core. In the core, we find that a subset of the core links often experience high utilization. Furthermore, the exact number of highly utilized core links varies over time, but never exceeds 25% of the core links in any data center.

- Losses occur within the data centers; however, losses are not localized to links with persistently high utilization. Instead, losses occur at links with low average utilization implicating momentary spikes as the primary cause of losses. We observe that the magnitude of losses is greater at the aggregation layer than at the edge or the core layers.

- We observe that link utilizations are subject to time-of-day and day-of-week effects across all data centers. However in many of the cloud data centers, the variations are nearly an order of magnitude more pronounced at core links than at edge and aggregation links.

To highlight the implications of our observations, we conclude the paper with an analysis of two data center network design issues that have received a lot of recent attention, namely, network bisection bandwidth and the use of centralized management techniques.

- **Bisection Bandwidth:** Recent data center network proposals have argued that data centers need high bisection bandwidth to support demanding applications. Our measurements show that only a fraction of the *existing bisection capacity* is likely to be utilized *within a given time interval* in all the data centers, even in the "worst case" where application instances are spread across racks rather than confined within a rack. This is true even for MapReduce data centers that see relatively higher utilization. From this, we conclude that load balancing mechanisms for spreading traffic across the existing links in the network's core can help manage occasional congestion, given the current applications used.

- **Centralization Management:** A few recent proposals [2, 14] have argued for centrally managing and scheduling network-wide transmissions to more effectively engineer data center traffic. Our measurements show that centralized approaches must employ parallelism and fast route computation heuristics to scale to the size of data centers today while supporting the application traffic patterns we observe in the data centers.

Data Center Study	Type of Data Center	Type of Apps	# of DCs Measured
Fat-tree [1]	Cloud	MapReduce	0
Hedera [2]	Cloud	MapReduce	0
Portland [22]	Cloud	MapReduce	0
BCube [13]	Cloud	MapReduce	0
DCell [16]	Cloud	MapReduce	0
VAL2 [11]	Cloud	MapReduce	1
Micro TE [4]	Cloud	MapReduce	1
Flyways [18]	Cloud	MapReduce	1
Optical switching [29]	Cloud	MapReduce	1
ECMP. study 1 [19]	Cloud	MapReduce	1
ECMP. study 2 [3]	Cloud	MapReduce Web Services	19
Elastic Tree [14]	ANY	Web Services	1
SPAIN [21]	Any	Any	0
Our work	Cloud Private Net Universities	MapReduce Webservices Distributed F'S	10

Table 1: Comparison of prior data center studies, including type of data center and application.

The rest of the paper is structured as follows: we present related work in Section 2 and in Section 3 describe the data centers studied, their high-level design, and typical uses. In Section 4, we describe the applications running in these data centers. In Section 5, we zoom into the microscopic properties of the various data centers. In Section 6, we examine the flow of traffic within data centers and the utilization of links across the various layers. We discuss the implications of our empirical insights in Section 7, and we summarize our findings in Section 8.

2. RELATED WORK

There is tremendous interest in designing improved networks for data centers [1, 2, 22, 13, 16, 11, 4, 18, 29, 14, 21]; however, such work and its evaluation is driven by only a few studies of data center traffic, and those studies are solely of huge (> 10K server) data centers, primarily running data mining, MapReduce jobs, or Web services. Table 1 summarizes the prior studies. From Table 1, we observe that many of the data architectures are evaluated without empirical data from data centers. For the architectures evaluated with empirical data, we find that these evaluations are performed with traces from cloud data centers. These observations imply that the actual performance of these techniques under various types of realistic data centers found in the wild (such as enterprise and university data centers) is unknown and thus we are motivated by this to conduct a broad study on the characteristics of data centers. Such a study will inform the design and evaluation of current and future data center techniques.

This paper analyzes the network traffic of the broadest set of data centers studied to date, including data centers running Web services and MapReduce applications, but also other common enterprise and campus data centers that provide file storage, authentication services, Line-of-Business applications, and other custom-written services. Thus, our work provides the information needed to evaluate data center network architecture proposals under the broad range of data center environments that exist.

Previous studies [19, 3] have focused on traffic patterns at coarse time-scales, reporting flow size distributions, number of concurrent connections, duration of congestion periods, and diurnal patterns. We extend these measures by considering additional issues, such as the applications employed in the different data centers, their transmission patterns at the packet and flow levels, their impact on link and network utilizations, and the prevalence of network hot-spots. This additional information is crucial to evaluating traffic engineering strategies and data center placement/scheduling proposals.

The closest prior works are [19] and [3]; the former focuses on a single MapReduce data centers, while the latter considers cloud data centers that host Web services as well as those running MapReduce. Neither study considers non-cloud data centers, such as enterprise and campus data centers, and neither provides as complete a picture of traffic patterns as this study. The key observations from Benson's study [3] are that utilizations are highest in the core but losses are highest at the edge. In our work, we augment these findings by examining the variations in link utilizations over time, the localization of losses to link, and the magnitude of losses over time. From Kandula's study [19], we learned that while most traffic in the cloud is restricted to within a rack and a significant number of hot-spots exist in the network. Our work supplements these results by quantifying the exact fraction of traffic that stays within a rack for a wide range of data centers. In addition, we quantify the number of hot-spots, show that losses are due to the underlying burstiness of traffic, and examine the flow level properties for university and private enterprise (both are classes of data centers ignored in Kandula's study [19]).

Our work complements prior work on measuring Internet traffic [20, 10, 25, 9, 8, 17] by presenting an equivalent study on the flow characteristics of applications and link utilizations within data centers. We find that data center traffic is statistically different from wide area traffic, and that such behavior has serious implications for the design and implementation of techniques for data center networks.

3. DATASETS AND OVERVIEW OF DATA CENTERS

In this paper, we analyze data-sets from 10 data centers, including 5 commercial cloud data centers, 2 private enterprise data centers, and 3 university campus data centers. For each of these data centers, we examine one or more of the following data-sets: network topology, packet traces from select switches, and SNMP polls from the interfaces of network switches. Table 2 summarizes the data collected from each data center, as well as some key properties.

Table 2 shows that the data centers vary in size, both in terms of the number of devices and the number of servers. Unsurprisingly, the largest data centers are used for commercial computing needs (all owned by a single entity), with the enterprise and university data centers being an order of magnitude smaller in terms of the number of devices.

The data centers also vary in their proximity to their users. The enterprise and university data centers are located in the western/mid-western U.S. and are hosted on the premises of the organizations to serve local users. In contrast, the commercial data centers are distributed around the world in the U.S., Europe, and South America. Their global placement reflects an inherent requirement for geo-diversity (reducing latency to users), geo-redundancy (avoiding strikes, wars, or fiber cuts in one part of the world), and regulatory constraints (some data can not be removed from the E.U. or U.S.).

Data Center Name	Number of Locations
EDU1	1
EDU2	1
EDU3	1
PRV2	4

Table 3: The number of packet trace collection locations for the data centers in which we were able to install packet sniffers.

In what follows, we first describe the data we collect. We then outline similarities and differences in key attributes of the data centers, including their usage profiles, and physical topology. We found that understanding these aspects is required to analyze the properties that we wish to measure in subsequent sections, such as application behavior and its impact on link-level and network-wide utilizations.

3.1 Data Collection

SNMP polls: For all of the data centers that we studied, we were able to poll the switches' SNMP MIBs for bytes-in and bytes-out at granularities ranging from 1 minute to 30 minutes. For the 5 commercial cloud data centers and the 2 private enterprises, we were able to poll for the number of packet discards as well.

For each data center, we collected SNMP data for at least 10 days. In some cases (e.g., EDU1, EDU2, EDU3, PRV1, PRV2, CLD1, CLD4), our SNMP data spans multiple weeks. The long time-span of our SNMP data allows us to observe time-of-day and day-of-week dependencies in network traffic.

Network Topology: For the private enterprises and university data centers, we obtained topology via the Cisco CDP protocol, which gives both the network topology as well as the link capacities. When this data is unavailable, as with the 5 cloud data centers, we analyze device configuration to derive properties of the topology, such as the relative capacities of links facing endhosts versus network-internal links versus WAN-facing links.

Packet traces: Finally, we collected packet traces from a few of the private enterprise and university data centers (Table 2). Our packet trace collection spans 12 hours over multiple days. Since it is difficult to instrument an entire data center, we selected a handful of locations at random per data center and installed sniffers on them. In Table 3, we present the number of sniffers per data center. In the smaller data centers (EDU1, EDU2, EDU3), we installed 1 sniffer. For the larger data center (PRV2), we installed 4 sniffers. All traces were captured using a Cisco port span. To account for delay introduced by the packet duplication mechanism and for endhost clock skew, we binned results from the spans into 10 microsecond bins.

3.2 High-level Usage of the Data Centers

In this section, we outline important high-level similarities and differences among the data centers we studied.

University data centers: These data centers serve the students and administrative staff of the university in question. They provide a variety of services, ranging from system back-ups to hosting distributed file systems, E-mail servers, Web services (administra-

Data Center Role	Data Center Name	Location	Age (Years) (Curr Ver/Total)	SNMP	Packet Traces	Topology	Number Devices	Number Servers	Over Subscription
Universities	EDU1	US-Mid	10	✓	✓	✓	22	500	2:1
	EDU2	US-Mid	(7/20)	✓	✓	✓	36	1093	47:1
	EDU3	US-Mid	N/A	✓	✓	✓	1	147	147:1
Private	PRV1	US-Mid	(5/5)	✓	X	✓	96	1088	8:3
	PRV2	US-West	> 5	✓	✓	✓	100	2000	48:10
Commercial	CLD1	US-West	> 5	✓	X	X	562	10K	20:1
	CLD2	US-West	> 5	✓	X	X	763	15K	20:1
	CLD3	US-East	> 5	✓	X	X	612	12K	20:1
	CLD4	S. America	(3/3)	✓	X	X	427	10K	20:1
	CLD5	S. America	(3/3)	✓	X	X	427	10K	20:1

Table 2: Summary of the 10 data centers studied, including devices, types of information collected, and the number of servers.

tive sites and web portals for students and faculty), and multicast video streams. We provide the exact application mix in the next section. In talking to the network operators, we found that these data centers "organically" evolved over time, moving from a collection of devices in a storage closet to a dedicated room for servers and network devices. As the data centers reached capacity, the operators re-evaluated their design and architecture. Many operators chose to move to a more structured, two-layer topology and introduced server virtualization to reduce heating and power requirements while controlling data center size.

Private enterprises: The private enterprise IT data centers serve corporate users, developers, and a small number of customers. Unlike university data centers, the private enterprise data centers support a significant number of custom applications, in addition to hosting traditional services like Email, storage, and Web services. They often act as development testbeds, as well. These data centers are developed in a ground-up fashion, being designed specifically to support the demands of the enterprise. For instance, to satisfy the need to support administrative services and beta testing of database-dependent products, PRV1 commissioned the development of an in-house data center 5 years ago. PRV2 was designed over 5 years ago mostly to support custom Line-of-Business applications and to provide login servers for remote users.

Commercial cloud data centers: Unlike the first two classes of data centers, the commercial data centers cater to external users and offer support for a wide range of Internet-facing services, including: Instant Messaging, Webmail, search, indexing, and video. Additionally, the data centers host large internal systems that support the externally visible services, for example data mining, storage, and relational databases (e.g., for buddy lists). These data centers are often purpose-built to support a specific set of applications (e.g., with a particular topology or over-subscription ratio to some target application patterns), but there is also a tension to make them as general as possible so that the application mix can change over time as the usage evolves. CLD1, CLD2, CLD3 host a variety of applications, ranging from Instant Messaging and Webmail to advertisements and web portals. CLD4 and CLD5 are primarily used for running MapReduce style applications.

3.3 Topology and Composition of the Data Centers

In this section, we examine the differences and similarities in the physical construction of the data centers. Before proceeding to examine the physical topology of the data centers studied, we present a brief overview of the topology of a generic data center. In Figure 1, we present a canonical 3-Tiered data center. The 3 tiers of the data center are the edge tier, which consists of the Top-of-Rack switches that connect the servers to the data center's network fabric; the aggregation tier, which consists of devices that interconnect the ToR switches in the edge layer; and the core tier, which consists of devices that connect the data center to the WAN. In smaller data centers, the core tier and the aggregation tier are collapsed into one tier, resulting in a 2-Tiered data center topology.

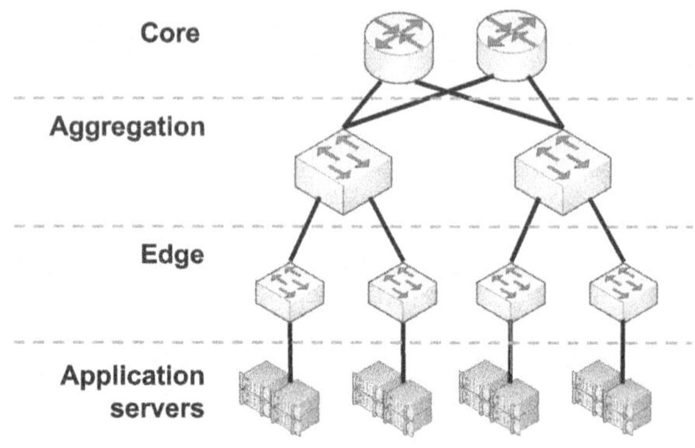

Figure 1: Canonical 3-Tier data center topology.

Now, we focus on topological structure and the key physical properties of the constituent devices and links. We find that the topology of the data center is often an accident of history. Some have regular patterns that could be leveraged for traffic engineering strategies like Valiant Load Balancing [11], while most would require either a significant upgrade or more general strategies.

Topology. Of the three university data centers, we find that two (EDU1, EDU2) have evolved into a structured 2-Tier architecture. The third (EDU3) uses a star-like topology with a high-capacity central switch interconnecting a collection of server racks – a design that has been used since the inception of this data center. As of this writing, the data center was migrating to a more structured set-up similar to the other two.

EDU1 uses a topology that is similar to a canonical 2-Tier architecture, with one key difference: while the canonical 2-Tier data centers use Top-of-Rack switches, where each switch connects to a rack of 20-80 servers or so, these two data centers utilize Middle-of-Rack switches that connect a row of 5 to 6 racks with the potential to connect from 120 to 180 servers. We find that similar conclusions hold for EDU2 (omitted for brevity).

The enterprise data centers do not deviate much from textbook-style constructions. In particular, the PRV1 enterprise data center utilizes a canonical 2-Tier Cisco architecture. The PRV2 data center utilizes a canonical 3-Tier Cisco architecture.

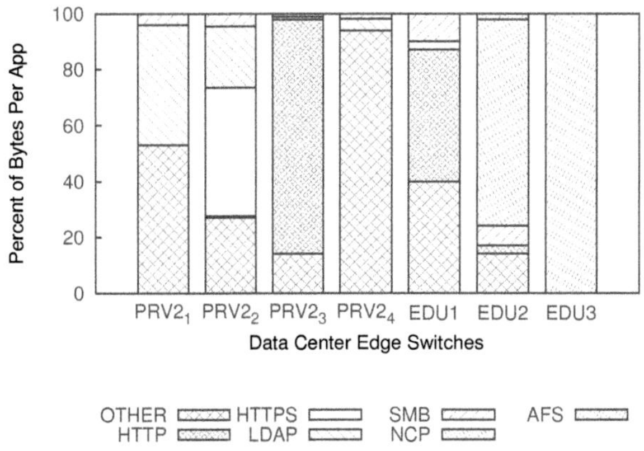

Figure 2: Classification of network traffic to application using Bro-Id. Each of the sniffers sees a very different mix of applications, even though the first 4 sniffers are located on different switches in the same data center.

Note that we do not have the physical topologies from the cloud data centers, although the operators of these data centers tell us that these networks uniformly employ the 3-Tier textbook data center architectures described in [11].

4. APPLICATIONS IN DATA CENTERS

We begin our "top-down" analysis of data centers by first focusing on the applications they run. In particular, we aim to answer the following questions: (1) What type of applications are running within these data centers? and, (2) What fraction of traffic originated by a switch is contributed by each application?

We employ packet trace data in this analysis and use Bro-Id [26] to perform application classification. Recall that we collected packet trace data for 7 switches spanning 4 data centers, namely, the university campus data centers, EDU1, EDU2, and EDU3, and a private enterprise data center, PRV2. To lend further weight to our observations, we spoke to the operators of each data center, including the 6 for which we did not have packet trace data. The operators provided us with additional information about the specific applications running in their data centers.

The type of applications found at each edge switch, along with their relative traffic volumes, are shown in Figure 2. Each bar corresponds to a sniffer in a data center, and the first 4 bars are from the 4 edges switches within the same data center (PRV2). In conversing with the operators, we discovered that this data center hosts a mixture of authentication services (labeled "LDAP"), 3-Tier Line-Of-Business Web applications (captured in "HTTP" and "HTTPS"), and custom home-brewed applications (captured in "Others").

By looking at the composition of the 4 bars for PRV2, we can infer how the services and applications are deployed across racks in the data center. We find that each of the edge switches monitored hosts a portion of the back-end for the custom applications (captured in "Others"). In particular, the rack corresponding to $PRV2_4$ appears to predominantly host custom applications that contribute over 90% of the traffic from this switch. At the other switches, these applications make up 50%, 25%, and 10% of the bytes, respectively.

Further, we find that the secure portions of the Line-of-Business Web services (labeled "HTTPS") are hosted in the rack corresponding to the edge switch $PRV2_2$, but not in the other three racks monitored. Authentication services (labeled "LDAP") are deployed across the racks corresponding to $PRV2_1$ and $PRV2_2$, which makes up a significant fraction of bytes from these switches (40% of the bytes from $PRV2_1$ and 25% of the byes from $PRV2_2$). A small amount of LDAP traffic (2% of all bytes on average) originates from the other two switches, as well, but this is mostly request traffic headed for the authentication services in $PRV2_1$ and $PRV2_2$.

Finally, the unsecured portions of the Line-of-Business (consisting of help pages and basic documentation) are located predominantly on the rack corresponding to the edge switch $PRV2_3$—nearly 85% of the traffic originating from this rack is HTTP.

We also see some amount of file-system traffic (SMB) across all the 4 switches (roughly 4% of the bytes on average).

Clustering of application components within this data center leads us to believe that emerging patterns of virtualization and consolidations have not yet led to applications being spread across the switches.

Next, we focus on the last 3 bars, which correspond to an edge switch each in the 3 university data centers, EDU1, EDU2 and EDU3. While these 3 data centers serve the same types of users we observe variations across the networks. Two of the university data centers, EDU2 and EDU3, seem to primarily utilize the network for distributed file systems traffic, namely AFS and NCP—AFS makes up nearly all the traffic seen at the EDU3 switch, while NCP constitutes nearly 80% of the traffic at the EDU2 switch. The traffic at the last data center, EDU1, is split 60/40 between Web services (both HTTP and HTTPS) and other applications such as file sharing (SMB). The operator of this data center tells us that the data center also hosts payroll and benefits applications, which are captured in "Others."

Note that we find file system traffic to constitute a more significant fraction of the switches in the university data centers we monitored compared to the enterprise data center.

The key take-aways from the above observations are that (1) There is a wide variety of applications observed both within and across data centers, such as "regular" and secure HTTP transactions, authentication services, file-system traffic, and custom applications and (2) We observe a wide variation in the composition of traffic originated by the switches in a given data center (see the 4 switches corresponding to PRV2). This implies that one cannot assume that applications are placed uniformly at random in data centers.

For the remaining data centers (i.e., PRV1, CLD1–5), where we did not have access to packet traces, we used information from operators to understand the application mix. CLD4 and CLD5 are utilized for running MapReduce jobs, with each job, scheduled to pack as many of its nodes as possible into the same rack to reduce demand on the data center's core interconnect. In contrast, CLD1, CLD2, and CLD3 host a variety of applications, ranging from messaging and Webmail to Web portals. Each of these applications is comprised of multiple components with intricate dependencies, deployed across the entire data center. For example, the Web portal requires access to an authentication service for verifying users, and it also requires access to a wide range of Web services from which data is aggregated. Instant Messaging similarly utilizes an authentication service and composes the user's buddy list by aggregating data spread across different data stores. The application mix found in the data centers impacts the traffic results, which we look at next.

5. APPLICATION COMMUNICATION PATTERNS

In the previous section, we described the set of applications running in each of the 10 data centers and observed that a variety of applications run in the data centers and that their placement is non-uniform. In this section, we analyze the aggregate network transmission behavior of the applications, both at the flow-level and at the finer-grained packet-level. Specifically, we aim to answer the following questions: (1) What are the aggregate characteristics of flow arrivals, sizes, and durations? and (2) What are the aggregate characteristics of the packet-level inter-arrival process across all applications in a rack — that is, how bursty are the transmission patterns of these applications? These aspects have important implications for the performance of the network and its links.

As before, we use the packet traces in our analysis.

5.1 Flow-Level Communication Characteristics

First, we examine the number of active flows across the 4 data centers where we have packet-level data, EDU1, EDU2, EDU3, and PRV2. To identify active flows, we use a long inactivity timeout of 60 seconds (similar to that used in previous measurements studies [19]).

In Figure 3(a), we present the distribution of the number of active flows within a one second bin, as seen at seven different switches within 4 data centers. We find that although the distribution varies across the data centers, the number of active flows at any given interval is less than 10,000. Based on the distributions, we group the 7 monitored switches into two classes. In the first class are all of the university data center switches EDU1, EDU2 and EDU3, and one of the switches from a private enterprise, namely $PRV2_4$, where the number of active flows is between 10 and 500 in 90% of the time intervals. In the second class, are the remaining switches from the enterprise, namely, $PRV2_1$, $PRV2_2$, and $PRV2_3$, where the number of active flows is between 1,000 and 5,000 about 90% of the time.

We examine the flow inter-arrival times in Figure 3(b). We find that the time between new flows arriving at the monitored switch is less than $10\mu s$ for 2-13% of the flows. For most of the switches in PRV2, 80% of the flows have an inter-arrival time under 1ms. This observation supports the results of a prior study [19] of a cloud data center. However, we found that this observation *does not* hold for the university data centers, where we see 80% of the flow inter-arrival times were between 4ms and 40ms, suggesting that these data centers have less churn than PRV2 and the previously studied cloud data center [19]. Among other issues, flow inter-arrival time affects what kinds of processing can be done for each new flow and the feasibility of logically centralized controllers for flow placement. We return to these questions in Section 7.

Next, we examine the distributions of flow sizes and and lengths in Figure 4(a) and (b), respectively. From Figure 4(a), we find that flow sizes are roughly similar across all the studied switches and data centers. Across the data centers, we note that 80% of the flows are smaller than 10KB in size. Most of the bytes are in the top 10% of large flows. From Figure 4(b), we find that for most of the data centers 80% of the flows are less than 11 seconds long. These results support the observations made in prior a study [19] of a cloud data center. However, we do note that the flows in EDU2 appear to be generally shorter and smaller than the flows in the other data centers. We believe this is due to the nature of the predominant application that accounts for over 70% of the bytes at the switch.

Finally, in Figure 5, we examine the distribution of packet sizes in the studied data centers. The packet sizes exhibit a bimodal pattern, with most packet sizes clustering around either 200 Bytes and 1400 Bytes. Surprisingly, we found application keep-alive packets as a major reason for the small packets, with TCP acknowledgments, as expected, being the other major contributor. Upon close inspection of the packet traces, we found that certain applications, including MSSQL, HTTP, and SMB, contributed more small packets than large packets. In one extreme case, we found an application producing 5 times as many small packets as large packets. This result speaks to how commonly persistent connections occur as a design feature in data center applications, and the importance of continually maintaining them.

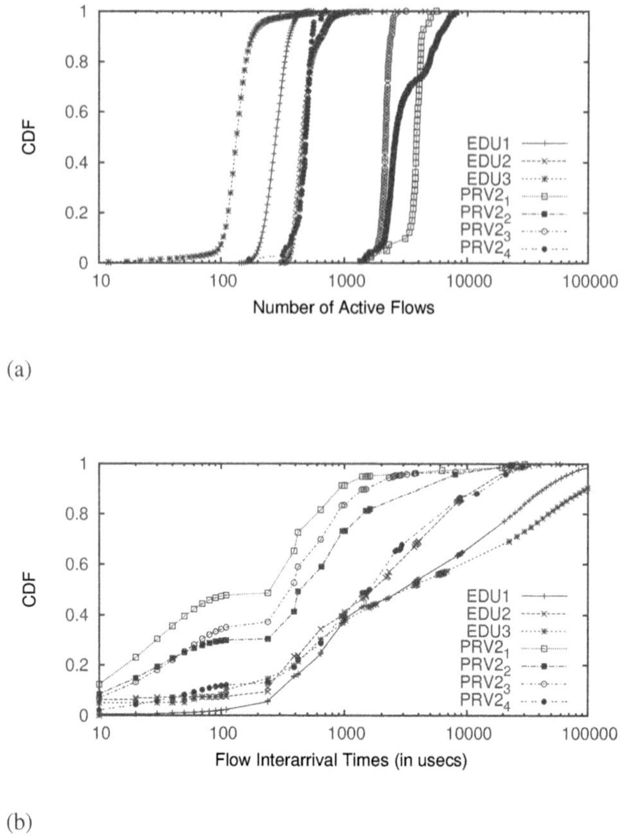

Figure 3: CDF of the distribution of the number of flows at the edge switch (a) and the arrival rate for flows (b) in EDU1, EDU2, EDU3, and PRV2.

5.2 Packet-Level Communication Characteristics

We first examine the temporal characteristics of the packet traces. Figure 6 shows a time-series of packet arrivals observed at one of the sniffers in PRV2, and the packet arrivals exhibit an ON/OFF pattern at both 15ms and 100ms granularities. We observed similar traffic patterns at the remaining 6 switches as well.

Per-packet arrival process: Leveraging the observation that traffic is ON/OFF, we use a packet inter-arrival time threshold to identify the ON/OFF periods in the traces. Let $arrival_{95}$ be the 95th percentile value in the inter-arrival time distribution at a particular switch. We define a $period_{on}$ as the longest continual period during which all the packet inter-arrival times are smaller than $arrival_{95}$. Accordingly, a $period_{off}$ is a period between two ON periods. To characterize this ON/OFF traffic pattern, we focus on three aspects: (i) the durations of the ON periods, (ii) the durations

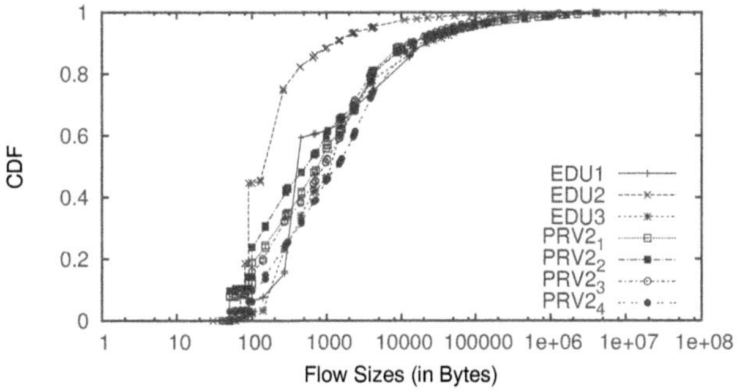

(a)

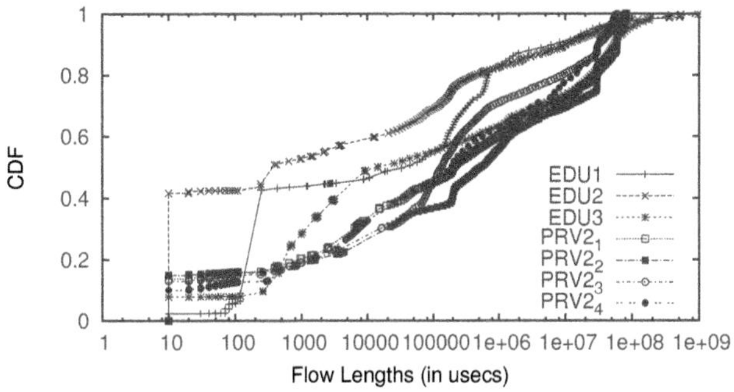

(b)

Figure 4: CDF of the distribution of the flow sizes (a) and of flow lengths (b) in PRV2, EDU1, EDU2, and EDU3.

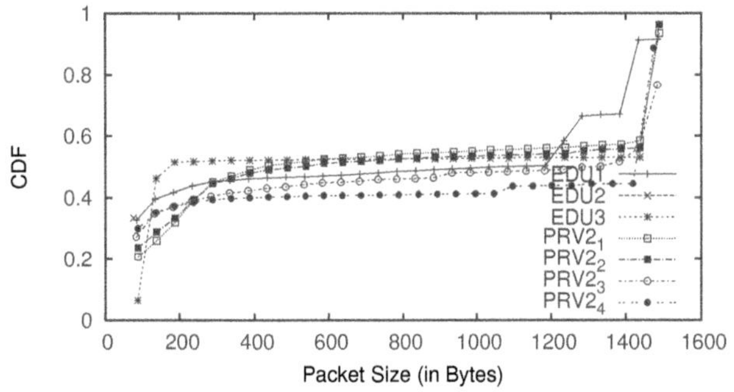

Figure 5: Distribution of packet size in the various networks.

of the OFF periods, and (iii) the packet inter-arrival times within ON periods.

Figure 7(a) shows the distribution of inter-arrival times within ON periods at one of the switches for PRV2. We bin the inter-arrival times according to the clock granularity of $10\mu s$. Note that the distribution has a positive skew and a heavy tail. We attempted to fit several heavy-tailed distributions and found that the lognormal curve produces the best fit with the least mean error. Figure 7(b)

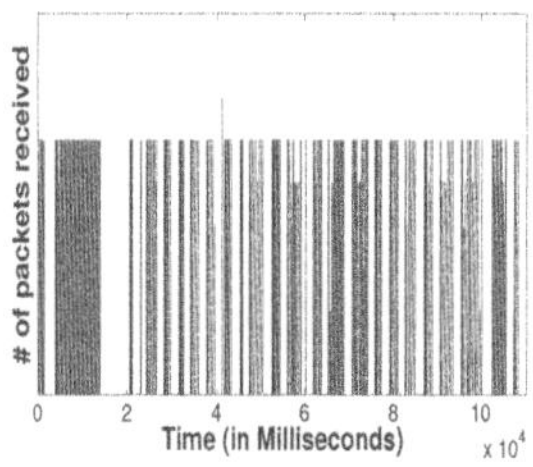

(a) 15ms

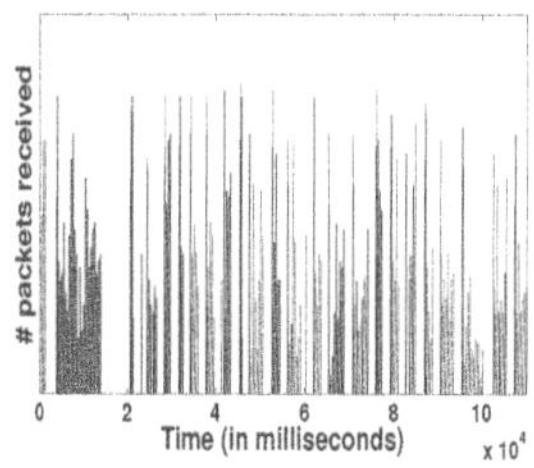

(b) 100ms

Figure 6: ON/OFF characteristics: Time series of Data Center traffic (number of packets per time) binned by two different time scales.

Data center	Off period Distribution	ON period Distribution	Interarrival Rate Distribution
$PRV2_1$	Lognormal	Lognormal	Lognormal
$PRV2_2$	Lognormal	Lognormal	Lognormal
$PRV2_3$	Lognormal	Lognormal	Lognormal
$PRV2_4$	Lognormal	Lognormal	Lognormal
EDU1	Lognormal	Weibull	Weibull
EDU2	Lognormal	Weibull	Weibull
EDU3	Lognormal	Weibull	Weibull

Table 4: The distribution for the parameters of each of the arrival processes of the various switches.

shows the distribution of the durations of ON periods. Similar to the inter-arrival time distribution, this ON period distribution also exhibits a positive skew and fits well with a lognormal curve. The same observation can be applied to the OFF period distribution as well, as shown in Figure 7(c).

We found qualitatively similar characteristics at the other 6 switches where packet traces were collected. However, in fitting a distribution to the packet traces (Table 4), we found that only the OFF period at the different switches consistently fit the lognormal distribution. For the ON periods and interarrival rates, we found that best distribution was either Weibull and lognormal, varying by data center.

Our findings indicate that certain positive skewed and heavy-tailed distributions can model data center switch traffic. This highlights a difference between the data center environment and the wide area network, where the long-tailed Pareto distribution typically shows the best fit [27, 24]. The differences between these distributions should be taken into account when attempting to apply models or techniques from wide area networking to data centers.

Per-application arrival process: Recall that the data centers in this analysis, namely, EDU1, EDU2, EDU3, and PRV2, are dominated by Web and distributed file-system traffic (Figure 2). We now examine the arrival processes for these dominant applications to see if they explain the aggregate arrival process at the corresponding switches. In Table 5, we present the distribution that best fits the arrival process for the dominant application. From this table, we notice that the dominant applications in the universities (EDU1, EDU2, EDU3), which account for 70–100% of the bytes at the respective switches, are indeed characterized by identical heavy-tailed distributions as the aggregate traffic. However, in the case of two of the PRV2 switches (#1 and #3), we find that the dominant application differs slightly from the aggregate behavior. Thus, in the general case, we find that simply relying on the characteristics of the most dominant applications is not sufficient to accurately model the aggregate arrival processes at data center edge switches.

Data center	Off period Distribution	Interarrival Rate Distribution	ON period Distribution	Dominant Applications
$PRV2_1$	Lognormal	Weibull	Exponential	Others
$PRV2_2$	Weibull	Lognormal	Lognormal	LDAP
$PRV2_3$	Weibull	Lognormal	Exponential	HTTP
$PRV2_4$	Lognormal	Lognormal	Weibull	Others
EDU1	Lognormal	Lognormal	Weibull	HTTP
EDU2	Lognormal	Weibull	Weibull	NCP
EDU3	Lognormal	Weibull	Weibull	AFS

Table 5: The distribution for the parameters of each of the arrival processes of the dominant applications on each switch.

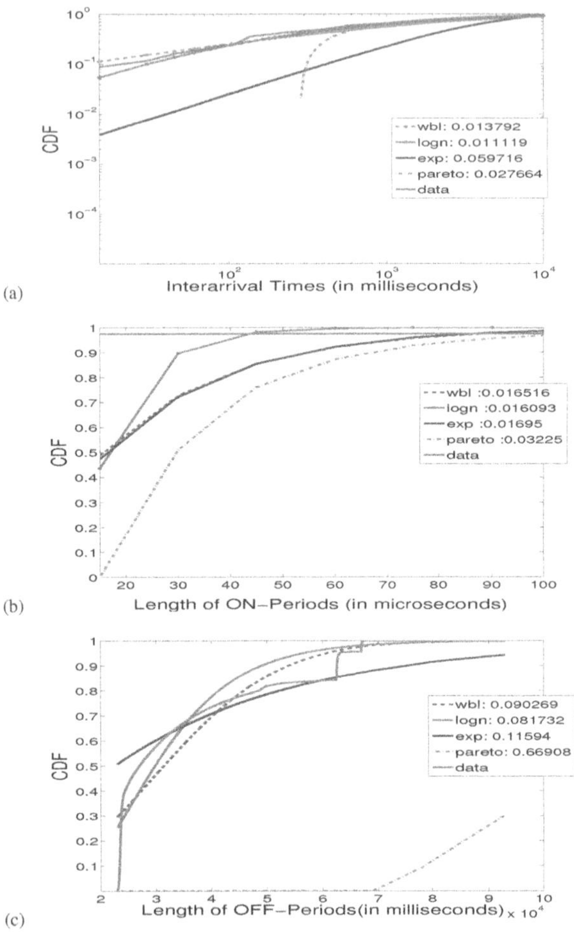

Figure 7: CDF of the distribution of the arrival times of packets at 3 of the switches in PRV2. The figure contains best fit curve for lognormal, Weibull, Pareto, and Exponential distributions, as well as the least mean errors for each.

Finally, we compare the observed distributions for HTTP applications in the data center against HTTP applications in the wide area and find that the distribution of ON periods in the data center *does* match observations made by others [7] in the WAN.

The take aways from our observations are that: (1) The number of active flows at a switch in any given second is, at most, 10,000 flows. However, new flows can arrive within rapid succession ($10\mu s$) of each other, resulting in high instantaneous arrival rates; (2) Most flows in the data centers we examined are small in size ($\leq 10KB$) and a significant fraction last under a few hundreds of milliseconds; (3) Traffic leaving the edge switches in a data center is bursty in nature and the ON/OFF intervals can be characterized by heavy-tailed distributions; and (4) In some data centers, the predominant application drives the aggregate sending pattern at the edge switch. In the general case, however, simply focusing on dominant applications is insufficient to understand the process driving packet transmission into the data center network.

In the next section, we analyze link utilizations at the various layers within the data center to understand how the bursty nature of traffic impacts the utilization and packet loss of the links at each of the layers.

6. NETWORK COMMUNICATION PATTERNS

In the two previous sections, we examined the applications employed in each of the 10 data centers, their placement, and transmission patterns. In this section, we examine, with the goal of informing data center traffic engineering techniques, how existing data center applications utilize the interconnect. In particular, we aim to answer the following questions: (1) To what extent does the current application traffic utilize the data center's interconnect? For example, is most traffic confined to within a rack or not? (2) What is the utilization of links at different layers in a data center? (3) How often are links heavily utilized and what are the properties of heavily utilized links? For example, how long does heavy utilization persist on these links, and do the highly utilized links experience losses? (4) To what extent do link utilizations vary over time?

6.1 Flow of Traffic

We start by examining the relative proportion of traffic generated by the servers that stays within a rack (Intra-Rack traffic) versus traffic that leaves its rack for either other racks or external destinations (Extra-Rack traffic). Extra-Rack traffic can be directly measured, as it is the amount of traffic on the uplinks of the edge switches (i.e., the "Top-of-Rack" switches). We compute Intra-Rack traffic as the difference between the volume of traffic generated by the servers attached to each edge switch and the traffic exiting edge switches.

In Figure 8, we present a bar graph of the ratio of Extra-Rack to Intra-Rack traffic in the 10 data centers we studied. We note that a predominant portion of server-generated traffic in the cloud data centers CLD1–5—nearly, 75% on average—is confined to within the rack in which it was generated.

Recall from Section 4 that only two of these 5 data centers, CLD4 and CLD5, run MapReduce style applications, while the other three run a mixture of different customer-facing Web services. Despite this key difference in usage, we observe surprisingly little difference in the relative proportions of Intra-Rack and Extra-Rack traffic. This can be explained by revisiting the nature of applications in these data centers: as stated in Section 4, the services running in CLD1–3 have dependencies spread across many servers in the data center. The administrators of these networks try to colocate applications and dependent components into the same racks to avoid sharing a rack with other applications/services. Low Extra-Rack traffic is a side-effect of this artifact. In the case of CLD4 and CLD5, the operators assign MapReduce jobs to co-located servers for similar reasons. However, fault tolerance requires placing redundant components of the application and data storage into different racks, which increases the Extra-Rack communication. Our findings of high Intra-Rack traffic within data centers supports observations made by others [19], where the focus was on cloud data centers running MapReduce.

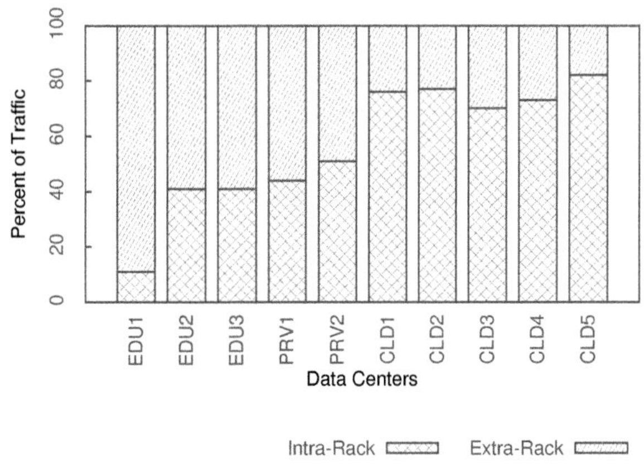

Figure 8: The ratio of Extra-Rack to Intra-Rack traffic in the data centers.

Next, we focus on the enterprise and university data centers. With the exception of EDU1, these appear to be both very different from the cloud data centers and qualitatively similar to each other: at least 50% of the server-originated traffic in the data centers leaves the racks, compared with under 25% for the cloud data centers. These data centers run user-facing applications, such as Web services and file servers. While this application mix is similar to CLD1–3 discussed above, the Intra/Extra rack usage patterns are quite different. A possible reason for the difference is that the placement of dependent services in enterprise and campus data centers may not be as optimized as the cloud data centers.

6.2 Link Utilizations vs Layer

Next, we examine the impact of the Extra-Rack traffic on the links within the interconnect of the various data centers. We examine link utilization as a function of location in the data center topology. Recall that all 10 data centers employed 2-Tiered or 3-Tiered tree-like networks.

In performing this study, we studied several hundred 5-minute intervals at random for each data center and examined the link utilizations as reported by SNMP. In Figure 9, we present the utilization for links across different layers in the data centers for one such representative interval.

In general, we find that utilizations within the core/aggregation layers are higher than those at the edge; this observation holds across all classes of data centers. These findings support observations made by others [3], where the focus was on cloud data centers.

A key point to note, not raised by prior work [3], is that across the various data centers, there are differences in the tail of the distributions for all layers–in some data centers, such as CLD4, there is a greater prevalence of high utilization links (i.e., utilization 70% or greater) especially in the core layer, while in others there are no high utilization links in any layer (e.g., EDU1). Next, we examine these high utilization links in greater depth.

6.3 Hot-spot Links

In this section, we study the hot-spot links—those with 70% or higher utilization—unearthed in various data centers, focusing on the persistence and prevalence of hot-spots. More specifically, we aim to answer the following questions: (1) Do some links frequently appear as hot-spots? How does this result vary across layers and data centers? (2) How does the set of hot-spot links in a layer change over time? (3) Do hot-spot links experience high packet loss?

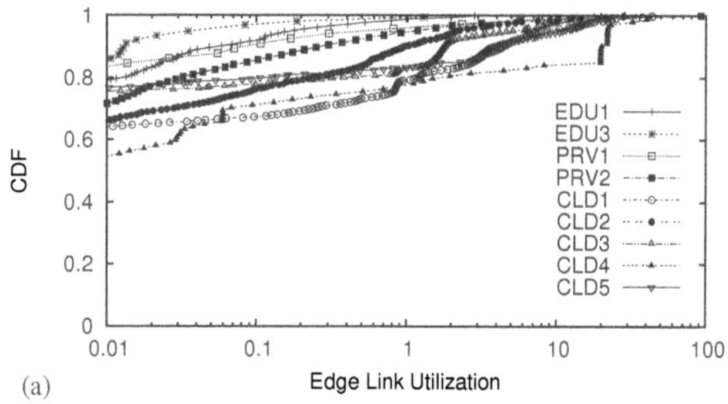

(a)

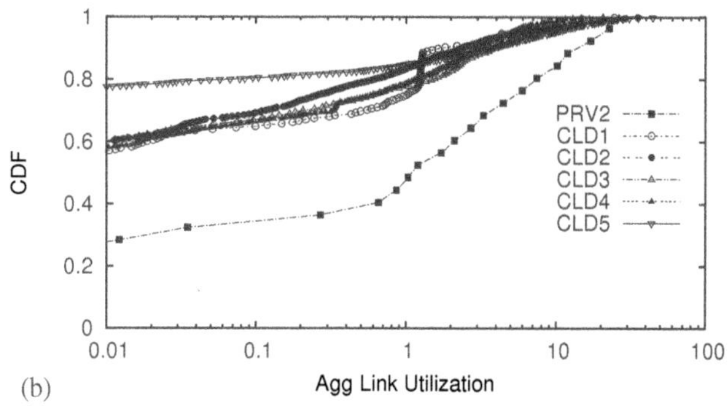

(b)

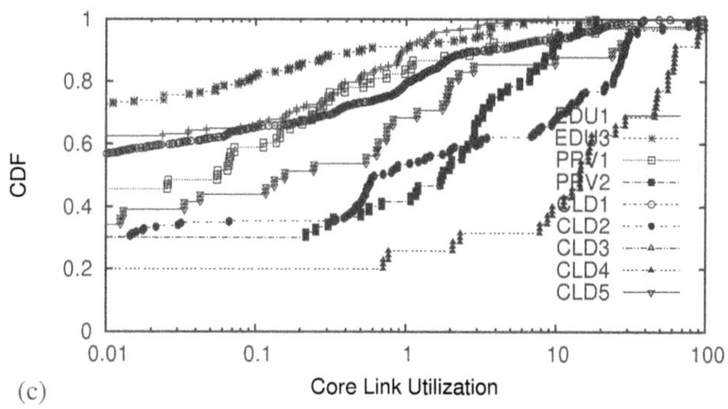

(c)

Figure 9: CDF of link utilizations (percentage) in each layer.

6.3.1 *Persistence and Prevalence*

In Figure 10, we present the distribution of the percentage of time intervals that a link is a hot-spot. We note from Figures 10(a) and (b) that very few links in either the edge or aggregation layers are hot-spots, and this observations holds across all data centers and data center types. Specifically, only 3% of the links in these two layers appear as a hot-spot for more than 0.1% of time intervals. When edge links are congested, they tend to be congested continuously, as in CLD2, where a very small fraction of the edge links appear as hot-spots in 90% of the time intervals.

In contrast, we find that the data centers differ significantly in their core layers (Figure 10(c)). Our data centers cluster into 3 hot-spot classes: (1) *Low Persistence-Low Prevalence:* This class of data centers comprises those where the hot-spots are not localized to any set of links. This includes PRV2, EDU1, EDU2, EDU3, CLD1, and CLD3, where any given core link is a hot-spot for no more than 10% of the time intervals; (2) *High Persistence-Low Prevalence:* The second group of data centers is characterized by hot-spots being localized to a small number of core links. This includes PRV1 and CLD2 where 3% and 8% of the core links, respectively, each appear as hot-spots in > 50% of the time intervals; and (3) *High Persistence-High Prevalence:* Finally, in the last group containing CLD4 and CLD5, a significant fraction of the core links

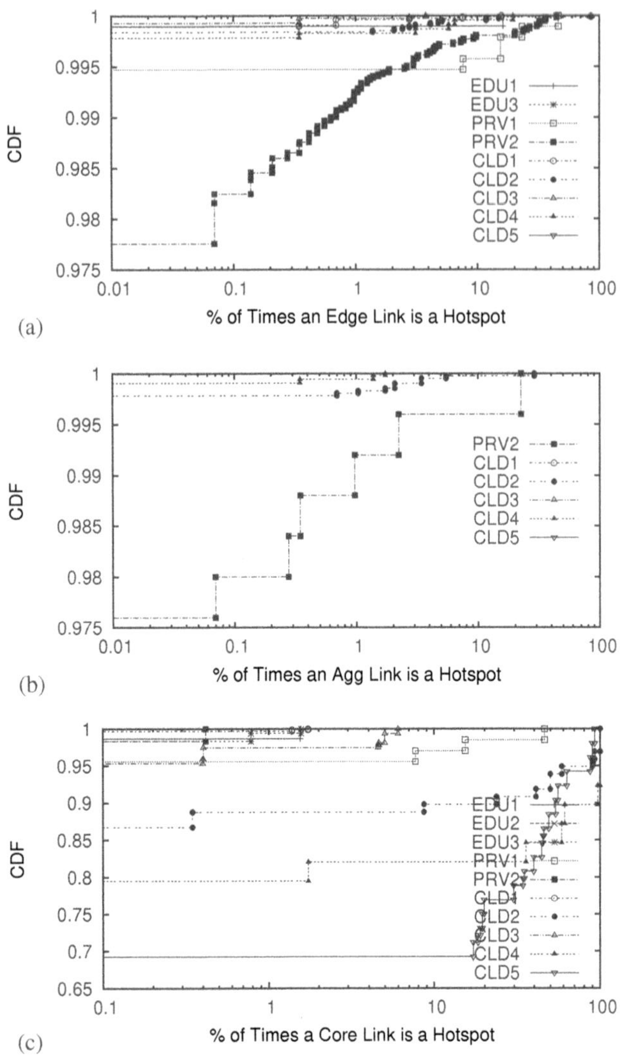

Figure 10: A CDF of the fraction of times that links in the various layers are hot-spots.

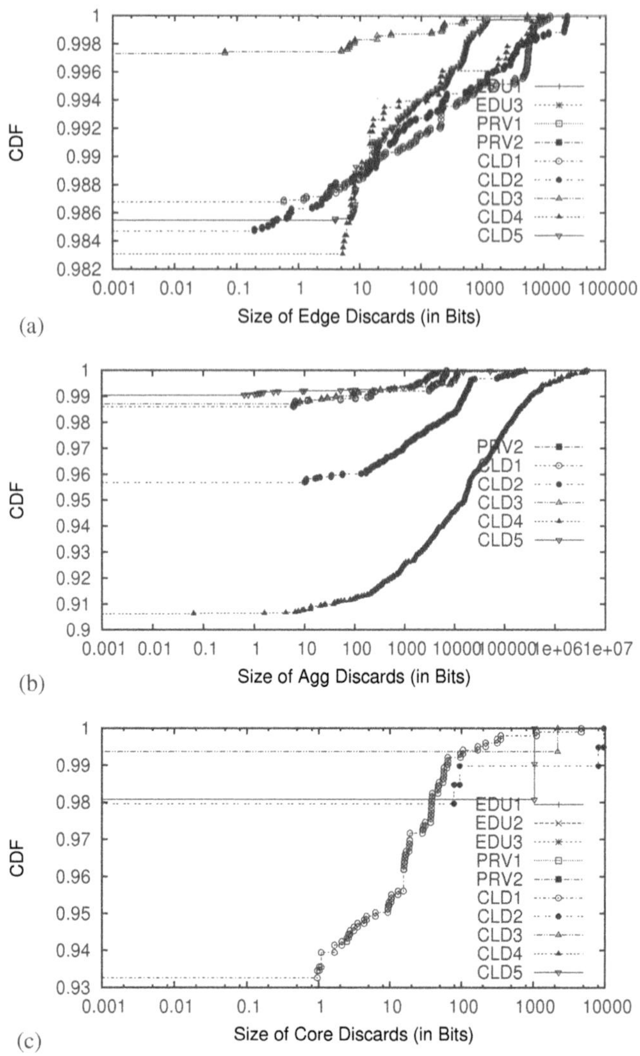

Figure 11: A CDF of the number of bits lost across the various layers.

appear persistently as hot-spots. Specifically, roughly 20% of the core links are hot-spots at least 50% of the time each. Note that both CLD4 and CLD5 run MapReduce applications.

Next, we examine the variation in the fraction of the core links that are hot-spots versus time. In Figure 13, we show our observations for one data center in each of the 3 hot-spot classes just described. From this figure, we observe that each class has a different pattern. In the low persistence-low prevalence data center, CLD1, we find that very few hot-spots occur over the course of the day, and when they do occur, only a small fraction of the core links emerge as hot-spots (less than 0.002%). However, in the high persistence classes, we observe that hot-spots occur throughout the day. Interestingly, with the high persistence-high prevalence data center, CLD5, we observe that the fraction of links that are hot-spots is affected by the time of day. Equally important is that only 25% of the core links in CLD5 are ever hot-spots. This suggests that, depending on the traffic matrix, the remaining 75% of the core links can be utilized to offload some traffic from the hot-spot links.

6.3.2 Hot-spots and Discards

Finally, we study loss rates across links in the data centers. In particular, we start by examining the discards for the set of hot-spot links. Surprisingly, we find that none of the hot-spot links experience loss. This implies that in the data centers studied, loss *does not* correlate with high utilization.

To understand where losses are prevalent, we examine Figures 11 and 12 that display the loss rates and link utilization for the links with losses. In the core and aggregation, all the links with losses have less than 30% average utilization, whereas at the edge, the links with losses have nearly 60% utilization. The fact that links with relatively low average utilization contain losses indicates that these links experience momentary bursts that do not persist for a long enough period to increase the average utilization. These momentary bursts can be explained by the bursty nature of the traffic (Section 5).

6.4 Variations in utilization

In this section, we examine if the utilizations vary over time and whether or not link utilizations are stable and predictable.

We examined the link utilization over a one week period and found that diurnal patterns exist in all data centers. As an example, Figure 14 presents the utilization for input and output traffic at a

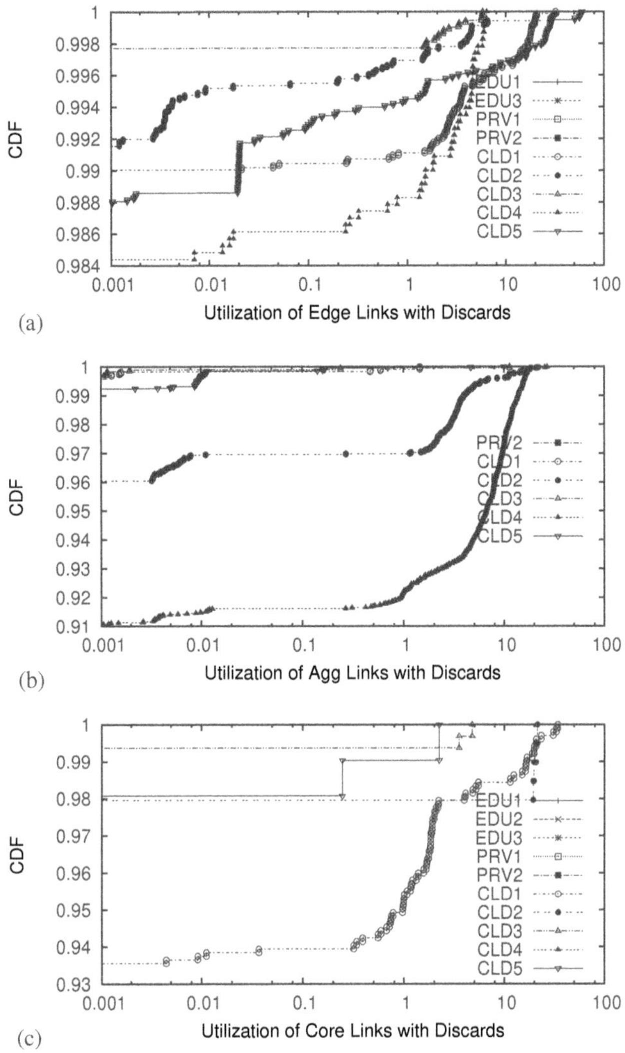

Figure 12: A CDF of the utilization of links with discards.

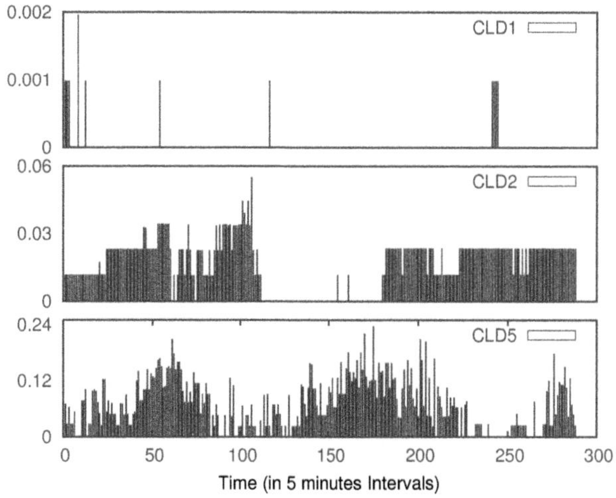

Figure 13: Time series of the fraction of links that are hot-spots in the core layer for CLD1, CLD2, and CLD5.

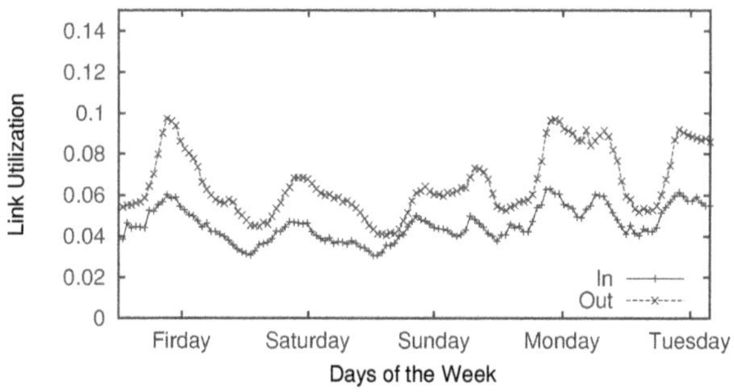

Figure 14: Time-of-Day/Day-of-Week traffic patterns.

router port in one of the cloud data centers. The 5-day trace shows diurnal and pronounced weekend/weekday variations.

To quantify this variation, we examine the difference between peak and trough utilizations for each link across the studied data centers. In Figure 15, we present the distribution of peak versus trough link utilizations across the various data centers. The x-axis is in percentage. We note that edge links in general show very little variation (less than 10% for a least 80% of edge links). The same is true for links in the aggregation layer (where available), although we see slightly greater variability. In particular, links in the aggregation layer of PRV2 show significant variability, whereas those in the other data centers do not (variation is less than 10% for a least 80% of edge links). Note that links with a low degree of variation can be run at a slower speed based on expected traffic volumes. This could result in savings in network energy costs [14].

The variation in link utilizations at the edge/aggregation are similar across the studied data centers. At the core, however, we are able to distinguish between several of the data centers. While most have low variations (less than 1%), we find that two cloud data centers (CLD4 and CLD5) have significant variations. Recall that unlike the other cloud data centers, these two cloud data centers run primarily MapReduce-style jobs. The large variations reflect differences between the periods when data is being reduced from the worker nodes to the master and other periods.

To summarize, the key take-aways from our analysis of network traffic patterns are as follows: (1) In cloud data centers, a significant fraction of traffic stays inside the rack, while the opposite is true for enterprise and campus data centers; (2) On average, the core of the data center is the most utilized layer, while the data center edge is lightly utilized; (3) The core layers in various data centers do contain hot-spot links. In some of the data centers, the hot-spots appear only occasionally. In some of the cloud data centers, a significant fraction of core links appear as hot-spots a large fraction of the time. At the same time, the number of core links that are hot-spots at any given time is less than 25%; (4) Losses are not correlated with links with persistently high utilizations. We observed losses do occur on links with low average utilization indicating that losses are due to momentary bursts; and (5) In general, time-of-day and day-of-week variation exists in many of the data centers. The variation in link utilization is most significant in the core of the data centers and quite moderate in other layers of the data centers.

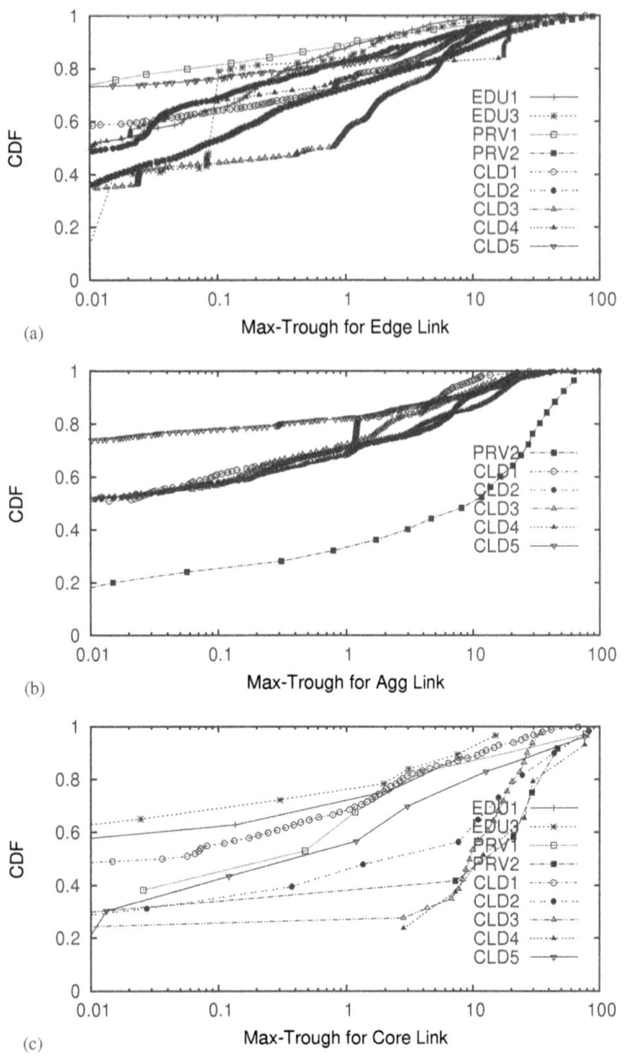

Figure 15: Difference between the peak and trough utilization.

7. IMPLICATIONS FOR DATA CENTER DESIGN

7.1 Role of Bisection Bandwidth

Several proposals [1, 22, 11, 2] for new data center network architectures attempt to maximize the network bisection bandwidth. These approaches, while well suited for data centers, which run applications that stress the network's fabric with all-to-all traffic, would be unwarranted in data centers where the bisection bandwidth is not taxed by the applications. In this section, we re-evaluate the SNMP and topology data captured from the 10 data centers and examine whether the prevalent traffic patterns are likely to stress the existing bisection bandwidth. We also examine how much of the existing bisection bandwidth is needed at any given time to support the prevalent traffic patterns.

Before explaining how we address these questions, we provide a few definitions. We define the *bisection links* for a tiered data center to be the set of links at the top-most tier of the data center's tree architecture; in other words, the core links make up the bisection links. The *bisection capacity* is the aggregate capacity of these links. The *full bisection capacity* is the capacity that would be required to support servers communicating at full link speeds with arbitrary traffic matrices and no oversubscription. The full bisection capacity can be computed as simply the aggregate capacity of the server NICs.

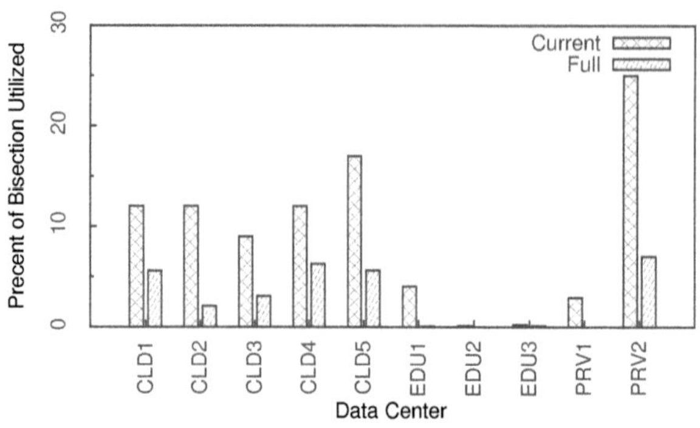

Figure 16: The first bar is the ratio of aggregate server traffic over Bisection BW and the second bar is the ratio of aggregate server traffic over full bisection capacity. The y-axis displays utilization as a percentage.

Returning to the questions posed earlier in this section, we use SNMP data to compute the following: (1) the ratio of the current aggregate server-generated traffic to the current bisection capacity and (2) the ratio of the current traffic to the full bisection capacity. In doing so, we make the assumption that the bisection links can be treated as a single pool of capacity from which all offered traffic can draw. While this may not be true in all current networks, it allows us to determine whether more capacity is needed or rather better use of existing capacity is needed (for example, by improving routing, topology, or the migration of application servers inside the data center).

In Figure 16, we present these two ratios for each of the data centers studied. Recall (from Table 2) that all data centers are oversubscribed, meaning that if all servers sent data as fast as they can and all traffic left the racks, then the bisection links would be fully congested (we would expect to find utilization ratios over 100%). However, we find in Figure 16 that the prevalent traffic patterns are such that, even in the worst case where all server-generated traffic is assumed to leave the rack hosting the server, the aggregate output from servers is smaller than the network's current bisection capacity. This means even if the applications were moved around and the traffic matrix changed, the current bisection would still be more than sufficient and no more than 25% of it would be utilized across all data centers, including the MapReduce data centers. Finally, we note that the aggregate output from servers is a negligible fraction of the ideal bisection capacity in all cases. This implies that should these data centers be equipped with a network that provides full bisection bandwidth, at least 95% of this capacity would go unused and be wasted by today's traffic patterns.

Thus, the prevalent traffic patterns in the data centers can be supported by the existing bisection capacity, even if applications were placed in such a way that there was more inter-rack traffic than exists today. This analysis assumes that the aggregate capacity of the bisection links forms a shared resource pool from which all offered traffic can draw. If the topology prevents some offered traffic from reaching some links, then some links can experience high utilization while others see low utilization. Even in this situation, however, the issue is one of changing the topology and selecting a routing algorithm that allows offered traffic to draw effectively from the existing capacity, rather than a question of adding more capacity. Centralized routing, discussed next, could help in constructing the requisite network paths.

7.2 Centralized Controllers in Data Centers

The architectures for several proposals [1, 22, 12, 2, 14, 21, 4, 18, 29] rely in some form or another on a centralized controller for configuring routes or for disseminating routing information to endhosts. A centralized controller is only practical if it is able to scale up to meet the demands of the traffic characteristics within the data centers. In this section, we examine this issue in the context of the flow properties that we analyzed in Section 5.

In particular, we focus on the proposals (Hedera [2], MicroTE [4] and ElasticTree [14]) that rely on OpenFlow and NOX [15, 23]. In an OpenFlow architecture, the first packet of a flow, when encountered at a switch, can be forwarded to a central controller that determines the route that the packet should follow in order to meet some network-wide objective. Alternatively, to eliminate the setup delay, the central controller can precompute a set of network paths that meet network-wide objectives and install them into the network at startup time.

Our empirical observations in Section 5, have important implications for such centralized approaches. First, the fact that the number of active flows is small (see Figure 4(a)) implies that switches enabled with OpenFlow can make do with a small flow table, which is a constrained resource on switches today.

Second, flow inter-arrival times have important implications for the scalability of the controller. As we observed in Section 5, a significant number of new flows (2–20%) can arrive at a given switch within 10μs of each other. The switch must forward the first packets of these flows to the controller for processing. Even if the data center has as few as a 100 edge switches, in the worst case, a controller can see 10 new flows per μs or 10 million flows per second. Depending on the complexity of the objective implemented at the controller, computing a route for each of these flows could be expensive. For example, prior work [5] showed a commodity machine computing a simple shortest path for only 50K flow arrivals per second. Thus, to scale the throughput of a centralized control framework while supporting complex routing objectives, we must employ parallelism (i.e., use multiple CPUs per controller and multiple controllers) and/or use faster but less optimal heuristics to compute routes. Prior work [28] has shown, through parallelism, the ability of a central controller to scale to 20 million flows per second.

Finally, the flow duration and size also have implications for the centralized controller. The lengths of flows determine the relative impact of the latency imposed by a controller on a new flow. Recall that we found that most flows last less than 100ms. Prior work [5] showed than it takes reactive controllers, which make decisions at flow start up time, approximately 10ms to install flow entries for new flows. Given our results, this imposes a 10% delay overhead on most flows. Additional processing delay may be acceptable for some traffic, but might be unacceptable for other kinds. For the class of workloads that find such a delay unacceptable, OpenFlow provides a proactive mechanism that allows the controllers, at switch start up time, to install flow entries in the switches. This proactive mechanism eliminates the 10ms delay but limits the controller to proactive algorithms.

In summary, it appears the number and inter-arrival time of data center flows can be handled by a sufficiently parallelized implementation of the centralized controller. However, the overhead of reactively computing flow placements is a reasonable fraction of the length of the typical flow.

8. SUMMARY

In this paper, we conducted an empirical study of the network traffic of 10 data centers spanning three very different categories, namely university campus, private enterprise data centers, and cloud data centers running Web services, customer-facing applications, and intensive Map-Reduce jobs. To the best of our knowledge, this is the broadest-ever large-scale measurement study of data centers.

We started our study by examining the applications run within the various data centers. We found that a variety of applications are deployed and that they are placed non-uniformly across racks. Next, we studied the transmission properties of the applications in terms of the flow and packet arrival processes at the edge switches. We discovered that the arrival process at the edge switches is ON/OFF in nature where the ON/OFF durations can be characterized by heavy-tailed distributions. In analyzing the flows that constitute these arrival process, we observed that flows within the data centers studied are generally small in size and several of these flows last only a few milliseconds.

We studied the implications of the deployed data center applications and their transmission properties on the data center network and its links. We found that most of the server generated traffic in the cloud data centers stays within a rack, while the opposite is true for campus data centers. We found that at the edge and aggregation layers, link utilizations are fairly low and show little variation. In contrast, link utilizations at the core are high with significant variations over the course of a day. In some data centers, a small but significant fraction of core links appear to be persistently congested, but there is enough spare capacity in the core to alleviate congestion. We observed losses on the links that are lightly utilized on average and argued that these losses can be attributed to the bursty nature of the underlying applications run within the data centers.

On the whole, our empirical observations can help inform data center traffic engineering and QoS approaches, as well as recent techniques for managing other resources, such as data center network energy consumption. To further highlight the implications of our study, we re-examined recent data center proposals and architectures in light of our results. In particular, we determined that full bisection bandwidth is not essential for supporting current applications. We also highlighted practical issues in successfully employing centralized routing mechanisms in data centers.

Our empirical study is by no means all-encompassing. We recognize that there may be other data centers in the wild that may or may not share all the properties that we have observed. Our work points out that it is worth closely examining the different design and usage patterns, as there are important differences and commonalities.

9. ACKNOWLEDGMENTS

We would like to thank the operators at the various universities, online services providers, and private enterprises for both the time and data that they provided us. We would also like to thank the anonymous reviewers for their insightful feedback.

This work is supported in part by an NSF FIND grant (CNS-0626889), an NSF CAREER Award (CNS-0746531), an NSF NetSE grant (CNS-0905134), and by grants from the University of Wisconsin-Madison Graduate School. Theophilus Benson is supported by an IBM PhD Fellowship.

10. REFERENCES

[1] M. Al-Fares, A. Loukissas, and A. Vahdat. A scalable, commodity data center network architecture. In *SIGCOMM*, pages 63–74, 2008.

[2] M. Al-Fares, S. Radhakrishnan, B. Raghavan, W. College, N. Huang, and A. Vahdat. Hedera: Dynamic flow scheduling for data center networks. In *Proceedings of NSDI 2010*, San Jose, CA, USA, April 2010.

[3] T. Benson, A. Anand, A. Akella, and M. Zhang. Understanding Data Center Traffic Characteristics. In *Proceedings of Sigcomm Workshop: Research on Enterprise Networks*, 2009.

[4] T. Benson, A. Anand, A. Akella, and M. Zhang. The case for fine-grained traffic engineering in data centers. In *Proceedings of INM/WREN '10*, San Jose, CA, USA, April 2010.

[5] M. Casado, M. J. Freedman, J. Pettit, J. Luo, N. McKeown, and S. Shenker. Ethane: taking control of the enterprise. In *SIGCOMM*, 2007.

[6] J. Dean and S. Ghemawat. MapReduce: simplified data processing on large clusters. volume 51, pages 107–113, New York, NY, USA, 2008. ACM.

[7] A. B. Downey. Evidence for long-tailed distributions in the internet. In *In Proceedings of ACM SIGCOMM Internet Measurment Workshop*, pages 229–241. ACM Press, 2001.

[8] M. Fomenkov, K. Keys, D. Moore, and K. Claffy. Longitudinal study of Internet traffic in 1998-2003. In *WISICT '04: Proceedings of the Winter International Symposium on Information and Communication Technologies*, pages 1–6. Trinity College Dublin, 2004.

[9] H. J. Fowler, W. E. Leland, and B. Bellcore. Local area network traffic characteristics, with implications for broadband network congestion management. *IEEE Journal on Selected Areas in Communications*, 9:1139–1149, 1991.

[10] C. Fraleigh, S. Moon, B. Lyles, C. Cotton, M. Khan, D. Moll, R. Rockell, T. Seely, and C. Diot. Packet-level traffic measurements from the Sprint IP backbone. *IEEE Network*, 17:6–16, 2003.

[11] A. Greenberg, J. R. Hamilton, N. Jain, S. Kandula, C. Kim, P. Lahiri, D. A. Maltz, P. Patel, and S. Sengupta. VL2: a scalable and flexible data center network. In *SIGCOMM*, 2009.

[12] A. Greenberg, P. Lahiri, D. A. Maltz, P. Patel, and S. Sengupta. Towards a next generation data center architecture: scalability and commoditization. In *PRESTO '08: Proceedings of the ACM workshop on Programmable routers for extensible services of tomorrow*, pages 57–62, New York, NY, USA, 2008. ACM.

[13] C. Guo, G. Lu, D. Li, H. Wu, X. Zhang, Y. Shi, C. Tian, Y. Zhang, and S. Lu. BCube: A High Performance, Server-centric Network Architecture for Modular Data Centers. *In Proceedings of the ACM SIGCOMM 2009 Conference on Data Communication, Barcelona, Spain*, August 17 - 21 2009.

[14] B. Heller, S. Seetharaman, P. Mahadevan, Y. Yiakoumis, P. Sharma, S. Banerjee, and N. McKeown. Elastictree: Saving energy in data center networks. April 2010.

[15] NOX: An OpenFlow Controller. `http://noxrepo.org/wp/`.

[16] C. Guo, H. Wu, K. Tan, L. Shi, Y. Zhang, and S. Lu. Dcell: a scalable and fault-tolerant network structure for data centers. In *SIGCOMM '08: Proceedings of the ACM SIGCOMM 2008 conference on Data communication*, pages 75–86, New York, NY, USA, 2008. ACM.

[17] W. John and S. Tafvelin. Analysis of Internet backbone traffic and header anomalies observed. In *IMC '07: Proceedings of the 7th ACM SIGCOMM conference on Internet measurement*, pages 111–116, New York, NY, USA, 2007. ACM.

[18] S. Kandula, J. Padhye, and P. Bahl. Flyways to de-congest data center networks. In *Proc. ACM Hotnets-VIII*, New York City, NY. USA., Oct. 2009.

[19] S. Kandula, S. Sengupta, A. Greenberg, P. Patel, and R. Chaiken. The Nature of Data Center Traffic: Measurements and Analysis. In *IMC*, 2009.

[20] W. E. Leland, M. S. Taqqu, W. Willinger, and D. V. Wilson. On the self-similar nature of ethernet traffic. In *SIGCOMM '93: Conference proceedings on Communications architectures, protocols and applications*, pages 183–193, New York, NY, USA, 1993. ACM.

[21] J. Mudigonda, P. Yalagandula, M. Al-Fares, and J. C. Mogul. Spain: Cots data-center ethernet for multipathing over arbitrary topologies. In *Proceedings of NSDI 2010*, San Jose, CA, USA, April 2010.

[22] R. Niranjan Mysore, A. Pamboris, N. Farrington, N. Huang, P. Miri, S. Radhakrishnan, V. Subramanya, and A. Vahdat. Portland: a scalable fault-tolerant layer 2 data center network fabric. In *SIGCOMM*, 2009.

[23] The OpenFlow Switch Consortium. `http://www.openflowswitch.org/`.

[24] V. Paxson. Empirically-Derived Analytic Models of Wide-Area TCP Connections. 2(4):316–336, Aug. 1994.

[25] V. Paxson. Measurements and analysis of end-to-end internet dynamics. Technical report, 1997.

[26] V. Paxson. Bro: a system for detecting network intruders in real-time. In *SSYM'98: Proceedings of the 7th conference on USENIX Security Symposium*, pages 3–3, Berkeley, CA, USA, 1998. USENIX Association.

[27] V. Paxson and S. Floyd. Wide area traffic: the failure of poisson modeling. *IEEE/ACM Trans. Netw.*, 3(3):226–244, 1995.

[28] A. Tavakoli, M. Casado, T. Koponen, and S. Shenker. Applying nox to the datacenter. In *Proc. of workshop on Hot Topics in Networks (HotNets-VIII)*, 2009.

[29] G. Wang, D. G. Andersen, M. Kaminsky, M. Kozuch, T. S. E. Ng, K. Papagiannaki, M. Glick, and L. Mummert. Your data center is a router: The case for reconfigurable optical circuit switched paths. In *Proc. ACM Hotnets-VIII*, New York City, NY. USA., Oct. 2009.

A First Look at Traffic on Smartphones

Hossein Falaki
CENS, UCLA

Dimitrios Lymberopoulos
Microsoft Research

Ratul Mahajan
Microsoft Research

Srikanth Kandula
Microsoft Research

Deborah Estrin
CENS, UCLA

Abstract—Using data from 43 users across two platforms, we present a detailed look at smartphone traffic. We find that browsing contributes over half of the traffic, while each of email, media, and maps contribute roughly 10%. We also find that the overhead of lower layer protocols is high because of small transfer sizes. For half of the transfers that use transport-level security, header bytes correspond to 40% of the total. We show that while packet loss is the main factor that limits the throughput of smartphone traffic, larger send buffers at Internet servers can improve the throughput of a quarter of the transfers. Finally, by studying the interaction between smartphone traffic and the radio power management policy, we find that the power consumption of the radio can be reduced by 35% with minimal impact on the performance of packet exchanges.

Categories and Subject Descriptors
C.2.5 [Computer-Communication Networks] Local and Wide-Area Networks – Internet

General Terms
Measurement, Performance

Keywords
Smartphone traffic, Power management

1. INTRODUCTION

Smartphone traffic represents an increasingly large share of Internet traffic. Cellular traffic is projected to grow 10 times faster than fixed Internet traffic [22] and most of this traffic is generated by smartphones [9]. By next year, smartphone sales are projected to surpass desktop PCs [18].

However, little is known today about the nature of smartphone traffic. Two recent studies have shed valuable light on some aspects of this traffic. Trestian *et al.* study the kinds of Web sites accessed at different times of the day [20]; and Maier *et al.* study HTTP traffic generated by mobile handheld devices (which include music players and personal gaming consoles in addition to smartphones) in homes [15]. Both studies are based on data gathered at a link in the middle of the network. As a result, while they can analyze traffic from a large number of devices, they do not capture a detailed, comprehensive view of individual devices. For instance, the second study misses traffic exchanged by devices through the cellular interfaces or outside of their homes.

In this paper, we report on our ongoing work on detailed characterization of smartphone traffic. Our approach is complementary to that of previous studies—we employ passive sniffers on the device and record all sent and received traffic. Given the difficulty of deploying continuous monitoring on a large number of end user devices, the breadth achievable using this method is limited. But the comprehensive view of smartphone traffic that it provides for monitored devices enables inferences that would otherwise be impossible to make. For instance, we can study how much total traffic a device generates in a day and interaction of its traffic patterns with radio power management.

The results in this paper are based on two datasets. Our primary dataset consists of 10 users across two smartphone platforms. For these users, we deployed a logger that captured packet-level traces. Our other dataset consists of 33 Android users. It contains bytes sent and received by each application in every two-minute window. We have from 1 to 5 months of data for each user.

Using these datasets, we shed light on several aspects of smartphone traffic. By analyzing commonly used ports and applications, we quantify traffic generated by various applications. We find that browsing contributes over half of the traffic, while each of messaging (email, IM), maps and media contribute roughly 10%.

We also find that most smartphone data transfers are small, with the median size being only 3 KB. Such small transfers have many implications. For instance, the overhead of lower layer protocols can be high. We show that for half of the transfers, header bytes constitute over 12% of the total bytes. In the presence of transport security, this overhead grows to 40%. For half of the transfers, lower layer handshakes constitute 20% of the total completion time.

Consistent with controlled experiments with probe traffic [12], we find that smartphone data transfers experience high delays and losses. Unlike controlled experiments, however, our data allows us to also study the impact of these path characteristics on actual smartphone workloads. Focusing on transfers with more than 10 data packets, we find that the median throughput is only 3.5 kbps in the downlink (from the network to the smartphone) and 0.8 Kbps in the uplink.

Analysis of what limits the throughput of smartphone data transfers [23] reveals that packet loss is the primary culprit. But interestingly, a quarter of the downlink transfers are bottlenecked by the size of the sender-side transport buffer. The throughput of such flows can be improved by simply increasing the buffer sizes at servers that communicate with smartphone clients.

Finally, we study the interaction of smartphone traffic with the radio power management policy. We find that the current sleep

IMC'10, November 1–3, 2010, Melbourne, Australia.

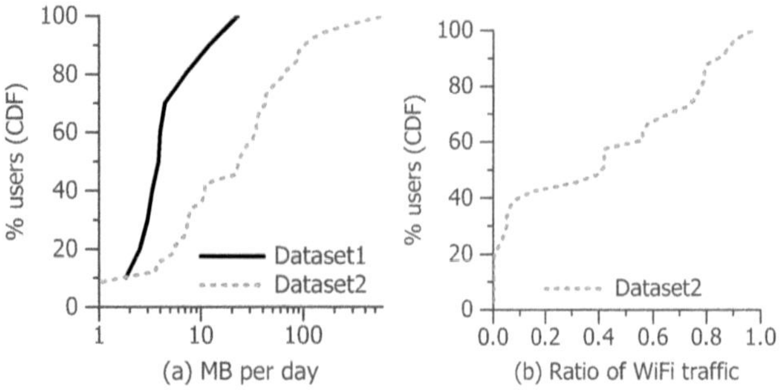

Figure 1: (a) Smartphone traffic per day. (b) Ratio of traffic sent on the WiFi interface.

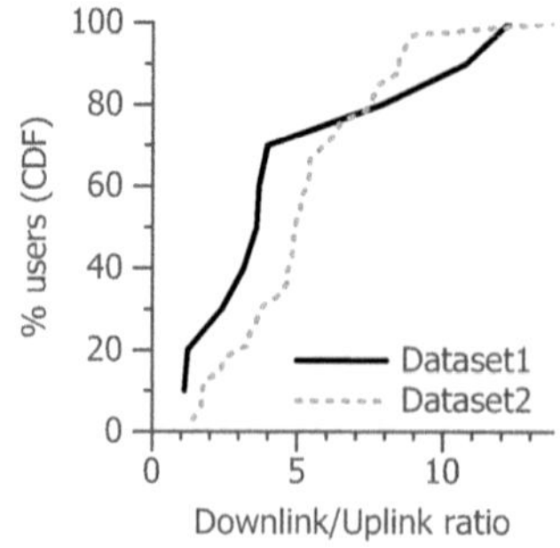

Figure 2: Ratio of downlink to uplink traffic.

timers, that is, the idle period after which the radio will go to sleep, are overly long. By reducing them based on current traffic patterns, radio power consumption can be reduced by at least 35% with minimal impact on performance.

2. DATASETS

Our results are based on two sets of traces. The first data set consists of packet level traces from 10 smartphone users across two different platforms. Our second data set contains application level traffic information from 33 Android users.

Dataset1 Our first dataset is from 8 Windows Mobile (HTC Touch) users and 2 Android (HTC Dream) users. It contains packet-level traces, including link layer headers, for data sent and received by the smartphone. We collected these traces using *Netlog* on Windows Mobile and *tcpdump* on Android. The traces were stored locally and uploaded at regular intervals using the USB connection.

All users are knowledge workers. Each had an unlimited data plan with their carrier (7 AT&T, 3 T-Mobile). The users were resident in two different cities in the USA.

Across all users, there is 532 days of data. For individual users, the data varies from 26 to 84 days.

Dataset2 Our second dataset is from 33 Android (HTC Dream) users. It was collected using a custom logging tool that provides an application-level view of smartphone traffic. Every two minutes, it records the number of bytes sent and received by every process that runs on the smartphone. This tool is available to other researchers by request and more details on its operation are available in [10].

The set of users consists of 17 knowledge workers and 16 high school students. As for user interactions [10], we did not find statistically valid differences among the two demographics with respect to traffic. We thus present their results jointly. Each participant was provided an unlimited voice, text and data plan through T-Mobile. The users were resident in the same city in the USA.

Across all users, there is 1660 days of data. For individual users, the data varies from 49-147 days.

A key limitation of our work is the small user populations of our datasets, even though they provide independent vantage points on smartphone traffic characteristics. Expanding our set of users is a subject of ongoing work.

3. TRAFFIC COMPOSITION

In this section, we study the basic makeup of smartphone traffic, starting with volume per user. Figure 1(a) shows how much traffic is exchanged per day by users. This amount is 2-20 MB in Dataset1 and 1-500 MB in Dataset2. Compared to residential broadband traffic this is roughly one order of magnitude smaller [1].

Two factors may explain the differences in the two datasets. One is that Dataset1 is dominated by Windows Mobile, while Dataset2 is exclusively Android. It is likely that the Android OS and users generate more traffic. The heaviest user in Dataset1 is in fact an Android user. In earlier work, we found that Android users interact with their devices more heavily than Windows Mobile users [10]. For instance, the median session length of Android users is more than twice that of Windows Mobile users.

The second factor, not unrelated to the first, is that many users in Dataset2 use WiFi heavily. Dataset1 does not provide direct information on the interface (WiFi or cellular) used by individual packets. But by observing interface addresses and path delays—cellular delays are much higher—we conclude that WiFi usage was minimal among those users. In Dataset2, we can reliably identify the share of WiFi traffic using information about interface state.

Figure 1(b) shows the ratio of WiFi traffic in Dataset2. We see that the median ratio is almost 0.5 but it varies widely across users. While the bottom 20% do not use WiFi at all, the top 20% use it for more than 80% of their traffic. These results also imply that depending on the user population smartphone studies based on only cellular traffic [20] or only WiFi traffic [15] can miss a significant fraction of device traffic.

We now study the composition of smartphone traffic from other perspectives.

Downlink vs. uplink Figure 2 shows the ratio of downlink (from the network to the smartphone) to uplink traffic. There is a wide variation among users, caused likely by diversity in application usage, from downlink traffic equaling uplink traffic to it being over 10 times the uplink traffic. The average across all users for downlink to uplink ratio is 6:1. This high asymmetry, indicating a strong bias towards downloads, has implications for provisioning access technologies for smartphones. It is comparable to asymmetry in residential broadband traffic in Europe [14] and Japan [11] but is well above the subset of "peer-type heavy-hitters"[11] whose ratio is close to 1:1.

Despite differences in total traffic exchanged the downlink to uplink ratios in the two datasets are similar. This suggests that the mix of activities that generate network traffic may not be disparate for the two cases. We study these next.

Common ports [Dataset1] Ports provide insight into user activities on smartphones. Identifying applications using ports may be inaccurate in some cases (e.g., peer-to-peer), but it is a simple indicator that works well overall [14].

Table 1 shows for Dataset1 all ports that carry over 0.1% of the

	Bytes (%)	Packets (%)
HTTPS (443)	43.88	31.66
HTTP (80)	37.48	22.16
IMAP4S (993)	15.21	39.32
DNS (53)	1.08	2.31
IM (5000-01)	0.69	0.32
Android-Mkt (5228)	0.48	1.10
IPv6local (5355)	0.22	0.88
DHCP (67)	0.22	0.24
NetBIOS (137-39)	0.17	0.60
other	0.57	0.37

Table 1: Ports (in parenthesis) used by IP packets in Dataset1.

	Bytes (%)
Browsing	58.02
Media	10.82
Messaging (Email, IM)	10.33
Maps	8.51
System	5.83
Social networking	4.18
Games	0.36
Productivity	0.15
unknown/other	1.79

Table 2: Traffic generated by applications in Dataset2.

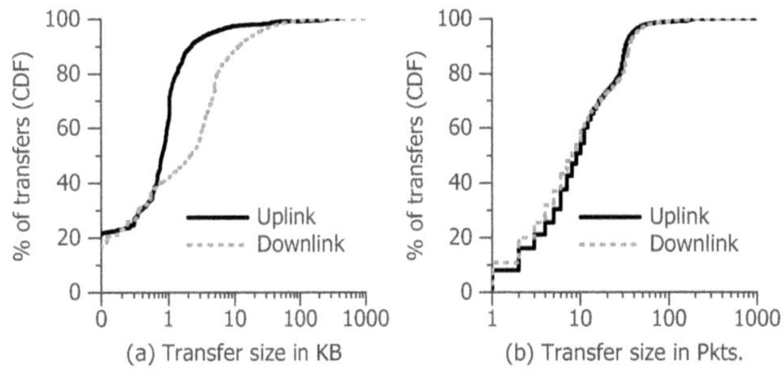

Figure 3: Transfer sizes in Dataset1. The x-axes are log scale.

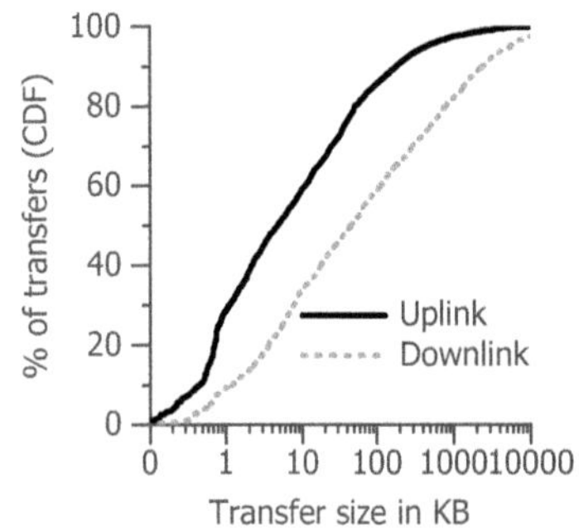

Figure 4: Transfer sizes in Dataset2. The x-axis is log scale.

bytes. We see that the dominant ports correspond to HTTPS, HTTP, and IMAP4S. These results suggest that the main traffic generators on smartphones of these users are browsing and email. HTTPS is used by secure Web sites and email servers (including Exchange). HTTP of course is used heavily as part of browsing and for downloading data of various kinds. IMAP4S is the secure version of the IMAP protocol for email. While IMAP4S has the most packets, it is third with respect to the number of bytes. This implies a bias towards small packets, likely generated as part of frequently polling for (often non-existent) new email. Many Dataset1 users had two configured email accounts—a push-based work account and a polling-based personal account. Increased adoption of push-based email, by which clients are notified when new email arrives, will change the nature of email traffic.

The 37% share of HTTP traffic that we find is roughly half of that observed for mobile handheld devices in homes [15] and 50% less than that in residential broadband traffic [14].

The large volume of traffic that uses HTTP or HTTPS perhaps indicates the trend among smartphone applications to tunnel their data through these protocols, even when such data would not normally be considered HTTP payload (e.g., music, video and, social apps).

Applications [Dataset2] Our second dataset lets us directly observe what applications are generating smartphone traffic. We partition applications into several categories that are shown in Table 2. "System" includes applications that are part of the OS (e.g., package manager, backup), and "Productivity" includes applications for calendars, alarms, and document handling (e.g., Office, PDF reader). The meanings of the other application categories are what their names suggest.

We see in the table that browsing dominates smartphone traffic. As in Dataset1, messaging is also a significant contributor. Media and maps are other major contributors. These applications tend to use HTTP and HTTPS for transport, but the application-level view lets us quantify their contribution independently.

4. TRANSFER SIZES

In this section, we study the sizes of individual data transfers, which impact throughput as well as power consumption [2]. We identify individual transfers using TCP flows. A TCP flow is identified using IP addresses and ports. Packets of a flow without an extended idle period (1 minute), are considered as part of one transfer; flows with long idle periods are considered separate transfers [6]. Long idle periods can arise within a TCP flow if the client (e.g., email application) maintains an open connection to the server, to avoid the TCP connection setup overhead for each transfer.

Figure 3 shows the CDF of transfer sizes in bytes and packets across all users in Dataset1. The size in bytes includes the bytes contributed by TCP and IP headers. While the mean transfer size is 273 KB sent and 57 KB received, most transfers are extremely small. When considering both directions cumulatively, 30% of them have fewer than 1K bytes and 10 packets. These results are consistent with those of Maier *et al.* for HTTP traffic from handheld devices [15].

Figure 4 shows that Dataset2 is dominated by small transfers as well. We define a transfer size differently in this case. Dataset2 has bytes sent and received by individual applications in 2-minute long intervals. For each application, we combine contiguous intervals with non-zero data exchanged as one transfer. If an application exchanges data over multiple TCP connections, this definition aggregates data across those connections into one transfer. Despite this aggregation, the graph shows that most transfers are small.

The small transfer sizes that we observe have many implications. Given the high amount of energy consumed by the 3G radio to go from sleep to ready state and from idle to sleep state (§6), there can

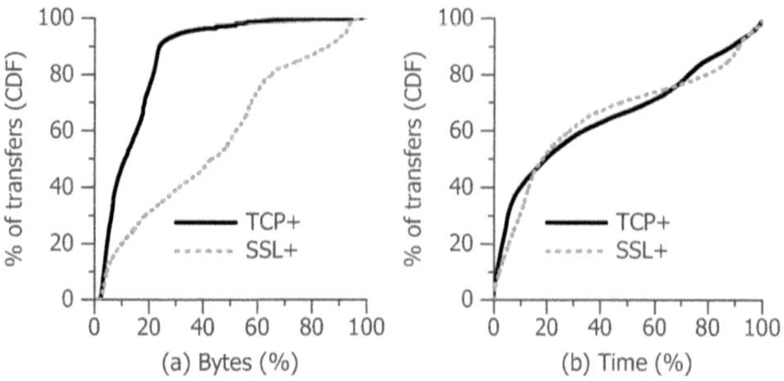

Figure 5: The overhead of layers below TCP and SSL (inclusive) in Dataset1.

be a high energy overhead associated with them. Another implication is that a scheme like Catnap [8] is unlikely to reduce radio power consumption. Catnap puts the radio to sleep during transfers but is effective only for long transfers. In §6, we present a simple method that can reduce radio power consumption by 35% by appropriately setting radio sleep timers.

Yet another implication of small transfers is that the already high overhead of lower-layer protocols can dominate. This overhead manifests as extra bytes that must be transmitted as headers as well as extra time that it takes to complete handshakes.

We quantify these overheads at the transport (TCP) and transport security (SSL) layers. According to our analysis 96% of smartphone traffic is TCP-based and more than half uses SSL (through HTTPS and IMAP4S). In Figure 5, "TCP+" captures overhead of TCP and all layers below it. "SSL+" captures overhead of SSL and all layers below it, and it is computed only for SSL-based transfers.

Figure 5(a) shows that the median TCP+ overhead at byte-level is 12%, i.e., more than one in ten bytes is devoted to TCP or lower layer headers. SSL further increases overhead. The median SSL+ overhead is 40%, and 20% of the transfers have an overhead that is twice that amount.

Figure 5(b) shows the time overhead. TCP+ is measured as the time between the first SYN and the first packet that contains non-TCP bytes. If the radio is asleep when the SYN is sent, this measure will include the time to wake up the radio. In the next section, we quantify the radio waking overhead separately. SSL+ is measured as the time between the first TCP SYN and the first packet that contains non-TCP, non-SSL bytes. Thus, in addition to the TCP handshake, it includes any time needed for SSL key exchange.

We see that the time overhead too is significant. The median overhead of TCP is 20%, i.e., a fifth of the total transfer time is spent waiting for TCP handshake to complete.

Surprisingly, SSL does not add much to the time overhead beyond TCP, which points to the effectiveness of SSL session key caching for smartphone workloads. Smartphones frequently talk using SSL to the same server (e.g., email server). Cached session keys enable quick connection establishment without the overhead of full key exchange. Most of the additional overhead due to SSL appears to be due to their larger headers. In Figure 5(b), the SSL+ overhead appears slightly lower than TCP+ in some cases because the two curves are computed over different sets of transfers.

In summary, we find that most smartphone transfers are small. Such transfers have a high energy cost and amplify the overhead of lower-layer protocols. One way to avoid this overhead, which we will investigate in the future, is to aggregate transfers across applications and across time. Using a proxy in the cloud can facilitate such aggregation.

5. PERFORMANCE

We now investigate the performance of TCP transfers. We study observed round trip time, throughput, and retransmission rate as well as estimate what limits the transfer throughput. We use only Dataset1 because Dataset2 does not have the granularity of information needed for this analysis. As almost all of Dataset1 traffic is 3G-based (§3), our analysis sheds light on the performance that is seen by smartphones when using the 3G interface in real operating conditions.

5.1 Round trip time

We estimate the RTT of a transfer as the difference between the SYN and SYN-ACK packets. Accurate inference of RTT using data and acknowledgment packets is complicated by delayed acknowledgments. If multiple SYN packets are transmitted for a transfer, we use the last SYN packet. In some cases, the SYN-ACK packet may be sent by a proxy in carrier network instead of the contacted server. Even in these cases, we get a good estimate if the dominant component of the RTT is the wireless delay [12].

We explicitly correct for a source of error that would otherwise significantly overestimate network RTT. If the radio is asleep when the transfer is initiated, it includes the times it takes for the radio to wake up and synchronize with the tower. To weed out this impact, we focus on transfers that are initiated when the radio is in full power mode. We identify such transfers as those that are initiated within 3 seconds of the previous transmission or reception. The idle period after which the radios go into a lower power mode is well above this threshold (§6).

The "Trailing" curve in Figure 6(a) shows the RTTs observed by such transfers. We see that the median is 125 ms but 10% of the transfers observe an RTT of over 0.5 seconds. Such high variance in RTT is consistent with controlled experiments [12]. A TCP flow that experiences high variance in RTT will suffer from delayed response to congestion among other things. Such variance can stem from a host of factors including link layer retransmissions (that are not visible to us), network congestion, and overloaded equipment inside the carrier network.

The "All" curve in the graph represents RTTs computed for all transfers, not just those initiated when the radio is awake. The difference in the two curves quantifies the overhead of radio wake-ups. The difference is 400 ms at the median and 1.7 seconds at 90th percentile. The variation stems from the variable amount of time the radio takes to fully synchronize with the tower and a wake-up may already be in progress because of another transfer.

5.2 Retransmission rate

We now study how frequently packets are retransmitted in TCP transfers. Retransmissions are identified using sequence numbers and provide a good estimate of path loss rate. Their rate can differ slightly from loss rate due to TCP dynamics such as spurious timeouts.

Across all transfers, the uplink retransmission rate is 3.7% and the downlink rate is 3.3%. These loss rates are much higher than those for wired paths. The median average loss rate seen from the SLAC laboratory during 2008 was less than 0.1% for North America and less than 1% for most of the world [7]. However, our observed wireless loss rate is similar to those inferred using controlled experiments [12]. We show below that packet loss is the main bottleneck for TCP throughput.

Figure 6(b) shows the retransmission rates for individual transfers. This graph is based only on connections that send more than 10 data packets in a given direction. We see that roughly 60% of the connections experience no retransmissions. But 25% of them

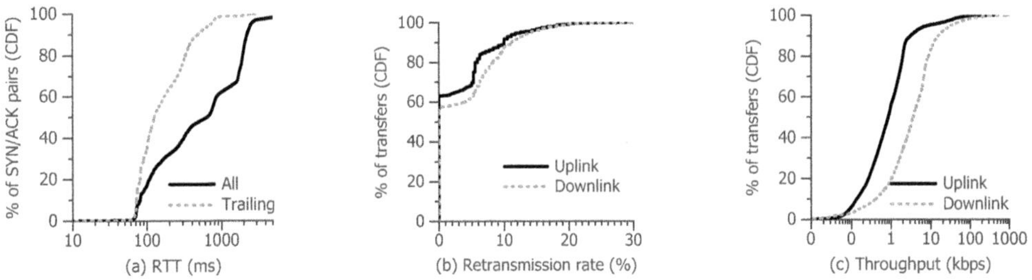

Limit	Uplink (%)	Downlink (%)
Packet loss	81.0	61.5
Sender window	4.1	27.4
Receiver window	6.8	3.4
Bandwidth	5.1	2.9
Transport	0.7	0.0
Application	0.0	0.0
Unknown	2.4	4.8

(d) Throughput limits

Figure 6: Performance of TCP transfers in Dataset1.

retransmit 5% of the packets and 10% of them retransmit more than 10% of the packets.

5.3 Throughput

As a final measure of smartphone traffic performance, we focus on the throughput observed by TCP connections in our data. Connection throughput is a function of not only path RTT and loss rate but also of application-level factors such as the amount of data.

Figure 6(c) shows the throughput of TCP transfers with at least 10 data packets in a given direction. We see that most transfers have very low throughput. The median is 0.8 Kbps for uplink and 3.5 Kbps for downlink. The 90th percentile values are 3 and 15 Kbps respectively.

Given that half the transfers in the analysis above have over 25 data packets, the lack of application data or slow TCP dynamics alone cannot explain the low throughputs that we observe. To understand the bottlenecks, we conduct the analysis of Zhang *et al.* [23]. This analysis estimates the factor that limits the throughput of a given TCP transfer, based on the timing and sequence of packets. We refer the reader to the original paper for details. The accuracy of this analysis has been evaluated in the wired case but not in a wireless setting. Manual inspection of several cases shows that it provides accurate answers for our data. This gives us confidence that it can yield an accurate aggregate characterization of the type that we present below. We will conduct a more rigorous evaluation in the future.

Figure 6(d) shows the results for transfers that have more than 100 data packets in the given direction. We find that with this threshold the analysis yields reliable, consistent estimates. Similar results are obtained with a threshold of 50.

We see that packet loss is the primary limiting factor in both directions, and the large transfers that we focus on are rarely bottlenecked by transport or application dynamics.

Interestingly, sender window limits over a quarter of the downlink transfers. This suggests that increasing the size of this window (which holds unacknowledged data) at servers will increase the throughput of downlink TCP transfers to smartphones. It is likely that the current buffer sizes are tuned to wired clients which tend to have much lower path delays. In future work, we plan to investigate this issue in detail.

6. INTERACTION WITH RADIO POWER MANAGEMENT

The radio is a major power consumer on a smartphone [17], and the nature of traffic determines the efficacy of its power management policy. In this section, we study the interaction between this policy and real smartphone traffic.

We first consider the power signature of current radios. Figure 7 shows the current drawn by an HTC Touch smartphone with Windows Mobile 6.1 when transmitting data over the 3G radio. We see

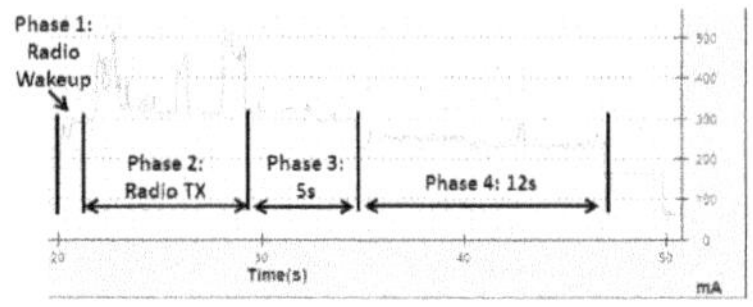

Figure 7: Current consumption (@4.2V) of HTC Touch.

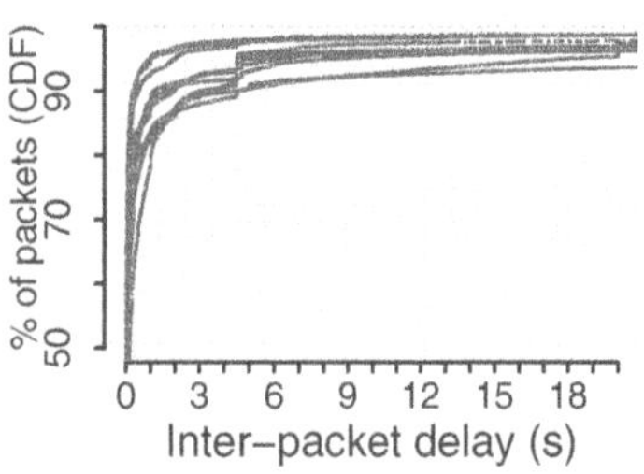

Figure 8: CDF of the inter-packet delays in Dataset1. Each line corresponds to a different user.

four distinct phases. The radio takes about 1.5 seconds to become operational from its sleep mode (Phase 1). After data transmission completes (Phase 2), the radio remains at its highest power level for 5 seconds (Phase 3) and at a lower level for 12 seconds (Phase 4). It then goes to sleep. This power signature is not unique to HTC or Windows Mobile. Similar behaviors hold across different manufacturers and OSes [2], though the exact timer values may be carrier dependent.

The goal of the tail in Phases 3 and 4 is to enable the radio to quickly resume packet exchange, without the time and energy cost of waking up. However, if it is too long, power is unnecessarily wasted when no transmissions occur. If it is too short, the radio will oscillate between the sleep and active states, which will waste energy due to the wake up cost. Given that each wake-up is accompanied by signaling to reserve resources for the radio in the carrier network, an overly short tail will also lead to a higher signaling overhead for the carrier.

The optimal length of the tail depends on the burstiness of smartphone traffic. More bursty traffic, with packet exchanges happening in clusters rather than being uniformly spread, calls for a shorter tail. To understand how bursty smartphone traffic is, we consider packet exchanges in Dataset1. Figure 8 shows the CDF of the delay between consecutive packets for all users. While there are differences among users, across all users 95% of the packets are received or transmitted within 4.5 seconds of the previous packet. The inter-

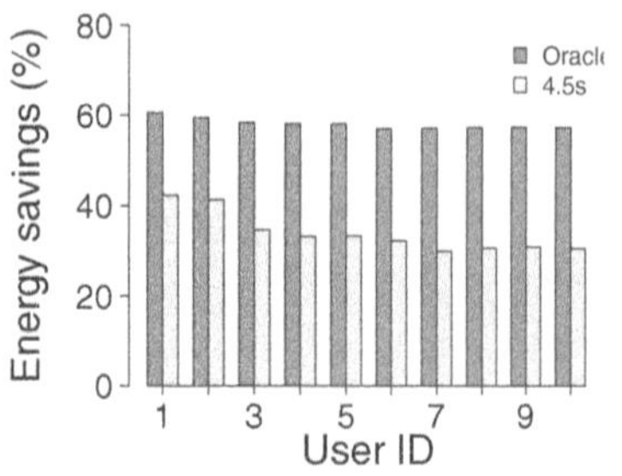

Figure 9: Reduction in energy consumed by the radio compared to the current radio power management policy.

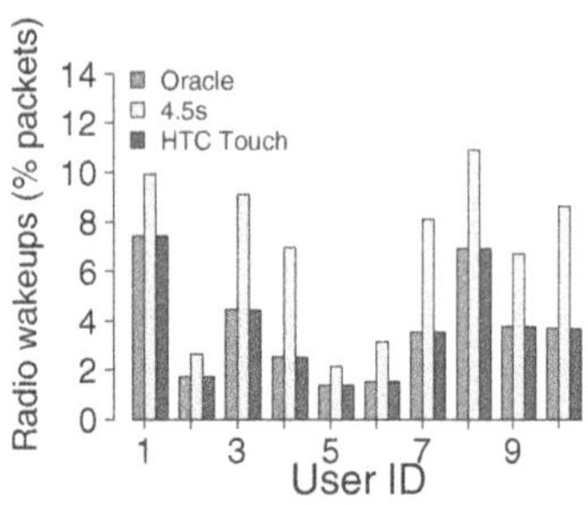

Figure 10: Percentage of overall packets that trigger a radio wake up across the different approaches.

packet delay for the rest of the packets appears to be roughly uniformly distributed over a longer time range.

This result suggests that a 4.5-second long tail before going to sleep can cover 95% of the packets; longer tails will have diminishing returns with respect to covering more packets while wasting more energy. But we saw above that the current tail is 17-second long, which suggests highly suboptimal power consumption.

To quantify this sub-optimality, we replay packet exchanges for every user, and we use the timing and power parameters from Figure 7 to compute the energy consumed by the 3G radio for different tail lengths. This computation includes the wake-up overhead. Figure 9 shows the energy savings from using a 4.5-second long tail compared to a 17-second long tail. It also shows the energy savings from using an oracle that has perfect knowledge of when the next packet exchange will occur and can therefore make an optimal decision of when and for how long the radio should go to sleep. This oracle can not be implemented in practice but indicates the maximum energy savings that can be achieved.

With an oracle, the energy consumption of the 3G radio can be reduced by 60%. A 4.5-second long tail reduces energy consumption by 35% on average across all users. To place these numbers in context, the radio typically accounts for a third to a quarter of energy drain on the phone [17].

We find that these energy savings have a minimal impact on the performance of packet exchanges. Figure 10 shows the number of times that the 3G radio has to wake up to exchange a packet as a percentage of all packets. With a 4.5-second tail, only an additional 2-5% of the packets are delayed by having to wake up the radio. This result also suggests that the additional signaling overhead due to a 4.5-second tail will be low.

In additional experiments, not reported in this paper, we find that the tail length needs to be carefully set based on both radio wake-up overheads and traffic characteristics. For instance, a tail length of 100 ms, which covers 50% of the packets, hurts energy consumption as well as performance. Energy usage doubles, and 35% of the packets are delayed due to radio the wake up overhead.

In summary, we show that current radio power management policies are highly inefficient. Because of temporal characteristics of smartphone traffic, simply reducing the tail length to 4.5 seconds can save 35% of the energy consumed by the radio. However, the oracle algorithm suggests that an additional 25% can be saved. We are currently investigating how to do so practically, by learning the traffic patterns of individual users and dynamically adjusting the radio sleep timers depending on various factors such as the application and the time of the day.

7. RELATED WORK

Given the challenge of conducting measurements on mobile devices, existing studies of mobile traffic are based on observations from the infrastructure [19, 15, 3, 13, 21, 20]. Recently, Maier *et al.* study packet-level traces from residential DSL connections at an aggregation point [15]. Using hints such as HTTP user-agent strings, they identify traffic from mobile hand-held devices and observe that this traffic is dominated by multimedia content and mobile application downloads. Trestian *et al.* study 3G authentication traces from a provider to measure the correlations between location, time-of-day and application usage [20]. Our approach of monitoring devices is complementary to these studies. It provides a comprehensive view of monitored devices and enables us to study aspects of smartphone traffic such as interaction with radio power management that would otherwise be difficult.

In recent work, we broadly characterized smartphone usage, including user interactions, traffic per day, and diurnal patterns [10]. The current paper studies smartphone traffic in detail, including its composition, transfer sizes, performance, and interaction with radio power management.

Also complementary to our work are studies that conduct active measurements using synthetic workloads [12, 4, 5, 16]. Such studies can analyze network characteristics in a range of conditions. But they do not provide a view of what users actually experience, which was our focus.

8. CONCLUSIONS

Based on monitoring the devices of 43 users, we presented a detailed look at smartphone traffic. We find that browsing contributes most traffic, lower layer protocols have a high overhead due to small transfers sizes, and packet loss is the primary bottleneck for traffic throughput. We also find that current server-side transfer buffers and radio power management policies are not well-tuned for smartphone workloads.

Our analysis points at several simple mechanisms that can improve the efficiency, performance, and power consumption of smartphone communication. Aggregating multiple small transfers through an in-cloud proxy can reduce the overhead of small transfers; increasing the socket buffer sizes at servers can improve throughput; and reducing radio sleep timers can reduce power consumption. In the future, we plan to investigate in the detail the efficacy of these mechanisms.

Acknowledgments We are grateful to the users who participated in our data collection efforts.

9. REFERENCES

[1] Trends in japanese residential traffic. http://www.isoc.org/isoc/conferences/bwpanel/docs/20091111_bandwidth_cho.pdf, 2009.

[2] N. Balasubramanian, A. Balasubramanian, and A. Venkataramani. Energy consumption in mobile phones: A measurement study and implications for network applications. In *IMC*, 2009.

[3] P. Benko, G. Malicsko, and A. Veres. A large-scale, passive analysis of end-to-end TCP performance over GPRS. In *INFOCOM*, 2004.

[4] R. Chakravorty, S. Banerjee, P. Rodriguez, J. Chesterfield, and I. Pratt. Performance optimizations for wireless wide-area networks: Comparative study and experimental evaluation. In *MobiCom*, 2004.

[5] J. Chesterfield, R. Chakravorty, J. Crowcroft, P. Rodriguez, and S. Banerjee. Experiences with multimedia streaming over 2.5 G and 3G Networks. In *BORADNETS*, 2004.

[6] K. Claffy. *Internet traffic characterization*. PhD thesis, University of California at San Diego, 1994.

[7] L. Cottrell and S. Khan. ICFA SCIC network monitoring report. http://www.slac.stanford.edu/xorg/icfa/icfa-net-paper-jan09/report-jan09.doc, 2009.

[8] F. Dogar and P. Steenkiste. Catnap: Exploiting High Bandwidth Wireless Interfaces to Save Energy for Mobile Devices. In *MobiSys*, 2010.

[9] Mobile data traffic surpasses voice. http://www.ericsson.com/thecompany/press/releases/2010/03/1396928.

[10] H. Falaki, R. Mahajan, S. Kandula, D. Lymberopoulos, R. Govindan, and D. Estrin. Diversity in smartphone usage. In *MobiSys*, 2010.

[11] K. Fukuda, K. Cho, and H. Esaki. The impact of residential broadband traffic on Japanese ISP backbones. *SIGCOMM CCR*, 35(1), 2005.

[12] J. Huang, Q. Xu, Z. Mao, M. Zhang, and P. Bahl. Anatomizing Application Performance Differences on Smartphones. In *MobiSys*, 2010.

[13] Y. Lee. Measured TCP Performance in CDMA 1xEV-DO Network. In *PAM*, 2006.

[14] G. Maier, A. Feldmann, V. Paxson, and M. Allman. On dominant characteristics of residential broadband internet traffic. In *IMC*, 2009.

[15] G. Maier, F. Schneider, and A. Feldmann. A First Look at Mobile Hand-Held Device Traffic. In *PAM*, 2010.

[16] K. Mattar, A. Sridharan, H. Zang, I. Matta, and A. Bestavros. TCP over CDMA2000 networks: A cross-layer measurement study. In *PAM*, 2007.

[17] A. Shye, B. Sholbrock, and M. G. Into the wild: Studying real user activity patterns to guide power optimization for mobile architectures. In *Micro*, 2009.

[18] L. Snol. More smartphones than desktop PCs by 2011. http://www.pcworld.com/article/171380/more_smartphones_than_desktop_pcs_by_2011.html.

[19] P. Svoboda, F. Ricciato, E. Hasenleithner, and R. Pilz. Composition of GPRS/UMTS traffic: Snapshots from a live network. *IPS MoMe 2006*, 4, 2006.

[20] I. Trestian, S. Ranjan, A. Kuzmanovic, and A. Nucci. Measuring serendipity: Connecting people, locations and interests in a mobile 3G network. In *IMC*, 2009.

[21] Y. Won, B. Park, S. Hong, K. Jung, H. Ju, and J. Hong. Measurement analysis of mobile data networks. *PAM*, 2007.

[22] N. Wood. Mobile data traffic growth 10 times faster than fixed over next five years. http://www.totaltele.com/view.aspx?ID=448681.

[23] Y. Zhang, L. Breslau, V. Paxson, and S. Shenker. On the characteristics and origins of Internet flow rates. In *SIGCOMM*, 2002.

Listen to Me if You can: Tracking User Experience of Mobile Network on Social Media

Tongqing Qiu
Georgia Tech
Atlanta, GA
tongqqiu@cc.gatech.edu

Junlan Feng
AT&T Labs – Research
Florham Park, NJ
junlan@research.att.com

Zihui Ge
AT&T Labs – Research
Florham Park, NJ
gezihui@research.att.com

Jia Wang
AT&T Labs – Research
Florham Park, NJ
jiawang@research.att.com

Jun (Jim) Xu*
Georgia Tech
Atlanta, GA
jx@cc.gatech.edu

Jennifer Yates
AT&T Labs – Research
Florham Park, NJ
jyates@research.att.com

ABSTRACT

Social media sites such as Twitter continue to grow at a fast pace. People of all generations use social media to exchange messages and share experiences of their life in a timely fashion. Most of these sites make their data available. An intriguing question is can we exploit this real-time and massive data-flow to improve business in a measurable way. In this paper, we are particularly interested in tweets (Twitter messages) that are relevant to mobile network performance. We compare tweets with a more traditional source of user experience, i.e., customer care tickets, and correlate both of them with a list of major network incidents. From our study, we have the following observations. First, Twitter users and users who call customer service tend to report different types of performance issues. Second, we observe that tweets typically appear more rapidly in response to network problems than customer tickets. They also appear to respond to a wider range of network issues. Third, significant spikes in the number of tweets appear to indicate short term performance impairments which are not reported in our current list of major network incidents. These observations together indicate that Twitter is an attractive, complementary source for monitoring service performance and its impact on user experience.

Categories and Subject Descriptors

C.2.3 [**Computer System Organization**]: Computer-Communication Networks—*Network Operations*

General Terms

Management, Measurement, Performance

*This work was supported in part by NSF grant CNS-0905169, funded under the American Recovery and Reinvestment Act of 2009 (Public Law 111-5), and NSF grant CNS-0716423.

IMC'10, November 1–3, 2010, Melbourne, Australia.

Keywords

Social Media, Twitter, User Experience

1. INTRODUCTION

Monitoring network performance is one of the key tasks in network operation. We detect service performance issues from both a systems perspective and from a customers' perspective. From the systems perspective, we infer the issues based on measurement of network delay, packet loss, etc. From a customers' perspective, we identify issues based on users' feedback. The traditional way to learn user feedback is through customer calls or emails. When a customer complains about a problem, we investigate and resolve it. In this paper, we propose to go beyond customer care data to exploit a different channel – online social media, for tracking user feedback regarding service performance.

Online social networks (OSN) have gained significant popularity during recent years [18]. Microblogging services such as Twitter, are one of popular means through which users share information and experiences on the web. Comparing with Facebook, LinkedIn, MySpace, YouTube, and other social networking services, messages on Twitter are short (less than 140 characters). Twitter messages are widely referred to as *tweets*. It takes only a few seconds for a user to write a tweet and have it distributed to the public and his followers. Users can send and receive tweets through various applications (such as web and instant messaging) and devices (such as mobile phones, TV and computers). According to comScore, Twitter finished 2009 with nearly 20 million visitors to its website, up from just 2 million visitors in 2008 [1].

In this paper, we analyze tweets related to one of the largest mobile service providers in the United States. We first identify tweets that relate to service performance issues, and compare them with customer care trouble tickets. Second, we correlate these two sources of customer feedback with a report of major network incidents. Our findings are threefold: (1) Issues reported on Twitter are complementary to customer care calls. (2) Twitter users are faster to report service performance issues compared to customers who call and complain to the customer care center. (3) Tweets report some short term and/or less severe problems, which are not recorded in the major network incidents report.

The remainder of the paper is structured as follows. Datasets for analysis are discussed in Section 2, followed by our presentation of results in Section 3. Section 4 reviews related work and Section 5 concludes the paper.

2. DATASETS

In this section, we discuss the methodology used to collect data and describe the data used in our work. Section 2.1 discusses Twitter data, Section 2.2 discusses customer care call data, and Section 2.3 discusses the major network incidents report data.

2.1 Twitter Data

We used Twitter APIs to retrieve publicly available data relevant to our task. We emphasize here that only information that was shared publicly by Twitter users was obtained and analyzed. First, we manually selected a few keywords that were deemed as good queries for retrieving tweets relevant to the mobile service provider in question. Second, we used the Twitter search API to obtain tweets and we archived the retrieved tweets along with the associated meta data. The meta data include the time that the tweet was submitted, the user who authored the tweets, etc. Third, we fetched user information through the Twitter REST API for those who authored the tweets that we archived. User information consists of the user profile such as user location to help localize issues reported.

After data archiving, our next step was to identify tweets related to mobile network performance issues. We used a few heuristic rules: (1) Tweets must contain mobile related words such as phone, mobile, 3G, edge, etc; (2) Tweets must contain performance related words such as slow, drop, intermittent, doesn't work, etc; and (3) Tweets should not contain words indicative of advertising, such as "Ads" and price symbols $. To verify the effectiveness of these rules, we randomly sampled 100 tweets, and manually annotated whether they were related to mobile performance issues. We observe an 87% agreement between rule-based prediction and human annotation. This is an acceptable level of accuracy[1] for our study. There are potential methods via natural language processing and machine learning which would likely improve the performance of this step. We leave this as future work.

2.2 Customer Care Calls

We obtained customer care tickets that had been created in response to customer calls for the mobile service provider. Note that these tickets are anonymized; no customer identification information is used from the tickets in this analysis. These tickets are tagged with the types of issues, i.e., billing and accounting, calling plan and features, mobile devices, service coverage, performance impairments and service outages. In this paper, we focus on the customer tickets relating to service impairments and outages. In addition, each ticket contains information regarding the type of service, the time that the call was received by the customer care team (the trouble ticket is often issued at the same time), the location, and a description of the performance issues that the customer experienced. The description usually provides detailed information on when and where the customer experienced the performance impairment as well as the device and application that the customer was using when the performance impairment occurred.

In our data, the performance related customer trouble tickets include issues such as no coverage, cannot make or receive calls, call disconnected/dropped, and poor voice quality, etc. It is important to note that not all customers will call the customer care team and report the performance impairments that they experienced. In addition, we will show later that customers may not call the customer service center immediately after they experience the performance impairments.

[1]In statistical scene, the estimation result 87% is within 95% confidence interval, with a margin error less than 0.1, given that we randomly selected 100 samples.

2.3 Major Network Incidents Report

The service provider has a top tier of operators that oversee the entire operation of the cellular network and service. They maintain a so called *Major Network Incidents Review* in a collaborative editing system. The network incident review keeps track of information regarding major network or service incidents as they are reported, diagnosed, resolved and concluded. The review report serves as a channel to communicate summary-level information about major incidents among the team members and senior management members.

The incidents in the report include a wide variety of network and service issues including hardware failures, major maintenance activities, outages due to adverse weather, congestion due to flash crowds (e.g., highway accident causing traffic congestion and unexpected high cellular network congestion), etc. Reading through the incidents report, we first filtered out those non-customer-impacting events from our study, such as planned system upgrade where redundant capacity is in use during the upgrade. We have also excluded very long incidents (e.g., greater than three hours) in the later part of the analysis so that the chance of falsely joining a network or service event to independent customer care tickets and tweets is low.

Each entry in the major network incidents report contains crucial information about an event. All entries contain temporal information (i.e., the start and end time of the incidents), and coarse spatial information, i.e., the primary market region where the incidents occurred (e.g, northeast, west, etc.). Moreover, all entries have facilitator/ incident manager contact details for follow up investigations, and the estimated scale of the customer impact. Most of the entries have *incident summaries* which describe the nature of the incidents in detail [2]. Some of the incidents contain root cause descriptions which explain the cause of the incidents in detail. In this paper, we only utilize the temporal and spatial information recorded for the incidents.

3. RESULTS

In this section, we first present the results on the major network incidents report, tweets and tickets data. Then we correlate both tweets and tickets with the incidents report. The data we analyze are based on a large cellular network provider in United States over the period of 16 days.

3.1 Major Network Incidents Report Results

We first analyze the temporal distribution of the major network incidents reported. Note that not all network incidents are included in the report - only those deemed most significant by the operations teams investigating. The report that we use contains only major network incidents. The vast majority of network incidents are fairly minor and not severe enough to be included in this report. Among these major incidents, we observe a very diverse duration ranging from seconds to over a day. As we mentioned in Section 2.3, in the later part of our analysis we focus on the incidents with duration of less than three hours.

3.2 Tweets vs. Customer Care Tickets

In this section, we compare two sources of user experience: tweets and tickets based on customer care calls. First, we conduct the comparison using the *raw* data, which include all tweets

[2]Although some descriptions contain certain kind of detail location information (for example, city, device, highway information), it is challenging to automatically and precisely extract them due to the loose structure of the description text.

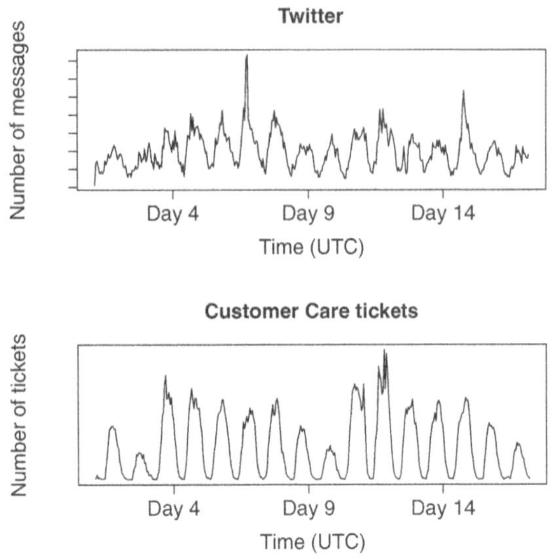

Figure 1: The number of tweets and tickets per hour. Due to privacy issues, the concrete number of tickets is not reported.

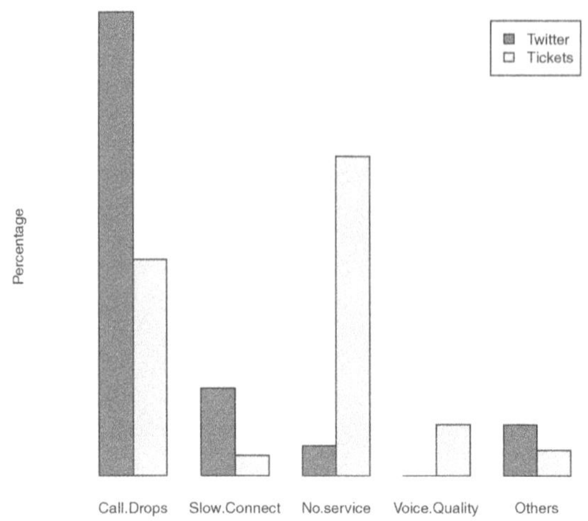

Figure 2: Classify performance related tweets/tickets based on the type of the issues. Due to privacy issues, the concrete percentages are not reported.

that we have archived and considered as relevant to the mobile service provider (i.e., some tweets are not performance related). Then we classify the data into different categories and drill down to the performance-related tweets. Finally, we examine the delay of user feedback, namely, how long it takes for a user to report a problem after he/she experienced it.

3.2.1 Time Series

We compare the volume of tweets and the volume of customer call tickets over a common period of time. Figure 1 shows the number of tweets and tickets per hour based on the *raw* data. From Figure 1, we observe the obvious daily pattern in both cases. It is easy to understand that customer calls have such pattern (common user behavior). It is also not surprising for tweets because of the daily pattern of social media access [2] and the fact that we focus on a US service provider. We will later (in Section 3.3) see that the diurnal pattern is weak when we focus on only performance related tweets. Another interesting observation from Figure 1 is the spike for Twitter data on Day 7. This spike is caused by discussions relating to new technology being made available to the consumer market.

3.2.2 Classification

We have investigated the *raw* data in the previous section. In this section, we move on to classify the data into different categories, and then focus on the performance related logs.

By manually inspecting the message content of the collected tweets, we observed the following three major types: (1) Comments and news regarding the product and customer service; (2) Advertisements (e.g. the promotion of a mobile phone); (3) Comments or complaints regarding performance related issues (which we are particularly interested in). Due to the loose organization of messages, it is difficult to precisely classify tweets automatically. But in general, the majority of the tweets are of type (1) or (2). On the other hand, since the tickets have a fixed structure and categorization, it is relatively easy to classify them. The majority (over 97%) of tickets are related to plan, bill or device issues. In the rest

Table 1: Location information of tweets.

Location Info.	No	Yes		
		City+State	State only	Others
Twitter Profile	37.2%	29.6%	20.5%	12.7%
Twitter Message	69.5%	20.5%	9.9%	1.0%

of the paper, we mainly focus on type (3), i.e., performance related tweets / tickets.

Among tweets extracted using the methodology described in Section 2.1, only about 1% of messages are related to performance issues. Similarly, only 1% to 2% of tickets are related to network performance. Figure 2 further breaks down the performance related issues into several categories. From this figure, we observe that issues reported by Twitter users and by customers who call customer care are very different. For Twitter users, call dropping is the most frequent complaint, followed by slow connection, no service and others (e.g., difficulty in sending messages or in posting something on websites). In contrast with the tweets, more tickets are related to lack of service or coverage issues (e.g. no coverage in some buildings). Very few of them are related to slow connection. Moreover, we also observe that many tickets are relate to voice quality, issues which are not typically seen in Twitter messages. This result illustrates that the types of performance issues reported by Twitter users are different from those reported by customer calls: the former tends to report short term and/or minor performance impairments, while the later tends to report more severe performance issues.

We also compare the tweets and tickets by locations. There are two ways to retrieve the location information of tweets: namely from the user profiles and from the message content itself. The message itself is a more valuable source because it presumably provides the location directly related to performance issues. Therefore, we first rely on the location information in messages. If there is no such information, then we consider the location in the user profile. Because both profile and messages are human language inputs without fixed structure, the location information could be missing

Table 2: The delay between the customers experience the incidents and the customers report the incidents.

Delay	0 day	1 day	> 1 day
Tweets	98.3%	1.2%	0.5%
Tickets	38.4%	21.2%	40.4%

or incomplete. There are three general categories of location information identified in our analysis: city + state, state only, others (e.g. city name only, street). Table 1 depicts the breakdown across these categories of the location information obtained from the user profiles and tweets analyzed. We observe that a large proportion of tweets have no location information at all - 37% of profiles have no location information and 69% of Twitter messages do not contain location specific information. It reduces the number of valid tweets for later correlation purposes. In contrast, the location information in tickets is well organized based on the *market* regions. A single market could include multiple states (e.g. Georgia + South Carolina) or cover just a part of one populous state (e.g. Northern California). Different data sources have different granularity of location information. Therefore, we use the most detailed common location for correlation purposes in Section 3.3 .

3.2.3 Timeliness

There is inherently a delay between the time when a customer experiences an incident and the time when the customer reports that incident. The reporting time is defined here to be the timestamp of when the Twitter message was posted or when the customer called customer care. It can be directly retrieved from the data. On the other hand, the time associated with when a customer experiences an incident is often hard to determine - if it is available, it will be embedded within a Twitter message or in a ticket's description. For example, in Twitter, the message may reference "a couple of call drops *today*"; in tickets, the description may mention"no service since *yesterday*". We extract such information from the tweets and tickets in a simple way: we identify the timing patterns like "now, today, yesterday, 3 days, 2010-04-03, this morning". We observed that over 90.1% of our collected tweets do have such timing information. In comparison, fewer than 23.7% of ticket descriptions contain explicit timing information. We then computed differences between the times when the issues were reported and the estimated incident times as extracted from the tweet and ticket contents. The resulting distribution is illustrated in Table 2. We observe that most tweets are posted on the same day as the customers experience the performance issues. In contrast, most tickets are opened one or more days after the incident being reported. The result indicates that Twitter users respond much faster than those reporting issues via customer care. However, we should notice that these two groups of users may care about different kinds of performance issues. Therefore we cannot conclude that Tweets are faster than tickets for any particular incident.

3.3 Correlation Results

In this section, we correlate both performance related tweets and tickets with events reported in the major network incidents report. Figure 3 shows the time series of the incidents, tweets and tickets. Different from Figure 1, performance related tweets demonstrate only a weak diurnal pattern as shown in Figure 3. This implies that most of these Twitter messages are incident-driven. But customer tickets still have the strong diurnal pattern, because of the customers' calling behavior and aforementioned delay in incident reporting.

To understand if there is a strong correlation between incident reports and customer feedback, we conduct a statistic correlation [12] between the incidents and tweets/tickets series, for each location. We compute Pearson's coefficient of correlation and conduct significance tests. Unfortunately, the test result shows no strong correlation between incidents and customers' experiences. One possible reason is the time lag from the time when the incidents start to the time when users report performance problems. Correction of this time lag by some time shifting should be applied for the correlation tests. The challenge is that the time lags vary case by case and cannot be compensated systematically. We will leave the design of new statistical significance test methodology under this particular situation for the future work.

Instead of using statistical correlation, we use the incidents in the report as the ground truth and investigate whether these incidents are reported within the collected tweets/tickets. More specifically, if we observe tweets / tickers during the incident and occurring within the same region (e.g. east, west, central, etc.), we deem these tweets or tickets to be *associated* with the incidents. We verify the incidents which last less than 3 hours. The reason to verify relatively short-term incidents is that we have more confidence with the joins when the time window is limited. In other words, the chance of falsely joining an incident to independent tickets/tweets is low. Because of this filtering process, the results we observe during the correlation are valid for relatively short term incidents. We find that 55.6% of incidents can be found in tweets, and only 37.0% of them found in customer care tickets.[3] One interesting observation is that the matches found in tickets can also be found in tweets. Moreover, we use the number of associated tweets/tickets divided by the accumulated duration of incidents to describe the chance of observing tweets/tickets when incidents happen, denoted as c_1. Similarly, the chance of observing tweets/tickets when no incident happens, say c_2, can be measured as the number of unassociated tweets/tickets divided by the accumulated duration of non-incidents during the measurement period. We find that the ratio c_1/c_2 is 8.3 for tweets and 6.8 for tickets. This suggests that the chance of having user feedback during an incident is significantly higher than that when there are no ongoing incidents.

In Section 3.2.3 we quantitatively studied the delay from the time when customers experience the service impact till the time when customers report the issue. In fact, there is another delay between the time when incidents take place and the time when users experience problems. However, the time when users experience the incidents is not an accurate timestamp, as we have discussed in Section 3.2.3. Therefore, we now quantitatively analyze the *total* delay from the time when the incidents start till the time when customers report the problem. Figure 4 shows the box statistics of two delay distributions. The bottom and top of the box are the 25th and 75th percentile, and the band near the middle of the box is the 50th percentile (the median). The ends of the whiskers represent the minimum and maximum value. The maximum value in both cases is approximately 80 minutes. Note that we filtered out all incidents exceeding 3 hours, which thus serves as the upper bound of the delay. We find that Twitter users respond approximately 10 minutes faster than customer who call the customer care team in general. The fastest Twitter users response is in several minutes. The implication of this observation is that it may be possible to utilize Twitter users' feedback to observe the impact of network performance issues more timely than using customer tickets.

Finally, let us revisit Figure 3. There are obvious spikes on Day 11 for both Twitter and customer care data, even though there

[3]Due to limited coarse location information, there are some potential mismatch cases or false positive.

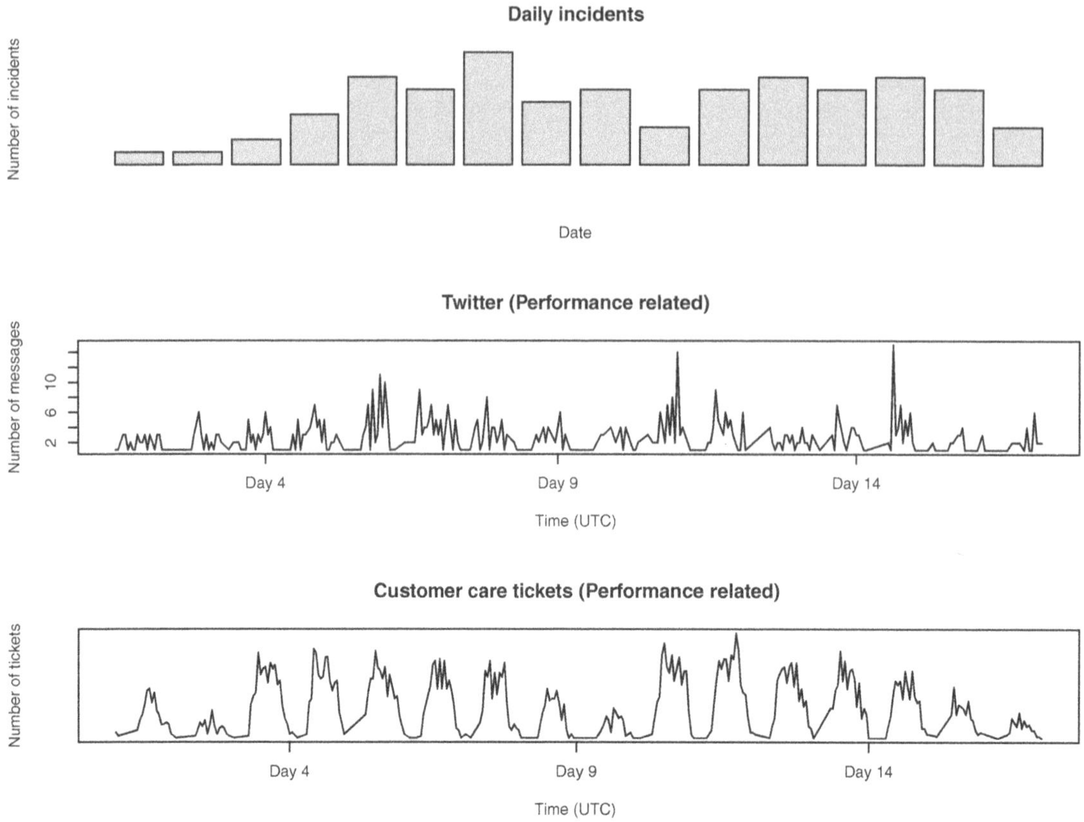

Figure 3: The time series of incidents, tweets and tickets. Due to privacy issues, the concrete numbers of incidents and tickets are not reported.

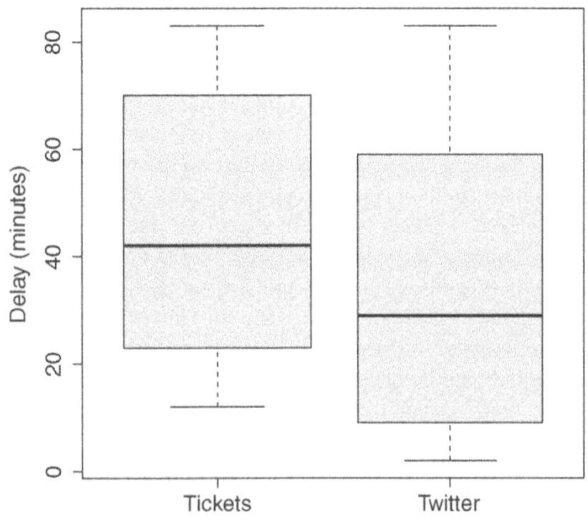

Figure 4: The CDF of delay distribution.

are very few incidents recorded in the same period of time. More specifically, there are many complaints from both Twitter and customer care regarding call drops during 8 PM to 10 PM in the central area. This may be an indication of certain short term network problems at that time, but yet none were reported in the major incident reports covering the area.

4. RELATED WORK

There have been a number of studies regarding the social network. However, most of them focus on the social network itself, e.g., users behavior [18, 13, 20, 2], the impact on network performance [21], community evolution [7, 14], information propagation [23, 5, 4], privacy issues [8, 6]. Very few studies focus on showing the value of social network content. Vieweg *et al.* shows the microblogging such as Twitter can contribute to the situation awareness during natural hazards events like floods and fire [22]. Motoyama *et al.* use Twitter data to infer on-line Internet service availability [19].

Correlating across data sources is a common methodology used in anomaly detection [15, 9, 3] and network problem diagnosis [12, 10, 17, 16, 11]. Most of these papers focus on the derivation of statistics methods. Our study in this paper takes the first step to reveal the possibility of utilizing social media content as a new source to understand user experience of mobile networks.

5. CONCLUSION AND FUTURE WORK

We have presented the primary study of exploiting the social network content for network performance monitoring. Our data suggest that users' feedback regarding network incidents is often observed in twitter messages in a timely fashion. Therefore, it is a complementary source for understanding network performance issues and their impact on user experience.

As future work, we plan to apply advanced natural language processing techniques to better understand tweets, as well as tickets and incident reports. For example, it is important to advance the technique for intelligently extracting performance related issues from tweets. It would also be interesting to quantify the severity level of performance related tweets by the scale of the responses and the sentiment in the messages (e.g. to detect urgent issues based on users' attitude).

6. REFERENCES

[1] comScore 2009 US Digital Year in Review, 2009. `http://www.comscore.com/Press_Events/Presentations_Whitepapers/2010/The_2009_U.S._Digital_Year_in_Review`.

[2] Fabrício Benevenuto, Tiago Rodrigues, Meeyoung Cha, and Virgílio A. F. Almeida. Characterizing user behavior in online social networks. In *Internet Measurement Conference*, pages 49–62, 2009.

[3] Daniela Brauckhoff, Xenofontas Dimitropoulos, Arno Wagner, and Kavè Salamatian. Anomaly extraction in backbone networks using association rules. In *Proc. ACM IMC*, 2009.

[4] Meeyoung Cha, Hamed Haddadi, Fabricio Benevenuto, and Krishna P. Gummadi. Measuring User Influence in Twitter: The Million Follower Fallacy. In *In Proceedings of the 4th International AAAI Conference on Weblogs and Social Media (ICWSM)*.

[5] Meeyoung Cha, Alan Mislove, and Krishna P. Gummadi. A measurement-driven analysis of information propagation in the flickr social network. In *WWW '09: Proceedings of the 18th international conference on World wide web*, pages 721–730, New York, NY, USA, 2009. ACM.

[6] Catherine Dwyer, Starr Roxanne Hiltz, and Katia Passerini. Trust and privacy concern within social networking sites: A comparison of facebook and myspace. In *Proceedings of the Thirteenth Americas Conference on Information Systems (AMCIS 2007)*, 2007. Paper 339.

[7] Sanchit Garg, Trinabh Gupta, Niklas Carlsson, and Anirban Mahanti. Evolution of an online social aggregation network: an empirical study. In *IMC '09: Proceedings of the 9th ACM SIGCOMM conference on Internet measurement conference*, pages 315–321, New York, NY, USA, 2009. ACM.

[8] Ralph Gross and Alessandro Acquisti. Information revelation and privacy in online social networks. In *WPES '05: Proceedings of the 2005 ACM workshop on Privacy in the electronic society*, pages 71–80, New York, NY, USA, 2005. ACM.

[9] Yiyi Huang, Nick Feamster, Anukool Lakhina, and Jim (Jun) Xu. Diagnosing network disruptions with network-wide analysis. *SIGMETRICS Perform. Eval. Rev.*, 35(1):61–72, 2007.

[10] Srikanth Kandula, Ranveer Chandra, and Dina Katabi. What is going on? learning communication rules in edge networks. In *Proc. ACM SIGCOMM*, 2008.

[11] Srikanth Kandula, Ratul Mahajan, Patrick Verkaik, Sharad Agarwal, Jitendra Padhye, and Paramvir Bahl. Detailed diagnosis in enterprise networks. In *Proc. ACM SIGCOMM*, 2009.

[12] R. R. Kompella, J. Yates, A. Greenberg, and A. C. Snoeren. Detection and localization of network blackholes. In *Proc. INFOCOM*, 2007.

[13] Balachander Krishnamurthy, Phillipa Gill, and Martin Arlitt. A few chirps about twitter. In *WOSP '08: Proceedings of the first workshop on Online social networks*, pages 19–24, New York, NY, USA, 2008. ACM.

[14] Haewoon Kwak, Yoonchan Choi, Young-Ho Eom, Hawoong Jeong, and Sue Moon. Mining communities in networks: a solution for consistency and its evaluation. In *IMC '09: Proceedings of the 9th ACM SIGCOMM conference on Internet measurement conference*, pages 301–314, New York, NY, USA, 2009. ACM.

[15] Anukool Lakhina, Mark Crovella, and Christophe Diot. Mining anomalies using traffic feature distributions. In *SIGCOMM '05: Proceedings of the 2005 conference on Applications, technologies, architectures, and protocols for computer communications*, pages 217–228, New York, NY, USA, 2005. ACM.

[16] A. Mahimkar, Z. Ge, , A. Shaikh, J. Wang J. Yates, Y. Zhang, , and Q. Zhao. Towards Automated Performance Diagnosis in a Large IPTV Network. In *Proc. ACM SIGCOMM*, 2009.

[17] A. Mahimkar, J. Yates, Y. Zhang, A. Shaikh, J. Wang, Z. Ge, and C. T. Ee. Troubleshooting chronic conditions in large ip networks. In *Proc. ACM CoNEXT*, 2008.

[18] Alan Mislove, Massimiliano Marcon, Krishna P. Gummadi, Peter Druschel, and Bobby Bhattacharjee. Measurement and analysis of online social networks. In *IMC '07: Proceedings of the 7th ACM SIGCOMM conference on Internet measurement*, pages 29–42, New York, NY, USA, 2007. ACM.

[19] Marti Motoyama, Brendan Meeder, Kirill Levchenko, Geoffrey M. Voelker, and Stefan Savage. Measuring online service availability using twitter. In *USENIX 3rd Workshop on Online Social Networks (WOSN)*, 2010.

[20] Atif Nazir, Saqib Raza, Dhruv Gupta, Chen-Nee Chuah, and Balachander Krishnamurthy. Network level footprints of facebook applications. In *IMC '09: Proceedings of the 9th ACM SIGCOMM conference on Internet measurement conference*, pages 63–75, New York, NY, USA, 2009. ACM.

[21] Fabian Schneider, Anja Feldmann, Balachander Krishnamurthy, and Walter Willinger. Understanding online social network usage from a network perspective. In Anja Feldmann and Laurent Mathy, editors, *Internet Measurement Conference*, pages 35–48. ACM, 2009.

[22] Sarah Vieweg, Amanda L. Hughes, Kate Starbird, and Leysia Palen. Microblogging during two natural hazards events: what twitter may contribute to situational awareness. In *CHI '10: Proceedings of the 28th international conference on Human factors in computing systems*, pages 1079–1088, New York, NY, USA, 2010. ACM.

[23] Bimal Viswanath, Alan Mislove, Meeyoung Cha, and Krishna P. Gummadi. On the evolution of user interaction in facebook. In *WOSN '09: Proceedings of the 2nd ACM workshop on Online social networks*, pages 37–42, New York, NY, USA, 2009. ACM.

The Effect of Packet Loss on Redundancy Elimination in Cellular Wireless Networks

Cristian Lumezanu
Georgia Tech
lume@cc.gatech.edu

Katherine Guo
Alcatel-Lucent Bell Laboratories
kguo@bell-labs.com

Neil Spring
University of Maryland
nspring@cs.umd.edu

Bobby Bhattacharjee
University of Maryland
bobby@cs.umd.edu

ABSTRACT

Network-level redundancy elimination (RE) algorithms reduce traffic volume on bandwidth-constrained network paths by avoiding the transmission of repeated byte sequences. Previous work shows that RE can suppress the transmission of 20-50% bytes when deployed at ISP access links or between routers. In this paper, we focus on the challenges of deploying RE in cellular networks. The potential benefit is substantial, since cellular networks have a growing subscriber base and network links, including wired backhaul, are often oversubscribed. Using three large traces captured at two North American and one European wireless network providers, we show that RE can reduce the bandwidth consumption of the majority of mobile users by at least 10%.

However, cellular links have much higher packet loss rates than their wired counterparts, which makes applying RE much more difficult. Our experiments also show that the loss of only a few packets can disrupt RE and eliminate the bandwidth savings. We propose *informed marking*, a lightweight scheme that detects lost packets and prevents RE algorithms from using them for future encodings. We implement RE with informed marking and deploy it in a real-world cellular network. Our results show that with informed marking, more than 60% of the bandwidth savings of RE are preserved, even when packet loss rates are high.

Categories and Subject Descriptors

C.2.1 [**Computer-communication networks**]: Network architecture and design; C.2.3 [**Computer-communication networks**]: Network operations; C.4 [**Performance of systems**]: Performance attributes

General Terms

Performance, design, measurement

Keywords

cellular networks, redundancy elimination, loss

IMC'10, November 1–3, 2010, Melbourne, Australia.

1. INTRODUCTION

Cellular wireless networks are increasingly becoming a ubiquitous medium for Internet access. Cellular devices are set to overtake PCs as the most common Web access devices worldwide [9]. The increasing subscriber base and increasingly rich applications strain the capacity of both the cellular wireless links and the wired backhaul network that connects cell towers to the Internet.

Network-level redundancy elimination (RE) [19, 20, 5] has emerged as an efficient way to reduce traffic volume on bandwidth-constrained network paths. Redundancy elimination algorithms rely on deploying a cache at each end of the network path. For each packet traversing the path, the ingress node finds common sequences of bytes within packets that were previously sent (and stored in its cache) and replaces them with fixed-size pointers to the cache. At the egress, packets are decoded by replacing encoded content with data from the cache. Previous work found that RE can suppress the transmission of 20-50% bytes at ISP access links [20, 4]. More recent work has shown that RE is feasible even as an end system service, when the only redundancy to be eliminated is that within (not across) pairs of hosts [2].

Cellular network links are clear candidates for the deployment of redundancy elimination: they are bandwidth constrained [18, 6] and are likely to remain so for several years. Because RE is successful as an end-system service [2], RE may provide savings on the constrained wireless link, not just in the infrastructure shared by many users. Yet, applying RE to cellular networks is not straightforward: loss in the radio network can cause the two caches to become unsynchronized and hinder the decoding of repeated content.

In this paper, we study the feasibility of network-level redundancy elimination in high-loss environments such as cellular wireless networks. Using packet-level simulation driven by three large cellular traces and live experimentation on a North American CDMA 1x-EvDO network, we show that even the loss of a few packets can eliminate the bandwidth savings obtained with RE. To alleviate the harm caused by packet loss on RE, we propose *informed marking*, a simple mechanism to detect lost packets and prevent RE from using them in future encodings. Compared with RE in a lossless environment, RE with informed marking is able to preserve more than 60% of the bandwidth savings in a real network with high loss rates (above 10%).

Our contributions are as follows: First, we present a measurement study on the effectiveness of redundancy elimination in cellular wireless networks using three real-world

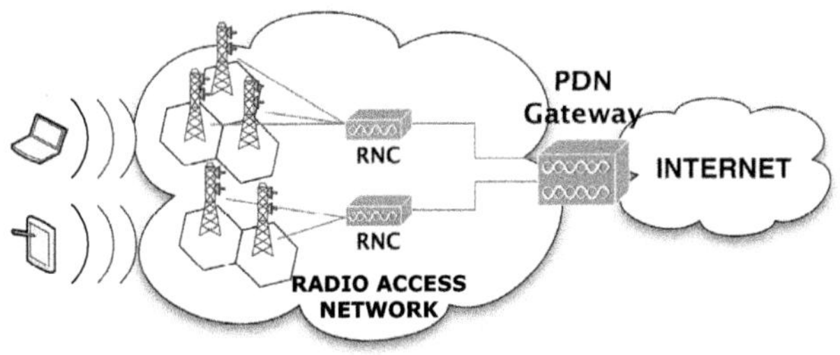

Figure 1: Simplified 3G/4G wide-area wireless network architecture.

packet traces gathered at wireless service providers in North America and Europe. Our analysis shows that most mobile users can save bandwidth with RE; some reduce their traffic volume by as much as 50%. Second, we observe that the high packet loss rates in cellular networks can pose problems for RE. We use simulations and live experimentation to understand how severe these problems are and show that even a few losses eliminate the benefit of RE. This is the first study on the effect of loss on redundancy elimination. Finally, we propose and evaluate informed marking, a lightweight mechanism that helps RE recover most of the bandwidth savings lost because of packet losses.

2. BACKGROUND

In this section, we describe the general architecture of cellular wireless networks, discuss existing RE techniques, and present the challenges that RE techniques face on cellular wireless links.

2.1 Cellular Wireless Networks

A cellular wireless network consists of a radio access network (RAN) that attaches to the Internet using a packet data network (PDN) gateway. We show a simplified example in Figure 1. We omit details and focus only on the path packets take from mobile station (MS) to the Internet. PDN gateways aggregate data from multiple radio network controllers (RNC) that receive mobile traffic over the air using base stations and wireless antennas. Data packets sent or received over the RAN are tunneled between the mobile devices and the PDN gateway.

The primary bandwidth bottleneck in wireless networks is in the airlink between the mobile users and the RNC [11]. WSPs have two solutions to keep the bandwidth demand below the available capacity: increase capacity or reduce traffic volume. Although 4G technologies, such as LTE, promise to increase the peak rates in the radio network to 100 Mbps, their deployment is expensive and will likely take several years, at which point they may remain bottlenecks.

2.2 Redundancy Elimination Overview

Network-level redundancy elimination (RE) is an efficient way of reducing traffic volume on bandwidth-constrained network paths. RE algorithms rely on deploying a packet cache at each end of a network path. The main idea is to compress outgoing packets by replacing sequences of bytes that have appeared in earlier packets with fixed-size pointers to the cached version of those packets. At the other end, packets are decoded by following the pointers and replacing encoded content with data from the cache. To function correctly and efficiently network-level RE requires the two caches to be synchronized.

RE works because network traffic contains a significant amount of repeated content. Spring *et al.* [20] found between 20% and 50% redundancy in traffic collected at an enterprise access link. More recently, Anand *et al.* [4] confirm these results by analyzing traffic from 11 enterprise networks. They also discover that most bandwidth savings come from repeated sequences of bytes within each user's traffic: a feature we exploit to deploy RE endpoints on cellular wireless clients.

Many commercial systems [16, 13, 14, 12] use RE in WAN optimization middleboxes placed on ISP access links. Recently, the EndRE system [2] proposed to push RE capabilities to end hosts. Neither middleboxes nor EndRE are suitable for cellular wireless networks. Although efficient for core Internet traffic, middleboxes cannot reduce traffic volume on last mile access links such as the radio access network for mobile users. On the other hand, EndRE can compress last mile traffic and, because it runs above the transport layer, is immune to losses in TCP traffic. However, potential packet loss will make it less effective for data streams that do not require reliable delivery (*e.g.*, UDP). Further, to effectively reduce traffic, EndRE must be installed on all servers that mobile users connect to. With the rapid increase in mobile users and applications, the destinations of mobile traffic become more diverse and application popularity becomes more dynamic. This makes the complete deployment of EndRE a difficult task. Even a partial deployment on popular servers is not trivial as it requires dynamic monitoring of server popularity.

2.3 RE over Cellular Wireless Links

To efficiently reduce the volume of traffic over the radio network, we must perform RE between each mobile user and the PDN gateway. This requires installing one cache on the mobile device and the other on the gateway. However, high packet loss rates in the radio network can create inconsistencies between caches and prevent RE from functioning correctly. A packet that enters the sender's cache, but is subsequently lost, will appear (to the sender) to be useful packet for encoding; if it does, the receiver will not be able to decode any subsequent packet that refers to the lost one.

How high can loss rates in wireless networks be? To answer this question, we connected a stationary laptop to the Internet through a CDMA 1xEV-DO USB wireless card and ran an experiment to measure the loss rates that TCP may experience. We used *wget* to download the front page of each of the 500 most popular web servers [3] and *tcpdump* to capture all network traffic (both uplink and downlink) during the downloads. We have chosen popular, well connected destinations to minimize the probability of losses on the wired section of the path. We compute the retransmission rate during the experiment. Because TCP may retransmit packets that are not necessarily lost, the retransmission rate can be viewed as an upper bound for the packet loss rate.

We present the results in Figure 2. We show, in log scale, the number of packets sent and retransmitted during every 1 minute interval for 100 minutes. The retransmission rate tends to oscillate between 0.001 and 0.10, with peaks of over 0.30. In Section 3.4, we analyze the effect of loss rates on the bandwidth savings obtained with RE and show that even small loss rates can affect the correctness of RE.

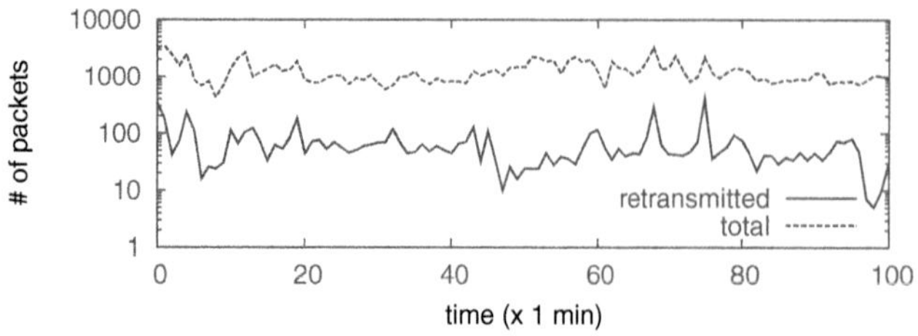

Figure 2: Number of total and retransmitted packets measured in a CDMA wireless network while downloading the front page of 500 most popular web sites (Total packets do not include retransmitted packets).

WSPs have made efforts to reduce the packet loss rate in their networks. This is mainly because high loss rates over the air interface also affect the performance of TCP, which interprets lost packets as a sign of congestion. Link layer retransmission protocols (such as RLP in CDMA [17] and RLC in UMTS [1]) ensure a link layer loss rate well below 1% [7]. However, when an IP packet is segmented into multiple link layer frames smaller than the maximum IP packet size, the IP loss rate is higher than link layer loss rate [10].

Existing RE schemes address loss by retransmitting the lost packets uncompressed. This may be sufficient in wired networks, where packet losses are few, and simply relying on retransmissions is enough. In wireless networks, however, this is not efficient: the large number of retransmissions may consume the bandwidth saved with RE, as we show in Section 3.

3. NORMAL REDUNDANCY ELIMINATION IN A LOSSY ENVIRONMENT

In this section, we analyze three cellular wireless traffic data sets and show that many mobile users can reduce their traffic volume with RE. We also show, using simulations and live experiments, that lost packets can significantly degrade the performance of RE.

3.1 Data Sets

We analyze three network traces, collected using *tcpdump*, at PDN gateways in two North American and one European 3G wireless service provider (WSP) networks. Table 1 shows the properties of each trace. Because we study the effects of RE for individual mobile users, we select the top k users that have sent or received the largest amount of traffic in each trace. We set k to 2,000 for WSP-1 and to 100 for WSP-2 and WSP-3. This ensures that the top k users are responsible for more than 80% of the traffic we capture in each network.

3.2 RE Algorithm Basics

We use the RE algorithm developed by Spring *et al.* [20] (commonly known as **modp**). For each packet, **modp** identifies content present in earlier packets by generating a list of fingerprints [15] associated with the packet. A fingerprint is a hash over a continuous sequence of bytes of length w. It is impractical to store all fingerprints that can be generated by a packet, since each byte in the packet generates a new fingerprint. Instead, **modp** chooses a fraction $1/p$, and stores only the fingerprints with value $0 \mod p$. This allows for the fingerprints to be chosen independently of their offset in the packet.

	WSP-1	WSP-2	WSP-3
when	10/2007	08/2008	05/2009
duration	30 min	1 hr	5 min
technology	CDMA	UMTS	UMTS
top users (k)	2,000	100	100
volume	0.5 GB	1.6 GB	0.8 GB
distribution:			
- TCP	59%	80%	97%
- UDP	36%	18%	2%
- ESP	1%	1%	0%
- others	4%	1%	1%
direction:			
- downlink	62%	89%	82%
- uplink	38%	11%	18%
avg packet size:			
- downlink	328B	952B	1001B
- uplink	199B	183B	322B
avg loss rate:			
- downlink	0.11	0.03	0.03
- uplink	0.12	0.09	0.14

Table 1: Properties of wireless data sets.

Next we describe the process of eliminating redundant traffic on the link between two nodes. For ease of exposition, we consider one direction of traffic and call the nodes sender and receiver. Both the sender and the receiver deploy a packet cache and a fingerprint store. The packet cache stores all packets that were sent or received by the node, while the fingerprint store keeps the fingerprints of all packets stored in the packet cache. For each outgoing packet, the sender computes its fingerprints and verifies whether they are present in the fingerprint store. Matches identify repeated sequences of size w (the size of window over which the fingerprint was computed). We then retrieve from cache the packet corresponding to the fingerprint and expand the matched region byte-by-byte in both directions to find the longest possible match. We replace each matched region with an 8-byte key, that indicates the location of the matched region in cache (packet id and offset) and its length. To obtain the original packet, the receiver identifies the keys in the encoded packet and replaces them with the regions in cache to which they point. Figure 3 is an illustration of the encoded packet and encoding keys.

The bytes of the encoding key represent the bandwidth cost that we have to pay to eliminate redundancy. Ideally, the size of the key is as small as possible. Our design of the 8-byte key improves over the existing **modp** algorithm which uses a 12-byte key. The first four bytes identify the packet in cache. Unlike Spring *et al.* [20], we choose to encode a hash of the packet in cache rather than the fingerprint associated with the repeated sequence, which reduces the size of the encoding key by four bytes. Similar to the original **modp** algorithm, we use the last four bytes to encode three 11-bit integers representing the offsets of the matched region in the current packet and in the cached packet as well as the length of the match. To accommodate the additional bit, we take advantage of the fact that the sum of either offset and the match length cannot be larger than 1,500.

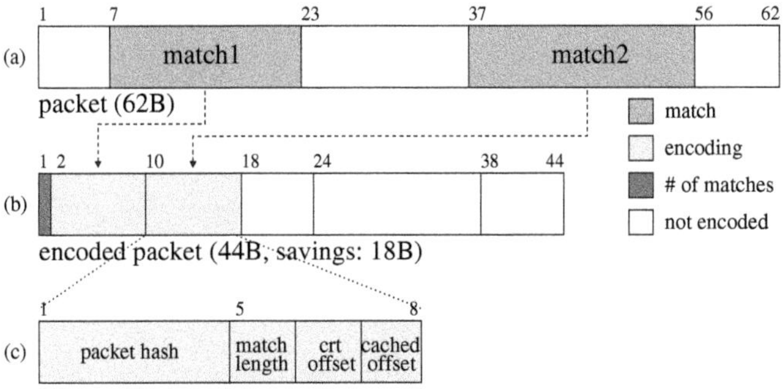

Figure 3: Encoding example: (a) incoming packet has two sequences of bytes seen in previous packets; (b) each match is replaced by an eight-byte encoding key; (c) each encoding key contains the hash of the packet in cache where the match was found (4 bytes), followed by the length of the match, offset in current packet, and offset in cached packet (all encoded in 9, 10, or 11 bits depending on their size.)

3.3 Bandwidth Savings

We define the *bandwidth savings* as the ratio between the volume of traffic saved after applying RE and the volume of traffic before RE. The bandwidth saved by each user depends on both the volume of redundant content that RE finds and the number of continuous repeated sequences of bytes (matches). This is regulated by parameters p and w of the **modp** algorithm. Recall that p determines how often we verify whether a fingerprint leads to a match and w represents the size of the smallest match. A small p has the potential to find more matches, but also strains the match-finding data structure.

We implement **modp** and run it for all users in each data set, for both uplink and downlink traffic. We vary the value of p from 1 (all fingerprints considered) to 256 (one in every 256 fingerprints considered). We present results for $p = 32$ because it generated the highest savings. We fix w to 8 because that is the size of the smallest possible match that would not waste bandwidth. We set the cache size to 64,000 packets. Unless otherwise noted, we use the same parameters throughout the rest of the paper.

Figure 4 (left) shows the cumulative distribution of bandwidth savings for all users in each data set. Uplink traffic is more redundant than downlink traffic. This is due to the increased number of identical or near-identical TCP ACKs and client requests sent on the uplink. WSP-1 has a higher overall redundancy than both WSP-2 and WSP-3. We speculate that this is because mobile data applications were not as diverse at the collection time of WSP-1 (October 2007).

3.4 The Effect of Loss

Loss in wireless is the result of transmission errors over the air interface, insufficient buffers at end points, or congestion. In Section 2, we showed that it is not unusual for wireless networks to experience high packet loss rates. Next, we study the effect of packet loss on bandwidth savings using simulations driven by our three data sets and live experiments on a US-based CDMA 1x-EvDO network.

3.4.1 Trace-based Simulations

To study the effect of loss under a controlled environment, we deploy RE on two computers connected through a wired network. One computer acts as the sender and the other as the receiver. We replay the traffic for each of the k mobile users in the trace between the sender and the receiver while simulating a lossy connection, where each packet is lost with probability pl.

We capture the effect of loss on RE with two measures: bandwidth savings and RE loss. We use the bandwidth savings (defined in Section 3.3) to capture the volume of traffic saved in the presence of loss. To capture the correctness of RE, we define the *RE loss* as the fraction of packets that cannot be decoded by the receiver because previous packets, on which they depend, are missing from the cache. Figure 4 (middle) shows the distribution of RE loss for all uplink traffic in WSP-3. Even when the loss rate is 0.01 ($\approx$ 1 in 100 packets is lost), 25% of the users cannot decode 20% of the packets they receive. Table 2 shows the results for all data sets.

We present the bandwidth savings for the uplink WSP-3 traffic in Figure 4(right) and for all data sets in Table 2. For the packets that receivers can decode, the bandwidth savings drop significantly (compared to a scenario where there is no loss): only around 20% of users see savings of more than 20% in uplink WSP-3 (compared to almost half when there is no loss). We also observe that the bandwidth savings and RE loss change with the loss ratio for WSP-1 but not for WSP-2 and WSP-3 (except for the RE loss rate for WSP-2 when $pl = 0.10$). We believe this is due to the lower volume of traffic that each user in WSP-1 sends or receives. In conclusion, packet loss affects both the performance and correctness of RE in wireless cellular networks.

3.4.2 Live deployment

To show the effect of loss on bandwidth savings under live network conditions, we deploy RE on a 3G-enabled laptop, as described in Section 2.3. The laptop tries to compress all outgoing packets, regardless of the destination, then tunnels them to a server on our campus network which decodes and forwards them to their destinations.

We run several experiments where we transfer, using UDP, parts of the Enron e-mail corpus [8] over the 3G connection. We transfer email because it is known to have higher repeated content. Each transfer takes 60 seconds and we send about 2MB of data. We demonstrate the effect of lost bandwidth savings due to loss, therefore we do not make any attempt to recover lost packets (*i.e.*, we assume that they could be retransmitted, without being compressed, by a higher layer).

Figure 5 shows the results of a representative experiment. The line labeled "expected savings" represents the evolution in time of the bandwidth savings expected by the sender, assuming no packet losses. The line labeled "actual savings" corresponds to the savings computed by the receiver from the packets it can decode (*i.e.*, bandwidth saved in the presence of packet loss). The average loss rate during the experiment, as measured with *iperf* was around 0.25. Although RE should be able to save around 63% of the bandwidth at the end of the experiment, due to loss, it saves much less—only 2%. This number is optimistic since it does not include the bandwidth lost by retransmitting the lost packets.

4. LOSS RECOVERY

Packet loss can compound when RE is used: missing packets will prevent receivers from being able to decode later

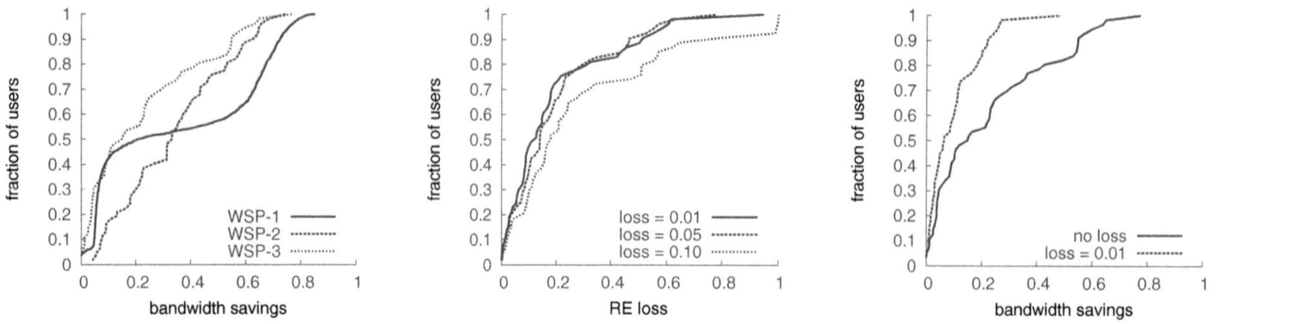

Figure 4: (left) Cumulative distribution of bandwidth savings without packet loss for uplink traffic, all data sets; (middle) Cumulative distribution of the fraction of packets that receiver cannot decode (RE loss), for various packet loss rates, uplink WSP-3; (right) cumulative distribution of bandwidth savings with and without packet loss, uplink WSP-3.

Data set	dir	no loss	loss					
		BW savings	BW savings			RE loss		
			pl=0.01	*pl*=0.05	*pl*=0.10	*pl*=0.01	*pl*=0.05	*pl*=0.10
WSP-1	down	0.50	0.46	0.04	0.00	0.00	0.78	0.95
	up	0.65	0.63	0.20	0.03	0.00	0.33	0.44
WSP-2	down	0.22	0.03	0.02	0.02	0.45	0.48	0.49
	up	0.46	0.15	0.14	0.10	0.23	0.26	0.55
WSP-3	down	0.08	0.01	0.01	0.01	0.27	0.26	0.30
	up	0.36	0.14	0.14	0.08	0.05	0.07	0.09

Table 2: 75th percentile values for bandwidth savings and RE loss for each data set with and without loss.

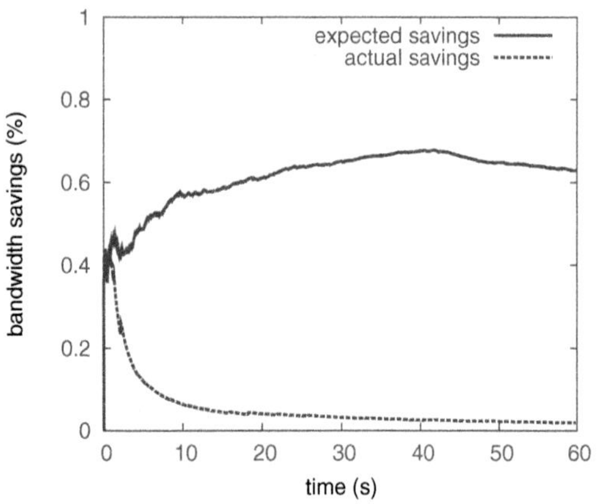

Figure 5: Expected bandwidth savings vs actual bandwidth savings when running RE in the presence of packet loss on a real 3G CDMA wireless network.

packets, which will then be dropped. We term this *RE loss*. Although we cannot prevent the original packet from being lost, we may be able to prevent the encoding from using lost packets and thus reduce or eliminate RE loss. For this, we must synchronize the sender's and receiver's caches. We consider two general solutions: (1) retransmit lost packets so that the receiver can decode future packets encoded based on them, and (2) detect lost packets and prevent the sender from encoding future packets based on them.

4.1 Loss recovery schemes

Existing RE schemes for wired networks [20] propose to retransmit lost packets. To detect loss, the receiver can wait for a packet that it cannot decode and request the missing packet from the sender or rely on sequence numbers assigned by the sender and request retransmissions of packets with missing sequence numbers. The potential of a retransmission-based scheme is high: it could offer bandwidth savings similar to when there was no loss. However, a retransmission-based RE scheme will likely waste significant additional bandwidth in a high-loss environment such as cellular networks.

Another solution for reducing the RE loss is to detect and blacklist lost packets such that they cannot be used in future encodings. We consider two detection methods: *ack snooping* and *informed marking*. Ack snooping relies on the fact that in TCP, all packets correctly received are acknowledged. The scheme requires the sender to monitor all traffic from the receiver and blacklist any packet not acknowledged after a predetermined interval. Ack snooping quickly detects loss without explicit feedback from the receiver and can reduce the RE loss rate to 0. However, it can generate false negatives by mistakenly considering slow packets lost. Moreover, it does not work with transport protocols that do not acknowledge received packets such as UDP, which is common in cellular wireless networks (see Table 1).

In search for a more general loss detection technique, we propose *informed marking*, where each receiver signals the sender whenever it cannot decode a packet due to a missing packet from its cache. The receiver sends a control packet with the hash of the missing packet and the sender blacklists the corresponding packet in its own cache; in future encodings, the sender ignores repeated content matched to any blacklisted packet. Informed marking reduces the RE loss rate to at most the value of network loss. This is because receivers need to receive one packet that they cannot decode to be able to notify the sender. Unlike ack snoop-

Data set	dir	retransmission	ack snooping			informed marking		
		pl=0.01, 0.05, 0.10	*pl*=0.01	*pl*=0.05	*pl*=0.10	*pl*=0.01	*pl*=0.05	*pl*=0.10
WSP-1	down	0.53	0.53	0.53	0.53	0.52	0.52	0.53
	up	0.65	0.65	0.64	0.65	0.65	0.65	0.65
WSP-2	down	0.22	0.22	0.19	0.19	0.22	0.20	0.20
	up	0.46	0.46	0.45	0.45	0.44	0.43	0.37
WSP-3	down	0.08	0.07	0.07	0.07	0.07	0.07	0.07
	up	0.36	0.36	0.37	0.37	0.35	0.35	0.34

Table 3: 75th percentile values for bandwidth savings for loss recovery methods based on retransmission, ack snooping, and informed marking (IM). In simulations, RE loss is 0 for retransmission and ack snooping and at most the network loss for informed marking.

ing, informed marking works with any type of traffic and is flexible because it does not introduce feedback overhead when there is no loss or when lost packets are not used in the encoding.

We evaluate the benefit of the three loss recovery schemes in simulation, by computing the bandwidth they save. We consider an ideal scenario where lost packets are immediately retransmitted or detected. Table 3 presents the 75th percentile values for bandwidth savings on the three data sets. We make two observations. First, all three schemes perform similarly and are able to remove the effect of loss rates on bandwidth savings observed when no recovery scheme is used (Table 2). Second, we obtain similar savings regardless of the network loss rate. The results show that it is more important to prevent senders from encoding based on lost packets than to retransmit the lost packets; RE loss has a much bigger effect on the bandwidth savings than network loss. By eliminating or limiting the RE loss, we are able to obtain savings similar to when there is no network loss at all.

Because it is more general and it does not introduce unnecessary feedback overhead, we implement informed marking and deploy it in a real cellular wireless network. We present the results of the deployment next.

4.2 Deployment of informed marking

In our simulations, receivers react immediately when they cannot decode a packet and instantaneously notify the senders. It is possible that, in a real wireless network, by the time a sender receives a request to blacklist packet A, it has already encoded another packet with pointers to A. To understand the extent to which this affects the bandwidth saved, we use the same experimental run as in Section 3.4.2. In Figure 6, we show the actual savings with informed marking and the expected savings (note that the expected savings are smaller than in Figure 5 due to packet blacklisting). The actual savings are about 25% smaller than expected.

The difference between expected savings and actual savings would be explained if there are many matches between packets sent very close to each other (*i.e.* traffic has temporal locality). Anand *et al.* have already shown that, for enterprise traces, 60-80% of matches are between packets in 10% of the cache. To verify whether such behavior exists in our data sets, we define the distance between two packets as the difference between their indices in cache. We compute the median distance for each user and find that 75% of all users have an median distance of at most 5. This means that half of their packets are encoded using recent packets.

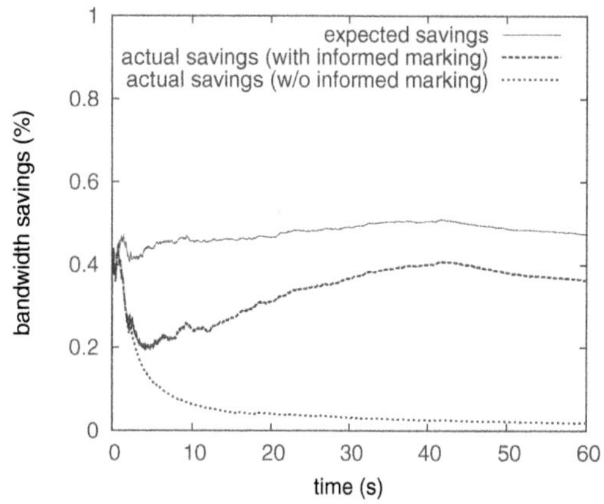

Figure 6: The benefit of informed marking on a real 3G CDMA wireless network.

If these recent packets are lost it is difficult to blacklist them in time to prevent RE loss.

5. CONCLUSIONS

We presented the first study on the effectiveness of traffic redundancy elimination in cellular wireless networks. Using real-world traces from three European and North American wireless service providers, we showed that the majority of mobile users sends or receives traffic with at least 10% redundant bytes. Yet, this redundancy cannot be exploited by redundancy elimination (RE) algorithms due to the high packet losses in cellular networks: even a few losses frustrate RE and prevent bandwidth savings. We proposed informed marking, a simple technique that allows RE to quickly detect and avoid lost packets. We evaluated informed marking both in simulation and in a live network and showed its effectiveness in reducing the effects of loss.

6. REFERENCES

[1] Third generation partnership project, RLC protocol specification 3G TS 25.322. `http://www.3gpp.org`, 1999.

[2] B. Aggarwal, A. Akella, A. Anand, A. Balachandran, P. Chitnis, C. Muthukrishnan, R. Ramjee, and G. Varghese. EndRE: An end-system redundancy elimination service for enterprises. In *NSDI*, 2010.

[3] Alexa. `http://www.alexa.com/`.

[4] A. Anand, C. Muthukrishnan, A. Akella, and R. Ramjee. Redundancy in network traffic: Findings and implications. In *Sigmetrics*, 2009.

[5] A. Anand, A. Gupta, A. Akella, S. Seshan, and S. Shenker. Packet caches on routers: The implications of universal redundant traffic eliminations. In *SIGCOMM*, 2008.

[6] R. Chakravorty, S. Banerjee, J. Chesterfield, P. Rodriguez, and I. Pratt. Performance optimizations for wireless wide-area networks: Comparative study and experimental evaluation. In *ACM Mobicom*, 2004.

[7] M. C. Chan and R. Ramjee. TCP/IP performance over 3G wireless links with rate and delay variation. In *Proc. MobiCom'02*, pp. 71–82, 2002.

[8] Enron Email Dataset. http://www.cs.cmu.edu/~enron/.

[9] Gartner Top End User Predictions for 2010: Coping with the New Balance of Power. http://www.gartnerinsight.com/download/Predicts2010_NewBalancePower.pdf.

[10] H. Lin and S. K. Das. Performance study of link layer and MAC layer protocols to support TCP in 3G CDMA systems. *IEEE Transactions on Mobile Computing*, 4(5), 2005.

[11] Motorola. Long Term Evolution (LTE): Overview of LTE air-interface technical white paper. http://business.motorola.com/experiencelte/pdf/LTEAirInterfaceWhitePaper.pdf.

[12] Netequalizer. http://www.netequalizer.com.

[13] Packeteer. http://www.bluecoat.com/packeteer.

[14] Peribit. http://www.juniper.net.

[15] M. Rabin. Fingerprinting by random polynomials. In *Harvard University, Technical Report*, pp. TR–15–81, 1981.

[16] Riverbed. http://www.riverbed.com.

[17] Data service options for spread spectrum systems: Radio link protocol type 3, TIA/EIA/IS-7-7-A-2.10. http://www.3gpp2.org, 2000.

[18] P. Rodriguez and V. Fridman. Performance of PEPs in cellular wireless networks. In *Web Caching and Content Distribution Workshop*, 2003.

[19] J. Santos and D. Wetherall. Increasing effective link bandwidth by supressing replicated data. In *Usenix Technical Conferences*, 1998.

[20] N. T. Spring and D. Wetherall. A protocol-independent technique for eliminating redundant network traffic. In *SIGCOMM*, 2000.

Performance Comparison of 3G and Metro-Scale WiFi for Vehicular Network Access

Pralhad Deshpande, Xiaoxiao Hou, and Samir R. Das
Computer Science Department, Stony Brook University
Stony Brook, NY 11794, USA
Email: {pralhad, xhou, samir}@cs.stonybrook.edu

ABSTRACT

We perform a head-to-head comparison of the performance characteristics of a 3G network operated by a nation-wide provider and a metro-scale WiFi network operated by a commercial ISP, from the perspective of vehicular network access. Our experience shows that over a wide geographic region and under vehicular mobility, these networks exhibit very different throughput and coverage characteristics. WiFi has frequent disconnections even in a commercially operated, metro-scale deployment; but when connected, indeed delivers high throughouts even in a mobile scenario. The 3G network offers similar or lower throughputs in general, but provides excellent coverage and less throughput variability. The two network characteristics are often complementary. It is conceivable that these properties can be judiciously exploited for a hybrid network design where 3G data can be offloaded to WiFi for better performance and to reduce 3G network congestion and to lower costs.

Categories and Subject Descriptors

C.2.1 [**Network Architecture and Design**]: Wireless Communications—*Vehicular Communications*; C.4 [**Performance of Systems**]: Measurement techniques.

General Terms

Performance, Measurement, Experimentation.

Keywords

Vehicular Internet Access, WiFi, 3G.

1. INTRODUCTION

3G cellular data and WiFi are the two wireless broadband access technologies widely available today. The two networks have significant differences. The former uses licensed bands and macrocells with large coverage areas. The base station and associated radio access network setup have significant capital and operational costs [25]. On the other hand, WiFi uses unlicensed spectrum. The access point (AP) coverage is relatively smaller and typically capital and operational costs are lower. Also, in comparison to 3G, most users expect that WiFi access would be free or inexpensive, and would provide a significantly higher bit rate (in the order of 10s of Mbps). However, they also expect that the coverage is available only in the local area, while 3G coverage is often ubiquitous.

Recent experiences with outdoor and vehicular access with WiFi [7, 11] have started to blur some of the differences between 3G and WiFi. Many metro-scale WiFi deployments [20] have also succeeded in making WiFi ubiquitous providing very good coverage in urban spaces. All these now make it viable to access WiFi in outdoors even in a mobile scenario at vehicular speeds. This makes us ask this question: *Can WiFi be used effectively in outdoors and mobile scenarios to reduce the load on the expensive 3G networks?* Demonstrating technical viability of this will certainly draw interest in developing networking protocols and applications that eventually lead to more efficient and cost effective wireless broadband access. We note that using WiFi to reduce the load on 3G networks is not new, and has been promoted by both networking [10, 27, 4] and policy researchers [16, 13]. Also, some carriers are known to incentivize such switching (e.g., TMobile @Home) to reduce load on their cellular networks. However, in spite of the general interest, systematic head-to-head comparisons of commercially operated metro-scale WiFi and 3G networks are still missing (except [4] where mostly open WiFi APs in the wild have been used).

Our paper makes the following contributions.

1. Provide an in-depth evaluation of WiFi access with vehicular mobility using a commercially operated metro-scale WiFi network. This is in contrast to prior studies that only considered open APs in the wild [11, 7, 4] or a limited WiFi deployment [12, 5, 9].

2. Provide a head-to-head comparison of WiFi and 3G access under vehicular mobility. This lays down the salient features of the two access networks and provide pointers as to how future hybrid network access could be designed by exploiting the better properties of the two networks.

The rest of the paper is organized as follows. In Section 2, we describe the related work. In Section 3, we describe the measurement setup including the networks considered, the testbed and the driving scenarios. The analysis of the mea-

IMC'10, November 1–3, 2010, Melbourne, Australia.

surement results are presented in Section 4. We conclude in Section 5.

2. RELATED WORK

2.1 Vehicular WiFi Access

Several experimental studies have explored the potential of using intermittently available WiFi connectivity from moving vehicles for data transfers. In the Drive-thru Internet project [23, 24] controlled experiments are done with a single car driving past a single access point to measure range and connectivity in an intermittent network. More recently, the CarTel project [7] has focused on upload performance while using open APs in the wild. In the ViFi project [5] the link layer performance is improved by exploiting macrodiversity (using multiple APs simultaneously), and opportunistic receptions by nearby APs. By the nature of the work, both CarTel and ViFi focus on upload.

Downloads and intermittent connectivity have been studied in a vehicular environment in a fleet of taxis in the Cabernet project [11] with an improved handoff scheme and a new transport protocol. In our prior work in this space [9], we also have focused on downloads. The emphasis there has been predictive methods for improving handoffs and use of prefetching in the APs for better download performance.

Improving handoffs with vehicular mobility has been an important area of research. Other than our work in [9], optimized handoffs techniques have also been developed and evaluated in the Cabernet project [11] and also in [12]. One or more of these strategies can nicely complement our work.

Applications that require maintaining a session face problems in vehicular WiFi access because of intermittent connectivity. Some papers address this issue by creating a transport layer protocol that maintains sessions transparently to changing IP addresses [11, 24].

Several other papers focus on sundry issues on vehicular WiFi access. For example, link and transport layer problems are examined in detail in [14]. Web applications are examined in presence of intermittent connectivity in [6]. Link layer measurements are reported in [18]. Use of directional antenna for better connectivity has been explored in [21].

2.2 Characterizing 3G Access

There has been less excitement about characterizing 3G access in mobile or stationary environment. This is likely because the 3G network is a closed system and under tight operator control. Thus, much of the work is measurement-based.

The important works in this space include cross-layer measurement study to evaluate TCP performance over 1xRTT networks in [19] and over EVDO networks in [15], capacity evaluation of UMTS networks in [26]. Mobile experiments are done in EVDO networks characterizing cross-layer aspects with TCP in [17]. Bandwidth predictability is evaluated for HSDPA networks in [28]. A measurement system for city-wide measurement of WiFi and EVDO networks was developed in [22].

2.3 Augmenting Mobile 3G using WiFi

A recent paper [4] has addressed the issue of augmenting mobile 3G by offloading data on WiFi whenever possible. However they mostly use open APs in the wild (more than 70% of times) and hence the median WiFi throughput numbers reported are much lower (about half) than in our 500 mile long drive case. Our work analyzes the performance of a single commercially operated WiFi network.

3. MEASUREMENT SETUP

3.1 Network

For our study we use a metro-scale WiFi deployment in the Long Island area in New York (population roughly 7 million). This service is called 'Optimum WiFi' [2] and is provided by Cablevision, a local cable TV provider and ISP. The WiFi network extends to most of populous areas of Long Island where our study is conducted. It also extends to parts of New York City, Pennsylvania, Connecticut and New Jersey, where Cablevision has service. The entire network has roughly 18,000 APs. WiFi access is provided free to all subscribers of Cablevision's TV or Internet services. We note that there are several hundreds of such metro-scale WiFi deployments in USA alone [20] While we expect that our general observations will be repeatable in another metro area deployment, we do note that more specific quantitative observations could be strongly tied to deployment density, radio characteristics of the APs and any handoff control on the APs.

For 3G access, we use Verizon's EVDO Rev. A service using the USB760 USB-based air interface available from Verizon. EVDO Rev. A service is capable of a maximum bit rate of 3 Mbps. Verizon's website [1] claims a maximum of 1.5 Mbps TCP throughout. In our experience we occasionally got a higher TCP throughput (about 2 Mbps).

3.2 Testbed

We use a Dell Latitude laptop running Linux as the client machine to be carried in the car. The original miniPCI WiFi interface from the laptop is removed and replaced by a carrier-grade interface (Ubiquity XR2 [3]) with transmit power set to 25 dBm. The interface uses Atheros chipset supported by the latest madwifi driver that we used. The WiFi card is connected to a high-gain (12 dBi) omni-directional antenna. We experimented with various other antennas (5 and 7 dBi) and transmit power choices (within FCC limits). However, the 12 dBi antenna provided the best connectivity. Note that due to the high gain, the beamwidth for this antenna on the vertical plane is relatively small (about 9°). Thus, assuming that the APs are deployed at the height of poletops, this antenna is likely to connect better to a distant AP relative to a very close AP. This is because the distant AP is much closer to the horizon relative to the car. The antenna is long – about 4ft. The antenna is carried inside the car with its top part sticking out from the sunroof.

The laptop also carries Verizon's USB-based USB760 EVDO Rev. A Modem as the second network interface. A USB-based Garmin GPS receiver is connected to the logging laptop. At startup the GPS receiver is initialized and the GPS location is logged every second.

A server program runs on a lab machine with a public IP address. The server accepts incoming connections from the WiFi/3G networks and transmits 1500 byte packets continuously to the client over TCP. as selected by the client. This enables download throughput tests to be reported in the next section.

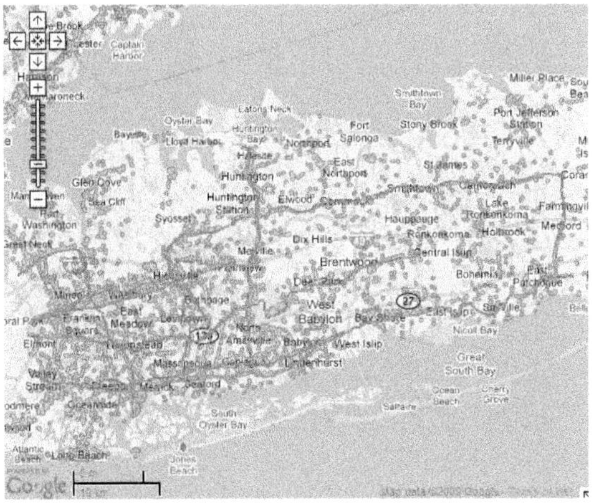

Figure 1: Map of the middle of Long Island – the area used in the long drive experiments. The route is shown in red. Approximate WiFi coverages are shown (from [2]).

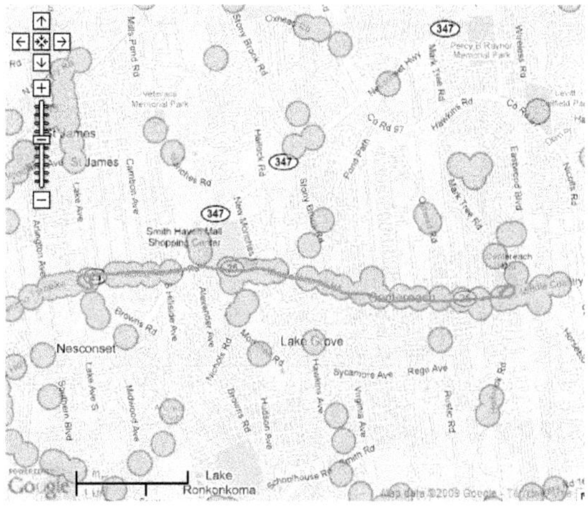

Figure 2: Map of the road stretch used for short repeated driving experiments (part of Route 25), along with the route shown in red. Approximate WiFi coverages are shown (from [2]).

We set the WiFi card's AP selection mode to automatic, i.e. the madwifi driver decides on the best AP to connect to. Auto rate control is disabled and a fixed bit rate of 11 Mbps is used. This is based on the observations in [11]. A few empirical tests indeed verified that this was the best policy in our setup.

DHCP is used to obtain the IP address. The Optimum WiFi network allows clients to retain the IP address between associations; thus DHCP delay is incurred only once at the beginning. This also allows us to retain the same TCP socket across associations. Optimum WiFi uses a browser-based authentication for the initial network access. This is done manually. Again this step is needed only once. Authentication is retained across associations.

Finally, a word about TCP. While using the stock TCP implementation on Linux we faced problems during our initial experiments when the WiFi link loses association for more than a few seconds. This sometimes makes the retransmission timeout really long (the timeout doubles at every step). This is a well-known issue for TCP in a mobile environment [8]. To tackle this problem, we simply set the maximum retransmission timer value on the server side TCP to 1 sec. We do note that this is not a general solution and more sophisticated client-side approaches are possible. However for the scope of this measurement study this solution worked reasonably well.

3.3 Driving Scenarios

Two driving scenarios are used for our evaluations.

- *Long Drive:* This is approximately a 500 miles drive shown in Figure 1 driven in a continuous fashion (close to 5 hours). The vehicle speed varied over a wide range depending on the road traffic. Each road is driven in both direction as the APs and their signal strengths visible from one side of the road are likely to be different from the other side of the road. This drive was performed only once. This long drive provides a reasonable sample of the quality of WiFi access from moving vehicles in a metro-scale deployment scenario. The association records for the long drive show over 900 unique APs.
- *Short Repeated Drives:* This is approximately a 9 mile drive on a selected stretch where the quality of the AP coverage is reasonably good. See Figure 2. Once again this drive constitutes a round-trip for the same reason. This drive was repeated 10 times to get a statistical confidence in the experimental results.

The Figures 1 and 2 show the approximate WiFi coverage taken from the provider [2]. Verizon coverage map for the same road stretch shows complete uninterrupted EVDO Rev. A coverage.

4. MEASUREMENT RESULTS

The laptop logs per second TCP throughputs (called instaneous throughputs) on both the connections along with GPS location and vehicle speed. The logs are postprocessed to develop the following analysis.

4.1 Quality of WiFi Coverage

To determine the quality of WiFi coverage we plot the CDF of run lengths (consecutive 1 sec segments) with zero and non-zero throughputs seen on WiFi. See Figure 3. Note that the 90-percentile zero throughput run length is 25 sec and 45 sec, for the short and long drives respectively. The same non-zero throughput numbers are 90 sec and 30 sec, respectively. The median numbers for non-zero throughputs are very short, however, just a few seconds. This reinforces the general experience that there are frequent disconnections on WiFi with vehicular mobility. However, we will note in the next subsection that we are nevertheless able to demonstrate impressive performance with respect to 3G.

It is important to note that this evaluation does not reflect true AP visibility; rather it shows whether there is actual connectivity and non-zero throughput on TCP. True AP visibility periods are likely to be longer than non-zero TCP throughput periods as we do not use any optimized

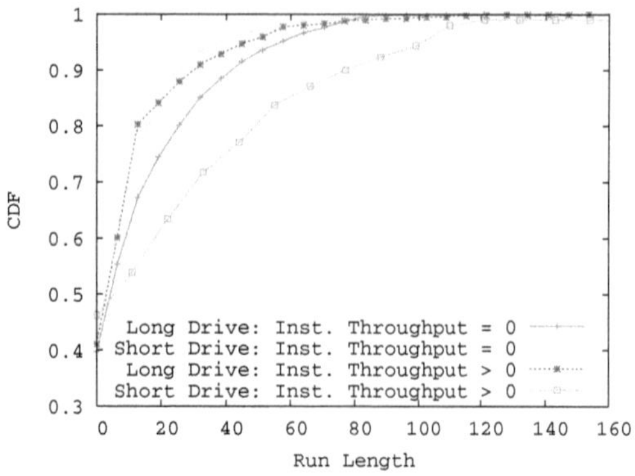

Figure 3: CDF of run lengths (consecutive 1 sec segments) with zero and non-zero throughputs seen on WiFi. Note that the short drive has zero throughput 25% of the times and the long drive 42% of the times.

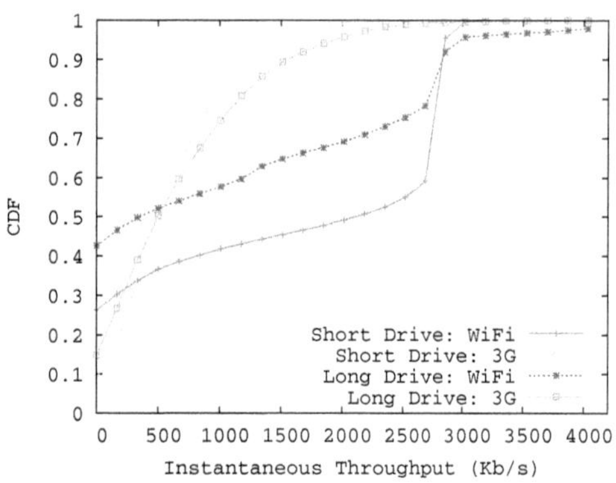

Figure 4: CDF of instantaneous TCP throughputs for WiFi and 3G.

handoff technique here. The TCP is also not optimized either except limiting the timeout period. Optimizing both of these will likely produce a much better WiFi experience [11]. Thus, our experience could be viewed as a lower bound for the WiFi performance.

4.2 Comparing WiFi and 3G Throughputs

In Figure 4 we compare the CDFs of instantaneous TCP throughputs on WiFi and 3G links. The long and short drives are shown separately. Note that WiFi throughputs are generally better in the short drive because of better coverage and slightly slower average driving speed experienced. However, 3G throughputs are very similar. While WiFi provides substantially better median throughput in the short drive (roughly 2400 Kbps vs. 500 Kbps) the median throughputs are similar in the long drive. However, WiFi has zero throughput on more occasions (roughly 25% vs. 10% for the long drive and 42% vs. 15% for the short drive). As noted before, this is expected as no special optimized handoff mechanism has been used. Also, WiFi coverage holes do exist (See Figures 1 and 2).

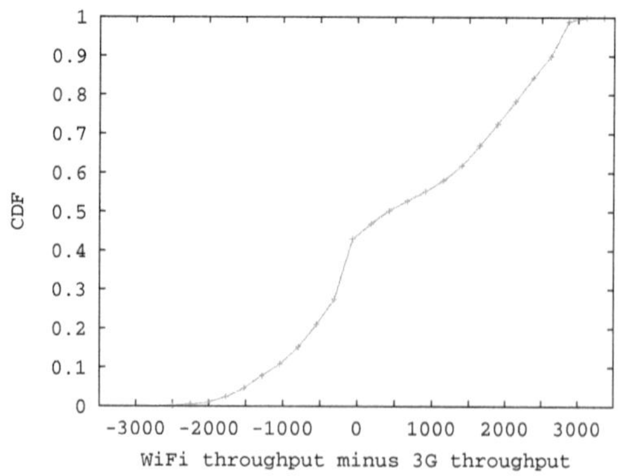

Figure 5: CDF of relative difference of instantaneous throughputs (in Kbps) between WiFi and 3G (i.e., WiFi minus 3G). Plot for the long drive only.

Also, notable is the fact that the *3G throughputs are well distributed in its entire range while WiFi demonstrates approximately tri-modal distribution* – zero or very low throughput, 0-2700 Kbps, higher upto about 3300 Kbps. Depending on the scenario each of these three modes persists for about 25%-40% of the times. The latter high throughput regions are specifically interesting for WiFi in our context.

Now we turn our attention to relative performance differentials between WiFi and 3G in the same time instants. See Figure 5 that plots the CDF of the algebraic difference between WiFi and 3G throughputs in the same time instants. This plot is done only for the long drive. Note that the fraction of times 3G performs better (45%) is only slightly higher than the times when WiFi has zero throughput (42%). In other words, when WiFi does have network layer connectivity, it is very likely that WiFi demonstrates better throughput. This again points to optimizing handoff making a serious impact.

Also, when WiFi outperforms 3G, it does it overwhelmingly so. The median difference is over 1500 Kbps. On the other hand, when 3G outperforms WiFi, the median difference is roughly 500 Kbps.

We have evaluated the correlation between WiFi and 3G throughputs for the same 1 sec intervals. *The correlation is very poor.* For the short drives it is 0.03 and for the long drive it is −0.03. This shows that these two networks can complement each other quite well.

4.3 Correlation with Vehicle Speed

It is also interesting to find out whether high throughputs are specifically correlated to slow vehicular speeds. In Figure 6 we present speedwise throughput statistics by breaking up the throughput data in the previous plot in three categories of speed – slow (0-20 Km/h), medium (20-40 Km/h) and high (40 Km/h and up). Note that the 3G throughput plots at different speeds are roughly similar. They also provide similar median throughputs. But the same cannot be claimed for WiFi, where slow speed has a clear advantage. This is expected as the WiFi physical layer is not built to support vehicular mobility, and the stock WiFi handoff implementations are not optimized for speed. The differences are much more for the short drive. This is likely because

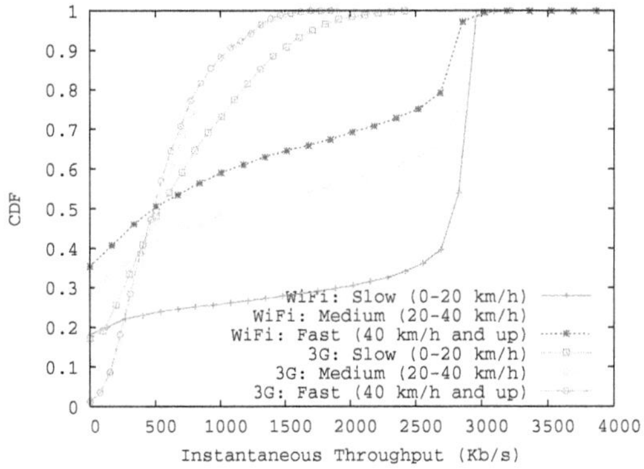

(a) Short drive.

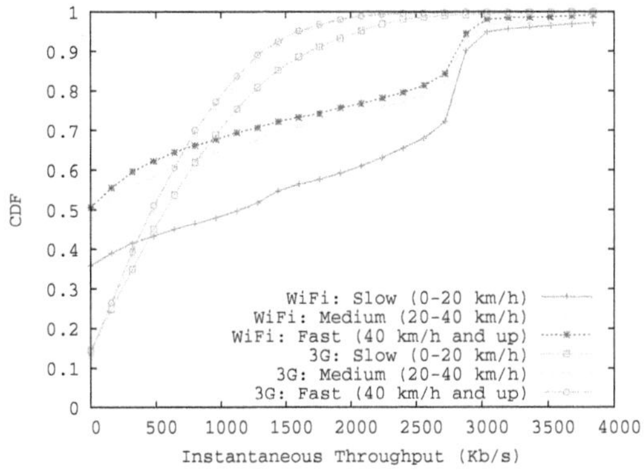

(b) Long drive.

Figure 6: CDF of Instantaneous TCP throughputs at different speeds for WiFi and 3G.

a better coverage better exposes the relationship between performance and speed.

Still at the fast speed, the median WiFi throughput is comparable to 3G for short drive. At slow speeds, it roughly doubles (for the long drive) or quadruples (for the short drive). WiFi is indeed impressive at slow speeds – providing over 2500 Kbps for over 60% or 35% of the times for short and long drives respectively. Thus, it is likely that WiFi would be much preferred in urban roadways in rush hour traffic, relative to high speed drives on rural highways. Incidentally, the former scenarios are likely to see metro-scale WiFi deployments.

4.4 Correlation with Location

Here, we evaluate how throughput is correlated with location. Previous research has indicated that WiFi signal strength in the same location has a reasonable degree stability and this property has been utilized to develop location-based handoff techniques [9]. However, throughput stability has not been evaluated. In regards to 3G, throughput stability has been evaluated to conclude that the entropy of the throughput distribution reduces significantly when conditioned on location [28]. However, no direct comparison between WiFi and 3G exists in this aspect.

For our analysis here, we use the general approach reported in [28]. The idea is to use the notion of *information entropy* that measures the level of uncertainty associated

	3G		WiFi	
Grid Size	Total H	Loc. H	Total H	Loc. H
10x10	1.56	1.19	2.26	1.44
20x20	1.52	1.16	2.25	1.56
30x30	1.51	1.12	2.23	1.71

Table 1: Comparison of total and location entropies for 3G and WiFi networks.

with a random process. The information entropy of a discrete random variable X is defined as,

$$H(X) = \sum_{x \epsilon X} p(x) \log_2 p(x), \qquad (1)$$

where $p(x)$ is the probability mass function, $0 \leq p(x) \leq 1$. The lower the entropy, the lower the uncertainty associated with the process. Hence, lower entropy indicates more predictability. Here, the random variable is the throughput. To address the influence of location on throughput we use the concept of *location entropy* as in [28]. Location entropy $H(X|l_i)$ is the entropy of throughput for a specific location l_i. This is defined as follows,

$$H(X|l_i) = \sum_{x \epsilon X} p(x|l_i) \log_2 p(x|l_i), \qquad (2)$$

where $p(x|l_i)$ is the probability mass function of throughput at location l_i. We use a similar technique as in [28] to calculate the entropy of instantaneous throughput measurements from the data corresponding to the short drives. Both total entropy (as in Equation 1) and location entropy (as in Equation 2) are computed.

The entire geographic space containing the drives is checkered with grids of different sizes: 10m×10m, 20m×20m and 30m×30m, with each grid square being indicative of a location. The grids simply discretize the space. The three different sizes are chosen to estimate what level of discretization is appropriate. The average instantaneous throughput per drive per grid square is treated as the realization of single independent random observation. Hence, each drive can produce at the most one observation per grid square. The total entropy is computed over all instantaneous throughput measurements for 3G and WiFi separately. The location entropy is computed similarly for each grid square and then averaged over all squares. The results are presented in Table 1. We can see that the total entropy of 3G is much lower than the total entropy of WiFi showing better predictability of 3G throughputs. Note that the size of grid squares makes little difference. We also see that the location entropy of both 3G and WiFi is lower than their respective total entropies. This result suggests that when conditioned on location, instantaneous throughput becomes more predictable in both networks. But the degree of improvement is somewhat similar.

4.5 Temporal Correlation

We also evaluate the temporal correlation of instantaneous throughput values. Figure 7 shows the autocorrelation for the long drive. Note the excellent temporal stability of 3G relative to WiFi. This is somewhat in contrast with measurements in [28], where the authors have found that the autocorrelation in HSDPA throughputs was quite small. Also,

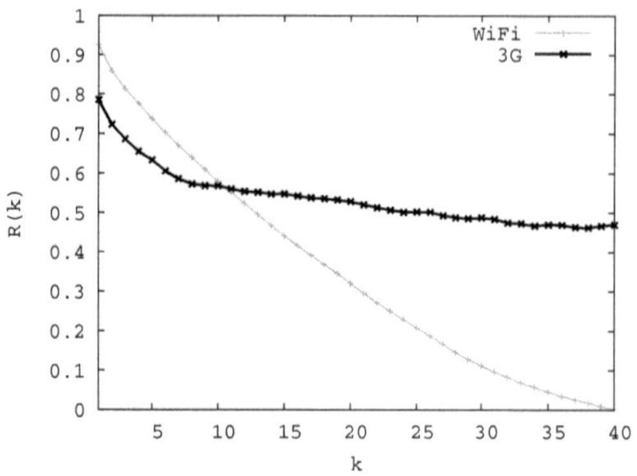

Figure 7: Autocorrelation $R(k)$ of the instantaneous throughputs measured in 1 sec intervals, where k denotes the time lag in seconds.

AR(k) Model	MSE(Y_{est})/VAR(Y)
AR(1)	0.120
AR(2)	0.119
AR(4)	0.119
AR(16)	0.117

Table 2: Prediction accuracy using AR(k) model.

interestingly for lower values of lag (k), the autocorrelation in WiFi throughputs is higher than that of 3G, though it decays promptly.

The knowledge of autocorrelation is useful is estimate how well the recent throughput experiences can predict the throughputs to be seen in near future. This could be useful in packet scheduling in a hybrid access scheme.

The prediction model can use one of several standard techniques such as autoregressive (AR) model, moving average (MA) model, autoregressive moving average (ARMA) model, etc. In [28] the authors have found that even the simplest of the models (AR) produces a very good estimate of the current throughput based on throughput measurements in the recent past. Thus, we have kept our analysis limited to AR models only. We have evaluated the performance of the AR(k) model for several values of k to see the quality of estimation. Table 2 shows the mean-squared estimation error divided by the sample variance (MSE/s^2). This is based on a standard AR(k) fitting method used in the mathematical software Octave, when applied on the time series WiFi throughput data.[1]

5. SUMMARY AND CONCLUSIONS

We now summarize the experiences we gathered from the measurement study.

- There is upto a factor of 4 improvement of median throughput on WiFi relative to 3G. This is somewhat drive specific.
- Instantaneous thoughputs on WiFi can be zero occasionally (very roughly one-third of the times). On the other hand, very roughly one-third of the times it can deliver significantly high throughput (over 2.5 Mbps).
- When WiFi is available, it is very likely (roughly 90%) that it outperforms 3G. Such outperformance is significant (a median difference of 1500 Kbps).
- There is more variability in WiFi throughputs relative to 3G. But variability reduces when conditioned on location. This is true for both networks.
- There is a good temporal correlation for the instantaneous throughputs on both networks, at least for short lags (more for WiFi).
- Slow speed means higher throughput on WiFi. But 3G is much less sensitive to speed.
- Correlation between WiFi and 3G throughputs are poor signifying that diversity techniques will be successful.

In conclusion, we have shown by experimental measurements that a metro-scale WiFi and 3G networks exhibit very different characteristics under vehicular mobility. WiFi has frequent disconnections even in a commercially operated, metro-scale deployment; but when connected indeed delivers high throughout even in a mobile scenario. The 3G network offers much lower throughputs, but provides much better coverage and less throughput variability. Our general experience indicates that a hybrid design that exploits the best properties of the two networks opportunistically can be very successful [4]. This can benefit the consumer with better throughput and as well as lower the cost for the provider by moving expensive 3G bits onto WiFi networks.

We do note that while our experiences are indeed provider specific, the general observations are not surprising and very likely would be repeated in other deployments. We expect that our work will encourage similar measurement studies. We also note that lack of access to the provider network lets us measure end-to-end throughput only, instead of the throughput on the wireless hop alone. The latter would certainly be more interesting to study. Our future work includes (i) understanding and improving handoff characteristics and TCP dynamics for vehicular WiFi access, specifically for metro-scale WiFi deployments, and (ii) designing hybrid access methods that exploit the best of 3G and WiFi, particularly targeting interactive use.

[1]If x_t is the average throughput at the t-th sec, the AR(k) model estimates x_t as $\hat{x_t} = c + \sum_{i=1}^{k} \phi_i x_{t-i} + \epsilon_t$, where c is a constant, ϕ_i's are the parameters of the model, and ϵ_t is white noise.

6. REFERENCES

[1] Coverage Locator – Verizon Wireless. http://www.verizonwireless.com/b2c/CoverageLocatorController?requesttype=NEWREQUEST.

[2] Optimum WiFi. http://www.optimum.net/MyServices/WiFi/.

[3] Ubiquity Networks, Inc. http://www.ubnt.com.

[4] A. Balasubramanian, R. Mahajan, and A. Venkataramani. Augmenting Mobile 3G Using WiFi. In *Proc. ACM MobiSys Conference*, 2010.

[5] Aruna Balasubramanian, Ratul Mahajan, Arun Venkataramani, Brian Neil Levine, and John Zahorjan. Interactive WiFi connectivity for moving vehicles. *ACM SIGCOMM Comput. Commun. Rev.*, 38(4):427–438, 2008.

[6] Aruna Balasubramanian, Yun Zhou, W. Bruce Croft, Brian Neil Levine, and Aruna Venkataramani. Web search from a bus. In *Proc. ACM CHANTS Workshop*, 2007.

[7] Vladimir Bychkovsky, Bret Hull, Allen Miu, Hari Balakrishnan, and Samuel Madden. A measurement study of vehicular Internet access using in situ Wi-Fi networks. In *Proc. ACM MobiCom Conference*, 2006.

[8] R. Caceres and L. Iftode. Improving the performance of reliable transport protocols in mobile computing environments. *IEEE Journal on Selected Areas in Communications*, 13(5):850–857, 1995.

[9] Pralhad Deshpande, Anand Kashyap, Chul Sung, and Samir R. Das. Predictive methods for improved vehicular WiFi access. In *Proc. ACM Mobisys Conference*, pages 263–276, 2009.

[10] A. Doufexi, EK Tameh, AR Nix, and A. Molina. Hotspot wireless LANs to enhance the performance of 3G and beyond cellular networks. *IEEE Communications Magazine*, 41, 2003.

[11] Jakob Eriksson, Hari Balakrishnan, and Samuel Madden. Cabernet: A WiFi-Based Vehicular Content Delivery Network. In *Proc. ACM MobiCom Conference*, 2008.

[12] Anastasios Giannoulis, Marco Fiore, and Edward W. Knightly. Supporting vehicular mobility in urban multi-hop wireless networks. In *Proc. ACM MobiSys Conference*, 2008.

[13] V. Gunasekaran and F.C. Harmantzis. Towards a Wi-Fi ecosystem: Technology integration and emerging service models. *Telecommunications Policy*, 32(3-4):163–181, 2008.

[14] David Hadaller, Srinivasan Keshav, Tim Brecht, and Shubham Agarwal. Vehicular opportunistic communication under the microscope. In *Proc. ACM MobiSys*, 2007.

[15] Y. Lee. Measured TCP performance in CDMA 1xEV-DO network. In *Proc. PAM Conference*, Adelaide, Australia, Mar. 2006.

[16] W. Lehr and L.W. McKnight. Wireless Internet access: 3G vs. WiFi? *Telecommunications Policy*, 27(5-6):351–370, 2003.

[17] X. Liu, A. Sridharan, S. Machiraju, M. Seshadri, and H. Zang. Experiences in a 3G network: interplay between the wireless channel and applications. In *Proc. ACM MobiCom Conference*, pages 211–222, 2008.

[18] Ratul Mahajan, John Zahorjan, and Brian Zill. Understanding WiFi-based connectivity from moving vehicles. In *Proc. Internet Measurement Conference (IMC)*, pages 321–326, 2007.

[19] K. Mattar, A. Sridharan, H. Zang, I. Matta, and A. Bestavros. TCP over CDMA2000 networks: A cross-layer measurement study. In *in Proc. Passive and Active Measurements (PAM) Conference*, 2007.

[20] Muniwireless.com. List of cities and counties with large WiFi networks. http://www.muniwireless.com/reports/Mar-28-2009-list-of-cities.pdf.

[21] Vishnu Navda, Anand Prabhu Subramanian, Kannan Dhanasekaran, Andreas Timm-Giel, and Samir R. Das. MobiSteer: using steerable beam directional antenna for vehicular network access. In *Proc. ACM MobiSys Conference*, 2007.

[22] J. Ormont, J. Walker, S. Banerjee, A. Sridharan, M. Seshadri, and S. Machiraju. A city-wide vehicular infrastructure for wide-area wireless experimentation. In *Proc. ACM WinTech Workshop*, pages 3–10, 2008.

[23] J. Ott and D. Kutscher. Drive-thru internet: IEEE 802.11b for automobile users. In *Proc. IEEE Infocom*, 2004.

[24] J. Ott and D. Kutscher. A disconnection-tolerant transport for drive-thru internet environments. In *Proc. IEEE Infocom Conference*, 2005.

[25] Qualcomm. The economics of wireless mobile data. http://www.wirelessdevnet.com/library/WirelessMobileData.pdf.

[26] Wee Lum Tan, Fung Lam, and Wing Cheong Lau. An empirical study on 3G network capacity and performance. In *Proc. IEEE INFOCOM*, pages 1514–1522, 2007.

[27] Peng Yang, Hui Deng, and Yuanchen Ma. Seamless integration of 3G and 802.11 wireless network. In *Proc. MobiWac*, pages 60–65, 2007.

[28] Jun Yao, Salil S. Kanhere, and Mahbub Hassan. An empirical study of bandwidth predictability in mobile computing. In *Proc. ACM WiNTECH*, pages 11–18, 2008.

An Empirical Study of Orphan DNS Servers in the Internet

Andrew J. Kalafut*
School of Computing
and Information Systems
Grand Valley State University
Allendale, MI, USA
kalafuta@gvsu.edu

Minaxi Gupta
School of Informatics
and Computing
Indiana University
Bloomington, IN, USA
minaxi@cs.indiana.edu

Christopher A. Cole
School of Informatics
and Computing
Indiana University
Bloomington, IN, USA
coleca@cs.indiana.edu

Lei Chen
School of Informatics
and Computing
Indiana University
Bloomington, IN, USA
lc6@cs.indiana.edu

Nathan E. Myers
School of Informatics
and Computing
Indiana University
Bloomington, IN, USA
natmyers@cs.indiana.edu

ABSTRACT

An *orphan DNS server* is a DNS server which has an address record in the DNS, even though the domain in which it resides has no DNS records itself and hence does not exist. For example, the DNS server `ns.foo.com` would be an orphan DNS server if it had an address record, but the domain `foo.com` did not exist. In this paper, we undertake the first systematic study of the prevalence of orphan DNS servers in the Internet. We also examine who is using them and what they are used for. We find that certain top-level domains (TLDs) account for a disproportionate number of orphans. We also find that some orphans are used for malicious activities and as placeholders for records from deleted domains, while others likely only exist due to simple configuration errors. Our study points to the need for better scrutiny of orphan DNS servers so they cannot be misused.

Categories and Subject Descriptors

C.2.2 [**Computer-Communication Networks**]: Network Protocols—*DNS*; C.2.5 [**Local and Wide-Area Networks**]: Internet

General Terms

Measurement, Security

Keywords

DNS, Top Level Domains

*This research was conducted while Andrew Kalafut was a Ph.D. student at Indiana University, Bloomington, IN, USA

IMC'10, November 1–3, 2010, Melbourne, Australia.

1. INTRODUCTION

The Domain Name System (DNS) [11, 12] is an important component of the Internet's infrastructure. Though it carries out a multitude of functions, its primary task is to translate host names to IP addresses. Internet users rely on the DNS every time they wish to address a host by its name.

The DNS is a hierarchical system, beginning at the root domain. Directly below the root, are the top-level domains (TLDs), such as `.com`. Below each TLD are domains falling within that TLD, such as `example.com`. The DNS servers for each TLD are responsible for storing records used to locate the DNS servers for each domain within that TLD. Clients need these records in order to find the addresses of hosts within those domains. For example, the DNS server for `.com` will store records for the name server[1] for `example.com`. Commonly, these records are of two types, those that contain the host name of the domain's name server (associating `example.com` with `ns1.example.com`), and those that contain its IP address (associating `ns1.example.com` with an address). This paper focuses on a special case of IP addresses records known to the TLD DNS servers: those where an IP address record exists for a DNS server whose parent domain has ceased to exist. An example of such a case is if there were an IP address record for `ns1.example.com` at the `.com` TLD when `example.com` itself was non-existent. Servers such as `ns1.example.com` have come to be referred to as *orphan name servers* in the operational community.

Orphan DNS servers have been found in use by malicious web sites [17]. This paper is motivated by curiosity about the existence of this phenomenon. Accordingly, we focus on studying the prevalence of orphan name servers in the Internet and to understand what, if anything, they are used for. We are also interested in understanding the impact of removing orphan servers. Specifically, if they are only used by malicious domains, it is actually beneficial to remove them. However, if they are used by legitimate domains as well, users of these name servers would see their DNS service degraded or interrupted if such servers were removed. To the

[1]The terms *DNS server* and *name server* are used interchangeably.

best of our knowledge, ours is the first work to investigate this phenomenon systematically. The questions we ask are:

- How prevalent are orphan DNS servers?
- How long do orphan name servers live?
- Are orphan name servers being used for purposes other than as DNS servers?
- Are orphan name servers commonly used for malicious purposes?

We examine an average of 106 million domains (60% of domains in the Internet at the time of our measurements) on a daily basis for a period of 31 days to investigate aspects of orphan DNS servers. Searching for orphans in these domains, we find that 1.7% of DNS servers we examine are orphans. Almost 1/3rd of these are being used as DNS servers by domains we can identify. Many others are used as web and email servers. We confirm that each of the 1% of domains using orphans as their DNS servers are web sites listed in phishing and malware blacklists, and a significant portion of IP addresses associated with orphans, 4.4%, are known to send spam. Benign uses of orphans include being used as placeholders for records from deleted domains. Due to a mix of uses, we conclude that orphans could not simply be removed but need to be monitored closely.

2. BACKGROUND

Here, we discuss the DNS records important to understanding orphan name servers. We also present a scenario which may lead to the creation of an orphan name server. Finally, we discuss related work.

2.1 DNS Background

The DNS server at each TLD maintains a *zone file* containing two types of records relevant for studying orphan name servers. These are the `NS` (name server) and `A` (address) records for each domain falling within that TLD. The `NS` records map a domain to the names of its DNS servers and `A` records provide IP addresses of those DNS servers. Figure 1 shows a sample portion of a zone file for `.com` TLD. Here, two name servers each for domains `fake.com` and `example.com` are listed in the `NS` records. However, names do not suffice. Clients need the corresponding IP addresses to contact name servers. Since the authoritative source for this IP address is the server itself, `A` records corresponding to the `NS` records are also needed in the zone file. These records are referred to as *glue* records. Notice, however, that the `A` records for `ns1.fake.us` and `ns2.fake.us` are not listed in Figure 1 because they may be obtained from the name servers for the `fake.us` domain, or possibly the name servers for `.us`.

2.2 Orphan Creation

We describe how orphans are created through a scenario. A domain, `orphan.com`, is created, leading to the addition of an `NS` record for this domain to the zone file: `orphan.com NS ns1.orphan.com`. The host `ns1.orphan.com` is in `orphan.com`, so its address record, `ns1.orphan.com A 1.2.4.4`, is also added to the zone file. Other domains may also use this server, resulting in the addition of `NS` records for them as well. If `bad.com` uses this server, then `bad.com NS ns1.orphan.com` will be added.

fake.com	NS	ns1.fake.us
fake.com	NS	ns2.fake.us
example.com	NS	ns1.example.com
example.com	NS	ns2.example.com
ns1.example.com	A	1.2.3.4
ns2.example.com	A	1.2.3.5

Figure 1: Sample portion of a TLD zone file

fake.com	NS	ns1.fake.us
fake.com	NS	ns2.fake.us
example.com	NS	ns1.example.com
example.com	NS	ns2.example.com
bad.com	NS	ns1.orphan.com
ns1.example.com	A	1.2.3.4
ns2.example.com	A	1.2.3.5
ns1.orphan.com	A	1.2.4.4

Figure 2: Sample portion of a TLD zone file containing an orphan name server record

Now imagine that some time later `orphan.com` is removed. In this case, the above mentioned `NS` record for the domain is deleted from the zone. However, what happens of the `A` record? One option is to delete it. Another option is to let this record live on, to account for cases when other domains in `.com` or other TLDs depend on it, for example, the above mentioned `bad.com`. Deleting the `ns1.orphan.com A` record would harm `bad.com`, perhaps taking it completely offline if this is its only DNS server. Keeping this `A` record prevents the deletion of this single domain from affecting others which may rely on the same server. This is an example of a common situation that leads to the creation of orphan DNS servers. The sample zone file from Figure 1 after these additions and deletions is shown in Figure 2.

The above scenario is of course not the only way an orphan server may appear. Some may arise out of configuration errors, such a simple typo where the name associated with an `A` record is not what it should have been and so this incorrect name does not match any existing domain. Others may occur due to lax registrar policies. While glue records are the only reason an `A` record *should* exist in a `TLD` zone, mechanisms may not be in place to actually enforce this. Lack of enforcement of such policy would allow such records to intentionally be added directly to the `TLD` zones.

2.3 Related Work

To our knowledge, there has been only a single other work that has looked into the problem of orphan name servers. This resulted in a recent presentation at an ICANN meeting [17], and was based on data collected by Karmasphere [8] and Internet Identity [7]. Their work begins with lists of malicious domains and checks if any name servers used by them are orphans. They find 3.4% of phishing domains and 59% of fast flux [10] domains use orphans. However, because they start with malicious domains, they are not able to identify orphans used for benign purposes. We believe that in deciding how best to solve the problem of orphan DNS servers, it is necessary to determine if they have legitimate uses. Therefore, we take a different approach, starting with TLD zone files instead of just with malicious domains, in order to find the general prevalence of orphans.

3. DATA AND METHODOLOGY

In this Section, we describe our methodology for locating orphan name servers and for finding who is using them.

3.1 Finding Orphan DNS Servers

We use three different techniques for discovering orphan name servers in order to be exhaustive where we have the necessary data, and still find some orphans where we have less data available. These techniques are direct analysis of zone files, DNS queries based on zone file information, and DNS queries based on malicious feeds.

3.1.1 Analysis of Zone Files

Analysis of the zone file for a top level domain (TLD) is the ideal way to find all orphans in that TLD. We have the TLD zones for 6 TLDs: `.asia`, `.com`, `.info`, `.mobi`, `.net`, and `.org` [1,3,14,18,25]. These TLDs accounted for 60% of the 177 million domains on the Internet at the time of our experiments [24]. We obtain these zones though file transfers from the organizations that administer them, so they should be up to date.

To find an orphan in a zone file, we use a simple algorithm. We first examine the entire list of `A` records in the zone file. For each host name listed in an `A` record, we extract the domain name. Since all of the TLDs considered here delegate zones to customers at the second level, directly under the TLD, the domain name in this context is always the TLD plus a single label. We then check if an `NS` record exists for the domain in order to verify if the domain itself exists. If such a record does not exist, then we classify the name from the `A` record as an orphan name server. Returning to Figure 2, when we come across the `A` record `ns1.orphan.com A 1.2.4.4`, we then search the NS records in the zone file for any `NS` records for the domain `orphan.com`. Since no such records exist, we classify `ns1.orphan.com` as an orphan.

To locate which domains are using the orphan name server, we search the zone files for `NS` records that point to orphans. In the case of Figure 2, we would find `bad.com`.

3.1.2 DNS Queries from Zone Files

While our TLD data contains the largest TLDs, a notable deficiency is that it does not contain any country code ccTLDs because operators of these TLDs are not willing to share them even for research purposes. Finding orphan name servers exhaustively for these TLDs is not possible. However, we can still find potential orphans through the zone files available to us.

Instead of looking at the `A` records, as we did earlier, we now look at the name servers pointed to by the `NS` records. If the name pointed to is in one of the TLDs we have a zone file for, we ignore it because if it were an orphan, it would have been identified though the previous method. If it is not, as is `ns1.fake.us` in Figure 2, we perform two DNS queries. We first extract the domain name from the name server's host name (in this case `fake.us`). For this purpose, we use the Public Suffix List [13], taking any suffix on the list, plus one additional label, as the domain name. We then and perform an `NS` query on this domain name. This query checks if the domain name that the server's host name is contained in exists. Orphans can only be present if the domain name does not exist. If this query fails, we perform an `A` query on the name server's host name (`ns1.fake.us`). If this query succeeds, the host name is an orphan. Otherwise, it is just a misconfiguration of a `NS` record pointing to a server that does not exist.

This method directly finds users of the orphans as well since the domain on the `NS` record used to find the orphan is a user of that orphan.

3.1.3 DNS Queries from Malicious Feeds

To get a glimpse of the use of orphans in hosting malicious web sites, including domains not seen by the above two methods, we bring in one more data source. We examine five different live feeds of phishing and malware-hosting sites [2,4,9,15,16]. We perform `NS` queries to identify their name servers, and then we perform DNS queries to check if these servers are orphans exactly the way we did in Section 3.1.2.

3.1.4 Data Collection Limitations

The above mechanisms allow us to find all orphan name servers contained in or used by domains in the DNS zones we can access. It also allows us to find ones used by domains in our malicious feeds. However, it is still not a complete picture of all orphans. Some orphans likely exist in zones we do not have access to. Some more may be used by domains not present in our feeds or zone files. The effect of this limitation is that we underestimate the prevalence of orphan name servers. Similarly, while all of these mechanisms automatically locate users of orphans, they will not identify any users not contained in the zone files or malicious feeds we have access to. This leads to an underestimation of the users of orphans as well.

3.2 Data Overview

We receive new zone files for each zone on a daily basis, and new malicious feeds every hour. We repeat the process described above each day on the new data. For this analysis we use 31 days of zone files and 14 days of the malicious feeds. Table 1 provides an overview of the data used to locate orphans.

Start date of zone files	2009-04-01
Days of zone files used	31 Days
Domains represented in zone files	106 million
`A` records in zone files	2.2 million
`NS` records in zone files	249 million
Out of zone name servers looked up	241,179
Start date of malicious feeds	2009-04-16
Days of malicious feeds used	14 Days
Hosts in malicious feeds	242,752
Domains in malicious feeds	9,554
Name servers for domains in malicious feeds	48,042

Table 1: Overview of data used for orphan detection. Numbers presented are daily averages

We see that as expected, there are over double the number of `NS` records than there are domains, since most domains use multiple name servers. Also as expected, there are far fewer `A` records than domains, since many domains share name servers. A majority of the name server IP addresses were contained in the zone files themselves. Only about

10% of them were out of the TLD zones and required a DNS look-up. The malicious feeds provided fewer servers to look up than the zone files, but are useful for providing more diversity in the potential orphan users.

4. CHARACTERISTICS OF ORPHANS

We now examine the prevalence, distribution, and lifetimes of the orphans name servers we found.

4.1 Prevalence of Orphan DNS Servers

We begin by examining the prevalence of the orphans. Overall, we find a total of 46,369 orphans. Each day, we record an average of 15,962 orphans. Many are present in our data for several days. 39,443 (85%) of orphans are in the TLDs we have zone files for, representing 1.7% of the `A` records in our TLDs, a small but significant percentage. For these, we know that they are all the orphans in these TLDs.

4.2 Distribution of Orphan DNS Servers

Now, to determine if certain entities on the Internet are responsible for disproportionate numbers of orphan name servers, we examine the distribution of orphans in terms of the domains, TLDs and autonomous systems (ASes) they belong to, as well as their IP addresses.

4.2.1 Distribution in Domains and TLDs

Although we saw 46,369 orphan name servers, they are likely not independent of each other. We can quantify relationship among them by looking at the number of zones that contained orphans. We find orphan servers in 23,153 domains, an average of 2.0 orphan servers per domain that contains them.

Since TLD policies may affect the presence of orphan servers, we examine the number of orphans contained in each TLD for which we have zone files. These results are seen in the top part of Table 2. Somewhat surprisingly, we see that *`.info` has a much higher percentage of its `A` records as orphans than any other TLD.* 26,111 (18.8%) of its 139,126 `A` records were orphans. In fact, `.info` contains four times as many orphans as the much larger `.com` which has an order of magnitude more `A` records. `.org`, also much smaller than `.com`, has more orphans than it as well. Notably, the two zones run by Verisign, `.com` and `.net`, have by far the least percentage of their `A` records as orphans as compared to the other TLDs. This indicates that perhaps Verisign makes policy decisions that discourage orphans.

We also checked the TLD distribution of domains containing orphans, to determine whether these high numbers were caused in part by many orphans in a few domains. The TLD distribution of these domains was similar to the distribution of the orphans themselves, including the same ordering of TLDs accounting for the most domains containing orphan name servers.

Owing to lack of zone files, we can not determine what percent of `A` records in other TLDs are orphans. We can also not determine the true number of orphans in other TLDs. However, even with the information we have, a few other TLDs stand out. Notably, 11 TLDs each have over 1,000 orphans, shown in the bottom part of Table 2, the most being 3,931 in `.us`. Since our methodology under-counts the number of orphans in these TLDs, the actual numbers are likely to be higher. In total, we find 123 TLDs containing orphans, although many of these contain only a few.

TLD	# orphans	A records	%
.info	26,111	139,126	18.8%
.mobi	433	4,062	10.7%
.asia	99	1,313	7.5%
.org	7,715	206,513	3.7%
.com	6,428	1,566,392	0.4%
.net	530	3,31896	0.2%
.us	3,931	n/a	n/a
.cm	2,771	n/a	n/a
.cn	2,715	n/a	n/a
.br	2,495	n/a	n/a
.de	2,413	n/a	n/a
.ws	2,344	n/a	n/a
.kr	2,118	n/a	n/a
.ru	1,801	n/a	n/a
.ca	1,368	n/a	n/a
.in	1,340	n/a	n/a
.jp	1,182	n/a	n/a

Table 2: Orphan name servers by TLD, as compared to the total `A` records in each TLD zone

4.2.2 IP Address Distribution

As with orphans in the same domain, orphans pointing to the same IP address are also related since these are using the same physical machine. Collectively, we find 14,411 IP addresses in use by orphans, an average of 3.2 orphan names pointing to the same physical machine.

To determine if certain network operators are responsible for disproportionate numbers of orphans, we translate these IP addresses into the corresponding AS numbers using the service offered by Team Cymru [23]. We find that 14,291 of these IP addresses belong to 1,960 ASes, an average of 7.3 IP addresses of orphans per AS that has them. This implies that about 6% of the approximately 30K ASes that originate routes on the Internet contain orphans. The remaining 120 are IP addresses with no corresponding AS, such as private IP addresses. These are in a sense doubly misconfigured, since they are orphans and point to addresses which are not publicly accessible.

Most ASes with orphans only have a few, with 89% having 10 or less, and 43% having just one. In these cases, it is likely that the operators of the AS themselves are not responsible for the presence of these orphans, at least not intentionally. Instead, these are either the result of mistakes, or set up intentionally by some other party. However, we also see four ASes each containing over 100 IP addresses of orphans. In these few cases with many orphans pointing to the same AS, the operators may be responsible for the behavior, but there may be another explanation. These four top ASes belong to commercial web-hosting companies; it is possible that this behavior is instead due to their customers creating such records pointing to the hosted address. However, if this were the case we would expect to see the same behavior in many more ASes.

4.3 Lifetimes of Orphan DNS Servers

Next, we examine the lifetimes of the orphan name servers in our data. Each day we check if orphans name servers recorded on the previous day are still present to examine how long each orphan persists. The results are shown in Figure 3.

We expected orphans to live for long periods of time, ow-

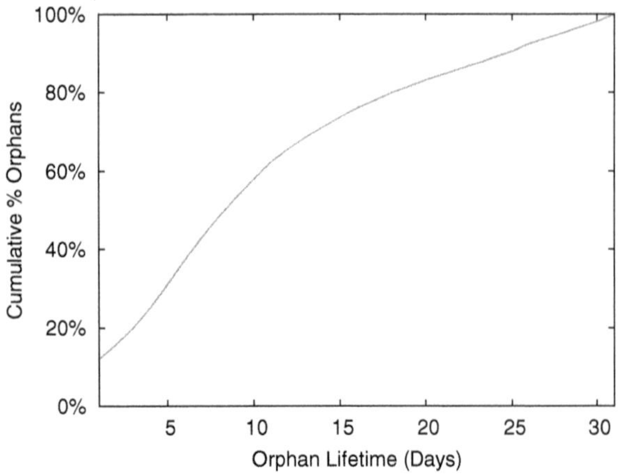

Figure 3: Orphan Lifetimes (CDF)

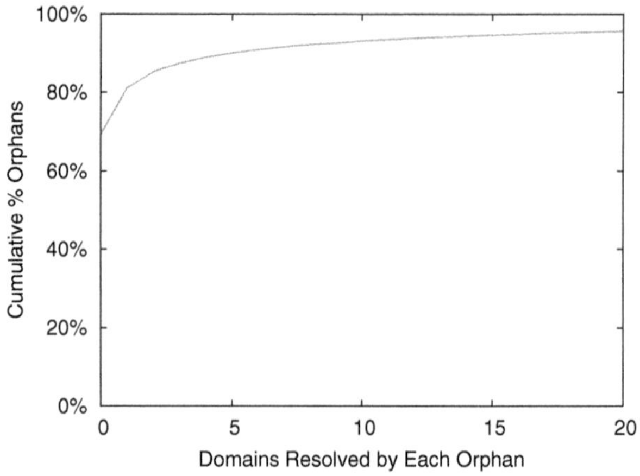

Figure 4: Number of domains using each orphan name server (CDF)

ing to the negligence in noticing them. In reality, many are shorter-lived. Specifically, 12% of them only live for a single day. These orphans may have been created unintentionally and then removed once somebody noticed the error. Less than 2% lasted for our entire 31-day data window. The median lifetime for an orphan is between 8 and 9 days, suggesting that many orphan name servers might exist for tasks that are completed in a short amount of time, such as hosting malicious web sites which are known to live only for a few days [10].

5. USES OF ORPHANS

In this section, we examine how orphan name servers are being used. We approach this question in a few ways. First, we examine their use in the most expected way, as a DNS server. Next, we examine the services running on each orphan. We also examine domains with a large number of orphans to learn how they are using orphans. Finally, we look specifically for malicious uses.

5.1 Use as DNS Servers

We now examine how many domains are actually using orphans as their DNS servers. In total, we see 212,850 domains using orphans as DNS servers, an average of 4.6 per orphan. Figure 4 shows that *almost 1/3rd of the orphans are actually in use as a name server by at least one domain.* We also find a few orphans being used by a large number of domains (not shown in the figure). Specifically, two orphans are each used by 30K domains and two by 15K. The rest of the orphans, 69%, are not being used as DNS servers by any users in our data, and thus appear to be present as a result of an oversight in keeping zone file contents up-to-date. We investigate if they are in use in some other manner in Section 5.2.

5.2 Running Services

Several host names of the orphan name servers begin with `www`. Because `www` is a common label for hosts that run an `http` server, we check if port 80 is open on each orphan. If so, the orphan may be used as a web server. We also check if port 25 is open to see if they may be running an `smtp` server. We find that 33% of the unique IP addresses of orphans have port 80 open, and thus appear to be running an `http` server. Additionally, 22% have port 25 open and appear to be running an `smtp` server, implying that they can potentially be used for sending e-mail.

From orphans with an open port 80, we select 1,000 which we do not see used as a name server, in order to determine if those not used as name servers had some other purpose. From these orphans we request a web page. We find that 42.9% of orphans return nothing despite having an open port. While we can not determine what content they are serving, we can not say they are serving nothing, since they may be using cloaking or ignoring our request since it does not have a standard user agent. 27.9% of the orphans we checked displayed the Apache welcome page. Although they may be serving content on a URL somewhere other than the root of their domain, but there is none at the root of the domain. Although some web sites may be set up in this manner, we have no good way of guessing which path may be used in order to check it.

The remaining 29.2% of orphans in our sample had content at the root of their domain. We classify the type of content on these orphans by performing keyword searches on the returned pages and manual inspection. We find that they primarily served advertisements or contained blogs or scam sites. The latter included the well known "Canadian Pharmacy" scam [19] shown in figure 5. The Canadian Pharmacy scam is one instance of a popular type of scam which claims to sell pharmaceuticals online but may be unlicensed, may not ever deliver the ordered products, or may fill orders incorrectly [5]. Such scams were on 1.4% of the orphans we checked.

5.3 Domains with the Most Orphans

Some domains contain a high number of orphans. The ten highest all contain more than 50 and the largest has 1,198. Although we can not determine for sure what all of them are doing, we do see one surprising activity.

A distinct behavior is seen among seven of the top ten domains containing the most orphans. The domain names of these tend to contain substrings like "delete" or "old". Such domains appear to contain name server records copied from domains that have or will soon expire. For example, we may see an orphan named `ns1.example.com.deleted.info`.

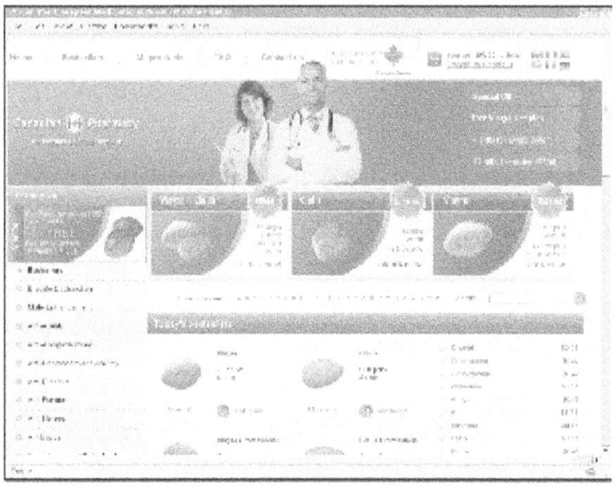

Figure 5: Screenshot of Canadian Pharmacy scam web site

Usually in this case, in addition to `deleted.info` not existing, the other domain implied in the host name, `example.com`, does not exist either. However, if we send this server DNS queries related to `example.com`, it responds as if the domain existed, and as if it was a name server for the domain. Checking IP addresses, if we ask this server for the IP address of `ns1.example.com` we get an address matching that of `ns1.example.com.deleted.info`.

Based on this behavior, we conjecture that registrars move name servers from expired domains to another domain as orphans to minimize disruption to other domains they administer. Other domains that use a server from the expired domain for name resolution can then have their `NS` record changed to point to the new orphan, perhaps automatically by the registrar, minimizing disruption to the service of these domains. This practice may help keep customers happy who own multiple domains using the same infrastructure, ensuring that the rest of their domains will still work after they cancel one. Since these are orphan name servers, they have the same resolution behavior as before the original domain expired. If they were not orphans, then an additional query would be needed to look up the authoritative name server for the domain to which the name server was moved.

5.4 Malicious Uses of Orphans

Given that orphans are being used to host scam sites, as we saw in Section 5.2, and the use of orphans by malicious sites found in [17], the connection between orphans and malicious activities deserves investigation. Orphan servers may be attractive to miscreants for a few reasons. For example, if they are using them for purposes other than DNS servers, having records for them on the TLD DNS server means the miscreants may not even have to run their own DNS server. Orphans related to malicious activity may also naturally arise from enforcement efforts by ISPs removing `NS` records of domains found to be malicious. The DNS server may already have been in use by other domains belonging to the same miscreant, and may continue to be used as such if the `A` record is left.

We look for malicious users of our orphan name servers in multiple sources. We use the Google Safe Browsing phishing and malware blacklists [6], three feeds of malware hosting sites [4, 9, 15], two of phishing sites [2, 16], and a feed of scam sites [22]. Results in this section are based on a longer data window than our general results, 40 days instead of 31.

Table 3 shows how many domains using orphans as their DNS server are involved in malicious activities. There are 212,850 total domains using orphans in our data. Of these users, 2,250 (1.1%), using a total of 86 orphan name servers, are in our phishing feeds. Similarly, 2,838 (1.3%), using a total of 53 orphan name servers are in our malware feeds. Other sources of malicious data also have orphans associated with them, as seen in the table. A small fraction of domains *containing* orphans appear in blacklists as well, the most significant being 76 appearing in the Google malware blacklist. We conclude that although miscreants are using orphans, orphans themselves are not often blacklisted.

Data Source	% of Orphan Users	# Domains
Google malware	0.4%	897
Google phishing	0.0%	4
Phishing Feeds	1.1%	2,250
Malware Feeds	1.3%	2,838
Scam Feed	0.0%	22

Table 3: Domains using orphans appearing in sources of malicious data

We additionally look for the IP addresses of orphans in the Spamhaus SBL blacklist [20] which tracks IP addresses associated with sending spam, and the Spamhaus XBL blacklist [21] which tracks IP addresses with types of exploits commonly used by spammers. 4% of IP addresses of orphans appear in the SBL and 0.4% in the XBL. When we look only at the 500 IP addresses hosting the most orphans, the SBL results are significantly different, 13.4% are blacklisted. We conclude that a significant fraction of orphans send spam.

6. CONCLUSION

Our study identifies three reasons for the existence of orphan name servers. These are typographical errors and misconfiguration in TLD zone files, malicious activity, and as placeholders for deleted domains. We find that a significant number of the orphans are being used to send spam, and a smaller number of orphans are used for other malicious activity including hosting scam sites and serving as the DNS servers for phishing and malware sites. Although these malicious uses are not widespread enough that use of orphans can be taken as an indicator of maliciousness on its own, they can certainly contribute to the determination when combined with other factors.

Many orphan name servers are used in benign roles. Because of this, disallowing them from being created, and removing all currently in existence, may do more harm than good. However, since a large percentage of orphan name servers were not serving any domains from the largest TLDs, we hypothesize that many orphans could be removed without any negative effects.

Finally, the disproportionate prevalence of orphan name servers in some TLDs and ASes indicates that perhaps the benign roles they serve are not necessary, or can be accomplished otherwise. Owing to this, we recommend that orphan DNS servers be better scrutinized to prevent misuse and to ensure that they really are providing a benefit.

7. REFERENCES

[1] Afilias Limited. How can I get access to Afilias' TLD zone file for .INFO domains? http://www.info.info/faq/how-can-i-get-access-afilias-tld-zone-file-info-domains.

[2] APWG. Anti-phishing working group. http://www.antiphishing.org/.

[3] DotAsia Organization Limited. .ASIA Zone File Access Agreement. http://www.dotasia.org/info/DAO.ZONE-2007-10-24.pdf.

[4] eSoft Inc. http://www.esoft.com/.

[5] Federal Trade Commission. Your health online. http://ftc.gov/bcp/edu/pubs/consumer/health/hea12.shtm.

[6] Google Code Labs. Google safe browsing API. http://code.google.com/apis/safebrowsing/.

[7] Internet Identity. http://www.internetidentity.com.

[8] Karmasphere, Inc. http://karmasphere.com/.

[9] Malware Patrol. Malware patrol - malware block list. http://www.malwarepatrol.net/lists.shtml.

[10] D. K. McGrath, A. Kalafut, and M. Gupta. Phishing infrastructure fluxes all the way. *IEEE Security and Privacy Magazine Special Issue on Securing DNS*, September/October 2009.

[11] P. Mockapetris. Domain names - concepts and facilities. IETF RFC 1034, Nov. 1987.

[12] P. Mockapetris. Domain names - implementation and specification. IETF RFC 1035, Nov. 1987.

[13] Mozilla Foundation. Public suffix list. http://publicsuffix.org.

[14] mTLD, Ltd. dotMobi Zone File Access Agreement. http://mtld.mobi/domain/zonefile.

[15] NETpilot GmbH. Viruswatch mailing list. http://lists.clean-mx.com/cgi-bin/mailman/listinfo/viruswatch.

[16] OpenDNS. PhishTank. http://www.phishtank.com/.

[17] D. Piscitello. Orphaned name servers. ICANN 35 Presentation, June 2009.

[18] Public Interest Registry. .ORG Registry - ZOne File Access. http://pir.org/index.php?db=content/Website&tbl=Registrars&id=7.

[19] Spamhaus Project. Register or known spam operations - canadian pharmacy. http://www.spamhaus.org/rokso/evidence.lasso?rokso_id=ROK8138.

[20] Spamhaus Project. SBL. http://www.spamhaus.org/sbl/index.lasso.

[21] Spamhaus Project. XBL. http://www.spamhaus.org/xbl/index.lasso.

[22] Support Intelligence, LLC. http://www.support-intelligence.com/.

[23] Team Cymru, Inc. IP to ASN mapping. http://www.team-cymru.org/Services/ip-to-asn.html.

[24] VeriSign. Domain name industry brief, Feb. 2009. http://www.verisign.com/static/044518.pdf.

[25] VeriSign, Inc. TLD Zone Access Program. http://www.versign.com/information-services/naming-services/page_001052.html.

FlowRoute: Inferring Forwarding Table Updates Using Passive Flow-level Measurements

Amogh Dhamdhere
CAIDA
University of California, San Diego
La Jolla, CA
amogh@caida.org

Lee Breslau, Nick Duffield, Cheng Ee, Alexandre Gerber, Carsten Lund, Subhabrata Sen
AT&T Labs-Research
Florham Park, NJ
{breslau, duffield, ctee, gerber, lund, sen}@research.att.com

ABSTRACT

The reconvergence of routing protocols in response to changes in network topology can impact application performance. While improvements in protocol specification and implementation have significantly reduced reconvergence times, increasingly performance-sensitive applications continue to raise the bar for these protocols. As such, monitoring the performance of routing protocols remains a critical activity for network operators. We design FlowRoute, a tool based on passive data plane measurements that we use in conjunction with control plane monitors for offline debugging and analysis of forwarding table dynamics. We discuss practical constraints that affect FlowRoute, and show how they can be addressed in real deployment scenarios. As an application of FlowRoute, we study forwarding table updates by backbone routers at a tier-1 ISP. We detect interesting behavior such as delayed forwarding table updates and routing loops due to buggy routers – confirmed by network operators – that are not detectable using traditional control plane monitors.

Categories and Subject Descriptors

C.2.3 [**Computer-Communication Networks**]: Network Operations, Network Management

General Terms

Design, Measurement, Performance

Keywords

Measurement, Netflow, Routing Update

1. INTRODUCTION

The behavior of networks during and after routing changes – when packets may be subject to looping, loss, and delay variation – is an important determinant of the performance that end users perceive. Historically, inter-domain routing convergence could take minutes [12], while intra-domain protocols (e.g., OSPF) could take tens of seconds. Subsequent improvements in protocol specification and implementation reduced the reconvergence times of these protocols. However, the recent rise of applications with stringent performance requirements means that routing reconvergence is still a subject of intense interest among service providers.

To study routing behavior, network operators often use specialized control plane monitors [19–21] that peer with and receive routing updates from one or more routers. Control plane monitors can indicate when a router received a routing update, i.e., *when the router should have updated its forwarding table, and what it should have updated to.* They cannot detect, however, *when the router actually implemented the change in its forwarding table, and what change it made.* The actual change may be delayed, or may differ from what is expected due to hardware or protocol implementation bugs in routers. Further, monitoring the control plane at one or a few routers may not indicate how close in time different routers update their forwarding tables. If these times diverge, we could see transient forwarding loops and poor end-to-end performance. One could study forwarding table updates using logs collected directly from routers. In today's networks, however, we cannot instrument routers to dump their forwarding tables after every update. Even if this were feasible, it would require transporting and processing gigabytes of data after every update. SNMP polling would also have to deal with the same data volume, and under current operational practices, would give us a 5-minute resolution for inferring forwarding table changes – too coarse for our needs. One could use active probing (e.g., traceroutes) to monitor forwarding table updates. Active probing faces two drawbacks, however; provisioning monitors to achieve high spatial coverage can be costly, and the temporal resolution is limited by probing rates, which we cannot increase indefinitely without causing excessive overhead.

We describe the design and implementation of FlowRoute, a tool that works *in conjunction with existing control plane monitors* to analyze forwarding table dynamics. FlowRoute can measure forwarding table update times across routers and help operators identify slow forwarding table updates, transient forwarding loops, and large traffic shifts. FlowRoute works offline, using *passive flow-level measurements* (e.g., Cisco's Netflow [4]) that operators routinely collect in today's networks; as such, it does not impose additional overhead on routers. FlowRoute is agnostic to the specific routing protocols in use and can be applied to both intra-domain and inter-domain routing.

As an application of FlowRoute, we study forwarding table updates at backbone routers in a large tier-1 ISP. We find unexpected cases wherein forwarding table updates at a single router are delayed following a routing event. Delayed updates, in turn, cause forwarding loops lasting tens of seconds in some cases. Using FlowRoute, we attributed these effects to specific routers that were often late in updating their forwarding tables. Network operators confirmed that those routers did indeed have protocol implementation bugs causing performance issues.[1] Such unexpected behavior is not detectable using traditional control plane monitors.

We believe that operators can apply FlowRoute to a broad set of other debugging/analysis problems. For example, by measuring forwarding behavior across routers, FlowRoute can help network operators examine the extent to which forwarding table updates are synchronized across routers. FlowRoute can also quantify the network-wide effects of routing changes, such as traffic shifts and changes in link utilization after a routing change.

2. RELATED WORK

The OSPFmon [21] deployment at AT&T, the IP monitoring project at Sprint [10] and commercial products such as Route Explorer [16] provide route monitoring services to ISPs. However, none of these systems can study forwarding table performance at the timescales that FlowRoute is capable of. Feldmann et al. [9] describe an approach to periodically dump router configuration files in order to identify configuration errors. Their approach provides a static view of the routing state at each router. Such an approach would face significant scalability problems if extended to studying routing table dynamics.

In theory, one could use traceroute-like active measurement tools [3] to infer forwarding table changes. Active measurement provides a view of the routing state at routers on a path *at the time the probes are sent.* To achieve a sufficiently high temporal resolution for studying forwarding table updates, we would need a high probing rate and a large number of vantage points. Previous studies have used a combination of active probing, route monitoring and passive measurements to quantify the effects of routing events on end-to-end loss rates [23] and delays [18]. FlowRoute allows us to study forwarding table dynamics, which we can use to investigate the effects of routing events on end-to-end performance.

Operators use flow-level measurements from ISP networks for a variety of applications such as estimating intradomain traffic matrices [13] and flow size distributions [8]. Teixeira et al. [22] use NetFlow and routing data from a large Tier-1 ISP to quantify the effects of routing changes on the intradomain traffic matrix. Agarwal et al. use passive data to measure the effect of BGP route changes on the ingress-egress traffic matrix [1], and to study how traffic to neighboring ASes shifts due to changes in a local AS' IGP link metrics [2]. To the best of our knowledge, no previous work used flow-level data to study forwarding table dynamics.

[1] These routers were subsequently retired from the network.

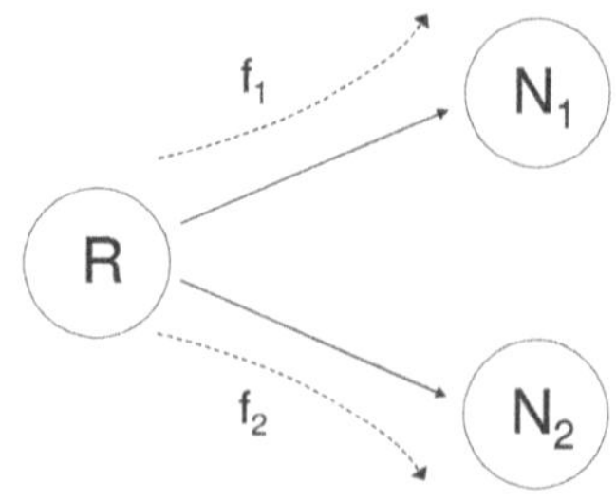

Figure 1: Basic model for routing change detection

3. FLOWROUTE DESIGN

We begin by describing, at a high level, the approach and algorithms embodied in FlowRoute. Figure 1 shows a single packet flow f_1 towards destination D. Suppose that router R forwards this flow towards next hop router N_1 at time t_1. The flow record at N_1 indicates that the previous hop was R, or, equivalently, that N_1 was R's next hop towards D at time t_1. If the next hop changes to N_2 at time $t_2 > t_1$, then a flow f_2 traversing R and destined to D will generate a corresponding flow record at N_2. By using these two flow records, we can infer when R started routing flows towards N_2. We next describe how we process the raw flow records from routers and infer routing changes. Note that FlowRoute processes flow records offline, on infrastructure that operators already use for network management, and does not impose additional overhead on routers.

3.1 Flow Records

We use flow records generated by Netflow [4], which is supported by multiple router vendors. Netflow records summarize flows, i.e., sets of packets which share common header fields (e.g., source and destination IP addresses). To infer routing changes, FlowRoute uses the following information that is present by default in Netflow records: the router R that observed the flow; the incoming and outgoing interfaces i and o at R; the times t_f and t_l of the first and last packets of the flow; and the destination D. We denote this flow record by the tuple (R, i, o, t_f, t_l, D).

While flow records report both incoming and outgoing interfaces, there is an important semantic difference between the two. The incoming interface is part of the flow key which defines a flow. A change in the incoming interface leads to the creation of a new flow record. Consequently, we know that each packet of a flow arrived on the input interface indicated by the flow tuple. In contrast, the outgoing interface o is not part of the flow key. Therefore, a change in the outgoing interface (next hop) while the flow is active will not generate a new flow record. Rather, the timestamp t_f in the flow record indicates the time when the flow record was created. Thus, we can only infer reliably that the reported outgoing interface was used for the first packet of the flow.

3.2 Inferring Routing Changes

We collect Netflow records and process them *offline* to obtain a stream of **Routing Flow Records** (RFRs). Each RFR is of the form (R_1, t_1, t_2, D, R_2), which states that during the interval $[t_1, t_2]$, router R_1 is forwarding packets to destination D via next hop R_2. In Figure 2, we describe how we construct two RFRs from each flow record

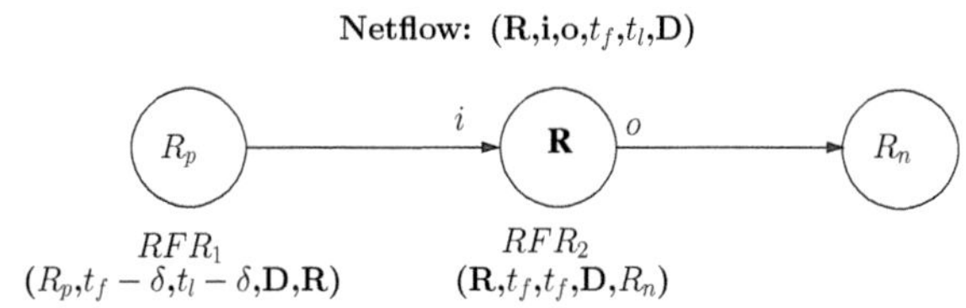

Figure 2: Construction of two Routing Flow Records from a flow record

(R, i, o, t_f, t_l, D) at router R. First, using the incoming interface i, we generate $RFR_1 = (R_p, t_f - \delta, t_l - \delta, D, R)$, which indicates that during the interval $[t_f - \delta, t_l - \delta]$, router R_p used R as the next hop to reach destination D.[2] To obtain timestamps at R_p from the packet observation times t_f and t_l at R, we subtract the propagation delay δ of the link between R_p and R. We ignore queuing delays, as they cannot be estimated using topology and configuration information alone. Moreover, queuing delays are typically negligible at backbone routers [17]. We also ignore clock skew across routers, as routers use NTP [14] for clock synchronization. Next, using the outgoing interface o, we generate $RFR_2 = (R, t_f, t_f, D, R_n)$. Due to the semantic difference between incoming and outgoing interfaces, the two timestamps in RFR_2 are the same.

Consider again the routers R, N_1 and N_2 in Figure 1. Suppose we have RFRs (R, t_1, t_2, D, N_1) and (R, t_3, t_4, D, N_2) with $t_1 < t_4$. The first RFR indicates that R used N_1 as the next hop to D during the interval $[t_1, t_2]$, and the second RFR indicates that R used next hop N_2 during $[t_3, t_4]$. Two scenarios are possible: if $t_3 < t_2$, this may mean that Equal-Cost Multi-Path (ECMP) routing [15] is sending similarly-destined flows over two different downstream links (We address the issue of ECMP in the following section). If, on the other hand, $t_2 < t_3$, then R changed its forwarding path to D at some point in the range $[t_2, t_3]$. Our fundamental unit of route change measurement is thus a **Range** $(R, [t, t'], D)$, indicating that R changed its next hop towards destination D at some point during the interval $[t, t']$.

4. PRACTICAL CONSIDERATIONS

In this section, we discuss some issues that must be addressed before FlowRoute can be deployed in operational networks.

4.1 Destination Granularity

FlowRoute needs to observe consecutive flows to the same destination, D, to be able to infer forwarding changes towards D. While the destination IP address of a flow is an obvious choice, a router may not observe sufficient flow volume towards the same destination to obtain a sufficient temporal resolution for the time window of the routing change. Aggregating at the level of destination prefixes yields more flows to each destination but requires some additional information to map a flow to its associated prefix. A third option is to use the iBGP next hop field [6] in Netflow, in which case routers need to have complete iBGP routing tables.

[2]We can map the incoming and outgoing interfaces in Netflow records to previous and next hop routers, and obtain link propagation delays using slowly changing information available from SNMP and configuration data.

Our motivation in developing FlowRoute was to understand the intra-AS routing dynamics of a large ISP. Such networks are often designed to have a *route free core*, meaning that routes consist of label-switched MPLS paths between ingress and egress routers. For routing within such a network, the address of the MPLS tunnel endpoint is the "destination" of a flow. In this work, we use FlowRoute to study intra-AS routing using MPLS tunnel endpoints as destinations. We emphasize, though, that *our method does not depend on the choice of MPLS tunnel endpoints as destinations.* An operator is free to choose the appropriate granularity of D.

4.2 Routing Change vs ECMP

We have assumed that consecutive RFRs with different next hops towards the same destination indicate a routing change. This may not hold when Equal-Cost Multi-Path (ECMP) [15] is enabled; a router may have two or more equal cost paths to the same destination and alternate between them on a per-flow basis. Consider a router R with two equal cost paths to destination D via next hops R_1 and R_2. Consecutive RFRs of the form (R, t_1, t_2, D, R_1), (R, t_3, t_4, D, R_2), and (R, t_5, t_6, D, R_1) would appear as a change in R's next hop from R_1 to R_2 in the time interval $[t_2, t_3]$, and from R_2 to R_1 in time interval $[t_4, t_5]$. Next-hop changes due to ECMP *do not appear as routing changes to a control plane monitor.* Further, the mapping of a flow tuple to next hop routers can be dynamic, meaning that our offline analysis cannot leverage known properties of the mapping function to detect ECMP. We therefore design a method to distinguish between routing changes and ECMP using the sequence of RFRs.

We find empirically – using data from a day on which a production control plane monitor reported no routing events – that in more than 99% of cases, a router forwards fewer than 20 flows to a certain next hop, before routing a flow to a different equal cost next hop. Using this observation, we devise the following ECMP filtering algorithm. We keep track of the current next hop $n_c(R, D)$ for router R towards destination D, and the number of consecutive flows $f_c(R, D)$ that R has routed towards the current next hop $n_c(R, D)$. Let $n_h(R, D)$ be the next hop for router R towards destination D obtained from the latest RFR. If $n_h(R, D)$ is different from $n_c(R, D)$, and if $f_c(R, D) > t_{ecmp}$, then we count this as a routing change; otherwise we assume it is an instance of ECMP. For the analysis in this paper, we use $t_{ecmp} = 20$.[3]

4.3 Traffic Rates and Sampling

FlowRoute produces a set of ranges, $(R, [t, t'], D)$, specifying the time window in which we infer a routing change to have occurred. The temporal resolution of our inference (the width of these ranges) depends on the frequency with which flows to destination D traverse router R, which itself depends on the popularity of D and the distance (in network hops) of R from D. Routers closer to destination D aggregate traffic from more sources on the sink tree towards D. Packet sampling in NetFlow also affects the temporal granularity of our inference. This effect is compounded by further sampling of flow records within the measurement collection infrastructure [7]. To quantify the effect of sampling, 1Gbps of backbone traffic would generate hundreds of Net-

[3]We would need to estimate t_{ecmp} specifically for the network on which we deploy FlowRoute.

Flow records per second with 1 in 500 packet sampling [11], giving us a temporal resolution of a few milliseconds. 1Mbps of traffic would yield a temporal resolution of a few seconds, still sufficient for many applications. FlowRoute achieves high temporal resolution on routes that have the most traffic, which are exactly the routes that operators care most about monitoring. Also, FlowRoute is not limited to using flow records generated by existing traffic. We can augment existing traffic on low-traffic routes with active packet probes. A router equipped with Flexible NetFlow [5] can instantiate a dedicated packet filter to select all active probe packets based on a predetermined IP address/port signature. The resulting temporal resolution can be as small as the inter-probe time.

Though the temporal resolution of our inferences depends on the flow rate and sampling, we emphasize that these factors *do not affect the correctness of the ranges we infer*. For example, the range $(R, [t, t'], D)$ denotes that we last observed a flow at R towards the old next hop (say N_1) at time t, and first observed a flow at R towards the new next hop (say N_2) at time t'. Due to sampling, we could have missed a flow at R towards N_1 at time $t + \delta_1$, and a flow towards N_2 at time $t' - \delta_2$. A larger flow volume or less sampling would thus lead to narrower ranges. In the absence of short-lived route flaps, the bounds provided by our inferred range $(R, [t, t'], D)$ are correct – R was routing flows to N_1 *at least until* t, and R started routing flows to the new next hop N_2 *no later than* t'.

5. RESULTS

In this section, we use FlowRoute to study how routers update their forwarding tables in response to routing events reported by a control plane monitor. We first describe our datasets and verify the consistency of the route change information obtained across routers.

5.1 Approach and Data

Our study uses two types of data collected from a Tier-1 ISP network during July and August 2008. Our first dataset consists of routing events reported by OSPFMon[16] in the form of Link State Advertisements (LSAs) that indicate changes in link status (up/down) or link weights which could result in routing changes. OSPF events lend themselves to *clustering*, since events such as the cost-in or cost-out of links often result in multiple subsequent events relating to changes in path metrics. For each OSPF event cluster, a range $[t_s, t_e]$ indicates the start and end time of the cluster. We use a clustering threshold of 50 seconds, after which two events are assigned to separate clusters. Our second dataset consists of packet sampled Netflow records (which were also subject to flow-level sampling [7]) collected from several hundred backbone routers during the same two month period. We use FlowRoute to measure the times when routers updated their next hops in response to measured OSPF events (after filtering out occurrences of ECMP).

5.2 Validation of Inter-Router Consistency

Recall from Section 3 that each Netflow record generated at a router R creates two RFRs: one describing the routing state at R (towards its next hop) and one describing the routing state at the previous hop (towards R). We may observe consecutive RFRs at router R, or two RFRs at different routers downstream of R, indicating that R changed its next hop.[4] We validate the consistency of routing changes inferred from the two vantage points, providing assurance that our methodology is sound, and that NTP time synchronization across routers is sufficient for FlowRoute's purpose.

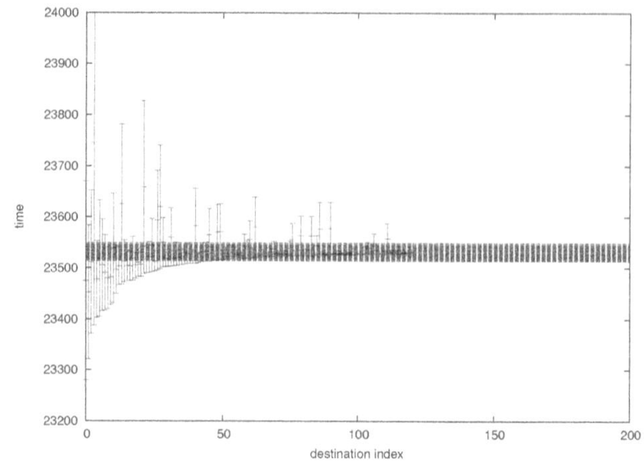

Figure 3: Router A: Updates of next hop to all destinations are consistent with OSPF events.

We separate the stream of RFRs into those obtained using input interfaces (I stream) and output interfaces (O stream). We apply the method of Section 3 to infer routing changes separately from the I and O streams. We compare cases where we infer a routing change for the same R, D pair using both I and O streams. For example, for a R, D pair, we infer the time windows $[t_1^i, t_2^i]$ and $[t_1^o, t_2^o]$ using the I stream and O stream, respectively. Using data from August 1, 2008, we find 2024 R, D pairs for which we inferred a routing change in both the I and O streams; *For each of these R, D pairs, the time windows are overlapping.* Thus, the I and O streams – which come from two independent sources – give consistent information about routing changes.

5.3 Delayed Forwarding Table Updates

We use FlowRoute to measure the times at which routers update forwarding tables in response to routing changes. Figure 3 shows the set of update ranges for a router A near the time of an OSPF event cluster on July 9, 2008. The OSPF event times are indicated by the horizontal band between 23,514 and 23,549 on the y-axis (denoting seconds since the start of the day.) The x-axis is the index of a destination D, and each vertical bar illustrates a range $(A, [t_1, t_2], D)$. The lower end of the bar (t_1) is the last time that we saw a flow routed towards to the old next hop, and the upper end of the bar (t_2) is the time we first saw a flow routed to the new next hop. We sort the destination indices in increasing order of t_1. For router A, the range for each destination overlaps the OSPF events; in this sense the FlowRoute view is consistent with the OPSFMon view. For some destinations, we obtain ranges that are narrower than one second, giving a fairly fine temporal resolution with which we can detect routing changes for those destinations.

Figure 4 shows the case of router B for an OSPF event

[4]While we may observe a routing change at both vantage points, often we only see it at one or the other location due to sampling.

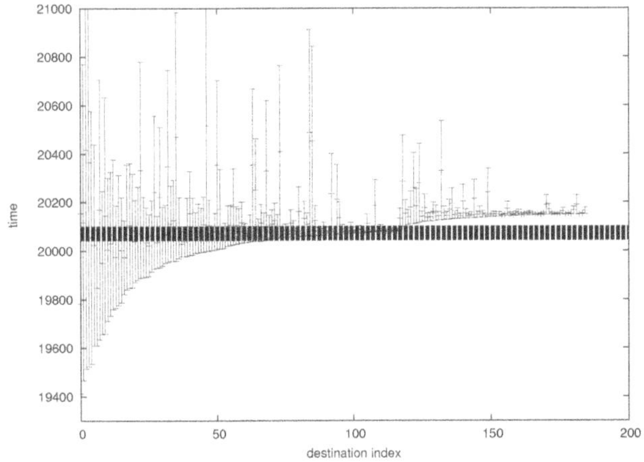

Figure 4: Router B: Updates of next hop to some destinations occur after last OSPF event.

cluster on July 4, 2008. The time range in which router B updated its route to some destinations (indices less than 100) overlaps the OSPF events; updates to these destinations could be consistent with the OSPF event cluster. For destinations with indices larger than 100, the *lower end of the range is up to 50 seconds after the last OSPF event.* The correctness of this observation is not affected by flow rates and sampling – the lower end of these ranges is *a lower bound* on when the router updated its forwarding table (see discussion in Section 4.3). We make two observations here. First, it appears that forwarding table updates for router B are spread out over time. Second, for destination indices greater than 100, router B was forwarding flows to the old next hop *at least until the lower end of the range* – more than 50 seconds after the OSPF event. This finding is significant because distributed routing protocols expect forwarding table updates to occur at about the same time across routers to ensure stability. Even a single router updating its forwarding table over an extended period (10s of seconds) could impact network-wide convergence. In Section 5.4, we describe cases where delayed forwarding table updates caused forwarding loops.

We measured the frequency of delayed forwarding table updates in the two month dataset from July and August 2008. Let $[t_1, t_2]$ be the window in which router R changed its next hop towards destination D in response to an OSPF event cluster from $[t_s, t_e]$. We say that a router R shows delayed forwarding table updates if $t_1 > t_e$ for at least N destinations. We use N=3 to avoid spurious conclusions due to a failure of our ECMP detection algorithm.[5] Across 2666 OSPF event clusters in the dataset, we found 97010 time ranges (one per R, D pair) that were consistent with the event cluster (i.e., like router A). We found 58 event clusters containing 117 time ranges where at least one router showed delayed forwarding table updates. Most routers showed this behavior only once over the two months; two routers, however, did so 14 times. We observed that most routers that showed delayed updates were of the same make/model. Discussions with network operators confirmed that those routers did indeed have protocol implementation bugs causing performance issues. The buggy routers have since been retired from the network.

[5]Different values of N yield qualitatively similar results.

5.4 Routing Loops

The delayed forwarding table updates described in the previous section can cause transient routing loops. We show how FlowRoute can detect such loops in practice. We use RFRs to identify routing loops using the following algorithm. Recall that an RFR (R_1, t_1, t_2, D, R_2) indicates that the next hop for router R_1 towards destination D was R_2 in the time interval $[t_1, t_2]$. To find routing loops, we search for RFRs of the form (R_1, t_1, t_2, D, R_2) and (R_2, t_3, t_4, D, R_1), where *the time windows* $[t_1, t_2]$ *and* $[t_3, t_4]$ *overlap.* This pair of RFRs indicates that a loop between adjacent routers R_1 and R_2 affected destination D during the intersection of time windows $[t_1, t_2]$ and $[t_3, t_4]$.[6] To study the duration of each such loop, we measure the number of consecutive seconds in which we saw overlapping RFRs for a pair of routers towards the same destination. We found 392 occurrences of one-hop loops during our two-month dataset. We found that more than 90% of these loops were short-lived, seen only in one or two consecutive seconds. We also found long-lived loops that lasted for 10s of seconds; the longest was seen in 67 consecutive seconds.

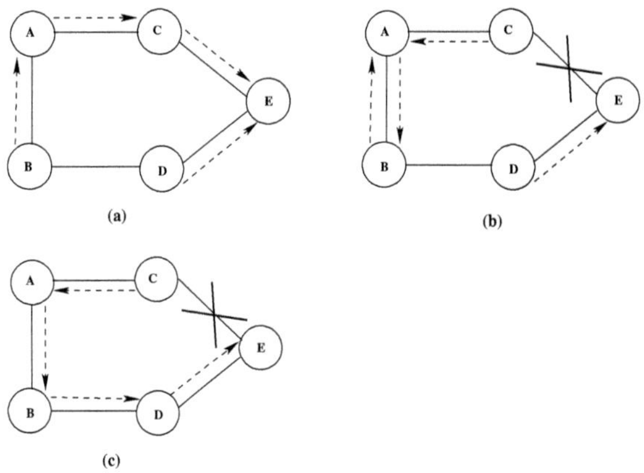

Figure 5: (a) Initial topology (b) A updates its next hop and forwards to B, but B is late to update, and continues to forward to A, resulting in a loop. (c) B updates its next hop and starts forwarding to D.

We next examine the relationship between the late forwarding table update phenomenon and transient routing loops. We found that of the 58 OSPF event clusters in which we observed late forwarding table updates, 33 were accompanied by transient one hop loops. Figure 5(a) shows the initial network topology for one such event. Figure 6 shows the route changes at routers A and B as they react to the OSPF event cluster which runs from approximately time 33280 to 33345 (seconds since the start of that day). This OSPF event cluster includes a cost-out event for link C-E, i.e., the link metric is increased such that it will not be part of any computed shortest path. The top graph in figure 6 shows that the forwarding table changes for router

[6]Our analysis focused on loops between adjacent routers; it can be easily extended to loops involving three or more routers.

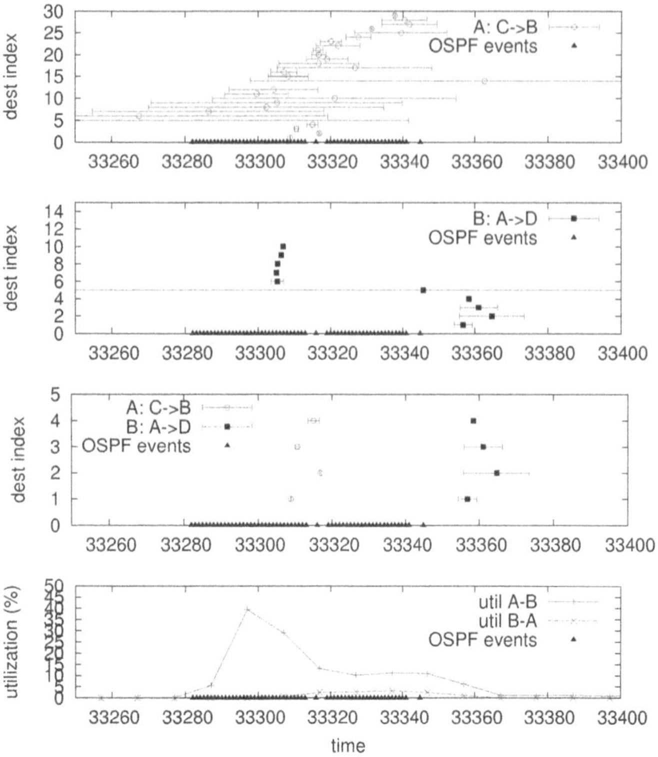

Figure 6: Updates by router A are consistent with OSPF events (top graph). Late updates by router B towards certain destinations (second graph). Update ranges for routers A and B for the same set of destinations (third graph). Spikes in the utilization of links A-B and B-A (bottom graph).

A are consistent with OSPF events (A changes its next hop from C to B). The second graph in Figure 6 shows that the forwarding table changes for router B towards certain destinations occur several seconds later (B changes its next hop from A to D). The third graph in Figure 6 shows the transition ranges for routers A and B towards the set of destinations for which B updated late. From time around 33320 to 33360, A is forwarding packets towards B (because it has already changed its next hop), and B is forwarding packets to A (because it has not yet changed its next hop). Figure 5(b) shows the situation from time around 33320 to 33360. Router A has updated its forwarding table to use B as its next hop. Router C has also updated its forwarding table to use A as its next hop. However, router B has not updated its forwarding table, causing a forwarding loop between A and B. Figure 5(c) shows the situation after time 33360, when router B has updated its forwarding table to use router D as its next hop; routing has stabilized.

The bottom graph in Figure 6 shows the utilization on links A-B and B-A, averaged over 10 second intervals during this event. Link utilization increases in both directions during the routing loop. Though route changes at other routers could impact utilization on these links (which could explain why the utilization in the direction A-B is higher than in the direction B-A), the fact that the spikes persist only during the loop suggest that they are primarily due to the routing loop.

6. DISCUSSION

We presented FlowRoute, a tool that uses passive flow-level measurements and works in conjunction with existing control plane monitors to study forwarding table dynamics. FlowRoute identified cases of delayed forwarding table updates and routing loops in a large tier-1 ISP network. These results are significant, as such anomalies are undetectable using control plane monitors alone. Before concluding, we mention ways in which the benefit of FlowRoute could be improved in the future.

6.1 Network-wide effects of routing changes

As FlowRoute uses data collected from hundreds of routers in the ISP's network, operators can use it to quantify the *network-wide* effects of routing changes. For example, we have used FlowRoute to measure how many routers in the network were "affected" by a routing change (in the sense that traffic traversing those routers was re-routed). Further, we have used FlowRoute to measure traffic shifts and changes in link utilization caused by routing events – at a finer time resolution than is possible with SNMP-based approaches. Due to space constraints, we could not present the results of measuring network-wide effects of routing changes.

6.2 Flexible Netflow

We expect that Flexible Netflow [5] will eventually make its way into production networks. Flexible Netflow allows operators to configure the fields that are part of the flow key. In particular, we could have the flow key consist of the input interface, output interface, and destination, where the destination refers to the iBGP next hop (see Section 4.1). Using this feature, the router can directly export a Routing Flow Record as defined in Section 3. These records, which would be generated directly by the router and which would include first and last packet timestamps, would allow us to get more detailed timing information about routing changes. Flexible Netflow can also help to overcome some of the problems of packet and flow sampling, which affect FlowRoute's temporal resolution. As mentioned in Section 4.3, we can augment existing traffic with additional active probes, and Flexible NetFlow can be configured to select all probe packets based on a pre-defined signature. We can then set the active probing rate to achieve a desired temporal resolution.

6.3 Online FlowRoute

FlowRoute, as described in this paper, uses an offline approach. The method relies on collecting Netflow records from different routers and creating Routing Flow Records using topology data collected by SNMP. Currently, FlowRoute requires on the order of a few hours to process a day's worth of Netflow data from several hundred routers. There is no reason *a priori* that this paradigm could not be extended to work in near real-time. Such a system would run a collector that aggregates and processes flow-level measurements from multiple routers and provides alerts about routing events. Tackling the systems and scalability issues involved in making FlowRoute near-online is a direction we plan to pursue in future work.

7. REFERENCES

[1] S. Agarwal, C.-N. Chuah, S. Bhattacharyya, and C. Diot. The Impact of BGP Dynamics on Intra-domain Traffic. *SIGMETRICS Performance Evaluation Review*, 32(1):319–330, 2004.

[2] S. Agarwal, A. Nucci, and S. Bhattacharyya. Measuring the Shared Fate of IGP Engineering and Interdomain Traffic. In *Proc. of the 13TH IEEE International Conference on Network Protocols (ICNP)*, pages 236–245, Sept. 2005.

[3] B. Augustin, X. Cuvellier, B. Orgogozo, F. Viger, T. Friedman, M. Latapy, C. Magnien, and R. Teixeira. Avoiding Traceroute Anomalies with Paris Traceroute. In *Proc. ACM SIGCOMM Internet Measurement Conference (IMC)*, Oct. 2006.

[4] Cisco. Cisco IOS Netflow. `http://www.cisco.com/en/US/products/ps6601/products_ios_protocol_group_home.html`.

[5] Cisco. IOS Flexible NetFlow Technology. `http://www.cisco.com/en/US/prod/collateral/iosswrel/ps6537/ps6555/ps6601/ps6965/prod_white_paper0900aecd804be1cc.html`.

[6] Cisco. NetFlow BGP Next Hop Support. `http://www.cisco.com/en/US/docs/ios/12_3/feature/guide/nfbgpnxt.html`.

[7] N. Duffield and C. Lund. Predicting Resource Usage and Estimation Accuracy in an IP Flow Measurement Collection Infrastructure. In *Proc. Internet Measurement Conference (IMC)*, Oct. 2003.

[8] N. Duffield, C. Lund, and M. Thorup. Estimating Flow Distributions from Sampled Flow Statistics. *IEEE/ACM Transactions on Networking*, 13(5):933–946, 2005.

[9] A. Feldmann and J. Rexford. IP Network Configuration for Intradomain Traffic Engineering. *IEEE Network Magazine*, 15:46–57, 2001.

[10] C. Fraleigh, C. Diot, B. Lyles, S. Moon, P. Owezarski, K. Papagiannaki, and F. Tobagi. Design and Deployment of a Passive Monitoring Infrastructure. In *Passive and Active Measurement (PAM) Workshop*, Amsterdam, Apr. 2001.

[11] Y. Gu, L. Breslau, N. Duffield, and S. Sen. On Passive One-Way Loss Measurements Using Sampled Flow Statistics. In *Proc. IEEE Infocom mini-conference*, Jul. 2009.

[12] C. Labovitz, A. Ahuja, A. Bose, and F. Jahanian. Delayed Internet Routing Convergence. *IEEE/ACM Transactions on Networking*, 9(3):293–306, 2001.

[13] A. Medina, N. Taft, K. Salamatian, S. Bhattacharyya, and C. Diot. Traffic Matrix Estimation: Existing Techniques and New Directions. *SIGCOMM Computer Communications Review*, 32(4):161–174, 2002.

[14] D. Mills. Network Time Protocol (Version 3) Specification, Implementation and Analysis. RFC 1305, 1992.

[15] J. Moy. OSPF Version 2. RFC 2328, April 1998.

[16] Packet Design. Route Explorer. `http://www.packetdesign.com/products/rex.htm`.

[17] K. Papagiannaki, S. Moon, C. Fraleigh, P.Thiran, and C. Diot. Measurement and Analysis of Single-Hop Delay on an IP Backbone Network. In *In IEEE Journal on Selected Areas in Communications, Special Issue on Internet and WWW Measurement, Mapping, and Modeling*, volume 21, 2003.

[18] H. Pucha, Y. Zhang, , Z. M. Mao, and Y. C. Hu. Understanding Network Delay Changes Caused by Routing Events. *SIGMETRICS Performance Evaluation Review*, 35(1):73–84, 2007.

[19] RIPE. RIPE Network Coordination Centre. `http://www.ripe.net`.

[20] Routeviews. University of Oregon Route Views Project. `http://www.routeviews.org`.

[21] A. Shaikh and A. Greenberg. OSPF Monitoring: Architecture, Design and Deployment Experience. In *Proc. USENIX Symposium on Networked Systems Design and Implementation (NSDI)*, Mar. 2004.

[22] R. Teixeira, N. Duffield, J. Rexford, and M. Roughan. Traffic Matrix Reloaded: Impact of Routing Changes. In *in Proc. Passive and Active Measurement (PAM) Workshop*, Mar. 2005.

[23] F. Wang, Z. M. Mao, J. Wang, L. Gao, and R. Bush. A Measurement Study on the Impact of Routing Events on End-to-end Internet Path Performance. *SIGCOMM Computer Communications Review (CCR)*, 36(4):375–386, 2006.

Digging into HTTPS: Flow-Based Classification of Webmail Traffic

Dominik Schatzmann
ETH Zurich
schatzmann@tik.ee.ethz.ch

Wolfgang Mühlbauer
ETH Zurich
muehlbauer@tik.ee.ethz.ch

Thrasyvoulos Spyropoulos
ETH Zurich
spyropoulos@tik.ee.ethz.ch

Xenofontas Dimitropoulos
ETH Zurich
fontas@tik.ee.ethz.ch

ABSTRACT

Recently, webmail interfaces, e.g., Horde, Outlook Web Access, and webmail platforms such as GMail, Yahoo!, and Hotmail have seen a tremendous boost in popularity. Given the importance of e-mail for personal and business use alike, and its exposure to imminent threats, there exists the need for a comprehensive view of the Internet mail system, including webmail traffic.

In this paper we propose a novel, *passive* approach to identify webmail traffic solely based on *network-level data* in order to obtain a *comprehensive* view of the mail system. Key to our approach is that we leverage *correlations* across protocols and time to introduce novel features for HTTPS webmail classification: First, webmail servers tend to reside close to legacy IMAP and POP mail servers, which are easy to identify. Second, the usage of webmail services results in distinct patterns on sessions' duration and on the diurnal/weekly traffic usage profile. Third, traffic flows to webmail platforms exhibit inherent periodicities since AJAX-based clients periodically check for new messages. We use these features to build a simple classifier and detect webmail traffic on real-world NetFlow traces from a medium-sized backbone network.

We believe that the major contribution of this paper – exploring a set of new features that could classify applications that run over HTTPS ports solely based on NetFlow data – will stimulate more general advance in the field of traffic classification.

Categories and Subject Descriptors

C.2.3 [**Computer-Communication Networks**]: Network Operations

General Terms

Measurement, Algorithms

Keywords

Traffic classification, HTTPS traffic, webmail, flow-level data

IMC'10, November 1–3, 2010, Melbourne, Australia.

1. INTRODUCTION

Speculations that web browsers could gradually supplant traditional operating systems as the default platform for user applications [21] go back to the first browser war in the mid 90's. According to recent reports [6] many Internet users prefer to access their e-mail via a web-based (webmail) interface such as Horde [11], Outlook Web Access (OWA) [25], or a webmail platform as provided by GMail, Yahoo!, or Hotmail. Similar trends also hold for many other applications, such as video, VoIP, and instant messaging, presently making browsers more than ever before the new operating system.

This trend however is detrimental for the field of Internet traffic classification, which over the past years has seen a plethora of proposals [16]. Evidently, *port-based* approaches are insufficient since many of today's applications use port 80 or HTTPS port 443 [23]. *Signature-based* solutions [5,9,14,23,30], which generally assume packet-level traces, fail if payload encryption is used, raise privacy or legal issues, and may not scale well enough to obtain a network-wide characterization of traffic. Even with hard to obtain, unencrypted full-packet traces, it is very difficult to identify the applications in use [8]. *Statistics-based* (e.g., [1,2,7,19,20,22,27]) and *host-behavior-based* [13–15] techniques avoid payload inspection. The former rely mainly on flow-level features such as flow duration, number and size of packets per flow and classify traffic flows. In our extensive experiments, we have found that flow-based features are not sufficient to classify individual HTTPS flows as webmail or not. Finally, host-based approaches (e.g., BLINC [14]) attempt to classify a host directly based on its communication pattern, and are the closest in spirit to our approach. Yet, to our best knowledge, host-based approaches have not been applied before to HTTP(S) traffic classification.

As a first step towards deciphering HTTP(S) traffic, we, in this work, address the challenging problem of extracting HTTPS-based webmail traffic from coarse-grained NetFlow data. Given its importance for personal and business use, and its exposure to imminent threats [3, 12], there exists a need for a comprehensive view of the Internet mail system [10, 26, 28], including webmail traffic. Measuring webmail traffic can enhance our understanding of shifting usage trends and mail traffic evolution. Surprisingly, we find that more than 66% of all HTTPS flows observed at the border routers of the SWITCH backbone network [31] are related to webmail. With GMail having recently enabled HTTPS by default (and other platforms expected to follow), this number will only increase in the future.

The most important contribution in this work is the introduction and evaluation of three novel features for identifying HTTPS mail traffic. Key to our approach is that we leverage *correlations across protocols and time*: (i) The Internet mail system is an interplay of multiple protocols (SMTP, IMAP, POP, webmail). We find that webmail servers tend to reside in the vicinity of legacy SMTP, IMAP, and POP servers, which can be identified easily and reliably [17] using port numbers, thus providing significant hints for detecting webmail servers. (ii) Moreover, clients of a mail server share certain characteristics (e.g., usage patterns) irrespective of the used mail delivery protocol, i.e., IMAP, POP, or webmail. (iii) Finally, webmail traffic exhibits pronounced periodic patterns due to application timers (and more generally AJAX-based technologies). This paper shows that these features can be harvested solely from coarse-grained NetFlow data to classify webmail traffic.

To get a first impression of the ability of the above features to uncover webmail traffic, we train a simple classifier based on a (manually) pre-labeled set of hosts. Although finding the best possible classifier is beyond the scope of this paper, our simple classifier already exhibits 93.2% accuracy and 79.2% precision in detecting HTTPS servers within SWITCH, which is remarkable given that we rely solely on NetFlow data. Moreover, our work shows that we can also effectively detect webmail traffic (e.g., GMail) towards mail servers *outside* the SWITCH network, for which only a small sample of their total traffic is visible.

As a final note, we expect our methodology to stimulate advance in the field of traffic classification in general. For example, for our third feature we distinguish between "machine-generated" and "user-invoked" traffic based on network-level data, which is a very general method that can be used for several different types of detection problems.

The rest of this paper is structured as follows. Section 2 explains our data set we have used. Section 3 introduces and discusses features to discriminate mail-related traffic from other web traffic. Then, Section 4 describes how we construct a classifier based on the features we identify and presents our first results. Finally, we give an overview of related work in Section 5 and conclude in Section 6.

2. DATA SETS AND GROUND TRUTH

Throughout this paper we will rely on NetFlow traces coming from SWITCH [31], a medium-sized ISP. SWITCH is a backbone operator connecting approximately 30 Swiss universities, government institutions, and research labs. For our studies we have collected a trace in March 2010 that spans 11 days and contains unsampled flows summarizing all traffic crossing the borders of SWITCH. This results in 50 to 140 million NetFlow records per hour, with approximately 3% being HTTPS. Over the 11 days, we observe more than 1 billion HTTPS records.

Instead of analyzing individual flows, we mainly consider *sessions*. Our flow collectors break up long-lived flows into smaller fragments. Therefore, we merge flows sharing the same 5-tuple (source address and port, destination address and port, transport protocol identifier) if traffic exchange does not stay silent for more than 900s. Moreover, we group merged flows with the same IP addresses into a session if they are not more than 1,800s apart in time. These values have been determined empirically, and found to work well in the past.

To train a classifier and to verify the accuracy of our classification in Section 4 we need a labelled data set. To this end, we first extract from a 1-hour trace recorded on Monday noon 2010-03-15 the 500 most popular internal HTTPS hosts/sockets (`top500`) in terms of unique IP addresses they communicate with. Then, we manually access each of the 500 obtained IP addresses with a web browser and determine the host type (e.g., Horde, OWA). In cases where this does not work (e.g., Skype), we use `nmap`. Table 1 summarizes the results of this time-consuming task.

class	type	# servers	# flows (mil.)
mail		77 (15.4%)	362.4 (66.0%)
	OWA	52	172.1
	Horde	10	84.9
	others	15	105.4
non mail		398 (79.6%)	159.0 (29.0%)
	WWW	137	88.9
	Skype	153	45.9
	VPN	15	8.3
	other	93	15.9
unknown		25 (5%)	27.7 (5.0%)
total		500	549.1

Table 1: `top500` data set

The fact that 66% of the observed HTTPS flows are related to Outlook Web Access, Horde, or other webmail interfaces (e.g., CommuniGate, SquirrelMail) is surprising and emphasizes the high popularity of webmail. Although the numbers may vary, we believe that our finding also holds for networks other than SWITCH. After all, e-mail is an omnipresent service in today's Internet. While we cannot label 5% of the `top500` hosts, we further differentiate 398 non-mail data sources into WWW content (e.g., e-shops, e-learning platforms), Skype, VPN services, etc.

3. FEATURES

We are now ready to discuss the features we propose for discriminating between mail related web traffic and other HTTPS traffic.

As mentioned earlier, classifying individual flows relying on flow-level statistics alone (e.g., packets and bytes per flow) does not work well. For example, cross-checking the distribution of number of bytes per flow does not reveal any significant differences between webmail and other HTTPS traffic flows.

An important challenge for feature extraction is to overcome the inherent heterogeneity of webmail traffic caused by the high number of different webmail implementations.

The features we present in the following are based on two main observations: first, the network-wide view provided by our flow-based data set allows to leverage correlations across hosts and protocols; second, periodic patterns due to regular timeouts are visible in flow data and provide useful application fingerprints.

To this end, this section sketches three approaches for distinguishing webmail from other HTTPS traffic. The key ideas are as follows: (i) classical mail services (POP, IMAP, SMTP) are frequently in the vicinity of webmail services (see Section 3.1), (ii) the client base of legacy mail services and the clients of its associated webmail service share common behavior in terms of user activity (Section 3.2), and (iii) traffic generated by AJAX-based webmail clients shows a pronounced periodicity that we can leverage to extract webmail traffic (Section 3.3). The following subsections explain these methods in detail, discuss their efficiency, and describe how to obtain features that can be used as input for a classifier.[1]

All three feature categories that we present in the following are broad in the sense that the key ideas are not limited to webmail classification. We believe that our features can be more generally applied towards demultiplexing HTTP(S) traffic into individual appli-

[1]We stress here that simplicity and interpretability, rather than optimality, have been our guiding principles in translating our observations into (scalar) features, used for our preliminary classification results.

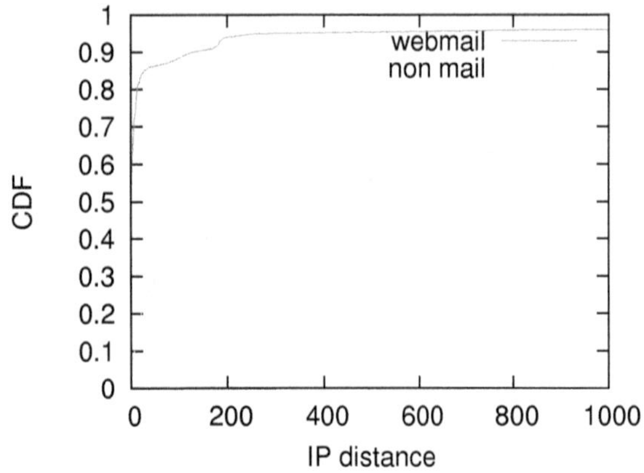

Figure 1: Distance to closest known legacy mail server.

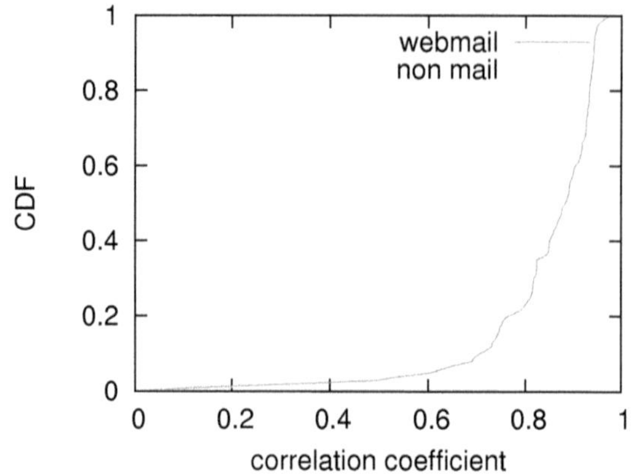

Figure 2: Correlation between activity profiles of web (mail or non-mail) servers and their closest legacy mail server.

cations. For example, inferring periodicity of sessions could translate into a powerful tool for distinguishing between "user-invoked" and "machine-generated" (e.g., AJAX) traffic and for extracting flow-level signatures associated with different applications. Also, studying the mix of well-known services within a subnet may provide hints for the existence of other unknown services in the same subnet. Finally, although we will focus on HTTPS traffic when introducing our features (motivated also by the earlier observations about webmail traffic), we stress that the techniques we describe are applicable to both HTTP and HTTPS flow traces.

3.1 Service proximity

The Internet mail system relies on the interplay of multiple services or protocols, including SMTP, IMAP, POP, and webmail. We have observed that if there exists a POP, IMAP, or SMTP server within a certain domain or subnet, there is a high chance to find a webmail server in the same subnet. This is often due to network planning reasons. Since legacy mail delivery traffic and respective servers can be easily and reliably identified using port-based classification [17], we can use their existence to infer webmail servers in the vicinity.

To verify our assumption of server proximity, we detect all mail servers in the SWITCH network relying on port numbers. Overall, we find 300 SMTP, 140 IMAP/S, and 176 POP/S servers. Moreover, we use our `top500` data set, see Section 2. For every HTTPS server we compute the IP address distance, which is simply the integer difference between two IP addresses towards the closest mail server. Our assumption is that legacy mail servers are closer to webmail than other HTTPS servers. Figure 1 shows the observed distance for webmail and non-mail HTTPS servers (e.g. WWW, VPN, Skype) found among the `top500` servers.

We observe that almost 60% of the webmail servers have a distance very close to the minimum, i.e., smaller than 10 IP addresses, while only 5% of the non-mail servers are in this range. Moreover, more than 90% of the webmail servers have a distance smaller than 200 IP addresses. These numbers indicate that webmail servers are substantially more likely than non-mail servers to be in the neighborhood of a legacy mail server.

3.2 Client base behavior

While Section 3.1 studies direct correlations between servers (i.e., how close they are), here we propose to analyze the entire client base of a server. We have found pronounced patterns for the following two properties: (i) the daily and weekly access patterns of HTTPS servers (Section 3.2.1), and (ii) the duration of client connections (Section 3.2.2).

3.2.1 Daily and weekly profile

It is well-known that Internet traffic as a whole has diurnal and weekly patterns. Different applications may also have their own specific access patterns. For example, people access their e-mail frequently and often in a scheduled way, i.e., first thing in the morning, whereas they access other web applications, such as online banking or Skype, in a substantially different way. More importantly, we expect client activity to be more balanced during the day for servers that have a worldwide user base (e.g., a web page) than for webmail servers with a local user base. For example, everyone can access the website of ETH Zurich, but only a limited group of people can use the webmail platform of ETH Zurich.

To quantify these differences, we use the activity profile of known IMAP and POP servers as a reference point and evaluate how it compares with the activity profile of unknown web servers in their vicinity. Our expectation is that IMAP and POP diurnal and weekly patterns will be more similar to webmail than to non-mail server patterns. In line with the observations of Section 3.1, we compare an unknown server to the closest legacy mail server in the same subnet. If there is no such server, we compare to the highest-volume legacy mail server in the same autonomous system.

Specifically, to compare two activity profiles, we partition a given time interval (in our case one week) into bins of one hour and count for every hour the number of client sessions that access the two servers. This way we derive two vectors of equal length that describe the profile of the servers. To measure statistical dependence between the profiles, we compute the Spearman's rank correlation coefficient [24] of the two vectors. The Spearman's coefficient has two useful properties. First, it is a rank correlation measure and therefore it effectively normalizes the two vectors. Second, it captures (non)-linear correlations between the two profiles, i.e., if the activity intensity of two profiles increases/decreases together. If two profiles are strongly correlated then the coefficient tends to 1. The resulting value is used as input to our classifier (Section 4).

To demonstrate the efficiency of this feature, Figure 2 plots the distribution of Spearman's correlation coefficient when comparing the activity profiles of all `top500` HTTPS services with the profile of the closest mail server. For more than 90% of the webmail servers the correlation coefficient is higher than 0.6 while this percentage is only about 50% for non-mail servers.

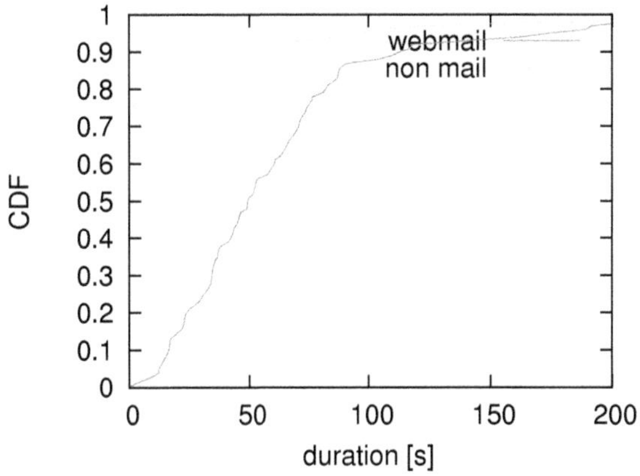

Figure 3: Median of session duration.

3.2.2 Session duration

A second characteristic of user behavior is how long clients normally use a service. We speculate that webmail users generally take some time to read and answer their e-mails and may even keep the browser window open to wait for incoming messages. Hence, access duration for a webmail service should be higher, on average, than the one for a normal webpage. To capture the access duration of a service we consider sessions as described in Section 2. By defining session duration as the time between the start of the first session flow and the start of the last session flow, we ignore potential TCP timeouts. Since we are interested in *typical* user behavior, we use the median across all session duration samples for a given server.

Figure 3 displays the distribution of the median duration for our `top500` servers. Again, we find significant differences between the client behavior of a webmail server and other non-mail servers. While the median session duration of a webmail service is shorter than 25s for only some 20% of the webmail servers, almost 90% of non-mail servers experience such short median access times. Although there exist some non-mail servers with long session durations (these are mainly VPN servers), the overall differences in access duration are sufficiently pronounced to use this as another feature for classifying webmail traffic.

3.3 Periodicity

The activity profiles of Section 3.2.1 capture fluctuations in client activity over long time periods such as one week. We now investigate the existence of higher frequency time patterns. The advent of AJAX-based technologies, which heavily rely on asynchronous interactions between clients and servers, has led to an increase in exchanged messages. Many of today's webmail solutions check periodically (e.g., every 5 minutes) for incoming messages and update the browser window if necessary. This is in line with the experience provided by mail programs such as Outlook or Thunderbird. Our idea is to leverage such periodicity that we expect to be visible in our flow-based data in order to classify e-mail related web traffic.

Using `Wireshark` and `Firebug` we analyze the communication triggered by different webmail implementations. We find evidence of distinct periodicity in the sense that even during idle times a synchronization message is sent at regular time intervals. This also results in a new observed flow between client and server at the same time intervals. Nevertheless, capturing this periodicity requires some signal processing.

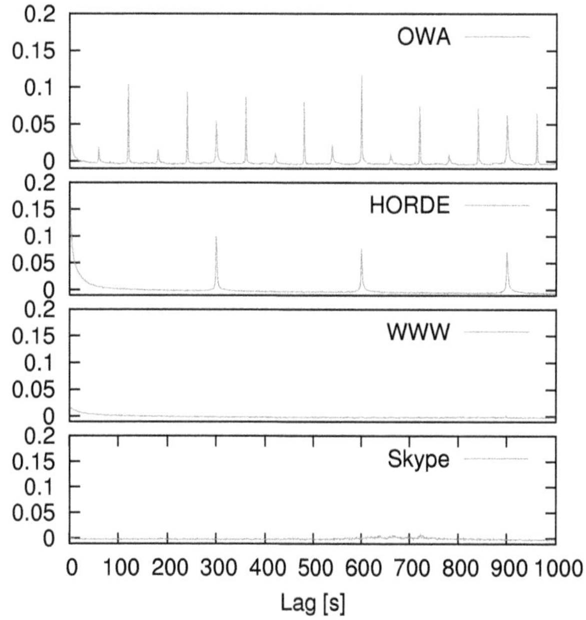

Figure 4: Autocorrelation of flow inter-arrival times.

We observe that webmail sessions are composed of noisy user-invoked traffic, resulting from activities such as sending e-mails or browsing folders, and evident machine-generated periodic traffic. To recover the periodicity buried in the signal, we start by filtering out all short sessions, since they are not useful for identifying periodic behaviors that repeat infrequently, e.g., every 5 minutes. For a server under study, we keep all sessions and respective flows with a duration higher than $1,800$s, which corresponds to six 5-minute intervals. We then split each session into time bins of 1s and count the number of flows that start within a bin. This is repeated for every client of the server under study. Then, we compute the autocorrelation function and average the autocorrelation signals over the entire client base of a particular server, in order to smooth the signal and obtain a server-level behavior.

The plots in Figure 4 display the results for four different types of servers from our `top500` class. Evidently, webmail applications show pronounced peaks at regular intervals, i.e., OWA at 60s and Horde at 300s, while web and Skype traffic does not show this pattern. Note that we observe similar periodic patterns for other webmail applications such as GMail or Yahoo!.

Although it is trivial to assess periodicity visually based on autocorrelation signals, we still need to introduce a simple metric that quantifies periodicity and can be used by a classifier. To this end, we consider the energies of different frequencies in the autocorrelation function. By cutting off small time lags (e.g., below 200s) and high time lags (e.g., above 400s), we mitigate the impact of noise. Then, we compare the maximum and median signal levels that we observe within this time interval. High ratios are a strong indicator for periodicity, i.e., for the existence of a webmail server.

We believe that the basic idea behind our approach could in general be used to distinguish between user- and machine-initiated traffic. Hence, a spectrum of other applications as well is likely to have a characteristic fingerprint related to flow timing (in fact, our preliminary results already hint to such a direction).

4. EVALUATION

The results of the preceding Section 3 are promising in the sense that it is apparently possible to discriminate between e-mail related web traffic and other HTTPS traffic leveraging correlations across protocols and time. In this section we explain how to build a classifier using our proposed features and present first results. Our main concern is not maximum accuracy. Rather we seek to demonstrate the general feasibility and the potential of our approach in a proof of concept study.

The general approach is as follows: We use the Support Vector Machine (SVM) library provided by [4]. For classification we rely on the four features presented in the preceding Section 3, namely service proximity, activity profiles, session duration, and periodicity. These features are used to discriminate between the two classes mail and non-mail. To estimate classification accuracy, we rely on 5-fold cross-validation: we partition the set of hosts into five complementary subsets of equal size. Four subsets are used as training data, the remaining subset serves as validation data. We repeat this process five times such that each of the five subsets is used exactly once as validation data.

Based on the `top500` data set, see Table 1, we classify webmail hosts that are inside the SWITCH network.

	Number of true HTTPS	
	mail servers	non mail servers
classified as mail	61	16
classified as non mail	16	382
accuracy (mean)	93.2% (±3)	

Table 2: Classification of internal HTTPS servers.

As shown in Table 2, our classification realizes a remarkably high mean accuracy of 93.2% (with standard deviation 3.0) across the five runs of our 5-fold cross-validation. In addition, the precision for the mail class is also reasonably good at 79.2% relying solely on flow data and can be further improved by optimizing the classifier. By manually scrutinizing the results of the classification, we find our classifier can effectively discriminate between webmail and Skype nodes mainly due to the service proximity feature of Section 3.1 and also between webmail and authentication services mainly due to the session duration feature of Section 3.2.2. However, it is challenging to distinguish between VPN and webmail servers, which is the main reason for false negatives when classifying webmail hosts.

Popular webmail platforms such as GMail, Yahoo!, or Hotmail do not maintain servers within the SWITCH network and, therefore, have been ignored in our discussion and analysis so far. Finally, we briefly illustrate that applying our approach to uncover arbitrary webmail applications is equally feasible, irrespective of whether hosts are internal or external.

To this end, we extract additional data from our trace collected in March 2010. Following the methodology outlined in Section 2, we select 500 popular *external* HTTPS hosts/sockets. Manually labeling this data set reveals 32 GMail servers[2]. For 452 additional HTTPS servers we established that they provide other non-mail services such as online banking, update, Facebook login servers, etc.

We now merge the original `top500` data set and the labeled external hosts creating a new data set with 1000 HTTPS servers. Based on our proposed features we build a classifier and again apply 5-fold cross-validation.

[2]Recall that GMail recently switched to HTTPS.

	Number of true HTTPS	
	mail servers	non mail servers
classified as mail	94	30
classified as non mail	19	820
accuracy (mean)	94.8% (±3)	

Table 3: Classification of internal and external HTTPS servers.

Table 3 shows that we are able to classify internal and external HTTPS servers with overall accuracy of 94.8% ± 3 and precision of 75.8% for the mail class. Although these results are preliminary, it appears possible to detect mail servers outside the SWITCH network using the same features, even though only a small sample of the total traffic of these servers is visible in our network. Moreover, our case study on GMail suggests that the techniques proposed in this paper are not limited to specific applications (e.g., Outlook Web Access, Horde).

5. RELATED WORK

Though extensive research has focused on traffic classification[3], only a comparably tiny portion has studied methods for dissecting WWW traffic. Schneider *et al.* [29] extracted traffic to four popular Ajax-based sites from full packet traces and characterized differences between Ajax and HTTP traffic. Li *et al.* used manually constructed payload signatures to classify HTTP traffic into 14 applications and discussed trends from the early analysis [18] of two datasets collected three years apart. Compared to previous studies, our work focuses on extracting mail traffic from WWW traces and operates on *flows*, solving a substantially more challenging problem than previous HTTP classification studies, which used full packet traces (e.g., [8]).

Some research has recently focused on the traffic characteristics of mail. Notably, Ramachandran *et al.* [26] characterized a number of network properties of spammers and emphasized that spammers can alter the content of spam to evade filters, whereas they cannot easily change their network-level footprint. This work suggested the plausibility of network-based spam filtering and was followed by the SNARE system [10], which uses a small number of simple traffic features to block spammers with reasonable accuracy.

Finally, compared to host-based classification, the novelty of our method can be mostly traced to the addition of the following two "dimensions": (i) we introduce a timing dimension, as this contains valuable information about user- and machine- behaviors; (ii) while earlier host-based approaches [14] attempt to identify a *common* communication pattern (graph) shared by all hosts of this application, we try to correlate the unknown host behavior to *known* hosts running a different, but *related* application; as a result, hosts with different patterns could be validly identified under one class.

6. CONCLUSION

In this paper, we have presented a number of flow-level techniques that can be used to separate webmail traffic from other HTTPS traffic. The novelty of our approach goes into two main directions: (i) we leverage correlations across (related) protocols (e.g. IMAP, POP, SMTP, and webmail) and among hosts sharing a similar client base, and (ii) we identify and exploit timing characteristics of webmail applications. Based on these, we have introduced novel features, investigated their efficiency on a large flow data set, and used them to produce preliminary classification results on internal and

[3]For a survey of traffic classification literature refer to [16].

external HTTPS servers. This is the first work to show that it is possible to uncover HTTPS webmail applications solely based on flow-level data with approximately 93.2% accuracy and 79.2% precision.

While the main focus of this paper has been the presented novel features, in future work, we intend to optimize our classifier and if needed to further extend our set of features (along the two directions discussed) to improve the precision of our classification. In the same direction, we would also like to test the effect of sampling on our techniques, as we believe that most of the features presented are likely immune to sampling. Furthermore, we believe that our features are of broader interest for traffic classification, and could be used, for example, to facilitate demultiplexing of HTTP(S) traffic in general. Finally, having a reliable method to extract webmail traffic, we intend to perform an extensive characterization of the long-term evolution of mail-related traffic including usage trends and traffic mix between classical delivery and web-mail protocols.

Acknowledgments

We are grateful to SWITCH for providing their traffic traces and to the anonymous reviewers for their helpful comments. Also, we want to thank Bernhard Tellenbach, Martin Burkhart and Brian Trammell for their contributions. Special thanks to Simon Leinen for assisting with flow collection and processing. Finally, we are grateful to our shepherd Mark Allman. Part of this work has been funded by the EC Marie Curie IRG project 46528.

7. REFERENCES

[1] T. Auld, A. Moore, and S. Gull. Bayesian Neural Networks for Internet Traffic Classification. *IEEE Transactions on Neural Networks*, 2007.

[2] L. Bernaille, R. Teixeira, and K. Salamatian. Early application identification. In *Proc. of ACM CoNEXT*, 2006.

[3] Trojan Now Uses Hotmail, Gmail as Spam Hosts. http://news.bitdefender.com/NW544-en-n-\-Trojan-Now-Uses-Hotmail-as-Spam-Hosts.html, 2007.

[4] C. Chang and C. Lin. *LIBSVM: a Library for Support Vector Machines*, 2001. www.csie.ntu.edu.tw/~cjlin/libsvm.

[5] T. Choi, C. Kim, S. Yoon, J. Park, B. Lee, H. Kim, and H. Chung. Content-Aware Internet Application Traffic Measurement and Analysis. In *Proc. of IEEE/IFIP NOMS*, 2005.

[6] Email client popularity. http://www.campaignmonitor.com/stats/email-clients.

[7] M. Crotti, M. Dusi, F. Gringoli, and L. Salgarelli. Traffic Classification Through Simple Statistical Fingerprinting. *ACM SIGCOMM CCR*, 2007.

[8] H. Dreger, A. Feldmann, M. Mai, V. Paxson, and R. Sommer. Dynamic Application-Layer Protocol Analysis for Network Intrusion Detection. In *Proc. of USENIX Security Symposium*, 2006.

[9] P. Haffner, S. Sen, O. Spatscheck, and D. Wang. Acas: Automated Construction of Application Signatures. In *Proc. of SIGCOMM MineNet Workshop*, 2005.

[10] S. Hao, N. Feamster, A. Gray, N. Syed, and S. Krasser. Detecting Spammers with SNARE: Spatio-Temporal Network-level Automatic Reputation Engine. In *Proc. of USENIX Security Symposium*, 2009.

[11] The Horde Project. www.horde.org.

[12] Scammers Exploit Public Lists of Hijacked Hotmail Passwords. http://www.computerworld.com/s/article/9139092/Scammers_exploit_public_lists_of_hijacked_Hotmail_passwords, 2007.

[13] M. Iliofotou, P. Pappu, M. Faloutsos, M. Mitzenmacher, and G. Varghese. Network Monitoring Using Traffic Dispersion Graphs. In *Proc. of ACM IMC*, 2007.

[14] T. Karagiannis, K. Papagiannaki, and M. Faloutsos. BLINC: Multilevel Traffic Classification in the Dark. In *Proc. of ACM SIGCOMM*, 2005.

[15] T. Karagiannis, K. Papagiannaki, N. Taft, and M. Faloutsos. Profiling the End Host. In *Proc. of PAM*, 2007.

[16] H. Kim, K. Claffy, M. Fomenkov, D. Barman, M. Faloutsos, and K. Lee. Internet Traffic Classification Demystified: Myths, Caveats, and the Best Practices. In *Proc. of ACM CoNEXT*, 2008.

[17] H. Kim, M. Fomenkov, K. Claffy, N. Brownlee, D. Barman, and M. Faloutsos. Comparison of Internet Traffic Classification Tools. In *Proc. of IMRG workshop on application classification and identification report*, 2009.

[18] W. Li, A. W. Moore, and M. Canini. Classifying HTTP Traffic in the New Age. In *ACM SIGCOMM, Poster Session*, 2008.

[19] Z. Li, R. Yuan, and X. Guan. Accurate Classification of the Internet Traffic Based on the SVM Method. In *Proc. of IEEE International Conference on Communications (ICC)*, 2007.

[20] A. McGregor, M. Hall, P. Lorier, and J. Brunskill. Flow Clustering Using Maching Learning Techniques. In *Proc. of PAM*, 2004.

[21] The Middleware Threats. http://biz.yahoo.com/msft/p7.html.

[22] A. Moore and D. Zuev. Internet Traffic Classification Using Bayesian Analysis Techniques. In *Proc. of ACM SIGMETRICS*, 2005.

[23] A. W. Moore and P. Konstantina. Toward the Accurate Identification of Network Applications. In *Proc. of PAM*, 2005.

[24] J. Myers and A. Well. *Research Design and Statistical Analysis (2nd edition)*. Routledge, 2002.

[25] Microsoft Outlook Web Access. www.microsoft.com/exchange/code/OWA/index.html.

[26] A. Ramachandran and N. Feamster. Understanding the Network-Level Behavior of Spammers. In *Proc. of ACM SIGCOMM*, 2006.

[27] M. Roughan, S. Sen, O. Spatschek, and N. Duffield. Class-of-Service Mapping for QoS: a Statistical Signature-Based Approach to IP Traffic Classification. In *Proc. of ACM IMC*, 2004.

[28] D. Schatzmann, M. Burkhart, and T. Spyropoulos. Inferring Spammers in the Network Core. In *Proc. of PAM*, 2009.

[29] F. Schneider, S. Agarwal, T. Alpcan, and A. Feldmann. The New Web: Characterizing AJAX Traffic. In *Proc. of PAM*, 2008.

[30] S. Sen, O. Spatscheck, and D. Wang. Accurate, Scalable In-Network Identification of P2P Traffic Using Application Signatures. In *Proc. of WWW*, 2004.

[31] The Swiss Education and Research Network (SWITCH). http://www.switch.ch.

Revisiting the Case for a Minimalist Approach for Network Flow Monitoring

Vyas Sekar
Carnegie Mellon University
Pittsburgh, PA
vyass@cs.cmu.edu

Michael K Reiter
UNC Chapel Hill
Chapel Hill, NC
reiter@cs.unc.edu

Hui Zhang
Carnegie Mellon University
Pittsburgh, PA
hzhang@cs.cmu.edu

ABSTRACT

Network management applications require accurate estimates of a wide range of flow-level traffic metrics. Given the inadequacy of current packet-sampling-based solutions, several application-specific monitoring algorithms have emerged. While these provide better accuracy for the specific applications they target, they increase router complexity and require vendors to commit to hardware primitives without knowing how useful they will be to meet the needs of future applications.

In this paper, we show using trace-driven evaluations that such complexity and early commitment may not be necessary. We revisit the case for a "minimalist" approach in which a small number of simple yet generic router primitives collect flow-level data from which different traffic metrics can be estimated. We demonstrate the feasibility and promise of such a minimalist approach using flow sampling and sample-and-hold as sampling primitives and configuring these in a network-wide coordinated fashion using cSamp. We show that this proposal yields better accuracy across a collection of application-level metrics than dividing the same memory resources across metric-specific algorithms. Moreover, because a minimalist approach enables *late binding* to what application-level metrics are important, it better insulates router implementations and deployments from changing monitoring needs.

Categories and Subject Descriptors

C.2.3 [**Computer-Communication Networks**]: Network Operations—*network monitoring, network management*

General Terms

Measurement, Management

Keywords

Traffic Monitoring, Sampling, Data Streaming, Anomaly Detection

IMC'10, November 1–3, 2010, Melbourne, Australia.

1. INTRODUCTION

Flow monitoring supports vital network management tasks such as traffic engineering [18], anomaly detection [28, 29], accounting [14, 17], identifying and analyzing end-user applications [12, 22], understanding traffic structure [43], detecting worms, scans, and botnet activities [44, 41, 35], and forensic analysis [42]. These require accurate estimates of different traffic metrics relevant to each application.

High traffic rates exceed the monitoring capabilities of routers,[1] and since traffic is scaling at least as fast as routers' capabilities, some form of sampling or data reduction is necessary in commodity solutions. (There are high-end solutions for full packet capture [3]. These are expensive and require specialized instrumentation.) The de-facto standard is NetFlow [11, 2] which uses packet sampling. Each packet is sampled with some probability and the selected packets are aggregated into flows.[2] NetFlow-style monitoring is sufficient for applications such as traffic volume estimation that require only a coarse view of traffic, but several studies have shown the inadequacy of packet sampling for many of the fine-grained monitoring applications mentioned earlier (e.g., see [34, 21, 15, 26, 7, 35, 17]).

A consequence of these results is that several research efforts have focused on developing application-specific monitoring techniques. This is exemplified by the proliferation of data streaming algorithms for computing specific traffic metrics, e.g., computing the flow size distribution [26], entropy estimation [30], superspreader detection [41], degree histogram estimation [44], change detection [25], and so on.

While this body of work has made valuable algorithmic contributions, this shift to application-specific approaches is undesirable for two practical reasons. First, having many application-specific proposals increases the implementation complexity and possibly the resource requirements of routers. Second, the set of applications is a moving target, as both normal and anomalous traffic patterns change over time. This requires router vendors and network managers to commit to a fixed set of application-level metrics without knowing if these will meet future requirements.

In this work, we reflect on these developments and ask a fundamental question:

Is such complexity and early commitment necessary?
Are there simpler alternatives that can provide the requisite fidelity and generality?

[1]Our arguments apply to non-router-based monitoring solutions as well.

[2]A flow is a sequence of packets with the same IP 5-tuple ⟨ srcip, dstip, srcport, dstport, protocol ⟩.

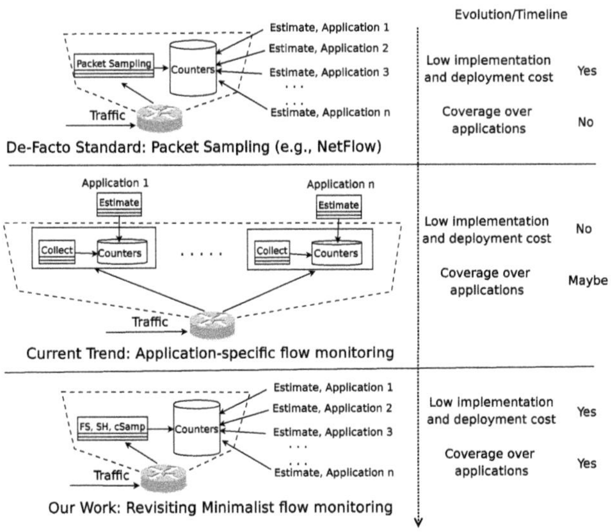

Figure 1: A minimalist approach runs a few collection algorithms. Applications can use the collected data later (possibly offline). NetFlow/packet sampling is a minimalist approach, but it is not well-suited for many applications. An application-specific architecture implements many focused algorithms. These work well for the specific applications, but increase complexity and are not robust to changing demands. We demonstrate a minimalist alternative that performs favorably compared to application-specific approaches over a wide spectrum of applications.

Approach and Intuition: We revisit the case for a *minimalist* approach that retains the simplicity of NetFlow, where routers only need to support a *few* monitoring primitives, but still provide coverage over a wide spectrum of applications.

To understand how we can achieve this, we can think of each monitoring application as being composed of two logical phases: (1) a *collection* phase that needs to operate at line rates and (2) an *estimation* phase to compute different traffic metrics that need not strictly work at line rates. Application-specific alternatives tightly couple these two components, only retaining counters and statistics relevant to a specific application context (Figure 1). In contrast, we envision a minimalist approach that *decouples* the collection and estimation phases as much as possible.

A key question is whether such an approach can provide estimation accuracy comparable to application-specific alternatives. One rationale to suggest that it can, is that the primary bottleneck for monitoring is keeping counters in fast memory (SRAM). Instead of splitting the available memory across different applications, we can aggregate it, and run a few simple primitives with high-enough sampling rates to obtain accurate estimates of traffic metrics for a wide spectrum of applications. In other words, when we look at each application in isolation, application-specific strategies are appealing. However, when we consider a portfolio of applications in aggregate, a minimalist approach might be a better alternative.

Contributions and Implications: Our goal is not to design an optimal minimalist approach. Rather, our objective is to establish a *feasible* instance.

We present a practical minimalist approach in Section 4 that combines sample-and-hold [17], flow sampling [21], and cSamp [39]. Our choice of these specific primitives is guided by the understanding that monitoring applications fall into two broad classes that analyze (1) *volume structure* (e.g., traffic engineering) or (2) *communication structure* (e.g., security applications). Flow sampling is ideally suited for the latter class [21, 34, 32] and sample-and-hold for the former [17]. cSamp provides a framework to efficiently leverage the available monitoring resources at routers to meet network-wide monitoring goals.

We use trace-driven analysis to evaluate this design against several application-specific approaches (Section 6): detecting heavy hitters [17], superspreaders [41], and large traffic changes [25]; computing entropy [30] and the outdegree histogram [44]; and estimating the flow size distribution [26]. When our approach has the same total memory resources as that used by the different application-specific algorithms in aggregate, it provides comparable or better estimation accuracy across the entire spectrum of applications. Moreover, by delaying the binding to specific applications, it enables computation of not-yet-conceived measures that will be interesting in the future.

Our work shows the promise of a minimalist approach even with a simple combination of existing techniques. We believe that this has significant implications for router vendors, network operators, and measurement researchers. First, it can reduce router complexity without compromising a vendor's ability to satisfy its customers' demands. Second, it helps insulate network deployments from the changing needs of monitoring applications. Finally, we hope that these results motivate further research in developing better minimalist primitives and estimation algorithms, and in understanding their fidelity for different applications.

2. BACKGROUND AND RELATED WORK

Packet sampling: Router vendors today use uniform packet sampling [11]: a router selects a subset of packets, and aggregates the sampled packets into flow reports. However, packet sampling has inherent limitations. There are known biases toward sampling larger flows (e.g., [21, 26, 34]) and several studies have questioned its accuracy for many management applications (e.g., see [34, 21, 15, 26, 7, 35, 17]).

Application-specific approaches: The limitations of packet sampling have motivated many application-specific data streaming algorithms. The high-level approach is to use a small number of SRAM counters that track traffic statistics pertinent to each application and then estimate the relevant application-level metrics from these counters. These include algorithms for estimating the flow size distribution [26, 36], identifying heavy hitters [17], entropy estimation [30], superspreader detection [41], degree histogram estimation [44], and change detection [25]. However, these approaches are tightly coupled to the specific applications and report summary statistics only relevant to these applications. Thus, it is difficult to estimate other measures of interest from these reports. Therefore, these lack the generality to serve as minimalist primitives.

Some data structures (e.g., sketches [13]) provide more generality. However, these have two limitations. First, they are designed primarily for coarse *volume queries* and less suited for fine-grained tasks like entropy estimation and superspreader detection. Second, sketches operate with a specific "flowkey" over one or more fields of the IP 5-tuple (srcip, dstip, srcport, dstport, protocol). Each flowkey of interest requires a separate instance. However, it is often necessary to analyze combinations of two or more fields for diagnostic purposes (e.g., for investigating anomalies). Having a separate instance for each combination incurs high overhead. Furthermore, this needs prior knowledge of which flowkeys will be useful, which may not be known until after the operator begins to investigate specific events.

Selective sampling: Some approaches assign different sampling rates for different classes of packets [27, 35]. Others only log flows with pre-specified patterns (e.g., [45, 1, 4, 33, 8]). While these approaches provide some flexibility, they need to know the specific classes and sampling rates to meet the applications' requirements. In contrast, we envision a minimalist approach that is largely agnostic to the specific types of analyses that may be performed.

Network-wide measurements: Many studies have stressed the importance of network-wide measurements to meet operational requirements as applications and attacks become more distributed [18, 28, 29]. For example, understanding peer-to-peer traffic [12], detecting botnets [35] and hit-list worms [32], understanding DDoS attacks [38], and network forensics [42] inherently require a network-wide view aggregated from multiple vantage points. In this respect, recent proposals show the benefits of moving beyond router-centric solutions to network-wide monitoring solutions [9, 39].

3. DESIGN CONSIDERATIONS

Given this background, we synthesize key requirements for a flow monitoring architecture and derive guiding principles for a minimalist approach, echoing the charter of the IETF PSAMP working group [5].

3.1 Requirements

Minimize router complexity: Given the hardware and development costs involved in modern router design, we want to keep router implementations as simple as possible.

Generalize to many applications: The monitoring infrastructure should cover a wide spectrum of applications and ideally be robust to future application needs.

Enable diagnostics: The monitoring architecture should support diagnostic "drill-down" tasks; e.g., by providing the capability to give different views into traffic structure.

Provide network-wide views: The monitoring architecture should provide network-wide capabilities as these are increasingly crucial for several aspects of network management and traffic analysis.

3.2 Design Principles

A few, simple, and generic primitives: A natural way to reduce router complexity is to have a few primitives that are easy to implement but powerful enough to support many management tasks.

Decouple collection and computation: Now, how can we provide generality and support diagnostics with a few monitoring primitives? We believe that this best achieved by *decoupling* the collection and computation phases involved in the monitoring tasks. Note that this is already implicit in network operations today: routers export NetFlow reports to a (logically) central collector and operators analyze this data. We retain this operational model; routers run some collection algorithms and export the collected flow reports. Once we have the flow-level reports, we can compute any traffic metric of interest and provide different views required for further diagnosis.

Network-wide resource management: To provide network-wide capabilities, we need a framework that assigns monitoring responsibilities across routers to satisfy network-wide monitoring goals. At the same time, this framework should be *resource-aware* and respect the constraints (e.g., SRAM capacity) of individual routers.

3.3 Challenges

Given the above considerations, two questions remain:

1. **Concrete Design:** What primitives should be implemented on routers to support a range of applications? How should monitoring responsibilities be assigned to meet network-wide measurement goals?

2. **Performance:** Does the intuitive appeal of a minimalist approach translate into quantitative benefits for a wide spectrum of applications?

In addressing these challenges, our goal is not to look for an "optimal" minimalist approach. (In fact, it is not clear if we can formally reason about optimality without committing to a fixed set of applications.) Rather, we want to look for a *feasible* instance that covers a broad spectrum of applications. We present one such proposal in the next section.

4. ARCHITECTURE

The first challenge above requires that we choose a small set of generic collection primitives that runs on each router and design a framework to manage them intelligently across a network of routers. Our specific proposal combines three ideas: flow sampling [21] and sample-and-hold [17] as single router sampling algorithms, and cSamp [39] for network-wide management. Keys et al. designed a system for providing traffic summaries and detecting "resource hogs" [23] using a combination of flow sampling and sample-and-hold, similar to our approach. We extend their work in two significant ways. First, we show how to combine these primitives with the network-wide capabilities of cSamp [39] in contrast to the single-vantage-point view in their work. Second, we look beyond simple traffic summaries and demonstrate that this combination can support a much wider range of applications.

4.1 Router Primitives

Choice of primitives: Flow monitoring applications can be divided into two broad classes: (1) those that require an understanding of *volume structure*; e.g., heavy-hitter detection and traffic engineering that require an understanding of the number of packets/bytes per-port or per-src and (2) those that depend on the *communication structure*; e.g., security applications and anomaly detection application that require an understanding of "who-talks-to-whom". Our choice of primitives is guided by these two broad classes. Flow sampling is well suited for security and anomaly detection applications that analyze communication structure [21, 34, 32]. Similarly, sample-and-hold is well suited for traffic engineering and accounting applications that analyze volume structure [17]. Thus, these two primitives effectively complement each other in their capabilities. We do note that there are other proposals for capturing the communication structure (e.g., [35, 27]) and volume structure (e.g., [13, 15, 24]), and flow sampling and sample-and-hold may not necessarily be the optimal primitives. Our goal is to pick a feasible point in this design space and quantitatively compare it to application-specific approaches.

For the following discussion, a flow is defined by the 5-tuple: $\langle$srcip, dstip, srcport, dstport, protocol$\rangle$. We use flow sampling and sample-and-hold at this 5-tuple granularity. The collected flows can be sliced-and-diced after the fact by projecting from this general definition to others (e.g., per destination port, per source address).

Sample-and-Hold (SH): Sample-and-hold (SH) [17] keeps near-exact counts of "heavy hitters" — flows with high packet counts. SH works as follows. For each packet, the router checks if it is tracking this packet's *flowkey*, defined over one or more fields of the IP 5-tuple. If yes, the router updates that counter. If not, the flowkey for this packet is selected with probability p, and the router keeps an exact count for this selected flowkey subsequently. Since this requires per-packet counter updates, the counters are kept in SRAM [17].

To configure SH, we specify the flowkey(s) (e.g., srcport, srcip, or 5-tuple), the anticipated total number of packets for a specific time interval ($numpkts$), and the number of flows that can be logged (L) depending on the SRAM constraint. To ensure that the number of flow entries created does not exceed the SRAM capacity, we use $numpkts$ in configuring SH to set the packet sampling probability $p = \frac{L}{numpkts}$.[3] In our minimalist design, we use one instance of SH and configure it to operate at the 5-tuple granularity.

Hash-based flow sampling (FS): Flow sampling (FS) picks flows rather than packets at random [21]. One way to implement FS is as follows. Each router has a *sampling manifest* — a table of one or more hash ranges indexed using a key derived from each packet header. On receiving a packet, the router computes the hash of the packet's 5-tuple (i.e., the flowkey). Next, it selects the appropriate hash range from the manifest and selects the flow if the hash falls within this range. If the flow is selected, then the router uses its hash as an index into a table of flows and updates the byte and packet counters for the flow. The hash function maps the input 5-tuple uniformly into the interval $[0, 1]$. Thus, the size of each hash range determines the flow sampling rate for each category of flows in the manifest.

Similar to SH, FS requires per-packet table lookups; the flow table must therefore be implemented in SRAM. It is possible to add a packet sampling stage to make DRAM implementations possible [24]. For simplicity, we assume that the counters are stored in SRAM.

4.2 Resource Management

Having chosen FS and SH as our minimalist primitives, we address the following question. Given a fixed amount of SRAM available for monitoring on each router, how should we divide it between these primitives?

Combining FS-SH on a single router: Consider a single router with a fixed amount of SRAM that can hold L flow counters. A simple way to split L is to give a fraction f to FS and the remaining $1 - f$ to SH. We show in Section 6 that $f \approx 0.8$ is a good choice.

Network-wide case: The above split works for the single router case. Next, we see how we can manage the monitoring resources across a network of routers. Network-wide management tasks are typically specified in terms of Origin-Destination pairs, specified by an ingress and egress router (or PoP). OD-pairs are convenient abstractions that naturally fit many of the objectives (e.g., traffic engineering) and constraints (e.g., routing paths, traffic matrix) in network management. A natural extension of the single router hybrid primitive to the network-wide case is to consider the resource split per OD-pair [9, 39].

Here, we observe a key difference between FS and SH. It is possible to coordinate FS instances by assigning non-overlapping responsibilities across routers on a path [39]. However, because SH logs heavy hitters, the same set of heavy hitters will be reported across routers on a path. Thus, replicating SH across routers on a path duplicates measurements and wastes router resources.

To address this issue, we make a distinction between ingress and non-ingress routers. Ingresses implement both FS and SH, sharing the aggregate memory as in the single router case. At each such ingress router, the SH resources are split between the OD-pairs originating at the ingress, in proportion to the anticipated number of packets per OD-pair.[4] Non-ingress routers only implement FS. In order to distribute FS responsibilities across the network, we use cSamp [39], which we describe next.

Overview of cSamp: We choose cSamp because, for a given set of router resource constraints, it provides a framework to optimize fine-grained network-wide monitoring goals; it leverages the available monitoring capacity efficiently by avoiding redundant measurements; and it naturally load balances responsibilities to avoid hotspots.

The inputs to cSamp are the flow-level traffic matrix (approximate number of flows per OD-pair), router-level path(s) for each OD-pair, the resource constraints of routers, and an ISP's objective function specified in terms of the fractional flow coverages per OD-pair (i.e., the fraction of flows on this OD-pair that are logged). These input parameters are typically available to network operators [18]. The output is a set of *sampling manifests* specifying the monitoring responsibility of each router in the network. Each sampling manifest contains entries of the form $\langle OD, [start, end] \rangle$, where $[start, end] \subseteq [0, 1]$ denotes a hash range and OD is an identifier for an OD-pair. In the context of the FS algorithm, this means that the OD-pair identifier is used as the "key" to get a hash range from the sampling manifest.[5]

The main idea is to bootstrap routers with the same hash function but assign *non-overlapping* hash ranges per OD-pair. Thus, the flows sampled by different routers do not overlap. This coordination also makes it possible to optimally achieve network-wide flow coverage goals. Next, we describe the optimization model used in cSamp to assign FS responsibilities across a network.

Each OD-Pair OD_i ($i = 1, \ldots, M$) is characterized by its router-level path P_i and the estimated number T_i of IP-level flows per measurement epoch (e.g., five minutes).[6] Each router R_j is constrained by the available *memory* for maintaining flow counters. L_j captures this constraint, and denotes the number of flows router R_j can record and report per epoch. d_{ij} denotes the fraction of flows of OD_i that router R_j logs. For $i = 1, \ldots, M$, let C_i denote the fraction of flows on OD_i that is logged.

cSamp can support a variety of network-wide objectives. Here we describe its use for one particular goal: achieving the best flow coverage subject to maximizing the minimum fractional flow coverage per OD-pair. First, the largest possible minimum fractional coverage per OD-pair, $\min_i\{C_i\}$, subject to the resource constraints is found. Next, this value is used as the parameter α to the linear program shown below (in Eq (1)–(4)) and the total flow coverage $\sum_i (T_i \times C_i)$ is maximized, i.e.,

[3]Estan and Varghese use SH to track heavy hitters who contribute more than a fraction $\frac{1}{x}$ to the total traffic volume. In their proposal, p is set to $\frac{O \times x}{numpkts}$, where O is an oversampling factor [17]. Our configuration can be viewed as determining x and O from the memory budget L.

[4]We use packets and not flows since the SH configuration depends on the number of packets in the traffic. In practice, we need only approximate estimates to divide the available memory resources.

[5]This formulation assumes that routers in the middle of the network can infer the OD-pair from packet headers using MPLS labels or ingress-egress prefix maps [6]. cSamp can also be implemented without OD-pair identifiers [40]. For clarity, we describe the simpler approach using OD-pairs.

[6]For simplicity, we assume that each OD-pair has one route, though cSamp accommodates multi-path routing [39].

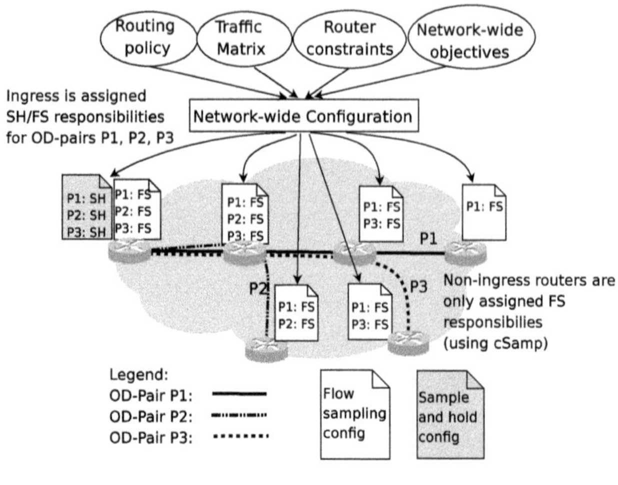

Figure 2: Overview of our network-wide approach

$$\text{Maximize} \sum_i (T_i \times C_i), \quad \text{subject to}$$

$$\forall j, \quad \sum_{i:R_j \in P_i} (d_{ij} \times T_i) \leq L_j \quad (1)$$

$$\forall i, \quad C_i = \sum_{j:R_j \in P_i} d_{ij} \quad (2)$$

$$\forall i, \forall j, \quad d_{ij} \geq 0 \quad (3)$$

$$\forall i, \quad \alpha \leq C_i \leq 1 \quad (4)$$

The rationale behind this objective is as follows. Maximizing the minimum coverage provides *fairness* in allocating resources across OD-pairs. Since it is hard to ascertain which OD-pairs might show interesting traffic patterns, allocating resources fairly is a reasonable choice. Given a fair allocation, we use the residual resources *efficiently* to achieve maximum aggregate coverage. The optimal solution $d^* = \{d^*_{ij}\}$ to this optimization problem is then translated into the *sampling manifests* specifying the FS responsibilities for each router.

Example configuration: Figure 2 shows how the different components are combined in the network-wide case. There are three OD-pairs P1, P2, and P3 originating at the left-most router. We envision a configuration module at the network operations center which disseminates configurations to the routers. This module takes into account the prevailing network conditions, routing policies, router constraints, and the flow monitoring objectives to generate the FS and SH configurations for each router. In the example, the ingress router is assigned SH responsibilities for P1, P2, and P3. The non-ingress routers are not assigned any SH responsibilities for these OD-pairs. (The other edge routers could be assigned SH responsibilities for OD-pairs for which they are the origin, but these are not shown.) The FS responsibilities are generated using cSamp. Each router is assigned FS responsibilities only for the paths of OD-pairs on which it lies, and these are specified as non-overlapping hash ranges per OD-pair.

5. EVALUATION METHODOLOGY

Our goal is to compare the minimalist design from the previous section against an application-specific architecture when both approaches are given the same total resource budget. In order to do so, we need to specify the different applications of interest, the corresponding application-specific algorithms, and the configurations for determining the resources provisioned for each algorithm.

First, we describe the different applications, the corresponding data streaming algorithms, and accuracy metrics in Section 5.1.

Application	Accuracy/Error Metric	Algorithm	Parameters (defaults)
FSD estimation (5-tuple)	WMRD	[26]	fsd (0.7)
Heavy hitter detection (5-tuple,sip,dip, sport,dport sip-dip)	Top-k detection rate	[17]	hh, k $(0.3, 50)$
Entropy estimation (5-tuple,sip, dip,sport,dport)	Relative Error	[30]	ϵ, δ $(0.5, 0.5)$
Superspreader detection	Detection accuracy	[41]	K, b, δ $(100, 4, 0.5)$
Change detection (sip,dip)	falsepos + falseneg	[25]	h, q, θ $(10, 1024, 0.05)$
Deg. histogram estimation	JS-divergence	[44]	–

Table 1: Summary of applications, accuracy metrics, algorithms, and default parameters. The parentheses in the first column specify the flowkey(s) for the application (e.g., FSD uses 5-tuple; heavy-hitter has six flowkeys). fsd and hh are expressed as a fraction of the number of distinct IP flows per epoch. ϵ, δ denote error tolerances. K, b means that any IP contacting $\geq K$ distinct IPs is a superspreader and any IP contacting $\leq \frac{K}{b}$ distinct destinations is a false positive. h is the number of hash functions and q is the number of counters per hash function in the sketch data structure, and θ is the change detection threshold.

Then, in Section 5.2, we describe how we normalize the resource usage of the minimalist and application-specific algorithms. We explain our assumptions and justify why these are conservative in that we underestimate the performance of an equivalently provisioned minimalist approach. Finally, in Section 5.3, we describe the configuration parameters for the different algorithms and the estimation phase for the minimalist approach in Section 5.4.

5.1 Applications and Accuracy Metrics

We pick a set of diverse monitoring applications that span the spectrum of traffic engineering, security, and anomaly detection tasks of interest to network operators. Table 1 summarizes the applications and the corresponding application-specific algorithms, accuracy metrics, and configuration parameters. The table also shows the default parameters we use in each case.

Flow size distribution (FSD) estimation: Let F denote the total number of flows in a traffic stream and F_l be the number of flows of size l pkts per flow. The FSD estimation problem is to determine $\forall l = 1 \ldots z, \phi_l = \frac{F_l}{F}$, where z is the largest flow size. Understanding the FSD is useful for many management tasks such as estimating gains from caches, configuring flow-switched networks, attack detection, and traffic matrix estimation [15, 26]. We use the data streaming and expectation-maximization algorithm proposed by Kumar et al. [26]. (We choose this because Kumar et al. show that their approach is significantly better than prior approaches based purely on packet sampling [15].)

The accuracy metric for FSD estimation is the weighted mean relative difference (*WMRD*) between the true FSD $\{F_l\}$ and the estimated FSD $\{\hat{F}_l\}$ [26]. The WMRD is defined as $\frac{\sum_l |F_l - \hat{F}_l|}{\sum_l \frac{F_l + \hat{F}_l}{2}}$.

Heavy-hitter detection: The goal here is to identify the top k items (e.g., srcip, srcport) with the most traffic volume. These are used by operators to understand application patterns and resource hogs, as well as for traffic engineering and accounting.

We use the SH algorithm [17] described earlier. We configure it to run with six instances, one each for the following flowkeys: source port, destination port, source address, destination address, 5-tuple, and source-destination address pairs. The accuracy metric is the *top-k detection rate* – the set intersection between the exact top-k and estimated top-k heavy hitters. Our minimalist approach also uses SH; the main difference is that we use only one instance of SH that runs at the 5-tuple granularity and use offline projections to determine heavy hitters for the other flowkeys.

Entropy estimation: The entropy of traffic distributions (e.g., distribution of pkts per dstport) is useful for anomaly detection [29] and traffic classification [43]. In particular, entropy-based analysis captures fine-grained properties that cannot be obtained with just volume-based analysis. The entropy of a random variable X is $H(X) = -\sum_{i=1}^{N} Pr(x_i)\log_2(Pr(x_i))$, where $x_1, \ldots, x_N$ is the range of values for X, and $Pr(x_i)$ is the probability that X takes the value x_i. It is useful to normalize the entropy between zero and one as $H_{norm}(X) = \frac{H(X)}{\log_2(N_0)}$, where N_0 is the number of distinct x_i values observed in a given measurement epoch [29].

We use the data streaming algorithm proposed by Lall et al. [30]. We consider five distributions: 5-tuple, src port, dst port, src address, and dst address. The accuracy metric is *relative error* — if the actual value is H_{norm} and the estimated value is $\hat{H}_{norm}$, the relative error is $\frac{|H_{norm} - \hat{H}_{norm}|}{H_{norm}}$.

Superspreader detection: Security applications like scan, worm, and botnet detection need to detect "superspreaders" - source IPs that contact a large number of distinct destination IPs. Note that this is different from heavy-hitter detection; we want to find sources talking to many *unique* destinations rather than sources generating a large volume of traffic.

We use the one-level superspreader detection algorithm proposed by Venkataraman et al. [41]. The algorithm has three parameters K, b, and δ; the goal is to detect all hosts that contact $\geq K$ distinct destinations with probability $\geq 1 - \delta$, and guarantee that a source that contacts $\leq \frac{K}{b}$ distinct destinations is reported with probability $\leq \delta$. The accuracy metric is the *detection accuracy*: the number of true superspreaders detected. (For brevity, we do not report the false positive rate since it was zero for the minimalist and application-specific approaches in almost all cases.)

Change detection: Change detection is used to detect DDoS attacks, flash crowds, and worms [25]. At a high-level, the goal is to detect IP addresses or ports whose behavior deviates significantly from some expected behavior based on a history-based forecast model. The problem can be formally described as follows.

Suppose we bin a traffic stream into measurement epochs ($t = 1, 2, \ldots$). Let $I_t = \beta_1, \beta_2, \ldots$ be the input traffic stream for epoch t. Each packet β_i is associated with a flowkey y_i and a count c_i (e.g., #bytes or just 1 if we are counting packets). $Obs_y(t) = \sum_{i:y_i=y} c_i$ denotes the aggregate count for flowkey y in epoch t. Let $Fcast_y(t)$ denote the forecast value (e.g., using exponentially weighted moving average, EWMA) for item y in epoch t. The forecast error for y then is $Err_y(t) = Obs_y(t) - Fcast_y(t)$. $F2Err_t = \sum_y Err_y(t)^2$ is the second moment of the forecast errors. The goal is to detect all ys with $Err_y(t) \geq \theta \times \sqrt{F2Err_t}$, where θ is a user-defined threshold. We define the *change detection accuracy* as the sum of the false positive (flowkeys whose volume did not change significantly but were incorrectly reported) and false negative rates (flowkeys that changed but were not reported).

We use the sketch-based change detection algorithm proposed by Krishnamurthy et al. [25] as sketches have a natural "linearity" property that makes them well-suited for change detection. We use an EWMA model $Fcast(t) = \gamma Obs(t) + (1 - \gamma)Fcast(t-1)$, with $\gamma = 0.9$. Note that since we are only interested in the relative performance of the minimalist vs. sketch-based approaches, the specific forecast model we use is not important. We consider two instances to identify changes in (1) the number of packets per source address and (2) the number of packets per destination address.

Degree histogram estimation: The outdegree d of a source IP is the number of distinct IPs it contacts in a measurement epoch. We construct the degree histogram as follows. For bucket i, let m_i denote the number of sources with outdegree d such that $2^i \leq d \leq 2^{i+1} - 1$. The goal is to estimate these m_i values. A specific application is to detect botnets involved in coordinated scans [44] by detecting changes in the outdegree histogram. The outdegree distribution is independently useful for understanding traffic structure. We use the sampling algorithm proposed by Gao et al. [44]. Given the exact distribution $\{m_1, m_2, \ldots\}$ and an estimated distribution $\{\hat{m}_1, \hat{m}_2, \ldots\}$, we use the *Jensen-Shannon (JS) divergence* between the two distributions as the accuracy metric.[7]

5.2 Assumptions and Justification

In order to compare the minimalist and application-specific approaches, we need to normalize their total resource footprints. We discuss our assumptions along three dimensions: hardware implementation, processing requirements, and memory use. We justify why our specific assumptions are *conservative* in that they underestimate the performance of our minimalist approach.

Hardware feasibility: We assume that both the application-specific algorithms and the minimalist primitives have feasible implementations that can operate at line rates. Some application-specific algorithms require a simple array of counters (e.g., [25, 44]), while others (e.g., [17, 30, 41]) and the minimalist primitives FS, SH [21, 17] involve key-value data structures. Previous work has demonstrated that it is possible to efficiently implement such key-value data structures in routers [20, 37, 31].

Processing requirements: There are two processing components: online collection and offline computation. By construction, the online collection overhead of the minimalist approach is lower. In the application-specific architecture, each packet requires as many counter updates as the number of application instances. (Further, each different flowkey for heavy-hitter detection, entropy estimation, and change detection requires separate updates.) With the minimalist approach, each packet requires only two updates, one for FS and one for SH.

We currently run estimation algorithms on the collected flow data without further sampling. Thus, the offline processing cost of the minimalist approach could be higher because the application-specific schemes only need to process compact summaries. We believe that offline processing costs are not a serious issue, given the costs/capabilities of commodity hardware today. That said, our

[7] Gao et al. [44] use the Kullback-Leibler (KL) divergence. However, it is not always well-defined. The JS divergence is based on KL divergence, but is always well-defined.

estimation procedures can be augmented with additional directed sampling, if necessary, to reduce the offline compute cost.

Memory consumption: For FS and SH, the flow record (the IP 5-tuple and other meta-data) need not be maintained in SRAM; these can be offloaded to DRAM. Only the counters tracking the byte or packet counts need to be in SRAM [31].

In terms of data structures, the above monitoring algorithms use either counter arrays or key-value structures. For example, FS and SH maintain key-value pairs, whereas sketch and FSD algorithms use a simple array of counters. In general, key-value structures use more memory than counter arrays. In order to normalize the resource consumption across the minimalist and application-specific approaches, we assume that each flow counter (i.e., the key-value pair) for the minimalist approach uses 4× the memory required by a counter used in the application-specific approaches. For example, if we have an aggregate SRAM capacity of 20000 bytes and each packet counter requires 2 bytes of SRAM, the application-specific approach can keep 10000 per-flow counters whereas the minimalist approach can only have 2500 per-flow counters. We justify why this 4× factor is *conservative*.

1. Each counter for the application-specific algorithms is typically at least 2 bytes [46]. We ran experiments with a sparse hash data structure [19] and found that it can store 10^6 flow counters in 8 MB, i.e., 8 bytes per counter. In other words, a *commodity, software only* implementation of a key-value structure uses only $\frac{8}{2} = 4\times$ the memory required by an array of counters.
2. Some of the application-specific algorithms (e.g., entropy estimation, heavy hitter detection) also require key-value style counters. We conservatively assume that these incur no overhead compared to an array of counters. That is, if each entry in a counter array is 2 bytes, we assume that it takes 8 bytes to store one key-value pair for the minimalist primitives but only 2 bytes to store one key-value pair for the application-specific algorithms.
3. With smarter hardware for storing flow counters such as counter braids [31], the memory requirement of the minimalist approach will be even lower. For example, maintaining 1 million flow counters using counter braids only requires 1.4 MB of memory, i.e., an effective overhead $\frac{1.4}{2}\times \ll 4\times$.

Summarizing the above discussion, we see that: the hardware requirements of our primitives are similar to the application-specific algorithms; the online processing overhead of the minimalist approach is strictly lower; and the minimalist primitives have at most a 4× memory overhead. Thus, for the rest of the paper, we only consider the conservative 4× memory overhead to generate an equivalent resource configuration for the minimalist approach. In other words, given the same amount of available SRAM the minimalist algorithms can only maintain one-fourth as many flow counters as the application-specific approach.

5.3 Configuring the different algorithms

Application-specific case: To configure the different algorithms, we follow the guidelines and recommended parameters from the literature:

1. The FSD estimation algorithm uses an array of $fsd \times F$ counters, where F is the number of distinct flows in a measurement interval. Following the guidelines of Kumar et al. [26], we set $fsd = 0.7$.
2. We configure the heavy-hitter detection algorithm with $hh \times F$ counters with $hh = 0.3$, divide these equally among the six instances, and focus on the top-50 detection rate.
3. The entropy estimation algorithm is an (ϵ, δ) approximation, i.e., the relative error is at most ϵ with probability at least $1-\delta$. The number of counters it uses increases as we require tighter guarantees (lower ϵ and δ). However, Lall et al. [30] show that in practice it works well even with loose bounds. Thus, we set $\epsilon = \delta = 0.5$.
4. For superspreader detection, we set $K = 100$ and $b = 4$. Again, since loose bounds work well in practice, we set $\delta = 0.5$.
5. The sketch data structure has three parameters: h, the number of hash functions; q, the size of the counter array per hash function; and the detection threshold θ. Following Krishnamurthy et al. [25], we set $h = 10$, $q = 1024$, and $\theta = 0.05$.
6. For degree histogram estimation, we use the same configuration as Gao et al. [44].

Minimalist case: The minimalist approach has two configuration parameters: the number of flow records it can collect (L) and, for ingress routers, the FS-SH split (f). To determine L, we configure the application-specific algorithms using the above guidelines. For each trace, we measure the total number of counters used across the different application-specific algorithms and scale it *down* by a factor of 4 as discussed earlier to calculate the value of L to be used for that setup. We set $f = 0.8$, giving 80% of the resources on each router to the FS component.

5.4 Estimation phase in minimalist approach

The estimation phase for the minimalist approach is conceptually simple. Since we have the actual flow records (i.e., the 5-tuples along with the packet counts), we can run exact estimation algorithms. For example, we can compute the flow size distribution of the reported flows and use that as our estimate of the true flow size distribution. Similarly, we can compute the observed (normalized) entropy of different flowkey combinations from the reported flows and use it as the estimate of the true (normalized) entropy.

The only issue is how to use the flow reports from the FS and SH components for the different estimation tasks. We use the following heuristic. First, we take the union of the flow records reported by SH (after normalizing packet counts by the sampling rate [17]) and the flow records reported by FS.[8] We compute the FSD and entropy, and detect heavy hitters or changes per-source (or destination), on this merged set of flow records. Second, we use the set of flow records reported by FS for detecting superspreaders and to compute the outdegree histogram. Again, we note that our procedures for merging the flow reports from the FS and SH components for various estimation tasks are only heuristics and may not be optimal. Finding the optimal estimator for specific application-level metrics from a given set of collection primitives is an interesting direction of future work.

Note that the minimalist approach exports the actual flow records. Thus, it is possible to run any estimation procedure on these flow records to compute any application metric, even unforeseen ones.

[8] If the same flow is reported by both FS and SH, we use the FS record because the packet count in FS is exact.

Trace	Description	Avg # pkts (millions)	Avg # flows (thousands)
Caida 2003	OC-48, large ISP	6	400
Univ-2	UNC, 2003	2.5	91
Univ-1	USC, 2004	1.6	93
Caida 2007-2	OC-12	1.3	45
Caida 2007-1	OC-12	0.7	30

Table 2: Traces used in the single router experiments; averages are over 5-minute epochs

6. TRACE-DRIVEN EVALUATION

In this section, we compare the minimalist approach against the different application-specific algorithms using packet and flow-level traces collected from different settings. We start with a single router evaluation and then proceed to a network-wide evaluation.

6.1 Single Router Case

Using trace-driven evaluations, we answer the following questions:

- How does the accuracy of the minimalist approach compare with the application-specific approaches when configured with the aggregate memory used by the application-specific algorithms? (Section 6.1.1)
- How sensitive is individual application performance to the amount of memory available to the minimalist approach? (Section 6.1.2)
- How does the success of the minimalist approach depend on the set of application-specific algorithms that are implemented on the router (we call this an *application portfolio*)? That is, when does it make sense to adopt a minimalist approach instead of implementing each application-specific alternative? (Section 6.1.3)
- How should we split resources between FS and SH? (Section 6.1.4)

Table 2 summarizes the five different one-hour packet header traces (binned into 5-minute epochs) used for the single-router evaluation.

6.1.1 Accuracy: minimalist vs. application-specific

We use the default parameters from Table 1 and run the minimalist approach configured with the total normalized memory used by the six algorithms. Then we compute the relative accuracy difference for each application. Let $Acc_{specific}$ denote the accuracy of the application-specific algorithm and let $Acc_{minimalist}$ denote the accuracy of the minimalist approach for that application. The *relative accuracy difference* is $\frac{Acc_{minimalist} - Acc_{specific}}{Acc_{specific}}$. By construction, a positive value indicates that the accuracy of the minimalist approach is better; a negative value indicates otherwise.[9]

All the algorithms are inherently randomized; we present the results over five independent runs with different seeds. Figure 3 shows the relative accuracy difference using a box-and-whiskers plot for the different traces. Each box shows the 25%ile, median, and 75%ile values. The whiskers extend to the most extreme data points not considered outliers. This corresponds to a length of at most 1.5× the difference between the 25%ile and 75%ile values.

The result shows that the median value of this metric is positive in most cases; i.e., the minimalist approach outperforms the application-specific alternative in most applications. Further, even the 25%ile is positive in many cases; i.e., the minimalist approach consistently outperforms the application-specific approaches. Only in heavy-hitter detection (Figure 3(b)) does the minimalist approach perform worse; even then the median accuracy gap is at most 0.08. This result gives a high-level answer to the second challenge from Section 3:

The minimalist approach provisioned with the total resources used by the six applications performs better than or comparable to the application-specific approaches.

We now proceed to answer to two natural questions: (a) what if we consider each application class in isolation and (b) what types of application portfolios does the minimalist approach perform favorably in. For brevity, we only present the results from the Caida 2003 trace.

6.1.2 Application Sensitivity

In the following experiments, we try 2-3 configurations for each application-specific algorithm. For each configuration, we consider a minimalist approach provisioned with G times as much memory as that used by the algorithm *in isolation*. For example, if the application-specific algorithm uses 10000 counters at 2 bytes/counter, the minimalist approach has $G \times 10000 \times 2$ bytes of SRAM.

As before, we focus on the relative accuracy difference between the minimalist and application-specific approach. Figure 4(a) plots the relative accuracy difference between the minimalist approach and the FSD estimation algorithm. We show three different configurations with the FSD algorithm using $fsd = 0.7$, 1, and 1.5. For some configurations (e.g., $fsd = 1.5$, $G = 1$), the minimalist approach performs worse. The large negative values of the metric result from the low WMRD values at these points. Since we normalize the difference by the WMRD of the application-specific case, the relative difference gets magnified. The absolute accuracy of the FSD algorithm improves (i.e., the WMRD goes down) as it is provisioned with more resources (not shown). For example, for the configuration $fsd = 1.5$ and $G = 1$, the WMRD for the FSD algorithm was 0.02 and the WMRD for the minimalist approach 0.05. Both values are small for many practical purposes [26].

Figure 4(b) shows similar results for heavy-hitter detection, with hh set to $0.3, 0.5$, and 0.7. For clarity, we average the relative accuracy difference across the six heavy-hitter instances. The minimalist approach is worse than the application-specific approach. However, as G increases, the accuracy gap closes significantly. One reason for the poor accuracy of the minimalist approach is that we configure the SH algorithm to operate at the 5-tuple granularity and then subsequently project results to other dimensions. In fact, the minimalist approach performs better if we only consider the 5-tuple granularity (Figure 3(b)). The relative accuracy for the other flowkeys is negative because the application-specific SH instances can directly determine heavy hitters without going through this projection step. We could also configure the SH algorithm in the minimalist approach to operate at multiple flowkeys. We trade-off a small reduction in accuracy for a significant reduction in online processing overhead complexity since we only need to run one instance of the SH algorithm instead of six instances.

Entropy estimation (Figure 4(c)) with $\epsilon = \delta$ set to 0.2 and 0.5 and superspreader detection (not shown) show similar trends. If we consider each application in isolation, the minimalist approach

[9]Some metrics denote "error" while others denote "accuracy". For error metrics (FSD, entropy, degree histogram, change detection) the relative accuracy as defined is negative when the minimalist approach performs better. For ease of presentation, we reverse the sign of the numerator in these cases.

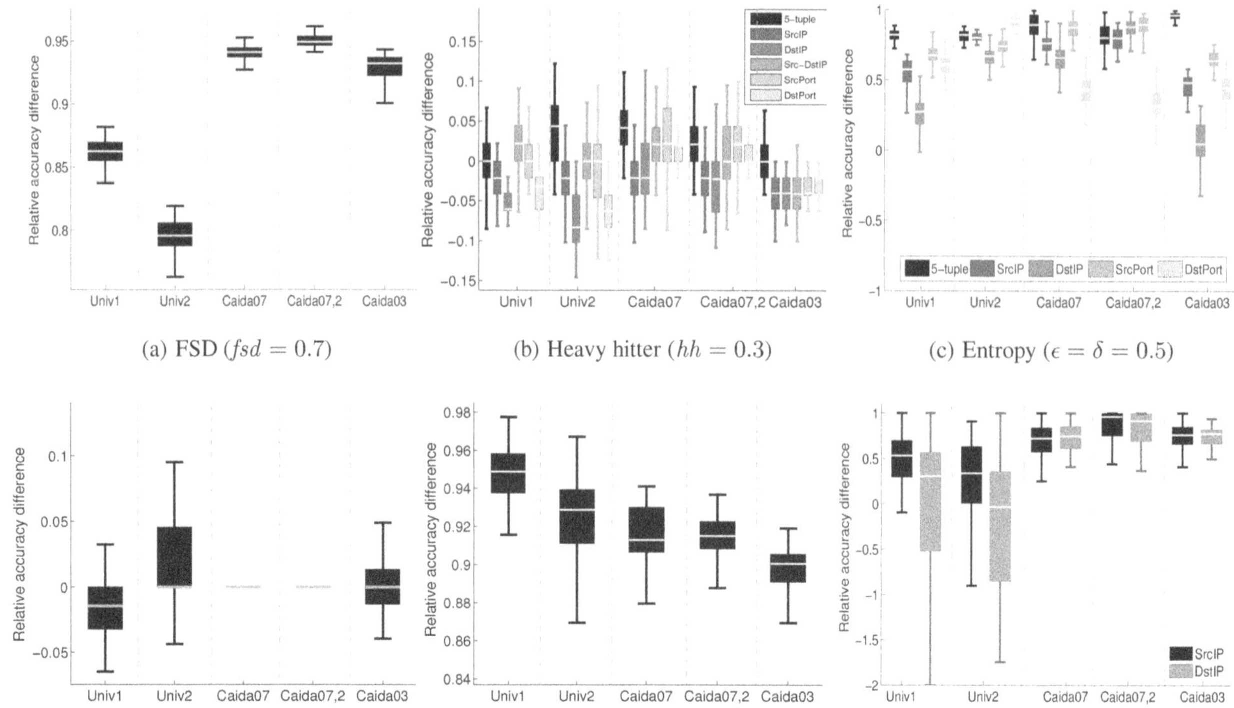

(a) FSD ($fsd = 0.7$) (b) Heavy hitter ($hh = 0.3$) (c) Entropy ($\epsilon = \delta = 0.5$)

(d) Superspreader (K, b, δ=100, 4, 0.5) (e) Degree histogram (f) Change Detection

Figure 3: Each result shows a box-whiskers plot with the median, 25%ile, 75%ile, and extreme values. A positive value on the y-axis means that the accuracy of the minimalist approach was better; a negative value indicates otherwise. For most applications, the minimalist approach outperforms the application-specific alternatives. In the cases where the performance is worse, it is only worse by a small relative margin.

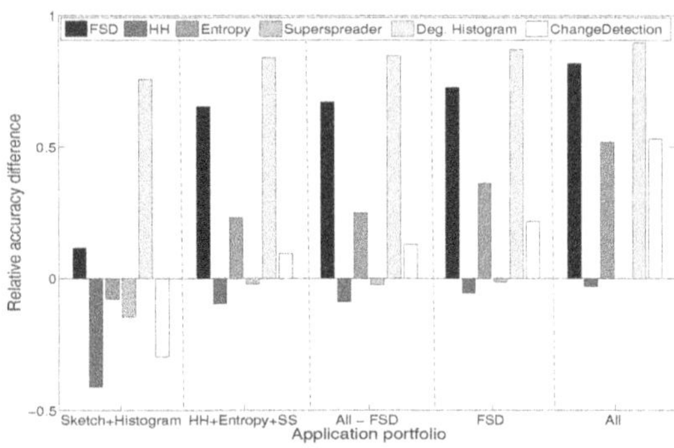

Figure 5: Effect of application portfolio on the relative accuracy difference. The portfolios are in increasing order of memory usage from left to right.

performs worse. But, the gap closes as G increases and the minimalist approach eventually outperforms the application-specific algorithm.

6.1.3 Sensitivity to Application Portfolio

Next, we evaluate the effect of varying the application portfolio. That is, we consider the case where the router implements only a subset of the six applications described earlier. For a fixed portfolio, we use the default configurations from Table 1 and run the minimalist approach configured with the aggregate resources contributed by only the applications within this portfolio. The relative accuracies are computed with respect to the default configurations for the different applications (even for those not in the portfolio). For example, the configuration labeled "Sketch + Histogram" uses resources only from sketch-based change detection and degree histogram estimation (the least resource-intensive applications). At the other extreme, the configuration labeled "All" uses the aggregate resources (as in Figure 3).

Figure 5 shows the portfolios in increasing order of memory usage. For clarity, we show averages across the different flowkeys for heavy-hitter detection, entropy estimation, and change detection. We observe two effects. First, for larger application portfolios (i.e., as the requirements of management applications increase), a minimalist approach is actually a better alternative as the relative accuracy difference becomes positive for almost all applications. Second, if there are some resource-intensive applications (e.g., FSD estimation), then it is better to adopt a minimalist approach because it benefits all potential applications, even those not specified in the current application portfolio.

6.1.4 Split between FS and SH

So far, we fixed the FS-SH split to be $f = 0.8$. Figure 6 shows the effect of varying f. The x-axis is f, the fraction of resources allocated to FS. For most applications, increasing f improves the accuracy of the minimalist approach, but there is a diminishing returns effect. For heavy-hitter detection, as expected, giving more resources to SH helps, but the improvement is fairly gradual. In light of this, the 80-20 split is a reasonable tradeoff across the different application classes.

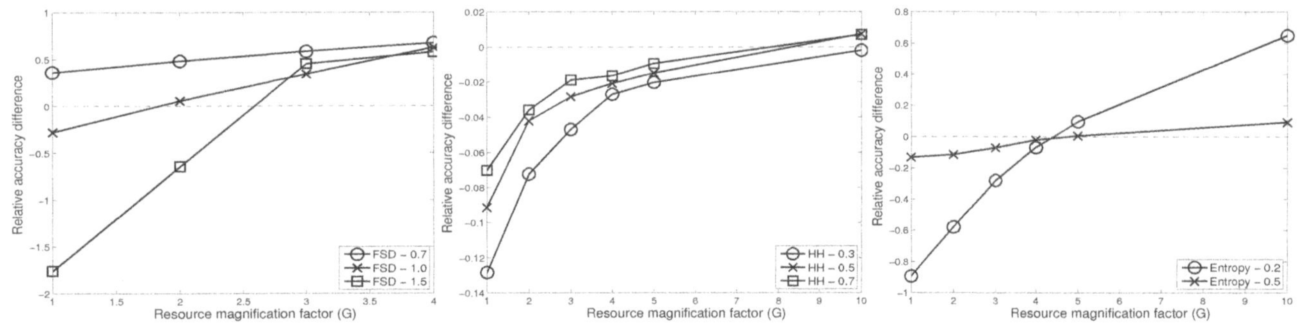

(a) FSD (b) Heavy hitter (c) Entropy

Figure 4: Exploring the sensitivity of applications in isolation. The zero line represents the point at which the minimalist approach starts to outperform the application-specific approach. The resource magnification factor captures the sharing effect of aggregating resources across applications.

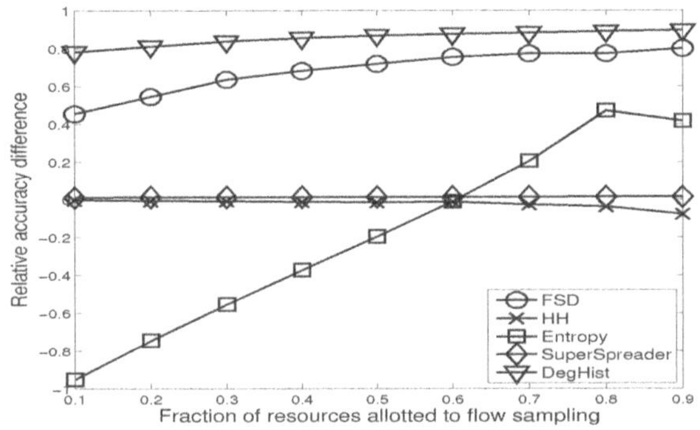

Figure 6: Varying the split between FS and SH

6.2 Network-wide evaluation

Dataset and Setup: We use a one-hour snapshot of flow data collected across eleven routers from the Internet2 backbone. There are roughly 1.4 million distinct flows and 9.5 million packets in aggregate per 5-minute interval. We map each flow entry to the corresponding network ingress and egress points [18]. Unlike the packet traces used earlier, these are flow records with sampled packet counts (with 1-in-100 sampling). We assume that the sampled flow records represent the actual traffic and use the sampled counts as the actual packet counts. Also, IP-addresses in the dataset are anonymized by zero-ing out the last 11 bits. We treat each anonymized IP as a unique IP. Thus, the entropy and outdegree measures are computed at this granularity. Since we are only interested in the *relative* performance, this dataset is still valuable for understanding network-wide effects.

In a network-wide setting, operators often want to compute the different traffic metrics such as FSD, entropy, heavy hitters, etc., over multiple *spatial views* [22, 43, 45, 29]. For example, we might want to understand traffic patterns on a per-ingress basis, or a per OD-pair basis, or over the entire network.

As such, we configure the application-specific algorithms on a per-ingress basis. That is, at each node, we run these algorithms only on packets originating from this node and ignore transit or terminating traffic. (In this topology, each node is an ingress for some traffic and there are no pure transit nodes that do not originate any traffic.) For example, the FSD algorithm at ATLA estimates the FSD for the traffic originating at ATLA and the superspreader algorithm at ATLA tracks only the source IPs that originate traffic at ATLA.

From this configuration, we obtain the total memory usage at each node by the application-specific algorithms. The coordinated minimalist approach from Section 4 operates on a per OD-pair granularity using this equivalent per-router memory (after scaling it down by the $4\times$ normalization factor). Given the flow records reported for each OD-pair, we estimate the traffic metrics over three spatial views: per-ingress, per-OD, and network-wide.

Per-ingress results: Figure 7 shows, for each ingress, the relative accuracy difference between the coordinated minimalist approach and the application-specific algorithms configured per ingress. Recall that a positive value indicates that the accuracy of the minimalist approach was better; a negative value indicates otherwise. As with the single router evaluation, we see that the minimalist approach outperforms the application-specific algorithms, except in heavy-hitter detection. (SNVA looks different from the others in the magnitude of the relative accuracy metric, but not in the qualitative sense that the minimalist approach is still better. While we have not been able to conclusively explain this observation, we noticed that the traffic volumes for SNVA were an order of magnitude lower than the rest. We suspect that this as a potential cause for the anomalous behavior.)

One potential concern is the high variability in the relative accuracy in some cases (e.g., DNVR and SNVA in Figure 7(c)). In each of these cases, we analyzed the raw accuracy values and found that the variability in fact comes from the application-specific case. That is, the accuracy of the minimalist approach has low variance, but the application-specific case can have a higher variance.[10]

Network-wide result: Next, we consider the application metrics on a *network-wide* basis. As a point of comparison, we consider an *uncoordinated minimalist* approach. Here, each node has the same resources as the coordinated case, but independently runs FS and SH on the traffic it sees.

Given the per-ingress results for the application-specific algorithms obtained earlier, we compute network-wide estimates by merging the reports from each ingress. While computing the network-wide FSD and the outdegree histogram, we need to normalize the per-ingress outputs by the number of flows and source IPs seen at each ingress. For example, to obtain the network-wide FSD, we take each per-ingress FSD and normalize it by the number of flows originating at that ingress. (One concern with merging per-ingress results to get the network-wide distributions is the risk of "double

[10]The high variance in the application-specific case is not an inherent flaw — the variance decreases with more memory. But as Figure 5 shows, adding a few memory-intensive applications makes the case for the minimalist approach stronger.

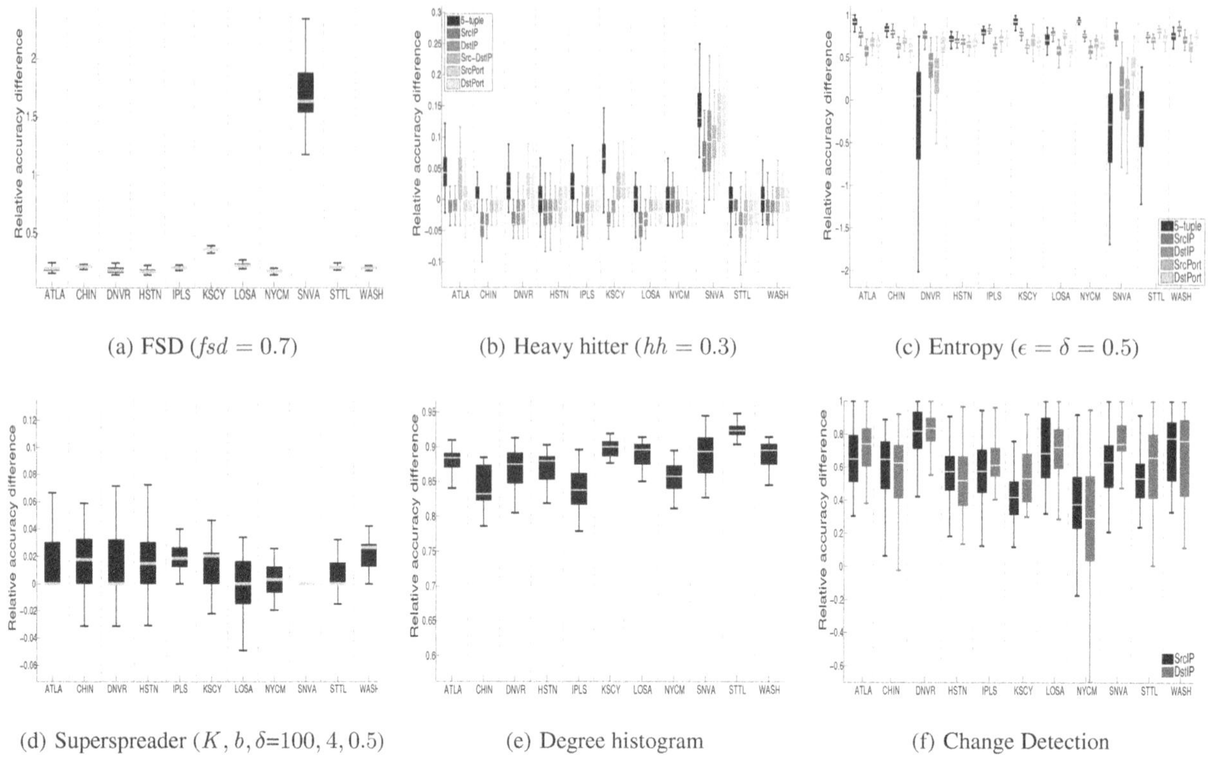

(a) FSD ($fsd = 0.7$)

(b) Heavy hitter ($hh = 0.3$)

(c) Entropy ($\epsilon = \delta = 0.5$)

(d) Superspreader (K, b, δ=100, 4, 0.5)

(e) Degree histogram

(f) Change Detection

Figure 7: Result showing the relative accuracy difference between the coordinated minimalist approach and the application-specific algorithms per ingress router (denoted by the abbreviated city names of the PoPs in the Internet2 backbone). A positive value indicates that the accuracy of the minimalist approach was better; a negative value indicates otherwise.

Application (error metric)	App Specific	Uncoord minimalist	Coord minimalist
FSD (WMRD)	0.16	0.19	0.02
Heavy hitter (miss rate)	0.02	0.3	0.04
Entropy (relative error)	n/a	0.03	0.02
Superspreader (miss rate)	0.02	0.04	0.009
Deg. histogram (JS)	0.15	0.03	0.02

Table 3: Absolute error for network-wide metrics. Lower values imply better performance.

counting" some flows or sources. Because the per-ingress setup implicitly partitions the network-wide traffic into non-overlapping subsets, we can simply merge reports from the different ingresses for each application without worrying about double counting.) However, we cannot estimate the network-wide entropy from the per-ingress entropy values as this does not give us sufficient information. For the coordinated approach, we simply take the union of the flow records obtained for each OD-pair and run the estimation procedures on this merged set of the flow records. The estimation step for the uncoordinated case proceeds similarly, but needs additional processing to remove duplicate flow reports.

Table 3 compares the application-specific, uncoordinated, and coordinated approaches for the network-wide case in terms of the *absolute error* values. (The entropy row is empty for the application-specific column because of the aforementioned reason.) There are two main observations. First, the coordinated approach has the lowest error overall. The benefits of coordination are particularly significant for the heavy-hitter and FSD estimation applications. Second, while the uncoordinated approach provides some generality (e.g., it can also provide per OD-pair estimates whereas the per-ingress application-specific algorithms cannot), it performs worse in this evaluation. One reason is that the per-ingress application-specific algorithms are implicitly coordinated and avoid ambiguity/biases when we merge the results for the network-wide case. The uncoordinated minimalist approach does not have this property and multiple sources of ambiguity/bias arise when we merge flow reports from multiple routers: (i) different routers may have different sampling rates as they see different traffic volumes, (ii) flows traversing longer paths get higher sampling probabilities, and (iii) large flows are reported multiple times by SH. An additional practical benefit of the coordinated approach is that the merging and estimation algorithms are simpler and more accurate.

Per OD-pair results: Finally, we consider the different application metrics on a *per OD-pair* basis. Note that the application-specific alternatives as configured cannot provide per OD-pair results. They work at a coarse per-ingress level and we cannot compute the application metrics on a more fine-grained per-OD basis. Again, this is not an inherent limitation of application-specific approaches; we can also configure them on a per-OD basis. However, this significantly increases the complexity since we need an instance per application per OD-pair. Thus, we only consider the minimalist approaches for this result.

Figure 8 shows four application metrics for the per OD-pair case. Since superspreader detection and change detection are meaningful only when viewed across all OD-pairs, we do not consider these. Also, we focus on the top-10 heavy hitters per OD-pair. The CDFs show that the coordinated approach performs well across most OD-pairs. The 80th percentile of the WMRD, heavy-hitter miss rate,

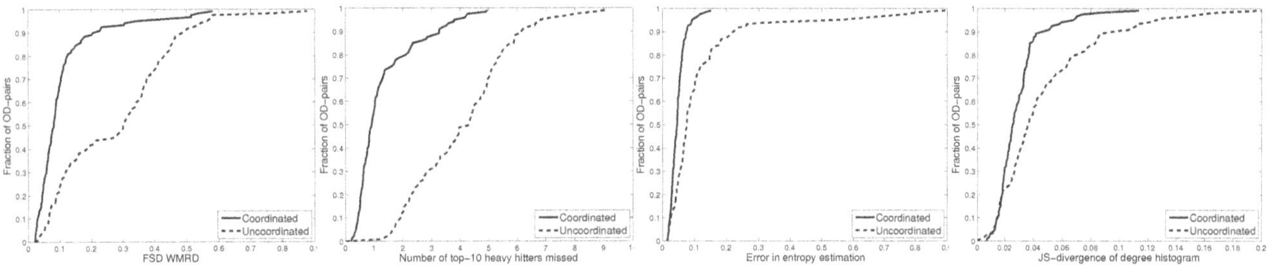

(a) FSD (b) Heavy hitter (c) Entropy (d) Degree histogram

Figure 8: Comparing the coordinated and uncoordinated approaches on a per-OD basis.

average relative error in entropy estimation, and JS-divergence for the degree histogram are $0.1, 2, 0.05$, and 0.03 respectively. The corresponding results for the uncoordinated case are $0.4, 5, 0.15$, and 0.06. Further, the OD-pairs where the coordinated approach has poor accuracy have low traffic volume (not shown), which indicates that it performs very well for the dominant traffic patterns. The results for network-wide and per OD-pair views demonstrate the benefits of a systematic coordinated approach for network-wide monitoring.

6.3 Summary of main results

- The accuracy of the minimalist approach configured with the aggregate resources used by the six different applications is better than or comparable to the application-specific approaches.
- With large application portfolios or if there are one or more resource-intensive applications in the portfolio, there is a clear win for a minimalist approach vs. application-specific approaches.
- A 80-20 split between FS and SH is a reasonable tradeoff across the spectrum of applications.
- In a network-wide setting, a coordinated minimalist approach provides more flexibility and better accuracy while projecting results to different spatial views compared to uncoordinated and application-specific approaches.

7. DISCUSSION

Bandwidth overhead: In the application-specific architecture, each router only reports summary estimates of the various traffic metrics (e.g., FSD, entropy). Thus the bandwidth overhead for aggregating these reports is negligible. A practical concern with our proposal is the bandwidth overhead for transferring flow records to a logically centralized collector. We give a back-of-the-envelope calculation to estimate the worst-case overhead. The Internet2 dataset has roughly 1.7GB of 1-in-100 packet-sampled flow data per PoP per day. This conservatively translates into 170 GB per PoP per day or 0.6GB per PoP per five minutes for full flow capture. (This is conservative because we are normalizing the number of flows by the packet sampling rate.) Suppose, we collect this data every five minutes with a near real-time requirement that the data be sent before the start of the next five-minute interval. The bandwidth per PoP required for full flow capture would be $\frac{0.6 \times 8 \text{ Gbits}}{300 \text{ seconds}} = 0.016$ Gbps. Given OC-192 backbone line rates of 10 Gbps today, it is not unreasonable to expect ISPs to use $\ll 1\%$ of the network bandwidth per PoP for measurement traffic to aid network management.

Adaptation: Another natural question is how does our minimalist approach deal with network dynamics. Estan et al. [16] and Keys et al. [23] have in-depth discussions on how to adapt the sampling rates for packet sampling, FS, and SH to changing traffic conditions. Our previous work discusses how cSamp can adapt to network dynamics [39]. We can leverage these existing techniques to make the minimalist approach robust to network dynamics.

Beyond monitoring 5-tuples: Some settings require more fine-grained monitoring capabilities that look beyond flow-level statistics. These include analyzing end-to-end performance metrics (e.g., loss, throughput, latency), deep packet inspection for signature matching, and on-demand analysis (e.g., analyze hosts that show specific patterns). Our minimalist primitives as described in this paper do not provide these capabilities. However, we believe that the broad principles underlying a minimalist approach will still apply and assume more importance with more complex monitoring requirements. One possible solution is to include other flexible primitives that provide such capabilities [10, 45] in the minimalist framework.

8. CONCLUSIONS

This paper is a reflection on recent trends in network monitoring. There is a growing demand for estimating a wide variety of traffic metrics to support different network management applications. The inadequacy of current packet-sampling-based solutions has given rise to a proliferation of many application-specific algorithms, each catering to a narrow application.

In contrast to these application-specific alternatives, we revisit the case for a minimalist architecture for flow monitoring. Such an architecture dramatically reduces router complexity and enables router vendors to focus their energies on building efficient implementations of a small number of primitives. Further it allows late binding to what traffic metrics are important, thus insulating router implementations from the changing needs of flow monitoring applications.

We demonstrated a proof-of-concept minimalist approach that combines flow sampling, sample-and-hold, and cSamp. We showed that this approach performs favorably across a wide spectrum of applications compared to application-specific approaches. Our proposal is by no means "optimal" or the final word in this problem space — the goal of this paper was to demonstrate the *feasibility* of a minimalist approach. In this respect, there are three avenues for future work: (i) developing better minimalist primitives, (ii) designing estimation algorithms that optimally leverage the data collected across different primitives, and (iii) providing formal models to reason about application requirements and performance. We hope that our work motivates further research in these directions.

Acknowledgments

We thank Ramana Kompella, Jeff Pang, and Amar Phanishayee for their feedback on this work. We would also like to thank Abhishek Kumar and Jim Xu for sharing their implementation of the FSD estimation algorithm. This work was supported in part by the National Science Foundation under grant numbers ANI-0331653, CNS-0756998, and CNS-0433540, the U.S. Army Research Office under grant number DAAD190210389.

9. REFERENCES

[1] Flexible Netflow. http://www.cisco.com/en/US/products/ps6965/products_ios_protocol_option_home.html,.

[2] Juniper cflowd. http://www.juniper.net/techpubs/software/junos/junos91/swconfig-policy/cflowd.html.

[3] Narus Intercept Solution. http://www.narus.com/index.php/solutions/intercept.

[4] NetFlow Input Filters. http://www.cisco.com/en/US/docs/ios/12_3t/12_3t4/feature/guide/gtnfinpf.html.

[5] Packet Sampling, IETF Working Group Charter. http://www.ietf.org/html.charters/psamp/charter/.

[6] K. Argyraki, P. Maniatis, O. Irzak, S. Ashish, and S. Shenker. Loss and Delay Accountability for the Internet. In *Proc. ICNP*, 2007.

[7] D. Brauckhoff, B. Tellenbach, A. Wagner, A. Lakhina, and M. May. Impact of Traffic Sampling on Anomaly Detection Metrics. In *Proc. IMC*, 2006.

[8] C. Cranor, T. Johnson, O. Spatscheck, and V. Shkapenyuk. Gigascope: A stream database for network applications. In *Proc. ACM SIGMOD*, 2003.

[9] G. R. Cantieni, G. Iannaccone, C. Barakat, C. Diot, and P. Thiran. Reformulating the Monitor Placement problem: Optimal Network-Wide Sampling. In *Proc. CoNeXT*, 2006.

[10] L. D. Carli, Y. Pan, A. Kumar, C. Estan, and K. Sankaralingam. PLUG: Flexible Lookup Modules for Rapid Deployment of New Protocols in High-speed Routers. In *Proc. SIGCOMM*, 2010.

[11] B. Claise. Cisco Systems NetFlow Services Export Version 9. RFC 3954.

[12] M. P. Collins and M. K. Reiter. Finding Peer-to-Peer File-sharing using Coarse Network Behaviors. In *Proc. ESORICS*, 2006.

[13] G. Cormode and S. Muthukrishnan. An improved data stream summary: the count-min sketch and its applications. *Journal of Algorithms*, 55, 2005.

[14] N. Duffield, C. Lund, and M. Thorup. Charging from sampled network usage. In *Proc. IMW*, 2001.

[15] N. Duffield, C. Lund, and M. Thorup. Estimating Flow Distributions from Sampled Flow Statistics. In *Proc. of ACM SIGCOMM*, 2003.

[16] C. Estan, K. Keys, D. Moore, and G. Varghese. Building a Better NetFlow. In *Proc. ACM SIGCOMM*, 2004.

[17] C. Estan and G. Varghese. New Directions in Traffic Measurement and Accounting. In *Proc. ACM SIGCOMM*, 2002.

[18] A. Feldmann, A. G. Greenberg, C. Lund, N. Reingold, J. Rexford, and F. True. Deriving Traffic Demands for Operational IP Networks: Methodology and Experience. In *Proc. ACM SIGCOMM*, 2000.

[19] Google sparse hash project. http://code.google.com/p/google-sparsehash/.

[20] H. Song, S. Dharmapurikar, J. Turner, and J. Lockwood. Fast Hash Table Lookup Using Extended Bloom Filter: An Aid to Network Processing. In *Proc. ACM SIGCOMM*, 2005.

[21] N. Hohn and D. Veitch. Inverting Sampled Traffic. In *Proc. IMC*, 2003.

[22] T. Karagiannis, D. Papagiannaki, and M. Faloutsos. BLINC: Multilevel Traffic Classification in the Dark. In *Proc. ACM SIGCOMM*, 2005.

[23] K. Keys, D. Moore, and C. Estan. A Robust System for Accurate Real-time Summaries of Internet Traffic. In *Proc. SIGMETRICS*, 2005.

[24] R. Kompella and C. Estan. The Power of Slicing in Internet Flow Measurement. In *Proc. IMC*, 2005.

[25] B. Krishnamurthy, S. Sen, Y. Zhang, and Y. Chen. Sketch-based change detection: Methods, evaluation, and applications. In *Proc. ACM IMC*, 2003.

[26] A. Kumar, M. Sung, J. Xu, and J. Wang. Data Streaming Algorithms for Efficient and Accurate Estimation of Flow Distribution. In *Proc. ACM SIGMETRICS*, 2004.

[27] A. Kumar and J. Xu. Sketch Guided Sampling – Using On-Line Estimates of Flow Size for Adaptive Data Collection. In *Proc. IEEE Infocom*, 2006.

[28] A. Lakhina, M. Crovella, and C. Diot. Diagnosing Network-Wide Traffic Anomalies. In *Proc. ACM SIGCOMM*, 2004.

[29] A. Lakhina, M. Crovella, and C. Diot. Mining anomalies using traffic feature distributions. In *Proc. ACM SIGCOMM*, 2005.

[30] A. Lall, V. Sekar, J. Xu, M. Ogihara, and H. Zhang. Data Streaming Algorithms for Estimating Entropy of Network Traffic. In *Proc. ACM SIGMETRICS*, 2006.

[31] Y. Lu, A. Montanari, B. Prabhakar, S. Dharmapurikar, and A. Kabbani. Counter Braids: A Novel Counter Architecture for Per-Flow Measurement. In *Proc. SIGMETRICS*, 2008.

[32] M. P. Collins and M. K. Reiter. Hit-list Worm Detection and Bot Identification in Large Networks Using Protocol Graphs. In *Proc. RAID*, 2007.

[33] H. Madhyastha and B. Krishnamurthy. A Generic Language for Application-Specific Flow Sampling. *ACM CCR*, 38(2):7–15, Apr. 2008.

[34] J. Mai, C.-N. Chuah, A. Sridharan, T. Ye, and H. Zang. Is Sampled Data Sufficient for Anomaly Detection? In *Proc. IMC*, 2006.

[35] A. Ramachandran, S. Seetharaman, and N. Feamster. Fast Monitoring of Traffic Subpopulations. In *Proc. IMC*, 2008.

[36] B. Ribeiro, D. Towsley, T. Ye, and J. Bolot. Fisher information of sampled packets: an application to flow size estimation. In *Proc. IMC*, 2006.

[37] S. Kumar and P. Crowley. Segmented Hash: An Efficient Hash Table Implementation for High Performance Networking Subsystems. In *Proc. ACM ANCS*, 2005.

[38] V. Sekar, N. Duffield, K. van der Merwe, O. Spatscheck, and H. Zhang. LADS: Large-scale Automated DDoS Detection System. In *Proc. USENIX ATC*, 2006.

[39] V. Sekar, M. K. Reiter, W. Willinger, H. Zhang, R. Kompella, and D. G. Andersen. cSamp: A System for Network-Wide Flow Monitoring. In *Proc. NSDI*, 2008.

[40] V. Sekar, A. Gupta, M. K. Reiter and H. Zhang. Coordinated Sampling sans Origin-Destination Identifiers: Algorithms and Analysis. In *Proc. COMSNSETS*, 2010.

[41] S. Venkataraman, D. Song, P. B. Gibbons, and A. Blum. New Streaming Algorithms for Fast Detection of Superspreaders . In *Proc. NDSS*, 2005.

[42] Y. Xie, V. Sekar, D. A. Maltz, M. K. Reiter, and H. Zhang. Worm Origin Identification Using Random Moonwalks. In *Proc. IEEE Symposium on Security and Privacy*, 2005.

[43] K. Xu, Z.-L. Zhang, and S. Bhattacharya. Profiling Internet Backbone Traffic: Behavior Models and Applications. In *Proc. ACM SIGCOMM*, 2005.

[44] Y. Gao, Y. Zhao, R. Schweller, S. Venkataraman, Y. Chen, D. Song and M.-Y. Kao. Detecting Stealthy Attacks Using Online Histograms. In *Proc. IWQoS*, 2007.

[45] L. Yuan, C.-N. Chuah, and P. Mohapatra. ProgME: Towards Programmable Network MEasurement. In *Proc. SIGCOMM*, 2007.

[46] Q. Zhao, J. Xu, and Z. Liu. Design of a novel statistics counter architecture with optimal space and time efficiency. In *Proc. ACM SIGMETRICS*, 2006.

Exact Temporal Characterization of 10 Gbps Optical Wide-Area Network

Daniel A. Freedman[§‡], Tudor Marian[§], Jennifer H. Lee[†], Ken Birman[§], Hakim Weatherspoon[§], Chris Xu[†]

[§]Department of Computer Science, Cornell University, Ithaca, New York, USA
[‡]Department of Physics, Cornell University, Ithaca, New York, USA
[†]Department of Applied and Engineering Physics, Cornell University, Ithaca, New York, USA

ABSTRACT

We design and implement a novel class of highly precise network instrumentation and apply this tool to perform the first exact packet-timing measurements of a wide-area network ever undertaken, capturing 10 Gigabit Ethernet packets in flight on optical fiber. Through principled design, we improve timing precision by two to six orders of magnitude over existing techniques. Our observations contest several common assumptions about behavior of wide-area networks and the relationship between their input and output traffic flows. Further, we identify and characterize emergent packet chains as a mechanism to explain previously observed anomalous packet loss on receiver endpoints of such networks.

Categories and Subject Descriptors

C.2.5 [**Computer-Communication Networks**]: Local & Wide-Area Networks—*Ethernet, High-speed, Internet*; C.4 [**Performance of Systems**]: *Measurement techniques, Performance attributes*

General Terms

Experimentation, Measurement, Performance, Reliability

Keywords

Wide-Area Network, Optical Network, 10 Gbps, Ethernet

1. INTRODUCTION

In this work, we advance the state-of-the-art in Internet measurement by presenting the design, implementation, and application of a novel form of precise instrumentation — BiFocals — that allows for the exact characterization of network traffic in flight. In addition to introducing our methodology, we employ BiFocals to empirically characterize a particular wide-area network path: a 15 000 km static route across the 10 Gbps National LambdaRail optical backbone [22]. We focus our measurements upon inter-packet timings, a fundamental metric of traffic flows from which many secondary characteristics can be derived (jitter, link capacity, etc.) [23]. Further, inter-packet timings are independently important as a practical metric [5, 2, 6, 9, 16].

Our measurements of National LambdaRail (NLR) shed light on the puzzling phenomenon of anomalous wide-area network (WAN) packet loss that we recently observed [20]: even low to moderate data rates across a WAN can provoke endpoint receiver packet loss, although the same endpoint can service such data rates within a local-area network. As we show, when a flow traverses a WAN, the routers perturb inter-packet spacing to such an extent that, within a few hops, a flow that entered the network with large, fixed inter-packet spacing has degenerated into a series of packet chains (see Figure 1). We observe this phenomenon on an otherwise lightly loaded WAN, *irrespective of input data rate*.

Internet traffic has already been shown to be bursty [14]. However, the presumption within the field is that sufficient burstiness to cause packet loss does not arise in networks with ample excess bandwidth. Thus, the key surprise in our study is the emphatic finding that this is *not* true here: an input flow, with packets homogeneously distributed in time, becomes increasingly perturbed, so that the egress flow is transformed into a series of minimally spaced packet chains. Packets within the chain have miniscule gaps, while the chains themselves are separated by huge idle gaps. For example, an ideal inflow, with constant data rate of 1 Gbps, degenerates into an extremely bursty outflow with data rates surging to 10 Gbps for short periods of time. Not surprisingly, these can trigger packet loss even in core network routers, and such surges can easily overwhelm an endpoint.

We should pause to explain why this matters. First, a wide range of protocol and application research implicitly assumes that it makes sense to measure networks with software running on end-hosts (tomography, Internet coordi-

Figure 1: Illustration of the perturbation of the time distribution of packets between homogeneous input to, and compressed output from, a wide-area network.

nates, various quality-of-service schemes, etc.). Our work provides "ground truth" properties of the WAN and contests this notion, demonstrating that previous timing characterizations could be susceptible to distortions on end-host receivers, which dwarf both fine and coarse structure.

Second, many protocols assume, more or less, that if a flow enters the network satisfying some profile or property, and background traffic along the network path is low, then it will emerge downstream with bounded properties [17]. For example, there has been a great deal of work on protocols such as Diffserv [3], which pre-negotiate resources along some route, then use edge-marking to associate packets with service classes. Overloaded core network routers preferentially retain in-profile packets while dropping out-of-profile and unmarked packets. Our work makes it clear that even if a conditioned flow were in profile at the point of ingress, within a few hops, it may be far outside of the negotiated parameters. Further, some congestion-detection schemes look at inter-packet spacing as a signal of congestion [4,1,24]; our work makes it clear that micro-bursts can develop even in a mostly idle network. Moreover, the chains generated by transitting a long path can overwhelm endpoints with bursts of high-rate data that overrun buffers. Thus, a deeper appreciation of the dynamics of deployed high-speed networks will likely be needed to arrive at the best possible application architectures.

We note that our particular findings reflect a lightly loaded 10 Gbps network, with Quality-of-Service routing features disabled and all packets traversing the identical path. The situation in other settings may be different. Just the same, our observations here suggest that similar effects are likely present in those portions of the public Internet backbone with similar architecture.

In summary, this work contributes to the science of network measurement as follows:

Instrumentation: We design and implement novel high-precision instrumentation, BiFocals, to enable the generation of extremely precise traffic flows, as well as their capture and analysis. We do *not* use computer endpoints or network adapters for traffic capture at all; rather, we generate and acquire analog traces in real-time directly off optical fiber using typical physics-laboratory test-equipment (oscilloscopes, frequency synthesizers, lasers, etc.). We combine these with off-line post-processing, so as to completely avoid the non-determinism and systemic noise that confound many conventional techniques. In doing so, we obtain six orders-of-magnitude improvement in timing precision over existing end-host software and two to three orders-of-magnitude relative to prior hardware-assisted solutions.

Measurements: We apply BiFocals to exactly characterize the delay distribution of network traffic after transit across two paths: a single isolated router, and a deployed, but lightly used, 10 Gbps WAN path across eleven enterprise routers and 15 000 km of optical fiber. While exceptionally precise, the measurements presented here are computationally non-trivial, requiring over **two trillion** individual samples and over **5000** processor-hours of off-line computation.

Observations: We observe that as a flow traverses a long sequence of routers, packets cluster into chains, irrespective of data rate. This finding clarifies previously unexplained observations [20] of packet loss on endpoints of a WAN. Further, it calls into question some basic premises of WAN paths, notably the common (although not universal) assumption that a well-conditioned packet flow will remain well-conditioned as it travels along a lightly loaded route. Additionally, we characterize the stability of such packet chains and their probability as a function of their length. Finally, we demonstrate that these observations would *not* be possible using common software techniques on commodity end-hosts.

Outlook: We provide support for the view that only high-fidelity experimental work can provide ground truth and answer some of the contentious questions about the behavior of networks.

2. MOTIVATION

In order to exactly measure timing in network packet flows, BiFocals departs substantially from existing techniques. This section presents a taxonomy of different approaches to measurement, of increasing precision, and motivates the resulting architectural decisions that inform our design of BiFocals.

As we shall see below, BiFocals' precision derives from its interaction with a much lower level of the network stack than existing methodologies. Thus, to understand this measurement taxonomy, we first must review the behavior of the Physical Layer — a portion of the network stack completely hidden from the end-host kernel and other software. For the ensuing discussion, we focus upon the Physical Layer of optical 10 Gigabit Ethernet (10GBase-R) [11], corresponding to our application in Section 3. Without loss of generality, this discussion could equally apply to other Ethernet standards, such as the 1000Base-X [11] also implemented by BiFocals.

2.1 Physical Layer background

In a commodity end-host computer, the Ethernet controller of a typical 10GBase-R network adapter accepts Ethernet packets from higher layers of the network stack in the kernel and prepares them for transmission across the physical medium of the optical fiber span. However, the network adapter does not transmit individual Ethernet packets across the network, but instead embeds the data *bitstream* of discrete network packets within a continuously transmitted *symbolstream*. The continuous characteristic of this symbolstream, along with the application of complex line-coding protocols and scrambling functions (described in more detail in Appendix B), provide critical guarantees for the proper performance of the transmission line.[1]

The crucial point here is that, while the higher-layer data bitstream involves discrete Ethernet packets, the lower-layer symbolstream is continuous. Every symbol is the same width in time (~100 picoseconds) and is transmitted at the precisely identical symbol rate (~10 GBaud), completely irrespective of the data rate of the actual network traffic.

Figure 2 depicts a comparison between the Physical Layer symbolstream and two hypothetical data bitstreams, motivating the likely loss of timing precision in the bitstreams. The top panel shows the actual symbolstream as transmitted on fiber, with its continuous flow of symbols of equal width at equal rate. The remaining panels demonstrate the absence of a continuous timebase once the Ethernet packets have been extracted: the middle shows the implausible scenario where the fidelity of packet timings has been main-

[1] Namely, clock recovery, DC-balance, reduction of intersymbol interference, etc.

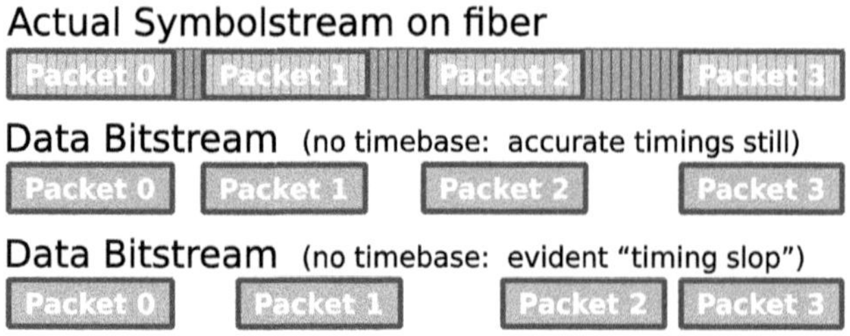

Figure 2: Comparison between an actual symbolstream on fiber (top panel) and two hypothetical examples of extracted data bitstreams, motivating both the potential (middle) and likely (bottom) loss of measurement precision due to the absence of a continuous timebase in the bitstreams.

tained, while the bottom demonstrates the most common case where timing information is perturbed. Namely, in the absence of the continuous timebase of the symbolstream, it is difficult to prevent "timing slop" of varying degree, with resulting errors in timing measurements, even though the network packets themselves are properly received and transferred to higher layers of the stack. This forms the crux of the issue of precise measurement of packet timings — the manner in which packets are time-stamped.

2.2 Sources of measurement error

With a renewed understanding of the Physical Layer of the network and the difference between symbolstreams and data bitstreams, we proceed to categorize the methods for time-stamping packets. The pertinent difference among these involves the "when" and "where" of time stamping as the packets transit the network and arrive at either the commodity end-host receiver, or our BiFocals tool, respectively. Here, we outline four approaches of increasing precision:

User-space software packet stamping: Software applications, executing in user-space context and deployed on commodity operating systems and computer end-hosts, serve overwhelmingly as the most common network measurement tools [7]. Embodying a balance among intrusiveness, cost, convenience, and accuracy, the canonical approach uses either an active or passive probe to observe traffic originating or terminating on the given end-host. Packets are assigned time-stamps as the user-space software processes them; such observations enable inference into traffic behavior on network paths.

While software tools are essential and productive elements of network research, it has long been recognized that they risk distortion of the metrics they seek to measure. The core problem involves the unmeasurable layers between the software and the optical fiber: network adapter (with hardware queues, on-chip buffering, and interrupt decisions), computer architecture (chipset, memory, and I/O buses), device driver, operating system (interrupt delivery and handling), and even measurement software itself. Each of these layers adds its own dynamics, distorts measurements in ways not deterministically reproducible, and contributes strongly to the timing errors as in Figure 2.

Kernel interrupt-handler stamping: Rather than having the user-space software application assign time-stamps to packets upon arrival, it is possible to modify the operating system kernel to internally time-stamp packets while servicing the network-adapter interrupts that announce the arrival of each packet. Such a technique removes ambiguities involved with kernel scheduling of the measurement application, as well as contention across memory buses. This method is not often used in practice due to the complexity of kernel and application modification; however, as discussed below, we implement an example of this approach to serve as a more stringent control against which we can compare our BiFocals instrumentation. Irrespective of its improvement over simple user-space software packet stamping, kernel interrupt-handler stamping still suffers from the non-determinism of the asynchronous interrupt-delivery mechanism[2] and manifests significant "timing slop" of the type seen in the bottom panel of Figure 2.

Network-adapter bitstream stamping: Both commercial solutions [8, 13] and academic projects [19] have been developed to address some of the sources of error above; the commercial varieties are primarily used by major router design firms and bear significant acquisition costs. These approaches involve specialized network adapters (generally, custom FPGAs) to enable packet time-stamping functionality in the network card hardware. While these designs aim to stamp the packets as early in their processing as possible, they still must first extract individual packets from the underlying Physical Layer symbolstream. However, as suggested by Figure 2, once they do so, the accompanying continuous timebase is lost, and the discrete packets may be subject to buffering and other error-inducing logic of FPGA gateware. (Vendor-released error estimates are addressed in Section 4.) As such, these techniques remain unable to exactly characterize the timing of network packets.

On-fiber symbolstream stamping: Our BiFocals instrumentation represents a substantial departure from the techniques enumerated above. Excluding the end-host completely and directly tapping the fiber transport, we record a contiguous portion of the entire Physical Layer symbolstream in real-time; only later, in off-line post-processing, do we extract the discrete Ethernet packets from this captured trace and assign time-stamps in relation to the symbolstream timebase. As our precision is significantly better than the width of a single symbol (~ 100 ps), our time-stamps are exact.

We recall, as in Figure 2, the difference between the discrete nature of the data bitstream, which causes "timing slop," and the presence of a continuous timebase in the symbolstream, where every symbol is the same width and transmitted at an identical symbol rate, irrespective of the data rate of the actual network traffic. Therefore, the fidelity of our instrumentation is agnostic to the data rate of the network traffic, as we always generate and capture traffic at the full 10GbE symbol rate of 10.3125 GBaud of the underlying Physical Layer. Whether the actual captured symbolstream is embedded with no data traffic (only infinitely repeating "idle" codewords) or maximal traffic density, our instrumentation responds identically and provides the exact time measurement of each packet.

2.3 Instrumentation architecture

Above, we articulate the key design decision within BiFocals to allow us to recover the exact timing of network packets in flight: we time-stamp packets using their associated on-fiber symbolstream. To understand how this criterion

[2]This is the classic "arbiter problem" of asynchronous events in a clocked digital system.

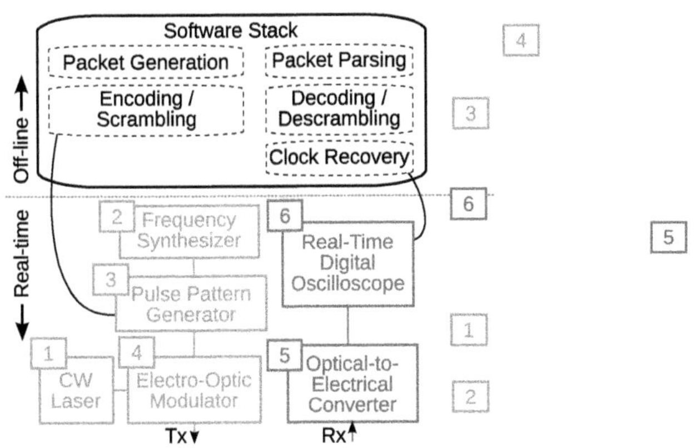

Figure 3: Diagram of BiFocals transmission and acquisition hardware and software (see detailed explication in the Appendices) connected across the network under test, with notations on the photograph of the hardware.

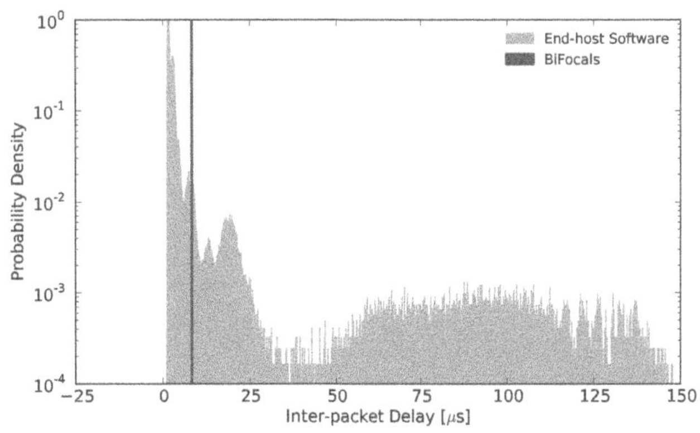

Figure 4: Timings for network traffic across a direct optical link between the sender and receiver: BiFocals presents an ideally homogeneous response, while kernel interrupt-handler stamping, a stringent type of end-host software, shows severe broadening and extensive distortion.

translates into practice, we briefly outline our instrumentation architecture here. In the Appendices, we detail the implementation and verification of BiFocals, expounding upon both the hardware foundation and software stack.

As depicted in Figure 3, BiFocals can be viewed as a special network adapter decomposed into two independent layers — an off-line software stack for the generation and deconstruction of symbolstreams, and separate physics test equipment (oscilloscopes, pattern generators, lasers, etc.) to faithfully send and receive these symbolstreams on the optical fiber. Note that this clean decomposition also separates what we implement in software (the bits we send) from what we implement in hardware (how we send them), enabling us to separately validate the fidelity of our hardware, independent of the software implementation of the Physical Layer. Further, this ensures that we can reproducibly send identical traffic on successive iterations, unlike common methods (`tcpreplay`, `iperf`, etc.) that introduce non-determinism.

On the software level, information is represented in binary Ethernet-compliant[3] symbolstreams, as sequences of ones and zeros (with each integer representing a distinct bit). On the hardware level, information is represented by light intensity: optical power modulated in time, off and on, to correspond to "0" and "1" bits, with unit length set by the symbol rate. This hardware implementation ensures that the binary symbolstreams are transmitted and acquired with perfect fidelity.[4]

2.4 Need for improved precision

It is worthwhile to question the extent of the need for the improved precision that BiFocals provides. Indeed, as we mention in the Introduction above, the packet chains that we ultimately observe in Section 3 show regimes of tiny timing delays interspersed by gaps of huge delays. This leads one to wonder: Could not such qualitative behavior be captured by existing techniques that use software on endpoints, without the difficulty of such specialized instrumentation as ours?

To probe this question quantitatively and further motivate our instrumentation, we conduct reference experiments comparing BiFocals to the above method of kernel interrupt-handler stamping, which we recall is a more rigorous and less error-prone evolution of the typical end-host software methodology. While space constraints preclude a full description of this comparison setup, we note in passing our use of high-end multicore servers as end-hosts, running a customized `iperf` [12] application and a modified Linux 2.6.27.2 kernel to read the time-stamp counter register (`RDTSC`) upon handling the network packet interrupt.[5]

Using both BiFocals and this reference kernel interrupt-handler stamping, we directly connect transmitter and receiver via fiber-optic link and measure the inter-packet delay. Figure 4 overlays the probability density histogram of inter-packet delays for each method and clearly depicts qualitative and quantitative distinctions between these techniques: BiFocals presents a perfect delta function where all packets have the same inter-packet delay, while the comparison end-host software shows severe broadening and excessive structure, with errors up to 150 μs. Any attempt to characterize the timing response across actual network paths with such a distortive tool would create grave difficulties in differentiating the response due to the actual network path from that of the measurement tool. We further note that the broadening of the timings from the end-host software is sufficient even to overwhelm the coarse structure of our results, as presented in Section 3.

3. MEASUREMENTS

We apply our BiFocals instrumentation to study network transit effects for a variety of traffic flows on 10 Gbps Ethernet over fiber-optic links. This paper focuses on two scenarios: an isolated enterprise router that we use as a control case, and a high-performance, semi-private WAN path, spanning 15 000 km of the NLR [22] backbone, circumscribing the United States and traversing eleven routers. In both scenarios, we directly sample the symbolstream off the fiber and present exact characterization of the network path itself.

[3]Here, IEEE 802.3-2008 Clauses 49 (PCS) and 51 (PMA) for 10 Gbps optical Ethernet [11].

[4]In accordance with IEEE 802.3-2008 Clause 52 [11].

[5]Further, we took care to maximize `RDTSC` precision by properly inserting explicit memory barriers to serialize instructions, binding `iperf` to the same processor core, and disabling any processor power-conservation features.

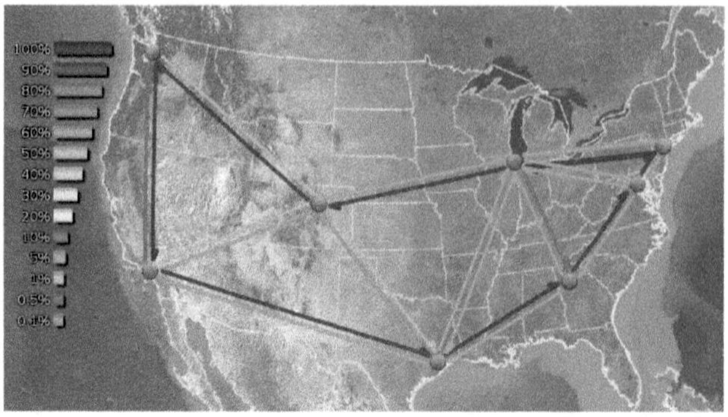

Figure 5: Map of the National LambdaRail (NLR), depicting high link utilization for BiFocals-generated traffic with a 9 Gbps data rate and 16 Mpps packet rate.

Packet size [Bytes]	Nominal data rate [Gbps]	Packet rate [kpps]	Inter-packet gap [bits]	Inter-packet delay [ns]
1500	1	82.0	109 784	12 199
1500	3	246.1	28 440	4 064
1500	9	740.5	1 304	1 350
46	1	1 755.6	5 128	570
46	3	5 208.3	1 352	192
46	9	15 625.0	72	64

Table 1: Ensembles of various packet sizes and data rates, with resulting packet rates and inter-packet gaps and delays, for network traffic homogeneous in time. Rows correspond to the six subfigures in Figures 6 and 7.

3.1 Experimental network setup

For the control router, we use a Cisco 6500, configured with IOS 12.2(33)SXI1 with tail-drop queueing, a CEF720 4-port 10-Gigabit Ethernet module, two 16-port Gigabit modules, and one Supervisor Engine 720. The 6500's centralized forwarding card forces all traffic to transit the router backplane, even though the two 10GbE ingress and egress interfaces share the same line card. While performing the control experiments, we isolated the router from any extraneous traffic.

Our main experimental path is a static route across the NLR PacketNet backbone, designed so that traffic originates and terminates at the same physical location at Cornell University. To reach the nearest NLR Point-of-Presence (POP), traffic is switched by a campus backbone switch (Cisco 6500) to an upstream campus router (Cisco 6500) in a New York City carrier-hotel and, there, routed onto the NLR backbone for subsequent transit across eight NLR routers spanning 15 000 kilometers. (Note that, in their primary failover role, neither of these campus Cisco 6500s handles commodity traffic, and they thus maintain light loads.) Figure 5 depicts the topology of our network path, as well as a real-time picture of one of our 9 Gbps traffic flows. All of these NLR optical links use Dense Wavelength Division Multiplexing technology and connect Cisco CRS-1 core routers, each with IOS XR 3.6.1[00] (tail-drop queueing), two 8-interface 10GbE line-cards, two modular service cards, and two 8-slot route processors. We note that Cisco recently upgraded the NLR infrastructure, so these routers are identical and contemporary, with passive optical components in ideal condition. We monitor the background traffic for all interfaces at each NLR POP and on both campus routers, using SNMP queries and RRDtool storage with 10-second resolution.

3.2 Measurement methodology

We characterize our traffic in terms of a number of quantities that we explicitly define here. The *packet size* refers to the size of the payload of our Ethernet packets.[6] We define the *data rate* as the data transmitted in the 64b/66b Physical Coding Sublayer (PCS) line code[7] over a given period of time, thus including the entire Ethernet packet as well as preamble and Start-of-Frame (SOF) delimiter. The packet rate is simply the number of Ethernet packets in a given period of time. Finally, in discussing the timings between packets, we define two separate quantities: *inter-packet delay* (IPD) is the time difference, or spacing, between identical bit positions in the Ethernet SOF delimiter for successive packets in the network flow, while the *inter-packet gap* (IPG) is the time between the end of one Ethernet packet and the beginning of the successive packet. More precisely, IPG is the bit-time measured from the last bit of the Ethernet Frame Check Sequence field of the first packet to the first bit of the preamble of the subsequent packet, thus including the idle (`/I/`), start (`/S/`), or terminate (`/T/`) control characters from the 64b/66b PCS line-code [11].

All experiments consist of the BiFocals apparatus generating UDP traffic at nominal data rates of 1 Gbps, 3 Gbps, and 9 Gbps for packet sizes of 46 Bytes (the minimum allowed) and 1500 Bytes (default Maximum Transmission Unit). For each data rate, the packets are homogeneously distributed in time: separated by a fixed number of 64b/66b line code bits (for example, `/I/` control characters), to exhibit identical IPG and IPD at the ingress point. Table 1 depicts the parameter space of packet size and nominal data rate, with resulting packet rate, IPG, and IPD.

We note that, while enforcing a homogeneous distribution of packets in time, the specifics of the 64b/66b line code prevent the generation of packet streams at arbitrary data rates.[8] Therefore, inter-packet gaps can only be transmitted as a certain discrete number of control characters, most of which are idles (`/I/`). The significance of this constraint is apparent below.

To measure the timings for over a million network packets for each packet size and data rate in Table 1, we had to acquire over two trillion samples from the optical fiber and process them off-line using resources exceeding 5000 processor-hours.

3.3 Results for control router

Our first experiment transmits data across a single isolated router, disconnected from any outside network. We observe neither packet loss nor packet reordering with one exception: 5% loss occurs for our smallest packet size at the highest data rate (46-Byte packets sent at 9 Gbps, corre-

[6]Each payload has an extra 25 Bytes of header and footer.
[7]The 64b/66b PCS [11] defines the specifics of the symbol-stream of the 10GBase-R Physical Layer; see Appendix B.

[8]Ethernet packets must be aligned at the start or middle of the 64-bit PCS frame.

sponding to ~16 Million packets per second). In this lossy scenario, it is interesting to recognize that input packets have an IPG of 72 bit-times: near the minimum allowed by the IEEE 10GBase-R standard, but above that value mandated for reception and below that for transmission.[9] Thus, the flow is legal. Nonetheless, it constitutes an edge case: any higher packet-rate traffic flow would violate the 10GbE specification.

Figure 6 depicts the distributions of inter-packet delay obtained in this experiment across the control router. Each subfigure represents one of the six ensembles, corresponding to various packet sizes and data rates enumerated above in Table 1. The large panel in each subfigure shows a probability density histogram of received packet delays, all with equivalent coordinate ranges and identical logarithmic vertical scales to allow for the visual comparison of the fine structure and broadening effects in the distribution. The upper-left inset of each subfigure shows the raw inter-packet delay of the received traffic as a function of time [packet #] for a small representative segment of the million-packet ensemble. The upper-right inset of each subfigure presents an enlarged graph of the histogram, centered around the peak of the distribution. For each ensemble, the inter-packet delay value of the injected homogeneous network traffic is also marked (red vertical dashed line). It is vital to understand what a "good" response looks like: the histogram should be nearly a vertical delta function, centered at the input data flow. The extent to which the output delay distribution deviates from this ideal serves as a measure of the router-induced dynamics.

We observe that:

1. Even this single isolated router broadens the inter-packet delay distribution (initial distribution has zero width, as input traffic arrives homogeneously in time). In effect, even though the packets arrive with perfect regularity, some manage to transit the router quickly, while others are delayed briefly.

2. At higher data rates, some packets emerge in closely packed chains with the spacing between packets reflecting the *minimum* legal number of IPG bits. We observed this effect for three of the measurement ensembles, only one of whose input stream itself included minimally spaced packets (namely, 46-Byte packets at 9 Gbps).

3. Packet loss is observed in the stream with the highest packet rate (46-Byte packets at 9 Gbps).

4. A fine-grain structure is evident, reflecting the architecture of the underlying 64b/66b PCS line code.

What should one take away from this experiment?

(1) Broadening of the delay distribution: We note that all ensembles (except the stream with highest packet rate) exhibit a significant broadening of the delay distribution with respect to that of the injected packet stream. Presumably, this is due to the store-and-forward nature of the router, as the router itself is a clocked device that undergoes some internal state transitions to determine its readiness to receive or send. Further, the half-width of most of these distributions — defined here as the range for −70 dB falloff from the distribution's peak — is approximately 200 ns. For these ensembles, the half-width represents a measure of the response delay to input packets evenly spaced in time. In contrast, the stream with the highest packet rate experiences negligible broadening of its distribution (see upper-right inset of Figure 6(f)); in this case, the input packets already arrive with minimum-allowed IPG. Thus, the distribution can only broaden in one direction (to higher IPD values), and any such broadening is associated with corresponding packet loss.

(2) Formation of packet chains: As previously mentioned, the inter-packet gap minimum is actually evident in the asymmetry of the delay distributions. Specifically, the IEEE 802.3ae-2002 standard [10] mandates a separation between packets to provide the receiver some latitude in processing the incoming packet stream. This property is expressed in terms of the inter-packet gap; as such, the corresponding minimum inter-packet delay is dependent on the packet size, yet independent of data rate. For example, given 1500-Byte packets, the minimum inter-packet delay (corresponding to an IPG of 96 bit-times) is actually 1230 ns, while, for 46-Byte packets, it is 66 ns.

In fact, we observe precisely these minimum inter-packet delay values in most of our measurements. For ensembles with smaller input IPDs (1500-Byte packets at 9 Gbps and 46-Byte packets at 3 and 9 Gbps), it is readily observable:[10] we note extremely sharp drop-offs in the probability densities (left side of subfigures), with −50 to −80 dB suppression over 3–6 ns. We measure a minimum IPD of 1226 ns for our ensemble with 1500-Byte packets at 9 Gbps (Figure 6(e)), a minimum IPD of 64 ns for our ensemble with 46-Byte packets at 3 Gbps (Figure 6(d)), and a minimum IPD of 64 ns for the final ensemble with 46-Byte packets at 9 Gbps (Figure 6(f)). These closely agree with the above theoretical predictions for lower constraints due to minimal IPGs: the first observation is within 0.3%, and the latter two are within 3.5%.

(3) Packet loss across the router: We observe packet loss for 46-Byte packets at 9 Gbps (see Figure 6(f), especially the upper-right inset, for asymmetric broadening). We note that alternative mechanisms independently confirm the same level of packet loss for this ensemble: a careful examination of router statistics (accessed via SNMP and averaged over long periods) shows that this loss is almost completely confined to packets that are discarded in the outbound router interface before acquisition by our instrumentation. This corresponds to 4.7% packet loss. An additional 0.02% of packets exhibit errors at the inbound router interface after transmission from our instrument, though no packets without errors are discarded at this interface. Further, we note that, during measurement of this ensemble, our packet stream elicits continuous router-log warnings of excessive backplane utilization.

Ultimately, it is not particularly surprising that we are able to provoke router drops, even with a single flow running across a single enterprise router, when we consider that this measurement ensemble is constructed with packet rates approaching 16 million packets per second and IPGs of only 72 bits, very close to the ultimate allowed minimum of 40 bits. In particular, the 10GbE standards allows for packet

[9]See Note 4 of Section 4.4.2 of IEEE 802.3ae-2002 [10].

[10]For larger input IPDs (1500-Byte packets at 1 and 3 Gbps and 46-Byte packets at 1 Gbps), small sample sizes mask the phenomenon.

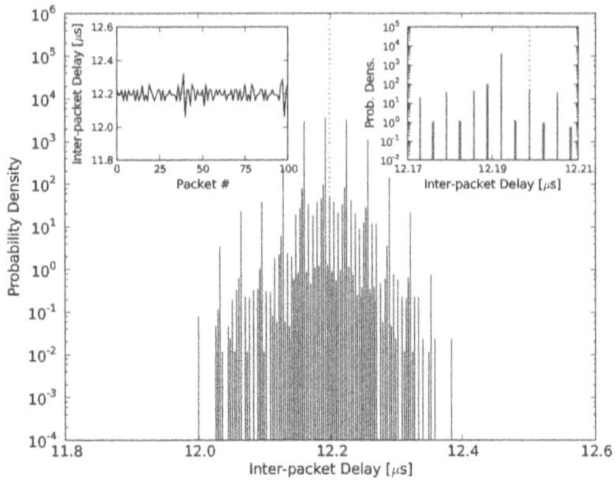

(a) 1 Gbps Data Rate (1500-Byte Packets)

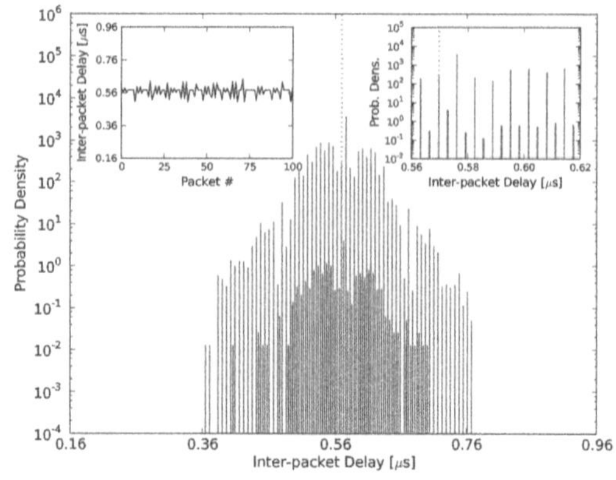

(b) 1 Gbps Data Rate (46-Byte Packets)

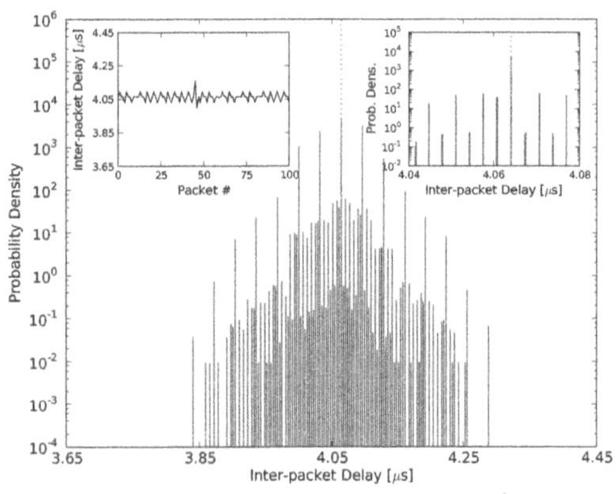

(c) 3 Gbps Data Rate (1500-Byte Packets)

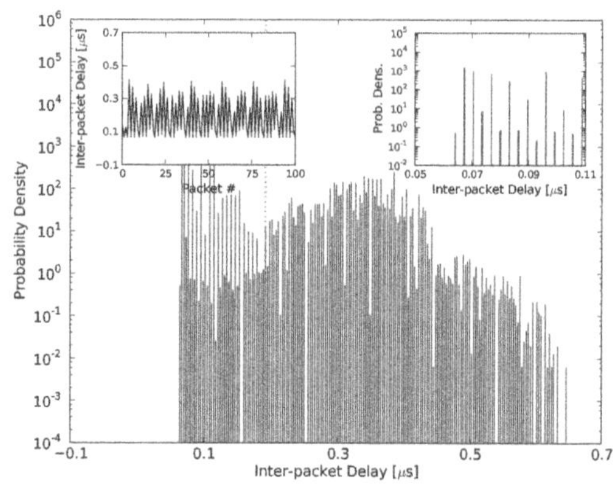

(d) 3 Gbps Data Rate (46-Byte Packets)

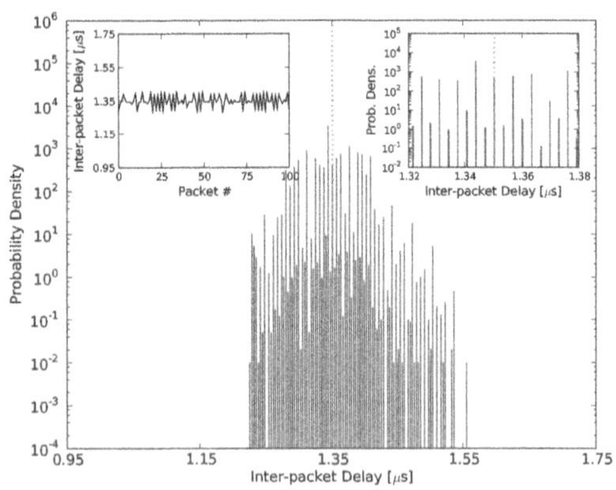

(e) 9 Gbps Data Rate (1500-Byte Packets)

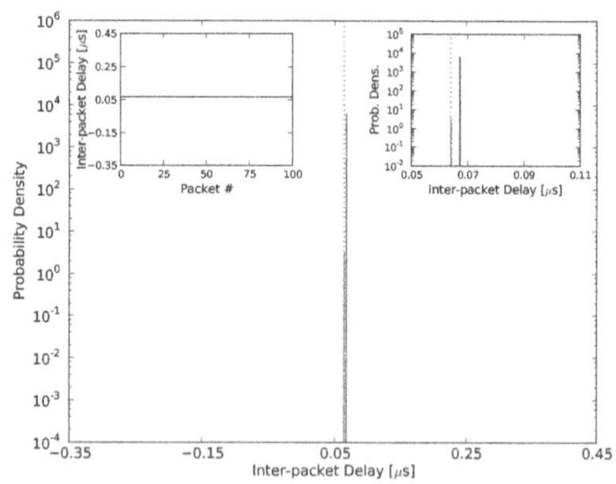

(f) 9 Gbps Data Rate (46-Byte Packets)

Figure 6: Comparison of packet delay across an isolated router (Cisco 6500) serving as the experimental control, with the input network traffic to the router perfectly homogeneous in time and the resulting delay distribution a response to transit across the router: subfigures show the probability density histograms of inter-packet delays [μs] for six ensembles (corresponding to the data rates and packet sizes enumerated in Table 1), with the delay for the input traffic marked with a dotted red line. Histogram coordinate axes are equivalent in their range (offset to center the distribution) to allow visual comparison of the broadening, and the ordinate axes are identical with a logarithmic scale to expose the fine-grained structure. Upper-left inset shows the raw delay [μs] as a function of time [packet #] for representative flows; while the upper-right inset is an enlarged view of the primary graph about its peak.

drops given that the minimum IPG of 40 bits for reception is lower than the minimum IPG of 96 bits for transmission; as a result, a router can drop packets due to this impedance mismatch between permissible IPGs.

Router drops often occur because a relentless, maximally dense stream of packets presents itself: if the router store-and-forward logic delays any packet for even the slightest amount of time, some packet will need to be dropped to compensate. This observation becomes particularly significant later for wide-area traffic; when we examine multihop data, as noted in the Introduction, we encounter a noticeable tendency for packets to form chains with minimal spacing, irrespective of the homogeneity of input packets in time. But now we recognize that packet chains can trigger router loss. It follows that long routes carrying high-speed data may be prone to loss, even in an otherwise lightly loaded network, if the receivers are not able to accept packets at the maximum-allowed rate.

(4) Fine-grained* n*-ary structure: Our final observation concerns the intriguing n-ary (secondary, tertiary, etc.) structure present in the packet delay histograms of all ensembles. This structure is most readily visible in the two ensembles comprised of 1500-Byte packets at 1 and 3 Gbps data rates. Per Table 1, these ensembles have the lowest packet rates and the largest inter-packet gaps. As seen in Figures 6(a) and 6(c), they manifest thirteen and fifteen local sub-peaks, respectively, superimposed atop a background distribution with typical monotonic fall-off from the central peak. These sub-peaks are substantial (100× the density of locally surrounding delay values) and uniformly distributed by the same delay offset of 32 ns.

This n-ary structure is closely related to the underlying 64b/66b Physical Coding Sublayer, as the timing separation between these peaks is almost precisely an integer multiple of 64b/66b frames; specifically, we measure 4.9992 frames. Furthermore, additional n-ary structure is seen, relating to single 64b/66b frames, as well as higher-order structure corresponding to half-frames (the former 100× more probable than the latter). We recognize that this structure results from the underlying PCS line code, which always aligns Ethernet frames with either the start or middle of a 64b/66b frame, thus explaining the fundamental half-frame period.

3.4 Results across Internet path

We next examine the same traffic flows transitting eleven routers and 15 000 km over NLR. The results appear in Figure 7, with the same six inputs of homogeneously spaced packet streams from Table 1.

Our observations here can be summarized:

1. *Irrespective of input data rate*, the delay distribution peaks at a value corresponding to a *minimum* IPD allowed by the IEEE standard, providing evidence for our contention that packets emerge from WANs in chains. So, after a sequence of 11 hops, even a 1 Gbps input flow evolves into a series of 10 Gbps bursts.

2. We observe packet loss, for the two highest packet-rate ensembles (5 and 16 Mpps: 46-Byte packets at 3 and 9 Gbps), of 1.9% and 32.4%, respectively.

3. We identify multiple secondary lobes in the delay distribution. These reflect the formation of packet chains, with lobe separation dependent upon data rate.

4. We again observe n-ary structure imposed by 64b/66b line coding.

(1) Formation of packet chains for all inputs: The first, and most striking, observation in Figure 7 is that the location of the primary peak does *not* depend upon the input data rate. In fact, it closely corresponds to an inter-packet delay reflecting the minimum-allowed inter-packet gap. (As above, this IPD value is actually a function of the sum of IPG and packet size and hence not identical for ensembles of different packet size). More packets emerge from WANs with the minimum-allowed inter-packet delay, than with any other inter-packet delay. Actually, as seen more clearly in the upper-right inset of each subfigure, the distribution peak is actually offset from the lowest recorded value by a single half-frame of 64b/66b line code. We conjecture that this is related to the subtle distinction in minimum IPGs by standard (between 40 bit-times for receive and 96 bit-times for transmit).

Now, as with the control measurements, we measure the inter-packet delay of the peak for both packet sizes: 1500-Byte packets show peak delays of 1226 ns, while 46-Byte packets have peak delays of 66 ns. Both of these values correspond almost precisely to the inter-packet delay between packets of this size at their maximum data rate (approaching 10 Gbps). In fact, if we assume that these packets are separated by the minimum-allowed inter-packet gaps (96 bit-times), we can find theoretical expectations for the delays: 1230 ns for 1500-Byte packets and 66 ns for 46-Byte packets. Our observed delays are within 0.3% and 0.5%, respectively, of such theoretical values.

This demonstrates that, irrespective of the input data rate, network flows are compressed as they transit a series of routers on a WAN. This compression reduces the spacing between sequential packets, causing chains to form, while introducing larger gaps between these chains. In the experiments of Section 3.3 on the control router, we noted a lower bound on packet spacing that created asymmetric delay distributions, and we now see this greatly amplified by the WAN. Indeed, one might speculate that this effect results from received packets being queued and later batch-forwarded along the path as quickly as possible (at line rate). Regardless of the cause, the engineering implication is that downstream routers and receiver endpoints must be capable of lossless receipt of bursts of packets arriving at the maximum possible data rate — 10 Gbps, here. Moreover, this effect occurs even when the original sender transmits at a much lower average data rate. Failing to adequately provision any component will thus trigger loss.

This finding now clarifies a phenomenon we measured earlier [20], though could not explain: commodity servers were receiving and then dropping network packets that had been sent, at low data rates, across a 10 Gbps WAN. One can now see why the network path itself, as a collection of store-and-forward routing elements, will skew even a perfectly homogeneous packet stream towards a distribution with a dominant peak around the maximum data rate supported by the 10GbE standard. As these chains of minimally spaced packets increase in length, packet loss is inevitable, unless all network elements are able to handle continuous line-speed receipt of packets.

(2) Packet loss on the WAN: We indeed observe packet loss on this NLR path for ensembles with the highest input packet rates (46-Byte packets at 3 Gbps and 9 Gbps): 1.9%

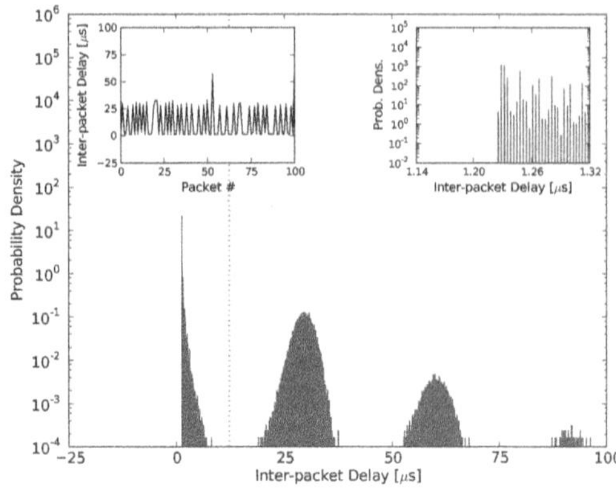

(a) 1 Gbps Data Rate (1500-Byte Packets)

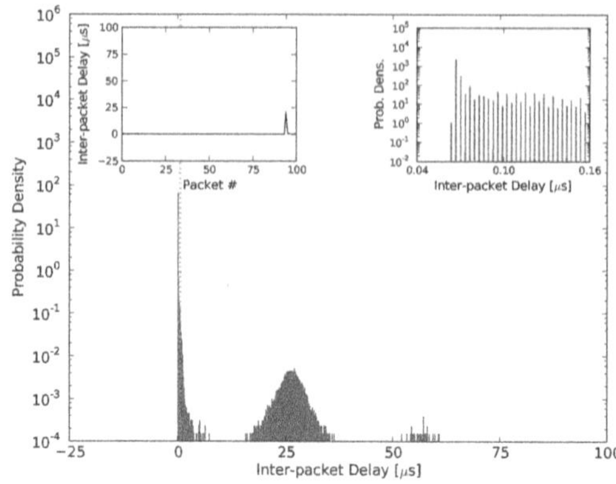

(b) 1 Gbps Data Rate (46-Byte Packets)

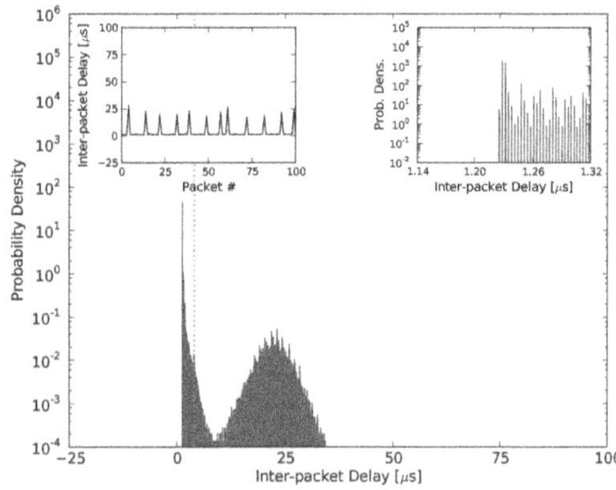

(c) 3 Gbps Data Rate (1500-Byte Packets)

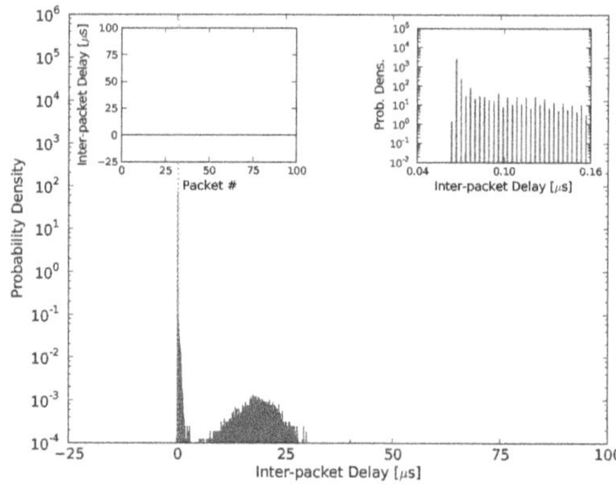

(d) 3 Gbps Data Rate (46-Byte Packets)

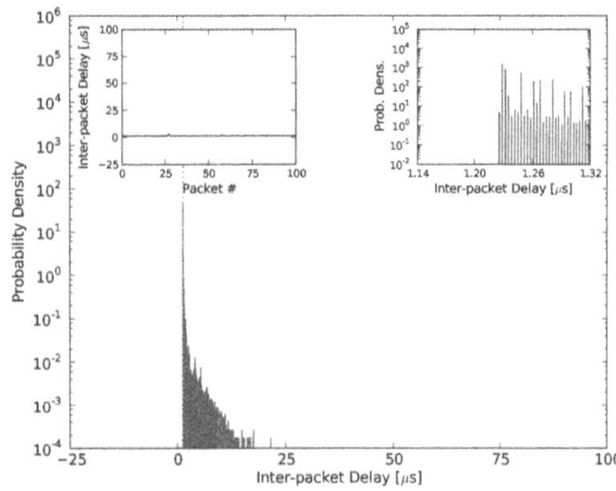

(e) 9 Gbps Data Rate (1500-Byte Packets)

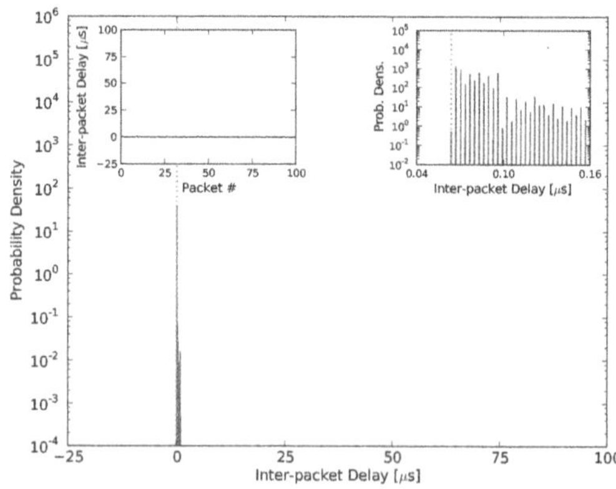

(f) 9 Gbps Data Rate (46-Byte Packets)

Figure 7: Comparison of packet delay across a lightly loaded 10 Gbps Internet path spanning 15 000 km of the National LambdaRail optical backbone and eleven routing elements (Cisco CRS-1 and 6500 routers), with the input traffic to the path perfectly homogeneous in time and the resulting delay distribution a response to transit across this wide-area network: subfigures and insets as specified earlier in Figure 6.

and 32.4%, respectively.[11] As noted above for the control router, it appears that this loss occurs as incoming traffic exceeds the backplane capacity of the routers and outbound buffers overflow, dropping packets before they can continue on the network path. We conjecture that the rate of loss might be related to the number of routing elements along the WAN path.

(3) Secondary lobes in delay distribution: Our third observation concerns the delay of the secondary lobes in Figure 7. For individual histograms with multiple lobes, the peaks are equidistant (separated by 30 μs in Figure 7(a), for example). For each packet size, we observe a negative linear correlation between data rate and peak separation (estimating the lobe location for ensembles without a distinct secondary lobe).

(4) Fine-grained n-ary structure: The final observation here mirrors the fourth point discussed for the control router. Once again, we see secondary (and tertiary) fine-grained structure atop the primary probability density distribution. While more difficult to discern for the ensembles with 46-Byte packets, we can readily measure it for the three ensembles with 1500-Byte packets. As above, we note a series of interwoven sub-peaks, with probability densities 100× above their surrounding background values; these sub-peaks are separated by delay values of 32 ns, with five tertiary peaks embedded between each. As in Section 3.3, this reflects the PCS substrate and its framing protocol.

3.5 Analysis of representative ensemble

While we report our measurements above for both control and Internet paths, we now further evaluate and analyze those data. Figures 6 and 7 present probability density histograms of inter-packet delays, showing the *statistical* behavior of network packet streams in our ensembles, but concealing the time correlations between neighboring packets. Here, we discuss these correlations and associate given delays with particular packets within an ensemble trace. Further, we connect our analysis to an investigation into the background traffic on the NLR backbone comprising our Internet path. Due to space constraints, the subsequent analysis examines only one such ensemble in detail: the 1500-Byte packet stream transmitted at a 1 Gbps data rate, described in Table 1 and presented in Figure 7(a), which is representative of traffic flows in this environment.

We find that:

1. Our results show *self-similar* behavior — measurements at differing time scales exhibit the same statistical properties — a recognized and critical property of network traffic [18].

2. Packet chains manifest similar characteristics irrespective of their particular definition; namely, chains of increasing length occur with exponentially less frequency.

3. The statistical distribution of inter-packet delays is relatively insensitive to background traffic.

We first must ensure that the statistical behavior seen in Sections 3.3 and 3.4 is not merely an anomaly, caused,

[11]Though NLR is a production network used by scientists nationwide, its routers might not be optimized relative to this particular sort of stress-test.

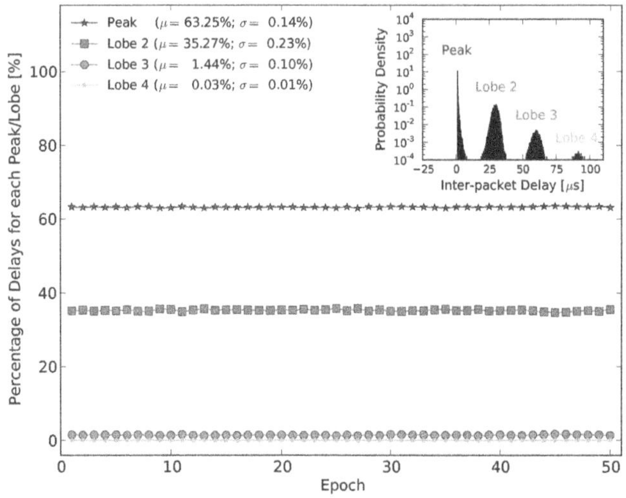

Figure 8: Self-similarity of inter-packet delays for network traffic: as a function of time-epoch, the percentage of delays associated with each peak or lobe of our 1 Gbps, 1500-Byte traffic (from Figure 7(a), reproduced as inset here, with labels); legend provides the mean and standard deviation.

for example, by the aggregation of distinct regimes of behavior in time (here, four separate regimes of different delays). To show the self-similarity of our observations, we start by proposing a metric of interest for our ensemble trace and by dividing this trace into some number of contiguous time-epochs, each containing the same number of packets. We then verify that this metric remains constant across all time-epochs. Figure 8 shows such a process: we employ fifty time-epochs (about 20 000 packets each) and compute, as a metric, the percentage of delays associated with the peak and each of the three lobes in Figure 7(a), reproduced here as inset. We immediately confirm that our metric holds constant across all epochs. Additionally, we report the mean and standard deviation of these values across epochs and note the relative proportion of delays among peak and lobe elements: $63.25 \pm 0.14\%$ of delays are in the peak, $35.25 \pm 0.23\%$ in the second lobe, $1.44 \pm 0.10\%$ in the third, and only $0.03 \pm 0.01\%$ correspond to the smallest fourth lobe. Though not illustrated here, we repeat this process for epochs of six alternate sizes, with each epoch containing between 2000 and 50 000 packets; in all cases, we observe identical mean percentage of delays for the peak and all three lobes, as well as similar constancy in time. This strongly affirms the self-similarity of the measured delays over the entire ensemble and provides assurance that our conclusions are not an artifact of the time or resolution of our measurements.

We now investigate the connection between the histograms of Section 3.4 and recognizable packet chains. We first define such a chain of packets by selecting a minimum inter-packet delay, below which packets are classified as a single packet chain. We set a delay threshold (1.25 μs) close to the minimum theoretical inter-packet delay (1.23 μs for this ensemble). Figure 9 shows the packet chains that emerge after transit across the NLR optical backbone; the figure presents the probability density for the occurrence of packet chains of prescribed lengths. For example, the histogram reveals that chains with ten packets occur approximately once per

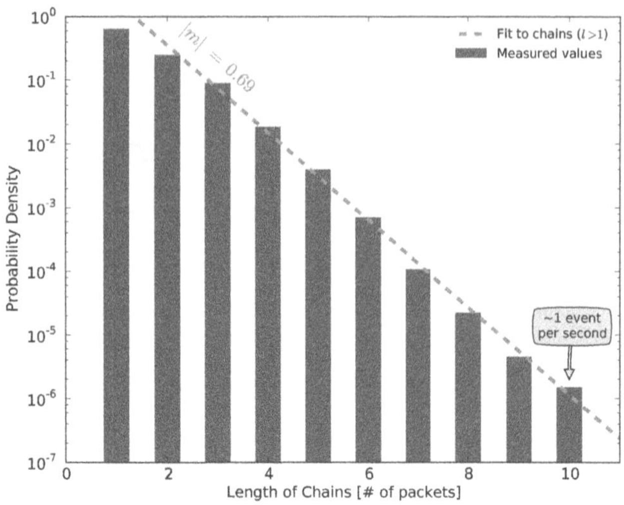

Figure 9: Transformation of a temporally homogeneous network packet stream into a series of packet chains, of varying lengths, after transit across the NLR optical backbone: probability density of the resulting packet chains as a function of chain length, showing exponential suppression of chains of increasing length (same ensemble as Figure 8).

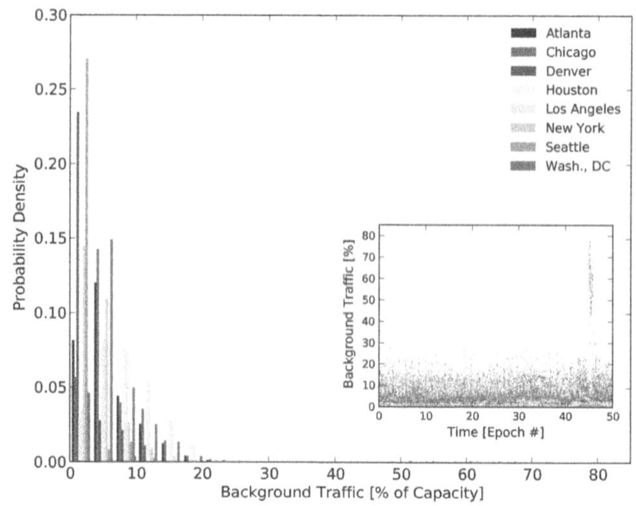

Figure 10: Background traffic across NLR routers during measurement: probability density of link utilization of background traffic transiting outbound NLR backbone interfaces, for each of eight NLR routers along our WAN path, simultaneous to our injected traffic at given time of measurement (same ensemble as Figure 8); inset depicts time-series, rather than statistical description, of traffic.

second. We observe the exponential suppression of packet chains of increasing length, $P(l) \propto 10^{-|m|l}$, and extract[12] the exponential coefficient, $|m| = 0.69$. This fit allows us to extrapolate the probability of chains longer than those we capture: 15-packet chains occur every forty-five minutes, while 20-packet chains are seen only once per ninety days, conveying the relative rarity of longer chains for this scenario. Finally, we analyze the sensitivity of packet chain formation to our particular choice of delay threshold. We increase the threshold by almost an order of magnitude, to a value of 12.20 μs, equivalent to the inter-packet delay of the input packet stream. Though not shown, we observe behavior almost identical to that of Figure 9, with an exponent only ~15% lower ($|m| = 0.59$), thus confirming that chains are robust and quite insensitive to how they are defined. Moreover, this also reinforces the magnitude of the separations between the chains, compared to that between packets within a chain. With such robust chain formation, further predictions become possible: one can combine this data with separate knowledge of the effect of packet chains on end-hosts attached to the WAN,[13] in order to develop expectations of packet loss and service reliability of the end-to-end path, including these attached endpoints.

Finally, we examine the influence of background traffic along NLR backbone links on our statistical observations of packet chains. First, we define *background traffic*: for each NLR POP, it is the difference between the total data rate of outbound traffic on that POP's interface along our Internet path, and the data rate of the inbound traffic we inject from Cornell into NLR's New York POP. For each of the NLR POPs, Figure 10 shows the probability density of the background traffic, in percentage utilization of the full 10 Gbps link capacity; the inset depicts the time-series of the traffic. The mean background traffic is quite low, in fact, registering only ~6% of the link capacity. The sole exception is a brief surge in background traffic to ~60% of link capacity (6 Gbps). Representing an order-of-magnitude more traffic and lasting 90% of a time-epoch (Epoch 46 in Figure 8), this traffic surge shows no effect on the statistical distribution of inter-packet delays, nor on their resulting packet chains. Such apparent independence, between the statistical properties of Section 3 and the background traffic, suggests that the explanation for our observations might rely on other factors. Still, our analysis does not yet enable us to precisely identify the cause of packet chains, and their emergence remains an open, and fascinating, research question.

This analysis shows that the exact characterization of packet timings provides meaningful insights into the behavior of Internet paths. While reliable and reproducible instrumentation and measurements are critical foundations, further investigations are clearly warranted here: varying WAN path lengths, modifying router model selection and configuration, controlling explicit background-traffic scenarios, and more. BiFocals provides a framework to conduct these in an empirically rigorous manner.

4. RELATED WORKS

Quantitative measurements of network traffic, both in the wild on the Internet and in isolation in the laboratory, hold a long established role within the systems and networking communities [7].

Our results showcase the application of BiFocals to exactly capture the time characteristics of network packets in flight — a landmark in Internet timing measurement. BiFocals achieves this precision by introducing on-fiber symbolstream time stamping to the taxonomy of measurement

[12] We fit $l > 1$ as, by definition, $P(l = 1)$ corresponds to the probability density of non-chain packets.

[13] For example, knowledge of chains' interactions with network-adapter buffers or other hardware or software specifics.

methods described in Section 2.2. Here, we compare our technique with the hardware-assisted method of network-adapter bitstream time stamping, used in the academic NetFPGA project [19] and the commercial Ixia [13] and DAG [8] frameworks. However, unlike BIFOCALS, these measurement techniques are simply unable to deliver the exact timings of packets, irrespective of their other benefits or drawbacks.

NetFPGA provides Verilog gateware and software for accurate packet transmission and acquisition, using rate limiters, delay modules, and time stamping at the gate-array level. Packet processing is done off-line, relying upon `PCAP` to generate and save traffic traces. Support for Ethernet standards differs from ours: NetFPGA currently implements 1000Base-T (with parallel symbolstreams at 125 MBaud), while BIFOCALS delivers the 100-fold higher symbol rate of 10GBase-R (10.3125 GBaud serial symbolstream). Further, our architecture allows for flexible interchange of standards (for example, we also support 1000Base-X) and seamless progression to higher-performance Ethernet (40GbE, 100GbE, etc.), while requiring minimal rewriting of our software and replacement of only certain individual pieces of test equipment (faster optics and electronics). In contrast, to adopt additional standards with higher symbol rates, NetFPGA would arguably require significant gateware revision, as well as likely a complete re-engineering of the data-path.

Similar to NetFPGA, Ixia network service modules use an FPGA-based domain-specific implementation to accurately generate and capture packets with high fidelity. (For example, the Ixia 10GBase-R solution possesses a resolution of 20 ns, yet this precision is still at least 200-fold worse than ours.) Ixia excels in providing a complete turn-key solution for the commercial market with strong support for application-load and content-processing modules. However, Ixia is a closed, expensive (~\$1M) platform with capabilities that cannot be independently expanded.

Endace's DAG (Data Acquisition and Generation) Network Monitoring Cards offer functionality comparable to that of Ixia, with lower cost and slightly better advertised time resolution (7.5 ns), although they lack Ixia's diversity of application testing modules. While similarly proprietary, DAG offers existing options for link monitoring, capacity planning, and forensics analysis. All told, DAG appears useful to the network operator, but less appropriate for precise measurement or network research.

Unlike such domain-specific technologies, our BIFOCALS instrumentation relies solely on conventional physics test equipment — oscilloscopes, pattern generators, lasers, etc. — to achieve exact timing characterization. Though our test equipment is not inexpensive (~\$200k), it is general in purpose and widely available within academic and research communities. In fact, when not serving as part of the BIFOCALS work, our hardware components are used for other Cornell University research, and no additional physics test equipment needed to be purchased to build our instrumentation. We envision that a similar environment of re-use would hold at other academic and research institutions and thus enable economical reproduction of this work.

5. CONCLUSIONS

BIFOCALS responds to the recognized need for principled, precise, and reproducible measurements [21], especially in the domain of packet timings for high-speed networks. Our instrumentation achieves remarkable levels of temporal precision to enable the exact characterization of the timing of network packets in flight on fiber. For 10GbE measurements, we achieve up to six orders-of-magnitude improvement in timing precision over existing end-host software. This is attained by eschewing computer endpoints and network adapters and instead generating and acquiring the symbolstream directly off optical fiber with real-time physics test equipment and off-line software.

Using BIFOCALS, we accomplish what we believe to be the most precise timing measurements ever made for various packet flows in relatively simple scenarios: through a single isolated router, and also across a statically routed wide-area network, spanning eleven routing elements and 15 000 km of the National LambdaRail optical backbone. We explore a range of traffic patterns, with packet sizes from 46 to 1500 Bytes, data rates up to 9 Gigabits per second, and single-flow packet rates up to 16 million packets per second.

Our instrumentation reveals phenomena previously obscured by the relatively imprecise methods available to classic network performance studies. In particular, we show that — irrespective of the input data rate — routers introduce burstiness. Thus, downstream routers and receiver endpoints must be prepared to accept extended chains of packets with the minimum legal 10GbE packet spacing, or, equivalently, the highest possible instantaneous data rate. Commodity receiver endpoints will often drop packets from flows with such bursts of minimally spaced packets. In fact, our prior observation of this anomalous behavior served originally to motivate this study [20].

In analyzing our data set, we probe the self-similarity of our results and exclude anomalous explanations for the observed probability densities of inter-packet delays. Further, we validate the stability of our definition of packet chains and find that chains of increasing length occur with exponentially less frequency. Finally, we comment upon the relative insensitivity of our distribution of packet delays to the background traffic along our WAN path.

All data collected here are available to the scientific community at `http://bifocals.cs.cornell.edu/`. Similarly, we freely distribute the software component of BIFOCALS under a two-clause BSD license.

6. ACKNOWLEDGEMENTS

We thank Jennifer Rexford for her insightful suggestions, David Bindel for his informative discourse, Robert Broberg and his colleagues at Cisco for their technical knowledge, and our referees for their anonymous, though no less thoughtful, input. We further recognize the engineers who helped establish and maintain the network infrastructure on which we performed these experiments: Eric Cronise, Dan Eckstrom, and Ed Kiefer (Cornell Information Technologies); Greg Boles, Brent Sweeny, and Joe Lappa (National LambdaRail); Scott Yoest and Larry Parmelee (Cornell Computer Science Technical Staff). Funding for this work was provided by the Air Force Research Laboratory (AFRL) and the National Science Foundation (NSF).

7. REFERENCES

[1] ANDERSON, T., COLLINS, A., KRISHNAMURTHY, A., AND ZAHORJAN, J. PCP: Efficient Endpoint Congestion Control. In *NSDI* (2006).

[2] Baccelli, F., Machiraju, S., Veitch, D., and Bolot, J. On Optimal Probing for Delay and Loss Measurement. In *IMC* (2007).

[3] Blake, S., Black, D., Carlson, M., Davies, E., Wang, Z., and Weiss, W. RFC 2475: An Architecture for Differentiated Services, 1998.

[4] Brakmo, L. S., and Peterson, L. L. TCP Vegas: End to End Congestion Avoidance on a Global Internet. *IEEE J. Sel. Area. Comm. 13* (1995), 1465–1480.

[5] Carter, R. L., and Crovella, M. E. Measuring Bottleneck Link Speed in Packet-Switched Networks. *Perform. Evaluation 27–28* (1996), 297–318.

[6] Choi, B., Moon, S., Zhang, Z., Papagiannaki, K., and Diot, C. Analysis of Point-To-Point Packet Delay In an Operational Network. *Comput. Netw. 51* (2007), 3812–3827.

[7] Crovella, M., and Krishnamurthy, B. *Internet Measurement: Infrastructure, Traffic and Applications.* Wiley, 2006.

[8] Endace DAG Network Cards. `http://www.endace.com/dag-network-monitoring-cards.html`.

[9] Hohn, N., Papagiannaki, K., and Veitch, D. Capturing Router Congestion and Delay. *IEEE ACM T. Network. 17* (2009), 789–802.

[10] IEEE Standard 802.3ae-2002. `http://grouper.ieee.org/groups/802/3/ae/`.

[11] IEEE Standard 802.3-2008. `http://standards.ieee.org/getieee802/802.3.html`.

[12] Iperf. `http://iperf.sourceforge.net/`.

[13] Ixia Interfaces. `http://www.ixiacom.com/`.

[14] Jiang, H., and Dovrolis, C. Why is the Internet Traffic Bursty in Short Time Scales? In *SIGMETRICS* (2005).

[15] Kaminow, I. P., and Li, T., Eds. *Optical Fiber Telecommunications: IV A & IV B.* Academic, 2002.

[16] Kompella, R. R., Levchenko, K., Snoeren, A. C., and Varghese, G. Every Microsecond Counts: Tracking Fine-Grain Latencies with a Lossy Difference Aggregator. In *SIGCOMM* (2009).

[17] Kurose, J. On Computing Per-session Performance Bounds in High-Speed Multi-hop Computer Networks. In *SIGMETRICS* (1992).

[18] Leland, W. E., Taqqu, M. S., Willinger, W., and Wilson, D. V. On the Self-Similar Nature of Ethernet Traffic (Extended Version). *IEEE ACM T. Network. 2* (1994), 1–15.

[19] Lockwood, J. W., McKeown, N., Watson, G., Gibb, G., Hartke, P., Naous, J., Raghuraman, R., and Luo, J. NetFPGA – An Open Platform for Gigabit-rate Network Switching and Routing. In *MSE* (2007).

[20] Marian, T., Freedman, D. A., Birman, K., and Weatherspoon, H. Empirical Characterization of Uncongested Optical Lambda Networks and 10GbE Commodity Endpoints. In *DSN* (2010).

[21] Mytkowicz, T., Diwan, A., Hauswirth, M., and Sweeney, P. F. Producing Wrong Data Without Doing Anything Obviously Wrong! In *ASPLOS* (2009).

[22] National LambdaRail. `http://www.nlr.net/`.

[23] Prasad, R., Murray, M., Dovrolis, C., and Claffy, K. Bandwidth Estimation: Metrics, Measurement Techniques, and Tools. *IEEE Network 17* (2003), 27–35.

[24] Wei, D. X., Jin, C., Low, S. H., and Hegde, S. FAST TCP: Motivation, Architecture, Algorithms, Performance. *IEEE ACM T. Network. 14* (2006), 1246–1259.

APPENDIX

A. HARDWARE FOUNDATION

We reference Figure 3 of Section 2.3 to depict both the transmission and acquisition hardware. All electrical and optical components used here are commercially available and commonly found in optical fiber communications labs. (Kaminow and Li [15] provide a comprehensive review of fiber components and systems.) The optical components for the transmitter consist of a continuous wave (CW) distributed feedback (DFB) laser (here: ILX Lightwave 79800E centered at $\lambda = 1555.75$ nm) and an electro-optic modulator (EOM, here: JDS Uniphase OC-192 Modulator). The CW laser outputs a constant light intensity, which is switched on and off by the EOM based upon a supplied electrical signal. This electrical impulse to the EOM is provided by the combination of a precise frequency synthesizer and a pulse pattern generator (PPG). The frequency synthesizer (here: Marconi 2042 Low Noise Signal Generator) is tuned to 5.15625 GHz, which is doubled (with a Narda 4453 frequency doubler) to 10.3125 GHz[14] to seed the clock of the PPG (here: Anritsu MP1800A / MU181020A with Picosecond Pulse Labs Model 5865 broadband RF amplifier). The PPG can be programmed with an arbitrary finite-length (here: 128 Mbit) bit sequence; it outputs an electrical waveform corresponding to these symbols continuously repeated, at a symbol rate of 10.3125 GBaud (as determined by the clock seed). The PPG output drives the EOM, resulting in an optical waveform with high light intensity representing "1" bits and no light intensity representing "0" bits. The amplitude and bias of the electrical signal can be adjusted to ensure maximal light intensity for the 1 bits and minimal for the 0 bits (here: this EOM can achieve 20 dB extinction of "on" to "off"). The optical signal from the EOM is output through a single-mode optical fiber, which completes the optical transmitter.

On the receiver side, the BiFocals acquisition hardware consists of a fast, broadband 12.3 Gbps optical-to-electrical (O/E) converter (here: Discovery Semiconductor DSC-R402) and a real-time digital oscilloscope (here: LeCroy SDA 11000-XL) with fast sampling (40 GSa/sec), high detection bandwidth (11 GHz), and deep memory (100 MSa). The O/E converter, a broadband photodetector with a built-in high-gain current-to-voltage amplifier, transforms the incident optical waveform into an electrical output signal. We employ the real-time oscilloscope as an analog-to-digital converter (ADC), sampling the output from the O/E converter in excess of the Nyquist rate. Leveraging a precisely calibrated timebase, this real-time oscilloscope captures waveform traces that precisely reflect the symbolstream on the fiber. Waveform traces are subsequently transfered for later off-line deconstruction by our software stack.

[14] In accordance with the nominal symbol rate specified in Table 52–12 of IEEE 802.3-2008 [11].

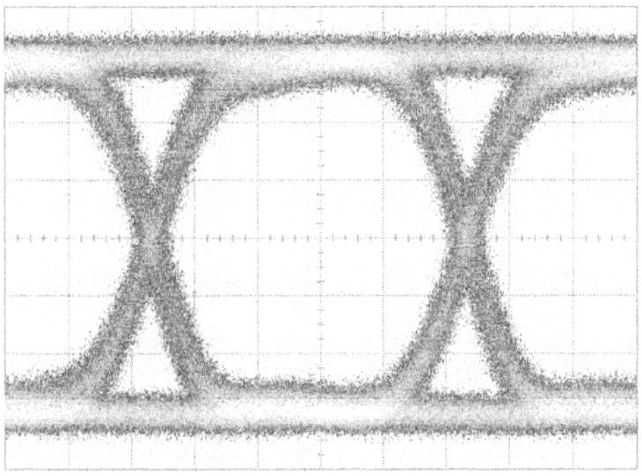

Figure 11: Eye diagram of the optical signal transmitted by BiFocals hardware: shows a large, open eye with negligible noise or jitter and conformance with 10GBase-R specifications for optical transmission power, rise time, eye mask, etc. Horizontal scale is 20 ps/div and vertical is 80 μW/div.

To validate the hardware instrumentation of BiFocals, we ascertain the quality of the transmitted optical signal (independent of the hardware receiver) by measuring its eye diagram, a standard measurement in digital communications. We connect the optical output of our transmitter directly to a wideband sampling oscilloscope (here: Agilent 86100A with 30 GHz 86109A optical module) and trigger it at the clock frequency of our transmitter, which overlays the sequence of samples in time, synchronized at a fixed point in the symbol frame, as shown in Figure 11. The degree to which the eye is "open" (in both time and amplitude) provides a direct metric of the quality of the signal. Vertical eye closure (indicative of high noise levels or weak signal) leads to ambiguity in the digitization of analog signals, while horizontal eye closure (from timing jitter or pulse walkoff) can result in symbol errors due to mis-sampling on a transition. The measured eye diagram for the BiFocals transmitter has lines that are thin and well-defined, indicating low amplitude and timing noise. Its central eye-opening is large and free of measured points, thus ensuring unambiguous "1" and "0" symbols in the signal. We also confirm via the measured eye diagram that our transmitter is in compliance with the time and amplitude standards for 10GBase-R.[15]

B. SOFTWARE STACK

With the description of the hardware layer of our BiFocals instrumentation complete, we now discuss the off-line software stack (shown also in Figure 3) that internalizes the intelligence and semantics of the Physical Layer and all other network layers. The transmission software stack involves two primary stages (analogous to PHY and MAC/IP/UDP layers): first, the creation of a sequence of discrete Ethernet packets; and second, the insertion of these packets into a continuous 64b/66b Physical Coding Sublayer (PCS) symbolstream suitable for transmission on the physical fiber media. Generation of a sequence of packets, in compliance with appropriate protocols, is a straightforward task of software engineering: our current implementation incorporates Ethernet, IP, UDP, and various application payloads.

The integration of these discrete packets into a standards-compliant 64b/66b PCS symbolstream, however, involves a number of subtleties. PCS wraps 64 bits of symbols into a 66-bit frame, resulting in a 3.125% overhead and requiring a 10.3125 GBaud symbol rate for a 10 Gbps data rate. The 64 bits are 8 octets of data or control information, while the two bits that delineate the frame ensure a signal transition every frame (as only "01" and "10" are allowed), easing clock recovery and frame synchronization. The content of these 64b/66b frames are mandated by the control code and data block formats allowed,[16] especially with respect to *Start* (`/S/`), *Terminate* (`/T/`), and *Idle* (`/I/`) control codes. The resulting sequence of the 64 payload bits from each frame is sequentially fed through a multiplicative self-synchronizing scrambler, defined by the polynomial $G(x) = 1 + x^{39} + x^{58}$ [11], to ensure that the resulting signal has desired DC-balance characteristics, irrespective of transmitted data. Self-synchronization ensures that the descrambler of the receiver does not need knowledge of any given initial state to implement $G(x)$.

Finally, when inserting discrete packets into the symbolstream, our encoder must minimize any boundary effects of the finite-length PPG memory depth by: (1) ensuring symbolstreams are integer numbers of 64b/66b frames (for PCS frame-sync); (2) positioning `/I/` codes at the start of the symbolstream (to mitigate the initial 58 bits necessary for self-synchronization of the descrambler at the beginning of the symbolstream); (3) maintaining identical numbers of `/I/` codes, as desired, across the periodic boundary of the symbolstream as it wraps around (for complete homogeneity of packets in time, required in this study); and (4) maximizing the length of the symbolstream, so as still to be able to fit it within the given finite PPG memory depth. To sum, our 64b/66b software encoder must comply with these requirements and implement all necessary functionality to generate a valid 64b/66b PCS symbolstream that can be understood by any deployed 10GBase-R implementation, such as commercial routers and switches.

In comparison with our software stack for symbolstream generation, our software for symbolstream deconstruction requires an additional clock recovery and waveform digitization step before conducting the inverse of the functions described above. (Note, on the transmission side, the hardware, rather than the software, handles the clock generation.) Accurate clock recovery is non-trivial and computationally expensive, but necessary for subsequent success at decoding symbolstreams and parsing packet streams. Our software clock recovery involves mathematical transformations (Fast Fourier Transforms, convolutions, etc.) of the acquired sampled waveform and a number of intermediary modules to iteratively refine our estimate for the symbol period associated with the actual symbol rate of the sender. These numerical calculations consume the bulk of the 5000+ processor-hours required for this data set.

The next two stages of our acquisition software provide 64b/66b PCS decoding and descrambling, as well as higher layer packet parsing, in exact analogue to the transmission scenario. Finally, we use the symbol period extracted during clock recovery, T_S, and convert the measured bit offsets, between successive packet Start-of-Frame (SOF) delimiters, into inter-packet delay times. Here, we measure $T_S = 96.9710 \pm 0.0001$ ps, with accuracy determined by BiFocals acquisition components.

[15]See Table 52–12 in IEEE 802.3-2008 [11].

[16]See Figure 49–7 of the IEEE 802.3-2008 standard [11].

TraceNET: An Internet Topology Data Collector

M. Engin Tozal
Department of Computer Science
The University of Texas at Dallas
Richardson, TX 75080 U.S.A.
engintozal@utdallas.edu

Kamil Sarac
Department of Computer Science
The University of Texas at Dallas
Richardson, TX 75080 U.S.A.
ksarac@utdallas.edu

ABSTRACT

This paper presents a network layer Internet topology collection tool called **tracenet**. Compared to **traceroute**, **tracenet** can collect a more complete topology information on an end-to-end path. That is, while **traceroute** returns a list of IP addresses each representing a router on a path, **tracenet** attempts to return all the IP addresses assigned to the interfaces on each visited subnetwork on the path. Consequently, the collected information (1) includes more IP addresses belonging to the traced path; (2) represents "being on the same LAN" relationship among the collected IP addresses; and (3) annotates the discovered subnets with their observed subnet masks. Our experiments on Internet2, GEANT, and four major ISP networks demonstrate promising results on the utility of **tracenet** for future topology measurement studies.

Categories and Subject Descriptors

C.2 [**COMPUTER-COMMUNICATION NETWORKS**]: Network Architecture and Design

General Terms

Measurement

Keywords

Internet, Network, Subnet, Topology, Traceroute

1. INTRODUCTION

Many successful research projects and efforts have been introduced attempting to derive an accurate and large scale topology map of the Internet [17, 18, 22, 16]. These efforts focus on different but correlated topology maps: *IP level* maps show IP addresses that are in use on the Internet; *router level* maps group the interfaces hosted by the same router into a single unit (via alias resolution); *subnet level* maps enrich the router level maps with subnet level connectivity info; and *AS level* maps demonstrate the adjacency relationship between ASes.

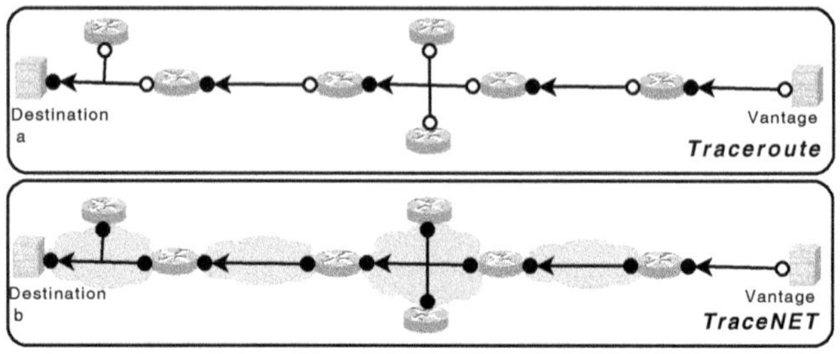

Figure 1: Traceroute vs tracenet on a path trace. Traceroute collects a single IP address vs tracenet collects a subnet at each hop.

Adverse to the benefits of having a network topology map, the main tools used to collect router or IP address level topology data are a few and operationally limited. **Traceroute** [12] and **ping** are the main data collection tools. **Traceroute** collects a list of IP addresses one for each router on the path between two hosts and **ping** is mainly used to check whether an IP address is in use or not. Almost all topology mapping projects use data collected by **traceroute** from multiple vantage points [19].

In this study, we propose a new end-to-end topology collection tool called **tracenet**. An accurate and complete Internet topology map at the router level requires identifying all routers and subnets among them. **Traceroute** attempts to collect an IP address at each router on a path between two hosts whereas **tracenet** attempts to collect a subnet at each router on the same path. In the worst case, **tracenet** returns the exact path that would be returned by **traceroute**, and, in the best case, it collects the complete topology of each subnet visited on the path. Consequently, a single session of **tracenet** (1) discovers new IP addresses that are missed by **traceroute**, (2) marks multi-access and point-to-point links, (3) reveals subnet relationship among IP addresses on the path, and (4) annotates the subnets with their observed subnet masks. **Traceroute**'s ability to collect a similar data is often limited in practice due to the difficulties of obtaining a reverse path trace and due to the dynamics of the underlying routing behavior between the two systems. As an example, consider the use of **traceroute** and **tracenet** to collect router level topology info between a vantage point

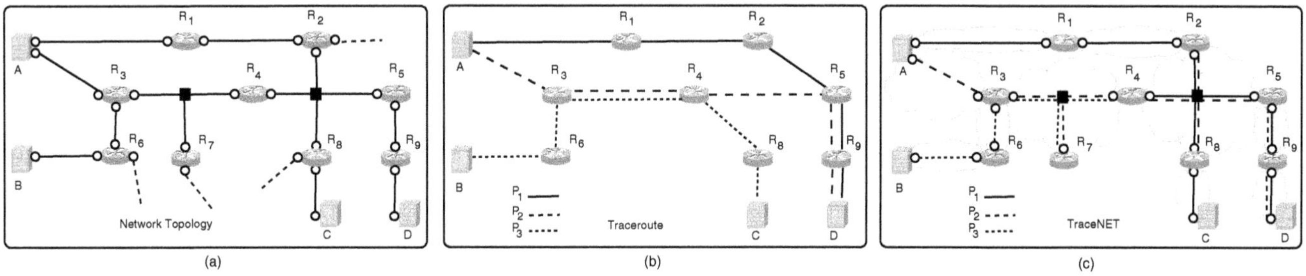

Figure 2: A network topology section among hosts A, B, C, and D with unweighed links. $P_1 = \{A, R_1, R_2, R_5, R_9, D\}$ and $P_2 = \{A, R_3, R_4, R_5, R_9, D\}$ are two paths from A to D. $P_3 = \{B, R_6, R_3, R_4, R_8, C\}$ is a path from B to C. Figures show the original network topology, `traceroute` view of the paths and `tracenet` view of the paths respectively.

and a destination as shown in Figure 1. Figures 1.a and 1.b show the data acquired by `traceroute` and `tracenet` respectively over a network segment. In the figure, small circles attached to the routers show the interfaces on the routers. An interface whose IP address is revealed during a trace is shown in black and otherwise is shown in white. The lines represent point-to-point or multi-access LANs and the arrows on the links show the routing direction of the trace between the vantage point and the destination. Note that in order for `traceroute` to return a similar topology information as `tracenet`, one needs to run `traceroute` in the reverse direction (from the destination to the vantage point) as well. However, a key limitation for `traceroute` is that one may not have access to the destination node to run a `traceroute` query in the reverse direction. Even if one has the required access, the paths between the two nodes may not be symmetric and therefore the reverse trace returned by `traceroute` might not capture the missing information from the first path trace. In fact, such a trace may return another incomplete network topology data for the reverse path. `Tracenet`, on the other hand, attempts to collect the complete topology information on the path in a single trace from the vantage point to the destination.

This valuable information comes with extra probing overhead. However, taking into account that acquiring similar information with `traceroute` requires extensive tracing conducted from many vantage points and a careful post processing [10, 8, 7], `tracenet` can be regarded as a cost effective solution in terms of bandwidth and computation.

Two important objectives in router level Internet topology mapping studies are *completeness* and *accuracy*. Completeness objective requires discovering each and every alive IP address on a given network and accuracy objective requires grouping together IP addresses that are on the same router and establishing both multi-access and point-to-point links between the routers.

A common goal in most topology discovery studies is to increase the coverage of the underlying network as much as possible. This is typically implemented by increasing the number of vantage points and destination addresses in topology discovery. However, the utility of this commonly followed approach was shown to be limited [6]. One of our primary goals in this work is to maximize the utility of our data collection process by focusing on discovering the complete topology of the visited subnets on the path. Naturally our approach allows us to collect more information at each path trace issued at a vantage point.

One critical observation about the existing topology discovery studies is that accuracy is always considered as a posterior process after data collection. Accuracy objective is achieved by addressing several functional steps in converting raw topology data to the corresponding topology maps and it involves IP alias resolution, anonymous router resolution, and subnet inference steps. Most of these tasks are shown to be computationally expensive due to the large volume of data [10, 8, 7]. `Tracenet` combines some of these functional steps, e.g., subnet inference, into topology collection phase significantly reducing the computational complexity in converting the raw data into corresponding topology maps.

Note that both completeness and accuracy conditions affect practical utility of the resulting topology maps. As an example, consider the use of a collected network topology map in designing resilient overlay network systems where the goal is to use the topology map to identify node and link disjoint overlay paths between two neighboring overlay nodes as shown in Figure 2. Figure 2.a shows the physical topology of a network that includes several point-to-point and multi-access links. Assume that our goal is to identify node and link disjoint paths between A and D as well as between B and C in this network. Figure 2.b shows the network topology collected by `traceroute` where P_1 and P_2 are two paths between A and D and P_3 is a single path between B and C. Based on this topology map one would infer that the use of P_1 for A to D path along with the use of P_3 for B and C path would satisfy the node and link disjointness requirement. However, this would be an inaccurate conclusion as routers R_2, R_4, R_5 and R_8 are sharing a multi-access link and P_1 and P_3 are not really link disjoint. On the other hand, a `tracenet` collected topology info as shown in Figure 2.c would include the subnet information hence, would help to avoid the incorrect conclusion above.

Our experimental evaluations of `tracenet` on Internet2 and GEANT topology, with data collected *from a single vantage point* at UT Dallas, resulted in a topology map with 86% similarity to the original Internet2 topology and 90% similarity to the original GEANT topology. (see Section 4.1). In addition, we ran `tracenet` over four major commercial ISPs from three vantage points and cross validated the obtained results (see Section 4.2). Figures show that around 60% of subnets observed by all three vantage points and roughly 80% of subnets observed by a particular vantage point is also observed from at least one other vantage point. Experimental results promote the use of `tracenet` in case studies involving network topology mapping and network analysis/debugging.

The remainder of the paper is organized as follows. Next section introduces the related work. Section 3 details the internals of `tracenet`. Section 4 presents our experimental evaluation results. Finally, Section 5 concludes the paper.

2. RELATED WORK

`Traceroute` [12] has been the main tool to collect router level topology data in the Internet. It sends TTL scoped packets in order to make the routers located at each hop between a vantage point and a destination to return ICMP TTL-Exceeded messages. Each router reports one of its IP addresses by setting it as the source address of the returned ICMP packet. All in all, `traceroute` returns a list of IP addresses each belonging to a router at each hop on the path. Certain load balancing practices may affect the accuracy of `traceroute` returned paths. A version of `traceroute`, called Paris `traceroute` [4], attempts to minimize the negative impact of such load balancing activities.

`Traceroute` can use ICMP, UDP, or TCP based probes. It has been reported that TCP `traceroute` is good at penetrating through firewalls whereas ICMP `traceroute` is more immune to path fluctuations [15, 9]. Discarte project [20] sets record-route option of probe packets to force the compliant routers to stamp the packets with outgoing IP address. As a result, it obtains two IP addresses per hop.

Various techniques have been used to discover more IP addresses in topology mapping studies. Skitter/ARK [17] traces the same set of destinations from multiple vantage points. Rocketfuel [21] aims to reveal the map of a single AS by carefully selecting the sources and the destinations to include the target AS network on the path traces. AROMA [13] advocates the selection of trace destinations from within the targeted network for better exploration of the network.

The well-known `ping` tool uses direct probing to check if a given IP address is in use or not. Census study [11] uses `ping` to determine alive IP addresses on the Internet.

Finally, our previous work [7] attempts to identify subnet relation among the IP addresses collected in a `traceroute` based topology collection study as a *post processing step* on the data set.

`Tracenet`, presented in this paper, is based on several observations related to IP address assignment practices and routing dynamics. Similar to `traceroute`, it obtains a single IP address at each hop, however, before moving to the next hop, it attempts to collect the IP addresses sharing the same LAN with the obtained IP address. *At the end of a `tracenet` run, we get a sequence of subnets between the source and destination hosts.* Unlike the approach presented in [7], `tracenet` discovers subnet topologies as part of the online data collection process.

3. TRACENET

In this section we develop necessary definitions, present several observations regarding operational and topological characteristics of the Internet, and describe internals of `tracenet`.

A router level Internet graph consists of routers and subnets. Each router and subnet hosts at least two interfaces. A router R is identified by the set of interfaces that it hosts: $R = \{l_1, l_2, \ldots, l_m\}$. Similarly, a subnet, S, is identified by a set of interfaces that are directly connected to it: $S = \{l_1, l_2, \ldots, l_n\}$. An interface l has an associated IP address defined as l^{ip} and a hop distance with respect to a certain vantage point v, shown as l^h_v. Whenever the vantage point v is obvious in a context, we drop v and use l^h. Finally, in our discussions we use $R.e$, $R.n$, $R.w$, and $R.s$ to refer to the interface located on (e)ast, (n)orth, (w)est, and (s)outh of a router R.

3.1 Definitions

In this section we introduce several definitions that we use in the rest of the paper.

(i) Direct Probing is the process of sending a probe packet with large enough TTL value destined to some IP address. It is used to test if the IP address is alive or not. In general a probe packet is an ICMP ECHO_REQUEST; a UDP packet destined to a likely unused port number; or the second packet of TCP handshake protocol. These probes force a responsive router to send back an ICMP ECHO_REPLY; an ICMP PORT_UNREACHABLE; or a TCP RESET packet, respectively.

(ii) Indirect Probing is the process of sending a probe packet with a small TTL value destined to some IP address in order to reveal an IP address of another router presumably located at TTL hops away on the path. The probe packet could be of type ICMP, UDP, or TCP. Whenever the TTL reaches zero, a responsive router would notify the originator of the probe message with an ICMP_TTL_EXCEEDED packet. The source address of this packet would be one of the IP addresses of the router based on its response configuration as explained next.

(iii) Router Response Configuration implies that a router is configured to remain reticent or reveal a certain interface's IP address in its response to a direct or indirect probe (query) packet. To the best of our knowledge, routers on the Internet are configured with five types of response policies: *nil interface routers* are configured not to respond to any probe packet; *probed interface routers* respond with the address of the probed interface; *incoming interface routers* respond with the address of the interface through which the probe packet has entered into the router; *shortest-path interface routers* respond with the address of the interface that has the shortest path from the router back to the probe originator; and *default interface routers* respond with a pre-designated default IP address regardless of the interface being probed. Usually, responsive routers are configured to behave as *probed interface routers* for direct probes and any other configuration for indirect probes. Observe that a router cannot be configured as *probed interface router* for indirect queries. Additionally, routers may be configured with multiple response configurations with respect to the protocol type of a probe packet i.e. ICMP, UDP, or TCP.

3.2 Observations

This section presents a set of operational and topological observations on the Internet.

(i) Hierarchical Addressing details the common IP address assignment practices and refers to the Classless Inter-Domain Routing (CIDR) on the Internet (RFC 4632). Given any subnetwork S on the Internet, the IP addresses assigned to the interfaces on S should share a common p bits prefix. Such a subnet S is said to have a $/p$ prefix (subnet mask) and is shown in this paper as S^p.

Any two IP addresses that have 31 or 30 bits common prefix are called *mate-31* or *mate-30* of each other.

(ii) Fixed Ingress Router implies that as long as there is no path fluctuations caused by routing updates, load balancing, or equal cost multi-path routing, there is a single path from a vantage point to any interface on a given subnet S. As an important result; two immediately successive probe packets released from the same vantage point and destined to two different interfaces on a subnet S are expected to reach the subnet through the same router. This fixed router is called *ingress router*. In Figure 3, R_2 is the ingress router of the subnet S with respect to the vantage (see Section 3.7 for more information on path fluctuations).

A fixed ingress router is resistant to intermediate path fluctuations as long as the fluctuated routes converge at or before the ingress router.

(iii) Unit Subnet Diameter implies that two interfaces on the same subnet are located at most one hop distance apart with respect to a vantage point. That is, for interfaces $i, j \in S \Rightarrow |i_v^h - j_v^h| \leq 1$. In Figure 3, interfaces $\{R_2.w, R_3.s, R_4.e, R_6.n\} \in S$ are at most one hop apart from each other with respect to the vantage.

(iv) Mate-31 Adjacency implies that given that i^{ip} and j^{ip} are alive and mate-31 of each other, then $i \in S \Rightarrow j \in S$.

3.3 Network Exploration (Growing)

In this section we detail how `tracenet` builds the subnet accommodating an IP address obtained at a particular hop and introduce the related algorithm. Similar to `traceroute`, `tracenet` gradually extends a trace path by obtaining an IP address l^{ip} (or anonymous) via indirect probing at each hop on the way from a vantage point to a destination. However, after obtaining IP address l^{ip} at a particular hop, `tracenet` collects other IP addresses that are hosted on the same subnet which accommodates interface l before moving to the next hop. We refer to the first step of acquiring an IP address at a certain hop via indirect probing as *trace collection* and refer to the second step of collecting other IP addresses sharing the same subnet as *subnet exploration*.

Given an acquired IP address l^{ip} at trace collection step, the main idea of subnet exploration is forming a subnet of /31 which covers l^{ip} and growing it as long as it does not conflict with one of the heuristics (Section 3.5) that we use for verifying the authenticity of the subnet.

Figure 3 freezes a `tracenet` session $P = \{\ldots, R_2.e, R_4.e\}$ at hop d. Interface $R_2.e$ was acquired at previous hop and interface $R_4.e$ is obtained at current hop via indirect probing in trace collection mode. Those two interfaces are called *ingress interface* and *pivot interface*, respectively. The router hosting the ingress interface (R_2 in Figure 3) is called the *ingress router*. In the figure, the interface $R_2.w$, which is located on the ingress router R_2 and accommodated on the same subnet with the pivot interface $R_4.e$, is called *contra-pivot interface*. Observe that the interface $R_4.e$ belongs to subnet S which hosts a number of other interfaces that we want to discover.

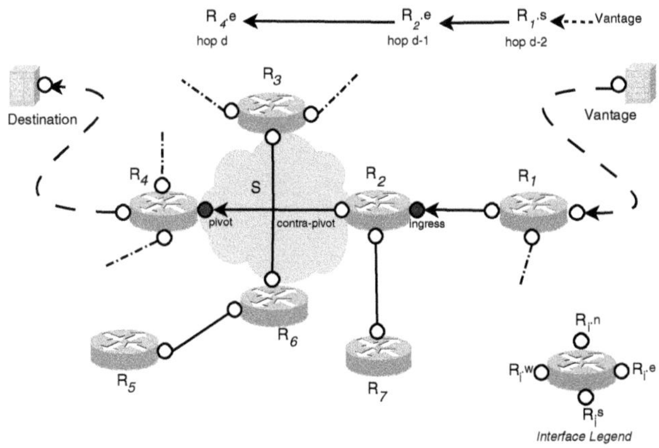

Figure 3: Subnet Exploration. Observed subnet is grown around the pivot interface discovered in trace collection mode by forming /31, /30, ... subnets.

To fully discover a subnet under investigation (S in Figure 3), `tracenet` forms a temporary subnet starting from /31 which covers the pivot interface and grows the subnet with decreasing prefix lengths (increasing subnet sizes). For each formed subnet, it directly probes the possible IP addresses within the range of the subnet to ensure that the probed IP address is assigned to an interface. Then, it applies the heuristics defined in Section 3.5 to decide whether or not the probed candidate IP address is on the subnet being explored. An investigated IP address breaking one of the heuristics implies that it is not on the subnet being built. As a result, subnet growing process immediately stops and the subnet gets shrunk to its last known valid state (i.e., the previous subnet prefix) by removing all interfaces that do not belong to the last valid state. Additionally, subnet growing stops if the number of successfully probed IP addresses for a subnet prefix is equal or less than half of the total number of IP addresses that such a subnet could accommodate.

Algorithm 1 shows the pseudocode for subnet exploration. Let $\hookrightarrow$ operator (read as "results in") be a syntactical element. $\langle i^{ip}, ttl\rangle \hookrightarrow \langle j^{ip}, RESPONSE\_MSG\_TYPE\rangle$ implies that probing of an IP address i^{ip} with TTL value of tll results in a response message of type $RESPONSE\_MSG\_TYPE$ with j^{ip} as the source IP address field of the message. If probing does not yield any response message, then j^{ip} and $RESPONSE\_MSG\_TYPE$ are set to *nil*. In cases where we are not interested in the value of j^{ip} but only the response message type, we use "..." in place of j^{ip}.

In the algorithm, the outer loop forms temporary growing of subnets S' starting from a /31 prefix. Inner loop traverses each candidate IP address in S' by first testing the aliveness of the IP address at distance d (line 6) and then applies the heuristics explained in Section 3.5 (line 7). As long as the heuristics hold for the current IP address, it is assumed to be part of subnet S being gradually built (line 12). Whenever any heuristic fails, the subnet gets shrunk to previous prefix (line 9). Obtaining an ICMP TTL-Exceeded message as a result of the test at line 6 implies that the subnet is overgrown and needs to be shrunk (lines 14-17). Lines 19-21 ensure that more than half of the potential IP addresses of S are utilized before growing S one more level further.

Algorithm 1 Subnet Exploration

```
Input: l_ingress, l_pivot /*ingress and pivot interfaces respectively*/
Output: S /*observed subnet*/
1  S ← ∅
2  S ← S ∪ {l_pivot}
3  for m ← 31 to 0 do
4    Form temporary S' covering l_pivot with prefix m
5    for each l^ip ∈ S' do
6      if ⟨l^ip, j^h⟩ ↪ ⟨..., ECHO_REPLY⟩ then
7        APPLY HEURISTICS TO l
8        if l breaks any heuristics then
9          S^p ← m + 1 /*Shrink S and STOP*/
10         return
11       else
12         S ← S ∪ {l}
13       end if
14     else if ⟨l^ip, j^h⟩ ↪ ⟨..., TTL_EXCD⟩ then
15       S^p ← m + 1 /*Shrink S and STOP*/
16       return
17     end if
18   end for
19   if m ≤ 29 and |S| ≤ (2^(32−m))/2 then
20     return
21   end if
22 end for
```

3.4 Subnet Positioning

As discussed in Section 3.1, routers usually report the queried IP addresses in their reply messages to direct probes. However, for indirect probes, a router may report the IP address of the incoming interface, a default interface or the interface on the shortest path from itself back to the vantage point. *Tracenet builds the subnet which accommodates the interface obtained with indirect probing at trace collection mode.* Therefore, it needs to correctly designate a pivot and an ingress interface, determine the distance to the pivot interface from the vantage point, and decide whether or not the subnet is on the trace path before growing the subnet (Section 3.3). Subnet positioning, discussed in this section, is the process of designating pivot and ingress interfaces, determining the distance of the pivot interface from the vantage point and deciding if the subnet is on the trace path.

In most cases, the perceived *direct* distance of a vantage point to an interface l that is obtained *indirectly* at hop d is also d. In some other cases, however, it might differ by one or a few hops. Consequently, direct distance to other interfaces on the subnet accommodating l changes. To determine the hop distance from the vantage point to an interface l obtained with indirect probing at hop d in trace collection mode, `tracenet` sends probe packets with increasing (forward) and decreasing (backward) TTL values starting from d until it locates the exact location of l.

Figure 4 shows portion of a `tracenet` session frozen at hop d passing through the routers R_1 and R_3. Different from Figure 3, it does not show the reported interfaces (filled black) by the routers in order to discuss various scenarios. Let u and v be the two successive interfaces obtained from R_1 and R_3 in trace collection mode at hops $d-1$ and d, respectively.

A subnet S to be explored in subnet exploration mode is said to be "on-the-trace-path" if the indirect probe packet in trace collection mode passes through it. For instance, in Figure 4, if router R_3 returns $R_3.e$ and the path to $R_3.e$ is P

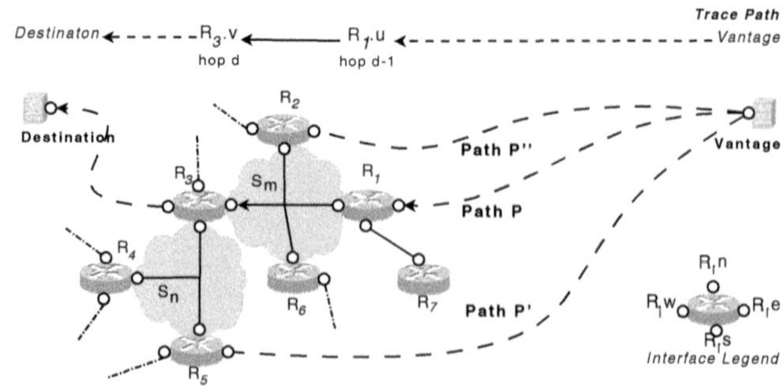

Figure 4: Subnet Positioning. Assuming path to S_m and S_n is P or P'', if $R_3.v = R_3.e$ then $l_{pivot} = R_3.e$, on the other hand, if $R_3.v = R_3.s$ then $l_{pivot} = mate31(R_3.e)$ or $l_{pivot} = mate30(R_3.e)$

or P'' then the subnet to be explored is S_m and it is on-the-trace-path. On the other hand, if it returns $R_3.s$ then the subnet to be explored is S_n and it is "off-the-trace-path". In Figure 4, `tracenet` assumes that a subnet to be explored at hop d is off-the-trace-path if the perceived direct distance to v is different from d. Instead, if the perceived direct distance to v is d and probing v^{ip} with TTL value $d-1$ results in an ICMP_TTL_EXCEEDED message with source IP address u^{ip}, i.e., $\langle v^{ip}, d-1\rangle \hookrightarrow \langle u^{ip}, TTL\_EXCD\rangle$ then the subnet to be explored is on-the-trace-path. On the other hand, if perceived direct distance to v is d and probing v^{ip} with TTL value $d-1$ results in an ICMP_TTL_EXCEEDED message with source IP address other than u^{ip} i.e., $\langle v^{ip}, d-1\rangle \hookrightarrow \langle l^{ip}, TTL\_EXCD\rangle$ where $l \neq u$, `tracenet` probabilistically concludes that the subnet to be explored is off-the-trace-path.

Under a stable path to a subnet S, the pivot interface is always selected among the farthest interfaces of a subnet to be explored with respect to the vantage point, i.e., $\exists l_{contra-pivot} \in S : \forall (l \neq l_{contra-pivot}), l^h = l^h_{contra-pivot} + 1$, $l \in S$, and $l_{pivot} \neq \{l_{contra-pivot}\}$ in S. To illustrate in Figure 4, in case R_3 returns $R_3.e$ and the path to subnet S_m is P or P'' then $R_3.e$ serves as pivot interface. Conversely, if R_3 returns $R_3.s$ and the path to subnet S_n is P or P'' then some other alive interface $l \in S_n$ (usually /31 mate or /30 mate of $R_3.s$) serves as pivot interface. Let $mate31(l^{ip})$ and $mate30(l^{ip})$ be functions returning /31 and /30 mate of a given IP address l^{ip}. `Tracenet` exploits mate-31 adjacency defined in Section 3.2 to determine the pivot interface. In Figure 4, if sending a probe packet to /31 mate of the IP address $v^{ip} \in R_3$ with TTL value of $v^h = d$ results in an ICMP response of $TTL\_EXCEEDED$, i.e. $\langle mate31(v^{ip}), v^h\rangle \hookrightarrow \langle \ldots, TTL\_EXCD\rangle$, then pivot interface is mate /31 or mate /30 of v^{ip}, otherwise pivot interface is v itself. Similar argument applies to /30 mate in case probing /31 does not yield any response.

After determining the pivot interface l_{pivot} at a distance d for the subnet to be explored, the ingress interface $l_{ingress}$ is obtained by sending a probe packet to the pivot interface with a TTL value of $d-1$ from the vantage point. Formally, $\langle l^{ip}_{pivot}, l^h_{pivot} - 1\rangle \hookrightarrow \langle l^{ip}_{ingress}, TTL\_EXCD\rangle$.

Algorithm 2 details the process of subnet positioning. In the algorithm $dst(l^{ip})$ is a function that determines the direct distance to the interface l from the vantage point. Lines

2-10 determine if the subnet to be explored is on-the-trace-path. Lines 11-21 designate the pivot interface and line 22 designates the ingress interface of the subnet to be explored.

Algorithm 2 Subnet Positioning

Input: u, v, d /*last two interfaces obtained in trace collection mode at hop $d-1$ and d*/
Output: $l_{pivot}, l_{ingress}$ /*pivot and ingress interfaces*/
1 $v^h \leftarrow dst(v^{ip})$
2 **if** $v^h \neq d$ **then**
3 Subnet to be explored is off-the-trace-path
4 **else**
5 **if** $\langle v^{ip}, v^h - 1\rangle \hookrightarrow \langle u^{ip}, TTL\_EXCD\rangle$ **then**
6 Subnet to be explored is on-the-trace-path
7 **else if** $\langle v^{ip}, v^h - 1\rangle \hookrightarrow \langle i^{ip}, TTL\_EXCD\rangle$ where $i^{ip} \neq u^{ip}$ **then**
8 Subnet to be explored is off-the-trace-path
9 **end if**
10 **end if**
11 **if** $\langle mate31(v^{ip}), v^h\rangle \hookrightarrow \langle \ldots, TTL\_EXCD\rangle$ **then**
12 **if** $mate31(v^{ip})$ is in use **then**
13 $l^{ip}_{pivot} \leftarrow mate31(v^{ip})$
14 **else if** $mate30(v^{ip})$ is in use **then**
15 $l^{ip}_{pivot} \leftarrow mate30(v^{ip})$
16 **end if**
17 $l^h_{pivot} \leftarrow v^h + 1$
18 **else**
19 $l^{ip}_{pivot} \leftarrow v^{ip}$
20 $l^h_{pivot} \leftarrow v^h$
21 **end if**
22 $l_{ingress} \leftarrow i$ where $\langle l^{ip}_{pivot}, l^h_{pivot} - 1\rangle \hookrightarrow \langle i^{ip}, TTL\_EXCD\rangle$

3.5 Heuristics

Heuristics given in this section are based on the common IP address assignment practices and routing behavior on the Internet. They are devised to capture a subnet regardless of its location at the core or edge of the Internet and regardless of its being a multi access LAN or a point to point link.

Let u and v be two consecutive interfaces obtained in trace collection mode and i and j be the ingress and pivot interfaces respectively determined by the subnet positioning algorithm. Note that $u = i$ and $v = j$ may or may not hold. Let l^{ip} be the IP address suspected to be sharing the same subnet with j^{ip} and S be the subnet we are trying to infer such that $j, v \in S$.

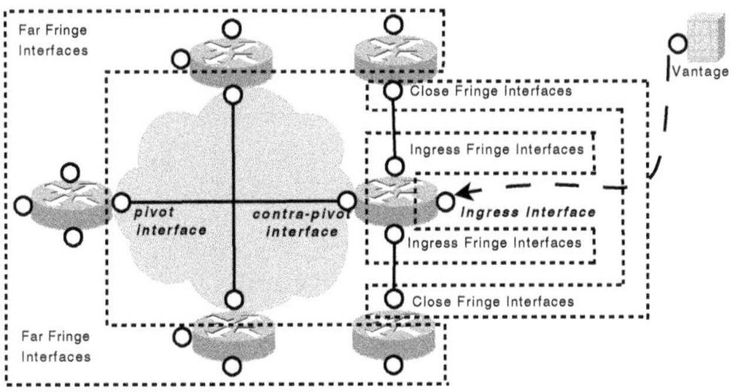

Figure 5: Fringe Interface Categorization

Figure 5 categorizes the false positive interfaces that are prone to be misinferred as members of the investigated subnet because they are located at the same distance from the vantage point as the interfaces of the subnet to be explored. None of the fringe interfaces are accommodated by the subnet being investigated and they must be caught and excluded from the observed subnet which is gradually being built. Additionally, trapping a fringe interface is a signal that the subnet exploration phase is growing the observed subnet beyond its bona-fide boundaries. As a result, `tracenet` stops growing the subnet and to shrinks it to its last known valid state.

Ingress fringe interfaces are the ones that are hosted by the ingress router. Far fringe interfaces are hosted by routers that are one hop distant from the ingress router but are not accommodated by any subnet that the ingress router has direct access. Similarly, close fringe interfaces are hosted by routers that are one hop distant from the ingress router but are accommodated by a subnet that the ingress router has direct access. Heuristics H3, H7, and H8 below catch the ingress, far fringe, and close fringe interfaces, respectively.

For each rule below, we give a description, a formal statement of a related observation on the Internet, and a code snippet demonstrating how `tracenet` utilizes the observation. Each code snippet is a test applied to address l^{ip}; keyword *apply-next-heuristic* implies l has passed the test and continue to apply the rest of the tests; keyword *stop-and-shrink* implies l has failed the test, hence, growing S should be stopped and S must get shrunk to its last known valid state; and keyword *continue-with-next-address* implies continue to grow S by getting the next candidate IP address to examine.

Although, the code snippets given for each heuristics lack details and have repetitions, our `tracenet` implementation is optimized to collect the subnets with the least number of probes and some of the rules are merged together.

Remember that in the following rules j^{ip} is the pivot IP address and l^{ip} is the candidate IP address that needs to be tested.

H1 prefix reduction: In the context of subnet exploration, whenever an IP address breaks the rules given below and causes the *stop-and-shrink* instruction to be executed, then subnet S is shrunk to last known intact status. That is S^p gets reduced to $S^p + 1$ and all false positive interfaces (i.e., interfaces conforming S^p but not $S^p + 1$), if ever passed the heuristics, gets omitted from subnet S. Obviously, as the subnet grows larger and larger the possibility of encountering a false positive causing *stop-and-shrink* instruction to be executed increases. This rule serves as a stopping condition of subnet exploration algorithm and increases our trust on the accuracy of large subnets.

H2 upper-bound subnet contiguity: This rule ensures that the examined IP address l^{ip} is in use and is not located farther from the investigated subnet with respect to the vantage point. More formally, $j, l \in S \Rightarrow \langle l^{ip}, j^h\rangle \hookrightarrow \langle \ldots, ECHO\_RPLY\rangle$.
Code snippet:

if $\langle l^{ip}, j^h\rangle \hookrightarrow \langle \ldots, ECHO\_RPLY\rangle$ **then**
apply-next-heuristic
else if $\langle l^{ip}, j^h\rangle \hookrightarrow \langle \ldots, TTL\_EXCD\rangle$ **then**
stop-and-shrink /*l located farther from S*/
else
continue-with-next-address
end if

H3 single contra-pivot interface: This rule ensures that the examined IP address l^{ip} is not one of the ingress

fringe interfaces. More formally, under a stable path to subnet S, $\exists l_{contra-pivot} \in S$ where $l^h_{contra-pivot} = j^h - 1$ and $\forall (l \neq l_{contra-pivot}), l^h = j^h$ where $l \in S$.
Code snippet:

```
if ⟨l^ip, j^h − 1⟩ ↪ ⟨..., ECHO_RPLY⟩ and l_contra−pivot = NIL then
    i_contra−pivot ← l
    apply-next-heuristic
else if ⟨l^ip, j^h −1⟩ ↪ ⟨..., ECHO_RPLY⟩ and l_contra−pivot ≠ NIL then
    stop-and-shrink /*Second contra-pivot detected*/
else
    continue-with-next-address
end if
```

Note that, regarding Figure 3, R_2 is the router hosting the contra-pivot interface $R_2.w$ and any other interface of R_2 seems to potentially pass the test given above. However, subnet exploration process demonstrated in Algorithm 1 starts to grow the subnet from prefix /31 and $R_2.w$ will be examined before any other interface hosted by R_2.

H4 lower-bound subnet contiguity: This rule increases our confidence level on contra-pivot interface before adding l to the subnet S if the examined IP address l^{ip} found to be a contra-pivot interface by H3. More formally, $\{l$ is found to be contra-pivot interface$\} \Rightarrow \langle l^{ip}, j^h - 2\rangle \hookrightarrow \neg\langle \ldots, ECHO_RPLY\rangle$.
Code snippet:

```
if l_contra−pivot = l and ⟨l^ip, j^h −2⟩ ↪ ⟨..., ECHO_RPLY⟩ then
    stop-and-shrink
else
    S ← S ∪ l
    continue-with-next-address
end if
```

H5 mate-31 subnet contiguity: This rule is a shortcut to add the examined IP address l^{ip} to subnet S if it is /31 mate of the pivot. The same rule is valid $l^{ip} = mate30(j^{ip})$ only if $mate31(j^{ip})$ is found not to be in use. More formally, $l^{ip} = mate31(j^{ip}) \Rightarrow l \in S$.
Code snippet:

```
if l^ip = mate31(j^ip) then
    S ← S ∪ l
    continue-with-next-address
else
    apply-next-heuristic
end if
```

H6 fixed entry points: This rule is used to test whether the examined IP address l^{ip} resides on a different subnet located at the same distance with S or not. More formally, $\{l$ is found not to be the contra-pivot interface$\} \Rightarrow (\langle l^{ip}, j^h - 1\rangle \hookrightarrow \langle i, TTL_EXCD\rangle$ or $\langle l^{ip}, j^h - 1\rangle \hookrightarrow \langle u, TTL\_EXCD\rangle$.
Code snippet:

```
if ⟨l^ip, j^h − 1⟩ ↪ ⟨i, TTL_EXCD⟩ then
    apply-next-heuristic
else if S is on-the-trace-path and ⟨l^ip, j^h −1⟩ ↪ ⟨u, TTL_EXCD⟩ then
    apply-next-heuristic
else if ⟨l^ip, j^h − 1⟩ ↪ ⟨k, TTL_EXCD⟩ where k ≠ i and k ≠ u then
    stop-and-shrink
else if ⟨l^ip, j^h − 1⟩ ↪ ⟨i, ECHO_RPLY⟩ then
    stop-and-shrink
end if
```

Remember that u is obtained in trace collection mode and i is obtained by subnet positioning algorithm. To minimize effects of path fluctuations both i and u are considered to be valid entry points to subnet S. Note that the rule is valid in case i and/or u are anonymous.

H7 upper-bound router contiguity: This rule is used to detect whether the examined IP address l^{ip} is one of the far fringe interfaces or not. More formally, $l \in S \Rightarrow \langle mate31(l^{ip}), j^h\rangle \hookrightarrow \neg\langle \ldots, TTL\_EXCD\rangle$.
Code snippet:

```
if ⟨mate31(l^ip), j^h⟩ ↪ ⟨..., TTL_EXCD⟩ then
    stop-and-shrink /*Far Fringe interface detected*/
else
    apply-next-heuristic
end if
```

A router hosting an interface that resides on S at distance j^h also hosts some other interfaces that are not on S. Those interfaces may pass all the rules given above and they must be eliminated.

To illustrate, in Figure 3, $R_6.w$ or $R_4.s$ behaves as if they are on the subnet. However, a probe directed to their /31 mates with $TTL = d$ result in a TTL-Exceeded message with a very high probability. Conversely, /31 mate of an interface that is really on subnet S, for example /31 mate of $R_6.n$ must result in an ICMP Echo-Reply or anonymous.

Note that if l is a far fringe interface, then the probe packet destined to its /31 expires one hop earlier. In case probing /31 mate of l^{ip} does not yield any response or yields an ICMP Host-Unreachable the same heuristic is performed with /30 mate.

H8 lower-bound router contiguity: This rule is used to detect whether the examined IP address l^{ip} is one of the close fridge interfaces or not. More formally, $l \in S \Rightarrow \langle mate31(l^{ip}), j^h - 1\rangle \hookrightarrow \neg\langle \ldots, ECHO\_RPLY\rangle$ such that $mate31(l^{ip}) \neq l^{ip}_{contra-pivot}$.
Code snippet:

```
if mate31(l^ip) ≠ l^ip_contra−pivot then
    if ⟨mate31(l^ip), j^h − 1⟩ ↪ ⟨..., ECHO_RPLY⟩ then
        stop-and-shrink /*Close Fringe interface detected*/
    else
        apply-next-heuristic
    end if
end if
```

To illustrate, in Figure 3, interface $R_7.n$ behaves as if it is on the subnet being investigated. However, a probe directed to its /31 mate with $TTL = d$ results in an ICMP Echo-Reply if the /31 mate is on the ingress router of the subnet being investigated. If probing /31 mate of l^{ip} does not yield any response or yields an ICMP Host-Unreachable, the same heuristic is performed with /30 mate. In case the subnet between R_2 and R_7 accommodates more than two interfaces, all false positive interfaces will be added to the investigated subnet until `tracenet` encounters an interface whose /31 or /30 mate is located on the ingress router. Remember that whenever `tracenet` traps a false positive interface, it shrinks S by removing all false positive interfaces from S.

H9 boundary address reduction: A final subnet that is populated with interfaces passing all the tests above cannot contain any of the boundary addresses, i.e., network address and broadcast address, unless $S^p = 31$. As a post processing task after collecting the subnet, as long as the subnet contains a boundary address, `tracenet` divides the subnet S into S_1 and S_2 where $S^p_1 = S^p_2 = S^p - 1$ drops S_i if $j \notin S_i$.

Remember that these nine heuristics are not designed for any specific type of network but are generic enough to work over various subnet configurations appearing on the Internet.

3.6 Probing Overhead

The exact number of probes for a `tracenet` session depends on the length of the trace, utilization/configuration of the IP addresses of the subnet being explored as well as its fringe subnets. In this section we give a model for lower and upper bounds on the probing complexity as a function of the size $|S|$ for a subnet S.

For each subnet S_i, *initial cost* is retrieving an IP address at the trace collection mode and determining pivot and ingress interfaces at the subnet positioning phase. The former requires a single probe and the latter requires one or three probes depending on the position of the subnet.

For each interface l on S_i; *intermediate cost* is incurred by heuristics and it depends on the type of l: no probing overhead for pivot interface; if l is /31 (or /30) mate of the pivot interface, then only H2 and H5 are applied; if l is contra pivot interface then, H2, H3, and H4 are applied; and otherwise, H2 to H4 and H6 to H8 are applied. Among those heuristics, H5 does not require probing, H7 and H8 may take one or two probes depending on the existence of $mate31(l^{ip})$, and the rest takes a single probe each where both H3 and H6 requires the same single probe.

For each subnet S_i; *final cost* is incurred by encountering a stopping condition and H9. Heuristic H9 has no probing overhead. On the other hand, stopping condition can be encountered because of either S_i being under-utilized (lines 19-21 of Algorithm 1) or trapping into a stop-and-shrink statement. The former has no probing cost, the latter depends on the number of heuristics applied until executing the stop-and-shrink statement.

The lower bound on probing overhead is when the discovered subnet S is a point-to-point link in which case only heuristics H2 and H5 are applied. Assuming, as the most typical case, the stopping condition is an immediate stop-and-shrink statement execution and the subnet is on-the-trace-path, the total cost is only four probes for discovering the point-to-point subnet.

The upper bound of probing overhead is when the discovered subnet S is off-the-trace-path and is a multi access LAN accommodating $|S| > 2$ interfaces. Each subnet has a single contra-pivot interface which requires three probes. Let $l^{ip} \neq mate31(i_{pivot})$, $\forall(l \in S)$, hence, $\forall(l \in S)$ requires all heuristics H2-H8 where heuristics H7 and H8 require two probes each. Also let the execution of the stopping condition is delayed until the last heuristic, i.e., H8. Under this scenario, exploring S has the *initial cost* of three probes, *final cost* of eight probes, and *intermediate cost* of three probes for contra-pivot interface and seven probes for other interfaces except pivot interface. As a result the upper bound probing cost would be $7|S| + 7$. Note that upper bound probing complexity is a worst case scenario with probability $p < 1/\binom{2^{\lceil \lg(2|S|-1) \rceil}}{|S|}$ of encountering and is only valid for multi access LANs. This scenario takes place when an administrator utilizes half of an IP address range where only the odd or even numbered IP addresses are assigned to interfaces.

3.7 Path Fluctuations

Path fluctuations [5] such as load balancing and equal cost multi-path routing on the Internet depend on local network traffic and router configuration that the packets pass through at a certain time. Although a single load balancing enabled router may potentially damage the authenticity of all trace paths passing on it, the effect is not the same for `tracenet` because *`tracenet` is based on the stable ingress router concept rather than stable path trace concept.* That is, as long as two packets destined to two different IP addresses on the same subnet enter into the subnet through the same ingress router we are not interested if they took the same path or not.

Heuristics defined above are meaningful at local sites identified by two neighboring routers and immune to path fluctuations taking place before and after the sites as long as the hop distance is preserved. On the other hand, path fluctuations with varying hop distances while exploring a subnet potentially causes the subnet being observed smaller than its actual size.

In case a path fluctuation occurs at a local site, only H6 among the rules given above gets affected. H6 expects that the packets destined to an interface on the subnet should enter into the subnet through certain router(s). The result of a path fluctuation in the context of H6 would be stopping to grow the subnet prematurely before it reaches its actual size. In order to minimize this negative effect we resort to the following methods: (1) our implementation of `tracenet` is completely based on ICMP probes which are shown to be the least affected by load balancing [15] and (2) `tracenet` always attempts to obtain at most two ingress routers to the subnet being investigated (one is in trace collection mode and the other is in subnet positioning phase) and applies the test H6 against both routers. As a result, any packet entering to the subnet through either of the routers does not cause early halt of subnet exploration phase.

Moreover, as long as the intermediate path fluctuations, if ever occur, converge to an ingress router determined by `tracenet`, H6 does not get affected from it and correctly grows the subnet. To increase the confidence level regarding path fluctuations on a collected subnet, the same subnet could be re-collected at a different time or from a different vantage point.

3.8 Limitations

`Tracenet` gradually enlarges a subnet around the IP address l_{pivot} after obtaining it via subnet positioning. Forming a subnet from a single IP address in a bottom-up fashion allows us to efficiently build large sized subnets compared to the top-down approach which assumes a very large subnet and shrinks it by testing if each IP address is within the boundaries of the assumed subnet. Since `tracenet` stops growing a subnet one level upwards in case it cannot fill at least half of the current level, sparsely utilized subnets might potentially get underestimated. A similar behavior would be observed when a consecutive portion of the IP addresses space of a subnet remain silent to `tracenet` probes. In our implementation we re-probe an IP address if we do not get a response for the first probe. Moreover, if the path length to the ingress router changes in the middle of subnet exploration mode then the resulting subnet would also be an underestimated subnet. Nevertheless, we believe that path length changes in the middle of subnet exploration mode is not very likely.

Trace collection mode of `tracenet` is similar to traditional `traceroute`. We plan to include the approach used in **Paris traceroute** in order to keep the end-to-end paths more stable. Finally, `tracenet` is designed mainly for IPv4 and its extension to IPv6 remains as a future work.

4. EVALUATIONS

In this section we measure accuracy and consistency of `tracenet` using two different types of experiments. In the first experiment set, we ran `tracenet` over Internet2 and GEANT and compare the collected subnets with the subnet list that we derived using the information provided by these research networks. Our comparisons are based on the rate of exact prefix length matches, similarity of subnet prefix lengths, and similarity of subnet sizes. For the second set of experiments, we ran `tracenet` from three different vantage points with a common target IP address set belonging to four commercial ISPs (Sprintlink, AboveNet, Level3, NTT America) and cross validate the collected subnets of each vantage point against the others. Finally, we ran `tracenet` from a single vantage point with ICMP, UDP, and TCP probe packets to see its behavior with different protocols. Note that the main focus in our experiments is limited to demonstrating the accuracy and consistency of `tracenet` rather than deriving complete [13, 21] or representative [14, 3] sample topologies of commercial ISPs.

Before continuing with the experiments and their evaluations we would like to point out a few issues regarding the authenticity of the subnets collected by `tracenet`. First of all, `tracenet` is based on active probing and completely unresponsive subnets, i.e., subnets located behind a firewall which blocks probe packets or their responses, cannot be captured. In this study we focus on sketching subnets at the core of the Internet which are mostly open for discovery. Secondly, a subnet sketched by `tracenet` is only an observable subnet. That is, if there is a partially unresponsive subnet, i.e., a subnet which consists of a mixture of responsive and unresponsive routers, `tracenet` can capture only the responsive portion of it. Related to observable subnet concept, in case there is a subnet utilizing only a portion of its whole IP address range, `tracenet` could only reveal what it observes. To illustrate, if a network administrator utilizes only a /30 portion of a subnet which is assigned a /29 subnet mask, `tracenet` collects it as a /30 subnet. Finally, Internet accommodates virtual subnets whose hosts connect to each other through tunnels. Even though such a tunnel is realized over a sequence of routers, `tracenet` captures it as a single subnet.

4.1 TraceNET Accuracy over Internet2 and GEANT

In this set of experiments, we run `tracenet` over Internet2 and GEANT and collect their subnet topologies. We measure the similarity of the collected topology against the derived subnet topologies of Internet2 and GEANT using four different metrics. In the first approach we directly compare the rate of exact matches i.e., rate of subnets that are collected exactly as announced in the original topologies. Results show that exact match rate of `tracenet` for Internet2 is 73.7% and for GEANT is 53.5%. In the second approach, we exclude those unresponsive subnets, i.e., the ones that do not reply back to our probes, and evaluate the exact match rate again. With this approach, our exact match rate raises to 94.9% and 97.3% for Internet2 and GEANT, respectively. In the third approach, we use each of the subnet prefix lengths in the original topology as a point in an n-dimensional euclidean space and measure the percentage of similarity of the collected topology to the original topology. This approach allows us to asses the amount of deviation from the original topology rather than looking upon it as a binary match/not-match value. Results show that the subnet prefix length similarity including unresponsive subnets for Internet2 and GEANT are 0.83 and 0.900 respectively. Our fourth approach is also based on the similarity in euclidean space, however, we use subnet size instead of prefix length as the coordinate space. We obtain similarity rates of 0.86 and 0.907 for Internet2 and GEANT respectively again including unresponsive subnets.

We first derive original Internet2[2] and GEANT[1] subnet topologies as our ground truth. `Tracenet` collects a subnet on-the-fly while tracing towards a destination if it appears on the end-to-end path. However, we cannot control the path taken by a packet and make it to pass through a certain subnet or router. Thus, we build destination IP address sets for Internet2 and GEANT by selecting a random IP address from each of their original subnets. Below we present the details of the experiments in the context of the aforementioned approaches.

4.1.1 *Exact Match Rate Evaluation*

Tables 1 and 2 show the original and collected subnet distributions of Internet2 and GEANT respectively. In both tables the first row (*orgl*) show the original subnet prefix distribution. The second row (*exmt*) shows the distribution of the subnets collected exactly as in the original topology. The third (*miss*) and fifth (*undes*) rows respectively show missing subnets that could not be discovered at all and underestimated subnets that inferred to be smaller than the originals. We further divide missing and underestimated distributions into two sets shown in fourth (*miss\unrs*) and sixth (*undes\unrs*) rows in order to observe whether the missing or underestimated subnets result from unresponsive hosts or incompetence of our heuristics. We believe that this distinction is important to show that a misinferred subnet which is behind a firewall that is filtering out our probe packets, e.g., *totally unresponsive subnet*, or utilizing only a sub-portion of its capacity, e.g., *partially unresponsive subnet* cannot be attributed as drawback of `tracenet`. The seventh (*ovres*), eighth (*splt*), and ninth (*merg*) rows show the overestimated subnets that are inferred to be larger than the original subnet, split, and merged subnets, respectively.

Given two subnets S_a and S_b that have their IP addresses from two consecutive address ranges, if the two subnets are incorrectly inferred to be a single subnet S_{ab} with the corresponding IP addresses, then they are considered to be merged. On the other hand, if one of them is collected accurately and the other one is collected as S_{ab} then the first one is considered to be an exact match and the second one is considered to be an overestimation.

The exact match rate of `tracenet` over Internet2 is 73.7% including unresponsive subnets and is 94.9% excluding totally unresponsive subnets. Internet2 topology is a special topology that consists of many small sized (mostly point-to-point) subnets at the backbone and a few larger subnets

Table 1: Internet2, Original and Collected Subnet Distribution

	/24	/25	/26	/27	/28	/29	/30	/31	total
orgl	6	1	0	2	26	20	101	23	179
exmt	0	0	0	0	2	16	92	22	132
miss	1	0	0	0	2	0	0	0	3
miss\unrs	4	1	0	2	1	4	8	1	21
undes	1	0	0	0	2	0	0	0	3
undes\unrs	0	0	0	0	19	0	0	0	19
ovres	0	0	0	0	0	0	1	0	1
splt	0	0	0	0	0	0	0	0	0
merg	0	0	0	0	0	0	0	0	0

behind some firewall that filters out ICMP messages or configured not to respond to any direct probe. After collecting the subnets we further probed every IP address within the address range of the missing and underestimated subnets to identify the unresponsive subnets. The results show that 19 out of 22 of the underestimated and 21 out of 24 of the missing subnets are caused by partially and totally unresponsive subnets, respectively. When we analysed the two underestimated /28 subnetworks shown in Table 1, we found that only 2 IP addresses were observed to be utilized in the first network and only 5 are observed to be utilized in the second network. Besides, the utilized IP addresses of the IP address range of the second network have large gaps, so line 19 of algorithm 1 stops growing the subnet prematurely.

Table 2: GEANT, Original and Collected Subnet Distribution

	/24	/25	/26	/27	/28	/29	/30	/31	total
orgl	0	0	0	0	24	109	138	0	271
exmt	0	0	0	0	0	41	104	0	145
miss	0	0	0	0	0	1	0	0	1
miss\unrs	0	0	0	0	10	53	34	0	97
undes	0	0	0	0	3	0	0	0	3
undes\unrs	0	0	0	0	11	14	0	0	25
ovres	0	0	0	0	0	0	0	0	0
splt	0	0	0	0	0	0	0	0	0
merg	0	0	0	0	0	0	0	0	0

The exact match rate of `tracenet` over GEANT is 53.5% including unresponsive subnets and is 97.3% excluding totally unresponsive subnets. Published GEANT topology mostly consists of /30 and /29 subnets. Although `tracenet`'s success rate with /30 networks is high, it misses most of /29 and /28 subnets. Studying those missed or underestimated subnets further by probing each and every possible IP address in the original subnet reveals the fact that those subnets mostly do not respond to the probes. That is, either our probe packets or their responses were filtered out or those subnets are not realized despite they are published to exist.

4.1.2 Similarity Rate Evaluation

To have an idea on the success rate other than exact match rate, we analyze the divergence of the collected Internet2/GEANT subnet topologies from the original ones. One can regard each subnet as a feature of the topology and subnet prefix as the value of that feature. Therefore, we can measure the similarity of the collected topology to the original topology in an n-dimensional euclidean space, where n is the number of subnets, by defining a proper distance function. We compute the distance factor of a given subnet S_i simply by taking the absolute value of the difference between its original and collected prefix lengths. Below is the *prefix distance factor* function:

$$d(S_i) = \begin{cases} 0 & S_i \in \text{exmt} \\ |s_i^o - s_i^c| & S_i \in \text{undes} \\ |s_i^o - s_i^c| & S_i \in \text{ovres} \\ \max\{|s_i^o - p_u|, |s_i^o - p_l|\} & S_i \in \text{miss} \\ |s_i^o - s_i^c| & S_i \in \text{merg} \\ |s_i^o - \max\{s_i^c\}| & S_i \in \text{splt} \end{cases} \quad (1)$$

such that s_i^o, s_i^c are the original and collected prefix values for subnet i, p_u and p_l are upper and lower prefix values found in the original or collected topology. Original Internet2 network has upper and lower boundary values of $p_u = 31$, $p_l = 24$ respectively and GEANT has $p_u = 30$, $p_l = 28$. For missing subnets we take the maximum of distances to the boundaries in favor of dissimilarity. Hereby, the dissimilarity of the topologies can be evaluated by the well known Minkowski distance of order k as

$$\left(\sum_i^n d(S_i)^k \right)^{1/k} \quad (2)$$

and normalized similarity equation with parameter $k = 1$ can be defined as

$$1 - \frac{\sum_i^n d(S_i)}{\sum_i^n \max\{(s_i^o - p_l), (p_u - s_i^o)\}}. \quad (3)$$

Based on equation (3) the similarity rate for Internet2 and GEANT are 0.83 and 0.900 respectively while zero means totally dissimilar and one means exactly the same. Compared to Internet2, GEANT, having a smaller prefix length range inherently makes its similarity to be larger.

Although equations (1), (2), and (3) present valuable insights related to similarity, they are not sensitive to the differences in the sizes of subnets (e.g., $|/29\ subnet| - |/30\ subnet| = 4$ vs $|/23\ subnet| - |/24\ subnet| = 256$ though both have a difference of one in terms of prefix length). To reflect this difference, we compute the distance factor of a given subnet S_i simply by taking the absolute value of the difference between its original and collected subnet sizes. Below, we define a new distance factor function called as *size distance factor* function:

$$\widehat{d}(S_i) = \begin{cases} 0 & S_i \in \text{exmt} \\ |2^{32-s_i^o} - 2^{32-s_i^c}| & S_i \in \text{undes} \\ |2^{32-s_i^o} - 2^{32-s_i^c}| & S_i \in \text{ovres} \\ \max\{(2^{32-p_l} - 2^{32-s_i^o}), \\ \quad (2^{32-s_i^o} - 2^{32-p_u})\} & S_i \in \text{miss} \\ |2^{32-s_i^o} - 2^{32-s_i^c}| & S_i \in \text{merg} \\ |2^{32-s_i^o} - \max\{2^{32-s_i^c}\}| & S_i \in \text{splt} \end{cases} \quad (4)$$

The corresponding similarity equation becomes

$$1 - \frac{\sum_i^n \widehat{d}(S_i)}{\sum_i^n \max\{(2^{32-p_l} - 2^{32-s_i^o}), (2^{32-s_i^o} - 2^{32-p_u})\}}. \quad (5)$$

Again for missing subnets we take the maximum of size distances to the boundaries in favor of dissimilarity.

Based on the equation (5), the subnet size similarities between the collected and the original Internet2 and GEANT topologies are 0.86 and 0.907 respectively while zero means totally dissimilar and one means exactly the same.

4.2 TraceNET Performance over the Internet

In this section we use `tracenet` on public Internet domains to evaluate its performance. A limitation regarding the verification of topology discovery tools over commercial ISPs is that their original topologies are considered to be proprietary and are not available to the public. In our work, we resort to cross validation by running `tracenet` at three different vantage points with the same target IP address set and demonstrate the level of agreement/disagreement among the observed subnets. The results show that all three vantage points agrees on around 60% of all collected subnets by a particular vantage point. Additionally, roughly 80% of the collected subnets by a particular vantage point is also verified by at least one other vantage point. On the other hand, analyzing the collected subnets further show that some subnets are inferred to be larger when collected from another vantage point. One explanation of this could be that like any other active probing based topology collection tool, `tracenet` is affected from rate limiting routers or ISPs. That is, routers or ISPs regulate their responsiveness to probes based on the traffic load or any other rate limiting policies. However, all three vantage points consistently infers that most of the subnets at the non-edge Internet are point-to-point links of /31 or /30 subnets. Then follows /29 subnets and a sharp continuing decrease after /29 with a small increase for /24 subnets. We believe that /24 is a de-facto standard subnet mask for small or medium organizations, however, most of the organizations are also behind probe blocking firewalls.

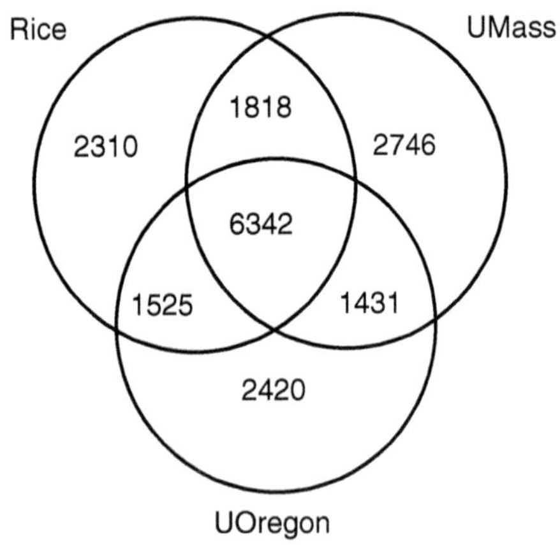

Figure 6: Distribution of exact math subnets among three different PlanetLab sites

As our experimental set-up, we designated PlanetLab sites at Rice University, University of Oregon and University of Massachusetts as our vantage points located at the south, west and east of the United States, respectively. We built a target set of 34084 IP addresses belonging to four major ISPs including Sprintlink, AboveNet, Level3, and NTT America. This target set does not contain IP addresses belonging to the customers of these major ISPs.

Figure 6 demonstrates the distribution of exactly matching subnets collected from three different PlanetLab vantage points. In the figure, almost 80% of subnets observed from a particular vantage point are also observed from one other vantage point. Besides, around 60% of subnets of a particular vantage point is observed from all three vantage points. Note that we selected those vantage points expecting that `tracenet` probes enter into each ISP from different border routers and take different paths towards a destination IP address. As a result, around 20% of subnets being observed uniquely by each vantage point is a natural outcome stemming from different border routers appearing in the paths and various paths being taken toward the destinations.

Next, for each vantage point, we assess the number of IP addresses in our target set, the number of IP addresses that are put into a subnet, and the number of IP addresses for which `tracenet` failed to grow a subnet. In Figure 7, the left aligned bars show the number of target IP addresses for our traces; central bars show the number of IP addresses that are found and placed into subnets of different sizes; and the right aligned bars show the number of IP addresses that are found but could not be placed into a subnet, i.e., these are the IP addresses for which we could not find a subnet larger than /32.

In Figure 7, SprintLink seems to be the least responsive ISP to our probes, the number of unsubnetized IP addresses are large compared to other ISPs consistently from all vantage points. Additionally, as observed from PlanetLab site at Rice, the total number of subnetized and unsubnetized IP addresses is less than the number target IP addresses. Further analysis of our data shows that not all target IP addresses has responded to our probe packets as a result they are not included in un-subnetized /32 IP address set. NTT America is the most responsive ISP. Note that, `tracenet` collects subnets along a path between a vantage point and a destination IP address, hence, path lengths as well as the number of responsive routers on the discovered subnets effect total number of subnetized IP addresses. Path length factor explains the fact that despite the number of un-subnetized IP addresses is large for SprintLink the number of subnetized IP addresses is close to that of Level3 and AboveNET on the average.

Figure 8 shows the distribution of total number of subnets per ISP at three vantage points. The numbers of collected subnets from each ISP are close to each other with respect to all vantage points. One counter intuitive observation takes place when we combine Figure 7 and Figure 8. In the former figure, NTT America has the largest number of subnetized IP addresses whereas in the latter figure it has the least number of subnets. Analyzing our data reveals the fact that NTT America accommodates large subnets of mask /20, /21, /22 whereas other ISPs mostly host small subnets of mask /30 and /31. That is, small number of large sized subnets hosts more IP addresses than large number of small sized subnets in our figures.

Figure 9 shows the distribution of subnet prefix length at three different vantage points in a logarithmic scale. The shape of the figure shows the fact that the distribution of collected subnets are coherent with each other. In the figure, there is a big decrease between /30 and /29 from 4499 to 1546 as observed at PlanetLab site at Rice and even bigger

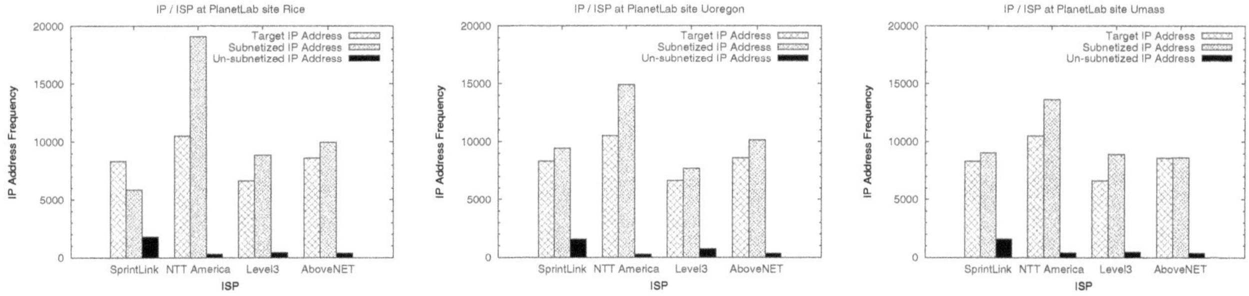

Figure 7: Target, Subnetized, Un-Subnetized IP address distribution at different Planetlab sites

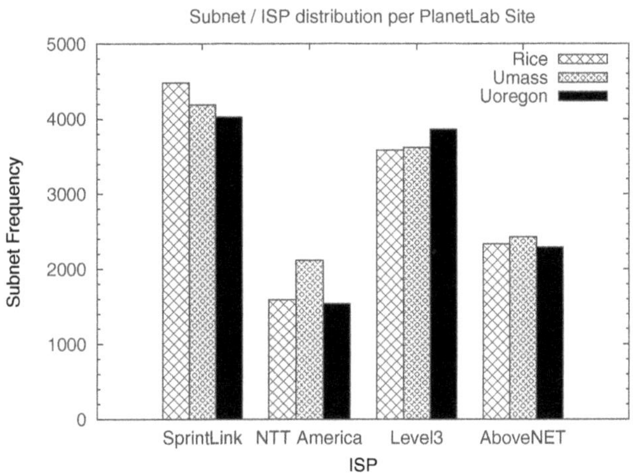

Figure 8: Subnet per ISP distribution at different PlanetLab sites

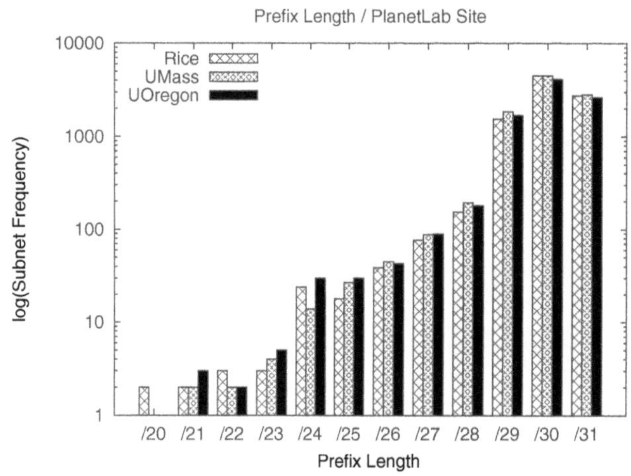

Figure 9: Subnet prefix length distribution at different PlanetLab sites

decrease between /29 and /28 from 1546 to 154. The figure shows that most of the links are point to point links (/31 and /30), then follows /29 multi access links, then the number of subnets decrease dramatically.

As our final experiment, we investigated performance of `tracenet` with different probing protocols. Table 3 shows the number of subnets collected by `tracenet` with ICMP, UDP, and TCP protocols over four ISPs. In the figure, ICMP protocol probing clearly outperforms UDP and TCP protocols in terms of the number of collected subnets. Our findings support the recent observations [9, 15] that routers respond better to ICMP probes compared to UDP and TCP probes. Additionally, the results collected with TCP probing is neglectable compared to ICMP and UDP.

5. CONCLUSIONS

Topology discovery studies make use of every bit of available data to sketch a complete and accurate map of a given network. BGP table dumps, `traceroute` paths, DNS tables, `ping` responses, registered prefix information of ASes, common IP assignment practices, and limitedly supported IP options such as loose source routing and record-route are among the sources of raw data. Among all, `traceroute` is the most prevalent tool used to reveal lists of IP addresses ordered by hop distance at a given network.

In this study, we have devised a set of heuristics to develop a router level Internet topology collector called `tracenet`. `Tracenet` collects topology information of each visited subnet on the path from a source to a destination whereas the traditional `traceroute` collects a single IP address at each visited router. With `tracenet`, we are able to (1) disclose a large number of IP addresses that could be exposed with traditional `traceroute` only if executed from many vantage points; (2) form multi-access and point-to-point links on the networks; (3) detect "being on the same LAN" association

Table 3: Tracenet under ICMP, UDP, TCP probing protocols at PlanetLab site Rice

	ICMP	UDP	TCP
SprintLink	4482	1834	13
NTT America	1593	106	4
Level3	3587	1062	11
AboveNET	2333	777	40
Total	11995	3779	68

among IP addresses; and (4) annotate subnets with their observed prefix values.

As a result, `tracenet` could be utilized as an effective data collection tool to improve completeness and correctness of current and future topology mapping studies. Finally, an implementation of `tracenet` is publicly available on our project web site at http://itom.utdallas.edu.

6. REFERENCES

[1] Geant2 looking glass. Available at http://stats.geant2.net/lg/.

[2] Internet2 observatory data collections. Available at http://www.internet2.edu/observatory/archive/data-collections.html.

[3] D. Achlioptas, A. Clauset, D. Kempe, and C. Moore. On the bias of traceroute sampling. In *ACM STOC*, Baltimore, MD, USA, May 2005.

[4] B. Augustin, X. Cuvellier, B. Orgogozo, F. Viger, T. Friedman, M. Latapy, C. Magnien, and R. Teixeira. Avoiding traceroute anomalies with Paris traceroute. In *ACM IMC*, Rio de Janeiro, Brazil, Oct 2006.

[5] B. Augustin, T. Friedman, and R. Teixeira. Measuring load-balanced paths in the internet. In *IMC Proceedings of the 7th ACM SIGCOMM conference on Internet measurement*, New York, NY, USA, 2007.

[6] P. Barford, A. Bestavros, J. Byers, and M. Crovella. On the marginal utility of network topology measurements. In *ACM Internet Measurements Workshop*, San Francisco, CA, USA, Nov 2001.

[7] M. Gunes and K. Sarac. Inferring subnets in router-level topology collection studies. In *ACM IMC*, San Diego, CA, USA, Oct 2007.

[8] M. Gunes and K. Sarac. Resolving anonymous routers in internet topology measurement studies. In *IEEE INFOCOM*, Phoenix, AZ, USA, Apr 2008.

[9] M. Gunes and K. Sarac. Analyzing Router Responsiveness to Active Measurement Probes. In *PAM*, Seoul, Korea, Apr 2009.

[10] M. Gunes and K. Sarac. Resolving IP aliases in building traceroute-based internet maps. *IEEE/ACM Transactions on Networking*, 17(6):1738–1751, Dec 2009.

[11] J. Heidemann, R. Govindan, C. Papadopoulos, G. Bartlett, and J. Bannister. Census and survey of the visible internet. In *ACM IMC*, Vouliag., Greece, Oct 2008.

[12] V. Jacobson. *Traceroute*. Lawrence Berkeley Laboratory (LBL), Feb 1989. Available from ftp://ee.lbl.gov/traceroute.tar.Z.

[13] S. Kim and K. Harfoush. Efficient estimation of more detailed Internet IP maps. In *IEEE ICC*, Glasgow, Scotland, Jun 2007.

[14] A. Lakhina, J. Byers, M. Crovella, and P. Xie. Sampling biases in IP topology measurements. In *IEEE INFOCOM*, San Francisco, CA, USA, Mar 2003.

[15] M. Luckie, Y. Hyun, and B. Huffaker. Traceroute probe method and forward IP path inference. In *ACM IMC*, Vouliag., Greece, Oct 2008.

[16] H. Madhyastha, T. Isdal, M. Piatek, C. Dixon, T. Anderson, A. Krishnamurthy, and A. Venkataramani. iPlane: An information plane for distributed services. In *OSDI*, Seattle, WA, USA, Nov 2006.

[17] D. McRobb, K. Claffy, and T. Monk. *Skitter: CAIDA's macroscopic Internet topology discovery and tracking tool*, 1999. Available from http://www.caida.org/tools/skitter/.

[18] Y. Shavitt and E. Shir. DIMES: Distributed Internet measurements and simulations. Project page http://www.netdimes.org.

[19] Y. Shavitt and U. Weinsberg. Quantifying the importance of vantage points distribution in internet topology measurements. In *IEEE INFOCOM*, Rio de Janeiro, Brazil, Apr 2009.

[20] R. Sherwood, A. Bender, and N. Spring. DisCarte: A disjunctive internet cartographer. In *ACM SIGCOMM*, Seattle, WA, USA, Aug 2008.

[21] N. Spring, R. Mahajan, D. Wetherall, and T. Anderson. Measuring ISP topologies with Rocketfuel. *IEEE/ACM Transactions On Networking*, 12(1):2–16, Feb 2004.

[22] University of Oregon. Route views project. http://www.routeviews.org.

Understanding Latent Interactions in Online Social Networks

Jing Jiang[§†], Christo Wilson[†], Xiao Wang[§], Peng Huang[§], Wenpeng Sha[§],
Yafei Dai[§] and Ben Y. Zhao[†]
[§]Peking University, Beijing, China
[†]U. C. Santa Barbara, Santa Barbara, CA, USA
{jiangjing,wangxiao,huangpeng,swp,dyf}@net.pku.edu.cn,
{bowlin,ravenben}@cs.ucsb.edu

ABSTRACT

Popular online social networks (OSNs) like Facebook and Twitter are changing the way users communicate and interact with the Internet. A deep understanding of user interactions in OSNs can provide important insights into questions of human social behavior, and into the design of social platforms and applications. However, recent studies have shown that a majority of user interactions on OSNs are *latent interactions*, passive actions such as profile browsing that cannot be observed by traditional measurement techniques.

In this paper, we seek a deeper understanding of both visible and latent user interactions in OSNs. For quantifiable data on latent user interactions, we perform a detailed measurement study on Renren, the largest OSN in China with more than 150 million users to date. All friendship links in Renren are public, allowing us to exhaustively crawl a connected graph component of 42 million users and 1.66 billion social links in 2009. Renren also keeps detailed visitor logs for each user profile, and counters for each photo and diary/blog entry. We capture detailed histories of profile visits over a period of 90 days for more than 61,000 users in the Peking University Renren network, and use statistics of profile visits to study issues of user profile popularity, reciprocity of profile visits, and the impact of content updates on user popularity. We find that latent interactions are much more prevalent and frequent than visible events, non-reciprocal in nature, and that profile popularity are uncorrelated with the frequency of content updates. Finally, we construct *latent interaction graphs* as models of user browsing behavior, and compare their structural properties against those of both visible interaction graphs and social graphs.

Categories and Subject Descriptors

J.4 [**Computer Applications**]: Social and behavioral sciences; H.3.5 [**Information Storage and Retrieval**]: Online Information Services

General Terms

Human factors, Measurement, Performance

Keywords

Latent interactions, Online social networks

1. INTRODUCTION

Not only are online social networks (OSNs) popular tools for interaction and communication, but they have the potential to alter the way users interact with the Internet. Today's social networks already count close to one billion members worldwide. Facebook, the most popular OSN, has more than 500 million active users [26], and has surpassed Google as the most visited site on the Internet [30]. Increasingly, Facebook and Twitter are replacing email and search engines as users' primary interfaces to the Internet [9, 15]. This trend is likely to continue, as networks like Facebook seek to personalize the web experience by giving sites access to information about their visitors and their friends, through new platforms such as OpenGraph [23].

A deep understanding of user interactions in social networks can provide important insights into questions of human social behavior, as well as the design of social platforms and applications. For example, gauging the level of reciprocity in social interactions can shed light on the factors that motivate interactions. In addition, understanding how interactions are distributed between friends can assist in tracking information dissemination in social networks, thus identifying "popular" or "influential" users to target in branding and ad campaigns [6, 11, 14]. Finally, lessons from studying how users interact through different communication tools can guide the design of new, more engaging mechanisms for social interaction.

Initial measurement studies [1, 22, 29] of OSNs focused on topological characteristics of the social graph, the underlying structures of these services that capture explicit relationships between users. To better understand the true nature of relationships between OSN users, more recent work has shifted focus to measuring observable social interactions [7, 19, 28, 29]. By examining records of interaction events across different links, the studies distinguish close-knit, active relationships from weak or dormant relationships, and derive a more accurate predictive model for social behavior.

Recently, two significant studies [3, 25] used clickstream data at the network level to capture the behavior of OSN users, and revealed that passive or *latent interactions* such as profile browsing often dominate user events in a social network [3].

Unfortunately, these studies have been constrained by several limitations of clickstream data. First, the type of data captured in a clickstream is highly dependent on the time range of the clickstream. Captured events are also from the perspective of the active user, making it challenging to correlate events across time and users. Second, clickstream data is also highly dependent on the structure of the OSN site, and can be extremely challenging to reduce large volumes of data to distinct user events. Finally, each application-level user event generates a large volume of clickstream data, and extremely large clickstreams are needed to capture a significant number of user events. These properties of verboseness and complexity mean that it is extremely difficult to gather enough clickstream data to study user interactions comprehensively at scale. However, a comprehensive and large study is necessary to answer many of the deeper questions about user behavior and interactions, such as: are user interactions reciprocal, do latent interactions such as profile browsing reflect the same popularity distributions as visible actions like user comments, what can users do to become "popular" and draw more visitors to their pages?

In this paper, we seek to answer these and other questions in our search for a deeper understanding of user interactions in OSNs. To address the challenge of gathering data on latent interactions, we perform a large-scale, crawl-based measurement of the Renren social network [24], the largest and most popular OSN in China. Functionally, it is essentially a clone of Facebook, with similar structure, layout and features. Like Facebook, Renren also evolved from a university-based social network (a predecessor called Xiaonei). Unlike Facebook, Renren has *two unique features* that make it an attractive platform to study user interactions.

First, while Renren users have full privacy control over their private profiles, their friend lists are public and unprotected by privacy mechanisms. This allowed us to crawl an exhaustive snapshot of Renren's largest connected component, producing an extremely large social graph with 42.1 million nodes and 1.66 billion edges. Second, and perhaps more importantly, Renren user profiles make a variety of statistics visible to both the profile owner and her visitors. Each user profile keeps a visible list of "recent visitors" who browse the profile, sorted in order, and updated in real-time. Each photo and diary entry also has its own page with a count of visits by users other than the owner. These records are extremely valuable, in that they expose latent browsing events to our crawlers, granting us an unique opportunity to gather and analyze large scale statistics on latent browsing events.

Our study. Our study of latent user interactions includes three significant components. *First*, we begin by characterizing properties of the large Renren social graph, and compare them to known statistics of other OSNs, including Facebook, Cyworld, Orkut and Twitter. Our *second* component focuses on questions concerning latent interactions, and constitutes the bulk of our study. We describe a log reconstruction algorithm that uses relative clocks to merge visitor logs from repeated crawls into a single sequential visitor stream. We repeatedly crawl users in the Peking University Renren network over a period of 90 days, extract profile visit history for 61K users, and examine issues of popularity, visitor composition, reciprocity, and latency of reciprocation. We compare user popularity distributions for latent and visible interactions, and use per-object visit counters to quantify the level of user engagement generated from user profiles, photos, and diary entries. We also study correlation of different types of user-generated content with a user's profile popularity. Finally, in our *third* component, we build *latent interaction graphs* from our visitor logs, and compare their structure to those of social graphs and interaction graphs. We also revisit the issue of experimental validation for social applications, and perform a case study of the impact of different social graphs on evaluating information dissemination algorithms.

Our study provides a number of insights into user behavior on online social networks, including:

- Users' profile popularity varies significantly across the population, and closely follows a Zipf distribution.
- Profile visits have extremely low reciprocity, despite the fact that Renren users have full access to the list of recent visitors to their profile.
- Compared to visible interactions, latent profile browsing is far more prevalent and more evenly distributed across a user's friends. Profile visits are less likely to be repeated than visible interactions, but are more likely to generate visible comments than other content such as photos and diary entries.
- For all users, regardless of their number of friends, profile popularity is not strongly correlated with frequency of new profile content.

Finally, we use our data to construct *latent interaction graphs* that capture browsing activity between OSN users. Our analysis finds that latent interaction graphs exhibit general Power-law features, fall between social and visible interaction graphs in terms of connectivity, but show less local clustering properties than both.

2. METHODOLOGY AND INITIAL ANALYSIS

Before diving into detailed analysis of user interaction events, we begin by providing background information about the Renren social network and our measurement methodology. We then give more specifics on our techniques for reconstructing profile browsing histories from periodic crawls. Using a random subset of user profiles, we perform sampling experiments to quantify the expected errors introduced by our approach. Finally, we analyze characteristics of the Renren social graph, and compare it to known graph properties of existing social graph measurements.

2.1 The Renren Social Network

Launched in 2005, Renren is the largest and oldest OSN in China. Renren can be best characterized as Facebook's Chinese twin, with most or all of Facebook's features, layout, and a similar user interface. Users maintain personal profiles, upload photos, write diary entries (blogs), and establish bidirectional social links with their friends. Renren users inform their friends about recent events with 140 character status updates, much like tweets on Twitter. Similar to the Facebook news feed, all user-generated updates and comments are tagged with the sender's name and a time stamp.

Renren organizes users into membership-based networks, much like Facebook used to. Networks represent schools, companies, or geographic regions. Membership in school and company networks require authentication. Students must offer an IP address, email address, or student credential from the associated university. Corporate email addresses are needed for users to join corporate networks. Renren's default privacy policy makes profiles of users in geographic networks private. This makes them difficult to crawl [29]. Fortunately, profiles of users in authenticated networks are public by default to other members of the same network. This allowed us to access user profiles within the Peking University network, since we could create nearly unlimited authenticated accounts using our own block of IP addresses.

Like Facebook, a Renren user's homepage includes a number of friend recommendations that encourage formation of new friend relationships. Renren lists 3 users with the most number of mutual friends in the top right corner of the page. In addition, Renren shows a list of 8 "popular users" at the very bottom of the page. These popular users are randomly selected from the 100 users with the most friends in the university network.

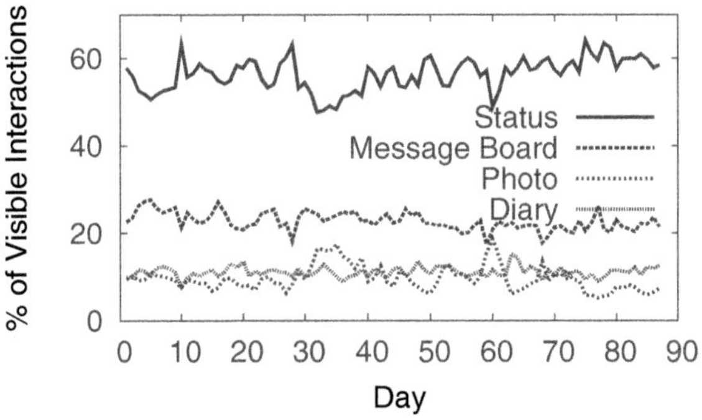

Figure 1: Daily distribution of comments across applications.

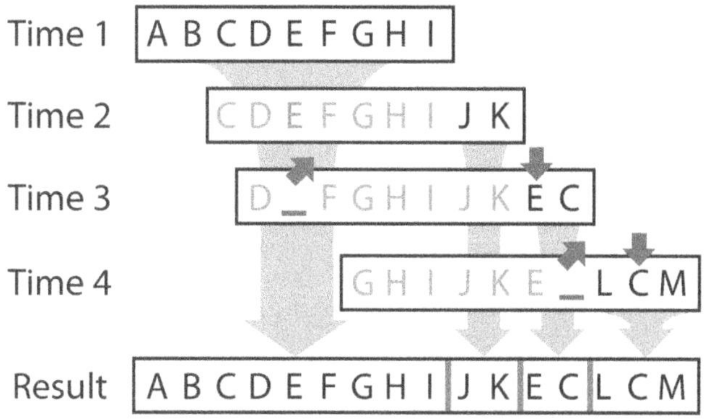

Figure 2: Integrating multiple visitor lists captured by multiple crawls of the same profile into a single history.

Unique features. Renren differs from Facebook in several significant ways. First, each Renren user profile includes a box that shows the total number of visitors to the profile, along with names and links to the last 9 visitors ordered from most to least recent. In addition, Renren also keeps on each individual photo and diary page a visible counter of visitors (not including the user himself). These lists and counters have the same privacy settings as the main profile. They have the unique property of making previously invisible events visible, and are the basis for our detailed measurements on latent user interactions.

A second crucial feature is that friend lists in Renren are always public. Users have no way to hide them. This allowed us to perform an exhaustive crawl of the largest connected component in Renren (42.1 million users). This contrasts with other OSNs, where full social graph crawls are prevented by user privacy policies that hide friendship links from the public. The exception is Twitter, which behaves more like a public news medium than a traditional social network [16].

In addition, comments in Renren are threaded, *i.e.* each new comment is always in response to one single other event or comment. For example, user A can respond to user B's comment on user C's profile, and only B is notified of the new message. Thus we can precisely distinguish the intended target of each comment. One final difference between Renren and Facebook is that each standard user is limited to a maximum of 1,000 friends. Users may pay a subscription fee to increase this limit to 2,000. From our measurements, we saw that very few users (0.3%) took advantage of this feature.

2.2 Data Collection and General Statistics

Like Facebook, Renren evolved from a social network in a university setting. Its predecessor was called Xiaonei, literally meaning "inside school." In September 2009, Renren merged with Kaixin, the second largest OSN in China, and absorbed all of Kaixin's user accounts.

Crawling the Renren social graph. We crawled the entire Renren network from April 2009 to June 2009, and again from September to November of 2009. We seed crawlers with the 30 most popular users' profiles, and proceeded to perform a breadth-first traversal of the social graph. During the crawl, we collect unique userIDs, network affiliations, and friendship links to other users. For our study, we use data from our last crawl, which was an exhaustive snapshot that included 42,115,509 users and 1,657,273,875 friendship links. While this is significantly smaller than the 70 million users advertised by Renren in September 2009, we believe the discrepancy is due to Kaixin users who were still organized as a separate, disconnected subgraph. We describe properties of the social graph later in this section.

Crawling the PKU network. We performed smaller, more detail oriented crawls of the PKU network between September and November of 2009 (90 days) to collect information about user's profiles and interaction patterns. This methodology works because the default privacy policy for authenticated networks is to make full profiles accessible to other members of the same network. Since we collected the network memberships of all users during our complete crawl, we were able to isolate the 100,973 members of the PKU network to seed our detailed crawl. Of these users, 61,405 users had the default, permissive privacy policy, enabling us to collect their detailed information. This covers the majority of users (60.8%) in the PKU network, and provides overall network coverage similar to other studies that crawled OSN regional networks [29].

As part of our PKU crawls, we gathered all comments generated by users in message board posts, diary entries, photos, and status updates. This data forms the basis of our experiments involving visible interactions. Our dataset represents the complete record of public visible interactions between users in the PKU network. In total, 19,782,140 comments were collected, with 1,218,911 of them originating in the September to November 2009 timeframe.

Figure 1 plots the percentage of comments in various applications each day. The most popular events to comment on are status updates, which accounts for roughly 55% of all daily comments. Message boards cover 25%, while diary and photo each account for roughly 10%.

Privacy and data anonymization. Our study focuses on the structure of social graphs and interaction events between users. Since we do not need any actual content of comments, photos, or user profiles, we waited for crawls to complete, then went through our data to anonymize userIDs and strip any private data from our dataset to protect user privacy. In addition, all user IDs were hashed to random IDs, and all timestamps are replaced with relative sequence numbers. We note that our group has visited and held research meetings with technical teams at Renren, and they are aware of our ongoing research.

2.3 Measuring Latent User Interactions

In addition to visible interactions generated by users in the PKU network, we also recorded the recent visitor records displayed on each user's profile. This data forms the basis of our study of latent interactions.

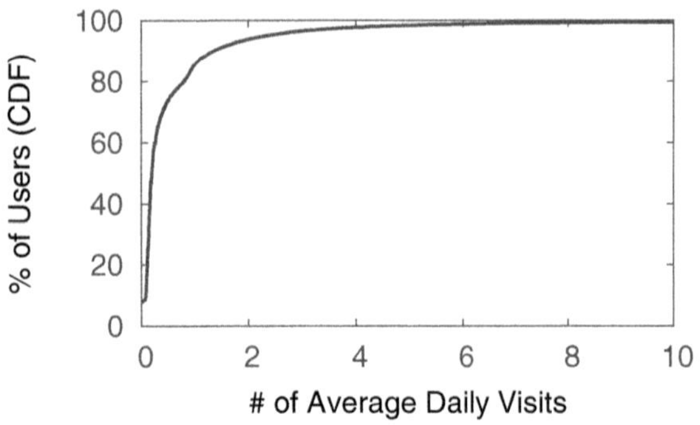

Figure 3: Average daily visit counts of user profiles.

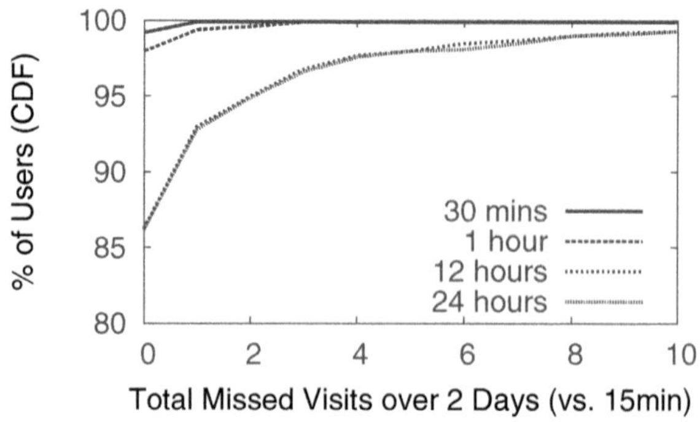

Figure 4: Number of visits missed when we lower crawler frequency from a high of once every 15 minutes.

Reconstructing Visitor Histories. Crawling Renren for recent visitor records is complicated by two things. First, each user's profile only lists the last 9 visitors. This means that our crawler must be constantly revisiting users in order to glean representative data, as new visitors will cause older visitors to fall off the list. Clearly we could not crawl every user continuously. Frequent crawls leave the ID of our crawler on the visitor log of profiles, which has generated unhappy feedback from profile owners. In addition, Renren imposes multiple per-account rate limits that slow our crawler significantly despite our large number of crawler accounts. Thus, we designed our crawler to be self-adapting. This means that we track the popularity and level of dynamics in different user profiles, and allocate most of our requests to heavily trafficked user profiles, while guaranteeing a minimum crawl rate (1/day) for low traffic users. The individual lists from each crawl contain overlapping results, which we integrate into a single history.

The second challenge to crawling recent visitor records is that each visitor is only shown in the list once, even if they visit multiple times. Repeat visits simply cause that user to return to the top of the list, erasing their old position. This makes identifying overlapping sets of visitors from the iterative crawls difficult.

To solve these two challenges, we use a log-integration algorithm to concatenate the individual recent visitor lists observed during each successive crawl. More specifically, some overlapping sets of visitors exist in successive crawl data, and our main task is to find new visitors and remove overlaps. There are two kinds of incoming visitors: new users, who do not appear in the previous list, and repeat users, who appear in the prior list at a different relative position. The first kind of incoming visitor is easily identified, since his record is completely new to the recent visitor list. New visitors provide a useful checkpoint for purposes of log-integration, since other users behind them in the list are also necessarily new incoming visitors. The second type of incoming visitor, repeat users, can be detected by looking for changes in sequence of the recent visitor list. If a user repeatedly visits the same profile in-between two visits of other users, nothing changes in the recent visitor list. Therefore, consecutive repeat visits are ignored by our crawler.

Figure 2 demonstrates our integration algorithm. We observe that visitors `ABCDEFGHI` viewed a user's profile at some time before our first crawl. New users view the profile and are added to the recent visitor list by the second crawl at time 2. We re-observe the old sequence `CDEFGHI`, and identify `JK` as new visitors, since `JK` do not exist in the previous visitor list. Next, we compare recent visitor lists at time 2 and 3. We find that `E` is before `K` in the recent visitor list crawled at time 2, but this order is changed at time 3. This means that at some time before the third crawl user `E` revisited the target and changed positions in the list. Thus we identify `E` as a new visitor. Since `C` is behind `E` at time 3, `C` is also identified as a new visitor. Our integration algorithm also works correctly at time 4. User `L` has not been observed before, and thus `L`, plus subsequent visitors `C` and `M`, are all classified as new visitors.

Overall, from the 61,405 user profiles we continuously crawled, we obtained a total of 8,034,664 total records of visits to user profiles in the PKU network. After integrating these raw results, we are left with 1,863,168 unique profile visit events. This high reduction (77%) is because most profiles receive few page views, and thus overlaps between successively crawled results are very high. Although Renren does not show individual recent visitors of user diaries and photos, it does display the total number of visits, which we crawled as well.

Impact of Crawl Frequency. We are concerned that our crawls might not be frequent enough to capture all visit events to a given profile. To address this concern, we took a closer look at the impact of crawler frequency on missing visits. First, we take all of the profiles we crawled for visit histories, and computed their average daily visit count between September and November 2009. We plot this as a CDF in Figure 3. Most users (99.3%) receive $<= 8$ visits per day on average. Since Renren shows 9 latest visitors, crawling a profile once every day should be sufficient to capture all visits. While our crawler adapts to allocate more crawl requests to popular, frequently visited profiles, we guarantee that every profile is crawled at least once every 24 hours.

Next, we select 1,000 random PKU users and crawl their recent visitors every 15 minutes for 2 days. We use the data collected to simulate five frequencies for crawling process, namely 15 minutes, 30 minutes, 1 hour, 12 hours and 1 day. Then we use the log-integration algorithm to concatenate the individual recent visitor lists at different crawling frequencies. For every person, we compute the number of visits missed by the crawler when we reduce the frequency, beginning with visits every 15 minutes. We plot CDF of these deviations in Figure 4. As we see, for 88% of users, there are no additional visits missed when we reduce the crawler rate from once every 15 minutes to once per day. Only for a very small group of users (0.7%) is the number of missing visits greater than 10 when crawling at once per day. Figure 3 also shows that less than 0.7% of all users receive more than 9 visits per day. Only these users would require more than one crawl per day to collect a full history of their visits. Since we allocate the bulk of our crawler requests to these high popularity users (and crawl once per day for

Network	Users Crawled	Links Crawled	Avg. Degree	Cluster Coef.	Assortativity	Avg. Path Len.
Renren	42,115K	1,657,273K	78.70	0.063	0.15	5.38
Facebook [29]	10,697K	408,265K	76.33	0.164	0.17	4.8
Cyworld [1]	12,048K	190,589K	31.64	0.16	-0.13	3.2
Orkut [22]	3,072K	223,534K	145.53	0.171	0.072	4.25
Twitter [13]	88K	829K	18.84	0.106	0.59	N/A

Table 1: Topology properties of social networks

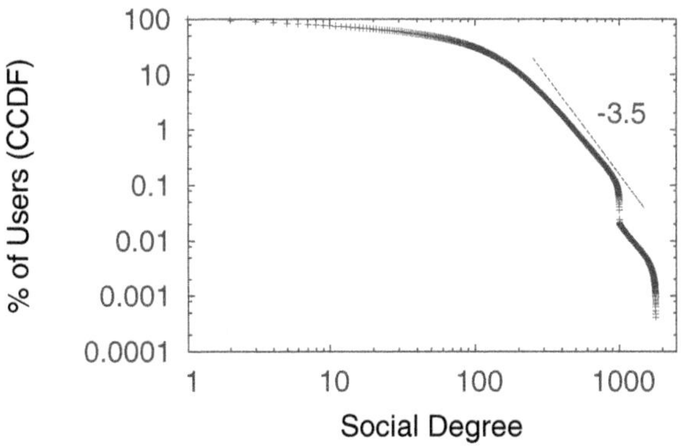

Figure 5: Node Degree Distribution in the Renren network

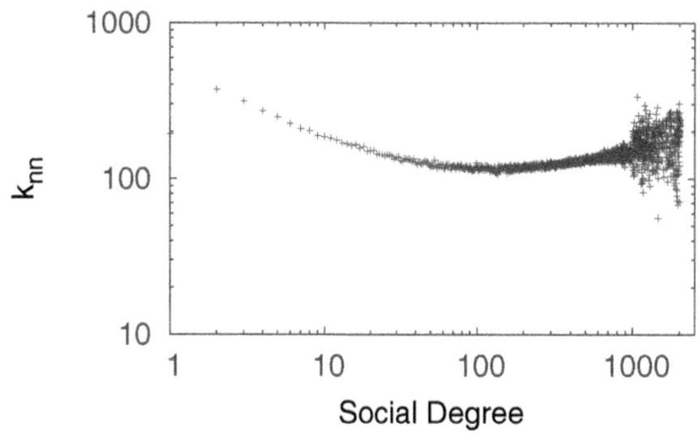

Figure 7: Renren k_{nn} Distribution

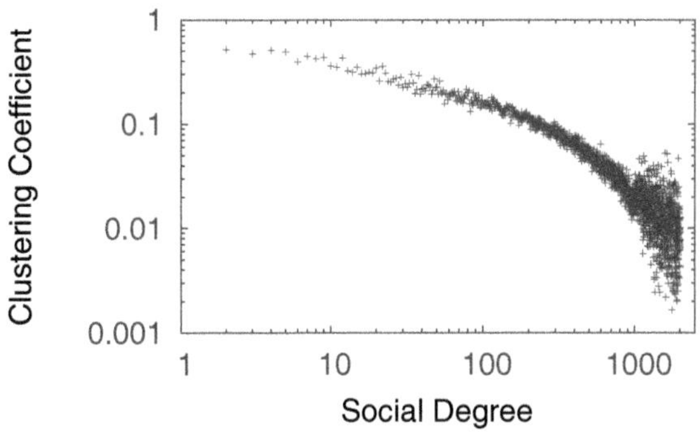

Figure 6: Renren Clustering Coefficient Distribution

the rest), we are relatively confident that very few visits are missed by our crawls.

2.4 Social Graph Analysis

In this section, we analyze the topological properties of the entire Renren social graph by focusing on salient graph measures. Table 1 shows some general properties of Renren, such as average degree, clustering coefficient, assortativity, and average path length as compared to other social networks. Our Renren dataset is larger than most previously studied OSN datasets, the exceptions being recent measurements of the Twitter network [4, 16]. However, our dataset shares similar properties with prior studies [7, 22, 29]. This confirms that Renren is a representative social network, and the behavior of its users is likely to be indicative of users in other OSNs like Facebook.

Figure 5 plots the complementary cumulative distribution function (CCDF) of user social degrees in the Renren network, and shows that Renren's network structure roughly follows a power-law [2]. We compute that the power-law curve fitting the social degree CCDF has an alpha value of 3.5, with fitting error of 0.02. This alpha value is significantly higher than that found for Facebook (1.5), Orkut (1.5), and Twitter (2.4).

We also look at Renren's clustering coefficient, which assesses the level of local connectivity between nodes. In undirected graphs, the clustering coefficient of a person is defined as the ratio of the number of links over all possible connections between one's friends. The clustering coefficient of the entire network is defined by the average of all individual clustering coefficients. Renren's average clustering coefficient is only 0.063, implying that Renren friend relationships are more loosely connected than the other social networks studied in Table 1. Figure 6 displays the distribution of clustering coefficient versus node degree. As expected for a social network, users with lower social degrees have higher clustering coefficients, thus demonstrating high levels of clustering at the edge of the social graph.

The assortativity coefficient measures the probability for users to establish links to other users of similar degree [29]. It is calculated as the Pearson correlation coefficient of the degrees of node pairs for all links in a graph. A positive assortativity coefficient indicates that users tend to connect to other users of similar degree, and a negative value indicates the opposite trend. Renren's assortativity is 0.15, implying that connections between like-degree users are numerous. Figure 7 displays node degree correlation (k_{nn}) versus node degree. k_{nn} is a closely related metric to assortativity. The positive correlation starting around degree 100 demonstrates that higher-degree users tend to establish links with other high-degree users. These chains of well-connected super-users form the backbone of the social network.

Average path length is the average of all-pairs-shortest-paths in the social network. It is simply not tractable to compute shortest path for all node pairs, given the immense size of our social graph. Instead, we choose 1000 random users in the network, perform Dijkstra to build a spanning tree for each user in the social graph, and compute the length of their shortest paths to all other users in the network. As shown in Table 1, the average path length in Renren is 5.38, which agrees with the six-degrees of separation hypothesis [20]. It is not surprising to see that average path length is

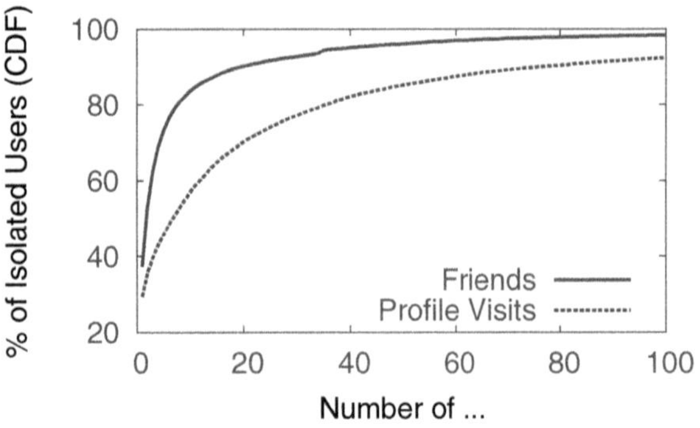

Figure 8: Social degree and total number of visits for isolated users

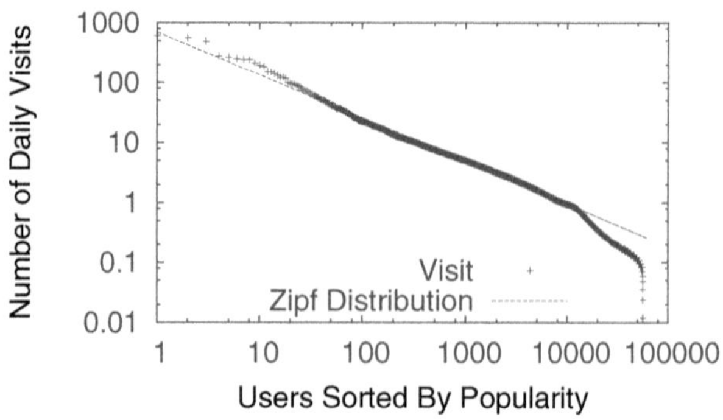

Figure 10: Average number of visits per day per user

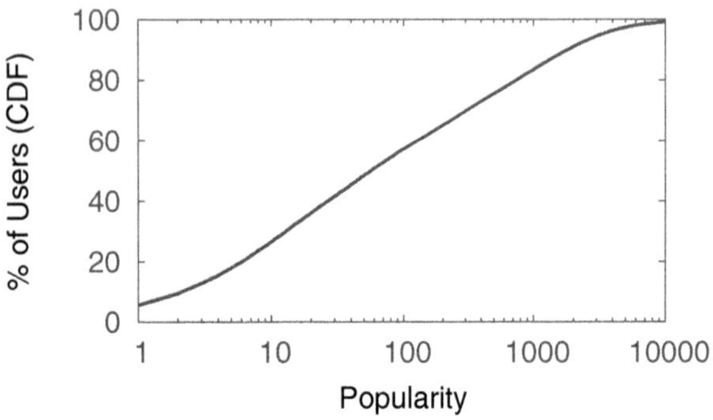

Figure 9: CDF of user profile popularity defined by visits

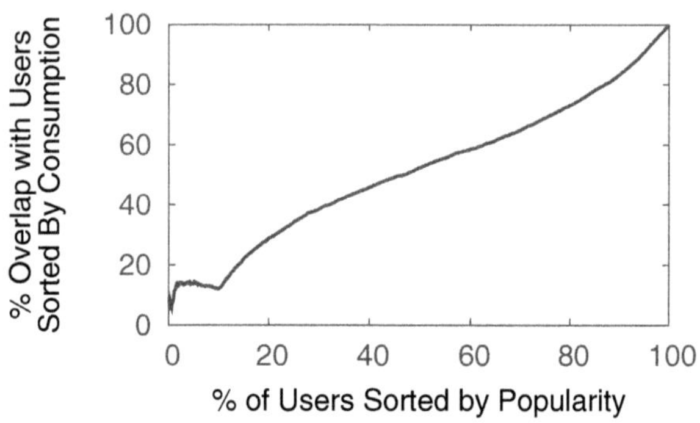

Figure 11: Overlap between users sorted by popularity vs. sorted by consumption

longer in Renren than prior results from Facebook [29], since those path lengths were computed over smaller subgraphs representing regional networks. It is surprising, however, when we compare it to results from Cyworld [7], since the two networks are similar in size and completeness. One reasonable explanation is that connectivity between Internet users in the Cyworld network is much stronger than connectivity between users in the Renren network.

Strongly Connected Component Analysis. User's online friendship links often correspond closely with their offline relationships [17]. Thus, it is natural to assume that college students would have many online friends in the same campus network. This behavior should manifest itself as a single, large, strongly connected component (SCC) that includes most users in the PKU network social graph. Surprising, we find that 23,430 (23.2%) of users in the PKU network have no friends in the PKU campus network, and are therefore disconnected from the SCC. We refer to these as *isolated users*. To confirm these results, we measured the SCC of 9 other large university networks and discovered similar numbers of isolated users.

Figure 8 shows social degrees and total number of profile visits for these isolated users. 83% of isolated users have social degrees less than 10. In addition, 70% of isolated users have less than 20 total profile visits, meaning their profiles are rarely browsed by others. These isolated users likely abandoned their accounts soon after registration, and did not have enough time to establish links with friends within the campus network. Further analysis into the behavior and activities of these isolated users is the subject of ongoing work.

3. PROPERTIES OF INTERACTION EVENTS

Our work focuses on the analysis of latent interaction events and the role they play in OSNs. In our measurement of the Renren OSN, we use histories of visits to user profiles to capture latent interactions. In this section, we take a closer look at latent interactions and compare them with visible interactions from a variety of perspectives.

3.1 Popularity and Consumption

We begin by analyzing the distribution of latent interactions across the Renren user-base. We define *popularity* as the number of views a user's profile receives; this is equivalent to the user's in-degree of latent interactions. Figure 9 shows the distribution of user popularity. As expected, popularity is not evenly spread across the population: only 518 people (1%) are popular enough to receive more than 10,000 views. Conversely, the majority of users (57%) exhibit very low popularity with less than 100 total profile views.

Figure 10 shows the average number of visits users receive on a daily basis. The distribution is fitted to a Zipf distribution of the form $\beta x^{-\alpha}$ where $\alpha = 0.71569687$ and $\beta = 697.4468225$. Popular users receive many more views per day: 141 users (0.2%) are viewed more than 20 times a day on average, with the most popular profile being viewed more than 600 times a day. Most users (85.5%) receive less than one visit per day on average. This reinforces our finding that latent interactions are highly skewed towards a very popular subset of the population.

Finally, we examine whether the popularity of users corresponds to their profile viewing behavior. We define *consumption* as the number of other profiles a user views; this is equivalent to the

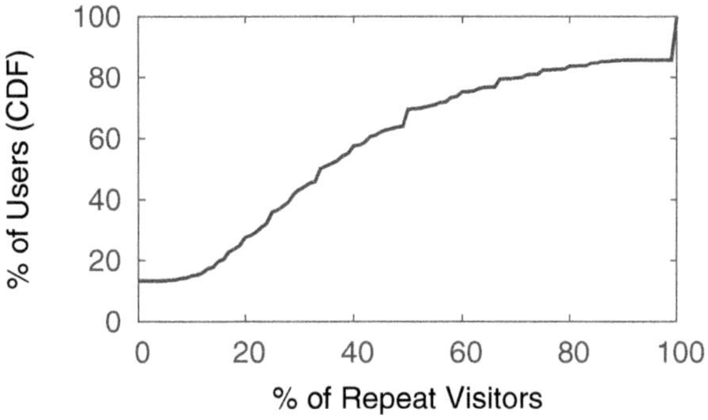

Figure 12: Ratio of repeat visitors

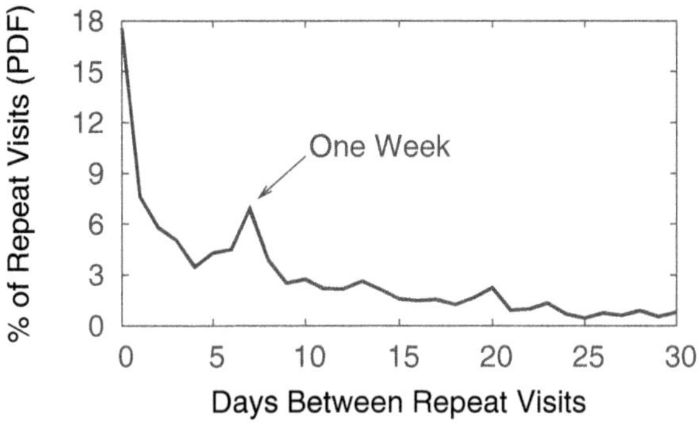

Figure 13: PDF of interval time between repeat visits

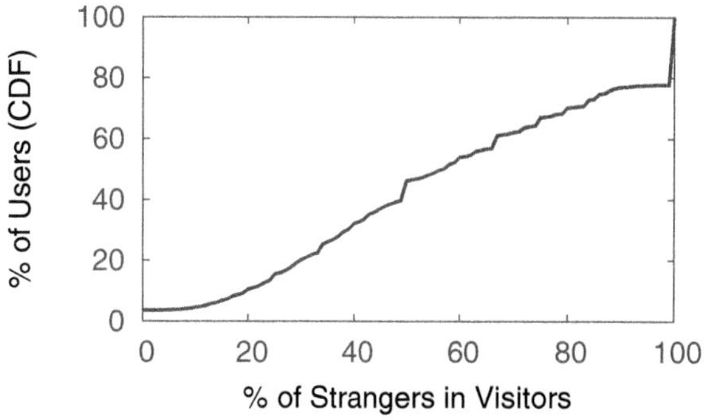

Figure 14: Percentage of strangers in visitors

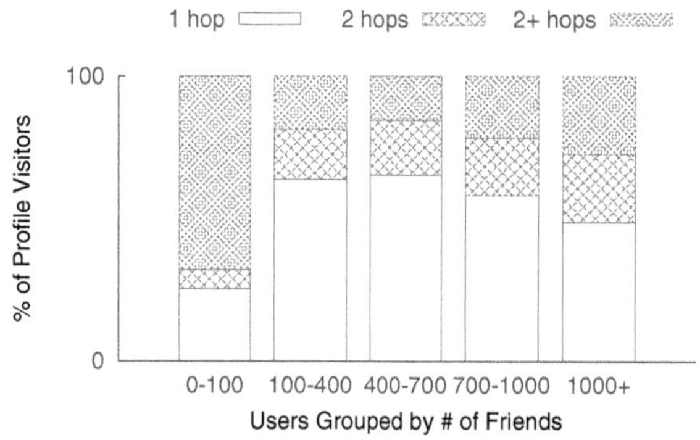

Figure 15: Breakdown of visitors by owner's social degree

user's out-degree of latent interactions. Figure 11 plots the overlap between the top users sorted by popularity, and top users sorted by consumption. The graph shows that the top 1% most popular users have 9% overlap with the top 1% biggest consumers. These users represent a hard-core contingent of social network users who are extremely active. For the most part however, users with high numbers of incoming latent interactions do not overlap with the people generating those interactions, *e.g.* profiles of celebrities are viewed by many users, but they are inactive in viewing others' pages. This necessarily means that many (presumably average, low-degree) users actively visit others, but are not visited in return. We examine the reciprocity of latent interactions in more detail in Section 3.3.

3.2 Composition of Visitors

Next, we want to figure out the composition of visitors to user profiles. We pose two questions: first, what portion of profile visitors are repeat visitors? Second, are visitors mostly friends of the profile owner, or are they unrelated strangers?

We begin by addressing the first question. We calculate the percentage of repeated visitors for each profile, and report the distribution in Figure 12. Roughly 70% of users have less than 50% repeat visitors, meaning that the majority of visitors do not browse the same profile twice. This seems to indicate the long tail of latent interactions is generated by users randomly browsing the social graph.

Next, we take a closer look at repeat profile visits. Figure 13 shows the probability density function (PDF) of the interval time between repeat visits. The graph peaks on day 0, meaning that users are most likely to return to a viewed profile on the same day. We will examine the causes for this behavior more closely in Section 4. The probability for repeated views decreases as the time delta expands, except for a noticeable peak at day 7. Interestingly, this shows that many users periodically check on their friends on a weekly basis. We confirmed that this feature is not an artifact introduced by our crawler or the use of RSS feeds by Renren users. Instead, we believe it may be due to the tendency for many users to browse their friends' profiles over the weekend.

We now move on to our second question: what users are generating latent interactions, friends of the profile owner, or *strangers*. We define a stranger as any user who is not a direct friend of the target user. Like Facebook, Renren's default privacy settings allow users in the same campus network to browse each other's profiles. Renren automatically recommends popular profiles to other users in the same network, which motivates people to view non-friends' profiles. However, they only recommend the 100 users in the network with the most users. Thus this feature should have minimal impact on our analysis of visitors to the average Renren user.

In order to answer our question, we calculate the percentage of visitors that are strangers and display the results in Figure 14. The results are fairly evenly divided: roughly 45% of users receive less than 50% of their profile visits from strangers. Or conversely, a slight majority of the population does receive a majority of their profile views from strangers.

We want to take a closer look at what component of a profile's visitors are strangers, and how far are they from the profile owner in the social graph. In Figure 15, we group the owners of profiles together by their social degree, and compute the average breakdown of their visitors into users who are friends (1-hop), friends-of-friends (2-hop) and other visitors (2+ hops). We see that for users with relatively few (< 100) friends, the large majority of their visitors are complete strangers, with very few friends-of-friends visit-

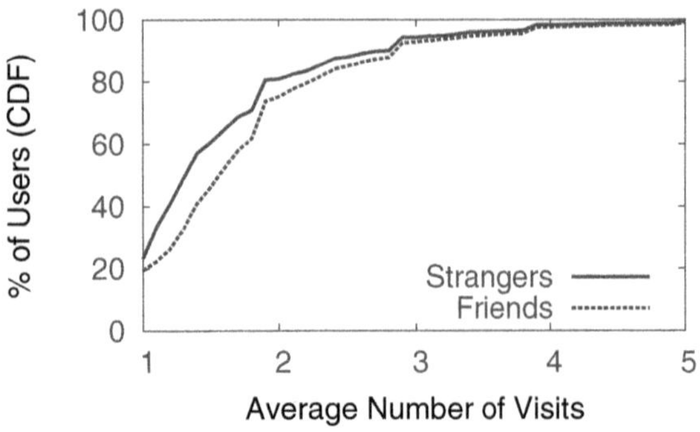

Figure 16: Average number of visits for friends and strangers

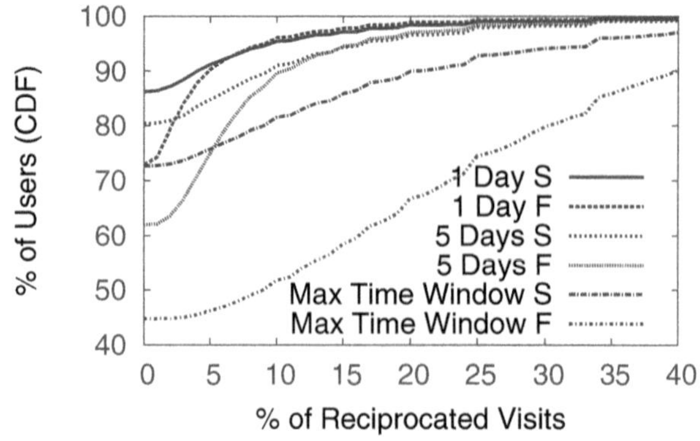

Figure 18: Probability of reciprocated profile views over various time windows for both strangers (S) and friends (F)

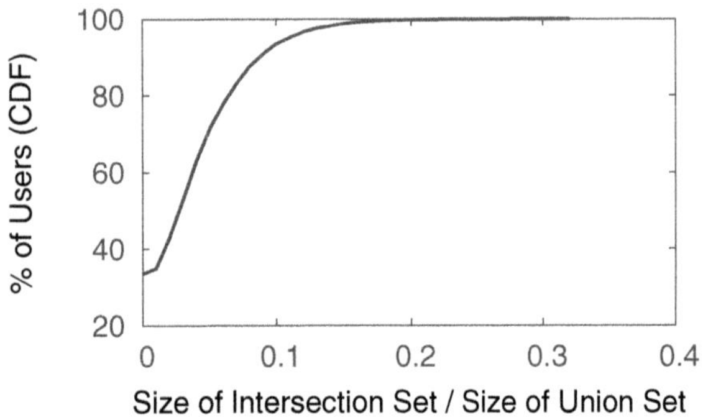

Figure 17: Ratio of reciprocated latent interactions over total latent relationships

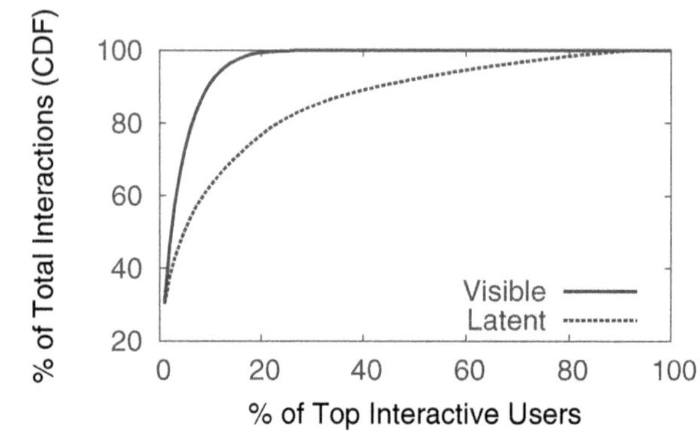

Figure 19: Distribution of total interactions

ing. For well-connected users with 100–1000 friends, the majority of their visitors are direct friends, and also a significant number of friends-of-friends. Finally, for extremely popular users with more than 1000 friends, their notoriety is such that they start to attract more strangers to visit their profiles. These results confirm those from previous work that discovered many Orkut users browse profiles 2 or more hops away on the social graph [3].

Unlike friends, strangers do not build long-term relationships with profile owners. Intuitively, this would seem to indicate that repeat profile viewing behavior should favor friends over strangers. To investigate this we compute the average number of visits for strangers and friends for each profile and plot the distribution in Figure 16. Surprisingly, our results indicate that the repeat profile viewing behavior for friends and strangers is very similar, with friends only edging out strangers by a small margin. This result demonstrates that when considering information dissemination via latent interactions, the significance of non-friend strangers should not be overlooked.

3.3 Reciprocity

Social norms compel users to reply to one another when contacted via visible interactions. Prior work has shown that these interactions are largely reciprocal on OSNs [29]. However, is this true of latent interactions? Since Renren users have full access to the list of recent visitors to their profile, it is possible for people to pay return visits to browse the profiles of their visitors. The question is, does visiting other user profiles actually trigger reciprocal visits?

As the first step towards looking at reciprocity of latent interactions, we construct the set of visitors who view each user profile, and the set of people who are visited by each user. Then, we compute the intersection and union of these two sets for every user. Intuitively, intersections include people who view a given user profile and are also visited by that user, *i.e.* the latent interactions are reciprocated. Unions contain all latent relationships for a given user, *i.e.* all users who viewed them, or they viewed. We calculate the ratio of intersection size to union size for each user and then plot the results in Figure 17. The ratio represents the number of reciprocated latent interactions divided by the total number of latent relationships. For more than 93% of users, less than 10% of latent relationships are reciprocated. This demonstrates that incoming profile views have little influence on user's profile browsing behavior. This is surprising, especially considering the fact that users know that their visits to a profile are visible to its owner through the visitor history feature.

Next we examine the time-varying characteristics of reciprocal profile visits for both strangers and friends. We compute the number of reciprocal visits that take place within t days after the initial visit. Figure 18 shows the results for threshold t values of 1 and 5 days plus the entire 90 days. As we look at increasingly larger window sizes, we see more profile visits being reciprocated. However, reciprocity remains low overall. Even across the entire measurement period, 73% of users receive no reciprocal page views from strangers, and 45% of users obtain no reciprocal page views from friends. This demonstrates that even with Renren's visitor history feature, visiting other user profiles is not sufficient to generate reciprocal visits. Compared to strangers, friends have relatively higher probability of reciprocal visits.

We take a further step and quantify the lack of reciprocity for latent interactions. For a data set of n users, if user i visits user j, then

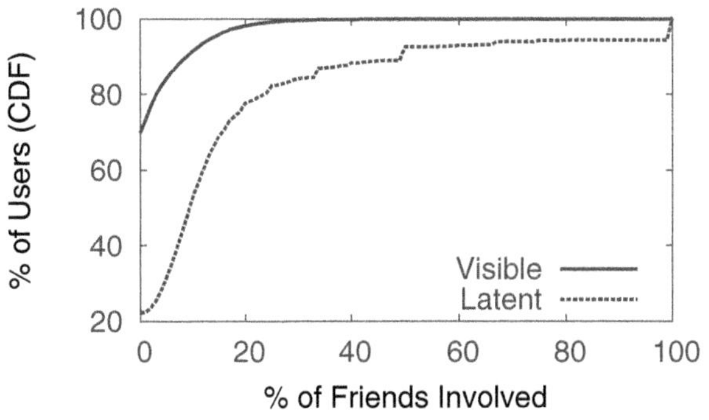

Figure 20: Distribution of interactions among each user's friends

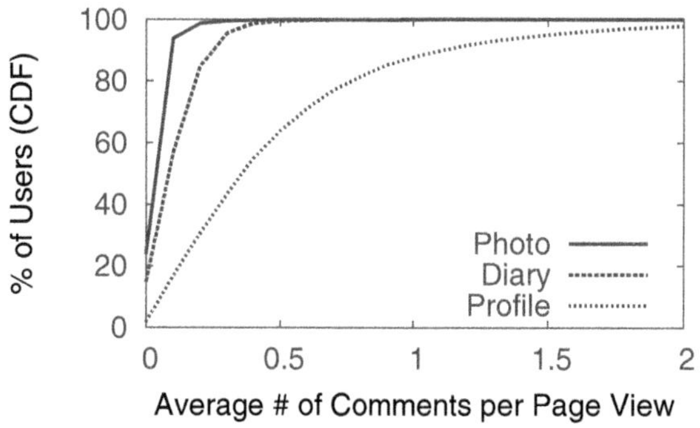

Figure 21: Average number of comments per page view for different types of pages

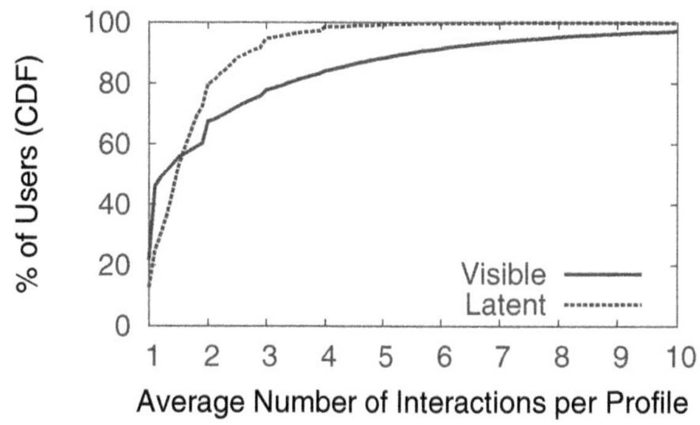

Figure 22: Average number of interactions per profile

$v_{ij} = 1$, otherwise $v_{ij} = 0$. The reciprocity coefficient [7] is defined as $\frac{\sum_{i \neq j}(v_{ij}-\bar{v})(v_{ji}-\bar{v})}{\sum_{i \neq j}(v_{ij}-\bar{v})^2}$, where $\bar{v} = \frac{\sum_{i \neq j} v_{ij}}{n(n-1)}$. The reciprocity coefficient is measured between -1 and 1, where positive values indicate reciprocity, and negative values anti-reciprocity. The reciprocity coefficient of profile visits on Renren is only 0.23. In contrast, reciprocity of visible comments on Renren is 0.49, and the reciprocity of visible interactions on Cyworld [7] is 0.78. Compared to these visible interactions, latent interactions show much less reciprocity.

3.4 Latent vs. Visible Interactions

In this section, we compare the characteristics of latent and visible interactions. To understand the level of participation of different users in both latent and visible interactions, Figure 19 plots the contribution of different users to both kinds of interactions. The bulk of all visible interactions can be attributed to a very small, highly interactive portion of the user-base: the top 28% of users account for all such interactions. In contrast, latent interactions are quite prevalent across the entire population, with more than 93% of all users contributing to latent interaction events. This confirms our original hypothesis that users are more active in viewing profiles than leaving comments, potentially because of a sense of anonymity in profile browsing. Given its widespread nature, this result also underscores the importance of understanding latent interactions as a way of propagating information across OSNs.

Next, we compare latent and visible interactions in coverage of friends. We compute for each user a distribution of their latent and visible interactions across their social links. We then aggregate across all users the percentage of friends involved in these events and plot the results in Figure 20. We see that roughly 80% of users only interact visibly with 5% of their friends, and no users interact with more than 40% of their friends. In contrast, about 80% of users view 20% or more of their friends' profiles, and a small portion of the population views all of their friends' profiles regularly. Thus, although not all social links are equally active, latent interactions cover a wider range of friends than visible interactions.

To get a sense of how many visible comments are generated by latent interactions, we examine the average number of comments per page view for a variety of pages on Renren, including profiles, diary entries, and photos. Figure 21 plots the results. Recall that along with visible comments, Renren keeps a visitor counter for each photo and diary entry. For diary entries and photos, the conversion rate is very low: 99% of users have less than 0.2 comments for every photo view, and 85% people have less than 0.2 comments for every diary view. This indicates that most users are passive information consumers: they view/read content and then move on without commenting themselves. In contrast, profile views have a higher conversion rate. Interestingly, 13% of users have a view/comment ratio greater than 1. This is because these users use profile comments as a form of instant messaging chat, leaving multiple responses and replies upon each visit.

Finally, we analyze the repeat activity frequency for latent and visible interactions on Renren. In particular, we want to examine the likelihood that users will repeatedly interact with the same page once they have viewed or commented on it once. Figure 22 plots the average number of interactions each user has with profile pages. 80% of users view a given profile <2 times. However, 80% of users leave 3.4 comments, almost twice the number of latent interactions. This result makes sense intuitively: for most types of data users only need to view them once to consume the data. However, comments can stimulate flurries of dialog on a given page, resulting in many consecutive interactions.

4. FACTORS INFLUENCING LATENT INTERACTIONS

As shown in Section 3.1, not all users in Renren are the target of equal numbers of latent interactions. In this section, we analyze factors that may impact latent interactions in order to quantify their effect on the popularity of individual users. We examine the following factors:

Friends. Does social degree directly correlate with popularity?

Lifetime. Are long lived accounts more likely to be popular than newer, less active accounts? We measure the number of days

Popularity	Friends	Lifetime	Diary	Photo	Status	Share	Comment
0-100	16 (0.15)	35 (0.55)	1 (0.51)	3 (0.47)	1 (0.5)	1 (0.5)	2 (0.54)
100-1000	131 (0.56)	423 (0.41)	11 (0.33)	41 (0.24)	27 (0.36)	43 (0.41)	96 (0.45)
1000-10000	401 (0.43)	792 (0.24)	50 (0.18)	125 (0.1)	115 (0.18)	155 (0.23)	596 (0.28)
>10000	708 (0.02)	869 (0.02)	117 (0.02)	251 (-0.03)	236 (0.01)	273 (-0.05)	1581 (0.01)
all users	112 (0.73)	263 (0.75)	12 (0.70)	34 (0.61)	28 (0.69)	39 (0.72)	134 (0.76)

Table 2: Average value of factors affecting user popularity. Spearman's rank correlation coefficient for each value is shown in parentheses.

in between a user joining and leaving Renren. Neither of these pieces of information is provided by Renren, and thus must be estimated. Join date can be approximated by the timestamp of the first comment received by a user, since the comment is likely to be a "welcome message" from a friend greeting the new user [29]. Because abandoned and inactive accounts can still receive comments, the best estimate of departure time is the timestamp of the last comment left by a user.

User-generated content. Do users who frequently update their profiles and upload new content attract the most visitors? This includes user's status updates, diary entries, photos, and shared links to content on the web.

Comments. Do users who comment frequently attract more users? Comments are snippets of text that user's can attach to other pieces of user-generated content.

We divide users into 4 groups based on their popularity, calculate the average value of these factors in each group, and display the results in Table 2. All factors increase along with popularity, *i.e.* the most popular users also have the most friends, the oldest accounts, and generate the largest amounts of content/visible interactions.

Given the drastic differences in size of each popularity group, and the average nature of the values in Table 2, it is difficult to infer definite correlations between any one factor and popularity. To analyze these correlations more specifically, we leverage a technique from prior work [4] called Spearman's rank correlation coefficient (Spearman's ρ). Spearman's ρ is a non-parametric measure of the correlation between two variables that is closely related to Pearson's correlation coefficient [18]. It is defined as $\rho = 1 - \frac{6\sum(x_i - y_i)^2}{n(n^2-1)}$, where x_i and y_i are the ranks of two different features in a data set of n users. $\rho > 0$ indicates positive correlation, while < 0 indicates negative correlation.

Table 2 shows Spearman's ρ in parenthesis beside the average value for each factor. Although all factors exhibit high correlation with the low popularity and "all users" categories, this is an artifact of the tied ranks among the (numerous) low activity users. All of these users exhibit very low interactivity and social degree, thus leading to high levels of correlation. Previous work has observed similar artifacts when analyzing all users in a large OSN dataset [4].

For the two median popularity groups (100-1000 and 1000-10000), number of friends has the highest correlation with popularity. Users in these categories can be broadly defined as normal social network users. They are not celebrities; they simply use the OSN for its intended purpose of sharing information with friends. This is reflected in the fact that users in these categories show relatively high levels of correlation across all user-generated content categories. Account lifetime is a less important factor for users in the 1000-10000 popularity range, given the ease with which users can quickly amass hundreds of friends on OSNs.

No factor has strong correlation with popularity for users in the high popularity group. Spearman's ρ for photos and shared links are even negative. This is an important finding, as it shows popularity is not trivially gained simply by having lots of friends, or producing copious amounts of user-generated content. Therefore, there must be other factors outside the scope of our measurements that contribute to determine user popularity. One possibility is that quality, rather than quantity, of content may be a significant draw to attract visitors. Another possibility is that real-world celebrity status is the most important determining factor of online popularity. Unfortunately, we cannot quantify these factors at present.

Recall that 100 of the most popular users in the university network are recommended to users by Renren. These 100 users account for less than 19.3% of the total users in the high popularity group, so the recommendation mechanism has limited impact on the high popularity group results.

5. LATENT INTERACTION GRAPHS

Previous studies have demonstrated that taking visible interactions into account has important implications for applications that leverage social graphs [29]. These changes can be modeled by *interaction graphs*, which are constructed by connecting users from the social graph who have visibly interacted one or more times.

We have already demonstrated significant differences between latent and visible interaction patterns on Renren. To summarize these key differences briefly, latent interactions are more numerous, non-reciprocal, and often connect non-friend strangers. These results are also likely to have profound implications on applications that leverage social graphs, and thus warrant the construction of a new model to capture the properties of latent interactions. We call this new model a *latent interaction graph*. In this section we formally define latent interaction graphs, analyze their salient properties, and compare them to the Renren social and visible interaction graphs.

5.1 Building Latent Interaction Graphs

A latent interaction graph is defined as a set of users (nodes) that are connected via edges representing latent interaction events between them. Unlike the social graph and visible interaction graph, we have shown that latent interaction is non-reciprocal (Section 3.3). Thus, we use directed edges to represent user's page views, unlike the social and visible interaction graphs, which are both undirected. The set of users (61,405 total) remains unchanged between the social and interaction graphs. We define *latent interaction in-degree* of a node as the number of visitors who have visited that user's profile; while *out-degree* is the number of profiles that user has visited.

We construct latent interaction graphs from our Renren data using profile views as the latent interactions. We use user comments as the visible interaction data to construct visible interaction graphs for Renren. In this paper we restrict our social, latent, and visible interaction graphs to only contain users from the PKU network, since these are the only users for which we have complete interaction records. Note that we only consider interactions that occur between users in the PKU network, as it is possible for interactions to originate from or target users outside the network for whom

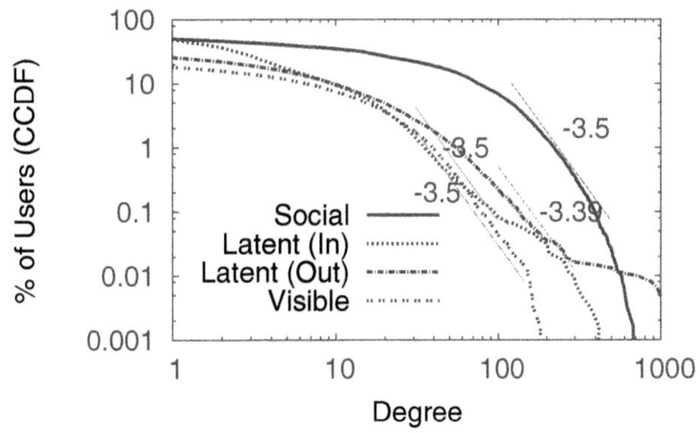

Figure 23: CCDF of node degree for latent interaction graph, visible interaction graph and social graph.

we have limited information. Also note that because non-friend strangers can view user's profiles, the latent interaction graph will contain edges between users who are not friends in the social graph.

Our formulation of interaction graphs uses an unweighted graph. We do not attempt to derive a weight scheme for interaction graphs analyzed in this paper, but leave exploration of this facet of latent interaction graphs to future work.

5.2 Comparing Social, Visible Interaction and Latent Interaction Graphs

In this section we compare the salient characteristics of the Renren social, visible, and latent interaction graphs using common graph metrics.

Degree distribution. Figure 23 plots the CCDFs of node degree for the three types of graphs. Since the latent interaction graph is directed, we plot both in-degree and out-degree. In Section 3.4 we show that latent interactions are more prevalent than visible interactions. This is reflected in the relative number of edges in the two interaction graphs, as shown in Table 3. This also leads to nodes in the latent graph having a noticeably higher degree distribution in Figure 23. However, neither of the interaction graphs have as many edges as the raw social graph, which leads to the social graph having the highest degree distribution. Interestingly, because a small number of Renren users are frequent profile browsers, *i.e.* they like to visit a large number of profiles (far greater than their circle of friends), the distribution of latent out-degrees flattens out at the tail-end and never approaches 0%.

Despite these differences, latent interaction graphs still exhibit power-law scaling. Table 3 shows similar in- and out-degree power-law fit alpha values for latent interaction graphs compared to the visible interaction graph and the social graph. Renren limits users to of 1,000 friends (2,000 for paying users), so all power-law curves decline quickly to zero, and alpha values are high.

Clustering coefficient. Table 3 shows that the average clustering coefficient is 0.03 for the latent interaction graph, and 0.05 for the visible interaction graph, which are both much less than that of the social graph. This is because not all social links are accurate indicators of active social relationships, and these links with no interactions are removed in interaction graphs. This produces loose connections between neighbors, and low clustering coefficients in these graphs. A portion of the latent interactions to a profile is from non-friend strangers who randomly browse the network. Thus, links between visitors in the latent interaction graph are less intensive than friends exchanging messages, which further lowers the clustering coefficients in latent interaction graphs.

Assortativity. Table 3 shows that the Renren latent interaction graph is slightly disassortative. This makes sense intuitively, as latent interactions are highly skewed towards a small subset of extremely popular users. In contrast, the other two graphs are both assortative, with the social graph being more so. This result contrasts with previous studies in which the interaction graph was more assortative than the social graph [29].

Average path length. The average path length of the latent interaction graph is between that of the visible interaction graph and the social graph. As the average number of links per node and the number of high-degree "super-nodes" decreases, the overall level of connectivity in the graph drops. This causes average path lengths to rise, especially in the visible interaction graph.

6. IMPACT ON SOCIAL APPLICATIONS

In the previous section, we analyzed salient properties of the Renren social, visible interaction, and latent interaction graphs. However, it remains unknown how different graph metrics impact the performance of real-world social applications. Social application tests present new perspectives since their performance on a particular graph cannot be easily correlated with a single graph metric.

Changes in user connectivity patterns can produce significantly different results for social network applications. In order to validate how much impact the choice of graphs can make on socially enhanced applications, we implement techniques from the paper "Efficient influence maximization" [6]. This work leverages graph properties in social networks to address information dissemination problems. We compare the effectiveness of these algorithms on the raw social graph, visible interaction graph, and latent interaction graph that are derived from our Renren measurements of the PKU network. These results allow us to validate whether socially enhanced applications require a model that takes latent interactions into account.

6.1 Efficient Influence Maximization

As OSNs become increasingly popular worldwide, they also become more critical platforms for information dissemination and marketing. Understanding how to fully utilize OSNs as marketing and information dissemination platforms is a significant challenge. The influence maximization problem seeks to determine the most influential individuals who will maximum the spread of information in an OSN.

Given the lack of publicly available social influence datasets, previous work [6, 14] builds statistical models based on raw social graph topologies, and designs algorithms to address influence maximization problems within these models.

Weighted cascade model. The weighted cascade model relies on social links for information propagation [14]. After receiving information, a user has a single chance of activating each currently inactive neighbor. In this model, the activation probability is related to node's degree: if a person w has d_w neighbors, it is activated by neighbors with probability $1/d_w$. Chen et al. propose instantiating the MixedGreedyWC algorithm to implement the weighted cascade model [6].

Latent cascade model. The weighted cascade model is based on social graphs, and relies on social relationships plus the activation probability to simulate the information dissemination process.

Network	Edges	Power-Law Fit Alpha	Cluster Coef.	Assortativity	Avg. Path Len.
Social Graph	753,297	3.5	0.18	0.23	3.64
Visible Interaction Graph	27,347	3.5	0.05	0.05	5.43
Latent Interaction Graph	240,408	3.5(in) 3.39(out)	0.03	-0.06	4.02

Table 3: Topology measurements for latent interaction, visible interaction and social graphs.

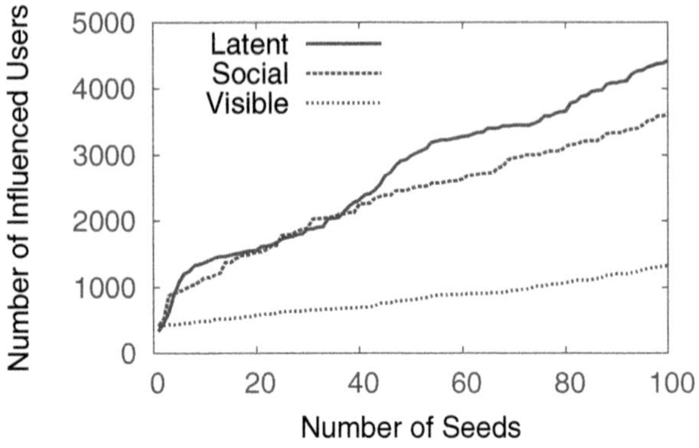

Figure 24: Influence spread using the MixedGreedyWC algorithm on different graphs.

However, we observe that information is not disseminated equally through social links. User profiles are usually only viewed by a small portion of friends, thus not all social links are active in information propagation. Moreover, a portion of the visits to profiles can be attributed to people not connected to the user, *i.e.* strangers.

When a user browses a profile, information in the web page is naturally propagated to that user. It is more accurate to represent information dissemination by links in latent interaction graphs than by passive friendship links in the social graph. Thus, to take latent interaction graphs into account we define the latent cascade model. When a person receives information, they have a single chance to activate inactive neighbors, who have directed links pointing to that person in the latent interaction graph. To transform the visitor counts from our month-long measurement into activation probabilities, we calculate the number of unique visitors for every user and determine the most popular user. We then compute the activation probability of every user by normalizing that user's number of unique visitors by the maximum value. This approximates an activation probability using the "visit rate" normalized to the most popular profile. We use visits from unique users and exclude repeated visits here, because the first visit contributes the most to the information propagation, and repeated follow-up visits are less likely to propagate information.

Visible cascade model. The visible cascade model is built atop visible interaction graphs, in a similar fashion to the latent cascade model. The information dissemination path is decided by visible interaction events, and the per node activation probability is determined using the same method as in the latent cascade model.

6.2 Experimental Results

For our experiments, we use the MixedGreedyWC algorithm [6] to find the most influential individuals in each of our three models, and then compute the number of people influenced. We vary the set of seed users to the MixedGreedyWC algorithm from 1 to 100 in our tests and observe the effects on influence spread.

Figure 24 shows influence spread versus seed set size for our three models. Influence in the weighted and latent cascade model both increase quickly in the beginning. Eventually, as more seeds are selected, the number of people influenced in latent cascade model surpasses the weighted model. The reason for this is that although social graphs have a large amount of links, the activation probability is generally low. This limits the spread of information to well connected components of the graph. Conversely, latent interaction graphs are constructed by page viewings, which correspond to higher activation probability. This is in accordance with real situations: people are likely to receive information when they browse profiles, while information cannot be disseminated through inactive social links. These high probabilities guarantee that information is progressively disseminated through the limited number of links in the latent interaction graph. Previous sections show that visible interaction graphs have the least number of links. Thus, although activation probabilities are relatively high, the visible cascade model reaches the smallest influence spread due to the dearth of links.

7. RELATED WORK

Much effort has been put into understanding the structure of large-scale online social networks [8]. Ahn et al. analyze topological characteristics of Cyworld, MySpace and Orkut [1]. Mislove et al. measure the structure of Flickr, YouTube, LiveJournal, and Orkut [22], and observe the growth of the Flickr social network [21]. Java et al. study the topological and geographical properties of Twitter [13]. Huang et al. measure user prestige and visible interaction preference in Renren [12]. To the best of our knowledge, our measurement of the Renren network provides the largest non-Twitter social graph to date, with 42,115,509 users and 1,657,273,875 friendship links. Most of Renren's topological properties are similar to those of other OSNs, including power-law degree distribution and small world properties.

Researchers have also studied the visible interaction network. Leskovec et al. analyze the instant messaging network, which contains the largest amount of user conversations ever published [19]. Valafar et al. characterize indirect fan-owner interactions via photos among users in Flickr [27]. Chun et al. observe that visible interactions are almost bidirectional in Cyworld [7]. Wilson et al. show the structure of the interaction graph differs significantly from the social network in Facebook [29]. Viswanath et al. observe that social links in the activity network tend to come and go quickly over time [28]. Finally, a recent study from Northwestern and UC Santa Barbara quantified the role of spam and phishing attacks in Facebook wall posts [10].

Benevenuto et al. collect detailed click-stream data from a Brazilian social network aggregator, and measure silent activities like browsing [3]. Schneider et al. extract click-streams from passively monitored network traffic and make similar measurements [25]. We analyze latent interactions from a different perspective than these existing works by leveraging data that is intrinsic to the OSN and not inferred from a third-party. Ideally, we would like to perform a detailed comparison between our dataset and prior studies using click-stream datasets. Unfortunately, the sensitive nature of these datasets make their distribution challenging. At publication time, we are currently unaware of any publicly available click-stream dataset.

Some researchers have performed initial studies on information propagation and user influence in OSNs. Cha et al. present a detailed analysis of popularity and dissemination of photographs on Flickr [5]. They find that popular users with high in-degree are not necessarily influential in terms of spawning subsequent, viral interactions in the form of retweets or mentions on Twitter [4]. Our Renren data confirms these results, as we show that factors like number of friends and amount of user-generated content produced are not strongly correlated with popularity.

8. CONCLUSIONS

Latent user interactions make up the large majority of user activity events on OSNs. In this paper, we present a comprehensive study of both visible and latent user interactions in the Renren OSN. Our data includes detailed visit histories to the profiles of 61,405 Renren users over a 90-day period (September to November 2009). We compute a single visitor history for each profile by using a novel technique to merge visitor logs from multiple consecutive crawls. We analyze profile visit histories to study questions of user popularity and reciprocity for profile browsing behavior, and the link between passive profile browsing and active comments.

Our analysis reveals interesting insights into the nature of user popularity in OSNs. We observe that user behavior changes for latent interactions: more users participate, users do not feel the need to reciprocate visits, and visits by non-friends make up a significant portion of views to most user profiles. We also see that visits to user profiles generate more active interactions (comments) than visits to photos or diary pages. Using profile browsing events, we construct *latent interaction graphs* as a more accurate representation of meaningful peer interactions. Analysis of latent interaction graphs derived from our Renren data reveal characteristics that fall between visible interaction graphs and social graphs. This confirms the intuition that latent interactions are less limited by constraints such as time and energy, but more meaningful (and thus sparser) than the social graph.

Finally, our measurement study also includes an exhaustive crawl of the largest connected component in the Renren social graph. The resulting graph is one of the biggest of its kind, with more than 42 million nodes and 1.6 billion edges. Other than the proprietary Cyworld dataset, this is the only social graph we know of that covers 100% of a large social graph component. Given its size and comprehensiveness, we are currently investigating different options for sharing this dataset with the research community.

Acknowledgments

We thank the anonymous reviewers for their valuable comments. This work is supported in part by National Science Foundation of China under project #60673183, #60873051, the National Basic Research Program of China under Grant No.2011CB302305, and Doctoral Funding of MOE #20060001044. The UCSB team is supported by the NSF under CNS-0546216, IIS-847925, and IIS-0916307. Any opinions, findings, and conclusions or recommendations expressed in this material are those of the authors and do not necessarily reflect the views of the National Science Foundation.

9. REFERENCES

[1] AHN, Y.-Y., HAN, S., KWAK, H., MOON, S. B., AND JEONG, H. Analysis of topological characteristics of huge online social networking services. In *Proc. of World Wide Web Conference* (2007).

[2] BARABASI, A.-L., AND ALBERT, R. Emergence of scaling in random networks. *Science 286* (1999).

[3] BENEVENUTO, F., RODRIGUES, T., CHA, M., AND ALMEIDA, V. Characterizing user behavior in online social networks. In *Proc. of ACM Internet Measurement Conference* (2009).

[4] CHA, M., HADDADI, H., BENEVENUTO, F., AND GUMMADI, K. Measuring user influence in twitter: The million follower fallacy. In *Proc. of International AAAI Conference on Weblogs and Social Media (ICWSM)* (May 2010).

[5] CHA, M., MISLOVE, A., AND GUMMADI, K. A measurement-driven analysis of information propagation in the flickr social network. In *Proc. of World Wide Web Conference* (2009).

[6] CHEN, W., WANG, Y., AND YANG, S. Efficient influence maximization in social networks. In *Proc. of ACM Conference on Knowledge Discovery and Data Mining* (June 2009).

[7] CHUN, H., KWAK, H., EOM, Y. H., AHN, Y.-Y., MOON, S. B., AND JEONG, H. Comparison of online social relations in volume vs interaction: a case study of cyworld. In *Proc. of ACM Internet Measurement Conference* (2008).

[8] FU, F., LIU, L., AND WANG, L. Empirical analysis of online social networks in the age of web 2.0. *Physica A 387*, 2–3 (2008), 675–684.

[9] GANNES, L. When social replaces search, what can you do to monetize? GigaOM, March 2010.

[10] GAO, H., HU, J., WILSON, C., LI, Z., CHEN, Y., AND ZHAO, B. Y. Detecting and characterizing social spam campaigns. In *Proc. of ACM Internet Measurement Conference* (Melbourne, Australia, November 2010).

[11] GRUHL, D., GUHA, R., LIBEN-NOWELL, D., AND TOMKINS, A. Information diffusion through blogspace. In *Proc. of World Wide Web Conference* (2004).

[12] HUANG, L., AND XIA, Z. Measuring user prestige and interaction preference on social network site. In *Proc. of ACIS-ICIS* (2009).

[13] JAVA, A., SONG, X., FININ, T., AND TSENG, B. L. Why we twitter: An analysis of a microblogging community. In *Proc. of WebKDD/SNA-KDD* (2007).

[14] KEMPE, D., KLEINBERG, J. M., AND TARDOS, Ï. Maximizing the spread of influence through a social network. In *Proc. of ACM Conference on Knowledge Discovery and Data Mining* (2003).

[15] KIRKPATRICK, M. Social networking now more popular than email, report finds. ReadWriteWeb, March 2009.

[16] KWAK, H., LEE, C., PARK, H., AND MOON, S. B. What is twitter, a social network or a news media? In *Proc. of World Wide Web Conference* (Raleigh, NC, April 2010).

[17] LAMPE, C., ELLISON, N., AND STEINFIELD, C. A familiar face(book): profile elements as signals in an online social network. In *Proc. of CHI* (2007).

[18] LEHMANN, E. L., AND D'ABRERA, H. J. M. *Nonparametrics: Statistical Methods Based on Ranks*. Prentice-Hall, 1998.

[19] LESKOVEC, J., AND HORVITZ, E. Planetary-scale views on a large instant-messaging network. In *Proc. of World Wide Web Conference* (2008).

[20] MILGRAM, S. The small world problem. *Psychology Today 1* (1967).

[21] MISLOVE, A., KOPPULA, H. S., GUMMADI, K. P., DRUSCHEL, P., AND BHATTACHARJEE, B. Growth of the flickr social network. In *Proc. of WOSN* (2008).

[22] MISLOVE, A., MARCON, M., GUMMADI, P. K., DRUSCHEL, P., AND BHATTACHARJEE, B. Measurement and analysis of online social networks. In *Proc. of ACM Internet Measurement Conference* (2007).

[23] Opengraph. `http://opengraphprotocol.org`.

[24] The renren social network. `http://www.renren.com`.

[25] SCHNEIDER, F., FELDMANN, A., KRISHNAMURTHY, B., AND WILLINGER, W. Understanding online social network usage from a network perspective. In *Proc. of ACM Internet Measurement Conference* (2009).

[26] SORKIN, A. R. Facebook tops 500 million users. New York Times Blog, June 2010.

[27] VALAFAR, M., REJAIE, R., AND WILLINGER, W. Beyond friendship graphs: A study of user interactions in flickr. In *Proc. of WOSN* (2009).

[28] VISWANATH, B., MISLOVE, A., CHA, M., AND GUMMADI, K. P. On the evolution of user interaction in facebook. In *Proc. of WOSN* (2009).

[29] WILSON, C., BOE, B., SALA, A., PUTTASWAMY, K. P. N., AND ZHAO, B. Y. User interactions in social networks and their implications. In *Proc. of ACM Eurosys* (2009).

[30] YAROW, J. Facebook was more popular in the u.s. than google last week. BusinessInsider.com, March 2010.

Measuring the Mixing Time of Social Graphs

Abedelaziz Mohaisen
University of Minnesota
Minneapolis, MN 55455, USA
mohaisen@cs.umn.edu

Aaram Yun
University of Minnesota
Minneapolis, MN 55455, USA
aaram@cs.umn.edu

Yongdae Kim
University of Minnesota
Minneapolis, MN 55455, USA
kyd@cs.umn.edu

ABSTRACT

Social networks provide interesting algorithmic properties that can be used to bootstrap the security of distributed systems. For example, it is widely believed that social networks are fast mixing, and many recently proposed designs of such systems make crucial use of this property. However, whether real-world social networks are really fast mixing is not verified before, and this could potentially affect the performance of such systems based on the fast mixing property. To address this problem, we measure the mixing time of several social graphs, the time that it takes a random walk on the graph to approach the stationary distribution of that graph, using two techniques. First, we use the second largest eigenvalue modulus which bounds the mixing time. Second, we sample initial distributions and compute the random walk length required to achieve probability distributions close to the stationary distribution. Our findings show that the mixing time of social graphs is much larger than anticipated, and being used in literature, and this implies that either the current security systems based on fast mixing have weaker utility guarantees or have to be less efficient, with less security guarantees, in order to compensate for the slower mixing.

Categories and Subject Descriptors

C.2.0 [**Computer Communication Networks**]: General – *Security and Protection*; C.4 [**Performance of Systems**]: Design studies

General Terms

Security, Design, Experimentation

Keywords

Social networks, Sybil defenses, Mixing time, Measurement

1. INTRODUCTION

Popularity of social networks have stimulated many ideas for using these networks to build revolutionary systems in many areas, including security and communication [24, 31, 3, 30, 12, 32, 11, 23, 25, 22, 29]. The systems built on top of social networks exploit algorithmic properties of the social graph, as well as the social trust. For instance, some security designs exploit the "fast mixing" property, an indicator of how quickly a random walk on a graph approaches the stationary distribution, to build Sybil [4] defenses [31, 3, 30, 12, 32, 11, 23]. Some other designs use node betweenness, an indicator of how a node is well-situated on the path between other nodes in the graph, for building Sybil defense as well [19]. There are also designs which use betweenness and similarity for building routing algorithms in disconnected networks [2], among many other designs based on different assumptions.

The applicability and effectiveness of these designs are critically dependent on the quality or degree of these properties in underlying social graphs. But, while they base their constructions and designs on these properties—assuming a high quality of the properties in the social graphs, they do not give conclusive evidences of the quality of these properties. It is claimed that these properties hold, based on mathematical models and indirect experiments, but it is hard to find a single work that evaluates the qualities of such properties *directly* in actual social networks. But doing that, it will be then possible to determine the exact quality of the property required for these designs to work.

For example, the mixing time of the social graph, which measures how quick a random walk on the graph reaches the stationary distribution, is claimed to be *fast*. Such claim implies that social graphs are well-enmeshed and any arbitrary destination in the social graph is reachable, with a probability driven according to the stationary distribution—a distribution that is proportional to nodes' degrees, from each possible source with a relatively small number of intermediaries. Furthermore, this property has been used widely without careful measurement of the mixing time [31, 3, 30, 12]. For example, Yu et al. [31] proposed SybilGuard, a Sybil defense protocol that exploits the fast mixing property of social graphs. Even though they performed experiments on social networks, their experiment was not about actual measurement of the mixing time of these graphs (see Section 2). Danezis and Mittal [3] proposed SybilInfer to detect Sybil nodes in social graph basing their design on the fast mixing property of social graph and cited [18] as an evidence to prove that social networks are fast mixing. We notice, however, that findings in [18] do not support the mixing time with the guarantees needed by SybilInfer. Lesniewski-Laas et al. [12] introduced Whānau, a Sybil-proof routing protocol that uses the fast mixing property and, while citing the existence of the property to a large body of previous work, they have attempted to estimate the mixing time in a few social graphs. However, their evidence is only circumstantial and it does not directly follow that these social graphs are really fast mixing (see Section 2).

In this paper, we evaluate the mixing time of social graphs. We systematically measure the mixing time of social graphs in a variety of real-world small to large-scale social networks (see Table 1),

IMC'10, November 1–3, 2010, Melbourne, Australia.

with designs based on these properties in mind. We use two methods for measuring the mixing time. First, we compute the Second Largest Eigenvalue Modulus (SLEM) of the social graphs which bounds the mixing time. Also, we sample initial points and compute the random walk with varying walk lengths. We find that in many actual large-scale social networks, the mixing time is much larger than suggested by those papers, which apply the fast mixing of social networks to design security systems. By experimenting with one of these systems—SybilLimit [30], we unveil that the quality of the mixing time required for such design is not as being claimed, yet in some real-world social graphs higher than anticipated, which calls for further investigation of the theory beyond these designs.

The rest of the paper is organized as follows. In section 2, we review some of the related work in literature. In section 3, we review the preliminaries including the network model, the random walk, and the mixing time. In section 4, we introduce the main results followed by discussion in section 5. Finally, in section 6 we draw concluding remarks and future work.

2. RELATED WORK

There are many systems built on top of social graphs and their properties. Daly et al. [2] proposed a social network-based scheme for routing in disconnected delay-tolerant mobile ad-hoc networks which uses both of the betweenness and similarity properties. Quercia et al. [19] used the betweenness property to defend against the Sybil attack in mobile networks. Yu et al. [30, 31] used the fast mixing property of a graph to build a defense mechanism against the Sybil attack. Danezis and Mittal [3] used the fast mixing property to build an inference (detection) mechanism for Sybil nodes in peer-to-peer Systems. Lesniewski-Laas et al. [12] introduced a routing protocol that uses the fast mixing property of the social graph. Kaustz et al. introduced ReferralWeb [7], a referral system that combines social networks and collaborative filtering and assumes a well-connected social network graph, a property that is very tied to the mixing time of the graph [6].

Schemes like SybilGuard [31] and SybilLimit [30] of Yu et al., and Whānau of Lesniewski-Laas et al. [12] are based on the fast mixing property of social networks, and they did perform experiments on some real social networks. But their experiments did not directly measure or estimate the mixing time of these social networks. Let us summarize contents of their experiments as follows.

Yu et al. [30] performed some experiments based on real-world social graphs. They ran their scheme with fixed, small walk length (e.g., 10 or 15), and checked whether their scheme works as well as expected (thereby indirectly trying to confirm that the graph is fast mixing). But, there are some deficiencies in their methodology. First, they manipulated the social graphs by trimming lower degree nodes in order to improve the mixing time. Second, their method used several parameters chosen heuristically without showing how these parameters are related to the mixing time. Last, they evaluated only three social graphs which would be too small for making a general conclusion for all social graphs. We would also like to point out that they measured only the false acceptance rate (i.e., the rate of accepted sybil nodes per honest nodes) and not other characteristics, like the rejection rate of honest nodes, which would be expected to increase with insufficient walk lengths. Experiments done in the SybilGuard [31] paper are similar.

Lesniewski-Laas et al. [12] also performed experiments on four large-scale social graphs. They produced CDF of tail edges of random walks with varying walk lengths, and expected that as the walk length approaches $O(\log n)$, probabilities that a random walk ends at a certain edge tend to approach $1/m$, the uniform probability over edges. But the convergence is very loose; they claim that as the walk length approaches 80[1], each CDF approaches the ideal uniform distribution, but among the social networks in their measurement, at least the LiveJournal result shows the distribution is very far from uniform at the walk length 80. The other three results also allow a lot of deviations from the uniform distribution which make it unlikely that the total variation distance between the distribution and the uniform distribution is close to 0. In short, they provided raw measurements but did not relate the distribution of the sampled tails to the stationary distribution itself, in terms of the variation distance.[2]

Recently, and concurrent to this work, Viswanath et al. conducted an experimental analysis of sybil defenses based on social networks in [27]. Their study aimed at comparing different defenses (namely, SybilGuard [32], SybilLimit [30], SybilInfer [3], and SumUp [23]) independent of the data sets being used, by decomposing these defenses to their cores. They show that the different Sybil defenses work by ranking different nodes based on how well-connected are these nodes to a trusted node (the verifier). Also, they show that the different Sybil defenses are sensitive to community structure in social networks and community detection algorithms can be used to replace the random walk based Sybil defenses. In conclusion, results on the poor performance of Sybil defenses when applied to community structure possessing social graphs agree with our findings, where we show that such networks are slow mixing.

3. PRELIMINARIES

In this section, we formalize the network model. We define the mixing time of a random walk on a graph, and we also define the fast mixing property of a graph.

3.1 Network model

The social network can be viewed as an undirected graph $G = (V, E)$ where V is the set of nodes (social actors) in the graph and E is the set of edges (relationships or interdependencies) between the nodes. The size of the graph $n = |V|$ and the number of edges in G is $m = |E|$. We define the degree of a node $v_i \in V$ as the number of nodes in V adjacent to v_i and denote it by $\deg(v_i)$. For G, we define the stochastic transition probability matrix $P = [p_{ij}]$ of size $n \times n$ where the $(i, j)^{\text{th}}$ entry in P is the probability of moving from node v_i to node v_j defined as

$$p_{ij} = \begin{cases} \frac{1}{\deg(v_i)} & \text{if } v_i \text{ is adjacent to } v_j, \\ 0 & \text{otherwise.} \end{cases} \tag{1}$$

3.2 Mixing time

In this subsection we recall definitions of some notions about random walks on graphs. For more detailed exposition, see [21].

The "event" of moving from a node to another in the graph is captured by the Markov chain which represents a random walk over the graph G. A random walk R of length k over G is a sequence of vertices in G begining from an initial node v_i and ending at v_t, the terminal node, following the transition probability defined in (1). The Markov chain is said to be *ergodic* if it is irreducible and aperiodic. In that case, it has a unique stationary distribution π and the distribution after random walk of length k converges to

[1]While 80 is much larger than $\log n$ when n is close to one million, one possibility is that this may be due to the hidden constant.

[2]While [12] uses a different measure, called the separation distance, and does not require ϵ to be too small, the necessary quality of the mixing time is not measured in [12].

π as $k \to \infty$. The stationary distribution of the Markov chain is a probability distribution that is invariant to the transition matrix P (i.e., $\pi P = \pi$). The mixing time of the Markov chain, T is defined as the minimal length of the random walk in order to reach the stationary distribution. More precisely, Definition 1 states the mixing time of a Markov chain on G parameterized by a variation distance parameter ϵ.

DEFINITION 1 (MIXING TIME). *The mixing time (parameterized by ϵ) of a Markov chain is defined as*

$$T(\epsilon) = \max_i \min\{t : |\pi - \pi^{(i)} P^t|_1 < \epsilon\}, \tag{2}$$

where π is the stationary distribution, $\pi^{(i)}$ is the initial distribution concentrated at vertex v_i, P^t is the transition matrix after t steps, and $|\cdot|_1$ is the total variation distance. We say that a Markov chain is rapidly mixing if $T(\epsilon) = poly(\log n, \log \frac{1}{\epsilon})$ where $n = |V|$.

In literature, the rapid mixing of the Markov chain is cited as "fast mixing" for the graph [3, 12, 30, 31]. In this work, we follow the tradition of referring to this bound as "fast mixing". Also, again following these previous work, we strengthen the definition by considering only the case $\epsilon = \Theta(\frac{1}{n})$, and requiring $T(\epsilon) = O(\log n)$.

THEOREM 1 (STATIONARY DISTRIBUTION). *For undirected unweighted graph G, the stationary distribution of the Markov chain over G is the probability vector $\pi = [\pi_{v_i}]$ where $\pi_{v_i} = \frac{\deg v_i}{2m}$. This is,*

$$\pi = \left[\frac{\deg(v_1)}{2m}\ \frac{\deg(v_2)}{2m}\ \frac{\deg(v_3)}{2m} \cdots \frac{\deg(v_n)}{2m}\right] \tag{3}$$

Notice that π is uniform for a regular graph with degree d since $m = \frac{n \times d}{2}$ and $\pi = [\frac{d}{2 \times \frac{n \times d}{2}}] = [\frac{1}{n}]$.

THEOREM 2 (SECOND LARGEST EIGENVALUE [21]). *Let P be the transition matrix of G with ergodic random walk, and λ_i for $1 \le i \le n$ be the eigenvalues of P. Then all of λ_i are real numbers. If we label them in decreasing order, $1 = \lambda_1 > \lambda_2 \ge \cdots \ge \lambda_{n-1} \ge \lambda_n > -1$ holds. We define the second largest eigenvalue μ as $\mu = \max(|\lambda_2|, |\lambda_{n-1}|)$. Then, the mixing time $T(\epsilon)$ is bounded by:*

$$\frac{\mu}{2(1-\mu)} \log(\frac{1}{2\epsilon}) \le T(\epsilon) \le \frac{\log(n) + \log(\frac{1}{\epsilon})}{1-\mu} \tag{4}$$

Mixing time versus connectivity: The mixing time is tightly related to the connectivity of the graph. This is, strongly-connected graphs are fast mixing (i.e., have small mixing time) while the weakly connected graphs are slow mixing and have large mixing time [21]. Also, the second largest eigenvalue used for measuring the mixing time bounds the graph conductance, a measure for the community structure [27]. In short, the conductance is $\Phi \ge 1 - \mu$.

3.3 Measuring the mixing time of social graphs

Measuring the mixing time, especially of large graphs, is a cumbersome task and that might be the reason why fewer efforts are made to measure this essential property in large social graphs. In order to measure the mixing time of a social graph, we begin by the definition itself in (2). We follow the definition, by starting from an initial distribution concentrated on a node v_i, and compute the distribution after the random walk of length t with t large enough so that the variation distance between the distribution after random walk and the stationary distribution is within ϵ. We repeat this for different initial points. This approach is feasible for not too small ϵ, because we may then expect long walk length for this computation.

Since the mixing time is defined as the maximum necessary walk length to achieve ϵ distance for different initial states, one such random walk would be enough to establish a lower bound of the mixing time. Since we are interested in how large the mixing time should be, in principle only one random walk could be enough, if the walk length is sufficiently large. But in order to understand the general tendency and distribution of walk lengths, we repeat this many times (i.e., 1000) by picking an initial node randomly and perform the above computation. The end result obtained using this technique gives intuition about the tendency of the mixing time.

As a complementary method for bounding the mixing time (for even smaller ϵ and also for comparing with the previous results), we also use the method described in Theorem 2. First, we compute the second largest eigenvalue modulus (SLEM) of the transition matrix P. Given that the matrix P is sparse, we found that the computation of SLEM is feasible for graphs with a million nodes (as is the case for largest graphs we used). Once we compute SLEM, we use the lower bound in (4) to bound the mixing time of the graph.

3.4 Social graphs—the data sets

The social graphs used in our experiments are in Table 1. These graphs are selected to feature two models of knowledge between nodes in the social networks. These networks are categorized as follows. (1) social networks that exhibit knowledge between nodes and are good for the trust assumptions of the Sybil defenses; e.g., physics co-authorships and DBLP. These are slow mixing, as we will see later. (2) Graphs of networks that may not require face-to-face knowledge but require interaction; e.g., Youtube and Livejournal. Closely related to those is the set of graphs that may not require prior knowledge between nodes or where the social links between nodes are less meaningful to the context of the Sybil defenses; e.g., Facebook and wiki-vote, which are shown to be fast mixing.

Table 1: Datasets, their properties and their second largest eigenvalues of the transition matrix

Dataset	Nodes	Edges	μ
Wiki-vote [8]	7,066	100,736	0.899418
Slashdot 2 [10]	77,360	546,487	0.987531
Slashdot 1 [10]	82,168	582,533	0.987531
Facebook [26]	63,392	816,886	0.998133
Physics 1 [9]	4,158	13,428	0.998133
Physics 2 [9]	11,204	117,649	0.998221
Physics 3 [9]	8,638	24,827	0.996879
Enron [9]	33,696	180,811	0.996473
Epinion [20]	4,158	13,428	0.998133
DBLP [13]	614,981	1,155,148	0.997494
Facebook A [28]	1,000,000	20,353,734	0.982477
Facebook B [28]	1,000,000	15,807,563	0.992020
Livejournal A [14]	1,000,000	26,151,771	0.999387
Livejournal B [14]	1,000,000	27,562,349	0.999695
Youtube [14]	1,134,890	2,987,624	0.997972

4. RESULTS

Equipped with the mathematical tools explained in section 3, we measure the mixing time of the different social graphs shown in Table 1. In order to apply the tools in section 3 for measuring the mixing time, we first convert directed graphs to undirected, which is similar to what is performed in other work [27, 3, 12, 11, 23, 30, 31, 32]. We further compute the largest connected component in each graph and use it as a representative social structure for measuring the mixing time, as the mixing time is undefined for disconnected graphs. For small to medium-sized graphs, we compute SLEM directly from the transition matrix of the graph. On the other hand, for feasibility reasons, we sample the representative subgraphs from each of the four large data sets (Facebook A, B and Livejournal A, B) using the breadth first search (BFS) algorithm beginning from a random node in the graph as an initial point.[3] We perform this sampling process to obtain graphs of 10K, 100K and 1000K nodes out of 3 to 5 million nodes in each original social graph. Bearing the different social graphs sizes in mind, as shown in Table 1, we proceed to describe the results of our experiments.

Figure 1 and Figure 2 plot the lower bound of the mixing time for the different graphs in Table 1. We choose to use the lower-bound, but not the upper bound, because it is more relevant to the context of our study. In particular, as we observe that the lower-bound of the mixing time to satisfy a given ϵ is large, it is obvious that the mixing time for social graphs is slower than anticipated. As shown in Figure 1, we also observe that the mixing time is very slow, in particular for social graphs that require physical acquaintance of the social actors, as can be seen in the general tendency of these graphs. For example, physics co-authorship, Enron, and Epinion, though the social network is small, a mixing time of 200 to 400 is required to achieve $\epsilon = 0.1$. Similarly for larger social graphs, as shown in Figure 2, the mixing time to achieve $\epsilon = 0.1$ is varying and depends on the nature of the data set. For example, while it is about 1500 to 2500 in case of Livejournal, it ranges from 100 to about 400 in case of DBLP, Youtube, and Facebook.

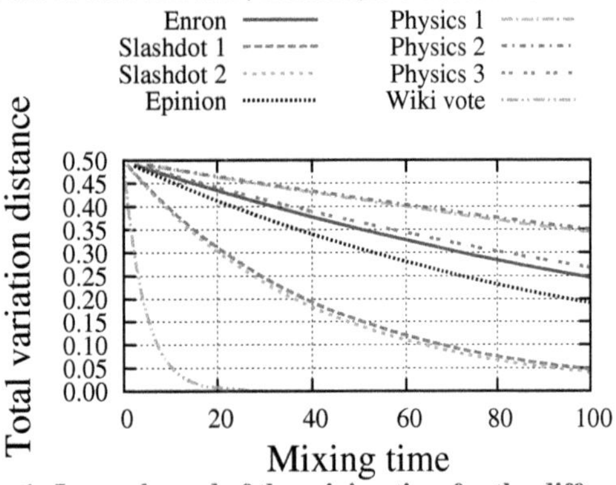

Figure 1: Lower bound of the mixing time for the different data sets used in our experiments — the case of small data sets.

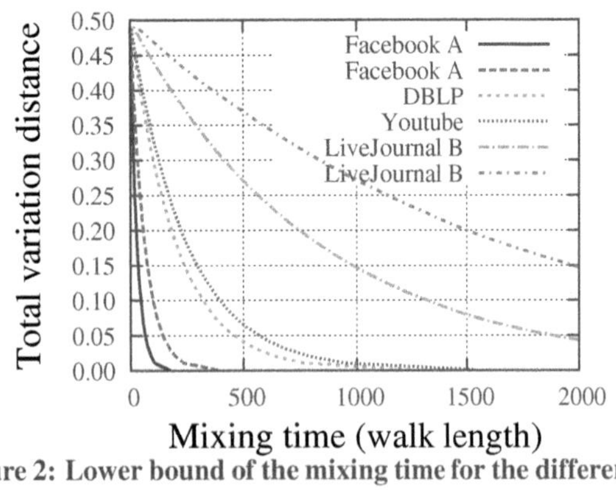

Figure 2: Lower bound of the mixing time for the different data sets used in our experiments — the case of large data sets

To see how tight are these measurements we perform the following experiment. We first compute the lower bound of the mixing time for the physics co-authorship data sets, which are also reasonably small and feasible to do exhaustive computations. Then we measure the mixing time using the model in (2) from every possible source in the graph (the CDFs of the raw measurements are shown in Figure 3 for small t and and in Figure 4 for large t). We aggregate these measurements into Figure 5, by sorting ϵ at each t and averaging values in various intervals as percentiles. We observe that while the mixing time of most sources in social graphs is better than that of the mixing time given by SLEM, the measurements using SLEM are correct since the mixing time is by definition maximum of walk lengths for given ϵ as shown in (2). However, even considering this effect, still for most sources the mixing time is slower than used by other papers (10 and 15 in SybilLimit).

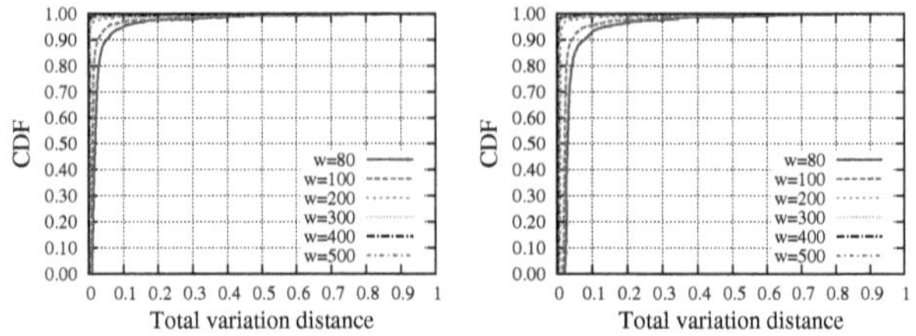

(a) Physics 2 (b) Physics 3

Figure 4: The CDF of mixing time (long walks) for the three physics datasets in Table 1. The variation distance is computed for every possible node in the graph, brute-forcefully.

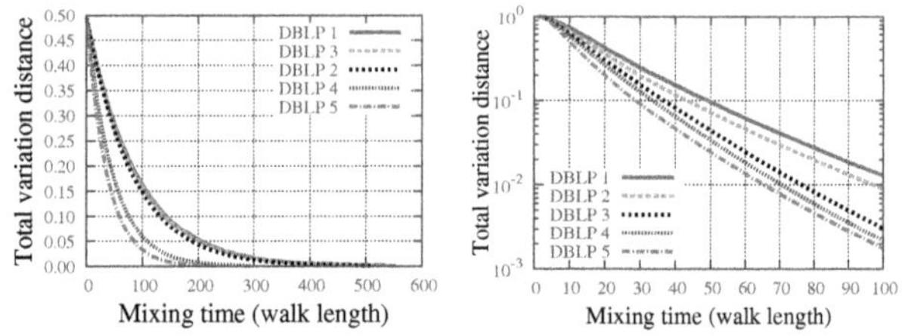

(a) Lower bound (b) Average mixing time

Figure 6: Lower-bound vs. the top the average mixing time for a sample of 1000 nodes in each data set, where DBLP x means the minimum degree in that data set is x.

To understand the relationship between the network size and the mixing time (of the same social graph) we use the different previously sampled subgraphs, using BFS, from Facebook and Livejournal data sets (10K, 100K, and 1000K). We further measure the mixing time using SLEM and the model in (2) for 1000 initial distributions. We further aggregate the top 10, median 20, and lowest 10 percentile of ϵ corresponding to the given random walk, and plot them along with the mixing time derived using SLEM where the results are shown in Figure 7. We observe that for a million nodes graph, while the mixing time in the top 10% in the sample we computed is 100 for an averaged $\epsilon = 10^{-5}$—an excellent value to the "theoretical" guarantees of the Sybil defenses, the SLEM-based mixing time results in only $\epsilon = 10^{-2}$ as shown in Figure 7(i). We attribute this difference to similar scenario as in the physics co-authorship graphs. Similar observations can be seen in each of the different large social graphs. It is worth mentioning that Livejournal (Figure 7(k) and Figure 7(l)) present poor mixing in relation with Facebook data sets, which are shown to be fast mixing.

Finally, to understand the methodology used for experimenting in Sybilguard and SybilLimit, we perform the same trimming technique by iteratively removing lower degree nodes (for 1 up to 5) from the DBLP data set and computed the mixing time of the resulting graphs at each time (results shown in Figure 6). We observe that the pruning of lower degree greatly improves the mixing time of the social graph: for fixed mixing time of 100, by successive trimming the variation distance is reduced from about 0.2 to 0.03 (Figure 6(a)), and from about 0.015 to 0.002 (Figure 6(b)). But this is with huge reduction of the graph size: DBLP 1 is of size 614,981 but after trimming up to 4 degree nodes, DBLP 5 is of size 145,497.

[3]Note that BFS algorithm may bias the sampled graph to have faster mixing. Since our goal is to show that the mixing time is slower than expected, this only strengthens our position.

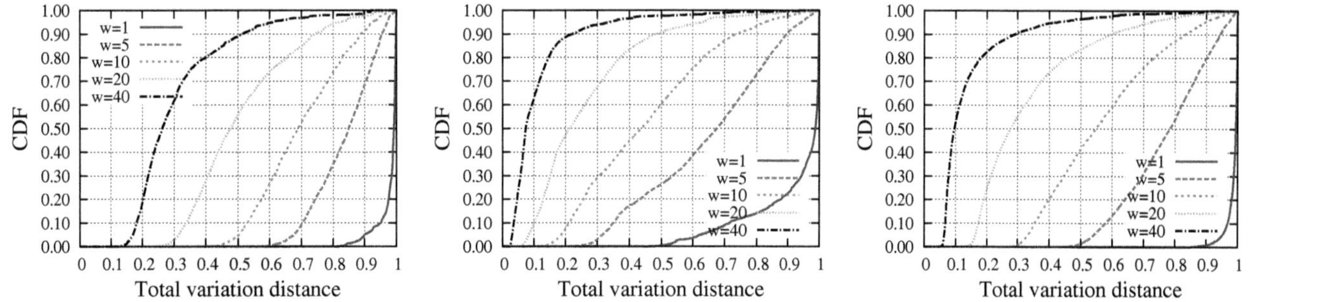

(a) Physics 1 (b) Physics 2 (c) Physics 3

Figure 3: The commutative distribution function (CDF) of mixing time for the three physics datasets in Table 1. The variation distance is computed for every possible node in the graph, brute-forcefully.

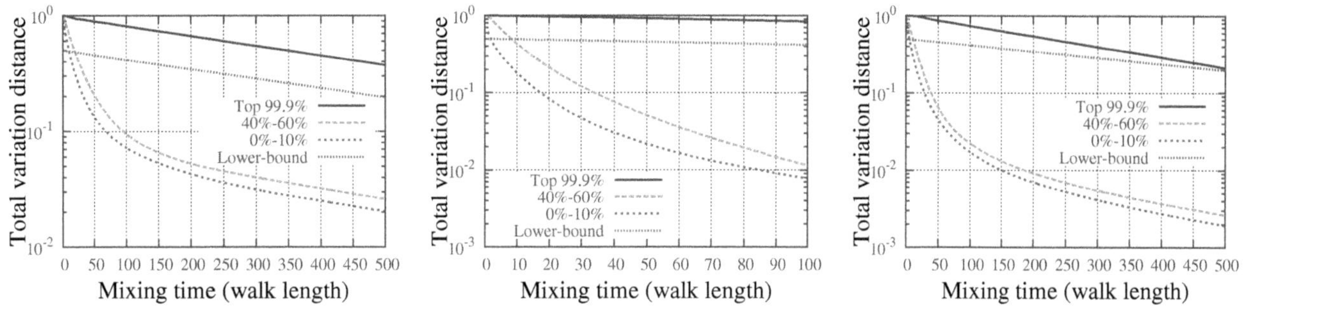

(a) Physics 1 (b) Physics 2 (c) Physics 3

Figure 5: Lower-bound of the mixing time compared to the mixing time when measured using the sampling method for the entire graphs brute-forcefully — different measurements meet the guarantees.

This means that about 75% of nodes are denied joining the service outright in order to boost the mixing time.

5. DISCUSSION

While the main finding in this study is that the mixing time of social graphs is higher than has been used in literature, we also conclude that different nodes approach the stationary distribution at different rates. This is, while the majority of walks initiated from different nodes reach closer to the stationary distribution at "higher" rate than that of the mixing time, which is defined as the maximum rate from any source, we still find—except in a few cases of online social networks—that the mixing time of the majority of nodes is larger than anticipated and used in the previous studies [30, 31, 12]. This has several implications and call for several actions.

First, since most of the theoretical guarantees of social graphs consider the model in (2), and since the majority of nodes in the social graphs measured in this paper have better mixing time than the bound in that model, this calls for rigorous study by basing such designs and analyses on the average case of the mixing, which is relatively small, instead of the worst case of the mixing time.

Second, the obvious implication of our findings is that one has to either give up some of the utility (service) guarantees—which are implied by that almost all honest nodes admit other honest nodes—by using relatively shorter walks, or give up part of the performance and security by enabling longer random walks in order to reach these isolated parts of the social graphs. Though this looks straightforward, going either way is not as simple as it seems. On the one hand, if one uses longer random walks in order to reach such isolated parts of the network it would be equally likely to escape to the Sbyil region which has a cut similar in its nature to that of the slower mixing part of the original social graph. On the other hand, using random walks shorter than the mixing time of the majority of nodes would would also be at the expense of the utility; not only for the isolated part but also the faster mixing part as well. The end detection guarantees of the design would work as long as g, the number of attack edges is less than $\frac{n}{w}$.

Third, papers introducing SybilGuard, SybilLimit, and Whānau all did experiments on their schemes. Despite the short mixing time that these experiments use, their results seem to support that their schemes work as expected. The explanation of this is two part. First, the trimming of lower-degree nodes would shorten the mixing time. Second, although they claim that the social networks are fast mixing and as a part of the definition—which is also used in parts of the proofs for the theoretical guarantees—they insist $\epsilon = \Theta(1/n)$, this is a very strong burden to achieve and perhaps somewhat larger ϵ might also be good enough for these schemes to work. Also, we suspect that the difference between the average mixing time and the worst-case mixing time may have some effects on the discrepancy between the analysis and the experiment. In practice, the majority of nodes with "fast" mixing would be served and those few other nodes with very slow mixing would be denied service, which then will not be a problem for the probabilistic average-case guarantees.

Finally, one of the assumptions in Sybil defenses based on social networks is that the used trust model requires physical acquaintance, which is the case in social networks such DBLP and Physics co-authorship networks, for which we show slower mixing time than other "online social networks" which are known to possess less strict trust models [5, 1], which by nature tolerate Sybil nodes. This calls for considering the trust model resulting from the underlying social network as a parameter, along with the mixing time, in order to evaluate the effectiveness of the social network-based defenses according to their real value. Our work in [16, 15] is a preliminarily result in this direction.

Performance Implications—the case of SybilLimit: in order to quantitively measure the impact of the findings of slower mixing time on the performance of Sybil defenses, we implement Sybil-

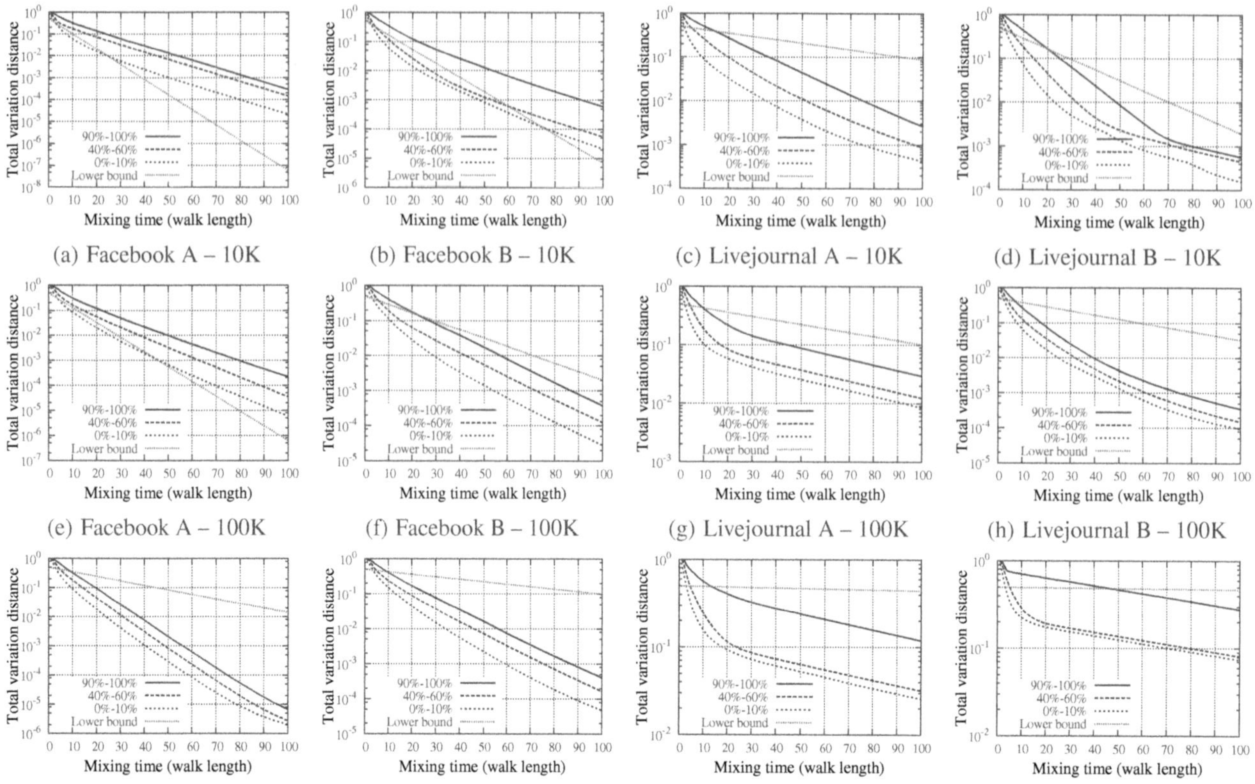

(a) Facebook A – 10K (b) Facebook B – 10K (c) Livejournal A – 10K (d) Livejournal B – 10K

(e) Facebook A – 100K (f) Facebook B – 100K (g) Livejournal A – 100K (h) Livejournal B – 100K

(i) Facebook A – 1000K (j) Facebook B – 1000K (k) Livejournal A – 1000K (l) Livejournal B – 1000K

Figure 7: Sampling vs. lower-bound measurements of the mixing time for 10K, 100K and 1000K of four large-scale datasets.

Limit and apply it to some of the different social networks with the following settings. Since we already know the social graphs size—both m and n, we select the proper r that guarantees high probability of intersection. We set r to $r_0\sqrt{m}$, where m is the number of undirected edges in the graph and r_0 is computed from the birthday paradox formula to guarantee a given intersection probability. In this experiment, we consider the case without an attacker, since SybilLimit bounds the number of the Sybil identities introduced based on the number of the attacker edges. Without considering Sybil attacker, we increase t until the number of accepted nodes by a trusted node (the verifier) reaches a almost all honest nodes in the social network. Then, with this t, we find the (average) total variation distance required in each graph, which is the necessary for the operation of these designs. It is then easy to compute the number of accepted Sybil identities which is $t \times g$, where g is the number of attack edges. SybilLimit works as long as $t < \frac{n}{w}$. The result of this experiment is in Figure 8. For more details, see [17]

6. CONCLUSION

In this paper, we measured mixing times of several on-line and and information social networks which may be used for building security defenses and communication systems. Our main finding shows that these social networks generally have much slower mixing time than the previous works anticipated. Meanwhile, we also observed that the average mixing time is better than the worst-case mixing time which is the standard definition of the mixing time of a random walk on a graph, although the average mixing time is again much higher than the ones being used. In the near future, we will investigate building theoretical models that consider the average case of the mixing time. We will also investigate cost models that consider the different mixing times of social graphs and their relation of the trust model exhibited in such networks to evaluate the overall effectiveness of design based on social networks. The later part of the future work is motivated by the observation that some social graphs are faster mixing than others while their underlying trust is different.

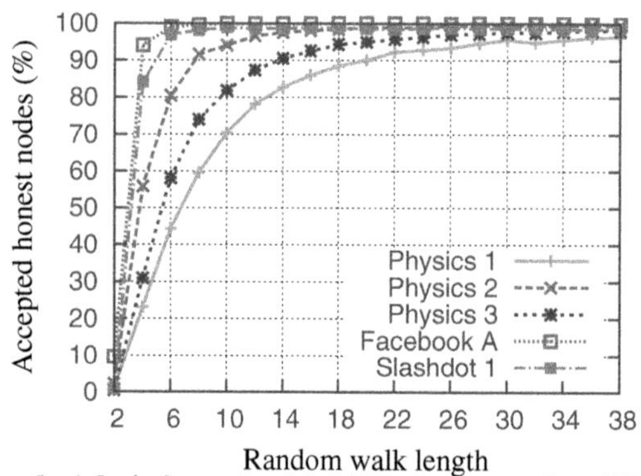

Figure 8: Admission rate of SybilLimit when using different t. Facebook (A) and Slashdot (1) have 10,000 nodes each.

Acknowledgement

We are grateful to Alan Mislove and Ben Y. Zhao for providing the data sets used in this study, Nicholas Hopper, John Carlis, and the anonymous reviewers for their useful feedback and comments, and Haifeng Yu and Chris Lesniewski-Laas for answering our questions on their schemes. This research was supported by NSF grant CNS-0917154 and a research grant from Korea Advanced Institute of Science and Technology (KAIST).

7. REFERENCES

[1] L. Bilge, T. Strufe, D. Balzarotti, and E. Kirda. All your contacts are belong to us: automated identity theft attacks on social networks. In *WWW '09: Proceedings of the 18th international conference on World wide web*, pages 551–560, New York, NY, USA, 2009. ACM.

[2] E. M. Daly and M. Haahr. Social network analysis for routing in disconnected delay-tolerant manets. In *MobiHoc '07: Proceedings of the 8th ACM international symposium on Mobile ad hoc networking and computing*, pages 32–40, New York, NY, USA, 2007. ACM.

[3] G. Danezis and P. Mittal. SybilInfer: Detecting sybil nodes using social networks. In *The 16th Annual Network & Distributed System Security Conference*, 2009.

[4] J. R. Douceur. The sybil attack. In *IPTPS '01: Revised Papers from the First International Workshop on Peer-to-Peer Systems*, pages 251–260, London, UK, 2002. Springer-Verlag.

[5] C. Dwyer, S. Hiltz, and K. Passerini. Trust and privacy concern within social networking sites: A comparison of Facebook and MySpace. In *Proceedings of AMCIS*, 2007.

[6] M. Jerrum and A. Sinclair. Conductance and the rapid mixing property for markov chains: the approximation of the permanent resolved (preliminary version). In *STOC*, pages 235–244. ACM, 1988.

[7] H. A. Kautz, B. Selman, and M. A. Shah. Referral web: Combining social networks and collaborative filtering. *Commun. ACM*, 40(3):63–65, 1997.

[8] J. Leskovec, D. P. Huttenlocher, and J. M. Kleinberg. Predicting positive and negative links in online social networks. In M. Rappa, P. Jones, J. Freire, and S. Chakrabarti, editors, *WWW*, pages 641–650. ACM, 2010.

[9] J. Leskovec, J. Kleinberg, and C. Faloutsos. Graphs over time: densification laws, shrinking diameters and possible explanations. In *KDD '05: Proceedings of the eleventh ACM SIGKDD international conference on Knowledge discovery in data mining*, pages 177–187, New York, NY, USA, 2005. ACM.

[10] J. Leskovec, K. J. Lang, A. Dasgupta, and M. W. Mahoney. Community structure in large networks: Natural cluster sizes and the absence of large well-defined clusters. *CoRR*, abs/0810.1355, 2008.

[11] C. Lesniewski-Laas. A Sybil-proof one-hop DHT. In *Proceedings of the 1st workshop on Social network systems*, pages 19–24. ACM, 2008.

[12] C. Lesniewski-Lass and M. F. Kaashoek. Whānau: A sybil-proof distributed hash table. In *7th USENIX Symposium on Network Design and Implementation*, pages 3–17, 2010.

[13] M. Ley. The DBLP computer science bibliography: Evolution, research issues, perspectives. In *String Processing and Information Retrieval*, pages 481–486. Springer, 2009.

[14] A. Mislove, M. Marcon, P. K. Gummadi, P. Druschel, and B. Bhattacharjee. Measurement and analysis of online social networks. In *Internet Measurement Comference*, pages 29–42, 2007.

[15] A. Mohaisen, N. Hopper, and Y. Kim. Designs to account for trust in social network-based sybil defenses. In *17th ACM Conference on Computer and Communications Security*, Chicago, IL, USA, 2010. ACM.

[16] A. Mohaisen, N. Hopper, and Y. Kim. Keep your friends close: Incorporating trust in social network-based sybil defenses. Technical report, University of Minnesota, 2010.

[17] A. Mohaisen, A. Yun, and Y. Kim. Measuring the mixing time of social graphs. Technical report, University of Minnesota, 2010.

[18] S. Nagaraja. Anonymity in the wild: Mixes on unstructured networks. In N. Borisov and P. Golle, editors, *Privacy Enhancing Technologies*, volume 4776 of *Lecture Notes in Computer Science*, pages 254–271. Springer, 2007.

[19] D. Quercia and S. Hailes. Sybil attacks against mobile users: friends and foes to the rescue. In *INFOCOM'10: Proceedings of the 29th conference on Information communications*, pages 336–340, Piscataway, NJ, USA, 2010. IEEE Press.

[20] M. Richardson, R. Agrawal, and P. Domingos. Trust management for the semantic web. In D. Fensel, K. P. Sycara, and J. Mylopoulos, editors, *International Semantic Web Conference*, volume 2870 of *Lecture Notes in Computer Science*, pages 351–368. Springer, 2003.

[21] A. Sinclair. Improved bounds for mixing rates of marcov chains and multicommodity flow. *Combinatorics, Probability & Computing*, 1:351–370, 1992.

[22] N. Tran, J. Li, L. Subramanian, and S. S. M. Chow. Brief announcement: improving social-network-based sybil-resilient node admission control. In A. W. Richa and R. Guerraoui, editors, *PODC*, pages 241–242. ACM, 2010.

[23] N. Tran, B. Min, J. Li, and L. Subramanian. Sybil-resilient online content voting. In *USENIX NSDI*, 2009.

[24] E. Vasserman. *Towards freedom of speech on the Internet: Censorship-resistant communication and storage*. PhD thesis, UNIVERSITY OF MINNESOTA, 2010.

[25] E. Vasserman, R. Jansen, J. Tyra, N. Hopper, and Y. Kim. Membership-concealing overlay networks. In *Proceedings of the 16th ACM conference on Computer and communications security*, pages 390–399. ACM, 2009.

[26] B. Viswanath, A. Mislove, M. Cha, and K. P. Gummadi. On the evolution of user interaction in facebook. In *Proceedings of the 2nd ACM SIGCOMM Workshop on Social Networks (WOSN'09)*, August 2009.

[27] B. Viswanath, A. Post, K. P. Gummadi, and A. Mislove. An analysis of social network-based sybil defenses. In *SIGCOMM*, 2010.

[28] C. Wilson, B. Boe, A. Sala, K. P. Puttaswamy, and B. Y. Zhao. User interactions in social networks and their implications. In *EuroSys '09: Proceedings of the 4th ACM European conference on Computer systems*, pages 205–218, New York, NY, USA, 2009. ACM.

[29] S. Xu, X. Li, and P. Parker. Exploiting social networks for threshold signing: attack-resilience vs. availability. In *ASIACCS '08: Proceedings of the 2008 ACM symposium on Information, computer and communications security*, pages 325–336, New York, NY, USA, 2008. ACM.

[30] H. Yu, P. B. Gibbons, M. Kaminsky, and F. Xiao. SybilLimit: A near-optimal social network defense against sybil attacks. In *IEEE Symposium on Security and Privacy*, pages 3–17, 2008.

[31] H. Yu, M. Kaminsky, P. B. Gibbons, and A. Flaxman. SybilGuard: defending against sybil attacks via social networks. In *SIGCOMM*, pages 267–278, 2006.

[32] H. Yu, M. Kaminsky, P. B. Gibbons, and A. D. Flaxman. SybilGuard: defending against sybil attacks via social networks. *IEEE/ACM Trans. Netw.*, 16(3):576–589, 2008.

Estimating and Sampling Graphs with Multidimensional Random Walks

Bruno Ribeiro
Computer Science Department
University of Massachusetts at Amherst
Amherst, MA, 01002
ribeiro@cs.umass.edu

Don Towsley
Computer Science Department
University of Massachusetts at Amherst
Amherst, MA, 01002
towsley@cs.umass.edu

ABSTRACT

Estimating characteristics of large graphs via sampling is a vital part of the study of complex networks. Current sampling methods such as (independent) random vertex and random walks are useful but have drawbacks. Random vertex sampling may require too many resources (time, bandwidth, or money). Random walks, which normally require fewer resources *per sample*, can suffer from large estimation errors in the presence of disconnected or loosely connected graphs. In this work we propose a new m-dimensional random walk that uses m *dependent* random walkers. We show that the proposed sampling method, which we call *Frontier sampling*, exhibits all of the nice sampling properties of a regular random walk. At the same time, our simulations over large real world graphs show that, in the presence of disconnected or loosely connected components, *Frontier sampling* exhibits lower estimation errors than regular random walks. We also show that *Frontier sampling* is more suitable than random vertex sampling to sample the tail of the degree distribution of the graph.

Categories and Subject Descriptors

G.3 [**Probability and Statistics**]: Statistical computing

General Terms

Experimentation

Keywords

Frontier Sampling, Random Walks, MCMC, Estimates, Power Laws, Assortativity, Global Clustering Coefficient

1. INTRODUCTION

A number of recent studies [7, 11, 15, 19, 20, 26, 30, 29, 36] (to cite a few) are dedicated to the characterization of complex networks. A complex network is a network with non-trivial topological features (features that do not occur in simple networks such as lattices or random networks). Examples of such networks include the Internet, the World Wide Web, social, business, and biological networks [7, 28]. This work represents a complex network as a directed graph with labeled vertices and edges. A label can be, for instance, the degree of a vertex or, in a social network setting, someone's hometown. Examples of network characteristics include the degree distribution, the fraction of HIV positive individuals in a population [24], or the average number of copies of a file in a peer-to-peer (P2P) network [16].

Characterizing the labels of a graph requires querying vertices and/or edges; each query has an associated cost in resources (time, bandwidth, money). Characterizing a large graph by querying the whole graph is often too costly. As a result, researchers have turned their attention to the estimation of graph characteristics based on incomplete (sampled) data. In this work we present a new tool, *Frontier Sampling*, to characterize complex networks. In what follows *random vertex (edge) sampling* refers to sampling vertices (edges) independently and uniformly at random (with replacement).

Distinct sampling strategies have different resource requirements depending on the network being sampled. For instance, in a network where each vertex is assigned a unique user-id (e.g., travelers and their passport numbers, Facebook, MySpace, Flickr, and Livejournal) it is a widespread practice to perform random vertex sampling by querying randomly generated user-ids. This approach can be resource-intensive if the user-id space is sparsely populated as the hit-to-miss ratio is low (e.g., less than 10% of all MySpace user-ids between the highest and lowest valid user-ids are currently occupied [30]). Another way to sample a network is by querying edges instead of vertices. Randomly sampling edges can be harder than randomly sampling vertices if edges are not be associated to unique IDs (or if edge IDs cannot be randomly queried). We summarize some drawbacks of random vertex and edge sampling:

- Random edge sampling may be impractical when edges cannot be randomly queried (e.g., online social networks like Facebook [15], MySpace [30], and Twitter or a P2P network like Bittorrent).
- Random vertex sampling may be undesirable when user-ids are sparsely populated (low hit-to-miss ratio) and queries are subject to resource constraints (e.g., queries are rate-limited in Flickr, Livejournal [26], and Bittorrent [18]). In a P2P network like Bittorrent, a client can randomly sample peers (vertices) by querying a tracker (server); however, trackers may rate-limit client queries [18].

IMC'10, November 1–3, 2010, Melbourne, Australia.

- Even when random vertex sampling is not severely resource-constrained, some characteristics may be better estimated with random edge sampling (e.g., the tail of the degree distribution of a graph).

An alternative, and often cheaper, way to sample a network is by means of a random walk (RW). A RW samples a graph by moving a particle (walker) from a vertex to a neighboring vertex (over an edge). By this process edges and vertices are sampled. The probability by which the random walker selects the next neighboring vertex determines the probability by which vertices and edges are sampled. In this work we are interested in random walks that sample *edges* uniformly. The edges sampled by RW can then be used to obtain unbiased estimates of a variety of graph characteristics (we present two examples in Section 4).

In this work we assume that a random walker has the ability to query a vertex to obtain all of its incoming and outgoing edges (Section 4 details the reason behind this assumption). This is possible for online networks such as Twitter, LiveJournal [26], YouTube [26], Facebook [15], MySpace [30], P2P networks [29], and the arXiv citations network. We revisit the theory behind random walks in Section 4.

Sampling graphs with random walks is not without drawbacks. The accuracy of the estimates depends not only on the graph structure but also on the characteristic being estimated. The graph structure can create distortions in the estimates by "trapping" the random walker inside a subgraph. An extreme case happens when the graph consists of two or more disconnected components (subgraphs). For instance, wireless mobile social networks exhibit connection graphs with multiple disconnected components [11]. But even connected graphs can suffer from the same problem. A random walker can get "temporarily trapped" and spend most of its sampling budget exploring the local neighborhood near where it got "trapped". In the above scenarios estimates may be inaccurate if the characteristics of the local neighborhood differ from the overall characteristic of the graph. This problem is well documented (see [21]) and our goal is to mitigate it.

Contributions

This work proposes a new m-dimensional random walk sampling method (*Frontier sampling*) that, starting from a collection of m randomly sampled vertices, preserves all of the important statistical properties of a regular random walk (e.g., vertices are visited with a probability proportional to their degree). While the vertices are visited with a probability proportional to their degree, we show that the joint steady state distribution of Frontier Sampling (the joint distribution of all m vertices) is closer to uniform (the starting distribution) than that of m independent random walkers, for any $m > 0$. This property has the potential to dramatically reduce the transient of random walks.

In our simulations using real world graphs we see that Frontier Sampling mitigates the large estimation errors caused by disconnected or loosely connected components that can "trap" a random walker and distort the estimated graph characteristic, i.e., Frontier sampling (FS) estimates have smaller Mean Squared Errors (MSEs) than estimates obtained from regular random walkers (single and multiple independent walkers, reviewed in Section 4.4) in a variety of scenarios.

We make two additional contributions: (1) we compare random walk-based estimates to those obtained from random vertex and random edge sampling. We show analytically that the tail of the degree distribution is better estimated using random edge sampling than random vertex sampling. We observe from simulations over real world networks (in Section 6.4) that FS accuracy is comparable to the accuracy of random edge sampling. These results help explain recent empirical results [29]; (2) we present asymptotically unbiased estimators using the edges sampled by a RW for the assortative mixing coefficient (defined in Section 4.2.2) and the global clustering coefficient (defined in Section 4.2.4).

Outline

The outline of this work is as follows. Section 2 presents the notation used in this paper. Section 3 contrasts random vertex with random edge sampling. Section 4 revisits single and multiple independent random walk sampling and estimation. Section 5 introduces *Frontier Sampling* (FS), a sampling process that uses m dependent random walkers in order to mitigate the high estimation errors caused by disconnected or loosely connected components. Section 5 also shows that FS can be seen as an m-dimensional random walk over the m-th Cartesian power of the graph (formally defined in Section 5). In Section 6 we see that FS outperforms both single and multiple independent random walkers in a variety of scenarios. We also compare (independent) random vertex and edge sampling with FS. Section 7 reviews the relevant literature. Finally, Section 8 presents our conclusions and future work.

2. DEFINITIONS

In what follows we present some definitions. Let $G_d = (V, E_d)$ be a labeled directed graph representing the (original) network graph, where V is a set of vertices and E_d is a set of ordered pairs of vertices (u, v) representing a connection from u to v (a.k.a. edges). We assume that each vertex in G_d has at least one incoming or outgoing edge. The in-degree of a vertex u in G_d is the number of distinct edges $(v_1, u), \ldots, (v_i, u)$ into u, and its out-degree is the number of distinct edges $(u, v_1), \ldots, (u, v_j)$ out of u. Some complex networks can be modeled as undirected graphs. In this case, when the original graph is undirected, we model G_d as a symmetric directed graph, i.e., $\forall (u, v) \in E_d$, $(v, u) \in E_d$.

Let $\mathcal{L}_v$ and $\mathcal{L}_e$ be a finite set of vertex and edge labels, respectively. Each edge $(u, v) \in E_d$ is associated with a set of labels $\mathcal{L}_e(u, v) \subseteq \mathcal{L}_e$. For instance, the label of edge (u, v) can be the in-degree of v in G_d. Similarly, we can associate a set of labels to each vertex, $\mathcal{L}_v(v) \subseteq \mathcal{L}_v$, $\forall v \in V$. Some edges and vertices may not have labels. If edge (u, v) is unlabeled then $\mathcal{L}_e(u, v) = \emptyset$. Similarly, if vertex v is unlabeled then $\mathcal{L}_v(v) = \emptyset$.

When performing a random walk, we assume that a random walker has the ability to retrieve incoming and outgoing edges from a queried vertex (and vertices are distinguishable). With this assumption we are able to build (on-the-fly) a symmetric directed graph while walking over G_d. Let $G = (V, E)$ be the symmetric counterpart of G_d, i.e.,

$$E = \bigcup_{\forall (u,v) \in E_d} \{(u, v), (v, u)\}.$$

Note that G may not be connected. As G is symmetric, we denote by $\deg(v)$ to be the in-degree or the out-degree of $v \in V$ as they are equal. Let $\text{vol}(S) = \sum_{\forall v \in S} \deg(v)$, $\forall S \subseteq V$, denote the volume of the vertices in S.

Let $\hat{\theta}_l$ be the estimated fraction of *vertices* with label l obtained by some estimator. The two error metrics used in most of our examples are the normalized root mean square error of $\hat{\theta}_l$, which is a normalized measure of the dispersion of the estimates, defined as

$$\text{NMSE}(l) = \frac{\sqrt{E[(\hat{\theta}_l - \theta_l)^2]}}{\theta_l} . \quad (1)$$

and the normalized root mean square error of the Complementary Cumulative Distribution Function (CCDF) $\gamma = \{\gamma_l\}$, where $\gamma_l = \sum_{k=l+1}^{\infty} \theta_k$, defined as

$$\text{CNMSE}(l) = \frac{\sqrt{E[(\hat{\gamma}_l - \gamma_l)^2]}}{\gamma_l} . \quad (2)$$

For the sake of simplicity, and unless stated otherwise, in the remainder of this paper we assume that all queries of edges and vertices have unitary cost and that we have a fixed sampling budget B.

3. VERTEX V.S. EDGE SAMPLING

We consider a straightforward estimation problem to illustrate a tradeoff between random edge and random vertex sampling. Consider the problem of estimating the out-degree distribution of G_d. Let θ_i be the fraction of vertices with out-degree $i > 0$ and d be the average out-degree. Let the label of vertex u, $\mathcal{L}_v(u)$, be the out-degree of u. We assume that d is known; also assume that from an edge (u, v) we can query $\mathcal{L}_v(u)$. In random edge sampling the probability of sampling a vertex with out-degree i is proportional i: $\pi_i = i\,\theta_i/d$. On the other hand, random vertex sampling samples a vertex with out-degree i with probability θ_i. A straightforward calculation shows that the NMSE (equation (1)) of B randomly sampled *edges* with out-degree i is

$$\text{NMSE}(i) = \sqrt{(1/\pi_i - 1)/B}, \quad i > 0. \quad (3)$$

Similarly, the NMSE(i) for random vertex sampling is

$$\text{NMSE}(i) = \sqrt{(1/\theta_i - 1)/B} . \quad (4)$$

Now note that $\pi_i/\theta_i = i/d$, which means that $\pi_i > \theta_i$ if $i > d$ and $\pi_i < \theta_i$ if $i < d$. From equations (3) and (4) we see that random edge sampling more accurately estimates degrees larger than the average ($i > d$) while random vertex sampling more accurately estimates degrees smaller than the average ($i < d$). This means random edge sampling exhibits smaller NMSE when estimating the tail of the out-degree distribution.

Above we have seen that random edge sampling is more accurate than random vertex sampling in estimating the tail of the out-degree degree distribution. A similar result happens with the in-degree distribution and the degree distribution of undirected networks. The above analysis explains real world experiments [29]. Unfortunately, as discussed in Section 1, random edge sampling is rarely practical. In what follows we see that, if G is connected, random walks exhibit similar statistical properties to random edge sampling.

4. RANDOM WALK SAMPLING

In this section we review random walk (RW) sampling and estimation over a non-bipartite, connected, directed, symmetric graph G. Sampling G with a RW is straightforward. The random walker has a sampling budget B and starts at vertex $v_0 \in V$. For the sake of simplicity, unless stated otherwise, we consider that all queries to vertices have unit cost and that we have a fixed sampling budget B.

Let $\{(u_i, v_i)\}_{i=1}^{B}$ be the a sequence of edges sampled by a RW, where $u_i = v_{i-1}$, $i = 2, \ldots, B$. Note that edges may be sampled multiple times. We refer to (u_i, v_i) as the i-th sampled edge. At the i-th step a walker at vertex v_i chooses an outgoing edge (v_i, u_i) uniformly at random from the set of outgoing edges of v_i and adds (v_i, u_i) to the sequence of sampled edges. At step $i + 1$ the random walker starts at vertex u_i and the sampling continues until $i = B$.

The RW described here is the most common type of RW found in the literature [22]. Other types of random walks differ in the way in which outgoing edges are sampled. The Metropolis-Hastings RW [38] is an example of a random walk that samples *vertices* (not edges) uniformly at random. However, experiments estimating a variety of metrics indicate that Metropolis-Hastings RW is less accurate than the random walk described in this work [15, 29]. For more details about other types of RW please refer to [32, Chapter 7].

An important property of a RW is its ability to reach a unique stationary regime. A necessary condition for stationarity is that G must be symmetric, connected, and non-bipartite (the non-bipartite assumption can be relaxed in a lazy random walk [22]). In a stationary RW, the sequence of sampled edges is a stationary sequence. A sequence $X_1, X_2, \ldots$ of random variables is said to be stationary if for any positive integers n and k, the joint distribution of $(X_n, \ldots, X_{n+k})$ is independent of n. Once the RW reaches steady state, it also shares two important properties with random edge (RE) sampling. First, both RW and RE sample edges uniformly at random [22], which means that the probability that a vertex v is sampled is $\deg(v)/\text{vol}(V)$. Second, both RW and RE obey the strong law of large numbers, as we see next.

4.1 Strong Law of Large Numbers

The following variation of the strong law of large numbers is a powerful tool to build (asymptotically) unbiased estimators of graph characteristics. We provide a trivial extension of a well known result [25, Theorem 17.2.1] to the case where we are interested in a subset of the graph edges. Let $E^\star \subseteq E$ be non-empty. Let (u_i, v_i) be the i-th RW sampled edge such that $(u_i, v_i) \in E^\star$; and let $B^\star(B)$ be the number of such samples, where B is the number of RW steps. $B^\star(B)$ is a random variable that represents the number of RW sampled edges that belong to $E^\star$. Note that $B^\star(B) \leq B$.

Theorem 4.1 (SLLN). *For any function f, where $\sum_{(u,v) \in E^\star} |f(u, v)| < \infty$,*

$$\lim_{B \to \infty} \frac{1}{B^\star(B)} \sum_{i=1}^{B^\star(B)} f(u_i, v_i) \to \frac{1}{|E^\star|} \sum_{\forall (u,v) \in E^\star} f(u, v) ,$$

almost surely, i.e., the event occurs with probability one.

PROOF. Let

$$h(u,v) = \begin{cases} 1 & \text{if } (u,v) \in E^\star \text{ , and} \\ 0 & \text{otherwise.} \end{cases}$$

As the RW is stationary (and edges are sampled uniformly)

$$\lim_{B\to\infty} \frac{\sum_{i=1}^{B} f(u_i,v_i)h(u_i,v_i)}{\sum_{i=1}^{B} h(u_i,v_i)} \to \frac{\sum_{\forall(u,v)\in E} f(u,v)h(u,v)}{\sum_{\forall(u,v)\in E} h(u,v)},$$

almost surely [25, Theorem 17.2.1]. The proof follows from noting that $B^\star(B) = \sum_{i=1}^{B} h(u_i,v_i)$ and that $h(u,v) = 0, \forall(u,v) \in E \backslash E^\star$. □

Theorem 4.1 allows us to construct estimators of graph characteristics that converge to their true values as the number of RW samples goes to infinity ($B \to \infty$). If we are trying to estimate vertex labels we set $E^\star = E$ and $B^\star = B$. In what follows we apply Theorem 4.1 to estimate graph characteristics; we also present four examples of estimators.

4.2 Estimators

An *estimator* is a function that takes a sequence of observations (sampled data) as input and outputs an estimate of a unknown population parameter (graph characteristic). In this section we see how we can estimate graph characteristics using the edges sampled by a RW.

We present estimators of the following four graph characteristics: the edge label density (the fraction of edges with a given label in the graph), the assortative mixing coefficient [27], the vertex label density, and the global clustering coefficient [34]. Designing these estimators is straightforward:

(1) First we find a function f that computes the characteristic of G using E;

(2) then we replace E with the sequence of edges sampled by a stationary RW.

In what follows we illustrate how to build an estimator of the edge label density.

4.2.1 *Edge Label Density*

We seek to estimate the fraction of *edges* with label $l \in \mathcal{L}_e$ in G_d among all edges (u,v) that have labels, i.e., $\mathcal{L}_e(u,v) \neq \emptyset$. Edge labels can be anything, from social networking labels to the amount of IP traffic over each link in a computer network. An edge label can be, for instance, a tuple $(\text{outdeg}(u), \text{indeg}(v))$ where $\text{outdeg}(u)$ is the out-degree of u and $\text{indeg}(v)$ is the in-degree of v in the original graph G_d.

For now we assume that we know E. Let $E^\star$ be the non-empty subset of E for which there are labels. Let p_l denote the fraction of edges in $E^\star$ with label l; it is clear that

$$p_l = \sum_{\forall(u,v)\in E^\star} \frac{\mathbf{1}(l \in \mathcal{L}_e(u,v))}{|E^\star|},$$

where

$$\mathbf{1}(l \in \mathcal{L}_e(u,v)) = \begin{cases} 1 & \text{if } l \in \mathcal{L}_e(u,v)\,, \\ 0 & \text{otherwise.} \end{cases}$$

Let $B^\star(B)$ be the number of RW sampled edges that belong to $E^\star$ and (u_i,v_i) be the i-th of such edges. Replacing $E^\star$ with the edges in $E^\star$ sampled by a stationary RW gives the following estimator

$$\hat{p}_l \equiv \sum_{i=1}^{B^\star(B)} \frac{\mathbf{1}(l \in \mathcal{L}_e(u_i,v_i))}{B^\star(B)}. \qquad (5)$$

It follows directly from Theorem 4.1 (with $f(u,v) = \mathbf{1}(l \in \mathcal{L}_e(u,v))$) that $\lim_{B\to\infty} \hat{p}_l \overset{\text{a.s.}}{\to} p_l$. Moreover, from the linearity of expectation, $E[\hat{p}_l] = p_l$ for all values of $B^\star(B) > 0$.

4.2.2 *Assortative Mixing Coefficient*

The assortative mixing coefficient [27] is a measure of the correlation of labels between two neighboring vertices. By appropriately assigning edge labels derived from vertex labels, we can use the density estimator of equation (5) to derive an estimator of the assortative mixing coefficient. In order to simplify our exposition, we restrict our analysis to the assortative mixing of vertex degrees in a directed graph (equation (25) of [27]). It is trivial to extend our analysis to other types of assortative mixing coefficients, e.g., equations (21) and (23) of [27].

Let $(\text{outdeg}(u), \text{indeg}(v))$ denote the label of a directed edge (u,v) in G that also exists in G_d; and let $E^\star$ be the set of all such edges ($E^\star = E_d$). Let p_{ij} denote the fraction of labeled edges with label (i,j). Let W_{out} (W_{in}) denote the maximum *observed* out-degree (in-degree) of G_d in the RW. The degree assortative mixing coefficient [27] of a directed graph can be estimated using

$$\hat{r} \equiv \frac{1}{\hat{\sigma}_{\text{in}}\,\hat{\sigma}_{\text{out}}} \sum_{i=0}^{W_{\text{out}}} \sum_{j=0}^{W_{\text{in}}} ij(\hat{p}_{ij} - \hat{q}_i^{\text{out}} \hat{q}_j^{\text{in}}),$$

where

$$\hat{p}_{ij} \equiv \sum_{k=1}^{B^\star(B)} \frac{\mathbf{1}(\text{outdeg}(u_k) = i\,,\, \text{indeg}(v_k) = j)}{B^\star(B)};$$

$$\hat{q}_i^{\text{out}} \equiv \sum_{k=0}^{W_{\text{in}}} \hat{p}_{ik} \;\; ; \;\; \hat{q}_j^{\text{in}} \equiv \sum_{k=0}^{W_{\text{out}}} \hat{p}_{kj} \;\; ;$$

$$\hat{\sigma}_{\text{in}} = \sqrt{\sum_{i=0}^{W_{\text{out}}} j^2 \hat{q}_j^{\text{in}} - \left(\sum_{i=0}^{W_{\text{out}}} j \hat{q}_j^{\text{in}}\right)^2} \;\; ; \text{ and}$$

$$\hat{\sigma}_{\text{out}} = \sqrt{\sum_{i=0}^{W_{\text{in}}} i^2 \hat{q}_i^{\text{in}} - \left(\sum_{i=0}^{W_{\text{in}}} i \hat{q}_i^{\text{out}}\right)^2}$$

where $\hat{\sigma}_{\text{in}}$ and $\hat{\sigma}_{\text{out}}$ are the standard deviation of the distribution $\hat{q}_i^{\text{in}}$ ($\hat{q}_j^{\text{out}}$). As the estimate $\hat{p}_{ij}$ (equation (5)) asymptotically converges almost surely to its true value, it is trivial to show that $\hat{q}_i^{\text{in}}$, $\hat{q}_j^{\text{out}}$, $\hat{\sigma}_{\text{in}}$, and $\hat{\sigma}_{\text{out}}$ also asymptotically converge almost surely to their true values. Thus, $\hat{r}$ asymptotically converges, almost surely, to the true assortative mixing coefficient of [27], as long as $\sigma_{\text{in}} > 0$ and $\sigma_{\text{out}} > 0$. This implies that $\hat{r}$ is an asymptotically unbiased estimator of the assortative mixing coefficient of G_d.

4.2.3 Vertex Label Density

Let $\mathcal{L}_v(v)$ be the set of labels associated with vertex v, $\forall v \in V$. The fraction of *vertices* with label l in G, θ_l, is

$$\theta_l = \frac{1}{|V|} \sum_{\forall(u,v)\in E} \frac{\mathbf{1}(l \in \mathcal{L}_v(v))}{\deg(v)}, \qquad (6)$$

as $G = (V, E)$ is directed and symmetric. By replacing E with a sequence of edges sampled by a stationary RW (here we have $E^\star = E$ and $B^\star = B$) and renormalizing, we arrive at the following estimator for θ_l

$$\hat{\theta}_l \equiv \frac{1}{S\,B} \sum_{i=1}^{B} \frac{\mathbf{1}(l \in \mathcal{L}_v(v_i))}{\deg(v_i)}, \qquad (7)$$

where $S = 1/B \sum_{i=1}^{B} 1/\deg(v_i)$. From Theorem 4.1 we have $\lim_{B\to\infty} S \to |V|/|E|$, almost surely. Using again Theorem 4.1 we have

$$\lim_{B\to\infty} \frac{1}{B} \sum_{i=1}^{B} \frac{\mathbf{1}(l \in \mathcal{L}_v(v_i))}{\deg(v_i)} \to \frac{1}{|E|} \sum_{\forall(u,v)\in E} \frac{\mathbf{1}(l \in \mathcal{L}_v(v))}{\deg(v)},$$

almost surely, which divided by $|V|/|E|$ yields equation (6). As S converges almost surely to $|V|/|E|$, we have $\lim_{B\to\infty} \hat{\theta}_l \to \theta_l$, almost surely. This also implies that $\hat{\theta}_l$ is an asymptotically unbiased estimator of θ_l.

4.2.4 Global Clustering Coefficient

In the literature the term *clustering coefficient* often refers to the local clustering coefficient [37]. In our example we estimate a different metric: the *global* clustering coefficient. In a social network the global clustering coefficient, C, is the probability that the friend of John's friend is also John's friend [34]. Let $V^\star$ be the set of vertices $v \in V$ with $\deg(v) > 1$. The global clustering coefficient of an undirected graph is defined as [34]

$$C \equiv \frac{1}{|V^\star|} \sum_{\forall v\in V} c(v), \qquad (8)$$

where

$$c(v) = \begin{cases} \Delta(v)/\binom{\deg(v)}{2} & \text{if } \deg(v) \geq 2 \\ 0 & \text{otherwise}, \end{cases}$$

where $\Delta(v) = |\{(u,w) \in E : (v,u) \in E \text{ and } (v,w) \in E\}|$ is the number of triangles that contain vertex v and $\binom{\deg(v)}{2}$ is the maximum number of triangles that a vertex v with degree $\deg(v)$ can belong to.

Note that finding $\Delta(v)$ for a given vertex $v \in V$ requires knowing all vertices within two hops of v, which can be a resource intensive task. To avoid the cost of computing Δ, we rewrite equation (8)

$$C = \frac{1}{|V^\star|} \sum_{\forall(v,u)\in E} \frac{f(v,u)}{\binom{\deg(v)}{2}},$$

where $f(v,u)$ gives the number of shared neighbors between u and v.

Let (v_i, u_i) be the i-th sampled edge in a stationary RW and let

$$\hat{C} \equiv \frac{1}{S\,B} \sum_{i=1}^{B} \frac{f(v_i,u_i)}{\binom{\deg(v_i)}{2}} \frac{1}{\deg(v_i)},$$

where

$$S = \frac{1}{B} \sum_{i=1}^{B} \frac{1}{\deg(v_i)}.$$

Corollary 4.2. *$\lim_{B\to\infty} \hat{C} \to C$, almost surely.*

PROOF. From Theorem 4.1

$$\lim_{B\to\infty} S \to |V^\star|/|E|,$$

almost surely. Also from Theorem 4.1

$$\lim_{B\to\infty} \frac{1}{B} \sum_{i=1}^{B} \frac{f(v_i,u_i)}{\binom{\deg(v_i)}{2}} \frac{1}{\deg(v_i)} \to \frac{1}{|E|} \sum_{\forall(v,u)\in E} \frac{f(v,u)}{\binom{\deg(v)}{2}},$$

almost surely, which together with the almost sure convergence of S implies that $\lim_{B\to\infty} \hat{C} \to C$, almost surely. □

Note that almost sure convergence implies that $\hat{C}$ is an asymptotically unbiased estimator of C.

4.3 Estimator Accuracy & Graph Structure

Sampling a graph using a RW is not without drawbacks. A random walker can get (temporarily) "trapped" inside a subgraph whose characteristics differ from those of the whole graph. Even if the random walker starts in steady state (i.e., is stationary), this scenario may increase the mean squared error of the estimates. If the random walker does not start in steady state, this scenario may cause an increase in the estimation bias as well as the mean squared error. Ideally, the random walker needs to mitigate the effect of these traps on the estimates.

The above two types of estimation errors are well documented in the literature and various solutions are available [14]. For instance, if the random walker does not start in a stationary regime (transient), it is common practice to discard the first w samples [14]. The value of w is called the *burn-in period*. There are two problems with this solution: (1) it only reduces the error related to the non-stationarity of the samples; (2) it is difficult to determine a good value for w if the sampling budget is small (compared to the size of the graph) and the size and structure of G are unknown.

A simple naive solution to the RW "trapping" problem (adopted in [15] to sample Facebook), is to sample the graph using multiple independent random walkers [14]. In what follows we see that this naive approach can lead to increased estimation errors. In Section 5 we propose a method to mitigate the random walk "trapping" problem using m *dependent* random walkers.

4.4 Multiple Independent Random Walkers

The main problem of estimating graph characteristics using a single walker is that the walker may get trapped inside a local neighborhood. But there is the question of what happens if we could start m independent random walkers (*MultipleRW*) at m independently sampled vertices in the graph. Note that when $m = 1$ we are back to sampling G using a single random walker, which we denote as *SingleRW*. Networks such as MySpace, Facebook, and Bittorrent admit random (uniform) vertex sampling at cost c higher than the cost of sampling the neighbors of a known vertex (which is what a RW does). In such networks random vertex sampling may help us start m random walkers at different parts of the graph. While the value of c can be large, initializing m random walkers with uniformly sampled vertices costs (only) mc units of our sampling budget (where one unity of the budget is the cost of sampling a vertex in a RW).

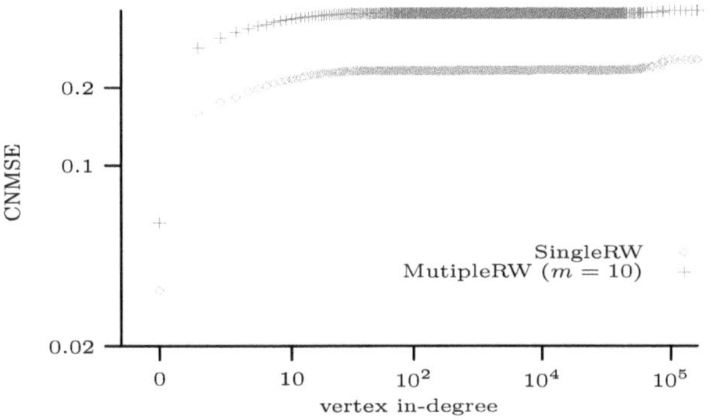

Figure 1: (Flickr) The log-log plot of the CNMSE of the in-degree distribution estimates with budget $B = |V|/10$.

Unfortunately, m independent random walkers starting at m randomly sampled vertices may decrease estimation accuracy. Consider the following experiment where each of the m random walkers (independently) performs $\lfloor B/m - c \rfloor$ steps. We seek to estimate the CCDF (complementary cumulative distribution function) of the in-degree of the Flickr graph (the Flickr dataset is summarized in Table 1). According to Table 1 the Flickr graph is disconnected. The goal of this simulation is to compare the estimation accuracy of SingleRW and MultipleRW when there are no disconnected components. For this we set $c = 1$. The sampling budget is $B = 171,525 = |V|/10$, which amounts to a sampling budget equivalent to 10% of the vertices in the graph. Figure 1 shows a log-log plot of the CNMSE, equation (2), of SingleRW and MultipleRW ($m = 10$) averaged over 10,000 runs. Note that the estimates obtained by SingleRW are, on average, more accurate than the estimates obtained by MultipleRW. Increasing the sampling budget B does not reduce the gap. In Section 6 we see, over other real-world graphs, that when starting random walkers from uniformly sampled vertices, MultipleRW has higher estimation errors than SingleRW.

4.5 Disconnected Graph Example

The following example shows a situation in which both MultipleRW and SingleRW have large estimation errors. In this example we initialize MultipleRW with m randomly (uniformly) sampled vertices. We simplify our exposition by assuming that each MultipleRW walker takes B/m steps, where B (the sampling budget) is a multiple of m. Let $G = (V, E)$ be an undirected graph that has two large disconnected components $G_A = (V_A, E_A)$ and $G_B = (V_B, E_B)$. Let $|V_A| = |V_B|$ and $\text{vol}(V_A) > \text{vol}(V_B)$. When initial vertices are uniformly sampled, the probability that each MultipleRW walker (independently) starts in G_A (G_B) is $h_A = |V_A|/|V|$ ($h_B = |V_B|/|V|$). Recall that G_A and G_B are disconnected. For each random walker, after B/m ($B \gg 1$) RW steps, an edge $(u_A, v_A) \in E_A$ is sampled with probability $p_A \approx h_A/\text{vol}(V_A)$. Similarly an edge $(u_B, v_B) \in E_B$ is sampled with probability $p_B \approx h_B/\text{vol}(V_B)$. Thus $p_A < p_B$, i.e., the edges in G_B are sampled with higher probability than the edges in G_A. As our estimators assume that all edges are sampled with the same probability, this imbalance between p_A and p_B has the potential to introduce large MSEs (and biases). Note that increasing m does not change p_A and p_B. Increasing B only mitigates this problem if G is connected and, in a loosely connected graph, only large values of B positively impact the MSE. Ideally we want a RW algorithm that does not rely on large sampling budgets B to achieve low estimation errors.

Now consider the same thought experiment where each random walker starts in G_A and G_B (independently) with probabilities $h_A = \text{vol}(V_A)/\text{vol}(V)$ and $h_B = \text{vol}(V_B)/\text{vol}(V)$, respectively. In this new scenario it is easy to see that $p_A = p_B = 1/\text{vol}(V) = 1/\text{vol}(V)$. Thus, we would like to start a RW at vertex v with probability $\deg(v)/\text{vol}(V)$, $\forall v \in V$. Section 6 shows that in practice this approach can successfully mitigate estimation errors caused by disconnected components. Unfortunately, it is difficult to sample m mutually *independent* vertices with probabilities proportional to their degrees. In the case where G is connected, this is equivalent to jointly start m independent random walkers in steady state. In networks such as MySpace, Facebook, and Bittorrent it is unclear how one can (efficiently) sample vertices with probabilities proportional to their degrees.

We want an m-dimensional random walk that, in steady state, samples **edges uniformly** *at random* **but,** *unlike MultipleRW, can benefit from starting its walkers at* **uniformly sampled vertices**.

5. FRONTIER SAMPLING (FS)

In this section we present a new and promising approach to an m-dimensional random walk that benefits from starting its walkers at uniformly sampled vertices. *Frontier Sampling* (FS) performs m *dependent* random walks in the graph. We refer to m as the dimension of the FS random walk. Let c be the cost of randomly sampling a vertex. The FS algorithm, given in Algorithm 1 is a centrally coordinated sampling algorithm that maintains a list of m vertices representing m random walkers. This way FS is less likely to get stuck in loosely connected components than a single random walker. However, in Section 5.2 we see that the joint steady state distribution of FS is much closer to the uniform distribution than is the steady state distribution of m independent random walkers. Section 5.3 describes how the FS algorithm can be made fully distributed. In Section 6 we see that, if the initial set of random walk vertices is chosen uniformly at random, FS estimates are more accurate than both single and m independent random walkers.

Algorithm 1: Frontier Sampling (FS).

```
n ← 0 {n is the number of steps}
Initialize L = (v_1, ..., v_m) with m randomly chosen
  vertices (uniformly)
repeat
  Select u ∈ L with probability deg(u)/∑_{∀v∈L} deg(v)
  Select an outgoing edge of u, (u, v), uniformly at
  random
  Replace u by v in L and add (u, v) to sequence of
  sampled edges
  n ← n + 1
until n ≥ B − mc
```

Frontier Sampling: An m-dimensional Random Walk

FS shares many of the same statistical properties of a single random walker. The key insight behind Theorem 5.2 below is that the FS stochastic process is equivalent to the stochastic process of a single random walker over the m-th Cartesian power of G, $G^m = (V^m, E_m)$, where

$$V^m = \{(v_1, \ldots, v_m) \mid v_1 \in V \wedge \cdots \wedge v_m \in V\}$$

is the m-th Cartesian power of V and $\forall \mathbf{v}, \mathbf{u} \in V^m$, $(\mathbf{v}, \mathbf{u}) \in E_m$ if exists an index i such that $(v_i, u_i) \in E$ and $u_j = v_j$ for $j \neq i$.

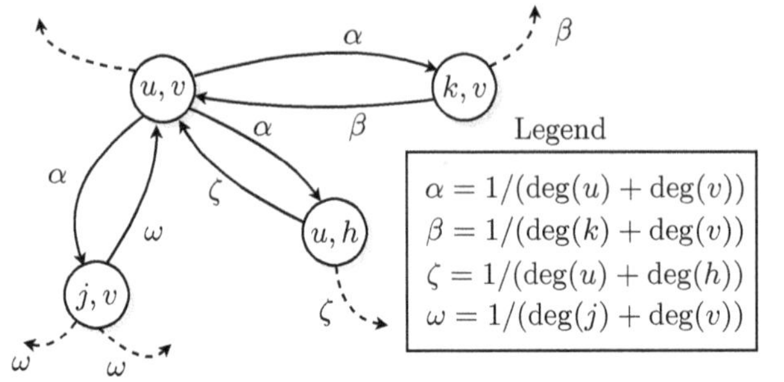

Figure 2: Illustration of the Markov chain associated to the Frontier sampler with dimension $m = 2$.

Lemma 5.1. *The Frontier sampling process is equivalent to the sampling process of a single random walker over G^m.*

Proof. Consider the $(n-1)$-st step of FS. The reader may find Figure 2 helpful in following the proof. Let $L_n = (v_1, \ldots, v_m)$ be the state of FS before the n-th step. Clearly $L_n \in V^m$. Let $e(L_n)$ denote the collection of all edges associated to the vertices in L_n. We refer to $e(L_n)$ as the edge frontier at the n-th step. We describe the transition from state L_n to state L_{n+1} as follows (lines (4) and (5) of the FS algorithm): Select a vertex $v \in L_n$ with probability proportional to $\deg(v)$ and then replace vertex v in L_n with one of its neighbors (selected uniformly at random). This is equivalent to randomly sampling an edge from $e(L_n)$ with probability

$$p = \frac{1}{|e(L_n)|} = \frac{1}{\sum_{\forall v \in L_n} \deg(v)}.$$

Therefore, L_n transits to state L_{n+1} iff $(L_n, L_{n+1}) \in E_m$ and the transition probability from L_n to L_{n+1} is $1/|e(L_n)|$. Thus, the Markov chain that describes FS is equivalent to the Markov chain of a single random walker over G^m. □

Theorem 5.2. *Recall that G is a directed symmetric graph. If G is connected and non-bipartite, then in steady state FS has the following properties:*

(I) edges are sampled uniformly at random and form a stationary sequence,

(II) has distribution, $L_\infty = (v_1, \ldots, v_m)$, equal to

$$\frac{\sum_{i=1}^{m} \deg(v_i)}{m|V|^{m-1}\mathrm{vol}(V)},$$

which is unique, and

(III) the sequence of sampled edges satisfies the Strong Law of Large Numbers (Theorem 4.1).

Proof. The proof is found in our technical report [31]. □

In Section 4.5 we observed that, when starting multiple RWs, the MSE is reduced when the number of walkers inside each subgraph matches the number obtained when the graph is connected and all walkers are in steady state. In what follows we see that, in steady state, the average number of MultipleRW walkers in V_A is far from the average number obtained with m uniformly sampled vertices. In contrast, Section 5.2 shows that as $m \to \infty$, by uniformly sampling the starting vertices, FS starts in steady state with respect to the number of random walkers in any subset of vertices $V_A \subseteq V$.

5.1 MultipleRW Steady State v.s. Uniform Distribution

Consider a MultipleRW process with m walkers and let $K_{mw}(m)$ be a random variable that denotes the steady state number of MultipleRW random walkers in V_A. Let $\alpha_A = E[K_{mw}(m)]/E[K_{un}(m)]$ be the ratio between the steady state number of MultipleRW in V_A and the number of random walkers that start in V_A from uniformly sampled vertices. As all random walkers are independent we have

$$E[K_{mw}(m)] = \frac{m\,|V_A| d_A}{|V| d}.$$

It is also easy to see that

$$E[K_{un}(m)] = \frac{m\,|V_A|}{|V|}.$$

From the above we have

$$\alpha_A = E[K_{mw}(m)]/E[K_{un}(m)] = d_A/d.$$

Note that the value of α_A may be quite large or close to zero depending on both (1) the choice of V_A and (2) the average degree of G.

5.2 FS Steady State v.s. Uniform Distribution

Let $G = (V, E)$ be a connected graph and $V_A \subset V$ be a proper subset of V; define $V_B = V \backslash V_A$. Let $d_A = \mathrm{vol}(V_A)/|V_A|$, $d_B = \mathrm{vol}(V_B)/|V_B|$, and $d = \mathrm{vol}(V)/|V|$ be the average degrees of the vertices in V_A, V_B, and V, respectively. Consider a FS process with m walkers and let $K_{fs}(m)$ be a random variable that denotes the number of random walkers in V_A in steady state. Let $K_{un}(m)$ be a random variable that denotes the number of sampled vertices, out of m uniformly (randomly) sampled vertices from V, that belong to V_A. $K_{un}(m)$ has distribution $P[K_{un}(m) = k] = \binom{m}{k} p^k (1-p)^{m-k}$, $\forall k \geq 0$, where $p = |V_A|/|V|$. In this section we show that $K_{fs}(m)$ and $K_{un}(m)$ converge to the same limiting distribution, i.e.,

$$\lim_{m\to\infty} P[K_{fs}(m) = k] = \lim_{m\to\infty} P[K_{un}(m) = k],\ \forall k \geq 0. \quad (9)$$

Recall that the FS algorithm starts m random walkers at m uniformly sampled vertices (sampled independently). Let $V_A \subseteq V$. As m increases, eq. (9), the number of FS walkers that are initially selected to be in V_A approaches the steady state distribution (assuming G is connected).

Let $L \in V^m$ be the state of FS; from (Theorem 5.2) we have

$$P[L = (v_1, \ldots, v_m)] = \frac{\sum_{i=1}^{m} \deg(v_i)}{m|V|^{m-1}\mathrm{vol}(V)}.$$

Graph	Flickr	LiveJournal	YouTube	Internet RLT
Description	Social Net.	Social Net.	Social Net.	Internet tracert.
Type of graph	Directed	Directed	Directed	Directed
# of Vertices	1,715,255	5,204,176	1,138,499	192,244
Size of LCC	1,624,992	5,189,809	1,134,890	609,066
# of Edges	22,613,981	77,402,652	9,890,764	609,066
Average Degree	12.2	14.6	8.7	3.2
$w_{\max}$	2232	1029	3305	335
% of Original Graph	26.9%	95.4%	NA	NA

Table 1: Summary of the graph datasets used in our simulations. "Size of LCC" refers to the size of the largest connected component and $w_{\max}$ is the value of the largest vertex degree divided by the average degree.

In the following lemma we find the probability that $K_{fs}(m) = k$, $0 \leq k \leq m$.

Lemma 5.3.

$$P[K_{fs}(m) = k] = \frac{1}{md}\binom{m}{k} p^k (1-p)^{m-k} (k\, d_A + (m-k) d_B)\,,$$

where $p = |V_A|/|V|$ *and* $0 \leq k \leq m$.

Proof. $P[K_{fs}(m) = k]$ is the sum of the probabilities $P[L = (v_1, \ldots, v_m)]$ over all states L in which exactly k vertices belong to V_A. Consider v_i, the i-th element of L. When $v_i \in V_A$, the contribution of v_i towards $P[K_{fs}(m) = k]$ is

$$|V_A|^{k-1} |V_B|^{m-k} \deg(v_i)/(m|V|^{m-1}\mathrm{vol}(V))\,;$$

when $v_i \in V_B$, the contribution of v_i towards $P[K_{fs}(m) = k]$ is

$$|V_A|^{k} |V_B|^{m-k-1} \deg(v_i)/(m|V|^{m-1}\mathrm{vol}(V)).$$

Summing over all elements in L and over all vertices yields

$$P[K_{fs}(m) = k] = \binom{m}{k} \frac{|V_A|^k |V_B|^{m-k}}{m|V|^{m-1}\mathrm{vol}(V)}$$
$$\times \left(\sum_{i=1}^{k} \sum_{\forall u_i \in V_A} \frac{\deg(u_i)}{|V_A|} + \sum_{j=1}^{m-k} \sum_{\forall t_j \in V_B} \frac{\deg(t_j)}{|V_B|} \right) \quad (10)$$
$$= \frac{1}{m\,d}\binom{m}{k} p^k (1-p)^{m-k} (k\, d_A + (m-k) d_B)$$

□

The previous lemma gives the probability that a subset of vertices V_A has $K_{fs}(m) \in \{0, \ldots, m\}$ FS random walkers. The following theorem shows that $K_{fs}(m)$ and $K_{un}(m)$ converge to the same limiting distribution.

Theorem 5.4.
$\lim_{m\to\infty} P[K_{fs}(m) = k] = \lim_{m\to\infty} P[K_{un}(m) = k]$, $\forall k \geq 0$.

Proof. From Lemma 5.3

$$P[K_{fs}(m) = k] = \frac{k\, d_A + (m-k) d_B}{m\, d} P[K_{un}(m) = k]. \quad (11)$$

Note that if $k = mp$ we have

$$\frac{mpd_A + (m - mp) d_B}{m\, d} = \frac{m\frac{\mathrm{vol}(V_A)}{|V|} + m\frac{\mathrm{vol}(V_B)}{|V|}}{m\, d} = 1\,. \quad (12)$$

As $m \to \infty$, the probability mass of $P[K_{un}(m) = k]$ gets highly concentrated around the interval $k \in [mp - c\sqrt{m}, mp + c\sqrt{m}]$, for large enough values of c. Let $k^-(m) = mp - z(m)\sqrt{mp(1-p)}$ and $k^+(m) = mp + z(m)\sqrt{mp(1-p)}$, where $z(m) = o(\sqrt[6]{m})$[1] is a slow increasing function of m. Note that

$$\frac{z(m)\sqrt{m}\sqrt{p(1-p)}(d_A - d_B)}{m\, d} = o(m^{4/6})/m$$

and, thus, eq. (12) yields

$$\lim_{m\to\infty} \frac{k^-(m)\, d_A + (m - k^-(m)) d_B}{m\, d} = 1 \quad (13)$$

and

$$\lim_{m\to\infty} \frac{k^+(m)\, d_A + (m - k^+(m)) d_B}{m\, d} = 1. \quad (14)$$

All that is left to show is that $\lim_{m\to\infty} P[K_{un}(m) < k^-(m)] = 0$ and $\lim_{m\to\infty} P[K_{un}(m) > k^+] = 0$. Using an extension of the *de Moivre-Laplace* limit theorem shown in [12, pg. 193] yields

$$\lim_{m\to\infty} P[K_{un}(m) < k^-(m)] = 0\,, \text{ and}$$
$$\lim_{m\to\infty} P[K_{un}(m) > k^+(m)] = 0. \quad (15)$$

Putting together eqs. (11), (13), (14), and (15), with

$$\lim_{m\to\infty} \frac{k(m)\, d_A + (m - k(m)) d_B}{m\, d} < \infty\,, \; k(m) = o(m)\,,$$

yields

$$\lim_{m\to\infty} P[K_{fs}(m) = k] = \lim_{m\to\infty} P[K_{un}(m) = k], \; \forall k \geq 0,$$

which concludes our proof. □

We have seen as m gets larger, FS gets closer to starting in steady state with respect to the number of FS random walkers inside V_A, $\forall V_A \subset V$.

We have seen that if we initialize m random walkers with uniformly sampled vertices, FS starts closer to steady state than MultipleRW. In what follows we show that FS is well suited to be used in large scale (parallel, asynchronous) experiments without incurring in any coordination or communication costs between the random walkers.

5.3 Distributed FS

FS is well suited to be used in large scale (parallel, asynchronous) experiments. Let B be the budget of FS. In the distributed version of FS the budget is not directly related to the number of sampled vertices obtained by the algorithm.

[1] $f(m) = o(h(m))$ implies $\lim_{m\to\infty} f(m)/h(m) = 0$.

This is because distributed FS is achieved using multiple independent random walkers where the cost of sampling a vertex v is an exponentially distributed random variable with parameter $\deg(v)$. In what follows we show, using the Uniformization principle of Markov chains [8, Chapter 7.5] and the Poisson decomposition property, that FS can be made fully distributed.

Theorem 5.5. *A MultipleRW sampling process where the cost of sampling a vertex v is an exponentially distributed random variable with parameter $\deg(v)$ is equivalent to a FS process.*

PROOF. Consider the following Distributed FS (DFS) process. Let $\chi = \{L(\tau) \in V^m : \tau \in \mathbb{R}^\star\}$ be the Markov chain associated with a random walker over $G^m = (V^m, E_m)$, the m-th Cartesian power of G, with transition rate matrix

$$\mathbf{Q} = \mathbf{A} - \mathbf{D},$$

where $\mathbf{A}$ is the adjacency matrix of G^m, $\mathbf{A}_{i,j} \in \{0,1\}$, $\forall i,j$, and $\mathbf{D}$ is a diagonal matrix with $\mathbf{D}_{i,i} = \sum_{\forall j} \mathbf{A}_{i,j}$. We observe this FS process over the interval $[0, B]$.

In the DFS process, the probability that the k-th random walker transitions out of vertex v_k at step $\tau + \Delta$ depends only on $\deg(v_k)$ and not on the state of $L(\tau)$. Thus, we can decompose the Poisson process describing a departure from the state $L'_n = (v_1, \ldots, v_m)$ into m independent stochastic processes, where the i-th process is a Poisson process with parameter $\lambda_i = \deg(v_i), i = 1, \ldots, m$. The above is equivalent to the stochastic process of a MultipleRW process with m random walkers and budget B, where the cost of sampling a vertex v is an exponentially distributed random variable with rate $\deg(v)$.

The DFS is equivalent to a FS process via the *Uniformization* property of Markov chains [8, Chapter 7.5]. The transition probability matrix of the Uniformized Markov chain (with unitary uniformization parameter) at the embedded transition points is

$$\mathbf{P} = I - \mathbf{D}^{-1}\mathbf{Q} = \mathbf{D}^{-1}\mathbf{A},$$

which is also the transition probability matrix of a FS process. □

6. RESULTS

In this section we compare FS with SingleRW and MultipleRW. We also contrast FS with random vertex and edge sampling. The experiments consist of executing these sampling methods on a variety of real world graphs. The datasets used in the simulations are summarized in Table 1: "Flickr", "Livejournal", and "YouTube" are popular photosharing, blog (weblog), and video sharing websites, respectively. Users are represented as vertices of a graph. In these websites a user can subscribe to other user updates; an edge (u, v) exists between users u and v if user u subscribes to user v. At "Livejournal" and "YouTube" it is possible to query the incoming and outgoing edges of a given user. Further details of these three datasets can be found in [26]. "Internet RLT" is a router-level Internet graph collected from traceroute measurements of 23 monitors distributed over the world [13]. Note that some of these graphs contain disconnected components (subgraphs).

In the following simulations the starting vertex of each random walker is chosen uniformly at random from the set of all vertices. Our results show that FS estimates are consistently more accurate than their SingleRW and MultipleRW counterparts. Moreover, when restricted to the largest connected component, FS reaches steady state faster than SingleRW and MultipleRW in the simulations presented in our technical report [31].

6.1 Assortative Mixing Coefficient

In our first experiment we treat the graphs in Table 1 as undirected graphs. In-degrees and out-degrees are represented as vertex labels and the assortative mixing coefficient is obtained using the estimator described in Section 4.2.2.

In our experiment we average the estimates and calculate their mean squared error (MSE) over 100 runs. The sampling budget is $|V|/100$ for all graphs. Let $\hat{r}$ denote the estimated value of r. Table 2 shows a summary of the relative bias of $\hat{r}$ $(1 - E[\hat{r}]/r)$ and $\hat{r}$'s NMSE with respect to the true value of r. We observe that FS is consistently more accurate than both MultipleRW and SingleRW. If we focus on Flickr, the FS bias is 7 fold smaller than the bias of both MultipleRW and SingleRW. In addition FS's NMSE is one order of magnitude smaller than the NMSEs of MultipleRW and SingleRW. The Internet graph ("Internet RLT") is the only graph we studied that shows little difference between FS and MultipleRW.

We also perform an extreme experiment that focuses on the impact of loosely connected components on the assortative mixing estimates. Consider a graph that consists of two instances of a random undirected Barabási-Albert [5] graph, G_A and G_B, with 5×10^5 vertices each and average degrees 2 and 10, respectively, joined by a single edge connecting the two smallest degree vertices in G_A and G_B (ties are resolved arbitrarily). Henceforth, we use G_{AB} to denote the above graph. It is worth noting that over the G_{AB} graph, SingleRW consistently finds $\hat{r} = 0$ over all 100 runs. This is because SingleRW only estimated the assortative mixing of either subgraph A or subgraph B, which are both zero. Over G_{AB} MultipleRW performs almost as bad as SingleRW while FS is able to accurately estimate r.

6.2 In- and Out-degree Distribution Estimates

We now focus on estimating the in-degree distribution. Let $\theta = \{\theta_i\}_{\forall i \in \mathcal{L}}$ denote the in-degree distribution, where θ_i is the fraction of vertices with in-degree i. In our simulations we estimate $\gamma_i = \sum_{k=i+1}^{\infty} \theta_k$, the CCDF of θ, using equation (7). We choose to estimate the CCDF instead of the density because the CCDF is the plot of choice when it comes to displaying degree distributions. Each simulation consists of 10,000 runs (sample paths) used to compute the empirical CNMSE (equation (2)). The CNMSE is used to compare the accuracy of the estimates obtained from FS (dimension $m \in \{10, 1000\}$), SingleRW, and MultipleRW ($m \in \{10, 1000\}$ walkers). For the sake of conciseness, we restrict our presentation to a handful of representative results.

Consider first two representative results from the Flickr graph, whose in-degree CCDF (complementary cumulative distribution function) log-log plot is shown in Figure 3. The sampling budget is $B = 17,152 = |V|/100$, which amounts to sampling 1% of the vertices. In the first simulation, we are restricted to the *Largest Connected Component* (LCC) (which contains 94% of the vertices). The objective is to test if FS can outperform SingleRW and MultipleRW even

Graph	r	FS		MultipleRW		SingleRW	
		Bias	|NMSE|	Bias	|NMSE|	Bias	|NMSE|
Flickr	0.007	8%	1.08	752%	7.65	−619%	27.32
LiveJournal	0.07	−0.5%	0.11	−12%	0.16	1%	0.17
Internet RLT	0.17	3%	0.33	2%	0.32	17%	0.44
Youtube	−0.03	0.001%	0.02	2%	0.03	−1%	0.1
G_{AB}	0.08	0.01%	0.12	70%	0.72	100%	1.00

Table 2: Assortative mixing coefficient estimate bias and the module of the estimator NMSE ; r is the true value of the global clustering coefficient and these values are estimated value over 100 runs. The sampling budget is $|V|/100$ for all graphs.

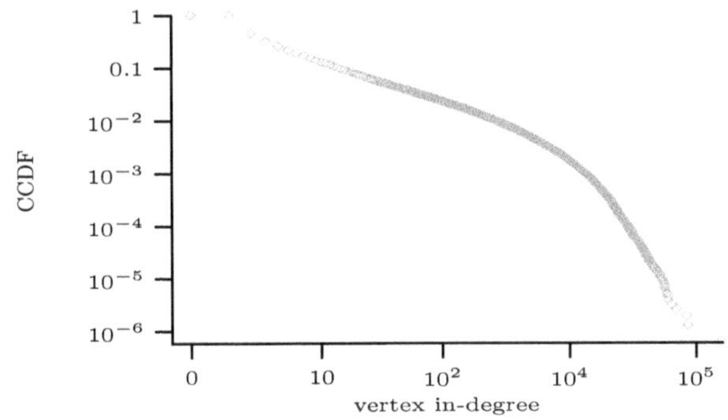

Figure 3: (Flickr) Log-log plot of the in-degree CCDF.

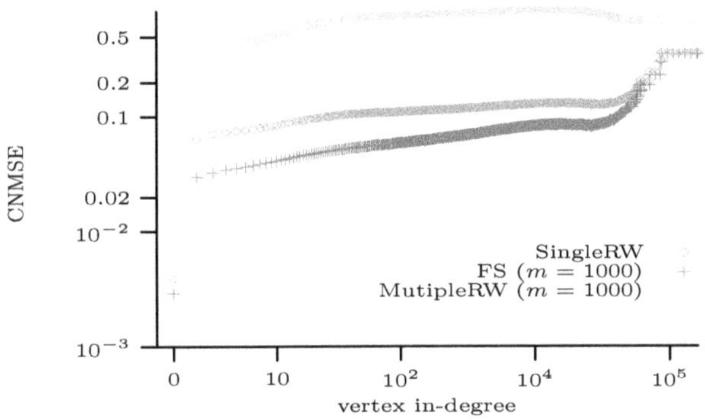

Figure 4: (LCC of Flickr) The log-log plot of the CNMSE of the in-degree distribution estimates with budget $B = |V|/100$.

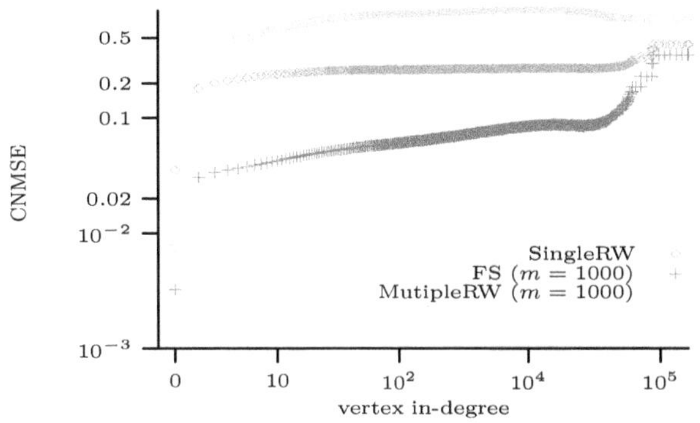

Figure 5: (Flickr) The log-log plot of the CNMSE of the in-degree distribution estimates with budget $B = |V|/100$.

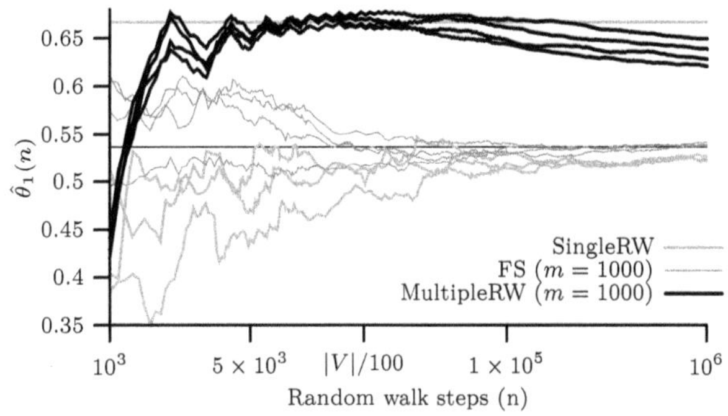

Figure 6: (LCC of Flickr) Four sample paths of $\hat{\theta}_1$ ($\theta_1 = 0.53$) as a function of the number of steps n (horizontal axis in log scale).

when there are no disconnected components. Figure 4 shows a log-log plot of the CNMSE of FS ($m = 1000$), SingleRW, and MultipleRW ($m = 1000$). In this experiment FS outperforms both SingleRW and MultipleRW. It is interesting to note that the estimates obtained by SingleRW are more accurate than the estimates obtained by MultipleRW. Now consider the complete Flickr graph. Figure 5 shows a log-log plot of the CNMSE of the in-degree distribution estimates. Contrasting the plots shown in Figures 4 and 5 we see that the gap between FS and both SingleRW and MultipleRW has significantly increased, favoring FS.

To better understand the differences between these sampling methods, Figure 6 focuses on four runs (sample paths) of the simulation over the complete Flickr graph. Figure 6 plots the evolution of $\hat{\theta}_1$ (the estimate of θ_1) as a function of n (the number of steps in the random walk). At each run of the simulator both FS and MultipleRW start at the same initial set of vertices (chosen using random vertex sampling). Figure 6 shows that all four FS sample paths (runs) quickly converge to the value of θ_1. For SingleRW, three of the four runs start inside the LCC. These runs do not converge to the value of θ_1 as some vertices with in-degree one lie outside the LCC. In one of the runs, SingleRW starts in a small disconnected component and, thus, grossly overestimates the value of θ_1. For a similar reason, i.e., walkers starting at small disconnected components, MultipleRW grossly overestimates the value of θ_1. The MultipleRW rapid increase of $\hat{\theta}_1$ at around $n = 10^3$ steps needs further investigation. It may be due to the transient of the random walk (discussed in Section 4.4). Even when $n \gg 1$ (not shown in Figure 6) the MultipleRW estimate is unable to converge to θ_1. Modifying both SingleRW and MultipleRW methods to cope with disconnected components is an interesting open problem.

For the sake of conciseness, we omit the results of the simulations over the remaining graphs (Table 1) as they are similar to the results observed over the Flickr graph. However, consider the *out-degree* distribution estimates of Livejournal. Figure 7 shows a log-log plot of the CCDF of the out-degrees. The log-log plot of the CNMSE is shown in Figure 8 for FS ($m = 100$), SingleRW, and MultipleRW ($m = 100$) with sampling budget $B = |V|/10$. From Figure 8 we see that estimates of vertices with small out-degrees

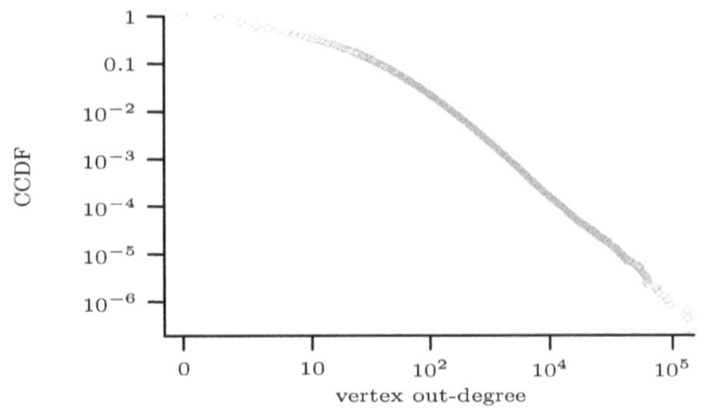

Figure 7: (Livejournal) Log-log plot of the out-degree CCDF.

in FS are up to one order of magnitude more accurate than those obtained from both SingleRW and MultipleRW.

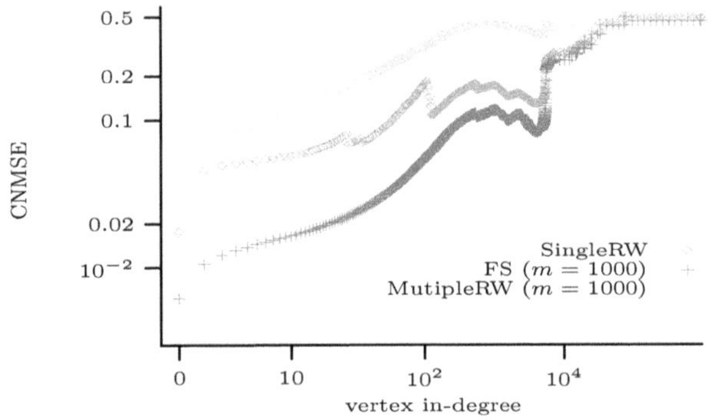

Figure 8: (Livejournal) The log-log plot of the CNMSE of the out-degree distribution estimation with sampling budget $B = |V|/100$ (CNMSE over 10,000 runs).

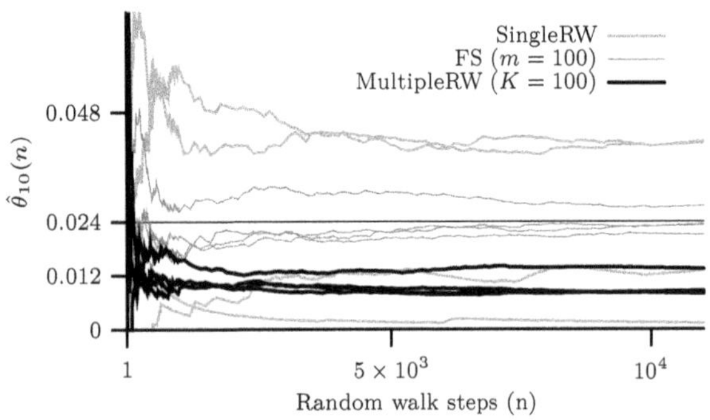

Figure 9: (G_{AB} graph) Four paths of $\hat{\theta}_{10}$ as a function of the number of steps n ($\theta_{10} = 0.024$).

The next experiment focuses on studying the impact of loosely connected components on the degree distribution estimates. For this we use the two Barabási-Albert joined graphs G_{AB} presented in Section 4.2.2. The experiment consists of estimating the degree distribution of G_{AB} using FS ($m = 100$), SingleRW, and MultipleRW ($m = 100$). Again, both FS and MultipleRW start at the initial set of vertices in each simulation (chosen uniformly at random). In this experiment the hypothesis is that, for small sampling budgets, each random walker will see the degree distribution of either G_A or G_B but not the degree distribution of G_{AB}. Moreover, as the starting vertex of each random walker is chosen uniformly at random, G_A, which has the same number of vertices as G_B but 1/5 of the edges, receives more random walkers than its *per edge* "share". Consequently, MultipleRW oversamples G_A.

Figure 9 shows the results of four simulation runs and plots the evolution of the estimates of θ_{10} ($\hat{\theta}_{10}$) as a function of the number of steps. In this simulation note that: (1) FS quickly converges to a value that is close to the correct value; (2) two out of the four SingleRW runs overestimate θ_{10} and the remaining two underestimate it; (3) three out of the four MultipleRW runs converge to the same, incorrect, fraction (underestimating the true value of θ_{10}). FS is designed to be robust to disconnected or loosely connected components. All of the FS runs quickly converge to a good estimates of θ_{10}. Figure 10 also shows that the CNMSE for FS is consistently lower than the CNMSE for SingleRW and MultipleRW.

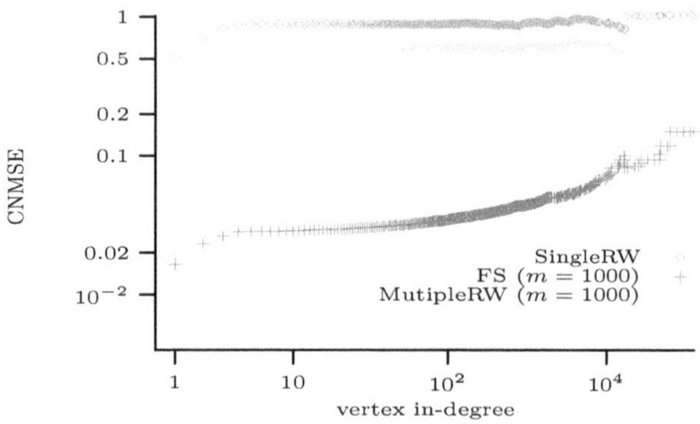

Figure 10: (G_{AB} graph) The log-log plot of the CNMSE of the degree distribution estimation with sampling budget $B = |V|/100$ (CNMSE over 10,000 runs).

6.3 FS v.s. Stationary MultipleRW & SingleRW

We now compare FS with SingleRW and MultipleRW, when the latter two start in steady state. Figure 11 shows the results (over the Flickr graph) of the same simulation scenario used to obtain the results in Figure 5, except that now MultipleRW and SingleRW both start in steady state. While SingleRW has improved slightly (most notably at the tail errors), the benefit of starting in steady state is most felt by the MultipleRW method. In this simulation we see that the large estimation errors of MultipleRW in the previous simulations were due to the starting vertices being sampled uniformly at random. It is interesting to observe that MultipleRW starting in steady state and FS have similar estimation errors.

6.4 FS v.s. Random Independent Sampling

In Section 3 we showed that, if the degrees of two neighboring vertices are independent, random edge sampling is more accurate than random vertex sampling when it comes to estimating the tail of the degree distribution. In this section we observe this to be true over large real world graphs; we also observe that the accuracy of FS closely matches the accuracy of random edge sampling. In the following simulations we estimate the in-degree distribution. Random edge sampling uses the estimator $\hat{\theta}_i$, equation (7) (the estimator used for sampled vertices is trivial).

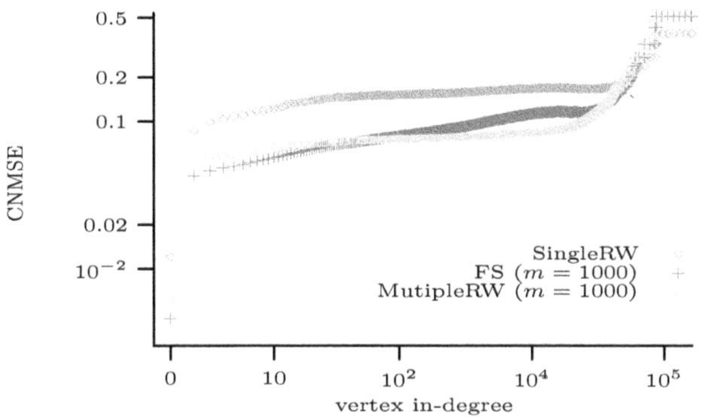

Figure 11: (Flickr) The log-log plot of the CNMSE of the in-degree distribution estimation of MultipleRW and SingleRW starting in steady state; sampling budget $B = |V|/100$ (NMSE over 10,000 runs).

In our first simulation we set the sampling cost of random vertex sampling to one and random edge sampling has cost two (as each edge samples two vertices). The sampling budget is $B = |V|/100$. We label this simulation "100% hit ratio" to indicate the unitary cost of randomly sampling vertices. Figure 12 shows a log-log plot of the NMSE (not the CNMSE) of our simulation over the (complete) Flickr graph. Here we use the NMSE (instead of the CNMSE) in order to be able to compare our results with the ones presented in equations (3) and (4). The vertical line indicates the average in-degree. Note that random edge sampling is more (less) accurate than random vertex sampling at estimating in-degrees larger (smaller) than the average in-degree, as predicted by equations (3) and (4) of our model in Section 3. We also observe that the accuracy of FS ($m = 1000$) closely matches the accuracy of random edge sampling.

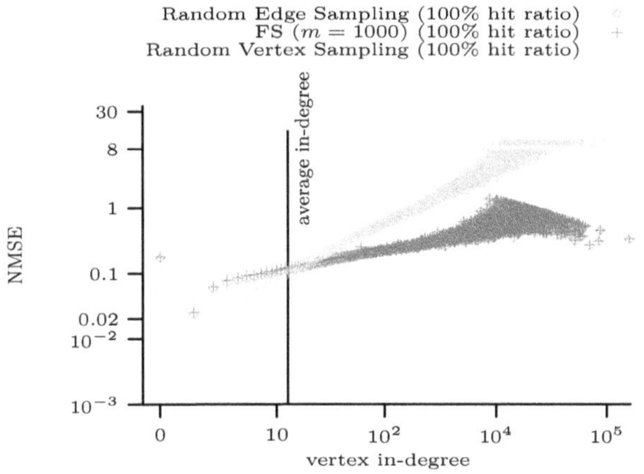

Figure 12: (Flickr) The log-log plot shows the NMSE of the in-degree distribution estimation with budget $B = |V|/100 = 18612$ (CNMSE over 10,000 runs).

Some complex networks exhibit a sparse user-id space. In this scenario a fraction of the sampling budget B can be spent querying invalid users-ids. Motivated by recent experiments over the MySpace network [30], the following experiment assumes that only 10% of the user-ids are valid, i.e., on average only one in every ten randomly sampled vertices are valid. We denote this value (10%) to be the *hit ratio*.

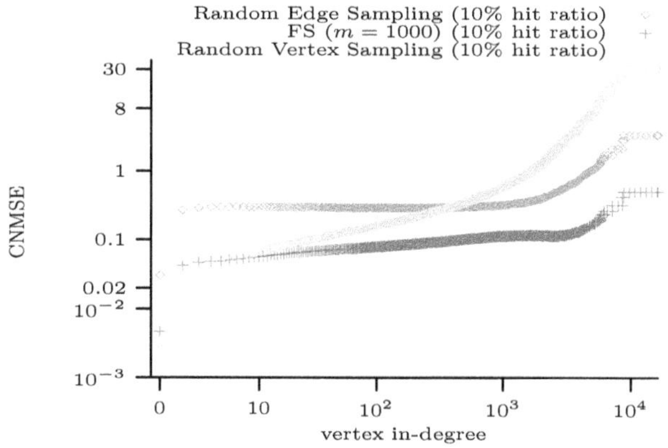

Figure 13: (Livejournal) The log-log plot shows the CNMSE of the in-degree distribution estimation with budget $B = |V|/100 = 52844$ (CNMSE over 10,000 runs).

For random edge sampling we assume a *hit ratio* of 1% (the choice of 1% is arbitrary). Figure 13 shows a log-log plot of the CNMSE of our simulation over the (complete) Livejournal graph with sampling budget $B = |V|/100 = 52844$. We observe that FS ($m = 1000$), which samples $m = 1000$ random vertices and (on average) crawls $B - 10\,m$ vertices, outperforms random edge sampling. Also note that FS estimates are more accurate than the estimates obtained from random vertex sampling for all but the three smallest in-degrees. This indicates that FS is more robust to low hit ratios than random vertex and edges sampling.

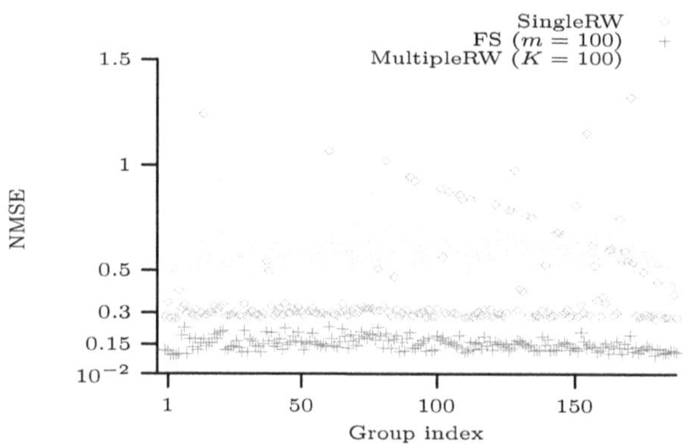

Figure 14: (Flickr) The NMSE of the density estimates of the most popular groups in the Flickr graph.

6.5 Density of Special Interest Groups

In a variety of complex networks, e.g. on-line social networks, each vertex (user) is associated with multiple labels that represent group affiliations, e.g. user interests, user geolocation, among others. For example, in the Flickr graph 21% of the users belong to one or more special interest groups [26]. Let $\mathcal{L}$ denote the set of groups in the Flickr graph and θ_l denote the fraction of vertices that belong to group $l \in \mathcal{L}$. In the simulations we estimate θ_l using FS ($m = 100$), SingleRW, and MultipleRW ($m = 100$) with budget $B = |V|/100$. Figure 14 shows the NMSE (from 10,000 runs) of the most popular 200 groups ordered in decreasing popularity. FS is clearly superior to both SingleRW and MultipleRW. Even when restricting the random walks to the largest connected component, FS still noticeably outperforms MultipleRW ($m = 100$) and SingleRW.

Graph	B	C	$E[\hat{C}]$ (NMSE) FS	SingleRW	MultipleRW
Flickr	1%	0.14	0.13 (0.04)	0.12 (0.33)	0.16 (0.18)
LiveJournal	1%	0.16	0.16 (0.02)	0.16 (0.02)	0.17 (0.06)

Table 3: Global clustering coefficient estimates. C is the true value of the global clustering coefficient and $\hat{C}$ is its estimated value.

6.6 Global Clustering Coefficient Estimates

In our last set of experiments we evaluate the accuracy of estimating the global clustering coefficient using FS, SingleRW, and MultipleRW. Our simulations show a small difference between FS ($m = 1000$), SingleRW, MultipleRW ($m = 1000$). Let C be the clustering coefficient and $\hat{C}$ denote its estimated value. Table 3 presents the empirical value of $E[\hat{C}]$ and the empirical NMSE of the clustering coefficient, given by

$$\text{NMSE} = \frac{\sqrt{E[(\hat{C} - C)^2]}}{C},$$

over 10,000 runs of FS, SingleRW, and MultipleRW over the Flickr and Livejournal graphs. From the results of Table 3 we see that FS accurately estimates the global clustering coefficient and has smaller error than both SingleRW and MultipleRW.

7. RELATED WORK

This section is devoted to review the related literature. FS can be classified as a Markov Chain Monte Carlo (MCMC) method. Other MCMC-based methods have been applied to characterize complex networks. Applications include, but are not limited to estimating characteristics of a population [36] (e.g. estimation of HIV seroprevalence among drug users [24]), content density in peer-to-peer networks [16, 23, 29, 35], uniformly sampling Web pages from the Internet [17, 33], and uniformly sampling Web pages from a search engine's index [4]. The above literature is mostly concerned with random walks that seek to sample vertices uniformly (also known as Metropolized Random Walks or Metropolis-RW) [16, 17, 33, 4, 35]. The accuracy of RW and Metropolis-RW (MRW) is compared in [15, 29], and in a variety of experiments RW estimates are shown to be consistently more accurate than or equal to MRW estimates.

The above literature does not consider the use of multiple random walks to address the problem of estimating characteristics of disconnected or loosely connected graphs. While multiple independent random walkers have been used as a convergence test in the literature, our simulations in Section 6 show that independent walkers are not suited to sample loosely connected graphs when the starting vertices are selected uniformly at random.

A number of real complex networks are known to have disconnected or loosely connected components. A large body of MCMC literature is dedicated to overcome the locality problem described in Section 4.3. However, the literature either assumes that the graph is very structured, e.g., a 2 dimensional lattice, or that the graph is completely known. These assumptions make the solutions inapplicable to our problem. A comprehensive list of MCMC methods and their characteristics can be found in [32].

Projecting a RW onto a higher dimensional space has been used in [9] to make the Markov chain associated to the random walker nonreversible, which can speed up the mixing of the original RW. Unfortunately, it is unclear if this method can be successfully used to estimate characteristics of complex networks.

In networks that cannot be crawled (e.g., the Internet topology), samples must be obtained along shortest paths, and vertex degrees cannot be queried, [1] shows that observed vertex degrees are biased. Our work, however, assumes a graph can be crawled and vertex degrees queried. Our scenario admits a RW with an unbiased estimator. Multiple random walks also find other applications besides the one presented in this work. They are used to collect Web data [10], search P2P networks [6, 38], and decrease the time to discover "new wireless nodes" [2]. Dependent multiple random walks are also used in percolation theory [3].

8. DISCUSSION AND FUTURE WORK

In this work we presented a new and promising random walk-based method (*Frontier sampling*) that mitigates the estimation errors caused by subgraphs that "trap" a random walker. Frontier sampling (FS) uses multiple (m) mutually *dependent* random walkers starting from vertices sampled uniformly at random. The FS samples are shown to be the projection (onto the original graph) of a special type of m-dimensional (single) random walker. Simulations over real world graphs in Section 6 show that Frontier sampling (FS) is more robust than single and multiple independent random walkers (starting out of steady state) to estimate in-degree distributions and the fraction of users that belong to a social group. We also present evidence, using an analytical argument (also substantiated by simulations), that random walks (in particular, FS) are better suited to estimate the tail (all degrees greater than the average) of degree distributions than random vertex sampling. FS can also be made fully distributed without incurring in any coordination or communication costs.

The ideas behind FS can have far reaching implications, from estimating characteristics of dynamic networks to the design of new MCMC-based approximation algorithms.

9. ACKNOWLEDGMENTS

We would like to thank Weibo Gong for many helpful discussions and Alan Mislove for kindly making available some of the data used in this paper. This research was sponsored by the ARO under MURI W911NF-08-1-0233, and the U.S. Army Research Laboratory under Cooperative Agreement Number W911NF-09-2-0053. The views and conclusions contained in this document are those of the author(s) and should not be interpreted as representing the official policies, either expressed or implied, of the U.S. Army Research Laboratory or the U.S. Government. The U.S. Government is authorized to reproduce and distribute reprints for Government purposes notwithstanding any copyright notation hereon.

10. REFERENCES

[1] Dimitris Achlioptas, Aaron Clauset, David Kempe, and Cristopher Moore. On the bias of traceroute sampling: Or, power-law degree distributions in regular graphs. *J. ACM*, 56(4):1–28, 2009.

[2] Chen Avin and Bhaskar Krishnamachari. The power of choice in random walks: An empirical study. *Comput. Netw.*, 52(1):44–60, 2008.

[3] P. Balister, B. Bollobás, and A. Stacey. Dependent percolation in two dimensions. *Prob. Theory and Related Fields*, 117(4):495–513, 2000.

[4] Ziv Bar-Yossef and Maxim Gurevich. Random sampling from a search engine's index. *J. ACM*, 55(5):1–74, 2008.

[5] A.-L. Barabási and R. Albert. Emergence of scaling in random networks. *Science*, 286:509–512, 1999.

[6] Nabhendra Bisnik and Alhussein A. Abouzeid. Optimizing random walk search algorithms in p2p networks. *Computer Networks*, 51(6):1499–1514, 2007.

[7] S. Boccaletti, V. Latora, Y. Moreno, M. Chavez, and D.-U. Hwang. Complex networks: Structure and dynamics. *Physics Reports*, 424(4-5):175–308, 2006.

[8] Christos G. Cassandras and Stephane Lafortune. *Introduction to Discrete Event Systems.* Springer-Verlag, Inc., 2006.

[9] Fang Chen, László Lovász, and Igor Pak. Lifting Markov chains to speed up mixing. In *Proc. of STOC*, pages 275–281, 1999.

[10] Junghoo Cho and Hector Garcia-Molina. Parallel crawlers. In *Proc. of the WWW*, pages 124–135, 2002.

[11] Nathan Eagle, Alex S. Pentland, and David Lazer. Inferring friendship network structure by using mobile phone data. *PNAS*, 106(36):15274–15278, August 2009.

[12] W. Feller. *An Introduction to Probability Theory and its Applications*, volume 1. John Wiley & Sons, New York, 3rd edition, 1968.

[13] Coperative Association for Internet Data Analysis. CAIDA's Internet topology data kit #0304, 2003.

[14] Charles J. Geyer. Practical Markov Chain Monte Carlo. *Statistical Science*, 7(4):473–483, 1992.

[15] Minas Gjoka, Maciej Kurant, Carter T. Butts, and Athina Markopoulou. A walk in Facebook: Uniform sampling of users in online social networks. In *Proc. of the IEEE Infocom*, March 2010.

[16] Christos Gkantsidis, Milena Mihail, and Amin Saberi. Random walks in peer-to-peer networks: algorithms and evaluation. *Perform. Eval.*, 63(3):241–263, March 2006.

[17] Monika R. Henzinger, Allan Heydon, Michael Mitzenmacher, and Marc Najork. On near-uniform url sampling. In *Proceedings of the WWW*, pages 295–308, 2000.

[18] Marlom A. Konrath, Marinho P. Barcellos, and Rodrigo B. Mansilha. Attacking a swarm with a band of liars: evaluating the impact of attacks on bittorrent. In *P2P '07: Proceedings of the Seventh IEEE International Conference on Peer-to-Peer Computing*, pages 37–44, Washington, DC, USA, 2007. IEEE Computer Society.

[19] Jure Leskovec and Christos Faloutsos. Sampling from large graphs. In *Proc. of the KDD*, pages 631–636, 2006.

[20] Jure Leskovec, Kevin J. Lang, Anirban Dasgupta, and Michael W. Mahoney. Statistical properties of community structure in large social and information networks. In *Proc. of the WWW*, pages 695–704, 2008.

[21] David A. Levin, Yuval Peres, and Elizabeth L. Wilmer. *Markov Chains and Mixing Times.* AMS, 2009.

[22] L. Lovász. Random walks on graphs: a survey. *Combinatorics*, 2:1–46, 1993.

[23] Laurent Massoulié, Erwan Le Merrer, Anne-Marie Kermarrec, and Ayalvadi Ganesh. Peer counting and sampling in overlay networks: random walk methods. In *Proc. of the PODC*, pages 123–132, 2006.

[24] Courtney McKnight, Don Des Jarlais, Heidi Bramson, Lisa Tower, Abu S. Abdul-Quader, Chris Nemeth, and Douglas Heckathorn. Respondent-driven sampling in a study of drug users in New York City: Notes from the field. *Journal of Urban Health*, 83(6):154–159, 2006.

[25] Sean Meyn and Richard L. Tweedie. *Markov Chains and Stochastic Stability.* Cambridge University Press, 2009.

[26] Alan Mislove, Massimiliano Marcon, Krishna P. Gummadi, Peter Druschel, and Bobby Bhattacharjee. Measurement and Analysis of Online Social Networks. In *Proc. of the IMC*, October 2007.

[27] M. E. J. Newman. Assortative mixing in networks. *Phys. Rev. Lett.*, 89(20):208701, Oct 2002.

[28] M. E. J. Newman. The structure and function of complex networks. *SIAM Review*, 45(2):167–256, 2003.

[29] Amir H. Rasti, Mojtaba Torkjazi, Reza Rejaie, Nick Duffield, Walter Willinger, and Daniel Stutzbach. Respondent-driven sampling for characterizing unstructured overlays. In *Proc. of the IEEE Infocom*, pages 2701–2705, April 2009.

[30] Bruno Ribeiro, William Gauvin, Benyuan Liu, and Don Towsley. On MySpace account spans and double Pareto-like distribution of friends. In *IEEE Infocom 2010 Network Science Workshop*, Mar 2010.

[31] Bruno Ribeiro and Donald Towsley. Estimating and sampling graphs with multidimensional random walks. arXiv:1002.1751v2, 2010.

[32] Christian P. Robert and George Casella. *Monte Carlo Statistical Methods.* Springer-Verlag, 2nd edition, 2005.

[33] Paat Rusmevichientong, David M. Pennock, Steve Lawrence, and Lee C. Giles. Methods for sampling pages uniformly from the world wide web. In *AAAI Fall Symposium on Using Uncertainty Within Computation*, pages 121–128, 2001.

[34] Thomas Schank and Dorothea Wagner. Approximating clustering-coefficient and transitivity. *Journal of Graph Algorithms and Applications*, 9(2):265–275, 2004.

[35] Daniel Stutzbach, Reza Rejaie, Nick Duffield, Subhabrata Sen, and Walter Willinger. On unbiased sampling for unstructured peer-to-peer networks. *IEEE/ACM Trans. Netw.*, 17(2):377–390, 2009.

[36] Erik Volz and Douglas D. Heckathorn. Probability based estimation theory for Respondent-Driven Sampling. *Journal of Official Statistics*, 2008.

[37] D.J. Watts and S.H. Strogatz. Collective dynamics of "small world" networks. *Nature*, 393:440–442, June 1998.

[38] Ming Zhong and Kai Shen. Random walk based node sampling in self-organizing networks. *SIGOPS Oper. Syst. Rev.*, 40(3):49–55, 2006.

The Impact of YouTube Recommendation System on Video Views

Renjie Zhou[†], Samamon Khemmarat[‡], Lixin Gao[‡]

[†] College of Computer Science and Technology
Harbin Engineering University, Harbin, China
renjie_zhou@hrbeu.edu.cn

[‡] Department of Electrical and Computer Engineering
University of Massachusetts, Amherst, USA
{khemmarat,lgao}@ecs.umass.edu

ABSTRACT

Hosting a collection of millions of videos, YouTube offers several features to help users discover the videos of their interest. For example, YouTube provides video search, related video recommendation and front page highlight. The understanding of how these features drive video views is useful for creating a strategy to drive video popularity. In this paper, we perform a measurement study on data sets crawled from YouTube and find that the related video recommendation, which recommends the videos that are related to the video a user is watching, is one of the most important view sources of videos. Despite the fact that the YouTube video search is the number one source of views in aggregation, the related video recommendation is the main source of views for the majority of the videos on YouTube. Furthermore, our results reveal that there is a strong correlation between the view count of a video and the average view count of its top referrer videos. This implies that a video has a higher chance to become popular when it is placed on the related video recommendation lists of popular videos. We also find that the click through rate from a video to its related videos is high and the position of a video in a related video list plays a critical role in the click through rate. Finally, our evaluation of the impact of the related video recommendation system on the diversity of video views indicates that the current recommendation system helps to increase the diversity of video views in aggregation.

Categories and Subject Descriptors

C.2.0 [**Computer-Communication Networks**]: General; H.3.5 [**Information Storage and Retrieval**]: Online Information Services

General Terms

Measurement, Human Factors

Keywords

Video Sharing Site, YouTube, Recommendation System, View Sources, View Diversity

1. INTRODUCTION

YouTube has been one of the most successful user-generated video sharing sites since its establishment in early 2005. It is estimated that there are over 100 million videos on YouTube [9], which makes the exploration of the desired videos a daunting task. In order to help users find interesting videos from a huge number of videos, YouTube provides several features such as search engine, front page highlight, and related videos recommendation.

YouTube can obtain the data on how users use these features, which can be useful for improving its service. However, the understanding of how video views are driven by these features is also helpful and interesting to outsiders such as researchers, advertisers, and content providers. For researchers, this is a case study of how contents in a large repository are discovered and the evidence for the importance of content discovery tools. For content providers and advertisers, this is useful for planning strategically to increase their videos' popularity and predicting the effectiveness of advertising. More recently, YouTube started to let video content providers be partners to cash in on the videos posted by sharing ad revenue and charging rental fees to viewers [2]. This underscores the need to understand how one can drive the views of a video.

In this paper, we perform a measurement study on data sets of hundreds of thousands of videos crawled from YouTube website. We study how videos are discovered by users, what are the major sources that drive the views of a video, and how well related video views are correlated. We summarize our findings as follows.

- The related video recommendation is one of the most important view sources of a video. Despite the fact that the YouTube video search is the number one source of views in aggregation, the related video recommendation is the main source of views for the majority of the videos on YouTube. In particular, for a large portion of videos with lukewarm popularity, the major source of their views is from users clicking related videos.
- There is a strong correlation between the view count of a video and the average view count of its top referrer videos. This means that if the top referrer videos are popular, then the video is also popular. This implies a video has a higher chance to become popular when

it is placed on the related video recommendation lists of popular videos. Furthermore, the position that a video is placed on the related video list plays a critical role in the click through rate of the video.

- We evaluate the impact of the video recommendation system on the diversity of video views. In contrast of recent results on the recommendation on book/CD sales [6], we find that YouTube recommendation provides more diversity on video views in aggregation than that without the recommendation. This means that YouTube recommendation helps viewers discover videos of their interest rather than popular videos only.

The rest of the paper is organized as follows. In section 2, we describe the data sets used in this study. In Section 3, we study the view sources for overall videos as well as individual videos. In Section 4, we investigate how the related video recommendation system affects video views. The evaluation of the impact of the related video recommendation system on the diversity of video views is studied in Section 5. Related work is described in Section 6 and finally, Section 7 concludes the paper.

2. DATA DESCRIPTION

Our study is based on the data sets crawled from YouTube. In this section, we first describe three elements of data provided by YouTube. We then describe how we collected the data sets.

2.1 Data Source

On YouTube, a video is viewed on a page named *watch page*, which not only shows the video itself, but also includes valuable data about the video. We focus on three elements of the data. The first element is *video metadata*, which includes the basic information about the video, such as title, upload time, and total view count. The second element is a *related video list*, which contains the related videos recommended by YouTube recommendation system. The third element is *view statistics & data*, which includes the particular video's view count sequence over time, top ten view sources, and the date of the first referral and the number of views from each source, as shown in Figure 1. By investigating the view statistics & data, we find that YouTube classifies the sources into 14 categories, such as YouTube Search, Related Video, and Mobile Device. Each of them indicates a specific kind of source, except for the Other/Viral category, which includes all the view sources that do not fall into other categories. For the category of Related Video, it also shows the video that leads users to the current video. We refer to this video as a *referrer video* of the current video.

2.2 Data Collection

In this section, we describe how we collected the two data sets in this study. We start by describing how the data can be obtained. The video metadata and related video list can be retrieved through HTML scraping as well as YouTube Data API, while the view statistics & data can only be retrieved through HTML because it is not supported by the API.

We used two different video sampling methods to obtain our data sets to minimize the bias from data sampling. Our results in the next section show that the trends of the results from the two data sets are consistent with each other despite

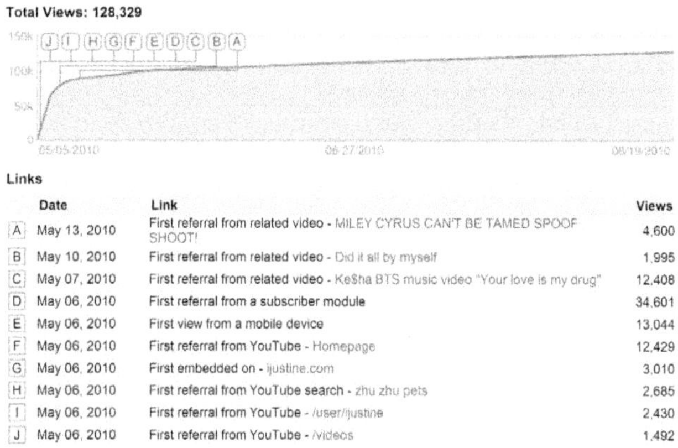

Figure 1: Snapshot of view statistics & data.

the different methods of video sampling. In the following, we describe the crawling process for each data set. For D1, we selected the videos by capturing and parsing YouTube video requests at a university network gateway, and the three elements of data associated with each video was collected through crawling. For D2, we retrieved 400 featured videos via API as the initial set, crawled their associated data, and then crawled the data for their related videos. We did this recursively in a breadth first search manner for three levels. Additionally, we crawled the metadata of referrer videos for both D1 and D2 and the related video lists of referrer videos for D2.

The data we collected and the approaches we used in the collection are shown in Table 1, and the amount of data we collected is shown in Table 2.

Collected Data	D1		D2	
	Crawl	Method	Crawl	Method
Metadata	Y	API	Y	API
Related Videos	Y	API	Y	API
Statistics & Data	Y	HTML	Y	HTML
Related Videos of Referrers	N	N/A	Y	API

Table 1: Collection method for each data set.

Data set	D1	D2
Start Date	28-Jan-10	17-Mar-10
Duration	21 days	14 days
# Videos with Metadata	498,233	202,428
# Videos with Related Videos	154,363	202,428
# Videos with S&D	111,351	55,280
# Referrer Videos	348,059	133,114

Table 2: General statistics of the data sets.

3. SOURCES OF VIDEO VIEWS

YouTube videos are accessed in a variety of ways, such as through Google search, Facebook, mobile device, and through the features provided on YouTube itself. In this section, we study which view source is the most frequently used and which one is the major contributor of views for the majority of the videos by investigating video view statistics & data. As mentioned in Section 2.1, view statistics & data contains the top ten view sources and the number of views from each source. We refer to the total views driven by the top ten sources as the *tracked views* of a video. It is necessary to verify first whether the tracked views are representative.

3.1 Representativeness of Tracked Views

To justify that the tracked views are representative, we use the percentage of tracked views from the total views of a video, and the correlation between them as the criteria. We calculate the percentage of tracked views for each video in D1 and D2, and the average is 56.7% and 63.1%, respectively. This means that, on average, the tracked views are the majority of the total views. Further, the Cumulative Distribution Function (CDF) of the percentage of tracked views is shown in Figure 2. From the figure, there are around 70% of videos whose tracked views are larger than 50% of the total views, which means that for the majority of videos, more than half of their views are recorded in view statistics & data.

In addition, we compute the Pearson's correlation coefficient between tracked views and total views to measure the linear correlation between them. The definition of Pearson's correlation coefficient is given by

$$\rho_{X,Y} = \frac{cov(X,Y)}{\sigma_X \sigma_Y} = \frac{E[(X-\mu_X)(Y-\mu_Y)]}{\sigma_X \sigma_Y},$$

where $\rho_{X,Y}$ is the correlation coefficient between total views X and tracked views Y with the expected value μ_X and μ_Y, and the standard deviation σ_X and σ_Y, respectively. The Pearson's correlation coefficients for D1 and D2 are 0.81 and 0.84, respectively. This indicates a strong linear correlation between tracked views and video views in both data sets. The correlation can be seen clearly in Figure 3, in which we plot the number of tracked views and total views for each video.

The high percentage of tracked views and the strong linear correlation between tracked views and total views lead to our conclusion that the tracked views can represent the total video views well. We believe that the view pattern explored by analyzing the tracked views is a good approximation of the overall view pattern on YouTube.

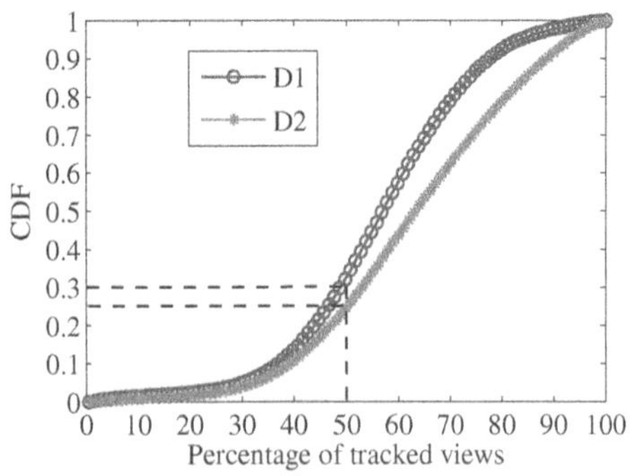

Figure 2: Distribution of percentage of tracked views.

3.2 Main Sources of Overall Views

To figure out the main sources of overall views on YouTube, we investigate the view statistics & data. The percentage of

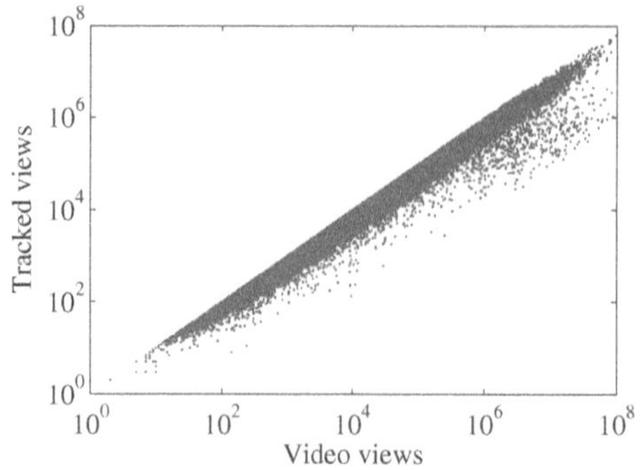

Figure 3: Video views vs. tracked views.

views from each category of view sources is shown in Figure 4, which clearly shows that YouTube Search and Related Video are the top two categories. Views from YouTube Search and Related Video together account for 66.88% and 56.06% of views in D1 and D2, respectively, while views from sources outside YouTube such as Google search, Google video search, Facebook and other sites only account for 7.6% and 5.6% of views in D1 and D2, respectively. From the figure, the percentage of views from Featured in D2 is much higher than that in D1. This is probably due to the fact that D2 was crawled with featured videos as the initial set. Comparing the contribution made by Related Video and YouTube Search, the results show that Related Video contributed a bit less views (2.6% in D1 and 1.2% in D2) than YouTube Search.

In conclusion, the related video recommendation is one of the main sources of the video views. It accounts for about 30% of the overall views on YouTube, and is only second to the YouTube Search by a small percentage.

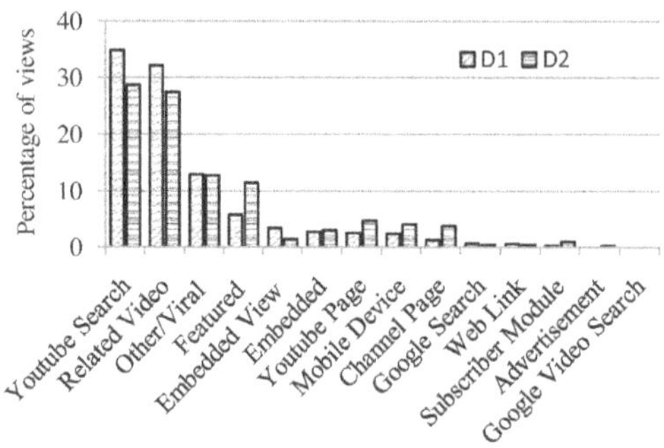

Figure 4: Percentage of tracked views from each category.

3.3 Dominant Sources for Individual Videos

Besides examining the main sources of overall views, we also investigate view sources for each individual video. For each video, we determine the category which contributes the largest proportion of views, and call it the *dominant category*. For example, if the YouTube Search contributes the largest proportion of views to a video among all sources, then YouTube Search is the dominant category of the video, in other words, the video is *dominated* by YouTube Search. The percentage of videos dominated by each category is shown in Figure 5. In contrast to Figure 4, Figure 5 shows that more videos are dominated by Related Video than YouTube Search. To show this clearly, we aggregate videos into three types, which are Related dominated, Search dominated, and Others. Table 3 shows the percentage of videos of each type for D1 and D2. We can see that the percentage of videos dominated by Related Video is the largest for both data sets.

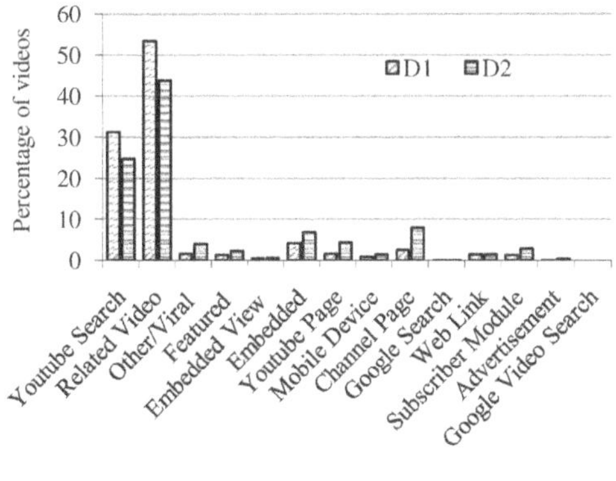

Figure 5: Percentage of videos dominated by each category.

For the disparity between the dominant category of overall views and individual video views, we further investigate the union set (D1&D2) of D1 and D2 to find out whether the dominant categories are different for videos with different popularity. We first aggregate videos into groups with view count range of one thousand views. Figure 6 shows the number of videos of each type for different view count ranges. Among the unpopular videos (left part of the figure), the number of Related dominated videos is the largest among the three types.

Category	D1 (%)	D2 (%)	D1&D2 (%)
Related Video	53.31	43.96	50.83
YouTube Search	31.18	24.71	28.79
Others	15.51	31.33	20.38

Table 3: Percentage of videos dominated by the three types.

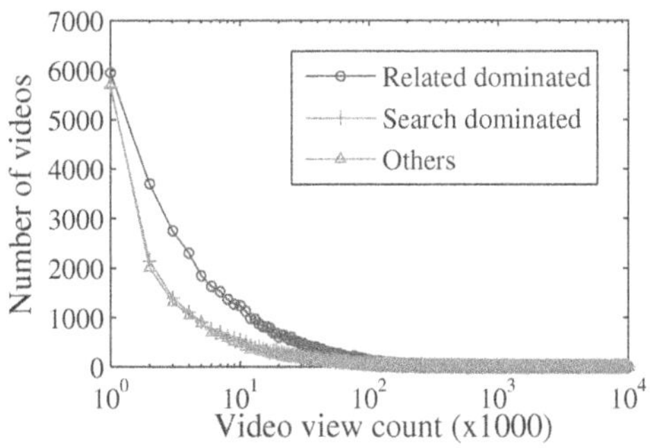

Figure 6: Number of videos for each type after aggregation with constant view count.

To understand which source is the dominant type for popular videos, we aggregate the videos using different view count range. Figure 7 shows the number of videos in each type for different view count ranges. From the figure, most

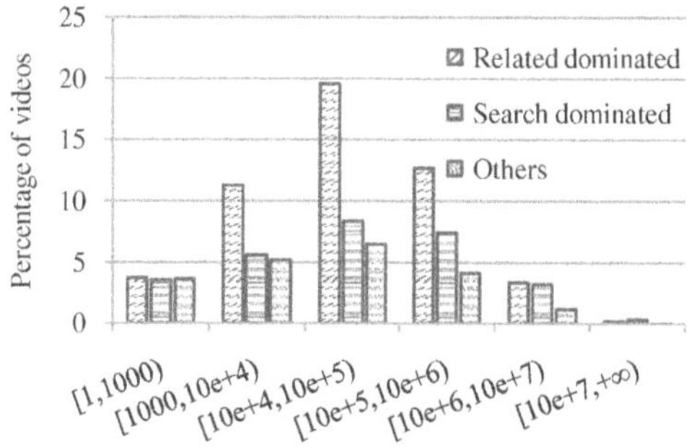

Figure 7: Number of videos for each type after aggregation with different view count.

videos have the view count in the range of one thousand to one million, and the number of Related dominated videos is distinctly the largest in this range. Similarly, we aggregate the videos by their view rates with the constant view rate range of 100 views per day and different view rate range. As shown in Figure 8 and 9, the number of Related dominated videos is always the largest, except for the extremely popular videos which account for 1.2% of total videos.

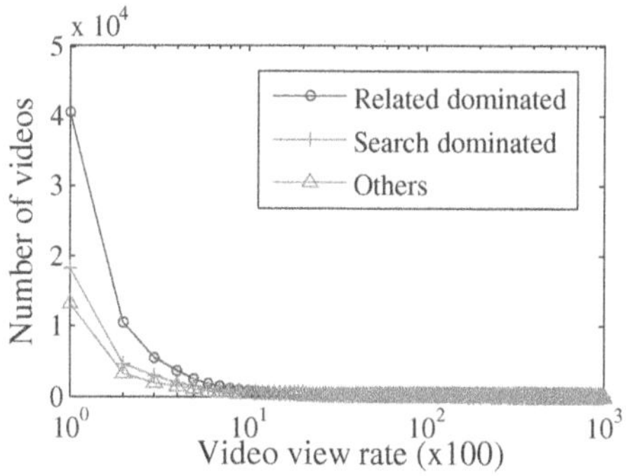

Figure 8: Number of videos for each type after aggregation with constant view rate.

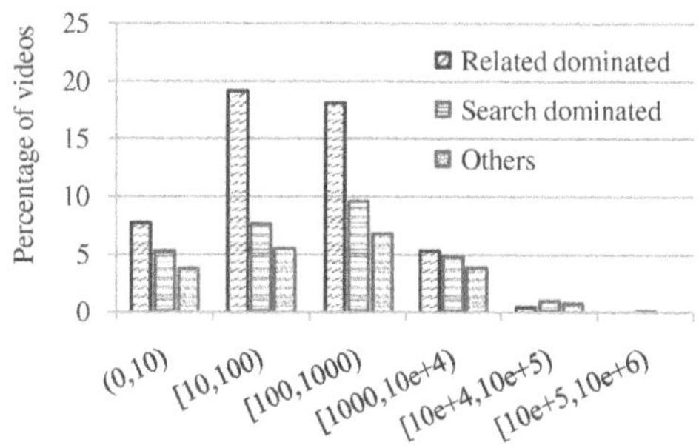

Figure 9: Number of videos for each type after aggregation with different view rate.

Based on the results of both view count and view rate, we conclude that the category of Related Video drives more views than other category of view sources for the majority of videos.

4. HOW RECOMMENDATION SYSTEM AFFECTS VIDEO VIEWS

In this section, we study how the recommendation system on YouTube affects the views of the videos. First, we look at the correlation of views and view rates between a video and its referrer videos. Then, we investigate how the positioning on the related video list affects the view propagation between the videos.

4.1 The Correlation Between Video Views and Referrer Video Views

As shown in Section 3.3, referrer videos are the dominant sources of views for the majority of videos. This suggests that there might be a strong correlation between the view or view rate of a video and its referrer videos. To verify this conjecture, we investigated the correlation of the view count of a video and the average view count of its top referrer videos. The *top referrer videos* of a video is a set of referrer videos that are the major view contributors to the video and are included in the top ten view sources list of the video. We further investigated the correlation of view rate of a video and the average video rate of its top referred videos.

In Figure 10 and Figure 11, we show the correlation between a video and its top referrer videos for view count and view rate, respectively, for the union set of D1 and D2. We observe the trend that the higher the average view count of the top referrer videos, the higher the view count of the video. The same trend can be observed for the view rate, but not as strong as that of the view count. This might be caused by the age difference of a video and its referrer videos.

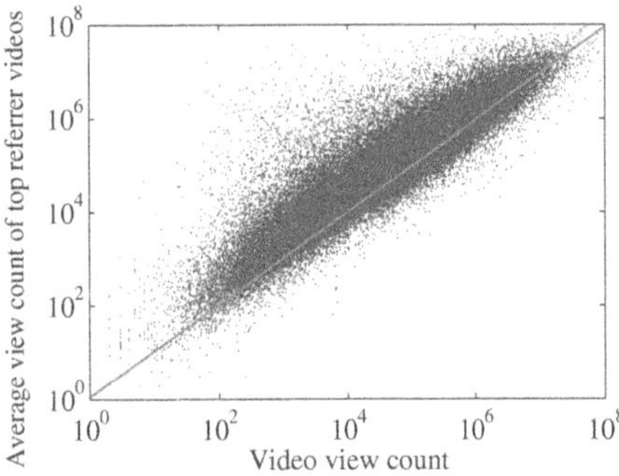

Figure 10: The view count of a video vs. the average view count of its top referrer videos.

We further investigate the correlation by computing the correlation coefficient of views and view rate between a video and its top referrer videos. The correlation coefficients are 0.60 and 0.44 for view count and view rate, respectively. The relatively high correlation coefficients are the additional evidence that the recommendation system has great impact on the views of videos. The implications from these results are that the group of referrer videos of a certain video is a good estimator and indicator for the view count of the video, and a video has a higher chance to become popular when it is placed on the related video lists of popular videos.

4.2 How the Position Affects Video Views

The related videos generated by the recommendation system are placed in order from the top to the bottom of the related video list shown on a video watch page. The understanding of how the position of a video in the related video list affects the click through rate (CTR) is important for understanding how videos drive views for their related videos.

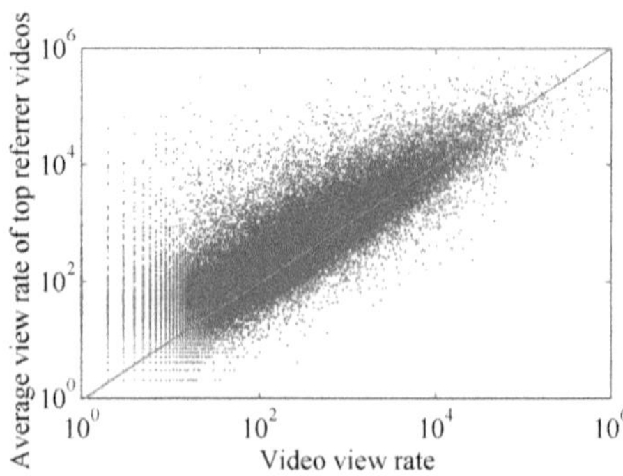

Figure 11: The view rate of a video vs. the average view rate of its top referrer videos.

We use the view statistics & data and the related video lists of referrer videos in D2 to investigate the CTR between related videos. For each pair (V, R) of a video V and its referrer video R, we figure out the position of V on R's related video list, the number of views that R contributed to V, and the number of views that R got after it contributed the first view to V. Then, we calculate the CTR for each pair (V, R), where V is in the Pth position of R's related video list ($1 \leq P \leq 20$). Finally, we compute the median of CTRs for each position P.

The result is shown in Figure 12. The figure shows that the CTR declines steadily in a log-log plot as the position lowers, and it fits the Zipf function $Y = \beta X^{-\alpha}$ quite well. The sum of the CTRs from all positions is 41.6%, with the first position having a CTR of 5.9% and the last position 1.0%. This means when a user views a certain video, there is a 41.6% chance that she will watch one of the related videos. The difference between the CTRs of the first and the last position indicates that the position in a related video list plays an important role in video view propagation. However, the CTR for YouTube videos decreases at a slower rate than that of Google advertisement, which was reported that the first position attracted about 39 times more clicks than the 10th position [1]. This reflects the difference in the usage patterns of the recommendation system on the video sharing sites and the web advertisement.

5. IMPACT ON VIDEO VIEW DIVERSITY

In this section, we investigate the impact of YouTube recommendation system on view diversity to understand whether the recommendation system helps users to discover videos of interest but not necessarily popular, or is more likely to recommend popular videos only.

To measure the view diversity, we use the Gini coefficient to measure the distributional inequality [5]. Ordering the videos ascendingly based on their number of views, the Gini coefficient for our case can be computed by

$$G = 1 - \sum_{k=1}^{n}(X_k - X_{k-1})(Y_k + Y_{k-1}),$$

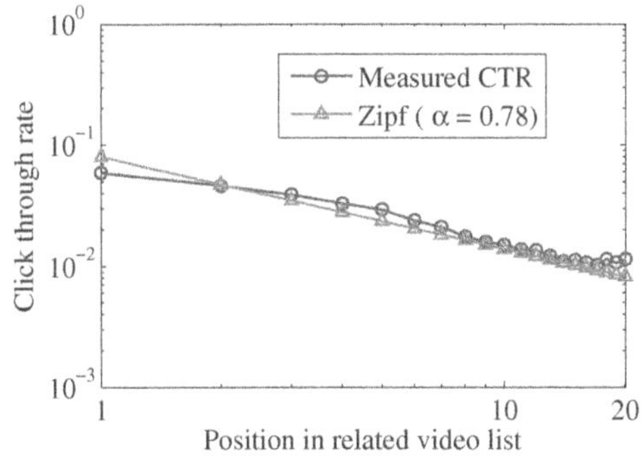

Figure 12: Click through rate for each position in related video lists.

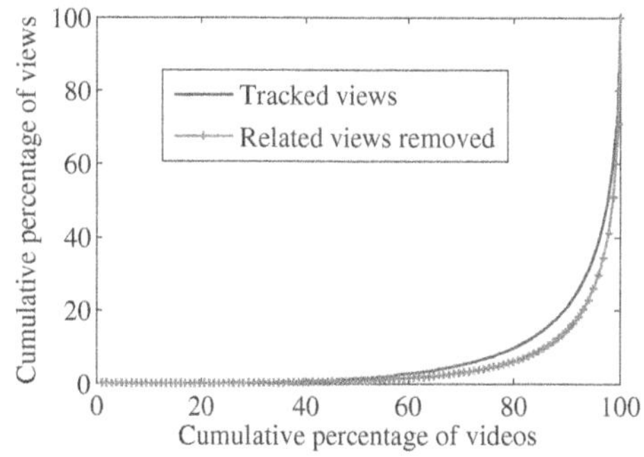

Figure 13: The Lorenz curves of the union set of D1 and D2.

where n is the number of total videos, X_k is the percentage of the first k videos, and Y_k is the percentage of the views from the first k videos.

We compare the Gini coefficients of two scenarios: where the recommendation system is presented and where it is not presented. For the first scenario, we simply use the tracked views to compute the Gini coeficients for data set D1, D2, and the union set of D1 and D2. For the second scenario, where the recommendation system is not presented, we remove the views contributed by referrer videos from the tracked views, and then recalculate the Gini coefficients.

The Gini coefficients and the Lorenz curves for the two scenarios are shown in Table 4 and Figure 13, respectively. From the table, we find that the Gini coefficient for each scenario is quite high, which means the gap between the views of popular videos and niche videos is huge. This is confirmed by the Lorenz curve, which shows more than 90% of the views are from 20% of the videos. Furthermore, when we remove the views from the recommendation system, the Gini coefficient becomes even higher. This indicates that the existence of the recommendation system helps to decrease the Gini coefficient or, in other words, increase the view diversity.

Dataset	Original views	Related removed
D1	0.87	0.90
D2	0.88	0.90
D1&D2	0.87	0.90

Table 4: Gini coefficient.

6. RELATED WORK

As one of the most popular and largest video sharing websites, there are several studies on the YouTube usage pattern and characteristics of videos on YouTube. In [7], Gill et al. study the traffic of YouTube from network edges, providing the insight on YouTube utilization. They analyze the traces to investigate the characteristics of user session on YouTube. Zink et al. also perform the analysis on YouTube usage based on the campus network traces in [12]. The relationship of related videos on YouTube has been studied by Cheng et al in [4]. Their result shows that the related video graph on YouTube exhibits small-world characteristics and has a large clustering coefficient. In [3], Cha et al. study various aspects about video popularity and video view on YouTube. They propose to use the history of video view to predict video popularity in near future. Our work compliments their work by showing that there is a correlation between a video's view count and its related videos' view count, and this should be another factor to consider in predicting video popularity.

Several previous works study the impact of recommendation system on the user behavior and the improvement for the recommendation system. In [5] and [6], Fleder and Hosanagar use analytical model and simulation to study the impact of the recommender on sales diversity. In [11], Zhou et al. propose the recommendation systems that aim to achieve both diversity and accuracy.

The propagation of video views to its related videos is related to influence spreading in social networks. Leskovec et al. study the influence patterns in user-to-user recommendation network in [8]. Zhao et al. present several mathematical models of influence spreading in [10].

7. CONCLUSION

In this paper, we perform a measurement study on the impact of related video recommendation system on video views. Through the measurement of view sources, we find that the related video recommendation accounts for about 30% of overall views. Moreover, it is the most important view source for the majority of videos. By investigating how video views are driven by the recommendation system, we find a strong correlation between the view count of a video and the average view count of its top referrer videos, and also discover that the position of a video on a related video list plays a critical role in the click through rate of the video. Finally, the evaluation of the impact of the video recommendation system on the diversity of video views shows that the existence of YouTube recommendation helps to increase the diversity of video views in aggregation, which means that YouTube recommendation helps viewers discover more videos of their interest rather than the popular videos only.

8. ACKNOWLEGEMENTS

The authors are grateful to the anonymous reviewers for their helpful comments and suggestions. This work is partially supported by U.S. NSF grants CNS-066618. Renjie Zhou was a visiting student at University of Massachusetts, Amherst, supported by China Scholarship Council, when this work was performed.

9. REFERENCES

[1] Google adwords click through rates per position. http://www.accuracast.com/seo-weekly/adwords-clickthrough.php, October 2009.

[2] S. Axon. Youtube to let users charge rental fees. http://www.cnn.com/2010/TECH/05/03/youtube.rental/index.html, May 2010.

[3] M. Cha, H. Kwak, P. Rodriguez, Y. Ahn, and S. Moon. I Tube, You Tube, Everybody Tubes: Analyzing the World's Largest User Generated Content Video System. In *Proceedings of ACM Internet measurement Conference(IMC), San Diego, CA, USA*, October 2007.

[4] X. Cheng, C. Dale, and J. Liu. Statistics and social network of youtube videos. In *International Workshop on Quality of Service (IWQoS'08)*, pages 229–238. IEEE, June 2008.

[5] D. Fleder and K. Hosanagar. Recommender systems and their impact on sales diversity. In *Proceedings of the 8th ACM conference on Electronic commerce*, page 199. ACM, 2007.

[6] D. Fleder and K. Hosanagar. Blockbuster culture's next rise or fall: The impact of recommender systems on sales diversity. *Management Science*, 55(5):697–712, 2009.

[7] P. Gill, Z. Li, M. Arlitt, and A. Mahanti. Characterizing Users Sessions on YouTube. In *Proceedings of SPIE/ACM Conference on Multimedia Computing and Networking (MMCN), Santa Clara, USA*, January 2008.

[8] J. Leskovec, A. Singh, and J. Kleinberg. Patterns of influence in a recommendation network. In *Pacific-Asia Conference on Knowledge Discovery and Data Mining (PAKDD*, pages 380–389. Springer-Verlag, 2005.

[9] P. White. How many videos are on youtube? http://www.associatedcontent.com/article/1927414/how_many_videos_are_on_youtube.html?cat=15, July 2009.

[10] B. Zhao, Y. Li, J. Lui, and D. Chiu. Mathematical Modeling of Advertisement and Influence Spread in Social Networks. In *NetEcon:Workshop on the Economics of Networks, Systems and Computation*, 2009.

[11] T. Zhou, Z. Kuscsik, J. Liu, M. Medo, J. Wakeling, and Y. Zhang. Solving the apparent diversity-accuracy dilemma of recommender systems. *Proceedings of the National Academy of Sciences*, 107(10):4511, 2010.

[12] M. Zink, K. Suh, Y. Gu, and J. Kurose. Watch Global, Cache Local: YouTube Network Traffic at a Campus Network - Measurements and Implications. In *Proceedings of SPIE/ACM Conference on Multimedia Computing and Networking (MMCN), Santa Clara, USA*, January 2008.

Selecting Representative IP Addresses for Internet Topology Studies*

Xun Fan
USC/Information Sciences Institute
4676 Admiralty Way, Suite 1001
Marina del Ray, CA, 90292
xunfan@isi.edu

John Heidemann
USC/Information Sciences Institute
4676 Admiralty Way, Suite 1001
Marina del Ray, CA, 90292
johnh@isi.edu

ABSTRACT

An *Internet hitlist* is a set of addresses that cover and can *represent* the the Internet as a whole. Hitlists have long been used in studies of Internet topology, reachability, and performance, serving as the destinations of traceroute or performance probes. Most early topology studies used manually generated lists of prominent addresses, but evolution and growth of the Internet make human maintenance untenable. Random selection scales to today's address space, but most random addresses fail to respond. In this paper we present what we believe is the first automatic generation of hitlists informed censuses of Internet addresses. We formalize the desirable characteristics of a hitlist: *responsiveness*, each representative responds to pings; *completeness*, they cover all the allocated IPv4 address space; and *stability*, list evolution is minimized when possible. We quantify the accuracy of our automatic hitlists, showing that only one-third of the Internet allows informed selection of representatives. Of informed representatives, 50–60% are likely to respond three months later, and we show that causes for non-responses are likely due to dynamic addressing (so no stable representative exists) or firewalls. In spite of these limitations, we show that the use of informed hitlists can add 1.7 million edge links (a 5% growth) to traceroute-based Internet topology studies Our hitlists are available free-of-charge and are in use by several other research projects.

Categories and Subject Descriptors

C.2.1 [**Computer-Communication Networks**]: Network Architecture and Design—*Network topology*; C.2.5 [**Computer-Communication Networks**]: Local and Wide-Area Networks—*Internet*; C.2.6 [**Computer-Communication Networks**]: Internetworking

*This work is partially supported by US DHS contract number NBCHC080035, and John Heidemann by NSF grant number CNS-0626696. The conclusions of this work are those of the authors and do not necessarily reflect the views of DHS or NSF.

IMC '10, November 1–3, 2010, Melbourne, Australia.

General Terms

Measurement

Keywords

Internet topology, Topology Representatives, IP Hitlist

1. INTRODUCTION

Smooth operation of the Internet is important to the global economy, so it is essential that Internet users, providers, and policy makers understand its performance and robustness. Although on the surface, individuals care only about their personal performance, a full diagnosis of "why is my web connection slow?" must consider not just the user's "first mile" connection, but dozens of servers that affect performance [9]. Web content providers invest great effort in optimizing page load times to sub-second values [23] and in building distributed content distribution networks that manage traffic (for example, [14]). Policy makers debate questions about universal access [33], a nation's relative availability for broadband access [24], and the robustness of what is recognized as critical infrastructure.

To answer these questions, network researchers, operations, and industry have developed a number of tools to map the Internet [17, 15, 26, 20, 22, 8], evaluate performance [32, 20, 23], consider questions about routing and reachability [31, 3], or the performance of replica placement (examples include [32, 10]), and evaluate topology robustness [1]. With the Internet's lack of centralization and multiple overlapping global "backbones", active probing plays an essential role in this process, with traceroute and ping and their variants providing the main source of router-level reachability. While one may add AS-level views [4], the Internet's router-level topology is the focus of this paper. Different router-level studies either target specific networks [26] or the whole Internet. Here we are most interested in observing the whole Internet—more than three billion allocated IPv4 addresses.

Studies of the entire Internet typically employ a *hitlist*—a list of IP address that can *represent* the billions of allocated addresses. The defining characteristic of a a hitlist is *completeness*, where a representative is chosen for every autonomous system or, in our case, for every allocated *block* of addresses defined by a /24 prefix, the smallest unit typically present in a default-free routing table. Representatives provide a 256-fold (or more) reduction in scanning size, allowing Internet-wide studies to take place in hours instead of months.

Although completeness is necessary to study the whole Internet, an ideally hitlist is also responsive and stable. A *responsive* representative replies to ICMP messages, allowing traceroute to confirm a path to the edge of the network, and ping to measure round-trip time to an edge host. To support longitudinal studies, the hitlist should be *stable*, with representative identities not changing frequently or arbitrarily.

Although hitlists are easy to define and have been used in topology studies for many years (we review related work in Section 2), they are surprisingly hard to create and maintain. Early hitlists were built manually from well known sites [20], but the size of the Internet and rate of churn in even well-known servers made manual maintenance untenable as it quickly became incomplete. More recent studies have typically used randomly chosen representatives. While randomness has some advantages (it can be statistically unbiased), it sacrifices secondary goals of stability and responsiveness.

The contribution of this paper is to provide a new, automated method of hitlist generation that provides complete coverage while maximizing stability and responsiveness.[1] Our hitlists are constructed (Section 3) by mining data from IP address censuses, complete, ping-based enumerations of the allocated IPv4 address space taken every two to three months [18].

The second contribution of our work is to evaluate our hitlists (Section 4). Our hitlists are 100% complete as of when they are constructed, although when we have no history (in about two-thirds of the blocks) we select representatives at random. We define the *accuracy* of our hitlists has how many representatives are responsive three months after the hitlist is taken. We find that two-thirds of the allocated address space never responds to ICMP probes and so never has responsive representatives. Of the remaining, responsive Internet, our hitlists select representatives that are responsive about 55% of the time. To our knowledge we are the first to study hitlist responsiveness and accuracy.

The final contribution of our work is what hitlists reveal about that nature of the Internet itself. We were surprised that, in spite of such complete input data, the responsiveness of our predicted representatives is not higher. We believe this upper bound on responsiveness characterizes the portion of the Internet that has an inherently high rate of address churn. One corollary of this limit to representative responsiveness is that no manual system could ever have been successful due to natural turnover of addresses in parts of the network. We also characterize the distribution of addresses in each block and show that it strongly reflects address allocation patterns (Section 5).

We make our hitlists available free-of-charge, and they are already being used by several research projects. In Section 6 we discuss the security and policy issues involved in sharing this data.

2. RELATED WORK

Hitlists are used in active probing for studies of topology [17, 15, 19, 26, 30, 22, 25, 8], performance [32, 20, 23], and reachability [31, 4]. and for other purposes [32, 1, 10]. Each of these studies uses some hitlist (sometimes called a seed or probe list) generated manually, randomly, or automated from several sources. We review each hitlist generation method next.

Early topology work used manually generated lists. Skitter is a well-known measurement tool developed at CAIDA, to study the IPv4-interface-level of the core Internet topology [19]. (With IP alias resolution, this can provide a router-level map.) It uses traceroutes from multiple locations to a hitlist of destinations. Their target address list was manually built from many sources, including tcpdump from the UCSD–CERF link, hostnames from search engines, and intermediate addresses seen from their own traces records. In 2000 their hitlist included about 313,000 destinations, and by 2004 it had grown to 971,080. While their hitlist was of high quality, they found it very labor-intensive to maintain, and responsiveness degraded over time as destinations changed. (They report that their initial, web-server based list shows a 2–3% reduction each month in reachable destinations [19].) The cost of manual list maintenance was one reason that prompted them to change to random probing with Archipelago. More recently, Maennel has maintained a manual list, derived from the Skitter list, but augmented with guided scanning to cover each AS and provide 306,708 representatives. They require reachable addresses study routing reachability [4]. We used a version of their list to seed our initial stable list, but our techniques provide much greater coverage at lower cost. Unlike all of these manual hitlists, our goal is to fully automate hitlist generation to allowing more complete and timely coverage.

Random representative selection allows low-cost generation of hitlists to much larger numbers of networks. Mercator developed *informed random probing* to adaptively adjust its probe list based on prior results [17]. By adaptively growing the hitlist, Mercator strives to quickly and efficiently discover a topology while minimizing hitlist size. Archipelago (Ark) is a measurement platform designed to support traceroute and other measurements [8], effectively a next-generation Skitter. Ark's hitlist covers all routed /24 blocks, choosing a random last-octet within each /24 block, The random hitlists in Mercator and Ark are essential to cover the millions of /24 networks in today's Internet, but Mercator's adaptive algorithm means completeness is uncertain (although efficiency, not completeness, was their goal), and random probing in both Mercator and Ark may sacrifice responsiveness of the destination address. Our hitlist provides complete coverage while maximizing responsiveness (both defined precisely in Section 3.1). In Section 4.5 we evaluate the degree to which informed hitlist generation may improve the number of links discovered in a topology study.

Rather than a random destination, DisCarte's hitlist selects the .1 address in each /24 block of the routed address space. DisCarte [25] adds record route information to traceroute probing to obtain more accurate and complete network topologies. DisCarte requires a responsive destination, and find 376,408 responsive representatives in the .1 address of each routed /24. Our work confirms that the .1 address is responsive twice as often as the address with median responsiveness (Section 5), but we suggest that census-informed representative selection can get much better responsiveness.

Finally, there has been some work in IPv6 topology discovery. The Atlas system uses a manually generated list built from 6bone destinations [30], then expanded it based on discoveries. The full address-space census that is the ba-

[1]We would like to thank Randy Bush for suggesting the idea that our address censuses data could support hitlist generation.

sis of our work is only applicable to the IPv4 address space, so combinations of active and passive methods as proposed in Atlas are essential for IPv6. As future work, comparison of both active and passive hitlist generation approaches in the IPv4 space may provide a basis for inferring coverage of passive studies of IPv6.

3. METHODOLOGY

We next describe the requirements of an IP hitlist (Section 3.1), and how we transform census data (reviewed in Section 3.2) using several possible prediction methods (Section 3.3) to get a good quality hitlist. We also provide some details on how our implementation copes with Internet-sized datasets.

3.1 Hitlist Requirements

Our goal is to provide representatives that are responsive, complete and stable.

By *responsive*, we mean each representative is likely to respond to an echo request with an echo reply instead of an ICMP error code. As we describe below, we select representatives that have responded frequently in the past. We do not guarantee that that address responded in the most recent census, but we bias our selection to favor recent results. We consider several prediction functions below in Section 3.3.

By *complete*, we mean we report one representative address for every allocated /24 block. Some groups have used other definitions of completeness, such as one representative per AS, or per routed BGP block. AS- or BGP-complete hitlists will be both sparser and smaller than /24-complete maps, since ASes typically include routes for many prefixes, and routed prefixes often cover blocks larger than /24s. Instead, we select one representative for each /24 block for two reasons. The main reason is so that the hitlist is decoupled from the routing system, to allow independent study of the routing system itself, and since routing tables vary depending on when and where they are taken. Second, it is relatively easy for researchers to derive custom hitlist from ours, perhaps selecting sparser representatives per AS or per routed prefix. We believe our per-/24 representatives thus provide a more general and reusable result than more "cooked" alternatives.

By *stable*, we mean that representatives do not change arbitrarily. We change representatives when a new representative would significantly improve the score for that block, typically because a representative has ceased to be reachable. We promote stability as a goal to simplify longitudinal studies, where frequent changes of representative would make comparisons across time more difficult. Stability also reduces the effects of transient routing outages or packet loss on the long-term hitlist. We implement stability by applying *inertia* as a threshold to changing a previously selected representative. Currently we switch representatives when the switch will improve its score significantly, with inertia of 0.34 (see Section 4.3).

The three goals of responsiveness, completeness, and stability can be in conflict. For example, completeness requires that we select representatives that may be non-responsive. To guarantee representatives for all allocated addresses, we select representatives even for blocks that have no recent responses. We also select representative for blocks that have never responded. In both cases, we annotate these representatives with distinguished scores. Stability and inertia can also decrease responsiveness; in Section 4.3 we examine how the inertia threshold reduces churn and how it affects responsiveness.

Censuses	Date	Duration (days)
it11w	2006-03-07	23
it12w	2006-04-13	24
it13w	2006-06-16	31
it14w	2006-09-14	31
it15w	2006-11-08	61
it16w	2007-02-14	50
it17w	2007-05-29	52
it18w	2007-09-14	47
it19w	2007-12-18	48
it20w	2008-02-29	86
it21w	2008-06-17	49
it22w	2008-09-11	35
it23w	2008-11-25	29
it24w	2009-02-03	29
it25w	2009-03-19	29
it26w	2009-05-27	31
it27w	2009-07-27	25
it28w	2009-09-14	30
it29w	2009-11-02	30
it30w	2009-12-23	29
it31w	2010-02-08	30
it32w	2010-03-29	29

Table 1: IPv4 censuses [29] used in this paper.

3.2 Background: Internet censuses

Our main goal with a hitlist is to predict the future: a representative should be responsive in the future. Our tool to make this prediction is data from past responses. Hitlists selection leverages Internet censuses that have been taken regularly since 2003 [18].

Each Internet census is the results of a ping (an ICMP ECHO REQUEST message) sent to every allocated IPv4 address. Censuses are far from perfect: a census must be taken carefully to avoid ICMP rate limiting or transient router errors, and firewalls reduce ping response rates by around 40%. Hitlist, however, prefer hosts that are ICMP responsive, since traceroute consists of iterated, TTL-limited ICMP messages. Firewall-limited censuses are therefore ideal for hitlist generation.

It takes 2–3 months to carry out a full census (the IPv4 space has more than 3 billion allocated unicast addresses, with 4 machines probing at about 6000 probes/s [18]). For this paper we consider censuses starting in Mar 2006 as shown in Table 1, since censuses before this date used a slightly different collection methodology. The results of this paper use all 22 censuses taken over the four years preceding analysis, but we expect to update our results as new censuses become available.

A census elicits a number of responses, including ECHO REPLY messages as well as a variety of errors. Each census is quite large, and more than 3 billion records per census, 22 censuses is over 260GB of raw data. We therefore preprocess all censuses into a *history map* convenient for analysis. A history map consists of a bitstring for each IP address where each 1 indicates a positive response, and a 0 indicates either a non-response or negative response.

In paper, we only consider echo replies ("positive" responses) as indicating a responsive address. We also explored treating both positive and negative responses (destination unreachable and similar error replies) as predicting a responsive address. However, we found that negative replies only rarely are helpful in predicting future responsiveness. We look at it28w and found 64% of positive responses were also responsive in the next census (165M in it28w, 107M of which respond in it29w). By contrast, of the 50M negative replies in it28w, only 2.7% (1.4M) respond positively in it29w. We therefore believe that negative responses are of little value in predicting future responsiveness.

We next show how this history map can predict future response rates.

3.3 Prediction Method

Of our hitlist goals of responsiveness, completeness, and stability, completeness and stability are under our control, but responsiveness requires predicting the future. Our guidance in this task is the prior history of each address. We next review several *prediction functions* that strive to select the best representative for each /24 block, where best is most likely to respond in the future.

Prediction functions take the prior history of address a as input and weights that history in different ways. Each bit of the history is presented by $r_i(a)$, the response (1 for positive, otherwise 0) of address a to the ith probe, numbered from 0 (oldest) to $N_h - 1$, the most recent observation. We consider several different weights $w(i)$ to get the scores $s(a)$ in the form:

$$s(a) = \sum_{i=0}^{N_h-1} r_i(a)w(i)$$

For each block of addresses, the address with the highest $s(a)$ is selected as the best representative. We may bias this by prior representatives to promote stability. In the case of ties and no prior representative we select any top scoring address in the block at random.

We considered several possible weights $w(i)$. The simplest is $w(i) = 1$, so all responses are *averaged*. To give more recent observations greater influence we consider two biased weights. With *linear* weighting, $w(i) = (i + 1) * 1/N_h$, and for a *power* function, $w(i) = \frac{1}{N_h - i}$. Weighting of each observation for an 8-observation history is shown in Figure 1.

In addition, we can normalize scores by to the maximum possible score (the minimum in all cases is zero), allowing all to fall in the range 0 to 1.

As an example of the different functions, Figure 2 shows scores for three different weights and different history lengths. For simplicity, we assume $N_h = 8$, shorter than we use in practice (in Section 4.1.2 we vary history duration). We consider three cases, all with 4 of 8 responding, but either responding most recently (Figure 2a), in the middle past (Figure 2b), or alternating response and non-response (Figure 2c). To a first approximation, all three weights are about the same, particularly with intermittent responsiveness in Figure 2c. The differences in decay rates are more obvious when responsiveness is consistent for blocks of time, with power and linear decay faster than average in Figures 2a and 2b. Finally, difference in history duration make a large difference when a block is non-responsive, comparing the left and right parts of Figures 2a and 2b, and these effects are even greater when comparing across weights (for example, compare history durations 1–4 of Figures 2a and 2b).

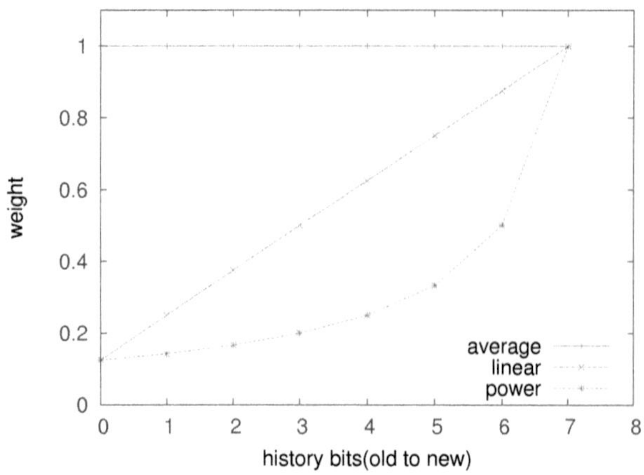

Figure 1: bits weight for different function

This framework provides flexibility, but requires setting several parameters. We later evaluate which weighting is best (Section 4.1.1), how much history is beneficial (Section 4.1.2), and the underlying reasons addresses are difficult to predict (Section 4.1.3).

3.4 Gone-Dark Blocks

Firewalls are probably the greatest impediment to active probing, since a conservative firewall can suddenly stop traffic an entire block. We will see in Section 4.1.3 that *gone dark* blocks are one cause of poor representative responsiveness. A gone-dark blocks is one that contained responsive addresses for some period of time, but then becomes unresponsive and stays that way, due to firewall or possibly renumbering. While we must select a representative for each allocated block, even if populated only by non-responsive addresses, we would like to indicate our low expectations for gone-dark blocks.

We define a block as *gone dark within history* N_d if, for the most recent N_d observations, no address in the block responded, even though we had some positive response before N_d observations.

We add gone-dark analysis to our hitlist generation by overriding the representative's score with a designated "gone-dark" value to indicate our skepticism that it will reply. We explored different values of N_d and ultimately select $N_d = N_h = 16$, identifying only those addresses whose responses have aged-out of our history as gone-dark. We use this large value of N_d because this value maximizes the absolute number of responsive representatives, while only decreasing the percentage of responsive, predicted representatives a small amount.

For gone-dark blocks, we still select the representative as the address with the best score. For allocated but never-responsive blocks, we select the .1 address as the representative because that is most likely to be first used (Section 5). In Section 4.1.3 we show the contribution of gone-dark blocks to responsiveness.

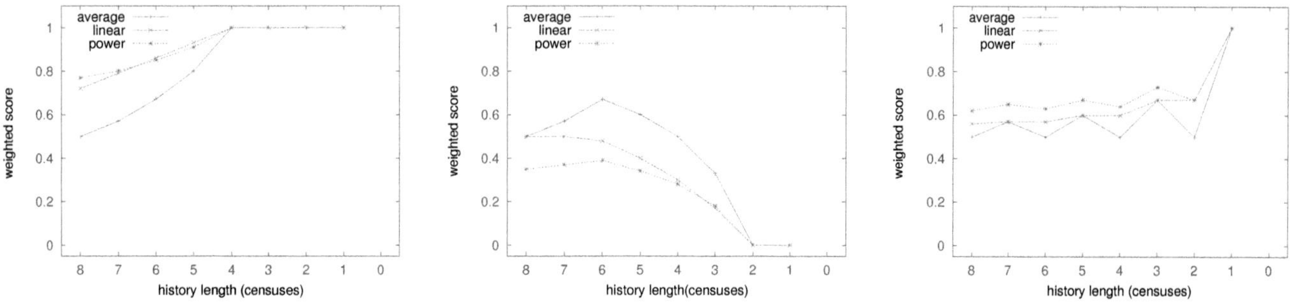

(a) 0000 1111. (b) 0011 1100. (c) 0101 0101.

Figure 2: Comparison of three history functions for selected addresses.

3.5 Hitlist Description

To summarize, our hitlist contain three kind of representatives for all allocated /24 blocks: informed and predicted representatives, where we select the best responder; gone-dark representatives, where some address once responded but has not recently; and allocated but never-responsive blocks, where we pick .1 as the representative.

Table 6 lists the hitlists we have publicly released to-date. We identify hitlists by the name of the last census used in their creation, and include the number of censuses in the history. Thus HL28/16 uses 16 hitlists through it28w. When necessary, we add the gone-dark window, so HL28/16-3 uses a window of 3. If no gone-dark window is specified, we disable gone-dark processing.

In addition to these public hitlists, Tables 2 and 3 show unreleased hitlists used to evaluate our methods.

4. EVALUATION

We next evaluate the success of our hitlist: how accurate are its predictions and how complete and stable is it? We first consider how responsiveness is affected by choices in our prediction mechanism. In Section 4.1.3 then look at causes of prediction failure. Finally, we consider completeness and stability.

4.1 Responsiveness

Our primary goal with prediction is *responsiveness*: how accuracy is our prediction that the representatives in a hitlist will respond in the future? We can define based on the number responding in the future, N_r, from the number of predicted representatives (including representatives of gone-dark and informed predicted blocks) N_p as:

$$\alpha = \frac{N_r}{N_p}$$

Responsiveness accuracy is affected by our choice of history weighting and length. We consider these next, and then consider structural reasons perfect accuracy is impossible to achieve.

Our general approach to test responsiveness is to generate a hitlist, then evaluate it against ICMP probes in the next census. For example, the first line of Table 2 evaluates HL19/8, generated from the eight censuses from it12w through it19w, tested against it20w. This approach has the advantage of supporting retroactive evaluation of hitlist

	weighting function		
hitlist	average	linear	power
HL19/8	0.50	0.51	0.51
HL21/8	0.53	0.54	0.55
HL23/8	0.53	0.54	0.54
HL25/8	0.53	0.54	0.54
HL27/8	0.54	0.55	0.55

Table 2: Fraction of responsive representatives across 5 different hitlists for three different history weights.

quality under different, controlled conditions. However, it also means each representative is only given one opportunity to be available. For this reason we report exact counts of results, without error estimates such as standard deviation. We evaluate repeatability of our results by considering multiple hitlists at different times.

4.1.1 Comparing History Weights

We first consider how our weighting of prior history affects accuracy. Here we assume a history duration of 8 prior censuses (a reasonable choice as evaluated next in Section 4.1.2), and from that history we predict the results of the next census for the three weights we defined in Section 3.3. Since the network is dynamic, our expectation is that biased weightings will perform best since they favor recent information over older information.

To answer this question, Table 2 compares our three weightings for several predictions. Each line evaluates a different hitlist as generated with three different weights, and evaluated for all predicted representatives (N_p). The most important observation is that *all weights* provide quite similar performance—the worst case responsiveness is only 5% worse than the best. Linear and power functions provide marginally better responsiveness. The examples of the weights in Figure 2 suggests on reason the difference is so small. For many histories, all three weights produce roughly the same relative scores.

4.1.2 Effects of History Duration

A second factor that can affect responsiveness is the duration of history considered in a prediction. Does more history provide more information, or does very old information become irrelevant or even misleading?

To study this question, we considered all history available to us at time of analysis—then we had 18 Internet censuses covering 3.5 years. We consider only the power weighting of history, and look at the responsiveness of our predictions.

Table 3 shows responsiveness of our predictions as a function of history length, for five predictions. We see that very short histories are insufficient: prediction rates are a 1–2% lower when fewer than 8 (about 1.5 years) observations are considered. On the other hand, we see no difference in prediction accuracy for histories from 8 to 16 censuses. (We also looked at history duration with the average function, and found there that long histories became slightly less accurate, although only by 1–2%. This observation argues in favor of a weighting that decays by history, like power.)

Finally, while longer histories may not improve the fraction that respond, it does provide information that allows *more* representatives to be selected. Table 3 shows the absolute number of responders as a function of history duration. Longer history allows 20k more responders with length 16 than with length 8. More history always increases the number responding, although with diminishing returns past a 12 censuses or so.

In practice, the incremental cost of longer history lengths is not large. So we use a history length of 16 censuses in our production lists.

Although 8 censuses provides slightly betters results, the faction responding, only 55%, seems lower than we might expect. We therefore next consider causes of non-responsiveness.

4.1.3 Causes of Failed Responses

We found the observation that our best methods get only 55% responsiveness seems somewhat surprising. Surely such a large amount of history (over three years of full censuses) can be explored somehow to select representatives with greater accuracy. To answer that question, we next explore the causes of why representatives fail to respond. Our conclusion is that *it is unlikely that any prediction can do better than about 70%* because of the use of dynamic address assignment and firewalls.

To support this claim, Table 4 counts prediction failures for HL28/16, tested against it29w (We found roughly similar results in examination of HL31/16 evaluated against it32w.) We see that 44% of representatives are non-responsive (1.8M of the 4M blocks). Two explanations account for the majority of our misses: blocks that use only dynamic address assignment, and "gone-dark" blocks. We consider each of these below.

While dynamic addressing and firewalls are target-specific causes of representative non-responsiveness, measurement error is a possible source of uncertainty. We believe that Internet census-taking methodology reduces these sources of error to random noise for reasons described in prior work [18]. To summarize briefly: we monitor the network hosting the probes for local routing outages. Probes are in pseudorandom order, so routing outages in the middle or near the destination result in lower responsiveness in proportion to outage rates, but randomly distributed. Pseudorandom probing is spread over two months, so the probe rate to any individual /24 is well below typical ICMP rate limits. We considered packet loss and routing outages in the middle or of the network or near probe sources are potential sources of error. For more complete discussion of sources of error in Internet census-taking, and validation studies, we refer to prior work [18].

Defining stable blocks: Blocks that lack stable addresses makes representative selection inherently difficult. In a block with a stable representative, it will likely remain responsive, but if all addresses in the block are unstable then the probability a representative will respond is equal to the occupancy of that block and independent of prior history. Addresses can lack stability either because the hosts using the addresses are only on intermittently, or because addresses in the block are allocated dynamically to a changing population of computers. Multiple groups have used different techniques to identify dynamically assigned addresses in the Internet [27, 34, 5]. A recent study estimates that about 40% of responsive Internet blocks are dynamic based on Internet address surveys using ICMP probes taken every 11 minutes for two weeks [5]. (We assume here that non-stable blocks are primarily due to dynamic addressing.)

To evaluate the prevalence of stable and non-stable blocks, we would like to identify them from the history that we collect. Prior analysis of surveys used address *availability* and *volatility* to identify dynamic addressing. Availability is the fraction of times the address responds in all probes, while volatility is the fraction of times the address changes between responsive and non-responsive [5]. While appropriate for survey data with 11-minute probes, volatility makes less sense when probes are months apart.

To identify stable blocks with infrequent probes, define a new metric, *truncated availability*, the fraction of time an address responds from its first positive response. More formally, if $r_i(a)$ is the response of address a to the ith probe, the raw and scaled availability, $A^*(a)$ and $A(a)$ (from [5]) and truncated availability, $A^t(a)$ are:

$$\begin{aligned} A^*(a) &= \sum_{1}^{N_h} r_i \\ A(a) &= A^*(a)/N_h \\ A^t(a) &= A^*(a)/L^*(a) \end{aligned}$$

where $L^*(a)$ is the length of a history, in observations, from the first positive response to the present.

While both volatility and truncated availability are correlated, we found that low volatility and high truncated availability are both good predictors a stable block. Low A^t values are a good predictor of intermittently used addresses. Continuing the examples in Figure 2, 00001111 has $A^t = 1$, while 01010101 has $A^t = 0.57$.

While A^t is good at differentiating between these solid (00001111) and intermittent (01010101) addresses, it interacts with gone-dark addresses, which will have a string of trailing 0s.

From these, we define a stable representative as $A^t \geq 0.9$. From Table 4 We find that 43% of all representatives are not stable by $A^t < 0.9$, a little higher than other independent observations 40% [5], and of 34–61% [34] (these values are for a random sample of DNS and for Hotmail users, respectively). We do not claim strong validation of this exact percentage because each work is a percentage of a different populations, and different definitions of what is dynamic or not stable. We claim only that our metric is in the right order of magnitude and so provides some insight into sources of non-responsive representatives.

hitlist	predicted representatives (N_p)	Responsive representatives and fraction 4	8	12	16
HL19/-	3,091,646 (100%)	1,558,620 (50%)	1,586,303 (51%)	—	—
HL21/-	3,386,540 (100%)	1,813,276 (54%)	1,846,019 (55%)	—	—
HL23/-	3,613,523 (100%)	1,925,322 (53%)	1,948,634 (54%)	1,950,960 (54%)	—
HL25/-	3,794,973 (100%)	2,007,138 (53%)	2,049,607 (54%)	2,059,019 (54%)	—
HL27/-	3,971,208 (100%)	2,135,337 (54%)	2,179,777 (55%)	2,193,062 (55%)	2,200,674 (55%)

Table 3: Responsive representatives with power weighting across 5 different hitlists for different history length.

	HL28/16			HL31/16		
predicted representatives (N_p)	4,055,193	100%		4,307,644	100%	
not stable	1,749,471	43%		1,820,806	42%	
gone dark	703,987	17%		772,014	18%	
responsive (N_r)	2,250,091	56%		2,560,420	59%	
non-responsive (N_n)	1,805,102	44%	[100%]	1,747,224	41%	[100%]
non-responsive and not stable (only)	590,472	14%	[33%]	565,654	13%	[32%]
non-responsive and gone dark only	0	0%	[0%]	0	0%	[0%]
non-responsive, not stable and gone-dark	693,832	17%	[38%]	766,338	18%	[44%]
non-responsive, just unlucky	520,798	13%	[29%]	415,232	10%	[24%]

Table 4: Causes of unsuccessful representatives predicted from HL28/16 and HL31/16, evaluated against responses in it29w and it32w. We don't apply gone-dark window on prediction here, gone-dark blocks are detected separately with gone-dark window size of 3.

Re-evaluating causes of non-responsive representatives: With these definitions, we return to Table 4. We see that both gone-dark and not-stable blocks contribute three-quarters of our misses. Almost one third are in not-stable only blocks, with almost 40% gone-dark. We therefore claim that three-quarters of our non-responses are due either to new firewalls or selection of representatives in not-stable blocks, neither of which can *ever* have always responsive representatives.

To support the claim that lower A^t values correlate with poorer response, Table 5 breaks out the 1.8M non-responsive representatives by two values of A^t. We see that 29% of non-responses come from stable blocks ($A^t > 0.9$). Representatives with poor truncated availability ($A^t < 0.9$) account for more than two-thirds of non-responses. We conclude there are many unstable blocks, such blocks simply cannot be expected to support stable representatives. Also note, by our definition of gone-dark, dark blocks also qualify as not stable (because $A^t < 0.9$).

To show our choice of threshold for A^t does not alter our conclusion, Figure 3 shows the cumulative distribution of A^t for both non-responsive and responsive representatives. It shows a large difference in responsiveness for any value of A^t.

4.2 Completeness

To evaluate completeness, Figure 4 shows the absolute number of representatives for using 16-deep histories through five different censuses, and Table 6 shows the raw data. We consistently see that about one-third of blocks have some history data allowing an informed selection of representatives (the white region of the graphs, with around 4.2M blocks). By contrast, about two-thirds of blocks have never responded (the top grey regions)

	non-responsive representatives
$A^t < 0.9$	1,284,304 (71%)
$A^t \geq 0.9$	520,798 (29%)
total	**1,805,102** (100%)

Table 5: Fraction of representatives that are non-responsive, based on A^t (HL28/16 tested against it29w).

In addition, this data shows gone-dark selection from Section 3.4. We identify about 0.3–1.5% of allocated blocks as formerly responsive (the black region in the middle of Figure 4).

To guarantee completeness, we select random representatives for never-responsive blocks. However, we can see that we can provide informed choices for only a third of blocks. Finally, we note that IANA only releases new allocation maps quarterly, and routing studies suggest this space becomes routable gradually [3], so we expect our hitlist to be useful for at least three months, about the frequency we update them.

4.3 Stability and Inertia

We next consider two aspects of hitlist stability: how much churn is there in the hitlist, with and without a representative inertia, and how much does inertia reduce prediction accuracy.

Recall that inertia is the amount I by which prediction score must improve to change representatives. An inertia $I = 0$ means we always pick the highest rank address in

class	HL28/16		HL29/16		HL30/16		HL31/16		HL32/16
allocated /24 blocks	12,774,056		12,774,056		12,905,128		13,036,541		13,167,613
never responding blocks	8,718,863		8,631,417		86,797,99		8,728,897		8,775,398
predicted blocks	4,055,193		4,142,639		4,225,329		4,307,644		4,392,215
gone-dark blocks	35,341		75,714		109,099		154180		195,216
informed prediction blocks	4,019,852	(100%)	4,066,925	(100%)	4,116,230	(100%)	4,153,464	(100%)	4,196,999
changed representatives	—	(5%)	218,419	(8%)	341,765	(7%)	292,079	(7%)	306,588
new representatives	—	(4%)	171,428	(2%)	82,690	(2%)	82,315	(2%)	84,571
responsiveness	2,250,091		2,344,539		2,411,662		2,451,351		—

Table 6: Released hitlists to-date, by last census used in prediction (top). The top group of rows show hitlist composition, including churn (changed) and new representatives relative to the prior hitlist. The bottom line, responsiveness, evaluates the hitlist against the census.

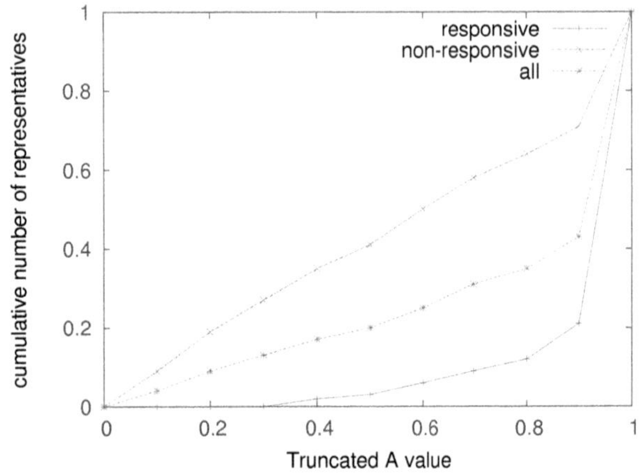

Figure 3: A^t cumulative distribution on responsive part of N_p, non-responsive part of N_p and all N_p

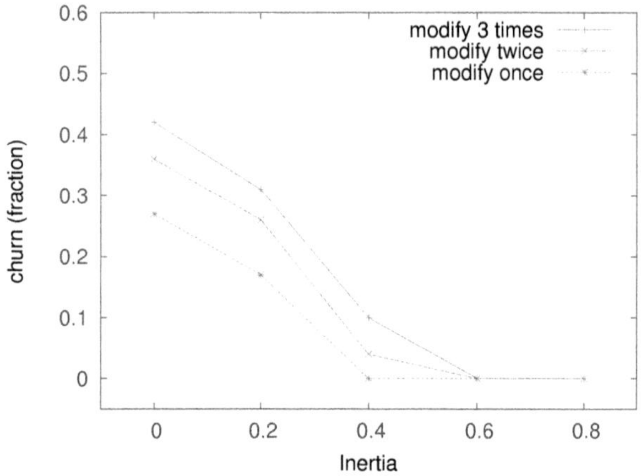

Figure 5: Effects of different inertia on representative churn (HL28/16 modified three times by it29w through it31w; modified twice by it29w, it30w; and once by only it29w).

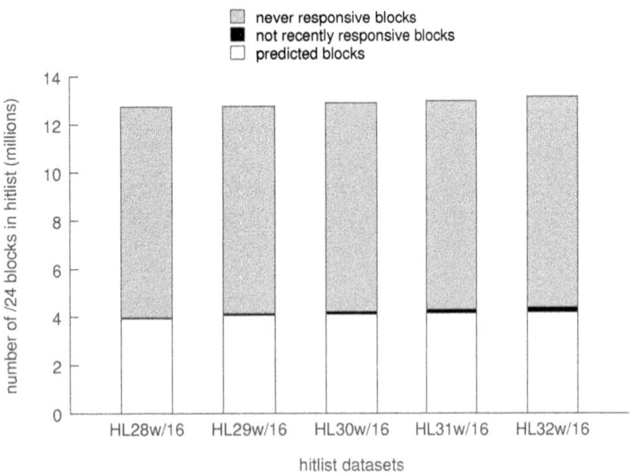

Figure 4: Relative size of hitlist components.

a block as the representative, independent of the representative in a hitlist based on a prior censuses. As inertia approaches 1, we will never switch representatives once chosen. For our production hitlists, we use $I = 0.34$ based on score changes due to weighting (Section 4.1.1) and the following analysis.

Inertia on churn: We first consider how much inertia affects churn. Churn is that rate at which we switch representatives for established blocks. Table 6 shows the amount of churn for four hitlists when using our standard inertia $I = 0.34$. Churn is shown in the "changed representatives" row, so in the HL32/16 column, we see that about 7% of all predictions (306,588 representatives) changed relative to the prior hitlist (HL31/16)). This Table 6 shows that the rate of churn is relatively stable over time, with 5–7% of all informed predictions changing each census.

While Table 6 shows churn over time for a fixed inertia, in Figure 5 we vary inertia to observe its effect on churn. To estimate the relationship shown in this figure, we generate HL28/16, then modify it three times with censuses it29w, it30w, and it31w with different levels of inertia. (Here we suspend gone-dark processing to focus only on inertia.) We then evaluate the hitlist against observations from census it32w. We evaluate inertia over several steps for two reasons. First, hitlist staleness is partially a function of time. Second, large values of inertia suppress changes in single or a few censuses.

As expected, Figure 5 shows that higher inertia suppresses churn, because it takes several new negative responses for a representative's score to change. In fact, weight selection means score can change only by 0.3 from one new census,

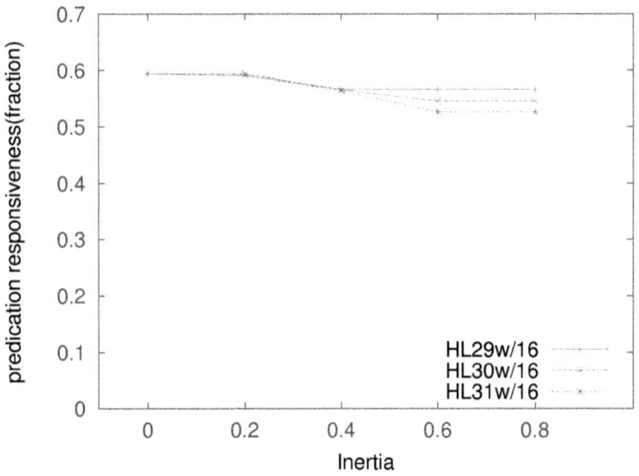

Figure 6: Effects of different inertia on responsiveness (HL28/16; modified once by it29w, then tested against it30w; modified twice by it29w, and it30w, then test against it31w; then modified three times by it29w through it31w and tested against it32w).

and decrease to 0.5 from two new censuses since the weight decrease in our pow weighting, so with three new observations here, an inertia of 0.2 has one observations that might cause change, while $I = 0.4$ has two; $I = 0.6$, three; and $I = 0.8$ requires more than eight observations to change.

Inertia on responsiveness: Inertia is selected to keep hitlists stable, reducing the amount of arbitrary representative turnover in long-running experiments. Such turnover can be eliminated by simply never changing representatives (setting $I = 1$), but prior experience shows that the responsiveness of a static hitlist will degrade over time as servers move, losing as much as 2–3% per month for the early Skitter web-server-based list [19]. We would therefore like to know the trade-off between inertia and representative responsiveness.

Figure 6 shows hitlist responsiveness for different values of inertia after this process. (This analysis was generated with the same multi-step process as Figure 5 described above.) We see that responsiveness degrades slightly for high inertia values, from 59% responsiveness with no inertia, to a low of 53% responsiveness when $I = 0.8$, when there are effectively no changes. We conclude that a moderate inertia has little effect on responsiveness costing at most 6 percentage points, even over eight months.

4.4 Effects of Probe Frequency

Hitlists are based on periodic censuses, so an important operational question is how the frequency of such censuses affect the quality of the hitlists. Intuitively, more frequent sampling can provide more information on address responsiveness, resulting in better predictions. Our current censuses are taken every two to three months (Table 1). More more frequent collection is possible, but should be justified because data collection entails some operational cost.

While Internet censuses cover the whole Internet very few months, we also have access to surveys that probe 1% of the Internet every 11 minutes for two weeks [18]. Here we turn to these much more frequent probes to evaluate the effects of different probe rates. A survey has about 1800

Probe Frequency	Responsive Representatives
Survey, 12 hours	15,484 (68%)
24 hours	15,362 (67%)
48 hours	15,197 (66%)
HL30/16 (3-months)	16,123 (70%)
total blocks analyzed	**22,861 (100%)**

Table 7: Prediction accuracy (in responsiveness) from different probe frequencies, for a given number of /24 blocks.

observations, but we downsample this information to get observations every 12, 24, or 48 hours, providing 28, 14, and 7 bits of history. We use survey 30 (taken at the same time as it30w in Dec., 2009) to do prediction, and test it against it31w. We use the average weighting function to evaluate these observations, since it seems unnecessary to favor recent observations when all are taken of a short, two-week period. In addition, in Section 4.1.1 we showed that weighting has relatively little effect on responsiveness. We then test the prediction from this history against the next census (it31w) to evaluate prediction accuracy. We compare the representatives found from the survey with those computed in HL30/16.

Table 7 compares responsiveness as a function of probe frequency. First, we see that, of the survey-derived hitlists, more frequent probing provides a slightly better prediction (68% responsive from 12-hour samples vs. 66% for 48 hours). This small improvement is because more frequent probing gives more information on host responsiveness. Second, we see that the census-derived hitlist is a better prediction than any of the survey-derived hitlists, by 2–4%. The main source of this difference is that the survey's hitlist finds some addresses that don't appear in the census-derived hitlist. These addresses seems less stable in the next census because the survey-derived hitlist considers only a short period of history, while the census-based hitlist considers many months history and so finds long-term stable addresses, if they exist. In addition, because our survey observations are taken at specific times of day, they may discover addresses that are only up during particular daily hours, while evaluating against the next census tests at random times of day.

4.5 Effects on Other Research

The above sections evaluate hitlists based on our goals: responsiveness, completeness, and stability. But hitlists are a tool to enable other research, so their ultimate benefits come by how they improve the quality of other network performance and topology studies.

Some network performance studies *require* responsiveness in their destinations. These studies include those that evaluate performance [32, 20, 23], consider questions about routing and reachability [31, 3], or the performance of replica placement (examples include [32, 10]). For studies that require end-to-end latency measurements, our representative selection methods optimize reachability within the constraints of sparse measurement. Our work also suggests directions for potential improvements: more frequent measurement could potentially better track reachable addresses in dynamically assigned blocks. In addition, our approach to stability assists evaluation of long-term performance trends.

Responsiveness is helpful but not essential for many other topology studies (such as [17, 15, 26, 20, 22, 8]). Most topology studies employ traceroutes to study *paths* across the Internet. A traceroute attempts to discover all IP addresses on the path towards a destination, and many such paths are aggregated with alias elimination [17, 26, 21] to produce a router-level map. However, in such studies, the presence or absence of the destination itself affects only the last hop. Topology studies thus *do not require* responsive representatives, but they may benefit from responsiveness. However, many have moved towards the use random or deterministically selected representatives. As one example, topology probing in Skitter [20] began with a manually generated hitlist, but later shifted to random probing in Archipelago [8]. Two reasons for this shift were difficulty in maintaining a responsive hitlist and the recognition that responsive targets are not essential.

Although responsiveness is not essential for topology studies that focus on the core of the Internet, it is important for studies that wish to explore the *edge* of the network. We can get a rough estimate on the number of edge links that are missed by randomly selected representatives: empirically, about 4–7% of the Internet responds to ICMP probes [18], so we expect that 93% of random representatives will not respond (approximating the distribution of responders as uniform, to get a rough estimate). If 55% of our hitlists respond, that will improve edge detection for 38% of blocks. With 1.3 million allocated /24 blocks (as of Nov. 2009), statistics suggest that responsive hitlists will detect about *630,000 additional* links compared to those found using a random hitlist. Some topology studies examining the core of the Internet find about 33M links, so this increases the size of the discovered Internet topology by 2% [6]. This simple analysis ignores correlation in the data, so it is only approximate.

To confirm this simple analysis, we consider CAIDA's Internet Topology Data Kit (ITDK-2010-01 [6]). ITDK combines the results of traceroutes from many traceroutes with alias resolution [17, 8] to produce a router-level map of the Internet. ITDK is formed from 42 *cycles* of data, each representing a traceroute to a randomly chosen representative in each /24 prefix.

Unfortunately, we cannot directly evaluate ITDK with different approaches to representative selection because it is the result of several levels of processing (aggregation of multiple cycles of data, and duplicate and alias elimination). In addition, direct comparison would be somewhat misleading since the goal of ITDK is to map the Internet's core, not edges. Instead, we obtained the raw IPv4 topology data [7] used to generate ITDK. We then compare the results of one cycle with random representatives, to using what we expect would have resulted using our HL29/16 (based on censuses from 2007 through Dec. 2009). We can evaluate the responsiveness of randomly selected representatives by looking at the raw data, while we test hitlist responsiveness by comparing to it30w completed in Jan. 2010. (Here report these results comparing to a single cycle, #739, of the raw IPv4 data. We got very similar results comparing to cycles 740 and 741.)

Table 8 summarizes our observations. First, we see that we only have data to make predictions for just under half of the blocks (N_p of 4,008,861). For the remaining 51%, we too fall back on random probing. (We actually predict about 100k additional prefixes because we use a more recent routing table compared to the IPv4 raw data, however, we omit these from the table to provide a more fair comparison.)

Second, we see that random probing finds responsive addresses about 9% of the time. This result is somewhat better than we predict (4-7% [18]), a difference probably because our prediction is over all allocated blocks, but here we study only *routable* blocks, and non-routable blocks cannot possibly predict representatives.

Finally, we find about 1.7 million additional edges if we use our hitlist compared to random probing, about 2.4× more edge links than random probing alone finds. For studies of edge links, this is a significant amount of additional coverage. Compared to the 33M links found in ITDK-2010-01, this use of informed probing would discover about 5% greater coverage. However, care must be taken in making this comparison for several reasons. First, ITDK is composed of 42 cycles, while we compare to only a single cycle. Because each cycle probes a different random destination, total coverage will improve as it eventually finds responsive destinations by chance. (In fact, with enough cycles, random probing may provide better coverage as it converges on probing all possible addresses.) Second, it is important to note that ITDK is designed to study the Internet core, not the edges, and this goal is well met with random probing alone. However, our results show they could get additional coverage with no additional probing effort by changing to representatives selected with a method such as ours.

4.6 Cost of Hitlist Generation

Finally, turning from hitlist quality, we consider the cost of generating hitlists. Hitlists are generated from a number of Internet censuses. We therefore review the cost of taking a census and then look at the cost of processing censuses to produce a hitlist.

Hitlists require Internet censuses as input. New censuses are started every two to three months; during most of that time four machines are actively probing the Internet, while there is a week or two of setup and data curation time at the beginning and end of a census [18]. Each census currently requires 12–15GB of archival storage Censuses are carried out as part of an ongoing Internet topology research project and are used for multiple purposes, but if carried out exclusively for hitlist generation they would represent an ongoing cost.

Processing hitlist from census data incurs several ongoing costs. First, we maintain a master history file with bitmaps of all censuses to date, indexed by IP address. Each census creates an observation file with about 1–2GB of new positive observations. We merge observations into an ongoing history file of all observations to date. Currently 22 observation files (32GB total) are merged into one 7.5GB history file, and the size of that file grows by about 300MB every new census.

We parallelize our computation with the Hadoop implementation [11] of map/reduce [12], running over a cluster of about 40 computers with about 120 CPU cores. With this parallelism, join in a new census into an existing history takes about half an hour, and evaluation of a new hitlist takes about another half hour. (our code is written in Perl and not optimized for speed). Our map function groups

/24 routable blocks studied	8,248,027	100%	
no prediction ($\overline{N_p}$)	4,239,166	51%	
prediction (N_p)	4,008,861	49%	[100%]
responsive	2,454,500		[61%]
random probing responsive	730,496	9%	
random probing responsive also in N_p	725,930		[18%]
extra edges found	1,728,570	21%	[43%]

Table 8: Evaluation of random and informed representatives on destinations from one cycle of IPv4 traceroute data.

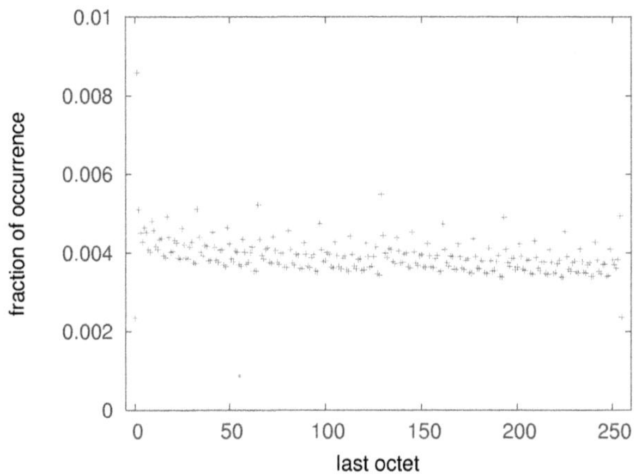

Figure 7: Frequency of responsiveness by last octet of the address (from it29w).

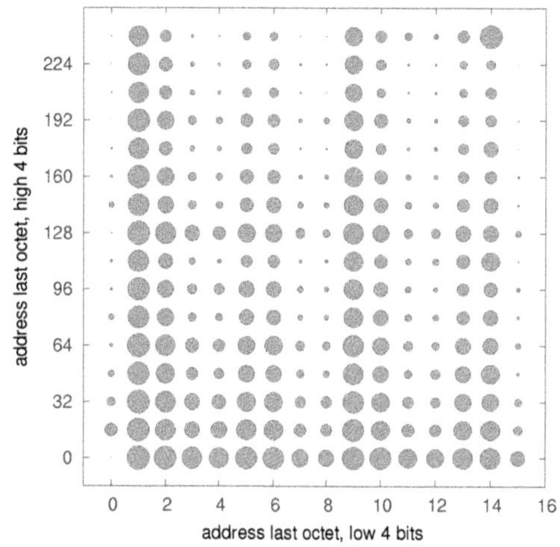

Figure 8: Rank (shown by circle area) of responsiveness by last octet, in a 16×16 grid by address (from it29w).

results by block, while the reducer carries out the join or evaluation.

5. OTHER OBSERVATIONS

Given no knowledge about a /24 block, which address is most likely to be responsive?[2] This question has some bearing on which representative we should select for gone-dark blocks, or for newly-allocated blocks with no census data yet.

Discussions with network operators suggest some network practices are common. Often addresses are allocated sequentially from the start of an block, and network managers often use the first or last address in a block for the routers. Since address blocks are allocated on powers-of-two according to CIDR [16], we expect to see uneven use of the address space. Recent work has confirmed visibility of allocation blocks in census data [5], but not last-octet usage.

To evaluate this question, Figure 7 shows the distribution of responsiveness for the last octet for all in it29w. (We got similar results on it28w and it30w censuses.) Consistent with expectation, the most responsive octet is .1, responding 0.86% of the time, more than twice as often as the median responsiveness (0.38%), and 1.5× more frequent than .129 (0.55%), the next most responsive last octet.

Figure 7 shows a pattern in responsiveness, with responses being most frequent at addresses that are one greater than a power of two. The top ten are ranked .1, .129, .65, .33, .2, .254, .17, .193, .97, .9, and of these only 2 and 254 do not follow this pattern. To show this trend more clearly, Figure 8 shows the rank of each last octet as the area of a circle, with the octets arranged in a sequential grid (so the x axis lists octets sequentially in groups of 16, while each step up the y axis is 16 more than the previous). The vertical lines correspond to more frequent responses, with $x = 1$ showing strong response from .1, .129, .65, etc., and $x = 9$ for .9, etc. The other prominent features are .254 and across $y = 0$ (.1, .2, .3, etc.). While showing ranks exaggerate what can be small absolute differences, these strong patterns show power-of-two allocations affect responsiveness.

6. SHARING HITLISTS

Our goal in generating hitlists is to share them with other research groups carrying out topology studies. We offer them free-of-charge to all, and to date we have provided them to four other projects. Although hitlists are not human subjects, networks are operated by and involve humans. Hitlist use by multiple prompts us to consider their distribution in the context of the Belmont protocols [28], weighing the benefits and potential costs of sharing and designing policies accordingly.

The benefits of sharing hitlists are similar to sharing of other research results. Shared data is a boon to researchers.

[2]We thank Kim Claffy for suggesting the question of last octet distribution for study.

A common data source can lower the barrier to entry for future research, and it also makes it easier for researchers to compare their results. (For example, the TREC benchmarks are seen as essential to rapid advances in the field of Information Retrieval [13], although our efforts are far more modest.) As importantly, we expect that the scrutiny of multiple researchers on a common dataset can often identify data or methodological errors that might be otherwise unnoticed. (In Internet topology, the problem of alias resolution is one that is still being refined [2, 21], nearly ten years after the first techniques [17].) For the hitlist creator, a shared result amortizes the operational costs of collection and processing of the input data (Internet censuses) needed to create hitlists. Finally, for the hitlist subjects, network operators in the Internet, a common source allows us to centralize "do-not-probe" blacklists and reduces raw data collection.

Shared hitlists have some costs, however. Most serious is that a hitlist can focus the probing of several researchers on a specific representative address in a network, while independently derived hitlists are more likely to distribute probing load. Second, eventually hitlists will be acquired by malicious users on the Internet. Potential harms are hiding malicious traffic mixed with research traffic, and the slight risk that any list of known active IP addresses may be at risk of additional malicious traffic such as worms or cracking attempts. While a risk, the effort to generate a hitlist is within the reach of a motivated individual, so strong restrictions on hitlists seem unwarranted.

Our current hitlist distribution policies are designed to balance risks with benefits. Although we share hitlists free-of-charge, we provide them subject to a usage agreement. Hitlist users may not redistribute hitlists so we can establish this agreement directly with all users. Tracking hitlist users allows us to estimate load on representatives. We also plan to seed the hitlist with representatives that we monitor to track load. We also hope controlled hitlist distribution delays their acquisition by malicious parties. We expect to review these policies as we gain more experience.

7. FUTURE WORK

Although we are providing our current hitlists for use currently, we see two directions for future work.

First, we would like to better understand the stability of Internet address usage. Our study shows only 50–60% of informed representatives respond three months later, implying a great deal of churn on Internet address usage. We would like to better understand why usage of the remaining addresses cannot be better predicted. More detailed analysis of gone-dark and unstable blocks may provide more information; and a combination of our data with information IANA assignments, RIR registration and block reassignment may explain causes for failure to respond. Alternatively, changes in firewalling may explain address instability.

Second, we expect to get more information about how hitlists are used. Several groups expressed concern that representatives may become overloaded as multiple groups target them with measurement traffic. We are in the process of seed our hitlist with monitors so we can observe hitlist use and compare it to normal "background radiation". Such an evaluation will help understand hitlist use and characterize general unsolicited Internet traffic. If representative load becomes high, it will suggest operational changes, such as multiple representatives per /24 block.

8. CONCLUSIONS

We have defined the properties that are important to hitlists: representatives that are responsive, stable, and provide complete coverage for the Internet. We have developed a fully automated algorithm that mines data from Internet censuses to select informed representatives for the visible Internet. We employ information that is available for about one-third of the Internet, and when an informed representative is available we see it is 50–60% likely to respond 2–3 months later. We showed that the primary reasons for prediction failure are blocks with dynamic addressing and gone-dark blocks that are probable firewalls.

Our hitlists are available free-of-charge and have already been distributed to four different research groups. Although we do not have external evaluation of how their use changes those studies, our evaluation of one prior study suggests the potential to discover 1.7 million additional edge links.

Acknowledgments

We thank Kim Claffy and Young Hyun for a detailed reading and comments that improved the paper, and for providing their raw data for comparison in Section 4.5. We also thank the anonymous reviewers for their comments. We are grateful to Yuri Pradkin for developing and operating the Internet census infrastructure that enables this work. We thank Randy Bush, Olaf Meannel, Beichuan Zhang, Ethan Katz-Bassett, and Harsha Madhyastha for their encouragement about this work.

9. REFERENCES

[1] R. Albert, H. Jeong, and A.-L. Barabási. Error and attack tolerance in complex networks. *Nature*, 406:378–382, July 27 2000.

[2] A. Bender, R. Sherwood, and N. Spring. Fixing Ally's growing pains with velocity modeling. In *Proceedings of the 8th ACM Internet Measurement Conference*, pages 337–342, Vouliagmeni, Greece, Oct. 2008. ACM.

[3] R. Bush, J. Hiebert, O. Maennel, M. Roughan, and S. Uhlig. Testing the reachability of (new) address space. In *Proceedings of the ACM Workshop on Internet Nework Management*, pages 236–241, Kyoto, Japan, Aug. 2007. ACM.

[4] R. Bush, O. Maennel, M. Roughan, and S. Uhlig. Internet optometry: assessing the broken glasses in internet reachability. In *Proceedings of the ACM Internet Measurement Conference*, pages 242–253. ACM, Nov. 2009.

[5] X. Cai and J. Heidemann. Understanding address usage in the visible internet. Technical Report ISI-TR-2009-656, USC/Information Sciences Institute, Feb. 2009.

[6] CAIDA. The internet topology data kit—2010-01. `http://www.caida.org/data/active/internet-topology-data-kit/`, Jan. 2010.

[7] CAIDA. The ipv4 routed /24 topology dataset 2009-12. `http://www.caida.org/data/active/ipv4_routed_24_topology_dataset.xml`, Jan. 2010.

[8] K. Claffy, Y. Hyun, K. Keys, M. Fomenkov, and D. Krioukov. Internet mapping: from art to science. In *Proceedings of the IEEE Cybersecurity Applications and Technologies Conference for Homeland Security*

(CATCH), pages 205–211, Alexandria, VA, USA, Mar. 2009. IEEE.

[9] D. D. Clark, C. Partridge, J. C. Ramming, and J. T. Wroclawski. A knowledge plane for the Internet. In *Proceedings of the ACM SIGCOMM Conference*, pages 3–10, Karlsruhe, Germany, Aug. 2003. ACM.

[10] E. Cronin, S. Jamin, C. Jin, A. R. Kurc, D. Raz, and Y. Shavitt. Constrained mirror placement on the Internet. *IEEE Journal of Selected Areas in Communication*, 20(7):1369–1383, Sept. 2002.

[11] D. Cutting. Scalable computing with Hadoop. `http://wiki.apache.org/lucene-hadoop-data/attachments/HadoopPresentatio%ns/attachments/yahoo-sds.pdf`, May 2006. Lecture note.

[12] J. Dean and S. Ghemawat. MapReduce: Simplified data processing on large clusters. In *Proceedings of the USENIX Symposium on Operating Systems Design and Implementation*, pages 137–150, San Francisco, California, USA, Dec. 2004. USENIX.

[13] A. Dekhtyar and J. H. Hayes. Good benchmarks are hard to find: Toward the benchmark for information retrieval applications in software engineering. In *Proceedings of the 22nd International Conference on Software Maintenance*, Philadelphia, Pennsylvania, USA, Sept. 2006. ACM.

[14] J. Dilley, B. Maggs, J. Parikh, H. Prokop, R. Sitaraman, and B. Weihl. Globally distributed content delivery. *IEEE Internet Computing*, 6(5):50–58, Sept. 2002.

[15] P. Francis, S. Jamin, C. Jin, Y. Jin, D. Raz, Y. Shavitt, and L. Zhang. IDMaps: A global internet host distance estimation service. *ACM/IEEE Transactions on Networking*, 9(5):525–540, Oct. 2001.

[16] V. Fuller, T. Li, J. Yu, and K. Varadhan. Classless inter-domain routing (CIDR): an address assignment and aggregation strategy. RFC 1519, Internet Request For Comments, Sept. 1993.

[17] R. Govindan and H. Tangmunarunkit. Heuristics for Internet map discovery. In *Proceedings of the IEEE Infocom*, pages 1371–1380, Tel Aviv, Israel, Mar. 2000. IEEE.

[18] J. Heidemann, Y. Pradkin, R. Govindan, C. Papadopoulos, G. Bartlett, and J. Bannister. Census and survey of the visible Internet. In *Proceedings of the ACM Internet Measurement Conference*, pages 169–182, Vouliagmeni, Greece, Oct. 2008. ACM.

[19] B. Huffaker, M. Fomenkov, D. Moore, and kc claffy. Macroscopic analyses of the infrastructure: measurement and visualization of internet connectivity and performance. `http://www.caida.org/outreach/papers/pam2001/skitter.xml`, Nov. 2001.

[20] B. Huffaker, M. Fomenkov, D. J. Plummer, D. Moore, and k claffy. Distance metrics in the internet. In *Proceedings of the IEEE International Telecommunications Symposium*. IEEE, 2002.

[21] K. Keys. IP alias resolution techniques. Technical report, CAIDA, 2008.

[22] H. V. Madhyastha, T. Isdal, M. Piatek, C. Dixon, T. Anderson, A. Krishnamurthy, and A. Venkataramani. iPlane: An information plane for distributed services. In *Proceedings of the 7th USENIX Symposium on Operating Systems Design and Implementation*, pages 367–380, Seattle, WA, USA, Nov. 2006. USENIX.

[23] H. V. Madhyastha, E. Katz-Bassett, T. Anderson, A. Krishnamurthy, and A. Venkataramani. iPlane Nano: Path prediction for peer-to-peer applications. In *Proceedings of the 6th USENIX Symposium on Network Systems Design and Implementation*, Boston, MA, USA, Apr. 2009. USENIX.

[24] E. Pfanner. Broadband speeds surge in many countries. *New York Times*, page B8, Oct. 1 2009.

[25] R. Sherwood, A. Bender, and N. Spring. DisCarte: A disjunctive Internet cartographer. In *Proceedings of the ACM SIGCOMM Conference*, pages 303–315, Seatle, Washington, USA, Aug. 2008. ACM.

[26] N. Spring, R. Mahajan, and D. Wetherall. Measuring ISP topologies with Rocketfuel. In *Proceedings of the ACM SIGCOMM Conference*, pages 133–145, Pittsburgh, Pennsylvania, USA, Aug. 2002. ACM.

[27] M. Sullivan and L. Munoz. Suggested generic DNS naming schemes for large networks and unassigned hosts. Work in progress (Internet draft draft-msullivan-dnsop-generic-naming-schemes-00.txt, Apr. 2006.

[28] The National Commission for the Protection of Human Subjects of Biomedical and Behavioral Research. The Belmont report: Ethical principles and guidelines for the protection of human subjects of research. Technical report, Department of Health, Education, and Welfare, Apr. 1979.

[29] USC/LANDER Project. Internet IPv4 address space census. PREDICT ID `USC-LANDER/internet_address_survey_it11w-20060307`. Retrieval information for this and other censuses is at `http://www.isi.edu/ant/traces/`, Mar. 2006.

[30] D. Waddington, F. Chang, R. Viswanathan, and B. Yao. Topology discovery for public IPv6 networks. *ACM Computer Communication Review*, 33(3):59–68, July 2003.

[31] F. Wang, Z. M. Mao, J. Wang, L. Gao, and R. Bush. A measurement study on the impact of routing events on end-to-end Internet path performance. In *Proceedings of the ACM SIGCOMM Conference*, Pisa, Italy, Aug. 2006. ACM.

[32] R. Wolski. Dynamically forecasting network performance using the network weather service. *Journal of Cluster Computing*, 1:119–132, Jan. 1998. Also released as UCSD technical report TR-CS96-494.

[33] E. Wyatt. Despite ruling, F.C.C. says it will move forward on expanding broadband. *New York Times*, page B3, April 15 2010.

[34] Y. Xie, F. Yu, K. Achan, E. Gillum, M. Goldszmidt, and T. Wobber. How dynamic are IP addresses? In *Proceedings of the ACM SIGCOMM Conference*, pages 301–312, Kyoto, Japan, Aug. 2007. ACM.

Speed Testing without Speed Tests: Estimating Achievable Download Speed from Passive Measurements

Alexandre Gerber, Jeffrey Pang, Oliver Spatscheck, Shobha Venkataraman
AT&T Labs - Research
180 Park Ave.
Florham Park, NJ
{gerber,jeffpang,spatsch,shvenk}@research.att.com

ABSTRACT

How fast is the network? The speed at which real users can download content at different locations and at different times is an important metric for service providers. Knowledge of this speed helps determine where to provision more capacity and helps detect network problems. However, most network-level estimates of these speeds today are obtained using active "speed tests" that place substantial load on the network and are not necessarily representative of actual user experiences due to limited vantage points. These problems are exacerbated in wireless networks where the physical locations of users play an important role in performance. To redress these problems, this paper presents a new technique to estimate achievable download speed using only flow records collected passively. Estimating achievable speed passively is non-trivial because the measured throughput of real flows is often not comparable to the achievable steady-state TCP rate. This can be because, for example, flows are small and never exit TCP slow start or are rate-limited by the content-provider. Our technique addresses these issues by constructing a *Throughput Index*, a list of flow types that accurately estimate achievable speed. We show that our technique estimates achievable speed more accurately than other techniques in a large 3G wireless network.

Categories and Subject Descriptors

C.2.3 [**Computer-Communication Networks**]: Network Operations

General Terms

Measurement

Keywords

throughput, passive, measurement, UMTS, 3G, wireless

IMC'10, November 1–3, 2010, Melbourne, Australia.

1. INTRODUCTION

The achievable throughput of a steady-state TCP flow at a given time and location in a network, hereafter referred to as *max-throughput*, has long been recognized as an important metric for service providers.[1] By measuring max-throughput a service provider can determine locations where provisioning more capacity would benefit users and detect temporary network problems. The increasing popularity of multimedia downloads and streaming only magnifies the importance of measuring max-throughput. Yet, the rapid shift from wired to wireless access links makes max-throughput more difficult to estimate using traditional active measurements. In this paper, we develop a new technique to estimate max-throughput passively. We show that our approach estimates max-throughput more accurately than other techniques in a large 3G wireless network.

A number of active probing techniques exist to estimate available capacity, but they are often insufficient to estimate max-throughput. For example, researchers have proposed lightweight active probing techniques based on measuring the inter-packet spacing between pairs of packets (e.g., [3, 5, 8]). These techniques do not work well in wireless networks because packets are often delayed for reasons other than congestion (e.g., due to physical layer loss or due to scheduling into Transmission Time Intervals of 10 ms or more [7]). Moreover, these techniques do not measure the final fair-share and loss-induced throughput that a TCP flow would achieve. Thus, the state-of-the-art for measuring max-throughput in such networks is to periodically download large files from a number of active probes while measuring their achieved throughput. While such experiments precisely characterize the max-throughput to each active probe, they have three obvious limitations: First, they place additional load on the network; second, they are expensive to deploy and maintain; and third, they do not capture the experience of real users at different vantage points.

Due to these limitations, active probes cannot scale to cover a representative portion of an entire wireless network. This paper examines whether passive measurements of real flows within a network are sufficient to estimate max-throughput. Estimating network metrics passively is not new: they have been used to determine bottleneck link capacities [9], to determine RTTs [12], and to find bottlenecks in a 3G core network [11]. However, using passive measure-

[1]Although other transport protocols exist, the throughput of TCP is the most important practical measure since the vast majority of flows use TCP (e.g., we find that 95% of flows in a large 3G network use TCP).

ments to estimate max-throughput poses unique challenges. First, because the network does not control either end-point, it can not control the duration of TCP flows. TCP flows take several round trips to ramp up to their fair-share capacity, so the observed throughput of small flows may not approximate max-throughput. The duration of TCP slow start is even longer in 3G networks because RTTs are typically 100s of milliseconds [12]. Second, flows may be throttled for reasons other than reaching the available network capacity. For example, content providers may rate limit streaming content. Finally, the enormous traffic volume of all TCP flows passing through a large network means that it is impractical to record and analyze every packet. In practice, only periodic flow samples can be recorded, and little processing can be done on those samples if we wish to monitor max-throughput in near real-time.

In this paper, we develop a novel technique to estimate max-throughput using only passively measured flow records. Our technique works by constructing a *Throughput Index* (TI) that includes only flow types that accurately estimate max-throughput. Only flows that match a flow type in the TI are used in estimates. We validate our technique in a large 3G wireless network by comparing our passive max-throughput estimates with active measurements. We make the following contributions:

- Compared to previous passive TCP parameter estimation techniques [2, 10, 11, 13, 14], our approach does not require packet traces and requires no online processing of flow records except for a simple, constant time filter. Therefore, our approach is amenable to very large-scale max-throughput monitoring and is already deployed as a prototype to monitor all data traffic in a large 3G network.

- To our knowledge, our approach is the first passive technique to estimate max-throughput that is validated on traffic in the wild. We find that our max-throughput estimates correlate well with measurements from active probes in several large metropolitan areas. In aggregate, we find a correlation coefficient of 0.88.

- Through the construction of a TI, we classify rate-limited content-providers and applications. Surprisingly, we find that nearly 60% of large flows are rate-limited and can never reach the peak network capacity.

2. BACKGROUND

To evaluate passive max-throughput estimation, we analyze traffic traces from a large UMTS wireless network. The majority of our analysis in this paper uses traces collected from April 1-7, 2010. We collected these traffic traces from an infrastructure [4] that monitored all traffic on the Gn interface between all Serving GPRS Support Nodes (SGSNs) and Gateway GPRS Support Nodes (GGSNs) in the packet-switched part of the UMTS Core Network [7]. Data traffic that originates from user handsets travels from the Radio Access Network (RAN) to the Gn interface before exiting to the Internet. Similarly, all traffic from the Internet to user handsets crosses the Gn interface. These traces contain traffic from all regions of the UMTS network roughly within the Pacific and Central timezones. The data that we use for this study does not contain personally identifiable information.

Flow Records. For our study, the measurement infrastructure collected one *flow record* for each flow every 1 minute for a random 3% of users. Flows are distinguished by the standard $(ipsrc, ipdst, sport, dport)$ tuple. For the purposes of our study, each flow record is annotated with two fields: *application*, the application protocol used in the flow, and *content-provider*, the service the flow is communicating with. Each record is also annotated with the following three statistics: *bytes*, the volume transferred during the 1 minute interval, *duration*, the time between the first and last packets in the interval, *total_bytes*, the volume transferred since the start of the flow. Note that the annotated flow records contain no personally identifying information. The *application* classification in our annotated flow records uses well known heuristics based on application headers and port numbers (see [6] for details). The *content-provider* for the annotation is identified by the HTTP Content-Provider header or the DNS name of the server when available. It is empty otherwise. HTTP traffic dominates the traffic as it is used for web browsing, downloads, and streaming. We define a *flow type* to be a (*application*, *content-provider*) pair; we find it useful to group flows records by flow type.

Device Categories. Different handset types have maximum air interface speeds that differ by several Mbps. In order to factor out the influence of different handset types and radio access technologies, this paper only considers downlink 3G flows from HSDPA category 6 devices, which are able to reach 3.6 Mbps in the download direction. In practice, we use our technique to estimate max-throughput for each class of devices and in each direction separately. The device type is identified by the Type Allocation Code of the device, which is available in the GTP tunnel carrying IP traffic between the GGSN the RAN [1].

Throughput Normalization. For proprietary reasons, all throughput values presented in this paper are normalized by an arbitrary constant (i.e., $normalized\_throughput = throughput/C$). Normalization does not change the dynamic range represented in figures.

3. METHODOLOGY

Our goal is as follows: given all TCP flow records that traversed a set of network paths during a time interval, output an estimate of the average max-throughput over that time interval when downloading from an unconstrained Internet source. The most trivial algorithm would be to apply a summary function over the *byte/duration* values in all flow records (e.g., the mean). However, most of these values will not reflect max-throughput because bytes transferred depends not only on available capacity, but also on total flow size, application protocol, and content-provider. This section describes our technique for filtering flow records to discard the effects of these other factors.

3.1 Why not Measure All Large Flows?

A TCP flow can transfer many bytes before achieving its steady-state throughput because it begins in a *slow-start* phase that incrementally probes for the available capacity. Therefore, an obvious first step to measure max-throughput is to only examine flows that have transferred enough bytes to exit slow-start. The volume transferred during slow-start depends on the RTT and the bottleneck capacity. These two parameters vary based on flow, but a first order ap-

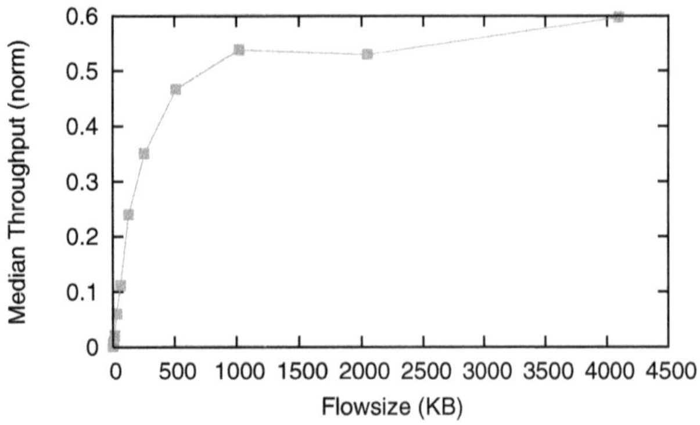

Figure 1: Median normalized throughput of non-rate-limited flow records vs. flow size. All flow records with size $2^i \leq total\_bytes < 2^{i+1}$ are aggregated in the bin 2^i.

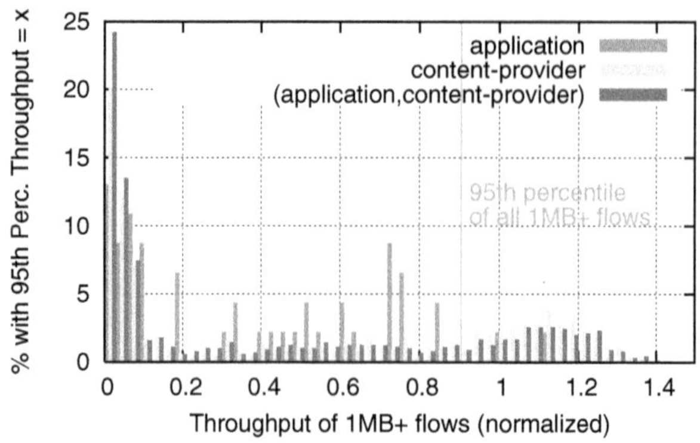

Figure 3: Histogram of the 95th percentile of throughput from each *application*, *content-provider*, and (*application*, *content-provider*) flow type, respectively.

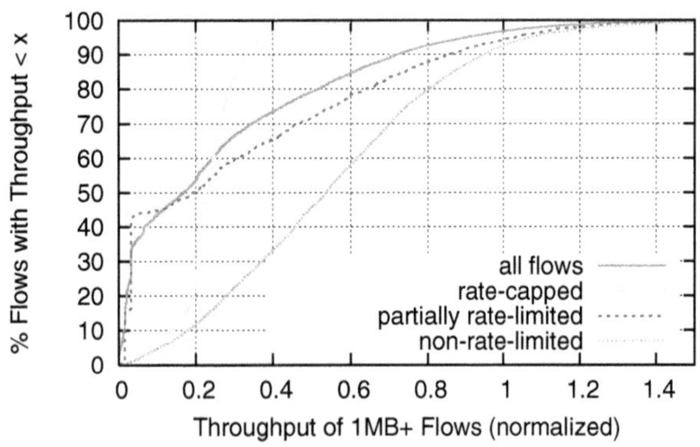

Figure 2: CDF of the measured throughput distribution of 1MB+ flows from: all flows, a (*application*, *content-provider*) that is rate-capped, one that is partially rate-limited, and one that is not rate-capped or partially rate-limited.

proximation is to find a flow size that allows most flows to exit slow-start.[2] Figure 1 shows that the median measured throughput of non-rate-limited flow records stabilizes at about flow size = 1MB. (We describe how we identify rate-limited flows in §3.2.)

Thus, the next most obvious algorithm is to apply a summary function over the *byte/duration* values in all flow records that have $total\_bytes \geq$ 1MB. For brevity, we call these records the *1MB+ flows*. However, this algorithm is not sufficient because measured throughput of identically sized large flows can still vary based on application protocol and content-provider. For example, Figure 2 shows the distribution of measured throughput values over 1MB+ flows for several (*application*, *content-provider*) flow types. The rate-capped type appears to be bottle-necked at or rate-limited by the content-provider since none of its flows achieve the higher throughputs possible, as shown in the tail of the all flows line. This is in contrast to the non-rate-limited type, which achieves throughput values throughout the possible spectrum. The partially rate-limited line shows that a flow type can exhibit bimodal behavior: rate-limited in some flows (0-40%) but non-rate-limited in others (40-100%). This can be because the same application protocol is used for control messages and bulk transfer. Our inspection of flow types showed that most fall into one of these three categories. This includes application protocols that are used only for control messages, which would appear to be rate-capped at a very low throughput value.

Note that a flow can appear to be rate-limited for a variety of reasons, including traffic shaping by the content-provider, application protocol bottlenecks, and persistent congestion or capacity problems on the Internet path to the server. In practice, we do not actually need to detect the cause of the rate-limiting, only its effect on the throughput distribution.

[2]Since our study examines a wireless network, TCP may exit slow start due to physical layer loss rather than congestion induced loss. Indeed, the throughput in Figure 1 continues to increase linearly at a slow rate even after the knee in the curve, which indicates that TCP AIMD sometimes finds more capacity available after slow-start. However, since our goal is to estimate the max-throughput that real users actually experience, we do not attempt to exclude the effects of physical layer loss.

3.2 Identifying Rate-Limited Flows

To obtain a more accurate measure of max-throughput, we must filter out the applications and content-providers that have flow distributions similar to the rate-capped and partially rate-limited flow types. We define a *rate-capped* flow type to be one that never reaches the available capacity of the network. We defined a *partially rate-limited* flow type to be one that has a significant fraction of rate-limited flows. We describe two heuristics to detect each flow type below.

To identify rate-capped flows, we note that the rate-capped flow distribution shown in Figure 2 never crosses the tail of the all flows distribution. In general, if we assume that at least 5% of all 1MB+ flows reach the available capacity, then a non-rate-capped flow type should have a 95th percentile throughput at least as large as the 95th percentile throughput of all 1MB+ flows. This is because all 1MB+ flows includes both rate-limited and non-rate-limited flow records. Figure 3 shows a histogram of the 95th percentile of each flow type, where we define flow type by *application* only, *content-provider* only, and (*application*, *content-provider*) pair. Only flow types with at least 100 flows are presented.

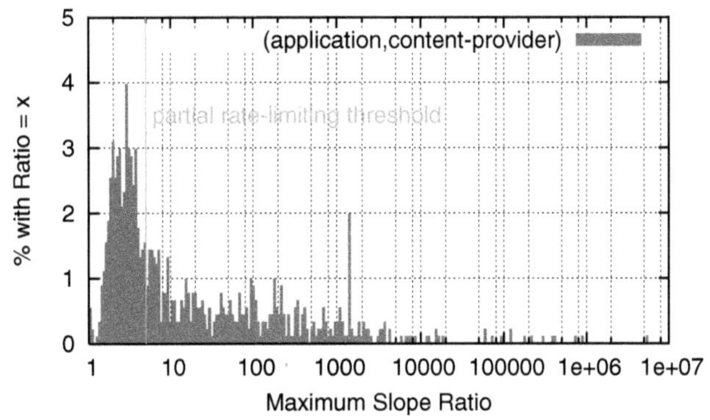

Figure 4: Histogram of the Maximum Slope Ratio of each (*application*, *content-provider*) flow type for details. See text in §3.2. Note the logarithmic scale of the x-axis.

Flow type	C	L	% 1MB+ Flows	Throughput (norm) Median	Mean
(streaming, C1)	•		11.79	0.229	0.237
(http other, C2)			**10.91**	**0.497**	**0.502**
(file download, C3)			**9.35**	**0.427**	**0.477**
(http other, C4)	•	•	6.78	0.032	0.028
(streaming, C5)			**6.36**	**0.539**	**0.559**
(p2p, C6)	•	•	3.03	0.014	0.029
(unknown, C7)	•	•	2.80	0.009	0.027
(email, C8)	•		1.19	0.056	0.116
(web browsing, C4)	•	•	0.95	0.032	0.026
(streaming, C5)		•	0.92	0.266	0.328
(http other, C9)			**0.90**	**0.566**	**0.576**
(email, C10)	•		0.80	0.147	0.175
(web browsing, C2)	•		0.76	0.421	0.415
(streaming, C4)	•	•	0.75	0.025	0.028
(email, C11)	•		0.61	0.072	0.155
...					
TI			38.7	0.503	0.524

Table 1: Top 15 (*application*, *content-provider*) flow types, the % of 1MB+ flows they comprise, and the normalized median and mean throughputs of their 1MB+ flows. Each content-provider is identified with a consistent Cx identifier. Column 'C' and 'L' indicate rate-capped flows and partially rate-limited flows, respectively. Bold rows are in the TI.

We see that for the *content-provider* and (*application*, *content-provider*) distributions, there is a clear mode to the right of the "95th percentile of all 1MB+ flows" line. This mode represents the non-rate-capped flows. The *application* distribution does not exhibit this mode, which suggests rate-capping is primarily a property of content-providers, not application protocols. We identify all flow types to the left of the line as rate-capped.

To identify partially rate-limited flows, we note that the partially rate-limited flow distribution shown in Figure 2 is bimodal: the first portion of the distribution has a very steep slope due to rate-limiting, while the later portion is less steep. In general, we want to detect these dramatic decreases in a flow type's CDF slope. We use the following heuristic: Let s_i and s_{i+5} be the slopes at percentile i and $i + 5$, respectively. We define the *slope ratio* of s_i and s_{i+5} to be s_i/s_{i+5}. Define the maximum slope ratio to be the greatest slope ratio over $i \in [7, 8, 9, \ldots, 93]$ (we ignore the top and bottom percentiles to guard against outliers). The maximum slope ratio will be large if there is a dramatic decrease in slope within any 5 percentile range. In practice, we approximate s_i as the difference between percentile $(i - 2.5)$ and percentile $(i + 2.5)$.

Figure 4 shows a histogram of the maximum slope ratio over each (*application*, *content-provider*) flow type. Again, only flow types with at least 100 flow records are presented. We see a primary mode to the left of line at maximum slope ratio = 5. This mode represents flow types without dramatic changes in slope. However, there is also a long tail to the right of this line. We identify flow types to the left of the "partial rate-limiting threshold" as partially rate-limited. The choice of a threshold = 5 conservatively captures the most of the flow types in the main mode. We note that our approach described in the next section is not very sensitive to this threshold value (we have tried thresholds up to 20 without noticeable differences).

3.3 Our Approach: A Throughput Index

To obtain a better estimate of max-throughput, our approach is to include only flow types that are non-rate-capped and non-rate-limited. We call the set of all (*application*, *content-provider*) types that satisfy these criteria the *Throughput Index* (TI). Table 1 shows the top 15 flow types by number of 1 MB+ flows, whether they are identified as rate-capped (C) and/or partially rate-limited (L), and their mean and median throughputs. The bold entries are included in the TI. We see that mean and median throughputs of TI flow types are much closer to each other than non-TI flow types, as expected of unconstrained vs. constrained downloads. One anomaly is the "web browsing" flow type third from last in the table, which has mean and median throughputs similar to the other TI flow types. A few of these potential "false negatives" exist because their 95th percentiles of throughput or maximum slope ratios fall just below or above our choice of thresholds. However, it is clear from Figure 3 and Figure 4 that modifying the thresholds slightly would not dramatically change the fraction of rate-capped or partially rate-limited flow types. Moreover, a perfect classification isn't necessary for the TI to be functional.

Table 1 also shows that inspecting the application protocol or content provider is not sufficient to determine which flow types are rate-limited. For example, the top two streaming applications use the exact same streaming protocol, but one is clearly rate-capped while the other is not. This is because the protocol can be configured so that the entire stream is downloaded at once. In addition, we see that identifying flow type by (*application*, *content-provider*) rather than just *application* or *content-provider* is important, since some content-providers have both non-rate-limited and rate-limited applications (e.g., C2 and C5). Table 2 shows the percentage of flows and flow types in each flow type category. Only the flow types with at least 100 flows are analyzed, but the remaining flow types comprise only 6% of flows. Surprisingly, nearly 60% of large flows are rate-capped and can never reach the peak network capacity. The TI includes 39% of flows and 23% of flow types.

In practice, we compute the TI offline based on a representative time period of flow records. Once computed, we process flows online using the TI as a filter to select flows for max-throughput estimates. We currently recompute the TI

	C	L	C+L	TI
% 1 MB+ Flows	25.8	1.9	33.5	38.7
% (*application*, *content-provider*)	24.3	3.0	49.6	23.1

Table 2: Percent of flows and (*application*, *content-provider*) types that are rate-capped (C), partially rate-limited (L), both (C+L), and in the TI.

once every few months since we have observed that the distributions of popular (*application*, *content-provider*) types do not change often.

A final question is how to aggregate the *byte/duration* measurements of flows in the TI. We evaluate two approaches: The first approach, TI-F, takes a mean over the throughputs of all flows records in the TI. This aggregate will be relatively robust to outlier users since it weights a very large number of flows from different users equally. However, it is also sensitive to non-network problems that impact the top 3 content-providers since they make up a majority of all flows in the TI. The second approach,TI-T, takes the mean of the means of each flow type. This aggregate weights each flow type equally so it is more robust to unexpected changes with individual content-providers, but it is more sensitive to unpopular flow types that may only be used by a small number of users. In the next section, we show that the estimate produced by each of these aggregates is comparable under typical circumstances.

4. EVALUATION

Evaluating the accuracy of any max-throughput estimation technique, whether passive or active, is difficult because "ground truth" measurements are not available from all user locations at all times. In this section, we evaluate our passive max-throughput estimation techniques by comparison with a set of active measurements. Although these active measurements do not necessarily represent ground truth, they do represent the current state-of-the-art for max-throughput estimation. The TI estimates of max-throughput are closer to these active measurements than alternative passive measurement techniques, which suggests that the TI estimates are more representative of max-throughput.

4.1 Setup

In this section we compare our passive max-throughput estimation techniques against active measurements in several 3G wireless network regions. Each region roughly covers a major metropolitan area. In addition, we compare against the aggregated measurements from all regions in roughly the Pacific and Central timezones.

We perform active throughput measurements from probes in several stationary locations. Each probe performs a throughput measurement by downloading a 3MB file via FTP from a well-provisioned server close to the Gn interface. 2 to 3 measurements per probe are collected each hour. Each region we consider in this section has probes in 3 to 12 different vantage points. The active max-throughput estimate we report each hour is the mean of all measurements from all probes in a region. We note that the active probes are generally placed in locations with good RF conditions. Thus, we expect that they would perform better than the average subscriber handset.

We select the flow types in the TI using traffic from March 24-30, 2010. Then, we compute the TI-F and TI-T estimates based on traffic observed on April 3-7, 2010. We also compute the naïve All 1MB+ Flows estimate, which corresponds to the mean throughput of all flow records with *total_bytes* $\geq$ 1 MB. We compare these passive max-throughput estimates to the active estimates for each hour during the same time period.

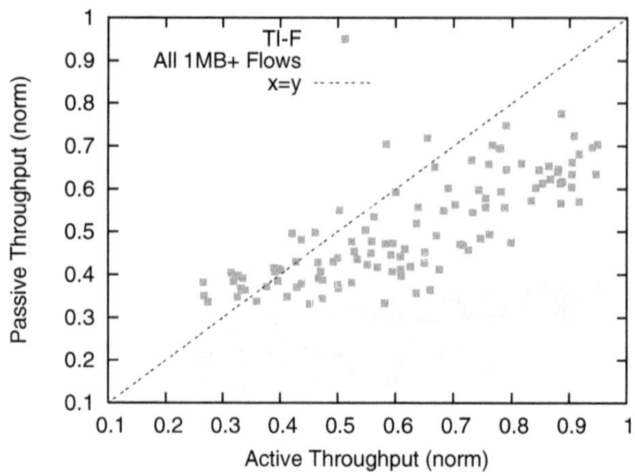

Figure 5: Comparison of active and passive estimates for region R1. Each point represents the estimate for one hour.

4.2 Results

Figure 5 shows a scatter plot comparing active and passive estimates. Each point represents the estimate for one hour in the largest region. If active and passive estimates report the same values, then the points would fall on the x=y line. We see that the All 1MB+ Flows approach produces estimates that are significantly less than the active measurements. TI-F produces estimates that are much closer, but are still generally less. This may be because some flows in the TI are still rate-limited by application behaviors that we do not detect. It may also be because the active measurement probes are in higher quality vantage points (i.e., better RF conditions) than most real users. During a few hours, the TI-F estimate is higher than the active measurement (i.e., the points above the diagonal). These cases can probably be attributed to variance in the small number of active measurement samples. Evaluating which set of measurements is closer to the "ground truth" is the subject of future work, but we are encouraged that both active estimates and the TI-F estimates show a similar trend over time.

Relative Difference. To see if this trend generalizes, we compare the relative difference between the passive and active estimates in other regions. Figure 6 compares the relative difference between each set of passive and active estimates for all regions and the 10 regions with the most active probe vantage points. The top of each bar indicates the median relative difference (over all hours) and the error bars show the 25th and 75th percentiles. We see that both the TI-F and TI-T estimates have roughly the same relative difference over all regions and both have relative differences substantially less than the All 1MB+ Flows approach. Most TI-F and TI-T estimates are less than 30% different than the active measurements, while most All 1MB+ Flows estimates

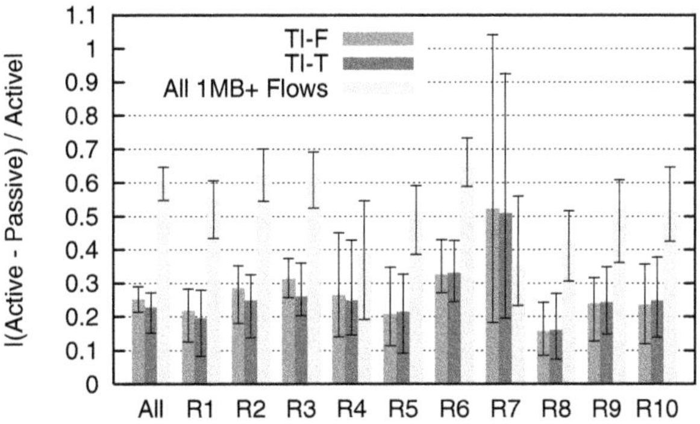

Figure 6: Relative difference of passive estimates to active throughput estimates in all regions and the 10 regions with the most active probe vantage points. That is, $|(active - passive)/active|$. The top of each bar shows the median relative difference over all hours and the error bars show the 25th and 75th percentiles.

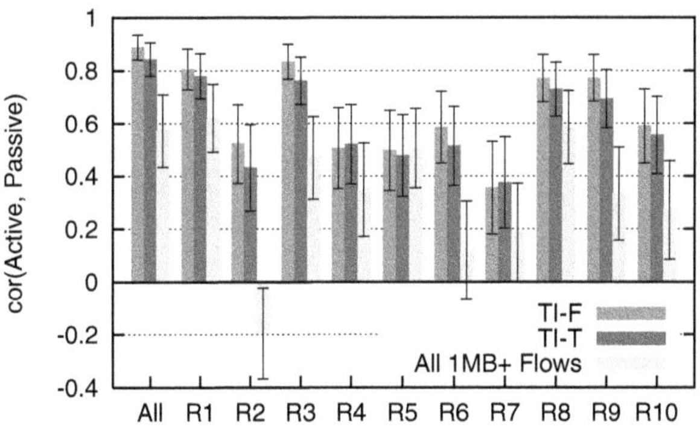

Figure 7: Correlation of passive estimates to active throughput estimates in all regions and the top 10 regions. Each error bar shows the 95% confidence interval of the corresponding correlation coefficient.

are more than 50% different. One anomaly is region R7, where the TI estimates have greater relative differences. We believe this is due to the active probes being in unrepresentative locations because this is the only location where the active estimates are lower than all passive estimates, on average.

Correlation. In addition to similar estimate values, we also expect good passive estimates to be correlated with the active estimates over time. That is, when the active estimate goes down (e.g., due to contention) we also generally expect the passive estimate to go down. Figure 7 shows Pearson's correlation coefficient between each passive estimate time series and the corresponding active estimate time series in all regions and the top 10. The error bars show 95% confidence intervals of the correlation coefficients. Two perfectly correlated signals would have a correlation of 1 and any correlation greater than 0.6 is well correlated. We see that both TI-F and TI-T are at least as correlated with the active estimates as the All 1MB+ Flows estimates. The correlation is substantially greater than the All 1MB+ Flows estimates in some regions, such as R2 and R6.

The regions where the TI estimates are less correlated with the active estimates, such as R2, R4, R5, and R7, are regions where there are fewer samples either in the TI or from the active probes. When many vantage points are aggregated, such as in the All case, the TI and active estimates' correlations are very high (close to 0.9). This suggests that when enough samples are available, the TI estimates correlate well to aggregate network-level effects such as shared congestion. To improve the TI's correlation of these effects at finer network granularities, we are currently increasing the sampling rate of flow types in the TI from 3% to 100% of users. This is feasible because the number of TI flows is small relative to the total flows that traverse the network.

5. CONCLUSION AND FUTURE WORK

Our results demonstrate that max-throughput can be estimated using passive measurements via judicious selection of flows. In this paper, we presented our initial attempt at such a selection by identifying non-rate-limited flow types to place in a Throughput Index.

By applying the TI approach to more real traffic, we hope to resolve a few outstanding issues. First, the the minimum flow size necessary to reach TCP steady-state depends on the RTT and the available capacity, both of which are dynamic quantities. We plan to explore how this flow size can be varied based on network conditions, which should improve the TI's max-throughput estimates when available capacity grows. Second, the filtering of certain flow records presents a trade-off between the number of samples and their aggregate accuracy. We plan to explore how to utilize the noisier rate-limited samples when an insufficient number of non-rate-limited samples exist. Third, application protocol and content-provider behavior can change over time. We plan to explore how to detect such changes dynamically by examining how each flow type contributes to the TI over time. Fourth, our approach assumes that most flows in the TI are typical and benign. In the future, we will explore how malicious and abnormal flows that skew the max-throughput estimate can be detected. Finally, while we believe the TI approach generalizes to wired networks, further study is needed to understand the impact of the greater heterogeneity in vantage points and TCP stacks.

6. REFERENCES

[1] 3GPP. Digital cellular telecommunications system (Phase 2+); Universal Mobile Telecommunications System (UMTS); General Packet Radio Service (GPRS); GPRS Tunnelling Protocol (GTP) across the Gn and Gp interface (3GPP TS 29.060 version 6.18.0 Release 6). ETSI TS 129 060 V6.18.0 (2007-10), 2007.

[2] J. But, U. Keller, and G. Armitage. Passive TCP Stream Estimation of RTT and Jitter Parameters. In *LCN '05: Proceedings of the The IEEE Conference on Local Computer Networks 30th Anniversary*, pages 433–441, Washington, DC, USA, 2005. IEEE Computer Society.

[3] R. L. Carter and M. E. Crovella. Measuring bottleneck link speed in packet-switched networks. *Perform. Eval.*, 27-28:297–318, 1996.

[4] C. Cranor, T. Johnson, O. Spatscheck, and V. Shkapenyuk. Gigascope: A stream database for network applications. In *SIGMOD '03: Proceedings of the 2003 ACM SIGMOD international conference on Management of data*, pages 647–651, New York, NY, USA, 2003. ACM.

[5] C. Dovrolis, P. Ramanathan, and D. Moore. Packet-dispersion techniques and a capacity-estimation methodology. *IEEE/ACM Trans. Netw.*, 12(6):963–977, 2004.

[6] J. Erman, A. Gerber, M. T. Hajiaghayi, D. Pei, and O. Spatscheck. Network-aware forward caching. In *WWW '09: Proceedings of the 18th international conference on World wide web*, pages 291–300, New York, NY, USA, 2009. ACM.

[7] H. Kaaranen, S. Naghian, L. Laitinen, A. Ahtiainen, and V. Niemi. *UMTS Networks: Architecture, Mobility and Services*. Wiley, New York, NY, 2001.

[8] R. Kapoor, L.-J. Chen, L. Lao, M. Gerla, and M. Y. Sanadidi. CapProbe: A simple and accurate capacity estimation technique. *SIGCOMM Comput. Commun. Rev.*, 34(4):67–78, 2004.

[9] S. Katti, D. Katabi, C. Blake, E. Kohler, and J. Strauss. MultiQ: automated detection of multiple bottleneck capacities along a path. In *IMC '04: Proceedings of the 4th ACM SIGCOMM conference on Internet measurement*, pages 245–250, New York, NY, USA, 2004. ACM.

[10] J. Pahdye and S. Floyd. On inferring TCP behavior. In *SIGCOMM '01: Proceedings of the 2001 conference on Applications, technologies, architectures, and protocols for computer communications*, pages 287–298, New York, NY, USA, 2001. ACM.

[11] F. Ricciato, F. Vacirca, and M. Karner. Bottleneck detection in UMTS via TCP passive monitoring: a real case. In *CoNEXT '05: Proceedings of the 2005 ACM conference on Emerging network experiment and technology*, pages 211–219, New York, NY, USA, 2005. ACM.

[12] P. Romirer-Maierhofer, F. Ricciato, A. D'Alconzo, R. Franzan, and W. Karner. Network-Wide Measurements of TCP RTT in 3G. In *TMA '09: Proceedings of the First International Workshop on Traffic Monitoring and Analysis*, pages 17–25, Berlin, Heidelberg, 2009. Springer-Verlag.

[13] S. Seshan, M. Stemm, and R. H. Katz. SPAND: Shared Passive Network Performance Discovery. In *USITS'97: Proceedings of the USENIX Symposium on Internet Technologies and Systems on USENIX Symposium on Internet Technologies and Systems*, pages 13–13, Berkeley, CA, USA, 1997. USENIX Association.

[14] M. Zangrilli and B. B. Lowekamp. Applying Principles of Active Available Bandwidth Algorithms to Passive TCP Traces. In *Passive and Active Network Measurement*, pages 333–336, 2005.

YouTube Traffic Dynamics and Its Interplay with a Tier-1 ISP: An ISP Perspective

Vijay Kumar Adhikari, Sourabh Jain, and Zhi-Li Zhang
Department of Computer Science & Engineering, University of Minnesota
Minneapolis, MN
viadhi@cs.umn.edu, sourj@cs.umn.edu, zhzhang@cs.umn.edu

Abstract

In this paper we conduct an extensive and in-depth study of traffic exchanged between YouTube data centers and its users, as seen *from the perspective of a tier-1 ISP* in Spring 2008 after YouTube was acquired by Google but before Google did any major restructuring of YouTube. Using flow-level data collected at multiple PoPs of the ISP, we first infer where the YouTube data centers are located and where they are connected to the ISP. We then deduce the load balancing strategy used by YouTube to service user requests, and investigate how load balancing strategies and routing policies affect the traffic dynamics across YouTube and the tier-1 ISP.

The major contributions of the paper are four-fold: (1) we discover the surprising fact that YouTube does not consider the geographic locations of its users at all while serving video content. Instead, it employs a location-agnostic, *proportional* load balancing strategy among its data centers to service user requests from all geographies; (2) we perform in-depth analysis of the PoP-level YouTube traffic matrix as seen by the ISP, and investigate how it is shaped by the YouTube load balancing strategy and routing policies utilized by both YouTube and the ISP; (3) with such knowledge, we develop a novel method to estimate *unseen* traffic (i.e. traffic that is carried outside the ISP network) so as to "complete" the traffic matrix between YouTube data centers and users from the customer ASes of the ISP; and 4) we explore "what if" scenarios by assessing the pros and cons of alternative load balancing and routing policies. Our study sheds light on the interesting and important interplay between large content providers and ISPs in today's Internet.

Categories and Subject Descriptors

C.2.4 [**Distributed systems**]: Distributed applications; C.4 [**Performance of systems**]: Performance attributes

General Terms

Measurement, Performance

Keywords

YouTube, proportional load balancing, unseen traffic estimation

1. INTRODUCTION

A significant portion of today's digital multimedia content is serviced by large content providers such as YouTube (now a subsidiary of Google), Yahoo, Google, and the like. These large content providers often employ several huge data centers – each of which is comprised of thousands of servers – to meet and serve growing user demands. For a variety of reasons, these data centers are typically located in different geographical sites, and connected to one or multiple ISPs at the nearby major Internet "interconnection regions" or Points-of-Presence (PoPs)[1]. In other words, the content serviced by a large content provider typically flows from one of its data centers through one of these PoPs to enter these ISPs, and is then carried to eventually reach various users. The dynamic *inter-dependence* and *interplay* between content providers and ISPs raise many interesting and important questions that have not been adequately studied.

Take YouTube as an example. As the most popular video sharing site on the Internet, YouTube attracts millions of users every day. Given the significant amount of traffic generated by YouTube videos, how YouTube manages its traffic dynamics and performs load-balancing among its data centers will have a considerable impact on the traffic flows across and within ISPs. Further, the (BGP) routing policies employed by both YouTube and ISPs also shape and drive the traffic dynamics between YouTube and those ISPs. Such dynamic *inter-dependence* and *interplay* therefore have significant implications in traffic management to both YouTube and the ISPs. For instance, can an ISP effectively estimate YouTube-specific traffic matrix so as to better manage its traffic dynamics?

In this paper we take a *measurement-oriented* approach to study the YouTube traffic dynamics *from the perspective of*

[1]For example, according to [11], there are eight major "interconnection regions" within the United States – namely, New York, Washington D.C. and Atlanta on the east coast, Dallas and Chicago in the central US, and Los Angles, the Bay Area and Seattle on the west coast – at which content providers typically buy transit from or peer with various ISPs.

a tier-1 ISP, with emphasis on the *interplay* between the two players, its effect on the traffic dynamics across them, and implications in traffic management for both players. Our study is based on sampled flow-level data collected at various PoPs of a tier-1 ISP.

From BGP routing tables, YouTube (AS36561) advertises 3 prefixes, namely, 64.15.112.0/20, 208.65.152.0/22, and 208.117.224.0/19. Using this information, we first extract all flows related to YouTube from the ISP flow-level measurement data. Through reverse DNS look-ups and other analysis, we infer and deduce that YouTube employs *seven* data centers[2] to service user demands, and that it is connected to the tier-1 ISP at six out of the eight Internet "interconnection regions" (or PoPs) mentioned in [11].

Using the extracted YouTube traffic, we perform an extensive and in-depth analysis of the traffic dynamics between YouTube and the ISP, and explore how load balancing strategies and routing policies employed by both players drive and affect the traffic dynamics between them. In the following we provide a brief overview of the major observations and contributions of our study along four inter-related lines of investigations.

Location-Agnostic Load Balancing: We analyze and infer the load balancing strategies used by YouTube to service user requests. We find that YouTube employs a *proportional* load balancing strategy among the seven data centers (as opposed to, say, a locality- or proximity-aware strategy), where the proportionality seems to be determined by the "size" of the data centers, e.g., as measured by the number of public IP addresses seen in the data that are associated with (front-end) video servers at each data center. This proportionality stays fairly constant over time and across different geographical locations (PoPs) of the tier-1 ISP, and holds for both the client-to-YouTube and YouTube-to-client traffic. *This finding is of particular interest, as it provides an important contrast to the findings of several earlier studies on CDNs [7, 9], which show the prevalence of* proximity-based *content distribution among several CDN services.*

Prevalence of Early-Exit Routing in the ISP Network: With knowledge of the YouTube load balancing strategy, we examine how the YouTube traffic flows between various PoPs of the ISP and the six PoP locations where YouTube is connected to the ISP. In other words, we estimate and analyze the *PoP-level YouTube traffic matrix* as seen by the ISP. Due to the routing asymmetry, we consider the client-to-YouTube and YouTube-to-client traffic separately. We find that the PoP-level *client-to-YouTube* traffic matrix is highly *geographically biased* in the sense that the client-to-YouTube traffic originated from a source PoP always leaves the ISP and enters YouTube at the "closest" of the six destination PoPs, *regardless of* which YouTube data center the traffic is destined to. For instance, the client-to-YouTube traffic originated at a source PoP near New York City, despite being proportionally load balanced across seven YouTube data centers, always exits the ISP and enters YouTube at the New York PoP itself. This observation suggests that YouTube somehow has to carry the client traffic from New York across its "internal" network to the destination data center. On the other hand, the *YouTube-to-client* traffic originated from six YouTube data centers always enters the ISP at the corresponding PoP that they are closest to. For instance, the YouTube-to-client traffic originated from the YouTube New York data center always enters the ISP at the New York PoP. In particular, the YouTube-to-client traffic from the Miami data center is *not* carried by the ISP, i.e., "unseen" by the ISP. This suggests that the YouTube-to-client traffic from the Miami data center is carried by another ISP to the clients. The asymmetry in the client-to-YouTube and YouTube-to-client traffic matrices can be attributed to the BGP routing policies such as "early exit" and route preferences set by the ISP and YouTube.

Estimating Unseen Traffic: Despite the highly asymmetric nature of the client-to-YouTube and YouTube-to-client traffic, the proportionality of traffic split across YouTube data centers (when seen by the ISP) still holds, even when we zero in on a specific customer AS (or prefix) of the ISP. This observation leads us to develop a novel method to estimate the *unseen* YouTube traffic (traffic that is being carried outside of *ISP-X* network), and "complete" the YouTube traffic matrices between YouTube data centers and client ASes of the ISP. This ability to estimate unseen traffic is useful and important both in theory and in practice: It allows us to infer and estimate the total traffic demand matrices between YouTube and various customer ASes of the ISP; it also enables an ISP to estimate the "new" traffic demand and prepare for the potential impact on its network, when routing changes lead YouTube to re-route this unseen traffic through the ISP instead.

Better Understanding of Interplay through "What If" Analysis: Using the YouTube traffic matrices estimated above, we investigate several "what if" scenarios to examine the pros and cons of different load balancing strategies and routing policies, and the impact of the resulting traffic dynamics on both YouTube and the ISP. For example, we find that due to uneven traffic demand distribution across the geographical locations, a locality-aware data center selection strategy [9], while may reduce the overall video download latency for users, can also lead to un-balanced loads across different data centers, especially when the capacities of data centers do not match the geographical load distribution. This plausibly explains why YouTube prefers a location-agnostic, proportional load balancing strategy, as server-load and network bandwidth are likely more critical than latency to the performance of video download/streaming services. We also explore how selective route announcements can shift traffic between YouTube and the tier-1 ISP, and how the ISP can prepare for such changes in YouTube traffic dynamics using the unseen traffic estimation.

To our best knowledge, our paper provides the first extensive study of traffic exchanged between YouTube data centers and users, as seen *from the perspective of a large (tier-1) ISP*. More importantly, while YouTube is one of many (albeit one of great importance) large content providers on the Internet, our work provides a valuable case study that demonstrates the importance of understanding the interplay between large content providers and ISPs. In particular, our study illustrates that the load balancing strategies employed by a content provider (be it proportional load-

[2]As inferred based on DNS names as well as traceroutes, the seven YouTube data centers are located respectively in New York City, Ashburn (near Washington D.C.), Miami, Chicago, Dallas, Los Angles, and the San Jose Bay Area. YouTube is connected to the tier-1 ISP in question at six PoP locations: New York City, Washington D.C., Chicago, Dallas, Los Angles, and the San Jose Bay Area.

balancing, locality-aware, latency-aware, or other more sophisticated strategies) *and* (BGP) routing policies can have a significant impact on the traffic dynamics across content providers and ISPs, and have important implications in traffic management and performance engineering for both content providers and ISPs. With the increasing prominence of data centers in content delivery and emergence of cloud computing, we believe that the interplay between large content (or application service) providers and ISPs will have broad ramifications in a number of key areas such as traffic engineering, network management, business agreements and economic models. Our work is only a first attempt in addressing this broad set of questions.

Caveat. The study presented in this paper provides a snapshot of YouTube traffic as seen by the tier-1 ISP in Spring 2008, shortly after Google acquired YouTube. Since then, Google has been expanding and restructuring YouTube. In Appendix A, we discuss some of the things that have changed after we collected the data used in this study and argue that our methodology and the insights gained from this work still apply to today's YouTube traffic.

The remainder of the paper is structured as follows. In Sec. 2 we overview the YouTube video delivery framework and datasets used in our study. In Sec. 3 we present the method used for inferring YouTube data centers, and in Sec. 4, we analyze and deduce the load balancing strategies used by YouTube among its data centers. In Sec. 5 we study the YouTube traffic matrices as seen by the ISP, and investigate the effects of load balancing and routing policies. In Sec. 6 we present a novel method for estimating the *unseen* traffic, and in Sec. 7 we explore "what-if" scenarios. The paper is concluded in Sec. 8.

2. OVERVIEW & RELATED WORK

2.1 A Quick Overview of YouTube

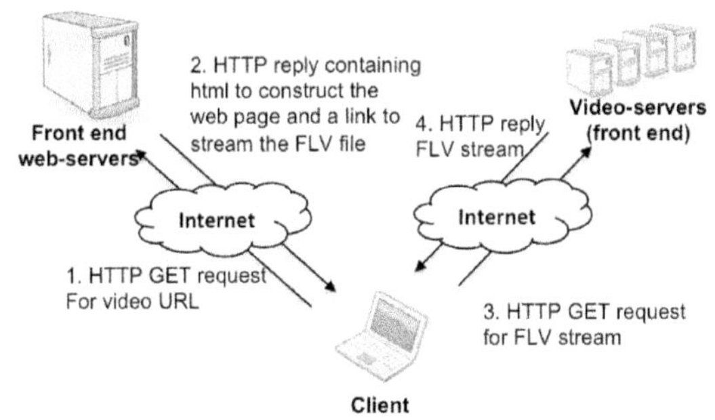

Figure 1: Overview of YouTube video delivery framework.

YouTube is the most popular video serving website that serves user-generated and other videos. It lets any user upload videos in a number of formats. YouTube then converts them in flash-video format and makes them available for viewing. Users with a browser that have Adobe Flash player (or some other compatible player) can watch those videos on YouTube.com or some other sites that embed those videos.

Fig. 1 schematically depicts a typical sequence of steps involved when a user watches a YouTube video. When a user goes to `www.youtube.com` to watch a video, a HTTP request is sent to one of the servers corresponding to `www.youtube.com`, which we refer to as the `(front-end) web-servers`, and a web page is returned that also contains a place-holder for the video. When the user clicks on the video or when the video starts playing automatically, the front-end web server instructs the browser (or the flash plug-in inside the browser) to stream video from another server within one of the YouTube data centers, which actually serves the Flash video content. We refer to these servers as the `(front-end) video-servers` – they are publicly visible in the sense each is assigned a public IP address (and a DNS name). Hence, to watch any YouTube video, a user's browser typically has to communicate with both one of the three front-end web servers and one of many (front-end) Flash video-servers. All parts of this communication - including the video streaming - happens over HTTP.

2.2 Datasets and General Statistics

In our study we use sampled Netflow records collected by a tier-1 ISP, which we will refer to as *ISP-X*, at various PoPs in the US and Europe. The collected flow data is augmented with BGP routing updates and other relevant information such as *AS Paths*, source and destination *IP prefixes* advertised by the neighbor ASes, *egress router* from which the destination prefix is learned (hence this is the router at which the flow exits *ISP-X* network), and so forth. The augmented routing information allows us to attribute the source and destination IP addresses contained in the IP headers to the source/destination ASes and the (specific) prefixes they own and announce via BGP. For our study, we use two flow datasets, each collected at 44 PoPs in US and Europe of the ISP for three consecutive days in two separate weeks in Spring, 2008. Using these datasets, we then extract all YouTube-related traffic, i.e., all flows containing IP addresses (either as source or destination IP) belonging to the 3 prefixes announced by YouTube.

Table 1 summarizes the basic statistics for the first dataset, where the statistics for the *client-to-YouTube* traffic is listed in the second column, and those for *YouTube-to-client* traffic in the last column. (The statistics for the second dataset is similar; we omit them here for lack of space.) In total, there are approximately 172 million sampled flows containing YouTube IP addresses, out of which 54 million flows are from clients (users) to YouTube, and 118 million flows from YouTube to clients. There are no flows from YouTube to YouTube traffic. The difference in the numbers of flows from clients to YouTube vs. YouTube to clients is partly due the *traffic asymmetry* in the two directions: the amount of traffic sent from YouTube to clients are in general far larger than the amount of traffic sent from clients to YouTube. (This traffic asymmetry also manifests in the disparate byte counts of flows in each direction, not shown here, see Sec. 5.) Another contributing factor is the effect of *routing asymmetry*: we see that the number of BGP prefixes for client IPs and the number of client AS numbers in the YouTube-to-client traffic are more than double of those in the client-to-YouTube traffic. Despite the routing and traffic asymmetries, there are ~3,000 ASes which are seen in both client-to-YouTube and YouTube-to-client traffic, and there are ~10,000 BGP advertised prefixes that are seen in both directions. Hence these client ASes (or prefixes) use *ISP-X* for connecting to YouTube in both directions.

In addition to the aforementioned augmented flow datasets, we also conduct reverse DNS look-ups and traceroutes to

Table 1: **Summary Statistics for Dataset I.**

	to YouTube	from YouTube
Total flows	$\sim 54 \times 10^6$	$\sim 118 \times 10^6$
Client IP addresses seen	$\sim 10 \times 10^6$	$\sim 20 \times 10^6$
BGP advertised client prefixes	$\sim 28,000$	$\sim 61,000$
Number of client ASes	$\sim 4,000$	$\sim 9,000$
YouTube IP addresses seen	$\sim 2,000$	$\sim 2,000$

classify YouTube traffic, infer and discover the locations of YouTube data centers, etc. We also collect several gigabytes of *tcpdump* [8] data by playing hundreds of randomly selected YouTube videos on a couple of our lab machines. Collected data includes IP, TCP, HTTP headers and as well as first 200 bytes of the payload. The *tcpdump* data is used to confirm and validate the YouTube traffic characteristics inferred from the sampled Netflow records.

2.3 Related Work

Existing studies of YouTube traffic characteristics have either focused on user behaviors or relied on data collected at end hosts or edge networks. For example, the authors in [3] examine video access patterns, user behavior, popularity life cycle of videos, etc., and compare these characteristics with the traditional web, whereas in [4] the authors explore the "social networks" of YouTube videos. The studies in [6, 16] utilize packet traces collected at campus networks to study the YouTube traffic characteristics from the perspective of an edge network. In a more recent work [12], Fahmy *et al.* analyze and compare the underlying distribution frameworks of three video sharing services, YouTube, Dailymotion and Metacafe, again using the traces collected at edge networks. The focus of the work is to investigate the variation in service delay experienced by users in different geographical locations, and when accessing videos of different popularity and ages. In contrast, using the flow-level data collected at multiple PoPs of a tier-1 ISP, we study the interplay between YouTube and the ISP by investigating the effects of load balancing strategies and routing policies (of both YouTube and the ISP) on the YouTube traffic dynamics. Our work also differs from existing studies (see, e.g., [1, 5, 14]) on characterizing large-scale *Content Distribution Networks* such as Akamai. With increasing reliance on large data centers for content delivery, our work sheds light on the interesting and important interplay between large content providers and ISPs.

3. CLASSIFICATION & LOCALIZATION OF YOUTUBE SERVERS

As explained in Sec. 2.1, YouTube has a two-tier video delivery framework, where servers can be divided into mainly two categories, *front-end* and *video-servers*. Although it might not be very difficult to get a list of data centers YouTube uses, it is a non-trivial task to identify the geographic locations and the roles played by individual YouTube servers in the video delivery framework. In this section we use the Netflow data along with DNS records to classify YouTube server IP addresses into these categories. We also use another dataset collected using the *tcpdump*, by playing a large number of videos on couple of client machines, to validate the classification. We explain how we map YouTube server IP addresses to different locations using reverse DNS mapping and traceroutes from multiple vantage points.

3.1 Classifying YouTube Server IP Addresses

We see a total of 2093 YouTube IP addresses in the datasets, and perform reverse DNS look-ups on each of them. Using the host names thus resolved, we classify YouTube IP addresses and corresponding flows into three categories: i) 3 YouTube IP addresses (i.e., *front-end web servers*) whose host names are all mapped to `www.youtube.com`; the corresponding flows are referred as the *web front-end* flows. ii) more than 2000 YouTube IP addresses (83% of the total YouTube IP addresses) whose host names are of the format `loc-`*v*`xx.loc.`
`youtube.com` (e.g., `dal-`*v*`26.dal.youtube.com`), where `loc` is one of the 8 city codes, `ash, chi, dal, lax, mia, nyc, sjc, sjl`, and `xx` is an integer. We deduce and later validate that these host names correspond to *front-end (Flash) video servers* within various YouTube data centers. iii) The remaining IP addresses are either mapped to host names with other formats (roughly 5%), containing keywords such as *smtp, dns, db, webcam*, or are not resolvable, i.e., with no public host names (roughly 11%). For flows associated with these IP addresses, many of them are either UDP, or are associated with TCP port numbers other than 80. Hence we deduce that these flows are unrelated to YouTube video delivery, and hence ignore them in the remainder of our study. For flows belonging to the first two categories, we further classify them based on the directions of the flows: *client-to-YouTube*, or *YouTube-to-client*.

Validating YouTube Server IP Address Classification using *tcpdump* Data. To validate the YouTube IPs and flow classification presented above, we also collect *tcpdump* data (packet traces) at end hosts by playing hundreds of randomly selected YouTube videos on these hosts. By examining the payload, we obtain the *ground-truth* regarding the role of the YouTube IP addresses seen in the *tcpdump* data. As above, we classify the flows into four (sub-)categories and characterize the overall traffic characteristics of each category: *i) Clients to (web) front-ends:* These packets carry the HTTP requests to front-ends for downloading various objects in the web-page. These packets are likely to be smaller but of variable sizes. *ii) Clients to Video servers:* These packets mainly carry the acknowledgments for the data sent by the video servers. These packets generally contain a smaller number of bytes. *iii) Front-ends to clients:* These flows carry packets mostly with HTML and javascripts etc which describes the downloaded web-page. These packets are likely to be larger packets, with varying number of bytes because of the varying sizes of the web objects. *iv) Video servers to clients:* These flows carry the video content, therefore are likely to be containing a constant but large number of bytes.

For flows of each category, we obtain the overall traffic characteristics of the flows obtained using the *tcpdump* data collected at the end hosts, and compare them with those obtained flows within the same category in the ISP (sampled) flow datasets. As an example, in Fig. 2, we plot the cumulative distribution of the packet sizes of flows in each category computed using the *tcpdump* data as well as the same distribution computed using the ISP datasets. The distribution of the former is shown as the dashed line, and the latter the solid line. We see that the two distributions in

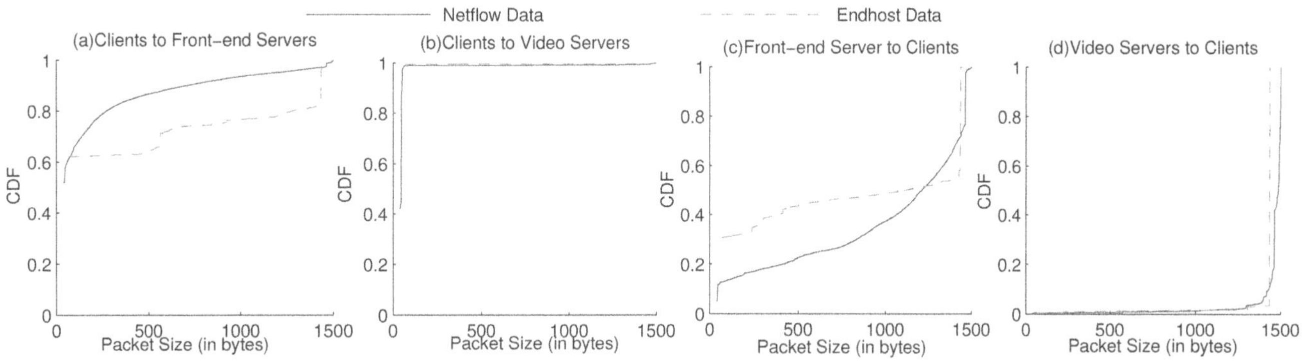

Figure 2: Packet size distribution.

each category match quite well, and are visibly distinct from those in the other categories. These results corroborate and confirm that the YouTube IP address and flow classification presented is indeed valid.

3.2 Locating YouTube Servers

The host names of video server IP addresses discovered through reverse DNS look-ups seem to suggest that there are eight data centers. We perform traceroutes from multiple vantage points to geo-locate and verify the locations for the IP addresses. We find that traceroute queries corresponding to the IP addresses located in the same city produce the same last-hop IP addresses. This traceroute-based analysis also reveals that the two city codes `sjc` and `sjl` point to the same (data center) location, namely within the San Jose Bay Area. We therefore group these two together as a single data center location. This yields a total of seven data centers, as shown in Table 2. The last column of the table also provides the percentage of video server IP addresses belonging to each data center, as seen in the ISP datasets.

We further associate the data center locations (city codes) with the PoP locations of the ISP. More specifically, we compare these origin PoP locations for each YouTube IP address with our 3-letter city code based classification. Except for those YouTube video server IP addresses containing the city code `mia`, in all other cases flows containing (as the source IP address) YouTube video server IP addresses originate from either a source PoP with the same city code or from a source PoP that is nearby. For instance, `nyc-v24.nyc.youtube.com` appears as a source IP address only in flows from New York PoP of the ISP, whereas `ash-v22.ash.youtube.com` appears as a source IP address only in flows from Washington D.C. PoP of the ISP. Furthermore, flows with the source IP addresses containing the city code `sjc` and `sjl` are only seen at the San Jose Bay Area PoP of the ISP. This analysis also reveals that YouTube is connected with the ISP at six PoP locations, Washington DC, New York City, Chicago, Dallas, Los Angles and San Jose.

Lastly, in terms of the three front-end web server IP addresses, they only show up in flows (as source IP addresses) originating from the San Jose PoP. Moreover, other YouTube IP addresses within the same /24 block are also mapped to the San Jose PoP. Traceroute analysis also reveals that these three front-end web server IP addresses are located within the San Jose Bay Area. Hence we deduce that all three

Table 2: Number of video servers at different locations

Code	City	% of IP addresses
ash	Ashburn, VA	24.77
chi	Chicago, IL	17.27
dal	Dallas, TX	07.89
lax	Los Angeles, CA	17.33
mia	Miami, FL	7.37
nyc	New York City	7.26
sjc, sjl	San Jose Bay Area	18.07

front-end web servers are located within the San Jose Bay Area.

4. LOAD BALANCING AMONG YOUTUBE DATA CENTERS

In this section we analyze and infer the load balancing strategy used by YouTube among its data centers to service user requests. The key discovery we make is that YouTube employs a *proportional* load balancing strategy among the seven data centers and not based on the geographical proximity to clients, where the proportionality seems to be determined by the "size" of the data centers; this is in contrast to several studies [7, 9] on CDNs which typically exploit *proximity-based* server selection strategy to reduce end-to-end latency[3].

4.1 Proportional Load Balancing of Client-to-YouTube Traffic

We now examine how client-to-YouTube traffic is distributed among the seven YouTube data centers. Our initial hypothesis is that YouTube does proximity-aware content distribution meaning clients are served videos primarily from the data-center that results in lowest latency. To our surprise, we found that this was not the case. For instance, when we examined a "/24" prefix belonging to New York Public Library, it was exchanging only about 7% of the total flows with YouTube NYC data-center. Similarly, another pre-

[3]In Sec. 7 we will discuss the pros and cons of using *proportional* load-balancing vs. *proximity-aware* load-balancing strategies. We also note that the authors in [9] find that simply relying on *proximity* for serving client requests lead to poor CDN performance for some users; the quality of paths should be also taken into account.

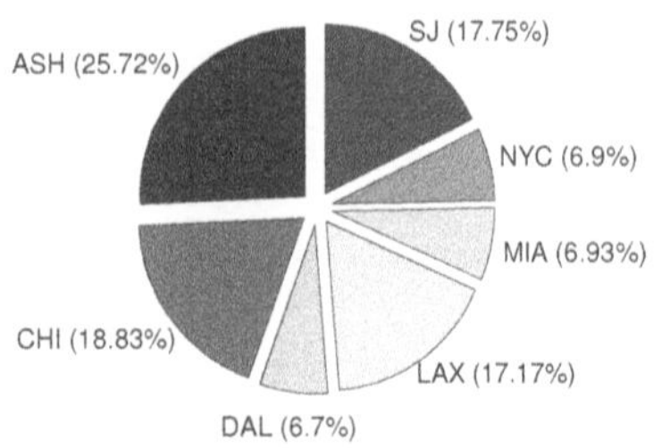

Figure 3: Distribution of client traffic to YouTube data centers.

fix owned by Illinois Century Network was only exchanging 19% of its traffic with YouTube Chicago data-center. It was also very clear that the flows were not being equally divided among data-centers because YouTube Ashburn data-center was receiving the highest share of traffic from both the networks and was significantly higher from traffic shares that other data-centers were getting. When we examined the traffic distribution more closely, we noticed that the traffic was being distributed at a fixed proportion to YouTube data-centers from all the *ISP-X* PoPs irrespective of which PoP was geographically closer to which data-center.

The distribution of the overall client-to-YouTube traffic is shown in Fig. 3. We can see that the client-to-YouTube traffic is clearly not equally divided among the data centers. In particular, we see that the ASH data center receives slightly more than a quarter of the traffic, while the LAX, CHI, and DAL data centers receive about 17% of the total traffic. On the other hand, the DAL, MIA and NYC data centers receive only ~7% of the total traffic each. This is very similar to what we observed in case of the two prefixes we discussed above.

Fig.3 shows how the total traffic is divided. Next, we look at how traffic coming from individual source PoPs of *ISP-X* is distributed. In Fig. 4, we show how client-to-video server traffic is distributed among 7 YouTube data centers for traffic originating at each *ISP-X* PoP. In this figure x-axis shows different PoP for *ISP-X*, and y-axis shows the fraction of total traffic going to different YouTube data centers. As seen in this figure, the fraction of traffic received by each YouTube data center from each PoP is the same for all PoPs. It implies that although PoPs of *ISP-X* and YouTube data centers are located at geographically diverse locations, they do not have any preferences to each other in terms of network/geographic "proximity". More specifically, traffic coming from clients is distributed to 7 YouTube data centers according to *fixed proportions*. We have also verified that these proportions hold at various other levels such as over time, at AS level, and individual IP prefix level (plots not shown due to space limitations).

4.2 Load Balancing among Three Web Servers

We now analyze how YouTube performs load balancing among the three front-end web servers. Since all the web-servers are located inside San Jose data-center, all the traffic to front-end web servers have to come to San Jose. An interesting but not so surprising discovery is that the traffic is equally distributed among those 3 front-end server IP addresses. This observation holds true at different time granularity, e.g., over different hours or over different days, as well as across different spatial granularity, e.g., at the level of individual PoPs of the ISP or with respect to individual client ASes. These observations are shown in Fig. 5, where Fig. 5(a) plots the traffic distribution among the three front-end web servers over different hours, Fig. 5(b) plots the traffic distributions among the three front-end web servers at various PoPs of the ISP, and Fig. 5(c) plots the traffic distributions among the three front-end web servers at various (large) client ASes of the ISP. That the traffic is equally distributed among the front-end web servers is expected, as YouTube front-ends employs the round-robin DNS resolution [2] for mapping `www.youtube.com` to the IP addresses of front-end web servers.

4.3 Proportional Load Balancing of YouTube-to-Client Traffic

In the discussion so far we used only one direction of the traffic. i.e, traffic going from clients to YouTube data centers. Our findings show that this traffic is proportionally distributed among various YouTube data centers. In the following, we analyze the traffic from the reverse direction, i.e., from YouTube data centers to clients. Comparing distributions in these two directions is inherently challenging because of asymmetric routing in the Internet. Routing in the Internet is not symmetric, that is the network path taken by the traffic going from a client to one of the YouTube data centers may not be the same as the path taken by the reply traffic coming from the YouTube data center to the client. Furthermore, since the network flow data available to us is only collected at various PoPs of the *ISP-X*, it may not have the YouTube to client traffic for some of the client-to-YouTube traffic, as the reply traffic from YouTube can go through different ISPs. Therefore, in order to analyze how the traffic from YouTube data centers to various *ISP-X* PoP is distributed, we only consider the IP prefixes for which we see the traffic coming from all the YouTube data center locations. In addition, some of the YouTube data centers may not use *ISP-X* to send the reply traffic to customers at all. In our data, we do not find any reply traffic from Miami YouTube data center. Hence we ignore traffic from Miami YouTube data center in the following analysis.

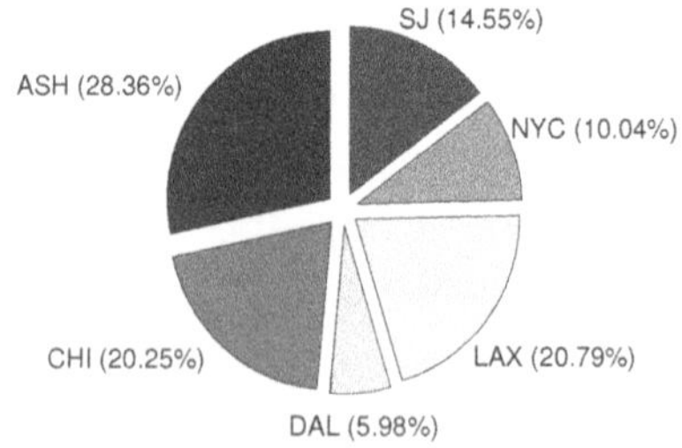

Figure 6: Traffic distribution from YouTube data centers to clients.

Fig. 6 shows how much traffic is sent by each of the YouTube data center to clients. As seen in this figure, the largest fraction of video traffic is sent by the YouTube ASH data center. While CHI and LAX send 20% of the traffic each, and remaining traffic is sent by the SJ, NYC and DAL data centers.

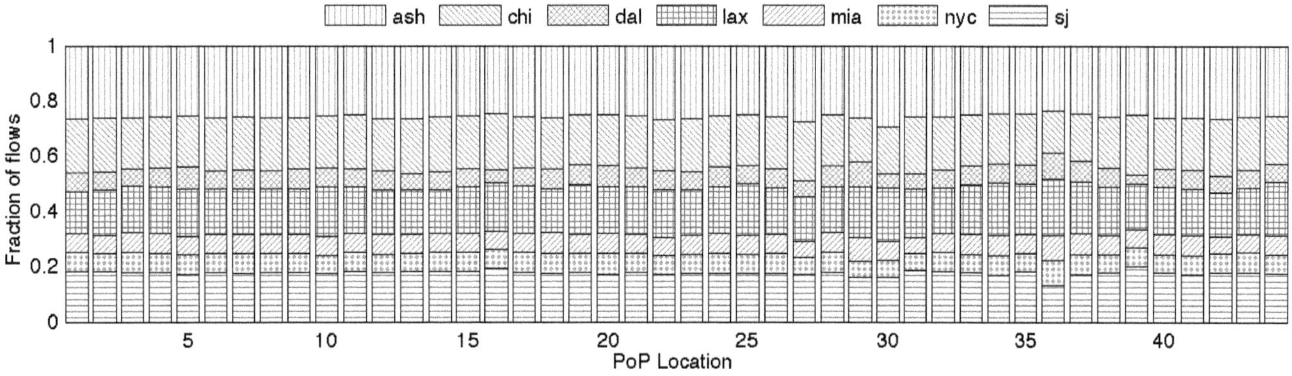

Figure 4: Client traffic distribution to different video serving data centers.

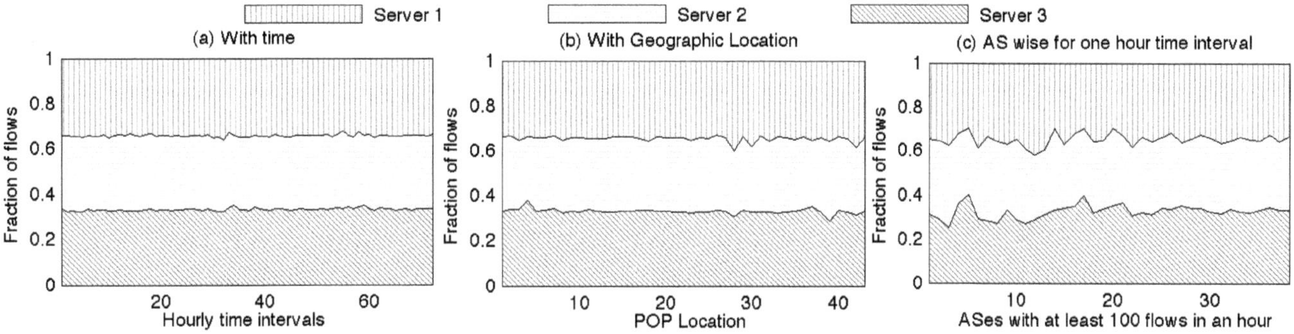

Figure 5: Load balancing among three front-end YouTube servers.

Next, we investigate if the proportional traffic distribution holds for the YouTube data center-to-client traffic at the PoP level. As mentioned before due to asymmetric routing in Internet, for this analysis, we consider traffic for only those IP prefixes which receive traffic from all the YouTube data centers (except Miami data center) through *ISP-X*. Furthermore, we group all the IP prefixes using *ISP-X* PoPs. For this we assign a PoP to each IP prefixes, which is the PoP from where traffic with the corresponding IP prefix enters in the ISP network.

We plot the fraction of traffic sent by each data center to various *ISP-X* PoPs in Fig. 7. In this figure different destination *ISP-X* PoPs are shown on the x-axis, and y-axis shows the fraction of the traffic as number of sampled flows received by the PoP, from a given YouTube data center. As seen in this figure, traffic from different YouTube data center to *ISP-X* PoP is distributed proportionally. In addition, these proportions are the same as the total proportions of the traffic sent by each data center shown in Fig. 6.

4.4 Proportional Load Balancing and "Size" of Data Centers

Our analysis has shown that YouTube does not do a proximity-aware load balancing. Instead, it does load balancing among its data centers in a fixed proportions. As we show next, the distribution of incoming video-requests to its data centers based on the "size" or the "resources" available at those data centers. Since we do not have any access to internal system design of each YouTube data center, we use the number of IP addresses seen at each location as the rough estimate of the size of a data center. We plot the fraction of traffic received by each YouTube data center along with the fraction of IP addresses seen from different data centers in Fig. 8(a). As we see in this figure, the amount of traffic received by each data center is directly proportional to number of IP addresses seen at that location. Furthermore, Fig. 8(b) shows

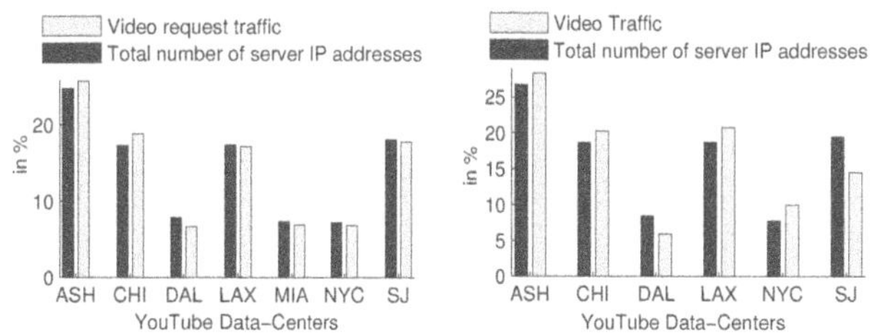

(a) Client to YouTube traffic (b) YouTube to client traffic

Figure 8: Distribution of traffic between clients and YouTube data centers.

that fraction of traffic sent by different YouTube data centers to *ISP-X* PoPs, is proportional to the fraction of total number of IP addresses seen at the corresponding data center. It shows that *YouTube performs load-sharing among its data centers based on their "size", not location.*

Extracting proportions using SVD: Next, we use the rank-1 approximation using SVD[4] [15] to estimate the pro-

[4]Albeit the proportionality can also be verified directly, the SVD automatically yields the proportionality (or a rank-1 matrix approximation) that best fits the data.

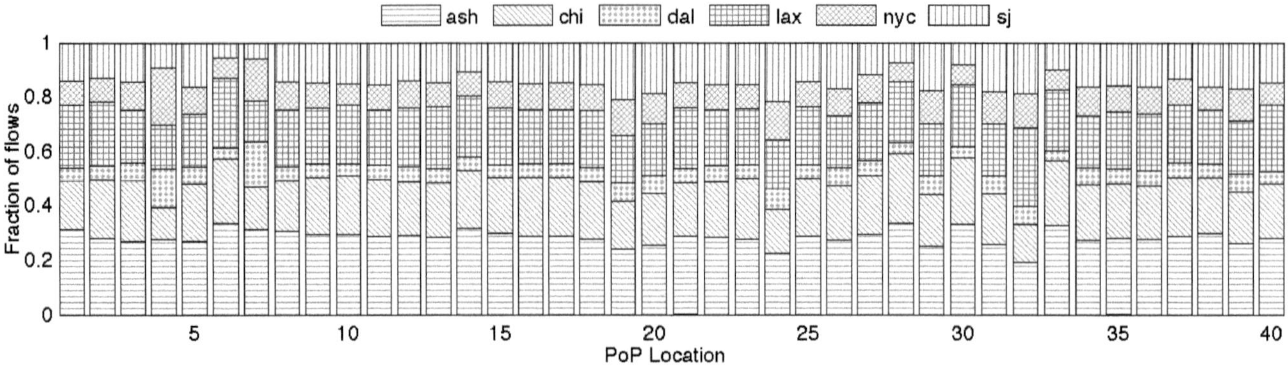

Figure 7: Traffic distribution from video servers to various client PoPs.

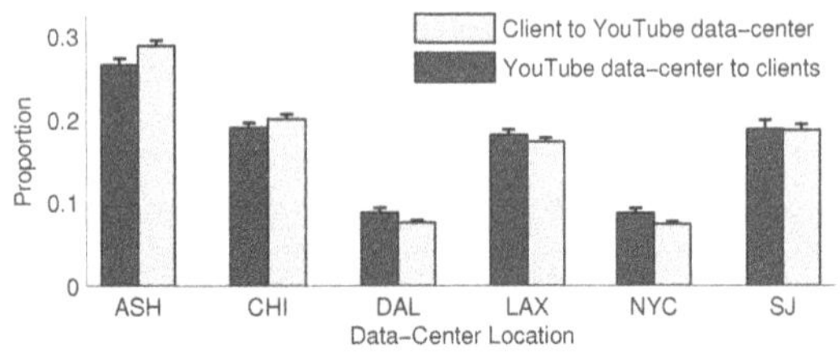

Figure 9: Traffic proportions extracted using SVD.

portions used to distribute the traffic among different data centers. For this analysis, we construct the traffic matrices C and S for client-to-YouTube and YouTubeto-client traffic respectively. Here C_{ij} is the traffic originating from ith /24 IP prefixes which is destined to jth data center, and S_{ij} is the traffic received by ith prefix from jth data center. It is possible that some IP prefixes may not be using *ISP-X* network to reach all the data centers and vice versa, therefore, for the unbiased estimate of proportions, we ignore the /24 IP prefixes which do not send data to all the data centers for the traffic matrix C, and prefixes which do not receive data from all the data centers for the traffic matrix S. Since we do not see traffic coming from YouTube Miami data center, we ignore it in this analysis so that we can compare the proportions seen in both directions of the traffic. We construct a large set of matrices c and s by randomly selecting 1000 rows from matrices C and S respectively to verify if the proportions hold for all the prefixes for different random selection of IP prefixes. We perform the SVD based rank-1 approximation on matrices c and s. Fig. 9 shows the proportions estimated for both client-to-YouTube and YouTube-to-client traffic using matrices c and s. In this figure, black horizontals line on top of each bar show the 95% confidence interval for the mean values shown in the figure. As seen in this figure, traffic is distributed in the same proportions for both matrices, with very little variances.

4.5 Traffic Volume Asymmetry

As we have already observed, the amount of client-to-YouTube flows is much smaller compared to YouTube-to-client flows(see Sec. 3). In this section we further analyze the YouTube-to-client and client-to-YouTube traffic ratios to get a better insights of the YouTube traffic. For this analysis, we define "two-way traffic pairs" as $\langle c2s(p, dc), s2c(p, dc)\rangle$ for different /24 IP prefixes p and YouTube data centers dc. We use term $c2s(p, dc)$ to represent the traffic sent by IP prefix p to dc data center of YouTube. Here we are interested in learning how the ratios $r(p, dc) = \frac{s2c(p,dc)}{c2s(p,dc)}$ are distributed.

Due to asymmetric routing in Internet some of the two-way traffic pairs may contain zero values. Therefore we only consider the pairs with non-zero values in our analysis. Fig. 10(a) shows the distribution of $r(p, dc)$ for all such two-way traffic pairs for the number of bytes exchanged between IP prefix p and data center dc, and Fig. 10(b) shows the distribution of $r(p, dc)$ using number of flows. As seen in this figure, the ratio of the bytes exchanged between IP prefixes and data centers stays between values 40 and 80 for more than 80% of the pairs, on the other hand the ratio of the flows exchanged is most of the times close to 2. *It demonstrates that traffic exchanged between IP prefixes and data centers is fairly consistent, and can be used for estimating the YouTube traffic that is not seen in the ISP-X network.* (See Sec. 6).

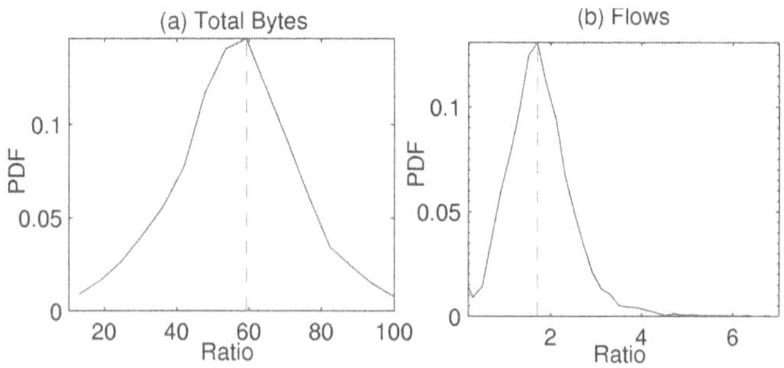

Figure 10: Distribution of ratios for the traffic exchanged between IP prefixes and YouTube data centers.

5. POP-LEVEL YOUTUBE TRAFFIC MATRICES

In Section 4, we made the observation that the YouTube traffic from clients at all locations are divided in a fixed proportion irrespective of whether a data-center is nearer to a client or very far from it. We also saw that the traffic from the data-centers to the clients also follow similar proportional distribution. This behavior of end-to-end traffic matrices naturally raises the question of whether the traffic also gets divided in a similar way inside the *ISP-X* backbone. In this section we look at the *entry PoP to exit PoP traffic-matrix* from the perspective of *ISP-X* with the objective to better understand how the traffic enters *ISP-X* network and gets divided to different exit PoPs.

To study this interaction, we generate *entry-exit* traffic matrices based on the entry and exit PoPs for the YouTube traffic from the perspective of *ISP-X*. We have following two entry-exit matrices based on the direction: (i) from clients to YouTube servers, and (ii) from YouTube servers to clients.

5.1 Single Preferred Exit in Client to YouTube Traffic

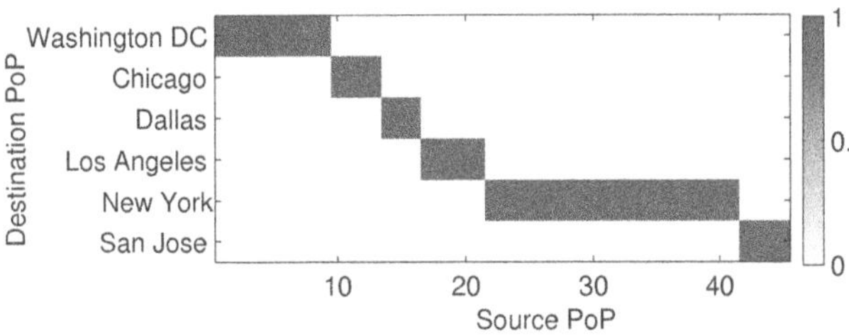

Figure 11: Entry PoPs to exit PoPs traffic distribution from client to YouTube traffic

For the clients to YouTube servers traffic we look at how much traffic enters from an *ISP-X* PoP and which PoP it exits from. We see that the traffic exits from only 7 of the *ISP-X* PoPs where YouTube is present. We also see that for each of the 44 PoPs from which the client to YouTube traffic enters *ISP-X*, all of the traffic from that PoP exits *ISP-X* from exactly one of the 7 exit PoPs. If we represent the entry PoPs as columns of the traffic matrix and exit PoPs as the rows, we see that each column has exactly one non-zero entry. A closer inspection of this matrix reveals that for any PoP P, it has a single exit-pop E_P such that E_P is the geographically closest *ISP-X* PoP where YouTube is present. Clearly, for the seven PoPs where YouTube data centers are present, $P = E_P$.

Next, we compare this entry-exit traffic matrix with the "end-to-end traffic demand and supply" matrices from YouTube's perspective seen in Sec. 4. We see that they are significantly different. For instance, the end-to-end traffic matrix which shows how the total traffic to YouTube video-servers are divided among different data centers, is a rank-one matrix, and follows the gravity model [10]. On the other hand the entry-exit traffic matrix seen by *ISP-X* is a full-rank sparse matrix where each column has exactly one non-zero row. From the point of view of *ISP-X*, traffic flows do not seem to be getting divided to different locations.

To understand the reason behind this difference between the two traffic matrices, we examined BGP routing information. From the BGP data, we see that YouTube aggregates all of its IP addresses in all the data centers in only 3 IP prefixes: 64.15.112.0/20, 208.65.152.0/22, and 208.117.224.0/19. All of these three prefixes are then announced to *ISP-X* at each of the 7 PoPs where YouTube is present. This allows *ISP-X* to do an early exit (or hot-potato) routing [13]. Since all the YouTube prefixes are announced from each of the locations where YouTube is present, *ISP-X* can transfer the YouTube-bound traffic at the exit PoP that is nearest to the source PoP irrespective of the final destination data center for the traffic.

Fig. 11 shows how the traffic entering from different *ISP-X* PoPs exits the ISP network. As we can see PoPs 1 to 9 send all of their YouTube-bound traffic towards Washington DC PoP. Similarly, there are 20 PoPs for which New York is the nearest exit PoP to reach YouTube. It shows that each *ISP-X* PoP has exactly one preferred exit PoP for all the YouTube traffic, irrespective of the final destination data center. We use this mapping of source PoPs to their nearest exit-PoP in Sec. 7 for some of the "what if" analysis.

Traffic carried by YouTube: The early-exit routing employed by *ISP-X* has another implication in terms of how the traffic reaches the final destination data center. Since *ISP-X* hands over all the YouTube-bound traffic to YouTube at local PoPs, YouTube has to deliver this traffic to the final destinations using its own "internal" network.

To estimate the amount of client to YouTube traffic that YouTube has to deliver to its different data centers, we look at how much traffic *ISP-X* hands over to YouTube at each location and how much of it is destined to the local YouTube data center. For instance, from all the clients in nearby PoPs, if *ISP-X* hands over 100 units of traffic to YouTube at New York PoP, then 7%, 7%, 17%, 7%, 18%, 16% and 17% of it are destined to New York, Miami, Los Angeles, Dallas, Chicago, Ashburn and San Jose data centers respectively. We see that only 7 units of traffic is actually delivered locally to New York data center, while remaining 93 units of the traffic still has to be carried somehow to other data centers. Overall, we see that only ~10% of the total traffic remains local, while remaining ~90% of the client to YouTube traffic is delivered to the final destination data centers by YouTube using its "internal" network.

5.2 High Locality-bias in YouTube to Client Direction

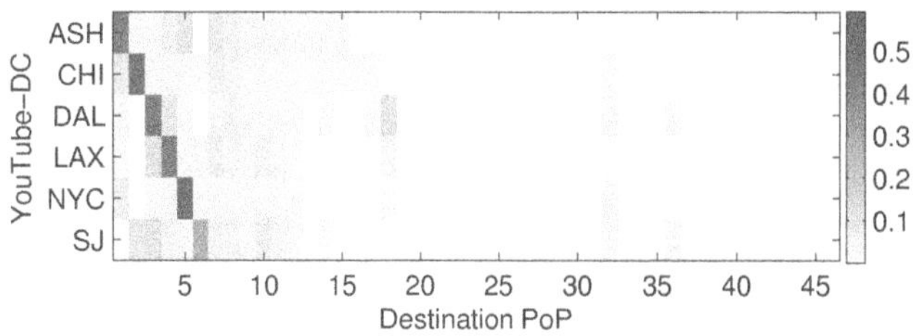

Figure 12: YouTube servers to exit-PoP traffic distribution

Although YouTube uses a proximity-agnostic mechanism to load balance the traffic between YouTube servers and client, the entry-exit traffic matrix at PoP level shows strong locality bias. In Fig. 12, each row represents the distribution of traffic originating from a YouTube data center, which enters the *ISP-X* network through the corresponding local PoP, to all the PoPs as a fraction of the total traffic coming from that data center. Also, in this figure first 6 destination PoP are the ones where the six data centers connect to the ISP in the same order as YouTube data centers shown in y-axis. This figure shows from each PoP from which YouTube to client traffic enters *ISP-X*, about 40% to 60% of the traffic exits *ISP-X* network from the local PoP itself, and only the remaining traffic enters the *ISP-X* backbone.

Not surprisingly, early-exit routing is again the reason behind high locality bias in the YouTube to client traffic. When we look at the BGP information available in the flows, a very large number of prefixes are announced from multiple *ISP-X* PoPs. Therefore, in many cases *ISP-X* selects an exit PoP from a list of PoPs where the destination prefix is announced and in general it prefers the PoP that is geographically closest to the entry PoP.

These results show that even when the content-providers do not do geography-aware load balancing, large ISPs still can still employ early-exit routing and carry less traffic in their backbone.

6. ESTIMATING UNSEEN TRAFFIC

As seen in Sec. 4, the proportionality of traffic split across YouTube data centers (as seen by the ISP) holds at various levels such as over different time intervals or at individual AS or IP prefix level. Furthermore, we showed that ratio of the traffic exchanged between YouTube data centers and individual client prefixes is fairly stable (See Fig. 10). These observations led us to develop a method to estimate the *unseen* and *partially seen* YouTube traffic – namely the (portion of) traffic carried by other ISPs – and "complete" the traffic matrix between YouTube data centers and users from the customer ASes of the ISP.

Basically we have two ways of estimating the unseen traffic: a) based upon the proportional distribution among data-centers, and b) based upon the ratio of client-to-YouTube and YouTube-to-client traffic. These approaches have different error characteristics. The proportions at which the traffic gets distributed to (and from) different data-centers have very small variations compared to the ratio of traffic in two direction (see Figures 9 and 10). Therefore, we try to use the proportionality of traffic distribution to do the estimate as much as possible. Only when its not possible to use that piece of information (such as when we see no client to YouTube data at all), we make use of the ratio of traffic in different directions.

• **Formulating a matrix completion problem:** To facilitate the discussion in this section, we represent the client-to-YouTube traffic matrix by C, where $C_{i,j}$ = Total bytes from ith IP prefix to jth data center, and the YouTube-to-client matrix by S, where $S_{i,j}$ = Total bytes to ith IP prefix from jth data center. Both C and S have unknown entries representing the traffic carried between corresponding client prefix and YouTube data center. To get a complete picture of how much traffic is actually exchanged between an IP prefix and and a YouTube data center including the traffic not carried by *ISP-X*, we need to estimate all such unknown values. The problem therefore can be viewed as a matrix completion problem where some entries are known and some unknown and we use the known entries to compute the values of the unknown entries.

• **Estimation using proportional distribution:** For our matrix completion problem, we first use the proportions at which the YouTube traffic is divided among its 7 data centers. First, we divide the rows of the matrices C and S to form three sub-matrices each: C^f and S^f which consist of all the rows for which all the column entries are known, C^p and S^p which consist of all the rows for which at least one column entry is known, and C^0 and S^0 which consist of all the rows for which none of the column entries are known.

Next we use the proportion $x_1 : x_2 : x_3 : x_4 : x_5 : x_6 : x_7$ (extracted in Sec. 4) to fill the missing entries of C^p as follows. For each row, we first get the known values, say $C^p_{i,j_1}, C^p_{i,j_2}, \ldots, C^p_{i,j_m}$ where $1 \leq m \leq 7$. Each of the unknown entry $C^p_{i,k}$ in that row can be estimated as $\frac{(C^p_{i,j_1}+C^p_{i,j_2}+\ldots+C^p_{i,j_m})\times x_k}{(x_{j_1}+x_{j_2}+\ldots+x_{j_m})}$. We apply the same mechanism to fill the missing entries in S^p by using the proportions.

For filling the values in C^0 and S^0 we use a slightly different approach. Since we do not have any known entries in any of the rows, we exploit the mean ratio between client-to-YouTube and YouTube-to-client traffic to estimate one entry per row for C^0 using the corresponding non-zero value from S^p or S^f. Since all of the IP prefixes in C and S must have either sent or received traffic from YouTube data centers through *ISP-X*, for each completely unknown row in C, the corresponding row in S must have at least one known entry. For each row in C^0, we pick one known field from the corresponding row in S and divide it by the mean ratio to get the corresponding column in C^0 and vice versa for S^0. Finally we combine the rows of C^f, C^p and C^0 to get the completed matrix C' for C, and S' by combining S^f, S^p and S^0 for in-complete initial traffic matrix S.

• **Results:** For the estimate of "unseen" traffic, we first extracted all the IP prefixes from the Netflow data, which were seen either in client-to-YouTube traffic or YouTubeto-client traffic or both. There are around 150,000 such IP prefixes in our Netflow data. Using these prefixes we prepared matrices C and S by extracting the total number of bytes exchanged by these prefixes with different YouTube data centers.

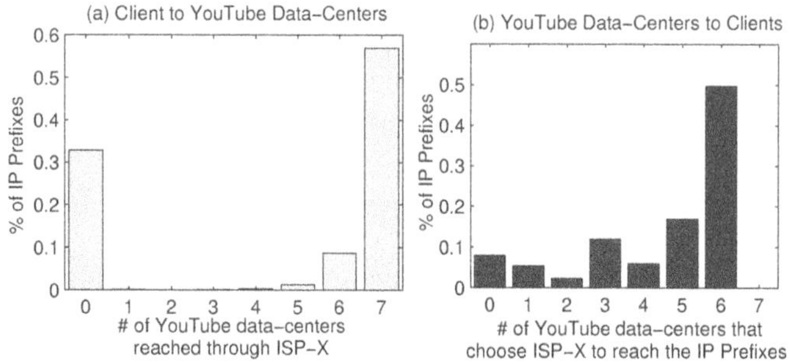

Figure 13: Distribution of IP prefixes on the basis of total number of YouTube data centers reached by them using *ISP-X*

Fig. 13 shows the distribution of IP prefixes seen in the YouTube traffic going through the *ISP-X*'s network, on the basis of the total number of YouTube data centers reached by them using *ISP-X*. In Fig. 13(a) we see that more than 50% prefixes use *ISP-X* to reach all 7 YouTube data centers, on the other hand less than 50% prefixes received traffic from 6 YouTube data centers through *ISP-X*. These figures show that there is a large amount of unseen traffic for these IP prefixes which is delivered through other ISPs.

We show the distribution of estimated unseen traffic for IP prefixes using our methodology in Fig. 14. In this figure, x-axis shows the IP prefixes and y-axis shows the corresponding unseen traffic as a fraction of total traffic received or sent by these prefixes to all the YouTube data centers. Moreover, for the client-to-YouTube data centers traffic we

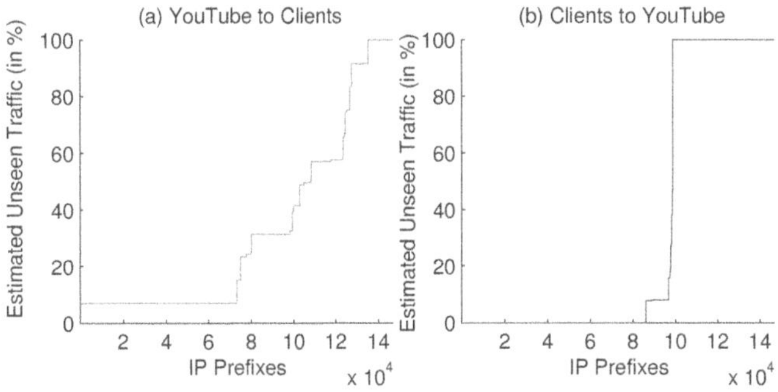

Figure 14: Distribution of estimated unseen traffic for IP prefixes

Table 3: Summary of traffic estimation. (We hide the original unit here due to the anonymity reasons.)

	to YouTube	from YouTube
Total seen traffic	0.59	39.7
Estimated unseen traffic	0.34	20.4

see that 36.5% of the estimated total traffic is not seen by *ISP-X*. Similarly, for the YouTube-to-client traffic 34% of the estimated total traffic is unseen. Overall the percentage of unseen traffic is 34.1% of the estimated total traffic. We summarize these results in Table 3.

We conclude from above that *ISP-X* does not see a huge portion of the traffic exchanged by its customer ASes with YouTube. Therefore, any changes in the routing policy used by its customer ASes and YouTube can have significant impact on the *ISP-X*'s network. Furthermore, this estimation of the unseen traffic can now enable the *ISP-X* to estimate the "new" traffic demand and prepare for the potential impact on its network, when routing changes lead to YouTube to re-route unseen traffic through the ISP instead.

7. "WHAT IF" ANALYSIS

In Section 4, we observed that YouTube does a location-agnostic proportional load-balancing. We also saw in Section 5 that YouTube announces all-inclusive large prefixes from all the locations where it peers with *ISP-X*. Finally, we were able to estimate some of the traffic that is exchanged between clients and YouTube that *ISP-X* does not see. These results give us insights on what is happening now. However, since the dynamics of the network change over time, it is natural to ask what happens if things change. In this section we use the insights gained about YouTube and its traffic characteristics with respect to *ISP-X* to investigate some of the "what if" scenarios to examine the pros and cons of different load-balancing strategies and routing policies, and the impact of the resulting traffic dynamics on both YouTube and the ISP.

- **Scenario 1: What if YouTube employs a location aware load balancing among its data centers?**

We investigate the scenario when instead of being location-agnostic, YouTube employs a "location based" load balancing scheme. One way YouTube can achieve this is by configuring its front-end web servers in such a way that they direct the clients' video requests to a data center that is nearest to the location of the requesting client.

We already know when the client to YouTube traffic enters *ISP-X* network from a PoP it exits from exactly one exit PoP where YouTube is attached. We will use this information to assign each PoP to its nearest YouTube data-center. For instance, YouTube data center near the New York PoP will be the only data center that will deliver video traffic to all the PoPs that use New York PoP as the exit PoP for YouTube bound traffic. We then evaluate how it affects the *ISP-X*'s traffic matrix and also the load at different YouTube data centers.

Effect on the ISP traffic matrix: Since all the client PoPs will fetch videos from the nearby YouTube data center in this scenario, the traffic that is carried in the ISP backbone will be reduced significantly. For instance, when we computed the amount of traffic that remains local at the source PoP under this approach, we see that about 44.5% of overall YouTube to client traffic does not even enter the ISP backbone compared to the same number for location-agnostic load balancing. Moreover, it eliminates most of the "long-distance" communication for the ISP. For example, Los Angeles data center will never have YouTube to client traffic going to Chicago PoP under the location based load balancing. *Hence, location based load balancing will have a positive impact on ISP-X's PoP level traffic matrix, since it reduces the traffic on ISP-X's backbone network significantly.*

Poor resource utilization under geographical load-balancing. Although geographical load-balancing helps in reducing the amount of traffic carried in the *ISP-X*'s backbone, it results in poorer resource utilization and increased peak load at each data center.

To analyze the impact of location based load balancing on YouTube data centers, we compute the amount of video requests served by each data center during different time of the day. We estimate the amount of video requests served by each data center by rearranging the client to YouTube data center matrix on the basis of nearest PoP. In Fig. 15, we compare the loads at six data centers under location based and resource based load balancing schemes. In each figure here, x-axis represents the time and y-axis represents the total number of flows received by the corresponding data center at different time. We observe that the load on New York and Dallas data center increases significantly as they are the nearest data centers for a large number of *ISP-X* PoPs.

Furthermore, let us assume that the maximum number of flows each data center receives in any hour indicates the load at that data center. Let L_i^j indicate the number of flows received by data center i in hour j, then we define the load $L_{max}(i), i = 1, 2, \ldots, 6$ as, $L_{max}(i) = \max_{j=1 \text{ to } 72} L_i^j$. Under these assumptions, the sum of peak load at each data center ($ML = \sum_{i=1}^{6} L_{max}(i)$) will represent the amount of computing resources needed during the peak load time to serve all the client requests. If we compare MLs under the two schemes, we see that the total units of resources that are needed in case of location based load balancing is about 30% higher than that of the current resource based load balancing.

The reason for this increase is the following. Since the peak load time for client requests coming from different PoP is different, the peak load at one of the PoPs of *ISP-X* is proportionally shared by all the data centers in the location agnostic load balancing. However, in case of location based load balancing it does not allow the distribution of peak

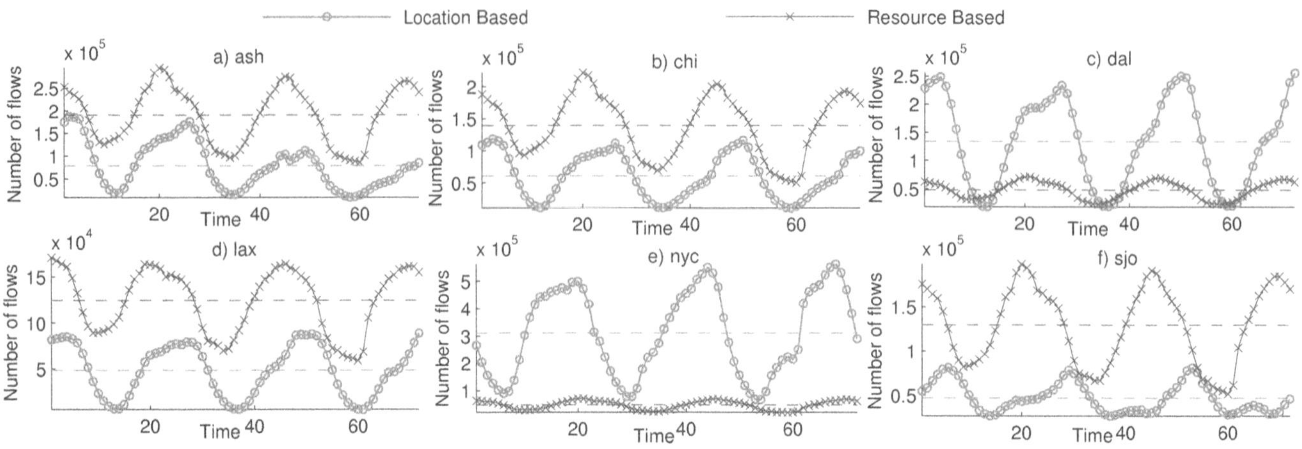

Figure 15: Comparison of traffic at different YouTube data centers for resource based and location based traffic distribution schemes.

load, and all the load accumulates at the nearest YouTube data center.

In summary, we see that while location based load balancing may reduce the load on *ISP-X*'s backbone network, it results in the poor resource utilization and creates more "hot-spots" for YouTube by increasing the load on the individual data centers during the peak load hours.

• Scenario 2: What if YouTube only announces IP prefixes specific to each data center at the corresponding location where it exchanges traffic with *ISP-X*?

Since YouTube announces larger all-inclusive prefixes at each location where it exchanges the traffic with *ISP-X*, the ISP can do early exit routing and dump all YouTube-bound traffic to YouTube at the nearest exit (see Sec. 5). This forces YouTube to carry that traffic internally to its different data centers. In this section, we investigate how traffic matrices will change if YouTube only announces specific prefixes from each of its location.

To see how the traffic matrix for *ISP-X* changes if YouTube starts announcing only the specific local prefixes at each location, we divided YouTube IP addresses in smaller prefixes so that each prefix has IP addresses belonging to only one YouTube data center. We combined smaller prefixes to form larger prefixes as long as the larger prefixes included IP addresses from a single data center. From the three large prefixes we obtained 2 /25s, 9 /24s and 5 /23s where each of the prefixes belonged to exactly one data center.

If YouTube announces only the specific prefixes from each location corresponding to the local data center, then *ISP-X* will have to carry the traffic corresponding to each YouTube prefix to the data center where it is present. This means most of client to YouTube server traffic will be carried in the ISP backbone.

However, as we have already seen in Sec. 4.5, the ratio between client-to-YouTube and YouTube to client traffic is approximately 1 : 59, the additional volume of traffic that is carried in *ISP-X* backbone will only increase by 2% for the total YouTube traffic.

• Scenario 3: What if due to BGP routing changes the number of prefixes YouTube reaches using *ISP-X* increases?

As seen in the Sec. 6, a significant portion of the traffic the customers of *ISP-X* exchange with YouTube is not visible to *ISP-X*. They are likely being carried by some other ISPs. If YouTube changes its routing policy and decides to send all that traffic through *ISP-X*, the amount of YouTube to client traffic handled by *ISP-X* would increase significantly: by about 50% of the current YouTube to client traffic volume. This might also happen if YouTube experiences routing failures in its other providers' network. Since YouTubetraffic amounts for about 5.8%, this results in about 2.9% increase in the total traffic carried by the ISP. On the other hand, being able to estimate this unseen traffic accurately, *ISP-X* can prepare and plan for such scenarios in advance.

8. CONCLUSIONS

In this paper, we presented the first extensive study of traffic exchanged between YouTube data centers and users, as seen *from the perspective of a large tier-1 ISP*. Using our trace-driven analysis of the interaction between YouTube and one of its large transit-providers, we inferred and analyzed the load balancing scheme employed by YouTube and how these choices affect the traffic dynamics across a large content provider and a tier-1 ISP. We further formulated and solved unseen traffic estimation problem that ISPs can use to get an estimate of the "new" traffic demand and prepare for the potential impact on its network, when routing changes lead their to re-route unseen traffic through the ISP instead. We also conducted several "what if" analysis to understand how the load balancing strategies chosen by content providers and routing policies used by the ISPs affect each other.

Although this paper focuses primarily on the traffic characteristics of YouTube, the methods used have general applicability. In fact, similar experiments can be easily carried out for any other content-providers to understand how their load-balancing and routing choices affect their and their ISPs routing matrices.

9. ACKNOWLEDGMENTS

We would like to thank the anonymous reviewers and our shepherd, Walter Willinger, for their helpful feedback on this paper.

We gratefully acknowledge the support of our sponsors. The work is supported in part by the NSF grants CNS-0626812, CNS-0721510, CNS-0905037, CNS-1017647 and the DTRA Grant HDTRA1-09-1-0050. The opinions expressed in this paper are solely those of the authors and do not necessarily reflect the opinions of any of the funding agencies or the University of Minnesota.

10. REFERENCES

[1] Z. Al-Qudah, S. Lee, M. Rabinovich, O. Spatscheck, and J. Van der Merwe. Anycast-aware transport for content delivery networks. In *WWW '09*, pages 301–310, New York, NY, USA, 2009. ACM.

[2] T. Brisco. DNS Support for Load Balancing. RFC 1794, April 1995.

[3] M. Cha, H. Kwak, P. Rodriguez, Y.-Y. Ahn, and S. Moon. I tube, you tube, everybody tubes: analyzing the world's largest user generated content video system. In *IMC '07*. ACM, 2007.

[4] X. Cheng, C. Dale, and J. Liu. Statistics and social network of youtube videos. In *Proc. of IEEE IWQoS*, 2008.

[5] J. Dilley, B. Maggs, J. Parikh, H. Prokop, R. Sitaraman, and B. Weihl. Globally distributed content delivery. *IEEE Internet Computing*, pages 50–58, 2002.

[6] P. Gill, M. Arlitt, Z. Li, and A. Mahanti. Youtube traffic characterization: a view from the edge. In *IMC '07*. ACM, 2007.

[7] C. Huang, A. Wang, J. Li, and K. W. Ross. Measuring and evaluating large-scale cdns (paper withdrawn). In *IMC '08*, pages 15–29, New York, NY, USA, 2008. ACM.

[8] V. Jacobson, C. Leres, and S. McCanne. Tcpdump Man Page. *URL http://www.tcpdump.org/tcpdump_man. html*, 2003.

[9] R. Krishnan, H. V. Madhyastha, S. Srinivasan, S. Jain, A. Krishnamurthy, T. Anderson, and J. Gao. Moving beyond end-to-end path information to optimize cdn performance. In *IMC '09*, pages 190–201, New York, NY, USA, 2009. ACM.

[10] A. Medina, N. Taft, K. Salamatian, S. Bhattacharyya, and C. Diot. Traffic matrix estimation: Existing techniques and new directions. *ACM SIGCOMM Computer Communication Review*, 32(4):174, 2002.

[11] W. Norton. The evolution of the US Internet peering ecosystem. Equinix White Papers, 2004.

[12] M. Saxena, U. Sharan, and S. Fahmy. Analyzing video services in web 2.0: a global perspective. In *NOSSDAV '08: Proceedings of the 18th International Workshop on Network and Operating Systems Support for Digital Audio and Video*, pages 39–44, New York, NY, USA, 2008. ACM.

[13] R. Teixeira, A. Shaikh, T. Griffin, and J. Rexford. Dynamics of hot-potato routing in IP networks. *SIGMETRICS Perform. Eval. Rev.*, 32(1):307–319, 2004.

[14] A. Vakali and G. Pallis. Content delivery networks: Status and trends. *IEEE Internet Computing*, 7(6):68–74, 2003.

[15] T. Will. Introduction to the Singular Value Decomposition. *La Crosse, WI*, 2003, 2003.

[16] M. Zink, K. Suh, Y. Gu, and J. Kurose. Characteristics of youtube network traffic at a campus network - measurements, models, and implications. *Comput. Netw.*, 53(4), 2009.

APPENDIX

A. CHANGES AFTER WE COLLECTED THE DATA

After this data was collected in Spring 2008, we have observed several ways in which YouTube video delivery has changed. Most importantly, we have seen that YouTube video delivery system now uses IPs that belong to Google (AS15169) and even the DNS names for the video hosting servers are using google.com domain. For example, `www.youtube.com` now has a CNAME record mapping it to `youtube-ui.l.google.com` which is then mapped to different IP addresses when accessed from different geographic locations. Since we do not have access to any new Netflow data, we did some active measurements. We tried to access `www.youtube.com` from hundreds of Planet-Lab nodes and based upon ICMP ping latency and traceroutes to the IPs the DNS servers return for `www.youtube.com`, we learned that IPs mapping to `www.youtube.com` are part of different geographic locations. Therefore, we conjecture that the traffic to the YouTube front-end servers is most likely being served by a data-center which is geographically closer to the user. We do not have any new information regarding the video traffic, other than the facts that (a) the video servers IPs have changed and most of video server IPs are coming from IP prefixes belonging to Google and (b) the packet size distribution shown in Fig. 2 still holds true.

On the Characteristics and Reasons of Long-lived Internet Flows *

Lin Quan
USC/Information Sciences Institute
4676 Admiralty Way, Suite 1001
Marina del Ray, CA 90292
linquan@isi.edu

John Heidemann
USC/Information Sciences Institute
4676 Admiralty Way, Suite 1001
Marina del Ray, CA 90292
johnh@isi.edu

ABSTRACT

Prior studies of Internet traffic have considered traffic at different resolutions and time scales: packets and flows for hours or days, aggregate packet statistics for days or weeks, and hourly trends for months. However, little is known about the *long-term* behavior of *individual flows*. In this paper, we study individual flows (as defined by the 5-tuple of protocol, source and destination IP address and port) over days and weeks. While the vast majority of flows are short, and most bytes are in short flows, we find that about 20% of the overall bytes are carried in flows that last longer than 10 minutes, and flows lasting 100 minutes or longer make up 2% of traffic. We show that long-lived flows are qualitatively different from short flows: they are generally slower, less bursty, and are due to different applications and protocols. We investigate the causes of short- and long-lived flows, and show that the traffic mix varies significantly depending on duration time scale, with computer-to-computer traffic more and more dominating in larger time scales.

Categories and Subject Descriptors

C.2.3 [**Computer-Communication Networks**]: Network Operations—*Network Monitoring*; C.2.5 [**Computer-Communication Networks**]: Local and Wide-Area Networks—*Internet*; C.2.6 [**Computer-Communication Networks**]: Internetworking

General Terms

Measurement

*Lin Quan and John Heidemann are partially supported by the US DHS, contract number NBCHC080035, and Heidemann by the NSF, grant number CNS-0626696. The conclusions of this work are those of the authors and do not necessarily reflect the views of DHS or NSF.

Keywords

Long Duration Flow, Computer-to-computer communication

1. INTRODUCTION

Traffic in the Internet is a complex mix of effects from protocols, routing, traffic engineering, and user behaviors. Understanding traffic is essential to modeling and simulation, traffic engineering and planning [3], router design [1], and better understanding of the Internet [17]. There has been a great deal of study of traffic at the protocol level [19, 20], and at time scales of seconds to hours [4–6, 17, 24], and over longer terms for planning [18, 22]. Yet prior work studies either protocol effects at small time scales (seconds to hours) or aggregate effects at large time scales (hours to weeks), but little attempt to bridge this division and understand protocol effects on long-lived traffic.

This paper explores how users and protocols affect long-lived network traffic. Unlike prior protocol studies, we explore traffic that lasts for multiple hours to days. Unlike prior long-term traffic studies, we explore the causes of traffic patterns at the flow-level in multiple time scales, instead of only trends of aggregate traffic. We use the standard flow definition of the 5-tuple of source and destination IP address and port, plus the protocol number, ended by a timeout [22].

There are several reasons that an understanding of long-lived flows is increasingly important. First, understanding long-lived flows is important for network management. While capacity planning can be done on measures of aggregate traffic, several kinds of on-line traffic control have been proposed: protocol trunking [16], optical trunking [11], lambda switching [2], and low-buffer operation [1]. Understanding the feasibility and impact of these approaches requires flow-level traffic characterization.

Second, a scientific understanding of the Internet must investigate the patterns and causes of long-lived traffic. What are the first-order statistical properties of long-lived flows, and how do they differ from short ones? In addition, short-term studies of network packet data have shown self-similar behavior in time scales of seconds to hours [7, 17], but most such analysis stops as diurnal effects dominate.

Finally, we wish to understand the *causes* of long-term flows. Protocol effects dominate sub-second time scales, and human behavior governs diurnal and weekend effects. Some human-centric traffic is no longer bound by human patience, such as "patient" peer-to-peer file sharing [10], and unattended streaming media, perhaps streaming Internet audio in a store, or automated, Internet-based, Tivo-like devices such as the Slingbox [14]. Computer-to-computer traffic is growing due to automated control and sensing, online backup, and distributed processing in the cloud and across distributed data centers. We hypothesize that at some point in the future, computer-to-computer traffic will eclipse human-driven traffic, just as data traffic has eclipsed voice.

The contribution of this paper is to begin to answer these questions. To this end, we describe new mechanisms for *multi-time-scale* flow analysis that allows efficient evaluation of network traffic from time scales of minutes to weeks (Section 3). We have operated this system for more than six months, taking data from a regional network. Second, we document the presence of long-lived flows, showing 21% of Internet traffic (by bytes) are carried by flows longer than 10 minutes, and nearly 2% are carried by 100 minutes or longer flows (Section 4.1). Finally, in Section 4.2 we begin to evaluate the causes of such traffic, exploring how protocol mix changes as a function of time scale.

2. RELATED WORK

An important aspect of understanding Internet traffic is packet sizes and protocols. Thompson et al. studied the packet size distribution and protocol mixes in one-day period, and diurnal patterns of aggregate traffic in 7-day period [22]. CAIDA has collected several 90-second traces each day, in a period of ten months, and studied the trends of packet lengths and protocol mixes [18]. We use the common 5-tuple flow definition [22], but we are more interested in flow characteristics and traffic mixes across different time scales.

Characteristics of Internet flows have also been studied extensively. Brownlee et al. studied lifetimes of streams (bi-directional flows) [4,5]. They found that at least 45% of the streams are *dragonflies* (lasting less than 2 seconds), 98% of the streams last less than 15 minutes and the rest 2% being *tortoises*. Similarly, we find that most of the Internet bytes are carried by the vast majority of short flows, but long flows also account for a considerable fraction of bytes (see 4.1.2). Later work studied flow characteristics systematically, showing the correlations between flow size, duration, rate and burstiness [6]. We adopt the similar ideas from this work, but compare flows behavior as a function of duration.

Because of the large volume of traffic, careful sampling techniques have been used to achieve better processing rates. Researchers from AT&T estimated flow statistics by sampling packet streams and exploiting protocol details [8]. Researchers at UCSD used adaptive sampling algorithms to increase Cisco NetFlow system robustness without compromising accuracy (in case of large volume of traffic) [9]. Zhang et al. studied the distributions and causes of different flow rates [24]. They collected sampled traces from a backbone ISP covering from 1 to 24 hours, and unsampled traces ranging from 30 to 120 minutes. They also studied the correlations between flow rates with size and duration, and gave careful analysis on the causes of different flow rates (such as congestion limited, sender/receiver window limited, and application limited). Our work builds on theirs: we continuously collect unsampled IP packet headers, and systematically study the relations between flow durations and other characteristics. We also provide the ability to investigate multi-time-scale flows for efficient analysis and give preliminary analysis of causes of long-lived flows.

Several other groups have exploited flow characteristics for traffic engineering purposes. Shaikh et al. studied load-sensitive routing, but they adopted a conservative, 10-or-more packet definition of long flows. We study several longer time scales and find interesting implications of the long flows. Trunking (with TCP or optical networks [2, 11, 16]) gathers together groups of flows to achieve throughput benefits. Our work identifies long-duration flows that could be used by trunking. Recent work in low-buffer routing has shown the possibility of using very few router buffers (two magnitudes fewer than current commercial practices), provided that traffic is "sufficiently" smooth [1]. We show that long-duration flows are smoother and could be a good candidate for such optimization.

3. DATA COLLECTION AND ANALYSIS

Network packet trace collection is well understood, but sequential processing becomes challenging as datasets stretch from minutes to months. In this section we review our approach to long-term collection of network flows and multi-time-scale analysis of that data.

3.1 Collection and Anonymization

Our campus network operators provide us anonymized packet headers at the main USC connection to our upstream regional network. We use the LANDER system [12] to process data at USC's HPCC compute cluster [23], coordinating parallel processing of 512MB fixed-length, Endace ERF-format, packet-header traces.

The default LANDER policy anonymizes traffic with keys that rotate at regular intervals. Such a scheme is useful because it insures that any accidental information disclosure in one period does not assist unanonymization in other periods. However, key rotation impedes analysis of flows longer than the rotation period. LANDER therefore re-anonymizes all flows with a common, long-term key. We reduce this greater risk through stricter policy controls: we control access to the long-term data and prohibit those with access to attempt unanonymization.

Although our work builds on packet-header traces, a potential direction for future is to start with NetFlow records as a data source. Another interesting direction is to compare characteristics of long flows at different places of the Internet.

3.2 Multi-time-scale IP Flow Analysis

Given our goal of observing long duration flows, we have four problems: what flows are and what to record for each flow; how to manage streaming data and incremental analysis; how to support analysis at very different time scales, from seconds to weeks or more. We consider each of these next.

We use the standard 5-tuple definition of flows: source and destination port and IP address, plus protocol. We convert LANDER's packet headers into flow records using a slightly modified Argus toolkit [13]. Argus flow records provide: the 5-tuple flow identifier (given above), flow start and finish time, number of packets, and number of bytes in the flow. Flows begin with the first packet with a unique 5-tuple, and continue until a timeout τ (currently set to 60 seconds).

We extend Argus to also capture information about flow burstiness, which is defined as variance of bytes over fixed time period T. We record the number of time periods ob-

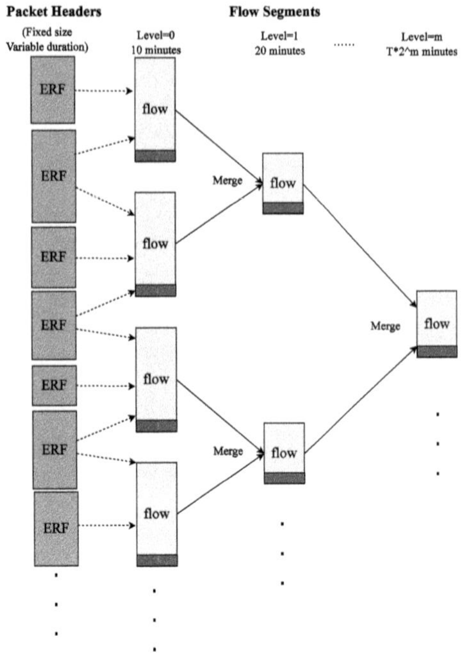

Figure 1: The structure of multi-level flow records: each level has primarily flows with exponentially longer durations, plus a "tail" to permit merging.

served, and the average and square sum of bytes over the time periods. Our base time period for variance is $T = 10$ minutes, the same as our base segment length as described below. This data allows us to compute standard deviation of bytes over T afterwords.

Because we expect to run data collection indefinitely, it is essential that we collect data concurrent with analysis, and that we store data in a manner that supports efficient queries. An easy algorithm would use an in-memory flow table (indexed by the 5-tuple), and update corresponding flow record upon seeing a flow. However, this algorithm can easily run out of memory due to a large number of concurrent flows, particularly with long timeouts. So we divide flow records into *segments* for efficient analysis. LANDER uses fixed-size segments (each 512MB of packet headers, or 1–2 minutes at our current capture rates), and these traces arrive asynchronously, invoking our segment processing engine as it arrives.

We convert these variable-duration segments to *hierarchical, fixed duration* segments to support efficient analysis and queries that span different timescales. We call the intial fixed duration segments *level-0 flow segments*, currently each at a duration of $T = 10$ minutes. When we determine that all packet-header traces needed to cover a flow segment are present, we process them to create the corresponding level-0 flow-segment. Care must be taken because each flow segment typically requires several packet-header traces, and the packet-header trace at the start or end of a flow segment typically span two flow segments. When a trace spans multiple segments, we place the packets corresponding to each segment in seperate flow records in each segment. These records will later be merged into a common flow record in hierarchical merging described next. The left-most column of Figure 1 shows packet headers (dark gray) being converted to level-0 flow-segments.

Each level-0 flow-segment contains 10 minutes of flow records, but long flows will span multiple, possibly hundreds or thousands of segments. Since we cannot sequentially process terabytes of data to make queries for different durations, we assemble level-0 flow-segments into *higher-level segments*. We assemble segments hierarchically in powers of two, so two adjacent level-0 segments are processed to produce one level-1 segment, and so on, with two level-i flows producing a level-$i+1$ flow.

To avoid segments growing in size indefinitely and to allow efficient queries at large timescales, we *prune* the flow contents at each level according to the following rule:

The pruning rule: A level-i segment starting at time t must preserve all flows of duration longer than $T2^{i-2}$ (the duration rule), and all flows that are active in the timeout period the last τ seconds of the trace (the tail rule).

The presence corollary: A level-i segment starting at time t guarantees to contain all flows of durations between $T2^{i-2}$ and $T2^{i-1}$ that start in the time $[t, t + T2^{i-1}]$. It may also contain some shorter flows at the end, and some longer flows (up to $T2^i$) which are not complete yet.

(When $i = 0$, the durations start at zero.)

The duration part of the pruning rule keeps each level file small, because each targets a specific time duration and guarantees coverage for that duration. All short flows that are not active at the end of the segment may be discarded. We can prove the presence corollary, because we guarantee coverage for flows that start in the first half of the segment and last for between a quarter and a half of the segment, since by definition those flows must terminate in the segment and are too long to be discarded. We do not guarantee all shorter flows are present, since they will be discarded to keep segment sizes manageable. We cannot guarantee that longer flows are complete since they may stretch into subsequent segments. We show the results of our multi-level storage below in Section 3.4.

The tail part of the pruning rule allows adjacent segments to be merged without loss of information. Only flows that are active in the last τ seconds of the segment are candidates to merge with the next segment, since by our definition of flows they will timeout if the gap is longer. By keeping *all* flows active in this window at the end of the trace we therefore guarantee no information about mergeable flows will be discarded, so we do not accidentally truncate the head of a new long-duration flow. Finally, the rule keeps flows that are *active* in the last τ seconds, more than flows *started* in the last τ seconds—a flow may start anywhere in the segment, and long-running flows will typically span most or all of the segments.

Several details in segment organization support merging and processing. When merging two adjacent level-i segments to create a level-$i+1$ segment, we combine and reorder flow records. We keep flow records sorted by flow start time, so if the level-i files are numbered n and $n+1$, the merge must scan all of file n but only the head of $n+1$. Variance can be combined across segments because we preserve the sum of observations and their squares, not just the computed variance.

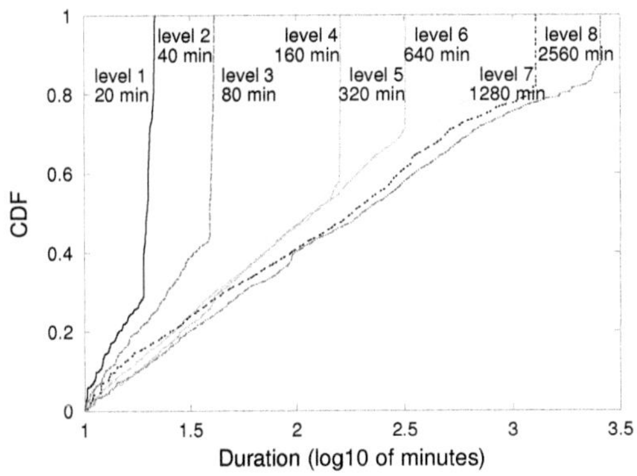

Figure 2: Durations of flows observed at 8 different time scale levels (from 2 days of dataset D1, flows less than 10 minutes truncated).

time scale	all	median	presence
0	4967M	2M	835k
1	652M	570k	7.1k
2	214M	276k	3.1k
3	105M	271k	1.5k
4	53M	274k	949
5	27M	268k	598
6	14M	265k	586
7	7M	300k	301
8	4M	308k	139
9	2.6M	265k	119
10	1M	243k	148
11	846k	846k	71

Figure 3: Number of flows at different time scales: all flows, median per segment, and *presence* flows in one segment (14 days from dataset D8).

Finally, all segment processing is done on a workstation cluster in parallel. Segments are processed and committed atomically (using filesystem rename as the commit method). Concurrent processing of the same file is discouraged by tagging in-process files with a flag, and we recover from crashed processing jobs by timing out flags. We periodically scan the segment tree to catch and correct any missed merges due to races.

3.3 Managing Outages

Very few network tasks can run uninterrupted forever without error—with power outages and scheduled maintenance, continuous operation more than a few months is good. While we tolerate several types of outages, we have experienced multiple gaps, primarily due to software errors in our experimental system. Since May 2009 we have taken 8 traces to date in durations of 8, 9, 15, 23, 40, 65, and 99 days. In the future we plan to bridge brief outages by computing both optimistic and pessimistic flow records around a gap.

3.4 Understanding the Methodology

To illustrate how different time scale flows are stored in different levels of our system, Figure 2 shows the cumulative distribution of flow durations for different levels of segments on a linear-log scale graph. Each line shows a different level segment, starting with level-1 at 20 minutes and doubling at each subsequent level.

Each level shows a range of flow durations. Because of the tail rule, all segments have some very short flows. Because there are relatively few very long flows, the size of high-level segments is dominated by shorter flows. Although each segments at level-i contain flows from zero to $T2^i$ in duration (some of them may not be complete yet), many short flows have been pruned away for clearer view of the longer flows.

In addition, each segment has a large number of flows near the segment duration limit. For example, 70% of level-1 flows are about 20 minutes long, and 57% of level-2 flows are 40 minutes long. These durations indicate flows that last the entire segment and are part of flows that span multiple segments. Their correct duration can only be identified at higher-levels.

To show the advantage of our multi-time-scale storage, Figure 3 shows the number of flows across all files at each level, the median for each level, and how many are valid by the presence rule. We see the number of valid, *presence* flows (bottom line) per segment drops quickly—the true number of long flows is small. The median number of flows plateaus around 300k per segement because segment size is limited by the tail rule and all flows active in the last τ seconds. Finally, the storage requirements (top line) drop exponentially, although they are again limited by the tail rule. We conclude that multi-scale storage is important to study long duration flows.

4. RESULTS

We next describe the results of our measurement system: how do long flows differ from short flows in their characteristics and causes? Since May 2009 we have colected 8 traces. For this paper, we focus on *D1*, a 2-day subset of 15-day capture starting 27 May 2009, and *D8*, a 14-day subset of a 65 day capture starting 19 Feb 2010.

4.1 Characteristics of Long Flows

We first compare flow characteristics: rate, size in bytes, and burstiness as a function of flow duration. Our goal is to understand what long flows are like, and how they differ from short flows. We therefore graph density plots, with darker shades indicating more flows. To quantify distributions at each time scale, we overlay box plots for each time scale, showing quartiles, minimum, and maximum.

Most graphs in this section are generated with *time-scale sampling*: we take one level-i segment for each level ($i \in [1, 11]$, omitting level 0), getting a representative sample from a fraction of the data (Section 3.4). We then select subset of that segment that we can guarantee full capture (flows with duration in $[T2^{i-2}, T2^{i-1}]$) and plot only those flows, discarding the rest. This approach implies that one can compare frequency of some characteristic across a given time scale (for a fixed x value). However, at different time scales (varying x), the absolute number of shorter duration flows are underrepresented relative to longer duration flows.

Figure 4 shows this difference: the left graph uses *both* level-0 segments and one level-1 segment (all flows), while the right uses only one of each level (sampled), so the left has higher absolute densities indicating more flows. Although time-scale sampling under-estimates the total num-

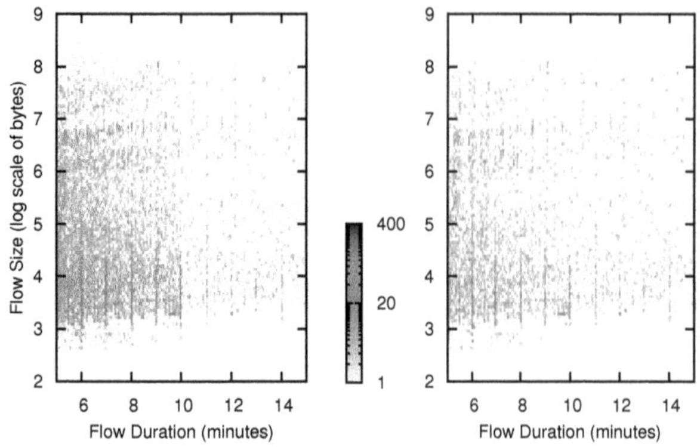

Figure 4: Density plot comparing all (left) and sampled flows (right), duration vs. size (from D8).

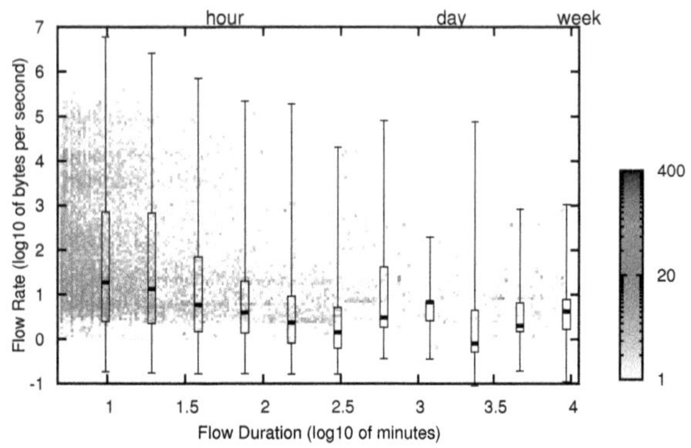

Figure 5: Density plot (log-scale) with quartile boxes of flow duration vs. rate (sampled from D8).

ber of flows in the sampled case, it correctly reports the overall trend of flow sizes. More importantly, it allows study of the long-tail of long-lived flows, while reducing computation spent on the already-well-studied shorter flows (computation that would otherwise overwhelm analysis). In summary, sampling allows efficient observation of the correct trends, but not absolute density scales across durations.

4.1.1 Flow Rates

We first look at flow rate vs. duration in Figure 5. We see that short-duration flows can be quite fast, spanning 6 orders of magnitude speed. By contrast, long flows are typically much slower. Quartiles show median rates are around 50 bytes/s for flows shorter than 40 minutes, with a broad distribution, while flows longer than 100 minutes or longer have medians closer to 10 bytes/s.

The slower rate of long flows may be helpful for traffic engineering, allowing longer time to react to long-lived but slow-moving flows. Although we see very different rates at different durations, rate alone does not show which flows contribute to traffic. To evaluate if "slow and steady wins the race", we next look at flow sizes across all time.

4.1.2 Flow Sizes

Prior studies of "slow but steady" tortoise flows can account for significant traffic [5, 6]. Having just shown long flows are slower than short flows, we next consider if their persistence makes up the difference.

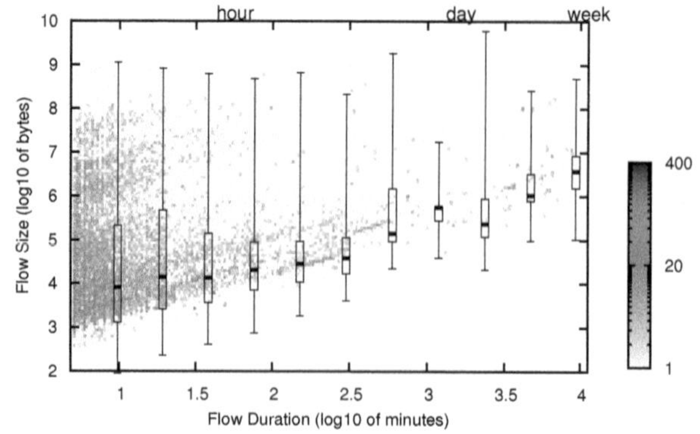

Figure 6: Density plot (log-scale) of flow duration vs. size (bytes) (sampled from D8).

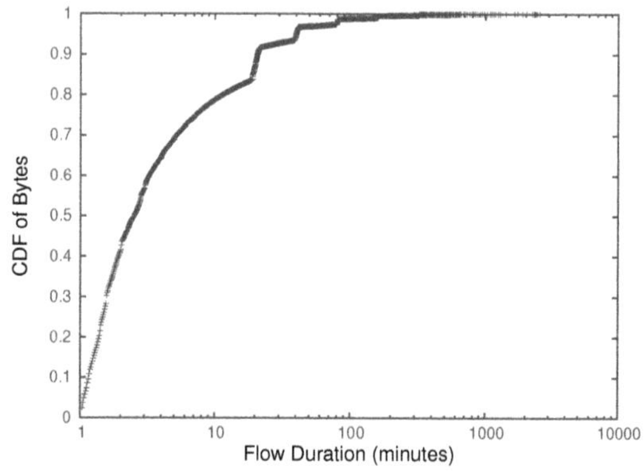

Figure 7: Cumulative distribution of flow sizes (in bytes) of all flows of two days from D1.

Figure 6 shows the flow sizes (in bytes) of D8. We see a strong correlation between flow duration and total number of bytes at a slower-than linear rate on the log-log plot. Linear regression of median shows an exponentially increase at a rate of 0.77 with a 0.958 confidence coefficient.

Although each long-duration flow sends many bytes, there are many more brief flows, so in the aggregate short flows may still dominate traffic by bytes. Figure 7 shows the cumulative number of bytes sent by *all* flows of a two day period in D1. (Unlike density plots, this CDF considers all flow segments of all time scales sent over the entire period.) This graph confirms that there are not enough long-duration flows to dominate Internet traffic. From the figure we can observe that although the short flows dominate the Internet traffic (in terms of bytes), 21.4% of the Internet traffic are carried by flows longer than 10 minutes, 12.6% are carried by flows longer than 20 minutes, and nearly 2% are carried by flows longer than 100 minutes. Even though short flows are the majority of traffic bulk, optimizations to long flows can still have a significant effect. Internet Service Providers may also be interested in this observation, since the contribution of long-running but slow flows supports the need to meter service by bytes, not by peak speeds.

4.1.3 Flow Burstiness

Burstiness measures the uniformity of traffic rate over time. From Figure 9, we can observe that long flows are generally less bursty than short flows (linear regression of me-

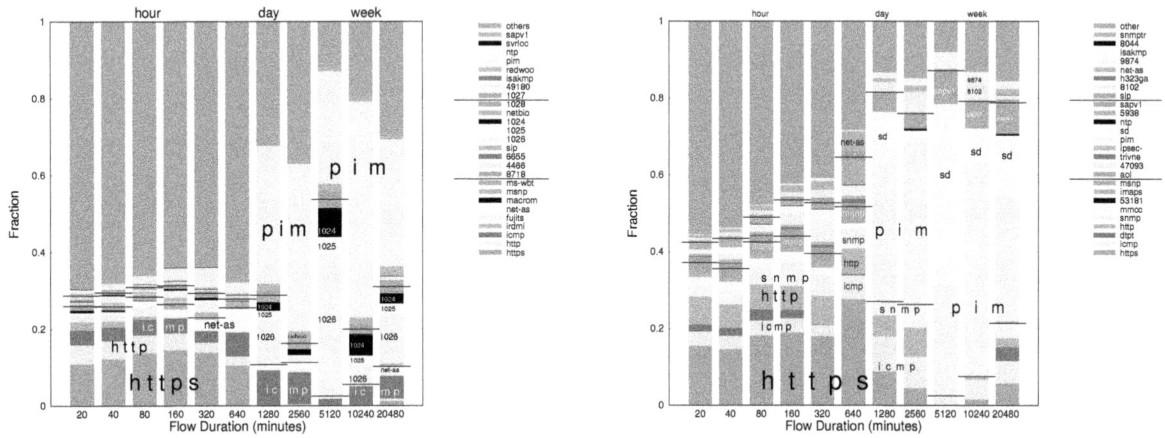

Figure 8: Source (left) and destination (right) port usage, plus PIM and ICMP, as a function of time scale (sampled from D8). Well-known ports are labeled with protocols and protocol colors differ.

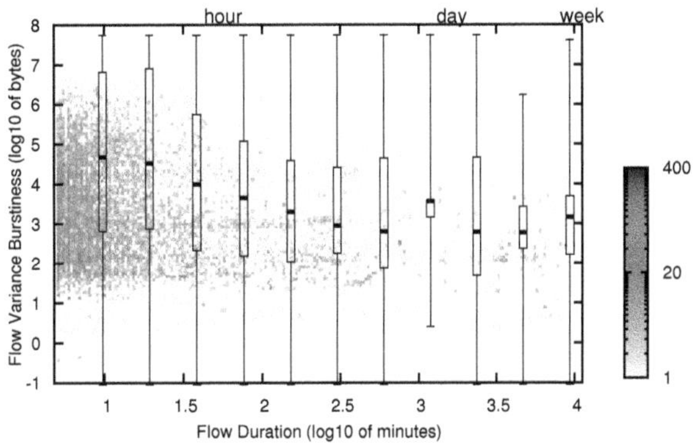

Figure 9: Density plot (log-scale) of flow duration vs. burstiness (log-scale variance, bytes) (sampled from D8).

dian shows an exponentially decrease at rate −0.296, with a −0.830 confidence coefficient). Our explanation, confirmed when we consider causes in Section 4.2, is that long flows are mostly computer-to-computer communications, and so are naturally less bursty. One implication of this observation is for very low-buffer routers, which assume input traffic is smooth [1,21]. Low burstiness could be provided with high probability in segregated long-duration flows.

4.2 Causes of Long-lived Flows

While we observe long-duration flows behave differently, we would like to know their causes. Although imperfect, port-based classification is our best tool and Figure 8 shows fraction of flows by port usage from minutes to weeks. We treat ICMP and Protocol Independent Multicast (PIM) as special "ports".

The result supports our hypothesis: the traffic mix switches from interactive, to background, to computer-to-computer as time scale increases. Hour time-scales are dominated by web (HTTP, HTTPS, ports 80 and 443) destinations. Web is also a frequent source port as well. Although at first it may seem suprising to think about port 80 as a source of traffic, this observation follows because our analysis treats each side of a bidirectional connection independently, so a port-80 source is the reply-side of a web request Day-long flows contain "background" traffic, with computer-driven but human-initiated protocols like chat and messaging (msnp, aol). We believe these represent regular application-level keep-alives and presence reports. Finally, week-long flows are almost all computer-to-computer protocols that run without human involvement, such as time synchronization (ntp) and multicast control (sd, pim, sapv1). This trend also shows with a very strong shift against TCP in the *protocol* mix at longer time scales: TCP is 66% through 10 hours, but falls to 16% at two weeks, where 30% is PIM and 43% UDP.

Another interesting result is that ports 1024 through 1026 are very common sources for long-lived flows. These are the first non-reserved ports and we believe indicate long-running, started-at-boot daemons.

Although we have identified the question of causes for long-lived Internet flows, we have only preliminary answers. Port-based classification schemes are well known to be inaccurate as many protocols today intentionally use random ports, so use of other techniques to identify applications is one direction (potentially those of Kim *et al.* [15]). Also, carrying out similar experiments in other locations, and more thorough evaluation of causes of long-running flows (protocols or applications) are both important future directions.

5. CONCLUSION

We propose an efficient multi-time-scale IP flow analysis methodology in this paper, targeting at the long-lived flows. The characteristics of different time scales of flows have been studied, with flow duration ranging from minutes to weeks. Our results show that long-lived flows are generally slow running and non-bursty ingredients of the Internet traffic, which is useful for traffic engineering purposes. We also study the causes of the long-lived flows, and found that unlike short flows with much human traffic, they are mostly computer-to-computer traffic for specific application purposes.

Acknowledgments

We would like to thank Yuri Pradkin for developing and operating the LANDER infrastructure that enables this work. We are also grateful to the anonymous reviewers for many valuable comments on this paper.

6. REFERENCES

[1] Guido Appenzeller, Isaac Keslassy, and Nick McKeown. Sizing router buffers. In *Proceedings of the ACM SIGCOMM Conference*, pages 281–292, Portland, Oregon, USA, August 2004. ACM.

[2] Daniel Awduche and Yakov Rekhter. Multiprotocol Lambda Switching: Combining MPLS Traffic Engineering Control with Optical Crossconnects. *IEEE Communications Magazine*, 39(3):111–116, March 2001.

[3] Chadi Barakat, Patrick Thiran, Gianluca Iannaccone, Christophe Diot, and Philippe Owezarski. A flow-based model for internet backbone traffic. In *Proceedings of the ACM SIGCOMM Internet Measurement Workshop*, pages 35–47, Marseille, France, October 2002. ACM.

[4] Nevil Brownlee. Some Observations of Internet Stream lifetimes. In *Passive and Active Measurement Workshop*, pages 265–277, 2005.

[5] Nevil Brownlee and kc claffy. Understanding Internet traffic streams: Dragonflies and tortoises. *IEEE Communications Magazine*, 40:110–117, 2002.

[6] Kun chan Lan and John Heidemann. A measurement study of correlation of Internet flow characteristics. *Computer Networks*, 50(1):46–62, January 2006.

[7] Mark E. Crovella and Azer Bestavros. Self-similarity in world wide web traffic: evidence and possible causes. *ACM/IEEE Transactions on Networking*, 5(6):835–846, December 1997.

[8] Nick Duffield, Carsten Lund, and Mikkel Thorup. Estimating Flow Distributions from Sampled Flow Statistics. In *Proceedings of the ACM SIGCOMM Conference*, pages 325–337, Karlsruhe, Germany, August 2003. ACM.

[9] Cristian Estan, Ken Keys, David Moore, and George Varghese. Building a better NetFlow. In *Proceedings of the ACM SIGCOMM Conference*, pages 245–256, Portland, Oregon, USA, August 2004. ACM.

[10] Krishna P. Gummadi, Richard J. Dunn, Stefan Saroiu, Steven D. Gribble, Henry M. Levy, and John Zahorjan. Measurement, modelling, and analysis of a peer-to-peer file-sharing workload. In *Proceedings of the 19th Symposium on Operating Systems Principles*, pages 314–329, Bolton Landing, NY, USA, October 2003. ACM.

[11] K.-P. Ho, H. Dal, C. Lin, S.-K. Liaw, H. Gysel, and M. Ramachandran. Hybrid wavelength-division-multiplexing systems for high-capacity digital and analog video trunking applications. *IEEE Photonics Technology Letters*, 10:297–299, February 1998.

[12] Alefiya Hussain, Genevieve Bartlett, Yuri Pryadkin, John Heidemann, Christos Papadopoulos, and Joseph Bannister. Experiences with a continuous network tracing infrastructure. In *Proceedings of the ACM SIGCOMM MineNet Workshop*, pages 185–190, Philadelphia, PA, USA, August 2005. ACM.

[13] Qosient Inc. Audit Record Generation and Usage System (ARGUS). `http://www.qosient.com/argus/`.

[14] Sling Media Inc. Slingbox: a tv streaming device. `http://en.wikipedia.org/wiki/Slingbox`.

[15] Hyunchul Kim, KC Claffy, Marina Fomenkov, Dhiman Barman, Michalis Faloutsos, and KiYoung Lee. Internet traffic classification demystified: myths, caveats, and the best practices. In *CoNEXT '08: Proceedings of the 2008 ACM CoNEXT Conference*, pages 1–12, New York, NY, USA, 2008. ACM.

[16] H. T. Kung and S. Y. Wang. TCP Trunking: Design, Implementation and Performance. In *IEEE International Conference on Network Protocols*, page 222, Washington, DC, USA, 1999. IEEE Computer Society.

[17] W.E. Leland, M.S. Taqqu, W. Willinger, and D.V. Wilson. On the self-similar nature of Ethernet traffic (extended version). *ACM/IEEE Transactions on Networking*, 2(1):1–15, February 1994.

[18] Sean McCreary and kc claffy. Trends in Wide Area IP Traffic Patterns - A View from Ames Internet Exchange. *CAIDA ITC Specialist Seminar*, 2000.

[19] J. Padhye, V. Firoiu, D. Towsley, and J. Kurose. Modelling TCP Throughput: A Simple Model and its Empirical Validation. In *Proceedings of the ACM SIGCOMM Conference*, pages 303–314, Vancouver, Canada, September 1998. ACM.

[20] Vern Paxson. Automated Packet Trace Analysis of TCP Implementations. In *Proceedings of the ACM SIGCOMM Conference*, pages 167–179, Cannes, France, September 1997. ACM.

[21] Anees Shaikh, Jennifer Rexford, and Kang G. Shin. Load-sensitive routing of long-lived IP flows. In *Proceedings of the ACM SIGCOMM Conference*, pages 215–226, Cambridge, MA, USA, September 1999. ACM.

[22] Kevin Thompson, Gregory J. Miller, and Rick Wilder. Wide-Area Internet Traffic Patterns and Characteristics (extended version). *IEEE Network Magazine*, 11(6):10–23, Nov/Dec 1997.

[23] USC. High-Performance Computing and Communications. `http://www.usc.edu/hpcc/`.

[24] Yin Zhang, Lee Breslau, Vern Paxson, and Scott Shenker. On the characteristics and origins of internet flow rates. In *Proceedings of the ACM SIGCOMM Conference*, pages 309–322, New York, NY, USA, 2002. ACM.

BasisDetect : A Model-based Network Event Detection Framework

Brian Eriksson
UW-Madison
bceriksson@wisc.edu

Paul Barford
UW-Madison
and Nemean Networks
pb@cs.wisc.edu

Rhys Bowden
University of Adelaide
rhysbowden@gmail.com

Nick Duffield
AT&T Research
duffield@research.att.com

Joel Sommers
Colgate University
jsommers@colgate.edu

Matthew Roughan
University of Adelaide
matthew.roughan@adelaide.edu.au

ABSTRACT

The ability to detect unexpected events in large networks can be a significant benefit to daily network operations. A great deal of work has been done over the past decade to develop effective anomaly detection tools, but they remain virtually unused in live network operations due to an unacceptably high false alarm rate. In this paper, we seek to improve the ability to accurately detect unexpected network events through the use of BasisDetect, a flexible but precise modeling framework. Using a small dataset with labeled anomalies, the BasisDetect framework allows us to define large classes of anomalies and detect them in different types of network data, both from single sources and from multiple, potentially diverse sources. Network anomaly signal characteristics are learned via a novel basis pursuit based methodology. We demonstrate the feasibility of our BasisDetect framework method and compare it to previous detection methods using a combination of synthetic and real-world data. In comparison with previous anomaly detection methods, our BasisDetect methodology results show a 50% reduction in the number of false alarms in a single node dataset, and over 65% reduction in false alarms for synthetic network-wide data.

Categories and Subject Descriptors

C.2.3 [**Computer-Communication Networks**]: Network Operations—*Network monitoring*

General Terms

Measurement, Performance

Keywords

Anomaly Detection

IMC'10, November 1–3, 2010, Melbourne, Australia.

1. INTRODUCTION

Networks are complex, dynamic and subject to external factors outside of their operators' control. Network operators must therefore vigilantly monitor their networks for faults and other events that could jeopardize their contractual commitments to customers. The problem is relatively easy when the type of fault is well understood (*e.g.,* link failures). There are standard protocols for alerting an operator to such faults, and although extending these methods particularly in the context of security is an ongoing effort, they are not the specific focus of this paper. Instead, this paper considers *unforeseen faults.* These faults are intrinsically more challenging to detect because we do not *a priori* know what we are looking for. These faults often manifest in unusual measurements that are commonly referred to as *anomalies.* Being able to find anomalies, and use them to diagnose network problems quickly and effectively would significantly enhance network operations. Developing a framework for effective and practical anomaly detection is the objective of our work.

A large number of studies over the past decade have been focused on developing methods to detect anomalous events in networks. The typical approach begins by measuring network traffic (*e.g.,* flow-export records) and then establishing a profile for "normal" behavior. Next, a method for detecting deviations from normality is applied. Most prior studies have largely taken a one-size-fits-all approach that has ultimately resulted in problems with accuracy and false alarm rate.

It is critically important in any anomaly detection system to have a very low false alarm rate. False alarms waste operator time and discredit results, leading to a "cry wolf" syndrome, where the anomaly detection system is quickly ignored. Most existing systems suffer from unduly high false-alarm rates. This is exacerbated by anomalies polluting the data used in determining the normal profile. In this paper, we seek to improve the accuracy of network event detection to the point where it becomes an effective tool for network operators.

To approach this problem of anomaly detection, we introduce the *BasisDetect* framework. The primary intuition behind the BasisDetect framework is that both normal traffic and anomalies have features that we can model and exploit for the purpose of automated detection. For instance, it is well known the traffic has strong diurnal and weekly cycles. Our hypothesis is that by considering traffic as a superposition of waveforms and then breaking these down into their component parts, we can build detection models that offer the opportunity to separate bundles of energy that can be semantically divided into to normal and anomalous traffic. The BasisDetect framework is divided into three components. The first step learns potential anomaly signal features from a small set of labeled network data provided to the algorithm. The second step uses a novel *basis pursuit* methodology to simultaneously decompose traffic into components of both non-anomalous behavior representing expected network traffic, and anomalous behavior learned from the previous step. This simultaneous estimation avoids the problem of anomalies polluting our normal profile data. The final step of the algorithm exploits known network structure to intelligently merge together the detected anomalous behavior using state-of-the-art statistical techniques.

Further objectives of our framework include developing an anomaly detection method that can be applied *(i)* to different data types since critical anomalies may be entirely invisible in some data, and *(ii)* in both a single node and network-wide context. Prior work has typically fallen into one or the other category due to detection methods that are primarily spatial or temporal. While our initial signal decomposition approach is temporal, we combine anomalies across the network using a *higher reasoning* framework. This combined, best-of-both-worlds approach offers a significant opportunity to improve detection accuracy. Intuitively, we treat network wide detection as a data fusion problem, where one can significantly reduce false alarms through the use of multiple time-series signals. It has the secondary advantage that it naturally incorporates different data types, without the need for strong relationships between the different time-series such as required, for example by PCA [1].

We use both synthetic and real world data to rigorously assess the capabilities of our model-based detection methodology. The first part of our evaluation considers NetFlow data collected at a single router along with a set of labeled anomalies that include DoS attacks, outages, scans, etc. We isolate a subset of the anomalies in the data and then apply the BasisDetect framework to learn anomalous models using a combination of signal components that isolate key elements of the events. We find that our BasisDetect methodology identifies all the labeled anomalies with 50% improvement in the false alarm rate when compared with the best competing methodology.

Next, we use a set of carefully generated synthetic data to assess the sensitivity of our model-based detection methodology. The data is designed to capture the key low and high frequency and spatial characteristics of non-anomalous traffic flows in a network-wide setting. We insert simple volume anomalies into this data and modulate the relative amplitude and frequency of these anomalies versus the non-anomalous traffic in order to assess sensitivity. While this synthetic data is not as rich as measurements collected in situ, we argue that it provides a powerful and meaningful starting point for assessing detection sensitivity. The results of our analysis show that the BasisDetect methodology detects all of the injected anomalies with false alarm rate over 65% less than the current state-of-the-art network-wide anomaly detection methodology.

Finally, we consider a set of Internet2 byte count data collected simultaneously across 11 PoPs. While this dataset does not have labeled anomalous events, we can compare the ability of the BasisDetect methodology and a state-of-the-art distributed method [2] to detect the most dominant anomalies detected by the standard PCA [1] anomaly detection methodology. Our results show that BasisDetect method will identify the PCA anomaly locations with 40% fewer false alarms than the competing state-of-the-art network-wide anomaly detection method. We believe that these results along with the results from single node and network-wide labeled data sets make a strong case for the utility of our model-based approach.

The remainder of this paper is as follows. In Section 2, we describe the background of detecting network anomalies and relevant related work. In Section 3, we describe the datasets used to test our method and competing anomaly detection algorithms. In Section 4 the BasisDetect framework is introduced. Then in Section 5, our temporal signal decomposition methodology is described with applications of anomaly extraction from a small training set, and anomaly detection. Then in Section 6, an intelligent data fusion methodology is described to localize anomalies given the results of our basis pursuit algorithm. Combining both methods, we summarize the BasisDetect methodology in Section 7. Finally, in Section 8 we evaluate the results of applying our method and several other well known methods to the given data sets. We summarize our work and discuss future directions in Section 9.

2. BACKGROUND AND RELATED WORK

Anomaly detection is now a large field, and we cannot hope to survey all papers within the field. We will focus on those of direct relevance to our work and describe them in detail since they help to highlight the uniqueness and potential benefits of our method. Our specific focus is on studies that consider anomaly detection on vector time-series data. This type of work gained its initial impetus with the consideration of how Principle Component Analysis (PCA) would perform in a network-wide setting [1, 3, 4]. Prior work relied primarily on performing some kind of temporal transform of the data, and assumed that anomalies will stand out against the traffic in the transformed space (examples transforms include wavelets in [5, 6], the Exponentially Weighted Moving Average or EWMA in [7, 8], and Fourier filtering in [6]). Anomalies are then generated for every individual set of measurements. The key benefits of the PCA methodology was that it took direct advantage of the non-scalar nature of network data, and that it sought to find an optimal linear transform of the data in order to reveal inconsistent data points. Following the initial work on PCA, Zhang *et al.* showed how much of the prior work on anomaly detection (including PCA) could be seen in a single framework [6], but more notably, that paper showed that the "sparseness" of anomalies could be exploited in aiding their discovery.

In more detail, the PCA framework described in [1] decomposes a traffic matrix into a set of vector components that capture the variance across all links or flows of the network. The components that resolve the highest variance across all links (*e.g.,* the most standard components) are considered to represent standard operating characteristics of the network observed in the link data matrix, the *"modeled traffic"*. Meanwhile, the less dominant components represent the *"residual traffic"* that is abnormal to the links in general. The amount of traffic energy in this residual component determines whether or not an anomaly has occurred in the observed traffic on each link.

The limitations of this PCA approach are well documented in [9]. In addition to having high sensitivity to tuning parameters, large anomalies in the network can corrupt the "modeled traffic" components and therefore cause obvious events to be ignored by the methodology. Also, detected anomalies found by PCA can not be localized to the specific anomalous link or router, and the PCA methodology can lead to *masking*, where one anomaly hides another. Finally, in PCA the "residual traffic" does not necessarily represent signal components specifying anomalies (possibly it is normal behavior found only on a single link), and therefore detecting events based on residual energy is prone to false alarms. Furthermore, the work in [10] shows how standard PCA-based anomaly detection methods are vulnerable to attacks. While the technique introduced in this paper builds on the idea of dividing the signal into modeled and residual components, the underlying methodologies used are completely different (PCA in the prior work, basis pursuit in this paper).

The authors of the Distributed Spatial Anomaly Detection technique described in [2] recognize that one of the main limitations of the PCA approach was the necessity of communicating all flow information back to some centralized computation point. Using non-parametric statistics and False Discovery Rate techniques (FDR) [11], each router in the network generates just a small test statistic that is communicated for anomaly detection. The use of more sophisticated multiple hypothesis detection techniques, like FDR thresholding, allows for a better statistical detection rate than more naive methodologies, such as Bonferroni Correction [12]. The biggest limitation of this approach is the complete decoupling of the measurements in the time domain. Therefore, any temporal correlation between network anomaly events (the measurements at time t helping inform the events from measurements at $t+1$) are ignored. In addition, the measurements considered are with respect to traffic volume only, with no discussion on how other link characteristic information (bytes, unique IP address, etc.) could be intelligently fused into the framework. Finally, the detected anomalies are not necessarily points of interest to a network administrator or anything that might represent the known structure of anomalies in networks. These detected anomalies are simply events of traffic volume that are abnormal compared with the remaining observed set of network data. A situation may occur when events are unlike the other observed network data and yet uninteresting from a network administration prospective. Other distributed approaches to anomaly detection exist [13, 14]. Although it should be noted that the BasisDetect framework is amenable to distribution, the focus of this paper will be to carefully treat the false alarm problem.

Our anomaly detection methodology will exploit the same non-parametric statistical techniques as [2] (originally developed in [15]). However, our methodology differs in that we use an estimated feature vector of detected anomaly energy instead of the raw packet counts. Data fusion from different data sources was shown some time ago to reduce false alarm rates (*e.g.*, [7]). In contrast, this paper develops an approach which can flexibly incorporate various different sources of data. By considering a general feature vector, we can potentially fuse a wide range of link characteristics, thereby improving results.

For the detection of anomalies in time-series data, our methodology will leverage the significant prior work on basis decomposition of signals [16, 17, 18]. This prior work focused on creating methodologies to exactly represent a signal given a sparse linear combination of components from the signal dictionary (*i.e.*, a matrix of signal components). In this paper, our goal is to resolve the gross characteristics of the signal, allowing for non-exact signal representation by our basis dictionary signals. In addition, our novel methodology will allow for the penalization of choosing selected dictionary signals, an application previously unexplored in the basis pursuit literature.

3. DATASETS

We use three different data sets to evaluate our model-based detection methodology. The intent of our analysis is to assess the capability of our approach as thoroughly as possible. To that end, we use empirical data sets for both single node with labeled anomalies and network-wide settings without labeled anomalies. We also use a synthetic data set in which we can precisely control both the normal and anomalous traffic in order to carefully assess the sensitivity of our method. Each of the data sets is described in detail below.

3.1 Synthetic Traffic Data

In order to accurately test anomaly detection algorithms, we need to be able to simulate reasonable datasets in a controlled way. Ringberg *et al.* [19] explain in detail why simulation must be used for accurate comparisons of anomaly detection techniques. In brief the reasons are: (i) accurate and complete ground truth information is needed to form both false-alarm and detection probability estimates; (ii) many more results are needed (than one can obtain from any realistic real dataset) to form accurate estimates of probabilities, and (iii) simulation allows one to vary parameters (say the anomaly size) in a controlled way in order to see the effect this has on anomaly detection.

Our approach to simulation is intended to highlight the features of the different techniques. We make no claim that the simulation is completely realistic, only that it illustrates clearly the properties of the different anomaly detection techniques. The simulations used here were generated in a similar manner to those in [20]. In particular, a spatial traffic matrix is generated using a gravity model and then extended into the temporal domain using a matrix product with a simple periodic signal. The resulting traffic is then enhanced by Gaussian noise with variance that is proportional to the traffic mean. The only differences with the previous study are that (i) we consider a range of sizes of networks, and (ii) consider a range of length of anomalies.

We should stress that the goal of these simulations is not to produce the most realistic test possible for the algorithms. However, the simulations allow us to obtain exact quantitative comparisons of algorithms in completely controlled circumstances, so we can explore the properties of the different approaches.

3.2 GEANT Data

The second set of data will be a collection of time-series data obtained from a GEANT network backbone router [21] located in Vienna, Austria. Collection of data began on January 14th 2009 and ended on February 24th 2009, for a total of 42 days of data acquisition. The dataset contains packet counts, byte counts, and IP entropy measured along this single link extracted using Juniper J-Flow records, sampled in aggregation bins of 1 minute for a total of 60,480 data samples observed. This dataset contains labeled anomalies, including Denial of Service (DoS) attacks, portscan events, and Distributed Denial of Service (dDoS) attacks. These events were found, validated, and annotated by network engineers.[1]

A limitation of this single node time-series is that it cannot show the power of strictly network-wide techniques (such as PCA or Distributed Spatial). Although we are restricted in the comparison methodologies available for this dataset, the single link information has the advantage that a great deal of effort has gone into classifying the anomalies in this data, so that we are closer to having ground truth than we are in any almost any other setting.

3.3 Abliene Real-World Data

The final set of data consists of byte counts recorded from the Abliene Internet2 backbone network.[2] Across 11 PoPs in the continental United States with 41 network links, byte counts were sampled into 10 minute time intervals from April 7th 2003 to April 13th 2003, resulting in 1008 byte count samples across each of the 41 links. Unfortunately, this dataset is completely unlabeled with no prior annotation of possible anomaly locations. To compensate for this deficiency in the dataset, we will use this real world network data to study how the new BasisDetect framework detects anomalies that are found by previous network-wide anomaly detection algorithms.

4. BASISDETECT OVERVIEW

Our automated BasisDetect framework for detecting network anomalies is divided into three distinct components. Practically speaking, these components are predicated on having a small initial set of network data with labeled anomalies from which event characteristics can be learned and the algorithm parameters are optimized against. The components of the BasisDetect framework are:

1. *Anomalous Dictionary Construction from Labeled Set* - Using a training set of labeled anomalies, we extract signal characteristics that have been pre-established as anomalous.

2. *Anomaly Decomposition using Penalized Basis Pursuit* - Using our novel Penalized Basis Pursuit methodology and the learned anomaly dictionary signals from the previous step, the BasisDetect methodology extracts anomaly energy from temporal network data for each data signal observed in the network.

3. *Network-wide Data Fusion* - Using knowledge of the network topology structure and the estimated anomaly energy for each link, our methodology classifies anomalous behavior at each router.

A visual description of the BasisDetect framework can be seen in Figure 1.

5. BASIS DECOMPOSITION OF NETWORK DATA

To begin, we establish an anomaly detection methodology on a single observed time-series signal (denoted $\mathbf{y}$). To detect anomalies on this signal, consider decomposing the signal into its anomalous and non-anomalous components. In contrast to previous methods, like PCA [1], we will not consider other concurrently observed signals as potentially non-anomalous behavior. Instead, we will decompose this signal by specifying characteristics that represent both anomalous and non-anomalous behavior for that link with respect to an established set of signal components. This avoids the drawback of PCA-related methods where anomalies pollute the representations of non-anomalous behavior.

In order to perform this decomposition, we introduce the idea of a signal *dictionary*, Φ, a matrix of signal components that will represent our observed data. The signal dictionary considered here will contain both anomalous and non-anomalous signal components,

$$\Phi = \left[\begin{array}{cc} \Phi_{non-anomaly} & \Phi_{anomaly} \end{array} \right] \quad (1)$$

While these anomalous dictionary components will not be known a priori, to begin we will assume they are known (with later discussion in Section 5.1 describing methodologies to extract these signals). We state that the observed traffic signal can be approximated by a linear combination of dictionary components. Therefore, the observed traffic signal can be stated as,

$$\begin{aligned} \mathbf{y} &\approx \Phi \mathbf{x} \quad (2) \\ &= \left[\begin{array}{cc} \Phi_{non-anomaly} & \Phi_{anomaly} \end{array} \right] \left[\begin{array}{c} \mathbf{x}_{non-anomaly} \\ \mathbf{x}_{anomaly} \end{array} \right] \end{aligned}$$

Where the coefficient $x_i \in \mathbf{x}$ is the contribution of dictionary element $\phi_i \in \Phi$ to the observed signal $\mathbf{y}$.

The amount of anomalous energy in the signal as a function of time is defined as the anomaly feature vector,

$$\mathbf{y}_{anomaly} = \Phi_{anomaly} \mathbf{x}_{anomaly} \quad (3)$$

It should be intuitive that if more coefficient energy is placed in the anomaly dictionary, then the more likely an anomaly has occurred. If there is little energy in the anomaly domain, then the non-anomalous, standard operating environment signal components are accurately approximating the signal, and therefore an anomaly is unlikely to have occurred. To discover this level of anomalous energy for each signal, it is necessary to resolve the unknown coefficient vector $\mathbf{x}$.

Given a dictionary of signal components Φ and the observed signal $\mathbf{y}$, we must determine which components are used to represent our observed flow record, specified by the coefficients in the vector $\mathbf{x}$ (such that $\mathbf{y} \approx \Phi\mathbf{x}$). In addition to representing the signal, we wish to also restrict the coefficient vector $\mathbf{x}$ to be sparse. This sparsity constraint will require as few dictionary elements as possible be used to represent the observed signal.

[1]We thank Fernando Silveira from Technicolor Research for supplying us with this dataset.
[2]We thank Mark Crovella for supplying us with this dataset.

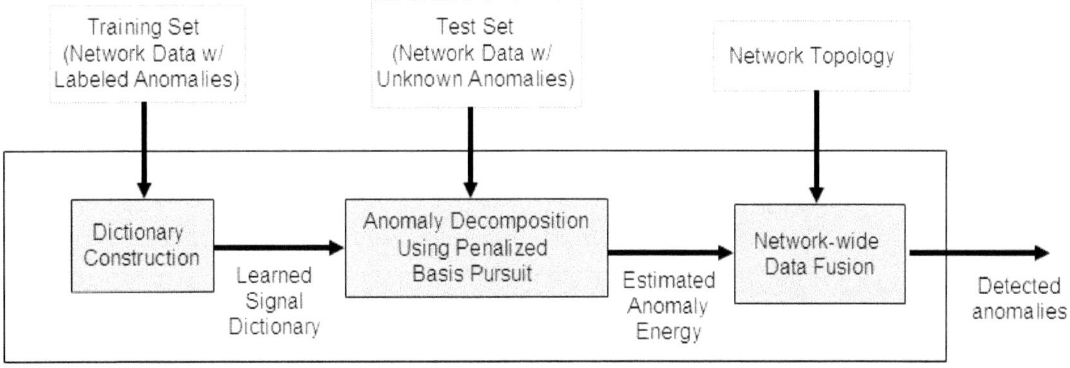

Figure 1: The BasisDetect Framework

The motivation for sparsity in the signal comes from two directions. First, as noted in [6], anomalies are sparse in a signal. Similar motivation comes from studies of the underlying causes of faults in networks [22, 23]. Motivation for sparsity of the normal traffic comes from simple consideration of Fourier analysis of traffic. Figure 2 shows a simple example of the excellent degree of approximation to traffic we can obtain using only a very small number of Fourier coefficients corresponding to daily periods. The figure shows the important components of the power-spectrum of one week of GEANT data, clearly highlighting the importance of the daily cycles. The approximation curve in Figure 2-(right) is generated using only the largest 30 terms from the Discrete Cosine Transform (DCT, which contains around 10,080 coefficients in total). The remaining coefficients of the power-spectrum (including those not shown in the figure) contain little power, so modeling the few critical components will enable us to obtain a reasonable initial model for the data.

While standard inverse problem techniques (linear least squares, etc.) could be used to resolve the coefficient vector, these standard techniques do not require the resulting coefficient vector to be sparse. This sparsity constraint is considered in the theory of *Basis Pursuit* [16], which defines the sparse optimization problem,

$$\min \|\mathbf{x}\|_0 \quad \text{such that} \quad \mathbf{y} = \Phi\mathbf{x} \tag{4}$$

Where we try to find the set of coefficients $\mathbf{x}$ such that the observed vector is reconstructed using the fewest number of dictionary components possible (where $\|\mathbf{x}\|_0 = \#$ of non-zero components in $\mathbf{x}$).

Unfortunately, solving the optimization problem in Equation 4 is combinatorial and therefore computationally intractable for signals of any practical size. In [16] it was shown that this optimization is equivalent to the ℓ_1 relaxation,

$$\min \|\mathbf{x}\|_1 \quad \text{such that} \quad \mathbf{y} = \Phi\mathbf{x} \tag{5}$$

(Where $\|\mathbf{x}\|_1 = \sum_{i=1}^{N} |x_i|$.) As a result of this relaxation, the problem can be restated as a simple linear optimization problem.

While this may be the best approach when we are trying to exactly reconstruct the observed signal, however, in the case of our anomaly detection problem, we are not interested in reconstructing every perturbation of the signal. The problem becomes how to approximate the general characteristics of the current system behavior. Considering the case where we wish to approximate the observed signal using relatively few elements of a signal dictionary, Orthogonal Matching Pursuit (OMP) [17] will offer a simple greedy approximation of the dictionary coefficients.

The Orthogonal Matching Pursuit algorithm starts with an all-zeros signal approximation ($\widehat{\mathbf{y}} = [0, 0, ..., 0]$), the signal component dictionary (Φ), and a null estimated dictionary space ($\widehat{\Phi} = []$). At each iteration of the OMP algorithm the residual signal ($\mathbf{r} = \mathbf{y} - \widehat{\mathbf{y}}$, the observed data minus the current approximation) is calculated. This residual can be considered the signal that is *orthogonal* to the current estimated dictionary space, $\widehat{\Phi}$. The best dictionary component signal, ϕ, not currently in the estimated dictionary space ($\phi \in \Phi$ and $\phi \notin \widehat{\Phi}$) is found. This component is then added to the current estimated dictionary space, $\widehat{\Phi}$. Finally, the best signal approximation is found given the specified current dictionary space, $\widehat{\mathbf{y}} = \widehat{\Phi}\mathbf{x}$ (for some vector $\mathbf{x}$). The process is repeated until either a specified number of components are found or the error of the signal approximation is below some threshold. In addition to the non-exact approximation of the signal, due to the greedy approach, the algorithm is significantly faster than the standard Basis Pursuit algorithm and offers considerable memory savings.

Using the orthogonal matching pursuit (OMP) algorithm in conjunction with a signal dictionary derived from the Discrete Cosine Transform (DCT), consider the decomposition of a vector of packet counts in Figure 2-(Left). The performance of describing the flow signal with this reconstructed signal is shown in Figure 3 for 24 hours of observed packet counts on the GEANT network. Note that by representing only the gross characteristics of the signal, the anomalous parts of the signal are becoming apparent in the residual between the observed data and the approximated signal.

5.1 Anomalous Dictionary Construction from Labeled Set

While the Orthogonal Matching Pursuit methodology will find the coefficient vector $\mathbf{x}$, it requires knowledge of the

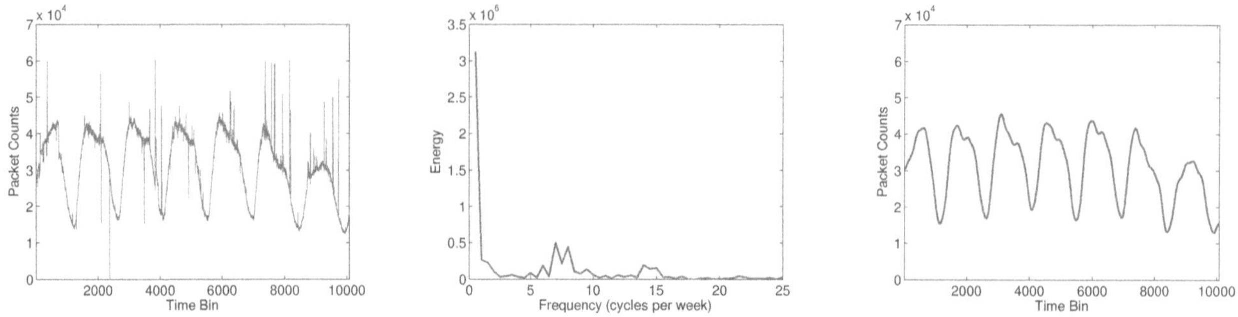

Figure 2: Fourier analysis of GEANT data (Left) - Observed one week of packet counts across a single link in the GEANT network. (Center) - Important region of Fourier power spectrum found using a Discrete Cosine Transformation (DCT). (Right) - Signal approximation using 30 largest DCT coefficients.

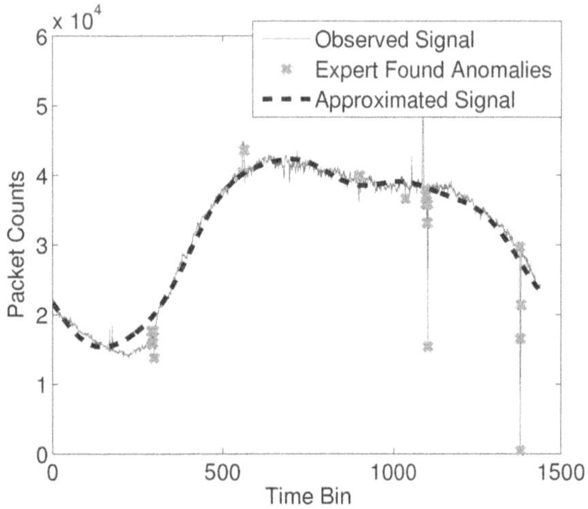

Figure 3: Approximation of 24 hours of GEANT data - Comparison of the observed signal with an approximation using the 30 largest Discrete Cosine Transform (DCT) coefficients. Expert annotated anomalies are marked with 'x'.

anomalous signal dictionary $\Phi_{anomaly}$, which is not known a priori. Through examining Figure 3, one can see that while the rough approximation from the matching pursuit algorithm is fitting most of the signal, the anomalous portions of the signal are not well represented by this simple approximation. If we knew for a subset of network data where anomalies were temporally located and had simple approximations of the signal based on expected signal behavior, we could extract examples of anomalous signal characteristics. Using this intuition and a small training set of labeled anomalies, we can estimated the anomaly dictionary $\widehat{\Phi}_{anomaly}$ and construct the complete signal dictionary $\Phi = \left[\begin{array}{cc} \Phi_{non-anomaly} & \widehat{\Phi}_{anomaly} \end{array} \right]$.

First, consider knowledge of the non-anomalous signal dictionary ($\Phi_{non-anomaly}$). Given the Fourier decomposition example from Figure 2, the most obvious non-anomalous signal type to represent the network data would be a set of sinusoids. This signal type can be created via a Discrete Cosine Transformation (DCT). Second, consider local variation that may not be represented by the global sinusoidal wave based representation of the Discrete Cosine Transform. Due to the need to represent non-anomalous localized variation characteristics in the network data, we will also add a discrete wavelet transform filter set to our non-anomalous signal dictionary (with motivation discussed in Section 8.2 as to the exact type of wavelet decomposition considered). Note that while the DCT/wavelet basis will be used as the non-anomalous signal dictionary in this paper, the BasisDetect framework is agnostic to the choice of non-anomalous signals and can be designed to operate with any chosen basis. We leave discovery of the optimal set of non-anomalous signal components as future work.

Given the constructed non-anomalous signal dictionary, we finally look to determine the anomalous signal dictionary $\Phi_{anomaly}$. Consider a single time-series signal $\mathbf{y}$ with known anomaly locations. In order to isolate anomalous signal characteristics, we first obtain a signal approximation $\widehat{\mathbf{y}}$ using Orthogonal Matching Pursuit, the observed signal $\mathbf{y}$, and the non-anomalous signal dictionary $\Phi_{non-anomaly}$. By examining the residual signal $\mathbf{r} = \widehat{\mathbf{y}} - \mathbf{y}$ (the difference between the approximated signal and the observed signal), we can see where the non-anomalous signal characteristics fail at representing the observed network data. By windowing the residual signal around areas of known anomalies, we can extract anomalous signal characteristics from the training set. A step-by-step description of this methodology can be seen in Algorithm 1.

5.2 Anomaly Decomposition using Penalized Basis Pursuit

In standard OMP all dictionary component signals are weighted equally, therefore there is no preference towards choosing one dictionary signal or another (with the exception of the contribution towards describing the original observed signal). In our anomaly detection problem, specific dictionary component signals may be more preferential than others. Generally, we want to use an anomaly dictionary signal component (and thereby classify that area of the observed data as anomalous) only if that anomaly signal is the sole dictionary component that can properly decompose that area of the signal. Therefore, we want to penalize choosing an anomaly dictionary element. This changes the OMP algorithm to a modified Penalized Basis Pursuit approach by choosing the next element in the signal dictionary $\phi_{\widehat{i}}$ as,

Algorithm 1 - Dictionary Construction Algorithm

Given:

- $\mathbf{Y} = \{\mathbf{y_1}, \mathbf{y_2}, ..., \mathbf{y_N}\}$ - Training set of network time-series data
- $\mathcal{I} = \{\mathcal{I}_1, \mathcal{I}_2, ..., \mathcal{I}_N\}$ - Index of known anomalies in each of the training set signals.
- $\Phi_{non-anomaly}$, Non-anomalous signal dictionary
- w, anomaly window size

Main Body

- Set $\widehat{\Phi}_{anomaly} = []$, the estimated anomalous signal dictionary
- For each network time-series signal, $\mathbf{y_i}$
  1. Obtain signal estimate $\widehat{\mathbf{y_i}}$ by using Orthogonal Matching Pursuit [17] with respect to time-series signal $\mathbf{y_i}$ and signal dictionary $\Phi_{non-anomaly}$.
  2. Find residual signal, $\mathbf{r_i} = \widehat{\mathbf{y_i}} - \mathbf{y_i}$.
  3. For each anomaly in the current signal, $j \in \mathcal{I}_i$
     (a) Set a new anomalous vector to the windowed component of the residual signal at the known anomaly, $\mathbf{a_j} = \left[\ r_i(j-w) \quad r_i(j-w+1) \quad ... \quad r_i(j+w)\ \right]$
     (b) Add $\mathbf{a_j}$ to anomalous signal dictionary $\widehat{\Phi}_{anomaly}$

Return:

- Return $\widehat{\Phi}_{anomaly}$

$$\widehat{i} = \arg \max_{i=\{1,2,...\}} \left(|\langle \phi_i, \mathbf{r}\rangle| - \lambda_i\right) \tag{6}$$

Where $\mathbf{r} = \widehat{\mathbf{y}} - \mathbf{y}$ the current residual signal with respect to the current signal dictionary, and defining the penalty vector $\Lambda = \{\lambda_1, \lambda_2, ..., \lambda_X\}$ (for a dictionary of X number of signal components), such that

$$\lambda_i = \begin{cases} \gamma & \text{if } \phi_i \in \widehat{\Phi}_{anomaly} \\ 0 & \text{if } \phi_i \notin \widehat{\Phi}_{anomaly} \end{cases} \tag{7}$$

For a large enough $\gamma > 0$, this prevents the algorithm from over-representing the signal from the anomalous dictionary. The full methodology is described in Algorithm 2.

Finally, using the Penalized Basis Pursuit methodology, we obtain the anomaly feature vector for the observed signal using the anomalous chosen dictionary signal components, $\mathbf{y}_{anomaly} = \widehat{\Phi}_{anomaly}\widehat{\mathbf{x}}_{anomaly}$. While we expect that a majority of anomalies will be detected using the anomaly dictionary representation, we also want to avoid the situation where limited training set anomalies result in missing true anomalies. To avoid missing anomalies, we also incorporate knowledge of the residual signal $\mathbf{r}$ into the anomaly energy.

Algorithm 2 - Penalized Basis Pursuit Algorithm

Given:

- $\mathbf{y}$ = observed N-length network data vector
- $\Phi = \left[\ \Phi_{non-anomaly} \quad \Phi_{anomaly}\ \right]$, the signal dictionary matrix
- γ, penalty for representing the signal using an anomalous signal component.
- N_{coef}, the specified number of coefficients used to represent the signal $\mathbf{y}$.
- ρ, the weight of the residual signal in the final anomaly energy output.

Main Body

1. Construct $\mathbf{\Lambda} = \{\lambda_1, \lambda_2, ..., \lambda_M\}$, the vector of penalty terms for each dictionary signal component using Equation 7.
2. Set $\widehat{\Phi} = []$, matrix of chosen dictionary signal components
3. Set $\mathbf{r} = \mathbf{y}$, current residual signal given chosen dictionary
4. For $\ell = \{1, 2, ..., N_{coef}\}$.
   (a) Find the most dominant dictionary component not yet considered,
   $$k = \arg \max_{i=\{1,2,...\}} \left(|\langle \phi_i, \mathbf{r}\rangle| - \lambda_i\right)$$
   (b) Remove ϕ_k from Φ, λ_k from Λ.
   (c) Add ϕ_k to $\widehat{\Phi}$
   (d) Find the dictionary coefficient for the current chosen dictionary signal components. Solve the least squares problem, setting $\widehat{\mathbf{x}} = \arg\min_{\mathbf{x}} \|\widehat{\Phi}\mathbf{x} - \mathbf{y}\|_2$
   (e) Recalculate the residual signal : $\mathbf{r} = \mathbf{y} - \widehat{\Phi}\widehat{\mathbf{x}}$

Return:

- Return the estimated anomaly energy, $\widehat{\mathbf{y}}_{energy} = \widehat{\Phi}_{anomaly}\widehat{\mathbf{x}}_{anomaly} + \rho\mathbf{r}$

$$\widehat{\mathbf{y}}_{energy} = \widehat{\Phi}_{anomaly}\widehat{\mathbf{x}}_{anomaly} + \rho\mathbf{r} \tag{8}$$

Where $\rho \in [0, 1]$.

6. NETWORK-WIDE DATA FUSION

While the penalized basis pursuit methodology will extract anomaly energy for a single time-series signal, we must add to our framework to detect network-wide anomalies. Given a network with known topology, containing N routers and M links, consider multiple observed time-series characteristics for each link (represented here by $\{c_1, c_2, ..., c_C\}$ for packet count, byte count, etc.). We observe time-series signal $\mathbf{y}^{(\ell,c)}$ for the data at link ℓ and for characteristic c.

After performing the Penalized Basis Pursuit Algorithm on the observed time-series network signal, $\mathbf{y}^{(\ell,c)}$, we obtain the estimated signal energy relating to the anomaly energy from Equation 8, denoted by $\widehat{\mathbf{y}}^{(\ell,c)}_{energy}$. Therefore, for each link ℓ, we would have an estimated anomaly energy vector for each observed characteristic of the link. For example,

$$\widehat{\mathbf{Y}}^{(\ell)}_{energy} = \begin{bmatrix} | & | & & | \\ \widehat{\mathbf{y}}^{(\ell,c_1)}_{energy} & \widehat{\mathbf{y}}^{(\ell,c_2)}_{energy} & \cdots & \widehat{\mathbf{y}}^{(\ell,c_C)}_{energy} \\ | & | & & | \end{bmatrix} \quad (9)$$

One could imagine aggregating the anomaly energy across all characteristics on this link and performing a simple energy thresholding mechanism for determining anomalies. One problem with this methodology is that it would ignore the spatial correlation between links. Given a router with links ℓ_A and ℓ_B, the appearance of anomaly energy on both links (at the same time) will strengthen our confidence that an anomaly has actually occurred. Meanwhile, the lack of anomaly energy on one of the links should weaken our belief in an abnormal event occurring at that time period.

Motivated by the work on distributed anomaly detection in [2], consider the multidimensional space where each dimension represents a link connected to the router. For a router r, with m links $\{\ell_1, \ell_2, ..., \ell_m\}$, and time-series observations at T time steps, we can form the $T \times Cm$ sized estimated router anomaly energy matrix,

$$\widehat{\mathbf{Y}}^{(r)}_{energy} = \begin{bmatrix} \widehat{\mathbf{Y}}^{(\ell_1)}_{energy} & \widehat{\mathbf{Y}}^{(\ell_2)}_{energy} & \cdots & \widehat{\mathbf{Y}}^{(\ell_m)}_{energy} \end{bmatrix} \quad (10)$$

Where row t' represents a specific time bin with the estimated anomaly energy on each of the m links connected to the router with respect to each observed link characteristic (*e.g.*, packet count, byte count, etc.). This Cm-length estimated anomaly energy vector, $\widehat{\mathbf{Y}}^{(r)}_{energy}(t')$ could be considered a point in some $\mathbb{R}^{Cm}$ estimated anomaly energy feature space. The anomaly energy vector's placement in this Cm-dimensional space will inform us whether or not an anomaly actually has occurred at router r at time t'. Intuitively, if every link and observed characteristic has very little anomaly energy estimated, there is likely not an anomaly at this router. Conversely, if several observed characteristics of this router have very large estimated anomaly energy values, then it is likely some anomaly is occurring at this time step. This reduces to a hypothesis testing problem of detecting whether or not the estimated anomaly energy vector $\widehat{\mathbf{Y}}^{(r)}_{energy}(t')$ is anomalous compared with the other estimated anomaly energy vectors.

Using the matrix of estimated anomaly energy for router r, $\widehat{\mathbf{Y}}^{(r)}_{energy}$, we can use the minimum volume level set methodology of [15] to assess which rows of the matrix are anomalous[3]. This methodology uses a nonparametric statistical technique to output the False Discovery Rate (FDR) of each vector, $p_{r,t}$, for each vector $\widehat{\mathbf{Y}}^{(r)}_{energy}(t)$. This False Discovery Rate value is the probability of observing a vector of estimated anomaly energy more extreme given the remaining matrix of estimated energy vectors. If the probability is very low that a more extreme vector would be observed, this vector is likely anomalous. The False Discovery Rate has been found [11] to be a more accurate metric than standard multiple hypothesis testing techniques (*e.g.*, Bonferroni Correction [12]). By thresholding based on these FDR $p_{r,t}$ values, we classify which entries are anomalous, and therefore where anomalies occur in the network, localized by both the specific router and the specific time of the anomaly.

[3]We thank the authors of this code for making the program readily available at http://www.eecs.umich.edu/~cscott/code/mnscann.zip

7. BASISDETECT ALGORITHM

Combining the novel basis pursuit methodology from Section 5 and the nonparametric statistical methodology described in Section 6, we can summarize our full BasisDetect framework in Algorithm 3. The non-anomalous signal dictionary, $\Phi_{non-anomaly}$, will be taken as the collection of waveforms from a combination of the Discrete Cosine Transform (DCT) and a Discrete Wavelet Transform using the discrete Meyer wavelet (as motivated in Section 8.2). Additionally, the BasisDetect methodology requires the detection parameter, ν, which determines the detection/false alarm rate of the anomaly detection. Throughout the experiments, this parameter is adjusted to present the spectrum of detection/false alarm rate for our BasisDetect methodology. Finally, the use of Algorithm 1 requires the tuning parameter w to adjust the time-series window for extracting the learned anomaly characteristics. While examination of our labeled anomalies resulted in setting this parameter to $w = 5$ (for consideration of 10 time bins around the labeled anomalies), this value will depend on link sampling rates and requires careful consideration through inspection of the training data.

The reliance on the Penalized Basis Pursuit Methodology of Algorithm 2 requires the additional input of three tuning parameters (N_{coef}, γ, ρ) into the BasisDetect algorithm. In order to find the optimal parameter values with respect to the number of false alarms declared, consider some initial estimate of these three parameters and running the BasisDetect algorithm using the training data as the test data. By using the training data as test, we are given a priori knowledge of where the anomalies are located and the performance of the BasisDetect methodology (in terms of the number of false alarms declared) with respect to the given input tuning parameters. Using a grid search of parameter values over feasible possible values, we can optimize the choice of tuning parameter values by choosing the set of parameter values (N_{coef}, γ, ρ) that minimize the total number of false alarms declared to detect all the anomalies in the training data.

8. RESULTS

We perform an extensive set of tests using three different data sources, which were described in Section 3. The intent of our experiments is to assess the capabilities of our model-based detection methods in both a single node and network-wide setting. We also compare and contrast our method with standard detection methods that have been described in prior studies. Finally, we assess the sensitivity of our detection method using synthetic traffic traces in which ground truth is intrinsic. For all experiments described, the tuning parameters required by the BasisDetect methodology and the training anomalies are discovered by hold out cross validation [24], where 20% of the data is held out as training data while the remaining 80% is used as test data. The results of our experiments are described below.

Algorithm 3 - BasisDetect Algorithm

Given:

- $\mathbf{y}^{(\ell,c)}$ = the observed link data from link ℓ and link characteristic c. Known for all network links $\ell = \{1, 2, ..., M\}$ and link characteristics $c = \{1, 2, ..., C\}$.
- Set of routers $r = \{1, 2, ..., N\}$.
- Router-level topology of the network.
- Training set of network data with labeled anomalies
- Test set of network data with unknown anomalies
- ν = detection threshold for anomaly FDR values
- $\Phi_{non-anomaly}$ = dictionary of non-anomalous signal components
- γ = penalty for representing the signal using an anomalous signal component.
- N_{coef} = the specified number of coefficients used to represent the signal $\mathbf{y}$.
- ρ = the weight of the residual signal in the final anomaly energy output.

Main Body

1. Using the training set with labeled anomalies, apply the Dictionary Construction approach in Algorithm 1 to learn the anomalous dictionary components, $\widehat{\Phi}_{anomaly}$. Construct the full dictionary array $\widehat{\Phi} = \left[\begin{array}{cc} \Phi_{non-anomaly} & \widehat{\Phi}_{anomaly} \end{array} \right]$.
2. Perform Penalized Basis Pursuit Method from Algorithm 2 to estimate the anomalous signal energy $\widehat{\mathbf{y}}^{(l,c)}_{energy}$ for each link $l = \{1, 2, ..., M\}$ and link characteristic $c = \{1, 2, ..., C\}$ using the learned dictionary $\widehat{\Phi}$.
3. Using knowledge of the network topology, construct the router anomaly energy matrix, $\widehat{\mathbf{Y}}^{(r)}_{energy}$ for each router $r = \{1, 2, .., N\}$ using Equation 10
4. Apply the nonparametric technique from [15], finding the False Discovery Rate value, $p_{r,t}$ for each router $r = \{1, 2, .., N\}$ at time index $t = \{1, 2, ..., T\}$.
5. For each element of $p_{r,t} < \nu$, label the router r as having an anomaly at time t.

8.1 GEANT Time-series Network Data

The first experiment will be on a collection of time-series data obtained from a Juniper J-Flow records from a GEANT router as described in Section 3.2. The dataset contains packet counts, byte counts, and IP entropy measured along the single link, sampled in aggregation bins of 1 minute evaluated for 42 days, resulting in a time-series signal of length 60,480. This dataset contains labeled anomalies (DoS, dDoS, portscan) found by network engineers.

In addition to our new BasisDetect methodology, we will compare against two time-series based forecasting techniques. Due to the availability of only single link data, the network-wide approaches of PCA and the Distributed Spatial methodology are not applicable here. Instead we will focus on two basic time-series anomaly detection methodologies, the Exponentially Weighted Moving Average (EWMA) Filter and Fourier thresholding.

8.1.1 EWMA Filter

The EWMA filter is a simple smoothing methodology that uses the previous observed values ($\{y_{t-1}, y_{t-2}, ...\}$) to forecast what the next observed value (y_t) should be.

$$\widehat{y}_{t+1} = \alpha_{ewma} y_t + (1 - \alpha_{ewma}) \widehat{y}_t \tag{11}$$

An anomaly is detected if the forecasted value deviates significantly compared with the observed value,

$$r_t^{ewma} = |y_t - \widehat{y}_t| \tag{12}$$

Where the threshold value α_{ewma} is found by the value that minimizes the false alarms declared to find all the anomalies in the training set.

8.1.2 Fourier Thresholding

The second time-series anomaly detection methodology consists of resolving the residual energy from Fourier analysis on the time-series signal. Given a Discrete Cosine Transformation of the time-series signal, we determine the vector of discrete cosine coefficients, α_{dct}, such that our observed time-series signal $\mathbf{y} = \Phi_{dct}\alpha_{dct}$. In order to generate a residual signal, we threshold the small components of the discrete cosine coefficients, such that,

$$\alpha'_{dct}(i) = \begin{cases} \alpha_{dct}(i) & : \text{if } |\alpha_{dct}(i)| \geq \alpha_{fourier} \\ 0 & : \text{if } |\alpha_{dct}(i)| < \alpha_{fourier} \end{cases} \tag{13}$$

Finally, the energy in the residual Fourier signal indicates whether or not an anomaly has occurred at each time step,

$$\mathbf{r}^{fourier} = \left|\mathbf{y} - \Phi_{dct}\alpha'_{dct}\right| \tag{14}$$

Where the threshold value $\alpha_{fourier}$ is found by the value that minimizes the false alarms declared to find all the anomalies in the training set.

8.1.3 GEANT Results

After performing anomaly detection using both the new BasisDetect algorithm and the two comparison time-series anomaly detection methodologies (EWMA and Fourier) on the GEANT dataset, the false alarm results for detecting the labeled true anomalies can be found in Figure 4. As seen in the figure, our BasisDetect framework consistently performs better than the two comparison methodologies with respect to the number of false alarms declared. The number of false alarms declared for specific percentages of true anomalies found can be seen in Table 1. The table shows that to find all of the labeled anomalies in our time-series signal, the BasisDetect method declares almost 50% fewer false alarms than the best competing methodology (the exponentially weighted moving average filter methodology (EWMA)), and over 75% fewer false alarms than the Fourier methodology.

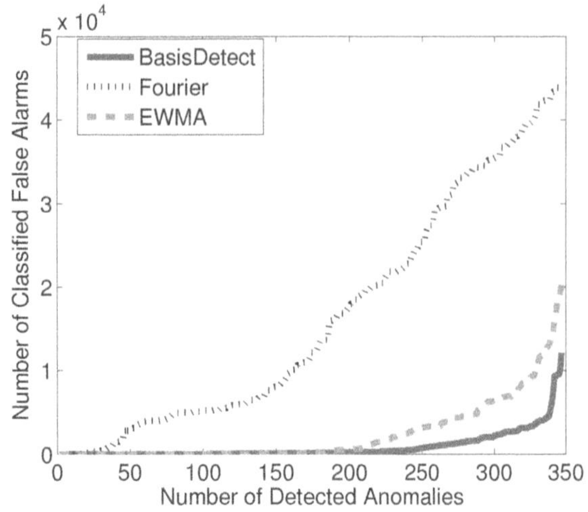

Figure 4: GEANT Network Data - False Alarm anomalies found for a specified level of true anomaly detection for the three time-series detection methodologies (Fourier, EWMA, BasisDetect).

Table 1: GEANT Network Data - Number of false alarms declared for a percentage of the true anomalies detected.

Methodology	Percentage of True Anomalies Found			
	70%	80%	90%	100%
BasisDetect	550	1,428	2,363	10,474
EWMA	2,825	4,558	7,138	20,275
Fourier	23,978	33,048	37,568	43,919

8.2 Wavelet Performance Analysis

To represent localized non-anomalous components of the observed data we use wavelets in the non-anomalous dictionary ($\Phi_{non-anomaly}$). The choice of which type of discrete wavelet signals to use is non-straightforward. The decision to use discrete Meyer wavelets in the signal dictionary was due to its performance against other wavelet types on the GEANT dataset. The results can be seen in Table 2, where in order to detect all the anomalies in the GEANT dataset, using the discrete Meyer wavelet results in almost 1,500 fewer false alarms declared against the next competing wavelet type (Haar wavelets). Intuitively, the Meyer wavelet represents localized sinusoidal behavior, which can commonly be found in non-anomalous network data. Meanwhile, Haar wavelets represent sharp signal discontinuities and Daubechies wavelets represent signal polynomial structure, neither of which should be expected to represent non-anomalous signal behavior well. The performance of the Meyer wavelet transform here motivates its use throughout the remainder of the experiments.

8.3 Tuning Parameter Performance Analysis

The BasisDetect framework uses a series of tuning parameters (γ, ρ) to optimize performance. In order to assess improvements in BasisDetect's false alarm rate due to these parameters, experiments were run on the GEANT dataset setting each of the tuning parameters to zero and observing

Table 2: GEANT Network Data - Number of false alarms declared in order to detect every anomaly in the GEANT dataset (with respect to various wavelet types).

Wavelet Type	Number of False Alarms
Discrete Meyer	10,474
Haar	12,096
Daubechies	14,210

performance. The results can be seen in Figure 5. As seen in the figure, the full BasisDetect methodology including both tuning parameters optimized by the training set significantly outperforms both parameter eliminated methods with respect to the number of false alarms declared. In the case of the eliminated anomaly signal component penalty ($\gamma = 0$) we revert to a standard greedy basis pursuit methodology, with this modified methodology consistently outperformed by the full BasisDetect methodology for the detection of every anomaly in the GEANT dataset. This indicates that our penalized methodology of BasisDetect offers a clear performance advantage over standard Basis Pursuit methodologies. In the case where the residual signal is ignored ($\rho = 0$), the results indicate better performance than the non-penalized BasisDetect method for a majority of the detected anomalies (while still worse than the full BasisDetect methodology), the method then fails at detecting the last fraction of anomalies in terms of the large number of false alarms declared to find that last fraction of anomalies. This represents a regime where the basis pursuit methodology is failing at fitting the anomalies to our estimated anomalous signal dictionary, likely due to limited training data for our learning-based methodology. These results motivate the use of both tuning parameters in our full BasisDetect framework.

8.4 Synthesized Network-wide Data

Using the synthetic network-wide traffic matrix technique described Section 3.1, we generate network-wide data with injected anomalies. To compare performance of our BasisDetect methodology, we will use two state-of-the-art network-wide anomaly detection techniques. The first methodology is the Principle Component Analysis (PCA) technique from [1], and the second will be the Distributed Spatial anomaly detection technique from [2]. In order to test the detection capabilities of all methods, the injected anomalies vary in both amplitude and length, while the level of added noise in the network data varies between network snapshots. Our detection methodologies will be tested to detect both the beginning and ending of each injected anomaly.

For the initial synthetic experiment, we evaluate performance of the three network-wide anomaly detection methodologies using data with constant injected anomaly amplitudes, $a_{anomaly}$ across all network snapshots. Using 20 synthesized network snapshots each with a single injected anomaly, we modify both the length of the anomaly injected (between 2 and 8 time bins) and the size of the network (between 3 and 5 fully connected routers, relating to 9 and 25 observed links respectively). Each network snapshot simulates 2.5 days of packet out link observations aggregated into 5 minute time bins, resulting in an observed 1024-length

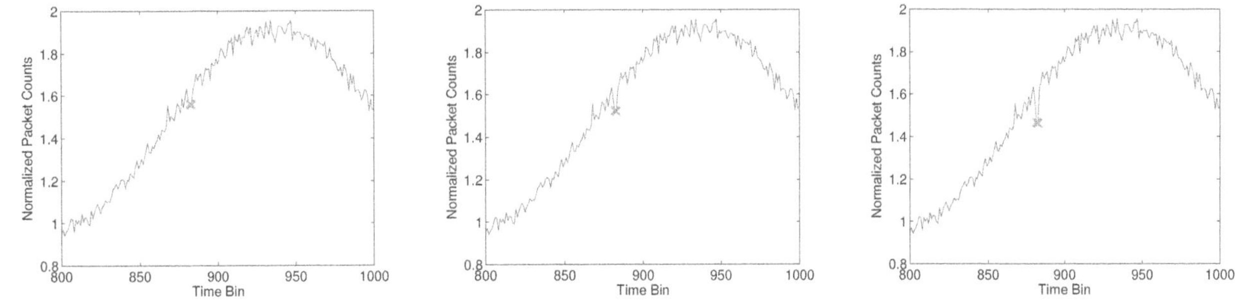

Figure 6: Three examples of injected anomalies with varying anomaly amplitudes. (Left) - $a_{anomaly} = 0.063$, (Center) - $a_{anomaly} = 0.1$, (Right) - $a_{anomaly} = 0.158$

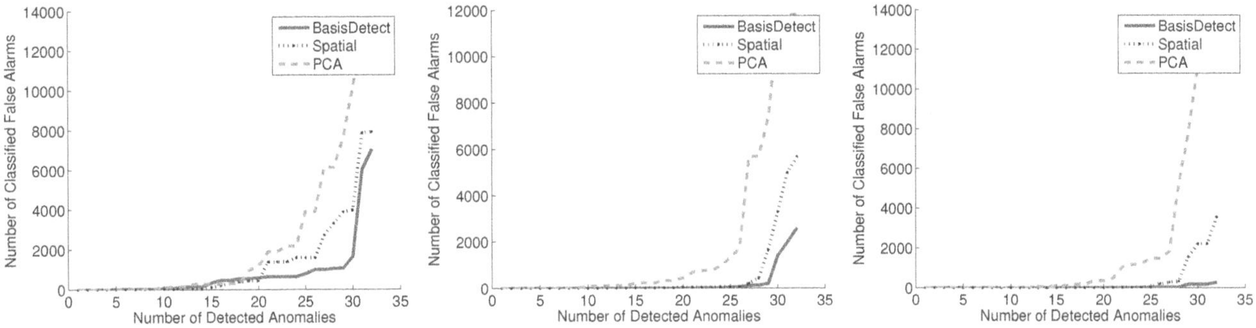

Figure 7: Synthetic Traffic Matrices with Constant Anomaly Amplitude - False Alarms declared for a specified level of true anomaly detection for the three network-wide detection methodologies (PCA, Distributed Spatial, BasisDetect). (Left) - $a_{anomaly} = 0.063$, (Center) - $a_{anomaly} = 0.1$, (Right) - $a_{anomaly} = 0.158$.

Table 3: Synthetic Traffic Matrices with Constant Anomaly Amplitude - Number of false alarms declared for a given number of the true anomalies detected.

Anomaly amplitude ($a_{anomaly}$)	0.063				0.1				0.158			
Number of true anomalies found	8	16	24	32	8	16	24	32	8	16	24	32
PCA	11	298	2,179	12,579	9	239	974	11,812	3	110	1,202	12,598
Spatial	21	216	1,594	7,932	2	10	55	5,690	0	1	24	3,545
BasisDetect	27	473	653	7,041	0	2	18	2,587	0	2	15	272

time-series vector at each synthetic link. Using hold-out cross validation, we use 4 of the network snapshots to train our BasisDetect methodology and then test detection performance across the remaining 16 networks. We consider three anomaly amplitude regimes, (low - $a_{anomaly} = 0.063$, medium - $a_{anomaly} = 0.1$, and high - $a_{anomaly} = 0.158$), with examples of these injected anomaly regimes for the observed network data shown in Figure 6.

In the experiment results in Figure 7, we see that for all three amplitude regimes our BasisDetect methodology outperforms the current state-of-the-art detection techniques in terms of the number of false alarms anomalies declared across all 16 test networks. In Table 3 we find a breakdown of the false alarms declared for various detection levels. As seen in the table, the BasisDetect methodology performs significantly better than both the PCA and Distributed Spatial methodology. In terms of the medium amplitude anomaly ($a_{anomaly} = 1$), BasisDetect finds all anomalies with over 54% fewer false alarms than Distributed Spatial and over 75% fewer false alarms than the PCA methodology. In terms of the high anomaly amplitude experiment ($a_{anomaly} = 0.158$), BasisDetect declares 90% fewer false alarms compared with the Distributed Spatial methodology and almost 99% fewer false alarms than the PCA approach, in order to find all the injected anomalies.

The second synthetic experiment tested anomaly detection performance on 30 network snapshots for a single anomaly injected into each snapshot, with each having varying anomaly amplitude levels ranging from $a_{anomaly} = 0.0316$ to $a_{anomaly} = 1$. In Figure 8 we see the results of detecting injected anomalies across all 24 test network snapshots with anomalies of various amplitude (holding out 6 of the network snapshots as training data for BasisDetect). Again, our BasisDetect methodology has uniformly better performance than both the Distributed Spatial and PCA anomaly detection methodologies. Selected results

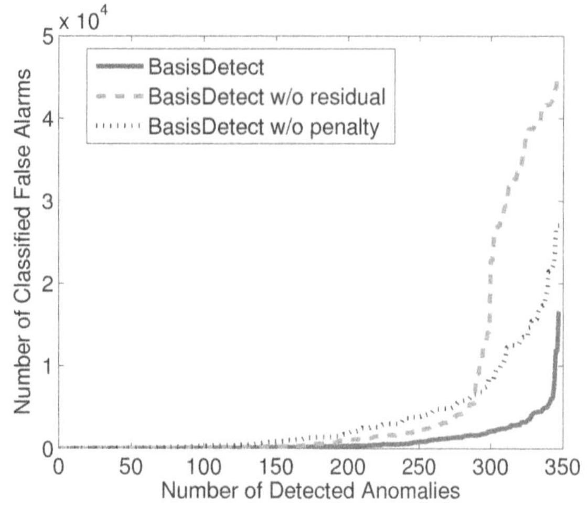

Figure 5: Tuning parameter performance experiment, examination of how well the BasisDetect algorithm performs as each of the tuning parameters are removed. Using the full BasisDetect algorithm (γ, ρ learned from training set), BasisDetect w/o residual (γ learned from training set, $\rho = 0$), and BasisDetect w/o penalty (ρ learned from training set, $\gamma = 0$)

highlighted in Table 4 show that with respect to the best competing methodology (the Distributed Spatial methodology), our BasisDetect algorithm declares over 65% fewer false alarms in order to detect all of the true anomalies. In comparison with the PCA algorithm, we find over 80% fewer false alarms in order to discover all of the true anomalies.

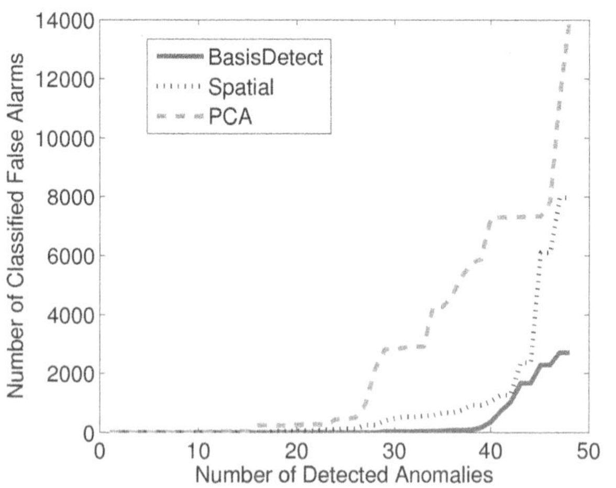

Figure 8: Synthetic Traffic Matrices with Varying Anomaly Amplitude - False Alarms declared for a specified level of true anomaly detection for the three network-wide detection methodologies (PCA, Distributed Spatial, BasisDetect).

One surprising result of both synthetic experiments is the very large number of false alarms declared in contrast with prior published results in [1, 2]. Note that our experiments consider a significantly larger dataset. While prior experiments examined network data with 1,008 time-series samples, we examined data with 16,384 and 24,576 time-series samples for the first and second synthetic experiments respectively. While the increase in the experiment size results in a significantly greater number of absolute false alarms declared, we feel that the larger experiments offer a greater understanding as to the performance characteristics of the three anomaly detection methodologies.

Table 4: Synthetic Traffic Matrices for Varying Anomaly Amplitude - Number of false alarms declared for a percentage of the true anomalies detected.

Methodology	Percentage of True Anomalies Found			
	70%	80%	90%	100%
PCA	4,266	5,874	7,325	13,966
Spatial	577	924	2,365	7,977
BasisDetect	43	166	1,673	2,716

Table 5: Abilene Network Data - Number of false alarms declared for a percentage of the PCA anomalies detected.

Methodology	Percentage of PCA Anomalies Found			
	70%	80%	90%	100%
Spatial	563	733	1,287	4,564
BasisDetect	327	495	747	2,746

8.5 Abilene Real-World Network Data

Finally, we test the performance of the BasisDetect framework on the Abilene real-world dataset. As mentioned in Section 2, there is no ground truth labeling of anomalies for this dataset. Instead, here we will use one of the two prior network-wide anomaly detection methodologies (PCA) to classify the most obvious anomalies for that methodology. Using these classified anomalies as the ground truth, we compare how the new BasisDetect methodology performs in comparison with the other competing network-wide anomaly detection methodology (*e.g.*, the Distributed Spatial methodology).

Using the PCA network-wide anomaly detection technique, we classify the 15 most dominant anomalies in the Abilene data. The performance of both the BasisDetect framework and the Distributed Spatial approach can be seen in Figure 9 on detecting these PCA classified anomalies using 5-way Cross Validation (thus expanding the total anomalies considered to 70 in the dataset). As seen in the figure, our BasisDetect methodology is detecting these PCA classified anomalies with lower false alarm rate than the Distributed Spatial approach, with almost 40% fewer false alarms declared to detect all the PCA anomalies. A specific breakdown of the false alarm rate can be seen in Table 5.

9. CONCLUSIONS AND FUTURE WORK

The ability to detect anomalies accurately and in a timely fashion in large networks would be a significant benefit in day to day network operations. It can be argued that cur-

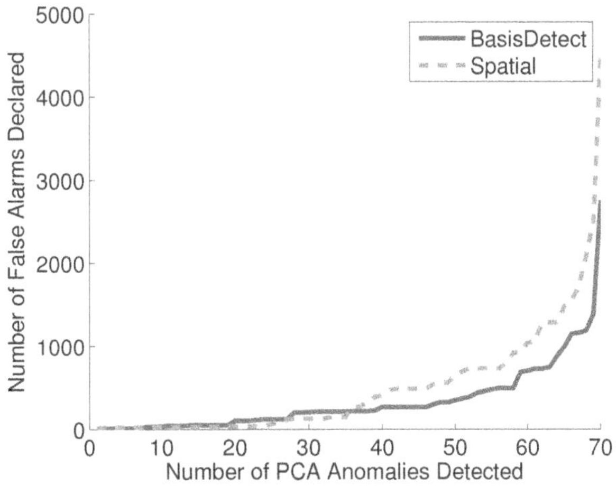

Figure 9: Abilene Real-World Network Data - Using 15 anomalies found by the PCA methodology, the false alarm rates are displayed for both BasisDetect and the Distributed Spatial methodology.

rent methods are not yet sufficiently capable based on the fact that they are not widely used today. The objective of our work is to develop an anomaly detection capability that is sufficiently accurate to be considered practical for operational deployment and use.

In this paper we present the BasisDetect framework, a model-based methodology for anomaly detection. We build temporal models by applying a novel basis pursuit algorithm to the key components of learned anomalies from a small training set. These temporal models are extended from anomaly detection on a single node to the network-wide context by applying a higher reasoning framework. This combined approach has additional benefits, such as the ability to be applied flexibly to a wide variety of data, extensibility to include a variety of filter functions, and low computational complexity.

We test and evaluate the BasisDetect methodology using both empirical and synthetic network data with labeled anomalies. In the single node case, when we compare with standard time-series based methods, our method identifies all of the labeled anomalies with over 50% fewer false alarms declared compared with the competing methodologies. In the case of unlabeled real-world network wide data, we show considerable improvements in detecting anomalies declared by previous network-wide anomaly detection methodologies. Finally, we use synthetic traces to examine in detail the sensitivity of our method over a range of anomalies to show that to find all of the labeled anomalies, our methodology will declare 65% fewer false anomalies than the best competing methodology. The results show that the model-based method is highly effective even when large amounts of noise are present.

The implication of our results is that our model-based methodology is indeed feasible for event detection in an operational environment. While we show that models from a small set of filters can be effective, we have not investigated optimizations of the filters that could enhance their ability. Furthermore, there are many practical issues revolving around where and how data is gathered in a network that must be systematically addressed to facilitate application of our methods. Ultimately, the best test of an anomaly detector is in a live environment. In the future, we plan to work closely with several network operations groups to deploy and test our techniques.

10. ACKNOWLEDGMENTS

This work was supported in part by NSF grants CNS-0716460, CNS-0831427 and CNS-0905186. Also support was provided by ARC Grant DP0665427. Any opinions, findings, conclusions or other recommendations expressed in this material are those of the authors and do not necessarily reflect the view of the NSF or ARC. We would also AT&T, Technicolor, Abilene and GÉANT networks for providing data.

11. REFERENCES

[1] A. Lakhina, M. Crovella, and C. Diot, "Diagnoising Network-Wide Traffic Anomalies," in *Proceedings of ACM SIGCOMM Conference*, Portland, OR, August 2004.

[2] P. Chhabra, C. Scott, E. Kolaczyk, and M. Crovella, "Distributed Spatial Anomaly Detection," in *Proceedings of IEEE INFOCOM Conference*, Phoenix, AZ, March 2008.

[3] A. Lakhina, M. Crovella, and C. Diot, "Characterization of Network-Wide Anomalies in Traffic Flows," in *Proceedings of ACM SIGCOMM Internet Measurement Conference*, Taormina, Sicily, Italy, October 2004.

[4] A. Lakhina, K. Papagiannaki, M. Crovella, C. Diot, E. D. Kolaczyk, and N. Taft, "Structural Analysis of Network Traffic Flows," in *ACM SIGMETRICS / Performance*, 2004.

[5] P. Barford, J. Kline, D. Plonka, and A. Ron, "A Signal Analysis of Network Traffic Anomalies," in *Proceedings of ACM SIGCOMM Internet Measurement Workshop*, Marseilles, France, November 2002.

[6] Y. Zhang, Z. Ge, M. Roughan, and A. Greenberg, "Network Anomography," in *Proceedings of the Internet Measurement Conference*, Berkeley, CA, USA, October 2005.

[7] M. Roughan, T. Griffin, M. Mao, A. Greenberg, and B. Freeman, "IP forwarding anomalies and improving their detection using multiple data sources," in *ACM SIGCOMM Workshop on Network Troubleshooting (NetTS)*, Portland, OR, September 2004, pp. 307–312.

[8] S. H. Steiner, "Grouped Data Exponentially Weighted Moving Average Control Charts," *Applied Statistics*, vol. 47, no. 2, 1998.

[9] H. Ringberg, A. Soule, J. Rexford, and C. Diot, "Sensitivity of PCA for Traffic Anomaly Detection," in *Proceedings of ACM SIGMETRICS Conference*, San Diego, CA, June 2007.

[10] B. Rubinstein, B. Nelson, L. Huang, A. Joseph, S. Lau, S. Rao, N. Taft, and J. Tygar, "ANTIDOTE: Understanding and Defending Against Poisoning of Anomaly Detectors," in *Proceedings of ACM SIGCOMM Internet Measurements Conference*, Chicago, Illinois, November 2009.

[11] Y. Benjamini and Y. Hochberg, "Controlling the False Discovery Rate," in *Journal of the Royal Statistical Society B*, vol. 57, no. 1, 1995, pp. 289–300.

[12] R. Miller, in *Simultaneous Statistical Inference.* Springer-Verlag, 1991.
[13] L. Huang, X. Nguyen, M. Garofalakis, J. Hellerstein, M. Jordan, M.Joseph, and N.Taft., "Communication-Efficient Online Detection of Network-Wide Anomalies," in *Proceedings of IEEE INFOCOM Conference*, Anchorage, Alaska, May 2007.
[14] Y. Liu, L. Zhang, and Y. Guan, "A Distributed Data Streaming Algorithm for Network-Wide Traffic Anomaly Detection," *SIGMETRICS Performance Evaluation Review*, vol. 37, no. 2, pp. 81–82, 2009.
[15] C. Scott and E. Kolaczyk, "Nonparametric Assessment of Contamination in Multivariate Data using Generalized Quantile Sets and FDR," in *Accepted for Publication in J. Computational and Graphical Statistics*, 2007.
[16] S. Chen, D. Donoho, and M. Saunders, "Atomic Decomposition by Basis Pursuit," in *SIAM Journal of Scientific Computing*, vol. 20, 1998, pp. 33–61.
[17] G. Davis, S. Mallat, and M. Avellaneda, "Greedy Adaptive Approximation," in *Journal of Constructive Approximation*, vol. 13, 1997, pp. 57–98.
[18] P. Huggins and S. Zucker, "Greedy Basis Pursuit," in *IEEE Transactions on Signal Processing*, vol. 55, no. 7, July 2007, pp. 3760–3771.
[19] H. Ringberg, M. Roughan, and J. Rexford, "The Need For Simulation In Evaluating Anomaly Detectors," *ACM SIGCOMM CCR*, vol. 38, no. 1, pp. 55–59, January 2008.
[20] Y. Zhang, M. Roughan, W. Willinger, and L. Qui, "Spatio-Temporal Compressive Sensing and Internet Traffic Matrices," in *Proceedings of ACM SIGCOMM Conference*, Barcellona, Spain, August 2009, pp. 267–278.
[21] "Geant Project Website," http://www.geant.net/.
[22] A. Markopoulou, G. Iannaccone, S. Bhattacharrya, C.-N. Chuah, and C. Diot, "Characterization of failures in an IP backbone," in *Proceedings of IEEE INFOCOM Conference*, Hong Kong, China, March 2004.
[23] D. Oppenheimer, A. Ganapathi, and D. A. Patterson, "Why do Internet services fail, and what can be done about it?" in *4th Usenix Symposium on Internet Technologies and Systems (USITS'03)*, 2003.
[24] L. Wasserman, "All of Nonparametric Statistics," in *Springer Texts*, 2006.

Temporally Oblivious Anomaly Detection on Large Networks Using Functional Peers*

Kevin M. Carter, Richard P. Lippmann, and Stephen W. Boyer
MIT Lincoln Laboratory
Lexington, MA USA
kevin.carter@ll.mit.edu, lippmann@ll.mit.edu, boyer@ll.mit.edu

ABSTRACT

Previous methods of network anomaly detection have focused on defining a temporal model of what is "normal," and flagging the "abnormal" activity that does not fit into this pre-trained construct. When monitoring traffic to and from IP addresses on a large network, this problem can become computationally complex, and potentially intractable, as a state model must be maintained for each address. In this paper, we present a method of detecting anomalous network activity without providing any historical context. By exploiting the size of the network along with the minimal overhead of NetFlow data, we are able to model groups of hosts performing similar functions to discover anomalous behavior. As a collection, these anomalies can be further described with a few high-level characterizations and we provide a means for creating and labeling these categories. We demonstrate our method on a very large-scale network consisting of 30 million unique addresses, focusing specifically on traffic related to web servers.

Categories and Subject Descriptors

C.2.3 [**Network Operations**]: Network Monitoring

General Terms

Measurement, Security

Keywords

Anomaly detection, network security, machine learning

1. INTRODUCTION

To complement *signature-based* intrusion detection systems (IDS) such as Snort [17] and Bro-IDS [16], there has been much research in the area of *anomaly-based* systems [22, 11], which do not match pre-defined signatures, but rather identify behavior which is rare compared to a data-driven model. This approach provides the benefit of being able to detect zero-day attacks – or deviations of known attacks without a signature – as long as they deviate from the normal traffic patterns. Sommer and Paxson [20] provide a detailed breakdown of several of the reasons why machine learning based anomaly detection methods have failed to reach wide adoption. We address two important weaknesses and develop an anomaly detection method that scales to large networks and provides context for decisions.

In this paper we present a method for anomaly detection on very large-scale networks which is temporally oblivious, e.g. we do not utilize any historic information about a host to determine if it is anomalous. In complete isolation, it is impossible to determine if a host is behaving in an anomalous fashion during a given moment without the historical context that is typically used for anomaly detection. However, in the presence of numerous functional peers – hosts providing similar services – we can identify those hosts exhibiting significantly different behaviors over a static snapshot in time. This intuition follows from the fact that many functions and services have inherent properties which govern their behavior. In our approach, the model used to detect anomalies consists of measurements over the group of peers and automatically compensates for variations in traffic patterns over time. While abnormal by definition, the anomalies detected can be further characterized by a small set of descriptions, and we provide an automated method of providing these qualitative assessments.

The contributions of this paper to network anomaly detection are as follows:

- Temporal modeling is not required, instead we use on-the-fly data driven statistics from other active network hosts performing similar functions.
- Computation is low because only NetFlow [1] features are used and instead of building one reference model per host, only one reference model is required for each general function. This supports scaling to very-large networks.
- After training, anomalies are automatically categorized by a small set of descriptive characterizations, requiring minimal additional computation in a live environment.

*This work is sponsored under Air Force Contract FA8721-05-C-0002. Opinions, interpretations, conclusions and recommendations are those of the authors and are not necessarily endorsed by the United States Government.

IMC'10, November 1–3, 2010, Melbourne, Australia.

Table 1: Anomaly Detection Features

Incoming	Outgoing	Ratio (Outgoing/Incoming)
Bytes / Packet (B/P)	B / P	Bytes
Packets / Flow (P/F)	P / F	Packets
Flows / Unique External Source IP (F/SIP)	F / DIP	Flows
# Unique External Source IP (SIP)	DIP	IP addresses

1.1 Previous Work

Some recently presented methods of network anomaly detection focus on detecting volume anomalies which show a sharp change (typically an increase) in the traffic volumes received by a network or host [2, 21, 22]. This approach may miss important traffic variations because the volume increases to an individual host are often masked by variations in normal network traffic [11]. There has been work to detect specific types of malicious volume activity such as port scanning [18], worm and botnet propagation [6, 8], and denial of service attacks [4, 23, 14]. These techniques use properties of machine learning, along with high-level network information (such as NetFlow records) to detect these very specific activities. Additional work has been done to classify internet traffic into specified applications [13]. While payload-oblivious techniques have their natural limitations [7], they scale to large networks. Statistical entropy has been used to detect a more general class of anomalies [10, 11, 12, 15], measuring the change in the distribution of network traffic. These methods have been shown to be very successful at identifying *when* an anomaly occurs on the network, but they require additional post-processing to identify the responsible parties, which has seen additional work [3].

2. DETECTING ANOMALOUS HOSTS

We define an anomalous host as one which exhibits behavior that is significantly dissimilar to other hosts on the monitored network performing similar function(s) during an observation window; stressing specifically that *anomalous* is not necessarily *malicious*. While network traffic is known to be highly variable over short periods for individual hosts, on large networks there are frequently many hosts performing similar functions. This makes it possible to detect anomalies among these functional peers by using the collection of hosts as a reference to detect the few which deviate from this behavior.

2.1 Data and Features

Given our goal for detection on large-scale networks, we utilize unsampled NetFlow data as full packet capture is often unfeasible. From the data, we extract a 12-dimensional feature vector x from each host on the monitored network during a T second observation window. These aggregated flow features are listed in Table 1, where SIP and DIP refer to the number of external unique source and destination IP addresses respectively, and the ratio of IP addresses is computed as DIP/SIP.

With the exception of the number of unique IP addresses communicating with the host, each feature is invariant to the scale of the network or service utilization. This was chosen specifically so that hosts with similar utilization patterns are observed as such, regardless of the number of external hosts accessing the service. However, it is still necessary to include the number of unique IP addresses connecting to the host in order to give some context to the access patterns.

2.2 Identifying Outliers

Measuring Dissimilarity

Given the collection of feature vectors for the N IP addresses on the network $\mathbf{X} = [x_1, x_2, \ldots, x_N]$, we identify anomalies by first defining a dissimilarity measure for each pair of hosts. As each measured feature from Table 1 covers a different range, we normalize each feature to the same relative scale. We choose to normalize each feature such that there is unit distance between the 10th and 90th percentiles of that feature. Specifically, let $f_p(y)$ be defined such that it returns the pth percentile of the data in vector y. For example, $f_{50}(y)$ would be equal to the median of y. We normalize each feature i in $\mathbf{X}$ such that

$$\mathbf{X}(i) = \mathbf{X}(i)/(f_{90}(\mathbf{X}(i)) - f_{10}(\mathbf{X}(i))),$$

where $\mathbf{X}(i) = [x_1(i), \ldots, x_N(i)]$. This normalization ensures that 80% of the mass of data will lie in the same range for the various features, but the outliers will still stand out as we are linearly scaling the data. Once normalized, we calculate pairwise distances between hosts with a standard Euclidean (L_2) distance $D(x_i, x_j) = \| x_i - x_j \|_2$.

Hierarchical Clustering

After calculating the pairwise dissimilarities between hosts, we employ hierarchical clustering [9] to identify outliers. Clustering is performed by first assigning each host to its own cluster or *node*. The two nodes with the smallest linkage cost between them are merged to form a new node, and the process is repeated until all hosts belong to the same node. For this task we use single-linkage clustering, which defines the cost of merging nodes A and B as $\min\{D(a,b) : a \in A, b \in B\}$; the minimum distance between any two hosts in the nodes. This is a logical linkage criterion for anomaly detection as we aim to find those samples which are most dissimilar from others. This method results in a hierarchical cluster tree in which the top of the tree is a single cluster containing all hosts, and the bottom of the tree contains a unique cluster for each host.

Intuition suggests that in the presence of outliers, the final nodes to merge would contain the potential outliers, as the linkage cost will be among the largest of any nodes in the set. We develop a stopping criterion intentionally designed to identify these outliers. Note that the linkage cost $L(i)$ is strictly non-decreasing over iterations i; we stop merging clusters at the point where $L(i) > \alpha L(i-1), \alpha > 1$. For a large enough value of α, this stopping criterion will identify the first significant jump in the linkage cost. When the cost of merging two nodes is a significant gain over the previous merge, any remaining clusters are distinctly different and any sample belonging to a cluster with less than n

members is flagged as an outlier. The threshold n may be defined either as a constant value, or some function of the set size N. By our definition of anomaly, if there is a cluster of activity with $\geq n$ members, those hosts will not be flagged because there is a large enough contingent of hosts exhibiting similar behaviors. Hence, certain activities which are not historically normal to the monitored network may go undetected. This does not mean the activity is not malicious or temporally anomalous, it is simply not anomalous for the monitored network *during this window T*.

2.3 A Network Illustration

We tested our anomaly detection method on seven continuous days of traffic on a monitored network consisting of 30 million hosts. Our data comes from gateway border routers that observe all traffic entering and leaving the network and transmit all flow records to a central repository. We use the SiLK system to query this database and compute aggregate statistics [5]. This centralized system alleviates concerns of asymmetric routing, as we are guaranteed to see both sides of the flow.

As a proof-of-concept, we limit our analysis to incoming traffic with destination port 80 and outgoing traffic with source port 80. This corresponds primarily, although not exclusively, to those IP addresses hosting web services. Note that we do not make a distinction between TCP and UDP for this analysis. On this monitored network, there are roughly 750 hosts receiving applicable traffic at any given time. While we lack appropriate labels for the data during this period, we do have knowledge of two large-scale SYN-flood distributed denial of service (DDoS) attacks against two network web servers during the monitored period.

Our detection parameters are set with the goal of identifying the most egregious anomalies on the network. We apply five-minute aggregation windows (T = 300s) to the data; a window large enough to benefit from consistency due to aggregation, yet small enough to still identify brief anomalies. Defining the optimal value T is a network-specific task and an area for future work. We set our stopping criterion variable at $\alpha = 3$ and our cluster size threshold at $n = 3$, reiterating our goal to find the most significant outliers.

As an illustration, we randomly select a five-minute window and demonstrate the detection results. In Fig. 1, we plot the dendrogram of the hierarchical cluster tree calculated from the extracted features, which shows the manner in which the tree is formed by merging nodes of increasing linkage costs. Due to the size of the network, we do not illustrate all of the unique leaf nodes, beginning instead with nodes that have already been merged. What is clear from Fig. 1 is that there exists a significant jump in the linkage cost near the top of the tree. We plot the cutoff threshold determined by $\alpha = 3$ with the dashed line, resulting in 3 remaining clusters, 2 of which contain only one sample. These two hosts are flagged as anomalous during this process. When run over the entire seven day window, this method resulted in 1,658 flagged anomalies out of a possible 1.5 million host samples, flagging an average of 0.11% of monitored hosts (0.8 hosts) as anomalous during a given observation period. In 47% of the observation windows, no hosts were flagged as anomalous.

3. GROUPING THE ANOMALIES

It is of particular interest to see if common anomalies occur at different time intervals and over different hosts in the network. This is not obvious, as by definition the behavior is not within the network norms. To determine this, we gather the feature vectors of all 1,658 anomalies flagged during the analysis of Section 2.2 in a set $\mathbf{Z}$, and perform additional clustering on this set. Each individual anomaly was detected in a temporally oblivious manner, and follow-on analysis determines if there are common themes amongst those detected.

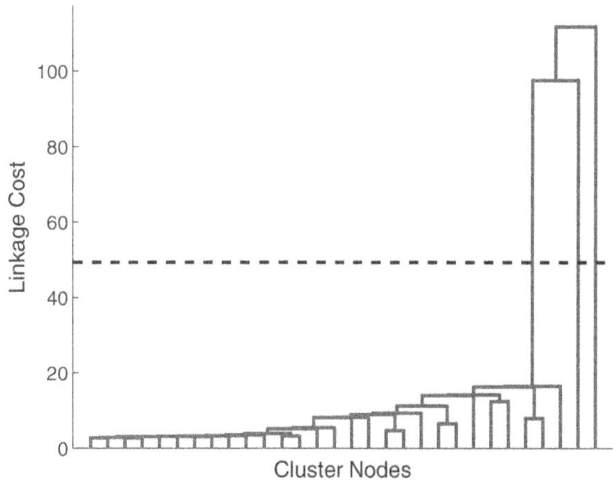

Figure 1: Dendrogram of the hierarchical cluster tree resultant from a single time window. The dashed line shows the stopping point, resulting in two detected outliers.

Normalizing the Data

To obtain categories for the collected outliers, it is necessary to normalize in a way that preserves the high-level description of the data. For example, if the vast majority of hosts receive less than F flows per unique external source IP, and two distinct hosts receive $100F$ and $500F$ flows in a five minute window, they should be treated as equals – they are anomalous due to large received F/SIP. To account for this issue, we normalize the data by a *sigmoid* function $s(x)$, which translates every value $x \in [-\infty, \infty]$ to $s(x) \in [0, 1]$:

$$s(x) = \frac{1}{1 + \exp(-(x - \mu)/b)}.$$

We omit the full details for brevity, but we set our parameters $\mu = f_{50}(\mathbf{Z}(i))$ and b such that the end of the linear portion of $s(x)$ (e.g. the bend point [19]) occurs at $x = f_{90}(\mathbf{Z}(i))$. We set the bend point to the 90th percentile of the data such that the extreme outliers will be truncated to near unity while still linearly scaling the majority of the data samples.

We demonstrate this scaling for the incoming B/P feature in Fig. 2, where we plot the scaled histogram of values alongside the sigmoid normalization function. This plot shows that the sample points far away from the mass of the distribution will be quantized to nearly 1, regardless of the magnitude of their distance.

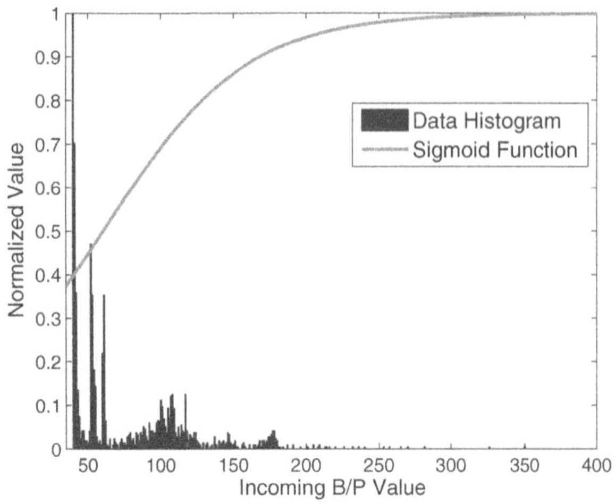

Figure 2: Normalizing the data features of the outliers using a sigmoid function. This offers linear scaling for the mass of the data while quantizing the extreme outliers.

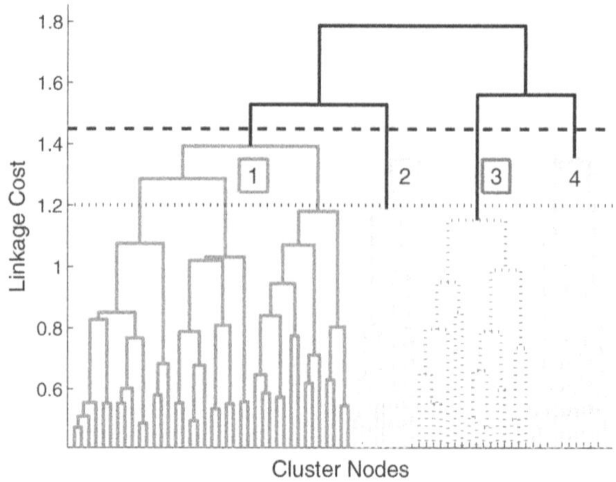

Figure 3: Dendrogram of the hierarchical cluster tree resultant from all anomalies over a 7 day period. The choice of cutoff threshold determines the cluster granularity.

Clustering the Anomalies

We proceed by performing hierarchical clustering on the normalized data using a complete-linkage criterion. The cost of merging nodes A and B is defined as $\max\{D(a,b) : a \in A, b \in B\}$, which is more useful for identifying similar clusters rather than outliers. Rather than assigning our cutoff threshold by identifying the jump in linkage cost as before, we qualitatively assess the dendrogram to determine the appropriate threshold. This has the benefit of enabling us to specify the level of detail which we are interested in describing the anomalies.

Visual inspection of the abbreviated dendrogram in Fig. 3 shows that we can glean a high-level description of the outliers by setting our threshold to 1.45, which results in 4 clusters covering all of the anomalies. In order to identify the common theme of each cluster in a quantitative sense we applied a 2-class decision tree for each cluster, in which members of the cluster belonged to the positive class, and all other vectors are given a negative label. While we omit the quantitative results, the decision rules were quite simple, accurately classifying the large amount of anomalies generally based on three primary features: byte ratio, IP ratio, and outgoing bytes/packet. We now provide a brief qualitative assessment of the type of traffic we see in each cluster:

Cluster 1: As the largest cluster, the hosts on this cluster exhibit several different patterns, and we noticed 3 distinct groups. However, the key feature is that 99% of the 1,008 host samples in the cluster sent traffic to more IP addresses than they received it from. The first group we observed in this cluster contains those hosts which received a large number of low-byte packets in a single flow from a single IP address, and responded with a much larger volume of traffic. An example of this would be a host that received a single flow with 26,000 packets each containing 40 bytes (1 MB total) from a single IP address, and responded to the same address with 30 MB of traffic.

The next group consists of hosts receiving a large amount of traffic from a single source IP through an abnormally large number of flow records, and responding in kind. An example of this would be a host which received 250 KB of data from a single IP across 350 flows. We can infer from this type of traffic that the source IP in question operates as a network address translation (NAT) or proxy server, and there are potentially numerous unique hosts using the same externally visible IP address.

Finally, the third group is clearly DDoS activity, as the hosts receive traffic from numerous unique source IP addresses each sending a significantly large number of flows containing only 2-3 packets. The servers are responding to more hosts than they are receiving traffic from, signifying that they are able to keep up for the time being. An interesting aspect about this cluster is that the DDoS attacks on the two servers mentioned earlier cluster together, even though they were carried out in different manners.

Cluster 2: The hosts in this cluster receive very low volumes of traffic from very few sources, yet send substantial volumes to more IP addresses than they received traffic from. In fact, 97% of the 94 hosts in this group sent outgoing traffic to more IP addresses than they received incoming traffic from. Example: A host received 735 bytes across 7 packets in a single flow from a single source and sent 195 MB of traffic across 140,000 packets in 2 flows to 2 unique IP addresses.

Cluster 3: The hosts in this cluster received high volumes, with a median of 595 MB of traffic during the observation period – for reference the median received traffic in the other clusters was 2.2 MB, 800 bytes, and 306 KB respectively. This could imply the hosts allow file uploads. Additionally, 99% of 402 hosts in this group sent outgoing traffic to less destinations than they received incoming traffic from. Within this cluster, we noticed subgroups containing high-volume unidirectional traffic entering the network which had no observed responses. This included DDoS traffic where the servers under attack had either crashed or stopped accepting traffic. There was additionally DDoS traffic for which there were responses, although the response volume was always less than the incoming traffic. This may imply a DDoS for which the server is unable to keep up with requests.

Cluster 4: The hosts in this cluster behaved similarly to those in Cluster 2; receiving low volumes of traffic while sending significantly larger ones. This cluster is differentiated by the fact that no host sent traffic to more IP addresses than it received traffic from. In fact, 66% of the 154 hosts sent traffic to fewer hosts. There was an additional group within this cluster of hosts that received traffic from a few sources, comprised of large numbers of small byte packets in a minimal number of flows, yet still sent a large volume of traffic in return, approaching the maximum transmission unit (MTU) size of the network (1,500 bytes/packet). This appears to be large file-transfer traffic, which would explain the large outgoing packet sizes, low flow counts, and small incoming packet sizes (which would simply by ACKs by the external host).

Our cluster descriptions provide a high-level understanding of the different types of detected anomalies. While there were many "repeat offenders", 172 of the 1,658 anomalies were attributed to unique IP addresses, and each cluster contained at minimum 39 unique IP addresses. A finer categorical granularity can be achieved by simply decreasing the cutoff threshold for the hierarchical cluster tree. For example, when reducing the threshold to 1.2, Cluster 1 is now split into the three clusters we previously observed as shown in Fig. 3

3.1 Classifying New Anomalies

If new anomalies could be detected without a new clustering analysis, the qualitative categorization presented would be of high value to analysts; abstracting them from the technical and statistical details concerning clustering. By training classifiers on anomalies detected over a period of time, we can provide a label along with a confidence for each newly detected anomaly. In the absence of ground truth, we develop our classifier by using the previously clustered anomalies as our training set. For this study, we train on the high-level cluster labels represented in Fig. 3 (four classes), and implement a simple linear classifier on the normalized anomaly data; choosing decision boundaries via linear discriminant analysis. This results in a 1.69% classification error on the training set. Note that this error is in classifying hosts which have already been flagged as anomalous, so there is a drastically lower cost for misclassification than with a traditional IDS.

We test this classifier over seven days of traffic occurring 8 weeks after the data we trained on. We normalize the newly flagged anomalous data in the same manner, still using the f_{50} and f_{90} values from the training data in order to preserve the appropriate scaling. There were 2,411 out of a possible 1.4 million hosts flagged during this testing period, yielding an average of 1.24 hosts being flagged as anomalous during an observation window. After classifying each anomaly, we note that the types of activity in each class are consistent with those during the training period. We can quantify the confidence $c(x)$ in these labels by using the posterior probability that a sample x_i belongs to a specific class C_j, which is denoted as $\mathrm{P}(C_j \mid x_i)$. As each sample is labeled according to the class C_j which maximizes this value, we can set the confidence of our classification label as $c(x_i) = \max_j \mathrm{P}(C_j \mid x_i)$. For the test data, 95.5% of the detected anomalies had $c(x) > 90\%$, confirming that the general categories of anomalies on the network did not change. It is worth noting that 66% of the anomalies detected during this testing phase were from IP addresses that were *never* flagged as anomalous during the training phase. It is not simply the same hosts consistently exhibiting the same anomalous behavior, but different hosts behaving in manners which fall under persistent categorizations. There was one sample with a confidence of $< 50\%$ ($c(x) = 42\%$). A sample with a confidence this low may represent a new category of anomaly, and a method for culling this information automatically is an area for future work.

4. DISCUSSION

We've presented what we deem to be very promising results, yet our work has a few shortcomings which we now address. First, while we provide intuition for our chosen parameter values, α and n, a more rigorous approach would be necessary for a full deployment. Given the nature of anomalies, and their lack of expert-defined labels, there is no straightforward way to define these parameters in an automated fashion. A network administrator deploying a system such as ours would have to train the parameters to yield an "acceptable" amount of alerts per observation period, as is done in many IDS and anomaly detection systems, and determine which classes of anomalous traffic are potentially benign. The detected anomalies could then be filtered based on their class and network knowledge (eg. NATs) to reduce the alerts an analyst must investigate.

There is a chance that a previously unseen anomaly could occur which is not accurately described by the previously trained classifier. This is the nature of anomaly detection, yet our system has the tools to account for this. Specifically, the classification confidence of such an anomaly would be predictably low (as shown in Section 3.1), and these types of anomalies could be saved for retraining the system. As with any classifier, periodic retraining is necessary if the statistics of the feature space change, and that will almost always be the case for network data. It is future work to determine how often this retraining would be necessary.

While our method is specifically *not* an IDS, we realize that anomaly detection is often used for that purpose and we want to detail how an adversary could circumvent this system. A sophisticated attack could have an adversary intentionally manipulate the traffic of multiple servers at the same time in the same manner, causing them to form a large enough group in the feature space that would not be deemed anomalous. This would require knowledge of the algorithm parameters, specifically the minimum cluster size n, and would also increase the required resources for the adversary.

5. CONCLUSIONS

In this paper we have described a temporally-oblivious approach for detecting anomalous hosts on large-scale networks. By modeling the behavior of functional peers, anomalies stand out and can be described by a small set of qualitative characterizations. The fact that anomalous activity, which by definition is significantly abnormal, is categorically consistent over time is intriguing. We utilized this discovery to develop a labeling system for anomalies discovered during new observation periods. This framework was trained over seven days and tested over an additional seven days nearly 2 months later, with very similar results.

This work is presented as a proof-of-concept of a novel method of detecting anomalies. We note that hierarchical clustering is an $O(N^2)$ operation, meaning that it will not purely scale to large N. This is why we operate our system on a *per service* basis, focusing on port 80 in this study. While port numbers do not restrict activity, many are reserved for specified functions, so this split is logical for anomaly detection. Since networks are made of a finite number of services of interest, this split also enables scaling to very large-scale networks. Determining a manner to cluster across services is an area for future work. Additionally, we would like to identify clusters of activity within the non-anomalous traffic, seeing whether these clusters remain consistent over time in a similar fashion as the clusters of anomalous activity. This naturally lends itself to many research areas in network behavioral analysis. The nature of the clusters themselves provides network situational awareness, and identifying the movement of hosts between clusters could provide additional information.

Acknowledgements

We would like to thank the reviewers for their thoughtful comments and William W. Streilein of MIT Lincoln Laboratory for his help with our normalization methods.

6. REFERENCES

[1] Cisco netflow. http://www.cisco.com.

[2] Barford, P., Kline, J., Plonka, D., and Ron, A. A signal analysis of network traffic anomalies. In *Internet Measurement Workshop* (2002), pp. 71–82.

[3] Brauckhoff, D., Wagner, A., and Salamatian, K. Anomaly extraction in backbone networks using association rules. In *Proceedings of 9th ACM SIGCOMM Internet Measurement Conference* (2009), pp. 28–34.

[4] Carl, G., Kesidis, G., Brooks, R. R., and Rai, S. Denial-of-service attack-detection techniques. In *IEEE Internet Computing* (Jan./Feb. 2006), vol. 10, pp. 82–89.

[5] CERT/NetSA at Carnegie Mellon University. *SiLK (System for Internet-Level Knowledge).* [Online]. Available: http://tools.netsa.cert.org/silk.

[6] Collins, M. P., and Reiter, M. K. Hit-list worm detection and bot identification in large networks using protocol graphs. In *Proceedings ofthe 10th International Symposium on Recent Advances in Intrusion Detection (RAID)* (2007).

[7] Collins, M. P., and Reiter, M. K. On the limits of payload-oblivious network attack detection. In *Proceedings of 11th International Symposium on Recent Advances in Intrusion Detection (RAID)* (2008), pp. 251–270.

[8] Gu, G., Perdisci, R., Zhang, J., and Lee, W. Botminer: Clustering analysis of network traffic for protocol- and structure-independent botnet detection. In *Proceedings of 17th USENIX Security Symposium* (2008), pp. 139–154.

[9] Hastie, T., Tibshirani, R., and Friedman, J. *The Elements of Statistical Learning.* Springer, July 2003.

[10] Lakhina, A., Crovella, M., and Diot, C. Characterization of network-wide anomalies in traffic flows. In *Proceedings of ACM/SIGCOMM Internet Measurement Conference* (2004), pp. 201–206.

[11] Lakhina, A., Crovella, M., and Diot, C. Diagnosing network-wide traffic anomalies. In *Proceedings of ACM SIGCOMM* (2004), pp. 219–230.

[12] Li, X., Bian, F., Crovella, M., Diot, C., Govindan, R., Iannaccone, G., and Lakhina, A. Detection and identification of network anomalies using sketch subspaces. In *Proceedings of 6th ACM SIGCOMM Conference on Internet Measurement* (2006), pp. 147–152.

[13] Moore, A. W., and Zuev, D. Internet traffic classification using bayesian analysis techniques. In *Proceedings of 2005 ACM SIGMETRICS International Conference on Measurement and Modeling of Computer Systems* (2005), pp. 50–60.

[14] Moore, D., Voelker, G., and Savage, S. Inferring internet denial-of-service activity. In *Proceedings of the 10th Usenix Security Symposium* (2001), pp. 9–22.

[15] Nychis, G., Sekar, V., Andersen, D. G., Kim, H., and Zhang, H. An emperical evaluation of entropy-based traffic anomaly detection. In *Proceedings of 8th ACM SIGCOMM Conference on Internet Measurement* (Oct. 2008), pp. 151–156.

[16] Paxson, V. Bro: A system for detecting network intruders in real-time. *Computer Networks 31*, 23–24 (1999), 2435–2463.

[17] Roesch, M. Snort - lightweight intrusion detection for networks. In *Proceedings of 13th LISA Conference* (1999), pp. 229–238.

[18] Schechter, S. E., Jung, J., and Berger, A. W. Fast detection of scanning worm infections. In *Proceedings of the 7th International Symposium on Recent Advances in Intrusion Detection (RAID)* (2004), pp. 59–81.

[19] Sebaugh, J. L., and McCray, P. D. Defining the linear portion of a sigmoid-shaped curve: Bend points. In *Pharmaceutical Statistics*, vol. 2. 2003, pp. 167–174.

[20] Sommer, R., and Paxson, V. Outside the closed world: On using machine learning for network intrusion detection. In *Proceedings of 31st IEEE Symposium on Security and Privacy* (May 2010).

[21] Subhabrata, B. K., Krishnamurthy, E., Sen, S., Zhang, Y., and Chen, Y. Sketch-based change detection: Methods, evaluation, and applications. In *Proceedings of ACM SIGCOMM Internet Measurement Conference* (2003), pp. 234–247.

[22] Thottan, M., and Ji, C. Anomaly detection in ip networks. *IEEE Transactions on Signal Processing 51* 8 (Aug. 2003), 2191–2204.

[23] Wang, H., Zhang, D., and Shin, K. G. Detecting syn flooding attacks. In *Proceedings of the IEEE Infocom* (2002), pp. 1530–1539.

What Happened in my Network? Mining Network Events from Router Syslogs

Tongqing Qiu
Georgia Tech
Atlanta, GA
tongqqiu@cc.gatech.edu

Zihui Ge
AT&T Labs – Research
Florham Park, NJ
gezihui@research.att.com

Dan Pei
AT&T Labs – Research
Florham Park, NJ
peidan@research.att.com

Jia Wang
AT&T Labs – Research
Florham Park, NJ
jiawang@research.att.com

Jun (Jim) Xu*
Georgia Tech
Atlanta, GA
jx@cc.gatech.edu

ABSTRACT

Router syslogs are messages that a router logs to describe a wide range of events observed by it. They are considered one of the most valuable data sources for monitoring network health and for troubleshooting network faults and performance anomalies. However, router syslog messages are essentially free-form text with only a minimal structure, and their formats vary among different vendors and router OSes. Furthermore, since router syslogs are aimed for tracking and debugging router software/hardware problems, they are often too low-level from network service management perspectives. Due to their sheer volume (e.g., millions per day in a large ISP network), detailed router syslog messages are typically examined only when required by an on-going troubleshooting investigation or when given a narrow time range and a specific router under suspicion. Automated systems based on router syslogs on the other hand tend to focus on a subset of the mission critical messages (e.g., relating to network fault) to avoid dealing with the full diversity and complexity of syslog messages. In this project, we design a SyslogDigest system that can automatically transform and compress such low-level minimally-structured syslog messages into meaningful and prioritized high-level network events, using powerful data mining techniques tailored to our problem domain. These events are three orders of magnitude fewer in number and have much better usability than raw syslog messages. We demonstrate that they provide critical input to network troubleshooting, and network health monitoring and visualization.

Categories and Subject Descriptors

C.2.3 [**Computer System Organization**]: Computer-Communication Networks—*Network Operations*

*This work was supported in part by NSF grant CNS-0905169, funded under the American Recovery and Reinvestment Act of 2009 (Public Law 111-5), and NSF grant CNS-0716423.

IMC'10, November 1–3, 2010, Melbourne, Australia.

General Terms

Management, Performance

Keywords

Syslog, Data Mining, Troubleshooting

1. INTRODUCTION

Router syslogs are messages that a router logs to describe a wide range of events observed by it. Although router syslogs are primarily designed and intended for router vendors to track and debug router software/hardware problems, they are also widely used by the network service providers as one of the most valuable data sources in monitoring network health and in troubleshooting network faults and performance anomalies. However, working with raw syslog messages is not easy from network service management prospectives. First, router syslog messages are essentially free-form text with only a minimal structure. The type of information that is logged and its formats vary among different vendors and router operating systems. Second, router syslog messages are often too low-level. They do not directly translate into what actually happened in the network (i.e., network events) without meaningful abstraction and aggregation. Third, not every router syslog message is an indication of an occurrence of an incident that could potentially impact network services. For example, some router syslog messages are generated purely for debugging purposes and have no implications on network services.

Although large ISP (Internet Service Provider) network, consisting of thousands of routers, is expected to observe millions of information-rich syslog message per day, the lack of sentence structures in log messages and relational structures across messages prevents router syslogs from being utilized to its fullest extent in various network management applications. Network monitoring systems typically rely on the input of domain knowledge to be able to focus on a rather small (yetdeemed important) subset of syslog messages. For example, commercial network management tools such as Lonix [1] and NetCool [2] focus on a small set of messages concerning network faults. The syntax and the relations of these syslog messages are explicitly captured to allow for automated parsing and understanding. When certain patterns of syslog messages are observed in the network, alarms are triggered and operation tickets are issued. The parsers and the message relationship models therein need to be constantly updated to keep up with network changes. For example, routers upgraded to a new operating system may introduce new syslog message formats and hence require a new parser. Network issues can also fly under the radar if they do not match syslog patterns already programmed. Meanwhile, when troubleshooting a network event, network operators have to focus on a narrow time-window and a specific router in examining the raw syslog messages in detail, in order to avoid being overwhelmed by the number of syslog messages. It is a very time-consuming and inefficient process when a complicated network incident involves a large number of messages. Moreover, by limiting to a small scope, operators lose the sight of "big picture", such as the information regarding the frequency or the scope of the kind of network events under investigation. Finally, network auditing and trend analysis systems have to rely on rather simple frequency statistics when it comes to router syslogs. For example, MERCURY [15] detects network behavior changes due to network upgrades by tracking the level-shift of message frequencies of individual syslogs. Knowing the relationship across syslog messages would make the result much more meaningful.

In this work, we focus on proactively mining network events from router syslogs. In particular, we design an automated system (called SyslogDigest) that transforms and compresses massive low-level minimally-structured syslog messages into a small number of meaningful and prioritized high-level network events. SyslogDigest is vendor/network independent and does not require domain knowledge on expected network behaviors. It automatically identifies signatures of different types of syslog messages in terms of both their syntax and temporal patterns (e.g., interarrival time of each type of syslog messages). In addition, SyslogDigest learns association rules between different types of syslog messages both on the same router and across routers. The combination of the signatures and association rules of syslog messages enables us to group them into meaningful network events. Furthermore, SyslogDigest prioritizes network events using a number of severity/importance measures. This allows network operators to quickly identify and focus on important network events. More importantly, this enables complex network troubleshooting, in which thousands to tens of thousands of syslog messages on multiple routers may be related to a single network event and may need to be identified out of millions of syslog messages for examination. SyslogDigest systematically classifies and groups these syslog messages into a single meaningful event, making obsolete the long and error-prone manual grouping process in the current practice. This automated grouping capability not only enables monitoring overall network health and tracking the appearance and evolvement of network events, but also allows for much better network visualization, since visualizing such network events provides a much clearer and more accurate big picture of what happened in the network than visualizing raw syslog messages.

It is also worth noting that, SyslogDigest greatly alleviates our reliance on the domain knowledge of (human) network operators in interpreting syslog messages. Instead, SyslogDigest is able to learn signatures and rules that capture how the network behaves over time. That is, SyslogDigest automatically learns network domain knowledge directly from the data. Such domain knowledge not only tells us what happens in the network, but also provides direct insights on "how the network behaves" vs. "how the network should behave". In addition, external domain knowledge, if available, can be easily input into SyslogDigest to further enhance or customize the system.

We apply SyslogDigest to router syslog messages collected from two large operational IP networks: one tier-1 ISP backbone network and one large IPTV backbone network. We show that SyslogDigest outputs prioritized network events that are over three orders of magnitude fewer in number and have much better usability than raw syslog messages. Using real applications, we further demonstrate that they provide critical input to not only network troubleshooting but also network health monitoring and visualization.

To summarize, we make four major contributions in this paper.

1. We designed an automated tool SyslogDigest that transforms massive volume of router syslog messages into a much smaller number of meaningful network events.

2. We developed effective techniques tailored to our problem domain to systematically identify signatures of syslog messages, learn association rules that capture network behaviors over time, group relevant raw syslog messages across multiple routers into network events, and label and prioritize network events based on their nature and severities.

3. We conducted large-scale experiments on real router syslog data collected from two large operational IP networks and demonstrated that SyslogDigest is able to transform millions of syslog messages into network events that are over three orders of magnitude fewer in number and smaller in size.

The remainder of this paper is organized as follows. Section 2 describes the syntax and semantics of router syslogs. Section 3 presents an overview of SyslogDigest system and Section 4 describes the detailed methodologies it uses. Section 5 presents the evaluation results based on router syslog data collected from two large operational IP networks. We present some applications of SyslogDigest in Section 6 and related work in Section 7. Finally, Section 8 concludes the paper.

2. ROUTER SYSLOG

In this section, we provide an overview of the syntax and semantics of router syslog messages. Similar to syslogs on computer servers, router syslogs are the messages that routers generate to record the hardware and software conditions observed by them, such as link and protocol-related state changes (e.g., down or up), alarming environmental measurements (e.g., high voltage or temperature), and warning messages (e.g., triggered when BGP neighbors send more routes than the router is configured to allow). Although syslog messages are intended primarily for tracking and debugging router software and hardware problems, they can be extremely valuable to network operators in managing networked services and troubleshooting network incidents. For this reason syslogs are usually collected on all routers inside a network, especially an ISP network, and a syslog (transmission) protocol [6] is standardized and widely supported by router vendors to transmit syslog messages from routers to one or more syslog collector(s).

While the syslog protocol – for transmitting syslog messages – is standardized, the syslog messages themselves are not. They are essentially free-form texts, the syntax and semantics of which vary among router vendors and router operating systems. Table 1 shows a few examples of syslog messages from two router vendors. We can observe only a minimal structure in a syslog message: (1) a timestamp indicating when the message is generated, (2) the identifier of the router that generates the message (called *originating router*), (3) message type, also known as the error code, indicating the nature of the problem, and (4) detailed message information generated by the router OS. In order to correlate syslog messages across routers, the clocks (for generating the timestamps) on these routers need to be synchronized often through the Network Time Protocol (NTP), which is the case in our studies.

Table 1: Syslog messages example

Vendor	Message timestamp	Router	Message-type/error-code	Detailed message
V1	2010-01-10 00:00:15	r1	LINEPROTO-5-UPDOWN	Line protocol on Interface Serial13/0.10/ 20:0, changed state to down
V1	2010-01-10 00:00:15	r5	LINK-3-UPDOWN	Interface Serial2/0.10/2:0, changed state to down
V1	2010-01-10 00:00:15	r8	SYS-1-CPURISINGTHRESHOLD	Threshold: Total CPU Utilization(Total/Intr): 95%/1%, Top 3 processes (Pid/Util): 2/71%, 8/6%, 7/3%
V1	2010-01-10 00:00:26	r8	SYS-1-CPUFALLINGTHRESHOLD	Threshold: Total CPU Utilization(Total/Intr) 30%/1%.
V2	2010-01-10 00:00:23	ra	SNMP-WARNING-linkDown	Interface 0/0/1 is not operational
V2	2010-01-10 00:00:24	rb	SVCMGR-MAJOR-sapPortStateChangeProcessed	The status of all affected SAPs on port 1/1/1 has been updated.
V2	2010-01-10 00:00:26	ra	SNMP-WARNING-linkup	Interface 0/1/0 is operational

The detailed message information (aforementioned field (4)) in router syslogs is quite ad hoc in nature. They are simply free-form texts "printf"-ed by router operating systems with detailed information such as the location, state/status, or measurement readings of a alarming condition embedded in them. For example, in Table 1 line 1, (`Line protocol on Interface Serial13/0.10/20:0, changed state to down`), the `Serial13/0.10/20:0` part indicates the network interface at which the layer-2 line protocol (PPP) has been impacted and the `down` part indicates the status/state of the line protocol. The rest of it, `Line protocol on Interface ..., changed state to ...`, can be viewed as the sub type for this type of syslog message. It is worth noting that there are often multiple sub types associated with the same syslog type (error code). The combination of syslog type and this sub type can be used as a *template* to uniquely identify the class of network conditions that the syslog message describes.

In some syslog versions, the error code field contains severity information. For example, in the first four lines (vendor V1 syslogs) of Table 1, the number between two "-" symbols is the severity level of the messages – the smaller the number is, the more important the message is *perceived by the originating router*. It is important to note, however, that the severity level of a syslog message is assigned by the equipment vendor based on the perceived impact of the observed event on the performance and proper functioning of the local network elements. It does not in general translate into the severity of the impact that this event will have on the performance and proper functioning of the overall network and therefore cannot be directly used for to rank-order the importance of events for network service management purposes. For example, syslog messages concerning router CPU utilization rising above or falling below a given threshold (lines 3 and 4 in Table 1) have been considered more important (smaller in severity number) than those concerning an adjacent link changing its state to "down" (line 2 in Table 1) in some router OS. Network operators would certainly disagree in this case.

Router configuration tools usually allow network operators to specify a threshold such that potential syslog messages with severity levels above or equal to it will be recorded. In this study, we collect syslogs at such "informational" level (usually the default setting). Depending on the network conditions, the amount of router syslog messages in an operational network varies. In the large-scale ISP network (hundreds to thousands routers) that we study in the paper, there are typically hundreds of thousands to millions of messages per day.

3. SYSTEM DESIGN OVERVIEW

The goal of the SyslogDigest system is to automatically transform and compress low-level minimally-structured syslog messages into meaningful and prioritized high-level network events. Our key observation is that one single (sometimes intermittent) condition on a network element, such as an network interface, router hardware, and router software, can often trigger a large number of different messages across time, protocol layers, and routers. For example, messages $m1$ to $m16$ in Table 2 are all triggered by the same network condition: the link between routers $r1$ and $r2$ flapped a couple of times. Based on this observation, our basic idea is to automatically construct a *network event* by grouping together *related* messages, *i.e.*, those triggered by the same network condition, and then prioritize network events using a number of severity/importance measures. Our goal is to be able to automatically determine such connections or the lack of them among syslog messages without relying on domain knowledge being manually input and updated (by network operators). SyslogDigest accomplishes this goal through a two-step process. In this first step, an *offline domain knowledge learning* component automatically extracts relevant domain knowledge from raw syslog data. In the second step, an *online processing* component will rely on such acquired domain knowledge and other available information (e.g., temporal closeness of messages) to finally group related messages into high-level events and present the prioritized results. In the rest of this section, we will provide a high-level overview of SyslogDigest's architecture, shown in Figure 1, and the functionalities of its components, by working out a running example shown in Table 2, where 16 syslog messages are eventually grouped into 1 high-level network event.

3.1 Offline Domain Knowledge Learning

The offline domain knowledge learning component automatically acquires domain knowledge such as the syntax/semantics of syslog messages, the relationships among various message templates, and the detailed location information pertained from raw syslog data. The offline domain knowledge learning proceeds as follows.

First, it automatically learns message templates from the historical syslog messages. To deal with the challenge posed by minimally-structured messages from different vendors and/or different OS versions that adopt different template syntax/semantics systems, we develop an effective signature identification technique in which messages are decomposed into whitespace-separated words and a frequent word (excluding those words denoting specific locations) sequence is considered as a template. For example, without going into the details of the signature identification technique, it is intuitive to see the following template can be extracted: **t1:** `LINK-3-UPDOWN Interface ..., changed state to down`, **t2:** `LINEPROTO-5-UPDOWN Line protocol on Interface ..., changed state to down`, **t3:** `LINK-3-UPDOWN Interface ..., changed state to up`, and **t4:** `LINEPROTO-5-UPDOWN Line protocol on Interface ..., changed state to up`.

Table 2: Toy Example. Router r1's interface Serial1/0.10/10:0 is connected to r2's inteface Serial1/0.20/20:0.

index	timestamp	router	message-type/error-code	detailed message
m1	2010-01-10 00:00:00	r1	LINK-3-UPDOWN	Interface Serial1/0.10/10:0, changed state to down
m2	2010-01-10 00:00:00	r2	LINK-3-UPDOWN	Interface Serial1/0.20/20:0, changed state to down
m3	2010-01-10 00:00:01	r1	LINEPROTO-5-UPDOWN	Line protocol on Interface Serial1/0.10/10:0, changed state to down
m4	2010-01-10 00:00:01	r2	LINEPROTO-5-UPDOWN	Line protocol on Interface Serial2/0.20/20:0, changed state to down
m5	2010-01-10 00:00:10	r1	LINK-3-UPDOWN	Interface Serial1/0.10/10:0, changed state to up
m6	2010-01-10 00:00:10	r2	LINK-3-UPDOWN	Interface Serial1/0.20/20:0, changed state to up
m7	2010-01-10 00:00:11	r1	LINEPROTO-5-UPDOWN	Line protocol on Interface Serial1/0.10/10:0, changed state to up
m8	2010-01-10 00:00:11	r2	LINEPROTO-5-UPDOWN	Line protocol on Interface Serial2/0.20/20:0, changed state to up
m9	2010-01-10 00:00:20	r1	LINK-3-UPDOWN	Interface Serial1/0.10/10:0, changed state to down
m10	2010-01-10 00:00:20	r2	LINK-3-UPDOWN	Interface Serial1/0.20/20:0, changed state to down
m11	2010-01-10 00:00:21	r1	LINEPROTO-5-UPDOWN	Line protocol on Interface Serial1/0.10/10:0, changed state to down
m12	2010-01-10 00:00:21	r2	LINEPROTO-5-UPDOWN	Line protocol on Interface Serial2/0.20/20:0, changed state to down
m13	2010-01-10 00:00:30	r1	LINK-3-UPDOWN	Interface Serial1/0.10/10:0, changed state to up
m14	2010-01-10 00:00:30	r2	LINK-3-UPDOWN	Interface Serial1/0.20/20:0, changed state to up
m15	2010-01-10 00:00:31	r1	LINEPROTO-5-UPDOWN	Line protocol on Interface Serial1/0.10/10:0, changed state to up
m16	2010-01-10 00:00:31	r2	LINEPROTO-5-UPDOWN	Line protocol on Interface Serial2/0.20/20:0, changed state to up

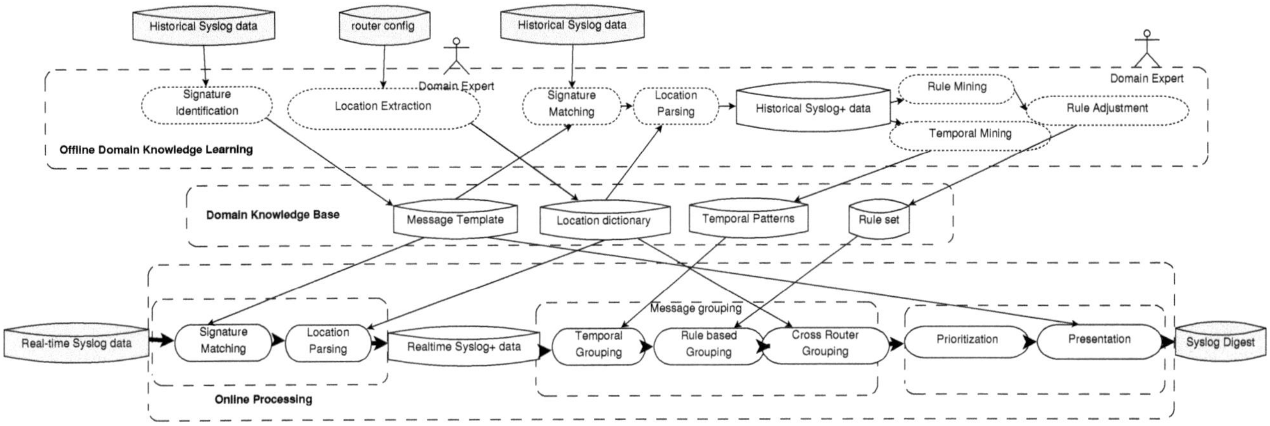

Figure 1: SyslogDigest Architecture. Bold arrows denotes the data flow. Dotted components run offline.

Second, to be able to parse the location information embedded and hidden in syslog messages, SyslogDigest learns and builds a "dictionary" for the locations in each router's syslog messages based on its configuration files (i.e., router configs). One might be tempted to parse the location information purely based on the vendor manual description for each message. This can however be overly expensive due to the high diversity of message formats and large number of messages. Our solution is based on one key observation: a router almost always writes to syslog messages only the location information it knows, i.e, those configured in the router. Our solution is therefore to parse router configs (much better formatted and documented than syslog messages) to build a dictionary of its locations offline. With router configs, we also build the mapping between different locations, e.g., from an interface name to its IP address, and the hierarchical location relationship between interfaces, ports and linecards, and network topology such as the interfaces connecting two routers. These mappings enable us to group syslog messages with related locations. In the example shown in Table 2, the location dictionary will contain interfaces `r1,Serial1/0.10/10:0` and `r2,Serial1/0.20/20:0` and also the information that these two interfaces are connected to each other.

Third, to learn the relationship among different templates, we first augment each historical syslog message with additional information, including message template and its location information, by matching it with the templates and locations previously learned. In our example, $m1$ is augmented as `m1|t1|r1,Serial1/0.10/10:0` (with template `t1` and location `r1,Serial1/0.10/10:0` appended), and $m4$ is augmented as `m4|t2|r2,Serial1/0.20/20:0`, and so on. The resulting messages are called **Syslog+** messages in our system. We then apply association rule mining techniques to Syslog+ messages to learn the relationships (i.e., associations) among different messages with different templates. A rule of thumb is that if two messages frequently occur *close* enough in time and at *related* locations (postpone the details to Section 4), they are considered *associated* and should be grouped together. For example, if syslog messages in templates $t1$ and $t2$ often happen close together, the association $t1, t2$ will be declared. Domain experts can be asked to comment on and/or adjust such associations (some of which can be "puzzling" or even "bizarre") but this is entirely optional.

Finally, SyslogDigest learns the temporal patterns of each template from Syslog+ message. The intuition is that messages with same template can appear periodically (e.g., due to various network timers), and if so, these events can be grouped together. Such kind of periodicity can be learned offline through measurements of corresponding interarrival times and predictions based on their linear regression.

The above domain knowledge learning process will be periodically run (offline) to incorporate the latest changes to router hardware and software configurations, and the acquired domain knowledge will be used as input to the online SyslogDigest System.

3.2 Online SyslogDigest System

The online system takes the real-time syslog message stream as well as the previously learned domain knowledge as input, and output meaningful prioritized network events, in a two-step process. The first step is to augment the real-time syslog messages with template and location information just like in the aforementioned offline process, and output the (augmented) Syslog+ messages in an online fashion.

The second step is to group related Syslog+ messages together to construct meaningful network events. We propose three grouping methods: **temporal grouping, rule-based grouping and cross-router grouping**. **Temporal grouping** targets at messages with the same template on the same router. It groups together messages that have the same template and happen periodically, where such periodicity (temporal patterns) is already detected during the offline temporal mining. In our example, it is intuitive to see that after the temporal grouping, $m1, m5, m9, m13$ (with common template $t1$ and common location `r1,Serial1/0.10/10:0`) are grouped together. So are $(m2, m6, m10, m14)$, $(m3, m7, m11, m15)$, and $(m4, m8, m12, m16)$. **Rule-based grouping** targets the messages with different templates on the same router. Based on the association rules learned by the offline learning component and saved in a domain knowledge base, this method groups messages that have different templates, but happen close together in time. In our example, after the rule-based grouping, messages $m1, m3, m5, m9, m11, m13, m15$ are grouped together due to association rule $\{t1, t2\}$ with common location `r1,Serial1/0.10/10:0`. Messages $m2, m4, m6, m8, m10, m12, m14, m16$ are grouped together due to association rule $\{t3, t4\}$ and common location `r2,Serial1/0.20/20:0`. Finally, the **cross-router grouping** method will group together messages with locations that are on different routers yet closely connected (e.g. two ends of one link, two ends of one BGP session), determined by the location dictionary in the domain knowledge base. They will be applied to the Syslog+ messages in this order (justifications explained later). After these three grouping methods are applied in the order that they are described above to the online syslog message stream, we obtain groups of messages, each of which is considered a single *network event*, which are much smaller in number compared to the raw syslog messages. In our example, $m1$ to $m16$ are eventually grouped together into a single network event.

The final step is to prioritize and present the network events based on their perceived importance to network operators. Various factors are considered together to determine the (relative) importance of an event, including the number of messages the event (group) contains, the frequency of this event type in the history and the perceived impact of this event on network health. Each event is presented as a well-formatted text line, with multiple fields summarizing the information contained in the raw syslog messages that are grouped into this event, including the start/end timestamps of this event, an location field that records where the event happens, an event type field that is more informative than its counterpart in individual raw syslog messages, and an index field that allows us to retrieve these raw syslog messages if necessary.

The presentation of Table 2 could be `2010-01-10 00:00:00|2010-01-10 00:00:31|r1 Interface Serial1/0.10/10:0 r2 Interface Serial1/0.20/20:0|link flap, line protocol flap`.

Table 3: The messages belong to the same message type (BGP-5-ADJCHANGE)

m_1	neighbor 192.168.32.42 vpn vrf 1000:1001 Up
m_2	neighbor 192.168.100.194 vpn vrf 1000:1002 Up
m_3	neighbor 192.168.15.78 vpn vrf 1000:1003 Up
m_4	neighbor 192.168.108.38 vpn vrf 1000:1004 Up
m_5	neighbor 192.168.0.26 vpn vrf 1000:1004 Down Interface flap
m_6	neighbor 192.168.7.6 vpn vrf 1000:1001 Down Interface flap
m_7	neighbor 192.168.0.238 vpn vrf 1000:1003 Down Interface flap
m_8	neighbor 192.168.2.114 vpn vrf 1000:1002 Down Interface flap
m_9	neighbor 192.168.183.250 vpn vrf 1000:1002 Down BGP Notification sent
m_{10}	neighbor 192.168.114.178 vpn vrf 1000:1003 Down BGP Notification sent
m_{11}	neighbor 192.168.131.218 vpn vrf 1000:1001 Down BGP Notification sent
m_{12}	neighbor 192.168.55.138 vpn vrf 1000:1000 Down BGP Notification sent
m_{13}	neighbor 192.168.1.13 vpn vrf 1000:1000 Down BGP Notification received
m_{14}	neighbor 192.168.12.241 vpn vrf 1000:1002 Down BGP Notification received
m_{15}	neighbor 192.168.155.66 vpn vrf 1000:1003 Down BGP Notification received
m_{16}	neighbor 192.168.254.29 vpn vrf 1000:1004 Down BGP Notification received
m_{17}	neighbor 192.168.35.230 vpn vrf 1000:1004 Down Peer closed the session
m_{19}	neighbor 192.168.171.166 vpn vrf 1000:1001 Down Peer closed the session
m_{19}	neighbor 192.168.2.237 vpn vrf 1000:1002 Down Peer closed the session
m_{20}	neighbor 192.168.0.154 vpn vrf 1000:1003 Down Peer closed the session

Table 4: Sub message types of BGP-5-ADJCHANGE

M_1	neighbor * vpn vrf * Up
M_2	neighbor * vpn vrf * Down Interface flap
M_3	neighbor * vpn vrf * Down BGP Notification sent
M_4	neighbor * vpn vrf * Down BGP Notification received
M_5	neighbor * vpn vrf * Down Peer closed the session

4. SYSLOG-MINING METHODOLOGIES

In this section, we present the detailed methodologies used in both the offline learning and the online digesting systems.

4.1 Offline Learning Methodologies

There are several basic aspects that we need to learn from syslog messages: message templates, location information, temporal patterns of message templates and template relationship.

4.1.1 Message Template Learning

As mentioned earlier, raw syslog messages have little structure. Although there is a message type field to describe the characteristics of messages, for each message type there can be multiple sub types. For example in Table 3, while all messages belong to the same type "BGP-5-ADJCHANGE" and correspond to BGP adjacency change in MPLS VPN, the details of these messages (and hence their sub types) can be different. At issue is how to automatically construct such sub types and combine them with the message type to form the template *without intervention from domain experts*. In our example, the neighboring IP addresses and the VRF[1] IDs (e.g. VRF 1000:1001 in m_1) differ from one message to another, but when these two fields are *masked* (i.e., replaced by the same symbol, say asterisk, as shown in Table 4), there are only five distinct "structure" types, or sub types as we call them. In practice, however, it is not easy to manually find all masked parts without domain knowledge, because all needed-masked parts do not have obvious pattern like IP address or VRF ID.

Our template learning approach is inspired by the signature abstraction used in spam detection [18]. The high level idea

[1]VRF stands for Virtual Routing and Forwarding. It is a technology that allows multiple instances of a routing table to co-exist within the same router at the same time. VRF is a common technique used in VPN environment. The VRF ID XXX:XXXX is a simple conceptional name.

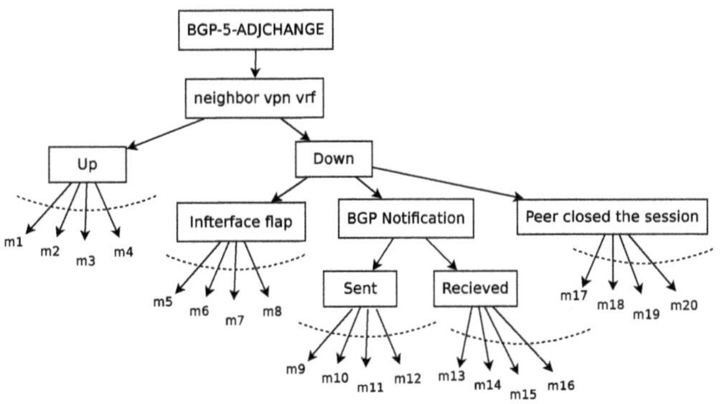

Figure 2: Sub type tree construction example.

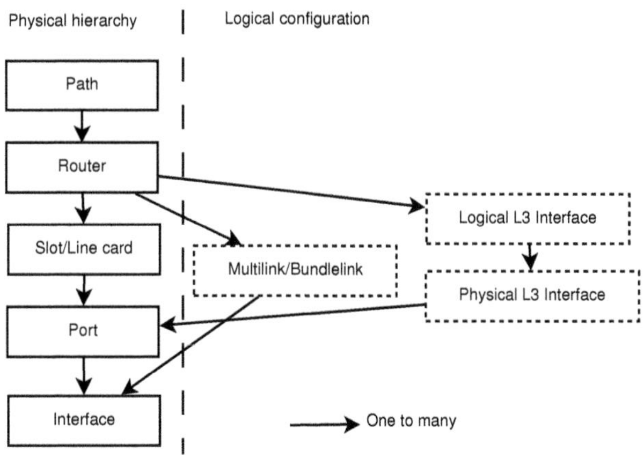

Figure 3: Location hierarchy

is that a signature, which corresponds to an aforementioned sub type node, is a combination of words with high frequency. We decompose messages into words separated by whitespace. For each type of message, we construct a tree structure to express the template (sub type) hierarchy based on the input messages (e.g. $m_1, m_2, \ldots, m_{20}$), shown in Figure 2. We say that a word *associates with* a message when the word appears in the message. The detailed construction algorithm follows breath-first search tree traversal. We first use the message type (e.g. BGP-5-ADJCHANGE) as the root of the tree. All messages are associated with this message type. Then given the parent node, we look for the most frequent combination of words which can associate with most messages that the parent node can associate with, and make this combination as a child node. We repeat this process to create child nodes based on remaining messages, until all messages have been associated. We then recursively proceed to the child nodes and repeat the process. Finally we prune the tree until it has the desired degree properties as follows. If a parent node has more than k children, we will discard all children to make the parent a leaf itself. Now each path from root to the each leaf become one template (type + sub type). The intuition of this pruning is that on the one hand, there are only a few sub types for each message type, on the other hand, usually there would be many more messages associated with each sub type. For example, there should be many IPs and VRF addresses associated with each sub type given enough data. In practice, We choose $k = 10$ based on our experience that no message type has more than 10 sub types.

Our template inference approach is quite generic because it is based on the words frequency as opposed to text semantic. However, we use an implicit assumption that the variable part of the syslog messages would appear as many distinct values given enough historical data. This assumption is surely not always true. For example, if certain protocol are enabled only on one type of network interface, say GigabitEthernet, then the "GigabitEthernet" part of the message may be falsely included in the syslog template of the protocol messages. However, this would have negligible impact on the final outcome of the grouping result, since the "GigabitEthernet" in this case contains as much information as the syslog sub type and hence there is no need to extract it out.

4.1.2 Location Information Learning

In a typical syslog message, we only have a router id field as the basic location information, but this is clearly not enough. For example, some events occur on a particular physical port while some other events occur on multiple logical links (e.g., IP links). Such detailed location information is essential for understanding what is going on in the network.

Figure 3 shows the generic location hierarchical structure. We classify the basic components here into physical ones and logical ones. The physical ones have a clear hierarchical structure from top to bottom. The arrow here illustrates a "one-to-many" relationship. For example, one router have multiple slots, each slot can have multiple ports and etc. Besides physical hierarchy, there are some logical configurations, but they will eventually map to some physical component. For example, one multilink/bundlelink can be mapped to multiple physical interfaces. Based on router configuration data, we can extract offline the hierarchy in Figure 3 specific to each router, cross-router location relationships such as neighbor links, etc.

The key question here is how to automatically exploit such kind of location information from each message. First, we know the particular format of these location information embedded into the messages. For example, the IP address has the format XXX.XXX.XXX.XXX, the port has the format X/X/X , etc. Compared with various parts of message we need to mask during template learning, the number of location format patterns are limited, which is manageable for extraction using predefined patterns. However, the naive pattern matching is not sufficient to extract needed location addresses, mainly because more than one location pattern (no matter whether they are all needed) can be found in each message. For example, multiple IP addresses can be found in one message. One could belong to the router itself, one could belong the neighbor router, and it is also possible there are some remote (e.g. remote session connection) or invalid IPs (e.g. scanning attacks). To understand the exact meaning of multiple location patterns, especially the belongings, we correlate these locations with router configuration data. For example we can verify if this IP belongs to the router or its neighbors. Note that the acquired location information and location hierarchy will be used during the offline rule mining and online grouping.

4.1.3 Learning Temporal Patterns of Templates

Once we identified the message templates, we learn the temporal patterns of the message templates, i.e, the interarrival patterns. This learned knowledge will be used in the online temporal grouping component.

We observe that if a particular template of message occurs periodically, the corresponding messages naturally form a number of clusters in the time series. For example, Figure 4 shows that one controller goes up down many times within a short interval because controller is unstable during the interval. Another example

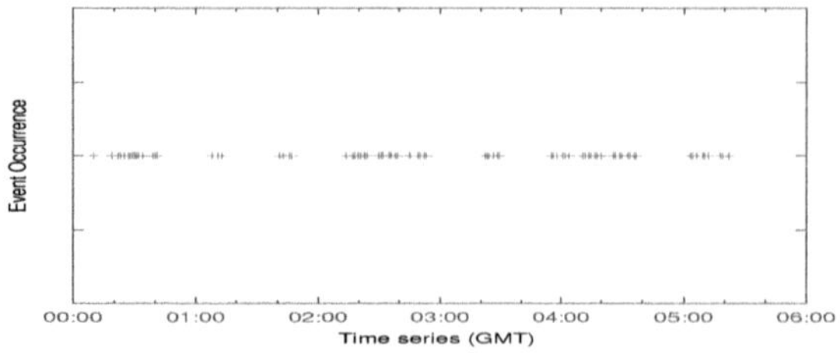

Figure 4: Controller up/down example.

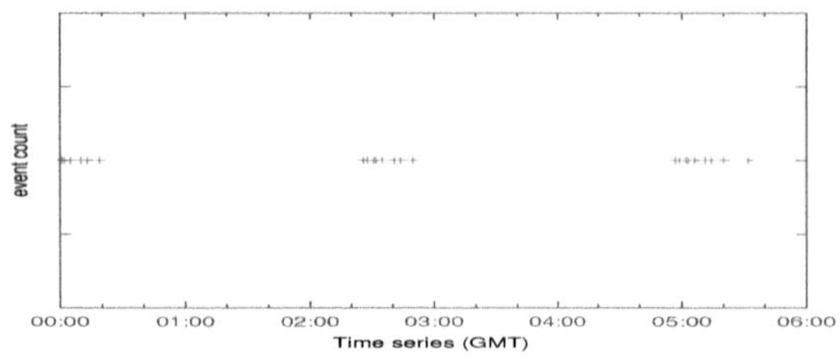

Figure 5: TCP bad authentication example

in Figure 5 shows that TCP bad authentication message has periodic occurrences, likely due to the underling timer configuration, or outside impact, e.g. scanning patterns.

In order to learn such temporal patterns, i.e. , the interarrival time within each cluster, we make a basic assumption, that is the impact of current message on the further message with the same template will exponentially decay. Such assumption is widely used for time series analysis and system measurement purpose [5, 21]. Our learning method is based on the interarrival sequence $S_1, S_2, \ldots$ for each message template. We compute the (predicted) exponential weighted moving average (EWMA) of interarrival time t, $\hat{S}_t$.

$$\hat{S}_t = \alpha \cdot S_{t-1} + (1 - \alpha) \cdot \hat{S}_{t-1}$$

where $\alpha \in (0, 1)$ is the weighting factor. A higher α discounts older observations faster. Intuitively, if the messages belong to the same cluster, in other words, there is a periodic pattern within the group, then the predicted value $\hat{S}_t$ should not be far away from the real one S_t. Consequently, we assume that if $S_t \leq \beta \cdot \hat{S}_t$ where $(\beta >= 1)$, which means the real interarrival time is no much larger than predicted one, we view that the message belongs to the same group. Otherwise, there is another new group. Here parameter β defines a threshold for grouping. Larger β means tolerating larger intervals in the group.

The offline learning component uses long-term historical data to infer the proper value of parameters α and β and can be updated periodically. The actually values of these parameters will be discussed in Section 5. These parameters are used in the online temporal grouping component.

4.1.4 Template Relationship (Rule) Learning

In order to group different messages together to extract network events, one natural thinking is to discover some implicit rules among different templates. Some rules are very intuitive. For example, layer-1 link failures (LINK-3-UPDOWN) often trigger layer-2 failures (LINEPROTO-5-UPDOWN). Some others are much more subtle. As we explained before, we cannot rely on domain experts to compile and update a complete rule set given the large number of templates. We need a systematic way to identify such rules. This turns out to be a typical association rule mining problem. Association rules describe items that occur frequently together in a dataset and are widely-used for market basket analysis. Following the original definition by Agrawal et al. [3] the problem of association rule mining is defined as: Let $I = \{i_1, i_2, \ldots, i_n\}$ be a set of n binary attributes called *items*. Let $D = \{t_1, t_2, \ldots, t_m\}$ be a set of transactions called the *database*. Each transaction in D has a unique transaction ID and contains a subset of the items in I. A $rule$ is defined as an implication of the form $X \Rightarrow Y$ where $X, Y \in I$ and $X \cap Y = \emptyset$. To select interesting rules from the set of all possible rules, constraints on various measures of significance and interest can be used. The best-known constraints are minimum thresholds on support and confidence. Support supp(X) of an itemset X is defined as the proportion of transactions in the data set which contain the itemset. The confidence of a rule is defined as

$$conf(X \Rightarrow Y) = \frac{supp(X \cap Y)}{supp(X)}$$

In our problem setting, each message template is one item. In order to construct the transactions, we use a sliding window W. It starts with the first message, and slides message by message (sorted messages on the time series). Each time there is one transaction. In one such transaction, the message templates in the window W are considered as the items showing up.

Note that we only consider pair wise association, or $|X| = |Y| = 1$. In other words, each rule only contains two templates. The reason is, first, the computation complexity is low, and second, it is relatively easy to verify the generated rule sets. Domain experts only need to verify the relationship of two templates per rule. The disadvantage of pair wise is that based on these rules we cannot group more than two templates each time, but since we assume the transition property during rule-based grouping discuss later in Section 4.2.2), the final digest will combine multiple templates together.

Until now, we assume that the rules are generated based on static dataset. But ideally we want to learn the rules continuously. In order to adaptively adjust the rules, we use the following conservative way. First, we training the a period of data to generate the basic rule sets. Then we keep change the rules periodically (e.g. each week). The new rules $X \Rightarrow Y$ should be added when $supp(X)$ and $conf(X \Rightarrow Y)$ are above the threshold. Old rules $X \Rightarrow Y$ should be deleted when updated $conf(X \Rightarrow Y)$ is below the threshold, no matter what $supp(X)$ is. Such conservative deletion approach ensures that we do not delete the rules because X are not common in this updating period (it is quite possible X become common again soon).

4.2 Online System Methodologies

The online system takes the real-time Syslog+ data (with message template and location information) and the offline-learned domain knowledge as input, groups related messages together and construct prioritized event. Roughly speaking, if two messages occur close in time and locations, they are related with high probability. While the temporal closeness between two messages can simply the characterized by the closeness of their timestamps, the characterization of spatial closeness is more subtle. We model various location types in the location hierarchy shown in Figure 3. We say the two locations are *spatially matched* when they can be mapped to same location in the hierarchy. For example, suppose one message happens on slot 2 and another one message on the same router happens on interface series 2/0/0:1. They are considered spatially matched because the later message's location (2/0/0:1) can be mapped upwards in Figure 3 to slot 2 (the first digit before the backslash interface series of 2/0/0:1).

4.2.1 Temporal Grouping

Online temporal grouping uses the same methodology as offline temporal patterns learning, presented in Section 4.1.3. Similar to Section 4.1.3 , if the real inter-arrival time $S_t \leq \beta \cdot \hat{S}_t$, then the messages belong to the same group, otherwise there is separate group.

We also introduce two thresholds S_{min} and S_{max}. S_{min} is the minimal interarrival time, and S_{max} is the maximum. The reason of introducing S_{max} is that the our algorithm cannot guarantee convergence. Each time we only guarantee that the S_t is not too large. But when $\hat{S}_t$ increase, S_t can grow exponentially. If the real interarrival time is smaller than S_{min}, then we consider the messages belong to the same group. If the real interarrival time is larger than the S_{max}, then we believe there is a separate group. We set S_{min} to be 1 second (this is the finest time granularity available in the syslog data we used) and S_{max} to be 3 hours (this is based on domain knowledge).

4.2.2 Rule based Grouping

In the temporal grouping part, we only consider grouping messages with the same template together. Now we try to discover the connections among messages with different message templates. The offline-learned rules using association mining contain pairwise message templates that occur frequently together. The rule based grouping component groups the messages which happen on the spatially matched locations and happen close enough in time (within the window W discussed in rule-learning part). Note that our rule based grouping does not consider the direction of rule since our system is not a troubleshooting system thus does not rely on causality inference. It is possible that we have $A \rightarrow B$ and $A \rightarrow C$ in the rule set, but we ignore the direction and can group A, B, C together, assuming temporal and spatial constraints are satisfied. This is because it is very likely they are triggered by the same network condition thus should be considered as one event, even though we ignore the detailed causal relationship among the messages.

4.2.3 Cross Router Grouping

The first two grouping methods all focus on a single router. A network event, however, can affect multiple routers. For instance, a link down event should involve two adjacent routers' links. To group such messages, our solution is a conservative one. Our offline location learning component already provides a dictionary for cross-router location relationship such as links, sessions, tunnels (a path) between different routers. Assuming that the propagation along the connects are fast enough, we group messages with the same template which happened on the same link, session, or path at almost the same time (e.g no larger than 1 second difference).

We perform three grouping methods in the order they are described. If any two messages in two different groups have been grouped together, then these two groups will be merged. Thus the changes of orders of these three parts have no impact on the final grouping results. We use this order because it is more natural to describe: from one signature to multiple ones, from single router to multiples ones.

4.2.4 Prioritization and Presentation

We now have a number of messages in each group. We first prioritize the messages so that the most important events will appear at the top of the digest. Recall from Section 2 that the severity level of a message provided by syslog shall not be trusted/used. Instead, we use a combination of the following three metrics. The first metric is the occurrence frequency of message signature on each router, say f_m for message m. The intuition is that we care more about rare events. We also consider the impact of the events. The event happened on the higher level of the hierarchy is more important. For example, an event happened on the router is more important than the one happened on the interface. Let l_m denote the location metric of message m, and we can assume that the value of l_m higher level is several (e.g. 10) times of lower level. Finally, we consider the number of messages in the grouped event, which in some sense reflects severity of the event. The group with more messages should be relatively important. Based on these three metrics, there is a score we assign for each event:

$$Score = \sum_{m=1}^{M} l_m / log(f_m)$$

where the event contains M messages. The reason for taking logarithm here is to prevent rare events with tiny f_m values from dominating the top of the ranked list. Note that our scoring method provides a baseline for ranking. The network operators can adjust the weights for each type of messages, based on their experience.

We rank all events based on the score in a decreasing order. After ranking, we (actually the SyslogDigest system) are ready to present the final result. There are many ways to display the event, and we choose the most concise way. First, we present the beginning and ending time of the event, which map to the time range of all messages in the group. Second, we present the location information of the event. For each router, we present the most common highest level location on hierarchy. For example, if the event contains two messages, one on the router level while the other on the interface level, we only show the router. Third, we present the type of event. One direct way is to present the combinations of message signatures within the group. Domain experts can certainly assign a name for each type of event. For example, we can assign a name "link flap" to a event which contains "LINK-DOWN" and "LINK-UP" messages.

5. EVALUATION

We evaluate SyslogDigest using real syslog data from two large operational networks. We first validate several design choices we made in the offline domain knowledge learning component. Then we report the results of the entire SyslogDigest system.

5.1 Evaluation Methodology

We use syslog data collected from two large operational IP networks in North America: a tier-1 ISP backbone network and a nation-wide commercial IPTV backbone network. Each of these two networks has around a couple of thousands of routers and records millions of syslog messages per day. We refer to these two syslog data as *Dataset A* and *Dataset B*, respectively. Note that these two networks use routers from different vendors and have different network design and protocol configurations for supporting different network applications/services – the ISP backbone network is for general/traditional IP/Internet service and the IPTV backbone is for commercial TV service. Both the types of messages and their signatures are very different in these two dataset. In our evaluation, we use three months of data collected from September to November 2009 for offline domain knowledge learning and two weeks' of data collected December 1-14, 2009 for online processing and reporting event digests.

We evaluate the effectiveness of SyslogDigest in the following two aspects. First, we use the metrics *compression ratio* to measure the ability of SyslogDigest to reduce the amount of information that operators need to receive and examine in order to know what happened in the network for each incident. We define the the compression ratio to be the number of events (compressed information

Table 5: Sensitivity of minimal support SP_{min} value

SP_{min}	Top % (A)	Coverage (A)	Top % (B)	Coverage (B)
0.001	13.4%	98.72%	14.2%	89.34%
0.0005	27.5%	99.92%	32.3%	99.95%
0.0001	42.5%	99.98%	54.3%	99.99%

size) divided by the total number of raw messages (uncompressed information size). Second, we validate the event digests output by SyslogDigest to see whether they are good representation of real network events. This validation process done manually by people who have rich network experiences and domain knowledge on these two operational networks.

5.2 Components Effectiveness

We first evaluate our design choices in message template identification, association rule mining and temporal mining components shown in Figure 1.

5.2.1 *Message Template Identification*

SyslogDigest automatically abstracts the template of each type of syslog messages. We validate our template abstraction method presented in Section 4.1 by comparing the syslog message templates identified by SyslogDigest with the "ground truth" templates obtained from hard-coding comprehensive domain knowledge on syslog. The domain knowledge we used here are very specific to certain router vendors. Hard-coding domain knowledge is clearly not scalable, and hence we use it only for validation purpose. Note that such kind of methods require the knowledge of all message format in advance, which is not practical specially when there are many messages types and facing different syslog data sources. We observe that 94% of message templates matches. It indicates our learning approach can extract the template fairly well.

5.2.2 *Association Rule Mining*

In order to generated rules, we use three months (Sep 2009 to Nov 2009) for mining for both datasets.

There are three parameters used by SyslogDigest in mining association rules between syslog messages: Window size W, the threshold of minimal support SP_{min}, and the minimal confidence $Conf_{min}$. We evaluate the sensitivity of these parameter setting on learning associations between syslog message. In particular, we vary W from 5 to 300 seconds and $Conf_{min}$ from 0.5 to 0.9. We also set SP_{min} at values 0.001, 0.0005, 0.0001. The implication of these settings of SP_{min} in our context is shown in Table 5. For example, when $SP_{min} = 0.005$, the top 27.5% types of messages will be used in rule mining and these types of messages cover over 99.9% of all messages in dataset A.

Figure 6 shows the number of association rules learned from dataset with fixing the value of W to be 1 minute and varying the values of SP_{min} and $Conf_{min}$. As we expected, the number of rules decreases as the value of $Conf_{min}$ increases. In addition, the higher the value of SP_{min} is, the fewer rules learned from the dataset. Similar observations hold different values of W. In our experiments, we set $Conf_{min} = 0.8$ and $SP_{min} = 0.0005$. With this setting, Figure 7 shows the number of generated rules by varying the value of W. We observe that the number of rules increases as W increases. However, the increase in the number rules diminishes at W = 120 seconds for dataset A and W = 40 second for dataset B. That is, the number of rules learned by SyslogDigest is less sensitive to the value of W when W is large. A detailed analysis on the rules reveals that the newly added rules by increasing W often captures implicit timing relationship between two types of messages. For example, in dataset A, we observe that when W changes from 10 to 30 seconds, there are several new rules added to the knowledge base. These rules associate the *controller flap*, *link flap* and*line protocol flap* messages, indicating that these types of messages usually occur together between 10-30 apart. Similarly, in dataset B we find that *ftp login failure* and *ssh login failure* messages are associated together when W is set to 30 - 40 seconds. Next, we present results on association rule mining with using W = 120 seconds for dataset A and W = 40 seconds for dataset B.

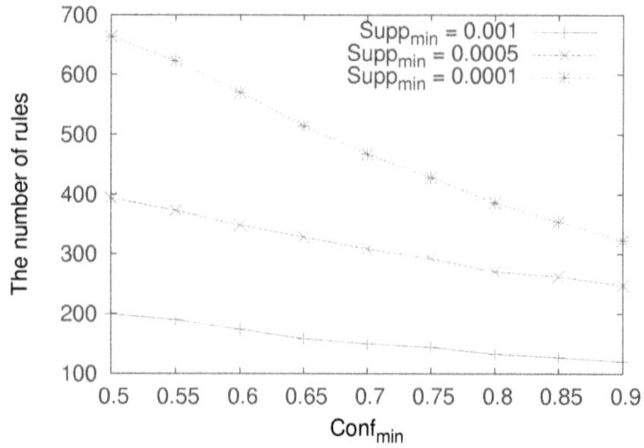

Figure 6: The impact of parameter SP_{min} and $Conf_{min}$, in dataset A.

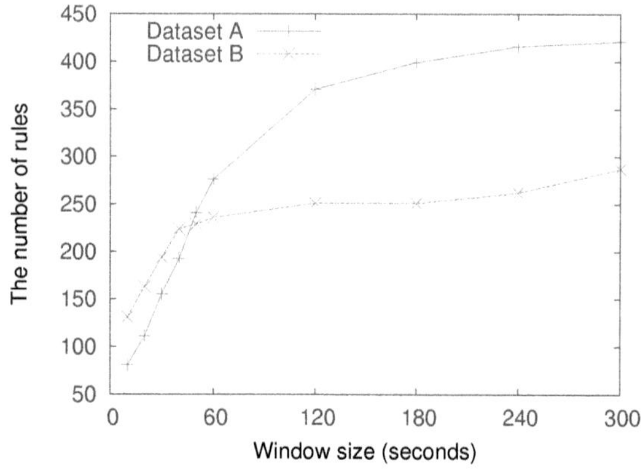

Figure 7: The impact of parameter W, when $Conf_{min} = 0.8$ and $SP_{min} = 0.0005$.

The association rule mining is performed weekly by SyslogDigest to (i) add new rules to the knowledge base, and (ii) identify invalid rules in the knowledge base and remove them using the method presented in Section 4.1.4. Figure 8 and Figure 9 show the total number of rules in the knowledge base as well as added/deleted rules for each week from week 2 to week 12. The number of rules in the knowledge base becomes stable after week 6 for dataset A and after week 8 for dataset B. This is because the number of added and deleted rules are close to zero after few weeks for both datasets.

We further validated the rule sets obtained at the end of week 12 with expert domain knowledge and vendor documentations. We found that almost all the rules are consistent with either the domain knowledge or the expected behaviors specified in vendor documentations. Thus, we believe that SyslogDigest successfully captures network behaviors using automatically learned rules. However, we did report a few "unexpected" rules (3 rules for dataset A and 16 rules for dataset B), which means the potential false positive rate

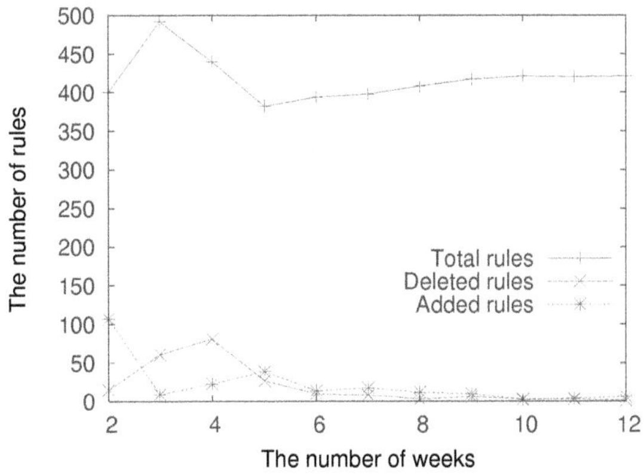

Figure 8: The number of rules over 12 weeks, dataset A.

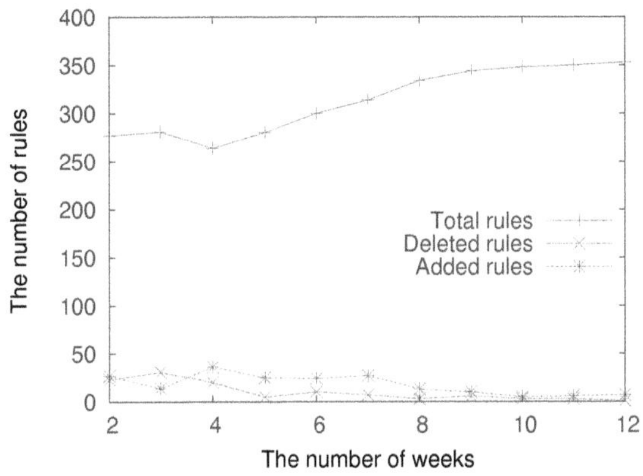

Figure 9: The number of rules over 12 weeks, dataset B.

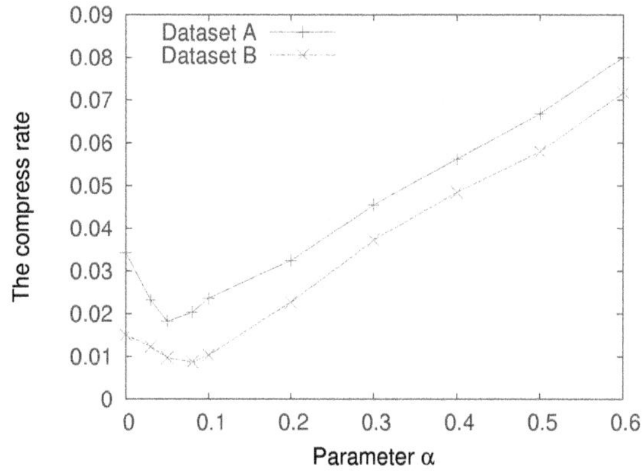

Figure 10: The impact of varying value of α on the compression ratio ($\beta = 2$).

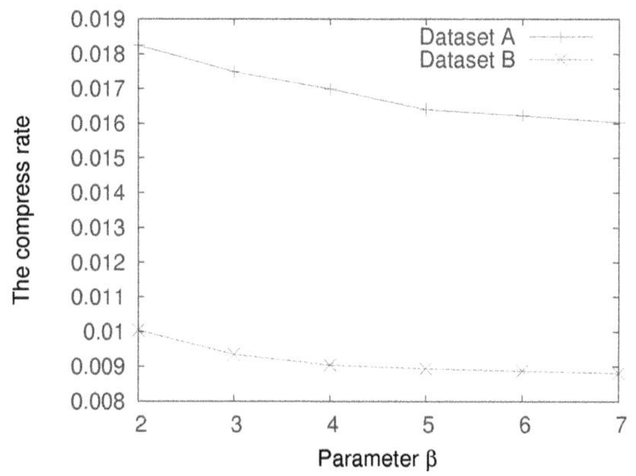

Figure 11: The impact of varying value of β on the compression ratio ($\alpha = 0.05$ for dataset A and $\alpha = 0.075$ for dataset B).

is less than 0.05 during rule mining. These unexpected rules are currently under investigation.

5.2.3 Temporal Pattern Mining

The goal of temporal pattern mining is essentially to find the proper parameter α and β, such that the underlying interarrival model can present the temporal patterns very well. In other words, we want to find α and β such that we can group messages appropriately (i.e. compression ratio would be optimal). Figure 10 shows the compression ratio of temporal grouping with α varying from 0 to 0.6 and β = 2 (i.e., if a new message arrives at an interval that is at least twice of the predicted interval, the message is put in a separate group). We observe that in both datasets, the larger the value of α is the higher the compression ratio is, except for very small value of α (e.g., $\alpha < 0.05$). The lowest (i.e., best) compression ratio is achieved when α = 0.05 for dataset A and α = 0.075 for dataset B. They will be used as the default value for α in the remaining experiments.

Figure 11 shows the impact of varying value of β (from 2 to 7) on the compression ratio with α being set at the default values. We observe that the compression ratio first decreases as we increase the value of β. This is consist to our intuition because a larger β value means larger intervals are used in temporal grouping of messages and hence fewer number of groups are output. We also observe that the improvement of compression diminishes when β increases. Thus, we set $\beta = 5$ for both datasets.

In summary, Table 6 shows the parameter settings in SyslogDigest. The rules of thumb are of choosing parameters are (1) to ensure the stability of rule sets and (2) to ensure the stability of the compress ratio, as we discussed through Section 5.2. These values in Table 6 will be used in the rest of our experiments presented in this paper.

Table 6: Parameter setting in SyslogDigest

Dataset	α	β	W (Dataset A/B)	SP_{min}	$Conf_{min}$
A	0.05	5	120	0.0005	0.8
B	0.075	5	40	0.0005	0.8

5.3 Performance of SyslogDigest

Using the domain knowledge base built by applying offline learning on three months of syslog data, we run SyslogDigest in online mode and generate event digests for 2 weeks of syslog data to evaluate the effectiveness of the entire system. Note that it generally takes less than one hour to digest one day's syslog. Table 7 shows compression ratios of different message grouping methodologies for both datasets. We found that the compression ratio varies by grouping method by dataset. Overall, the number of event digests is over three orders of magnitude smaller than the number of raw syslog messages. This is fairly substantial information compression/reduction.

Figure 12 shows the number of events and number of messages per day during these two weeks for dataset A (the numbers are normalized by a fixed factor due to proprietary information). Again, we obverse the three orders of magnitude compression. In addition, the number of events per day is relatively stable across days

Table 7: Effectiveness (compression ratio) of three digest methodologies. T: temporal based, R: rule based, C: cross router

Methodology	Ratio (Dataset A)	Ratio (Dataset B)
T	1.63×10^{-2}	9.08×10^{-3}
T+R	5.15×10^{-3}	2.26×10^{-3}
T+R+C	3.27×10^{-3}	0.91×10^{-3}

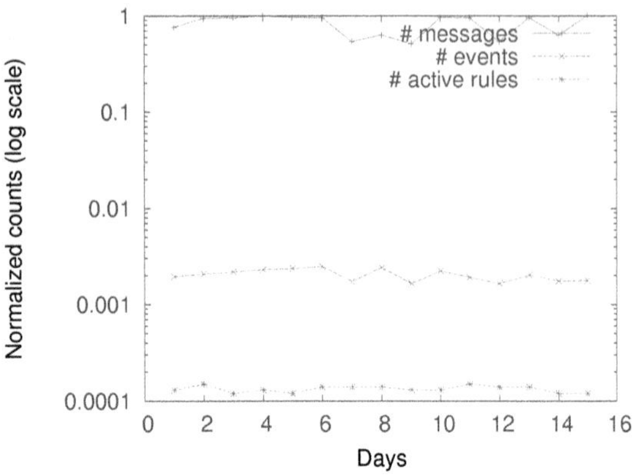

Figure 12: Number of event digests and active rules per day for dataset A.

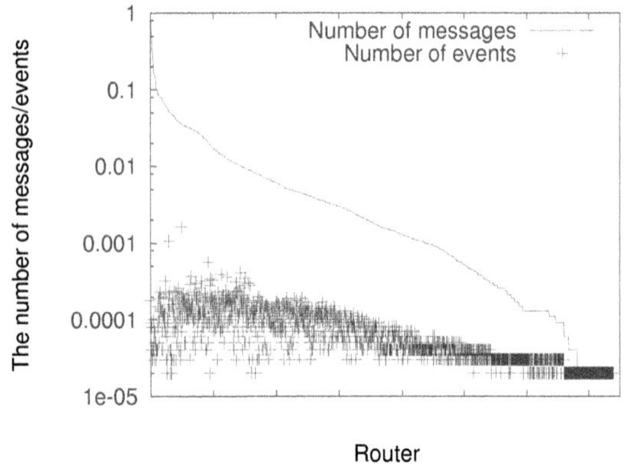

Figure 13: The digest result per router of dataset A.

for both datasets. In addition to the events digest, SyslogDigest also tracks the association rules that are used in message grouping (we call them "active rules"). The number of active rules is also stable: $100 \sim 200$ per day. The observations on dataset B is similar and omitted due to space limit.

Figure 13 show normalized number of raw messages and number of events on each individual router for datasets A[2]. We observe that the distribution of events across routers are less skew than that of raw syslog messages. In addition, routers that have more syslog messages usually have a better compression ratio. The best compression ratio is achieved on the router which has the largest number of raw message.

In order to verify that SyslogDigest system does not miss important network events during extraction, we compare the event digests output by SyslogDigest with known network events obtained from the trouble tickets. We obtained trouble tickets for both dataset A and dataset B, each of which is associated with a unique case identifier, timestamp of which the ticket is created and/or updated, and type and location of the event. While an extensive and systematic evaluation is undergoing, we show our preliminary results in this paper. In our preliminary evaluation, we rank the tickets based on the number of times a ticket is investigated and the corresponding record is updated. The intuition is that the more times that a ticket is investigated, the more likely the corresponding event is more important (and/or complicated). Hence, we use the number of times a ticket is investigated and updated as an approximation of the important of an event. We select the top 30 tickets regarding dataset B and correlate them with event digests output by SyslogDigest. We say there is *match* between a trouble ticket and an event digest if (i) the duration of the event digest covers the creation time of the trouble ticket and (ii) the event location of specified in the event digest is consistent with that described in the trouble ticket (at the state level, e.g. TX, GA, etc.). We found that all 30 tickets match with event digests that are ranked as top 5% or even higher by SyslogDigest. This initial evaluation shows that SyslogDigest does not miss important incidents.

[2]Due to page limitation, very similar result for dataset B is not shown here

6. APPLICATIONS

In this section, we demonstrate that SyslogDigest can be used an essential building block for many critical applications in network operations, such as troubleshooting and network health monitoring and visualization.

6.1 Complex network troubleshooting

Router syslog is one of the most important data source for network troubleshooting, and SyslogDigest provides network operators the gist of the syslogs – high-level network events. This is very important especially for diagnosing complex events that involve protocol interactions across multiple network layers and locations.

We next examine a real-world example on PIM neighbor loss event in the IPTV network – an event that was identified by SyslogDigest and is intriguingly complex.

In the commercial IPTV network, live TV streams are delivered using native IP multicast (i.e., PIM in this example). A change or loss of PIM neighbor session (e.g., caused by link failures) can disrupt delivery of IPTV data streams. Hence, there are several mechanisms implemented in the layer 2 and layer 3 network to enhance the service reliability. Particularly, two static layer 2 paths are configured between each pair of routers on the multicast tree – the primary path is the single-hop one directly connecting these two routers and the secondary path is a multi-hop path through routers in different VHOs. When there is a physical link failure on the primary path, the secondary path will be used to deliver IPTV data streams through the MPLS tunnels. The fast re-route (FRR) is done in layer 2 so that layer 3 routing (i.e., OSPF) is oblivious of this fail-over event, avoiding lengthy route-reconvergence impacting the PIM neighbor session. In this design, PIM neighbor session should only be impacted when there are dual failures on both primary path and secondary path. Such dual failures are extremely rare in operational networks.

In a troubleshooting task, operators investigated a PIM neighbor session flap event between a pair of nodes in two VHOs. The event was somewhat unexpected because the PIM neighbor session loss appeared to be triggered by a single link failure on the primary path between two routers. In theory, the PIM neighbor session should not be impacted. The event signature output by SyslogDigest revealed that the secondary path had not been set up successfully and was undergoing connection retries every five minutes. Con-

Figure 14: Visualization based on SyslogDigest output.

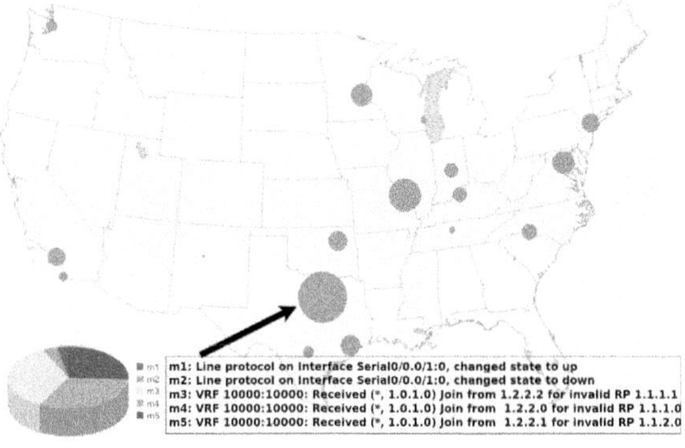

Figure 15: Visualization based on raw syslog data.

sequently, the PIM neighbor session was immediately interrupted when the primary path failed. In the event signature, hundreds of syslog messages recorded on a dozen of routers in multiple VHOs are associated to this SyslogDigest event. These syslog messages are of 15 distinct error codes involving 6 network protocols across three network layers.

If without SyslogDigest, it would easily take operators hours to manually identify these messages among tens of thousands of syslogs recorded at these routers and close in time to the PIM loss event. As a matter of fact, it is not clear what time duration should the network operators focus on in searching for related syslogs, simply because different protocols operate (or react to network changes) at different time granularities (ranging from sub-seconds to minutes or longer). In this particular event, the syslog messages that indicates a failure in setting up the secondary path, i.e., the connection retries, are several minutes apart from the link failure. Without knowing the exact protocols and timer involved, it is difficult to find the right time window to focus on – a short window (e.g., ± 60 seconds) would risk missing the failure information of the secondary path, while a long window (e.g., ± 3600 seconds) would certainly increase the amount of syslogs to be analyzed, slowing down operators' investigation.

By contrast, SyslogDigest was able to uncover the complete stream of this complex event. This is because SyslogDigest "learns" both the types and the co-occurrence time patterns of related syslog messages, and consequently associate such syslogs together when they do co-occur.

Furthermore, even with other automated troubleshooting systems (e.g., [8]) in place, working with pre-processed high-level events can greatly improve the efficiency compared to working with large numbers of raw syslog events.

6.2 Network health monitoring and visualization

It is imperative for network operators to keep track of "what happened in my network?". Visualization is often an effective way to achieve this as operators are able to "see" what happened in the network and how things evolve over time. The digest events from SyslogDigest can greatly improve network health visualization.

Figures 14 and 15 show the snapshots of network status map at 2009/12/5 16:00:00 (in 10 minute updating window) using SyslogDigest and using raw syslog messages, respectively. Network topology and link load status are removed from the graph to protect proprietary information. The circles in the map indicate events (or messages) observed at these routers with larger circles indicating more events (or messages) observed. We observe that only a small number of events took place in the network then, while the corresponding syslog messages range from dozens to a couple of hundreds on each of these routers. Making sense of the raw syslogs visualization requires decoding plenty of supplement information (e.g., the pie chart shown in Figure 15 reporting the mixture of syslog types and counts for all events on the router). It is worth noting that high syslog message counts do not necessarily imply more network events or "bigger trouble" – the big circle in Figure 15 was one moderate level event compare to others in Figure 14. Visualization the raw syslog messages can potentially mislead operators to focus on routers with more messages and delay their investigation on more sever issues.

7. RELATED WORK

Commercial softwares, like NetCool [2] Lonix [1], that are capable of parsing and making log data. These tools, however, require intensive domain knowledge to describe the format of logs. Xu *et al.* propose a general methodology to mine the console logs and to automatically detect system running time problem [19]. But they assume that they have the access to source code which generate the logs. It is not a practical assumption in the environment of router syslogs.

Troubleshooting network problems is one of the most important management tasks. Many approaches have been proposed recent years [12, 11, 17, 7, 14, 13, 10]. The general idea is to apply advanced statistical methodologies to multiple raw data sources. Our system is not specifically designed for troubleshooting, but as illustrated in Section 6, it can benefit complex troubleshooting task significantly.

Rule learning has been widely applied in acquiring insight on different network problems. Kandula *et al.* [9] mine the rules in edge networks based on the network traffic data. Brauckhoff *et al.* [4] use association rule mining techniques to extract anomaly in backbone network. Their data sources, detailed mining methodologies and utilities of final mining results are different from our system. Yamanishi *et al.* [20] provides a dynamic syslog mining technique on server syslogs. They focus on generating predicative alarm for system failures. Our goal is more broad – to represent the network events. Moreover, their syslog data are essentially logs on the end host devices, rather than router syslogs.

The idea of extracting high level information from raw data has been used in network traffic analysis. A few tools aggregate traffic volumes and visualize the resulting aggregates. For example, FlowScan [16] analyzes and reports on Internet Protocol (IP) flow data exported by routers, based on the application, the IP prefix, or the AS identifier. eXpose [9] identifies temporally correlated clusters of flows. NICE [14] is a correlation tool focusing on the chronic network conditions. In comparison, our system is the first one used for extracting network events from logs.

8. CONCLUSION

In this paper, we develop a system called SyslogDigest that groups massive volume of syslog messages into small number of meaningful network events using data mining techniques. SyslogDigest systematically identifies signatures of syslog messages, learns association rules that capture network behaviors over time, groups related raw syslog messages across multiple routers into network events, and labels and prioritizes network events appropriately. We evaluated SyslogDigest using real syslog data collected from two large operational networks and demonstrated how SyslogDigest can be applied on complex network troubleshooting and network health monitoring and visualization. Though we focused on syslog data in this paper, our techniques can also be applied on other network data. We believe SyslogDigest will be an essential building block for many network management tools. Applying SyslogDigest on other network data and integrating it into various network management tools are among our future work.

9. REFERENCES

[1] Emc lonix website. `http://www.emc.com/products/family/ionix-family.htm`.

[2] Ibm netcool website. `http://www-01.ibm.com/software/tivoli/welcome/netcool`.

[3] Rakesh Agrawal, Tomasz Imielinski, and Arun Swami. Mining association rules between sets of items in large databases. In *Proc. ACM SIGMOD*, 1993.

[4] Daniela Brauckhoff, Xenofontas Dimitropoulos, Arno Wagner, and Kavè Salamatian. Anomaly extraction in backbone networks using association rules. In *Proc. ACM IMC*, 2009.

[5] Peter J. Brockwell and Richard A. Davis. *Introduction to Time Series and Forecasting*. Springer, 2002.

[6] R. Gerhards and Adiscon GmbH. The Syslog Protocol. In *IETF RFC*, 2009.

[7] Yiyi Huang, Nick Feamster, Anukool Lakhina, and Jim (Jun) Xu. Diagnosing network disruptions with network-wide analysis. *SIGMETRICS Perform. Eval. Rev.*, 35(1):61–72, 2007.

[8] Charles R. Kalmaneka, Zihui Ge, Seungjoon Lee, Carsten Lund, Dan Pei, Joseph Seidel, Jacobus Van der Merwe, and Jennifer Yates. Darkstar: Using exploratory data mining to raise the bar on network reliability and performance. In *Proc. the 7th international workshop on Design of Reliable Communication Networks (DRCN)*, October 2009.

[9] Srikanth Kandula, Ranveer Chandra, and Dina Katabi. What's going on? learning communication rules in edge networks. In *Proc. ACM SIGCOMM*, 2008.

[10] Srikanth Kandula, Ratul Mahajan, Patrick Verkaik, Sharad Agarwal, Jitendra Padhye, and Paramvir Bahl. Detailed diagnosis in enterprise networks. In *Proc. ACM SIGCOMM*, 2009.

[11] R. R. Kompella, J. Yates, A. Greenberg, and A. C. Snoeren. Detection and localization of network blackholes. In *Proc. INFOCOM*, 2007.

[12] Anukool Lakhina, Mark Crovella, and Christophe Diot. Mining anomalies using traffic feature distributions. In *SIGCOMM '05: Proceedings of the 2005 conference on Applications, technologies, architectures, and protocols for computer communications*, pages 217–228, New York, NY, USA, 2005. ACM.

[13] A. Mahimkar, Z. Ge, , A. Shaikh, J. Wang J. Yates, Y. Zhang, , and Q. Zhao. Towards automated performance diagnosis in a large iptv network. In *Proc. ACM SIGCOMM*, 2009.

[14] A. Mahimkar, J. Yates, Y. Zhang, A. Shaikh, J. Wang, Z. Ge, and C. T. Ee. Troubleshooting chronic conditions in large ip networks. In *Proc. ACM CoNEXT*, 2008.

[15] Ajay Mahimkar, Han Hee Song, Zihui Ge, Aman Shaikh, Jia Wang, Jennifer Yates, Yin Zhang, and Joanne Emmons. Detecting the performance impact of upgrades in large operational networks. In *Proc. ACM SIGCOMM*, 2010.

[16] Dave Plonka. Flowscan: A network traffic flow reporting and visualization tool. In *Proc. USENIX System Admin. Conf.*, 2000.

[17] M. Tariq, A. Zeitoun, V. Valancius, N. Feamster, and M. Ammar. Answering what-if deployment and configuration questions with wise. In *Proc. SIGCOM*, 2008.

[18] Yinglian Xie, Fang Yu, Kannan Achan, Rina Panigrahy, Geoff Hulten, and Ivan Osipkov. Spamming botnets: Signatures and characteristics. In *Proc. ACM SIGCOMM*, 2008.

[19] Wei Xu, Ling Huang, Armando Fox, David Patterson, and Michael I. Jordan. Detecting large-scale system problems by mining console logs. In *SOSP '09: Proceedings of the ACM SIGOPS 22nd symposium on Operating systems principles*, pages 117–132, New York, NY, USA, 2009. ACM.

[20] Kenji Yamanishi and Yuko Maruyama. Dynamic syslog mining for network failure monitoring. In *Proc. ACM KDD*, August 2005.

[21] Nong Ye, S. Vilbert, and Qiang Chen. Computer intrusion detection through EWMA for autocorrelated and uncorrelated data. In *IEEE transactions on reliability*, October 2003.

Author Index

www.ingramcontent.com/pod-product-compliance
Ingram Content Group UK Ltd.
Pitfield, Milton Keynes, MK11 3LW, UK
UKHW051414290926
15471UKWH00009B/1599

9 781450 300575